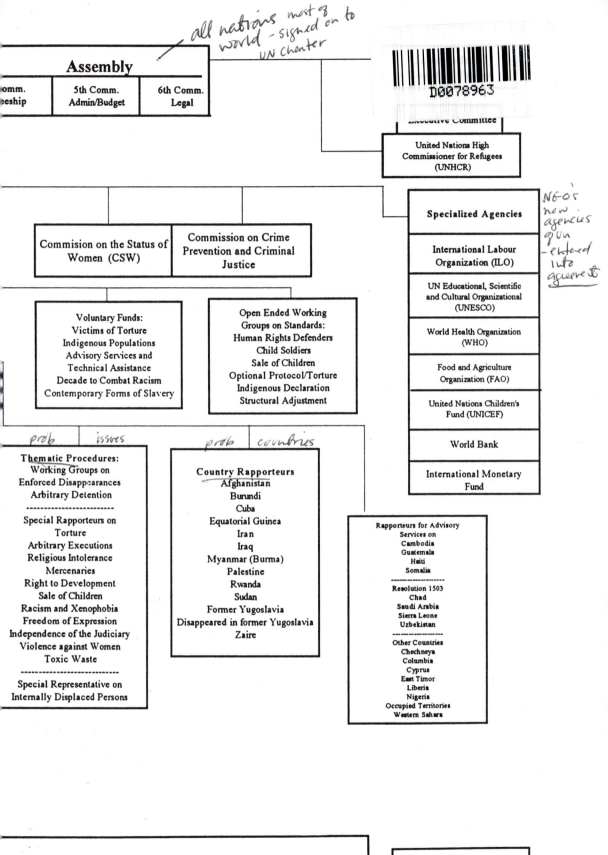

all nations most g world – signed on to UN Charter

Assembly

| ...omm. ...eeship | 5th Comm. Admin/Budget | 6th Comm. Legal |

D0078963

Executive Committee

United Nations High Commissioner for Refugees (UNHCR)

Specialized Agencies

NGO's now agencies g UN – entered into agreemt

International Labour Organization (ILO)

UN Educational, Scientific and Cultural Organizational (UNESCO)

World Health Organization (WHO)

Food and Agriculture Organization (FAO)

United Nations Children's Fund (UNICEF)

World Bank

International Monetary Fund

Commision on the Status of Women (CSW)

Commission on Crime Prevention and Criminal Justice

Voluntary Funds:
Victims of Torture
Indigenous Populations
Advisory Services and Technical Assistance
Decade to Combat Racism
Contemporary Forms of Slavery

Open Ended Working Groups on Standards:
Human Rights Defenders
Child Soldiers
Sale of Children
Optional Protocol/Torture
Indigenous Declaration
Structural Adjustment

prob · issues

Thematic Procedures:
Working Groups on
Enforced Disappearances
Arbitrary Detention

Special Rapporteurs on
Torture
Arbitrary Executions
Religious Intolerance
Mercenaries
Right to Development
Sale of Children
Racism and Xenophobia
Freedom of Expression
Independence of the Judiciary
Violence against Women
Toxic Waste

Special Representative on
Internally Displaced Persons

prob · countries

Country Rapporteurs
Afghanistan
Burundi
Cuba
Equatorial Guinea
Iran
Iraq
Myanmar (Burma)
Palestine
Rwanda
Sudan
Former Yugoslavia
Disappeared in former Yugoslavia
Zaire

Rapporteurs for Advisory
Services on
Cambodia
Guatemala
Haiti
Somalia

Resolution 1503
Chad
Saudi Arabia
Sierra Leone
Uzbekistan

Other Countries
Chechneya
Columbia
Cyprus
East Timor
Liberia
Nigeria
Occupied Territories
Western Sahara

Human Rights Bodies

© 1996 Newman & Weissbrodt

INTERNATIONAL HUMAN RIGHTS:

LAW, POLICY, AND PROCESS

ANDERSON'S

Law School Publications

ADMINISTRATIVE LAW ANTHOLOGY
by Thomas O. Sargentich

ADMINISTRATIVE LAW: CASES AND MATERIALS
by Daniel J. Gifford

ALTERNATIVE DISPUTE RESOLUTION: STRATEGIES FOR LAW AND BUSINESS
by E. Wendy Trachte-Huber and Stephen K. Huber

AN ADMIRALTY LAW ANTHOLOGY
by Robert M. Jarvis

ANALYTIC JURISPRUDENCE ANTHOLOGY
by Anthony D'Amato

AN ANTITRUST ANTHOLOGY
by Andrew I. Gavil

APPELLATE ADVOCACY: PRINCIPLES AND PRACTICE (Second Edition)
Cases and Materials
by Ursula Bentele and Eve Cary

BASIC ACCOUNTING PRINCIPLES FOR LAWYERS:
With Present Value and Expected Value
by C. Steven Bradford and Gary A. Ames

A CAPITAL PUNISHMENT ANTHOLOGY (and Electronic Caselaw Appendix)
by Victor L. Streib

CASES AND PROBLEMS IN CRIMINAL LAW (Third Edition)
by Myron Moskovitz

THE CITATION WORKBOOK
by Maria L. Ciampi, Rivka Widerman, and Vicki Lutz

CIVIL PROCEDURE: CASES, MATERIALS, AND QUESTIONS
by Richard D. Freer and Wendy C. Perdue

COMMERCIAL TRANSACTIONS: PROBLEMS AND MATERIALS
Vol. 1: Secured Transactions Under the UCC
Vol. 2: Sales Under the UCC and the CISG
Vol. 3: Negotiable Instruments Under the UCC and the CIBN
by Louis F. Del Duca, Egon Guttman, and Alphonse M. Squillante

COMMUNICATIONS LAW: MEDIA, ENTERTAINMENT, AND REGULATION
by Donald E. Lively, Allen S. Hammond, Blake D. Morant, and Russell L. Weaver

A CONSTITUTIONAL LAW ANTHOLOGY
by Michael J. Glennon

CONSTITUTIONAL LAW: CASES, HISTORY, AND DIALOGUES
by Donald E. Lively, Phoebe A. Haddon, Dorothy E. Roberts, and Russell L. Weaver

THE CONSTITUTIONAL LAW OF THE EUROPEAN UNION
by James D. Dinnage and John F. Murphy

THE CONSTITUTIONAL LAW OF THE EUROPEAN UNION,
DOCUMENTARY SUPPLEMENT
by James D. Dinnage and John F. Murphy

CONSTITUTIONAL TORTS
by Sheldon H. Nahmod, Michael L. Wells, and Thomas A. Eaton

CONTRACTS
Contemporary Cases, Comments, and Problems
by Michael L. Closen, Richard M. Perlmutter, and Jeffrey D. Wittenberg

A CONTRACTS ANTHOLOGY (Second Edition)
by Peter Linzer

CORPORATE AND WHITE COLLAR CRIME: AN ANTHOLOGY
by Leonard Orland

A CRIMINAL LAW ANTHOLOGY
by Arnold H. Loewy

CRIMINAL LAW: CASES AND MATERIALS
by Arnold H. Loewy

A CRIMINAL PROCEDURE ANTHOLOGY
by Silas J. Wasserstrom and Christie L. Snyder

CRIMINAL PROCEDURE: ARREST AND INVESTIGATION
by Arnold H. Loewy and Arthur B. LaFrance

CRIMINAL PROCEDURE: TRIAL AND SENTENCING
by Arthur B. LaFrance and Arnold H. Loewy

ECONOMIC REGULATION: CASES AND MATERIALS
by Richard J. Pierce, Jr.

ELEMENTS OF LAW
by Eva H. Hanks, Michael E. Herz, and Steven S. Nemerson

ENDING IT: DISPUTE RESOLUTION IN AMERICA
Descriptions, Examples, Cases and Questions
by Susan M. Leeson and Bryan M. Johnston

ENVIRONMENTAL LAW (Second Edition)
Vol. 1: Environmental Decisionmaking: NEPA and the Endangered Species Act
Vol. 2: Water Pollution
Vol. 3: Air Pollution
Vol. 4: Hazardous Waste
by Jackson B. Battle, Robert L. Fischman, Maxine I. Lipeles, and Mark S. Squillace

AN ENVIRONMENTAL LAW ANTHOLOGY
by Robert L. Fischman, Maxine I. Lipeles, and Mark S. Squillace

ENVIRONMENTAL PROTECTION AND JUSTICE
Readings and Commentary on Environmental Law and Practice
by Kenneth A. Manaster

AN EVIDENCE ANTHOLOGY
by Edward J. Imwinkelried and Glen Weissenberger

FEDERAL EVIDENCE COURTROOM MANUAL
by Glen Weissenberger

FEDERAL RULES OF EVIDENCE (1996-97 Edition)
Rules, Legislative History, Commentary and Authority
by Glen Weissenberger

FEDERAL RULES OF EVIDENCE HANDBOOK (1996-97 Edition)
by Publisher's Staff

FIRST AMENDMENT ANTHOLOGY
by Donald E. Lively, Dorothy E. Roberts, and Russell L. Weaver

INTERNATIONAL ENVIRONMENTAL LAW ANTHOLOGY
by Anthony D'Amato and Kirsten Engel

INTERNATIONAL HUMAN RIGHTS: LAW, POLICY AND PROCESS (Second Edition)
by Frank C. Newman and David Weissbrodt

SELECTED INTERNATIONAL HUMAN RIGHTS INSTRUMENTS AND
BIBLIOGRAPHY FOR RESEARCH ON INTERNATIONAL HUMAN RIGHTS LAW (Second Edition)
by Frank C. Newman and David Weissbrodt

INTERNATIONAL INTELLECTUAL PROPERTY ANTHOLOGY
by Anthony D'Amato and Doris Estelle Long

INTERNATIONAL LAW ANTHOLOGY
by Anthony D'Amato

INTERNATIONAL LAW COURSEBOOK
by Anthony D'Amato

INTRODUCTION TO THE STUDY OF LAW: CASES AND MATERIALS
by John Makdisi

Continued

JUDICIAL EXTERNSHIPS: THE CLINIC INSIDE THE COURTHOUSE
by Rebecca A. Cochran

JUSTICE AND THE LEGAL SYSTEM
A Coursebook
by Anthony D'Amato and Arthur J. Jacobson

THE LAW OF DISABILITY DISCRIMINATION
by Ruth Colker

ADA HANDBOOK
Statutes, Regulations and Related Materials
by Publisher's Staff

THE LAW OF MODERN PAYMENT SYSTEMS AND NOTES
by Fred H. Miller and Alvin C. Harrell

LAWYERS AND FUNDAMENTAL MORAL RESPONSIBILITY
by Daniel R. Coquillette

MICROECONOMIC PREDICATES TO LAW AND ECONOMICS
by Mark Seidenfeld

PATIENTS, PSYCHIATRISTS AND LAWYERS
Law and the Mental Health System
by Raymond L. Spring, Roy B. Lacoursiere, M.D., and Glen Weissenberger

PROBLEMS AND SIMULATIONS IN EVIDENCE (Second Edition)
by Thomas F. Guernsey

A PRODUCTS LIABILITY ANTHOLOGY
by Anita Bernstein

PROFESSIONAL RESPONSIBILITY ANTHOLOGY
by Thomas B. Metzloff

A PROPERTY ANTHOLOGY
by Richard H. Chused

THE REGULATION OF BANKING
Cases and Materials on Depository Institutions and Their Regulators
by Michael P. Malloy

A SECTION 1983 CIVIL RIGHTS ANTHOLOGY
by Sheldon H. Nahmod

SPORTS LAW: CASES AND MATERIALS (Second Edition)
by Raymond L. Yasser, James R. McCurdy, and C. Peter Goplerud

A TORTS ANTHOLOGY
by Lawrence C. Levine, Julie A. Davies, and Edward J. Kionka

TRIAL PRACTICE
by Lawrence A. Dubin and Thomas F. Guernsey

TRIAL PRACTICE AND CASE FILES
by Edward R. Stein and Lawrence A. Dubin

TRIAL PRACTICE AND CASE FILES with *Video* Presentation
by Edward R. Stein and Lawrence A. Dubin

FORTHCOMING PUBLICATIONS

A CONFLICT OF LAWS ANTHOLOGY
by Gene R. Shreve

A CORPORATE LAW ANTHOLOGY
Franklin A. Gevurtz

CONSTITUTIONAL CONFLICTS
by Derrick A. Bell, Jr.

A FEDERAL INCOME TAX ANTHOLOGY
by Paul L. Caron, Karen C. Burke, and Grayson M.P. McCouch

Continued

INTERNATIONAL HUMAN RIGHTS:

LAW, POLICY, AND PROCESS

Second Edition

FRANK NEWMAN (1917-1996)

Justice, Supreme Court of California (retired)
Ralston Professor of International Law (emeritus)
University of California Law School, Berkeley

DAVID WEISSBRODT

Briggs & Morgan Professor of Law
University of Minnesota Law School

ANDERSON PUBLISHING CO.
CINCINNATI, OHIO

INTERNATIONAL HUMAN RIGHTS: LAW, POLICY, AND PROCESS
SECOND EDITION

Anderson Publishing Co.
2035 Reading Road / Cincinnati, Ohio 45202
800-582-7295 / e-mail andpubco@aol.com / Fax 513-562-5430

ISBN: 0-87084-370-2

SUMMARY OF CONTENTS

Page

TABLE OF CONTENTS xi
PREFACE xxv
ACKNOWLEDGMENTS xxxiii
FRANK C. NEWMAN xxxv
CONTRIBUTIONS xxxvii

1. Introduction to International Human Rights 1

TREATIES

2. Ratification and Implementation of Treaties: The Covenant on Economic, Social and Cultural Rights 27
3. State Reporting Under International Human Rights Treaties (United States) 89
4. State Reporting Under International Human Rights Treaties (Iran); Cultural Relativism 127

GROSS VIOLATIONS

5. What U.N. Procedures are Available for Violations of Human Rights?: ECOSOC Resolutions 1235 and 1503; Thematic Procedures 173
6. Collective and Unilateral Humanitarian Intervention 217
7. Can Human Rights Violations be Punished and Victims Assured Redress? 255
8. International Human Rights Fact-Finding 307
9. How can the U.S. Government Influence Respect for Human Rights in Other Countries? 373

USE OF ADJUDICATIVE REMEDIES

10. How are Pronouncements of Human Rights in International Instruments Interpreted? The *Baby Boy* Case in the Inter-American Commission 423
11. What Can U.S. Lawyers Learn From the European Human Rights System? 467
12. U.S. Adjudicative Remedies for Violations Occurring Outside the U.S.: *Filartiga* and its Progeny 499
13. U.S. Remedies for Human Rights Violations Within the U.S.: Alien Children in Detention 553
14. Refugee and Asylum Law; Jurisprudence of Human Rights; Cultural Relativism 631

CAUSES OF HUMAN RIGHTS VIOLATIONS

15. What seem to be the Causes of Human Rights Violations and
    How Might Knowledge as to Causation be Useful?   699

TABLE OF AUTHORITIES   755

INDEX   813

DOCUMENTARY SUPPLEMENT

Selected International Human Rights Instruments   3

Bibliography for Research on International Human Rights Law   207

TABLE OF CONTENTS

Page

SUMMARY OF CONTENTS   ix
PREFACE   xxv
ACKNOWLEDGMENTS   xxxiii
FRANK C. NEWMAN   xxxv
CONTRIBUTIONS   xxxvii

CHAPTER 1: INTRODUCTION TO INTERNATIONAL HUMAN RIGHTS

A. Brief Historical Introduction   2
    1. Early Developments   2
    2. World War I and the League of Nations   3
    3. The Inter-War Years   4
    4. World War II and the Beginning of the Modern Human Rights Movement   5
       a. The Nuremberg and Tokyo Tribunals, and Control Council Law No. 10   6
       b. The Creation of the United Nations: Dumbarton Oaks and San Francisco   7
       c. The United Nations and Multilateral Protection of Human Rights   7
          i. Codification   8
          ii. Development of Human Rights Law within the U.N. Structure; Charter-based human rights bodies   9
          iii. Development of Human Rights Law through six treaty-based human rights committees   13

B. Human Rights in International Law   13
    1. The U.N. and International Human Rights Law   13
       a. Human Rights under the U.N. Charter   13
       b. International Bill of Human Rights   14
       c. Other U.N. Treaties   14
       d. Related U.N. Instruments   15
    2. Other Worldwide Treaties and Instruments   16
    3. Customary International Law   18
    4. Regional Organizations and Law-Making   19
       a. European System   19
       b. Inter-American System   20
       c. Organization of African Unity   21
    5. Domestic Implementation of Human Rights   21

C. Conclusion   23

CHAPTER 2: RATIFICATION AND IMPLEMENTATION OF TREATIES: THE COVENANT ON ECONOMIC, SOCIAL AND CULTURAL RIGHTS

A. **Introduction**   28

B. **Questions**   28

C. **Ratification of Treaties**   29

    1. **How Do Governments Become Bound?**   29
        Vienna Convention on the Law of Treaties   29
        Anne M. Williams, United States Treaty Law   30
    2. **Reservations**   31
        Vienna Convention on the Law of Treaties   31
        Dinah Shelton, International Law   33
    3. **U.S. Ratification of Human Rights Treaties**   34
        Nigel Rodley, On the Necessity of United States Ratification of
          the International Human Rights Conventions   35
        Genocide Convention   39
        Treaty against Torture   40
        Covenant on Civil and Political Rights   41
        Race Convention   42
        Women's Convention   43
        American Convention on Human Rights   45

D. **The Covenant on Economic, Social and Cultural Rights**   49

    1. **What Are Economic, Social, and Cultural Rights?**   49
        Philip Alston & Gerard Quinn, The Nature and Scope of States
          Parties' Obligations Under the International Covenant on Eco-
          nomic, Social and Cultural Rights   51
    2. **Should the U.S. Ratify the Covenant on Economic, Social and Cultural Rights?**   58
        Philip Alston, U.S. Ratification of the Covenant on Economic,
          Social and Cultural Rights: The Need for an Entirely New
          Strategy   58
    3. **Ratification—With or Without Qualifications?**   66
        Four Treaties Pertaining to Human Rights: Message From the
          President of the United States   66
        Burns Weston, U.S. Ratification of the International Covenant on
          Economic, Social and Cultural Rights: With or Without Qualifi-
          cations   68

E. **Implementation and Enforcement**   72

    1. **U.N. Committee on Economic, Social and Cultural Rights**   72
        Philip Alston, Out of the Abyss: The Challenges Confronting the
          New U.N. Committee on Economic, Social and Cultural Rights   72
        Committee on Economic, Social and Cultural Rights, Report on
          the Eighth and Ninth Sessions   75
    2. **Coordination with Other Bodies**   79

F. Recognition of New Rights   **81**

Stephen Marks, Emerging Human Rights: A New Generation for the 1980s?   81

CHAPTER 3: STATE REPORTING UNDER INTERNATIONAL HUMAN RIGHTS TREATIES (UNITED STATES)

A. Introduction   **89**

B. Questions   **90**

C. Reporting Procedures   **91**

    1. The Civil and Political Covenant's Human Rights Committee   **91**
    2. Reporting and Consideration Procedures   **91**
      a. The Initial Report   92
      b. Periodic Reports   94
      c. Supplementary Reports   95
      d. Emergency Reports   96
    3. Distribution of Committee Reports and Comments   **96**

D. The Initial U.S. Report   **100**

    1. The Report   **100**
    John Shattuck, Introduction to U.S. Report   100
    Wall Street Journal, The State of PC   103
    International Covenant on Civil and Political Rights, Article 2   104
    U.S. Understanding Regarding Article 2   105
    U.S. Report Under the CCPR (Article 2)   105
    U.S. Report Under the CCPR (Land and People)   113
    Human Rights Watch & American Civil Liberties Union, Human Rights Violations in the United States: A Report on U.S. Compliance with the International Covenant on Civil and Political Rights   115
    Kevin Reed, Race, Criminal Justice and the Death Penalty   118
    Stan R. Gregory, Note, Capital Punishment and Equal Protection   121
    2. The Examination   **122**
    Comments of the Human Rights Committee   123

CHAPTER 4: STATE REPORTING UNDER INTERNATIONAL HUMAN RIGHTS TREATIES (IRAN); CULTURAL RELATIVISM

A. Introduction   **128**

B. Questions   **129**

C. The Situation in Iran   **130**

    1. Creation of the Islamic Republic of Iran   **130**
    Amnesty International, Iran: Violations of Human Rights   131
    2. Human Rights Committee   **134**
    Human Rights Committee, Consideration of Reports Submitted

by States Parties Under Article 40 of the Covenant: Iran (1982) 135

Report of the Human Rights Committee, Comments by the Iranian Representative during the Committee's examination of the report (1982) 136

Report of the Human Rights Committee, General Comments on Article 7 of the Covenant 137

Human Rights Committee, Consideration of Reports Submitted by States Parties Under Article 40 of the Covenant: Iran (1992) 138

Human Rights Committee, Observations and Questions Presented during the Committee's Examination of the second Iranian report 139

    1194th Meeting 139

    1196th Meeting 139

    1230th Meeting 140

3. Country Rapporteur Process of the U.N. Commission on Human Rights 142

Report by the Commission's Special Representative on the Human Rights Situation in Iran (1985) 143

4. Iranian Violations of International Law 146

D. The International Law Prohibition of Torture and Other Cruel, Inhuman or Degrading Treatment or Punishment 147

Standard Minimum Rules for the Treatment of Prisoners 147

Declaration on the Protection of All Persons from Being Subjected to Torture and Other Cruel, Inhuman or Degrading Treatment or Punishment 148

Convention Against Torture and Other Cruel, Inhuman or Degrading Treatment or Punishment 148

Body of Principles for the Treatment of Detainees 150

1. Human Rights Committee Consideration of Communications Under the Optional Protocol 150

    a. Committee Procedures 151

    Report of the Human Rights Committee re: Consideration of Communications Under the Optional Protocol 151

    b. Committee Jurisprudence 155

    Manfred Nowak, U.N. Covenant on Civil and Political Rights: CCPR Commentary 155

    Human Rights Committee Views on Communication No. 414/1990 157

2. European System 159

    Ireland v. United Kingdom, European Commission 159

    Ireland v. United Kingdom, European Court 161

    Tyrer Case, European Court 162

    Geneva Conventions of 1949, Common Article 3 165

    Restatement (Third) of the Foreign Relations Law of the United States 165

3. U.N. Response to Amputations Under the Islamic Penal Code of Sudan 166

E. **Theoretical Foundations of Human Rights: Natural Law, Positivism, and Islamic Principles**   **166**

> Myres S. McDougal, Harold D. Lasswell, & Lung-Chu Chen, Human Rights and World Public Order: The Basic Policies of an International Law of Human Dignity   167
>
> S. Farooq A. Hassan, The Islamic Republic: Politics, Law and Economy   168

F. **Cultural Relativism and International Human Rights Law**   **171**

CHAPTER 5: WHAT U.N. PROCEDURES ARE AVAILABLE FOR VIOLATIONS OF HUMAN RIGHTS?

ECOSOC Resolutions 1235 and 1503; Thematic Procedures

A. **Introduction**   **174**

B. **Questions**   **174**

C. **Background on Burma (Myanmar)**   **176**

> Stan Sesser, A Rich Country Gone Wrong   176
>
> Human Rights Watch, Burma (Myanmar)   180

D. **U.N. Procedures for Responding to Human Rights Violations**   **181**

> 1. **Development of Major U.N. Procedures**   **182**
>   ECOSOC Resolution 728F   182
>   ECOSOC Resolution 1235   184
>   ECOSOC Resolution 1503   185
> 2. **Overview of the 1503 Procedure in Practice**   **187**
> 3. **Theme Procedures**   **191**
>   David Weissbrodt, The Three "Theme" Special Rapporteurs of the UN Commission on Human Rights   192
>   Report on the visit to Peru by two members of the Working Group on Enforced or Involuntary Disappearances   202
>   Report on a second visit to Peru by two members of the Working Group on Enforced or Involuntary Disappearances   205
> 4. **Further Remarks on 1235, 1503, and the Theme Procedures**   **208**
>   Marc Bossuyt, The Development of Procedures of the U.N. Commission on Human Rights   211
>   Sandra Coliver, U.N. Machineries on Women's Rights   214
>   Amnesty International, Oral Statement on Thematic Mechanisms   214
> 5. **Freedom of Information Act (FOIA) and Confidentiality Under ECOSOC 1503 in regard to the U.S.**   **216**

CHAPTER 6: COLLECTIVE AND UNILATERAL HUMANITARIAN INTERVENTION

A. **Introduction**   **217**

B. **Questions**   **217**

C. **U.N. Missions to Maintain or Restore International Peace and Security**   **218**

> United Nations, The Blue Helmets: A Review of United Nations Peace-keeping   219
>
> U.N. Secretary-General, An Agenda for Peace: Preventive Diplomacy, Peacemaking and Peace-keeping   223

Amnesty International, Peace-keeping and Human Rights 224
Claire Palley, Sub-Commission on Prevention of Discrimination and
Protection of Minorities, Implications of Humanitarian Activities
for the Enjoyment of Human Rights 229
Nancy D. Arnison, The Law of Humanitarian Intervention 234
U.N. Secretary-General, Supplement to an Agenda for Peace 235

D. Unilateral Action 243

Richard B. Lillich, A United States Policy of Humanitarian Interven-
tion and Intercession 243
Abraham D. Sofaer, International Law and the Use of Force 245
Tom J. Farer & Christopher C. Joyner, The United States and the
Use of Force: Looking Back to See Ahead 247

**CHAPTER 7: CAN HUMAN RIGHTS VIOLATIONS BE PUNISHED
AND VICTIMS ASSURED REDRESS?**

A. Introduction 256

B. Questions 256

C. Responding to past Human Rights Violations 259

Diane F. Orentlicher, Settling Accounts: The Duty to Prosecute Human Rights Violations of a Prior Regime 259
José Zalaquett, Balancing Ethical Imperatives and Political Constraints: The Dilemma of New Democracies Confronting Past Human Rights Violations 262
David Weissbrodt & Paul W. Fraser, Political Transitions and Commissions of Inquiry 264
Thomas Buergenthal, The United Nations Truth Commission for El
Salvador 267

D. Nuremberg Principles 276

1. The Nuremberg and Tokyo Tribunals 276
2. Control Council Law No. 10 and "Minor" Tribunals 277
3. Nuremberg's Legacy 278

E. The International Tribunal for the Former Yugoslavia 280

1. Historical Background 280
**2. U.N. Response: War Crimes Tribunal for the former Yugo-
slavia** 281
Diane F. Orentlicher, Legal Basis of the Tribunal for the former
Yugoslavia 283
Statute of the International Criminal Tribunal for the former
Yugoslavia 284
3. Efficacy of the Tribunal for the Former Yugoslavia 288
Aryeh Neier, War Crimes Tribunal is an Imperative 288
Herman Schwartz, War Crimes Trials—Not a Good Idea 289
Françoise J. Hampson, Violation of Fundamental Rights in the
Former Yugoslavia: The Case for a War Crimes Tribunal 291
David P. Forsythe, Politics and the International Tribunal for the
Former Yugoslavia 292

F. Creating a Permanent International Criminal Court   **298**

M. Cherif Bassiouni, The Time Has Come for an International Criminal Court   298

Michael P. Scharf, The Jury is Still Out on the Need for an International Criminal Court   300

CHAPTER 8: INTERNATIONAL HUMAN RIGHTS FACT-FINDING

A. Introduction   **308**

B. Questions   **308**

C. Background on Rwanda   **311**

Rwanda, Human Rights Watch   313

Andrew Clapham & Meg Henry, Peacekeeping and Human Rights in Africa and Europe   314

Rwanda and Burundi, A Call for Action by the International Community   316

D. Fact-Finding Procedures   **319**

    1. Preparation for an On-Site Investigation   **320**

    2. Methods of On-Site Fact-Finding   **322**

    3. Analysis, Verification, Follow-up, and Reporting   **330**

    4. U.S. State Department Country Reports   **332**

E. Experience of the Inter-American Commission on Human Rights   **334**

Inter-American Commission on Human Rights, Report on the Situation of Human Rights in Argentina   334

Thomas Buergenthal, Robert Norris, & Dinah Shelton, Protecting Human Rights in the Americas: Selected Problems   341

Inter-American Commission, Case 9265   343

Edmundo Vargas, Visits on the Spot: The Experience of the Inter-American Commission on Human Rights   348

F. Fact-Finding Without On-Site Observation: Democratic People's Republic of Korea   **351**

G. Impact of Fact-Finding Investigations   **358**

    1. Americas Watch, Asia Watch & Helsinki Watch, Four Failures: A Report on the U.N. Special Rapporteurs on Human Rights in Chile, Guatemala, Iran, and Poland   **358**

    2. Assessing the Impact of Fact-Finding   **361**

    Maria Bartolomei & David Weissbrodt, The Impact of Fact-Finding International Pressures on the Human Rights Situation in Argentina, 1976-1983   361

    3. Fact-Finding for United States Violations of Human Rights   **371**

CHAPTER 9: HOW CAN THE U.S. GOVERNMENT INFLUENCE RESPECT FOR HUMAN RIGHTS IN OTHER COUNTRIES?

A.	**Introduction**	374
B.	**Questions**	374
C.	**International Duties**	375
	1. **U.S. Duties as a U.N. Member-Nation**	375
	a. The U.N. Charter	375
	b. International Human Rights Treaties	375
	2. **President Clinton's Early View of U.N. Human Rights Obligations**	376
	Address to the 49th U.N. General Assembly	377
D.	**Incorporating Human Rights Goals into U.S. Foreign Policy**	379
	Warren Christopher, Human Rights and the National Interest	379
	Department of State, Country Reports on Human Rights Practices for 1988	383
	James Baker, Hearing of the Senate Foreign Relations Committee	385
	Warren Christopher, Remarks at the World Conference on Human Rights	386
E.	**Defining and Implementing U.S. Human Rights Policy**	391
	1. **The Role of Congress**	391
	Donald M. Fraser, Congress's Role in the Making of International Human Rights Policy	392
	Olufunmilayo B. Arewa & Susan O'Rourke, Country-Specific Legislation and Human Rights: The Case of Peru	396
	2. **The Role of the Administration**	399
	Human Rights Watch & Lawyers Committee for Human Rights, Critique: A Review of the Department of State's Country Reports on Human Rights Practices for 1988	399
	Stephen B. Cohen, Conditioning U.S. Security Assistance on Human Rights Practices	403
	David D. Newsom, The Diplomacy of Human Rights: A Diplomat's View	411
	3. **Economic Sanctions**	415
	Barry E. Carter, International Economic Sanctions: Improving the Haphazard U.S. Legal Regime	415

CHAPTER 10: HOW ARE PRONOUNCEMENTS OF HUMAN RIGHTS IN INTERNATIONAL INSTRUMENTS INTERPRETED?

The *Baby Boy* Case in the Inter-American Commission

A.	**Introduction**	424
B.	**Questions**	424

C. Jurisprudence of the Inter-American Commission 426

    1. Case 2141 (the *Baby Boy* Opinion) 426
    2. Regulations of the Inter-American Commission 436
    3. Additional Cases Raising Difficult Interpretive Issues 437
    4. Typical Cases in the Inter-American Commission 440

D. The Inter-American Commission on Human Rights 444

    Juan Méndez & José Vivanco, Disappearances and the Inter-American Court: Reflections on a Litigation Experience 444

E. Treaty Interpretations and Reservations 450

    The Vienna Convention on the Law of Treaties 450
    Four Treaties Pertaining to Human Rights: Message from the President of the United States 452
    Restatement (Third) of the Foreign Relations Law of the United States 453

F. Advisory Jurisdiction of the Inter-American Court of Human Rights 454

    Thomas Buergenthal, The Inter-American Court of Human Rights 454
    Thomas Buergenthal, The Advisory Practice of the Inter-American Human Rights Court 457
    Restrictions to the Death Penalty, Advisory Opinion OC-3/83 459

G. Other Regional Systems 463

    1. The Organization of African Unity 464
    2. Human Rights in Asia 466

CHAPTER 11: WHAT CAN U.S. LAWYERS LEARN FROM THE EUROPEAN HUMAN RIGHTS SYSTEM?

A. Introduction 467

B. Questions 468

C. Areas of Protection in the European Court of Human Rights 470

    1. Homosexuality 470
    Dudgeon v. United Kingdom 470
    2. Death Penalty 476
    Soering v. United Kingdom 476
    3. Corporal Punishment 478

D. Remedies in the European Court of Human Rights 478

    1. Bringing a Case 479
    2. Damage Awards 481
    Sporrong and Lönnroth v. Sweden 482
    3. Parallel Remedies Outside the European System 486
    Inter-American Court of Human Rights 486
    U.N. Compensation Commission 488
    U.S. Courts 488

E. Interstate Human Rights Cases in the European System: The Greek Case 489

F. Human Rights Law in Europe Apart From the European
    Convention   491

    1. European Union (EU)   491
    2. Organization for Security and Cooperation in Europe
        (OSCE)   494
    3. North Atlantic Treaty Organization (NATO)   496

CHAPTER 12: U.S. ADJUDICATIVE REMEDIES FOR VIOLATIONS OCCURRING OUTSIDE THE U.S.

Filartiga and its Progeny

A. Introduction   500

B. Questions   500

C. Alien Tort Litigation   504

    1. Jurisdiction   504
        Filartiga v. Peña-Irala (1980)   505
        Forti v. Suarez-Mason (*Forti I*)   510
        Forti v. Suarez-Mason (*Forti II*)   515
        Joan Fitzpatrick, The Future of the ATCA   521
    2. International Rules Governing Rape   523
        Geneva Conventions of 1949   523
        Protocol I   525
        Protocol II   525
        Covenant on Civil and Political Rights   526
        Convention on the Elimination of All Forms of Discrimination
            Against Women   527
        Declaration on the Elimination of Violence Against Women 528
        Theodor Meron, Rape as a Crime Under International Humanitar-
            ian Law   528

D. Obstacles to Adjudication Under the Alien Tort Claims   533
    Act

    1. Foreign Sovereign Immunities Act   534
    2. Acts of State and of Heads of State   541
        Liu v. Republic of China   542
    3. Statute of Limitations, Damages, and Choice of Law   547
        Filartiga v. Peña-Irala (1984)   547

E. Torture Victim Protection Act Litigation   550

    28 U.S.C. § 1350   550

CHAPTER 13: U.S. REMEDIES FOR HUMAN RIGHTS VIOLATIONS WITHIN THE U.S.

Alien Children in Detention

A. Introduction   554

    Justice Harry Blackmun, Comments   555

B.	**Questions**	**557**
C.	**U.S. Law**	**560**
	1. **Constitution**	**560**
	Article VI, § 2	560
	Amendment V	560
	Amendment VIII	560
	2. **Federal Statutes and Regulations**	**560**
	8 U.S.C. § 1252	560
	8 U.S.C. § 1357	561
	8 C.F.R. § 242.24	561
	3. **Judicial Interpretation**	**562**
	Reno v. Flores	562
D.	**International Standards**	**568**
	1. **U.S.-Ratified Treaties**	**568**
	Covenant on Civil and Political Rights	568
	2. **Treaties Which the U.S. Has Not Ratified**	**572**
	Convention on the Rights of the Child	572
E.	**Approaches to Using International Human Rights Law**	**574**
	Judge Hans Linde, Comments	576
F.	**Treaties**	**580**
	Vienna Convention on the Law of Treaties	580
	1. **Treaties in U.S. Law**	**581**
	United States v. Palestine Liberation Organization	*581*
	2. **Treaties Which the U.S. Has Not Ratified**	**585**
	3. **The Doctrine of Self-Executing Treaties**	**585**
	Kathryn Burke, et al., Application of Human Rights Law	586
	Matter of Medina, Board of Immigration Appeals	589
	Matter of Medina, ACLU Amicus Brief	591
	4. **Reservations**	**594**
	5. **Implementing Legislation: The U.S. Refugee Act of 1980**	**597**
G.	**Customary International Law**	**598**
	1. **Proving a Customary Norm**	**599**
	2. **General Principles of Law Recognized by the Community of Nations**	**601**
	3. **Peremptory Norms**	**601**
H.	**Using International Law to Guide Interpretation of U.S. Law**	**602**
	1. **Prison Conditions**	**602**
	Lareau v. Manson	*602*
	2. **U.S. Supreme Court Opinions**	**607**
	3. **Protesting International Crimes**	**608**
	Declaration of Frank Newman, in *People v. Wylie*	*608*
	4. **Rights of Aliens**	**610**

5.	Other Rights	611
I.	**Incorporating International Law in U.S. Statutes**	**612**
	Sandra Coliver & Frank Newman, Using International Human Rights Law	612
J.	**Obstacles to Application of International Law**	**613**
1.	Challenges to U.S. Foreign Policy: Political Questions, Sovereign Immunity, Standing, and Failure to State a Cause of Action	614
	Committee of U.S. Citizens in Nicaragua v. Reagan	*614*
2.	Challenges to U.S. Policies: Customary Norms and Executive, Legislative, and Judicial Acts	622
K.	**Strategy Issues: When to Invoke International Law in U.S. Courts; When to Seek Relief Through Administrative Processes; When to Seek Incorporation of International Law in U.S. Statutes?**	**624**
	Conference Report: Human Rights in American Courts	624

CHAPTER 14: REFUGEE AND ASYLUM LAW; JURISPRUDENCE OF HUMAN RIGHTS; CULTURAL RELATIVISM

A.	**Introduction**	**632**
B.	**Questions**	**632**
C.	**Introduction to Refugee Law**	**636**
1.	**Procedural Issues: Claiming Refugee Status**	**636**
	Deborah Anker, The Law of Asylum in the U.S.	636
2.	**Definition of Refugee**	**640**
3.	**Interpreting the Refugee Definition: Exactly What is a Well-Founded Fear of Persecution?**	**642**
	UNHCR Handbook	643
D.	**The Role of the UNHCR**	**646**
1.	**Purpose, Function, and Responsibility**	**646**
	Statute of the Office of the UNHCR	646
	Lawyers Committee, The UNHCR at 40	646
2.	**Participation in U.S. Asylum Proceedings**	**649**
	Letter from UNHCR Associate Legal Counselor	649
E.	**Gender-Based Refugee Claims**	**650**
1.	**Gender as a Social Group**	**651**
	Fatin v. INS	*651*
	UNHCR Guidelines on the Protection of Refugee Women	656
	Women Refugees Project Guidelines	657
	INS Guidelines for Consideration of Gender-Related Asylum Claims	658
2.	**Are FGM and Spousal Abuse Persecution?**	**666**
	UNHCR Position on FGM	668

	3.	Internal Flight	675
		INS Basic Law Manual	675
F.	**Obstacles to FGM- and Spousal Violence-Based Asylum Claims**		**677**
	1.	**Cultural Relativism**	**677**
		Katherine Brennan, The Influence of Cultural Relativism	677
		Jack Donnelly, Cultural Relativism and Universal Human Rights	678
	2.	**Theoretical Foundations of Human Rights**	**683**
		Hilary Charlesworth et al., Feminist Approaches to International Law	683
		Nigel Purvis, Critical Legal Studies in Public International Law	687
		Anthony D'Amato, Is International Law Really "Law"?	694

CHAPTER 15: WHAT SEEM TO BE THE CAUSES OF HUMAN RIGHTS VIOLATIONS AND HOW MIGHT KNOWLEDGE AS TO CAUSATION BE USED?

A.	**Introduction**		**700**
B.	**Questions**		**701**
C.	**Political and Economic Factors**		**705**
	1.	**Political and Economic Theories and Research**	**705**
		Neil Mitchell & James McCormick, Economic and Political Explanations of Human Rights Violations	705
		Reinhard Heinisch, Political Explanations of Basic Human Rights Performance	712
		Steven Poe & C. Neal Tate, Repression of Human Rights to Personal Integrity in the 1980s: A Global Analysis	715
	2.	**Military Expansion and Conflict**	**721**
D.	**Sociological Aspects of Power**		**723**
		James Scott, The Value and Cost of the Public Transcript	723
E.	**Psychological Factors**		**729**
		Robert Jay Lifton, Socialization to Killing	732
F.	**Sociocultural Factors**		**738**
	1.	**Group Identity and Scapegoating**	**738**
		Philip Mayer, Witches	739
		Robert Jay Lifton, Genocide	742
	2.	**Change, Uncertainty, and Political Manipulation**	**743**
		J.R. Crawford, The Consequences of Allegation	743
		H.R. Trevor-Roper, The European Witch-Craze	743
		Joyce Bednarski, The Salem Witch-Scare Viewed Sociologically	745
		A. Rebecca Cardozo, A Modern American Witch-Craze	747
G.	**Additional Readings**		**749**
	1.	**General research on human rights violations**	**749**
	2.	**Economic & Political Factors**	**749**
		a. Economic Development	749

	b.	Political Theories	750
	c.	Military Expansion & Conflict	750
	d.	U.S. Foreign Policy	751
3.		**Sociocultural & Psychological Factors**	**752**
	a.	Ingrouping & Outgrouping	752
	b.	Group Conformity & Obedience to Authority	752
	c.	Sociological Aspects of Political Power	752
	d.	Socialization to Violence & War	752
	e.	Torture—Effects on Victims	752
4.		**Violations of Human Rights in Latin America**	**753**

TABLE OF AUTHORITIES — 755

INDEX — 813

PREFACE

This book provides an introduction to international human rights law, policy, and process. At the outset new readers may ask why they should study international human rights? Readers who are familiar with our first edition may inquire why a second edition was needed. This preface responds to those two questions and also seeks to help new readers.

This preface also presents a series of questions to guide readers through the book, describes the second edition's organizational design, and discusses the authors' rationale for choosing their approach.

Why study international human rights?

There are several reasons for pursuing a course on international human rights law. *First,* the subject deals with many concerns that also are the focus of civil liberties and civil rights law. People whose national liberties and rights are violated (or threatened) often can benefit from international legal assistance. Readers of this book should expect to learn about a system of laws, policies, and procedures that have been designed to protect people from torture, other inhuman treatment, arbitrary killing, unjustified discrimination, forced eviction, and countless other abuses—wherever they may occur.

Second, lawyers and law students who expect to practice civil liberties or civil rights law should know that if they do not prevail in national forums—legislative, executive, or judicial—there may be international tribunals or other bodies to which they can take their case. Even the U.S. Supreme Court is not the last resort for advocates working to protect human rights. Advocates should also be aware that there are arguments based on international law that clearly should be raised in U.S. federal and state courts, as well as in legislatures and administrative agencies. Civil liberties and civil rights attorneys arguably breach their professional responsibilities if they represent clients and stay ignorant of international laws and procedures. At the very least those attorneys would not afford their clients the most zealous and competent representation possible.

The present status of international human rights law is comparable to earlier stages in the progress of civil liberties and civil rights law in the United States. A century or more ago the judicial impact of the Bill of Rights in the U.S. Constitution and similar provisions in state constitutions was minimal. It has taken two centuries to develop legal protections for the rights of U.S. citizens and to train lawyers how to protect those rights effectively. The varied developments included the 1791 adoption of the Bill of Rights, the Civil War, post-war amendments to the Constitution of 1865-70 (including the Equal Protection Clause), and then nearly a century of litigation to help effectuate the new rules. It was not until the twentieth century that the Supreme Court decided that the Bill of Rights applied to the states as well as to the federal government and that *Brown v. Board of Education*[1] finally held segregated schools to be a violation of the Equal Protection Clause.

---

[1] 349 U.S. 483 (1954).

The *Brown* decision was followed by the Civil Rights Movement of the 1960s, the struggle for equal rights for women, and other movements for much-enhanced protection for rights and liberties. The struggle for equality resulted in landmark legislation, including the Equal Pay Act of 1963,[2] the Civil Rights Act of 1964,[3] the Age Discrimination in Employment Act of 1967,[4] Title IX in the Education Amendments of 1972,[5] the Rehabilitation Act of 1973,[6] the Age Discrimination Act of 1975,[7] and the Americans with Disabilities Act of 1990.[8] And by no means have those efforts achieved all their objectives.

By comparison, international human rights law has developed with more deliberate speed. The invigorated, worldwide, human rights movement was proclaimed during 1945 in the United Nations Charter, was concretized during 1948 by the Universal Declaration of Human Rights (the first segment of the International Bill of Human Rights), and was dramatically extended in succeeding years by scores of treaties and related instruments. As a result, there exist in some situations more protection for human rights under international law than under U.S. law and other national law. Lawyers and others who practice in the area of civil rights and civil liberties need training on how to invoke the broader protections and profit from international insights as to how law may be improved.

Third, this book can help train human rights professionals and assist readers to be more effective human rights volunteers. Lawyers, law students, and others can help victims and benefit from international human rights law in many ways. They can assist clients affected by human rights abuses. They may also work as government officials, members of human rights organizations, informal groups, and sometimes as individuals working alone. They litigate, advocate in non-adjudicative forums, negotiate, draft, write letters, advise, and participate in investigations throughout the world. As individuals, they petition, protest, speak, and write. This book considers all those functions and helps evaluate their worth.

As you read through the book, consider questions like these:

1) As a human rights advocate what are your objectives?
2) What resources (of skill, time, finances, etc.) do you have at hand?
3) In pursuing your objectives, should you seek the support or collaboration of nongovernmental human rights organizations (NGOs) at the national level? Of your and/or other governments?
4) How might international norms and activities help you achieve your objectives?
    a) Which international norms might be useful?
        1) In seeking legislative change?
        2) In local courts?
        3) In dealing with administrative agencies?
    b) When might it be inappropriate to use international norms? Has there been

---

[2] 29 U.S.C. § 206 (1988).

[3] Pub. L. No. 88-352, 78 Stat. 241 (codified as amended at 42 U.S.C. §§ 2000e-2000e-17 (1988 & Supp. IV 1992)).

[4] 29 U.S.C. §§ 621-634 (1988 & Supp. III 1991).

[5] 20 U.S.C. §§ 1681-1686 (1982).

[6] 29 U.S.C. §§ 701-796 (1988).

[7] 42 U.S.C. §§ 6101-6107 (1982).

[8] 42 U.S.C. §§ 12101-12117 (Supp. V 1993).

a violation of international human rights law? What exactly does international law prescribe? Do the facts show that international law has been violated?

5) How can international organizations, both governmental and nongovernmental, help you to achieve your objectives?

a) Do international organizations consider sufficiently the above questions?

b) Which international procedures should you select? Which might be harmful to your efforts?

c) How should the international procedures be invoked to enable you to achieve the most from them?

Fourth, there are countless international human rights jobs in governments, intergovernmental organizations, NGOs, and elsewhere. For instance, many professionals are sent to observe and protect human rights as part of U.N. peacekeeping actions throughout the world. Many lawyers apply the principles of human rights law as part of their more general practice. For example, lawyers represent applicants for political asylum or refugee status, do civil liberties or civil rights work in which international human rights norms or procedures can be used, or may be retained by human rights victims.

Readers should not, however, pursue this course of study with the expectation that paid employment will generally be available after graduation in the field of international human rights. The work of numerous volunteers is crucial in this field. An increasing number of lawyers volunteer for *pro bono publico* work in international human rights. Lawyers, students, and others can write letters to governments accused of human rights violations, carry out research on human rights abuses, assist in publicizing specific violations, and undertake other activity. Such work is valuable, not only because the volunteers are helping victims, but also because they are saying something about themselves. Writing letters, investigating wrongs, and speaking out, indeed, are better than remaining silent in the face of repression. As Elie Wiesel said when he accepted the Nobel Peace Prize in 1986, it is sometimes necessary to "speak truth to power." The study of international human rights law provides a theoretical foundation for such activity. Similarly, learning to use international human rights procedures affords mechanisms for action. While many volunteers may not need an understanding of the legal basis for their efforts, those who are familiar with international human rights law and procedure, may help develop, improve, and even direct the work of others.

Fifth, as with any course about a legal system different from one's own, this book provides insights that often encourage a renewed understanding of one's own legal system. International human rights law, like international law generally, is not all that different from other kinds of law, such as torts and constitutional law. The main focus of human rights law is not, however, on appellate court opinions, as are many other courses. Instead, the course in international human rights law focuses on constitutive instruments such as the U.N. Charter, the International Bill of Human Rights, the Charter of the Organization of American States, and many related documents. The student will learn to apply these sources of law to various fact situations, much as in other law courses, and will learn how to advocate effectively for compliance with the human rights norms contained in those instruments.

Sixth, a course in international human rights law covers one aspect of public international law and deals with several of the same issues: the nature of international law; drafting, ratification, and interpretation of treaties; customary international law; intergovernmental and nongovernmental organizations; the protection of aliens; international fact-finding, etc. The first, introductory chapter discusses how international human rights law fits into the larger domain of international law.

Why a second edition?

This second edition reflects many significant developments that have occurred since publication of the first edition in 1990. The most significant development in the protection of human rights has been the emergence of the U.N. Security Council as a principal actor in the human rights field, including its authorization of on-site U.N. work to deal with emergency situations, its establishment of a Compensation Commission to compensate victims of the Iraqi invasion of Kuwait, and its establishment of *ad hoc* international criminal tribunals to deal with violations in the former Yugoslavia and Rwanda. *See* chapters 6 and 7, *infra*.

Another important development has been the long-awaited ratification by the United States of three of the most important human rights treaties: the International Covenant on Civil and Political Rights; the International Convention on the Elimination of All Forms of Racial Discrimination; and the Convention against Torture, and Other Cruel, Inhuman or Degrading Treatment or Punishment. The ratifications, however, were limited by extensive reservations. Ratification is discussed in chapter 2, *infra*.

A third major development was the increased tension between the developed nations of the North and the less developed nations of the South. The North-South division has encouraged the South to renew its campaign for the right to development and for an increased focus on economic, social and cultural rights. Some countries of the South have intensified their arguments that human rights must be interpreted in the cultural context of each region and that Western European definitions of human rights should not be rigidly imposed. The South has also shown growing concern about the increased activity of the U.N. Security Council, the evident capacity of the United States to influence U.N. actions, and a decreased respect for national sovereignty. *See* chapters 2, 4, 6, and 14, *infra*.

A fourth major development has been the unleashing of ethnic hatred, intercommunal strife, and strident nationalism in many parts of Central and Eastern Europe as well as a disturbing increase in racism and xenophobia in Western Europe, North America, and elsewhere. During most of the post-World War II era, the Soviet Empire suppressed the ethnic divisions in Central and Eastern Europe, which have now resurfaced most visibly in the territory of the former Yugoslavia, Ngorno-Karabagh, Georgia, and the Baltic States. Those conflicts and tensions have led to greater numbers of refugees and internally displaced persons, placing increased burdens on countries that had previously welcomed or at least accepted people fleeing from repression. In Germany, France, and elsewhere in Western Europe foreigners are far less welcome and racist incidents have become more frequent. The United States has adopted new measures to restrict asylum seekers (such as requiring a work authorization waiting period) and has seen a rise in xenophobia. *See* chapter 14, *infra*.

A fifth significant development has been the establishment of hundreds of nongovernmental human rights organizations in many parts of the world where no popular forces for human rights had previously been able to operate. While there had been an increasing number of and membership in human rights organizations and institutions in Western Europe and North America during the 1970s, many such organizations were established in Latin America during the 1980s. In the late 1980s and early 1990s, many new human rights groups have also arisen in Asia and Africa. With the convening of the World Conference on Human Rights in June 1993, it was evident that a worldwide human rights movement had become a transnational constituency for mutual support when violations are threatened. *See* chapter 5, 8, 12-14, *infra.*

Not only must those principal developments be reflected in this second edition, but they require a rethinking of the entire subject.

How is the book organized?

The book is divided into six parts: (A) this preface and an introduction, (B) human rights treaties (chapters 2-4), (C) procedures for responding to gross violations (chapters 5-9), (D) the use of adjudicative remedies (chapters 10-14), (E) causes of human rights violations (chapter 15), and (F) a supplement with the principal human rights instruments and a research bibliography. Accordingly, the book begins with a brief introduction to the history of international human rights law and how human rights fit within the domain of international law. The rest of the book is organized around several problems or factual situations that can inspire discussion and opportunities for role playing in the classroom. Since chapter 1 deals with the historical development of international human rights law, chapter 2 focuses upon the acceptance of the principal source of human rights law through the ratification of treaties. Chapter 3 introduces the main obligation governments undertake in ratifying major human rights treaties, that is, periodic state reporting and review. Chapter 4 uses the procedural context of state reporting and review to consider the jurisprudential sources of human rights law and cultural differences; chapter 4 also summarizes another important treaty-based procedure available for individual complaints of violations. Having dealt with the principal treaty-based procedures, chapter 5 begins a new part of the book by explaining the mechanisms for responding to consistent patterns of gross violations under the U.N. Charter-based procedures of the U.N. Commission on Human Rights and its Sub-Commission. Chapters 6, 7, and 8 look at the ways the U.N. Security Council and General Assembly have handled human rights emergencies through humanitarian intervention and humanitarian law (chapter 6); criminal sanctions, civil remedies, and advisory services (chapter 7); and on-site observation (chapter 8). Chapter 9 examines the way individual governments can influence the human rights practices of other countries where gross violations are occurring. Chapter 10 considers the contribution of the Inter-American human rights system and other regional mechanisms for protecting human rights— principally through adjudicative remedies. Chapter 11 describes the European human rights structure and how its extensive jurisprudence might be useful to U.S. lawyers and decisionmakers. Chapter 12 explores the use of courts inside the U.S. to influence violations of human rights and humanitarian law in other countries. Chapter 13 considers how U.S. courts can provide relief for human rights violations inside the United States. Chapter 14 examines the use of refugee and asylum law to protect human rights; it also explores more fully the jurisprudential sources of human rights law and cultural relativism. Chapter 15 provides an insight into the extremely difficult question of what causes human rights violations and how such an inquiry can assist in improving techniques for preventing or responding to violations.

The supplement contains *Selected International Human Rights Instruments* and the *Bibliography for Research on International Human Rights Law*. The *Selected International Human Rights Instruments* contains several major international human rights treaties and other instruments. Readers may also find the bibliography in the supplement useful—particularly if research papers are assigned as part of the course.

The problems draw on five different aspects of the study of international human rights to provide a representative sampling of the subject: (1) various procedural postures, (2) diverse institutional settings, (3) a geographical spread of countries, (4) several substantive human rights norms, and (5) changing approaches to learning.

The problems touch on each of the major procedural channels for implementing international human rights: on-site observation, state reporting, individual complaints, emergency procedures, state v. state complaints, litigation in domestic courts, legislative hearings, fact-finding, public discourse and decision in international forums, the work of nongovernmental organizations, criminal prosecution, procedures for compensating victims, etc. The problems are set in most of the major international institutions, and include procedures of the U.N., the Human Rights Committee, the Inter-American Commission on and Court of Human Rights, the European human rights system, international criminal tribunals, and nongovernmental organizations. The principal focus is on factual contexts in the United States or efforts that can be mounted from this country, but chapters also relate to abuses in such diverse settings as Burma (Myanmar), Ghana, Iran, Rwanda, and the former Yugoslavia.

The problems deal with economic rights and the right to development (chapter 2); racial discrimination (chapter 3); torture and other ill-treatment (chapter 4); minority rights and the right to a free and fair election (chapter 5), human rights in armed conflict (chapter 6); crimes against humanity, indigenous rights, and impunity (chapter 7); arbitrary killing and disappearance (chapter 8), the relationship between foreign aid/foreign policy and human rights violations (chapter 9); abortion, the right to life, and discrimination against women (chapter 10); the right to be free from discrimination on the basis of sexual orientation (chapter 11); rape and violence against women (chapter 12); detention of alien children (chapter 13); domestic violence and rights of refugees (chapter 14); and causes of human rights violations (chapter 15).

The format also calls for diversity in teaching style. Some overview lectures will be appropriate. Other classes can involve advising a client, role-playing, the dialogue method, drafting, preparation of congressional testimony, advocacy in litigation, and many other skills.

All problems contain assigned readings and questions that may serve as a basis for student preparation and class discussion. Each chapter begins with an introduction, to establish the setting and suggest major questions for discussion. The chapters also contain materials with information students will need to deal with the problems. Further questions are occasionally posed to indicate the materials' relevance and to focus attention on particular issues.

The materials for the book were initially used for a weekly law school seminar of two hours during a semester. The book has also been used for courses meeting three hours per week during a semester. In any case, the chapters are designed so readers would expect to cover one chapter for each week of the course.

Some teachers may wish to assign chapters in an order different from their placement in the book. For example, teachers who have a civil rights and civil liberties orientation may want to start with chapters 12 and 13 on the use of U.S. courts to protect human rights outside and inside this country. Other teachers may find chapter 15 on the causes of human rights violations a challenging place to begin.

While the book was designed for use in law schools, the first edition has also been used in political science and international relations courses for undergraduate and graduate students.

ACKNOWLEDGMENTS

We trace the origins of this book to the first seminar on international human rights offered at the University of California Law School, Berkeley, during the summer of 1968. Thomas Buergenthal, Frank Newman, Egon Schwelb, and Karel Vasak co-taught the course. Several of the participants became law teachers—including Dinah Shelton, Jon van Dyke, and David Weissbrodt.

We are very grateful for the comments we received from teachers, who used the first edition and various drafts of the second or who gave useful advice, including Philip Alston (European University Institute, Florence), Connie de la Vega (San Francisco), Robert Drinan (Georgetown), Stephanie Farrior (Dickinson), Joan Fitzpatrick (University of Washington), Arvonne and Donald Fraser (Minnesota), Barbara Frey (Minnesota), Larry Garber (American), Robert Goldman (American), Claudio Grossman (American), Harold Koh (Yale), Virginia Leary (Buffalo), Bert Lockwood (Cincinnati), Samuel Murumba (Brooklyn), Diane Orentlicher (American), Steve Schnably (Miami), Dinah Shelton (Santa Clara/Notre Dame), Ronald Slye (Yale), John Weeks (Hamline), Burns Weston (Iowa), and others.

We wish to thank Deborah Ellingboe, Lee Friedman, Cathy Gillman, Lisa Gordon, Cynthia Maas, Wendy Mahling, and Paula Schwartzbauer, as well as other students and staff at the Universities of California and Minnesota who assisted with this edition.

We wish also to thank Penny Bailey, Katherine Brennan, Deborah Ellingboe, Carlos Figueroa, Sharla Flora, Mark Gardner, Ruth Gaube, Zara Kivi Kinnunen, Rachel Lager, Peter-Christian Olivo, Jennifer Prestholdt, Ramona Price, Rebecca Raliegh, Cynthia Reed, Sonia Rosen, Peter Schuman, Linda Sennholtz, Maria Treby, Ann Marie Trost, Deepika Udagama, and Jamie Wilson who assisted in production of the first edition and the 1994 supplement, from which materials were drawn for this edition.

We are specially indebted to Angie Hoeft and Kathryn Sikkink for their significant contribution to chapter 15 as well as Marci Hoffman, Lyonette Louis-Jacques, and Susan Snyder for their very fine work on the bibliographical supplement. Brian Kluge, Florence McKnight, and Mary Thacker did excellent secretarial work to make the book possible.

Frank Newman & David Weissbrodt
February 1996

Frank Newman died on February 18, 1996. He had just completed editing the last chapter of the revised edition of this book. It was a privilege to be Frank's student, co-author, and colleague. I hope that this book will be a tribute to him and to the two generations of human rights teachers, scholars, and advocates he enthusiastically encouraged and supported.

David Weissbrodt
May 1996

FRANK C. NEWMAN (1917-1996)

Frank C. Newman was born in Eureka, California, and spent his early days in South Pasadena. He attended Dartmouth College, where he played piano in the College's dance band. He studied law at the University of California at Berkeley (Boalt Hall), receiving his degree in 1941. During World War II he served as an officer in the U.S. Navy's Office of General Counsel and as an attorney with the Office of Price Administration. After the war he continued his legal studies at Columbia University and received his J.S.D. in 1953.

Newman joined the Boalt Hall faculty in 1946 and served as Dean from 1961 to 1966. He initially taught legislation and administrative law. His sabbatical year in 1967 was spent in Switzerland, where he became acquainted with the emerging field of international human rights law. He helped establish new U.N. procedures for responding to gross violations of human rights and drafted human rights legislation that formed the basis for President Jimmy Carter's human rights campaigns. He also initiated the first human rights law course at Berkeley.

In 1977 Frank Newman was appointed to the Supreme Court of California. During his five years on the bench, Newman wrote a number of important constitutional decisions on freedom of expression and the right to privacy. Some of his opinions also referred to international human rights law.

Newman's first book on human rights was written with Richard Lillich of Virginia in 1979. After retiring from the Court in 1982, Newman returned to teaching and scholarship at Boalt Hall, Golden Gate University, University of San Francisco, and universities in Asia and Europe. He also continued to play an active role in pursuing human rights protections at the United Nations and with the U.S. government.

CONTRIBUTIONS

The authors wish to express their thanks to copyright holders for graciously permitting us to include excerpts from their works (in alphabetical order by author):

Philip Alston, *Out of the Abyss: The Challenges Confronting the New U.N. Committee on Economic, Social and Cultural Rights,* 9 HUM. RTS. Q. 332 (1987). Copyright by Johns Hopkins University Press. Reprinted by permission.

Philip Alston & Gerard Quinn, *The Nature and Scope of States Parties' Obligations Under the International Covenant on Economic, Social and Cultural Rights,* 9 HUM. RTS. Q. 156 (1987). Copyright by Johns Hopkins University Press. Reprinted by permission.

Philip Alston, *U.S. Ratification of the Covenant on Economic, Social and Cultural Rights: The Need for an Entirely New Strategy,* 84 AM. J. INT'L L. 365 (1990). Reproduced with permission from 84 AJIL 365 (1990), © The American Society of International Law.

Americas Watch, Asia Watch, & Helsinki Watch, *Four Failures: A Report on the U.N. Special Rapporteurs on Human Rights in Chile, Guatemala, Iran and Poland* 15 (1986). Reprinted by permission.

Amnesty International, *Bosnia-Herzegovina: Gross Abuses of Basic Human Rights,* AI Index: EUR 63/01/92 (1992). Reprinted by permission.

Amnesty International, *Iran: Violations of Human Rights: Documents Sent by Amnesty International to the Government of the Islamic Republic of Iran* 45, AI Index: MDE 13/09/87 (1987). Reprinted by permission.

Amnesty International, *Peace-keeping and Human Rights,* AI Index: IRO 40/01/94 (1994). Reprinted by permission.

Amnesty International, *Rwanda and Burundi, A Call for Action by the International Community,* AI Index: AFR 02/24/95 (1995). Reprinted by permission.

Amnesty International, *United Nations: Oral Statement on Thematic Mechanisms,* AI Index: IOR 41/WU 02/1994 (1994). Reprinted by permission.

DEBORAH E. ANKER, ET AL., THE LAW OF ASYLUM IN THE UNITED STATES: A GUIDE TO ADMINISTRATIVE PRACTICE AND CASE LAW (2d ed. 1991). Copyright © 1991. American Immigration Law Foundation. Reprinted by permission.

Olufunmilayo B. Arewa & Susan O'Rourke, *Country-Specific Legislation and Human Rights: The Case of Peru,* 5 HARV. HUM. RTS. J. 183 (1992). Copyright © 1992 by the President and Fellows of Harvard College. Reprinted by permission.

Nancy D. Arnison, *The Law of Humanitarian Intervention, in* REFUGEES IN THE 1990s: NEW STRATEGIES FOR A RESTLESS WORLD 37 (Harlan Cleveland ed., 1993). Reprinted by permission.

Asia Watch & Minnesota Lawyers International Human Rights Committee, Human Rights in the Democratic People's Republic of Korea (North Korea) (1988). Reprinted by permission.

Peter R. Baehr, *Amnesty International and its Self-Imposed Limited Mandate*, 12 N.Q.H.R. 5 (1994). Reprinted by permission.

M. Cherif Bassiouni, *The Time Has Come for an International Criminal Court*, 1 IND. INT'L & COMP. L. REV. 1 (1991). Reprinted by permission.

Joyce Bednarski, *The Salem Witch-Scare Viewed Sociologically, in* WITCHCRAFT AND SORCERY 151 (Max Marwick ed., 1970). Abridged version of Joyce Bednarski, *The Salem Witch-Scare Viewed Sociologically,* 1968, original MS.

Harry A. Blackmun, *The Supreme Court and the Law of Nations: Owing a Decent Respect to the Opinions of Mankind,* ASIL Newsl. (American Soc'y of Int'l Law, Wash., D.C.), Mar.-May 1994, at 1 (1994). Reproduced with permission from *ASIL Newsletter* (March-May 1994), © 1994 by The American Society of International Law.

Marc Bossuyt, *The Development of Special Procedures of the United Nations Commission on Human Rights,* 6 H.R.L.J. 179 (1985). Reprinted with permission of the Human Rights Law Journal, N.P. Engel, Publisher.

Katherine Brennan, *The Influence of Cultural Relativism on International Human Rights Law,* 7 LAW & INEQ. J. 367 (1991). Reprinted by permission.

Thomas Buergenthal, *The Advisory Practice of the Inter-American Human Rights Court,* 79 AM. J. INT'L L. 1 (1985). Reproduced with permission from 79 AJIL 1 (1985), © The American Society of International Law.

Thomas Buergenthal, *The Inter-American Court of Human Rights,* 76 AM. J. INT'L L. 231 (1982). Reproduced with permission from 76 AJIL 231 (1982), © The American Society of International Law.

Thomas Buergenthal, *The United Nations Truth Commission for El Salvador*, 27 VAND. J. TRANSNAT'L L. 497 (1994). Reprinted by permission. THOMAS BUERGENTHAL, ROBERT NORRIS, & DINAH SHELTON, PROTECTING HUMAN RIGHTS IN THE AMERICAS: SELECTED PROBLEMS, 179 (1986). Reprinted by permission.

Kathryn Burke et al., *Application of International Human Rights Law in State and Federal Courts,* 18 TEX. INT'L L.J. 291 (1983). Reprinted by permission.

Burma (Myanmar), HUMAN RIGHTS WATCH WORLD REPORT 132 (1995). Reprinted by permission.

A. Rebecca Cardozo, *A Modern American Witch-Craze, in* WITCHCRAFT AND SORCERY 369 (Max Marwick ed., 1970). Reprinted by permission.

Barry E. Carter, *International Economic Sanctions: Improving the Haphazard U.S. Legal Regime,* reprinted from *California Law Review,* Vol. 75, No. 4, July 1987, pp. 1159-1278, by permission. © 1987 by California Law Review, Inc. There is a book with the same title by Professor Carter (1988: Cambridge University Press).

Hilary Charlesworth, Christine Chinkin & Shelley Wright, *Feminist Approaches to*

Philip P. Frickey, *Domesticating Federal Indian Law* (1996) (manuscript, on file with author). Reprinted by permission.

Deborah R. Gerstel & Adam G. Segall, *Conference Report: Human Rights in American Courts,* 1 AM. U. J. INT'L L. & POL'Y 137 (1986). Reprinted by permission.

Ruth Bader Ginsburg, *Some Thoughts on Autonomy and Equality in Relation to Roe v. Wade,* 63 N.C.L. REV. 375 (1985). Reprinted by permission.

Stan R. Gregory, Note, *Capital Punishment and Equal Protection: Constitutional Problems, Race and the Death Penalty,* 5 ST. THOMAS L. REV. 257 (1992). Reprinted by permission.

Françoise J. Hampson, *Violation of Fundamental Rights in the Former Yugoslavia: The Case for a War Crimes Tribunal,* OCCASIONAL PAPER 3, at 1 (The David Davies Memorial Inst. of Int'l Stud., 1993). Reprinted by permission.

S. FAROOQ A. HASSAN, THE ISLAMIC REPUBLIC: POLITICS, LAW AND ECONOMY (1984). Reprinted by permission.

Reinhard Heinisch, *Political Explanations of Basic Human Rights Performance,* Paper Prepared for the Annual American Political Science Association Meeting, New York City (1994). Reprinted by permission.

HUMAN RIGHTS WATCH & AMERICAN CIVIL LIBERTIES UNION, HUMAN RIGHTS VIOLATIONS IN THE UNITED STATES: A REPORT ON U.S. COMPLIANCE WITH THE INTERNATIONAL COVENANT ON CIVIL AND POLITICAL RIGHTS (1993). Reprinted by permission.

HUMAN RIGHTS WATCH & LAWYERS COMMITTEE FOR HUMAN RIGHTS, CRITIQUE: A REVIEW OF THE DEPARTMENT OF STATE'S COUNTRY REPORTS ON HUMAN RIGHTS PRACTICES FOR 1988 (1989). Reprinted by permission.

Menno Kamminga, *The Thematic Procedures of the U.N. Commission on Human Rights,* 34 NETH. INT'L L. REV. 299 (1987). Reprinted by permission.

NANCY KELLY, WOMEN REFUGEES PROJECT OF CAMBRIDGE AND SOMERVILLE LEGAL SERVICES AND HARVARD IMMIGRATION AND REFUGEE PROGRAM, GUIDELINES FOR WOMEN'S ASYLUM CLAIMS (1994). Reprinted by permission.

Harold H. Koh, *Transnational Public Law Litigation*, 100 YALE L.J. 2347 (1991). Reprinted by permission of The Yale Law Journal Company and Fred B. Rothman & Company from The Yale Law Journal, Vol. 100, pages 2347-2402.

LAWYERS COMMITTEE FOR HUMAN RIGHTS, CRITIQUE: REVIEW OF THE U.S. DEPARTMENT OF STATE'S COUNTRY REPORTS ON HUMAN RIGHTS PRACTICES 1991 (1992). Reprinted by permission.

LAWYERS COMMITTEE FOR HUMAN RIGHTS, HUMAN RIGHTS AND U.S. FOREIGN POLICY: BUREAUCRACY AND DIPLOMACY, 1988 PROJECT SERIES NO. 4 (1989). Reprinted by permission.

LAWYERS COMMITTEE FOR HUMAN RIGHTS, THE UNHCR AT 40: REFUGEE PROTECTION AT THE CROSSROADS (1991). Reprinted by permission.

Robert Jay Lifton, *Socialization to Killing, in* THE NAZI DOCTORS: MEDICAL KILLING AND THE PSYCHOLOGY OF GENOCIDE 195 (1986). Excerpts as submitted from THE NAZI

Ralph G. Steinhardt, *The United Nations and Refugees: 1945-1988, in* THE UNIVERSAL DECLARATION OF HUMAN RIGHTS 1948-1988: HUMAN RIGHTS, THE UNITED NATIONS AND AMNESTY INTERNATIONAL (1988). Reprinted by permission.

H.R. Trevor-Roper, *The European Witch-Craze, in* WITCHCRAFT AND SORCERY 121 (Max Marwick ed., 1970). Excerpts from H.R. Trevor-Roper, *Religion, Reformation and Social Change,* Macmillan, 1967, chapter 3, 'The European Witch-Craze of the Sixteenth and Seventeenth Centuries', pp.90-192.

UNITED NATIONS, THE BLUE HELMETS: A REVIEW OF UNITED NATIONS PEACE-KEEPING (2d ed. 1990). Reprinted by permission.

Edmundo Vargas, *Visits on the Spot: The Experience of the Inter-American Commission on Human Rights, in* INTERNATIONAL LAW AND FACT-FINDING IN THE FIELD OF HUMAN RIGHTS 137 (B. Ramcharan ed., 1982). Reprinted by permission.

David Weissbrodt & Paul W. Fraser, Book Review, 14 HUM. RTS. Q. 601 (1992) (reviewing National Commission on Truth and Reconciliation, Report of the Chilean National Commission on Truth and Reconciliation (1991)). Copyright by Johns Hopkins University Press. Reprinted by permission.

David Weissbrodt, *The Three "Theme" Special Rapporteurs of the UN Commission on Human Rights,* 80 AM. J. INT'L L. 685 (1986). Reproduced with permission from 80 AJIL 685 (1986), © The American Society of International Law.

Burns Weston, *U.S. Ratification of the International Covenant on Economic, Social and Cultural Rights: With or Without Qualifications, in* U.S. RATIFICATION OF THE HUMAN RIGHTS TREATIES: WITH OR WITHOUT RESERVATIONS? 27 (Richard B. Lillich ed., 1981). Edited for the International Human Rights Law Group by R. Lillich. Reprinted by permission of the International Human Rights Law Group.

Anne M. Williams, *United States Treaty Law, in* U.S. RATIFICATION OF THE INTERNATIONAL COVENANTS ON HUMAN RIGHTS 35 (Hurst Hannum & Dana D. Fischer ed., 1993). Reproduced with permission, © The American Society of International Law.

José Zalaquett, *Balancing Ethical Imperatives and Political Constraints: The Dilemma of New Democracies Confronting Past Human Rights Violations,* 43 HASTINGS L.J. 1425 (1992). © 1992 by University of California, Hastings College of the Law. Reprinted from HASTINGS LAW JOURNAL, Vol. 43, No. 6, pp. 1425, 1429-32, by permission.

CHAPTER 1

INTRODUCTION TO INTERNATIONAL HUMAN RIGHTS

A. **BRIEF HISTORICAL INTRODUCTION**   Page   2

    1. **Early Developments**   2

    2. **World War I and the League of Nations**   3

    3. **The Inter-War Years**   4

    4. **World War II and the Beginning of the Modern Human Rights Movement**   5

       a. The Nuremberg and Tokyo Tribunals, and Control Council Law No. 10   6

       b. The Creation of the United Nations: Dumbarton Oaks and San Francisco   7

       c. The United Nations and Multilateral Protection of Human Rights   7

          i. Codification   8

          ii. Development of Human Rights Law within the U.N. Structure; Charter-based human rights bodies   9

          iii. Development of Human Rights Law through six treaty-based human rights committees   13

B. **HUMAN RIGHTS IN INTERNATIONAL LAW**   13

    1. **The U.N. and International Human Rights Law**   13

       a. Human Rights under the U.N. Charter   13

       b. International Bill of Human Rights   14

       c. Other U.N. Treaties   14

       d. Related U.N. Instruments   15

    2. **Other Worldwide Treaties and Instruments**   16

    3. **Customary International Law**   18

    4. **Regional Organizations and Law-Making**   19

       a. European System   19

       b. Inter-American System   20

       c. Organization of African Unity   21

    5. **Domestic Implementation of Human Rights**   21

C. **CONCLUSION**   23

This chapter sketches human rights law in an historical context and considers how it fits within the domain of international law. Most of the topics mentioned here are considered at greater length in later chapters.

A. BRIEF HISTORICAL INTRODUCTION

This section examines the origins of human rights concepts and traces the evolution of human rights law, first, in the establishment of the U.N. and its human rights machineries, and, second, in several regional human rights structures.

1. Early Developments

Concepts of human rights can be traced to antiquity—*e.g.* the Ten Commandments, the Code of Hammurabi's approach to law as a means of preventing the strong from oppressing the weak, and the Rights of Athenian Citizens. Early efforts often came in response to atrocities of war and refugee problems. Religious, moral, and philosophical origins can be identified not only in biblical and classical history but also in Buddhism, Confucianism, Hinduism, Judaism, Shinto, and other faiths. Rights concepts also emerged in national documents such as the Magna Carta of 1215. Following the revolution of 1688 in England, Parliament enacted the Declaration of the Rights of Man (1689) to protect citizens from violations by the monarchy.

Starting with the Reformation and religious wars of the 16th and 17th centuries, peace treaties began to include clauses aimed at protecting religious minorities. A state's mistreatment of minorities also could provoke intervention by other states. Via its own military a state might punish or replace an abusive government. Intrusion on sovereignty was believed permissible when a government's treatment of its own subjects "shocked the conscience of humankind."

With the rise of nation states in the 17th century, however, classical international law rejected the notion of human rights and favored state sovereignty. Beginning in 1648, with the Treaty of Westphalia, states would agree to protect some individual rights; but the agreements typically reflected the view that individuals were mere objects of international law whose rights existed as a byproduct of states' sovereignty.

Developments in the 18th and 19th centuries reflect incremental steps to recognize individual rights and diminish the importance of sovereignty. They included, for instance, diplomatic efforts to protect rights of aliens abroad. Early enforcement of aliens' rights took the form of reprisal: a citizen with a grievance against a foreigner could seize the foreigner's goods. Reprisals in the 19th century were gradually replaced by negotiations between governments of aggrieved individuals and of the territory where the wrongs occurred. A state's right to intervene on citizens' behalf rested on two principles—the rights of aliens to be treated in accordance with "international standards of justice" and to be treated equally with nationals of the country wherein they resided.

During the 18th and early 19th centuries, governments took further measures to recognize inherent rights of the individual under national laws. The 1776 American Declaration of Independence proclaimed, "as self evident," the "unalienable rights" of all men to "life, liberty and the pursuit of happiness." Those rights were based on 18th century theories of natural law philosophers like Locke and Rousseau, who argued that fundamental rights were beyond state control and that individuals are autonomous in nature. Entering society, each individual's autonomy combined to form the people's sovereignty. Rights of self-government, including the right to choose and change the government, became the first inalienable right; but each individual retained some personal autonomy in the form of inviolable rights.

Belief in such rights produced the French Declaration of the Rights of Man and of the Citizen in 1789 and led federated states to insist on adding the Bill of Rights to the U.S. Constitution between 1789 and 1791. A number of nations followed the French and U.S. examples in their constitutions: the Netherlands (1798), Sweden (1809), Spain (1812), Norway (1814), Belgium (1831), Liberia (1847), Sardinia (1848), Denmark (1849), and Prussia (1850).

In addition, 19th century efforts to abolish the slave trade and protect workers' rights evidenced a growing international concern for human rights. The slave trade was first condemned by treaty in the Additional Articles to the Paris Peace Treaty of 1814 between France and Britain. In 1885 the General Act of the Berlin Conference on Central Africa affirmed that "trading in slaves is forbidden in conformity with the principles of international law."

To reduce casualties of war, the 1863 Geneva Conference founded the International Committee of the Red Cross (ICRC). The ICRC was instrumental in preparing initial drafts of what became the first multilateral treaty protecting victims of armed conflict: the 1864 Geneva Convention for the Amelioration of the Condition of the Wounded and Sick in Armies in the Field. It aimed to protect military hospitals and provided for equal medical treatment for combatants on both sides of a conflict. The fifteen Hague Conventions of 1899 and 1907 emphasized limits on methods and means of warfare. For example, they banned poisonous gases and other weapons calculated to cause unnecessary suffering.

2. World War I and the League of Nations

Further concern for human rights developed after World War I. President Wilson's 1918 address to Congress presented his "Fourteen Points program" to end war and create a world dedicated to justice and fair dealing. He called, *inter alia*, for rights to self-determination through newly drawn national borders and statehood for nationalities seeking autonomy. The Senate repudiated the program; Secretary of State Lansing criticized the principle of national self-determination; and other countries withheld support.

Nonetheless, during peace talks Wilson's influence was undeniable. The war ended after the Paris Peace Conference in 1919 produced the Versailles Treaty. The treaty created the League of Nations and the International Labour Organization. The Covenant of the League did not explicitly mention human rights, but the following excerpt notes pertinent concerns:

President Wilson had proposed at the Paris Peace Conference to include in the Covenant an obligation of all League members to respect religious freedom and to refrain from discrimination on the basis of religion (draft Article 21). The British delegate Lord Robert Cecil considered this not strong enough and proposed to give the Council of the League a right of intervention against states that would disturb world peace by a policy of religious intolerance. For President Wilson this proposal went too far. In the course of the discussion the Japanese delegate Baron Makino proposed to add to draft Article 21 an obligation of all member states to refrain from discrimination on the basis of race or nationality against foreigners who would be nationals of League members. The Japanese proposal obtained majority support at the commission level but was rejected by the United Kingdom and the United States. In this situation the American delegation also withdrew its own proposal concerning

religious freedom. As a result, no obligations regarding human rights were incorporated in the Covenant of the League.

Jan Herman Burgers, *The Road to San Francisco: The Revival of the Human Rights
Idea in the Twentieth Century*, 14 HUM. RTS. Q. 447, 449 (1992) (footnotes omitted).

The League of Nations did not ignore human rights, and "self-determination"
became a basic component of agreements that the League administered in countries
and regions including Austria, Bulgaria, Czechoslovakia, Greece, Hungary, Poland,
Rumania, Turkey, and Yugoslavia. Known as minorities-treaties, they purported to
guarantee protection of life and liberty for all inhabitants of the countries or regions
party to the treaties, as well as nationals' equality before the law and in the enjoyment of civil and political rights. The League also required Albania, Estonia, Finland,
Latvia, and Lithuania to pledge protection of minority rights before becoming members.

League protection extended only to nationals of countries and regions party to
the treaties. In 1922 the Assembly of the League expressed hope that countries and
regions not party to the treaties would even extend the same protection to their
nationals. Thrice, however, the Assembly rejected proposals to draft a new treaty,
applicable to all members, that would prescribe each member's obligations towards
minorities.

The League also created a mandate system to protect freedom of conscience
and religion in former colonial territories of Germany and Turkey. Governments
controlling non-self-governing mandated-territory promised to promote the material
and moral well-being, as well as the social progress, of inhabitants. The goal was
to prepare the colonies for independent statehood, and they would be ready for
autonomy when they could guarantee protection of religious, linguistic, and ethnic
minorities as well as rights of aliens and freedom of conscience. The territories
included Palestine and Transjordan administered by Britain, Syria and Lebanon
administered by France, the Cameroons and Togoland administered by Britain and
France, and Rwanda administered by Belgium. The mandate system subsequently
evolved into the U.N. trusteeship system. (See the U.N. Charter's Chapter XII.)

3. The Inter-War Years

Scholarly internationalists were responsible for much of the human rights development prior to and during the inter-war years. Alejandro Alvarez of Chile, for
example, was among the first to advocate international rights for individuals. Co-
founder of the American Institute of International Law, he submitted a 1917 draft
declaration on future international law that included a section on individual rights.

Another noted scholar, Russian jurist Andre Nicolayevitch Mandelstam, emigrated to Paris after the Bolsheviks came to power. In 1921 he persuaded the
International Law Institute to establish a commission to study protection of minorities and human rights generally. He served as rapporteur and, in 1929, persuaded
the commission to adopt a *Declaration of the International Rights of Man*. It included
a preamble and six articles. The first three defined a state's duty to recognize the
equal rights of each person within its territory to life, liberty, property, and religious
freedom; the remaining articles defined states' duties towards their citizens.

In an October 1939 letter to the Times, British novelist H.G. Wells spoke of rights
to food and medical care, education, access to information, freedom of discussion,
association, and worship, and also discussed rights to work, freedom of movement,
and protection from violence, compulsion, and intimidation. Wells and colleagues

eventually wrote a document known as the Sankey Declaration. Throughout 1940 and 1941 he promoted the Declaration at meetings and in various publications. In 1940 he published *The Rights of Man, or What Are We Fighting For?*, which contained the Declaration and his commentary. Reportedly 30,000 copies were circulated in Britain and it was translated into ten languages and offered for world syndication. He received reactions from numerous human rights pioneers, including Ghandi and Nehru as well as Jan Masaryk, Chaim Weizmann, and Jan Christiaan Smuts (who in 1945 drafted Articles 55 and 56 of the U.N. Charter). Burgers, *supra*, at 467.

While scholars and others were promoting human rights, events in Europe undermined their work. Most notorious was the rise of Adolf Hitler. He and the Nazis took control of Germany in 1933 and quickly began implementing their agenda of anti-Semitism. In May 1933, illustratively, the League of Nations heard a complaint from a German who claimed he had been fired from his job because of an April 1933 decree to discharge all Jewish civil servants, to exclude Jewish lawyers from legal practice and Jewish doctors from practice for health insurance funds, and to limit admission of Jewish students to German schools. Germany assured the League that it would protect the life and liberty of its citizen without discrimination, and assertedly that led the League to close the case. The League reconsidered Germany's anti-Semitic policies at the end of 1933, and Germany responded by withdrawing from the League.

4. World War II and the Beginning of the Modern Human Rights Movement

The modern human rights movement began during World War II. The war represented the ultimate extension of state sovereignty concepts that had dominated international relations for three centuries. The Nazis, seeking international preeminence, acted with unprecedented brutality and demonstrated that previous attempts to protect individuals from ravages of war were hopelessly inadequate. The war demonstrated that unfettered national sovereignty could not continue to exist without untold hardships and, ultimately, the danger of total destruction of human society.

Germany's tactics were based on speed, surprise, and terror. In the Battle of Britain bombers from Germany pounded English population centers and for 61 nights in October and November 1940 sought to destroy British cities. During the heaviest bombing, from July to December 1940, more than 23,000 civilians were killed and 32,000 injured. The German assault on the Soviet Union was even more brutal. That conflict raged for nearly four years and resulted in Soviet military casualties of 6.5 million. Including civilians, an estimated 20 million Soviets were killed during the attempted German conquest of the Soviet Union.

The most infamous brutality during the war was the Holocaust. The extermination of Jews began in the summer of 1941 when Reichsfuhrer Himmler gave the order for the liquidation of Russian Jews encountered during the invasion of the Soviet Union. In the course of the first year, the German army killed an estimated 90,000 Jews. Massive deportations of Jews to death camps began in 1942. From all over Europe they were brought by train; and, when the trains arrived, Germans unloaded the prisoners—primarily Jews but also gypsies, homosexuals, and assorted political dissidents—and stood them in lines for inspection by SS doctors. From trainloads of 1,500 people the doctors generally selected 1,200-1,300 for immediate extermination by firing squads or gas chambers. By the end of the war the Germans in the death camps had exterminated an estimated 6,000,000 Jews and nearly that many non-Jews. Another 2 million died outside the camps as a result of the German policy of extermination. This total amounted to nearly two-thirds of the population of pre-war European Jewry.

The war in Asia and the Pacific was brutal too. The Japanese occupation of China, for instance, proved to be as vicious as Germany's conquest and control of Eastern Europe. Among the worst atrocities was the occupation commonly known as the "Rape of Nanking." When the Japanese conquered the city an estimated 500,000 civilians resided there. During the first few months, when acts of brutality were at their highest, the army killed at least 43,000 civilians; and soldiers raped countless women. One observer of the Japanese occupation of Nanking estimated that at least 1,000 rapes took place each night.

In response to those and other horrors, world leaders spoke out in defense of peace and protection of human rights. On January 6, 1941, President Roosevelt, in his State of the Union address to Congress, outlined his vision of the future based on the "four essential human freedoms"; and that speech was one of many strong statements as to the crucial importance of human rights in the international community. On August 14, 1941, Roosevelt and Prime Minister Churchill set forth aims of the allied war effort in a Joint Declaration known as the Atlantic Charter. It stated general principles regarding the structure of the post-war world. Among the principles Article 6 stressed the importance of human rights:

> After the final destruction of Nazi tyranny they hope to see established a peace which will afford to all nations the means of dwelling in safety within their own boundaries, and which will afford assurance that all men in all the lands may live out their lives in freedom from fear and want.

During 1941 the Atlantic Charter received endorsements from all the European allies, which were followed by the "Declaration of the United Nations" on January 1, 1942, in which 26 nations pledged alliance in the war against the German/Italian/Japanese axis.

After the war political leaders and scholars continued to look to the protection of human rights as both an end and a means of helping to ensure international peace and security. The victors responded to the War and the Holocaust by forming the United Nations. Soon thereafter, intergovernmental organizations in Europe and the Americas also established their standards for the protection and promotion of human rights.

a. The Nuremberg and Tokyo Tribunals, and Control Council Law No. 10

During the war and the immediate post-war period, most human rights advocates focused on the prosecution of perpetrators of war-time abuses. The allied governments had received innumerable reports of German and Japanese atrocities and, in response, the allies vowed to punish the individuals responsible. The International Military Tribunal, which sat at Nuremberg, was created by the London Agreement of August 8, 1945. See *Selected International Human Rights Instruments* at 198 for the principal provisions of the London Agreement. The International Military Tribunal for the Far East was set up at Tokyo on January 19, 1946. Both tribunals served the immediate function of punishing the leading war criminals. The Control Council for Germany (Britain, France, the Soviet Union, and the United States) issued Control Council Law No. 10 in 1946 to expand the London Agreement and authorize the trial of thousands of cases not pursued by the International Tribunal at Nuremberg. See *Selected International Human Rights Instruments* at 198 for the text of Control Council Law No. 10 and chapter 7, *infra,* for much more on humanitarian law and war crimes tribunals.

b.   The Creation of the United Nations: Dumbarton Oaks and San Francisco

In 1944 Britain and the U.S. met with the Soviet Union (and later with China) at Dumbarton Oaks in Washington, D.C. to formulate a "proposal for the establishment of a general international organization." The initial plan proposed by the U.S. State Department included an international bill of rights that member governments of the organization would agree to accept. The proposal envisioned that the organization's structure would include means to help ensure protection of human rights.

By the time U.S. delegates reached Dumbarton Oaks they had decided, however, to include only a general statement on human rights. Even that approach met with resistance from the British and Soviet delegations. Eventually the U.S. persuaded Britain and the Soviets to include a brief statement demonstrating support for human rights in a draft U.N. Charter issued by the Conference on October 7, 1944. It mentioned human rights only once, stating that "the Organization should facilitate solutions of international economic, social and other humanitarian problems and promote respect for human rights and fundamental freedoms." *See* JACOB ROBINSON, HUMAN RIGHTS AND FUNDAMENTAL FREEDOMS IN THE CHARTER OF THE UNITED NATIONS: A COMMENTARY, From War to Peace Series No. 4, at 17 (1946).

After the Dumbarton Oaks Conference various nongovernmental organizations (NGOs) lobbied for a stronger and more specific statement on human rights. A proposal made by several Jewish groups advocated explicit reference in the Charter to protection of human rights. They proposed also that either the Security Council or the Economic and Social Council be empowered to establish human rights guidelines and take action to enforce compliance with the guidelines. *See* Robinson, *supra*, at 32. A coalition of 22 NGOs, including the National Council of Women, the National Board of the YWCA, the AFL-CIO, and the NAACP, similarly pressed for an active U.N. role to counter human rights abuses. *See* ROBINSON, *supra*, at 34; THOMAS M. FRANCK, NATION AGAINST NATION 9 (1985). They proposed that each member nation pledge to secure progressively, for its inhabitants, rights including life, liberty, and freedom of religion. In a strong statement on duties of a state with respect to its own citizens, the American Jewish Committee declared:

> [N]o plea of sovereignty shall ever again be allowed to permit any nation to deprive those within its borders of fundamental rights on the claim that they are matters of internal concern. It is now a matter of international concern to stamp out infractions of basic human rights. A.J.C. News Release, June 13, 1945.

In spite of the early difficulties, government representatives from North and South America arrived at the U.N. Conference in San Francisco in the Spring of 1945 with apparent intent to fulfill President Roosevelt's vision of the future and to incorporate human rights clauses in the U.N. Charter.

c.   The United Nations and Multilateral Protection of Human Rights

The U.N. Charter established human rights as a matter of international concern.

The U.N. set forth these rights in the International Bill of Human Rights, and began the process of internationalizing human rights.

i. Codification

The Charter's preamble states that the "Peoples of the United Nations" are determined "to reaffirm faith in fundamental human rights, in the dignity and worth of the human person, in the equal rights of men and women and of nations large and small." The Charter was promulgated in 1945 to maintain international peace and security; to develop friendly relations among nations based on respect for the principle of equal rights and self-determination; and to achieve international cooperation in solving international problems of an economic, social, cultural, or humanitarian character. According to Article 1 of the Charter, the U.N. seeks "[t]o achieve international cooperation . . . in promoting and encouraging respect for human rights and for fundamental freedoms[1] for all without distinction as to race, sex, language, or religion." Article 55 of the Charter requires that the United Nations shall promote "conditions of economic and social progress and development; solutions of international economic, social, health, and related problems; and international cultural and educational cooperation; and universal respect for . . . human rights . . . without discrimination. . . ." In accordance with Article 56 members pledge "joint and separate action . . . for the achievement of the purposes set forth in Article 55." *See Selected International Human Rights Instruments* at 13. In 1948 the U.N. General Assembly adopted the Universal Declaration of Human Rights, articulating the importance of rights which were placed at risk during the decade of the 1940s: the rights to life, liberty, and security of person; freedoms of expression, peaceful assembly, association, religious belief, and movement; and protections from slavery, arbitrary arrest, imprisonment without fair trial, and invasion of privacy. The Universal Declaration also contains provisions for economic, social, and cultural rights. The Declaration's force, however, is unfortunately limited by very broad exclusions and the omission of monitoring and enforcement provisions.

Following adoption of the Universal Declaration, the U.N. Commission on Human Rights drafted the International Bill of Human Rights, which contains the Covenant on Economic, Social and Cultural Rights, the Covenant on Civil and Political Rights, and an Optional Protocol to the Civil and Political Covenant. The three instruments were adopted by the General Assembly in 1966 and entered into force in 1976. The International Bill of Human Rights comprises the most authoritative and comprehensive prescription of human rights obligations that governments undertake in joining the U.N.

The two Covenants distinguish between implementation of civil and political rights—on the one hand—and economic, social, and cultural rights—on the other. Civil and political rights, such as freedom of expression and the right to be free from torture or arbitrary arrest, are immediately enforceable. Economic, social, and cultural rights are to be implemented "to the maximum of available resources, with a view to achieving progressively the full realization of the rights . . . by all appropriate means, including particularly the adoption of legislative measures." In other words,

---

[1] [Ed. note: Although it is unclear whether the drafters intended to draw a distinction between "human rights" and "fundamental freedoms," traditional constructions of "human rights" seem to encompass the concept of "fundamental freedoms." In this book, the authors will use only the inclusive phrase "human rights."]

governments that ratify the Covenants must immediately cease torturing their *stop tortin imed* citizens, but they are not immediately required to feed, clothe, and house them. These latter obligations are generally to be accomplished only progressively as resources permit. *But cf., e.g.,* Economic, Social and Cultural Covenant Art. 15(3) (a provision requiring immediate implementation). For more on the Covenants, see chapters 2 - 4, *infra*; for texts of the Covenants, see *Selected International Human Rights Instruments* at 26, 33.

In addition to the International Bill of Human Rights, the United Nations has drafted, promulgated, and now helps to implement more than 80 human rights treaties, declarations, and other instruments dealing with genocide, racial discrimination, discrimination against women, religious intolerance, the rights of disabled persons, the right to development, and the rights of the child. Human rights law has thus become the most codified domain of international law.

One early focus of the United Nations emphasized self-determination through the elimination of colonial domination of the developing world. The constitutions of most nations that have become established since the formation of the U.N. include reference to the rights that are protected by the Universal Declaration of Human Rights and the remainder of the International Bill of Human Rights.

ii.   Development of Human Rights Law within the U.N. Structure; Charter-based human rights bodies

Human rights are implemented by various bodies under the authority of the United Nations Charter, and by six expert committees created by specialized human rights treaties. These two kinds of U.N. human rights institutions—Charter-based bodies and expert treaty-based committees—are illustrated by the chart in the frontispiece of this book. Most of the Charter-based bodies are comprised of government representatives and will be discussed first.

Under the authority of the U.N. Charter, human rights activities are principally undertaken by the Security Council, General Assembly, Economic and Social Council, Commission on Human Rights, Sub-Commission on Prevention of Discrimination and Protection of Minorities, the Commission on the Status of Women, and the Commission on Crime Prevention and Criminal Justice.

The *Security Council* is the principal organ of the U.N., on which the Charter confers primary responsibility for the maintenance of international peace and security. The Council is composed of fifteen members, including five permanent members (China, France, Russia, the United Kingdom, and the United States) and ten non-permanent members elected for two-year terms by the General Assembly. Under Chapter VII of the Charter, the Security Council makes recommendations or decides what measures should be taken to maintain or restore international peace and security. Council measures may include humanitarian aid, economic sanctions, and military intervention. With the end of the Cold War, the Security Council's role has *end cold war* become more visible as the permanent members have more frequently agreed on action.

The Security Council's activism becomes apparent when contrasting the number of actions taken during and after the Cold War. During the Cold War, the Security Council considered on five occasions whether human rights violations qualified as threats to the peace so as to justify measures under Chapter VII. Furthermore, from 1945 to 1987, the Security Council established only 13 peacekeeping operations. The Council established more than twice that number of operations between 1987 and 1996. In addition, based principally upon Security Council decisions, on-site U.N. activities with a significant human rights dimension have taken place in more than a dozen countries since 1989, including Angola, Burundi, Cambodia, El Salvador, Guatemala, Haiti, Iraq, Mozambique, Namibia, Nicaragua, Rwanda, Somalia, South Africa, Western Sahara, and the former Yugoslavia. The role of the Security Council is discussed more fully in chapter 6, *infra.*

In 1993, the Security Council further contributed to the development of human rights law when it authorized an international tribunal to prosecute persons responsible for serious violations of international humanitarian law committed in the former Yugoslavia. Security Council resolution 827 of 25 May 1993. The judges on the tribunal and the prosecution have been selected, and the tribunal has begun to issue indictments and to undertake its first prosecutions. In addition, following widespread killings in Rwanda during April 1994, the Security Council established a second tribunal using the same basic approach as in the former Yugoslavia. The Yugoslav Tribunal is located in The Hague, Netherlands, and the Rwanda Tribunal was established in Tanzania. The tribunals and proposals for establishing a permanent international criminal court are discussed in greater detail in chapter 7, *infra.* The Security Council has also created a Compensation Commission to assist victims of the Iraqi invasion of Kuwait, which is discussed in chapter 11, *infra.*

The *General Assembly* is the most authoritative source of international declarations and conventions. Human rights issues are generally discussed in the Assembly's Third Committee. The General Assembly is also the most representative decision-making organ of the U.N., where all members of the U.N. are entitled to vote. Furthermore, the General Assembly elects the ten nonpermanent members of the Security Council, elects the members of the Economic and Social Council (ECOSOC), regularly reviews ECOSOC recommendations, and receives reports from several of the human rights treaty bodies.

The General Assembly usually meets from September through December and considers resolutions on several hundred matters. For example, in recent sessions the General Assembly passed resolutions lifting sanctions against South Africa, adopting the Declaration on the Elimination of Violence against Women, appealing for international emergency assistance to Azerbaijani refugees, proclaiming 1995 the United Nations Year for Tolerance, proclaiming the U.N. Decade for Human Rights Education, and creating the post of the High Commissioner for Human Rights.

Despite a longstanding tension between Charter Article 2(7)'s prohibition against invading states' domestic jurisdiction and human rights protections in Charter Articles 1, 55, and 56, the General Assembly has increasingly drawn attention to the situation of human rights in several countries. That tension was broken in the mid-1970s when the General Assembly and the Commission on Human Rights developed a consensus that a Working Group must be established to investigate human rights violations in Chile.[2] Following that period, almost all governments have accepted the propositions that human rights constitute a matter of international concern, and that U.N. investigations and hortatory resolutions do not, in any case, invade a country's domestic jurisdiction. Domestic jurisdiction arguments under Article 2(7) are occasionally raised by specific governments accused of violations, but are not met with broad approval. In fact, offending governments often

---

[2] *See* MENNO T. KAMMINGA, INTER-STATE ACCOUNTABILITY FOR VIOLATIONS OF HUMAN RIGHTS 95-99 (1990).

undermine their arguments by supporting condemnatory resolutions with regard to other offending countries. Since the mid-1970s the General Assembly and other U.N. organs have more regularly expressed concern and taken other actions with regard to country situations, including Afghanistan, Cambodia, Cuba, El Salvador, Estonia and Latvia, Haiti, Iraq, the Islamic Republic of Iran, Kosovo, Myanmar (Burma), Rwanda, Somalia, the Sudan, and the former Yugoslavia.

The *Economic and Social Council* (ECOSOC) oversees the Commission on Human Rights and the Commission on the Status of Women. The Council is also responsible for monitoring compliance with the Covenant on Economic, Social and Cultural Rights through the Committee on Economic, Social and Cultural Rights. In addition, it has issued such human rights standards as the Standard Minimum Rules for the Treatment of Prisoners and the Principles on the Effective Prevention of Extra-Legal, Arbitrary and Summary Executions. For more on ECOSOC procedures, see chapter 5, *infra*.

The *Commission on Human Rights*, composed of 53 member-states elected by the Economic and Social Council for three-year terms, meets annually in Geneva for six weeks in the spring. As its name suggests, the Commission is the most important U.N. body concerned with human rights. It may initiate studies and fact-finding missions, draft conventions and declarations for approval by higher bodies, discuss specific human rights violations in public or private sessions, and initiate suggestions for improving the U.N.'s human rights procedures. Nongovernmental organizations (NGOs) such as Amnesty International, Human Rights Watch, the International Commission of Jurists, the Lawyers Committee for Human Rights, and the International League for Human Rights are allowed to express their concerns to the Commission during the six-week session. The Commission has established three principal approaches to serious and widespread violations of human rights: establishment of country rapporteurs and working groups under the authority of ECOSOC resolution 1235, consideration of country situations under the confidential procedure of ECOSOC resolution 1503, and review through thematic procedures relating to forced disappearances, summary or arbitrary executions, torture, religious intolerance, mercenaries, arbitrary detention, internally displaced persons, violence against women, etc. Those procedures are explored in chapter 5, *infra*; see also *Selected International Human Rights Instruments* at 142-45 for texts of ECOSOC resolutions 1235 and 1503.

The *Sub-Commission on Prevention of Discrimination and Protection of Minorities* is unusual because it is composed of 26 persons elected by the Commission, for four-year terms, in their individual capacities rather than as governmental representatives. The Sub-Commission considers information regarding human rights violations and reports its findings to the U.N. Commission on Human Rights. The Sub-Commission often is the source of resolutions and ideas that are considered and adopted by the Commission. With the assistance of the U.N. Centre for Human Rights, members of the Sub-Commission also prepare studies on human rights problems. Representatives of NGOs actively participate in the Sub-Commission's sessions.

The *Commission on the Status of Women* was established by the Economic and Social Council in 1946. The Commission is composed of representatives from 45 United Nations member states, elected by the Council for four-year terms. Its functions are to prepare recommendations and reports to the Council on promoting women's rights in political, economic, civil, social, and educational fields. The Commission may also make recommendations to the Council on problems in the field of women's rights that require immediate attention. The Commission has a procedure for receiving confidential communications on human rights violations, but that procedure has not been well-publicized, is not often invoked, and has not been particularly efficacious. The Commission's objects are to implement the principle that men and women shall have equal rights, to develop proposals that give effect to its recommendations, and to adopt its own resolutions and decisions. The Inter-American Commission of Women and the Commission on the Status of Arab Women submit reports to each session of the Commission on the Status of Women.

The U.N.'s crime prevention and criminal justice program was, until 1992, administered by the Committee on Crime Prevention and Control, a subsidiary organ of ECOSOC. The Committee, composed of twenty-seven experts, planned the quinquennial Congresses on the Prevention of Crime and the Treatment of Offenders, submitted proposals, and implemented the Congresses' recommendations. The Committee's primary roles were to foster the exchange of information concerning criminal justice and to generate standards against which state performance may be judged. *See* ROGER S. CLARK, THE UNITED NATIONS CRIME PREVENTION AND CRIMINAL JUSTICE PROGRAM 19-23 (1994).

In 1992 ECOSOC, pursuant to a request by the General Assembly, disbanded the Committee and replaced it with the *Commission on Crime Prevention and Criminal Justice*. The Commission is composed of forty government representatives rather than the independent experts that served on the Committee. The Commission's functions are similar to those of the Committee, with the additional responsibility of mobilizing U.N. member states' support for the crime prevention and criminal justice program. *See* Clark, *supra*, at 4, 58-62.

There are many other U.N. organs whose expertise touches on the protection of human rights. In 1993, for example, the General Assembly voted to create the post of the High Commissioner for Human Rights. According to the General Assembly mandate, the High Commissioner for Human Rights has principal responsibility for U.N. human rights activities, including "[p]romoting and protecting the effective enjoyment by all of all civil, cultural, economic, political and social rights." High Commissioner for the Promotion and Protection of All Human Rights, G.A. res. 48/141, 48 U.N. GAOR (No. 49) at 411, U.N. Doc. A/48/49 (1993).

Other U.N. organs that work to protect human rights include the International Labour Organization (ILO), the oldest intergovernmental organization, which has promulgated 183 recommendations and 176 conventions, including several treaties relating to human rights (*e.g.*, on freedom of association, forced labor, and indigenous rights). The ILO's Committee on Freedom of Association adjudicates complaints by trade unions that their rights have been infringed, and its Committee of Experts reviews periodic states reports under the ILO standard-setting treaties. The ILO also contributes to the deliberations of the treaty bodies, such as the Human Rights Committee. The U.N. Educational, Scientific and Cultural Organization (UNESCO) has promulgated a few treaties related to human rights (*e.g.*, as to discrimination in education). UNESCO has also established a Committee on Conventions and Recommendations, which examines allegations of human rights violations against artists, authors, scientists, and teachers. The U.N. High Commissioner for Refugees repatriates, resettles, and assists refugees as well as other displaced persons fleeing political persecution, war, poverty, and famine. The Food and Agriculture Organization (FAO), the United Nations Children's Fund (UNICEF), and World Health Organization (WHO) also take actions relating to human rights within their respective fields of action. Indeed, the International Monetary Fund, the World Bank, and other intergovernmental organizations also make decisions which have substantial human rights consequences.

iii. Development of Human Rights Law through six treaty-based human rights committees

Increasingly, the six monitoring bodies established under specific human rights treaties are playing a significant role. These expert bodies include the Human Rights Committee, which considers states reports under the International Covenant on Civil and Political Rights and adjudicates individual cases under the Optional Protocol to the Civil and Political Covenant. The five other treaty bodies oversee the implementation of multilateral conventions in their respective domains: the Committee on the Elimination of All Forms of Racial Discrimination, the Committee on the Elimination of Discrimination against Women, the Committee against Torture, the Committee on the Rights of the Child, and the Committee on Economic, Social and Cultural Rights. These expert bodies are discussed below in this chapter at B.1.b., *infra*, and in chapters 2-4, *infra*.

B. HUMAN RIGHTS IN INTERNATIONAL LAW

Having placed international human rights in its historical context, there remains the task of introducing human rights as an aspect of international law.

1. The U.N. and International Human Rights Law

Treaties constitute the primary sources of international human rights law. The United Nations Charter is both the most prominent treaty and contains seminal human rights provisions. Charter Article 103 establishes the primacy of the U.N. Charter: "In the event of a conflict between the obligations of the Members of the United Nations under the present Charter and their obligations under any other international agreement, their obligations under the present Charter shall prevail." Art. 103, U.N. Charter, 59 Stat. 1031, T.S. 993, 3 Bevans 1153, *entered into force* Oct. 24, 1945.

a. Human Rights under the U.N. Charter

The Charter identifies the promotion and encouragement of respect for human rights as among the principal objectives of the United Nations:

Article 1:   The Purposes of the United Nations are: . . . To achieve international cooperation in solving international problems of an economic, social, cultural, or humanitarian character, and in promoting and encouraging respect for human rights and for fundamental freedoms for all without distinction as to race, sex, language or religion . . . .

[handwritten margin notes: *broad* / *there are HR + we will respect*]

Articles 55 and 56 of the Charter establish the primary human rights obligations of all 185 U.N. member states:

Article 55:   With a view to the creation of conditions of stability and well-being which are necessary for peaceful and friendly relations among nations based on respect for the principle of equal rights and self-determination of peoples, the United Nations shall promote:

[handwritten margin notes: *again vague but building blocks.*]

a. higher standards of living, full employment, and conditions of economic and social progress and development;

b. solutions of international economic, social, health, and related problems; and international cultural and educational cooperation; and

c. universal respect for, and observance of, human rights and fundamental freedoms for all without distinction as to race, sex, language, or religion.

Article 56:   All members pledge themselves to take joint and separate action in cooperation with the Organization for the achievement of the purposes set forth in Article 55.

b. International Bill of Human Rights

The United Nations General Assembly defined the human rights obligations of member states in the International Bill of Human Rights, which is comprised of:

* Universal Declaration of Human Rights — *in sup. incorp into UN charter*
* International Covenant on Economic, Social and Cultural Rights
* International Covenant on Civil and Political Rights
* Optional Protocol to the International Covenant on Civil and Political Rights

US signed but not ratified

The Covenant on Civil and Political Rights establishes an international minimum standard of conduct for all participating governments, *ensuring* the rights of self-determination; legal redress; equality; life; liberty; freedom of movement; fair, public, and speedy trial of criminal charges; privacy; freedom of expression, thought, conscience, and religion; peaceful assembly; freedom of association (including trade union rights); family; and participation in public affairs; but *forbidding* torture; "cruel, inhuman or degrading treatment or punishment"; slavery; arbitrary arrest; double jeopardy; and imprisonment for debt.

By ratifying the Covenant on Economic, Social and Cultural Rights, a government agrees to take steps for the progressive realization of the following rights to the full extent of its available resources: the right to gain a living by work; to have safe and healthy working conditions; to enjoy trade union rights; to receive social security; to have protection for the family; to possess adequate housing and clothing; to be free from hunger; to receive health care; to obtain free public education; and to participate in cultural life, creative activity, and scientific research. *See Selected International Human Rights Instruments* at 26-46.

c. Other U.N. Treaties

The U.N. has further codified and more specifically defined international human rights law in a number of treaties relating to various subjects initially identified by the International Bill of Human Rights. Treaties create legal obligations for those nations that are party to them, but are generally not binding on the international community as a whole. *But cf.* U.N. Charter Art. 2(6). Treaties may, however, create general international law when such agreements are intended for adherence by states generally, are in fact widely accepted, and restate general principles of law. *See* RESTATEMENT OF THE LAW (THIRD) THE FOREIGN RELATIONS LAW OF THE UNITED STATES § 102(3) (1987 & Supp. 1988) [hereinafter RESTATEMENT].

Once drafted by the United Nations, treaties are adopted by General Assembly and are then opened for ratification or other forms of acceptance by governments, often including those governments not involved in the drafting process. For example, the United States participated in drafting and adopting the International Covenant on Civil and Political Rights, which the U.S. ratified in 1992, albeit with several significant reservations as to its application. The U.S. also participated in drafting and adopting, but has only signed and has not yet ratified the International Covenant on Economic, Social and Cultural Rights.

Aside from the Charter and the International Bill of Human Rights, the most significant U.N. treaties that have received enough ratifications or accessions to enter into force include (in order of their date of entry into force): *more specific treaties — easier to enforce*

* Convention on the Prevention and Punishment of the Crime of Genocide
* Convention relating to the Status of Refugees
* Protocol relating to the Status of Refugees
* International Convention on the Elimination of All Forms of Racial Discrimination
* Convention on the Elimination of All Forms of Discrimination Against Women
* Convention Against Torture and Other Cruel, Inhuman or Degrading Treatment or Punishment
* Convention on the Rights of the Child
* Second Optional Protocol to the International Covenant on Civil and Political Rights, aiming at the abolition of the death penalty

wide support — many countries sign.

Treaties so drafted are interpreted as international legislation. The most authoritative collection of rules concerning the interpretation of treaties is the Vienna Convention on the Law of Treaties, 1155 U.N.T.S. 331, T.S. No. 58 (1980), 8 I.L.M. 679 (1979), *entered into force* January 27, 1980. The principal sources of interpretation include the terms of the treaty, agreements or instruments made in connection with conclusion of the treaty, subsequent agreements between the parties, subsequent practice in the application of the treaty, relevant rules of international law applicable to relations between the parties, and any special meaning intended by the parties. *Id.* Art 31. Article 32 of the Vienna Convention provides that supplementary means of interpretation include preparatory work (*traveaux preparatoires*), which is similar to legislative history for statutes.

Pursuant to six of the principal human rights treaties, committees have been established to provide authoritative interpretive materials. Those six treaty bodies are the Human Rights Committee (under the Civil and Political Covenant); the Committee on Economic, Social and Cultural Rights; the Committee on the Elimination of Racial Discrimination; the Committee on the Elimination of Discrimination Against Women; the Committee Against Torture; and the Committee on the Rights of the Child. The six treaty bodies regularly review reports by States parties as to their compliance with the respective treaties and most issue general comments and recommendations that reflect their experience in reviewing the States reports and thus provide authoritative interpretations of the treaty provisions. The treaty bodies also issue conclusions as to each State report that provide useful interpretive indications. Further, three of the treaty bodies—the Human Rights Committee, the Committee on the Elimination of Racial Discrimination, and the Committee Against Torture—may receive communications complaining about violations of those treaties and thus issue adjudicative decisions interpreting and applying treaty provisions.

d. Related U.N. Instruments

In addition to treaties, the United Nations has promulgated dozens of declarations, codes, rules, guidelines, principles, resolutions, and other instruments that interpret the general human rights obligations of member states under Articles 55 and 56 of the U.N. Charter and may reflect customary international law. The Universal Declaration of Human Rights is the most prominent of those human rights instruments, which not only provides an authoritative, comprehensive, and nearly contemporaneous interpretation of the human rights obligations under the U.N. Charter, but also has provisions which have been recognized as reflective of customary international law. Among the other prominent human rights instruments are:

* Standard Minimum Rules for the Treatment of Prisoners
* Declaration on the Rights of Disabled Persons
* Code of Conduct for Law Enforcement Officials
* Declaration on the Right to Development
* Body of Principles for the Protection of All Persons under Any Form of Detention or Imprisonment
* Principles on the Effective Prevention and Investigation of Extra-Legal, Arbitrary and Summary Executions
* Declaration on the Protection of All Persons from Enforced Disappearances
* Declaration on the Rights of Persons Belonging to National or Ethnic, Religious or Linguistic Minorities
* Declaration on the Elimination of Violence Against Women
* Beijing Declaration and Platform of Action

2.   Other Worldwide Treaties and Instruments

The United Nations is not the only global organization which has issued or facilitated the issuance of worldwide human rights standards. Others include U.N. specialized agencies (such as the International Labour Organization (ILO) and the U.N. Educational, Scientific, and Cultural Organization (UNESCO)) as well as the International Committee of the Red Cross.

As the oldest intergovernmental organization, the International Labour Organization (ILO) has promulgated 183 recommendations and 176 conventions, including several treaties relating to human rights. For example, the ILO has promulgated the following treaties:

* Convention concerning Forced or Compulsory Labour (ILO No. 29)
* Convention concerning Freedom of Association and Protection of the Right to Organise (ILO No. 87)
* Convention concerning the Application of the Principles of the Right to Organise and to Bargain Collectively (ILO No. 98)
* Convention concerning Equal Remuneration for Men and Women Workers for Work of Equal Value (ILO No. 100)
* Abolition of Forced Labour Convention (ILO No. 105)
* Discrimination (Employment and Occupation) Convention (ILO No. 111)
* Convention concerning the Promotion of Collective Bargaining (ILO No. 154)
* Forced Labour Convention (ILO No. 155)
* Convention concerning Indigenous and Tribal Peoples in Independent Countries (ILO No. 169)

Those treaties are principally interpreted by the ILO's Committee on Freedom of Association, which adjudicates complaints by trade unions that their rights have been infringed, and the ILO Committee of Experts, which reviews periodic states reports under the ILO standard-setting treaties.

The U.N. Educational, Scientific and Cultural Organization (UNESCO) has promulgated several treaties related to human rights, for example, the Convention against Discrimination in Education, 429 U.N.T.S. 93, *entered into force* May 22, 1962.

The International Committee of the Red Cross has since the mid-19th century convened governmental conferences to draft treaties protecting soldiers and sailors wounded in armed conflict, prisoners of war, and civilians in times of war. These treaties constitute the core of international humanitarian law which is designed to limit human rights violations during periods of international and non-international armed conflict. In the context of armed conflicts, international humanitarian law provides a stronger and far more detailed basis for the protection of human rights than the International Bill of Human Rights and other U.N. human rights instruments.

The principal multilateral treaties that legislate international humanitarian law—the four Geneva Conventions of 1949—have been ratified by more governments than other human rights treaties aside from the U.N. Charter and the Convention on the Rights of the Child. The four Geneva Conventions are:

* Geneva Convention for the Amelioration of the Condition of the Wounded and Sick in Armed Forces in the Field
* Geneva Convention for the Amelioration of the Condition of Wounded, Sick and Shipwrecked Members of Armed Forces at Sea
* Geneva Convention Relative to the Treatment of Prisoners of War
* Geneva Convention Relative to the Protection of Civilian Persons in Time of War

The two Geneva Protocols of 1977 extend and make more specific the protections of the 1949 Geneva Conventions to international and non-international armed conflicts:

* Protocol Additional to the Geneva Conventions of 12 August 1949 Relating to the Protection of Victims of International Armed Conflicts (Protocol I)
* Protocol Additional to the Geneva Conventions of 12 August 1949, and Relating to the Protection of Victims of Non-International Armed Conflicts (Protocol II)

Many provisions of the four Geneva Conventions, the two Protocols, and the Hague Conventions of 1899 and 1907 are broadly accepted as restating customary international humanitarian law applicable to all countries.[3] Humanitarian law applies specifically to emergency situations; international human rights law permits significant derogations during these same periods.[4]

Since there are inconsistencies and gaps between the protections afforded by various human rights and humanitarian law instruments, as well as by national and local laws, the individual should be entitled to the most protective provisions of applicable international, national, or local laws. Accordingly, if humanitarian law affords better rights protections than human rights law, humanitarian law should

---

[3] *See, e.g.,* SALLY MALLISON & WILLIAM MALLISON, ARMED CONFLICT IN LEBANON 1982: HUMANITARIAN LAW IN A REAL WORLD SETTING 67-68 (1983).

[4] *See* Joan Hartman, *Derogations from Human Rights Treaties in Public Emergencies*, 22 HARV. INT'L L.J. 1 (1981).

be applied—and *vice versa*.[5] Humanitarian law is treated more fully in chapters 6, 7, and 12, *infra*.

3. Customary International Law

International custom is a source of international law where it is evidence of a general practice accepted as law. Only widespread, rather than unanimous, acquiescence is needed, and acquiescence may occur in a short period of time. IAN BROWNLIE, PRINCIPLES OF PUBLIC INTERNATIONAL LAW 6-7 (3d ed. 1979); RESTATEMENT § 102, comment b (1987) ("there is no precise formula to indicate how widespread a practice must be, but it should reflect wide acceptance among the states particularly involved in the relevant activity"). Often there is disagreement as to precisely when a rule has ripened into a norm, but consensus that a norm in fact has evolved does emerge. For example, the U.S. Court of Appeals in *Filartiga v. Pena-Irala*, 630 F.2d 876 (2d. Cir. 1980), determined that the right to be free from torture had become customary international law.

Governmental practice in negotiating and approving international instruments has been accorded an increasingly important role in the development of customary law. In the human rights field widespread acceptance of treaties, declarations, resolutions, and other instruments arguably has become more significant than actual practice in creating binding law. RESTATEMENT § 702 (1987). Authority for that development seems to inhere in Article 38(1)(c) of the International Court's Statute, which directs the Court to apply "the general principles of law recognized by civilized nations."

A customary norm binds all governments, including those that have not recognized the norm, so long as they have not expressly and persistently objected to its development. RESTATEMENT § 102, comment d; *Military and Paramilitary Activities in and Against Nicaragua* (Nicar. v. U.S.), 1986 I.C.J. 14 (Judgment of June 27); *North Sea Continental Shelf Cases* (W. Ger. v. Den.; W. Ger. v. Neth.), 1969 I.C.J. 3, 41-44 (1969).

The Restatement of the Foreign Relations Law of the United States lists several prohibitions as giving rise to customary international law: (a) genocide; (b) slavery or slave trade; (c) the murder or causing the disappearance of individuals; (d) torture or other cruel, inhuman or degrading treatment or punishment; (e) prolonged arbitrary detention; (f) systematic racial discrimination; or (g) consistent patterns of gross violations of internationally recognized human rights.[6]

A *jus cogens* norm is a peremptory rule of international law that prevails over any conflicting international rule or agreement.[7] A *jus cogens* norm permits no derogation, and can be modified only by a subsequent international law norm of the same character.[8]

The concept of *jus cogens* is of relatively recent origin, although it is incorporated in the Vienna Convention on the Law of Treaties.[9] Its content is disputed, and thus far, only the UN Charter's principles prohibiting the use of force are generally

---

[5] *See* Frank Newman, *Civil and Political Rights*, in THE INTERNATIONAL DIMENSIONS OF HUMAN RIGHTS 135, 161 (Karel Vasak & Philip Alston eds., 1982).

[6] 1 RESTATEMENT § 702 (1987).

[7] 1 RESTATEMENT § 102 comment k (1987).

[8] *Id.*

[9] Vienna Convention on the Law of Treaties, *supra*, Arts. 53, 64.

agreed to be *jus cogens*.[10] The International Court of Justice appeared to find that a peremptory norm of international law establishes the inviolability of envoys and embassies in its judgment concerning Iranian treatment of the U.S. diplomatic and consular staff in Tehran.[11] Commentators have suggested that prohibitions against genocide, slavery, racial discrimination, and other gross human rights violations also have acquired *jus cogens* status.[12]

4. Regional Organizations and Law-Making

In addition to the U.N. mechanisms for implementing human rights, regional structures now operate in Europe, the Americas, and Africa. The rights protected by these structures derive from, and are similar to, those of the International Bill of Human Rights, but each of the structures has developed unique approaches to seeking assurance that the rights are put into practice.

The Organization for Security and Cooperation in Europe, which arose from the 1975 Helsinki Accords and follow-up efforts, now has 53 members from the U.S. and Canada on the West to Russia and Kazakhstan in the East. It has created the office of High Commissioner for Minorities and has begun to employ a staff in Prague and Warsaw to encourage democracy and deal with ethnic strife and other serious human rights problems in Central Europe. Relatively little has been done, however, to establish a regional human rights system in Asia. Regional systems are discussed generally in chapters 10 and 11, *infra*.

a. European System

The European system is the most fully developed of the regional human rights structures. In 1950 the Council of Europe promulgated the European Convention for the Protection of Human Rights and Fundamental Freedoms, which entered into force in 1953. The Convention created two principal bodies for human rights implementation: the European Commission of Human Rights and the European Court of Human Rights. Parties to the Convention may refer alleged violations by other states to the Commission. They also may accept the competence of the Commission to hear applications brought by individuals. The Commission usually will refer, to the Court, cases that Commission members believe raise important questions for interpretation of the Convention. The Council of Europe has promulgated 11 protocols to expand the protections offered under the European Convention. The 11th protocol (1994) will, when fully implemented, create a unified European Court of Human Rights to replace the current Commission-and-Court procedure.

---

[10] 1 RESTATEMENT § 102 reporter's note 6.

[11] *See United States Diplomatic and Consular Staff in Tehran* (U.S. v. Iran), 1980 I.C.J. 41 (Judgment of May 24). "Whatever extenuation of the responsibility to be attached to the conduct of the Iranian authorities may be found in the offence felt by them because of the admission of the Shah to the United States could not affect the imperative character of the legal obligations incumbent upon the Iranian Government which is not altered by a state of diplomatic tension between the two countries." *See also id.* at 42 (citing *United States Diplomatic and Consular Staff in Tehran* (U.S. v. Iran) 1979 I.C.J. 19 (Interim Order of Dec. 15)): "There is no more fundamental prerequisite for the conduct of relations between States than the inviolability of diplomatic envoys and embassies, so that throughout history nations of all creeds and cultures have observed reciprocal obligations for that purpose."

[12] 1 RESTATEMENT § 102 reporter's note 6 (1987). *See also* Ian Brownlie, Principles of Public International Law at 513 (1979).

The European system has compiled impressive jurisprudence and has achieved a high degree of compliance with its decisions.

In addition to the European Convention, there are several other European human rights treaties, including the European Social Charter, the Additional Protocol to the European Social Charter, and the European Convention for the Prevention of Torture and Inhuman or Degrading Treatment or Punishment. There also are several relevant European institutions with a human rights role, including the European Committee for the Prevention of Torture, the European Court of Justice in Brussels, and the European Parliament. For more on the European system, see chapter 11, *infra*.

b. Inter-American System

The Inter-American system for protecting human rights has two principal legal sources: the American Declaration of the Rights and Duties of Man, an instrument adopted by the Organization of American States (OAS) along with its Charter in 1948, and the American Convention on Human Rights, adopted by the OAS in 1969, which came into force in 1978. The OAS created the Inter-American Commission on Human Rights in 1959, but until 1970 the Commission derived its existence only from OAS General Assembly resolutions of uncertain legal force. In 1970, revisions in the OAS Charter transformed the Inter-American Commission into one of the principal organs of the OAS. The Inter-American Commission and the Inter-American Court of Human Rights are the bodies charged with the implementation of the American Convention.

The Commission's main functions are to promote respect for, and to defend, human rights. In fulfilling its functions, the Inter-American Commission on Human Rights has done impressive fact-finding work on grave country situations and has issued many individual decisions, but has had difficulty in achieving compliance.

The Commission initiates country studies if it receives a large number of complaints charging a particular government with serious and widespread human rights violations. The Commission prepared its first country reports on Cuba, Haiti, and the Dominican Republic in the 1960s. Although the governments of Cuba and Haiti refused to admit the Commission into their countries, the Dominican Republic allowed the Commission to visit and thus became the subject of the Commission's first on-site investigation. Since then, the Commission has conducted on-site investigations in a number of other OAS countries, including Argentina, Bolivia, Chile, Colombia, El Salvador, Guatemala, Haiti, Honduras, Nicaragua, Panama, Paraguay, Suriname, and Uruguay.

The Commission can also receive individual petitions alleging human rights violations by OAS member-states, whether or not the state in question has ratified the American Convention. The Commission determines admissibility, engages in fact-finding, and attempts to arrange friendly settlements. The Commission may also refer cases involving state parties to the American Convention to the Inter-American Court of Human Rights. A state party to the Convention must specifically recognize the Court's competence to interpret the Convention before the Court may hear a complaint against that state. The Court has handled a few individual cases and has issued several significant advisory opinions. In addition to the OAS Charter, the American Declaration, and the American Convention, the OAS has promulgated several other treaties and protocols relating to economic, social, and cultural rights;

the death penalty; disappearances; torture, and violence against women. For more on the Inter-American system, see chapter 10, *infra*.

c.   Organization of African Unity

The Organization of African Unity (OAU) is a regional intergovernmental organization that brings together governments of the African continent and its surrounding islands. The Charter of the OAU was adopted in 1963 and reaffirms adherence to the principles of the U.N. Charter and the Universal Declaration of Human Rights. In 1981 the OAU adopted its human rights treaty, the African Charter on Human and Peoples' Rights. The African Charter entered into force in 1986. The African Charter creates the African Commission on Human and Peoples' Rights, the body charged with supervising implementation of the African Charter. The OAU has also promulgated the 1969 Convention governing the specific aspects of refugee problems in Africa, which contains a broader definition of refugee than the U.N. Refugee Convention and Protocol, as well as the 1990 African Charter on the Rights and Welfare of the Child.

5.   Domestic Implementation of Human Rights

From the perspective of impact on the individual, the most important means of implementing international law is through the national legislation, courts, and administrative agencies.

In the United States, the best example of a statute which incorporates international human rights law is the Refugee Act of 1980, which was codified in Immigration and Nationality Act § 101(a)(42), the definition of refugee from the Convention and Protocol relating to Refugees. In interpeting § 101(a)(42), the Supreme Court in *INS v. Cardoza-Fonseca*, 480 U.S. 421 (1987), referred not only to its origins in the Refugee Convention and Protocol, but also to the authoritative interpretation of those treaty provisions in the Office of the U.N. High Commissioner for Refugees, Handbook on Procedures and Criteria for Determining Refugee Status. The Handbook in turn uses the Universal Declaration and the two Human Rights Covenants as interpretive tools for defining refugee both in regard to the meaning of "persecution" and also as to the five grounds for asylum or refugee status. Hence, U.S. law has incorporated a large body of international law into national law. *See* chapter 14, *infra*. Similarly, Section 502B of the Foreign Assistance Act, adopted as a standard for limiting U.S. military aid, the definition of a gross and consistent violation of human rights from Economic and Social Council Resolution 1503. *See* chapters 5, 9, *infra*.

Even if there is no statute or regulation which specifically incorporates international human rights law into domestic law, courts in many countries have directly incorporated the international law in their national legal structures. This direct incorporation approach, known as the monist approach, accepts international law, including particular treaty obligations, as an integral part of domestic law.[13] Austria is one country which appears to exemplify the monist view. Other countries have adopted the dualist approach that considers international obligations as entirely a matter of a government's relations with other nations. In the dualist view a govern-

---

[13] 1 Lassa Oppenheim, International Law: A Treatise 37-39 (Hersch Lauterpacht, ed. 8th ed. 1955).

ment may violate its international obligations, but such a violation would not have any domestic impact. In order for a treaty, for example, to have domestic effect, it must be incorporated specifically in national legislation. The United Kingdom generally follows the dualist approach, although in regard to its obligations in the European Union it has directly incorporated international law into its domestic legal order.

The United States has accepted certain aspects of both the monist and dualist approaches to international law and, therefore, to international human rights law. Under the U.S. Constitution "treaties made or which shall be made under the authority of the United States" constitute "the supreme law of the land" and "the judges in every State shall be bound thereby, anything in the Constitution or law of any State to the contrary notwithstanding."[14] U.S. Supreme Court decisions, particularly during the early 19th century, considered international customary law and some treaties as integral parts of national law. In *Foster v. Neilson*, the Supreme Court distinguished between treaties which are and are not self-executing:

> Our Constitution declares a treaty to be the law of the land. It is, consequently, to be regarded in the courts of justice as equivalent to an act of the legislature, whenever it operates of itself without the aid of any legislative provision. But when the terms of the stipulation import a contract, when either of the parties engages to perform a particular act, the treaty addresses itself to the political, not the judicial department; and the legislature must execute the contract before it can become a rule of the Court.[15]

Over the years, courts have used, and commentators have advocated, various standards for determining the extent to which a treaty ought to be considered self-executing. For example, in the much cited opinion of *Foster v. Neilson*, Chief Justice Marshall looked principally at the language of a bilateral treaty in determining that it was not sufficiently definite and compulsory to be self-executing. Only four years later, however, Marshall reversed his conclusion as to the same bilateral treaty, based upon a review of the history of negotiations indicating that the parties apparently intended the treaty to be self-executing.[16]

In regard to multilateral treaties, including almost all international human rights treaties, it is doubtful whether the intent of the parties manifested either at drafting or in ratification should serve as the appropriate standard of evaluation. Professor Stefan Riesenfeld has suggested, instead, that a multilateral treaty ought to be deemed self-executing if it "(a) involves the rights and duties of individuals; (b) does not cover a subject for which legislative action is required by the Constitution; and (c) does not leave discretion to the parties in the application of the particular provision."[17]

Most, but not all of the human rights treaties ratified by the United States have been accompanied by a declaration that it considers the substantive provisions of those treaties not self-executing. In introducing such declarations, however, the Legal Adviser of the State Department explained to the Senate that the declarations applied only to efforts by courts to imply a private cause of action from treaty

---

[14] U.S. Const. art. VI, § 2.

[15] Foster v. Neilson, 27 U.S. (2 Pet.) 253, 314 (1829).

[16] United States v. Percheman, 32 U.S. (7 Pet.) 51, 88 (1833).

[17] Stefan Riesenfeld, *The Doctrine of Self-Executing Treaties and GATT: A Notable German Judgment*, 65 Am. J. Int'l L. 548, 550 (1971).

provisions. Otherwise, it is the obligation of the courts to determine the applicability of treaty provisions in U.S. law.

In addition to the enactment of legislation which specifically incorporates international law into domestic law (as has been done with the Refugee Protocol) and through the direct application of treaties in domestic law as self-executing, courts have also interpreted existing legislation and the Constitution in the light of international human rights law. Probably, the most visible examples of that approach can be found in *Filartiga v. Peña-Irala*, 630 F.2d 876 (2d Cir. 1980), and *Kadic v. Karadzic*, 74 F.3d 377 (2d Cir. 1995), in interpreting the Alien Tort Claims Act, 28 U.S.C. § 1350. Similarly, U.S. courts would not want to interpret U.S. constitutional protections for such rights as religious freedom and due process in a way less protective of human rights than are guaranteed around the world through international human rights law.

Accordingly, the most important means of implementing and thus developing international human rights law is through its application in national and local law. International human rights law can be applied in four ways: (1) by the enactment of legislation which specifically incorporates international law into domestic law; (2) through the direct application of treaties in domestic law as self-executing; (3) through the interpretation and application of existing legislative or constitutional provisions; and (4) as customary international law. These matters are explored more fully in chapters 12 and 13, *infra*.

C. CONCLUSION

The years since World War II have brought nearly unanimous recognition of individual rights as an appropriate subject of international concern. The U.N. responded by adopting the International Bill of Human Rights, by promulgating scores of other multilateral human rights instruments, and by developing procedures for human rights implementation and enforcement.

In addition to the human rights machinery of the U.N., regional organizations have promulgated human rights treaties, incorporating many of the norms found in U.N. instruments, and have developed regional mechanisms to enforce the treaties. Nongovernmental organizations dedicated to protecting human rights have increased in number and sophistication. These organizations have contributed to the drafting of human rights standards, have assisted intergovernmental organizations with their investigations, and have intervened directly to protect the victims of human rights abuses.

Earlier in this century, the term "human rights" was defined as those rights guaranteed by the International Bill of Rights. Over the years, however, international and regional human rights instruments have made more explicit the rights set forth in the International Bill of Rights. "Human rights" are now defined with far more detail and specificity. International human rights law is, therefore, more protective of vulnerable individuals and groups, including children, indigenous groups, refugees and displaced persons, and women. In addition, in some cases, human rights instruments have expanded the definition by elaborating new rights.[18]

International humanitarian law can be defined as the international law of hu-

---

[18] *See, e.g.*, the Declaration on the Rights of Disabled Persons, G.A. res. 3447 (XXX), 30 U.N. GAOR Supp. (No. 34) at 88, U.N. Doc. A/10034 (1975); and the Declaration on the Right to Development, G.A. res. 41/128, Annex, 41, U.N. GAOR Supp. (No. 53) at 186, U.N. Doc. A/41/53 (1986).

man rights that is applicable in situations of international armed conflict, and, to a much more limited extent, in some situations of internal armed conflict. International humanitarian law should be viewed as the intersection of human rights law with the law of war. Growing from customary international law and treaties adopted at the Hague Peace Conferences of 1899 and 1907, international humanitarian law has its principal sources in the four Geneva Conventions of 1949 and the two Protocols Additional to these Conventions.

While most human rights are perceived as individual rights vis-a-vis the government, human rights norms may also apply to non-state actors (such as armed opposition groups, businesses, and individuals who perpetrate domestic violence) who commit human rights abuses. The campaign to abolish slavery, one of the oldest efforts to protect human rights, was an attempt to prevent private actors from keeping slaves.[19] By Common Article 3 of the 1949 Geneva Conventions and their 1977 Protocols, international humanitarian law applies to armed opposition groups. Further, a series of treaties exist relating to hijackers, kidnappers of diplomats, etc. More recently, international human rights norms have been addressing the responsibility of governments to restrain individuals from committing human rights abuses in the areas of domestic violence, female genital mutilation, etc.

In sum, currently the term "human rights" should be viewed as incorporating both the rights traditionally defined by the International Bill of Rights, as well as the expansion of that definition to include rights guaranteed by international humanitarian law. Further, human rights norms are now perceived to be enforceable against non-state actors.

The worldwide recognition of human rights law should lead to more widespread acceptance of human rights and, in turn, to increased protection of rights. The remainder of this book deals with the various ways international human rights law is implemented by governments (courts, administrative agencies, and legislatures), intergovernmental organizations, nongovernmental organizations, and individuals.

NOTES AND QUESTIONS

For further reading on the development of international human rights law, see:

PHILIP ALSTON, THE UNITED NATIONS AND HUMAN RIGHTS, A CRITICAL APPRAISAL (1992);

SYDNEY D. BAILEY, THE UN SECURITY COUNCIL AND HUMAN RIGHTS (1994);

THOMAS BUERGENTHAL, INTERNATIONAL HUMAN RIGHTS IN A NUTSHELL (2d ed. 1995);

Jan Herman Burgers, *The Road to San Francisco: The Revival of the Human Rights Idea in the Twentieth Century*, 14 HUM. RTS. Q. 447 (1992);

JACK DONNELLY, THE CONCEPT OF HUMAN RIGHTS (1985);

DAVID FORSYTHE, THE INTERNATIONALIZATION OF HUMAN RIGHTS (1991);

GUIDE TO INTERNATIONAL HUMAN RIGHTS PRACTICE (Hurst Hannum ed., 2d ed. 1992);

HUMAN RIGHTS IN INTERNATIONAL LAW: LEGAL AND POLICY ISSUES (Theodor Meron ed., 1985);

HUMAN RIGHTS IN THE WORLD COMMUNITY: ISSUES AND ACTION (Richard Pierre Claude & Burns H. Weston, eds., 1992);

---

[19] *See* General Act and Declaration of Brussels of 1890, Convention of Saint-Germain-en-Laye of 1919, and the Slavery Convention of 1926, 60 L.N.T.S. 253, *entered into force* March 9, 1927.

HUMAN RIGHTS OF WOMEN, NATIONAL AND INTERNATIONAL PERSPECTIVES (Rebecca J. Cook ed., 1994);

Dorothy W. Jones, *The League of Nations Experiment in International Protection*, 8 ETHICS & INTERNATIONAL AFFAIRS 77 (1994);

RICHARD LILLICH & HURST HANNUM, INTERNATIONAL PROTECTION OF HUMAN RIGHTS: LAW, POLICY & PRACTICE (3d ed. 1995);

DOMINIC MCGOLDRICK, THE HUMAN RIGHTS COMMITTEE, ITS ROLE IN THE DEVELOPMENT OF THE INTERNATIONAL COVENANT ON CIVIL AND POLITICAL RIGHTS (1991);

JAMES W. NICKEL, MAKING SENSE OF HUMAN RIGHTS: PHILOSOPHICAL REFLECTIONS ON THE UNIVERSAL DECLARATION OF HUMAN RIGHTS (1987);

ARTHUR H. ROBERTSON, HUMAN RIGHTS IN THE WORLD: AN INTRODUCTION TO THE STUDY OF THE INTERNATIONAL PROTECTION OF HUMAN RIGHTS (3d ed. 1989);

JACOB ROBINSON, HUMAN RIGHTS AND FUNDAMENTAL FREEDOMS IN THE CHARTER OF THE UNITED NATIONS (1946);

LOUIS B. SOHN, THE HUMAN RIGHTS MOVEMENT: FROM ROOSEVELT'S FOUR FREEDOMS TO THE INTERDEPENDENCE OF PEACE, DEVELOPMENT AND HUMAN RIGHTS (1995);

UNITED NATIONS CENTRE FOR HUMAN RIGHTS, HUMAN RIGHTS MACHINERY, FACT SHEET NO. 1 (1987);

UNITED NATIONS CENTRE FOR HUMAN RIGHTS, UNITED NATIONS ACTION IN THE FIELD OF HUMAN RIGHTS, U.N. Doc. ST/HR/2/Rev.4 (1994);

GREGORY J. WALTERS, HUMAN RIGHTS IN THEORY AND PRACTICE, A SELECTED AND ANNOTATED BIBLIOGRAPHY (1995);

Burns Weston, *Human Rights,* in ENCYCLOPEDIA BRITANNICA (15th ed. 1985);

JOSEPH M. WRONKA, HUMAN RIGHTS AND SOCIAL POLICY IN THE 21ST CENTURY (1992).

CHAPTER 2

RATIFICATION AND IMPLEMENTATION OF TREATIES: THE COVENANT ON ECONOMIC, SOCIAL AND CULTURAL RIGHTS

A. INTRODUCTION   Page   28

B. QUESTIONS   28

C. RATIFICATION OF TREATIES   29

   1. **How Do Governments Become Bound?**   29
      Vienna Convention on the Law of Treaties   29
      Anne M. Williams, United States Treaty Law   30

   2. **Reservations**   31
      Vienna Convention on the Law of Treaties   31
      Dinah Shelton, International Law   33

   3. **U.S. Ratification of Human Rights Treaties**   34
      Nigel Rodley, On the Necessity of United States Ratification of
         the International Human Rights Conventions   35
      a. Genocide Convention   39
      b. Treaty against Torture   40
      c. Covenant on Civil and Political Rights   41
      d. Race Convention   42
      e. Women's Convention   43
      f. American Convention on Human Rights   45

D. THE COVENANT ON ECONOMIC, SOCIAL AND CULTURAL RIGHTS   49

   1. **What Are Economic, Social, and Cultural Rights?**   49
      Philip Alston & Gerard Quinn, The Nature and Scope of States
         Parties' Obligations Under the International Covenant on Eco-
         nomic, Social and Cultural Rights   51

   2. **Should the U.S. Ratify the Covenant on Economic, Social and
      Cultural Rights?**   58
      Philip Alston, U.S. Ratification of the Covenant on Economic,
         Social and Cultural Rights: The Need for an Entirely New
         Strategy   58

   3. **Ratification — With or Without Qualifications?**   66
      Four Treaties Pertaining to Human Rights: Message From the
         President of the United States   66

Burns Weston, U.S. Ratification of the International Covenant on Economic, Social and Cultural Rights: With or Without Qualifications   68

E. IMPLEMENTATION AND ENFORCEMENT   72

1. U.N. Committee on Economic, Social and Cultural Rights   72
Philip Alston, Out of the Abyss: The Challenges Confronting the New U.N. Committee on Economic, Social and Cultural Rights   72
Committee on Economic, Social and Cultural Rights, Report on the Eighth and Ninth Sessions   75

2. Coordination with Other Bodies   79

F. RECOGNITION OF NEW RIGHTS   81
Stephen Marks, Emerging Human Rights: A New Generation for the 1980s?   81

A. INTRODUCTION

Treaties constitute a primary source of international human rights law. The decision to ratify is a critical step in making truly effective treaties. This chapter examines ratification of a treaty with regard to a crucial group of rights characterized as economic, social, and cultural. Some readers may not be familiar with them, but several international instruments prescribe them. Here we focus on the Covenant on Economic, Social and Cultural Rights (ESC Covenant), which complements the Covenant on Civil and Political Rights, which is discussed in chapter 3. Together with the Universal Declaration of Human Rights, the two Covenants and a procedural protocol to the Civil and Political Covenant constitute the International Bill of Human Rights.

We begin with an overview of treaty ratification procedures and then discuss qualifications that nations sometimes assert when they ratify. We next examine the nature of economic, social, and cultural rights; their implementation and enforcement; and whether the U.S. delay in ratifying the ESC Covenant is justifiable.

We also consider the work of the Committee on Economic, Social and Cultural Rights, which monitors the Covenant's implementation and enforcement. Its procedures are compared with those of the Human Rights Committee, discussed in chapters 3 and 4.

B. QUESTIONS

The class is to conduct itself as a Senate committee that has scheduled hearings to determine whether the Senate should consent to U.S. ratification of the ESC Covenant. One student should testify in favor of ratification, another against. Others, as committee members, will question the two witnesses and debate the issues. In deciding whether to recommend that the Senate consent, consider these questions:

1. What are basic differences between (1) civil and political rights and (2) economic, social, and cultural rights?

a. Do you think that one set is positive, the other negative?
b. In what ways do implementation and enforcement of the two sets differ?
c. Are there conflicts between achievement of civil and political rights and achievement of economic, social, and cultural rights?

2. Should the U.S. ratify the ESC Covenant?
   a. What advantages might be gained by ratifying?
   b. Are there disadvantages?
   c. Are there disadvantages of nonratification?

3. Exactly what obligations would the U.S. undertake by ratifying?
   a. Do you think it likely that the U.S. would be found in violation of the Covenant? If so, which clauses?
   b. How is compliance monitored?

4. How might advocates of ratification most effectively proceed?
   a. What are advantages and disadvantages of a "stealth" approach?
   b. What are advantages and disadvantages of advocating ratification via open discussion of the Covenant's perceived impact on U.S. laws and practices?

5. Are reservations and other qualifications desirable?
   a. Should the Senate accept all of President Carter's proposals? Should it propose some of its own?
   b. What effect would the qualifications have on other parties to the Covenant? Might they argue that some of the proposed qualifications are invalid?
   c. Is it worth ratifying a treaty with so many reservations?
   d. What impact might the U.S. practice of extensively qualifying the treaties it ratifies have on other countries?

C.   RATIFICATION OF TREATIES

1.   How Do Governments Become Bound?

Vienna Convention on the Law of Treaties, 1155 U.N.T.S. 331, U.S. No. 58 (1980), *reprinted in* **8 I.L.M. 679 (1969),** *entered into force* **Jan. 27, 1980:**

Article 9

Adoption of the text

1. The adoption of the text of a treaty takes place by the consent of all the States participating in its drawing up except as provided in paragraph 2.
2. The adoption of the text of a treaty at an international conference takes place by the vote of two-thirds of the States present and voting . . .

Article 11

Means of expressing consent to be bound by a treaty

The consent of a State to be bound by a treaty may be expressed by signature, exchange of instruments constituting a treaty, ratification, acceptance, approval or accession, or by any other means if so agreed. . . .

Article 16

Exchange or deposit of instruments of ratification, acceptance, approval or accession

Unless the treaty otherwise provides, instruments of ratification, acceptance, approval or accession establish the consent of a State to be bound by a treaty upon:

a. their exchange between the Contracting States;
b. their deposit with the depositary; or
c. their notification to the Contracting States or to the depositary, if so agreed.
    . . .

Article 18

Obligation not to defeat the object and purpose of a treaty prior to its entry into force

A State is obliged to refrain from acts which would defeat the object and purpose of a treaty when:

(a) it has signed the treaty or has exchanged instruments constituting the treaty subject to ratification, acceptance or approval, until it shall have made its intention clear not to become a party to the treaty; or

(b) it has expressed its consent to be bound by the treaty, pending the entry into force of the treaty and provided that such entry into force is not unduly delayed.

*   *   *   *   *

Anne M. Williams, *United States Treaty Law*, in U.S. RATIFICATION OF THE INTERNATIONAL COVENANTS ON HUMAN RIGHTS 35, 39-43 (Hurst Hannum & Dana D. Fischer ed., 1993) (footnotes omitted):

[I]n an impressive number of instances, the Senate or its committees dealing with foreign affairs have participated in the negotiating process in advance of the conclusion of a treaty, lending at least advisory assistance but leaving the ultimate power of consent or non-consent to the formal Senate vote. The House of Representatives has likewise participated in such an advisory role. . . .

Once negotiations are complete, the President signs the treaty as an indication that the text represents the agreement reached by the parties. At that stage, the President decides whether to submit the treaty to the Senate for its advice and consent to ratification. If it is submitted to the Senate, the President usually sends an accompanying report explaining the treaty's provisions and the circumstances which make its ratification desirable.

Once the Senate receives the treaty, it is referred to the Committee on Foreign Relations. . . .

The Committee may or may not decide to report the treaty to the full Senate for its advice and consent. Sometimes the Executive Branch may request that the Committee withhold or suspend action on the treaty. When the treaty is submitted to the full Senate, the advice and consent of the Senate must be given by a vote of two-thirds of the Senators present. Few treaties have been defeated in recent years by a direct vote, and non-action is the usual method of withholding consent to controversial treaties. . . .

After the Senate gives its advice and consent, a treaty is returned to the President for ratification. The President may either ratify the treaty as presented by the Senate, or if he believes any Senate action taken is undesirable, the treaty may be returned to the Senate for further consideration. The President may also decide not to ratify the treaty.

After a treaty is ratified, which is a domestic action, some form of international action must be taken to bring the treaty into force. Usually the treaty specifies this action as the exchange or deposit of a certain number of instruments of ratification.

NOTES AND QUESTIONS

1.   There are several steps in the ordinary treaty ratification process, most of which are identified in the preceding excerpts. For multilateral treaties, the U.N. or a similar international body begins the ratification process by creating and announcing the proposed text of the treaty. The President endorses the text by signing it. The President then submits it to the Senate, sometimes with recommendations for reservations, declarations, and understandings. The Senate refers the treaty to its Foreign Relations Committee, which conducts hearings to monitor public reaction. The full Senate ordinarily withholds advice and consent until the Committee recommends the treaty. The Committee may also recommend various qualifications, which the full Senate may accept, reject, or revise. Once the Senate gives advice and consent, any limitations must be fulfilled before the President submits the formal ratification documents to the U.N. For example, the Senate may ask that legislation to implement the treaty be enacted before ratification. Three months after the ratification documents are deposited with the U.N., the U.S. normally becomes a party to the treaty.

2.   Does the House of Representatives have a role (*e.g.* if compliance will be costly)?

3.   The Vienna Treaties Convention also articulates a consensus on how treaties should be construed. The U.S. has not, however, ratified it. In a Letter of Submittal to the President, however, the State Department said that "the Convention is already generally recognized as the authoritative guide to current treaty law and practice." S. Exec. Doc., 92d Cong., 1st Sess. 1 (1971).

2.   Reservations

Vienna Convention on the Law of Treaties, 1155 U.N.T.S. 331, U.S. No. 58 (1980), *reprinted in* **8 I.L.M. 679 (1969),** *entered into force* **Jan. 27, 1980:**

Article 2

Use of Terms . . .

1.   For purposes of the present Convention: . . .

(d)   "reservation" means a unilateral statement, however phrased or named, made by a State, when signing, ratifying, accepting, approving or acceding to a treaty, whereby it purports to exclude or to modify the legal effect of certain provisions of the treaty in their application to that State . . ..

Article 19

Formulation of reservations

A State may, when signing, ratifying, accepting, approving or acceding to a treaty, formulate a reservation unless:

(a)   the reservation is prohibited by the treaty;

(b)   the treaty provides that only specified reservations, which do not include the reservation in question, may be made; or

(c)   in cases not falling under sub-paragraphs (a) or (b), the reservation is incompatible with the object and purpose of the treaty.

Article 20

Acceptance of and objection to reservations

1.   A reservation expressly authorised by a treaty does not require any subsequent acceptance by the other Contracting States unless the treaty so provides.

2.   When it appears from the limited number of the negotiating States and the object and purpose of a treaty that the application of the treaty in its entirety between all the parties is an essential condition of the consent of each one to be bound by the treaty, a reservation requires acceptance by all the parties.

3.   When a treaty is a constituent instrument of an international organisation and unless it otherwise provides, a reservation requires the acceptance of the competent organ of that organisation.

4.   In cases not falling under the preceding paragraphs and unless the treaty otherwise provides:

a.   acceptance by another Contracting State of a reservation constitutes the reserving State a party to the treaty in relation to that other State if or when the treaty is in force for those States;

b.   an objection by another Contracting State to a reservation does not preclude the entry into force of the treaty as between the objecting and reserving States unless a contrary intention is definitely expressed by the objecting State;

c.   an act expressing a State's consent to be bound by the treaty and containing a reservation is effective as soon as at least one other Contracting State has accepted the reservation. . . .

Article 21

Legal effects of reservations and of objections
to reservations

1.   A reservation . . .

a.   modifies for the reserving State in its relations with that other party the provisions of the treaty to which the reservation relates to the extent of the reservation; and

b.   modifies those provisions to the same extent for that other party in its relations with the reserving State.

2.   The reservation does not modify the provisions of the treaty for the other parties to the treaty *inter se*.

3.   When a State objecting to a reservation has not opposed the entry into force of the treaty between itself and the reserving State, the provisions to which the reservation

relates do not apply as between the two States to the extent of the reservation.

Article 22

Withdrawal of reservations and of objections to reservations

1.   Unless the treaty otherwise provides, a reservation may be withdrawn at any time and the consent of a State which has accepted the reservation is not required for its withdrawal.
2.   Unless the treaty otherwise provides, an objection to a reservation may be withdrawn at any time.

*   *   *   *   *

Dinah Shelton, *International Law*, in U.S. RATIFICATION OF THE INTER- NATIONAL COVENANTS ON HUMAN RIGHTS 27, 29-33 (Hurst Hannum & Dana D. Fischer ed., 1993) (footnotes omitted):

In the process of becoming party to a treaty, States may file reservations to their consent to be bound unless the treaty provides otherwise. . . .
. . . Prior to 1945, reservations were generally held to be valid only if the treaty concerned permitted reservations and if all other parties accepted the reservations. In essence the reservation constituted a counter-offer which required a new acceptance. This rule rested on the notion of the absolute integrity of the treaty as adopted.
While scattered support for this principle remains, practice in regard to multilateral treaties demonstrates considerable variation on the acceptability and effect of reservations. When questions arose on the admissibility of reservations to the Genocide Convention, a request was made for an advisory opinion from the International Court of Justice. The Court in its opinion stressed the divergence of practice as well as the unique character of the Genocide Convention, including the intent of the drafters and parties that the Convention be universal in scope. Although its findings were expressly limited to the Genocide Convention, the Court's often-cited holding was that "a State which has made . . . a reservation which has been objected to by one or more of the parties to the Convention but not by others, can be regarded as being a party to the Convention if the reservation is compatible with the object and purpose of the Convention. . . ."
The Compatibility test is incorporated in the Vienna Convention in Articles 19-21 . . ..
The effect of a reservation is to modify relations between the reserving State and other States Parties to the treaty to the extent of the reservations. This applies on a reciprocal basis, meaning that no State may invoke a provision to which it has reserved until the reservation is withdrawn. Reservations may be withdrawn at any time, as may objections to reservations. . . .
. . . Neither Covenant [(*i.e.* the Covenant on Civil and Political Rights and the Covenant on Economic, Social and Cultural Rights)] expressly addresses the issue of reservations, so the question is one of compatibility with the object and purpose of the treaties.
In regard to the ESC Covenant, 18 States expressed reservations out of the 90 that had ratified as of the end of 1987. The reservations of 17 of the 18 States concern substantive rights, but in many cases the reservations are postponements of application rather than permanent exemptions. Nearly half of the permanent reservations limit in some way the right to strike guaranteed in Article 8(1)(d);

three States do not accept the requirement to pay for public holidays, five temporarily or permanently limit the right to education; and one provides regional preferences for workers. . . .

Past United States practice is consistent with the generally limited use of reservations to human rights treaties. The United States submitted one reservation to the 1926 Slavery Convention, none to the Supplementary Convention on Slavery, and none to the two Conventions on the Political Rights of Women. All four treaties were unanimously approved by the Senate.

NOTES AND QUESTIONS

1.   As previously discussed, the President often has proposed qualifications to a treaty when submitting it for advice and consent. President Carter proposed many limitations on the Civil and Political Covenant when he submitted it to the Senate in 1978. President Carter also proposed qualifications to the other three treaties submitted at the same time: the ESC Covenant, the International Convention on the Elimination of All Forms of Racial Discrimination, and the American Convention on Human Rights.

2.   Regarding Shelton's statement concerning the United States' "limited use of reservations," see *infra* at 37 for discussion of qualifications attached to treaties to which the Senate has given advice and consent since 1989. Do you agree with Shelton's characterization of U.S. reservations?

---

3.   U.S. Ratification of Human Rights Treaties

Despite its active participation in the drafting of many U.N. human rights instruments, the U.S. found itself unable to ratify them because of congressional opposition during the 1950s. Several members of Congress, including notably Senator Bricker, feared that the Genocide Convention and various drafts (which later became the two Covenants, as well as the Racial Discrimination treaty) might lead to international scrutiny of U.S. practices, particularly racial discrimination, and might infringe on prerogatives of state governments. As a result, a series of proposals known as the Bricker Amendment was introduced to amend the U.S. Constitution restricting the government from entering into treaties that might infringe on powers of the states or be applicable in domestic courts without implementing legislation.

One version of the Bricker Amendment failed in 1954, by only one vote, to pass the Senate. To secure defeat, Secretary of State Dulles was moved to promise that this country did not plan to become a party to any human rights treaties or present any such treaties for consideration by the Senate. He also indicated that the U.S. would neither sign the Convention on the Political Rights of Women nor seek ratification of the Genocide Convention.

The Kennedy Administration sought to relax the Dulles doctrine by submitting three minor human rights treaties to the Senate. Only one, the Supplementary Slavery Convention, was approved. The two U.N. Covenants were first submitted to the Senate in 1977 by the Carter Administration.

With the enactment of major civil rights statutes, the efforts of courts to eradicate the worst injustices of racial discrimination, a decrease of interest in states rights, and an increasing interest in international human rights, the climate for ratification of multilateral treaties gradually improved. In 1976 the U.S. ratified the Inter-American Convention on Granting of Political Rights to Women and the U.N. Convention on the Political Rights of Women. In 1987 the Senate finally, with certain qualifications, consented to U.S. ratification of the Genocide Convention, which President Truman had signed almost 40 years earlier.

Keep that historical overview in mind as you read the following excerpt:

Nigel S. Rodley, *On the Necessity of United States Ratification of the International Human Rights-Conventions, in* U.S. RATIFICATION OF THE HUMAN RIGHTS TREATIES: WITH OR WITHOUT RESERVATIONS? 3, 4-13 (Richard B. Lillich ed., 1981) (footnotes omitted):

One of the most important activities of the UN has been the elaboration of the International Bill of [Human] Rights consisting of the Universal Declaration of Human Rights, the International Covenant on Economic, Social, and Cultural Rights, the International Covenant on Civil and Political Rights, and the Optional Protocol to the latter covenant. The withdrawal in 1953 of the U.S. from the process of drafting these instruments and its continuing aloofness from participating in their operation demonstrate a degree of inconsistency that it is fair to say the U.S. must rectify if it is to maximize its declared commitment in favor of human rights, a commitment that we are assured is being sustained and is "the soul" of American foreign policy. . . .

I. Disadvantages of Nonparticipation

One of the disadvantages of nonparticipation in the promotion of human rights through the development of international standards became apparent when the U.S. opted out of the process of negotiating the texts of the international covenants on human rights. But even where the U.S. has participated in the development of such standards, as for example in the conclusion of the Convention on the Elimination of All Forms of Racial Discrimination or, more recently, in the development of international standards (including a convention) against torture, the impact of that participation may well have been weakened by the possible perception on the part of representatives of other states that for the U.S. such activity is, in terms of future legal obligations, more academic than real.

Similarly, U.S. credibility is at stake in efforts to develop mechanisms to monitor compliance at the international level. The U.S. has taken strong and positive positions on the strengthening of the existing UN mechanisms providing for thorough studies or investigations of situations appearing to reveal consistent patterns of gross and reliably attested violations of human rights pursuant to Economic and Social Council Resolution 1503 (XLVIII). It has similarly sought to promote the establishment within the UN of a High Commissioner for Human Rights. Both of these efforts are designed to advance UN involvement in the protection of human rights by developing fact-finding techniques that would function on an objective basis. The development of such mechanisms would inhibit manipulation according to the preferences of fluctuating government majorities. Indeed, no delegation at the UN has been more vocal in the last few years than that of the U.S. in denouncing the apparent double standard with which the UN assesses various allegations of violations of human rights. Yet it is precisely the mechanisms established under the various international human rights instruments that are designed to institutionalize a more objective, consistent, and depoliticized approach to assessing such allegations. By standing aloof from participation in such UN human rights mechanisms, the credibility of the U.S. position is impaired when it eloquently complains about alleged double standards in actual UN investigations.

What is also damaging about the failure of the U.S. government to integrate itself into the standard-setting and compliance-assessment systems provided by the international instruments is that the U.S. opens itself to the charge that, despite concern for the protection of human rights in other countries, it is not willing to enter into an international obligation to protect human rights at home. You may not consider it a particularly fair argument or even a particularly cogent one, but as far as arguments go in the field of international politics it is an extremely telling one. . . .

Of course, the damaging effect of noninvolvement in the international treaty protection systems is not just evident at the multilateral level; it also must inevitably limit the amount of influence the U.S. government can bring to bear bilaterally. This would be particularly true in the case of governments with which the U.S. does not already have a tradition of influence, especially of governments that have themselves ratified the instruments. . . .

Indeed, the double-standard charge against the U.S. takes on particular significance in the context of some of the interesting legislation that has over the past few years been adopted by the Congress whereby U.S. aid policy is made subject to the taking into account of and compliance with "internationally recognized human rights." There are a number of places one might go to look for internationally recognized human rights, but the International Bill of [Human] Rights, and not just the Declaration, would certainly be one such place. It can hardly enhance the integrity of the U.S. posture when it is prepared to incorporate into its own legislation standards for application against others that it is not prepared to apply juridically to itself. . . .

II. The Advantages of Participation

. . . I shall now turn to the advantages that I see would flow from its ratification of the same conventions. Perhaps it goes without saying that the principal advantage would be avoidance of the disadvantages that I have already described. The major reproaches of inconsistency, hypocrisy, and the exercise of a double standard would lose their force. . . .

More particularly, the U.S. may feel it has something to contribute to the work of the [Human Rights] Committee. It could not have a governmental delegate on the Committee; that, indeed, is the Committee's strength. However, it would be one of the electors of the Committee, and it could nominate an expert who might be able to bring something of the rich tradition of American jurisprudence and legal creativity to bear upon the work of the Committee.

Meanwhile, there would be far greater opportunities for U.S. participation in the appropriate forums of the UN in discussion of the annual reports of the Human Rights Committee. At the moment, any such participation by the U.S., or any other country that has not become a party to the covenant, is hardly likely to carry much weight . . ..

I do not hesitate to deal with what some would perceive to be the disadvantages of the U.S. being subjected to criticism by others in an international forum. This should indeed be listed amongst the manifest advantages of the U.S. being a party to the covenants and subject to the substantive and procedural obligations of those instruments. In my view, it is good for any and every country to be subjected to criticism. It is healthy and constructive, and this is so even if the criticism itself is not. For, in the final analysis, a forum for rational discussion of criticism, well- or ill-founded, is precisely the value that is afforded by the work of the Human Rights Committee. . . . [T]here are no doubt areas of human rights where the U.S. would think it had reason to be fairly satisfied with its performance. I think there are other areas where that may not so easily be the case, and obviously here I have in mind to some extent the field of economic, social, and cultural rights. . . . I am also mindful that . . . the history of the U.S., as of other countries, does not demonstrate continuous and uniform commitment to certain very fundamental civil and political rights. President Carter has recently acknowledged that "the struggle for full human rights for all Americans—black, brown and white, male and female, rich and poor—is far from over." Not only is there further to go, it is necessary to build safeguards against retrogression. Systematic international scrutiny is one such safeguard. . . .

It may also be cause for some satisfaction that what the U.S. does or does not do is frequently influential on the behavior of other countries. In the final analysis there can surely be no more desirable way to influence the behavior of others than by the example of one's own behavior. This is not mere rhetoric. I can assure you that in at least one Third World country it has been a matter of deep disappointment to those who are seeking to persuade their government of the importance of ratifying the covenants that the U.S. has itself not done so. It has been a partial answer that an administration of the U.S. has at least declared an intention to secure ratification. A complete answer would have been better. . . .

NOTES AND QUESTIONS

For illustrative arguments in favor of and against U.S. ratification, see Natalie Hevener Kaufman & David Whiteman, *Opposition to Human Rights Treaties in the United States: The Legacy of the Bricker Amendment*, 10 HUM. RTS. Q. 309, 321-37 (1988); Frank C. Newman, *United Nations Human Rights Covenants and the United States Government: Diluted Promises, Foreseeable Futures*, 42 DEPAUL L. REV. 1241 (1993); Nadine Strossen, *United States Ratification of the International Bill of Rights: A Fitting Celebration of the Bicentennial of the U.S. Bill of Rights*, 24 U. TOLEDO L. REV. 571 (1992); David Weissbrodt, *United States Ratification of the Human Rights Covenants*, 63 MINN. L. REV. 35 (1978).

The U.S. is now a party to many human rights treaties. The number of States parties listed here represents the number as of February 1996. The parenthetical notes as to reservations, declarations, understandings, etc., pertain to U.S. qualifications only.

(a) U.N. Charter, 59 Stat. 1031, T.S. 993, 3 Bevans 1153, *entered into force* Oct. 24, 1945 (185 States parties);

(b) Slavery Convention, 60 L.N.T.S. 253, *entered into force* Mar. 9, 1927, *for the U.S.* Mar. 21, 1929 (91 States parties) (1 reservation);

(c) Four Geneva Conventions for the Protection of Victims of Armed Conflict, 75 U.N.T.S. 31, 85, 135, 287, *entered into force* Oct. 21, 1950, *for the U.S.* Feb. 2, 1956 (186 States parties) (Convention I - 1 reservation; Convention IV - 1 reservation);

(d) Protocol Amending the Slavery Convention, 182 U.N.T.S. 51, *entered into force* July 7, 1955, *for the U.S.* Mar. 7, 1956 (57 States parties);

(e) Supplementary Convention on the Abolition of Slavery, the Slave Trade and

Institutions and Practices Similar to Slavery, 226 U.N.T.S. 3, *entered into force* Apr. 30, 1957, *for the U.S.* Dec. 6, 1967 (114 States parties);

(f) Protocol Relating to the Status of Refugees, 606 U.N.T.S. 267, *entered into force* Oct. 4, 1967, *for the U.S.* Nov. 1, 1968 (127 States parties) (2 reservations);

(g) O.A.S. Charter, 119 U.N.T.S. 3, *entered into force including for the U.S.* Dec. 13, 1951, *amended* 721 U.N.T.S. 324, *entered into force* Feb. 27, 1970 (35 States parties);

(h) Convention on the Political Rights of Women, 193 U.N.T.S. 135, *entered into force* July 7, 1954, *for the U.S.* July 7, 1976 (108 States parties);

(i) Convention on the Prevention and Punishment of the Crime of Genocide, 78 U.N.T.S. 277, *entered into force* Jan. 12, 1951, *for the U.S.* Feb. 23, 1989 (121 States parties) (2 reservations, 5 understandings, 1 declaration);

(j) International Covenant on Civil and Political Rights, G.A. res. 2200A (XXI), 21 U.N. GAOR Supp. (No. 16) at 52, U.N. Doc. A/6316 (1966), 999 U.N.T.S. 171, *entered into force* Mar. 23, 1976, *for the U.S.* Sept. 8, 1992 (132 States parties) (5 reservations, 5 understandings, 4 declarations, 1 proviso);

(k) Abolition of Forced Labour Convention (ILO No. 105), 320 U.N.T.S. 291, *entered into force* Jan. 17, 1959, *for the U.S.* Sept. 25, 1992 (117 States parties);

(l) Convention Against Torture and Other Cruel, Inhuman and Degrading Treatment or Punishment, G.A. res. 39/46, Annex, 39 U.N. GAOR Supp. (No. 51) at 197, U.N. Doc. A/39/51 (1984), *entered into force* June 26, 1987, *for the U.S.* ratification deposited Nov. 20, 1995 (94 States parties) (2 reservations, 5 understandings, 2 declarations);

(m) International Convention on the Elimination of All Forms of Racial Discrimination, G.A. res. 2106 (XX), Annex, 20 U.N. GAOR Supp. (No. 14) at 47, U.N. Doc. A/6014 (1966), 660 U.N.T.S. 195, *entered into force* Jan. 4, 1969, *for the U.S.* Nov. 20, 1994 (146 States parties) (3 reservations, 1 understanding, 1 declaration, 1 proviso).

* * * * *

The U.S. has signed these treaties, but has not become a party:

(a) Convention on Consent to Marriage, Minimum Age for Marriage and Registration of Marriages, 521 U.N.T.S. 231, *entered into force* Dec. 9, 1964 (45 States parties);

(b) International Covenant on Economic, Social and Cultural Rights, G.A. res. 2200A (XXI), 21 U.N. GAOR Supp. (No. 16) at 49, U.N. Doc. A/6316 (1966), 993 U.N.T.S. 3, *entered into force* Jan. 3, 1976 (133 States parties);

(c) American Convention on Human Rights, O.A.S. Off. Rec. OEA/Ser.L/V/II.23, doc. 21, rev. 6 (1979), *entered into force* July 18, 1978 (25 States parties);

(d) Additional Protocols I and II to the Geneva Conventions of 12 August 1949, 1125 U.N.T.S. 3, 609, *entered into force* Dec. 7, 1978 (Protocol I—143 States parties, Protocol II—134 States parties); (Protocol I—2 understandings attached at signing; Protocol II—1 understanding attached at signing);

(e) Convention on the Elimination of All Forms of Discrimination Against Women, G.A. res. 34/180, 34 U.N. GAOR Supp. (No. 46) at 193, U.N. Doc. A/34/46, 1249 U.N.T.S. 13, *entered into force* Sept. 3, 1981 (151 States parties);

(f) Convention on the Rights of the Child, G.A. res. 44/25, Annex, 44 U.N. GAOR Supp. (No. 49) at 167, U.N. Doc. A/44/49 (1989), *entered into force* Sept. 2, 1990 (187 States parties).

* * * * *

The U.S. has neither signed nor ratified a number of significant treaties, including:

(a)   Convention Relating to the Status of Refugees, 189 U.N.T.S. 150, *entered into force* Apr. 22, 1954 (127 States parties);

(b)   Optional Protocol to the International Covenant on Civil and Political Rights, G.A. res. 2200A (XXI), 21 U.N. GAOR Supp. (No. 16) at 59, U.N. Doc. A/6316 (1966), 999 U.N.T.S. 302, *entered into force* Mar. 23, 1976 (87 States parties);

(c)   Second Optional Protocol to the International Covenant on Civil and Political Rights, aiming at the abolition of the death penalty, G.A. res. 44/128, Annex, 44 U.N. GAOR Supp. (No. 49) at 207, U.N. Doc. A/44/49 (1989), *entered into force* July 11, 1991 (29 States parties);

(d)   International Convention on the Protection of the Rights of All Migrant Workers and Members of Their Families, G.A. res. 45/158, Annex, 45 U.N. GAOR Supp. (No. 49A) at 262, U.N. Doc. A/45/49 (1990), *entered into force* xxxx xx, 19xx (7 States parties);

(e)   Inter-American Convention to Prevent and Punish Torture, 25 ILM 519, Dec. 9, 1985, *entered into force* Feb. 28, 1987 (13 parties);

(f)   Inter-American Convention on the Prevention, Punishment and Eradication of Violence Against Women, 27 U.S.T. 3301, *entered into force* Apr. 22, 1949 (18 States parties).

a.   Convention on the Prevention and Punishment of the Crime of Genocide (Genocide Convention)

The Genocide Convention, adopted on December 9 and signed by President Truman on December 11, 1948, was transmitted to the Senate in 1949. The Foreign Relations Committee reported favorably to the Senate in 1970, 1971, 1973, and 1976; but not until 1986 did the Senate give advice and consent to ratification. 132 CONG. REC. S1377 (daily ed., Feb. 19, 1986). Ratification was qualified by two reservations, five understandings, and one declaration. The qualifications are reproduced in *Selected International Human Rights Instruments*. One reservation required specific consent to submitting a dispute involving the treaty to the International Court of Justice. Another articulated the supremacy of the U.S. Constitution over any treaty obligation. The five understandings limited the meaning of several clauses, and the Senate declared that implementing legislation would be required before the administration could deposit the ratification documents. The statute was finally enacted on November 5, 1988. Genocide Convention Implementation Act of 1987, P.L. 100-606; 102 Stat. 3045.

The U.S. deposited notice of ratification on November 25, 1988. Eleven nations have objected to or commented unfavorably on the reservation that claimed supremacy of the U.S. Constitution. Four objected to the U.S. reservation regarding jurisdiction of the ICJ. *See* Lawrence J. LeBlanc, *The Intent to Destroy Groups in the Genocide Convention: The Proposed U.S. Understanding*, 78 AM. J. INT'L L. 369, 369-70 (1984); Lawrence J. LeBlanc, *The ICJ, the Genocide Convention, and the United States*, 6 WISC. INT'L L.J. 43, 43-45 (1987); INTERNATIONAL HUMAN RIGHTS INSTRUMENTS 130.1-.16 (Richard Lillich ed., 1986); Comment, *International Convention on the Prevention and Punishment of the Crime of Genocide: United States Senate Grant of Advice and Consent to Ratification*, 1 HARV. HUM. RTS. Y.B. 227 (1988).

b. Convention against Torture and Other Cruel, Inhuman or Degrading Treatment or Punishment (Treaty against Torture)

The General Assembly adopted the Treaty against Torture on December 10, 1984. On April 18, 1988, the U.S. signed, and on May 20, 1988, President Reagan submitted the treaty to the Senate. He attached a letter from the Secretary of State suggesting reservations, understandings, and declarations that might be attached to the treaty. *Letter from Secretary of State George Shultz to President Reagan (May 10, 1988), Message from the President of the United States transmitting the Convention against Torture and Other Cruel, Inhuman or Degrading Treatment or Punishment*, 100th Cong., 2d Sess. (1988).

In 1989 the Bush Administration indicated that the Treaty against Torture had higher priority for ratification than any other human rights treaty. In that year the Bush Administration withdrew several of the Reagan/Shultz proposals and forwarded its own package of 3 reservations, 8 understandings, and 2 declarations.

One newly proposed reservation limited the treaty's proscription of "cruel, inhuman or degrading treatment or punishment" to the narrower protections afforded by the 5th, 8th, and/or 14th Amendments to the U.S. Constitution. A Reagan/Shultz reservation limiting the impact of the treaty on state governments, as distinguished from the federal government, was reasserted. Also reasserted was a Reagan/Shultz reservation requiring the State Department to decide on a case-by-case basis whether to refer a dispute under the treaty between two governments to the International Court of Justice.

The Reagan Administration letter had recommended that the U.S. not accept the competence of the Committee against Torture for complaints initiated by one state against another state, individual complaints, or *sua sponte* visits. The Bush package withdrew the proposed reservation as to U.S. participation in regard to state v. state complaints but did not imply that the U.S. would permit individual complaints to the Committee.

The Bush package also kept the Shultz proposal that the treaty be considered not self-executing. Just prior to hearings in the Senate Foreign Relations Committee on January 30, 1990, the Bush Administration proposed another declaration stating that the treaty would not restrict U.S. use of the death penalty. Senator Helms also proposed a reservation similar to the reservation he had attached to the Genocide Convention, stating:

> Nothing in the Convention requires or authorizes legislation or other action by the United States of America prohibited by the Constitution of the United States, as interpreted by the United States.

The State Department opposed his proposed reservation because it might lead other governments to make similar reservations, thus inappropriately indicating that national law should be invoked as a justification for failure to perform a treaty.

When the Senate gave its advice and consent, it made only minor modifications to the package and adopted 2 reservations, 5 understandings, and 2 declarations. 136 CONG. REC. S17486-92 (daily ed., Oct. 27, 1990); reprinted in *Selected International Human Rights Instruments*. Senator Helms' proposed reservation was not included, and he agreed to withdraw and resubmit it as a proviso. The "sovereignty proviso," included in the resolution of ratification, requires the President to notify all present and prospective parties to the Treaty against Torture that nothing in the treaty authorizes legislation prohibited by the Constitution. *Id.* The U.S. deposited its instrument of ratification on October 21, 1994, and the treaty came into force with regard to the U.S. on November 20, 1994.

c. Covenant on Civil and Political Rights

The U.S. ratified the Covenant on Civil and Political Rights on June 8, 1992; the treaty entered into force for the U.S. on September 8, 1992. It was encumbered by five reservations, five understandings, four declarations, and one proviso. 102 Cong. Rec. S4781-4784 (daily ed., April 2, 1992); reprinted in *Selected International Human Rights Instruments.* The first reservation preserved the higher protection of free speech and association guaranteed by the U.S. Constitution. The second ensured that the U.S. could continue to impose the death penalty as punishment for persons under the age of 18 convicted of appropriate crimes. The third reservation, similar to a reservation imposed on the Treaty against Torture, limited the proscription of "cruel, inhuman or degrading treatment or punishment" to the definition under the 5th, 8th, and 14th Amendments. The fourth preserved the U.S. rule allowing imposition of any higher penalty in force at the time an offense was committed. The final reservation preserved the right to treat juveniles as adults in exceptional circumstances, and reserved certain provisions with respect to individuals who volunteer for military service prior to age 18.

There also were five understandings. The first reflected the U.S. practice of permitting distinctions based on people's varying characteristics when they are rationally related to a legitimate governmental objective or when they have a disproportionate effect on persons of a particular status. The second ensured that victim compensation for unlawful arrest, detention, or miscarriage of justice might be subject to the "reasonable requirements of domestic law." The third preserved certain practices concerning accused and convicted persons, while the fourth limited governmental responsibilities to criminal defendants. The final understanding limited the obligation of the federal government to enforce the terms of the Covenant in the federal system.

The Senate also added four declarations. As it had done with the Treaty against Torture, the Senate declared the Covenant not to be self-executing. Second, the Senate declared that states should not use the words of the Covenant to reduce higher human rights standards protected by relevant national law. The U.S. also accepted the competence of the Human Rights Committee to receive and consider reports under the Covenant. The Senate then attached a proviso, similar to the reservation to the Genocide Convention and the proviso attached to the Treaty against Torture regarding the sovereignty of U.S. law.

For additional discussion of U.S. reservations to the Civil and Political Covenant and the response of the Human Rights Committee, see *infra* chapter 3.

Many commentators have criticized the U.S. package of qualifications as excessive. *See, e.g.,* M. Christian Green, *The 'Matrioshka' Strategy: U.S. Evasion of the International Covenant on Civil and Political Rights*, 10 So. Afr. J. Hum. Rts. 357 (1994); *Lawyers Committee for Human Rights, Statements on U.S. Ratification of the CCPR*, 14 Hum. Rts. L.J. 125 (1993). The State Department defended them. *See* David Stewart, *U.S. Ratification of the Covenant on Civil and Political Rights: The Significance of the Reservations, Understandings, and Declarations*, 14 Hum. Rts. L.J. 77 (1993). Stewart, an Assistant Legal Advisor in the Department, argued that the U.S. has accepted the Covenant with few substantive limitations. He stated that the reservations are not contrary to the object and purpose of the Covenant. *Id.* See also the notable contribution by Stefan Riesenfeld & Frederick Abbott, *Foreword: Symposium on Parliamentary Participation in the Making and Operation of Treaties*, 67 CHI-KENT L. REV. 293 (1992).

Several parties to the Covenant objected to various limitations. Eleven European countries, for instance, objected to the reservation preserving the right to impose the death penalty on juvenile offenders. They contended that it is incompatible with the object and purpose of the treaty. Eight countries objected to the reservation limiting the meaning of "cruel, inhuman or degrading treatment or punishment." Finland and Sweden objected to the understanding allowing distinctions based on certain characteristics if rationally related to a legitimate governmental objective. Sweden also objected to the reservation preserving the right to apply the penalty in effect at the time an offense was committed.

See U.N., MULTILATERAL TREATIES DEPOSITED WITH THE SECRETARY-GENERAL: STATUS AS AT 31 DECEMBER 1993, at 134 (1994).

d.   Convention on the Elimination of All Forms of Racial Discrimination (Racial Convention)

The Racial Convention was adopted in 1965. Though President Johnson signed on September 28, 1966, it was not transmitted to the Senate until President Carter did so in 1978. Neither Presidents Reagan nor Bush supported ratification. The Clinton Administration, however, recommended ratification and proposed three reservations, one understanding, and one declaration, as follows:

I.   The Senate's advice and consent is subject to the following reservations:

(1)   That the Constitution and laws of the United States contain extensive protections of individual freedom of speech, expression and association. Accordingly, the United States does not accept any obligation under this Convention, in particular under Articles 4 and 7, to restrict those rights, through the adoption of legislation or any other measures, to the extent that they are protected by the Constitution and laws of the United States.

(2)   That the Constitution and the laws of the United States establish extensive protections against discrimination, reaching significant areas of non-governmental activity. Individual privacy and freedom from governmental interference in private conduct, however, are also recognized as among the fundamental values which shape our free and democratic society. The United States understands that the identification of the rights protected under the Convention by reference in Article 1 to the fields of "public life" reflects a similar distinction between spheres of public conduct that are customarily the subject of governmental regulation, and spheres of private conduct that are not. To the extent, however, that the Convention calls for a broader regulation of private conduct, the United States does not accept any obligation under this Convention to enact legislation or take other measures under paragraph (1) of Article 2, subparagraphs (1)(c) and (d) of Article 2, Article 3 and Article 5 with respect to private conduct except as mandated by the Constitution and laws of the United States.

(3)   That with reference to Article 22 of the Convention, before any dispute to which the United States is a party may be submitted to the jurisdiction of the International Court of Justice under this article, the specific consent of the United States is required in each case.

II.   The Senate's advice and consent is subject to the following understanding, which shall apply to the obligations of the United States under this Convention:

That the United States understands that this Convention shall be implemented by the Federal Government to the extent that it exercises jurisdiction over the matters covered therein, and otherwise by the state and local governments. To the extent that state and local governments exercise jurisdiction over such matters, the Federal Government shall, as necessary, take appropriate measures to ensure the fulfillment of this Convention.

III.   The Senate's advice and consent is subject to the following declaration:

That the United States declares that the provisions of the Conventionare not self-executing.

140 CONG. REC. S7634 (daily ed., June 24, 1994). The Foreign Relations Committee added this proviso:

IV.   The Senate's advice and consent is subject to the following proviso, which shall not be included in the instrument of ratification to be deposited by the President:

Nothing in this Convention requires or authorizes legislation, or other action, by the United States of America prohibited by the Constitution of the United States as interpreted by the United States.

Id. Note that as part of a compromise, Senator Helms agreed that the proviso would not be included in the instrument of ratification deposited with the U.N.

Many human rights activists criticized the qualifications, particularly the declaration that the treaty was not self-executing. The International Human Rights Law Group, for example, declared that most of the qualifications were unnecessary or undesirable. The American Bar Association supported most of the qualifications, but believed the third reservation was more restrictive than necessary to achieve its goal of gradual acceptance of ICJ jurisdiction through successive agreements with specific states. See Hearing on the International Convention on the Elimination of All Forms of Racial Discrimination Before the Committee on Foreign Relations of the United States Senate, S. HRG. REP. NO. 659, 103d Cong., 2d Sess. (1994). Nonetheless, on June 24, 1994, the Senate gave its advise and consent to ratification with the quoted qualifications. 140 CONG. REC. S7634 (daily ed., June 24, 1994). The U.S. deposited its instrument of ratification on October 21, 1994, and the treaty came into force with regard to the U.S. on November 20, 1994.

e.   Convention on the Elimination of All Forms of Discrimination against Women (Women's Convention)

The Women's Convention was adopted by the U.N. General Assembly on December 18, 1979, signed by the U.S. on July 17, 1980, and submitted to the Senate by President Carter on November 12, 1980. Neither Reagan nor Bush advocated ratification. The Senate Foreign Relations Committee held no hearings until August 2, 1990, and then did not send the Convention to the full Senate. In 1993, however, 68 senators asked President Clinton to take steps necessary for ratification. In October 1994, the Committee voted 13-4 in favor of forwarding the Convention to the full Senate, and no action was taken.

The Committee recommended four reservations, four understandings, and two declarations, as follows:

I.   The Senate's advice and consent is subject to the following reservations:

(1)   That the Constitution and laws of the United States establish extensive protections against discrimination, reaching all forms of governmental activity as well as significant areas of non-governmental activity. However, individual privacy and freedom from governmental interference in private conduct are also recognized as among the fundamental values of our free and democratic society. The United States understands that by its terms the Convention requires broad regulation of private conduct, in particular under Articles 2, 3 and 5. The United States does not accept any obligation under the Convention to enact legislation or to take any other action with respect to private conduct except as mandated by the Constitution and laws of the United States.

(2)   That under current U.S. law and practice, women are permitted to volunteer for military service without restriction, and women in fact serve in all U.S. armed services, including in combat positions. However, the United States does not accept an obligation under the Convention to assign women to all military units and positions which may require engagement in direct combat.

(3)   That U.S. law provides strong protections against gender discrimination in the area of remuneration, including the right to equal pay for equal work in jobs that are substantially similar. However, the United States does not accept any obligation under this Convention to enact legislation establishing the doctrine of comparable worth as that term is understood in U.S. practice.

(4)   That current U.S. law contains substantial provisions for maternity leave in many employment situations but does not require paid maternity leave. Therefore, the United States does not accept an obligation under Article 11(2)(b) to introduce maternity leave with pay or with comparable social benefits without loss of former employment, seniority or social allowances.

II.   The Senate's advice and consent is subject to the following understandings:

(1)   That the United States understands that this Convention shall be implemented by the Federal Government to the extent that it exercises jurisdiction over the matters covered therein, and otherwise by the state and local governments. To the extent that state and local governments exercise jurisdiction over such matters, the Federal Government shall, as necessary, take appropriate measures to ensure the fulfillment of this Convention

(2)   That the Constitution and laws of the United States contain extensive protections of individual freedom of speech, expression and association. Accordingly, the United States does not accept any obligation under this Convention, in particular under Articles 5, 7, 8 and 13, to restrict those rights, through the adoption of legislation or any other measures, to the extent that they are protected by the Constitution and laws of the United States.

(3)   That the United States understands that Article 12 permits States Parties to determine which health care services are appropriate in connection with family planning, pregnancy, confinement and the post-natal period, as well as when the provision of free services is necessary, and does not mandate the provision of particular services on a cost-free basis.

(4)   That nothing in this Convention shall be construed to reflect or create any right to abortion and in no case should abortion be promoted as a method of family planning.

III.   The Senate's advice and consent is subject to the following declarations:

(1)   That the United States declares that, for purposes of its domestic law, the provisions of the Convention are non-selfexecuting.

(2)   That with reference to Article 29(2), the United States declares that it does not

consider itself bound by the provisions of Article 29(1). The specific consent of the United States to the jurisdiction of the International Court of Justice concerning disputes over the interpretation or application of this Convention is required on a case-by-case basis.

140 CONG. REC. S13927-28 (daily ed. Oct. 3, 1994).

f. American Convention on Human Rights (American Convention)

The American Convention was adopted in 1968. President Carter signed on June 1, 1977, and submitted it to the Senate six months later. In a letter accompanying the transmission of the Convention to President Carter, Deputy Secretary of State Warren Christopher acknowledged:

> The American Convention on Human Rights is a significant advance in the development of the international law of human rights and in the development of human rights law among the American States. United States ratification of the Convention is likely to spur interest in this important document among other American States. United States adherence is in the national interest and in that of the world community. It is our hope that the Senate, after full consideration, will give prompt approval to the Convention, and that the United States will become a party to it.

The Senate Committee held hearings in 1979 but took no action, and the U.S. still has not ratified. At the June 1993 World Conference on Human Rights in Vienna, Secretary Christopher declared that the U.S. "strongly support[s] the general goals" of the American Convention. He said that the Clinton Administration would support ratification after the Senate had acted on the Racial Convention.

NOTES AND QUESTIONS

1. Think about the reservations, understandings, and declarations attached to each of the treaties described above. What were the purposes of the qualifications?

2. Should the U.S. attach similar qualifications if it ratifies the ESC Covenant? Would we suggest that any other countries take our approach to ratification? Do you think ratification with so many qualifications is worthwhile? Might other countries argue the qualifications are not effective? What is the effect of an objection?

3. At the 1993 World Conference on Human Rights in Vienna, the U.S. joined a consensus declaration that urged all states "to avoid, as far as possible, the resort to reservations." Has U.S. practice since then been justifiable?

4. In November 1994, the Human Rights Committee issued a General Comment, in accordance with its power under Article 40 of the Civil and Political Rights Covenant criticizing the increasing number of reservations States add to treaties before ratifying. Human Rights Committee, *General Comment No. 24*, U.N. Doc. CCPR/C/21/Rev.1/Add.6 (1994). After noting that, as of November 1, 1994, 46 of the 127 parties to the Civil and Political Covenant entered a total of 150 reservations, the Committee concluded that "[t]he number of reservations, their content and their scope may undermine the effective implementation of the Covenant and tend to weaken respect for the obligations of States Parties." *Id.* ¶ 1. The Committee also noted that it is often difficult to distinguish between reservations and declarations, and declared that it would acknowledge distinctions based on the intent of the party rather than on the form of the instrument:

If a statement, irrespective of its name or title, purports to exclude or modify the legal effect of a treaty in its application to the State, it constitutes a reservation. Conversely, if a so-called reservation merely offers a State's understanding of a provision but does not exclude or modify that provision in its application to that State, it is, in reality, not a reservation.

Id. ¶ 3 (footnote omitted). The Committee acknowledged that reservations "serve a useful function" by enabling States that might otherwise have difficulty guaranteeing all the rights in the Covenant to nonetheless ratify, but stressed its desire that states accept the full range of obligations imposed by the treaty. *Id.* ¶ 4. Paragraphs 6 and 16 of the Comment state that the Committee will accept only reservations that are compatible with the object and purpose of the treaty, pursuant to Article 19(3) of the Vienna Convention on the Law of Treaties and the ICJ *Reservations to the Genocide Convention Case* (1951). The Committee went on to assess the compatibility of certain types of reservations, discuss its authority to make determinations concerning compatibility, and propose consequences for "unacceptable" reservations:

8.   Reservations that offend peremptory norms would not be compatible with the object and purpose of the Covenant. . . . [P]rovisions in the Covenant that represent customary international law . . . may not be the subject of reservations. Accordingly, a State may not reserve the right to engage in slavery, to torture, to subject persons to cruel, inhuman or degrading treatment or punishment, to arbitrarily deprive persons of their lives, to arbitrarily arrest and detain persons, to deny freedom of thought, conscience and religion, to presume a person guilty unless he proves his innocence, to execute pregnant women or children, to permit the advocacy of national, racial or religious hatred, to deny to persons of marriageable age the right to marry, or to deny to minorities the right to enjoy their own culture, profess their own religion, or use their own language. And while reservations to particular clauses of Article 14 may be acceptable, a general reservation to the right to a fair trial would not be.
. . .

10.   The Committee has further examined whether categories of reservations may offend the "object and purpose" test. In particular, it falls for consideration as to whether reservations to the non-derogable provisions of the Covenant are compatible with its object and purpose. While there is no hierarchy of importance of rights under the Covenant, the operation of certain rights may not be suspended, even in times of national emergency. . . . While there is no automatic correlation between reservations to non-derogable provisions, and reservations which offend against the object and purpose of the Covenant, a State has a heavy onus to justify such a reservation.

11.   The Covenant consists not just of specified rights, but of important supportive guarantees. These guarantees provide the necessary framework for securing the rights in the Covenant and are thus essential to its object and purpose. Some operate at the national level and some at the international level. Reservations designed to remove these guarantees are thus not acceptable. Thus, a State could not make a reservation to article 2, paragraph 3 of the Covenant, indicating that it intends to provide no remedies for human rights violations. Guarantees such as these are an integral part of the structure of the Covenant and underpin its efficacy. The Covenant also envisages, for the better attainment of its stated objectives, a monitoring role for the Committee. Reservations that purport to evade that essential element in the design of the Covenant, which is also directed to securing the enjoyment of the rights, are also incompatible with its object and purpose. . . . Accordingly, a reservation that rejects the Committee's competence to interpret the requirement of any provisions of the Covenant would also be contrary to the object and purpose of that treaty.

12.   The intention of the Covenant is that the rights contained therein should be ensured to all those under a State party's jurisdiction. . . . Of particular concern are widely formulated reservations which essentially render ineffective all Covenant

rights which would require any change in national law to ensure compliance with Covenant obligations. No real international rights or obligations have thus been accepted. And when there is an absence of provisions to ensure that Covenant rights may be sued on in domestic courts, and, further, a failure to allow individual complaints to be brought to the Committee under the first Optional Protocol, all the essential elements of the Covenant guarantees have been removed. . . .

16.   The Committee finds it important to address which body has the legal authority to make determinations as to whether specific reservations are compatible with the object and purpose of the Covenant. As for international treaties in general, . . . a State which objected to a reservation on the grounds of incompatibility . . . could, through objecting, regard the treaty as not in effect as between itself and the reserving State. . . . Essentially, a reservation precludes the operation, as between the reserving and other States, of the provision reserved; and an objection thereto leads to the reservation being in operation as between the reserving and objecting State only to the extent that it has not been objected to. . . .

18.   It necessarily falls to the Committee to determine whether a specific reservation is compatible with the object and purpose of the Covenant. This is in part because . . . it is an inappropriate task for States parties in relation to human rights treaties, and in part because it is a task that the Committee cannot avoid in the performance of its functions. . . . The normal consequence of an unacceptable reservation is not that the Covenant will not be in effect at all for a reserving party. Rather, such a reservation will generally be severable, in the sense that the Covenant will be operative for the reserving party without benefit of the reservation.

Id. ¶¶ 8-12, 16, 18 (footnotes omitted). Under the Committee's interpretation should any U.S. qualifications really be considered reservations? Do you think some of the U.S. reservations are invalid?

5.   Conrad Harper, Legal Adviser of the State Department, transmitted certain U.S. "observations with respect to General Comment 24." Letter from Conrad Harper to Francisco Jose Aguilar-Urbina, Chairman, U.N. Human Rights Committee (Mar. 28-29, 1995):

There can be no serious question about the propriety of the Committee's concern about the possible effect of excessively broad reservations on the general protection and promotion of the rights reflected in the Covenant . . .. General Comment 24, however, appears to go much too far. The United States would therefore like to set forth in summary fashion a number of observations concerning the General Comment as follows.

1.   Role of the Committee

[The last statement of paragraph 11] can be read to present the rather surprising assertion that it is contrary to the object and purpose of the Covenant not to accept the Committee's views on the interpretation of the Covenant. This would be a rather significant departure from the Covenant scheme, which does not impose on States Parties an obligation to give effect to the Committee's interpretations or confer on the Committee the power to render definitive or binding interpretations of the Covenant. The drafters of the Covenant could have given the Committee this role but deliberately chose not to do so. . . .

Moreover, the Committee appears to dispense with the established procedures for determining the permissibility of reservations and to divest States Parties of any role in determining the meaning of the Covenant . . . and of the extent of their treaty obligations. . . .

The Committee's position, while interesting, runs contrary to the Covenant scheme and international law.

2.   Acceptability of Reservations: Governing Legal Principles

The question of the status of the Committee's views is of some significance in light of the apparent lines of analysis concerning the permissibility of reservations in paragraphs 8-9. . . .

It is clear that a State cannot exempt itself from a peremptory norm of international law by making a reservation to the Covenant. It is not at all clear that a State cannot [choose] to exclude one means of enforcement of particular norms by reserving against inclusion of those norms in its Covenant obligations.

The proposition that any reservation which contravenes a norm of customary international law is *per se* incompatible with the object and purpose of this or any other convention, however, is a much more significant and sweeping premise. It is, moreover, wholly unsupported by and is in fact contrary to international law. As recognized in paragraph 10 analysis of non-derogable rights, an "object and purpose" analysis by its nature requires consideration of the particular treaty, right, and reservation in question. . . .

3. Specific Reservations

The precise specification of what is contrary to customary international law, moreover, is a much more substantial question than indicated by the Comment. Even where a rule is generally established in customary international law, the exact contours and meaning of the customary law principle may need to be considered.

Paragraph 8, however, asserts in a wholly conclusory fashion that a number of propositions are customary international law which, to speak plainly, are not. . . .

4. Domestic Implementation

The discussion in paragraph 12, as it stands, is very likely to give rise to misunderstandings . . .. The Committee here states, with regard to implementing the Covenant in domestic law, that such laws "may need to be altered properly to reflect the requirements of the Covenant; and mechanisms at the domestic level *will be needed to allow the Covenant rights to be enforceable at the local level.*" (Emphasis added in original.)

. . . [T]his statement may be cited as an assertion that States Parties *must* allow suits in domestic courts based directly on the provisions of Covenant. Some countries do in fact have such a scheme of "self-executing" treaties. In other countries, however, existing domestic law already provides the substantive rights reflected in the Covenant as well as multiple possibilities for suit to enforce those rights. . . .

As a general matter, deciding on the most appropriate means of domestic implementation of treaty obligations is, as indicated in Article 40, left to the internal law and processes of each State Party. . . .

5. Effect of Invalidity of Reservations

It seems unlikely that one can misunderstand the concluding point of this General Comment, in paragraph 18, that reservations which the Committee deems invalid "will generally be severable, in the sense that the Covenant will be operative for the reserving party without benefit of the reservation." Since this conclusion is so completely at odds with established legal practice and principles and even the express and clear terms of adherence by many States, it would be welcome if some helpful clarification could be made.

The reservations contained in the United States' instrument of ratification are integral parts of its consent to be bound by the Covenant and are not severable.

If it were to be determined that any one or more of them were ineffective, the ratification as a whole would thereby be nullified.

Articles 20 and 21 of the Vienna Convention set forth the consequences of reservations and objections to them. Only two possibilities are provided. Either (i) the remainder of the treaty comes into force between the parties in question or (ii) the treaty does not come into force at all between these parties. In accordance with

Article 20, paragraph 4(c), the choice of these results is left to the objecting party. The Convention does not even contemplate the possibility that the full treaty might come into force for the reserving state.

6. If the Committee is correct, what would be the implications for U.S. ratification of future human rights treaties? Do you agree with Conrad Harper or the Human Rights Committee?

7. Other countries have submitted to the Human Rights Committee observations regarding General Comment 24. *See, e.g.,* Letter from Michel de Bonnecorse, French Ambassador to the United Nations, to the Center for Human Rights (Sept. 11, 1995) (copy on file with authors); *Report of the Human Rights Committee,* 50 U.N. GAOR Supp. (No. 40) at 135, U.N. Doc. A/50/40 (1995) (containing the United Kingdom's observations).

8. On December 9, 1993, the U.N. General Assembly endorsed a decision of the U.N. International Law Commission to consider and report on "the law and practice relating to reservations to treaties." U.N. Doc. A/RES/48/31 (1993). At its forty-sixth session, the ILC appointed Alain Pellet as Special Rapporteur for this topic. *Report of the International Law Commission on the Work of its Forty-Sixth Session, Official Records of the General Assembly, Forty-ninth session, Supplement No. 10,* U.N. Doc. A/49/10 (1994). Mr. Pellet's initial report was issued in May 1995. International Law Commission, *First Report on the Law and Practice Relating to Reservations to Treaties, by Alain Pellet, Special Rapporteur,* U.N. Doc. A/CN.4/470 (1995).

9. U.S. consideration of treaty ratifications is ongoing. In late February 1996, the U.S. was in the final stages of considering ILO Convention No. 111 (concerning Discrimination in Respect of Employment and Occupation) for submission to the President and eventually the Senate.

D. THE COVENANT ON ECONOMIC, SOCIAL AND CULTURAL RIGHTS

1. What Are Economic, Social, and Cultural Rights?

On January 6, 1941, while German bombers continued their nightly blitz of British cities and Hitler planned the conquest of the Soviet Union which ultimately would leave 20 million people dead, President Roosevelt, in his annual State of the Union address to Congress, outlined his vision of the future based upon "four essential human freedoms." He declared:

> In the future days, which we seek to make secure, we look forward to a world founded upon four essential human freedoms.
> The first is the freedom of speech and expression everywhere in the world.
> The second is the freedom of every person to worship God in his own way everywhere in the world.
> The third is the freedom from want, which, translated into world terms, means economic understandings which will secure to every nation a healthy peace-time life for its inhabitants everywhere in the world.
> The fourth is freedom from fear—which, translated into world terms, means a world-wide reduction of armaments to such a point and in such a thorough fashion that no nation will be in a position to commit an act of physical aggression against any neighbor—anywhere in the world.

Franklin D. Roosevelt, "Four Freedoms" Speech, 87-I CONG. REC. 44, 46-47 (1941).

Later during World War II, President Roosevelt's State of the Union message on January 11, 1944, more specifically addressed the freedoms he had previously enumerated:

It is our duty now to begin to lay the plans and determine the strategy for the winning of a lasting peace and the establishment of an American standard of living higher than ever before known. We cannot be content, no matter how high that general standard of living may be, if some fraction of our people—whether it be one-third or one-fifth or one-tenth—is ill-fed, ill-clothed, ill-housed, and insecure.

This Republic had its beginning and grew to its present strength, under the protection of certain inalienable political rights—among them the right of free speech, free press, free worship, trial by jury, freedom from unreasonable searches and seizures. They were our rights to life and liberty.

As our Nation has grown in size and stature, however,—as our industrial economy expanded—these political rights proved inadequate to assure us equality in the pursuit of happiness.

We have come to a clear realization of the fact that true individual freedom cannot exist without economic security and independence. "Necessitous men are not free men." People who are hungry and out of a job are the stuff of which dictatorships are made.

In our day these economic truths have become accepted as self-evident. We have accepted, so to speak, *a second Bill of Rights* under which a new basis of security and prosperity can be established for all—regardless of station, race or creed.

Among these are:

The right to a useful and remunerative job in the industries or shops or farms or mines of the Nation;

The right to earn enough to provide adequate food and clothing and recreation;

The right of every farmer to raise and sell his products at a return which will give him and his family a decent living;

The right of every businessman, large and small, to trade in an atmosphere of freedom from unfair competition and domination by monopolies at home or abroad;

The right of every family to a decent home;

The right to adequate medical care and the opportunity to achieve and enjoy good health;

The right to adequate protection from the economic fears of old age, sickness, accident, and unemployment;

The right to a good education.

All of these rights spell security. And after this war is won, we must be prepared to move forward, in the implementation of these rights, to new goals of human happiness and well-being.

America's own rightful place in the world depends in large part upon how fully these and similar rights have been carried into practice for our citizens. For unless there is security here at home there cannot be lasting peace in the world.

Franklin D. Roosevelt, State of the Union Message, 90-I Cong. Rec. 55, 57 (1944) (emphasis added).

After World War II the international community began to focus on the rights discussed by President Roosevelt in the excerpts above. Several international instruments issued during the post-War period protect economic, social, and cultural rights to some extent. Notably, Article 55 of the U.N. Charter prescribes:

[T]he United Nations shall promote higher standards of living, full employment, and conditions of economic and social progress and development; solutions of international economic, social, health, and related problems; and international cultural and educational co-operation; and universal respect for, and observance of human rights and fundamental freedoms for all without distinction as to race, sex, language, or religion.

In Article 56, all members pledge "to take joint and separate action . . . for the achievement of the purposes set forth in Article 55."

The 1948 Universal Declaration of Human Rights added specificity to those goals. In its Article 22, the General Assembly proclaimed that:

> Everyone, as a member of society, has the right to social security and is entitled to realization, through national effort and international cooperation and in accordance with the organization and resources of each State, of the economic, social and cultural rights indispensable for his dignity and the free development of his personality.

The Declaration also proclaims that everyone has the right to: work and join trade unions (Article 23); rest and leisure (Article 24); an adequate standard of living (Article 25); education (Article 26); and participate freely in cultural life (Article 27).

Though the earlier agreements broadly defined the scope of economic, social, and cultural rights, the principal source of international obligations now is the International Covenant on Economic, Social and Cultural Rights, G.A. res. 2200A (XXI), 21 U.N. GAOR Supp. (No. 16) at 49, U.N. Doc. A/6316 (1966), 993 U.N.T.S. 3, *entered into force* Jan. 3, 1976. Originally the drafters intended to create one document covering all rights enunciated in the Universal Declaration. In the course of drafting, however, they decided to employ separate documents: the ESC Covenant; and the Civil and Political Covenant.

Professor David Trubek suggests one reason for that decision might have been a belief that it was impossible to develop one system to implement both sets of rights. He notes that civil and political rights can be implemented more immediately through passing laws and revising constitutions, while economic, social, and cultural rights require action over time, including establishment of social programs. The difference in temporal implementation suggests a similar difference in implementation methodology. He also noted that some states might be unwilling to accept an obligation to ensure economic, social, and cultural rights. David M. Trubek, *Economic, Social, and Cultural Rights in The Third World: Human Rights Law and Human Needs Programs, in* HUMAN RIGHTS IN INTERNATIONAL LAW: LEGAL AND POLICY ISSUES 205 (Theodor Meron ed., 1984).

The following excerpt further illuminates the nature of economic, social, and cultural rights in the context of the ESC Covenant. Before reading the excerpt, please be sure to read through the substantive provisions of the ESC Covenant that are reprinted in *Selected International Human Rights Instruments*. As you read the excerpt, note how U.S. interpretation of the Covenant's words leads to some objections concerning ratification.

Philip Alston & Gerard Quinn, *The Nature and Scope of States Parties' Obligations Under the International Covenant on Economic, Social and Cultural Rights*, 9 HUM. RTS. Q. 156, 157-92 (1987) (footnotes omitted):

I. INTRODUCTION

The concept of economic, social, and cultural rights has long generated controversy among philosophers, as indeed has the very notion of human rights itself. From a legal perspective, however, this controversy should have been laid to rest by the adoption [in 1966] of the International Covenant on Economic, Social and Cultural Rights by the United Nations General Assembly. . . . Nevertheless, the debate remains at least as polarized today as it ever was in the days when the international community had yet to recognize formally the legitimacy of economic, social, and cultural rights. . . .

The purpose of this article is to examine the nature and scope of the obligations of states parties under Parts I, II, and III of the Covenant. . . . [I]t is hoped that a clearer understanding of the obligations contained in the Covenant will serve to destroy some of the fallacies and misperceptions which in the past have too often served to distort and obfuscate the debate. . . .

A. *An Overview of Common Perceptions of Economic, Social and Cultural Rights*

Before embarking on a textual analysis of the Covenant it is appropriate first of all to take note of some of the ways in which economic, social, and cultural rights are commonly perceived. For the most part the relevant characterizations are put forward in the context of comparisons between civil and political rights on the one hand and economic, social, and cultural rights on the other.

The first and most commonly drawn distinction is between positive and negative rights. Thus civil and political rights are characterized as negative in that they require only that governments should abstain from activities that would violate them. Economic, social and cultural rights require active intervention on the part of governments and cannot be realized without such intervention. Closely linked to this is a distinction between resource-intensive and cost-free rights. Thus it is said that civil and political rights can be realized without significant costs being incurred, whereas the enjoyment, of economic, social, and cultural rights requires a major commitment of resources. Largely for that reason the former are considered to be capable of immediate and full realization whereas the latter constitute no more than long term aspirational goals.

A further distinction arises from the fact that in direct contrast to the obligations attaching to economic, social, and cultural rights those relating to civil and political rights are considered to be capable of relatively precise definition, to be readily justiciable, and to be susceptible of enforcement. Similarly civil and political rights relate to widely shared values to which governments are genuinely committed and raise issues that are manageable and within reach. By contrast, economic, social and cultural rights have attracted no real governmental commitment, and concern issues that are considered to be inherently intractable and unmanageable and are thus much too complex to be dealt with under the rubric of rights.

Finally, civil and political rights are seen as essentially non-ideological in nature and are potentially compatible with most systems of government. By contrast, economic, social, and cultural rights are often perceived to be of a deeply ideological nature, to necessitate an unacceptable degree of intervention in the domestic affairs of states, and to be inherently incompatible with a free market economy.

. . . In the final analysis the central underlying question concerns the extent to which the concept of economic, social, and cultural rights can or should be artificially moulded so as to fit a predetermined conception of rights which by definition has been tailored to reflect the perceived characteristics of civil and political rights. . . .

II.   THE NATURE OF STATES PARTIES' DOMESTIC OBLIGATIONS UNDER THE COVENANT . . .

Article 2(1) reads as follows:

Each State Party to the present Covenant undertakes to take steps, individually and through international assistance and co-operation, especially economic and technical, to the maximum of its available resources, with a view to achieving progressively the full realization of the rights recognized in the present Covenant by all appropriate means, including particularly the adoption of legislative measures.

A. *An Analysis of the Words and Phrases Used in Article 2(1)*

(i) *"undertakes to take steps"*

The original proposal under which states parties would have undertaken "to promote" the rights recognized was replaced almost immediately by this phrase. . . .

During the preparatory work most states' representatives indicated a preference for the phrase "to take steps" rather than "to guarantee." The former had the "virtue" of avoiding a formal undertaking to guarantee the rights, a commitment that would have been too "onerous in the circumstances." It was a more "guarded" expression and more realistically reflected what could be expected of states. Proposals to use the terms "to ensure" and "to pledge themselves" were unacceptable to the majority of the members of the Commission on Human Rights.

In essence the undertaking is akin to assuming an obligation of conduct . . .. While the resulting obligation is clearly to be distinguished from, and is less demanding than a guarantee, it nonetheless represents a clear legal undertaking. The key point is that the undertaking to take steps is of immediate application. Thus, at least in this respect, the Covenant imposes an immediate and readily identifiable obligation upon states parties.

While the full realization of the relevant rights may be achieved progressively, steps towards that goal must be taken either before or within a reasonably short time after ratification.

(ii) *"by all appropriate means, including particularly the adoption of legislative measures"*

As a general rule, the ratification of a treaty need not necessarily entail domestic legal consequences provided, of course, that the treaty itself does not explicitly call upon states parties to take legal measures. In the case of the International Covenant on Civil and Political Rights the nature of the obligation imposed upon states parties by Article 2 makes it abundantly clear that legal measures are required. However, in the case of the International Covenant on Economic, Social, and Cultural Rights it is unclear whether states parties are required to take such action. . . .

[The authors conclude that Article 2 permits but does not require parties to incorporate the Covenant into national law. The Covenant similarly does not require parties to adopt legislation to give effect to their obligations under Article 2. Such an obligation to legislate was rejected by the drafters of the Covenant because of the various ways in which parties choose to fulfill their responsibilities under international treaties—"by legislation, administrative action, common law, custom or otherwise." The authors then conclude legislation alone is insufficient to fulfill a state's obligation under Article 2 to use "all appropriate means." The drafters of the Covenant clearly intended to require parties to do more than simply take legislative action to implement the Covenant.

The guidelines governing the form and content of states' reports under the Covenant also support that construction of the framers' intent "clearly indicate that states should provide details not only of relevant laws but also of relevant agreements, court decisions, policies, programs, techniques, measures, etc."]

. . . [T]he mere enactment of legislation does not *ipso facto* constitute a discharge of the relevant obligations. What is required is "to make the provisions of the

Convention effective in law and in fact. . . . Full conformity of the law . . . is therefore essential, but taken alone is not enough." . . .

Judicial Remedies. A requirement that judicial remedies for violations be provided in national law is a characteristic of the great majority of international human rights treaties. . . .

For some commentators, the formal justiciability of a right is an indispensable element. Thus for Kelsen "the essential element [of a right] is the legal power bestowed upon the [individual] by the legal order to bring about, by a law suit, the execution of a sanction as a reaction against the nonfulfillment of the obligation." While some other writers do not go so far, it is frequently contended that a claim must be enforceable if it is to qualify as a human right. The issue then is how enforceability differs from justiciability. . . .

When the Covenant on Civil and Political Rights was being drafted it was contended that the provision of effective remedies was implicit in the general obligation imposed upon states parties and that an explicit statement to this effect was unnecessary. That view was rejected, however, and Article 2(3) is both explicit and detailed. No counterpart to it was proposed during the drafting of the Economic and Social Covenant although the issue was touched upon on occasion. . . .

It is clear from the preparatory work therefore that the provision of judicial remedies cannot be considered to be an indispensable element of the obligation contained in Article 2(1). . . .

Other Appropriate Means. In addition to the various possible means of implementation referred to above, mention should also be made of what have traditionally been termed promotional measures. These might include measures to disseminate the text of the Covenant, to translate it into local languages, to promote teaching and discussion, to provide training courses for judges and lawyers, etc. . . .

(iii) *"achieve progressively"*

The concept of progressive achievement is in many ways the linchpin of the whole Covenant. Upon its meaning turns the nature of state obligations. Most of the rights granted depend in varying degrees on the availability of resources and this fact is recognized and reflected in the concept of "progressive achievement." The concept thus mirrors the inevitably contingent nature of state obligations. The question that arises is whether the nature of the obligation is so contingent as to deprive it of any normative significance. . . .

. . . Commentators invariably contrast the concept of progressive achievement with that of immediate implementation which is said to be required by Article 2 of the Civil and Political Rights Covenant. . . . [T]he reality is that the full realization of civil and political rights is heavily dependent both on the availability of resources and the development of the necessary societal structures. The suggestion that realization of civil and political rights requires only abstention on the part of the state and can be achieved without significant expenditure is patently at odds with reality. . . .

In the context of the preparatory work for Article 2 the need to reflect economic circumstances in determining the nature of state obligations was recognized by most as legitimate. As one representative put it, the "covenant would recognise rights whose content would differ greatly from country to country, depending on available resources, and it therefore could not impose absolute obligations on the states parties to it." The commitment "was conditional and depended upon factors outside [state] control, such as international co-operation, available resources and progressive action." . . .

(iv) *"to the maximum of its available resources"*

It is the state of a country's economy that most vitally determines the level of its obligations as they relate to any of the enumerated rights under the Covenant. From an evaluation of these circumstances flows a picture of a state's abilities and from this may be determined the thresholds it must meet in discharging its obligations. In ascertaining the quantum of resources to be set aside to promote realization of the rights, the state is of course entitled to a wide measure of discretion. Nevertheless such discretion cannot be entirely open-ended or it would have the *de facto* effect of nullifying the existence of any real obligation.

The main dilemma that arises in connection with the use of this phrase is clearly posed by the following analysis contained in the commentary on the tentative draft of the Restatement of the Foreign Relations Law of the United States[1]:

> By adhering to this Covenant the United States would be obligated to take legislative, executive and other measures, federal or State, generally of the kind which are already common in the United States, "to the maximum of its available resources," "with a view to achieving progressively the full realization" of those rights. Since there is no definition or standard in the Covenant, the United States would largely determine for itself the meaning of "full realization" and the speed of realization, and whether it is using "maximum of its available resources" for this purpose.

The word "largely" is used in a controlling sense so as to convey the impression that the United States would determine entirely for itself whether it had satisfied the obligation contained in Article 2(1). It would, in other words, be the sole judge of its own compliance.

This interpretation, however, raises the fundamental question as to why it is necessary, or even appropriate, to have an international treaty if each state party is only to be held accountable, with respect to the central element in the obligation, to itself. An open-ended, self-evaluated obligation of this type would seem more characteristic of a declaration or recommendation than of a convention or covenant.

It is therefore not surprising that the interpretation offered by the drafters of the Restatement is not supported by the *traveaux preparatoires*. To the contrary, a number of delegations indicated that they did not consider that a state party's subjective determination as to what constitutes an adequate resource allocation is entitled to complete deference. . . . Rather, it may be appropriate to probe beyond those allocations and take account of the country's "real" resources. . . .

States must therefore, as the French representative put it, "without exceeding the possibilities open to them . . . do their utmost in implementing the rights." In avoiding excessive idealism and in accommodating the test to the changing realities of economic circumstances the framers did not thereby intend to let states arbitrarily and artificially determine for themselves the level of commitment required by the Covenant. Moreover the reference to resources was deemed by many to include whatever international as well as national resources were available. . . .

By the same token it is clear from the *traveaux* that states parties are presumed to have considerable discretion in determining what resources are in fact available for use in economic, social, and cultural rights-related concerns. . . .

The discretion to which a state is entitled is, however, not unlimited, and its position is clearly not immune from scrutiny by the international body charged with

---

[1] [Ed. note: Virtually identical language is contained in Reporter's Note 8, RESTATEMENT (THIRD) OF FOREIGN RELATIONS LAW § 701 (1987).]

responsibility for supervising states parties' compliance with their treaty obligations.

While the Covenant itself is, inevitably, devoid of specific allocational benchmarks, there is presumably a process requirement by which states might be requested to show that adequate consideration has been given to the possible resources available to satisfy each of the Covenant's requirements, even if the effort was ultimately unsuccessful. If a state is unable to do so then it fails to meet its obligation of conduct to ensure a principled policy-making process one reflecting a sense of the importance of the relevant rights. . . .

III.   THE NATURE OF STATES PARTIES' INTERNATIONAL OBLIGATIONS; THE MEANING OF THE PHRASE: "INDIVIDUALLY AND THROUGH INTERNATIONAL ASSISTANCE AND CO-OPERATION, ESPECIALLY ECONOMIC AND TECHNICAL"

The Covenant contains three provisions that could be interpreted as giving rise to an obligation on the part of the richer states parties to provide assistance to poorer states parties in situations in which the latter are prevented by a lack of resources from fulfilling their obligations under the Covenant to their citizens. The first is the phrase quoted above, which appears in Article 2(1). The second is the provision in Article 11(1) according to which states parties agree to "take appropriate steps to ensure the realization of this right [to an adequate standard of living], recognizing to this effect the essential importance of international co-operation based on free consent." Similarly in Article 11(2) states parties agree to take, "individually and through international co-operation," relevant measures concerning the right to be free from hunger.

Almost inevitably, dramatically diverging interpretations of the significance of these provisions have been put forward. On the one hand they have been said to give rise to quite specific international obligations on the part of industrialized countries and to provide the foundations for the existence of a right to development. On the other hand, the Carter administration, in seeking the advice and consent of the U.S. Senate to U.S. ratification of the Covenant, proposed a reservation to the effect that: "It is also understood that paragraph 1 of article 2, as well as article 11 . . . import no legally binding obligation to provide aid to foreign countries."

. . . [T]he phrase under consideration is of direct and immediate relevance to the nature of the obligations implicit in the phrase "to the maximum of its available resources." As noted above, it was made clear during the preparatory work that the word "its" is to be interpreted as including both the resources available to a country internally as well as externally, i.e., from international sources. . . .

During the preparatory work it was conceded by virtually all delegations that the developing states would require some forms of international assistance if they were to be able to promote effectively the realization of economic and social rights. . . .

Those arguing in favor of imposing a strong obligation on the developed countries invoked a wide range of justifications. Perhaps the least controversial was the argument based on interdependence. . . .

On occasion, however, this argument was closely linked to the view that international cooperation was owed to the formerly colonized states in reparation for "the systematic plundering of their wealth under colonialism." As another representative put it, "nations that were or had been colonized did not go begging, but called for the restoration of their rights and property." . . . It was also argued that the absence of a provision relating to international cooperation would render the undertakings of developing countries "purely academic" because they would be unable to afford to implement them.

The only formal suggestion of the existence of a binding obligation came from the Chilean representative who observed "that international assistance to under-developed countries had in a sense become mandatory as a result of commitments assumed by States in the United Nations."

The arguments against that proposition took a variety of forms and came from a significant range of states. France argued simply that "multilateral assistance could not be mandatory" and an almost identical argument was made by the Soviet Union. In the view of the representative of Greece "developing countries like her own had no right to demand financial assistance through such an instrument; they could ask for it, but not claim it." . . .

. . . [O]n the basis of the preparatory work it is difficult, if not impossible, to sustain the argument that the commitment to international cooperation contained in the Covenant can accurately be characterized as a legally binding obligation upon any particular state to provide any particular form of assistance. It would, however, be unjustified to go further and suggest that the relevant commitment is meaningless. . . .

In conclusion, it seems appropriate to assume that states are likely to accept a far greater level of international obligation *in practice* than they will ever formally accept *in writing*.

NOTES AND QUESTIONS

1. Several other international treaties that affect economic, social, and cultural rights are excerpted in *Selected International Human Rights Instruments. See*

   a. Articles 1, 7, 17, and 23-30 of the Universal Declaration of Human Rights;
   b. Preamble and Article 22 of the Covenant on Civil and Political Rights;
   c. Articles 16, 29-31, 40, 42-45, 47-48, and 52(d) of the O.A.S. Charter;
   d. Preamble and Articles XI-XVI, XXIII, XXVIII, and XXXV-XXXVII of the American Declaration of the Rights and Duties of Man;
   e. Articles 21 and 26 of the American Convention on Human Rights.

Are the rights enumerated in those documents similar to the rights discussed in the excerpt above?

2. What are differences between economic, social, and cultural rights and civil and political rights? How do the two Covenants differ in the obligations they impose on parties with respect to those rights? Might the differences explain why the U.S. has not ratified the ESC Covenant when it has ratified the Civil and Political Covenant? Are there other explanations? What obstacles to ratification are implied in the Alston and Quinn excerpt?

3. For further reading see:

ADVISORY COMMITTEE ON HUM. RTS. AND FOREIGN POL'Y, ECONOMIC, SOCIAL AND CULTURAL HUMAN RIGHTS, Advisory Report No. 18 (1994);

FONS COOMANS, NETHERLANDS INST. HUM. RTS., ECONOMIC, SOCIAL AND CULTURAL RIGHTS, Netherlands Inst. Hum. Rts. SIM Special No. 16 (1995) (report commissioned by the Advisory Committee on Hum. Rts. and Foreign Pol'y of the Netherlands);

MATTHEW C.R. CRAVEN, THE INTERNATIONAL COVENANT ON ECONOMIC, SOCIAL, AND CULTURAL RIGHTS: A PERSPECTIVE ON ITS DEVELOPMENT (1995);

Connie de la Vega, *Protecting Economic, Social and Cultural Rights*, 15 WHITTIER L. REV. 471

(1994) (discussing the ways in which international human rights standards may be used to promote welfare and education rights);

ECONOMIC, SOCIAL AND CULTURAL RIGHTS: A TEXTBOOK (Asbjorn Eide, Catarina Krause, & Allan Rosas eds., 1995);

Vladimir A. Kartashkin, *Economic, Social and Cultural Rights*, *in* INTERNATIONAL DIMENSIONS OF HUMAN RIGHTS 111 (Karel Vasak & Philip Alston eds., 1982);

Realization of Economic, Social and Cultural Rights, Report Submitted by Mr. Danilo Turk, Special Rapporteur, U.N. Doc. E/CN.4/Sub.2/1992/16 (1989) (report of a study for the Sub-Commission on Prevention of Discrimination and Protection of Minorities);

United Nations Action in the Field of Human Rights, at 163-83, U.N. Doc. ST/HR/2/Rev.3 (1988).

---

2. Should the U.S. Ratify the Covenant on Economic, Social and Cultural Rights?

Philip Alston, *U.S. Ratification of the Covenant on Economic, Social and Cultural Rights: The Need for an Entirely New Strategy*, 84 AM. J. INT'L L. 365, 365-92 (1990) (footnotes omitted):

In January 1989, in the follow-up to the Conference on Security and Co-operation in Europe (the so-called Helsinki process), the United States signed the Vienna Declaration, in which it recognized "that the promotion of economic, social, cultural rights . . . is of paramount importance for human dignity and for the attainment of the legitimate aspirations of every individual." To that end, the United States in signing the declaration undertook, *inter alia*, to guarantee "the effective exercise" of economic, social and cultural rights and to consider acceding to the International Covenant on Economic, Social and Cultural Rights. These undertakings seem to warrant renewed consideration of proposals that have been made at various times over the past quarter of a century for the United States to ratify the Covenant on Economic, Social and Cultural Rights.

. . . The thrust of the analysis that follows is to endorse the call for U.S. ratification of the Covenant on Economic, Social and Cultural Rights but to suggest at the same time that the strategy that will be required if success is to be achieved is very different from that pursued so far by the proponents of ratification.

In the past, the tendency has been to portray the Covenant as though it did not differ significantly from the other treaties whose ratification was being advocated. Two different reasons suggest themselves as possible explanations for that tendency. The first is that it was assumed that the best hope of achieving ratification of a potentially controversial Covenant was to smuggle it through as part of a "package" of treaties, the majority of which would presumably be endorsed fairly readily because of their similarity to the U.S. Bill of Rights. A second, alternative, explanation is that it was assumed that the Covenant could be "sold" as part of a package deal largely because it could convincingly be portrayed as being devoid of any substantive practical or legal significance. . . .

There is good reason, however, to question whether the Covenant can, or should, be "sold" to the U.S. Senate on the basis of either of these two approaches. In the first place, despite having been around since 1966, the Covenant has failed to attract any significant domestic support, even from within the human rights community . . .. Of even greater relevance is the extent to which it seems to be viewed with suspicion by many Americans, who tend to think of it less as an international treaty seeking to promote the satisfaction of basic material needs than as a "Covenant on Uneconomic, Socialist and Collective Rights." Only by facing that reality, and by taking it as a starting point for an open and animated public debate, is there any real prospect of securing the broad-based support and momentum without which the Senate is unlikely ever to act. . . .

. . . [T]he obstacles to be overcome to secure ratification of the Covenant on Economic, Social and Cultural Rights are . . . formidable. They arise essentially from the absence of clear agreement on values between the United States and the international community when it comes to the very concept of economic, social and cultural rights. The lack of the necessary community of values is most clearly attested to by the fact that the U.S. Government [in the Reagan and Bush administrations], for almost a decade, has categorically denied that there is any such thing as an economic, a social or a cultural human right. . . .

The second obstacle is rather more complex and will prove considerably more difficult to overcome. It derives from the conjunction of two factors. The first is that the nature of the obligations contained in the Covenant on Economic, Social and Cultural Rights, while by no means the object of precise agreement among governments or scholars, is nevertheless considerably more substantial and demanding than has been assumed in most of the ratification debate in the United States so far. Moreover, as the "jurisprudence" relating to individual economic, social and cultural rights becomes clearer, and as the recently established Committee on Economic, Social and Cultural Rights begins to generate a deeper and more widely shared understanding of the nature of the obligations in the Covenant, a decision by the United States to ratify will take on more and more significance. The second complicating factor is the lack of consensus within the United States as to the desirability, or philosophical and political acceptability, of the domestic recognition of economic, social and cultural rights. . . .

I. AN OVERVIEW OF THE RIGHTS AND OBLIGATIONS

The Covenant is sometimes described by its critics as though it were really a "holidays with pay treaty." . . . [A]lthough the right to take an occasional break from work (a sabbath, in religious terms) is an important one, it is perhaps less self-evidently fundamental than several of the other rights dealt with. They include the right to work, which, notwithstanding allegations to the contrary, has always been interpreted by international organizations so as to avoid the implication that a job is guaranteed by the state to all and sundry. The relevant provision, however, does indicate that the job in question should be freely chosen or accepted (Art. 6(1)) and that appropriate policies should be pursued "under conditions safeguarding fundamental political and economic freedoms to the individual" (Art. 6(2)). The link between the two sets of rights is thus strongly reaffirmed.

Articles 7 and 8 deal with conditions of work . . .. Article 9 provides for the right to social security—exactly the term the United States has opted for since the Great Depression. Article 10 confirms the importance of the family as a social group and calls for special protection for children and young persons and for mothers during a reasonable period before and after childbirth. None of these provisions appear to be controversial or out of step with widespread practice in the United States. The same can be said of Article 15, which in most respects raises issues that seem more relevant to the Covenant on Civil and Political Rights. . . .

The remaining articles (Arts. 11-14), however, are more problematic from a U.S.

perspective. In essence, they deal with the rights to food, clothing and housing, the right of access to physical and mental health care, and the right to education. In terms of the "ratifiability" of the Covenants by the United States, the issues raised by that cluster of rights are twofold. Is the United States prepared to commit itself to the general proposition that there is indeed a human right to each of these social goods or, put differently, to the satisfaction of each of these basic human needs? And, even if it is, is it prepared to accept the specific level of obligation in that regard provided for by the Covenant? . . .

The Covenant makes clear that the responsibility for monitoring and promoting the implementation of the various rights is principally incumbent upon the state party itself. . . . The sole international implementation mechanism provided for in the Covenant consists of the duty assumed by each state party to report . . . .. The procedure is based on the assumption that a constructive dialogue between the Committee and the state party, in a nonadversarial, cooperative spirit, is the most productive means of prompting the government concerned to take the requisite action. . . . Although . . . the principal thrust of the implementation provisions of the Covenant is to emphasize the responsibility of the state party itself, the element of international accountability is not thereby rendered irrelevant or meaningless. . . .

II. THE FOREIGN POLICY OBSTACLE: U.S. REJECTION OF ECONOMIC, SOCIAL AND CULTURAL "RIGHTS" AS RIGHTS

In the early days of the Reagan administration, an internal memorandum of the Department of State on human rights policy was leaked to the press and reprinted in full in the New York Times. The memorandum, which was apparently approved by then Secretary of State Alexander Haig, has subsequently been shown to have had a major impact on U.S. policy. It . . . endorsed the unqualified rejection of economic, social and cultural "rights" as rights. Human rights were to be explicitly defined for the purposes of future U.S. policy as "meaning political rights and civil liberties." To entrench this highly restrictive definition, the memorandum urged that the administration "move away from 'human rights' as a term, and begin to speak of 'individual rights,' 'political rights' and 'civil liberties.' "

This strategy of simply defining economic rights out of existence was rapidly put into place by deleting the sections dealing with "economic and social rights" from the first of the State Department's annual Country Reports on Human Rights Practices . . . .. This deletion was strongly defended by Assistant Secretary of State Elliott Abrams in a congressional hearing to review the report. His arguments were buttressed by both pragmatic and philosophical considerations. The former, which have been repeated in every subsequent issue of the Country Reports, consisted of two strands. The first was that recognition of economic and social rights "tends to create a growing confusion about priorities in the human rights area and a growing dispersion of energy in ending human rights violations."

The second was that the rights in question are "easily exploited to excuse violations of civil and political rights." Leaving aside the validity of these arguments, it could be contended that they need not per se preclude ratification of the Covenant by the United States since they appear to be directed primarily at foreign, rather than domestic, policy considerations.

Abrams's historical and political arguments, however, constitute the most significant obstacle to acceptance of the very concept of economic and social rights and hence to ratification of the Covenant. In brief, Abrams invoked the public/private distinction:

"The great men who founded the modern concern for human rights . . . established separate spheres of public and private life . . .. Social, economic and cultural life was left in the private sphere . . .." Without so labeling them, Abrams used the distinction between positive and negative categories of rights and concluded that "the rights that no government can violate [i.e., civil and political rights] should not be watered down to the status of rights that governments should do their best to secure [i.e., economic, social and cultural rights]." . . . [E]ven though Abrams's assessment of the unacceptability of economic, social and cultural rights was unqualified, as well as clearly reflected in U.S. policy, the administration tended initially to avoid unnecessarily confrontational tactics on the issue. The result was that few, if any, U.S. human rights groups treated the issue with any degree of priority or urgency, and scholars could write, as late as 1986, that the Reagan administration "has not actually repudiated [the Covenants] in public (unless one so construes the 'rumblings of discontent' expressed by . . . Abrams at various times about the Economic and Social Covenant)." In fact, however, the signals had been sufficiently clear and consistent . . ..

After 1986, the language of rejection became even more straightforward, and unquestionably consistent. . . .

Another strand in the arguments used against economic and social rights in recent years by U.S. officials has been to portray the issue as one of East versus West. This argument has been expressed by Assistant Secretary Schifter in the following terms:

> Critics of the Western democracies used to contend that, while emphasizing free speech and a free press, the democracies ignored such basic needs as food, jobs, housing and medical care. These critics, particularly those affiliated with the Soviet bloc, stressed that their governments guaranteed citizens the right to obtain these basic needs. Supporters in democracies responded that, people needed, not guarantees of food, jobs, housing and medical care, but delivery of these benefits.

But the "critics" of whom he speaks have not assailed "the Western democracies" in general, since, with the sole exception of the United States, all the Western democracies have accepted the validity and equal importance of economic, social and cultural human rights, at least in principle. [The author cited Australia, the Netherlands, Greece, Portugal, Spain, Switzerland, the Scandinavian countries, and 13 Latin American countries as examples of Western democracies which have championed the economic, social, and cultural rights enumerated in various documents.]

. . . If . . . the debate needs to be pursued in geopolitical terms, it is between the United States on the one hand, and most of the rest of the world on the other. It is not principally between East and West.

A final element that is open to challenge . . . is the suggestion that a choice must be made between formal guarantees and the actual delivery of things such as medical care and housing. . . .

No specific analysis is offered to support the assumption that formal guarantees will inevitably be hollow and meaningless and that a society which makes such undertakings will therefore fail to honor them. . . . [T]he dichotomy is a false one. There will always be governments that make empty promises and some will even clothe those promises in the garb of formal guarantees. But many other governments have given carefully worded guarantees and delivered as well. They include the United States with respect to a limited, but nonetheless important, range of social benefits. . . .

III. THE DOMESTIC POLICY OBSTACLE

The Nature of the Obligations Imposed by the Covenant

[The Carter Administration proposed the following understanding when it transmitted the Covenant to the Senate for its advice and consent: "The United States understands paragraph (1) of Article 2 as establishing that the provisions of Articles 2 through 15 of this Covenant describe goals to be achieved progressively rather than through immediate implementation." Some commentators even believed the obligations contained in Article 2(1) of the Covenant violated the U.S. Constitution, on the grounds that the treaty power does not extend to welfare matters traditionally left to the political arena. Critics argued Carter's proposed understanding undermined the basic character of the Covenant, which created obligations in addition to establishing goals.]

. . . A careful analysis of the Covenant reveals that the most general obligation of an immediate nature is . . . "to begin immediately to take steps towards full realization of the rights contained in the Covenant." . . . But the proposed U.S. understanding would remove even the need for the adoption of formal legal provisions. . . . The starting point for a program to implement economic and social rights is to ascertain, as precisely as possible, the nature of the existing situation with respect to each right, so as to identify more clearly the problems that need to be addressed and provide a basis for principled policy making. Thus, to take the case of the right to adequate food, an immediate and feasible step that the United States could take would be to adopt legislation requiring the various levels of government to collaborate periodically on a detailed survey of the nutritional status of the American people, with particular emphasis on the situation of the most vulnerable and disadvantaged groups and regions. Such a survey could then constitute the basis for carefully targeted legislative, administrative and practical measures aimed at enhancing realization of the right.

[The author next discussed the "guarantee" language of Article 2(2) and the "ensure" language of Article 3. The author also discussed the obligations imposed in Part III of the Covenant. For a discussion of that terminology, see Alston & Quinn, excerpted *supra* at 51.] The undertakings "to guarantee" and "to ensure" cannot reasonably be construed as mere declarations of goals to be achieved in the distant future. . . .

In sum, the understanding proposed by the Carter Administration to the effect that all of the substantive provisions of the Covenant "describe goals to be achieved progressively rather than through immediate implementation" is manifestly incorrect and would be incompatible with the basic object and purpose of the Covenant. Accordingly, it cannot serve as an appropriate basis for future public or congressional debate over ratification of the Covenant. Rather, the starting point for such a debate in the 1990s must be recognition of the fact that a significant range of obligations would flow from ratification.

Domestic Acceptability of an Economic, Social and Cultural Rights Ideology

Another issue that was treated in a rather cavalier fashion . . . is the extent to which acceptance of even a fairly low level of obligation with respect to economic, social and cultural rights is likely to be acceptable in domestic political terms in the United States. That issue, in turn, is linked to whether existing U.S. domestic policies can be said to reflect a commitment to securing, even on the basis of progressive realization, the enjoyment of a full range of economic, social and cultural rights for each and every American citizen. . . .

. . . [T]he acceptability within the United States of a "rights psychology" in the economic and social domain is much less apparent. However, before moving to that issue, it is important to dispose of a separate, although related, issue that can sometimes mistakenly dominate discussions of this subject. [Alston noted that several U.S. officials believe U.S. domestic policy and practice ensures, to a large extent, the economic, social, and cultural rights enshrined in the Covenant.] In fact, such claims stand in marked contrast to the findings of most serious studies of U.S. economic and social policy. . . .

Nevertheless, the performance of the United States . . . is not, and should not be permitted to become, the principal issue in the present context. If universally applicable minimum standards were required to be met before a state could qualify to ratify the Covenant, those standards either would preclude ratification by the great majority of states or would be ludicrously low . . .. But, for the most part, there are no such universal benchmarks, and each state is required, in effect, to do its utmost in light of its own situation at the time of ratification.

The issue at hand, therefore, concerns not the actual extent to which economic, social and cultural rights are currently being enjoyed in the United States but, rather, the acceptability of using the notion of human rights (with whatever implications that may have) as one of the principal underpinnings of future American policy endeavors in this domain. . . . [C]onsiderable evidence points to a deep-seated reluctance on the part of the U.S. Government to embrace the concept of economic, social and cultural rights, let alone to do so within the framework of an international treaty that imposes a degree of accountability in that regard. . . .

The conclusion to be drawn . . . is not necessarily that the concept of economic, social and cultural rights is, by definition, incompatible with the philosophy of the American people or even of recent U.S. administrations. Rather, it is that the acceptability to the American people and their political representatives in the U.S. Senate of the assumptions implicit, and the obligations explicit, in the Covenant cannot readily be assumed. . . .

IV. SOME CONSEQUENCES OF NONRATIFICATION OF THE COVENANT

For the past decade, the debate has been largely instrumentalist in character, in the sense that the proponents of ratification have promoted the Covenant less on the basis of its intrinsic merits than on that of other goals its ratification could serve indirectly.

The most important such goal has been to ensure that the United States retains its credibility as a proponent of international concern for human rights, a status that is widely assumed to require U.S. ratification of each of the basic standards in the field. . . . [I]t is appropriate to consider here the consequences of nonratification of the Covenant on Economic, Social and Cultural Rights combined with ratification of the Covenant on Civil and Political Rights. Such a course of action . . . from a tactical viewpoint . . . would reduce the possibility that the former Covenant would act as a lightning rod for criticism from conservative groups, which would threaten the prospects for both Covenants, and it would greatly simplify the range of issues that would need to be addressed by the U.S. Senate. However, it also has some drawbacks, particularly if coupled with the continuing rejection in principle of economic, and social and cultural rights. The major problem is that any reference to "internationally recognized human rights" (a phrase commonly used in U.S. legislation dating from the 1970s, most of which is still in force) cannot legitimately be interpreted as referring only to half of the single, "indivisible and interdependent" package of human rights (consisting of economic, social and cultural as well as civil and political rights) that has consistently, and without exception, been endorsed by the international community. . . .

The inconsistency of purporting to base U.S. policy on internationally agreed human rights norms, on the one hand, and dismissing the relevance and even the legitimacy of half of those very norms, on the other hand, leads inevitably to a convoluted and ultimately indefensible position. . . .

Perhaps most troubling of all about this approach is the set of political and historical misrepresentations on which it is based. Take the following assertion:

> Much of the confusion in Western thinking about what is and is not a human right stems from the gradual abolition, under Jimmy Carter's Administration, of the demarcation line between the Anglo-American concept of the Rights of Man (political and civil liberties) and the Soviet-Third World concept of "social and economic rights."

This analysis is wrong on every count. The confusion in question is not in "Western" thinking but in American policy since 1981, a policy that has not been supported by even a single other Western government. . . . Similarly, it was not Jimmy Carter who abolished the distinction between the two concepts but Franklin Delano Roosevelt, who actively advocated the recognition of economic and social rights, and Harry Truman, whose administration voted to adopt the Universal Declaration of Human Rights (in 1948), which accepted the equality of the two sets of rights. References to "the Anglo-American concept of the Rights of Man" not only ignore that part of U.S. history, but also overlook the enthusiastic support by British governments of various political persuasions for economic and social rights (embodied in the concept of the welfare state), as well as the nature of the French, German, Mexican and other contributions to the original concept. Finally, the suggestion that the concept of economic and social rights is a "Soviet-Third World" creation does a gross injustice to the Catholic and many other churches (at least since the late 19th century) and those many Western European states, not to mention Australia and New Zealand, which have consistently championed economic and social rights . . ..

The principal purpose of the present analysis, however, is . . . to emphasize the long-term lack of viability of seeking to rely on international human rights standards in the context of both East-West and North-South relations and at the same time misrepresenting and undermining those standards. While ratification of the Covenant is not indispensable to remedying that situation, its continuing rejection and active disparagement will compound an already unacceptable position.

V.   THE U.S. HUMAN RIGHTS COMMUNITY AND RATIFICATION OF THE COVENANT . . .

[One] principal shortcoming of the debate so far has been the tendency to present the issue as though acceptance of an obligation to recognize, and to move purposefully toward the progressive implementation of, a wide range of economic, social and cultural rights were, to put it colloquially, "no big deal." In fact, such a decision would be a very big deal in the light of the attitudes and approaches that have prevailed in the United States, especially over the last decade.

The Carter administration's proposed "understanding," which was explicitly designed to neutralize any impact that ratification might have been expected to have in the normal course of events, could only with the utmost difficulty be characterized as having been put forward in good faith. On careful examination, it is inconsistent with the legal language used in the Covenant and it cannot readily be reconciled with the very nature and purpose of the act of assuming international human rights obligations. The understanding seems to have been accepted by some of the proponents of ratification largely for tactical reasons, on the grounds that it would be easier to give substance to the obligations of the Covenant after ratification was achieved, rather than before. But there is no reason to believe that recognition of the rights in question can be achieved by stealth, and no justification for believing that it should be.

On the contrary, the ratification debate of the 1990s is going to have to confront the hard issues with a much greater degree of openness and sophistication than has so far been the case. To take but one example: Is there reason to conclude, as an eminent international lawyer and human rights advocate has argued, "that the full achievement of . . . economic and social rights entails a loss of individual liberties which is unacceptable to the western liberal democracies?" And, if so, on what basis and by what means can the obligations contained in the Covenant be interpreted and applied so as to avoid, or at least minimize, such undesirable consequences? It is on issues such as these that the future debate will need to focus.

NOTES AND QUESTIONS

1.   According to Alston what are the advantages of ratification for the U.S.? What are the disadvantages?   What obstacles must be overcome to secure ratification?

2.   Not all commentators agree with Alston's strategy to encourage U.S. ratification of the treaty. Many proponents of ratification advocate the "stealth" method criticized by Alston at the beginning of his article. They argue that stealth is necessary to avoid alarming conservative contingents in the Senate and elsewhere, which might mount a vigorous campaign to oppose the Senate's consenting to the treaty. Also, a vigorous public debate may make it impossible to obtain the Senate's advice and consent to ratification, because the Senate usually acts on treaties by consensus or not at all. Moreover, they argue that lack of an organized and powerful lobby in favor of ratification makes Alston's strategy unlikely to succeed. Proponents of the stealth strategy encourage ratification, even if it is achieved only through the use of reservations, declarations, and understandings, because those qualifications may be ineffective after ratification to the extent they are inconsistent with the object and purpose of the treaty. Does Alston convincingly counter those arguments?

3.   Do you think that economic, social, and cultural concerns are goals, not rights? Does the recognition of rights encourage governments to conform their practices accordingly?
Do methods of implementing rights under the ESC Covenant fully address the Reagan and Bush administrations' argument that capability for immediate implementation is necessary for claims to be defined as rights? *See* HARVARD LAW SCHOOL HUMAN RIGHTS PROGRAM, *Applying Rights Rhetoric to Economic and Social Claims*, in ECONOMIC AND SOCIAL RIGHTS AND THE RIGHT TO HEALTH 1 (An Interdisciplinary Discussion Held at Harvard Law School in September 1993) (1995); HARVARD LAW SCHOOL HUMAN RIGHTS PROGRAM, *Institutionalizing Economic and Social Rights*, in ECONOMIC AND SOCIAL RIGHTS AND THE RIGHT TO HEALTH 35 (An Interdisciplinary Discussion Held at Harvard Law School in September 1993) (1995).

4.   The Reagan and Bush administrations argued that viewing economic and social goals as rights leads governments to deny civil and political rights in the search for economic stability. Were that assertion true, is it a valid objection to recognizing economic, social, and cultural rights? Or does it merely reflect the view that civil and political guarantees are more important than economic stability? Should governments strive to provide both civil and political rights *and* economic, social, and cultural rights? *See* Rhoda Howard, *The Full Belly Thesis: Should Economic Rights Take Priority Over Civil and Political Rights*, 5 HUM. RTS. Q. 467 (1983); Barbara Stark, *Urban Despair and Nietzsche's "Eternal Return:" From the Municipal Rhetoric of Economic Justice to the International Law of Economic Rights*, 28 VAND. J. TRANSNAT'L L. 185 (1995).

5.   The U.S. view of economic, social, and cultural rights has not always been negative. President Carter signed the ESC Covenant and submitted it to the Senate for advice and consent. His administration viewed human rights as falling into three broad categories: rights that protect the integrity of the person; rights that guarantee fulfillment of basic economic and social needs; and rights that protect civil and political liberties. The administration promoted protection of all categories of rights as being complementary and mutually reinforcing. *See* Cyrus Vance, *Human Rights and Foreign Policy*, 7 GA. J. INT'L & COMP. L. 223 (1977).

6.   Recall Alston's discussion of the East-West and North-South division. He is criticizing the view, first expressed during the Cold War, that "economic and social rights" are an Eastern creation. Since the breakup of the Soviet Union and the dismantling of Eastern European governments the East-West split largely has disappeared. In its place is a growing debate over human rights between the developed countries of the North and those of the South. The South has argued for the right to development and for greater attention to economic, social, and cultural rights. Some governments also assert that human rights must be interpreted in the cultural context of each region and that a Western European definition of human rights should not be rigidly imposed on the South. For a discussion of the North- South debate over human rights, see PHILIP ALSTON, HUMAN RIGHTS IN 1993: HOW FAR HAS THE UNITED NATIONS COME AND WHERE SHOULD IT GO FROM HERE? (memorandum distributed at the Vienna Conference on Human Rights, June 1993).

7.   If the U.S. were a party to the ESC Covenant, would the U.S. violate its obligations by:

    (a) failing to provide adequate housing for the homeless?
    (b) reducing the distribution of food stamps?
    (c) reducing Medicare benefits for the elderly?
    (d) spending vast sums on national defense and notably less on aid to families with dependent children?

8.   In light of General Comment No. 24 and the U.S. response, *supra* at 45, is U.S. ratification of the ESC Covenant more or less likely?

9.   For support of U.S. ratification of the ESC Covenant, see J. Kenneth Blackwell, *Howard Tolley, Jr., The U.N. Commission on Human Rights*, 14 HUM. RTS. Q. 485 (1992) (book review). For further reading, see Natalie Hevener Kaufman & David Whiteman, *Opposition to Human Rights Treaties in the United States Senate: The Legacy of the Bricker Amendment*, 10 HUM. RTS. Q. 309 (1988); A. GLENN MOWER, HUMAN RIGHTS AND AMERICAN FOREIGN POLICY: THE CARTER AND REAGAN EXPERIENCE 37-40 (1987). For criticism of the inclusion of economic, social, and cultural rights, see JOSHUA MURAVCHIK, THE UNCERTAIN CRUSADE: JIMMY CARTER AND THE DILEMMAS OF HUMAN RIGHTS POLICY 88-105 (1986).

---

3.   Ratification—With or Without Qualifications?

Four Treaties Pertaining to Human Rights: Message From the President of the United States, 95th Cong., 2d Sess. at VIII-XI (1978).

[Ed. Note: In its transmission of the ESC Covenant to the Senate for advice and consent, the Carter Administration suggested the following reservations, understandings, and declarations.]

The International Covenant on Economic, Social and Cultural Rights sets forth a number of rights which, while for the most part in accord with United States law and practice, are nevertheless formulated as statements of goals to be achieved progressively rather than implemented immediately. . . .

Article 1 affirms in general terms the right of all peoples to self-determination, and the right to freely dispose of their natural wealth and resources without prejudice to any obligations arising out of international economic cooperation, based upon the principle of mutual benefit, and international law. This is consonant with United States policy.

Paragraph (1) of Article 2 sets forth the basic obligation of States Parties "to take steps," individually and through international assistance and cooperation, "to the maximum of its available resources, with a view to achieving progressively the full realization of the rights recognized" by the Covenant "by all appropriate means, including legislative measures." In view of the terms of paragraph (1) of Article 2, and the nature of the rights set forth in Articles 1 through 15 of the Covenant, the following statement is recommended:

"The United States understands paragraph (1) of Article 2 as establishing that the provisions of Articles 1 through 15 of this Covenant describe goals to be achieved progressively rather than through immediate implementation."

It is also understood that paragraph (1) of Article 2, as well as Article 11, which calls for States Parties to take steps individually and through international cooperation to guard against hunger, import no legally binding obligation to provide aid to foreign countries.

Paragraph (2) of Article 2 forbids discrimination of any sort based on [enumerated characteristics]. United States and international law permit certain limited discrimination against non-nationals in appropriate cases (*e.g.*, ownership of land or of means of communication). It is understood that this paragraph also permits reasonable distinctions based on citizenship. Paragraph (3) of Article 2 provides that developing countries, with due regard to human rights and their national economy, may determine to what extent they will guarantee the economic rights recognized in the Covenant to non-nationals. Of related significance is Article 25, which provides that nothing in the Covenant is to be interpreted as impairing the "inherent right of all peoples to enjoy and utilize fully and freely their natural wealth and resources." With respect to paragraph (3) of Article 2 and to Article 25, the following declaration is recommended:

"The United States declares that nothing in the Covenant derogates from the equal obligation of all States to fulfill their responsibilities under international law. The United States understands that under the Covenant everyone has the right to own property alone as well as in association with others, and that no one shall be arbitrarily deprived of his property."

This declaration and understanding will make clear the United States position regarding property rights, and expresses the view of the United States that discrimination by developing countries against nonnationals or actions affecting their property or contractual rights may only be carried out in accordance with the governing rules of international law. Under international law, any taking of private property must be nondiscriminatory and for a public purpose, and must be accompanied by prompt, adequate, and effective compensation. . . .

Paragraph (1) of Article 5 provides that nothing in the Covenant may be interpreted as implying for any State, group or person any right to engage in any activity or to perform any act aimed at the destruction of any of the rights or freedoms recognized in the Covenant, or at their limitation to a greater extent than provided for in the Covenant.

This clause raises in indirect fashion the problem of freedom of speech, and accordingly, the following statement is recommended:

"The Constitution of the United States and Article 19 of the International Covenant on Civil and Political Rights contain provisions for the protection of individual rights, including the right to free speech, and nothing in this Covenant shall be deemed to require or to authorize legislation or other action by the United States which would restrict the right of free speech protected by the Constitution, laws, and practice of the United States." . . .

Articles 6 through 9 of the Covenant list certain economic rights, including the right to work (Article 6), to favorable working conditions (Article 7), to organize unions (Article 8), and to social security (Article 9). Some of the standards established under these articles may not readily be translated into legally enforceable rights, while others are in accord with United States policy, but have not yet been fully achieved. It is accordingly important to make clear that these provisions are understood to be goals whose realization will be sought rather than obligations requiring immediate implementation.

Similarly, Articles 10 through 14 detail certain social rights, among them the right to protection of the family, including standards for maternity leave (Article 10), the right of freedom from hunger (Article 11), the right to physical and mental health (Article 12), and the right to education (Articles 13 and 14). Article 15 provides for certain cultural rights, all of which are appropriately protected by United States law and policy. . . .

Articles 26 through 31 are the final clauses. Article 28 states that "The provisions of the present Covenant shall extend to all parts of federal States without any limitations or exceptions." In view of the nature of the United States federal system, this Article is not acceptable as formulated. With respect to Article 28, the following reservation is recommended:

"The United States shall progressively implement all the provisions of the Covenant over whose subject matter the Federal Government exercises legislative and judicial jurisdiction; with respect to the provisions over whose subject matter constituent units exercise jurisdiction, the Federal Government shall take appropriate measures, to the end that the competent authorities of the constituent units may take appropriate measures for the fulfillment of this Covenant."

In addition, it is further recommended that a declaration indicate the non-self-executing nature of Articles 1 through 15 of the Covenant.

NOTES AND QUESTIONS

1.   Is the first paragraph of the above excerpt accurate in stating that the Covenant is "for the most part in accord with United States law and practice"? What about the final sentence of the second paragraph?

2.   Do you agree that the qualifications are consistent with the object and purpose of the treaty?

Burns Weston, *U.S. Ratification of the International Covenant on Economic, Social and Cultural Rights: With or Without Qualifications, in* U.S. RATIFICATION OF THE HUMAN RIGHTS TREATIES: WITH OR WITHOUT RESERVATIONS? 27, 30-38 (Richard B. Lillich ed. 1981):

I. *The Two Reservations*

A. *Free Speech*

The first proposed reservation pertains to Article 5(1) of the [Economic, Social and Cultural Rights] covenant . . .. Correctly, the Carter Administration has perceived a potential conflict with the First Amendment free-speech guarantees of our Constitution.

Accordingly, because a treaty cannot be ratified by the Senate if it conflicts with the Constitution, the administration has recommended [a] reservation . . .. The trouble with th[e] reservation is that, while appropriate in referring to the Constitution, it goes too far in referring also to the "laws and practice of the United States."

In the first place, this additional reference is unnecessary. Free speech laws and practices in the U.S. are constitutionally protected; therefore, they would be protected by a reservation limited in reference to the U.S. Constitution only. Secondly, as our colleague David Weissbrodt from the University of Minnesota has recently pointed out, this additional reference could be used perversely to authorize U.S. "laws and practice" that would be *less* protective of free speech than Article 19 of the International Covenant on Civil and Political Rights. Because Article 19 could be interpreted to prohibit "laws and practice" that heretofore have been sanctioned by our Supreme Court—for example, authorization of police surveillance of peaceful demonstrations—the proposed reservation actually may offer less free-speech protection than is afforded by the covenants.

Accordingly, the reservation could be used to prevent any treaty-based improvement in U.S. laws and practice.

In sum, insofar as the free speech reservation refers to "laws and practice of the United States," it is superfluous and probably very shortsighted. Furthermore, because it signals to the world that we will abide by the covenant so long as such adherence does not require any improvement in our own free speech practices, it encourages other countries to make similar status quo reservations—reservations that, in turn, would seriously jeopardize the protection of free speech as envisioned in the Civil and Political Covenant. Therefore, the proposed reservation should be revised so as to exclude reference to the "laws and practice of the United States."

B. *States' Rights*

The second reservation pertains to Article 28 of the . . . covenant, which stipulates that "the provisions of the present Covenant shall extend to all parts of federal States without any limitation or exceptions." According to the Carter Administration, which seems to fear some violation of states' rights or some inconsistency with our federal system, this provision requires [a] reservation . . . limit[ing] the impact of the covenant on state governments within the U.S.

In thus proceeding, however, the Carter Administration has forgotten our constitutional history and consequently has reopened old wounds. In a phrase, this proposed states' rights reservation constitutes a legal/historical anachronism. In addition to the fact that the U.S. Supreme Court has unequivocally upheld the power of the federal government to make treaties in respect of matters that otherwise would be the sole prerogative of the separate states, the recent trend of constitutional decision, at least since the early 1950s, has been to resolve virtually all states' rights doubts in favor of federal power—via the commerce clause and via the thirteenth, fourteenth, and fifteenth amendments. Moreover, there is absolutely no question that the U.S. government has the authority to enter into human rights treaties per se.

But the real objection to the proposed states' rights reservation is that it could be not just a silly anachronism but a *costly* one, both domestically and internationally.

Domestically, there is the possibility that it would refuel politically retrogressive (perhaps even racist) divisions that, in turn, could call into question even the limited international human rights commitments that have so far been made by the U.S. And internationally, because the reservation is so explicitly contrary to the language and intent of Article 28, it could vitiate the covenant in major part. . . . Thus, assuming that the states' rights reservation were to be perceived—as well it might—as fundamentally incompatible with Article 28, it could be legitimately maintained that no agreement has been reached and therefore no binding treaty established.

As I see it, then, the proposed states' rights reservation should be ruled out entirely. So also should any equivalent alternatives, since the matter of federalism, especially in the human rights field, is best left up to our courts on a case-by-case basis.

II. *The Three Understandings*

A. *Progressive Implementation*

. . . The Carter Administration's stipulated understanding of [Article 2(1)] is that Articles 1 through 15 of the covenant "describe goals to be achieved progressively rather than through immediate implementation." In the end, this proposed understanding might prove only redundant, and therefore harmless for being superfluous. However, by adding the language of nonimmediacy—*i.e.*, "rather than through immediate implementation"—it is possible that it could be interpreted to justify unwarranted delays, much too deliberate speed, in taking immediate steps toward the progressive achievement of the goals enumerated. Also, at the very least, it communicates an embarrassing foot-dragging that scarcely is in keeping with a full and constructive commitment to the human rights cause. Accordingly, the understanding should be dropped entirely.

B. *Foreign Aid*

Again with reference to Article 2(1) . . ., the Carter Administration asserts an understanding that the covenant does not require foreign economic aid . . .. Because Article 2(1) does not actually impose a duty to give foreign economic aid, this understanding surely would instill or reinforce an impression of Scrooge-like churlishness on the part of the U.S. in relation to the meeting of basic human needs, and it provides unfortunate grist for the anti-American propaganda mill. This proposed understanding, too, should be stricken from the record.

C. *Citizenship Discrimination*

The third and final understanding proposed by the Carter Administration relates to Article 2(2) . . . forbidding discrimination in implementation of the covenant . . .. The proposed understanding is that this language "permits reasonable distinctions based on citizenship"—for instance, in ownership of land or of means of communication (two examples expressly mentioned in the Carter transmittal message). Presumably, this proposed understanding is designed to protect domestically based U.S. industries and assets from foreign control. This seems clear. Not so clear, however, is how one should respond to it—bearing in mind that, if retained, it would invite equivalent and probably even more far-reaching understandings from other States Parties to the Covenant. The answer, I believe, must necessarily depend on one's views about the global economic system. If one believes that it is desirable to foster conditions conducive to direct U.S. capital investment abroad, particularly in the developing world where anti-U.S. and anticapitalist sentiment may be strong, then probably the understanding should be discarded . . .. If, on the other hand, one believes that the export of U.S. capitalism is not always or even usually in the best interests of the host countries involved, then probably it should be retained. The decision here is more ideological than legal.

III. *The Two Declarations*

A. *Private Property Rights . . .*

In response to [Articles 2(3) and 25], the Carter Administration proposes [a] combined declaration and understanding . . .. In other words the right to own private property, one of the fundamental—and often stridently espoused—tenets of U.S. law and policy, is given special protection.

Of course, there can be no objection to requiring all states to fulfill their responsibilities under international law. However, considering the dangers of ethnocentrism, I have serious misgivings when it comes to insisting that "everyone has the right to own property," particularly in an increasingly ideologically divided world. Also, for similar reasons, I have misgivings about the Department of State's express gloss on the declaration, namely, that "under international law, any taking of private property . . . must be accompanied by prompt, adequate, and effective compensation." My point is that the international law of state responsibility, early fashioned by a Western capital-exporting world and now subject to the pressures of a Third World movement for a "new international economic order," is changing rapidly. It is by no means clear that the Department's views of international law in this realm are today either accurate or justified.

On the other hand, given the exemption extended to the "developing countries" under Article 2(3) of the covenant, some safeguards do seem justified. The ultimate purpose of international legal decision—and so, international human rights decision—is and should be the reconciliation and accommodation of competing points of view and interests.

Accordingly, I would revise the Carter Administration's property rights declaration and understanding to read as follows: "The United States declares that nothing in the Covenant derogates from the equal obligation of all States to fulfill their responsibilities under international law relative to foreign private wealth ownership, including the duty to ensure that no one shall be arbitrarily deprived of his property." Such a declaration, I believe, would be judiciously appropriate.

B. *Non-Self-Executing Treaty*

Finally, despite a constitutional supremacy clause tradition that says that treaties, as part of the supreme law of our land, may sometimes be considered applicable by the courts without special implementing legislation, the Carter Administration proposes to declare that "the provisions of Articles 1 through 15 of the ECOSOC Covenant are not self-executing."

More than any other qualifying statement, this one, in my view, does the most harm. In effect, it [undermines] the covenant . . .. Contrary to the language of the covenant that conveys a clear self-executing intent, in particular as regards the obligation to take steps toward the progressive realization of the rights enumerated, the proposed declaration would require intermediate legislative action to implement the covenant's provisions, and, accordingly, the covenant would have little or no effect beyond that of a lofty policy pronouncement. No one could sue in court to enforce its provisions; no one could use the covenant as a source of genuinely binding law. For these and related reasons, therefore, this declaration should be stricken—assuming, that is, that it is not already too late. By attempting to remove the issue of the self-executing nature of the covenant from the courts, where traditionally this issue ultimately has resided, President Carter may have given away too much too soon and thereby have dealt a severe blow to the human rights movement with which he has become so closely identified.

NOTES AND QUESTIONS

1.   Do you agree with Weston's recommendations? Hurst Hannum commented on those views in U.S. RATIFICATION OF THE HUMAN RIGHTS TREATIES: WITH OR WITHOUT RESERVATION 39-40 (Richard Lillich ed. 1981). Other views of interest are those of Louis Henkin, *id.*, at 20; Clyde Ferguson, *id.*, at 41; Thomas Buergenthal, *id.*, at 47; the general discussion, *id.*, at 68-81; and especially Arthur Rovine and Jack Goldklang, *id.*, at 54 (defending the reservations, understandings, and declarations).

2.   How do Weston's comments compare with Alston's in his article urging U.S. ratification of the Covenant? Do you think Alston is too critical with respect to the U.S. qualifications? Or is Weston too accepting?

E.   IMPLEMENTATION AND ENFORCEMENT

1.   U.N. Committee on Economic, Social and Cultural Rights

Philip Alston, *Out of the Abyss: The Challenges Confronting the New U.N. Committee on Economic, Social and Cultural Rights*, 9 HUM. RTS. Q. 332, 332-52 (1987) (footnotes omitted):

I.   INTRODUCTION

In May 1986, the United Nations created a new expert Committee on Economic, Social and Cultural Rights. Its task is to assist the Economic and Social Council in monitoring states parties' compliance with their obligations under the International Covenant on Economic, Social and Cultural Rights. . . .

II.   AN OVERVIEW OF THE COVENANT'S IMPLEMENTATION PROCEDURES

Before embarking on an analysis of the background to the establishment of the new Committee it is necessary to provide at least a broad overview of the relevant implementation provisions contained in Part IV of the Covenant. Articles 16-22 may be summarized as follows: The states parties are required to report, in accordance with a program to be determined by the Economic and Social Council after consultation with the specialized agencies concerned and the states parties, on the measures they have adopted and the progress made in achieving the observance of the right recognized in the Covenant. The reports may indicate factors and difficulties affecting the degree of fulfillment of the obligations. They are to be submitted to the Secretary-General, who is required to transmit copies to the Council and copies of all the relevant parts to the agencies. Where information has already been furnished to an agency, it is sufficient for the report to refer thereto. Provision is made for arrangements between the Council and agencies whereby the latter will report on progress achieved in the observance of the Covenant. The Commission on Human Rights may receive from the Council copies of both the state and agency reports and may make "general" recommendations thereon. The agencies and states parties are entitled to submit comments on any such recommendations to the Council. The Council, in turn, may submit reports to the General Assembly with recommendations of a general nature and a summary of the information received. It may also bring to the attention of the agencies matters that might warrant the provision of technical assistance or the taking of other international measures. The role of the new Committee is to assist the Council in fulfilling all of its responsibilities and, in particular, those provided for in Articles 21 and 22 of the Covenant.

III. BACKGROUND TO THE ESTABLISHMENT OF THE COMMITTEE

The context in which the decision to establish the Committee was taken is, in several respect[s], without precedent in the UN system. In the first place, the creation of such a committee had been debated at length when the Covenant was being drafted but two specific proposals, championed by the United States and Italy respectively, conspicuously failed to win support. As a result, the Covenant makes no provision for the establishment of any specialist supervisory body.

Secondly, the decision to establish an expert committee was taken after relatively limited and somewhat inconclusive consultations with states parties and with surprisingly few objections having been raised in advance. Thirdly, and perhaps most significantly, the decision can be seen, in a sense, as a last ditch effort to establish a meaningful international implementation system for the Covenant in the wake of the failure of earlier approaches. . . .

[Alston described earlier attempts at forming an implementation system. The Economic and Social Council first created a "Sessional Working Group" to review states reports due under the Covenant. When membership changed to include persons with specialist expertise, the Council renamed the Group the Sessional Working Group of Governmental Experts. Many commentators were dissatisfied with the Group's supervision of the implementation of the Covenant under either formulation. Most significantly, the Group failed to make any] recommendations on other than procedural matters. It has, as a result, not provided the Council with anything of substance on the basis of which the latter could, if it wished, to have exercised its right under Article 21 of the Covenant to "submit from time to time to the General Assembly reports with recommendations of a general nature and a summary of the information received from the States Parties . . . and the specialized agencies. . . ."
. . .

IV. THE COMPOSITION AND TERMS OF REFERENCE OF THE COMMITTEE

The new Committee resembles in several respects the Committee on Human Rights established under the Covenant on Civil and Political Rights. Thus, for example, its members are designated as "experts with recognized competence in the field of human rights, serving in their personal capacity." . . . [T]hey are . . . not acting as representatives of governments. Also like its counterpart, the Committee will have eighteen members with "due consideration" being given in their election to "equitable geographical distribution and to the representation of different forms of social and legal systems." However, this general principle has been translated into a relatively inflexible formula whereby each of the five geopolitical regional groupings has three members and an additional three seats are allocated "in accordance with the increase in the total number of States parties per regional group." . . .

Only states parties to the Covenant can nominate persons for election to the Committee. Although there appears to be nothing to prevent the nomination of an individual who is not a national of a state party, there have been no precedents and the chances of election would probably be slight. Unlike elections for the Human Rights Committee, in which only states parties can vote, all members of the Economic and Social Council, whether or not they are parties to the Covenant, are entitled to take part in the secret ballot by which the members of the Committee are elected.

Members of the Committee are elected for four years with elections for half the membership being held every two years. Members are eligible for reelection. These provisions are of particular importance in view of the detrimental consequences flowing from the unduly high rate of turnover in membership of the old Working Group. It may be hoped that a significant degree of continuity will thus be ensured.

The Committee is scheduled to meet annually in Geneva for up to three weeks and its members' expenses will be paid by the United Nations, thus underlining their independence from the governments that nominated them.

The principal differences between the new Committee and the Human Rights Committee relate to their status and independence as committees. Whereas the latter is a treaty-based organ whose mandate is laid down in the Covenant on Civil and Political Rights and which is responsible directly only to the states parties to that Covenant, the former exists entirely at the pleasure of ECOSOC. Its terms of reference, its composition, and its working arrangements can thus be altered at any stage by the Council. Moreover, its mandate is in a sense only an indirect one in that its task is "to assist the Council" in fulfilling the Council's role under the Covenant rather than to be directly responsible, in its own right, for supervisory activities. . . .

V.   THE PRINCIPAL CHALLENGES CONFRONTING THE COMMITTEE

A.   *Norm Clarification*

One of the most striking features of the Covenant is the vagueness of the normative implications of the various rights it recognizes. While some of the formulations are no more vague or ill-defined than some of those in the other Covenant, the difference in the extent of elaboration of their normative content undertaken both before and after the adoption of the Covenant is immense. Several factors account for this discrepancy. In the first place, the content of the Covenant on Economic, Social and Cultural Rights was not based upon any significant bodies of domestic jurisprudence as was the case with civil and political rights. Thus, phrases like "cruel, inhuman or degrading treatment or punishment" had been the subject of in-depth judicial and academic analysis long before their inclusion in the Covenant on Civil and Political Rights. By contrast, the range of rights recognized in the other Covenant was, with the exception of labor-related rights, considerably in advance of most national legislation. Indeed, this is still the case today so that the international lawyers seeking enlightenment as to the meaning of rights such as those pertaining to food, education, health care, clothing, and shelter will find little direct guidance in national law.

The second reason for the discrepancy lies in the failure of the international community to develop jurisprudence of any significance on many of the principal economic rights since the Covenant's adoption in 1966. By contrast, the meaning and precise policy implications of specific civil and political rights have been the subject of detailed legal analysis and of carefully-honed judicial and quasi-judicial interpretation, as well as being spelled out in much greater detail in specialized instruments such as the Standard Minimum Rules for the Treatment of Prisoners and the Convention Against Torture. Economic, social, and cultural rights have been the beneficiaries of remarkably few such endeavors and those that have been undertaken have not been very revealing. . . .

As a result, even a state that is deeply committed to achieving the fullest possible implementation of the Covenant will be hard pressed to determine for itself exactly what the Covenant requires of it with respect to a given right. For the same reason, the Committee itself will face equally intractable dilemmas until such time as it consciously and systematically addresses itself to the normative issue.

*   *   *   *   *

Committee on Economic, Social and Cultural Rights, *Report on the Eighth and Ninth Sessions*, Supp. No. 3, at 14-20, U.N. Doc. E/1994/ 23 (1994) (paragraph numbers omitted):

. . . Since its first session, in 1987, the Committee has made a concerted effort to devise appropriate working methods which adequately reflect the nature of the tasks with which it has been entrusted. In the course of its nine sessions it has sought to modify and develop these methods in the light of its experience. It may be expected that these methods will continue to evolve, taking account of: the intro-duction of the new reporting system which requires that a single global report be submitted every five years, the evolution of the procedures developing within the treaty regime as a whole and the feedback which the Committee receives from States parties and the Economic and Social Council. . . .

A. *Examination of State parties' reports* . . .

Since the third session, a pre-sessional working has met, usually for five days, prior to each of the Committee's sessions. It is composed of five members of the Committee nominated by the Chairperson, taking account of the desirability of a balanced geographical distribution.The principal purpose of the working group is to identify in advance the questions which might most usefully be discussed with the representatives of the reporting States. . . .

In terms of its own working methods, the working group . . . allocates to each of its members initial responsibility for undertaking a detailed review of a specific number of reports and for putting before the group a preliminary list of issues. . . . Each draft is then revised and supplemented on the basis of observations by the other members of the group and the final version of the list is adopted by the group as a whole. This procedure applies equally to both initial and periodic reports. . . .

In order to ensure that the Committee is as well informed as possible, it provides opportunities for non-governmental organizations to submit relevant information to it. They may do this in writing at any time . . .. The Committee's pre-sessional working group is also open to the submission of information in person or in writing from any NGOs . . .. In addition, the Committee sets aside part of the first afternoon at each of its sessions to enable NGO representatives to provide oral information. . . .

The lists of issues drawn up by the working group are given directly to a represen-tative of the States concerned, along with a copy of the Committee's most recent report . . ..

In accordance with the established practice of each of the United Nations human rights treaty monitoring bodies, representatives of the reporting States are entitled, and indeed are strongly encouraged, to be present at the meetings of the Committee when their reports are examined. The following procedure was followed in this regard at the Committee's ninth session. The representative of the State party was invited to introduce the report by making brief introductory comments and introducing any written replies, or otherwise responding orally, to the list of issues drawn up by the pre-sessional working group. A period of time was then allocated to enable the representatives of the specialized agencies to provide the Committee with any observations relevant to the report under consideration. During the same period, members of the Committee were invited to put questions and observations to the representative of the State party. A further period of time, preferably not on the same day, was then allocated to enable the representative to respond, as precisely as possible, to the questions asked. It was generally understood that questions that could not adequately be dealt with in this manner could be the subject of additional information provided to the Committee in writing.

The final phase of the Committee's examination of the report consists of the drafting and adoption of the Committee's concluding observations. . . . The agreed structure of the concluding observations is as follows: implementation of the Covenant; principal subjects of concern; and suggestions and recommendations. . . .

F. *Other consultations*

The Committee has sought to coordinate its activities with those of other bodies to the greatest extent possible and to draw as widely as it can upon available expertise in the fields of its competence. For this purpose, it has consistently invited individuals such as special rapporteurs of the Sub-Commission on Prevention of Discrimination and Protection of Minorities, chairpersons of Commission on Human Rights working groups and others to address it and engage in discussions.

The Committee has also sought to draw upon the expertise of the relevant specialized agencies and United Nations organs, both in its work as a whole and, more particularly, in the context of its general discussions.

In addition, the Committee has invited a variety of experts who have a particular interest in, and knowledge of, some of the issues under review, to contribute to its discussions. These contributions have added considerably to its understanding of some aspects of the questions arising under the Covenant.

G. *General Comments*

In response to an invitation addressed to it by the Economic and Social Council, the Committee decided to begin, as from its third session, the preparation of general comments based on the various articles and provisions of the International Covenant on Economic, Social and Cultural Rights with a view to assisting the States parties in fulfilling their reporting obligations.

By the end of its ninth session, the Committee and the Sessional Working Group of Governmental Experts . . . had examined 146 initial reports, 63 second periodic reports . . . and 13 global reports. This experience covered a significant number of States parties to the Covenant . . .. They represented all regions of the world, with different political, legal, socio-economic and cultural systems. Their reports submitted so far illustrated many of the problems which might arise in implementing the Covenant, although they had not yet provided any complete picture of the global situation with regard to the enjoyment of economic, social and cultural rights.

The Committee endeavours, through its general comments, to make the experience gained so far through the examination of those reports available for the benefit of all States parties in order: to assist and promote their further implementation of the Covenant; to draw the attention of the States parties to insufficiencies disclosed by a large number of reports; to suggest improvements in the reporting procedures and to stimulate the activities of the States parties, the international organizations and the specialized agencies concerned in achieving progressively and effectively the full realization of the rights recognized in the Covenant. . . .

The Committee has so far adopted the following general comments: General Comment number 1 (1989) on reporting by States parties; General Comment number 2 (1990) on international technical assistance measures; General Comment number 3 (1990) on the nature of States parties' obligations; and General Comment number 4 (1991) on the right to adequate housing.

NOTES AND QUESTIONS

1. As noted above, the Committee on Economic, Social and Cultural Rights at its Sixth Session issued a General Comment regarding the right to adequate housing:

> Pursuant to article 11(1) of the Covenant, States parties "recognize the right of everyone to an adequate standard of living for himself and his family, including adequate food, clothing and housing, and to the continuous improvement of living conditions". The human right to adequate housing, which is thus derived from the right to an adequate standard of living, is of central importance for the enjoyment of all economic, social and cultural rights. . . .
>
> Despite the fact that the international community has frequently reaffirmed the importance of full respect for the right to adequate housing, there remains a disturbingly large gap between the standards set in article 11(1) of the Covenant and the situation prevailing in many parts of the world. While the problems are often particularly acute in some developing countries which confront major resource and other constraints, the Committee observes that significant problems of homelessness and inadequate housing also exist in some of the most economically developed societies. The United Nations estimates that there are over 100 million persons homeless worldwide and over 1 billion inadequately housed. There is no indication that this number is decreasing. It seems clear that no State party is free of significant problems of one kind or another in relation to the right to housing. . . .
>
> The right to adequate housing applies to everyone. While the reference to "himself and his family" reflects assumptions as to gender roles and economic activity patterns commonly accepted in 1966 when the Covenant was adopted, the phrase cannot be read today as implying any limitations upon the applicability of the right to individuals or to female-headed households or other such groups. . . .
>
> In the Committee's view, the right to housing . . . should be seen as the right to live somewhere in security, peace and dignity. This is appropriate for at least two reasons. In the first place, the right to housing is integrally linked to other human rights and to the fundamental principles upon which the Covenant is premised. . . . Secondly, the reference in article 11(1) must be read as referring not just to housing but to adequate housing. As both the Commission on Human Settlements and the Global Strategy for Shelter to the Year 2000 have stated: "Adequate shelter means . . . adequate privacy, adequate space, adequate security, adequate lighting and ventilation, adequate basic infrastructure and adequate location with regard to work and basic facilities—all at a reasonable cost."

Committee on Economic, Social and Cultural Rights, *Report on the Sixth Session, General Comment No. 4 (1991)*, Supp. No. 3, Annex III, at 114-15, U.N. Doc. E/1992/23 (1992) (footnotes omitted). The Comment identifies seven aspects of the right to adequate housing: legal security of tenure; availability of services, materials, facilities, and infrastructure; affordability; habitability; accessibility; location; and cultural adequacy. *Id.* at 115-17. The Comment concludes:

> [T]he Committee considers that instances of forced eviction are *prima facie* incompatible with the requirements of the Covenant and can only be justified in the most

exceptional circumstances, and in accordance with the relevant principles of international law. *Id.* at 119.

2.   The Committee's work on adequate housing is founded in part on codifications of the right to housing included in U.N. instruments such as the Universal Declaration, the International Convention on the Elimination of All Forms of Racial Discrimination, the International Convention on the Elimination of All Forms of Discrimination Against Women, and the Convention on the Rights of the Child. A right to housing is also espoused in the American Declaration on the Rights and Duties of Man and the Charter of the Organization of American States. Because of its ability to monitor compliance, however, the Committee on Economic, Social and Cultural Rights may have more influence on the definition and protection of housing rights than monitors of the other instruments. *See* Scott Leckie, *The UN Committee on Economic, Social and Cultural Rights and the Right to Adequate Housing: Towards an Appropriate Approach*, 11 HUM. RTS. Q. 522 (1989).

3.   The U.N. Commission on Human Rights reaffirmed at its 49th Session that "the practice of forced evictions constitutes a gross violation of human rights, in particular the right to adequate housing." Res. 1993/77, *adopted* Mar. 10, 1993. Despite the international prohibition, however, forced evictions are not uncommon. The Centre on Housing Rights and Evictions reported such evictions between 1992 and 1994 in 27 countries, including France and the United Kingdom. CENTRE ON HOUSING RIGHTS AND EVICTIONS, FORCED EVICTIONS: VIOLATIONS OF HUMAN RIGHTS 6-17 (6th compilation, 1994). The Centre reported planned or possible evictions in 22 countries. *Id.* at 18-25. In describing positive developments, the report noted "[o]f all United Nations human rights bodies, the [ESC] Committee has become the premier international legal mechanism in the struggle against forced evictions." *Id.* at 28. That opinion was based in part on Committee reports from the 7th, 8th, 9th, and 10th Sessions regarding housing rights in Belgium, Canada, Italy, Kenya, Mauritius, Mexico, and Nicaragua *Id.* at 28-32. The report concluded that:

> [W]hile such pronouncements may on the surface of things seem inconsequential, once the Committee begins explicitly addressing housing rights issues within countries, a broad series of domestic political and legal processes are brought into motion, leading in some instances to favourable changes in national laws and policies, reconsideration of the practice of forced evictions and awareness throughout countries that the international community is concerned about and closely monitoring the human rights situation. The intense scrutiny given by this Committee to housing rights in both developing as well as developed countries reveals, as well, that such matters are anything but purely internal affairs, as is argued by a select few governments. Housing rights everywhere are, without doubt, matters of universal concern and relevance.

Id. at 28.

4.   Might the Committee's work on adequate housing and forced evictions be used as an argument against U.S. ratification of the Covenant? How might the standards discussed in the preceding notes be used to challenge U.S. practices if it ratified the Covenant?

5.   In 1993, Professor Alston, who now serves as Chairman of the Committee on Economic, Social and Cultural Rights, argued in favor of an Optional Protocol to the ESC Covenant. It would allow the Committee to receive complaints alleging violations of the Covenant. In this way, he stated, the Committee could "fill the existing vacuum, as a result of which international procedures effectively exclude these rights from their purview. . . ." In addition, an Optional Protocol would allow the Committee to develop "meaningful jurisprudence on economic, social and cultural rights." *See* Philip Alston, *Human Rights in 1993: How Far Has the United Nations Come and Where Should it Go from Here?* (memorandum distributed at the Vienna Conference on Human Rights, June 1993). *See also Draft Report of the Committee on Economic, Social and Cultural Rights to the Economic and Social Council*, Annex V, U.N. Doc. E/C.12/1992/CRP.2/Add.3 (1992) (discussing the draft of an Optional Protocol). As of

February 1996, the Committee on Economic, Social and Cultural Rights was considering a draft optional protocol to the ESC Covenant. U.N. Doc. E/CN.4/1996/96 (1996).

6. For further reading on the work of the Committee on Economic, Social and Cultural Rights, see:

Philip Alston, *The Committee on Economic, Social and Cultural Rights*, in THE UNITED NATIONS AND HUMAN RIGHTS: A CRITICAL APPRAISAL (Philip Alston ed., 1992);

Philip Alston & Bruno Simma, *First Session of the UN Committee on Economic, Social and Cultural Rights*, 81 AM. J. INT'L L. 747 (1987);

Philip Alston & Bruno Simma, *Second Session of the UN Committee on Economic, Social and Cultural Rights*, 82 AM. J. INT'L L. 603 (1988);

U.N. Centre for Human Rights, The Committee on Economic, Social and Cultural Rights, Fact Sheet No. 16 (1991).

7. For further reading on the right to adequate housing, see:

CENTRE ON HOUSING RIGHTS AND EVICTIONS, FORCED EVICTIONS & HUMAN RIGHTS: A MANUAL FOR ACTION (1993);

CENTRE ON HOUSING RIGHTS AND EVICTIONS & HABITAT INTERNATIONAL COALITION, FORCED EVICTIONS: VIOLATIONS OF HUMAN RIGHTS (1993);

SCOTT LECKIE, HABITAT INTERNATIONAL COALITION, WHEN PUSH COMES TO SHOVE: FORCED EVICTIONS AND HUMAN RIGHTS (1995).

---

2. Coordination with Other Bodies

In June 1993, the U.N. sponsored a World Conference on Human Rights, in Vienna, to encourage cooperation among various U.N. agencies and organizations. The Conference produced the Vienna Declaration and Programme of Action to serve as a basis for common efforts to protect human rights. The first paragraph of the Declaration noted the focus:

> The World Conference on Human Rights reaffirms the solemn commitment of all States to fulfill their obligations to promote universal respect for, and observance of all human rights and fundamental freedoms for all in accordance with the Charter of the United Nations, other instruments relating to human rights, and international law. The universal nature of these rights and freedoms is beyond question.
>
> In this framework, enhancement of international cooperation in the field of human rights is essential for the full achievement of the purposes of the United Nations.

The Plan of Activities of the Centre for Human Rights for the Implementation of the Vienna Declaration and Programme of Action outlined a strategy to achieve such cooperation:

> The Vienna Declaration and Programme of Action provides for the enhancement of international coordination in the field of human rights as essential for the full achievement of the programme of the United Nations. The World Conference thus recommended increased coordination in support of human rights and fundamental freedom within the United Nations system. The vital role of the relevant specialized agencies, bodies and institutions of the United Nations system was recognized and the Conference urged all United Nations organs, bodies and the specialized agencies whose activities deal with human rights to cooperate in order to strengthen, rational-

ize and streamline their activities taking into account the need to avoid unnecessary duplication.

The Conference thus recommended to the Secretary-General that high level officials of the United Nations bodies and agencies at their annual meeting coordinate their activities and also assess the impact of their strategies and policies on the enjoyment of all human rights.

The Committee on Economic, Social and Cultural Rights has been advocating such cooperation since its inception. In 1993, in conjunction with the World Conference, Alston prepared a report on possible long-term approaches to improving the effectiveness of human rights treaty-bodies. He recommended universal participation in the principal treaties as well as increased scrutiny of States whose reports are overdue. With regard to reports, he recommended reducing overlap among treaty-bodies:

> The overlapping competences of different treaty bodies can result in a situation in which a State may be required to report on virtually the same issue to several different treaty bodies. In an effort to reduce such duplication each State party should be encouraged to identify for its own purposes the instances in which cross-referencing can effectively and appropriately be used in preparing its reports. . . . The treaty bodies and the ILO should also contribute to the development of more effective approaches.

He also suggested reducing the number of treaty bodies, allowing States to produce a single "global" report for all cognizant bodies, and replacing comprehensive periodic reports with specifically tailored reports. World Conference on Human Rights, *Interim Report on Updated Study by Mr. Philip Alston*, at 9, U.N. Doc. A/CONF.157/PC/62/Add.11/Rev.1 (1993).

NOTES AND QUESTIONS

1.   Do you think Alston's suggestions would improve the effectiveness of treaty bodies. Are there practical barriers to consider?

2.   The Committee on Economic, Social and Cultural Rights has begun to implement some of Alston's suggestions; *e.g.,* the first meeting of Chairpersons of U.N. human rights treaty bodies held at Geneva in 1984. Meetings of the Chairpersons were also in 1988, 1990, 1992, and 1994. Fifth Meeting of Chairpersons of Treaty Bodies, *Improving the Operation of the Human Rights Treaty Bodies: Report of the Secretary-General*, at 1, U.N. Doc. HRI/MC/1994/2 (1994). The delegates at the Fifth Meeting addressed a number of concerns, including: developing effective responses in emergency situations; integrating human rights into the totality of U.N. activities; funding the treaty bodies and the Centre for Human Rights; establishing an integrated network of country information; reducing the number of reservations upon ratification; creating new human rights instruments; urging universal ratification of existing agreements; coordinating reporting requirements; and coordinating the flow of information between and among treaty bodies. *Id.*

Another product of coordination is a consolidated report summarizing the status of overdue reports. *See* Fifth Meeting of Chairpersons of Treaty Bodies, *Status of the International Human Rights Instruments and the General Situation of Overdue Reports*, U.N. Doc. HRI/MC/1994/3 (1994).

3.   The Vienna Declaration also urges universal acceptance of international human rights instruments. It sets a target date of ratification for only two instruments: the Convention on the Elimination of All Forms of Discrimination Against Women (2000) and the Convention on the Rights of the Child (1995). In addition, the Declaration calls for states to minimize

their reservations and declarations on future treaties and to withdraw such qualifications on already-ratified treaties.

4.   One scholar advocates the establishment of *national* human rights commissions to focus on the promotion and protection of economic, social, and cultural rights. He suggests that such commissions could define socioeconomic rights, submit national reports, scrutinize public policy, and work with NGOs. Mario Gomez, *Social Economic Rights and Human Rights Commissions*, 17 HUM. RTS. Q. 155 (1995).

F.   RECOGNITION OF NEW RIGHTS

As previous sections have demonstrated, some U.S. commentators view economic, social, and cultural rights as goals rather than rights. Nonetheless, established international instruments, such as the Universal Declaration and the ESC Covenant prescribe those rights. Even more controversial are new rights that are currently being developed. This section discusses the development and proclamation of new rights by international organizations. In addition, the section examines a few of those new rights.

Stephen P. Marks, *Emerging Human Rights: A New Generation for the 1980s?*, 33 RUTGERS L. REV. 435, 439-52 (1981) (footnotes omitted):

[Ed. note: The author outlines three generations of human rights. The first generation (civil and political rights) derives from the 18th century. The second generation (economic, social, and cultural rights) came into prominence at the end of the 19th century and beginning of the 20th century. The author then advocates:]

. . . A NEW GENERATION OF HUMAN RIGHTS . . .

The distinguishing characteristics of the new generation of human rights have been expressed by the person who in fact forged the notion of a "third generation of human rights," Karel Vasak . . . [when] he said that the new human rights of the third generation:

> are new in the aspirations they express, are new from the point of view of human rights in that they seek to infuse the human dimension into areas where it has all too often been missing, having been left to the State, or States. . . . [T]hey are new in that they may both be *invoked against* the State and *demanded* of it; but above all (and herein lies their essential characteristic) they can be realized only through the concerted efforts of all the actors on the social scene: the individual, the State, public and private bodies and the international community.

Vasak has further distinguished the three generations of human rights as corresponding successively to each of the elements of the motto of the French revolution: *liberte, egalite, fraternite*. The third generation is the generation of human rights predicated on brotherhood (*fraternite*), in the sense of solidarity. Vasak has, in fact, called these rights "solidarity rights" or "rights of solidarity." . . .

Six areas are currently under consideration: environment, development, peace, the common heritage, communication, and humanitarian assistance.

The case of *environment* is perhaps the most "classical" case of a set of claims which have been given a holistic formulation in terms of human rights. All the features of a right of the new generation are there: elaboration of a specialized body of law, an easily identifiable international legislative process, incorporation of the right as a human right within municipal legal systems, and need for concerted efforts of all social actors. . . .

At the international level the first formulation in human rights terms was in the Stockholm Declaration, adopted by the U.N. conference on the Environment in 1972. Principle I of the Declaration reads as follows: "Man has the fundamental right to freedom, equality and adequate conditions of life, in an environment of a quality that permits a life of dignity and well-being, and he bears a solemn responsibility to protect and improve the environment for present and future generations." . . .

Like other solidarity rights, this one has both an individual and a collective dimension. The individual right is the right of any victim or potential victim of an environmentally damaging activity to obtain the cessation of the activity and reparation for the damage suffered. The collective dimension implies the duty of the state to contribute through international cooperation to resolving environmental problems at a global level. As with all solidarity rights, the collective aspect means, in the last analysis, that the state and all other appropriate social actors have the duty to place the human interest before the national or individual interest.

The right to *development* as a human right has been the subject of extensive reflection and proposed formulations for nearly a decade and is well advanced in acquiring the status of an internationally recognized human right. . . .

. . . SOME OBJECTIONS AND A TENTATIVE CONCLUSION

Much hostility has been voiced against the idea of a new generation of human rights. Not only is proliferation of rights considered to be dangerous, but also the use of the term "generation" implies, the detractors say, that the rights belonging to earlier generations are outdated. It is also frequently said that the rights of the new generation are too vague to be justiciable and are no more than slogans, at best useful for advancing laudable goals of the U.N., at worst useful for the propaganda of certain countries.

Indeed, it would weaken the idea of human rights in general if numerous claims or values were indiscriminately proclaimed as human rights. It is also true that the essential normative task in the field of human rights was accomplished during the first three decades after the founding of the U.N., and that the more urgent task now is implementation. Nevertheless, I have tried to stress the dynamic nature of the process by which these rights are recognized and the consequent emergence of new human rights in the 1980s. . . .

. . . [T]he human rights specialist is, to a certain extent, faced with the choice of resisting the rights which, whether he likes it or not, are emerging, or understanding and contributing to the process by which a limited number of new rights will succeed in attaining international recognition because (a) the need for them is sufficiently great and (b) the international community is ready to recognize them as human rights. He should seek to apply rigorous standards to the definition of new rights, and in particular, . . . see that they have a clearly defined object and an identifiable subject and can be reasonably expected to be enforced. Many human rights already recognized for several decades fall short of these standards. The proclamation of these rights nevertheless increased the likelihood that they would be translated into law and practice. As long as emerging rights are not so unrealistic or trivial as to be treated with mockery, their recognition does serve the advancement of the cause of human rights without endangering the rights of earlier generations.

NOTES AND QUESTIONS

1.   Is the concept of generations of rights useful? Some commentators are critical of the concept. Using "generation" to refer to different categories of rights, they say, might mislead people into thinking that the new generation may gradually replace the old. Nor is the concept historically correct. Civil and political rights and economic, social, and cultural rights were often developed together, rather than as one set neatly following the other. *See* Philip Alston, *A Third Generation of Solidarity Rights: Progressive Development or Obfuscation of International Human Rights Law?*, 29 NETH. INT'L L. REV. 367 (1982). *See also* Burns Weston, *Human Rights, in* 20 NEW ENCYCLOPEDIA BRITANNICA 714 (1989).

Alston has expressed concern that a proliferation of new rights might undermine the normative force of labeling a concept to be a right. He bases his concern on lack of deliberation or meaningful consultation with member states and U.N. bodies before proclaiming new rights. He acknowledges the need for a dynamic approach to proclaiming new rights in response to changing views. Nonetheless, he proposes guidelines for international organizations to follow when proclaiming new rights, in order to protect the legitimacy of rights already proclaimed.

His proposal, in general terms, calls for the preparation of studies on the content of proposed new rights and their relation to existing rights, solicitation of comments from governments and concerned intergovernmental and nongovernmental organizations, revision of studies on the proposed rights (reflecting comments received), appointment of a committee to report on proposals and, finally, proclamation by the appropriate body. *See* Philip Alston, *Conjuring Up New Human Rights: A Proposal for Quality Control*, 78 AM. J. INT'L L. 607 (1984).

The General Assembly has adopted a resolution that provides guidelines for governments and U.N. bodies when they articulate new rights. Proposed new human rights instruments should:

(a)   Be consistent with the existing body of international human rights law;
(b)   Be of fundamental character and derive from the inherent dignity and worth of the human person;
(c)   Be sufficiently precise to give rise to identifiable and practicable rights and obligations;
(d)   Provide, where appropriate, realistic and effective implementation machinery, including reporting systems;
(e)   Attract broad international support.

G.A. res. 41/120, 41 U.N. GAOR Supp. (No. 53) at 178, U.N. Doc. A/41/53 (1987).

2.   Another method of dealing with proliferation of new rights is to establish a hierarchy. Some rights would be deemed "fundamental" or "peremptory," and governments could not violate them. The hierarchical concept is founded in part on the existence of certain nonderogable rights in human rights instruments which governments cannot restrict, even in emergencies. *See, e.g.,* Article 4(2) of the Civil and Political Covenant. Another basis for hierarchical concepts is the principle of *jus cogens* (peremptory norms) in international law. Under customary international law codified in Article 53 of the Vienna Convention on the Law of Treaties, agreements that conflict with peremptory norms are void.

For discussion of the hierarchical concept, including an examination of possible legal bases, see Theodor Meron, *On a Hierarchy of International Human Rights*, 80 AM. J. INT'L L. 1 (1986).

Do you find the hierarchical concept of rights useful? Can you foresee problems with implementing the concept?

3.   Some commentators criticize international organizations for expending limited time and resources proclaiming new rights while too many existing rights remain vague. The action

governments should take to fulfill many rights discussed in this chapter (rights to food and health, for instance) are only now to be defined. *See, e.g.*, HARVARD LAW SCHOOL HUMAN RIGHTS PROGRAM, *Defining the Right to Adequate Health, in* ECONOMIC AND SOCIAL RIGHTS AND THE RIGHT TO HEALTH 17 (An Interdisciplinary Discussion Held at Harvard Law School in September 1993) (1995); Virginia A. Leary, *The Right to Health in International Human Rights Law*, 1 HEALTH & HUM. RTS. 25 (1994); THE RIGHT TO COMPLAIN ABOUT ECONOMIC, SOCIAL AND CULTURAL RIGHTS Netherlands Inst. Hum. Rts. SIM Special No. 16 (Fons Coomans & Fried van Hoof eds., in cooperation with Kitty Arambulo, Jacqueline Smith, & Brigit Toebes, 1995) (articles on rights to education, food, health, and housing); THE RIGHT TO FOOD: GUIDE THROUGH APPLICABLE INTERNATIONAL LAW (Katarina Tomasevski ed., 1987); THE RIGHT TO KNOW: HUMAN RIGHTS AND ACCESS TO REPRODUCTIVE HEALTH INFORMATION (Sandra Coliver ed., 1995).

Many new rights discussed by Marks are even broader and less well defined. *See Interrelationship Between Human Rights and International Peace*, U.N. Doc. E/CN.4/Sub.2/1988/2 (1988); *Agora: What Obligation Does Our Generation Owe to the Next? An Approach to Global Environmental Responsibility*, 84 AM. J. INT'L L. 190 (1990) (articles by Anthony D'Amato, Edith Brown Weiss, Lothar Gundling); W. PAUL GORMLEY, HUMAN RIGHTS AND ENVIRONMENT: THE NEED FOR INTERNATIONAL COOPERATION (1976). *See also Earth Rights and Responsibilities: Human Rights and Environmental Protection Symposium*, 18 YALE J. INT'L L. 215 (1993); ELLI LOUKA, THE TRANSNATIONAL MANAGEMENT OF HAZARDOUS AND RADIOACTIVE WASTES (1992); Robert E. Lutz et al., *Environment, Economic Development and Human Rights: A Triangular Relationship?*, 82 AM. SOC'Y INT'L L. PROC. 40 (1988); Melissa Thorme, *Establishing Environment as a Human Right*, 19 DEN. J. INT'L L. & POL'Y 301 (1991); Theo Van Boven, *Fundamental Rights and Nuclear Arms*, 19 DEN. J. INT'L L. & POL'Y 55 (1990).

Nonetheless, at least one of the new rights—the right to development—has served as a potent symbol inspiring some governments to improve the human rights of their citizens. Though contours of the right to development are vague, it encompasses many of the economic, social, and cultural rights discussed in this chapter that are themselves ill-defined. *See* Philip Alston, *Making Space for New Human Rights: The Case of the Right to Development*, 1 HARV. HUM. RTS. Y.B. 3 (1988); *The Regional and National Dimensions of the Right to Development as a Human Right*, U.N. Doc. E/CN.4/1488 (1981); *The International Dimensions of the Right to Development as a Human Right*, U.N. Doc. E/CN.4/1334 (1979).

Do you think a formal U.N. declaration on the right to development would be helpful? Would it help encourage U.S. ratification of the ESC Covenant?

4.   The Sub-Commission on Prevention of Discrimination and Protection of Minorities has undertaken an extensive study of human rights and the environment. The final report underscored the importance of environmental concerns:

> [I]t is . . . important to establish the legal framework for pursuing what have become the essential demands of this century, in order to take up the legitimate concerns of our generation, to preserve the interests of future generations and mutually to agree upon the components of a right to a health and flourishing environment.
>   . . . . [P]roviding the various agents and beneficiaries of this evolving right with the legal framework and means of expression, communication, participation and action will . . . make it possible to go beyond reductionist concepts of "mankind first" or "ecology first" and achieve a coalescence of the common objectives of development and environmental protection. This would signify a return to the principal objective that inspired the Universal Declaration of Human Rights, whose article 28 states: "Everyone is entitled to a social and international order in which the rights and freedoms set forth in this Declaration can be fully realized".

U.N. Commission on Human Rights, Sub-Commission on Prevention of Discrimination and Protection of Minorities, *Human Rights and the Environment: Final Report Prepared by Mrs. Fatma Zohra Ksentini, Special Rapporteur*, at 3-4, U.N. Doc. E/CN.4/Sub.2/1994/9 (1994). Ksentini's report reviewed environmental protections in existing treaties, emphasized the indivisibility and interdependence of all human rights, particularly the right to development and environmental protection, and summarized the impact of environmental degradation on vulnerable social groups (*e.g.* women, youth, disabled persons, and environmental refugees). *Id.* at 8-41. She concluded that the environment affects enjoyment of many other fundamental rights. *Id.* at 42-57. She recommends that treaty bodies examine the environmental dimension of the human rights of concern to them. She also recommends that the U.N. coordinate efforts of those treaty bodies and others through the Centre for Human Rights and appoint a special rapporteur to oversee protection of the environment. Her report also included a Draft Declaration of Principles on Human Rights and the Environment and urged the U.N. to adopt a set of norms consolidating the right to a satisfactory environment as an international human right. *Id.* at 62-64.

Below are selected paragraphs from the Declaration on the Right to Development, adopted by the U.N. General Assembly. G.A. res. 41/128, 41 U.N. GAOR Supp. (No. 53) at 186, U.N. Doc. A/41/53 (1986):

Article 1

1. The right to development is an inalienable human right by virtue of which every human person and all peoples are entitled to participate in, contribute to and enjoy economic, social, cultural and political development, in which all human rights and fundamental freedoms can be fully realized. . . .

Article 2

1. The human person is the central subject of development and should be the active participant and beneficiary of the right to development.

2. All human beings have a responsibility for development, individually and collectively, taking into account the need for full respect of their human rights and fundamental freedoms as well as their duties to the community, which alone can ensure the free and complete fulfillment of the human being, and they should therefore promote and protect an appropriate political, social and economic order for development.

3. States have the right and the duty to formulate appropriate national development policies that aim at the constant improvement of the well-being of the entire population and of all individuals, on the basis of their active, free and meaningful participation in development and in the fair distribution of the benefits resulting therefrom.

Article 3

1. States have the primary responsibility for the creation of national and international conditions favourable to the realization of the right to development.

2. The realization of the right to development requires full respect for the principles of international law concerning friendly relations and co-operation among States in accordance with the Charter of the United Nations.

3. States have the duty to co-operate with each other in ensuring development and eliminating obstacles to development. States should fulfill their rights and duties in such a manner as to promote a new international economic order based on sovereign equality, interdependence, mutual interest and co-operation among all States, as well as to encourage the observance and realization of human rights.

Article 4

1. States have the duty to take steps, individually and collectively, to formulate

international development policies with a view to facilitating the full realization of the right to development.

2. Sustained action is required to promote more rapid development of developing countries. As a complement to the efforts of developing countries effective international co-operation is essential in providing these countries with appropriate means and facilities to foster their comprehensive development. . . .

Article 6

1. All States should co-operate with a view to promoting, encouraging and strengthening universal respect for and observance of all human rights and fundamental freedoms for all without any distinction as to race, sex, language and religion.

2. All human rights and fundamental freedoms are indivisible and interdependent; equal attention and urgent consideration should be given to the implementation, promotion and protection of civil, political, economic, social and cultural rights.

3. States should take steps to eliminate obstacles to development resulting from failure to observe civil and political rights as well as economic, social and cultural rights. . . .

Article 8

1. States should undertake, at the national level, all necessary measures for the realization of the right to development and shall ensure, *inter alia*, equality of opportunity for all in their access to basic resources, education, health services, food, housing, employment and the fair distribution of income. Effective measures should be undertaken to ensure that women have an active role in the development process. Appropriate economic and social reforms should be made with a view to eradicating all social injustices.

2. States should encourage popular participation in all spheres as an important factor in development and in the full realization of all human rights.

Article 9

1. All the aspects of the right to development set forth in this Declaration are indivisible and interdependent and each of them should be considered in the context of the whole. . . .

Article 10

Steps should be taken to ensure the full exercise and progressive enhancement of the right to development, including the formulation, adoption and implementation of policy, legislative and other measures at the national and international levels.

NOTES AND QUESTIONS

1. In 1993, the U.N. Commission on Human Rights established the Working Group on the Right to Development. The Working Group's assignment is to identify obstacles to implementing the Declaration on the Right to Development.

2. The right to development was discussed at the 1993 World Conference on Human Rights, and paragraph 6 of the Vienna Declaration reaffirmed the right "as a universal and inalienable right and an integral part of fundamental human rights." Paragraph 6 of the Declaration also urges States to promote international cooperation so that the right to development may be realized. Vienna Declaration and Programme of Action (June 25, 1993).

3. In 1993, the Economic and Social Council decided to establish the Commission on Sustain-

able Development. *See* Commission on Sustainable Development, *Adoption of the Agenda*, at 1, U.N. Doc. E/CN.17/1993/1 (1993). The Commission monitors the implementation of Agenda 21 as well as the integration of environmental and developmental goals throughout the U.N. system. *Id.* at 2. Agenda 21 embodies the Rio Declaration on Environment and Development, approved at the U.N. Conference on Environment and Development at Rio de Janeiro In 1992. *See Enhancing International Cooperation for Development: The Role of the United Nations System*, at 7, U.N. Doc. E/1992/82 (1992).

4.   For more on the right to development, see:

Russel Barsh, *Democratization and Development*, 14 HUM. RTS. Q. 120 (1992);

Commission on Human Rights, *Report of the Seminar on Extreme Poverty and the Denial of Human Rights—Note by the Secretariat*, U.N. Doc. E/CN.4/1995/101 (1994);

DILYS HILL, DEVELOPMENT ASSISTANCE AND HUMAN RIGHTS: PRINCIPLES, CRITERIA AND PROCEDURES (1991);

Dietrich Kappeler, *Human Rights and Development: International Views*, 85 AM. J. INT'L L. 735 (1991) (book review);

John O'Manique, *Human Rights and Development*, 14 HUM. RTS. Q. 78 (1992);

THE RIGHT TO DEVELOPMENT IN INTERNATIONAL LAW (Subrata Chowdhury ed., 1992);

Richard Siegel, *A Policy Approach to Human Rights: The Right to Development*, *in* HUMAN RIGHTS: THEORY AND MEASUREMENT (D. Ciagconelli ed., 1988);

Frances Stewart, *Basic Needs Strategies, Human Rights, and the Right to Development*, 11 HUM. RTS. Q. 347 (1989).

CHAPTER 3

STATE REPORTING UNDER INTERNATIONAL HUMAN RIGHTS TREATIES (UNITED STATES)

A. INTRODUCTION   Page   89

B. QUESTIONS   90

C. REPORTING PROCEDURES   91

   1. The Civil and Political Covenant's Human Rights Committee   91

   2. Reporting and Consideration Procedures   91
      a. The Initial Report   92
      b. Periodic Reports   94
      c. Supplementary Reports   95
      d. Emergency Reports   96

   3. Distribution of Committee Reports and Comments   96

D. THE INITIAL U.S. REPORT   100

   1. The Report   100
      John Shattuck, Introduction to U.S. Report   100
      Wall Street Journal, The State of PC   103
      International Covenant on Civil and Political Rights, Article 2   104
      U.S. Understanding Regarding Article 2   105
      U.S. Report Under the CCPR (Article 2)   105
      U.S. Report Under the CCPR (Land and People)   113
      Human Rights Watch & American Civil Liberties Union, Human Rights Violations in the United States: A Report on U.S. Compliance with The International Covenant on Civil and Political Rights   115
      Kevin Reed, Race, Criminal Justice and the Death Penalty   118
      Stan R. Gregory, Note, Capital Punishment and Equal Protection   121

   2. The Examination   122
      Comments of the Human Rights Committee   123

A. INTRODUCTION

Once a government has ratified a human rights treaty, it must comply with the treaty norms and procedures of implementation. This chapter focuses on one of the most commonly used procedures for treaty implementation, that is, periodic reporting and review. The U.N. has promulgated seven principal human rights treaties which are in force and in which the States parties have agreed to submit periodic reports on their compliance with their treaty obligations. Those treaties include: the Covenant on Civil and Political Rights (Article 40); the Covenant on Economic, Social and Cultural Rights (Article 16); the Convention on the Elimination of All Forms of Racial Discrimination (Article 9); the Convention on the Elimination of All Forms of Discrimination against Women (Article 18); the Convention against Torture and Other Cruel, Inhuman or Degrading Treatment or Punishment (Article 19); the Convention on the Suppression and Punishment of the Crime of *Apartheid* (Article VII); and the Convention on the Rights of the Child (Article 44). Each government that is a party to those treaties must submit reports on the measures it has adopted to give effect to the rights recognized in the treaties and on progress made in the enjoyment of those rights. The reporting procedures, together with individual communications under three of those treaties, are the primary means for monitoring implementation of U.N. human rights treaties.

This chapter will focus principally upon the reporting obligations and procedures under the Covenant on Civil and Political Rights (Article 40). Many of our observations apply also to other treaties. We begin with a discussion of the Civil and Political Covenant procedures, then excerpt portions of the initial U.S. report submitted to a human rights treaty body, and finally present the treaty body's response to the U.S. report.

B.   QUESTIONS

1.   The U.S. ratified the Convention on the Elimination of All Forms of Racial Discrimination, and the Convention Against Torture and Other Cruel, Inhuman or Degrading Treatment or Punishment, on October 21, 1994. What can the U.S. learn, from the preparation and defense of its initial Article 40 report, that might help in preparing a report under the Race Convention or the Treaty against Torture (due November 19, 1995) as well as its second report to the Human Rights Committee? In answering this question, consider the following aspects of the first Article 40 report of the U.S. to the Human Rights Committee:

  a.   Did the U.S. present sufficient facts in its report?
  b.   Did the U.S. sufficiently consult with states and nongovernmental organizations while preparing the report and before its issuance?
  c.   What other advice might you give the State Department as it prepares its next report under a human rights treaty?

2.   For a role-playing exercise, members of the class should be designated as either members of the Human Rights Committee or representatives of the United States, convening in the year 2000 to discuss the second U.S. report. To encourage a manageable discussion, assume the Committee will focus on racial discrimination provisions of the Covenant.

The following questions are written from the vantage points of Committee members, but students should keep in mind that the members are citizens of a wide range of governments.

  a.   What procedures did the U.S. seem to follow in preparing the initial report?
  b.   Did the U.S. comply with requirements for the second part of its initial

report? Should the Committee have requested additional information in a supplementary report?

c.   What concerns expressed in the 1995 Committee comments would you expect to see the U.S. address in its second report? Did the Committee give adequate attention to racial and other kinds of discrimination?

d.   As a Committee member, what questions in addition to, or in place of, those asked during the examination of the initial report would you ask U.S. representatives during examination of the second report?

C.   REPORTING PROCEDURES

DWP – US

1.   The Civil and Political Covenant's Human Rights Committee

Article 28 of the Covenant establishes a Committee of 18 members, "persons of high moral character and recognized competence in the field of human rights" who are nationals of state parties but serve as independent experts. Article 31 requires that the Committee not include more than one national from any State party. In addition, "consideration shall be given to equitable geographical distribution of membership and to the representation of the different forms of civilization and of the principal legal systems." In 1994 the elected members were from the following countries:

Australia	France	Jamaica
Chile	Germany	Japan
Costa Rica	Hungary	Mauritius
Cyprus	India	United Kingdom
Ecuador	Israel	United States
Egypt	Italy	Venezuela

All state parties convene every two years to elect half of the Committee, from candidates nominated by governments. Each member serves four years and may be re-elected.

Article 41 of the Covenant empowers the Committee to receive and consider complaints from one State party that another party is not fulfilling obligations under the Covenant. No complaints have been filed as of January 1996.

Under the Covenant's Optional Protocol the Committee may hear complaints from individuals subject to the jurisdiction of a State party to the Protocol who claim to be victims of violations of rights prescribed by the Covenant. We discuss that procedure in chapter 4.

2.   Reporting and Consideration Procedures

The main aim of the reporting requirement is to help governments bring their laws and practices into conformity with the Covenant's obligations. The requirement encourages governments and citizens to focus their discussions regarding nations' human rights performance. Governments then may remedy problems that become evident while preparing reports and, thus, reaffirm their commitment to comply with treaty obligations.

a. The Initial Report

Article 40(1) of the Covenant requires each State party to report within one year after the treaty comes into force for that party. The initial report should discuss measures the government has taken to give effect to rights set forth in the Covenant, progress made in the enjoyment of those rights, and difficulties, if any, affecting implementation. The report should stress legal aspects and assess the government's capacity to review legislation and practices to assure compliance with the obligations. Typically the initial review is drafted by the Ministry of Foreign Affairs—in the U.S., the Department of State—and may or may not involve other government agencies.

*   *   *   *   *

The Committee's guidelines concern form and content (*Report of the Human Rights Committee*, 46 U.N. GAOR Supp. (No. 40), Annex VII, at 206, U.N. Doc. A/46/40 (1992)) and suggest that initial reports be in two parts. The general part is to be prepared in accordance with guidelines established for submitting reports under various human rights treaties including the Covenant. In particular, it should discuss:

(a) the land and its people, including information, disaggregated by sex if possible, regarding the ethnic and demographic characteristics of the population and socio-economic and cultural indicators (*e.g.* per capita income, gross national product, inflation rate, unemployment rate, religion). It also should include information on the population by mother tongue, life expectancy, infant mortality, maternal mortality, fertility rate, relative age of population, percentage of population in rural and urban areas, and percentage of households headed by women;

(b) the State's general political structure, including its political history and framework, the type of government, and the organization of the executive, legislative, and judicial bodies;

(c) the general legal framework within which human rights are protected, including information on:

(1) which judicial, administrative, or other competent authorities have jurisdiction affecting human rights;

(2) what remedies and systems of compensation and rehabilitation are available to individuals whose rights are violated;

(3) whether any rights referenced in the human rights treaty are protected by the constitution and what provisions are made for derogation in times of emergency;

(4) how human rights instruments are made part of the national legal system;

(5) whether the treaty provisions may be invoked before, or directly enforced by, the courts, administrative authorities, or other tribunals; and

(6) whether any institutions are responsible for overseeing the implementation of human rights; and

(d) information and publicity, including the nature and extent of dissemination and discussion of the text of the treaty and whether any special efforts have been made to promote awareness of human rights guarantees contained in the treaty

The second part of the report should deal with each article of the Covenant and provide information about:

(a) legislative, administrative, and other measures in force relative to each right;

(b) any restrictions or limitations (even of a temporary nature) imposed by law or practice affecting the enjoyment of each right;

(c) other factors or difficulties affecting the enjoyment of each right;

(d) any other information on progress made as to the enjoyment of the right.

* * * * *

Governments are encouraged to augment their reports with copies of principal statutes and other texts referenced in the report, and the Committee welcomes information on new developments.

One problem has been that initial reports rarely are submitted on time. Gabon's report, for instance, was due in 1984 but still had not been received as of the date this book went to press. There is, though, a fairly uniform set of procedures for response to late reports. *First*, the Committee issues increasingly firm reminders. (Gabon had been sent 21 reminders as of the October 1994 meeting.) *Second*, the Committee through its chairperson, a member from the same geographical region as the state concerned, or the Director of the U.N. Centre for Human Rights seeks to make personal contact with the government. If those steps do not induce compliance, the Committee has developed sanctions including sending a letter to the meeting of all state parties regarding non-compliance, citing non-compliers in the Annual Report to the General Assembly, and sending a "Chairman's letter" directly to the government's Minister of Foreign Affairs. DOMINIC MCGOLDRICK, THE HUMAN RIGHTS COMMITTEE: ITS ROLE IN THE DEVELOPMENT OF THE INTERNATIONAL COVENANT ON CIVIL AND POLITICAL RIGHTS ¶ 3.9 (1991).

Another problem is that initial reports which have been submitted often are self-congratulatory and not self-critical. The mechanism for not taking those reports at face value is scrutiny by the Committee.

The Committee currently meets for three-week sittings three times per year, once in New York (generally March) and twice in Geneva (generally July and October). At its March 1995 meeting in New York it considered the initial reports of the U.S. and Paraguay, the second periodic reports of Argentina and Yemen, the third report of New Zealand, and special reports from Haiti and Rwanda. Presentation of an initial report—including the government's introduction, questions and comments by members, the government's reply, and further observations—may take two or three days.

The procedures are set forth in Committee rules. Pursuant to Rule 68 each reporting government is invited to send a representative to the public meeting who may orally introduce the report and place it in legal, social, economic, and political context. The representative also may update information submitted earlier. MCGOLDRICK, *supra*, ¶ 3.19.

After the introduction Committee members, in turn, engage in a dialogue with the representative by asking questions about the report and the government's fulfillment of treaty obligations. Though the focus of the initial report is on legal developments relevant to the Covenant, the Committee also expects descriptions of actual practices. Government representatives are given time to prepare oral replies or, alternatively, to refer questions back to the government. After the replies, Committee members may again question the representatives. *Id.* ¶ 3.20.

Committee members are not limited to information in the state's report but may utilize their own expertise, information available from other sources, and materials submitted informally by NGOs. Members from governments under consideration generally have not questioned their own governments, but, informally, may provide information to colleagues on the Committee. *Id.* ¶ 3.20.

* * * * *

Prior to 1992 the Committee announced no "conclusions" as to the human rights situation in a country or the adequacy of its report and of government replies to questions. Individual members made observations after government replies, indicating matters they still would like to have clarified; but the Committee sought no consensus.

The Committee does issue authoritative and useful "General Comments" discussing the desired form and content of reports, common implementation problems, its interpretation of various treaty provisions, and its experience gained as a result of considering State reports. The Comments provide guidance to States parties, and are often cited to by Committee members when they pose their own questions.

In 1992, the Committee decided to supplement members' oral comments by issuing consensus comments on each report. At its March 1992 meeting

> the Committee decided that comments would be adopted reflecting the views of the Committee as a whole at the end of the consideration of each State party report. That would be in addition to, and would not replace, comments made by members, at the end of the consideration of each State party report. A rapporteur would be selected in each case to draft a text, in consultation with the Chairman and other members, for adoption by the Committee. Such comments were to be embodied in a written text and dispatched to the State party concerned as soon as practicable before being publicized and included in the annual report of the Committee. They were to provide a general evaluation of the State party report and of the dialogue with the delegation and to underline positive developments that had been noted during the period under review, factors and difficulties affecting the implementation of the Covenant, as well as specific issues of concern regarding the application of the provisions of the Covenant. Comments were also to include suggestions and recommendations formulated by the Committee to the attention of the State party concerned.

Report of the Human Rights Committee, 47 U.N. GAOR Supp. (No. 40) at 18, U.N. Doc. A/47/40 (1992). The decision was formally incorporated into Rule 70(3) of the Committee's rules of procedure.

b. Periodic Reports

Article 40(1) of the Covenant also provides that the Committee may request such additional reports as it may decide. To further its aim of "engaging in a constructive dialogue with each reporting State" the Committee established a policy of requiring periodic reports. *Report of the Human Rights Committee*, 36 U.N. GAOR Supp. (No. 40), Annex IV, at 102, U.N. Doc. A/36/40 (1981).

Parties now submit periodic reports every five years from the date their initial or last periodic report was due. That decision was made, however, without prejudice to moving to a shorter periodicity at a later time if appropriate. The decision to require periodic reports did not inhibit the Committee's power to request a subsequent report whenever it deems appropriate. *Id.* Annex V, at 104.

The Committee has issued guidelines governing the form and content of periodic reports. *Report of the Human Rights Committee*, 46 U.N. GAOR Supp. (No. 40), Annex VII, at 206, U.N. Doc. A/46/40 (1992). Like initial reports, periodic reports should contain two parts. The first should contain general information prepared in accordance with the consolidated guidelines for the initial reports submitted under the various international human rights instruments, summarized *supra* at 92. The second part should contain information relating to each article of the Covenant, concentrating primarily on:

(a)   updating information regarding implementation measures and providing additional information requested in questioning before the Committee related to previous reports;

(b)   information taking into account the Committee's General Comments;

(c)   changes made or proposed in laws and practices relevant to the Covenant;

(d)   action taken as a result of experience gained in cooperation with the Committee;

(e)   factors affecting and difficulties experienced in implementing the Covenant; and

(f)   the progress made since the last report in the enjoyment of rights recognized by the Covenant.

The periodic reports thus can relay information previously requested by the Committee, information relevant to General Comments, changes made by the State party in response to the Committee's concerns, and difficulties in implementing the Covenant. If the state is a party to the Covenant's Optional Protocol, the Committee also wants to know what remedies have been provided for cases under the Optional Protocol. *Report of the Human Rights Committee*, 36 U.N. GAOR Supp. (No. 40), Annex IV, at 102, U.N. Doc. A/36/40 (1981).

The Committee has developed a practice of assigning second periodic reports to a group of four members. The members meet during the week preceding the Committee's sessions, review information received, and prepare a list of questions to be addressed during consideration of the report. The list then is given to each Committee member to enrich the oral examination process. The Committee follows a similar procedure while considering third periodic reports but urges governments to concentrate on developments occurring after submission of the second report. *Report of the Human Rights Committee*, 48 U.N. GAOR Supp. (No. 40), Annex X, at 218, U.N. Doc. A/48/40 (1993).

The list of questions prepared by the four-member group is submitted to governments prior to the session so that each has an opportunity to prepare its comments. *Id.*

During the consideration of periodic reports a dialogue often develops between the government and the Committee, in which concerns are articulated and sometimes repeated. The focus in later reports should be on progress made in responding to those concerns. The questioning and requests for information often are challenging—particularly if the government representatives are not adequately prepared.

As with initial reports, Committee members make final observations and consensus comments at the conclusion of the dialogue.

c.   Supplementary Reports

Governments often have found reporting requirements to be substantial, requiring extensive effort and considerable expenditure. The Committee is not satisfied with anecdotal information. Hence, the government must establish mechanisms for its own monitoring of treaty obligations so that it can prepare reports which provide accurate descriptions and factually based material. Statistics must be in such detail that Committee members obtain a realistic sense of situations facing the entire nation, as well as regions and significant groups. Incomplete reports are not uncommon; and during questioning the government representative may be unable fully to answer questions posed and may choose to refer them back to the government. Additional information and responses to unanswered questions are supplied through supplementary reports. Rule 70 of the Rules of Procedure authorizes requests for additional information from states whose reports seem inadequate.

The Committee has not yet issued guidelines for supplementary reports. Its consideration of them largely mirrors the approach established with respect to both initial and periodic reports. The Committee's procedure for handling additional information and for dealing with cases where information has been promised but not submitted is as follows:

> (a) Whenever additional information is received at the same time as the next periodic report or shortly before the next periodic report is due, to consider the additional information together with the periodic report;

> (b) When additional information is received at other times, to decide, on a case-by-case basis, whether it should be considered, and to notify the State party concerned of any eventual decision to examine the additional information;

> (c) Where promised additional information has not been received, the Bureau of the Committee will consider sending appropriate reminders to the States parties. The Secretariat, in corresponding with States parties concerning the date for submission of their next periodic reports, is also to remind them of their promise, during consideration of their previous reports, that additional information would be supplied to the Committee.

Report of the Human Rights Committee, 41 U.N. GAOR Supp. (No. 40) at 9-10, U.N. Doc. A/41/40 (1986).

d. Emergency Reports

The Committee occasionally has used its authority under Article 40 to request reports regarding emergency situations. It considers emergencies to be "recent or current events indicating that the enjoyment of human rights protected under the Covenant ha[s] been seriously affected." *Report of the Human Rights Committee*, 48 U.N. GAOR Supp. (No. 40), Annex X, at 219, U.N. Doc. A/48/40 (1993).

For example, at the time of issuing its own 1993 Annual Report the Committee had requested emergency reports from Iraq (April 11, 1991), the Federal Republic of Yugoslavia (November 4, 1991), Peru (April 10, 1992), Bosnia and Herzegovina, Croatia, and the Federal Republic of Yugoslavia (October 6, 1992). All parties complied and participated in the consideration of those reports. *Id.* At its October 1993 meeting, the Committee requested emergency reports from Burundi and Angola.

3. Distribution of Committee Reports and Comments

Article 40(4) requires that the Committee transmit all its reports and General Comments to each party to the Covenant. In addition, the article authorizes the Committee to send copies to the Economic and Social Council (ECOSOC). While

Article 40(5) authorizes states to submit observations on comments made under 40(4), there is no precise indication of ECOSOC's required or permitted role in response to Committee communications.

Article 45 provides that the Committee "shall submit to the General Assembly. . ., through the Economic and Social Council, an annual report on its activities." These reports include Committee views on individual cases under the Optional Protocol, the General Comments promulgated during the year, and a summary of its considerations of state reports. As with ECOSOC the General Assembly's role is unclear. Also, because the Committee technically is not an organ of the U.N. but is a treaty body, its duty to follow Assembly recommendations is unclear. In general, however, perhaps because the Committee depends on U.N. funding and staff assistance, Committee members carefully consider Assembly observations while planning and executing their work. McGOLDRICK, *supra*, ¶ 3.40.

NOTES AND QUESTIONS

1.   The International Labour Organization (ILO) also utilizes reporting to monitor compliance with its treaties. One ILO counterpart to the Human Rights Committee is its Committee of Experts on the Application of Conventions and Recommendations, formed in 1927. Like the Human Rights Committee it is composed of independent experts from various countries. Unlike the Human Rights Committee, which reviews reports only under the Civil and Political Covenant, the ILO Committee reviews consolidated reports that discuss practices under numerous ILO treaties. As of the date this book went to press, more than 170 ILO treaties were in force. The Committee of Experts uses government reports and other information to analyze states' compliance with ILO treaties and then comments formally on compliance.

The ILO also sponsors a Conference Committee on the Application of Conventions and Recommendations, which is larger than the Committee of Experts and composed of representatives of governments, employers, and workers. It is established by the International Labour Conference after each annual meeting, and it uses the Committee of Experts' report to select governments as to which a more-detailed analysis of discrepancies and implementation measures seems appropriate.

The second main difference between the Human Rights Committee and ILO committees is that the ILO is largely staff-driven whereas the Human Rights Committee is largely member-driven. For example, ILO comments are drafted by staff and circulated to Committee members, who then make comments and changes. In contrast, the Human Rights Committee drafts its own comments and questions with relatively little assistance from staff.

For further additional information on ILO procedures, see: Virginia Leary, *Lessons from the Experience of the International Labour Organisation, in* THE UNITED NATIONS AND HUMAN RIGHTS: A CRITICAL APPRAISAL 580 (Philip Alston ed., 1992); NICOLAS VALTICOS, INTERNATIONAL LABOUR LAW (1979).

2.   Contrast the Civil and Political Covenant's reporting procedures with those of the Convention on the Elimination of All Forms of Racial Discrimination (Racial Treaty):

Article 8

1.   There shall be established a Committee on the Elimination of Racial Discrimination . . . consisting of eighteen experts of high moral standing and acknowledged impartiality elected by States Parties from among their nationals, who shall serve in their personal capacity, consideration being given to equitable geographical distribution and to the representation of the different forms of civilization as well as of the principal legal systems. . . .

Article 9

1.   States Parties undertake to submit to the Secretary-General of the United

Nations, for consideration by the Committee, a report on the legislative, judicial, administrative or other measures which they have adopted and which give effect to the provisions of this Convention: (a) within one year after the entry into force of the Convention for the State concerned; and (b) thereafter every two years and whenever the Committee so requests. The Committee may request further information from the States Parties.

2.   The Committee shall report annually, through the Secretary-General, to the General Assembly of the United Nations on its activities and may make suggestions and general recommendations based on the examination of the reports and information received from the States Parties. Such suggestions and general recommendations shall be reported to the General Assembly together with comments, if any, from States Parties.

The Civil and Political Covenant was adopted on December 16, 1966, one year after the Racial Convention, adopted on December 21, 1965. What differences do you note in the words of the reporting provisions? Are the differences significant?

3.   The Convention on the Rights of the Child (Children's Treaty), adopted in 1989, contains the most recent codification of reporting requirements. Compare the reporting procedures of the Covenant and the Racial Treaty with those of the Children's Convention that are excerpted below. Note that the Children's Treaty contains more explicit instructions. Why might U.N. drafters decided to codify these provisions as part of the treaty itself rather than as part of committee rules of procedure?

Article 42

1.   For the purpose of examining progress made by States Parties in achieving the realization of the obligations undertaken in the present Convention, there shall be established a Committee on the Rights of the Child, which shall carry out the functions hereinafter provided.
2.   The Committee shall consist of ten experts of high moral standing and recognized competence in the field covered by this Convention. The members of the Committee shall be elected by States Parties from among their nationals and shall serve in their personal capacity, consideration being given to equitable geographical distribution, as well as the principal legal systems. . . .

Article 44

1.   States Parties undertake to submit to the Committee, through the Secretary-General of the United Nations, reports on the measures they have adopted which give effect to the rights recognized herein and on the progress made on the enjoyment of those rights:

a.   Within two years of the entry into force of the Convention for the State Party concerned;
b.   Thereafter every five years.

2.   Reports made under the present article shall indicate factors and difficulties, if any, affecting the degree of fulfillment of the obligations under the present Convention. Reports shall also contain sufficient information to provide the Committee with a comprehensive understanding of the implementation of the Convention in the country concerned.
3.   A State Party which has submitted a comprehensive initial report to the Committee need not, in its subsequent reports submitted in accordance with paragraph 1(b) of the present article, repeat basic information previously provided.
4.   The Committee may request from States Parties further information relevant to the implementation of the Convention.

5.   The Committee shall submit to the General Assembly, through the Economic and Social Council, every two years, reports on its activities.

6.   States Parties shall make their reports widely available to the public in their own countries.

Article 45

In order to foster the effective implementation of the Convention and to encourage international co-operation in the field covered by the Convention:

a.   The specialized agencies, the United Nations Children's Fund, and other United Nations organs shall be entitled to be represented at the consideration of the implementation of such provisions of the present Convention as fall within the scope of their mandate. The Committee may invite the specialized agencies, the United Nation's Children's Fund and other competent bodies as it may consider appropriate to provide expert advice on the implementation of the Convention . . . [and] to submit reports on the implementation of the Convention;

b.   The Committee shall transmit, as it may consider appropriate, to the specialized agencies, the United Nation's Children's Fund and other competent bodies, any reports from States Parties that contain a request, or indicate a need, for technical advice or assistance, along with the Committee's observations and suggestions, if any, on these requests or indications;

c.   The Committee may recommend to the General Assembly to request the Secretary-General to undertake on its behalf studies on specific issues relating to the rights of the child;

d.   The Committee may make suggestions and general recommendations based on information received pursuant to articles 44 and 45 of the present Convention. Such suggestions and general recommendations shall be transmitted to any State Party concerned and reported to the General Assembly, together with comments, if any, from States Parties.

Note that the Children's Treaty, by specifying desired roles, avoids debate (under the Civil and Political Covenant) involving the proper role of U.N. specialized agencies. *See* Committee on the Rights of the Child, *Report on Seventh Session*, U.N. Doc. CRC/C/34 (1994). Addenda to that report reprint several countries' initial reports.

4.   The body charged with monitoring, implementing, and enforcing the Economic, Social and Cultural Covenant is the Economic and Social Council (ECOSOC), which has delegated its responsibility to the Committee on Economic, Social and Cultural Rights. For discussion of reporting and examination procedures under that Covenant, see Committee on Economic, Social and Cultural Rights, *Report on the Seventh Session*, at 12-19, U.N. Doc. E/1993/22 (1993) and chapter 2, *supra*.

5.   For general reading, see:

Ineke Boerfijn, *Towards a Strong System of Supervision: The Human Rights Committee's Role in Reforming the Reporting Procedure under Article 40 of the Covenant on Civil and Political Rights*, 17 Hum. Rts. Q. 766 (1995);

Sandra Coliver, *International Reporting Procedures, in* Guide to International Human Rights Practice 245 (Hurst Hannum ed., 2d ed. 1992);

José L. Gomez del Prado, *United Nations Conventions on Human Rights: The Practice of the Human Rights Committee and the Committee on the Elimination of Racial Discrimination in Dealing with Reporting Obligations of States Parties*, 7 Hum. Rts. Q. 492 (1985);

Dana D. Fischer, *Reporting Under the Covenant on Civil and Political Rights: The First Five Years of the Human Rights Committee*, 76 Am. J. Int'l L. 142 (1982);

Farrokh Jhabvala, *The Practice of the Covenant's Human Rights Committee, 1976-82: Review of State Party Reports*, 6 HUM. RTS. Q. 81 (1984);

Sarah Joseph, *New Procedures Concerning the Human Rights Committee's Examination of State Reports*, 12 NETH. Q. HUM. RTS. 5 (1995) (discussing and assessing the Committee's new procedures of adopting consensus comments and requiring emergency reports);

MANFRED NOWAK, U.N. COVENANT ON CIVIL AND POLITICAL RIGHTS: CCPR COMMENTARY (1993) (discussing the Covenant by article);

MICHAEL O'FLAHERTY, HUMAN RIGHTS AND THE UN: PRACTICE BEFORE THE TREATY BODIES (1996);

Michael O'Flaherty, *The Reporting Obligation under Article 40 of the International Covenant on Civil and Political Rights: Lessons to be Learned from Consideration by the Human Rights Committee of Ireland's First Report*, 16 HUM. RTS. Q. 515 (1994);

Torkel Opsahl, *The Human Rights Committee, in* THE UNITED NATIONS AND HUMAN RIGHTS 369 (Philip Alston ed., 1992);

UNITAR/CENTRE FOR HUMAN RIGHTS, MANUAL ON HUMAN RIGHTS REPORTING, HR/PUB/91/ 1 (1991) (Revised and republished in 1995 with a "Trainers' Guide");

UNITED NATIONS, WORKSHOP ON INTERNATIONAL HUMAN RIGHTS INSTRUMENTS AND REPORTING OBLIGATIONS: PREPARATION OF REPORTS TO UNITED NATIONS HUMAN RIGHTS TREATY BODIES, HR/ PUB/91/5 (1992).

D. THE INITIAL U.S. REPORT

1. The Report

The United States submitted its initial report under the Civil and Political Covenant in July 1994. The preface is excerpted below, followed by an editorial that criticizes the approach of the preface.

John Shattuck, Assistant Secretary of State for Democracy, Human Rights, and Labor, *Introduction, in* CIVIL AND POLITICAL RIGHTS IN THE UNITED STATES: INITIAL REPORT OF THE UNITED STATES OF AMERICA TO THE U.N. HUMAN RIGHTS COMMITTEE UNDER THE INTERNATIONAL COVENANT ON CIVIL AND POLITICAL RIGHTS i-vi (July 1994):

I am pleased to introduce the initial report prepared by the United States Government concerning its compliance with the International Covenant on Civil and Political Rights. The report was submitted in July to the U.N. Human Rights Committee established by the Covenant. This is also the first report submitted by the United States in accordance with its obligations under an international human rights treaty. Written to United Nations specifications, and prepared through the collaborative efforts of the U.S. Departments of State, Justice and other Executive Branch departments and agencies, with input from nongovernmental organizations and concerned individuals, it represents a government-wide commitment to creative interaction with the emerging global framework of international human rights law. It is meant to offer to the international community a sweeping picture of human rights observance in the United States and the legal and political system within which those rights have evolved and are protected. . . .

The antecedents of contemporary human rights law stretch far back into history—to natural law traditions, the ethical teachings of the world's great religions—both East and West—Greco-Roman law, and the pioneering philosophical work of Hugo Grotius and John Locke. The concept of universal rights developed by 18th century political theorists nourished international law, as it also set the stage for American constitutionalism. Indeed international human rights law and the constitutional law of the United States are at bottom profoundly related: both seek to limit the authority of states to interfere with the inalienable rights of all individuals without discrimination. . . .

The Covenant on Civil and Political Rights contributes to the promotion of international human rights by codifying many of the principles we in the United States hold dear—political freedom; self-determination; freedom of speech, opinion, expression, association and religion; and protection of the family against governmental intrusion. The unfortunate fact that these principles are disregarded in many countries in no way diminishes their commanding authority.

US principdles

The United States as a nation was founded on the principle of inalienable individual rights. The history of this country is in many ways the story of an ongoing struggle to fulfill the promise of that conception of rights, a struggle to overcome old and new injustices in our own democracy that continues today. As part of that struggle the United States is also firmly committed to promoting respect for human rights and fundamental freedoms around the globe.

As this report shows, United States law provides extensive protection against human rights abuses by government authorities. Under the U.S. Constitution, government authority is distributed and diffused through the separation of powers between the three branches of government. From the beginning of this nation's history, the United States Supreme Court has exercised the power of judicial review to check unconstitutional action by the executive and legislative branches.

Freedoms of speech and religion are protected by law, police power is subject to significant constitutional limitations, and America's political leadership at all levels is held accountable to its citizens.

Our Constitution laid out a blueprint for the interpretation and realization of the idea of civil and political rights and freedoms, but it has taken the labors of generations of citizens from all parts of our society to build the institutions which carry the promise of these rights and freedoms. This process has unfolded over more than two centuries, through many chapters of history, some noble and others dark, and the task continues to this day.

Over the course of its history, America has experienced egregious human rights violations in this ongoing American struggle for justice, such as the enslavement and disenfranchisement of African Americans and the virtual destruction of many Native American civilizations.

US hum. rts violatias

The profound injustices visited on African Americans were only partially erased after the Civil War (1861-1865), and then a century later by the civil rights movement of the 1950s and 1960s, a movement that combined heroic leadership with grass-roots organizing and dogged legal marches through courthouses and legislatures; a movement that helped shape the interpretation and implementation of constitutional law to ensure that human rights could be respected in practice.

Those efforts to undo the bitter legacy of slavery continue today. The lessons learned from our nation's unfinished battle with racial discrimination can be shared with other members of the international community. Simply put, our national experience demonstrates that legal guarantees of human rights are a prerequisite to social progress, not the other way around.

native americans

Native Americans have suffered a fate similar to that of many indigenous civilizations: destruction and displacement of their cultures and societies. The lessons of those injustices, and the responsibilities the people of the United States are charged with as a result, are also central legacies of American history.

immigration

The members of other minority groups have suffered injustices in the United States. The United States is largely a nation of immigrants. We continue to draw wave after wave of men and women from around the world seeking a better life, with annual immigration now surpassing 900,000. However, immigrants to our shores, like immigrants everywhere, have often met with discrimination and resistance that have deepened the personal dislocations of migration. The openness of our society has permitted, with time, mobility and release from poverty and marginalization. In the process, immigrant groups themselves have deeply enriched our national identity, as the 19th century's notion of a "melting pot" of assimilation has gradually given way to a broader vision of pluralism.

women

The ongoing struggle for full realization of the rights of women is a central feature of the human rights process in America. Women did not have the vote in the United States until 1920, a century and a half after the founding of the republic. With growing strength, women have moved to claim their equal place in the political, economic and social life of the country. Efforts are underway in all sectors of American life to broaden women's opportunities and end remaining discrimination.

There are many other human rights challenges in our nation's historical and contemporary experience. As we have continued to find new challenges, we have worked with varying degrees of success to strengthen the capacity of our institutions to address them.

As an open democracy, the United States tends to address its most difficult and divisive human rights issues in public and in the courts. The result is a number of long-standing human rights issues with a large body of case law as well as many newer issues on which legal ground is being broken. Among the former are such areas as freedom of religion, immigrants and refugees, race discrimination, and freedom of expression. More recent areas of concern include gender discrimination,

recent areas

the death penalty, abortion, police brutality, and language rights.

As a matter of domestic law, treaties as well as statutes must conform to the requirements of the Constitution. No treaty provision will be given effect as U.S. law if it conflicts with the Constitution. In the case of the Covenant on Civil and Political Rights, the U.S. Constitution offers greater protection of free speech than does the Covenant; on those and some other provisions of the Covenant, the United States has recorded its understanding of a particular provision or made a declaration of how it intends to apply that provision or undertaking.

It is of little use to proclaim principles of human rights protection at the international level unless they can be meaningfully realized and enforced domestically. In the words of the renowned human rights and constitutional scholar Louis Henkin: "The international law of human rights parallels and supplements national law... but it does not replace, and indeed depends on, national institutions." Thus it is up to the various organs of federal, state and local government here in the United States to bring those international commitments to fruition.

As observers have noted ever since the great French thinker and statesman Alexis de Tocqueville penned his classic "Democracy in America" in the 1830s, the United States possesses a strikingly robust legal and judicial system, and it is in and through that system that legal protection for human rights has taken shape. This report of the United States to the UN Human Rights Committee thus focuses on the law of human rights protection as it has evolved in the distinctive mix of statutory and common law that exists at the federal level.

The broad conception of rights that has evolved in the course of U.S. history has come to serve as the basis for much of international human rights law, and, ironically but fittingly, to set the standard by which the United States is judged by other members of the international community.

While the state of human rights protection in the United States has advanced significantly over the years, many challenges and problems remain. The elaborate structure of human rights law set forth in this report emerged in the course of long and painful struggle in the United States, in a sweeping historical narrative displaying cruelty and injustice alongside vision and courage. It has been a distinguishing characteristic of our political and legal system to weave the constant possibility of change into the fabric of constitutional democracy.

In publishing this report and giving it wide domestic distribution we hope to enhance public awareness of human rights protection and foster human rights education in the United States. We hope it will find a wide readership in schools and universities, among civil and political groups and with concerned citizens.

We will be issuing subsequent reports under the Covenant, and under additional human rights agreements to which the United States is a party.

Here as elsewhere the realization of universal human rights is a work-in-progress. While the U.S. system has done much over time to advance and champion human rights—as this report demonstrates—much remains to be done. The U.S. Government welcomes spirited dialogue and debate on the advancement of human rights in the United States and throughout the global community that is taking shape on the horizon of the twenty-first century.

*   *   *   *   *

Review & Outlook: The State of PC, WALL ST. J., Sept. 9, 1994, at A14:

Political correctness was once merely the bane of campus life. Now, incredibly, it has been enshrined as official U.S. foreign policy. That, at least, is the only conclusion we can reach from the release this week of a remarkable report from the Clinton State Department purporting to expose human rights abuses *within* the United States.

The U.S. has for years campaigned against human-rights abuses in places ranging from South Africa to the Soviet Union. Leonid Brezhnev and the Soviet press were famous for pushing the standard party line of foreign dictators caught in the most heinous offenses: What about America's treatment of blacks or Indians?

Democratic presidencies in our time seem to have a knack for attracting officials with a taste for fashionable sackcloth: Andrew Young, President Carter's U.N. ambassador, caused quite an uproar when he said in 1976 that the U.S. held "hundreds, maybe thousands of people I would categorize as political prisoners." Mr. Young had to retract that statement, but now the Brezhnev view comes dressed up as official State Department policy.

This week, the State Department released a "preface" to its first report on human rights abuses within the U.S. . . . The report itself, a technical document mandated by a U.N. treaty signed by the Bush Administration, came out on July 28. But the preface took longer, reports the Washington Post, because it caused so much dissension inside the government.

Little wonder: The document, signed by John Shattuck, the assistant secretary of state for human rights, is a PC view of U.S. history as found only on campuses or among Smithsonian curators. It details "egregious human rights violations" ranging from the treatment of African-Americans to the "ongoing struggle for full realization of the rights of women."

"While the state of human rights protection in the United States has advanced significantly over the years, many challenges and problems remain," the preface concludes. Such as? Well, the report's "areas of concern" include "gender discrimination, the death penalty, abortion, police brutality and language rights."

We look forward to a "60 Minutes" expose of America's "language" dungeons. Meanwhile, someone might ask Bill Clinton about the death penalty's appearance on this list. The President, after all, just spent a good chunk of his political capital to pass a crime bill strengthening the death penalty. Does that make Mr. Clinton a human-rights offender like Haiti's junta?

Supposedly something like the State Department flagellating the U.S. as a systematic human rights violator causes heartburn for the administration's more serious types. But we've also just had the example of HUD supporting over-the-top prosecutions of ordinary citizens under the Fair Housing Act. How many of these left-liberal misfires by Clinton operatives have to occur before it's clear they're not anomalies but are instead part of this administration's political worldview?

NOTES AND QUESTIONS

1. The Wall Street Journal editorial was nearly the only substantive commentary in the U.S. media on either the U.S. report or the U.S. appearance before the Human Rights Committee. Do you agree with the Wall Street Journal criticism?

2. If you were the cognizant State Department official, would you include a preface to the next U.S. report under the Covenant? Do you think it helps either the Human Rights Committee or interested members of the general public?

3. Think about the bind in which U.S. officials are placed. Cooperating with the Committee and being critical of U.S. practices may ingratiate members of Committee and make the process smoother. Open critique of U.S. history and policy, however, incites criticism from certain groups and legislators. How would you resolve the dilemma?

In the second part of its initial report the U.S. discussed, article by article, laws protecting rights advanced in the Covenant. Excerpted below are two articles of the Covenant and an "understanding" attached by the U.S. upon ratification.

International Covenant on Civil and Political Rights, G.A. res. 2200A (XXI), 21 U.N. GAOR Supp. (No. 16) at 52, U.N. Doc. A/6316 (1966), *entered into force* Mar. 23, 1976:

Article 2

1.   Each State Party . . . undertakes to respect and to ensure to all individuals within its territory and subject to its jurisdiction the rights recognized in the present Covenant, without distinction of any kind, such as race, colour, sex, language, religion, political or other opinion, national or social origin, property, birth or other status.

2.   Where not already provided for by existing legislative or other measures, each State Party . . . undertakes to take the necessary steps, in accordance with its constitutional processes and with the provisions of the present Covenant, to adopt such legislative or other measures as may be necessary to give effect to the rights recognized in the present Covenant.

3.   Each State Party to the present Covenant undertakes:

a.   To ensure that any person whose rights or freedoms as herein recognized are violated shall have an effective remedy, notwithstanding that the violation has been committed by persons acting in an official capacity;

b.   To ensure that any person claiming such a remedy shall have his rights thereto determined by competent judicial, administrative or legislative authorities, or by any other competent authority provided for by the legal system of the State, and to develop the possibilities of judicial remedies. . . .

Article 26

All persons are equal before the law and are entitled without any discrimination to the equal protection of the law. In this respect, the law shall prohibit any discrimination and guarantee to all persons equal and effective protection against discrimination on any ground such as race, colour, sex, language, religion, political or other opinion, national or social origin, property, birth or other status.

*   *   *   *   *

Following is the "understanding" attached by the U.S. upon ratification of the Covenant. For more on U.S. treaty reservations, see section D.2 below and chapter 2.

138 CONG. REC. S4783 (daily ed., April 2, 1992):

II.   The Senate's advice and consent is subject to the following understandings, which shall apply to the obligations of the United States under this Covenant:

(1)   That the Constitution and laws of the United States guarantee all persons equal protection of the law and provide extensive protection against discrimination. The United States understands distinctions based upon race, color, sex, language, religion, political or other opinion, national or social origin, property, birth or any other status—as those terms are used in Article 2, paragraph 1 and Article 26—to be permitted when such distinctions are, at minimum, rationally related to a legitimate governmental objective. . . .

*   *   *   *   *

Following is the U.S. report on protections under Article 2.

Consideration of Reports Submitted by States Parties Under Article 40 of the Covenant; Initial Report of the United States of America, at 20-29, U.N. Doc. CCPR/C/81/Add.4 (1994) (several citations omitted):

As a general principle, all individuals within the United States are afforded the enjoyment of the rights enumerated in the Covenant on Civil and Political Rights as a matter of law without regard to race, colour, sex, language, religion, political or other opinion, national or social origin, property, birth or other status. Judicial interpretation of the guarantees in the U.S. Constitution has led to the development of an extensive body of decisional law covering a broad spectrum of governmental activity according to a number of well-accepted canons. The right of individuals to challenge governmental actions in court, and the power of the judiciary to invalidate those actions that fail to meet the constitutional standards, provides an effective method for ensuring equal protection of the law in practice. In addition, a number of significant anti-discrimination statutes provide additional protection for the civil and political rights of persons within the United States. . . .

Equal Protection. Most of the substantive rights enumerated in the Covenant have exact or nearly-exact analogues in the U.S. Constitution. . . . In addition, and of particular relevance to Article 2, the Constitution guarantees "equal protection" to all. This principle derives from the Fourteenth Amendment's guarantee that no state may "deny to any person within its jurisdiction the equal protection of the laws," and the Fifth Amendment's guarantee that "no person shall be deprived of life, liberty, or property, without due process of law," which has been read to incorporate an "equal protection" component. These constitutional provisions limit the power of government with respect to all persons subject to U.S. jurisdiction. As interpreted and applied by the U.S. Supreme Court, the doctrine of equal protection applies not only with respect to the rights protected by the Covenant, but also to the provision of government services and benefits such as education, employment and housing.

The substantive guarantees of the Constitution are often implemented without reference to equal protection. For example, the Supreme Court recently held that a local government could not constitutionally prohibit animal sacrifices that are part of a religious ritual, although the government could pass neutral laws to protect animals from torture, or to protect public health. While the group that practices the sacrifices may be identifiable racially and ethnically, the case was decided squarely under the First Amendment protection for religious freedom. The Court did not discuss the issues in terms of ethnic nondiscrimination and equal protection.

Classifications. Under the doctrine of equal protection, it has long been recognized that the government must treat persons who are "similarly situated" on an equal basis, but can treat persons in different situations or classes in different ways with respect to a permissible state purpose. The general rule is that legislative classifications are presumed valid if they bear some reasonable relation to a legitimate governmental purpose. The most obvious example is economic regulation. Both state and federal governments are able to supply different rules to different types of economic activities, and the courts will review such regulation under a very deferential standard. Similarly, the way in which a state government chooses to allocate its financial resources among categories of needy people will be reviewed under a very deferential standard.

Suspect Classifications. On the other hand, certain distinctions or classifications have been recognized as inherently invidious and therefore have been subjected to more exacting scrutiny and judged against more stringent requirements. For example, classification on the basis of racial distinctions is automatically "suspect" and must be justified as necessary to a compelling governmental purpose. Laws which purposely discriminate against racial minorities, whether in the fields of housing, voting, employment, education or other areas, have rarely been upheld under this higher standard. When intentional discrimination on the basis of race or national origin can be inferred from a legislative scheme or discerned in legislative history, it is as forbidden as overt use of a racial classification. Unlawful intentional discrimination has sometimes been inferred simply from the impact of a law. For example, . . . the Supreme Court found impermissible discrimination where all of some 200 Chinese applicants were denied permits to operate laundries while virtually all non-Chinese applicants were granted permits under the same statute. . . .

Fundamental Interest. Where a so-called "fundamental interest" is at stake, the Supreme Court has subjected legislative classifications to "strict scrutiny" despite the absence of a suspect classification. This explains why, in the cases involving the right to vote (including fair apportionment) and in due process cases (right to counsel, etc.), the Court has found invidious discrimination even though the basis for that discrimination is not race, national origin, sex, or any other suspect class. What makes a right "fundamental" is not always clear. The fundamental rights are not necessarily those found in other provisions of the Constitution; indeed, those other rights can be protected without reference to equal protection. More likely, the rights are the ones *not* found in the Constitution by inference, such as the right to procreation.

Corrective or Affirmative Action. In recent years, the question has frequently arisen whether legislation may classify by race for purposes of compensating for past racial discrimination. The general rule that has evolved is that because race is a "suspect classification," in this context as in all others, it will be subject to "strict scrutiny" by the courts. However, where an employer or other entity has engaged in racial discrimination in the past, it will generally be permitted (and may sometimes be required) to accord narrowly-tailored racial preferences for a limited period of time, to correct the effects of its past conduct. Greater latitude for racially-based remedies has been permitted when Congress has acted under the enabling clause of the Fourteenth Amendment than when states or political subdivisions have given a racial preference.

Specific Issues. Although, as noted above, issues of discrimination involving rights protected by the Covenant are often addressed through suits to vindicate a constitutional right other than equal protection, equal protection has sometimes been invoked directly in connection with certain guarantees specified in the Covenant. . . .

Race and due process. Even in the nineteenth century it was clear that racial discrimination in jury selection affected the due process rights of African Americans. Reading the Equal Protection clauses in conjunction with the constitutional guarantee of Due Process, the Supreme Court has repeatedly held that it is a violation to discriminate in preparation of jury lists on the basis of race or national origin. That prohibition has been extended to the exercise of peremptory challenges in petit jury selection, and, most recently, to peremptory challenges on the basis of sex. . . .

Race and the death penalty. Legal attacks on the death penalty have generally been based on the Eighth Amendment's prohibition of cruel and unusual punishment. In recent years, however, there have been efforts to demonstrate that in operation, the death penalty is unequally applied on the basis of race. Numerous defendants have attempted, so far without success, to show that the discretionary elements in the process of sentencing a defendant to death have had the effect of discrimination by race of defendant or race of victim. *See McCleskey v. Kemp,* 481 U.S. 279 (1987) (where petitioner could not demonstrate that he personally had been discriminated against, statistics suggesting systemic inequities could not be used to overturn death sentence). This issue is also the subject of considerable public debate and political consideration. . . .

Race and the right to form families. The Supreme Court has relied upon the Equal Protection Clause to invalidate state bans on intermarriage, and to prevent courts dealing in child custody from implementing societal prejudices.

State Action. Operating alone, the constitutional equal protection clauses protect one only against discriminatory treatment by a government entity, or by persons acting "under color of law." Thus, the doctrine does not reach purely private conduct in which there is no governmental involvement. Whether or not in any particular situation there is sufficient "state action" to bring a discriminatory practice under the constitutional Equal Protection clauses represents a complicated jurisprudence in its own right.

Federal Statutes. Congress has supplemented the constitutional guarantees of equal protection to encompass certain private actions. . . . After the Civil War, Congress implemented the Thirteenth Amendment by passing laws prohibiting private racial discrimination in property and contractual relationships. Most of the federal civil rights laws were passed in and after 1964. . . . These statutes prohibit discrimination in the areas beyond those covered by the Covenant, including privately-owned public accommodations, private and federal, state or local governmental employment, federally-assisted programs, and private and public housing. Where the statutes cover ground already protected by the Constitution, they add remedies that did not exist before. . . .

Virtually every federal agency is involved in promoting or enforcing equal protection guarantees. Although the federal civil rights statutes and implementing regulations are too numerous to provide an exhaustive list, some of the principal statutes are described below. Because these statutes were passed at different times to address different problems, no two cover precisely the same ground. For example, Title II of the Civil Rights Act of 1964, prohibiting discrimination in places of public accommodation and amusement (hotels, restaurants, cinemas) does not mention "sex" as a protected category. Title II, moreover, does not protect against discrimination by race in ordinary retail stores. . . . Some of the gaps in coverage are filled in by state and local constitutions, laws, and ordinances.

Title VI of the Civil Rights Act of 1964 prohibits public and private employers (with certain exceptions including the federal government and small private businesses) from discriminating on the basis of race, color, religion, sex or national origin in their employment practices. . . .

. . . Executive Order 11246, as amended, prohibits most federal contractors and subcontractors and federally assisted contractors and subcontractors from discriminating in employment decisions on the basis of race, color, sex, religion or national origin. . . .

The Fair Housing Act . . . prohibits discrimination based on race, color, religion, sex, national origin, handicap and familial status in activities relating to the sale, rental, financing and advertising of housing and in the provision of services and facilities in connection with housing. The Act applies both to public and private housing. . . .

Additionally, many federal agencies administer programs designed to enhance opportunities for women, minorities, and other groups. For example, the U.S. Department of Education administers grant programs designed to encourage and assist the participation of minorities and women in elementary, secondary and higher education programs. These include bilingual education programs, magnet schools, desegregation assistance centers, women's educational equity programs, financial aid for students who are minorities or women, and grants to strengthen historically

African-American colleges and universities. The U.S. Department of Labor monitors and enforces compliance with the nondiscrimination provisions applicable to federal contractors and apprenticeship programs, including affirmative action programs for women and minorities, and promotes the placement of Native Americans with federal contractors. . . .

State Constitutions. Roughly 27 states currently have "equal protection clauses" in their constitutions. . . . As a practical matter, the Fourteenth Amendment provides a minimum below which no state can go in according equal protection. The states can extend but not contract what the federal Constitution demands.

Remedies. U.S. law provides extensive remedies and avenues for seeking compensation and redress for alleged discrimination and denial of constitutional and related statutory rights, including:

1.   A person claiming to have been denied a constitutional or, in some instances, a statutory right, may bring a civil action in federal court under 42 U.S.C. § 1983 . . ..

Only "state actions" or actions "under color of state law" are subject to Section 1983. These include actions by federal, state and local officials. Some officials, however, are subject to absolute or qualified immunity. Judges, for example, enjoy absolute immunity. Other officials enjoy qualified immunity, which is designed to protect the discretion of officials in the exercise of their official functions. Qualified immunity will not be afforded, however, if the officials violated clearly established statutory or constitutional rights of which a reasonable person would have known. While prosecutors enjoy absolute immunity from suit for their involvement in the judicial phase of the criminal process, they are afforded only qualified immunity for law enforcement functions.

The Fourteenth Amendment's Due Process and Equal Protection clauses, as well as other constitutional rights, are enforced under Section 1983 in hundreds of federal suits every year. The most common relief under Section 1983 is damages, subject only to rules about official immunity. Injunction relief is also available and widely used as relief under this provision.

All states have judicial procedures by which official action may be challenged. . . .

2.   Federal officials may be sued directly under provisions of the Constitution, subject only to doctrines of immunity.

3.   Conspiracies to deny civil rights, apart from being subject to criminal prosecution, may be attacked civilly under 42 U.S.C. § 1985. However, where the right is one enumerated in the Constitution as being secured only from "state action," there must be official actors in the conspiracy, or it cannot be reached under that statute.

4.   Section 2 of the Voting Rights Act of 1965 . . . may be enforced by a private suit to vindicate . . . intentional denials or limitations on the right to vote or to exercise an effective vote. . . .

5.   Where Congress has so provided, the federal government, through the Attorney General, may bring civil actions to enjoin acts or patterns of conduct that violate some constitutional rights. . . .

Publicity and Education. People in the United States are very aware of their rights. . . . [T]he text of the Covenant, as well as its legislative history in the United

States and numerous commentaries, are available to any interested person through libraries, Congressional and other publications and computer databases. Throughout the United States, students at all levels receive extensive instruction in fundamental civil and political rights. The federal government has sent copies of the Covenant to the Attorneys General of each state and constituent unit in the United States, with the request that they be further distributed to all relevant officials, and U.S. government officials have participated in a number of public presentations highlighting the significance of U.S. ratification. This report will be widely distributed by the U.S. Government, bar associations, and human rights organizations.

* * * * *

As stated in the U.S. report, the United States Constitution is the principal basis for all rights and liberties in the United States. In addition to the specific individual rights protected by the first ten amendments to the Constitution, the Thirteenth, Fourteenth, and Fifteenth Amendments, ratified shortly after the Civil War of 1861-1865, provide additional procedural and substantive safeguards against racial discrimination. Those three amendments were principally intended to secure equal rights for the African Americans who had been slaves, but have been interpreted by the courts to protect the rights of all persons in the United States. JEROME A. BARRON & C. THOMAS DIENES, CONSTITUTIONAL LAW, PRINCIPLES AND POLICY 996-97 (1981).

Section one of the Thirteenth Amendment prohibits slavery and involuntary servitude. It also gives Congress the power to enact laws to prevent all the "badges and incidents" of slavery and has been held to forbid abuses by individuals as well as government authorities. *The Civil Rights Cases*, 109 U.S. 3 (1883). Despite the promise of the new amendment, however, a number of southern states enacted Black Codes which restricted the newly freed slaves' ability to make and enforce contracts or to hold or convey property. In addition to legal discrimination, extra-legal discrimination by both private citizens and government officials was common. Though the slaves were technically free from slavery, this discrimination continued to relegate African Americans to second-class status. PAUL BREST & SANFORD LEVINSON, PROCESSES OF CONSTITUTIONAL DECISIONMAKING 408-09 (2d ed. 1983). Nonetheless, it was under the power granted by the Thirteenth Amendment that Congress began enacting the civil rights legislation discussed in the U.S. report.

Doubt concerning the adequacy of the Thirteenth Amendment to protect African Americans led to the ratification of the Fourteenth Amendment on July 9, 1868. The Equal Protection clause of the Fourteenth Amendment, as discussed in the U.S. report, prohibits the State from "deny[ing] to any person within its jurisdiction the equal protection of the laws." U.S. CONST. amend. XIV. The Equal Protection Clause is the constitutional foundation for most judge-made law against racial discrimination in the United States.

It is widely agreed that "the central purpose of the Fourteenth Amendment was to eliminate racial discrimination emanating from official sources in the States." *McLaughlin v. Florida*, 379 U.S. 184, 192 (1964). Courts usually invalidate laws which on their face purposefully discriminate against racial minorities—whether in voting, housing, employment or other fields. For example, the Supreme Court unanimously voided statutes that excluded blacks from jury duty in *Strauder v. West Virginia*, 100 U.S. 303 (1879), and reached the same result when blacks were excluded by law from residence on any block occupied by a white majority. *Buchanan v. Warley*, 245 U.S. 60 (1917).

Laws which are facially neutral but which are applied in a discriminatory manner are also usually invalidated. Thus, a law which allows for an element of subjectivity on the part of those implementing the law and which is applied discriminatorily will usually be struck down. In *Yick Wo v. Hopkins*, 118 U.S. 356, 374 (1886), for example, the Court invalidated a San Francisco ordinance which prohibited operating laundries in buildings constructed of a material other than brick or stone without a special permit, where all 240 Chinese applicants were denied the permit but where 79 of 80 non-Chinese applicants were granted the permit. The Supreme Court noted:

> Though the law itself be fair on its face and impartial in appearance, yet if it is applied and administered by public authority with an evil eye and an unequal hand, so as practically to make unjust and illegal discriminations between persons in similar circumstances, material to their rights, the denial of equal justice is still within the prohibition of the Constitution.

Id. at 373-74.

In contrast to facially neutral laws applied in a discriminatory manner, facially neutral laws which have a racially disproportionate effect are unconstitutional only on proof of intentional discrimination. In *Washington v. Davis*, 426 U.S. 229 (1976), and *Village of Arlington Heights v. Metropolitan Housing*, 429 U.S. 252 (1977), the Supreme Court held that it is not unconstitutional for government action to have racially differentiated effects, unless the action can be "ultimately traced to a racially discriminatory purpose." While discriminatory impact is evidence of a discriminatory purpose, other factors must be present for the discrimination to be found illegal. Courts have looked to the historical background of the allegedly racist action, the presence of procedural departures from the normal course of conduct, and the legislative history of the action. *Village of Arlington Heights*, 429 U.S. at 267-68. Intentional discrimination can be difficult to prove in many situations, resulting in calls for greater protections for minorities. Debra Evenson, *Competing Views of Human Rights: The U.S. Constitution from an International Perspective*, INT'L REV. CONTEMPORARY LAW 18 (1990).

Because of the difficulty inherent in proving intentional discrimination in constitutional Equal Protection litigation, much of the civil rights legislation adopts a more lenient standard of proof. For example, complaints of both employment discrimination and housing discrimination require the same burden of proof. The Supreme Court has held that minority plaintiffs must prove that they were qualified to secure the job (or home), that they were refused, and that subsequently the employer (or landlord) sought other applications from persons with qualifications similar to the qualifications of members of the rejected minority. When the plaintiff establishes such a prima facie case, "the burden then must shift to the employer [or landlord] to articulate some legitimate, nondiscriminatory reason for the employee's rejection." *McDonnell Douglas Corp. v. Green*, 411 U.S. 792, 802 (1973). The plaintiff next has an opportunity to show that the nondiscriminatory reason offered is a mere pretext. *Id.* at 804.

NOTES AND QUESTIONS

1. Is the Covenant well-known in the U.S.? In his statement before the Human Rights Committee, John Shattuck, Assistant Secretary of State for Democracy, Human Rights and Labor, reported that the U.S. has published the Covenant in the Federal Register in addition to sending copies to each state's Attorney General. It also reprinted the report to make hard copies available to the general public as well providing access to the report in electronic form

via the Internet. Hard copies of the report were distributed to non-governmental organizations, libraries, federal agencies and offices, state bar associations, and interested academics. In light of these measures and those indicated in the U.S. report, has the U.S. undertaken a program of dissemination? Are U.S. efforts in this regard adequate? What would be?

2.   Notice that the U.S. report focuses on U.S. law rather than on specific Covenant provisions. Is that focus correct for the initial report? In its examination of the report, one member of the Human Rights Committee noted that the report should have focused on the consonance of human rights in the U.S. with the Covenant rather than the consonance of domestic and constitutional law with the Covenant. Do you agree?

3.   Did the U.S. report properly address the states' role in U.S. protection of rights under the Covenant? Could the U.S. report have adequately covered laws and practices in all of the fifty states?

4.   The U.N.'s Special Rapporteur on Contemporary Forms of Racism, Racial Discrimination, Xenophobia and Related Intolerance issued a report, on January 16, 1995, that sharply criticized the United States:

> [T]here is no lack of legislation against racism and racial discrimination in the United States. . . . [T]he Special Rapporteur has drawn on numerous accounts and documents provided by reliable sources and has concluded that all too often the law is circumvented or violated by federal or State agents and individuals. In addition, economic and social conditions inherited from the past, which the law has not yet succeeded in totally eliminating, restrict its impact. As a result, de facto segregation may persist, for economic reasons, in housing and education . . . [and] in access to health care.

Report by Mr. Maurice Glélé Ahanhanzo, Special Rapporteur on Contemporary Forms of Racism, Racial Discrimination, Xenophobia and Related Intolerance On His Mission to the United States of America, at 29, U.N. Doc. E/CN.4/1995/78/Add.1 (1995). For additional analyses of discrimination and segregation in the U.S., see DOUGLAS MASSEY & NANCY DENTON, AMERICAN APARTHEID: SEGREGATION AND THE MAKING OF THE UNDERCLASS (1993); Daniel A. Farber, *Poverty and Discrimination: Notes on American Apartheid*, 11 CONST. COMMENT. 455 (1994-1995). For an analysis of competing theories of congressional representation of African Americans, see Daniel A. Farber, *Book Review: Black Races, Black Interests: The Representation of African Americans in Congress. By Carol M. Swain*, 11 CONST. COMMENT. 613 (1994-95).

5.   The Covenant does not sufficiently define the term "discrimination" to determine whether it prohibits only purposeful discrimination or also discrimination in effect. In a General Comment, the Human Rights Committee attempted to clarify the requirements of non-discrimination:

> . . . [T]he term "discrimination" as used in the Covenant should be understood to imply any distinction, exclusion, restriction or preference which is based on any [enumerated] ground . . ., and which has the purpose or effect of nullifying or impairing the recognition, enjoyment or exercise by all persons, on an equal footing, of all rights and freedoms.
>   The enjoyment of rights and freedoms on an equal footing, however, does not mean identical treatment in every instance. . . .
>   Reports of many States parties contain information regarding legislative as well as administrative measures and court decisions which relate to protection against discrimination in law, but they very often lack information which would reveal discrimination in fact. When reporting on articles 2(1), 3 and 26 of the Covenant, States parties usually cite provisions of their constitution or equal opportunity laws with respect to equality of persons. While such information is of course useful, the Committee wishes to know if there remain any problems of discrimination in fact,

which may be practised either by public authorities, by the community, or by private persons or bodies. The Committee wishes to be informed about legal provisions and administrative measures directed at diminishing or eliminating such discrimination. . . .

Finally, the Committee observes that not every differentiation of treatment will constitute discrimination, if the criteria for such differentiation are reasonable and objective[1] and if the aim is to achieve a purpose which is legitimate under the Covenant.

General Comment 18 Adopted by the Human Rights Committee, *reprinted in Compilation of General Comments and General Recommendations Adopted by Human Rights Treaty Bodies*, at 27-28, U.N. Doc. HRI/GEN/1/Rev.1 (1994). Does the General Comment shed any light on the appropriate interpretation? Recall that the U.S. added an understanding to the Covenant allowing it to make distinctions based on race when those distinctions "are, at minimum, rationally related to a legitimate governmental objective." Do you think the U.S. practice of upholding laws that have discriminatory effects would comport with the Covenant? With the Covenant as supplemented by the U.S. understanding?

Excerpted below is the first part of the U.S. report. In that part, the U.S. cited several statistics which might be helpful in analyzing the effectiveness of existing U.S. laws protecting rights enumerated in the Covenant. Following the excerpt from the U.S. report are excerpts from other articles discussing racial statistics in the criminal law area.

Core Document Forming Part of the Reports of States Parties: United States of America, at 1-5, U.N. Doc. HRI/CORE/1/Add.49 (1994) (several citations omitted):

I. LAND AND PEOPLE

A. Population. . .

The United States is home to a wide variety of ethnic and racial groups. . . . Overall, 80 percent of all people are white. Among the minority groups, 12 percent are African Americans, 9 percent are of Hispanic origin, 3 percent are of Asian or Pacific Island origin, and less than 1 percent are Native Americans. . . .

About three-quarters of all people in the United States live in urban areas, with "urban" defined as 2500 or more residents in an area incorporated as a city, village or town. While almost 30 percent of all whites reside in rural areas, minorities reside predominantly in urban areas (87.2 percent of all African Americans, 95 percent of all Asians, 91 percent of all Hispanics). . . .

B. Vital Statistics

According to 1989 figures, overall life expectancy in the United States was 75.3 years. . . . Whites have a longer life expectancy than minorities. For example, the life expectancy for whites is 76 years, but for African Americans it is only 69.2, and only 64.8 for African-American men. However, studies show these figures to be

---

[1] [Ed. note: The Committee also articulated the "reasonable and objective criteria" standard in *Cavalcarti Araujo-Jongen v. The Netherlands*, No. 418/1990, U.N. Doc. A/49/40 (1994).]

improving for all racial groups. Preliminary 1990 figures show the life expectancy for all of the United States to be 75.4, 76 for whites, and 70.3 for African Americans.

The total fertility rate for the United States, according to 1991 figures, was 2073 births per 1000 women aged 10-49. In other words, women in the U.S. on average have 2.1 births over the course of their child-bearing years. . . . Once again, there is significant disparity between racial groups: the white fertility rate is 1885, with the rate decreasing, but the African-American fertility rate is 2583, with the rate increasing. Overall, nearly 30 percent of all births in the United States are currently to unmarried women.

The overall mortality rate in 1992 was 853.3 per 100,000, slightly lower than the previous year. The infant mortality rate was 9.8 deaths per 1000 live births. However, there is a significant disparity between the rates for African Americans and whites. For example, the rate for whites was 8.2 per 1000, but the rate for African Americans was more than double that, at 17.7. Lack of adequate prenatal care, socio-economic conditions, drug and alcohol abuse, and lack of education are cited as factors contributing to the difference. A similar pattern exists for the maternal mortality rate: the overall rate was 7.9 maternal deaths per 1000 births, but the rate for whites was 5.6, compared to the 18.4 rate for African Americans.

. . . In recent years, owing to the increasing acceptance of divorce and single-parenthood, more children are living with only one parent. Among all children under age eighteen, 27 percent lived with a single parent in 1992, more than double the 12 percent of children who lived with only one parent in 1970. Most children who live with one parent live with their mother. For instance, in 1992 approximately 88 percent of children who lived with one parent lived with their mother. The proportion of children living with one parent varies according to race. Among children under eighteen, 21 percent of white children lived with one parent, whereas 57 percent of African-American children and 32 percent of Hispanic children lived with one parent. Children in every group were far more likely to live with their mother than their father. Among children living with their mother or father only, 84 percent of white children, 94 percent of African-American children, and 89 percent of Hispanic children lived with their mother. In total, approximately three percent of children under eighteen live with a relative other than their parents or with a nonrelative. While similar data is not available for Asians, in 1992 approximately 15 percent of Asian family households were headed by women. . . .

C.   Socio-Economic Indicators . . .

In 1992, 67 percent of the population 16 years and older . . . was in the workforce, including 16.8 million working mothers. The overall unemployment rate was 7.4 percent. . . . Whites' rate of unemployment was 6.5 percent, African-Americans' rate was 14.1 percent, and Hispanics' rate was 11.4 percent. The minimum wage in 1992 was $4.25 per hour. Women and minorities continue to be over-represented in low-paying jobs.

In 1992, 14.5 percent of the population was below the poverty level, the federally established figure below which a person is considered to have insufficient income for his or her basic needs. For a household of four in 1992, this was equal to $14,335. Of all households headed by females, 34.9 percent were below the poverty level. The poverty rates for white, African American, and Hispanic households headed by women were, respectively, 28.1 percent, 49.8 percent, and 48.8 percent. Among children, 21.9 percent lived below the poverty line, including one in four children under six years old.

The rate of poverty varies significantly among racial groups in the United States.

While 11.6 percent of whites (9.6 percent when Hispanics are not included) are below the poverty line, 33.3 percent of African Americans, 29.3 percent of Hispanics, and 12.5 percent of Asian/Pacific Islanders fall below the poverty level. Among the poor in 1992, 73.2 percent received some form of federal welfare assistance. Assistance may include cash as well as noncash benefits. In 1992, 42.7 percent of the poor received means-tested cash assistance. In 1989, the United States spent $956 billion on social welfare expenditures for an average of $3,783 per person in current 1989 dollars.[2]

According to the 1990 Census, 78.4 percent of the population had four years or more of high school education, 39.8 percent had one or more years of college, and 21.4 percent had four or more years of college. . . . Educational levels differed more widely, however, on the basis of race. Rates for high school and four or more years of college were 79.9 percent and 22.2 percent for whites versus 66.7 percent and 11.5 percent for African Americans, and 51.3 percent and 9.7 percent for Hispanics. . . .

NOTES AND QUESTIONS

The U.S. report indicates that "the United States spent $956 billion on social welfare expenditures for an average of $3,783 per person in current 1989 dollars." Do you find such statistics misleading? Reread the footnote detailing the components of that total. If you were a member of the Human Rights Committee, would you want more details on the wealth transfers?

for criticism

HUMAN RIGHTS WATCH & AMERICAN CIVIL LIBERTIES UNION, HUMAN RIGHTS VIOLATIONS IN THE UNITED STATES: A REPORT ON U.S. COMPLIANCE WITH THE INTERNATIONAL COVENANT ON CIVIL AND POLITICAL RIGHTS 11-23 (1993) (citations & several footnotes omitted):

Although formal protection from racial discrimination is quite high in the U.S., fulfillment of these legal rights and obligations has not been forthcoming. This is where implementation of the ICCPR would have its biggest impact, for, in addition to requiring that each State Party "give effect to the rights recognized in the . . . Covenant," Article 2 also mandates that each State Party provide an effective remedy for violation of Covenant rights, and that these remedies be enforced. . . .

Thus, while U.S. laws on race discrimination are at least equal to the ICCPR, the Covenant provides a crucial legal obligation to fulf[i]ll the requirements of the law and provide effective remedies to victims of discrimination. In order to enforce

---

[2] [Ed. note: The $956 billion total includes federal outlays of $563 billion and state outlays of $393 billion. Those federal and state outlays consist of the following amounts, rounded to the nearest billion:

Item	Federal	State
Social insurance	$ 387	$ 81
Public aid	80	48
Health & medical programs	24	33
Veterans programs	30	0
Education	19	220
Housing	15	3
Other social welfare	8	8

BUREAU OF THE CENSUS, U.S. DEP'T OF COMMERCE, STATISTICAL ABSTRACT OF THE UNITED STATES 1992, Table

this obligation in U.S. courts, legislation implementing the ICCPR must be passed.
. . .

Education

In its landmark decision, *Brown v. Board of Education*, the U.S. Supreme Court declared that "separate but equal" public schools were "inherently unequal" and therefore unconstitutional. "An [educational] opportunity is a right which must be made available to all on equal terms," said the court. Sadly, the promise in *Brown* of an equal educational opportunity to all children has since been rendered an empty one under U.S. constitutional law; almost forty years after *Brown*, minority and poor children in this country continue to suffer the inequalities attendant to segregated public school systems. . . .

Most African-American children remain in schools that are separate and decidedly unequal. Approximately two-thirds of all minority children in this country are enrolled in schools that are predominantly minority; more than 17 percent attend classes that are over 99 percent minority. The most telling examples of racial isolation exist in the largest urban areas of the nation. The 25 largest central city school districts in 1986 enrolled 27.5 percent of the nation's African-American students, but only 3.3 percent of the nation's white students. Due to their increasing isolation in largely segregated school systems, and the continued resistance both to full integration and to adequate funding of all school districts, many black and poor children continue to be deprived of training in even the most basic skills.

Children attending school in racially-isolated poorer districts routinely endure classes that are badly overcrowded. In these classes, both student and teacher are forced into an environment where keeping order in the classroom takes precedence over the interactive learning that takes place in wealthier school districts. Given such conditions, it is not surprising that minority children are twice as likely to drop out of school as white children. Moreover, disproportionate numbers of minority children continue to leave school functionally illiterate and unemployable.

Not surprisingly, black and Latino children, who comprise the majority of children living below the poverty line in this country,[3] fare far worse than their white counterparts at all levels of education. In 1989, both black and Latino 3- and 4-year-olds were less likely than white children to attend nursery classes. At the elementary level, black and Latino children are generally more likely to be below the appropriate grade for their age than white children. At the secondary level, the graduation rates for black students have improved, but are still lower than rates for white students; Latino students, however, still lag far behind.[4] Lastly, in higher

---

560, at 354. Social insurance includes workers' compensation, unemployment benefits, state temporary disability insurance, and public employment and railroad employee retirement, in addition to old-age, survivors, and disability benefits. Public aid includes items such as public assistance, Medicaid, social services, and food stamps. Health and medical programs include hospital and medical care for civilians and defense department personnel, maternal and child health programs, medical research, and construction of medical facilities. Education consists of spending on elementary, secondary, and higher education and facilities, as well as adult vocational education. Other social welfare includes amounts expended for child nutrition, child welfare, institutional care, and vocational rehabilitation. *Id.*, Table 561, at 355.

The total expenditures represented 53% of all government outlays for 1989, or 49.3% of federal outlays and 60.2% of state outlays. *Id.*, Table 562, at 356.]

[3] In 1990, 44 percent of black children and 38 percent of Latino children compared to only 15 percent of white children lived in families with income below the poverty line.

[4] In 1991, 56 percent of Latino persons 25- to 29-years-old had completed high school, compared to 81 percent of blacks and 90 percent of whites.

education the rate of college education among black and Latino high school graduates remains far lower than whites.[5] . . .

In 1973,the Supreme Court delivered an opinion in one of the most important equal educational opportunity decisions since *Brown*. In the case, *San Antonio School District v. Rodriguez*, the Supreme Court declared that the use of property taxes for financing public school education was not violative of the equal protection clause, even though such funding scheme resulted in grossly unequal per-pupil expenditures between school districts.[6] . . .

Housing

As we approach the 21st century, residential segregation is alive and well and prevalent across the United States. Indeed, there is little debate that, despite nearly 30 years of congressional, executive, and judicial activities aimed at eliminating racial segregation and discrimination in housing, racial minorities continue to face discrimination in their attempts to secure minimally adequate and affordable housing in racially and ethnically-integrated communities. According to one analysis of the 1990 Census data, the majority of the nation's 30 million African-Americans were as segregated in 1991 as they were at the height of the civil rights movement in the 1960s. In particular, the survey of 219 major metropolitan areas found that African-Americans were highly segregated in 31—or two-thirds—of the 47 metropolitan areas where they make up at least 20% of residents, including Detroit, Michigan, Chicago, Illinois, Miami, Florida, and Birmingham, Alabama.

One piece of federal legislation created to address the problem of residential segregation and discrimination is Title VIII of the Civil Rights Act of 1968, or the Fair Housing Act. Title VIII prohibits discrimination in the sale or rental of housing on a number of bases, including race, color, religion, national origin and sex. The statute bars both private and public discrimination; it also prohibits banks and other lending institutions from discriminating in issuing loans. In 1990, nearly a quarter of a century after the passage of the Act, Drew Days, then law professor at Yale Law School and presently Solicitor General of the United States, offered the following comments with regard to the Fair Housing Act:

> There is little doubt that the 1968 Act has made an important difference in the lives of the many who have benefitted from successful litigation to increase housing opportunities. It is also true that housing discrimination has proven far more intractable a national problem than the sponsors of the Fair Housing Act of 1968 anticipated. . . . Increased residential segregation has complicated efforts at school desegregation. Businesses have also followed the movement to the suburbs, leaving center city residents far from meaningful employment opportunities.
>
> To place major responsibility for this situation at the feet of the 1968 Act, however, would be unwarranted. Certainly no legislation can be expected to counteract entirely

---

[5] In 1991, 41 percent of black high school graduates 25- to 29-years-old had completed 1 or more years of college, compared to 55 percent of their white counterparts. The percentage of Latino high school graduates with at least some level of college education has stabilized at about 43 percent. Interestingly, Latino high school graduates who go on to college are more likely to enroll in a 2-year college than black and white graduates.

[6] For example, the Edgewood Independent School District, the poorest of the seven school district[s] in metropolitan San Antonio, has an assessed property value of $5,960 per student. By imposing a property tax of $1.05 per $100 of assessed property value—the highest rate in the metropolitan area—the district was able to raise only $26 per student in local funds. In contrast, the Alamo Heights Independent School district, the wealthiest school district in the area, had an assessed property value of $49,000 per student and with a tax rate of only 85 cents per $100 they were able to raise $333 per student.

the complex forces that contribute to the creation and maintenance of residential segregation in the United States. . . .

The most recent nationwide study of housing discrimination conducted by [the Department of Housing and Urban Development (HUD)] found that African-Americans encountered discrimination 59 percent of the time when trying to buy a house and 56 percent of the time when seeking rental housing. Latinos suffered discrimination 56 percent of the time when they tried to purchase housing and 50 percent of the time when they tried to rent.

HUD has responsibility for enforcing the Fair Housing Act and also is under a general mandate to combat housing discrimination through Secretary-initiated investigations and supervision of federally-sponsored and federally-funded programs. Yet HUD's own statistics reveal a huge gap between the known scope of discrimination and HUD's enforcement of claims. For example, while HUD's surveys show that African-Americans suffer discrimination over 50 percent of the time that they attempt to buy or rent a home, HUD found "cause" in less than one-half of one percent of all race discrimination cases filed in 1990. Additionally, in the cases that HUD settles, it fails to obtain substantial remedies—remedies important to compensate the victims and deter future discrimination. . . .

Discrimination in housing also takes the form of "redlining," a practice by which banks and other financial institutions discriminate against residents of minority neighborhoods by denying them mortgages or housing insurance. Recent studies show a large discrepancy between the mortgage application denial rates of whites and African-Americans, even when incomes are similar. In addition to private banks and financial institutions, which have been instrumental in the perpetuation of redlining, the U.S. government has itself been a major offender. . . .

Federally funded housing created for low-income persons is another area in which discriminatory practices are pervasive. When first developed, many housing projects were subject to explicit racially-segregated admission policies. In addition, poor African-Americans and other minorities receiving public housing or other federally assisted housing have been subjected to unit, project, and neighborhood conditions that are not only extremely segregated, but also vastly inferior to the unit, project and neighborhood conditions of white public housing recipients.

* * * * *

Kevin Reed et al., *Race, Criminal Justice and the Death Penalty*, 15 WHITTIER L. REV. 395, 395-99 (1994) (footnotes omitted):

. . . [T]he statistics on crime are very telling. In the thirteen years since 1980, although the incarceration rate ha[s] doubled, the crime rate in the United States has remained the same. In fact, violent crime has increased over the last five years. Also within that time, the number of people subject to imprisonment and the death penalty has dramatically increased. The nation's prison population has more than doubled since the 1980s: in 1991 there were 800,000 people in prison. . . . According to the National Council on Crime and Delinquency, if the current trend continues there will be over 1.1 million Americans in prison alone in 1994. This is more than three and a half times the number in 1980.

As a result of the policies of the last thirteen years, the United States has the world's highest known rate of incarceration. The length of prison terms has also increased as has the number of individuals on death row. Since 1980, the number of persons on death row has more than tripled, increasing from 718 in 1980 to approximately 2600 [in 1993]. Yet, as mentioned before, the crime rates have not changed. . . .

This increase has had a greater impact on communities of color than on the white communities in this country. Incarceration rates have been vastly disproportionate. As of 1988, African Americans were incarcerated at the rate of 965 per 100,000 compared to 155 per 100,000 for whites.[7] These statistics show that African Americans were incarcerated at a rate six and a quarter times greater than white Americans. The rate of incarceration for African-American men in the United States was more than four times greater than the rate of incarceration for black men in South Africa.

Additionally, this disproportionate rate of incarceration of African Americans holds true throughout the age spectrum. African-American juveniles are incarcerated at a rate five times greater than white juveniles, and this disproportion has increased dramatically within the last twelve years. In the juvenile justice system, between 1984 and 1988, the percentage of white youths incarcerated in detention centers dropped 2% while that of non-white juveniles rose by 269%. Because of the increasingly disproportionate rates of incarceration, nearly 50% of the nation's entire prison and jail population is now African American and Latino.

Some recent studies have focused on the criminal justice system and its impact on urban areas. The Sentencing Project found that in 1989 nearly one in four African-American men between the ages of twenty and twenty-nine were in jail, prison, or on probation or parole on any given day in the United States. If you compare that to the number of African-American men in college, you see that 609,690 African American men were in jail in 1990 while only 436,000 were in college. By comparison, just over one million young white men were in the criminal justice system while 4.6 million were in college.

Other studies that focused on urban areas show that among African-American men in some urban areas, more than eight out of ten will have some sort of adverse contact with the criminal justice system in their lifetime. Nearly all African-American men enter the criminal justice system in some form. . . . [A] study [published] in 1992 . . . showed that on any given day in Baltimore in 1991, 56% of the African-American men between the ages of eighteen and thirty-five years of age were in jail, in prison, or on parole or probation.

These statistics also hold true for the death penalty. The General Accounting Office did a study in 1990 that reviewed all the post-*Furman*[8] studies of race and found a pattern of evidence indicating racial disparities in the charging and imposition of death penalties. . . .

Much of this trend has been caused by the increase in rhetoric and resources put on the war on drugs. In fact, statistics show that the war on drugs has a devastating effect on young African-American men. In 1984, twice as many whites as African Americans were arrested for drug offenses in this country: 10,250 to 5,000. By 1989, however, the yearly number of arrests of African Americans has

---

[7] [Ed. note: At the end of 1993, there were 1,432 African-American inmates per 100,000 African-American U.S. residents, and 203 white inmates per 100,000 white residents.

Briefing Paper: Prison Conditions, Human Rights Violations in the United States: U.S. Compliance with the International Covenant on Civil and Political Rights (1994).]

[8] [Ed. note: *Furman v. Georgia*, 408 U.S. 238 (1972) (invalidating all existing death penalty statutes, specifically Georgia's, which the Court held to be arbitrary and in violation of the Eighth Amendment's prohibition against cruel and unusual punishment).]

increased by 183%, reaching a total of 14,000, while drug arrests for whites increased by only 36%. In some cities, the statistics are even more striking. For example, in 1991, the percentage of African Americans among all individuals arrested for drug offenses in Columbus, Ohio was 90%[9] and in New York City 92% were either African American or Latino.[10]

Some have argued that these statistics must reflect a higher prevalence of drug use within the African American or Latino communities, but this is not reflected in the available data. The National Institute on Drug Abuse has done a survey and reported that 77% of this nation's drug users are white, 15% are African American, and 8% are Latino. These numbers indicate that drug use is roughly proportionate along racial lines. Therefore, it is apparent that the criminal justice system itself produces racially disparate results.

[Focusing] on two factors that contribute to this problem[:] One is the activities of law enforcement officers in this country, and the second is the exercise of prosecutorial discretion and its increase in the last thirteen years.

The police have had an enormous impact on the criminalization of young men of color in Los Angeles and throughout the nation. It has been reported in the city that the Los Angeles County Sheriff's Department and the Los Angeles Police Department keep a database of all persons known to be members of criminal street gangs. But, if you depose the sheriff, his captains, or any deputy and ask what it means to be a member of the street gang, you will find that they do a[n] unsatisfactory job of defining who is a member and who is not. They focus on factors such as dress, modes of walk, and association. What you find is that in the databases of these law enforcement agencies, an enormous proportion of young African-American and Latino men—over 50%—between the ages of fourteen and twenty are listed as street-gang members. This over-inclusion provides enormous incentive for law enforcement contact, law enforcement involvement, and the sweeping into the criminal justice system of young men of color. The war on gangs in the city has certainly contributed to the criminalization of the city's youth.

The second element mentioned is prosecutorial discretion. It has recently been established in a federal court proceeding in data that the United States Attorney's Office for the Second District of California was ordered to produce, that when local law enforcement conducts joint ventures with federal law enforcement agencies, discretionary decisions are made about whether people arrested for drug offenses will go to the state system or to the federal system for charging and prosecution.

---

[9] [Ed. note: According to the 1990 census, the population of the city of Columbus was 632,910. Of the total, 467,352 identified themselves as white, non-Hispanic (73.8%) and 141,919 as African-American (22.4%). BUREAU OF THE CENSUS, U.S. DEPT OF COMMERCE, 1990 CENSUS OF POPULATION: GENERAL POPULATION CHARACTERISTICS OHIO, Table 6, at 44 (June 1992). Looking at the entire Columbus metropolitan area population of 1,377,419, the concentration of racial minorities is even smaller. White, non-Hispanic persons comprised 85.5% of the metropolitan population, while African-Americans made up 12%. BUREAU OF THE CENSUS, U.S. DEPT OF COMMERCE, 1990 CENSUS OF POPULATION: GENERAL POPULATION CHARACTERISTICS UNITED STATES, Table 266, at 466 (Nov. 1992).]

[10] [Ed. note: According to the 1990 census, the population of New York City was 7,322,564. Of the total, 3,163,125 identified themselves as white, non-Hispanics (43.2%), 1,847,049 as African-American (25.2%), and 1,783,511 as Hispanics (24.4%). BUREAU OF THE CENSUS, U.S. DEPT OF COMMERCE, 1990 CENSUS OF POPULATION: GENERAL POPULATION CHARACTERISTICS NEW YORK, Table 6, at 152 (May 1992). Looking at the entire New York metropolitan area population of 18,087,251, the concentration of racial minorities is even smaller. White, non-Hispanic persons comprised 63.2% of the metropolitan population, African-Americans 18.2%, and Hispanics 15.4%. BUREAU OF THE CENSUS, U.S. DEPT OF COMMERCE, 1990 CENSUS OF POPULATION: GENERAL POPULATION CHARACTERISTICS UNITED STATES, Table 266, at 468 (Nov. 1992).]

The difference is very significant because under the federal system, mandatory minimum sentencing and the inflexible system of federal sentencing guidelines guarantee much stiffer penalties for individuals. In the area covered by the Central District of California, 100% of all African Americans who are arrested for crack cocaine offenses by the joint ventures were put into the federal system and not into the state system.

* * * * *

Stan R. Gregory, Note, *Capital Punishment and Equal Protection: Constitutional Problems, Race and the Death Penalty*, 5 St. Thomas L. Rev. 257, 257-59 (1992) (footnotes omitted):

The death penalty has long been imposed upon blacks at proportionately higher rates than whites. The year with the most executions in the United States was 1935, in which 199 persons were executed: 77 blacks, 119 whites and 3 of other races. Between 1930 and 1989, 2115 of the 3979 persons executed by legal means were black.

Many studies have shown an anti-black animus in the imposition of the death penalty in America. Between 1864 and 1967, blacks sentenced to death were more likely than whites to die without receiving an appeal. Furthermore, several studies prior to 1967 showed that whites on death row were more likely to receive commuted sentences than blacks. Between 1924 and 1961, in Florida alone, 40 blacks were convicted for raping whites, 2 whites were convicted for raping whites, but no whites were convicted for raping blacks. While the victims are the same race as their assailants in 95% of all murders, states which exercise the death penalty seek redress primarily for white victims, especially where the assailant is black.

Finally, one study conducted in the earlier part of this century suggests that black defendants had a much higher probability of being executed than white defendants. Notwithstanding the implementation of procedural safeguards in the past two decades to eliminate discrimination in death penalty sentencing, it vehemently continues to exist today.

In addition to exhibiting discrimination against black death row inmates, statistics confirm the reality that blacks on death row are not equally protected under the Fourteenth Amendment. While the Fourteenth Amendment guarantees all persons "the equal protection of the laws," the Supreme Court refuses to allow the use of statistical evidence to prove violations of the Equal Protection Clause.

NOTES AND QUESTIONS

1.   Based on the criminal justice and death penalty statistics discussed in the preceding excerpts, do you think African Americans are equally protected under the Fourteenth Amendment? Does the Civil and Political Rights Covenant offer more protection? As noted below, the Human Rights Committee expressed its concern about the racial disparity in the U.S. criminal justice system? What changes might you hope to see reflected in the second U.S. report?

2.   Most governments give themselves an A+ in their reports. Did the U.S. follow this self-congratulatory approach? If not, what grade did the U.S. give itself? Why didn't the U.S. give itself an A+? How does the U.S.'s self-grading compare with the opinions expressed in the Committee comment excerpted below?

---

2. The Examination

The Human Rights Committee met in New York on March 29 and 31, 1995, to consider the initial U.S. report under the Covenant. The first day of the examination began with statements by five senior U.S. officials. John Shattuck, Assistant Secretary of State for Democracy, Human Rights and Labor, emphasized the historic significance of the occasion, the first U.S. presentation to a United Nations treaty body. He spoke of the U.S.'s longstanding commitment, reflected in the Constitution, to the protection of human rights, but also acknowledged the ongoing work to address such problems as crime, drugs, poverty, discrimination, and violence against women. Conrad Harper, Legal Adviser of the U.S. Department of State, spoke next, reviewing the reservations, understandings, and declarations on which the U.S. conditioned its ratification of the Covenant. Deval Patrick, Assistant Attorney General for the Civil Rights Division of the Department of Justice, addressed the Committee regarding the Civil Rights Division's prominent role as promoter and enforcer of federal civil rights laws. JoAnn Harris, Assistant Attorney General in charge of the Criminal Division of the Department of Justice, addressed violent crime in the U.S., and discussed the Criminal Divison's efforts to develop policy and law-enforcement strategies to protect citizens. Ada Elizabeth Deer, Assistant Secretary of the Interior for Indian Affairs, concluded the U.S. delegation's remarks with a brief history of U.S. Indian policy. She explained the destructive impact of termination policies in the 1950s and 1960s, the crucial return to self-determination policies in the 1970s, and the 1994 enactment of the Tribal Self-Governance Act, which ushered in the latest era in federal Indian policy. *See* INTRODUCTION OF REPORT OF UNITED STATES, U.N. Press Release HR/CT/1/400 (1995); United States Mission to the United Nations, Press Releases, *Statements of John Shattuck, Conrad K. Harper, and Ada Elizabeth Deer Before the United Nations Human Rights Committee at its Fifty-third Session*, USUN 48-(95)-50-(95) (1995).

After the prepared opening remarks, the expert from Australia began the questioning. Committee members praised the comprehensiveness and usefulness of the U.S. report and the U.S. role in protecting human rights throughout the world. The Committee's questioning covered a variety of subjects, but focused primarily on U.S. reservations, declarations, and understandings. The Committee was extremely concerned because the reservations seemed to indicate that the U.S. did not intend to modify its laws to comply with the Covenant. For example, when asked about the U.S. declaration that the Covenant is not self-executing, a U.S. representative stated that U.S. law already satisfied the Covenant. Treaty reservations are discussed more fully in chapter 2.

Many Committee members expressed concern about the U.S. reservation of the right to execute juvenile offenders age 16 or 17 at the time of the commission of the crime. The Covenant forbids the death penalty for juvenile offenders under the age of 18. In addition, the Committee noted that 27 U.S. states oppose applying the death penalty to criminals under age 17. U.S. representatives argued that the majority of U.S. citizens favor the death penalty, including for some juvenile offenders. *See* chapter 13, *infra*, for further discussion of the pre-Covenant U.S. position on the execution of juveniles.

The Committee also expressed concern about the prolonged detention of excludable aliens, including Haitians detained at Guantanamo Bay, and about the conditions of imprisonment for all U.S. prisoners. The Supreme Court's position on the detention of alien children pending deportation is discussed in chapter 13, *infra*.

Several inquiries focused on self-determination. Committee members questioned how often residents of Puerto Rico, Guam, and the Virgin Islands were given an opportunity to approve their constitutional relationship with the United States, and asked why native Hawaiians were not a federally recognized Indian tribe or group as Alaskan natives were. Members also questioned U.S. representatives about the status and sovereignty of Native American tribes.

A few Committee members touched on the racial discrimination, discussed *supra* Part 1, beginning at 18. They focused on the disproportionate impact of the criminal justice system on racial minorities and English-only rules governing the workplace and schools. They also questioned the reduced emphasis on affirmative action programs. One member emphasized that the Covenant promoted substantive equality, not merely formal equality, such that unequal treatment of unequally situated persons is required.

Several members questioned the implementation of the Covenant at the state level. They noted the dearth of discussion in the U.S. report about state policies and practices and questioned how the federal government planned to ensure that state laws were brought into conformity with the Covenant. U.S. representatives responded that they had told states of ratification of the treaty and asked them to tell the federal government of any deficiencies in their laws. No states had reported any deficiencies.

On April 6, 1995, the Committee adopted official comments in response to the U.S. initial report.

Consideration of Reports Submitted by States Parties Under Article 40 of the Covenant: Comments of the Human Rights Committee, U.N. Doc. CCPR/C/79/Add.50 (1995).

Following are excerpts that reflect the Committee's primary critiques:

A. Introduction

2.   The Committee expresses its appreciation at the high quality of the report submitted by the State party, which was detailed, informative, and drafted in accordance with the guidelines. The Committee regrets, however, that, while containing comprehensive information on the laws and regulations giving effect to the rights provided in the Covenant at the federal level, the report contained few references to the implementation of Covenant rights at the state level. . . .

4.   The Committee notes with appreciation that the Government gave publicity to its report, thus enabling non-governmental organizations to become aware of its contents and to make known their particular concerns. . . .

B. Factors and Difficulties Affecting the Implementation of the Covenant

5.   The Committee notes that, despite the existence of laws outlawing discrimination, there persist within society discriminatory attitudes and prejudices based on race or gender. Furthermore, the effects of past discrimination in society have not yet been fully eradicated. This makes it difficult to ensure the full enjoyment of the rights provided for under the Covenant to everyone within the State party's jurisdiction. The rise in crime and violence also affects the enjoyment of the rights provided in the Covenant.

6.   The Committee also notes that under the federal system prevailing in the

United States, the States of the Union retain extensive jurisdiction over the application of criminal and family law in particular. This factor, coupled with the absence of formal mechanisms between the federal and state levels to ensure appropriate implementation of the Covenant rights by legislative or other measures may lead to a somewhat unsatisfactory application of the Covenant throughout the country.

C. Positive Aspects

7. The Committee recognizes the existence at the federal level of effective protection of human rights available to individuals under the Bill of Rights and Federal laws. . . .

8. The Committee notes with satisfaction that the United States has recently ratified or acceded to some international human rights instruments,. . . . These ratifications reflect a welcome trend towards acceptance of international scrutiny, supervision and control of the application of universal human rights norms at the domestic level. . . .

12. The Committee further notes with satisfaction the assurances of the Government that its declaration regarding the federal system is not a reservation and is not intended to affect the international obligations of the United States.

D. Principal Subjects of Concern . . .

14. The Committee regrets the extent of the State party's reservations, declarations and understandings to the Covenant. It believes that, taken together, they intended to ensure that the United States has accepted what is already the law of the United States. . . .

16. The Committee is concerned about the excessive number of offenses punishable by the death penalty in a number of States, the number of death sentences handed down by courts, and the long stay on death row, which in some instances, may amount to a breach of article 7 of the Covenant. It deplores the recent expansion of the death penalty under federal law and the reestablishment of the death penalty in certain States. It also deplores provisions in the legislation of a number of States which allow the death penalty to be pronounced for crimes committed by persons under 18. . . .

17. The Committee is concerned at the reportedly large number of persons killed, wounded or subjected to ill-treatment by members of the police force in the purported discharge of their duties. It also regrets the easy availability of firearms to the public. . . .

18. The Committee is concerned that excludable aliens are dealt with by lower standards of due process than other aliens. . . . The situation of a number of asylum-seekers and refugees is also a matter of concern to the Committee. . . .

20. The Committee is concerned about conditions of detention of persons deprived of liberty in federal and state prisons. . . . The Committee is particularly concerned at the conditions of detention in certain maximum security prisons which are incompatible with article 10 of the Covenant. . . .

22. The Committee is concerned at the serious infringement of private life in some states which classify as a criminal offence sexual relations between adult

consenting partners of the same sex carried out in private, and the consequences thereof for their enjoyment of other human rights without discrimination.

23.   The Committee is concerned about the impact which the current system of election of judges may, in a few states, have on the implementation of the rights provided under article 14 of the Covenant. . . .

25.   The Committee is concerned that aboriginal rights of Native Americans may, in law, be extinguished by Congress. . . .

26.   The Committee notes with concern that . . . disproportionate numbers of Native Americans, African Americans, Hispanics and single parent families headed by women live below the poverty line. . . . It is concerned that poverty and lack of access to education adversely affect persons belonging to these groups in their ability to enjoy rights under the Covenant on the basis of equality.

E. Suggestions and Recommendations

27.   The Committee recommends that the State party review its reservations, declarations and understandings with a view to withdrawing them. . . .

30.   The Committee emphasizes the need for the government to increase its efforts to prevent and eliminate persisting discriminatory attitudes and prejudices against persons belonging to minority groups and women including, where appropriate, through the adoption of affirmative action. State legislation which is not yet in full compliance with the non-discrimination articles of the Covenant should be brought systematically into line with them as soon as possible.

31.   The Committee urges the State party to revise the federal and State legislation with a view to restricting the number of offenses carrying the death penalty strictly to the most serious crimes. . . .

32.   The Committee urges the State party to take all necessary measures to prevent any excessive use of force by the police. . . . Regulations limiting the sale of firearms to the public should be extended and strengthened.

33.   The Committee recommends that appropriate measures be adopted as soon as possible to ensure to excludable aliens the same guarantees of due process as are available to other aliens. . . .

34.   The Committee expresses the hope that measures be adopted to bring conditions of detention of persons deprived of liberty in federal [or] state prisons in full conformity with article 10 of the Covenant. . . .

36.   The Committee recommends that the current system in a few states in the appointment of judges through elections be reconsidered with a view to its replacement by a system of appointment on merit by an independent body.

37.   The Committee recommends that steps be taken to ensure that previously recognized aboriginal Native American rights cannot be extinguished. . . .

38.   The Committee expresses the hope that, when determining whether currently permitted affirmative action programmes for minorities and women should be withdrawn, the obligation to provide Covenant's rights in fact as well as in law be borne in mind.

39.   The Committee recommends that measures be taken to ensure greater public awareness of the provisions of the Covenant and that the legal profession as well as judicial and administrative authorities at federal and State levels be made familiar with these provisions in order to ensure their effective application.

NOTES AND QUESTIONS

1.   The Human Rights Committee was not the only group to critique the U.S. report. Various U.S. NGOs collaborated to produce and submit an analysis of the report to the Committee, in order to aid the Committee's assessment of U.S. efforts to comply with the Covenant. THE STATUS OF HUMAN RIGHTS IN THE UNITED STATES: AN ANALYSIS OF THE INITIAL U.S. GOVERNMENT REPORT TO THE HUMAN RIGHTS COMMITTEE OF THE UNITED NATIONS UNDER THE INTERNATIONAL COVENANT ON CIVIL AND POLITICAL RIGHTS (Morton Sklar ed., March 2, 1995). The NGOs' major findings included:

A.   Refugee and Asylum Rights: "Asylum proceedings are often not conducted 'in accordance with the law,' under the meaning of the Covenant." *Id.* at iii.

B.   Criminal Justice Issues: "Contrary to the objectives of the Covenant, the death penalty continues to be applied on a widespread basis." *Id.*

C.   Native American Rights: "Although increased recognition of Native American rights has taken place in recent years in some jurisdictions and with respect to some aspects of Native American life, abusive, discriminatory treatment . . . remains a serious problem." *Id.* at iv.

D.   Discrimination Based on Sex: "Today, despite significant gains and legal advancements such as the right to vote, own property, enter into contracts and gain custody of children in divorce, women still experience discrimination due to the failure of existing laws to address or resolve persisting gender inequities." *Id.*

E.   Discrimination Based on Race and Ethnicity: "[E]specially since more conservative political policies were adopted in the 1980's calling for a less intrusive federal government, significant vestiges of racism and discriminatory treatment remain." *Id.* at v.

2.   For additional NGO reviews of the initial U.S. report, see Amnesty International, *United States of America—Human Rights Violations: A Summary of Amnesty International's Concerns,* AI Index: AMR 51/25/95 (1995); HUMAN RIGHTS WATCH CHILDREN'S RIGHTS PROJECT, UNITED STATES: A WORLD LEADER IN EXECUTING JUVENILES, VOL. 7, No. 2 (1995); INT'L LABOR RIGHTS EDUCATION AND RESEARCH FUND, BRIEFING PAPER, U.S. COMPLIANCE WITH LABOR RIGHTS PROVISIONS OF ARTICLE 22 OF THE ICCPR (1994); NOW LEGAL DEFENSE AND EDUCATION FUND, FACT SHEET: SEX DISCRIMINATION UNDER THE INTERNATIONAL COVENANT ON CIVIL AND POLITICAL RIGHTS (1994). What, if any, contribution did the NGOs make to the preparation of the initial U.S. report? What role should they play in the preparation of the next report? To what extent did the Human Rights Committee's questions and comments to the U.S. reflect the NGOs' concerns? How much influence should the NGOs have in shaping the Committee's examination process?

3.   Readers are encouraged to review the extensive discussion in chapter 2 of U.S. reservations to the Civil and Political Covenant, and the Human Rights Committee's response.

CHAPTER 4

STATE REPORTING UNDER INTERNATIONAL HUMAN RIGHTS TREATIES (IRAN); CULTURAL RELATIVISM

A. INTRODUCTION   Page   128

B. QUESTIONS   129

C. THE SITUATION IN IRAN   130

1. **Creation of the Islamic Republic of Iran**   130
    Amnesty International, Iran: Violations of Human Rights   131

2. **Human Rights Committee**   134
    Human Rights Committee, Consideration of Reports Submitted
       by States Parties Under Article 40 of the Covenant: Iran (1982)   135
    Report of the Human Rights Committee, Comments by the Iranian
       Representative during the Committee's examination of the re-
       port (1982)   136
    Report of the Human Rights Committee, General Comments on
       Article 7 of the Covenant   137
    Human Rights Committee, Consideration of Reports Submitted
       by States Parties Under Article 40 of the Covenant: Iran (1992)   138
    Human Rights Committee, Observations and Questions Pre-
       sented during the Committee's Examination of the second Ira-
       nian report   139
          1194th Meeting   139
          1196th Meeting   139
          1230th Meeting   140

3. **Country Rapporteur Process of the U.N. Commission on Hu-
    man Rights**   142
    Report by the Commission's Special Representative on the Human
       Rights Situation in Iran (1985)   143

4. **Iranian Violations of International Law**   146

D. **THE INTERNATIONAL LAW PROHIBITION OF TORTURE AND
    OTHER CRUEL, INHUMAN OR DEGRADING TREATMENT OR
    PUNISHMENT**   147
    Standard Minimum Rules for the Treatment of Prisoners   147
    Declaration on the Protection of All Persons from Being Subjected
       to Torture and Other Cruel, Inhuman or Degrading Treatment
       or Punishment   148

Convention Against Torture and Other Cruel, Inhuman or Degrading Treatment or Punishment   148

Body of Principles for the Treatment of Detainees   150

1. **Human Rights Committee Consideration of Communications Under the Optional Protocol**   150

    a. Committee Procedures   151

       Report of the Human Rights Committee re: Consideration of Communications Under the Optional Protocol   151

    b. Committee Jurisprudence   155

       Manfred Nowak, U.N. Covenant on Civil and Political Rights: CCPR Commentary   155

       Human Rights Committee Views on Communication No. 414/1990   157

2. **European System**   159

    Ireland v. United Kingdom, European Commission   159

    Ireland v. United Kingdom, European Court   161

    Tyrer Case, European Court   162

    Geneva Conventions of 1949, Common Article 3   165

    Restatement (Third) of the Foreign Relations Law of the United States   165

3. **U.N. Response to Amputations Under the Islamic Penal Code of Sudan**   166

E. **THEORETICAL FOUNDATIONS OF HUMAN RIGHTS: NATURAL LAW, POSITIVISM, AND ISLAMIC PRINCIPLES**   166

    Myres S. McDougal, Harold D. Lasswell, & Lung-Chu Chen, Human Rights and World Public Order: The Basic Policies of an International Law of Human Dignity   167

    S. Farooq A. Hassan, The Islamic Republic: Politics, Law and Economy   168

F. **CULTURAL RELATIVISM AND INTERNATIONAL HUMAN RIGHTS LAW**   171

A. INTRODUCTION

Preceding chapters have examined the need for international human rights law, the process for ratifying human rights treaties, and principal techniques for applying treaty norms through periodic reporting and review. Some commentators have questioned whether it is possible to create human rights norms that apply universally to all cultures. The debate between universality of rights, on the one hand, and cultural relativism, on the other, derives from conflicting views about the source of authority for human rights.

This chapter examines the juridical basis of international human rights law, using one particular right—to be free from torture or cruel, inhuman, or degrading treatment or punishment—as a focus of discussion. That right appears in many human rights instruments, but this chapter focuses principally on its presence in

Article 5 of the Universal Declaration of Human Rights and Article 7 of the Covenant on Civil and Political Rights.

Some teachers may choose to begin the course with this chapter as a means of introducing students to jurisprudential sources of international human rights law. The authors have instead placed it here based on their conviction that students cannot effectively study sources of rights law without first knowing about the law and procedures that *already exist*. Readers are urged to take note that learning about international human rights law does not occur on a *tabula rasa*.

The chapter begins with a description of several punishments prescribed by the Islamic Penal Code of Iran adopted after the Islamic revolution of 1979. The questions ask readers to consider whether those punishments violate international human rights law. In order to provide an institutional and procedural context for discussion, readers are asked to engage in a role-playing exercise in which they serve either as members of the Human Rights Committee or as representatives of Iran. A majority of Committee members will argue that the Iranian punishments violate Article 7 of the Covenant and will seek to persuade the Iranian government to comply with its obligations. The government's representatives will argue that the punishments, as part of Islamic law that Iranians view as the source of human rights in their culture, do not constitute torture or other cruel, inhuman or degrading treatment or punishment. This conflict requires that readers examine the origins of the rights prescribed in international instruments as well as current interpretations of those rights.

To aid analysis, the chapter provides examples of how the Human Rights Committee and other bodies have interpreted the prohibition against torture or other cruel, inhuman, or degrading treatment or punishment. Using those interpretations forces readers to confront the issue of whether international human rights norms are valid for people in all cultures or whether rights can only apply when interpreted within particular cultural contexts. Issues of cultural relativism and sources of international legal jurisprudence are discussed in chapter 14 as well as here; and teachers may want to discuss these issues here and/or upon reading that chapter. Readers also must discuss whether international human rights law is law that sovereign states must obey or simply sets forth norms that states may choose to follow or disregard as they wish.

B.   QUESTIONS

This chapter provides an opportunity for a role-playing exercise. Members of the group should be assigned roles as either members of the Human Rights Committee[1] or representatives of Iran. A wide range of countries should be represented in the membership of the committee, with at least one member espousing each of the theories of rights identified in question *five*. (The following questions are written from the point of view of the members of the Human Rights Committee. Students should also consider these issues from the perspective of the representatives of Iran.)

1.   As a member of the Human Rights Committee, what questions would you ask the Iranian representative?

---

[1] Note that the Human Rights Committee selects one member to serve as the principal questioner of the presenting government.

a.   How would you argue to the Iranian government that it should refrain from crucifying its citizens, amputating their fingers, or whipping them?

b.   How would you try to convince the government to comply with the Covenant on Civil and Political Rights?

[In preparing questions and responses, consider the following:]

2.   Would you want to cite Shari'a provisions that appear to be consistent with international norms?

3.   What are the precise norms Iran arguably has violated?

a.   Is there a specific norm against chopping off fingers?

b.   Might precision or lack thereof in the international norms affect your success in convincing Iran to comply?

4.   When did Iran ratify the Covenant on Civil and Political Rights? Is that date significant?

a.   Do you think the incumbent government wants to comply?

b.   Could they get out of it? (See Article 40 reproduced in *Selected International Human Rights Instruments*) Have they tried?

5.   Assume that these are the leading human rights theories: the natural law approach, the positivist view, the cultural relativist position, the critical-legal view, the Chinese view, and the feminist view. *See* chapter 14, *infra*, at 677-697. Which might be most helpful in convincing Iran?

6.   Is there anything distinctive about the source of authority upon which rights theories are based that will assist or hinder you in persuading Iran to comply with international norms?

a.   What generally is the source of rights in U.N. human rights instruments, and what influence might that source have on Iran?

b.   What in fact is the benefit of calling something a right?

c.   Is there no right without a remedy?

d.   What source of remedy does international human rights law provide?

7.   Why do governments obey or disobey laws? Why do individuals obey or disobey laws?

8.   Is it reasonable to anticipate universal compliance with international human rights law? Is there universal respect for ordinary legal norms, such as the prohibition of burglary?

9.   Should the international community expect countries with varying civil, political, economic, social, and cultural traditions to respect human rights standards in the same way? Is there room for diversity?

C.   THE SITUATION IN IRAN

1.   Creation of the Islamic Republic of Iran

In January 1979, the Shah of Iran was compelled to abdicate under pressure of violent resistance to his continued rule. In place of the Shah's westernized government the resistance instituted a republic founded on tenets of Islam. To implement the transformation the new government created a system of revolutionary courts, military police, and provisional laws. Readers should keep that history in mind when reading the material on Iran that follows. One of the major projects of the new government was to adopt an Islamic penal code, which forms the basis of discussion in this chapter. The following excerpt examines three parts of the Islamic Penal Code of Iran: *Ta'azirat*, *Hodoud*, and *Qesas*.

Amnesty International, *Iran: Violations of Human Rights: Documents Sent by Amnesty International to the Government of the Islamic Republic of Iran* 45-48, 56-60, AI Index: MDE 13/09/87 (1987) (footnotes omitted and the order of the text slightly changed for clarity):

The Universal Declaration of Human Rights (Article 5)[2], the International Covenant on Civil and Political Rights (Article 7)[3], and several other international human rights instruments forbid torture or cruel, inhuman, or degrading treatment or punishment.

Article 38 of the Constitution of the Islamic Republic of Iran is consistent with these international norms in specifying:

> "Any form of torture for the purpose of extracting confessions or gaining information is forbidden. It is not permissible to compel individuals to give testimony, make confessions, or swear oaths, and any testimony, confession, or oath obtained in this fashion is worthless and invalid. Punishments for the infringement of these principles will be determined by law."

There are a few provisions in the Islamic Penal Code of Iran which forbid torture: for example, article 58 of the *Ta'azirat* forbids physical ill-treatment in order to obtain a confession, thus rendering the infliction or ordering of such acts punishable offences. Similarly, Article 49 of the Law of *Hodoud* and *Qesas* states, "Retribution by a blunt and unsharp instrument causing torment to the criminal is not permitted."

The Islamic Penal Code of Iran, however, contains several provisions which impose punishments constituting torture or cruel, inhuman, or degrading treatment or punishment. The punishments include stoning, crucifixion, mutilation and flogging.

A. *Stoning*

Article 119 of the Law of *Hodoud* and *Qesas* makes clear that the purpose of the punishment of stoning is the intentional infliction of grievous pain leading to death.

Article 119 states with respect to the penalty for adultery:

> "In the punishment of stoning to death, the stones should not be too large so that the person dies on being hit by one or two of them; they should not be so small either that it could not be defined as stones."

---

2 [Ed. note: Article 5 states that "[n]o one shall be subjected to torture or to cruel, inhuman or degrading treatment or punishment."]

3 [Ed. note: Article 7 states that "[n]o one shall be subjected to torture or to cruel, inhuman or degrading treatment or punishment. In particular, no one shall be subjected without his free consent to medical or scientific experimentation."]

B. *Crucifixion*

Article 207 of the Law of *Hodoud* and *Qesas* also makes clear that the purpose of crucifixion is the intentional infliction of severe pain or suffering which may lead to death. Article 207 states:

> "The crucifixion of a *mohareb* [at enmity with God] and *mofsed fil arz* [corrupt on earth] shall be carried out by observing the following conditions:
>
> a)   The manner of tying does not cause his death;
> b)   He does not remain on the cross for more than three days; but if he dies during the period of three days, he may be brought down after his death;
> c)   If he remains alive after three days, he must not be killed."

C. *Mutilation*

The Law of *Hodoud* and *Qesas* contains provisions calling for amputation of limbs and mutilation of other parts of the body for such offences as being *mohareb* and *mofsed fil arz* under Article 208, theft under Article 218, and intentional mayhem or inflicting of injury to a limb under Articles 55-80. . . .

The Islamic Penal Code of Iran, in stipulating a number of offences that are punishable by amputation, also prescribes the manner in which this should be inflicted.

Article 218 (*Hodoud* and *Qesas*) states:

> "Punishment of *hadd* for theft for the first time is the dismembering of four fingers of the right hand of the thief from the fingers' extremity so that only the thumb and palm of the thief remain; for the second time the dismembering of the left foot of the thief from the lower part of the protrusion so that half his foot and part of the place of anointment remain; for the third time the thief is condemned to life imprisonment; for the fourth time, if he commits theft in the prison, he shall be condemned to death.

> "Note 1:   A number of thefts, so long as the *hadd* is not inflicted, shall be regarded as one theft.

> "Note 2:   Where the fingers of the thief's hand are dismembered and after the infliction of this punishment another theft committed by him prior to the infliction of the punishment is proved, his left foot shall be dismembered."

Amnesty International does not have a complete record of the number of amputations carried out. However, during 1985 and the first half of 1986, it recorded 11 cases (all of which were reported in Iranian newspapers) involving individuals convicted of repeated theft.

In an interview published by *Keyhan International* on 16 February 1986, Hojatoleslam Moqtadaie, spokesman of the Supreme Judicial Council, stated that there had been "numerous cases of severing of hands in Tehran and other provincial cities."

Amputations are believed at the moment to be inflicted by the Judicial Police. According to an interview reported in *Keyhan* on 21 November 1984, the head of the Judicial Police, Abbas Hashemi Ishaqpour, said:

> "The Judicial Police have already prepared a device which very speedily severs the hand of the thief. . . . To facilitate the enactment of Islamic law on severance of thieves' hands, help has been sought from relevant competent authorities, such as the Coroner's Office, the Ministry of Health, and the Medical Faculties of Tehran and Beheshti Universities."

The machine was reportedly installed in February 1985 in Qasr Prison and, Amnesty International believes, is still being used to amputate fingers. . . .

D. *Flogging*

The Law of *Hodoud* and *Qesas* contains a number of provisions imposing the punishment of flogging on those who commit such offences as adultery (Articles 100-104), taking alcohol (Articles 123-136), sodomy (Article 152), lesbianism (Articles 159, 164), pimping (Article 168), and *qazf* (malicious accusation) (Articles 176, 178, 187). Article 102, for example, provides, "Punishment for fornication by a man or woman who is not qualified as married is one hundred (100) lashes." Article 178 prescribes flogging for a "discerning" minor who maliciously accuses someone. Article 131 provides, "Punishment for drinking liquor is eighty (80) lashes, whether it is a man or woman." Article 132 provides, "A man is whipped while standing and his body naked except a cover on his privy parts but a woman is whipped while sitting and her dress tied to her body." (See the similar provisions in Article 115 for adultery.) While Article 187 slightly ameliorates the kind of flogging imposed for malicious accusation, that provision gives some indication of the intent to inflict severe pain and suffering by flogging: "Lashes are inflicted over the normal clothes and with average force, not with the force used in the punishment of fornication." . . .

The reports of flogging received by Amnesty International have not mentioned any medical examination either before or after the infliction of the prescribed number of lashes, and it has received reports of women who, having been flogged when pregnant, have subsequently had miscarriages. This is evidently a breach of Article 107 of the Islamic Penal Code of Iran (*Hodoud* and *Qesas*) which states:

> "If the infliction of whipping is likely to harm the foetus or suckling baby, the whipping of a pregnant or nursing woman should be delayed.". . .

Amnesty International has interviewed both a number of former prisoners who were themselves flogged as a judicial punishment and many others apparently flogged in order to extract information or confessions. . . . From these interviews the organization has concluded that flogging methods have been harsher than those prescribed by law. Although some victims have claimed that the lashes were delivered with minimal force, others have told Amnesty International that they were lashed very hard by several officers in turn, and that the pain was so intense that they lost consciousness. Indeed, Amnesty International knows of cases in which the physical results of such lashings lasted for many months; in some cases prolonged medical treatment has been necessary because of damage to internal organs. . . .

The *Ta'azirat* provisions of the Islamic Penal Code contain more than 50 articles prescribing lashing of up to 74 strokes. The provisions include Article 29 (forgery), . . . 40 (negligent failure of an officer to arrest an accused), . . . 72 (impersonating a government officer), . . . 82 (destruction of officially held documents), 87 (insulting high government officials), 88 (collusion to commit crimes against foreign or internal security), 89 (destruction of evidence or obstruction of justice), 97, 98 (refusal to return a child), 99 (abandonment of a child), 100 (tampering with a grave), 102 (failure of women to wear veils and other offences in public places), 103 (encouraging prostitution), 105 (failure to support wife), 106 (medical personnel revealing patients' secrets), . . . 115 (fraudulent bankruptcy), 116 (fraud), 117 (defrauding a minor), 118 (misuse of an official seal), 119 (failure to return property), 120-122 (other business fraud and deception including trade mark infringement), . . . 140, 141 and 143 (defamation), 145 (transactions involving alcohol), 146, 147 (establishment of and keeping a place for gambling or alcohol), 156 (driving without a licence), and

158 (tampering with a speedometer). There are a few other *Ta'azirat* provisions which carry the penalty of lashing: Article 86 (up to 30 lashes for vulgar insults) and Article 101 (up to 99 strokes for kissing by an unmarried couple).

*   *   *   *   *

The Islamic Penal Code of Iran embodies Muslim concepts of Islamic law. Islamic law is set forth in two primary sources—the Qur'an and the Sunnah. The Qur'an reflects a verbatim recitation of revelations made by God to the Prophet Muhammed, while the Sunnah reflects Muhammed's interpretation of God's word. According to those sources, Islamic law is comprised of three main categories of offenses: *Hadd*, *Qesas*, and *Ta'zir*.

In the Islamic Penal Code of Iran, *Hadd* crimes are set forth in the *Hodoud*. *Hadd* are offenses for which the Qur'an and the Sunnah designate specific punishments. The punishments are believed to be stipulated by God and, as such, may not be altered by Islamic judges (known as "jurists"). Islamic scholars differ on the precise nature of *Hadd* crimes, but the Islamic Penal Code of Iran includes the following in the *Hodoud*: theft, robbery, adultery, apostasy, consumption of alcohol, and rebellion against Islam.

Qesas offenses are also covered by the Qur'an and the Sunnah, and include homicide, manslaughter, battery, and mutilation. Islamic law dictates that such crimes may be punished by retribution. The decision to inflict such retribution, however, rests not with the state but with the victim or the victim's family. The victim or family may also demand alternative punishments, such as compensation (known as "blood money") or forgiveness.

Ta'zir offenses are those for which the Qur'an and the Sunnah do not mention specific penalties. Punishment of *Ta'zir* offenses, therefore, is left to the discretion of Islamic judges. In the Islamic Penal Code of Iran, the range of punishments for *Ta'zir* crimes is set forth in the *Ta'azirat*, which somewhat limits judicial discretion.

While Islamic law embodies Muslim teachings, the term "Islamic law" cannot be applied generically to the systems of all Muslim nations. The Muslim nations interpret tenets differently and have created six distinct schools of law within the Islamic world. Even *Hadd* and *Qesas* crimes can carry different penalties within the different schools, depending upon the interpretation given to relevant passages in the Qur'an and Sunnah. Therefore, readers should keep in mind that although the Iranian penal code is based on Islamic law, some provisions may be particular to Iran and are not immutable interpretations of Muslim concepts.

2.   Human Rights Committee

Chapters 1 and 2 introduced the Human Rights Committee and chapter 3 examines in detail the Covenant's only obligatory implementation mechanism—the submission of reports from States parties for examination—and the Committee's practice of issuing general comments on the reports. Before proceeding, students should read carefully the "Reporting Procedures" section of that chapter. In order to illustrate the process, this section includes excerpts from Iran's 1982 and 1992 reports, and the Committee's discussion of those reports.

The Committee's interpretations of its role in commenting on reports further illustrate the goal of cooperation and assistance. Article 40 instructs the Committee to transmit "its reports, and such general comments as it may consider appropriate, to the States Parties."

This chapter also contains the Committee's general comments on Article 7 of the Covenant—the article prohibiting torture and other cruel, inhuman, or degrading treatment or punishment—as an example of the Committee's comments on provisions of the Covenant and to provide aid in evaluating the actions of Iran at issue here.

*   *   *   *   *

Human Rights Committee, *Consideration of Reports Submitted by States Parties Under Article 40 of the Covenant: Initial Reports of States Parties Due in 1977. Addendum Iran* **at 2-5, U.N. Doc. CCPR/ C/1/Add.58 (1982):**

In implementation of article 40 of the International Covenant which reads: "The States Parties to this Covenant undertake to submit reports on the measures they have adopted which give effect to the rights recognized herein and on the progress made in the enjoyment of those rights. . .", and with a view to submitting a report on the law and regulations approved to guarantee the individual's rights and liberties, I have the honour to inform you as follows:. . .

The Islamic Revolution of Iran is based on the belief that so long as man is not liberated from ideological, cultural, political and economic enslavement and dependence, freedom and independence will not be possible and without freedom and independence respect for human rights will not have any correct and proper applicability. Accordingly, the intention of the Islamic Revolution is to liberate man from slavery and servitude to another "slave", and to bestow upon him human growth and grandeur ("In order to liberate man from servitude of man and direct him to servitude of God"). It is on the basis of this belief that the third principle of the Constitution of the Islamic Republic of Iran reads as follows:

Principle 3: The Government of the Islamic Republic of Iran is bound to take into consideration all its possibilities to achieve the objectives referred to under Principle 2 above for:

1. Creation of a favourable atmosphere for furtherance of moral virtues based on the faith and righteousness and struggle against all manifestations of corruption and ruin;. . .

6. Putting an end to any despotism, autocracy and oligarchy;

7. Ensuring political and social freedom within the domain of the law;. . .

[A]ll the laws which for long years governed the deprived people of this country, were enacted in such a way as to bring about the domination of a small group over the rest of the people while disregarding the equality, liberties and rights of human beings. Since the Revolution therefore, the Ministry of Justice of the Islamic Republic of Iran has set out to review and amend these laws or to rewrite or change them in a rational and reasonable manner so as to guarantee the individual's rights and liberties. . . .

[B]ills and laws have been approved and enacted to determine and ensure the rights and liberties of the people. The measures taken in this regard may be summarized as follows:. . .

Laws and regulations approved to ensure rights and liberties

1. *The Constitution of the Islamic Republic of Iran*

The Constitution of the Islamic Republic of Iran, every word, or better, every letter of which is the crystallization of the drops of the pure blood of the martyrs who have freely and consciously chosen martyrdom, is persuasive evidence of respect for and guarantee of human rights and liberties. . . .

2. *State General Inspection Act*

This Act, which, on the basis of Principle 174 of the Constitution of the Islamic Republic of Iran, was passed, in 14 articles and several notes, by the Islamic Consultative Assembly, enables the Judiciary to investigate, in its continuous and extraordinary inspections, any discord or offence committed by civil and military organs and all the Revolutionary Institutions, and to pursue the matter through legal channels until the attainment of the final results. . . .

3. *Administrative Court of Justice Act*

. . .Principle 173 of the Constitution of the Islamic Republic of Iran. . .provides:

> To investigate litigations, complaints and protests of the public against Government officials, units or regulations and to administer justice in such cases a tribunal known as the 'Administrative Court of Justice' shall be formed under the control of the Supreme Judicial Council. The jurisdiction and procedure for the functioning of this tribunal shall be established by law.

Enactment of a law in such a manner is unprecedented in the history of the Iranian Ministry of Justice. If ever such a law has been enacted under other titles it has never been put into practice. The approval of the Administrative Court of Justice Act permits and enables any individual of the nation to lodge a complaint with one of the benches of the Administrative Court of Justice against any injustice or oppression committed by Government employees or units, through regulations or decrees, against people and cause justice [to] be administered. . . .

It must be acknowledged that in a Revolutionary society in which all former criteria and rules are reversed, much time is needed to establish a new order. This is natural and ordinary in any revolution. For this very reason and in order to see us through this critical period, the Leader of the Revolution declared the year 1360 (1981) as the Year of the Law and, in his orders and edicts, instructed all to comply with laws and protect the rights of individuals.

*   *   *   *   *

Report of the Human Rights Committee, 37 U.N. GAOR Supp. (No. 40) at 66-74, U.N. Doc. A/37/40 (1982):

Iran

298. The Committee considered the report of Iran (CCPR/C/1/add.58) at its 364th, 365th, 366th and 368th meetings held on 15, 16 and 19 July 1982 (CCPR/C/SR.364, 365, 366 and 368).

299.   The report was introduced by the representative of the State party who explained the ideological foundation of the Islamic Revolution in Iran. . . .

300.   The representative stated that, although many of the articles of the Covenant corresponded to the teachings of Islam, in the case of differences between the two sets of laws, the tenets of Islam would prevail. . . .

324.   [The Iranian representative] stressed that the criteria for determining the validity of any law would be the values given by God and transmitted to earth, that since human traits were considered to be in harmony with revealed values, values derived from human civilization and from reason were held to be close to Islamic values, and that whenever divine law conflicted with man-made law, divine law would prevail. He explained that the Koran contained guidance on a comprehensive range of matters involving morals, historical analysis, a criminal code and precepts regarding the distribution of wealth, teachings on community growth and spiritual values, and when a nation recognized and accepted the principles of Islam, as the basis for its existence, Islamic precepts would be followed in resolving problems. However, in Shi'ite canon law the basic requirements governing the continuity of community life could be viewed in historical terms, and the divine laws could be interpreted and implemented accordingly. Unfortunately, the conspiracies that had occurred in Iran since the revolution had prevented the Government from having sufficient time to develop new laws along those lines. Nevertheless, an attempt was being made to establish, at an early date, the three separate powers of the judiciary, the executive and the legislative in conformity with Islamic law. After the legislative power had been established, the relative conformity of each law with Islamic precepts would be determined. In this connexion, he explained his Government's position on the incorporation of international instruments on human rights in Islamic law and stated that if the intention was that such instruments should complement and add to the Islamic laws with a view to harmonizing them in a single legal system, then his Government would have to respond negatively, since it considered that the Islamic laws were universal and Shi'ite canon law would take any new needs of society into account. If, however, it was intended that international instruments on human rights and Islamic laws should be taken together in an effort to achieve mutual understanding and to explore what they had in common, then such an endeavour would be accepted with pleasure. He pointed out that laws of non-religious inspiration were not necessarily contrary to the Moslem faith; however, any laws contrary to the tenets of Islam would not be acceptable.

* * * * *

Report of the Human Rights Committee, General Comments on Article 7 of the Covenant, 37 U.N. GAOR Supp. (No. 40) at 94-95, U.N. Doc. A/37/40 (1982):

[Ed. Note: The following selection consists of general comments on Article 7 of the International Covenant on Civil and Political Rights issued by the Human Rights Committee pursuant to Article 40 of the Covenant.]

1.   In examining the reports of States parties, members of the Committee have often asked for further information under article 7 which prohibits, in the first place, torture or cruel, inhuman or degrading treatment or punishment. The Committee recalls that even in situations of public emergency such as are envisaged by article 4 (1) this provision is non-derogable under article 4 (2). Its purpose is to protect the integrity and dignity of the individual. The Committee notes that it is not sufficient for the implementation of this article to prohibit such treatment or punishment or to make it a crime. Most States have penal provisions which are applicable to cases of torture or similar practices. Because such cases nevertheless occur, it follows from article 7, read together with article 2 of the Covenant, that States must

ensure an effective protection through some machinery of control. Complaints about ill-treatment must be investigated effectively by competent authorities. Those found guilty must be held responsible, and the alleged victims must themselves have effective remedies at their disposal, including the right to obtain compensation. Among the safeguards which may make control effective are provisions against detention incommunicado, granting, without prejudice to the investigation, persons such as doctors, lawyers and family members access to the detainees; provisions requiring that detainees should be held in places that are publicly recognized and that their names and places of detention should be entered in a central register available to persons concerned, such as relatives; provisions making confessions or other evidence obtained through torture or other treatment contrary to article 7 inadmissible in court; and measures of training and instruction of law enforcement officials not to apply such treatment.

2.   As appears from the terms of this article, the scope of protection required goes far beyond torture as normally understood. It may not be necessary to draw sharp distinctions between the various prohibited forms of treatment or punishment. These distinctions depend on the kind, purpose and severity of the particular treatment. In the view of the Committee the prohibition must extend to corporal punishment, including excessive chastisement as an educational or disciplinary measure. Even such a measure as solitary confinement may, according to the circumstances, and especially when the person is kept incommunicado, be contrary to this article. More-over, the article clearly protects not only persons arrested or imprisoned, but also pupils and patients in educational and medical institutions. Finally, it is also the duty of public authorities to ensure protection by the law against such treatment even when committed by persons acting outside or without any official authority. For all persons deprived of their liberty, the prohibition of treatment contrary to article 7 is supplemented by the positive requirement of article 10 (1) of the Covenant that they shall be treated with humanity and with respect for the inherent dignity of the human person.

Iran's second report was due in 1983, but the government did not submit it until May 12, 1992. Excerpts from that report are provided below.

Human Rights Committee, *Consideration of Reports Submitted by States Parties Under Article 40 of the Covenant: Second Periodic Reports of States Parties Due in 1983. Addendum Islamic Republic of Iran* at 1-2, 18-19, U.N. Doc. CCPR/C/28/Add.15 (1992):

2.   According to article 2 of the Constitution, the Islamic Republic is a system based on belief in: . . .

6.   The exalted dignity and value of man and his freedom coupled with responsibility before God in which equity, justice, political, economic, social, cultural independence and national solidarity are secured by recourse to:

(a)   Continuous *Ijtehad* (exegesis of divine law) of *Fughaha* (Islamic Jurist) possessing necessary qualifications;

(b)   Science and arts and the most advanced results of human experience . . . ;

(c)   Negation of all forms of oppression . . . ..

3.   According to article 4 of the Constitution: "All civil, penal, financial, economic, administrative, cultural, military, political and other laws and regulations must be based on Islamic criteria. This principle applies absolutely and generally to all articles of the Constitution, as well as to all other laws and regulations, and the *Fughaha* of the Guardian Council are to supervise this matter."

4.   Article 91 of the Constitution provides that "with a view to safeguard the Islamic ordinances and the Constitution, in order to examine the compatibility of the legislation passed by the Islamic Consultative Assembly with Islam, the Guardian Council will consist . . . of six *fughaha* . . . and six jurists . . .." . . .

6.   The provisions of the Covenant are incorporated in the Constitution as well as in other laws and put into force accordingly. . ..

. . . *Article 7*

77.   The laws of the Government of the Islamic Republic of Iran are based on negation of any form of mistreatment of all individuals. This overriding principle has been accorded due attention in the Constitution. In order to ensure effective respect for this principle, not only has the Constitution provided for the punishment of those who ignore the prohibitions and commit acts of mistreatment and torture, but provisions have also been made for the legal protection of the victims of torture. . . .

80.   Another measure taken by the legislature to prevent torture and mistreatment of individuals, is outlined in article 62 of the *Ta'azirat* (Reproof) Law. According to this article, "If any judicial or non-judicial employee or official, in discharging his duties or due to such actions, subjects someone to mistreatment or orders such an act without legal authorization, he will be sentenced to retribution or blood-money or 74 lashes, as the case may be." . . .

*   *   *   *   *

The Human Rights Committee examined Iran's second report in 1993. Excerpts of the observations and questions of Committee members are reproduced below.

Human Rights Committee, *Summary Record of the 1194th Meeting* at 2, U.N. Doc. CCPR/C/SR.1194 (1993):

4. With regard to the implementation of the Covenant in general, [Committee Member Prado Vallejo, of Ecuador] noted that, under article 4 of the Constitution, all civil, penal, financial, economic, administrative, cultural, military, political and other laws and regulations must be based on Islamic criteria. . . . While that in itself was a perfectly respectable option, the developments that had occurred in the world since the emergence of Islam made it permissible to ask whether the fact of ordering the whole life of a country on the basis of such ancient precepts could not give rise to certain problems. . . .

*   *   *   *   *

Human Rights Committee, *Summary Record of the 1196th Meeting* at 11-14, U.N. Doc. CCPR/C/SR.1196 (1993):

33. [Committee Member] *Mr. DIMITRIJEVIC* [of Yugoslavia] wished first of all to

clarify a certain point. In his view, the Iranian delegation was using a false assumption as a point of departure in stating that the Covenant could be interpreted according to the principle of cultural relativity. It was not the first time that representatives for a State party had stated in the Committee that the Covenant should be interpreted in the light of the culture of a specific country and that that culture should influence the application of the Covenant to the extent that the Committee was unable to understand the human rights situation in that country. He challenged that point of view since the Covenant was the result of a multicultural effort. . . . He recalled that the Iranian authorities had freely ratified the Covenant because they had considered it to be compatible with the basic cultural values of their country. . . . Generally speaking, and regardless of cultural heritages, it could be generally agreed that the Covenant constituted a zone of convergence for all cultures in an extremely important sphere. . . . On a whole series of rights the Covenant left a certain amount of leeway to the State party which could, to a varying extent, restrict those rights subject to certain conditions. Yet there were some fundamental principles from which no derogation was possible. . . .

37.   *Mr. PRADO VALLEJO* [of Ecuador] . . . reverted specifically to the matter of punishment which had been referred to at length by other members of the Committee. He quoted the head of the judiciary, who had allegedly stated in 1991 that punishments, and in particular lapidation [stoning], were an integral part of Islam. In his own opinion, no concept could justify the punishments that had been mentioned. . . .

39.   The practice of torture was contrary to article 7 of the Covenant. The Committee could never accept the idea that torture, amputations or flogging should be provided for by the law or recognized as normal practice. If a State's legislation, practice and customs were contrary to the Covenant, it should change them. . . .

47.   The Islamic Republic of Iran was not the only State party to the Covenant whose Constitution was based on Islamic law. There was considerable leeway in the interpretation of Islamic law by Islamic theologians and experts, and the Islamic Republic of Iran should be able, without difficulty, to bring its legislation and practice into line with the Covenant and thereby to comply with its international obligations. It should, for example, be possible to replace punishments such as amputation or lapidation by others which were in conformity not only with Islamic law but also the international Covenants. . . .

*   *   *   *   *

Human Rights Committee, *Summary Record of the 1230th Meeting* at 5-6, U.N. Doc. CCPR/C/SR.1230 (1993):

14.   [The Iranian representative, in response to questions regarding whether Iranian authorities would consider bringing their legislation into line with the Covenant, stated that] Iranian criminal law provided for certain forms of corporal punishment, including flogging and stoning. If a court decided that a person who had been found guilty should be flogged, the flogging was not considered to be torture, since that form of punishment existed under Islamic law. . . .

19.   Mr. Dimitrijevic had argued that the Covenant was an expression of fundamental humanitarian principles that were beyond interpretation according to any particular culture. That was also his Government's understanding of the Covenant, as

an embodiment of universal principles of justice and humaneness. It was on specific issues, however, that interpretations would differ from culture to culture—for example, in the definition of certain crimes or of the civil rights of individuals. Those who practised justice did so in a humanitarian way, but their interpretation of how the laws should be executed would differ.

20.   The Islamic Republic of Iran had, like the previous regime, accepted the Covenant. The Republic, however, had an inescapable obligation to the majority of its people, who had by their vote established that Iran must have a Government based on Islamic law. All legislation in the country must therefore be based on Islamic laws and ratified as such. . . . Regardless of the Committee's categorical interpretation of the provisions of the Covenant, his Government, when an Islamic decree was at odds with a provision of the Covenant, could not take sides without alienating its people and its elected parliament, who had voted for the decree. . . .

NOTES AND QUESTIONS

1.   In 1992, the Human Rights Committee adopted new general comments on Article 7 of the Covenant on Civil and Political Rights. The new general comments retain the language of the previous comments, while elaborating on concepts not directly pertinent to this chapter. The new comments focus particularly on States parties' reporting obligations. *See International Covenant on Civil and Political Rights: Note by the Secretary-General*, U.N. Doc. E/ 1992/58 (1992).

2.   Readers should note that Iran made no reservations when it ratified the Covenant on Civil and Political Rights. Regarding reservations, see chapter 3.

3.   While the reporting requirement is valuable in that it helps Governments bring their laws and practices into conformity with treaty obligations, the process is not without flaws. For example, reports are often too self-congratulatory. Further, governments frequently are late in submitting the reports.

4.   Compare Committee discussion of Iran's 1982 report with its responses to the 1992 report. How has the Committee's approach changed? Is the new approach appropriate? Effective?

5.   For further reading, see:

Sandra Coliver, *International Reporting Procedures*, *in* GUIDE TO INTERNATIONAL HUMAN RIGHTS PRACTICE 245 (Hurst Hannum ed., 2d ed. 1992);

Dana D. Fischer, Note, *Reporting Under the Covenant on Civil and Political Rights: The First Five Years of the Human Rights Committee*, 76 AM. J. INT'L L. 142 (1982);

Human Rights Committee, *General Comments*, U.N. Doc. CCPR/C/21/Rev.1 & Add.1 (1990);

Human Rights Committee, *Guidelines Regarding the Form and Content of Periodic Reports from States Parties*, U.N. Doc. CCPR/C/20/Rev.1 (1991);

Jose L. Gomez del Prado, *United Nations Conventions on Human Rights: The Practice of the Human Rights Committee and the Committee on the Elimination of Racial Discrimination in Dealing with Reporting Obligations of States Parties*, 7 HUM. RTS. Q. 492 (1985);

Farrakh Jhabvala, *The Practice of the Covenant's Human Rights Committee, 1976-82: Review of State Party Reports*, 6 HUM. RTS. Q. 81 (1984);

DOMINIC MCGOLDRICK, THE HUMAN RIGHTS COMMITTEE: ITS ROLE IN THE DEVELOPMENT OF THE INTERNATIONAL COVENANT ON CIVIL AND POLITICAL RIGHTS (1991);

UNITAR/CENTRE FOR HUMAN RIGHTS, MANUAL ON HUMAN RIGHTS REPORTING, HR/PUB/91/1 (1991) (Revised and republished in 1995 with a "Trainers' Guide").

3. Country Rapporteur Process of the U.N. Commission on Human Rights

Following this note is an excerpt from the preliminary report of the U.N. Commission on Human Rights' ("Commission") Special Representative on Iran. The Commission is a body comprised of 53 governmental representatives as contrasted with the 18 experts on the Human Rights Committee. The Commission has developed the process of appointing rapporteurs and representatives as part of its broader efforts to monitor the human rights situation in specific countries where serious problems have arisen. The Commission has appointed these country rapporteurs and representatives pursuant to ECOSOC resolution 1235 which grants it authority to "make a thorough study of situations which reveal a consistent pattern of violations of human rights." The Commission has established several approaches to implementing ECOSOC resolution 1235 that are examined in chapter 5 of this book. At this point, however, it is only important to note that the Special Representative to Iran acts under the Commission's authority, while the Human Rights Committee acts under authority granted by the Covenant on Civil and Political Rights. Consequently, the Special Representative's report relies on a broad range of U.N. instruments in evaluating the human rights situation in Iran; whereas the Human Rights Committee only has authority to monitor implementation of the Covenant.

The Commission has not developed specific guidelines for its rapporteurs and representatives to follow in carrying out their investigative duties. Rather, the resolution establishing each rapporteur specifies the rapporteur's/representative's mandate in broad terms, usually involving a direction to study the human rights situation in the country at issue and prepare a report to the Commission, including conclusions and recommendations. The mandate of the Special Representative to Iran, described in this excerpt from his report, is typical. As part of their fact-finding, several rapporteurs and representatives have conducted on-site missions in the countries which they were assigned to investigate. Such factfinding efforts are discussed in chapter 8 of this book. Though the Special Representative on Iran was authorized in 1984, Iran did not permit an on-site visit until January 1990. Since January 1990, the Special Representative on Iran has made at least two more on-site visits.

Resolutions establishing special rapporteurs and representatives generally authorize the Chair of the Commission, after consultation with regional representatives, to appoint a recognized international human rights expert. Often the Chair will consult with the country under consideration as well, to enhance the likelihood of that country's cooperating with the special rapporteur. Most mandates are of only a year's duration, but the Commission usually will renew the mandate on a yearly basis until the country resolves the situation or the Commission decides to drop the case. Several countries have been the subject of rapporteur investigations, including: Afghanistan, Bolivia, Chile, Guatemala, El Salvador, Iran, and Romania. For particularly egregious human rights violations—such as *apartheid* in South Africa—the Commission has appointed a working group of experts rather than a single rapporteur to study the human rights situation. For additional information on the country-specific rapporteur process and practice, see Marc Bossuyt, *The Development of*

Special Procedures of the United Nations Commission on Human Rights, 6 HUM. RTS. L.J. 179 (1985); HOWARD TOLLEY, JR., THE U.N. COMMISSION ON HUMAN RIGHTS 111-24 (1987); *see also* chapter 5, *infra.*

* * * * *

Preliminary Report by the Special Representative of the Commission on Human Rights on the Human Rights Situation in the Islamic Republic of Iran at 3-9, U.N. Doc. E/CN.4/1985/20 (1985) (footnotes omitted):

1. At its fortieth session, on 14 March 1984, the Commission on Human Rights adopted resolution 1984/54 on the human rights situation in the Islamic Republic of Iran. By that resolution the Commission requested the Chairman to appoint, after consultation within the Bureau, a special representative of the Commission whose mandate would be to establish contacts with the Government of the Islamic Republic of Iran and to make a thorough study of the human rights situation in that country based on such information as he might deem relevant, including comments and materials provided by the Government, containing conclusions and appropriate suggestions, to be presented to the Commission at its forty-first session. The Commission further requested the Government of the Islamic Republic of Iran to extend its co-operation to the Special Representative of the Commission and decided to continue its consideration of the situation of human rights and fundamental freedoms in the Islamic Republic of Iran at its forty-first session.

2. Pursuant to resolution 1984/54, the Chairman of the Commission on Human Rights, on 19 October 1984 designated Mr. Andrés Aguilar as Special Representative of the Commission. . . .

10. The Special Representative has received from various sources, including non-governmental organizations in consultative status with the Economic and Social Council, communications and documents containing information on alleged violations of human rights in the Islamic Republic of Iran. The Special Representative, due to his recent designation and to the lack of direct contact with the authorities of the Islamic Republic of Iran, has not yet been in a position to evaluate the information received from these sources and the allegations contained therein. . . .

11. It may be recalled in this context that Iran, on 4 April 1968, signed the International Covenant on Civil and Political Rights and the International Covenant on Economic, Social and Cultural Rights. It ratified both Covenants on 24 June 1975. . . .

12. In its resolution 1984/54 which established the mandate of the Special Representative, the Commission on Human Rights was expressly guided by the principles embodied in the Charter of the United Nations, the Universal Declaration of Human Rights and the International Covenants on Human Rights. The Commission further reaffirmed that all Member States had an obligation to promote and protect human rights and fundamental freedoms and to fulfill the obligations they had undertaken under the various international instruments in that field.

13. This position of principle, as expressed in the above-mentioned resolution, is in line with the Charter of the United Nations of which Iran is an original member. The purposes of the United Nations as spelled out in Article 1, paragraph 3, of the

Charter expressly include the achievement of international co-operation in solving international problems of an economic, social, cultural, or humanitarian character, and in promoting and encouraging respect for human rights and for fundamental freedoms for all without distinction as to race, sex, language, or religion. Moreover, under Article 56 of the Charter all Member States pledge themselves to take joint and separate action in co-operation with the Organization for the achievement of the purposes set forth in Article 55 which in turn includes the promotion of universal respect for, and observance of, human rights and fundamental freedoms for all without distinction as to race, sex, language, or religion.

14.   The Universal Declaration of Human Rights gave expression to the human rights principles contained in the Charter of the United Nations. The Universal Declaration is thus an emanation of the Charter providing as it does common standards of achievement for *all* peoples and *all* nations. Through practice over the years, the basic provisions of the Universal Declaration of Human Rights can be regarded as having attained the status of international customary law and in many instances they have the character of *jus cogens*. This is, for example, the case with the right to life, freedom from torture, freedom of thought, conscience and religion and the right to a fair trial.

15.   Such fundamental guarantees of the Universal Declaration of Human Rights cannot be open to challenge by any State as they are indispensable for the functioning or an international community based on the rule of law and respect for human rights and fundamental freedoms.

16.   States of all political, economic, social, cultural, and religious persuasions participated in the drafting of the Charter, the Universal Declaration of Human Rights and the International Covenants on Human Rights. The Universal Declaration of Human Rights and the International Covenants thus contain norms which, distilled from the collective experience and the common heritage of the world's peoples, represent universal standards of conduct for all peoples and all nations.

17.   Within the framework of the International Covenants on Human Rights, States of all religious, cultural or ideological persuasions co-operate in the implementation of universal standards of human rights in their respective countries. The General Assembly has repeatedly emphasized the importance of the strictest compliance by States parties with their obligations under the International Covenants and has further stressed the importance of uniform standards of implementation of the International Covenants.

18.   Therefore it must be concluded that no State can claim to be allowed to disrespect basic, entrenched rights such as the right to life, freedom from torture, freedom of thought, conscience and religion, and the right to a fair trial which are provided for under the Universal Declaration and the International Covenants on Human Rights, on the ground that departure from these standards might be permitted under national or religious law.

19.   It is the firm conviction of the Special Representative that the following fundamental principles are applicable to the situation in the Islamic Republic of Iran as indeed to the situation, present or future, in any other country:

   (a)   States members of the United Nations are bound to abide by universally accepted standards of conduct in so far as the treatment of their population is concerned, particularly as regards the protection of human life, freedom from torture and other cruel, inhuman or degrading treatment or punishment, freedom of thought, conscience and religion and the right to a fair trial;

(b)   In so far as the basic rights and freedoms of the individual are concerned, the Universal Declaration of Human Rights gives expression to the human rights principles of the Charter of the United Nations and essential provisions such as those referred to above represent not only rules of international customary law but rules which also have the character of *jus cogens*;

(c)   The International Covenants on Human Rights give added conventional force to those provisions of the Universal Declaration of Human Rights which already reflect international customary law. Since the Islamic Republic of Iran is a party to the International Covenants on Human Rights, the latter's provisions in their entirety are legally binding upon the Government of the Islamic Republic of Iran. They must be complied with in good faith.

NOTES AND QUESTIONS

1.   Following Mr. Aguilar's submission of the preliminary report, the Commission on Human Rights extended his mandate for one year and requested a final report to be presented at the Commission's forty-second session in 1986. *See* CHR res. 1985/39, at 81, U.N. Doc. E/CN.4/1985/66 (1985). Mr. Aguilar resigned in January 1986, however, and was not able to complete the final report. *See* U.N. Doc. E/CN.4/1986/25 (1986).

In July 1986, the Commission appointed Mr. Reynaldo Galindo Pohl, a lawyer from El Salvador, as Special Representative to Iran and he submitted his first report to the Commission at its forty-third session in January 1987. *See* Commission on Human Rights, *Report on the Human Rights Situation in the Islamic Republic of Iran by the Special Representative of the Commission, Mr. Reynaldo Galindo Pohl*, U.N. Doc. E/CN.4/1987/23 (1987). His report detailed allegations of human rights violations, but did not reach any significant conclusions regarding either those allegations or the overall situation in Iran because the Iranian government refused to allow an on-site visit or even reply to Mr. Pohl's requests for information.

Mr. Pohl subsequently conducted several on-site visits and submitted reports to the Commission in 1989, 1991, 1992, 1993, 1994, and 1995. *See* U.N. Doc. E/CN.4/1989/26 (1989); U.N. Doc. E/CN.4/1991/35 (1991); U.N. Doc. E/CN.4/1992/34 (1992); U.N. Doc. E/CN.4/1993/41 (1993); U.N. Doc. E/CN.4/1994/50 (1994); U.N. Doc. A/49/514 and Add.1-2 (1994); U.N. Doc. E/CN.4/1995/55 (1995). The Commission has continued to extend the Special Representative's mandate on a yearly basis through the date of publication of this book.

2.   The Special Representative to Iran, in the preceding excerpt, stresses the legal obligation of Iran to observe the provisions of the Covenant on Civil and Political Rights in good faith. The concept that states have an obligation to observe treaties to which they are parties is based on the doctrine of *pacta sunt servanda* (treaties are to be observed). The doctrine is a norm of customary international law that developed as the growing intercourse among nations necessitated respect for international agreements.

Modern formulations of the doctrine add the element of good faith. One example can be found in Article 26 of the Vienna Convention on the Law of Treaties. "Every treaty in force is binding upon the parties to it and must be performed by them in good faith." Vienna Convention on the Law of Treaties, Art. 26, 1155 U.N.T.S. 331, T.S. No. 58, 8 I.L.M. 679 (1969), *entered into force* Jan. 27, 1980. The Restatement (Third) of the Foreign Relations Law of the United States follows the language of the Vienna Convention, substituting the phrase "international agreement" for the word "treaty." RESTATEMENT (THIRD) OF THE FOREIGN RELATIONS LAW OF THE UNITED STATES § 321 (1987). The U.N. Charter imposes a similar obligation of good faith in Article 2(2). "All members . . . shall fulfil in good faith the obligations assumed by them in accordance with the present Charter."

3.   The issue of cultural relativism arose consistently during the Committee's discussion of Iran's second periodic report. The issue also was addressed by the Special Representative in his 1985 report, as seen in the excerpt from that report. In addition, he discussed relativism in his 1993 report, stating:

> 319.   On the question of the structure and organization of the systems for supervision of compliance with the international human rights instruments, the Special Representative again feels obliged to point out that regional and national developments must be fully consistent, and maintain continuity, with the system lawfully established by the United Nations, and that no such development is admissible if it runs counter to, or deviates from the international order. In the event of such a discrepancy, the regional and national systems must conform to the international system. . . .

Final Report on the Situation of Human Rights in the Islamic Republic of Iran by the Special Representative of the Commission on Human Rights, Mr. Reynaldo Galindo Pohl at 56-57, U.N. Doc. E/CN.4/1993/41 (1993) [hereinafter *1993 Report on Iran*].

4.   Iranian Violations of International Law

The Iranian penal sanctions discussed in this chapter provide a useful basis for an exploration of relativism in the application of human rights norms. Yet by presenting this material the authors do not wish to imply that these penal sanctions represent the most significant aspect of Iran's violations of human rights law during the period from the institution of the Islamic Republic of Iran to the publication of this book.

Reynaldo Galindo Pohl's first report in 1987, for example, contained allegations of numerous violations, including summary executions; torture and other ill-treatment; warrantless arrests; lengthy detentions without formal charge or trial; expedited trials with no access to counsel or right to call witnesses, to testify, or to appeal; and harassment, discrimination, and persecution of religious minorities, especially members of the Baha'i faith. Commission on Human Rights, *Report on the Human Rights Situation in the Islamic Republic of Iran by the Special Representative of the Commission, Mr. Reynaldo Galindo Pohl*, U.N. Doc. E/CN.4/1987/23 (1987).

Reporting in January 1993, Mr. Pohl further outlined human rights violations in Iran:

> 322.   On the specific question of the current situation of human rights in Iran, it should be mentioned that: there is continued uncertainty about the official reaction to dissidence; self-censorship is widespread in the media; several guarantees of due process are still merely the letter of the law or the subject of proposed legislation; the right of free association has been denied, with the express banning of the Freedom Movement; the International Committee of the Red Cross continues to be prevented from performing its function in the prisons; the restrictions on non-Islamic religious groups are manifold; and the situation of women leaves much to be desired.

> 323.   Furthermore, with regard to the right to life, the number of judicial executions continues greatly to exceed the very restrictive terms of the International Covenant on Civil and Political Rights and there have been cases of torture and cruel, inhuman or degrading treatment or punishment. The guarantees of due process and legal defence by means of a qualified lawyer are not complied with in trials before the Islamic revolutionary courts; this is serious and irreversible when these trials result in the defendant being sentenced to death or amputation.

1993 Report on Iran at 57. In his 1994 and 1995 reports, Mr. Pohl summarized allegations that he received concerning human rights violations in Iran including:

* Continuing use of the death penalty
* Enforced or involuntary disappearances
* Torture of prisoners
* Lack of transparency and predictability in the application of Iranian law
* Obstacles to a free press
* Systematic persecution, harassment and discrimination against members of the Baha'i faith
* Discrimination against women

See U.N. Doc. E/CN.4/1995/55 (1995); U.N. Doc. A/49/514 and Add.1-2 (1994); U.N. Doc. E/CN.4/1994/50 (1994).

Many human rights organizations have increasingly focused on the human rights situation for women in Iran. In February 1994, several NGOs circulated a statement discussing what they described as the "despicable condition of women in Iran," and urging the Commission on Human Rights to "adopt more effective measures to force the Iranian regime to end the brutal persecution of women in that country." U.N. Doc. E/CN.4/1994/NGO/40, at 1-3 (1994). For additional reading on the human rights situation for women in Iran, see DOCUMENTATION, INFORMATION AND RESEARCH BRANCH, IMMIGRATION AND REFUGEE BOARD OF CANADA, HUMAN RIGHTS BRIEFS: WOMEN IN THE ISLAMIC REPUBLIC OF IRAN (1994).

Iran has also been accused of perpetrating numerous human rights violations in connection with its war against Iraq. *See, e.g., Armed Conflict and Iran*, U.N. Doc. E/CN.4/1987/NGO 51 (1987) (written Statement submitted to the Commission on Human Rights by Human Rights Advocates, an NGO in consultative status); *Report of the Mission Dispatched by the Secretary-General on the Situation of Prisoners of War in the Islamic Republic of Iran and Iraq*, U.N. Doc. S/20147 (1988).

For further reading on human rights in Iran, see MIDDLE EAST WATCH, GUARDIANS OF THOUGHT: LIMITS ON FREEDOM OF EXPRESSION IN IRAN (1993).

D. THE INTERNATIONAL LAW PROHIBITION OF TORTURE AND OTHER CRUEL, INHUMAN OR DEGRADING TREATMENT OR PUNISHMENT

The following readings concern the prohibition against torture and other cruel, inhuman or degrading treatment or punishment. The selections should be useful in interpreting the prohibition, ascertaining whether a consensus exists as to its scope, and determining whether Iran's actions have violated the prohibition.

Standard Minimum Rules for the Treatment of Prisoners, *adopted* **Aug. 30, 1955, by the First United Nations Congress on the Prevention of Crime and the Treatment of Offenders, U.N. Doc. A/CONF/6/1, Annex I, A (1956);** *adopted* **July 31, 1957, by Economic and Social Council, E.S.C. res. 663C, 24 U.N. ESCOR Supp. (No. 1) at 11, U.N. Doc. E/3048 (1957),** *amended* **E.S.C. res. 2076, 62 U.N. ESCOR Supp. (No. 1) at 35, U.N. Doc. E/5988 (1977) (adding Article 95):**

31. Corporal punishment, punishment by placing in a dark cell, and all cruel,

inhuman or degrading punishments shall be completely prohibited as punishments for disciplinary offences.

32. (1)   Punishment by close confinement or reduction of diet shall never be inflicted unless the medical officer has examined the prisoner and certified in writing that he is fit to sustain it.

(2)   The same shall apply to any other punishment that may be prejudicial to the physical or mental health of a prisoner. In no case may such punishment be contrary to or depart from the principle stated in rule 31.

(3)   The medical officer shall visit daily prisoners undergoing such punishments and shall advise the director if he considers the termination or alteration of the punishment necessary on grounds of physical or mental health.

NOTES AND QUESTIONS

The Standard Minimum Rules also contain specific protections for insane and mentally abnormal prisoners (Rule 82), prisoners under arrest or awaiting trial (Rules 84-93), civil prisoners (Rule 94), and persons arrested or detained without charge (Rule 95).

For further reading about the Standard Minimum Rules and other U.N. standards in the area of crime prevention and criminal justice, see *United Nations, Human Rights and Pre-Trial Detention*, U.N. Doc. HR/P/PT/3 (1994).

Declaration on the Protection of All Persons from Being Subjected to Torture and Other Cruel, Inhuman or Degrading Treatment or Punishment, G.A. res. 3452, 30 U.N. GAOR Supp. (No. 34) at 91, U.N. Doc. A/10034 (1976):

Article 1

1.   For the purpose of this Declaration, torture means any act by which severe pain or suffering, whether physical or mental, is intentionally inflicted by or at the instigation of a public official on a person for such purposes as obtaining from him or a third person information or confession, punishing him for an act he has committed or is suspected of having committed, or intimidating him or other persons. It does not include pain or suffering arising only from, inherent in or incidental to, lawful sanctions to the extent consistent with the Standard Minimum Rules for the Treatment of Prisoners.

2.   Torture constitutes an aggravated and deliberate form of cruel, inhuman or degrading treatment or punishment.

*   *   *   *   *

Convention Against Torture and Other Cruel, Inhuman or Degrading Treatment or Punishment, G.A. res. 39/46, 39 GAOR Supp. (No. 51) at 197, U.N. Doc. A/39/51 (1985), *entered into force* June 26, 1987:

Article 1

1.   For the purposes of this Convention, the term "torture" means any act by

which severe pain or suffering, whether physical or mental, is intentionally inflicted on a person for such purposes as obtaining from him or a third person information or a confession, punishing him for an act he or a third person has committed or is suspected of having committed, or intimidating or coercing him or a third person, or for any reason based on discrimination of any kind, when such pain or suffering is inflicted by or at the instigation of or with the consent or acquiescence of a public official or other person acting in an official capacity. It does not include pain or suffering arising only from, inherent in or incidental to lawful sanctions.

2.   This article is without prejudice to any international instrument or national legislation which does or may contain provisions of wider application. . . .

Article 16

1.   Each State Party shall undertake to prevent in any territory under its jurisdiction other acts of cruel, inhuman or degrading treatment or punishment which do not amount to torture as defined in article 1, when such acts are committed by or at the instigation of or with the consent or acquiescence of a public official or other person acting in an official capacity. . . .

NOTES AND QUESTIONS

1.   The Torture Convention created the Committee Against Torture to help implement the Convention's provisions. Established in 1987, the Committee

> consists of 10 experts of high moral standing and recognized competence in the field of human rights, elected by States parties to the Convention from among their nationals. Members are elected for a four-year term by secret ballot at a meeting of States parties, and serve in their personal capacity.
>
> The tasks of the Committee, as set out in articles 19 to 24 of the Convention, are: to study reports on the measures taken by States parties to give effect to their undertakings under the Convention; to make confidential inquiries, if it decides that this is warranted, concerning well-founded indications that torture is being systematically practised in the territory of a State party; to perform certain functions with a view to settling disputes among States parties concerning the application of the Convention, providing that those States parties have recognized the competence of the Committee against Torture to undertake such functions; to establish when necessary *ad hoc* conciliation commissions to make available its good offices to the States parties concerned with a view to a friendly solution of inter-State disputes; to consider communications from or on behalf of individuals subject to the jurisdiction of States parties concerned who claim to be victims of a violation of the provisions of the Convention, provided that those States parties have recognized the competence of the Committee to that effect; and to submit annual reports on its activities to the States parties and to the General Assembly of the United Nations. . . .
>
> By [the end of February 1996], there were [94] States parties to the Convention against Torture and Other Cruel, Inhuman or Degrading Treatment or Punishment, [38] of which had accepted the competence of the Committee against Torture under articles 21 and 22 to consider matters relating to inter-State disputes and communication from or on behalf of individuals. [11] of the States parties have [current and effective declarations] that they do not recognize the competence of the Committee under article 20 of the Convention to undertake confidential inquiries or fact-finding missions on their territories.

UNITED NATIONS CENTRE FOR HUMAN RIGHTS, HUMAN RIGHTS MACHINERY, FACT SHEET NO. 1 at 15-16 (1988) (updated to the end of February 1996).

2.   As of February 1996, Iran had not ratified the Convention against Torture and Other Cruel, Inhuman or Degrading Treatment or Punishment, and so the Committee has no power to consider complaints from individuals who claim to be victims in that country. The Special Rapporteur on torture, however, may investigate such claims within his mandate from the U.N. Commission on Human Rights.

In his December 1992 report, for example, Special Rapporteur Peter Kooijmans outlined complaints received about Iran, stating:

> Common methods of physical torture include suspension for long periods in contorted positions, burns from cigarettes and severe and repeated beating with cables or other instruments on the back and the soles of the feet. Sometimes, a blanket or cloth is stuffed into the victims' mouths to stop them screaming, making it hard to breathe properly. Usually the victims have been blindfolded, and strapped to a kind of bedstead or held down by guards sitting on their backs. Other arbitrary punishments reportedly include being kicked or punched, made to stand without moving for hours at a time, cancellation of family visits or reducing food.

Report of the Special Rapporteur [on torture], Mr. Peter Kooijmans at 65, U.N. Doc. E/CN.4/ 1993/26 (1992).

Body of Principles for the Protection of All Persons Under Any Form of Detention or Imprisonment, G.A. res. 43/173, 43 U.N. GAOR Supp. (No. 49) at 297, U.N. Doc. A/43/49 (1988):

Principle 1

All persons under any form of detention or imprisonment shall be treated in a humane manner and with respect for the inherent dignity of the human person. . . .

Principle 6

No person under any form of detention or imprisonment shall be subjected to torture or to cruel, inhuman or degrading treatment or punishment.[4] No circumstance whatever may be invoked as a justification for torture or other cruel, inhuman or degrading treatment or punishment.

1.   Human Rights Committee Consideration of Communications Under the Optional Protocol

In addition to the reporting and examination mechanism through which the Human Rights Committee implements the Civil and Political Covenant, the Optional Protocol to the Covenant contains a mechanism whereby the Committee considers communications from individuals alleging Covenant violations by States parties.

---

[4] The term "cruel, inhuman or degrading treatment or punishment" should be interpreted so as to extend the widest possible protection against abuses, whether physical or mental, including the holding of a detained or imprisoned person in conditions which deprive him, temporarily or permanently, of the use of any of his natural senses, such as sight or hearing, or of his awareness of place and the passing of time.

The Protocol grants authority to reach views on the merits, but the Committee does not issue judgments. Rather, it forwards its views to the individual and State party concerned. The Committee has, however, published views on some of the communications it has evaluated. The Optional Protocol is reproduced in *Selected International Human Rights Instruments*. The following materials discuss the Committee's procedures under the Optional Protocol and examine its interpretation of Article 7's prohibition of torture and cruel, inhuman or degrading treatment or punishment.

a. Committee Procedures

Report of the Human Rights Committee, 39 U.N. GAOR Supp. (No. 40) at 110-17, U.N. Doc. A/39/40 (1984):

III. CONSIDERATION OF COMMUNICATIONS UNDER THE OPTIONAL PROTOCOL

Introduction

558. Under the Optional Protocol to the International Covenant on Civil and Political Rights, individuals who claim that any of their rights enumerated in the Covenant have been violated and who have exhausted all available domestic remedies may submit written communications to the Human Rights Committee for consideration. . . . No communication can be received by the Committee if it concerns a State party to the Covenant which is not also a party to the Optional Protocol. . . .

Procedure

559. Consideration of communications under the Optional Protocol takes place in closed meetings (art. 5(3) of the Optional Protocol). All documents pertaining to the work of the Committee under the Optional Protocol (submissions from the parties and other working documents of the Committee) are confidential. The texts of final decisions of the Committee, consisting of views adopted under article 5(4) of the Optional Protocol, are however made public. As regards decisions declaring a communication inadmissible, which are also final, the Committee has decided that it will normally make these decisions public, substituting initials for the names of the alleged victim(s) and the author(s).

560. In carrying out its work under the Optional Protocol, the Committee is assisted by Working Groups on Communications, consisting of not more than five of its members, which submit recommendations to the Committee on the action to be taken at the various stages in the consideration of each case. The Committee has also designated individual members to act as Special Rapporteurs in a number of cases. The Special Rapporteurs place their recommendations before the Committee for consideration.

561. The procedure for the consideration of communications received under the Optional Protocol consists of several main stages.

(a) *Registration of the communication*

Communications are received by the Secretariat and are registered . . ..

(b) *Admissibility of communication*

Once a communication has been registered, the Committee must decide whether it is admissible under the Optional Protocol. The requirements for admissibility, which are contained in articles 1, 2, 3 and 5(2) of the Optional Protocol, are listed in rule 90 of the Committee's provisional rules of procedure. Under rule 91(1) the Committee or a Working Group may request the State party concerned or the author of the communication to submit, within a time-limit which is indicated in each such decision (normally between six weeks and two months), additional written information or observations relevant to the question of admissibility of the communication. Such a request does not imply that any decision has been taken on the question of admissibility (rule 91(3)). The decision to declare a communication admissible or inadmissible rests with the Committee. The Committee may also decide to terminate or suspend consideration of a communication if its author indicates that he wants to withdraw the case or if the Secretariat has lost contact with the author. A decision to declare a communication inadmissible or otherwise to terminate or suspend consideration of it may, in a clear case, be taken without referring the case to the State party for its observations.

(c) *Consideration on the merits*

If a communication is declared admissible, the Committee proceeds to consider the substance of the complaint. In accordance with article 4 of the Optional Protocol, it requests the State party concerned to submit to the Committee explanations or statements clarifying the matter. Under article 4(2), the State party has a time-limit of six months in which to submit its observations. When they are received, the author is given an opportunity to comment on the observations of the State party. The Committee then normally formulates its views and forwards them to the State party and to the author of the communication, in accordance with article 5(4) of the Optional Protocol. The State party may be requested to transmit a copy of the views to an imprisoned victim. In exceptional cases, further information may be sought from the State party or the author by means of an interim decision before the Committee finally adopts its views. A Committee member may also write an individual opinion, which is appended to the Committee's views.

Duration of procedure

562.   Since the Committee, which meets three times a year, must allow both the author and the State party sufficient time to prepare their submissions, a decision on admissibility can only be taken between six months and a year after the initial submission; views under article 5 (4) may follow one year later. The entire procedure normally may be completed within two to three years. The Committee tries to deal expeditiously with all communications. . . .

Issues considered by the Committee

569.   The following summary illustrates the nature and results of the Committee's activities under the Optional Protocol. It does not constitute an exhaustive restatement. . . .

1. *Procedural issues*

570.   A number of questions relating to the admissibility of communications have been dealt with in the Committee's earlier reports to the General Assembly or in the Committee's decisions on particular communications. These issues always depend, directly or indirectly, on the terms of the Optional Protocol, and concern, *inter alia*, the following matters.

(a) *The standing of the author*

571.   Normally, a communication should be submitted by the individual himself or by his representative; the Committee may, however, accept to consider a communication submitted on behalf of an alleged victim when it appears that he is unable to submit the communication himself (rule 90(1)(b)). In practice, the Committee has accepted communications not only from a duly authorized legal representative, but also from a close family member acting on behalf of an alleged victim, but in other cases the Committee has found that the author of a communication lacked standing. In case No. 128/1982, the author was a member of a non- governmental organization and had taken interest in the alleged victim's situation. He claimed to have authority to act because he believed "that every prisoner treated unjustly would appreciate further investigation of his case by the Human Rights Committee". The Committee decided that the author lacked standing and declared the communication inadmissible. The Human Rights Committee has thus established through a number of decisions on admissibility that a communication submitted by a third party on behalf of an alleged victim can only be considered if the author justifies his authority to submit the communication.

572.   The Committee has also held that an organization as such cannot submit a communication. In case No. 163/1984 . . . it stated: "According to article 1 of the Optional Protocol, only individuals have the right to submit a communication. To the extent, therefore, that the communication originates from the [organization], it has to be declared inadmissible because of lack of personal standing". . . .

(b) *The victim*

573.   The Committee has clarified in case No. 35/1978 that "a person can only claim to be a victim in the sense of article 1 of the Optional Protocol if he or she is actually affected. It is a matter of degree how concretely this requirement should be taken. However, no individual can in the abstract, by way of an *actio popularis*, challenge a law or practice claimed to be contrary to the Covenant. If the law or practice has not already been concretely applied to the detriment of that individual, it must in any event be applicable in such a way that the alleged victim's risk of being affected is more than a theoretical possibility". That is, a person is not a victim unless he has personally suffered a violation of his rights. In case No. 61/1979 the Committee stressed "that it has only been entrusted with the mandate of examining whether an individual has suffered an actual violation of his rights. It cannot review in the abstract whether national legislation contravenes the Covenant, although such legislation may, in particular circumstances, produce adverse effects which directly affect the individual, making him thus a victim in the sense contemplated by articles 1 and 2 of the Optional Protocol".

(c) *Date of entry into force of the Covenant and the Optional Protocol*

574.   The Committee has indicated frequently that it "can consider only an alleged violation of human rights occurring on or after 23 March 1976 (the date of entry into force of the Covenant and the Protocol for [the State party]) unless it is an alleged violation which, although occurring before that date, continues or has effects which themselves constitute a violation after that date". . . .

(e) *Preclusion under article 5 (2) (a) of the Optional Protocol if the same matter is being examined under another procedure of international investigation or settlement*

577.   The Optional Protocol precludes the competence of the Committee to consider

cases which are simultaneously being examined under other procedures of international investigation or settlement, such as the procedures of the Inter-American Commission on Human Rights (IACHR) and the European Commission of Human Rights. When this situation arises, the practice of the Committee has been to instruct the Secretariat to explain to the author that consideration by the Committee is precluded under article 5(2)(a) of the Optional Protocol. . . .

581.   In the first case placed before it under the Optional Protocol, the Committee had occasion to determine that the examination of a particular human rights situation in a given country under Economic and Social Council resolution 1503 (XLVIII), which governs a procedure for the examination of situations which appear to reveal "a consistent pattern of gross and reliably attested violations of human rights and fundamental freedoms", does not within the meaning of article 5(2)(a) of the Optional Protocol constitute an examination of the "same matter" as a claim by an individual submitted to the Human Rights Committee under the Optional Protocol. The procedure governed by Economic and Social Council resolution 1503 (XLVIII) therefore does not bar the Human Rights Committee from considering an individual case. Also in one of the early cases considered, the Human Rights Committee determined that a procedure established by a non-governmental organization (such as the Inter-Parliamentary Council of the Inter-Parliamentary Union) does not constitute a procedure of international investigation or settlement within the meaning of article 5(2)(a) of the Optional Protocol.

582.   At its twenty-first session, the Committee also observed, when declaring admissible a number of similar and related cases concerning the same country, "that a study by a intergovernmental organization either of the human rights situation in a given country (such as that by the IACHR) or a study of the trade union rights situation in a given country (such as the issues examined by the Committee on Freedom of Association of the ILO), or of a human rights problem of a more global character (such as that of the Special Rapporteur of the Commission on Human Rights on summary or arbitrary executions), although such studies might refer to or draw on information concerning individuals, cannot be seen as being the same matter as the examination of individual cases within the meaning of article 5(2)(a) of the Optional Protocol." . . .

(g) *Exhaustion of domestic remedies*

584.   Under article 5(2)(a) of the Optional Protocol, the Committee shall not consider any communication unless it has ascertained that the author has exhausted all available domestic remedies. Numerous communications before the Committee have been declared inadmissible on this ground. In its decisions on admissibility, the Committee has clarified the meaning of article 5(2)(b) of the Optional Protocol, explaining, *inter alia*, that "exhaustion of domestic remedies can be required only to the extent that these remedies are effective and available" and further clarified that "an extraordinary remedy, such as seeking the annulment of decision(s) of the Ministry of Justice" does not constitute an effective remedy within the meaning of article 5(2)(b) of the Optional Protocol.

* * * * *

In 1990, the Human Rights Committee created a formal follow-up procedure to urge compliance with its decisions adopted under the Optional Protocol. It appointed Dr. Janos Fodor as the first Special Rapporteur for the Follow-Up on Views with responsibility for communicating with States parties and victims and monitoring compliance with its decisions. In 1993, Dr. Fodor was succeeded by Andreas Mavrommatis.

In 1994, the Committee sought to increase the effectiveness of the follow-up procedure by endowing the Special Rapporteur with authority to conduct on-site fact-finding missions and, in 1995, the first on-site investigative mission took place in Jamaica. Following the Special Rapporteur's visit, the Jamaican government agreed to comply with several Committee rulings that called for criminal sentences other than the death penalty. Beginning in 1995, the Committee sought to increase awareness of its follow-up efforts by including in its Annual Report a "black list" identifying all States parties that fail to cooperate with follow-up activities. *See* Markus G. Schmidt, *Individual Human Rights Complaints Procedures Based on United Nations Treaties and the Need for Reform*, 41 INTL & COMP. L.Q. 645, 650-53 (1992); Markus G. Schmidt, *Portée et suivi des constatations du Comité des droits de l'homme*, Remarks at the Colloquium of the Faculty of Law at the University of Montpellier (Mar. 6-7, 1995).

b. Committee Jurisprudence

Although adjudicative remedies are treated extensively beginning with chapter 10, this subsection discusses the Human Rights Committee's adjudicative functions as an important component of implementing the Civil and Political Covenant. The following materials focus on the Committee's interpretation of Article 7 of the Covenant.

MANFRED NOWAK, U.N. COVENANT ON CIVIL AND POLITICAL RIGHTS: CCPR COMMENTARY 128-35 (1993) (footnotes omitted):

II.   Prohibition of Torture or Cruel, Inhuman or Degrading Treatment or Punishment . . .

2.   *Delineation of the Individual Offences*

. . . Art[icle] 7 . . . prohibit[s] not only torture, inhuman and degrading punishment and treatment but also cruel treatment and punishment. Insofar as the various terms are used in a particular order, a certain classification as to the kind and purpose of treatment can be seen, especially as regards the intensity of the suffering imposed: this runs from "mere" degrading treatment or punishment, to that which is inhuman and cruel, up to torture as the most reprehensible form. The Committee has correctly pointed out that it is unnecessary to draw sharp distinctions between these various categories with respect to whether Art. 7 has been violated. Thus, in its holdings in individual communications, it has usually avoided qualifying the attacked actions in detail. Only in recent years can a greater willingness to differentiate be seen.

With respect to the (at least moral) impropriety of an action of its organs, it is however not irrelevant for the State Party concerned whether it is charged with torture or "mere" degrading treatment. . . .

3.   *Torture.* . .

Only in a relatively few cases has the Committee found that torture was committed. These involved *communications against Uruguay*, and on occasion against *Colombia* and *Bolivia*, where the victims had been subjected to a variety of practices during interrogations in the initial period of (usually "incommunicado") detention: systematic beatings, electroshocks, burns, extended hanging from hand and/or leg chains, repeated immersion in a mixture of blood, urine, vomit and excrement ("submarino"), standing for great lengths, threats, simulated executions or amputations, etc. . . . .

4. *Inhuman and/or Cruel Treatment*

These two terms include all forms of imposition of severe suffering that are unable to be qualified as torture for lack of one of its essential elements. They also cover those practices imposing suffering that does not reach the necessary intensity. . . . In [*Viana Acosta v. Uruguay*], the Committee expressly deemed forced psychiatric experiments, such as injections against the will of the imprisoned victim, to be inhuman treatment. . . . In the case of *Tshisekedi v. Zaire*, deprivation of food and drink for four days after arrest was considered inhuman treatment. . . . .

5. *Degrading Treatment*

Degrading treatment is the weakest level of a violation of Art. 7. The severity of the suffering imposed is of less importance here than the humiliation of the victim, regardless of whether this is in the eyes of others or those of the victim himself or herself. . . . In *Conteris v. Uruguay*, the Committee expressly designated as degrading treatment within the meaning of Art. 7 certain arbitrary prison practices in the *"Libertad Prison"* in Montevideo aimed at humiliating prisoners and making them feel insecure (repeated solitary confinement, subjection to cold, persistent relocation to a different cell). . . . .

6. *Cruel, Inhuman or Degrading Punishment*

Since all punishment contains an element of humiliation and perhaps also inhumanity, an additional element of reprehensibleness must also be present in order for it to qualify as a violation of Art. 7. . . . .

Under the current standard, such punishment as the *pillory* or *caning* represent degrading punishment at the least. Further, the Committee has placed under the prohibition of Art. 7 excessive chastisement as an educational or disciplinary measure.

7. *Summary of the Case Law of the Committee in Individual Communications*

Only in a few cases has the Committee expressly qualified specific treatment as degrading, inhuman, cruel or as torture. In most cases, it was satisfied with a simple determination of a violation of Art. 7. . . . The majority of these cases deal with Uruguay, which, in their cumulative effect, reveal a systematic practice of disregard for human dignity and personal integrity during the period of military rule. . . . Apart from Uruguay, the Committee ha[d as of 1993] found violations of Art. 7 only in some cases against Colombia, Bolivia, Ecuador and the Dominican Republic as well as against Zaire and Madagascar.

*   *   *   *   *

Following is an excerpt, from an opinion that the Committee issued subsequent to publication of Nowak's book, that illustrates how the Committee considers individual communications.

Views of the Human Rights Committee under article 5, paragraph 4, of the Optional Protocol to the International Covenant on Civil and Political Rights (Fifty-first session) concerning Communication No. 414/1990 at 2-6, U.N. Doc. CCPR/C/51/D/414/1990 (1994) (made public by decision of the Human Rights Committee):

Submitted by:	Primo José Essono Mika Miha
Victim:	The author
State party:	Equatorial Guinea
Date of communication:	28 May 1990 (initial submission)
Date of adoption of Views:	8 July 1994 . . .

Adopts its Views under Article 5, paragraph 4, of the Optional Protocol.

1.   The author of the communication is Primo José Essono Mika Miha, a citizen of Equatorial Guinea born in 1940. . . . The Optional Protocol entered into force for Equatorial Guinea on 25 December 1987.

The facts as presented by the author:

2.1   The author is a former official of past governments of the Republic of Equatorial Guinea. . . . After the election and the installation of President Macias, the author resigned from his post and left the country together with his family for Spain, where he requested political asylum.

2.2   After the death of President Macias, the author returned to his country and took up [a government position]. In 1982, he once again left the country and sought refuge in Spain, as he feared persecution at the hands of the clan of Mongomo, to which Obiang Nguema (who had replaced President Macias) belongs.

2.3   On an unspecified date in the summer of 1988, the author returned to Equatorial Guinea, so as to actively support the activities of the opposition party (Partido de Progreso) of which he is a member. . . . [H]e was abducted by members of the security forces in a street of Malabo, the country's capital. He claims that he was handcuffed, blind-folded, and that a handkerchief was pushed into his mouth in order to silence him. He was told that President Obiang had ordered his arrest, but no further explanations were given. . . .

2.4   After his arrest, the author was detained on board of a ship and allegedly deprived of food and drink for one week. He was then transferred to the prison of Bata on the mainland where he allegedly was tortured for two days. . . .

2.5   The author does not specify the nature of the injuries sustained during torture but claims that he was subsequently kept in detention for well over one month without any medical assistance. . . .

2.7   As to the requirement of exhaustion of domestic remedies, the author submits that such judicial remedies as exist in Equatorial Guinea are totally ineffective. According to the author, the judiciary is directly controlled by President Obiang Nguema himself . . ..

The State party's observations:

4.1   . . . [T]he State party challenges the admissibility of the communication, arguing that it violates elemental norms of international law and constitutes an interference into domestic affairs of Equatorial Guinea . . ..

4.2   In this context, the State party explains that the author voluntarily relinquished his Equatorial-Guinean citizenship in 1982 and instead opted for Spanish nationality. . . .

The Committee's admissibility decision:

5.1   . . . [The Committee] dismissed the State party's contention that the author was not subjected to its jurisdiction . . . and further noted that the State party's acceptance of the Committee's competence under the Optional Protocol implied that considerations of domestic policy could not be advanced to prevent the Committee from considering claims from individuals subject to the State party's jurisdiction. . . .

5.4   On 16 October 1992, the Committee declared the communication admissible in so far as it appeared to raise issues under [article] 7 . . . of the Covenant.

Examination of the merits: . . .

6.2   The Committee notes with regret and concern that the State party has not cooperated with it as far as the provision of information on the substance of the author's claims is concerned. . . . Accordingly, due weight must be given to the author's allegations, to the extent that they have been substantiated.

6.3   The Committee has noted the State party's contention that the Communication constitutes an interference into its domestic affairs. The Committee strongly rejects the State party's argument and recalls that when ratifying the Optional Protocol, the State party accepted the Committee's competence to consider complaints from individuals subject to the State party's jurisdiction.

6.4   The author has claimed, and the State party has not refuted, that he was deprived of food and water for several days after his arrest . . ., tortured during two days after his transfer to the prison of Bata, and left without medical assistance for several weeks thereafter. The author has given a detailed account of the treatment he was subjected to and submitted copies of medical reports that support his conclusion. On the basis of this information, the Committee concludes that he was subjected to torture at the prison of Bata, in violation of article 7; it further observes that the deprivation of food and water . . . , as well as the denial of medical attention after the ill-treatment . . . amounts to cruel and inhuman treatment within the meaning of article 7 . . . ..

8.   Under article 2 of the Covenant, the State party is under an obligation to provide Mr. Mika Miha with an appropriate remedy, including appropriate compensation for the treatment to which he has been subjected.

9.   The Committee would wish to receive information, within 90 days, on any measures taken by the State party in respect of the Committee's views.

NOTES AND QUESTIONS

1.   Do you think the Optional Protocol provides an adequate procedure for implementing rights prescribed in the Covenant?

2.   How effective do you think the Committee's decision under the Optional Protocol will be in enabling Mr. Mika Miha to obtain remedies for actions of the government of the Republic of Equatorial Guinea?

3.   How can a body such as the Committee get governments to adhere to its requirements and decisions?

4.   By the end of February 1996, 132 states had ratified the Covenant on Civil and Political Rights but only 87 had also ratified the Optional Protocol.

5.   As of February 1996, Iran had not ratified the Optional Protocol. What might be the ramifications if it had?

6.   For additional reading, see Fionnuala Ni Aolain, *The Emergence of Diversity*, 19 FORDHAM INT'L L.J. 101 (1995); Alfred de Zayas, Jacob Th. Móller, & Torkel Opsahl, U.N. Centre for Human Rights Geneva, Application of the International Covenant on Civil and Political Rights under the Optional Protocol by the Human Rights Committee (1990); Human Rights Committee, *Selected Decisions under the Optional Protocol—Volume 2 (Seventeenth to thirty-second sessions)*, U.N. Doc. CCPR/C/OP/2 (1990); Human Rights Committee, *Selected Decisions under the Optional Protocol (Second to sixteenth sessions)*, U.N. Doc. CCPR/C/OP/1 (1985); DOMINIC MCGOLDRICK, HUMAN RIGHTS COMMITTEE: ITS ROLE IN THE DEVELOPMENT OF THE INTERNATIONAL COVENANT ON CIVIL AND POLITICAL RIGHTS (1991); Manfred Nowak, *U.N. Human Rights Committee: Survey of Decisions Given Up Till July 1990*, 10 HUM. RTS. L.J. 139 (1990); EGON SCHWELB, *The International Measures of Implementation of the International Covenant on Civil and Political Rights and the Optional Protocol*, 12 TEX. INT'L L.J. 141 (1977).

2.   European System

European human rights bodies produce the greatest body of jurisprudence on many issues including the meaning of torture and inhuman or degrading treatment or punishment. Hence, victims and their advocates often refer to the European jurisprudence even if problems do not arise in Europe. The first three readings below are excerpts of European decisions. The first is from a decision of the European Commission of Human Rights; the other two are from decisions of the European Court of Human Rights. All three interpret Article 3 of the European Convention on Human Rights which states that "[n]o one shall be subjected to torture or to inhuman or degrading treatment or punishment." While Article 3 of the European Convention is similar to Article 7 of the Civil and Political Covenant, the two provisions are not identical. Chapter 11, *infra*, discusses the structure and jurisprudence of the European system in a bit more detail; at this point it is necessary only to note that the decisions are official interpretations of Article 3. For further reading, see P.J. Duffy, *Article 3 of the European Convention on Human Rights*, 32 INT'L & COMP. L.Q. 316 (1983); NIGEL RODLEY, THE TREATMENT OF PRISONERS UNDER INTERNATIONAL LAW 71-95 (1987).

Ireland v. United Kingdom, 1976 Y.B. Eur. Conv. on Hum. Rts. 512, 748, 788-94 (Eur. Comm'n of Hum. Rts.) (extracts from commission's report) (citations omitted):

[Ed. Note: This case involved the detention and interrogation of persons in Northern Ireland by British authorities. The authorities used a combination of five techniques including: forcing detainees to stand for periods of several hours leaning against a wall, keeping black hoods over the detainees' heads at all times except during interrogation, holding detainees pending interrogation in a room where there was a continuous loud hissing noise, depriving detainees of sleep pending interrogation, and depriving detainees of adequate food and drink during the period of detention.

The government of Ireland lodged an application with the European Commission, alleging that these interrogation practices violated Article 3 of the European Convention.]

2.   *The interpretation of Art. 3*

The ordinary meaning and purpose of Art. 3 of the Convention which provides that "no one shall be subjected to torture or to inhuman or degrading treatment or punishment" does not seem difficult to assess.

Difficulties arise, however, when it comes to defining the scope of the terms concerned and to applying them to the circumstances of particular acts purported to be in breach of that provision.

In the First Greek Case the Commission considered the notions of "torture," "inhuman treatment" and "degrading treatment" first in relation to each other and found that "all torture must be inhuman and degrading treatment and inhuman treatment also degrading." Describing each notion separately, it started from the notion of "inhuman treatment" which covered "at least such treatment as deliberately causes severe suffering, mental or physical, which, in the particular situation, is unjustifiable." As regards "torture" the Commission considered that it was "often used to describe inhuman treatment, which has a purpose, such as the obtaining of information or confessions, or the infliction of punishment, and it is generally an aggravated form of inhuman treatment." Finally, "[t]reatment or punishment of an individual may be said to be degrading if it grossly humiliates him before others or drives him to act against his will or conscience."

The Commission also explained further what constituted nonphysical torture, namely "the infliction of mental suffering by creating a state of anguish and stress by means other than bodily assault."

Finally, the Commission distinguished in the Greek Case between acts prohibited by Art. 3 and what it called "a certain roughness of treatment." The Commission considered that such roughness was tolerated by most detainees and even taken for granted. It "may take the form of slaps or blows of the hand on the head or face. This underlines the fact that the point up to which prisoners and the public may accept physical violence as being neither cruel nor excessive varies between different societies and even between different sections of them."

Concerning the five techniques in the present case, the Commission considers that it should express an opinion only as to whether or not the way in which they were applied here, namely in combination with each other, was in breach of Art. 3. It observes that, if they were considered separately deprivation of sleep or restrictions on diet might not as such be regarded as constituting treatment prohibited by Art. 3. It would rather depend on the circumstances and the purpose and would largely be a question of degree.

In the present case, the five techniques applied together were designed to put severe mental and physical stress, causing severe suffering, on a person in order to obtain information from him. It is true that all methods of interrogation which go beyond the mere asking of questions may bring some pressure on the person concerned, but they cannot, by that very fact, be called inhuman. The five techniques are to be distinguished from those methods.

Compared with inhuman treatment [as defined in the *Greek Case*] the stress caused by the application of the five techniques is not only different in degree. The combined application of methods which prevent the use of the senses, especially the eyes and the ears, directly affects the personality physically and mentally. The will to resist or to give in cannot, under such conditions, be formed with any degree of independence. Those most firmly resistant might give in at an early stage when subjected to this sophisticated method to break or even eliminate the will.

It is this character of the combined use of the five techniques which, in the opinion of the Commission, renders them in breach of Art. 3 of the Convention in the form not only of inhuman and degrading treatment, but also of torture within the meaning of that provision. . . .

*   *   *   *   *

Ireland v. United Kingdom, 25 Eur. Ct. H.R. (ser. A) 65-67 (1978):

[Ed. Note: After the Commission delivered its report in *Ireland v. United Kingdom*, the Irish government referred the case to the European Court of Human Rights. The following is an excerpt from the Court's decision.]

162.   As was emphasized by the Commission, ill-treatment must attain a minimum level of severity if it is to fall within the scope of Article 3. The assessment of this minimum is, in the nature of things, relative; it depends on all the circumstances of the case, such as the duration of the treatment, its physical or mental effects and, in some cases, the sex, age and state of health of the victim, etc. . . .

164.   In the instant case, the only relevant concepts are "torture" and "inhuman or degrading treatment", to the exclusion of "inhuman or degrading punishment". . . .

167.   The five techniques were applied in combination, with premeditation and for hours at a stretch; they caused, if not actual bodily injury, at least intense physical and mental suffering to the persons subjected thereto and also led to acute psychiatric disturbances during interrogation. They accordingly fell into the category of inhuman treatment within the meaning of Article 3. The techniques were also degrading since they were such as to arouse in their victims feelings of fear, anguish and inferiority capable of humiliating and debasing them and possibly breaking their physical or moral resistance.

On these two points, the Court is of the same view as the Commission.

In order to determine whether the five techniques should also be qualified as torture, the Court must have regard to the distinction, embodied in Article 3, between this notion and that of inhuman or degrading treatment.

In the Court's view, this distinction derives principally from a difference in the intensity of the suffering inflicted.

The Court considers in fact that, whilst there exists on the one hand violence which is to be condemned both on moral grounds and also in most cases under the domestic law of the Contracting States but which does not fall within Article 3 of the Convention, it appears on the other hand that it was the intention that the Convention, with its distinction between "torture" and "inhuman or degrading treatment", should by the first of these terms attach a special stigma to deliberate inhuman treatment causing very serious and cruel suffering.

Moreover, this seems to be the thinking lying behind Article I *in fine* of Resolution 3452 (XXX) adopted by the General Assembly of the United Nations on 9 December 1975, which declares: "Torture constitutes an *aggravated* and deliberate form of cruel, inhuman or degrading treatment or punishment".

Although the five techniques, as applied in combination, undoubtedly amounted to inhuman and degrading treatment, although their object was the extraction of confessions, the naming of others and/or information and although they were used systematically, they did not occasion suffering of the particular intensity and cruelty implied by the word torture as so understood.

168.   The Court concludes that recourse to the five techniques amounted to a practice of inhuman and degrading treatment, which practice was in breach of Article 3.

*   *   *   *   *

Tyrer Case, 26 Eur. Ct. H.R. (ser. A) 14-17 (1978) (citations omitted):

[Ed. Note: This case involved a 15-year-old citizen of the United Kingdom and a resident of the Isle of Man. He assaulted a schoolmate and was sentenced to three strokes of a birch in accordance with Manx law. He appealed his case, but the appeal was dismissed. Subsequently, police officers birched him at a police station in accordance with his sentence. They forced him to take down his trousers and underwear and bend over a table in preparation for the birching. Two officers held him while another officer administered the punishment. The birching raised his skin but did not cut it. He was sore for approximately 10 days after the birching.

He then lodged an application with the European Commission, claiming a violation of Article 3 and other articles of the European Convention. The Commission concluded that the corporal punishment inflicted was degrading and violated Article 3. The Commission then referred the case to the Court of Human Rights.]

29.   The Court shares the Commission's view that Mr. Tyrer's punishment did not amount to "torture" within the meaning of Article 3. The Court does not consider that the facts of this particular case reveal that the applicant underwent suffering of the level inherent in this notion as it was interpreted and applied by the Court in its judgment of 18 January 1978 (Ireland v. the United Kingdom, Series A no. 25, pp. 66-67 and 68, §§ 167 and 174).

That judgment also contains various indications concerning the notions of "inhuman treatment" and "degrading treatment" but it deliberately left aside the notions of "inhuman punishment" and "degrading punishment" which alone are relevant in the present case (ibid., p. 65, § 164). Those indications accordingly cannot as such, serve here. Nevertheless, it remains true that the suffering occasioned must attain a particular level before a punishment can be classified as "inhuman" within the meaning of Article 3. Here again, the Court does not consider on the facts of the case that that level was attained and it therefore concurs with the Commission that the penalty imposed on Mr. Tyrer was not "inhuman punishment" within the meaning of Article 3. Accordingly, the only question for decision is whether he was subjected to a "degrading punishment" contrary to that Article.

30.   The Court notes first of all that a person may be humiliated by the mere fact of being criminally convicted. However, what is relevant for the purposes of Article 3 is that he should be humiliated not simply by his conviction but by the execution of the punishment which is imposed on him. In fact, in most if not all cases this may be one of the effects of judicial punishment, involving as it does unwilling subjection to the demands of the penal system.

. . . It would be absurd to hold that judicial punishment generally, by reason of its usual and perhaps almost inevitable element of humiliation, is "degrading" within the meaning of Article 3. Some further criterion must be read into the text. Indeed, Article 3, by expressly prohibiting "inhuman" and "degrading" punishment, implies that there is a distinction between such punishment and punishment in general.

In the Court's view, in order for a punishment to be "degrading" and in breach of Article 3, the humiliation or debasement involved must attain a particular level and must in any event be other than that usual element of humiliation referred to in the preceding subparagraph. The assessment is, in the nature of things, relative: it depends on all the circumstances of the case and, in particular, on the nature and context of the punishment itself and the manner and method of its execution.

31. The Attorney-General for the Isle of Man argued that the judicial corporal punishment at issue in this case was not in breach of the Convention since it did not outrage public opinion in the Island. However, even assuming that local public opinion can have an incidence on the interpretation of the concept of "degrading punishment" appearing in Article 3, the Court does not regard it as established that judicial corporal punishment is not considered degrading by those members of the Manx population who favour its retention: it might well be that one of the reasons why they view the penalty as an effective deterrent is precisely the element of degradation which it involves. As regards their belief that judicial corporal punishment deters criminals, it must be pointed out that a punishment does not lose its degrading character just because it is believed to be, or actually is, an effective deterrent or aid to crime control. Above all, as the Court must emphasise, it is never permissible to have recourse to punishments which are contrary to Article 3, whatever their deterrent effect may be.

The Court must also recall that the Convention is a living instrument which, as the Commission rightly stressed, must be interpreted in the light of present-day conditions. In the case now before it the Court cannot but be influenced by the developments and commonly accepted standards in the penal policy of the member States of the Council of Europe in [abolishing corporal punishment]. Indeed, the Attorney-General for the Isle of Man mentioned that, for many years, the provisions of Manx legislation concerning judicial corporal punishment had been under review.

32. As regards the manner and method of execution of the birching inflicted on Mr. Tyrer, the Attorney-General for the Isle of Man drew particular attention to the fact that the punishment was carried out in private and without publication of the name of the offender.

Publicity may be a relevant factor in assessing whether a punishment is "degrading" within the meaning of Article 3, but the Court does not consider that absence of publicity will necessarily prevent a given punishment from falling into that category: it may well suffice that the victim is humiliated in his own eyes, even if not in the eyes of others. . . .

33. Nevertheless, the Court must consider whether the other circumstances of the applicant's punishment were such as to make it "degrading" within the meaning of Article 3.

The very nature of judicial corporal punishment is that it involves one human being inflicting physical violence on another human being. Furthermore, it is institutionalised violence, that is in the present case violence permitted by the law, ordered by the judicial authorities of the State and carried out by the police authorities of the State. Thus, although the applicant did not suffer any severe or long-lasting physical effects, his punishment—whereby he was treated as an object in the power of the authorities—constituted an assault on precisely that which it is one of the main purposes of Article 3 to protect, namely a person's dignity and physical integrity. Neither can it be excluded that the punishment may have had adverse psychological effects.

The institutionalized character of this violence is further compounded by the whole aura of official procedure attending the punishment and by the fact that those inflicting it were total strangers to the offender.

Admittedly, the relevant legislation provides that in any event birching shall not take place later than six months after the passing of sentence. However, this does not alter the fact that there had been an interval of several weeks since the applicant's conviction by the juvenile court and a considerable delay in the police station where the punishment was carried out. Accordingly, in addition to the physical pain he experienced, Mr. Tyrer was subjected to the mental anguish of anticipating the violence he was to have inflicted on him. . . .

35.   Accordingly, viewing these circumstances as a whole, the Court finds that the applicant was subjected to a punishment in which the element of humiliation attained the level inherent in the notion of "degrading punishment" as explained at paragraph 30 above. The indignity of having the punishment administered over the bare posterior aggravated to some extent the degrading character of the applicant's punishment but it was not the only or determining factor.

The Court therefore concludes that the judicial corporal punishment inflicted on the applicant amounted to degrading punishment within the meaning of Article 3 of the Convention.

NOTES AND QUESTIONS

1.   In the *Tyrer* case the European Court of Human Rights stated that for corporal punishment to be degrading, it must "attain a particular level" of severity. The Court found that the punishment at issue did attain this "particular level" but otherwise gave little guidance regarding the definition of "degrading."

In 1993, the Court again examined a case of corporal punishment alleged to have been degrading. *See Case of Costello-Roberts v. United Kingdom*, 247-C Eur. Ct. H.R. (ser. A), No. 89/1991/341/414 (1993). The Court held that the corporal punishment inflicted in that case did not constitute "degrading punishment" because it did not reach the required "minimum threshold of severity." Slip op. at 11.

In *Costello-Roberts*, the punishment at issue occurred in October 1985. Jeremy Costello-Roberts, then seven years old, was a student at a private boarding school. At the school, students receive demerit marks for misbehavior. Upon receiving five demerit marks, they are "slippered," whereby the school's headmaster "whacks" them on the bottom three times with a rubber-soled gym shoe. Jeremy received his fifth demerit mark for talking in the hall. About a week later the headmaster "slippered" him. *Id*. at 3.

Jeremy wrote to his mother about the slippering. *Id*. She then contacted the school to express disapproval. She also complained to the police, and to the National Society for the Prevention of Cruelty to Children, but was told no action could be taken without any visible bruising on the child. She then lodged a complaint with the European Commission of Human Rights.

The Commission referred the case to the Court. By 5-4 vote, the Court decided that the school's actions did not constitute degrading punishment. The Court discussed Tyrer's "minimum level of severity," then stated:

The assessment of this minimum level of severity depends on all the circumstances of the case. Factors such as the nature and context of the punishment, the manner and method of its execution, its duration, its physical and mental effects and, in some instances, the sex, age and state of health of the victim must all be taken into account.

Applying this standard to Jeremy, the Court found that he "adduced no evidence of any severe or long-lasting effects as a result of the treatment complained of." Therefore, though the Court disapproved of the "automatic nature of the punishment," the Court found that the punishment did not violate Article 3. *Id.*

2.   In *Tyrer*, the Court found that punishment could be degrading even when the recipient does not suffer "severe or long-lasting *physical* effects." *Tyrer*, at para. 33 (emphasis added). Did the Court step away from this standard in *Costello-Roberts*? What do you suppose the Court there meant by "severe or long-lasting effects"? Was there a crucial difference between *Tyrer* and *Costello-Roberts*?

3.   Should the European interpretation of degrading treatment be applied elsewhere? In the United States, Congressman Major Owens (D-NY) introduced a bill, in January 1996, that would deny federal funding to schools and other educational programs that allow corporal punishment. H.R. 2918 would allow school personnel to use reasonable physical restraint in order to prevent injury to themselves or others, to obtain possession of a weapon or dangerous object from a child, or to protect property from serious damage. Owens previously introduced similar bills, but they were not enacted.

Geneva Conventions for the Protection of Victims of Armed Conflict, 75 U.N.T.S. 31, 85, 135, 287, Common Article 3, *entered into force* Oct. 21, 1950:

In the case of armed conflict not of an international character occurring in the territory of one of the High Contracting Parties, each Party to the conflict shall be bound to apply, as a minimum, the following provisions:

1.   Persons taking no active part in the hostilities, including members of armed forces who have laid down their arms and those placed *hors de combat* by sickness, wounds, detention, or any other cause, shall in all circumstances be treated humanely, without any adverse distinction founded on race, colour, religion or faith, sex, birth or wealth, or any other similar criteria.

To this end, the following acts are and shall remain prohibited at any time and in any place whatsoever with respect to the above-mentioned persons:
   (a)   violence to life and person, in particular murder of all kinds, mutilation, cruel treatment and torture;
   (b)   taking of hostages;
   (c)   outrages upon personal dignity, in particular humiliating and degrading treatment. . . .

*   *   *   *   *

RESTATEMENT (THIRD) OF THE FOREIGN RELATIONS LAW OF THE UNITED STATES (1987):

§ 702.   Customary International Law of Human Rights

A state violates international law if, as a matter of state policy, it practices, encourages, or condones

(a)   genocide,
(b)   slavery or slave trade,
(c)   the murder or causing the disappearance of individuals,
(d)   torture or other cruel, inhuman, or degrading treatment or punishment,
(e)   prolonged arbitrary detention,
(f)   systematic racial discrimination, or
(g)   a consistent pattern of gross violations of internationally recognized human rights.

3.   U.N. Response to Amputations Under the Islamic Penal Code of Sudan

The penal code of Sudan has prescribed the amputation (right hand or right hand and left foot) for offenses of theft and persistent or armed robbery. The penal sanctions are based on Islamic law (Shari'a). Over 120 such amputations were carried out in a two-year period by the previous government which was overthrown in 1985. The code was not changed by the new government and offenders continued to be sentenced to amputation although the sentences were not carried out. Amnesty International, *Amputation Sentences* (1987) (AI Index: AFR 54/01/87); INTERNATIONAL COMM'N JURISTS, THE RETURN OF DEMOCRACY IN SUDAN 72-73 (1986).

In response to this situation, the U.N. Sub-Commission on Prevention of Discrimination and Protection of Minorities adopted a resolution in 1984 which recommended that the Commission on Human Rights urge governments to abolish amputation as a penal sanction. The Sub-Commission recalled Article 5 of the Universal Declaration of Human Rights as the basis for the resolution. *Report of the Sub-Commission on Prevention of Discrimination and Protection of Minorities, 37th Session* at 95, U.N. Doc. E/CN.4/1985/3; E/CN.4/Sub.2/1984/43 (1985).

The original draft of the resolution called directly on Sudan to abolish the infliction of amputation as a penalty. A number of Sub-Commission members, however, questioned the appropriateness of challenging Islamic law, judging internal penal policies, or singling out Sudan for condemnation. The revised text omitted references to Islamic law and Sudan and was readily adopted. NIGEL RODLEY, THE TREATMENT OF PRISONERS UNDER INTERNATIONAL LAW 246 (1987). The Sub-Commission's parent body, the Commission on Human Rights, took no action, however, in response to this resolution.

E.   THEORETICAL FOUNDATIONS OF HUMAN RIGHTS: NATURAL LAW, POSITIVISM, AND ISLAMIC PRINCIPLES

Several theoretical bases of human rights are examined in detail in chapter 14, *infra*, at 677-697. Before proceeding, students should read carefully those materials. The following excerpt supplements them by discussing natural law, positivist, and Islamic approaches.

Myres S. McDougal, Harold D. Lasswell, & Lung-Chu Chen, Human Rights and World Public Order: The Basic Policies of an International Law of Human Dignity 68-71, 73-75 (1980) (footnotes omitted):

The Natural Law Approach

The natural law approach begins with the assumption that there are natural laws, both theological and metaphysical, which confer certain particular rights upon individual human beings. These rights find their authority either in divine will or in specified metaphysical absolutes. The natural law constitutes a "higher law" which is the ultimate standard of fitness of all . . . national or international [law]; decisions by state elites which are taken contrary to this law are regarded as mere exercises of naked power.

The great historic contribution of the natural law emphasis has been in the affording of this appeal from the realities of naked power to a higher authority which is asserted to require the protection of individual rights. The observational standpoint assumed by those who take this approach has commonly been that of identification with the whole of humanity. A principal emphasis has been upon a common human nature that implies comparable rights and equality for all. For many centuries this approach has been an unfailing source of articulated demand and of theoretical justification for human rights. . . .

The principal inadequacies of the natural law approach stem from its conception of authority. When authority is conceived in terms of divine will or metaphysical absolutes, little encouragement is given to that comprehensive and selective inquiry about empirical processes which is indispensable to the management of the variables that in fact affect decision. It is not to be expected, further, that scholars and decision makers, whose primary concern is to put into effect on earth either divine will or the import of transcendental essences, will devote much attention to the formulation of human rights problems in terms of the shaping and sharing of values or to the location of such problems in the larger community processes which affect their solution. Similarly, the establishment of the most basic, overriding, and abstract goals of the community by the use of exercises in faith, rather than by the empirical exploration of common interest, can only provoke the assertion of different, and perhaps opposing, goals by those who profess a different faith.

The intellectual task most relied upon in the natural law approach is syntactic derivation. Though appropriate concern is exhibited for the establishment and clarification of goals, the method by which clarification is sought for decision in particular instances is not by the disciplined, systematic employment of a variety of relevant intellectual skills, but rather by derivation from postulated norms achieved by techniques such as the revelation of divine will, messages obtained by consultation of oracles or entrails, transcendental cognition of absolutes, and participation in natural reason. . . . The abiding difficulty with the natural law approach is that its assumptions, intellectual procedures, and modalities of justification can be employed equally by the proponents of human dignity and the proponents of human indignity in support of diametrically opposed empirical specifications of rights, and neither set of proponents has at its disposal any means of confirming the one claim or of disconfirming the other. . . .

The Positivist Approach

The positivist approach assumes that the most important measure of human rights is to be found in the authoritative enactment of a system of law sustained by organized community coercion. Within this approach authority is found in the perspectives of established officials, and any appeal to a "higher law" for the protection of individual rights is regarded as utopian or at least as a meta-legal aspiration. . . .

The great contribution of the positivists has been in recognizing the importance of bringing organized community coercion, the state's established processes of authoritative decision, to bear upon the protection of human rights. By focusing upon deprivations in concrete situations and by stressing the importance of structures and procedures, as well as prescriptions, at phases of implementation, the positivists have enhanced the protection of many particular rights and strengthened explicit concern for more comprehensive means of fulfillment.

The fatal weakness of the positivist approach is in its location of authority in the perspective of established officials. The rules of law expressing these perspectives are commonly assumed to have a largely autonomous reference, different from community policy in context. . . . Actually, in the positivist approach the task of specifying the detailed content of the human rights protected in a community goes forward very much as in the natural law approach—by logical, syntactic derivation. The difference is that, while the natural lawyer takes off from theological or metaphysical absolutes, the positivist takes off from assumptions about the empirical reference of traditional legal concepts.

The difficulties inherent in clarifying the content of human rights, either as a whole or in particular, by relying on logical derivation from highly abstract and traditional legal concepts are multiple. The most obvious difficulty is that the inherited concepts may embody not the values of human dignity, but those of human indignity.

*   *   *   *   *

S. FAROOQ A. HASSAN, THE ISLAMIC REPUBLIC: POLITICS, LAW AND ECONOMY 106-21 (1984) (footnotes and citations omitted):

Shariah: Basic Constitutional Concepts

Prophet Mohammed showed a path to mankind, the path of a universal law, i.e. the Shariah. Contrary to the rigid limitations of race, national frontiers, language, and geographical configuration, it contains many commandments about the political setup of an ideal Islamic community. . . .

The Shariah contains many principles for public, private, social, national, and international conduct; these principles govern all human action for life in this world and also for life hereafter. . . . Shariah is . . . a complete science which is not specialized for a particular period of time, but is meant for all periods and times. It cannot be amended or modified . . . for it is given by God, who is Perfect and Creator of the universe and all things. The principles laid down by the Shariah are above every man-made society and, being perennial, are adoptable for every new situation. . . .

The system of the Shariah is based upon divine principles and its institutions are sacred. The infringement of the moral rules of the system, as opposed to secular rules, includes unlawful conduct, and it is also a sin against religion and God. There is a double protection of human rights. The rules of law work not only for the prevention of injurious conduct towards others, but they also go deeper than other systems through internal conscience. It is not only an offense but is also a sin to injure or damage the rights of other individuals.

The basic and most fundamental right is the protection of life. (Article 3 of the Universal Declaration of Human Rights, 1948). The Quran declares: "If anyone slew a person unless it be for murder or for preventing mischief in the land, it would be as if he slew the whole people; and if anyone saved a life, it would be as if he saved the life of the whole people". Moreover, the Quran declares: "And slay not the life which Allah hath forbidden save with right". Apart from this right, Constitutional laws and various international documents attempt to guarantee other rights, like that of property, reputation or family. The provisions of the Quran are more clear on this subject. Thus, dishonoring others, hoarding, smuggling, defamation, back biting, and destroying others' property are declared offenses and sins.

The conception of freedom recognized by the Shariah is much wider than is commonly perceived. The rules of Shariah provide for the freedom of religion, conscience, expression, speech, avocation, movement, education, assembly, etc. . . . The freedom given to man is related to the establishment of right and justice. The Quran makes it the duty of every individual to speak the truth without any fear. . . . This freedom is given through limitations set up in public interest, and anything which disturbs the public in general is not permitted. All possible methods of demonstration against evil by expression are possible, but they must be under the limits of the rules of morality. Freedom of speech must observe the constitutional means for expression. It should not be violent and injurious and should not give rise to other evils or wrongs. Nevertheless, the Shariah makes provision for rising against authority when there is a violation of the sacred principles on its part. The traditions of the Prophet make it clear that orders or directions to do what is sinful are not to be obeyed. . . .

The conception of *pacta sunt servanda* [treaties are to be observed] has a special place in any law, so the Muslims are bound by their stipulations. . . . The social and economic rights of the community are safeguarded by the particular guarantee of freedom of contract. In addition to the secular operation of contracts between the parties, it is a divine institution. . . . The moral sanctity in Islam of contracts makes redundant the modern international law recourse to the doctrine of *pacta sunt servanda*. Thus treaties, like contracts, are binding because Providence has commanded in His law to make all agreements binding.

The contemporary declarations on human rights especially provide and preach for the right to equality and equal protection of the law. In addition to Article 1 of the Universal Declaration (also Article 2), similar elements are contained in most modern constitutions. To what extent these declarations are implemented is another question. The principles of justice in the Shariah incorporate perfect observation of equality before law and equal protection thereof without any kind of discrimination whatsoever. . . . The exercise of justice and its principles is a vital rule of religion, and it is a duty of every Muslim to abide by these principles. The Quran further says that there is to be no discrimination between the sexes; that man is one nation and no discrimination is allowed on the basis of race, region, caste, color, religion, etc. The traditions of the Prophet contain many principles of justice and equality in treatment of men and women. The notion of justice in the Shariah binds a Muslim not only to God but also to his fellow men including the non-Muslims. This principle is applied not only to private matters but also in public transactions and even in international relations. There is a sacred duty to administer justice without any fear or prejudice, and the history of Islam has many remarkable examples in the dispensation of justice.

The modern approaches, in protecting human rights, operate upon the principles of rights of the people. The concept of democracy which establishes a State by the people, must work for the betterment of human life. The Shariah's conception of Umma is a system which has the same goals for an Islamic State. But it was centuries before the modern notions came to be established. . . . The principles of the Shariah lay down the limitations of any ruler. When the ruler violates the rules of the Shariah, particularly those dealing with human rights, it is a person's duty to disobey such ruler's authority. The concepts of imamate and caliphate are based upon the theory of the trust of the public. The moment the ruler or the government violates the mandate of God and His book, the change of government is essential. . . . It leads to the natural result that the Shariah principles imply the protection of human rights in a most comprehensive manner. Only some of them have been reproduced in the above pages. They are enough to show the vast field covered by the list of human rights of the Shariah.

NOTES AND QUESTIONS

1.   Farooq Hassan, author of the preceding excerpt, is a professor of law, a member of the International Institute of Strategic Studies in London, and a member of the bar of the United Kingdom, Pakistan, and the United States. In his preface, the author states that he prepared the text in part to respond to interest in the concept of an ideal Islamic state generated by the emergence of the Islamic Republic of Iran. He bases his work in the primary sources for Islamic jurisprudence—the Qur'an and the Sunnah—and avoids citing post-tenth-century authors. Yet, he states that his interpretations fall in the Sunni school of Islamic law. The Islamic Republic of Iran, however, is founded on the views of the Shi'a school.

2.   For further reading on the theoretical basis of human rights in Islam, see

PARVEEN SHAUKAT ALI, HUMAN RIGHTS IN ISLAM (1980);

ABDULLAHI AHMED AN-NA'IM, TOWARD AN ISLAMIC REFORMATION: CIVIL LIBERTIES, HUMAN RIGHTS, AND INTERNATIONAL LAW (1990);

Karima Bennoune, *As-Salamu 'Alaykum?—Humanitarian Law in Islamic Jurisprudence*, 15 MICH. J. INT'L L. 605 (1994);

CONFERENCES ON MOSLEM DOCTRINE AND HUMAN RIGHTS IN ISLAM (1974);

KEVIN DWYER, ARAB VOICES: THE HUMAN RIGHTS DEBATE IN THE MIDDLE EAST (1991);

Ahmad Farrag, *Human Rights and Liberties in Islam, in* HUMAN RIGHTS IN A PLURALIST WORLD (J. Berting et al. eds., 1990);

Suhail Hashmi, *Is There an Islamic Ethic of Humanitarian Intervention?*, 7 ETHICS & INT'L AFF. 55 (1993);

Riffat Hassan, *On Human Rights and the Qur'anic Perspective*, 19 J. ECUMENICAL STUD. 51 (Summer 1982);

HUMAN RIGHTS IN ISLAM: REPORT OF A SEMINAR HELD IN KUWAIT, December 1980 (1982) (Islamic scholars from various countries, including at least one Iranian, participated in the seminar.);

Note, *Human Rights Practices in the Arab States: The Modern Impact of Shari'a Values*, 12 GA. J. INT'L & COMP. L. 55 (1982);

INTERNATIONAL INSTITUTE OF HIGHER STUDIES IN CRIMINAL SCIENCES, DRAFT CHARTER OF HUMAN AND PEOPLE'S RIGHTS IN THE ARAB WORLD (1987);

INTERNATIONAL INSTITUTE OF HUMAN RIGHTS, POUR UNE COMMISSION D'ETUDE SUR LA PROTECTION DES DROITS DE L'HOMME DANS LE CONTEXT MUSULMAN (1971);

INTERNATIONAL INSTITUTE OF HUMAN RIGHTS, SÉLECTION BIBLIOGRAPHIQUE DES OUVRAGES CONCERNANT DE DROIT EN GÉNÉRAL ET LES DROITS DE L'HOMME DANS LES PAYS ISLAMIQUES (1971);

La Commission Arabe des Droits de L'Homme, 3 HUM. RTS. J. 101 (1970);

TORE LINDHOLM & KARI VOGT, ISLAMIC LAW REFORM AND HUMAN RIGHTS: CHALLENGES AND REJOINDERS (1993);

Ann Elizabeth Mayer, *Universal Versus Islamic Human Rights: A Clash of Cultures or a Clash with a Construct?*, 15 MICH. J. INT'L L. 307 (1994);

ANN ELIZABETH MAYER, ISLAM AND HUMAN RIGHTS: TRADITION AND POLITICS (1991);

Seyyed Hossein Nasr, *The Concept and Reality of Freedom in Islam and Islamic Civilization, in* THE PHILOSOPHY OF HUMAN RIGHTS: INTERNATIONAL PERSPECTIVES 95 (Rosenbaum ed. 1980) (The author is a former director of the Iranian Academy of Philosophy.);

Abdul Aziz Said, *Human Rights in Islamic Perspectives, in* HUMAN RIGHTS: CULTURE AND IDEOLOGICAL PERSPECTIVES 86 (A. Pollis & P. Schwab eds. 1979) (The author was Professor of International Relations at the American University, Washington, D.C. at the time the book was published.);

Leila P. Sayeh & Adriaen M. Morse, Jr., *Islam and the Treatment of Women: An Incomplete Understanding of Gradualism*, 30 TEX. INT'L L.J. 311 (1995).

F. CULTURAL RELATIVISM AND INTERNATIONAL HUMAN RIGHTS LAW

Cultural relativity advocates argue that traditional cultures often justify deviations from international human rights standards. This position and several counter-arguments are discussed in detail in chapter 14.

The issue of cultural relativism arises in many contexts. For example, the Ayatollah Khomeini, leader of Iran, in 1989 issued an order for followers to kill a British author, Salman Rushdie, for writing a book called *The Satanic Verses*. Rushdie had been raised in the Islamic faith, but Khomeini found parts of the book heretical. In the faith as it is practiced in Iran the killing of heretics presumably was acceptable.

In a similar case in Bangladesh, fundamentalist Islamic groups called for the death of Taslima Nasrin for her publication of *Lajja*, a novel criticizing Islam. Authorities issued a warrant for her arrest on charges of blasphemy. *See* Mary Anne Weaver, *A Fugitive from Injustice*, NEW YORKER, Sept. 12, 1994, at 48. For additional reading on the rise in threats and violence against Arab artists and performers, see S.L. Bachman, *Women Lessen Impact of Muslim Conservatives*, NEW ORLEANS TIMES-PICAYUNE, July 30, 1995, at A38; Yasmine Bahrani, *The Rushdie Specter: For Muslim Intellectuals the Danger Deepens*, WASH. POST, Aug. 14, 1994, at C1; Kim Murphy, *Islamic Militants Target Arab Intellectuals, Artists*, LOS ANGELES TIMES, Nov. 28, 1994, at A1.

NOTES AND QUESTIONS

In 1994, Michael Fay, an 18-year-old U.S. citizen, received four lashes with a rattan cane as punishment for vandalism in Singapore. The government reduced the punishment from six lashes to four in a gesture of goodwill toward the U.S. but refused to commute the sentence. Fay originally confessed to vandalism but later recanted, claiming that the confession was coerced and that he had been subjected to ill-treatment by the police.

Should the argument for cultural relativism in human rights extend to the killing of heretics? To other extreme forms of punishment? Where would you draw the line? What kind of standard might keep cultural variations within limits? Might additional arguments be raised when the victim is not a member of the culture condoning the practice?

CHAPTER 5

WHAT U.N. PROCEDURES ARE AVAILABLE FOR VIOLATIONS OF HUMAN RIGHTS?

ECOSOC Resolutions 1235 and 1503; Thematic Procedures

A. INTRODUCTION   Page   174

B. QUESTIONS   174

C. BACKGROUND ON BURMA (MYANMAR)   176
     Stan Sesser, A Rich Country Gone Wrong   176
     Human Rights Watch, Burma (Myanmar)   180

D. U.N. PROCEDURES FOR RESPONDING TO HUMAN RIGHTS VIOLATIONS   181

   1. Development of Major U.N. Procedures   182
     ECOSOC Resolution 728F   182
     ECOSOC Resolution 1235   184
     ECOSOC Resolution 1503   185

   2. Overview of the 1503 Procedure in Practice   187

   3. Theme Procedures   191
     David Weissbrodt, The Three "Theme" Special Rapporteurs of the UN Commission on Human Rights   192
     Report on the visit to Peru by two members of the Working Group on Enforced or Involuntary Disappearances   202
     Report on a second visit to Peru by two members of the Working Group on Enforced or Involuntary Disappearances   205

   4. Further Remarks on 1235, 1503, and the Theme Procedures   208
     Marc Bossuyt, The Development of Procedures of the U.N. Commissionon Human Rights   211
     Sandra Coliver, U.N. Machineries on Women's Rights   214
     Amnesty International, Oral Statement on Thematic Mechanisms   214

   5. Freedom of Information Act (FOIA) and Confidentiality Under ECOSOC 1503 in regard to the U.S.   216

A. INTRODUCTION

The preceding chapters have introduced how governments ratify or accede to human rights treaties and have dealt with the most prevalent technique for implementing human rights treaties, that is, periodic reporting and review by treaty bodies, such as the Human Rights Committee and the Committee on Economic, Social and Cultural Rights. Chapter 4 also introduced another technique for implementing human rights treaty obligations, that is, individual complaints against a government. Individual human rights complaints and other adjudicative techniques will be discussed more fully in chapters 10 through 14, *infra*.

The periodic reporting and review mechanisms are available, however, only for governments which have ratified human rights treaties. The individual complaint procedures also require that governments specifically accept those procedures. While the reporting and review mechanisms are very thorough and painstaking, they generally require a country to report only once every two to five years. While there are provisions for more urgent reports, the treaty bodies are generally not very visible and are not particularly well adapted to handling emergency situations. Similarly, the individual complaint mechanisms cannot provide an adequate international response for human rights emergencies involving large numbers of persons.

This chapter deals with the U.N. procedures which have been established to handle consistent patterns of gross human rights violations throughout the world. The procedures do not rely upon a specific treaty, but are based on resolutions of the Economic and Social Council (ECOSOC)—principally, resolutions 1235 and 1503. The chapter also deals with the closely associated "thematic" procedures, which concentrate on violations occurring in any country and take a subject-oriented approach.

The chapter asks the reader to relate the U.N. procedures to human rights conditions in Myanmar (previously known as Burma).[1] The situation in that country has undergone much change and likely will continue changing. Hence, the material in the book must be taken as a snapshot of the conditions in the country as of a particular moment, that is, early 1996.

This chapter gives the reader an opportunity to look at the facts and to identify the human rights norms that may have been violated. The reader must also determine how best to approach the U.N. since there are three basic alternatives: the public procedure established by ECOSOC resolution 1235 including the establishment of country rapporteurs, the confidential procedure established by ECOSOC resolution 1503, and the thematic procedures of the U.N. Commission on Human Rights.

B. QUESTIONS

Citizens of Myanmar have requested your assistance in presenting their government's human rights violations to the U.N. Consider the following questions. (This problem requires careful construction of U.N. resolutions. Be prepared to use operative language from the resolutions in answering the questions.)

---

[1] Although the country formerly known as the Socialist Republic of the Union of Burma changed its name to the Union of Burma and then to Myanmar, the chapter will use Burma and Myanmar interchangeably.

1.   The U.N. receives thousands of human rights communications each year. Before ECOSOC resolution 728F (1959), the U.N. either discarded the letters (and sometimes, postcards) or filed them without response. In comparison to this initial process, what did 728F achieve?

2.   What did ECOSOC resolution 1235 (1967) add? What does it require be done with communications mentioned in 728F?

3.   What do the materials suggest about the evolution of practice under 1235?

4.   How has ECOSOC resolution 1503 (1970) helped the protection of human rights?

5.   How have the thematic procedures begun in 1980 contributed to the protection of human rights?

6.   What rights in the <u>International Bill of Human Rights</u> has Myanmar arguably violated?   *torture*

7.   Would those violations fall within the scope of resolution 1503? What is the basis for finding "a consistent pattern of gross and reliably attested violations of human rights"? Which thematic procedure might be applicable to the situation in Myanmar?

8.   Which violations alleged under 1503 are most likely to produce a successful complaint? Why? What constitutes success?

   a.   What violations are "gross" under resolutions 1235 or 1503?

   b.   Does Article 4 of the Covenant on Civil and Political Rights, which permits the derogation of certain rights during periods of emergency, suggest which rights ought to be considered "gross"?   *p35 sup*

   c.   Is it more likely that a situation involving the violation of nonderogable rights will be considered "gross"?   *yes*

   d.   Should some violations of derogable rights be considered "gross"?

   e.   Does the International Bill of Human Rights indicate that certain rights ought to be considered more "fundamental" and, thus, their violation might be "gross"?

   f.   In construing what constitutes a "gross" violation under resolutions 1235 and 1503, should primary reference be made to the International Bill of Human Rights? (*See also* Sub-Commission resolution 1 in the accompanying handbook, *Selected International Human Rights Instruments.*)

9.   Do any of the articles of the International Bill of Human Rights arguably provide a defense for Myanmar?

10.   Are violations perpetrated by private individuals or armed opposition groups the responsibility of Myanmar under the International Bill of Human Rights?

11.   What must be kept confidential under resolution 1503? (*See also* Sub-Commission resolution 1.) May a complainant issue a press release announcing submission of a claim under 1503? May the complainant publish the communication?

12.   How may governments respond to complaints made under the 728F procedure? 1235 procedure? 1503 procedure? thematic procedures?   *— publicity*

13.   What are the mechanisms available under the 1235 procedure for inducing a government to improve its human rights record? How do those differ from the mechanisms available under 1503?   *— recommendation - secretive*

14.   In what ways may nongovernmental organizations (NGOs) participate in the 1235 procedure? 1503 procedure? thematic procedures?

15.   If an NGO is presenting a human rights complaint against Myanmar to the U.N., should it choose 1235, 1503, or a thematic procedure? Why?

16.   What is the significance of a "successful" 1503 complaint?

17.   Why have there been so few "successful" 1503 complaints?

18.   Does the 1503 process do more to protect the violating country than to exert pressure for improvement?

19.   For U.S. complainants could 1503 be used with the Freedom of Information Act to pursue litigation and legislative efforts?

20.   To what extent can 1235, 1503, and thematic procedures be used simultaneously or in sequence? Should an NGO mention its 1503 complaint when it presents an oral or written intervention in the Human Rights Commission or the Sub-Commission under resolution 1235?

21.   If an NGO wants to build the kind of consensus needed to establish a country rapporteur or to achieve significant progress under 1235, how could the thematic procedures be useful?

22.   Consider the marked increase in use of thematic procedures in recent years.

a.   Have the thematic procedures covered all or almost all of the "gross violations" to which the 1503 procedure was intended to apply?

b.   Are the thematic procedures more rapid, less subject to political considerations, less complex, more transparent, and more responsive than the 1503 procedure?

c.   In view of the advent of country rapporteurs under resolution 1235 and thematic procedures, is there still a need for the 1503 procedure?

d.   Has the Commission strayed from its original purpose—to offer protection against notably grievous violations—in creating new thematic procedures?

e.   Is there sufficient consensus on the content of all the themes, such as the right to development and discharge of toxic waste, to permit the procedures to take effective action?

f.   Are there practical constraints, such as insufficient staffing and insufficient time for consideration of the thematic reports at the Commission sessions?

g.   Has the Commission on Human Rights begun to use thematic procedures so much and apply them in such diverse areas that the procedures have become less effective?

C.   BACKGROUND ON BURMA (MYANMAR)

Stan Sesser, *A Reporter at Large: A Rich Country Gone Wrong*, NEW YORKER, Oct. 9, 1989, at 55 *et seq.*:

Burma is a nation that does not have to worry about air pollution, because it has little industry. The country also avoids the plague of traffic congestion, because there are few cars. No one complains about urban overcrowding, because in Burma —a country the size of Texas, with forty million people—there are no jobs in the cities to attract migrants. No one needs to organize a historic-preservation movement, because hardly a new building has gone up since the British withdrew, in 1948. Rangoon and Mandalay, the only large cities, boast not a single skyscraper, and in the entire country there are just a handful of elevators and one escalator, which is boarded up. For twenty-seven years, Burma has stood isolated in the world, governed by a brutal and xenophobic military dictatorship, which, though it has maintained diplomatic relations with all major nations and has not refused foreign aid, is as suspicious of anything Russian or Chinese as of anything American. In the nineteen-sixties, the government, to guard against the taint of foreign ideas, limited visitors to a stay of one day. That limit gradually grew with the need for hard currency, jumping from seven days to fourteen in May of this year. But this liberalization came with a significant catch: all tourists must now hire an official government guide, whose duties include restricting contacts with the Burmese people.

For many years, the few visitors who have come have been fascinated by Burma—a nation that for three decades has shut itself off so tightly from the modern world it has all but faded from view. Then, during the summer of 1988, an uprising of unprecedented scale propelled Burma onto the front pages of American newspapers. A people's movement arose with what seemed like total spontaneity. Without any identifiable leadership, without a program or a platform beyond a demand for freedom, students and Buddhist monks took to the streets daily. They rallied their countrymen to the point where even government workers and policemen left their posts to join the demonstration. By September, the entire nation stood allied, opposed only by the government and the Army. America—a remote nation whose wealth and liberty people could only dream about—became a symbol of what the protesters wanted for Burma. Each day in Rangoon, the capital, crowds gathered downtown in front of a former bank building that houses the American Embassy. Hundreds of thousands of Burmese—many of whom did not understand English—marched under English-language banners calling for "DEMOCRACY."

But on September 19th, in an action that now seems almost a blueprint for what happened in China nine months later, soldiers took to the streets and the roofs and gunned down anyone in sight. At the American Embassy, frightened employees huddled on the floor as troops outside fired into groups of demonstrators. At Rangoon General Hospital, the bodies of the dead and the wounded piled up in corridors. The government decreed that from that day on outdoor political gatherings of more than four people would be fired upon. It kept its word. Life in Rangoon changed in many other ways as well, with the closing of all schools, a 10 P.M. curfew, and thousands of political arrests—arrests so numerous that in July the jails were emptied of most common criminals to make room for new political prisoners. . . .

* * * * *

General Saw Maung's military brigade, the State Law and Order Restoration Council (SLORC), has maintained control of the Myanmar government since the September 1988 crackdown on Burmese dissidents. Its rule, however, has been turbulent. Civil unrest has continued to demand the attention of the military leaders, while international condemnation of the SLORC's human rights abuses has forced the government to take steps to try to improve its international reputation.

The SLORC faced its first international challenge when a number of nations— including Japan, the United States, and the European Community—cut off aid to

Myanmar after the military coup. In response, the SLORC in December 1988 promised to hold free elections by May 1990. After the SLORC made this announcement, political leaders established three main opposition parties: the National League for Democracy (NLD), the National Unity Party (NUP, reconstituted from the Burmese Socialist Programme Party), and the League for Democracy (LDP). Domestic and international optimism regarding the prospect of free elections, however, soon faded.

Faith in the electoral process dimmed with the July 1989 arrest of most top opposition leaders. Among those detained was Daw Aung San Suu Kyi, the popular head of the National League for Democracy (NLD). The SLORC also enacted various measures aimed at controlling the outcome of the elections. Those measures required all speeches delivered through the state-controlled media to be submitted seven days in advance, and prohibited all meetings of more than five people that did not have government approval. In addition, the SLORC kept Myanmar's universities closed to reduce student influence on the elections, and postponed elections in some provinces in order to reduce the voting power of ethnic minorities.

Despite these efforts to assure a victory for the SLORC-backed National Unity Party (NUP), the NLD overwhelmingly prevailed at the May 1990 elections, winning over eighty percent of the 485 parliament seats. The SLORC, however, refused to transfer power to the NLD. Instead, the SLORC set up an Election Commission to consider the results of the elections. The SLORC also announced the creation of a Constitutional Convention, which would decide the procedures for drafting a new constitution.

Following the SLORC's refusal to recognize the winners of the May 1990 elections, a number of countries began calling for embargoes and sanctions against Myanmar. The European Community, for example, suggested a worldwide arms embargo against Myanmar, while the United States imposed a series of economic sanctions on the ruling government.

International scrutiny of SLORC rule increased at the end of 1991, when NLD leader Daw Aung San Suu Kyi was awarded the 1991 Nobel Peace Prize. Daw Aung San Suu Kyi, still under house arrest after her detention during the election campaign, was unable to travel to Oslo to accept the award. Her continued imprisonment led a group of Nobel Peace Laureates to call on Myanmar's military rulers to release her, and spurred the United Nations to take a more critical look at Myanmar's human rights record. In addition, the United States cut off all aid to the country, and Japan, which continues to finance humanitarian projects within Myanmar, warned the ruling government that its human rights record must improve.

Domestic strife also increased following the announcement that Daw Aung San Suu Kyi had won the 1991 Nobel Peace Prize. In mid-December of 1991, about 2,000 students gathered outside Rangoon University to protest the military government and to voice support for Daw Aung San Suu Kyi. The SLORC responded by sending troops to quell the protest. The SLORC also announced that Daw Aung San Suu Kyi would never be allowed to lead the country because of her marriage to a foreigner, English professor Michael Aris, and stated that she would not be released from her house arrest until she agreed to leave the country.

In spite of international rebukes and domestic protests, the SLORC further tarnished its human rights record at the beginning of 1992, when its program of persecution sent Myanmar Muslims streaming into neighboring Bangladesh. An estimated 250,000 Muslims sought refuge in Bangladesh after Burmese troops burned their homes, stole their belongings, raped Muslim women, and killed those who protested. The Muslims, known as Rohingyas, said the Myanmar government launched the campaign of persecution against them after refusing to recognize them as Myanmar nationals. In March 1992, a United Nations official, U.N. High Commissioner for Refugees (UNHCR) Director Jamshed Anver, decried Myanmar's claim that Rohingyas are not its nationals. Anver stated that the UNHCR would not accept the expulsion of minority populations from their homelands.

In response, Myanmar officials attempted to improve the country's international reputation by meeting with Bangladesh officials in April 1992 to sign an agreement for the safe, voluntary return of the Muslim refugees. Also in April 1992, the SLORC began releasing political prisoners, and allowed Daw Aung San Suu Kyi to receive a visit from her husband, the first visit for the couple since her arrest three years earlier. In September 1992, the SLORC announced it would lift the last of the martial law decrees that were imposed in 1989, and it allowed the country's universities to re-open after a four-year closure.

These moves by the SLORC did little to appease the international community. Asia Watch, a New York-based human rights group, reported that the changes were cosmetic, and that the human rights situation in Myanmar did not fundamentally improve. At the end of 1992, the United Nations General Assembly condemned the Myanmar government. In addition, the United Nations Commission on Human Rights went ahead with its March 1992 resolution to send a special rapporteur into Myanmar to observe human rights conditions. The special rapporteur, Professor Yozo Yokota (Japan), visited Myanmar in December 1992. Prior to 1992, Myanmar had only been treated by the Commission's confidential procedure.

In January 1993, the Constitutional Convention promised by the SLORC after the May 1990 elections finally met to consider drafting a new constitution for Myanmar. The SLORC did allow members of the National League for Democracy (NLD) to attend the convention, but limited the number of NLD members to 88. NLD members had won 392 parliament seats in the 1990 elections, but most of those NLD members were either under arrest at the time of the convention or were removed from the roster of election winners by the Election Commission. Discussion at the convention, which continues to meet intermittently, is controlled by the military authorities. The convention has been denounced as a sham by Burmese dissidents.

In February 1993, the United Nations Commission on Human Rights received Professor Yokota's report on Myanmar. The report stated that Myanmar's military authorities were "responsible for carrying out arbitrary executions, death under custody and death due to torture within the context of armed conflict." The report further stated that members of Myanmar's ethnic minority groups were the country's main victims of repression. Professor Yokota stated that the SLORC had submitted most minorities to forced labor, and said many were dying of ill-treatment. The report denounced the SLORC for creating "an atmosphere of pervasive fear," and called on the SLORC to free Nobel Peace Laureate Daw Aung San Suu Kyi and to comply with international conventions banning arbitrary executions, torture, and forced child labor. In response to Professor Yokota's report, the Commission adopted a 10 March 1993 resolution condemning Myanmar for its human rights abuses. The Commission also extended Professor Yokota's mandate for another year.

Also during the 1993 session, the Commission on Human Rights heard a proposal from a group of Nobel Peace Laureates to suspend Myanmar from the United Nations. Myanmar's neighbors, including China, Thailand, and the Association of Southeast Asian Nations (ASEAN), have actively opposed the proposal. The ASEAN group, comprising Brunei, Indonesia, Malaysia, the Philippines, Singapore, and Thailand, has maintained diplomatic and trade ties with Myanmar, stating that it can better influence Myanmar with continued contacts. China, meanwhile, has supplied the SLORC with an estimated $1.2 billion worth of military equipment, and Japan has extended about $100 million in developmental aid to Myanmar.

Burma (Myanmar), HUMAN RIGHTS WATCH WORLD REPORT 132-37 (1995):

Human Rights Developments . . .

Some seventy political prisoners were released during the year under SLORC Order 11/92, though there were no details of those released, and it was likely that at least some had served their full sentences.

The National Convention, the constitutional forum established by the SLORC in January 1993, continued with no clear end in sight. Members of political parties elected in May 1990 made up only 14 percent of the 700 delegates, the rest being hand-picked by the SLORC. . . .

Arrest and harassment of the political opposition continued. At least seven people were arrested in May when they stood to watch two foreigners who held aloft banners calling for the release of Aung San Suu Kyi. It is not known if they were later freed or tried. On July 8 and 11, seven people were arrested for distributing pamphlets calling for the release of Aung San Suu Kyi. Although their names are known, no details were available on their trials or sentences. In September, a former UNICEF employee, Khin Zaw Win, and four members of the National League for Democracy (NLD), the opposition party headed by Aung San Suu Kyi, were arrested for passing "fabricated news" to foreign media and embassies and distributing "documents of expatriate groups." On October 9, Khin Zaw Win was sentenced to fifteen years in prison, and San San Nwe, a well-known writer and NLD member, to ten years. The others were all sentenced to eight years. They were tried under the 1950 Emergency Provisions Act and the 1957 Unlawful Associations Act. Most political prisoners in Burma are held under these two laws. . . .

Forced labor took place on a massive scale across the country. Journalists visiting Burma noted that people, including shackled prisoners, were forced to dredge the moat in Mandalay, Burma's second largest city. In Bassein in southern Burma, 30,000 villagers forced to build a new airport reportedly received no wages, food, or medical supplies, despite a cholera outbreak at the site in June. . . .

The trafficking of women into sex slavery in Thailand and elsewhere in Asia continued to be a major problem. There was also a rise in prostitution inside Burma, as the government-promoted tourism industry tried to attract tourists through promoting sexuality of young girls and women. . . .

The U.N. special rapporteur, Professor Yozo Yokota, on his mission in November 1993 was allowed access to prisoners in detention for the first time, although one man, Dr. Aung Khin Sint, cut short the visit for fear of reprisals later.

*   *   *   *   *

In his 1994 report to the Commission, the Special Rapporteur, Yozo Yokota, stated that "the people of Myanmar do not enjoy freedom of thought, opinion, expression, publication or peaceful assembly and association. The Government should consider accession to human rights treaties and domestic law should be made compatible with international standards regarding the protection of physical rights, including the right to freedom of assembly and expression." The Commission extended the rapporteur's mandate for another year.

In July 1995, Daw Aung San Suu Kyi was released from house arrest after more than six years, but the SLORC remains in power and the other human rights problems continue. The government of Myanmar has declared 1996 to be "Visit Myanmar Year." Though this could be viewed as an opening up of the country, human rights activists remain skeptical. Many steps the government has taken to encourage tourism have involved human rights violations, such as the use of forced labor to prepare tourist sites and roadways. *Report of the United Nations Special Rapporteur, Situation of Human Rights in Myanmar*, 2 BURMA DEBATE 24, 27 (Nov.-Dec. 1995). In his 1996 report to the U.N. Commission, the Special Rapporteur, Yozo Yokota, emphasized that widespread torture continues, that citizens do not enjoy freedom of expression or political association, and that hundreds of people remain in prison for political reasons. *Report on the Situation of Human Rights in Myanmar*, U.N. Doc. E/CN.4/1996/65 (1996).

NOTES AND QUESTIONS

1.   Myanmar has ratified the U.N. Charter, the Geneva Conventions of 1949, the Genocide Convention, and the Convention on the Rights of the Child. Myanmar is not a party to the International Covenant on Civil and Political Rights; the International Covenant on Economic, Social and Cultural Rights; the Convention against Torture, Cruel, Inhuman or Degrading Treatment or Punishment; or the 1977 Protocols to the Geneva Conventions.

2.   Readers should review the material in chapter *1* at *14-16*, introducing U.N. structures including ECOSOC, the Commission on Human Rights, and the Sub-Commission.

3.   For further reading, see:

Amnesty International, *Myanmar, Conditions in Prisons and Labour Camps*, AI Index: ASA 16/22/95 (1995);

Amnesty International, *Suggested Further Action on Myanmar and Daw Aung San Suu Kyi*, AI Index: ASA 16/21/95 (1995);

Amnesty International, *Union of Myanmar (Burma), Human Rights Violations Against Muslims in the Rakhine (Arakan) State*, AI Index: ASA 16/06/92 (1992);

AMNESTY INTERNATIONAL REPORT 1993; EDITH MIRANTE, BURMESE LOOKING GLASS: A HUMAN RIGHTS ADVENTURE AND A JUNGLE REVOLUTION (1993);

ARTICLE 19, STATE OF FEAR: CENSORSHIP IN BURMA (1991);

ASIA WATCH, BURMA (MYANMAR): WORSENING REPRESSION (1990);

DEPARTMENT OF STATE, COUNTRY REPORTS ON HUMAN RIGHTS PRACTICES FOR 1994, 104th Cong., 1st Sess. 539 (1995).

D. U.N. PROCEDURES FOR RESPONDING TO HUMAN RIGHTS VIOLATIONS

The U.N. has created several procedures to deal with the thousands of communications they receive regarding violations of human rights each year. The mechanisms include the 1235 procedure, the 1503 procedure, country rapporteurs, and thematic procedures. These procedures have evolved slowly from the U.N.'s initial approach that the Commission had "no power" to become involved in human rights or respond to communications.

1. Development of Major U.N. Procedures

In Articles 55 and 56 of the U.N. Charter, all member governments "pledge themselves to take joint and separate action" to "promote . . . higher standards of living . . . development . . . solutions of international economic . . . and related problems; and . . . universal respect for, and observance of, human rights and fundamental freedoms. . . ." Participants in the San Francisco Conference of 1945 proposed that the Charter should assure not only promotion and observance but also protection of human rights. That proposal was defeated because the United Kingdom and the United States believed that such language would inappropriately raise expectations of U.N. action on specific human rights problems. In 1947 the newly established U.N. Commission on Human Rights decided that it had "no power to take any action in regard to any complaints regarding human rights." ECOSOC confirmed that position but also requested the U.N. Secretariat to prepare an annual list of the complaints received.

Numerous efforts were made between 1947 and 1959 to alter the "no power" rule, but none were successful. In 1959 ECOSOC reaffirmed its "no power" rule in adopting resolution 728F, which consolidated the procedures for handling human rights communications. Resolution 728F does provide for the Secretary-General to prepare and distribute to the members of the U.N. Commission on Human Rights and its subsidiary body, the Sub-Commission on Prevention of Discrimination and Protection of Minorities, a "confidential list containing a brief indication of the substance of other communications concerning human rights, however addressed, and to furnish this list to members of the Commission [and Sub-Commission], in private, without divulging the identity of the authors of communications. . . ." Resolution 728F also encourages governments to reply to the communications.

ECOSOC res. 728F (XXVIII), 28 U.N. ESCOR Supp. (No. 1) at 19, U.N. Doc. E/3290 (1959):

COMMUNICATIONS CONCERNING HUMAN RIGHTS

The Economic and Social Council, . . .

1. *Approves* the statement that the Commission on Human Rights recognizes that it has no power to take any action in regard to any complaints concerning human rights;

2. *Requests* the Secretary-General:. . .

(b) To compile before each session of the Commission a confidential list containing a brief indication of the substance of other communications concerning human rights, however addressed, and to furnish this list to members of the Commission, in private meeting, without divulging the identity of the authors of communications except in cases where the authors state they have already divulged or intend to divulge their names or that they have no objection to their names being divulged;

(c) To enable the members of the Commission, upon request, to consult the originals of communications dealing with the principles involved in the promotion of universal respect for, and observance of, human rights;

(d) To inform the writers of all communications concerning human rights, however addressed, that their communications will be handled in accordance with this resolution, indicating that the Commission has no power to take any action in regard to any complaint concerning human rights;

(e) To furnish each Member State concerned with a copy of any communication concerning human rights which refers explicitly to that State or to territories under its jurisdiction, without divulging the identity of the author, except as provided for in sub-paragraph (b) above;

(f) To ask Governments sending replies to communications brought to their attention in accordance with sub-paragraph (e) whether they wish their replies to be presented to the Commission in summary form or in full;

* * * * *

Resolution 728F still applies to communications. Complainants are sent a letter referring to the "no power to take any action" rule along with a copy of resolution 728F, 1235, and 1503. That letter remains the last information an author officially receives about the communication. In 1977 the Secretariat stopped issuing non-confidential lists of communications with very brief indications of their substance, but has continued to circulate confidential lists with somewhat more substantial summaries of the communications. In accordance with resolution 728F, communications referring explicitly to a member state are furnished to that state without divulging the identity of the author.

Instead of responding to communications alleging specific human rights violations, the Commission on Human Rights devoted its energies to establishing the principal norms of international human rights during its early years. Those norms included the Universal Declaration of Human Rights (1948), the Convention on the Prevention and Punishment of the Crime of Genocide (1948), the Covenant on Civil and Political Rights (1966), and the International Covenant on Economic, Social and Cultural Rights (1966).

In 1966, however, as the Commission on Human Rights completed its work in drafting the two covenants, it requested authority from ECOSOC to review its functions and to be empowered to make recommendations about specific violations brought to its attention. ECOSOC asked the General Assembly to let the Commission review the organization of its work and expanded the session of the Commission from four to six weeks. Shortly thereafter the General Assembly, in resolution 2144A of October 26, 1966, invited ECOSOC and the Commission to consider ways in which the U.N. could work to eliminate human rights violations. At its next session, in early 1967, the Commission adopted resolution 8 (XXIII), which requested specific authority to examine communications on the lists prepared pursuant to Council resolution 728F.[2]

a. Resolution 1235

The Economic and Social Council, in resolution 1235 (XLII) of June 6, 1967,[3] approved the Commission's request. Resolution 1235 allowed the Commission to examine allegations of gross violations of human rights found in the 728F lists of

---

[2] C.H.R. res. 8 (XXIII), U.N. Doc. E/CN.4/940, at 131 (1967). Also in 1967, the Commission sought ECOSOC authority for the establishment of the *Ad Hoc* Working Group of Experts to investigate and study the policies and practices which violate human rights in South Africa and Namibia.

[3] E.S.C. res. 1235 (XLII), 42 U.N. ESCOR Supp. (No.1) at 17, U.N. Doc. E/4393 (1967) (reproduced in the accompanying handbook *Selected International Human Rights Instruments* at 142).

communications. It further authorized the Commission to make a "thorough study" of cases revealing consistent patterns of human rights violations. Resolution 1235 also permitted the Sub-Commission to establish a similar agenda item. The resolution did not define the procedure for examining the communications. The adoption of 1235 was a significant step, because it was the first time the Commission had been authorized to take action in response to communications, thus weakening the "no power" doctrine.

ECOSOC res. 1235 (XLII), 42 U.N. ESCOR Supp. (No. 1) at 17, U.N. Doc. E/4393 (1967):

The Economic and Social Council, . . .

1. *Welcomes* the decision of the Commission on Human Rights to give annual consideration to the item entitled "Question of the violation of human rights and fundamental freedoms, including policies of racial discrimination and segregation and of *apartheid,* in all countries, with particular reference to colonial and other dependent countries and territories," . . .; and concurs with the requests for assistance addressed to the Sub-Commission on Prevention of Discrimination and Protection of Minorities and to the Secretary-General;

2. *Authorizes* the Commission on Human Rights and the Sub-Commission on Prevention of Discrimination and Protection of Minorities, . . ., to examine information relevant to gross violations of human rights and fundamental freedoms, as exemplified by the policy of *apartheid* . . ., and to racial discrimination . . ., contained in the communications listed by the Secretary-General pursuant to Economic and Social Council resolution 728 F (XXVIII) of 30 July 1959;

3. *Decides* that the Commission on Human Rights may, in appropriate cases, . . . , make a thorough study of situations which reveal a consistent pattern of violations of human rights, . . . , and report, with recommendations thereon, to the Economic and Social Council;

*   *   *   *   *

In practice, resolution 1235 has served as the basis for annual debate during the sessions of the Commission and Sub-Commission on human rights violations in specific countries. These debates began as rather reserved discussions in which governments claimed that they could not be criticized by name. By the late 1970s, however, governments and nongovernmental organizations (NGOs) accepted this agenda item as the occasion for lively public discussion of violations committed by named governments. Based on those debates, the Commission and Sub-Commission began to adopt resolutions expressing concern about human rights violations in particular countries. In 1995, for example, the Commission adopted 16 resolutions addressing specific country situations.

For the first time, in 1995, the U.S. was the subject of substantial discussion under 1235. A resolution was introduced which endorsed the report of the Special Rapporteur on racism and xenophobia regarding the situation in the U.S., and expressed concern about persisting racial discrimination in the U.S. The proposed resolution was rejected by a wide margin, with only three countries voting in favor. Commission on Human Rights, *Violation of Human Rights in the United States as a Result of Racism and Racial Discrimination Persisting in United States Society,* U.N. Doc. E/CN.4/1995/L.26/Rev.2 (1995). *See also* Penny Parker, A Summary of the Major Developments at the 1995 Session of the U.N. Commission on Human Rights, Held in Geneva, Switzerland, From January 30 to March 10, 1995, World Wide Web (http://www.umn.edu/humanrts) (1995).

In addition to adopting resolutions, the Commission developed a practice under resolution 1235 of appointing special rapporteurs, special representatives, experts, working groups, and other envoys to monitor human rights violations in particular countries. The countries have included Afghanistan, Bolivia, Burundi, Cambodia, Chile, Cuba, Democratic Kampuchea, El Salvador, Equatorial Guinea, Guatemala, Haiti, Iran, Iraq, Myanmar, Palestine, Poland, Romania, Rwanda, Somalia, Southern Africa, Sudan, Togo, former Yugoslavia, and Zaire. Special rapporteurs or experts were appointed to investigate situations in twelve countries in 1995. The special rapporteurs, representatives, and others collect information on human rights violations and prepare annual reports to the Commission, and if requested, to the General Assembly. Information can be gathered from individuals, groups, organizations, and governments. The experts or rapporteurs often attempt to obtain the relevant information by visiting the countries. Difficulties arise, however, when governments refuse to grant permission for these visits.

b. Resolution 1503

Although resolution 1235 refers to the communications listed pursuant to resolution 728F, the Commission may not refer to the substance of those communications directly because they remain confidential pursuant to resolution 728F. Moreover, resolution 1235 does not provide a mechanism for consideration or analysis of the communications themselves. Accordingly, in 1968 the Sub-Commission proposed that the 728F communications should be subjected to a three-stage screening process by a working group of the Sub-Commission, the whole Sub-Commission, and the Commission. In its resolution 17 (XXV) of 1969 the Commission essentially accepted the Sub-Commission's recommendation to the Economic and Social Council, but gave governments a year to consider the proposal. On May 27, 1970, ECOSOC adopted resolution 1503 (XLVIII).[4] The resolution established a procedure separate from the public debate conducted under resolution 1235 in the Commission and the Sub-Commission; the public discussion continued despite the adoption of resolution 1503.

ECOSOC res. 1503 (XLVIII), 48 U.N. ESCOR (No. 1A) at 8, U.N. Doc. E/4832/Add.1 (1970):

Procedure for dealing with communications relating to violations of human rights and fundamental freedoms

The Economic and Social Council, . . .

1. *Authorizes* the Sub-Commission on Prevention of Discrimination and Protection of Minorities to appoint a working group consisting of not more than five of its members, with due regard to geographical distribution, to meet once a year in private meetings for a period not exceeding ten days immediately before the sessions of the Sub-Commission to consider all communications, including replies of Government thereon, received by the Secretary-General under Council resolution 728 F (XXVIII) of 30 July 1559 with a view to bringing to the attention of the Sub-Commission

---

[4] E.S.C. res. 1503 (XLVIII), 48 U.N. ESCOR Supp.(No.1A) at 17, U.N. Doc. E/4832/Add.1 (1970).

those communications, together with replies of Governments, if any, which appear to reveal a consistent pattern of gross and reliably attested violations of human rights and fundamental freedoms within the terms of reference of the Sub-Commission;
. . .

4. *Further requests* the Secretary-General:

(a)   To furnish to the members of the Sub-Commission every month a list of communications prepared by him in accordance with Council resolution 728 F (XXVIII) and a brief description of them together with the text of any replies received from Governments;

(b)   To make available to the members of the working group at their meetings the originals of such communications listed as they may request, having due regard to the provisions of paragraph 2(b) of Council resolution 728 F (XXVIII) concerning the divulging of the identity of the authors of communications;

(c)   To circulate to the members of the Sub-Commission, in the working languages, the originals of such communications as are referred to the Sub-Commission by the working group;

5. *Requests* the Sub-Commission on Prevention of Discrimination and Protection of Minorities to consider in private meetings, in accordance with paragraph 1 above, the communications brought before it in accordance with the decision of a majority of the members of the working group and any replies of Governments relating thereto and other relevant information, with a view to determining whether they refer to the Commission on Human Rights particular situations which appear to reveal a consistent pattern of gross and reliably attested violations of human rights requiring consideration by the Commission;

6. *Requests* the Commission on Human Rights after it has examined any situation referred to it by the Sub-Commission to determine:

(a)   Whether it requires a thorough study by the Commission and a report and recommendations thereon to the Council in accordance with paragraph 3 of Council resolution 1235 (XLII);

(b)   Whether it may be a subject of an investigation by an *ad hoc* committee to be appointed by the Commission which shall be undertaken only with the express consent of the State concerned and shall be conducted in constant co-operation with that State and under conditions determined by agreement with it. In any event, the investigation may be undertaken only if:

(i)   All available means at the national level have been resorted to and exhausted;
(ii) The situation does not relate to a matter which is being dealt with under other procedures prescribed in the constituent instruments of, or conventions adopted by, the United Nations and the specialized agencies, or in regional conventions or which the State concerned wishes to submit to other procedures in accordance with general or special international agreements to which it is a party. . . .

8. *Decides* that all actions envisaged in the implementation of the present resolution by the Sub-Commission on Prevention of Discrimination and Protection of Minorities or the Commission on Human Rights shall remain confidential until such time as the Commission may decide to make recommendations to the Economic and Social Council;

* * * * *

The 1503 procedure has evolved since 1970. While the new practices may not be specifically authorized by resolution 1503, they appear to have become regular attributes of the procedure. For example, In 1974 the Commission decided to inform governments that they had been the subject of a situation referred by the Sub-Commission, to send them the relevant documents, and to invite the governments to submit any observations. Also in 1974 the Commission decided to establish its own Working Group on Situations to meet just before the next annual session of the Commission and to consider the disposition of situations referred by the Sub-Commission to the Commission. The Commission's Working Group on Situations met for the first time in 1975 and continued to meet annually. In 1990 ECOSOC approved the permanent establishment of the Working Group on Situations.

In 1978 the Commission formalized a number of practices which had developed under the 1503 process. For example, the Commission decided to invite the Chair of the Sub-Commission's Working Group on Communications to participate in sessions of the Commission on 1503 matters. The Commission also gave accused governments the opportunity to respond during the confidential discussions of the Commission. Further, the Commission decided that the Sub-Commission and its Working Group should be given access to the confidential records of the Commission's meetings on 1503 matters.

For the first time, in 1978, the Chair of the Commission announced the names of the governments which had been the subject of discussion during the 1503 deliberations, but the Chair did not explain the substance of the complaints or the decisions reached. In 1984 the Commission's Chair announced not only the names of the countries discussed, but whether the Commission had decided to keep the matter under consideration or to terminate the consideration of particular countries.

The secrecy surrounding the 1503 procedure, which is one of its principal features, has been an obstacle to adequate knowledge about the functioning and effectiveness of the procedure. In 1985 and 1986 the new governments in Argentina, the Philippines, and Uruguay successfully requested that the records of the 1503 proceedings in their respective cases should be released to the public. The availability of this material has made it possible for a new evaluation of the 1503 procedures based upon more comprehensive information. Also, human rights advocates can now be given some useful advice as to how they should present their 1503 communications.

2.   Overview of the Resolution 1503 Procedure in Practice

The 1503 process has a year-long cycle. The resolution provides that any communications alleging a consistent pattern of gross and reliably attested violations shall be considered initially by the Sub-Commission, and it has in turn delegated the first review of the thousands of communications received by the U.N. each year to a Working Group of five members of the Sub-Commission. The five members are selected for the following year by the Chair of the Sub-Commission at the end of each Sub-Commission session. The Chair consults with the Sub-Commission members from each of the five regions represented in the U.N.: Africa, Asia, Eastern Europe, South America, and "Western Europe and Other."

The Working Group meets for two weeks before the commencement of the Sub-Commission session in August each year. The Working Group considers communications submitted during the previous year as well as any responses that the governments concerned may wish to provide. The Working Group usually receives 20,000-

25,000 communications per year, although postcard campaigns on certain countries may raise the number of complaints in a single year over 350,000. Of the thousands of communications received by the U.N. only about two dozen may be sufficiently well prepared to be given serious consideration by the Working Group. Though there is authority within 1503 for consolidating individual communications, including postcards and letters, to assess whether there exists a consistent pattern of gross violations of human rights in a country, the Group only reviews with care those communications that muster sufficient facts to support a finding that a government is responsible for a consistent pattern of gross and reliably attested violations.

The Working Group meets in secret session with only its members and the staff of the Communications Unit of the Centre for Human Rights present. Each member of the Group takes responsibility for identifying communications for referral to the Sub-Commission. The members ordinarily divide their responsibilities by categories of rights in the Universal Declaration. For example, the member from the "Western European and Other" group of nations may be responsible for raising cases involving torture, arbitrary killing, and other violations of personal integrity. The African member may take responsibility for communications regarding discrimination. The member from Eastern Europe may accept primary responsibility for communications raising violations of the right to leave and return. The assignments are not rigid, and any member may request consideration of any communication. The staff of the Centre assists the Working Group members in identifying communications appropriate for discussion.

A majority of the members of the Group, that is, three out of five, must vote in favor of referring a communication to the Sub-Commission. Difficulties in obtaining the three votes required for action have arisen when one or even two of the members of the Group have not arrived in Geneva in time for all or part of the Group sessions. The Group takes separate votes on the referral of each communication. Often several communications are referred to the Sub-Commission in regard to a particular country. The Working Group usually forwards communications involving 8-10 countries to the Sub-Commission. The Group has also developed a practice of holding a few additional cases for consideration during the following year. While not constituting a formal action under the 1503 process, this practice may indicate that the Working Group will seriously consider referral if the situation does not improve by the following year. As soon as the Group completes its deliberations, the Centre for Human Rights arranges for the translation of the communications referred by the Group, so that they can be considered by the Sub-Commission in the principal languages of the U.N. The Group reports its conclusions to the Sub-Commission in a confidential document.

The Sub-Commission meets in private session about two to three days in late August to consider the communications referred by its Working Group. The Sub-Commission refers some communications to the Commission by a majority vote, refuses to refer other situations, and has developed a practice of keeping others under consideration until the following year's session.

The Sub-Commission's decisions are confidential—at least vis-a-vis the authors of communications who do not officially know what happened to their communications. The Centre for Human Rights informs affected governments in October that communications have been transmitted to the Commission or have been kept under review by the Sub-Commission. The governments are invited to submit written observations on the situation in question.

The Commission has established a two-stage process like that of the Sub-Commission. The Working Group on Situations is comprised of five members of the

Commission, representing governments from different geographical areas. The Group meets in private session for one week before the Commission session each year to draft recommendations as to how each situation referred by the Sub-Commission should be handled by the Commission. In contrast to the Sub-Commission's working group, however, the Working Group on Situations may not decide which situations the Commission will consider.

The Commission meets in private session to consider situations brought to its attention by the Sub-Commission under resolution 1503. Through 1995 the Commission met from late January or early February through mid-March. Beginning in 1996, the Commission is meeting from mid-March through late April. The discussion ordinarily begins with an introduction of each situation by the Chair of the Commission's Working Group or its special rapporteur on the situation, appointed at a previous session. The government concerned is then permitted to respond. The Chair of the Sub-Commission's Working Group may participate in the proceedings, if requested, to explain the rationale for the Sub-Commission's referral of the situation. In practice, however, the Sub-Commissions's representative is rarely asked to speak and is present more as an observer to inform the Sub-Commission of the Commission's actions. In the presence of the government representative, the Commission decides whether to accept the Working Group's recommended decision. The government may comment on the Commission's decision after the vote.

Under resolution 1503 the Commission is authorized to recommend to ECOSOC the mounting of a "thorough study" or an even more intensive inquiry by an *ad hoc* fact-finding body. The Commission has recommended a "thorough study" on only two occasions[5] and has never recommended the use of an *ad hoc* fact-finding body. Instead, the Group has proposed and the Commission has developed an expanding repertoire of approaches, including posing written questions to the governments concerned, sending a member of the Commission to make direct contacts with the government, sending a U.N. staff person to the country, keeping the case under consideration, transferring the case to the public procedure, dismissing the situation, or some other approach. For example, during the late 1980s the Commission selected a special rapporteur to pursue direct contacts with the government of Myanmar (Burma) and to report the results of her investigations to the Commission in confidential session. After several annual confidential reports produced no appreciable results and little cooperation from the government, the Commission decided in 1992 to appoint a Special Rapporteur under the public procedure authorized by resolution 1235.

When the Commission returns to public session, the Chair announces the list of countries that have been dropped or continued under the 1503 process and any other actions taken. Countries which are continued on the Commission agenda will be considered the following year whether or not they are the subject of new communications. Since the initiation of the 1503 procedure, the Commission has discussed the human rights situation in over 50 countries.

a.   Deadline for and Length of Submissions

Communications must be submitted prior to the annual meeting of the Sub-Commission's Working Group on Communications. Prior to 1989, the Working Group considered all communications received by June 30, although successful communica-

---

[5] The subjects of the "thorough studies" were Uganda and Equatorial Guinea. The Equatorial Guinea situation was later transferred to the public procedure. The Uganda study ended before it reached any concrete result.

tions were usually received by the end of May. In 1990, the Sub-Commission decided that governments should be given 12 weeks to respond. Hence, communications must be submitted by late April of each year in preparation for the Working Group's meeting during late July.

Because the Working Group receives so many communications, the most successful are usually comprehensive but brief (for example, 10 to 20 pages) and indicate the scope of the violations while also providing details of some individual cases. Because the U.N. has limited resources, only the principal communications are translated. Generally, appendices will not be translated—particularly if they are voluminous.

b. Admissibility Requirements

At its 1971 session the Sub-Commission adopted standards and criteria for the admissibility of 1503 communications.[6] The Sub-Commission decided that communications "shall be admissible only if . . . there are reasonable grounds to believe that they may reveal a consistent pattern of gross and reliably attested violations of human rights and fundamental freedoms, including policies of racial discrimination and segregation and of *apartheid* in any country, including colonial and other dependent countries and peoples." Sub-Commission resolution 1 (XXIV) also stated that admissible

> communications may originate from a person or group of persons who . . . are victims of the violations . . . , any person or group of persons who have direct and reliable knowledge of those violations, or non-governmental organizations acting in good faith in accordance with recognized principles of human rights, not resorting to politically motivated stands contrary to the provisions of the Charter of the United Nations and having direct and reliable knowledge of such violations.

Anonymous communications are not admissible, but the author of a communication may request that his or her name not be revealed to the government.

The communication must contain a "description of the facts and must indicate . . . the rights that have been violated." Second-hand information may be included, so long as accompanied by "clear evidence." "Communications shall be inadmissible if their language is essentially abusive and . . . if they contain insulting references to the State against which the complaint is directed." There is a provision for consideration of communications after the removal of abusive language. Communications are also inadmissible if they have "manifestly political motivations" or are "based exclusively on reports disseminated by mass media."

Communications shall be inadmissible if they would prejudice the functioning of U.N. specialized agencies (such as the International Labour Organization), if there exist domestic remedies which have not been exhausted and which are not "ineffective or unreasonably prolonged," if the matter has been satisfactorily settled, or if the communication is not submitted within "a reasonable time after the exhaustion of domestic remedies. . . ."

c. Confidentiality of the 1503 procedure

In order to use the 1503 process effectively, an advocate needs to know whether the government answered the communication, what the government responded, whether the Sub-Commission's Working Group referred the communication to the

---

[6] Sub. Comm'n res. 1 (XXIV), U.N. Doc. E/CN.4/1070, at 50-51 (1971).

Sub-Commission, whether the Sub-Commission referred the matter to the Commission, what recommendation was made by the Commission's Working Group, the nature of the defense raised by the government at the Commission, and the Commission's resolution of the issue. At most stages of the process there are opportunities for advocacy with the Sub-Commission and Commission members who are responsible for decisions. Those opportunities are exploited by the concerned governments and can be used by the complainant if the requisite information can be gathered.

Despite the rather daunting language of ECOSOC 1503 and considerable effort by responsible U.N. officials to keep the process secret, most authors of communications who participate in the meetings of the Sub-Commission and Commission are able to obtain the relevant information. Some Sub-Commission members inform at least their own governments about the results of each step in the 1503 process—particularly if their government has been accused of violating human rights. Once the members disclose anything, it is not surprising that word travels fast.

Most of the successful 1503 communications are prepared by lawyers or researchers for NGOs that send representatives to the Sub-Commission. Most participants in the public sessions of the Sub-Commission who wish to know the 1503 decisions can discover them without effort. Indeed, the tentative list of countries developed by the Sub-Commission is often published in the *International Herald Tribune* or *Le Monde*.

Similarly, at the Commission on Human Rights, with dozens of government delegations privy to confidential information, those attending Commission sessions who wish to know what is happening under 1503 often are able to learn.

    d.   *What Constitutes a Consistent Pattern of Gross and Reliably Attested Violations?*

It is possible to infer from the names of the countries mentioned by the Chair of the Commission on Human Rights at the end of the Commission's 1503 deliberations and from publicly available information about those countries what sort of situation constitutes a "consistent pattern of gross and reliably attested violations." As of 1995 fifty-four countries had been considered under the 1503 process. The governments of those countries were responsible for a large number of cases involving torture, political detention, summary or arbitrary killing, and disappearance.[7]

3. Theme Procedures

In addition to the country-oriented approach of responding to human rights communications, the Commission on Human Rights has set up theme-oriented procedures for dealing with human rights violations. Thematic procedures, like country procedures, allow rapporteurs or working groups to seek and receive information on human rights violations. Thematic rapporteurs or working groups, however, may also respond to information received in an effort to eliminate certain human rights abuses. The ability to respond promptly to complaints separates thematic procedures from mere studies or country procedures. Additionally, the special rapporteurs and working groups act on individual cases of human rights abuses, rather than only on situations revealing patterns of gross violations.

The Human Rights Commission has created fourteen thematic procedures—

---

[7] *See* Howard Tolley, *The Concealed Crack in the Citadel: The United Nations Commission on Human Rights' Response to Confidential Communications*, 6 HUMAN RTS. Q. 420, 448 (1984).

Working Group on Enforced or Involuntary Disappearances (established in 1980); Special Rapporteur on summary or arbitrary executions (1982); Special Rapporteur on torture (1985); Special Rapporteur on religious intolerance (1986); Special Rapporteur on mercenaries (1987); Special Rapporteur on the sale of children (established in 1990 and recognized as a thematic procedure in 1992); Working Group on Arbitrary Detention (1991); Special Representative on internally displaced persons (established in 1992 and recognized as a thematic procedure in 1993); Special Rapporteur on racism and xenophobia (1993); Special Rapporteur on freedom of opinion and expression (1993); Working Group on the Right to Development (1993); Special Rapporteur on violence against women (1994); Special Rapporteur on the independence of judges and lawyers (1994); and Special Rapporteur on toxic waste (1995). The rapporteurs and working groups are generally appointed for three-year terms.

Thematic rapporteurs and working groups gather information about human rights violations around the world, based on a particular subject. The thematic mechanisms work as a communication process between governments and victims of human rights abuses. In regard to most of these themes, the Commission has authorized a Special Rapporteur or a Working Group to receive complaints from individuals; to make direct, urgent appeals to governments; to visit countries; to make detailed recommendations to governments; and ultimately to seek an end to specific violations. Gathering information can be difficult, because governments often do not reply to requests for information or deny the allegations against them, and many refuse to allow visits. The rapporteurs and working groups also make annual public reports to the Commission, which include a summary of their activities, summaries of correspondence, analyses of situations, and recommendations. Recently, some reports have included specific country situations, detailing how a country has acted in relation to the subject, rather than focusing only on individual cases. The thematic special rapporteurs have actually stopped torture, helped to locate disappeared people, and otherwise had a very important impact.

David Weissbrodt, *The Three "Theme" Special Rapporteurs of the UN Commission on Human Rights,* 80 AM. J. INT'L L. 685, 685-95 (1986) (footnotes omitted):

In March 1982, the United Nations Commission on Human Rights initiated the appointment of a Special Rapporteur on summary or arbitrary executions. The Special Rapporteur on summary or arbitrary executions has done far more than merely study that grave human rights problem; he has received complaints about impending and past executions, issued appeals to governments about threatened executions and the need to investigate past killings, and reported publicly on much of his activity. The Commission on Human Rights not only has renewed the Special Rapporteur on summary or arbitrary executions in its subsequent annual sessions, but has followed this precedent by appointing in 1985 a similar Special Rapporteur on torture and in 1986 a Special Rapporteur on intolerance and discrimination based on religion or belief.

The development of the "theme" special rapporteur is a relatively new and remarkably flexible approach to implementing international human rights norms. Although the concept grew out of the practice of the Working Group on Enforced or Involuntary Disappearances, the special rapporteur, as a single individual of recognized international standing, is ordinarily less expensive and less visible, as well as more efficient, than the five-member working group in achieving similar objectives.

The Working Group on Enforced or Involuntary Disappearances

The Working Group on Enforced or Involuntary Disappearances, which was initiated by the Commission on Human Rights in 1980, has developed an effective approach to coping with the human rights violations within its narrow mandate. The evolution of the working group not only has given guidance to the special rapporteurs, but has presaged how their activities will develop.

The resolution that established the Working Group on Enforced or Involuntary Disappearances gave that body of five members authority (1) to "examine questions relevant to enforced or involuntary disappearances"; (2) to "seek and receive information from governments, intergovernmental organizations, humanitarian organizations and other reliable sources"; and (3) "to bear in mind the need to be able to respond effectively to information that comes before it and to carry out its work with discretion." It was directed to report to the Commission's next session. While the mandate of the working group to "examine questions" might at first glance appear to suggest an academic study of the issue, the working group relied principally upon its authority to "respond effectively" in raising specific cases of disappearances and in requesting responses from governments without seeking any publicity about the cases.

After receiving the working group's first report, the Commission extended the group's tenure for another year, but made several significant changes in its mandate to reflect both approval of and some limitations on its activities. The Commission noted that governments had not always given the working group the full cooperation "warranted by its strictly humanitarian objectives and its working methods based on discretion." The working group had embarrassed the Argentine Government by reprinting its reply in full, and thus the group was reminded "to discharge its mandate with discretion"; on the one hand, it should "protect persons providing information," and on the other, "limit the dissemination of information provided by Governments."

While the Commission simply extended the working group's mandate in 1982 and 1983 without making significant changes, it did express "complete confidence" in the group. In 1984 the Commission for the first time requested that the working group "help eliminate the practice of enforced or involuntary disappearances" and encouraged governments to permit the group to make site visits to fulfill "its mandate more effectively." The Commission continued this approach in 1985. . . .

The Working Group on Enforced or Involuntary Disappearances has developed incrementally into an effective human rights implementation mechanism on no broader a consensual basis than a consensus of the Commission on Human Rights and without the authority of any human rights treaty beyond the United Nations Charter. The special rapporteurs are gradually following in the footsteps of the working group.

The Special Rapporteur on Summary or Arbitrary Executions

The Special Rapporteur on summary or arbitrary executions was the first special rapporteur on a theme or particular kind of human rights violation. The 1982 mandate of the special rapporteur was styled to some extent upon the 1980 resolution that established the working group, that is, to "examine the questions related to summary or arbitrary executions" and to report annually to the Commission on the rapporteur's activities. . . .

Although his position was initiated in March 1982 and his authority confirmed by the Economic and Social Council in May 1982, the first Special Rapporteur on summary or arbitrary executions, Amos Wako of Kenya, was not actually appointed by the Chairman of the Human Rights Commission until August of that year. Rather than take the incremental approach handed down by the Working Group on Enforced or Involuntary Disappearances, Mr. Wako's first report attempted to begin at the level of activity that the working group had achieved after several years. He evidently failed to note that the authorizing resolution did not instruct him to "respond effectively" but only to gather information, examine the question and report to the Commission. Instead, he had ambitiously identified 37 governments that had allegedly been responsible for summary or arbitrary executions; he had then sent the allegations to those governments, and the responses of 16 of them were summarized forthrightly in his report.

This first report was roundly criticized by members of the Commission—particularly by representatives of the governments that had been discussed. Consequently, Mr. Wako was again in 1983 not given authority to "respond effectively" to summary or arbitrary killings. His second and third reports omitted most references to countries, except for reprinting the telexes he had continued to send, without clear authority, in an attempt to avert specific summary or arbitrary executions. Accordingly, the special rapporteur's reports became less controversial; his mandate was more easily renewed in 1984 and 1985, and he was finally given authority to "respond effectively to information that comes before him."

The fourth report largely returned to the practice of identifying the governments that had allegedly engaged in summary or arbitrary executions. Indeed, the greatest part of the report contained the substance of the special rapporteur's appeals against summary or arbitrary executions during the previous year, the requests made by the special rapporteur for information about past executions and the responses of governments. This laudable record demonstrated that the special rapporteur had finally achieved the credibility he had sought at first and that his initially weak authority had been enhanced by the Commission. The report indicates that the special rapporteur has been quite active in pursuing his mandate and in attempting to prevent summary or arbitrary executions. The report makes no effort, however, to resolve the issues raised by the allegations and the replies of governments, and it makes only a rudimentary effort to synthesize the material presented and to draw useful conclusions and recommendations.

The Special Rapporteur on summary or arbitrary executions has not been as careful and successful in developing his mandate as the Working Group on Enforced or Involuntary Disappearances. Nevertheless, he has generally followed the approach of the working group and has been given the additional responsibility of helping to develop standards on such important subjects as international norms for the investigation of summary or arbitrary killings. As will be seen below, the Special Rapporteur on torture has benefited both from the mistakes of the Special Rapporteur on summary or arbitrary executions and from the guidance afforded by the Working Group on Enforced and Involuntary Disappearances.

The Special Rapporteur on Torture

During its session in 1985, the Commission on Human Rights established a Special Rapporteur on torture with the authority to "respond effectively to credible and reliable information" on torture. It was understood at the time that the Chairman of the Human Rights Commission would appoint Professor P. H. Kooijmans of the Netherlands. . . .

In many ways, the special rapporteur's report is a model first step in what promises to be a very effective United Nations approach to a serious human rights problem. Professor Kooijmans describes the nature of the problem, his mandate, international legal norms against torture and his activities, including the material he received from governments, the Organization of American States and nongovernmental organizations such as Amnesty International. He established his authority to transmit allegations of torture to national authorities by sending such information to 33 governments. The special rapporteur avoids angering these governments unnecessarily in his initial report by identifying only those nations which were already on the Commission's agenda, that is, Afghanistan, Chile, El Salvador, Guatemala and Iran.

Professor Kooijmans also records that he engaged in consultations with governments, nongovernmental organizations and individuals; without identifying those involved, he thus established his authority to undertake such consultations. In addition, he reports his decision to make eight urgent appeals to governments to prevent the occurrence of torture in Chile, the Comoros, Ecuador, Honduras, Indonesia, South Africa, Uganda and the USSR. The special rapporteur identifies some of these urgent situations very briefly and is careful to describe the governmental response, if any. For example, the report states, "The Special Rapporteur was informed that the USSR rejected the allegation sent to it as baseless and false and pointed out that the action of the Special Rapporteur violated the provisions of the Commission resolution 1985/33." While the report does not contain even a vague description of the problem that prompted this brusque reply, it appears to have been reports of psychiatric abuse in the USSR.

The remainder of the report largely deals with national legislative provisions forbidding torture; the barring of statements induced by torture as evidence in proceedings; the provision of remedies, such as *amparo* or habeas corpus, for torture allegations; and legislative provisions on matters creating a risk of torture, such as incommunicado detention, states of emergency and trade in implements of torture. Although countries are very rarely identified, except in a positive light, the United States is mentioned because of the export regulations regarding "specially designed implements of torture." The report concludes by listing the kinds of torture that have been identified, analyzing briefly the relationship between torture and other sorts of human rights violations (such as disappearances, arbitrary killings) and submitting a set of recommendations.

In general, the special rapporteur's work was well received by the Commission in March 1986. . . .

When the Commission debated the agenda item entitled "Question of the human rights of all persons subjected to any form of detention or imprisonment," which includes a review of the work of the Special Rapporteur on torture, the Australian delegation introduced an idea borrowed from the Special Rapporteur on summary or arbitrary executions: that international standards be set for investigations into "cases of suspicious death, and that these investigations should include an adequate autopsy." Australia pointed to "the general need for accurate information to determine the cause of death where there is suspicion of torture" and reiterated the advantages international standards would confer on practitioners that were mentioned in the debate on summary and arbitrary executions. Although these sentiments were not reflected in the Belgian resolution to prolong the special rapporteur's mandate for another year, the Commission is definitely beginning to see the theme special rapporteurs as a mechanism not only for implementing human rights norms but also for developing standards. . . .

The Special Rapporteur on Intolerance and Discrimination Based on Religion or Belief

The most significant single development at the 42nd session of the Human Rights Commission was its decision in March 1986 to establish a Special Rapporteur on intolerance and discrimination based on religion or belief. The newest special rapporteur will presumably follow the same approach as his predecessors, that is, to study the phenomenon of intolerance and discrimination based on religion or belief; to "respond effectively to credible and reliable information that comes before him and to carry out his work with discretion and independence"; and to report to the Commission at its next session in 1987 about his activities.

The decision to establish a Special Rapporteur on intolerance and discrimination based on religion or belief arose from a long history of United Nations activity on this issue culminating in the proclamation by the General Assembly in 1981 of the Declaration on the Elimination of All Forms of Intolerance and of Discrimination Based on Religion or Belief. The Declaration was the product of 20 years of drafting work in the Commission on Human Rights and the very thorough Study on Discrimination in the Matter of Religious Rights and Practices, released in 1960. The new special rapporteur has been asked to "examine" incidents and governmental actions in all parts of the world which are inconsistent with the provisions of the Declaration.

* * * * *

WORKING GROUP ON ENFORCED OR INVOLUNTARY DISAPPEARANCES

The mandate of the Working Group, with chairman Ivan Tosevski of the former Yugoslav Republic of Macedonia, was renewed for another three years at the 1995 Commission session. The Group's 1995 report to the Commission stated that the number of countries involved in disappearances has increased to 73, almost double what it was five years ago. The Group has visited several countries including, for example, the former Yugoslavia in 1994. The Group reported in 1995 that when "the political situation becomes so unstable as to result in internal conflict, many Governments resort to the technique of disappearance as a means of bringing the situation under control. Far from doing so, it leads to an inevitable reaction and therefore to more oppression and more disappearances." U.N. Doc. E/CN.4/1995/36 (1995).

The Group has a humanitarian, rather than adjudicatory, approach. It is a channel of communication between governments and individuals, but makes no decisions on specific human rights violations. In 1995 the Group requested that the Commission establish a more judgmental monitoring procedure. *Id.*

SPECIAL RAPPORTEUR ON EXTRAJUDICIAL, SUMMARY OR ARBITRARY EXECUTIONS

Bacre Waly N'diaye (Senegal) was appointed in 1994 as the Special Rapporteur on summary or arbitrary executions, and in 1995 his mandate was extended for three years. The Special Rapporteur has visited several countries and has made joint visits with country rapporteurs and the Special Rapporteur on torture. In 1994, for example, he visited Colombia, Rwanda, Indonesia, and East Timor. In 1994 the Special Rapporteur warned of massive killings in Rwanda, but his report received scant attention until after 500,000 people were killed for ethnic and political reasons in April 1994. His 1995 report listed 75 countries which have engaged in summary or arbitrary executions. The Special Rapporteur has developed a system of reviewing individual cases, sending a questionnaire to governments concerning the cases, and following-up with letters to both the governments and the complainants.

SPECIAL RAPPORTEUR ON TORTURE AND OTHER CRUEL, INHUMAN OR DEGRADING TREATMENT OR PUNISHMENT

The Special Rapporteur on torture, Nigel Rodley (U.K.), has also visited countries alone and with other special rapporteurs. In 1994 he stated that "he will not as a rule seek to visit a country in respect of which the United Nations has established a country specific mechanism such as a special rapporteur on the country, unless a joint visit seems to both to be indicated." U.N. Doc. E/CN.4/1994/31 (1994).

His 1995 report to the Commission included allegations of torture in 79 countries around the world. The Commission has directed him to focus specifically on torture against women, and he has found that rape and sexual abuse are common mechanisms of torture. In 1995 the Commission again invited him to "examine questions concerning torture directed primarily against women and children and conditions conducive to such torture, and to make appropriate recommendations concerning the prevention of gender-specific forms of torture and the torture of children." C.H.R. res. 1995/37, U.N. Doc. E/CN.4/1995/L.52 (1995).

SPECIAL RAPPORTEUR ON RELIGIOUS INTOLERANCE

The Special Rapporteur's mandate now includes recommending specific remedial measures as well as examining incidents of religious intolerance. This rapporteur, Abdelfattah Amor (Tunisia), has followed the methods of the previous rapporteurs by engaging in country visits and making recommendations to governments. In 1995, the report of the Special Rapporteur and the Commission resolution noted that religious intolerance rarely occurs independent of other human rights violations. The Commission stated "the rights violated on religious grounds include the rights to life, the right to physical integrity and to liberty and security of person, the right to freedom of expression, the right not to be subjected to torture or other cruel, inhuman or degrading treatment or punishment and the right not to be arbitrarily arrested or detained." C.H.R. res. 1995/23, U.N. Doc. E/CN.4/1995/L.31 (1995).

SPECIAL RAPPORTEUR ON MERCENARIES

In 1987 the Commission decided to appoint a rapporteur "to examine the question of the use of mercenaries as a means of violating human rights and of impeding the exercise of the right of peoples to self-determination." The Commission did not authorize the rapporteur to respond effectively to information received, a right that other theme procedures have used to justify transmittal of complaints to governments. *See* C.H.R. res. 1987/16, U.N. Doc. E/CN.4/1987/60, at 60 (1987).

In a 1988 report, his first, the Special Rapporteur (Enrique Bernales Ballesteros of Peru) examined international law relating to mercenaries and summarized information received from governments, IGOs, and NGOs. In addition, he examined the issue of how to define the word mercenary and outlined three broad types of mercenaries. He concluded that mercenary practices still are present in the world and recommended further study. *See* U.N. Doc. E/CN.4/1988/14 (1988).

In his 1989 report, he once again summarized information received; the bulk of the report is devoted to his visit to Nicaragua. The aim was to conduct an on-site study of effects the use of mercenaries has on human rights, especially the right to self-determination. He also visited Angola and sent letters to governments involved in an apparent use of mercenary aggression against the government of Maldives. The report contained several recommendations, including a proposal that states should adopt penal legislation prohibiting and punishing mercenary activities. *See* U.N. Doc. E/CN.4/1989/14 (1989).

The Special Rapporteur has continued to investigate activities involving mercenaries. In 1995 the Commission extended the mandate of the Special Rapporteur for three years. C.H.R. res. 1995/5, U.N. Doc. E/CN.4/1995/L.12 (1995). The U.S. was the only country to vote against that resolution.

SPECIAL RAPPORTEUR ON THE SALE OF CHILDREN, CHILD PROSTITUTION AND CHILD PORNOGRAPHY

In 1990 the Commission appointed a rapporteur to "consider matters relating to the sale of children, child prostitution and child pornography, including the problem of adoption of children for commercial purposes." *See* C.H.R. res. 1990/68, U.N. Doc. E/CN.4/1990/94, at 145 (1990).

The Special Rapporteur (Vitit Muntarbhorn of Thailand) presented his first full report at the Commission's 1992 session. The report summarized three types of information—documentary evidence offered by government and non-government sources; questionnaire responses from governments, individuals, and NGOs; and data collected from visits to the Netherlands and Brazil. The report also described an "urgent action" intervention that the Special Rapporteur sent to the government of Pakistan on behalf of a girl alleged to have been kidnapped in Bangladesh and taken to Pakistan. *See* U.N. Doc. E/CN.4/1992/55 (1992).

In the report the Special Rapporteur outlined factors that lead to the sale of children, child prostitution, and child pornography. He stressed poverty as the leading factor and also cited family breakdowns, increased materialism, consumerism, and sexism. *Id*. at 2. He also offered discussions on the sale of children, child prostitution, and child pornography, giving the current state of laws and practices relating to each, and emphasized the need for better enforcement of existing laws regarding abuses of children. *Id*. at 8-26, 62. He recommended adopting preventive programs including education, medical care, family planning, job opportunities, and social security. *Id*. at 61.

The reports of the Special Rapporteur reveal difficulties faced in collecting reliable information and accurately documenting abuse. The 1992 report stated that the Special Rapporteur often lacked key information and that some information came from unreliable sources. For example, he relied exclusively on press reports for information on organ transplants and apparently did not seek to verify the information or reflect the contradictory data he received about the press reports.

In 1994 Vitit Muntarbhorn resigned and was replaced by Ofelia Calcetas-Santos of the Philippines. In 1995 the Special Rapporteur noted increased violations of the rights of the child and emphasized the need to focus on the causes of those violations. The Commission was also concerned with the plight of street children and children in armed conflicts. The Commission invited the Special Rapporteur to cooperate with the Sub-Commission's Working Group on Contemporary Forms of Slavery, the Committee on the Rights of the Child, and other U.N. bodies to elaborate on guidelines for an optional protocol to the Convention on the Rights of the Child concerning the sale of children, child prostitution, and child pornography. The Commission extended her mandate for another three years. U.N. Doc. E/CN.4/1995/L.103 (1995).

WORKING GROUP ON ARBITRARY DETENTION

In 1991 the Commission created the Working Group on Arbitrary Detention, assigning to it the task of "investigating cases of detention imposed arbitrarily or otherwise inconsistently with the relevant international standards set forth in the

Universal Declaration of Human Rights or in the relevant international legal instruments." *See* C.H.R. res. 1991/42, U.N. Doc. E/CN.4/1991/91, at 105 (1991). Headed by Chairman/Rapporteur Louis Joinet (France), the group was given a three-year mandate.

The Group initially adopted the humanitarian approach of the Working Group on Enforced or Involuntary Disappearances, accepting complaints, investigating, and receiving government replies. Its 1993 report, however, indicated that it had begun to take an adjudicative approach to its cases: "The Group takes the view that . . . investigation should be of an adversarial nature. . . ." U.N. Doc. E/CN.4/1993/24, at 102 (1993). It thus renders decisions and makes recommendations on individual complaints it accepts. The Working Group on Enforced or Involuntary Disappearances does not render decisions, though it does invite authors of complaints to comment on government responses to their cases.

The Working Group on Arbitrary Detention has dealt with hundreds of cases in its first four years. In October 1991, after its first session, the Group sent communications regarding 223 alleged cases of arbitrary detention to seventeen governments. After its second session the Working Group sent another 15 communications to 9 governments, including one "urgent action" communication to the government of the Lao People's Democratic Republic. After its third session the Working Group sent 34 communications to 24 governments. The Group also sent 11 "urgent action" messages to 10 governments. In 1993 the Group sent 18 urgent appeals to governments. The Commission in 1994 extended the mandate of the Working Group for another three years.

In 1994 The Working Group considered 300 cases and issued several urgent appeals. The Group also made its first on-site visits, to Bhutan and Vietnam. *See* U.N. Doc E/CN.4/1995/31 (1995).

SPECIAL REPRESENTATIVE ON INTERNALLY DISPLACED PERSONS

In 1992, the Commission on Human Rights requested the Secretary-General to designate a representative to gather information from governments on internally displaced persons. C.H.R. res. 1992/73, U.N. Doc. E/CN.4/1992/84, at 173 (1992). The Secretary-General appointed Francis M. Deng (Sudan).

Deng submitted his comprehensive study to the Commission at its 1993 session. His report summarized information received from governments, intergovernmental bodies, and non-governmental organizations. The report also contained data gathered in the course of on-site visits to five countries—the former Yugoslavia, the Russian Federation, Somalia, the Sudan, and El Salvador. With this information, Deng was able to give an overview of internal displacement, including its causes and consequences as well as its scope. Deng also analyzed existing law and legal institutions and offered proposals for improving both areas. U.N. Doc. E/CN.4/1993/35 (1993).

The Commission approved of Deng's ambitious efforts and decided to extend the mandate of the Representative of the Secretary-General for another two years, essentially converting the Representative's work from a study into a theme procedure. The Commission assigned the Representative the task of obtaining "a better understanding of the general problems faced by internally displaced persons and their possible long-term solutions, with a view to identifying, where required, ways and means for implementing protection for and assistance to internally displaced persons." *See* C.H.R. res. 1993/95, U.N. Doc. E/CN.4/1993/L.11/Add.9, at 3 (1993); *see also* Norwegian Refugee Council & Refugee Policy Group, Norwegian Government

Roundtable Discussion on United Nations: Human Rights Protection for Internally Displaced Persons (1993).

In his 1994 address to the Commission, Deng stated that the number of internally displaced persons had risen from 20 to 24 million in the last three years. He attributed the displacement to internal conflicts, communal violence, forced relocations, and a lack of a code of conduct focusing on the needs of internally displaced people.

In 1995 the Commission extended his mandate for an additional three years and commended Deng for his careful work on the subject. The Representative visited Burundi, Colombia, and Rwanda in 1994, bringing the total number of countries he has visited to nine.

SPECIAL RAPPORTEUR ON CONTEMPORARY FORMS OF RACISM, RACIAL DISCRIMINATION AND XENOPHOBIA

In 1993, the Commission on Human Rights created a Special Rapporteur on racism and xenophobia. The Special Rapporteur is to report to the Commission on an annual basis regarding contemporary forms of racism, racial discrimination, and xenophobia. The Commission gave the Special Rapporteur a three-year mandate. C.H.R. res. 1993/20, U.N. Doc. E/CN.4/1993/L.11/Add.3, at 6 (1993).

The Special Rapporteur, Maurice Glélé-Ahanhanzo (Benin), made his first country visit in 1994 to the U.S. He reported that racism existed in the U.S. with "sociological inertia, structural obstacles and individual resistance hindering the emergence of an integrated society based on the equal dignity of the members of the American nation." U.N. Doc. E/CN.4/1995/78.

WORKING GROUP ON THE RIGHT TO DEVELOPMENT

Also in 1993, the Commission on Human Rights created a 15-member Working Group on the Right to Development. The Working Group, in accord with its three-year mandate, is to "identify obstacles to the implementation and realization of the Declaration on the Right to Development, on the basis of information furnished by Member States and other appropriate sources." The Working Group must also "recommend ways and means towards the realization of the right to development by all States." C.H.R. res. 1993/22, U.N. Doc. E/CN.4/1993/L.11/Add.4, at 3 (1993).

The Working Group has identified several obstacles to the right to development including violence, conflict, the use or threat of force, structural inequalities in the international trading system, and the lack of democracy in the international financial institutions. FRIENDS WORLD COMMITTEE FOR CONSULTATION, SOCIETY OF FRIENDS, REPORT ON THE 1995 UN COMMISSION ON HUMAN RIGHTS 4 (1995). The Working Group meets each April and September for two-week sessions.

SPECIAL RAPPORTEUR ON FREEDOM OF OPINION AND EXPRESSION

In 1993 the Commission on Human Rights initiated a three-year mandate for a Special Rapporteur on freedom of opinion and expression, and appointed Abid Hussain of India. The Special Rapporteur must "gather all relevant information wherever it may occur of discrimination against, threats or use of violence and harassment, including persecution and intimidation, directed at persons seeking to promote the exercise of the right to freedom of expression and opinion. . . ." The Special Rapporteur must also, "as a matter of high priority, . . . gather all relevant information . . . of discrimination against, threats or use of violence and harassment, including persecution and intimidation, against professionals in the field of information seeking to exercise or to promote the exercise of the right to freedom of expression and opinion. . . ." C.H.R. res. 1993/45, U.N. Doc. E/CN.4/1993/L.11/Add.5, at 57 (1993).

According to its mandate, the Special Rapporteur is to seek and receive information from governments, NGOs, and other parties who have knowledge of relevant cases. He also is to report on the work of other United Nations agencies regarding the right to freedom of opinion and expression. *Id.* at 61. The Special Rapporteur is Abid Hussain of India.

SPECIAL RAPPORTEUR ON THE INDEPENDENCE OF JUDGES AND LAWYERS

The Commission created a Special Rapporteur on interference with the independence and impartiality of the judiciary and the independence of the legal profession in 1994. The mandate of that rapporteur is to "(a) enquire into substantial allegations transmitted to him; (b) identify and record . . . attacks on the independence of the judiciary, . . .; and (c) study important and topical questions of principle with a view to protecting and enhancing the independence of the judiciary and lawyers." C.H.R. res. 1994/41. Mr. Dato Param Cumaraswamy of Malaysia was appointed to this position.

The Special Rapporteur's first report identified several areas of focus for future years. The areas included transition to democracy, separation of powers, independence of military courts, states of emergency, independence in relation to terrorism, and the media. U.N. Doc. E/CN.4/1995/39 (1995). His mandate extends through 1997.

SPECIAL RAPPORTEUR ON VIOLENCE AGAINST WOMEN

The Special Rapporteur on violence against women was also created in 1994. This rapporteur is mandated to seek information on violence against women and make recommendations to eliminate it at all levels. The mandate also calls for the Special Rapporteur to work with other rapporteurs and working groups, as well as the Centre for Human Rights, the Division for the Advancement of Women, the Commission on the Status of Women, the Committee on the Elimination of Discrimination against Women, and other organizations. C.H.R. res. 1994/45. In her first report, the Special Rapporteur, Radhika Coomaraswamy (Sri Lanka), addressed violence against women in three areas: family, community, and the state. She also addressed traditional laws and practices which institutionalize violence against women. U.N. Doc. E/CN.4/1995/42 (1995).

SPECIAL RAPPORTEUR ON TOXIC WASTE

This procedure was established in 1995 to monitor the effects of dumping toxic wastes, primarily in developing countries. The rapporteur is directed to receive communications, make recommendations, and submit lists of countries and organizations that engage in the dumping of toxic waste. Several Western countries were opposed to creating this procedure, arguing that toxic waste only indirectly affects human rights and is beyond the scope of the Commission. C.H.R. res. 1995/81. The Commission appointed Fatma Zohra Ksentini of Algeria to this position.

NOTES AND QUESTIONS

1. For further reading on theme procedures, see:

NIGEL RODLEY, THE TREATMENT OF PRISONERS UNDER INTERNATIONAL LAW 191-218 (1987);

Marc Bossuyt, *The Development of Special Procedures of the United Nations Commission on Human Rights*, 6 HUM. RTS. L.J. 179, 194-99 (1985);

John Crook, *The Fiftieth Session of the UN Commission on Human Rights*, 88 AM. J. INT'L L. 806 (1994);

Joan Fitzpatrick, *UN Action With Respect to "Disappearances" and Summary or Arbitrary Executions*, 5 AIUSA LEGAL SUPPORT NETWORK NEWSLETTER 35 (Fall 1988).

Menno Kamminga, *The Thematic Procedures of the U.N. Commission on Human Rights*, 34 NETHERLANDS INT'L L. REV. 299 (1987);

Penny Parker, A Summary of the Major Developments at the 1995 Session of the U.N. Commission on Human Rights, Held in Geneva, Switzerland, From January 30 to March 10, 1995 World Wide Web (http://www.umn.edu/humanrts) (1995);

Nigel Rodley, *United Nations Action Procedures Against "Disappearances," Summary or Arbitrary Executions, and Torture*, 8 HUM. RTS. Q. 700 (1986);

Special Rapporteur on Violence Against Women Submits Preliminary Report, 9 INTERIGHTS BULLETIN 7 (Spring 1995);

U.N. CENTRE FOR HUMAN RIGHTS, ENFORCED OF INVOLUNTARY DISAPPEARANCES, FACT SHEET NO. 6 (1989).

As an example of how the thematic procedures operate, two reports of the Working Group on Enforced or Involuntary Disappearances are reproduced below.

***Report of the Working Group on Enforced or Involuntary Disappearances*, Addendum at 1-2, 30-32, U.N. Doc. E/CN.4/1986/18/Add.1 (1986) (footnotes omitted):**

Report on the visit to Peru by two members of the Working Group on Enforced or Involuntary Disappearances (17-22 June 1985)

I. INTRODUCTION

1. Upon the invitation of the Government of Peru, two members of the Working Group on Enforced or Involuntary Disappearances, Mr. Toine van Dongen and Mr. Luis Varela Quirós, visited Peru from 17 to 22 June 1985 on the Group's behalf. The purpose of the present report on their mission should be understood as an effort to provide the Commission on Human Rights, as the Working Group's parent body, with an analysis of the situation of disappearances in Peru. It must be emphasized that the report relates primarily to the situation as the mission's members found it in June 1985. It therefore only covers facts and developments until that point in time.

2. In the conduct of the visit the two members of the Working Group were received by the President of the Republic, the Prime Minister and Minister for Foreign Affairs, the Ministers of the Interior and Justice, the President of the Supreme Court, the Attorney-General (*Fiscal de la Nación*), the Joint Command of the Armed Forces, the Political-Military Commander of National Security Sub-Zone Nr. 5 and other high officials of the Government as well as by local authorities in Ayacucho and Huanta. The members also met a great number of witnesses, relatives of missing persons and representatives of their associations as well as organizations

dealing with human rights in general. Dignitaries of the Roman Catholic Church and its Episcopal Social Action Committee (CEAS), representatives of universities, educational and national development institutions, academicians and members of the Peruvian Parliament, the bar and the media were also heard. During the short time available, every effort was made to obtain from different segments of peruvian political, legal, religious and intellectual life a maximum of views on the complex socio-political environment in which enforced or involuntary disappearances developed. The meetings both with officials and non-governmental sources were not only limited to the capital of Lima, but further expanded during the Group's visit to the cities of Ayacucho and Huanta on 20 and 21 June. The mission's members wish to stress that they received every co-operation and assistance from the Peruvian Government in the organization of their meetings with officials and did not encounter any obstacles in receiving private informants, witnesses, or relatives of missing persons. They were, however, not allowed to visit military compounds.

3.   As the Working Group's mandate is limited to the examination of questions relevant to enforced or involuntary disappearances, the present report focuses on that phenomenon. Thus, allegations of summary or arbitrary executions and torture, that were brought to the attention of the two members of the Working Group could not be dealt with on their merits in the framework of this report.

4.   Chapter II discusses the context of violence in which disappearances have occurred. Chapter III briefly explains the nation's legal and institutional framework in which the problem has to be considered. Chapter IV describes the main characteristics of individual cases of disappearances which were brought to the Group's attention, the mechanics involved as reported by relatives and witnesses, and the steps taken by them before the authorities; it further gives an appreciation of the quality of the evidence by quoting some typical testimonies and provides a detailed statistical summary; the chapter also contains a graph showing the development of the phenomenon, based on the date of the cases of disappearances which the Group has transmitted to the Government of Peru. In chapter V the position of the Government of Peru and of other official sources, such as the Office of the Attorney General, is reflected; chapter VI describes the different non-governmental sources from which the Working Group has received information; chapter VII contains observations on social and economic consequences. Finally, concluding observations are presented in chapter VIII of the report.

5.   It should be born in mind that, as a matter of principle, the Working Group on Enforced or Involuntary Disappearances discharges its mandate in a humanitarian spirit, taking a non-accusatory approach. The mission two of its members have undertaken in Peru should be viewed in the same light. . . .

VIII.   CONCLUDING OBSERVATIONS

101.   The Working Group thanks the Government of Peru and appreciates its invitation to come and visit the country, during what are, no doubt, trying times, and the measure of co-operation that the members of the mission received.

102.   The Working Group is not a court of law and hence is not called upon to establish the guilt or innocence of individuals in relation to specific allegations. Instead, in addition to clarifying cases, it is called upon, at a higher level of abstraction, to establish what the mechanics are and who is involved in a given question of enforced or involuntary disappearances, with a view to informing the Commission accordingly. Therefore, the standards of evidence to be met by prosecutors and to

be applied by judges in criminal cases do not come into play. Nonetheless, the Group is bound to evaluate any situation of disappearances in the light of all material and testimonies available to it after carefully weighing their veracity.

103.   The situation of Peru is not an enviable one. In addition to climatic disasters and a heavily mortgaged economy, the country has been beset by a brutal guerrilla organization [Sendero Luminoso]. Under the circumstances, the country requires extraordinary leadership, deeply committed to human rights, to wage an effective fight against Sendero Luminoso's terror without resorting to counter-terror. That task is in any event a formidable one.

104.   Ironically, Sendero Luminoso resorted to actual use of violence for the first time on the eve of democratic government following 12 years of military rule over the country. There can be no doubt that since then a great many disappearances have taken place in Peru. Indeed, the vast majority of cases denounced to the Attorney-General in the course of the ensuing five years would seem to be genuine cases of missing persons, even if one deducts the number of cases where people listed as missing evidently registered on the Peruvian electoral roll after the alleged date of disappearance.

105.   There is considerable evidence that Sendero Luminoso has abducted people, although mainly with a view to forcing them to join its ranks and less as a method of reprisal. Generally, disappearances do not seem to figure prominently among the methods of elimination Sendero has applied. However, [given] the attraction the movement is shown to have, particularly for the young, it seems likely that a number of people listed as missing may in reality have enrolled with Sendero Luminoso voluntarily.

106.   It appears from the overwhelming number of testimonies and statements from a wide variety of sources that the largest proportion of disappearances occurred in the course of the counter-insurgency campaign undertaken by the various branches of the armed forces and the police since the end of 1982. . . .

107.   A state of emergency has been declared in Peru, formally suspending four rights and freedoms from which derogation may indeed be made under the terms of the International Covenant on Civil and Political Rights, to which Peru is a party. The area, to which the state of emergency applies in particular, centers on Ayacucho City and encompasses all provinces where Senderistas have spread their subversive activities. Under the law, the Political-Military Command in the area has taken full control not only over all armed forces and the entire police, but also over all civil authorities as well. From there only a slim line of authority runs to the Government in Lima. Thus, as of 1982 the armed forces were granted a great deal of latitude in fighting Sendero Luminoso and in restoring public order as they saw fit, while their actions were no longer subject to ordinary democratic controls. As a result the stage was set for a situation where disappearances and concomitant violations of human rights were almost bound to take place sooner or later.

108.   Relatives of missing persons have in most cases turned to the authorities and denounced the disappearance; yet to little avail. Indeed, some sort of institutional paralysis in matters pertaining to the protection of human rights seems to have settled on the emergency zone. Prosecutors are being criticized for not carrying out proper investigations to identify the responsible parties or ensure the release of persons believed to be detained. Prosecutors, for their part, maintain that their efforts are frustrated by the military and police authorities and that they lack proper

resources. They further point to the fact that the Investigatory Police (PIP), which is supposed to assist them in their work, is placed under military command. The military authorities contend that they are not responsible for disappearances and remain silent about their actions under the state of emergency. The judiciary refers all cases involving military personnel to military courts. It appears, therefore, that theoretically a solid system of law, which when strictly applied ought to ensure protection of human rights, is not made to function properly. As a result, few of those who have disappeared are actually acknowledged to have been arrested and there are no known cases of those thought responsible having been convicted.

109.   Human rights organizations and family associations left a favourable impression, generally having provided the mission and the Working Group with solid and well-documented information. Despite the climate of fear that is said to have permeated the Ayacucho area, hundreds of witnesses openly came to see the mission's members, invariably under the eyes of the military. Amazing too was the unbridled freedom of the media, which reported extensively on the mission's activities. . . .

110.   The question of violence in Peru reflects a serious and complex interrelationship of socio-economic and political factors which are a legacy from centuries ago. In Ayacucho, the severe underdevelopment of the area has been a major contributing factor. It would appear, therefore, that only through a comprehensive development strategy can one hope to render the social fabric of the affected population more resilient in the long run. Then perhaps people would better withstand the perverting influence of violent movements and lead a normal life at last.

111.   In the short term, it would occur to the members of the mission that a number of measures could be considered that might alleviate some of the aspects of the problem of disappearances. First of all, security and personal safety seem of the essence, so that the people in the towns and countryside will no longer feel threatened by violence from all sides. Secondly, members of the police and the armed forces operating in the area should be taught the basic concepts of the Peruvian legal system and be trained in human rights matters. Thirdly, both the judiciary and the Office of the Attorney-General need to be effectively guaranteed the co-operation of all branches of the executive, notably the armed forces, as well as the resources to carry out their functions properly. Lastly, in the light of the acute hardship of the many relatives of disappeared people, it would appear that some form of relief programme is called for in order to ease their sorry lot.

*   *   *   *   *

Report of the Working Group on Enforced or Involuntary Disappearances, **Addendum at 1, 13-14, U.N. Doc. E/CN.4/1987/15/Add.1 (1986):**

Report on a second visit to Peru by two members of the Working Group on Enforced or Involuntary Disappearances (3-10 October 1986)

I.   INTRODUCTION

1.   In June 1985, two members of the Working Group, Mr. Toine van Dongen and Mr. Luis Varela Quirós, visited Peru in response to an invitation addressed to the

Group by the Government of President Fernando Belaúnde Terry to send a mission to Peru. The Government of President Alan García Pérez, which assumed power on 28 July 1985, extended a further invitation to the Working Group for a second visit to the country. Mr. van Dongen and Mr. Varela Quirós again represented the Working Group on that visit, which took place from 3 to 10 October 1986.

2.   The two members of the Working Group again received ample co-operation from the Government of Peru in the conduct of the visit and were able freely to meet all witnesses, relatives of missing persons and other private sources they wished to hear. They were received on behalf of the Government by the Ministers for Foreign Affairs, Justice and the Interior, the President of the Senate and members of the human rights commissions of both houses of the Peruvian parliament, the Attorney-General (Fiscal de la Nación), the Joint Command of the Armed Forces, the Acting Political-Military Commander in Ayacucho and members of parliament and officials of the Executive and the Judiciary, in both Lima and Ayacucho. The members of the mission heard many relatives of missing persons, as well as representatives of organizations dealing with human rights in general. They also met dignitaries of the Roman Catholic Church and its Episcopal Social Action Committee (CEAS), academic staff of the University of Huamanga (Ayacucho) and representatives of the bar and the media. The members again paid a one-day visit to Ayacucho. They were not permitted to visit military compounds.

3.   The present report updates the report on the Group's first visit to Peru (E/CN.4/1986/18/Add.1) and should be read in conjunction with it. The present report relates the developments which have occurred since President García Pérez took office as they were conveyed to the members of the mission. . . .

V.   CONCLUDING OBSERVATIONS

42.   The Working Group is grateful to the Peruvian Government for providing an opportunity to review the progress made in combating the phenomenon of disappearances in Peru, following its first visit in June of 1985.

43.   As already stated in last year's report, in assessing the situation of missing persons in Peru, the Working Group has to pay due regard to the overall context of violence in which disappearances have been reported to it. For, in both intellectual and practical terms, it is not feasible to divorce the issue of disappearances completely from related violations of human rights or from the socio-political processes that have engendered them. If it did so, the Group would not be exercising its mandate properly in the manner consistently supported over the years by the Commission on Human Rights.

44.   Being faced with a terrorist movement such as Sendero Luminoso amidst a variety of urgent economic and social problems is not an enviable position for any government to be in. Terrorist violence rages unabated, without the least respect for life, limb or property. Worse still, although for a long time it was confined to some provinces of Ayacucho and neighbouring departments, insurgence has now spread to the Departments of Cerro de Pasco (north of Ayacucho) and of Cuzco and Puno (to the south) and the capital itself has become affected. In consequence, the area covered by the state of emergency has been extended.

45.   Clearly, in its contacts with the Working Group, the previous Government was loath to admit that disappearances had indeed occurred in significant numbers and avoided apportioning responsibility for any excesses to the armed forces or the police.

It was heartening, therefore, to note that the new President declared upon taking office that his administration would not fight "barbarism with barbarism". Indeed, that promise as well as concrete action bear witness to a firm resolve to call a halt to disappearances and other violations of human rights by government forces. Civil participation has been sought in finding long-term solutions for internal strife and in promoting the cause of human rights. Establishing the National Council for Human Rights is but one example. The present Government has also resolutely opened its doors to international scrutiny of Peru's human rights record. It has taken a much more co-operative attitude towards the Group, swiftly responding to cases transmitted to it and making immediate efforts to clarify them.

46.   In parliament, interest for human rights seems to have increased markedly and this had led to the introduction of legislation designed to remedy lacunae in Peruvian human rights law.

47.   One of the major concerns expressed in the previous report concerned the wide latitude granted by the central Government to the armed forces and the police to fight Sendero Luminoso and restore public order in the manner they saw fit. At the same time it was argued that such latitude would almost inevitably lead sooner or later to disappearances and concomitant violations of human rights. It would seem that the present administration has made great strides towards regaining control over the counter-insurgency strategy followed by the armed forces. Consequently, the incidence of disappearances has decreased considerably, particularly since the end of 1985. . . .

48.   However, disappearances still continue to occur in Peru on an appreciable scale, and other forms of violence at the hands of government forces appear to have increased, particularly since the middle of 1986. The Working Group has transmitted to the Government some 160 cases that occurred in the emergency zone between August 1985 and November 1986. About half of these cases have subsequently been clarified: detention was acknowledged or subjects were turned over to the police by the armed forces or released. While this shows a welcome increase in the measure of responsiveness of the armed forces, it is also indicative of the practice of short-term disappearances as a method of counter-insurgency in breach of Peruvian law.

49.   In last year's report attention was drawn to what was described as some sort of institutional paralysis pertaining to the protection of human rights in the emergency zone. Little progress can be reported in that regard. In the majority of cases prosecutors are still obstructed in their efforts to follow up on denunciations of disappearances. The Judiciary seems ill at east with *habeas corpus* proceedings, which in any case meet with lack of co-operation from the respondents. Almost without exception civilian courts refer cases involving military and police personnel to military courts, despite the fact that the Code of Military Justice does not cover homicide, maltreatment and the like. The broad powers concentrated in the hands of the military in the emergency zone further diminish the role which civil institutions might otherwise play in applying the rule of law.

50.   Establishing a Human Rights Office under the auspices of the Attorney-General has admirably expedited the processing of cases of missing persons. Yet that fact in itself has not substantially enhanced the measure of protection extended to citizens at large. Undoubtedly, adequate access to registers of arrests maintained by the armed forces would have not only a curative but also a preventive effect. At any rate, the armed forces must be prevailed upon to co-operate more closely in the emergency zone

with prosecutors and judicial authorities. Moreover, the latter are in dire need of material and human resources, as was pointed out in last year's report.

51.   The situation of the victims among the indigenous population in the affected areas remains dismal. Humanitarian aid from national and international sources is an increasingly vital necessity. A long-term development strategy, designed to eliminate the poverty and neglect which are among the root causes of the Ayacuchan drama, is slowly getting under way, even though efforts have been set back by terrorist onslaughts.

52.   Violence cannot be countered with violence alone. Only when the structural factors that contributed to the spiral of terror and counter-terror are properly dealt with, can there be any hope of preventing a recurrence of the excesses of the past. The Peruvian Government seems keenly aware of that fact. Its task remains a formidable one.

NOTES AND QUESTIONS

1.   The Group conducted three on-site visits prior to the visits to Peru. On the first visit to Mexico in 1982 one commentator observed:

> The Working Group's first mission to *Mexico* in 1982, was an embarrassing failure. Although the delegates met both senior government representatives and domestic human rights groups, in reality it appears that they were 'taken for a ride' by the Government. The Working Group was apparently so much taken by the 'co-operation' shown by the Mexican Government that it agreed not to further pursue 'disappearance' cases in Mexico. In return, the Government promised to inform the families of the 'disappeared' of the results of any investigations. Not surprisingly, no such information has been forthcoming and for several years the 'Mexican deal' remained one of the most serious blots on the record of the Working Group. By 1986, the Working Group's patience had finally run out and it transmitted 177 newly reported cases, much to the annoyance of the Mexican Government.

Menno Kamminga, *The Thematic Procedures of the U.N. Commission on Human Rights*, 34 NETHERLANDS INT'L. REV. 299, 312 (1987).

Do you think undue concern with obtaining governmental cooperation biased the Working Group's conclusions on its visits to Peru?

Kamminga was less critical of the Group's reports on the visits to Peru. In his view "the reader is left in little doubt that the delegates hold the Peruvian Government responsible for the large majority of 'disappearances' that have occurred." He goes so far as to conclude that the Working Group "came tantalizingly close to abandoning its traditional nonjudgmental style." *Id.* at 313. *See also* NIGEL RODLEY, THE TREATMENT OF PRISONERS UNDER INTERNATIONAL LAW 211-14 (1987) (discussing the Group's on-site visits and concluding that the Group in its Peruvian visit reports dropped its traditional agnosticism, unmistakably implying that the government was responsible for many disappearances).

Do you agree with that analysis of the Peru reports? Must the Working Group's nonjudgmental posture necessarily hinder its on-site visits? Which purposes do the Working Group's visits seek to achieve?

---

4.   Further Remarks on 1235, 1503, Country Rapporteurs, and the Theme Procedures

In cases of human rights violations, advocates must choose between: (1) making an oral presentation to the Commission or Sub-Commission under resolution 1235, (2) seeking the establishment of a country rapporteur or expert under 1235, (3) providing information to a country rapporteur or expert already established by resolution 1235, (4) submitting a communication under the confidential procedure established by resolution 1503, and (5) providing information to a thematic working group or special rapporteur. Each mechanism has the purpose of promoting and protecting human rights and can be used in regard to any country, regardless of whether they have ratified a particular treaty or consented to the monitoring procedures.

Resolution 1235 is effective in situations wherein prompt publicity, public action, and continuous monitoring are required. Oral presentations to the Commission or Sub-Commission can be made by accredited nongovernmental organizations (NGOs). An oral presentation will be more effective than submitting a communication through the 1503 process when prompt attention is needed. Positive results of making an oral presentation include general hortatory resolutions passed by the Commission and publicity. The publicity may motivate the government to solve the problem on its own.

Quick, public action results from a successful campaign to establish a country mechanism. Country rapporteurs have been successful at publicizing human rights violations, collecting information, and encouraging governments to end human rights violations. Establishing a country rapporteur, however, is a difficult task.

The U.N. Secretariat may refuse to circulate a written NGO intervention about a country, unless that country is already on the 1235 agenda for the Sub-Commission or Commission. A written intervention about violations in a country not already on the agenda will ordinarily be received as a complaint under resolution 1503. Also, to mention the complaint in public discussion under 1235 risks an objection that the advocate has violated the confidentiality assured by 1503. In addition, one should note that country rapporteurs have limited monetary and human resources available, which affects their ability to carry out their mandate adequately.

Providing information to an established country rapporteur or expert, while an indirect way of influencing U.N. action, is a relatively simple procedure. Individuals, groups, NGOs, and governments may offer information on human rights violations. If a 1235 procedure has been established, this option is often better than submitting a communication under 1503, as it is faster and can draw public attention. It is also available to individuals, unlike the 1503 procedure.

The 1503 process may encourage governments to engage in an exchange of views and possibly to improve the situation without the glare of substantial publicity. It affords an incremental technique for placing gradually increasing pressure on offending governments. Many governments, including the U.S., regularly respond to 1503 communications. They may not provide a substantive answer to public criticism heard at the Commission or its Sub-Commission, because they have insufficient opportunity during the busy debate (under resolution 1235) to research and submit a good response. Also, unless there is a substantial consensus for action under 1235, governments may realize the public criticism can safely be ignored. In addition, a few governments are so offended by public criticism that they stubbornly refuse to take action to improve the situation. Hence, the 1503 procedure may sometimes afford a better opportunity for constructive dialogue than the public 1235 process. Until 1989 Iran was an example of a country which was intransigent in the face of public actions under 1235. It is doubtful, however, that Iran would have been more responsive under 1503. *See supra* chapter 4.

Resolution 1503 was created to handle continuing patterns of gross violations of human rights. If a consistent pattern can be shown, therefore, the confidential procedure may be a good choice. Although 1503 was not designed to deal with individual cases, however, U.N. officials familiar with the 1503 process indicate that large numbers of individuals have petitioned the U.N. pursuant to resolution 1503 and have obtained relief. The 1503 process may be helpful to individual victims, even though the communications will not likely be referred to the Commission. For example, until the opening of the Berlin Wall in 1989, a large number of individual complaints were filed on behalf of residents of the German Democratic Republic who were detained for attempting to emigrate. The G.D.R. government reportedly responded to such complaints on a number of occasions by releasing the individuals. Also, those individuals were often the subject of buying-out arrangements with the Federal Republic of Germany such that they were able to leave the G.D.R. At minimum resolution 1503 affords a mechanism for complaints to be received through the official channels of the U.N. and for governments to be able to respond, if they so desire.

The 1503 process, however, is painfully slow, complex, secret, and vulnerable to political influence at many junctures. The confidentiality of the process can be used as a barrier to effective U.N. action in the case of governments that do not respond to incremental pressure and continue to engage, over several years, in grave and widespread violations of human rights. Resolution 1503 cannot offer prompt assistance in emergency situations. To use the 1503 procedure, communications must be submitted by the end of April. A year passes, however, before the communication can even be considered in the Commission, which meets in March-April. Often, communications are held over by the Working Group on Communications, the Sub-Commission, or the Commission for consideration the next year. Situations arising after the submission deadline, for example, in May, could not be considered by the Commission for almost two years. If the objective is to obtain prompt publicity or public action for serious human rights violations, the 1503 process is inappropriate.

The thematic procedures are likely the most effective and prompt choice for cases involving individual victims of human rights abuses and for emergency situations. Since 1503 was created to respond to patterns of gross violations, the Working Group and Sub-Commission are not likely to forward a communication regarding an individual victim of a human rights violation. In emergency cases, requiring immediate attention, the thematic rapporteurs and working groups can achieve prompt action. They have had success with urgent appeals to governments concerning individual human rights abuses.

The drawbacks of the thematic procedures include a lack of human and financial resources to effectively carry out their mandates. The special rapporteurs have become overwhelmed with their increasing workload and limited resources. Another problem is that since their reports are so broad, and list violations occurring around the world, situations in particular countries often do not receive the attention they deserve. In addition to the different strengths and weaknesses of the procedures, their functions often overlap. For example, thematic rapporteurs have submitted specific country reports along with their comprehensive annual reports. One author described that trend as follows:

> Last year the Special Rapporteur on Torture and the Working Group on Disappearances both published a report on the Philippines in addition to their regular reports and in this way in fact acted like some sort of country rapporteurs, be it only on torture and disappearances. This year the Working Group issued a report on disappearances in Sri Lanka and the Rapporteur on Torture issued one on Indonesia and East Timor.

The consolidation of this practice of country reports by thematic mechanisms can in my view only be welcomed, since the "real" country rapporteurs seem to be under a lot of pressure in recent years. A specific advantage of this approach is that no new mandate and therefore no new decision by the Commission is needed for country reports by thematic rapporteurs; the process of getting agreement on new country rapporteurs has always proved to be cumbersome.

Koen Davidse, *The 48th Session of the UN Commission on Human Rights and UN Monitoring of Violations of Civil and Political Rights*, 10 NETH. Q. HUM. RTS. 283, 290 (1992) (citations omitted).

Another potential area of duplication involves resolution 1503 and the thematic procedures. Both mechanisms were established to handle human rights violations in areas such as torture, disappearances, and arbitrary detention, and both may be concentrating time and resources on the same situations. Their functions are distinct, however, inasmuch as the confidential procedure responds to situations of human rights violations in a country, and the thematic procedures respond to individual cases, on a global level.

The excerpts below illustrate how resolutions 1235 and 1503 and the thematic procedures have been used.

Marc Bossuyt, *The Development of Special Procedures of the United Nations Commission on Human Rights*, 6 HUM. RTS. L. J. 179, 181-94, 202-03 (1985) (footnotes omitted):

I.   THE CONFIDENTIAL PROCEDURE . . .

The confidential nature of the 1503 procedure is often criticized. It is, however, not without justification that the communications are kept confidential in the initial phase of the procedure, and that discussions of the Working Group and of the Sub-Commission on those communications are held in closed sessions. After all, the pre-trial enquiry and the deliberations of judges in a judicial trial are generally also confidential. Nevertheless, the emphasis on confidentiality in the 1503 procedure is grossly exaggerated. At least decisions of the Sub-Commission, taken with respect to communications forwarded by the Working Group, should be made public at the end of the closed meetings. If the Commission was able to establish such a practice beginning in 1978, there is absolutely no reason why the Sub-Commission should not be able to adopt exactly the same practice.

Being confidential, the 1503 procedure has all the advantages of established procedure, consisting of successive steps taken by the organs involved. A progressive adoption of these steps, which individually are considered to constitute sanctions, may induce the government concerned to accept a dialogue with the UN-organ involved. Before reaching the level of the Commission, the governments concerned are invited to present written replies; at the level of the Commission they are moreover invited to participate in the discussion of the human rights situation in their country. At every level of the procedure, it may be assumed that the cooperation shown by the government concerned in replying to these invitations, will generally dispose the organ involved favourably, and eventually increase the chances of the government of escaping further review. Whatever the organ may be, it is quite probable that cooperation will be appreciated and neglect resented.

Everything which induces a government to cooperate is particularly important because the efficacity of United Nations procedures in the field of human rights depends to a large extent, on the measure of dialogue which can be established between the United Nations and the government of the country concerned. The procedure is useful as long as it is a means of exercising pressure on the country concerned. By expressing regrets when communications are kept pending—particularly when this happens at the level of the Sub-Commission—instead of being forwarded to the superior organ, human rights friends overlook the point that there is no real solution to the problem at the end of the procedure. The succession of steps composing the procedure is more influential than the actual step itself. Keeping a communication pending at the level of the Sub-Commission can be more effective for inducing a government to start a dialogue with the United Nations than forwarding the communication to the Commission, where it can be rejected as soon as it gets there.

The possible effects of the 1503 procedure are often minimized because of its confidential nature. However, one should be aware of the limits of the confidentiality of the procedure. As a matter of fact, with the exception of the deliberations of the Sub-Commission's Working Group on communications which are really secret, not only the 26 independent experts of the Sub-Commission, but also the. . .Governments which compose the constantly renewed Commission, know exactly what happens under the confidential procedure. Consequently, all decision makers in the United Nations in the field of human rights are aware of the available information on the human rights situation in the countries concerned. This fact can be quite embarrassing to the governments concerned, particularly when they are invited to explain themselves before the Commission. There is no doubt that a continuous review of the human rights situation in a country progressively erodes its human rights reputation at the United Nations.

The main usefulness of the procedure is twofold:

(a)   confronting the human rights situation in a given country within the framework of the confidential procedure may facilitate the Commission's eventual decision to deal with it in public session. As will be demonstrated below, most "country oriented" (public) procedures have been preceded by a decision of the Sub-Commission to forward communications to the Commission within the framework of the confidential procedure;

(b)   situations in countries neglected by world public opinion can be brought to the attention of the Sub-Commission—and eventually the Commission—within the framework of the confidential procedure, although it is highly unlikely that these organs would ever address themselves to these situations if there was no such procedure.

However, since the adoption of ECOSOC resolution 1503 (XLVIII) of 27 May 1970, a tremendous development has taken place in the form of new public procedures. Particularly the "thematic" procedures, which grew out of the "country oriented" procedures—to which development the confidential procedure contributed substantially—could decrease somewhat the importance of the confidential procedure. The "thematic" working group and special rapporteurs can act much more swiftly than the organs involved in the confidential procedure. The confidential procedure probably suffers more from its inability to react immediately on urgent information and from the difficulty of breaking through the majority requirements of the Sub-Commission's Working Group on Communications, than from its confidential nature.

II.   THE PUBLIC PROCEDURE

Within the framework of the public procedure on "violation of human rights," which is based on ECOSOC-resolution 1235 (XLII) of 6 June 1967, the members of the Commission and the Sub-Commission can, during a debate in public session, refer to violations of human rights in any part of the world. This procedure may lead to the adoption of resolutions and in exceptional cases to [the] establishment of special procedures. There has been a genuine breakthrough of those procedures since 1975. Before 1975, there was only the procedure concerning the Republic of Viet-Nam (in 1963) and the ongoing procedures concerning the "outcasts" of the United Nations in human rights: Southern Africa (since 1967) and the Israeli occupied territories (since 1969). . . .

[Since 1975] several additional procedures concerning a variety of countries came into existence. These procedures concern Chile (1975), Equatorial Guinea (1979), Bolivia, El Salvador and Guatemala (1981), Poland and Iran (1982), and Afghanistan (1984). Along with this "country oriented" approach, a "thematic" approach came into existence and expanded with procedures regarding missing persons (1980), mass exoduses (1981), summary executions (1982) and torture (1985).

III.   ANALYTICAL ASSESSMENT . . .

2.   Interaction with the confidential procedure

There are also interactions between the confidential and the public procedure. Confidential procedure being confidential, it is not always possible to demonstrate these interactions. In exceptional cases it is nevertheless possible to give indications, particularly since the Chairman of the Commission started in 1978, to announce which countries are dealt with by the Commission within the framework of this procedure.

The interaction between the confidential and the public procedure is obvious in the case of Equatorial Guinea, since [ECOSOC] has, on the recommendation of the Commission, decided on 10 May 1979 (decision 1979/35) to make the relevant material public. The forwarding in 1975 of communications by the Sub-Commission to the Commission was not successful in 1976, but it was in 1977. When the government concerned refused to establish direct contacts with the Secretary-General on the matter, the Commission requested its Chairman in March 1979 to appoint a special rapporteur, as announced within the framework of the confidential procedure in 1978.

The situation of human rights in Bolivia, El Salvador and Guatemala had already been submitted to the Commission by the Sub-Commission within the framework of the confidential procedure when the Commission decided in 1981 to start with a public procedure. The Sub-Commission had decided thus in 1977 for Bolivia, and in 1980 for El Salvador and Guatemala.

The Commission's review of the situation in Afghanistan under the confidential procedure from 1981 onward, did not prevent the Commission—nor the Sub-Commission—from adopting public resolutions with respect to the human rights situation in that country. When the Commission decided in its resolution 1984/55 of 15 March 1984 to request its Chairman to appoint a special rapporteur, its Chairman announced the following day that the Commission had decided to discontinue its review of the situation in Afghanistan within the framework of the confidential procedure.

The situation of human rights in Haiti, which was also under review by the Commission within the framework of the confidential procedure since 1981, led in March 1984 to a public request by the Commission to the Secretary-General to hold consultations with the Government of Haiti. It appears from the report of the expert appointed by the Secretary-General on his visit to Haiti, that previously he had already accomplished several missions to Haiti within the framework of the confidential procedure. . . .

*   *   *   *   *

Sandra Coliver, *United Nations Machineries on Women's Rights: How Might They Better Help Women Whose Rights are Being Violated?* **in** NEW DIRECTIONS IN HUMAN RIGHTS **25, (Ellen Lutz, Hurst Hannum, & Kathryn Burke eds., 1989) (footnotes omitted):**

The 1235 and 1503 procedures derive their effectiveness from the Commission's ability to "mobilize shame." They are most likely to have an impact when the investigated government is sensitive to international scrutiny and condemnation, when publicity or the threat of publicity is substantial, and when the Commission identifies concrete steps that must be taken if the government is to escape scrutiny. A few countries appear impervious to UN condemnation but most are not. On several occasions governments have announced planned reforms during Commission or Sub-Commission meetings as concessions to escape further criticism. Most governments respond to requests from rapporteurs concerning specific cases; even when they deny allegations, their treatment of victims often improves.

*   *   *   *   *

Amnesty International, *United Nations: Oral Statement on Thematic Mechanisms,* **AI Index: IOR 41/WU 02/1994 (Feb. 17, 1994):**

In addition to the country mechanisms, the thematic mechanisms are among the most worthwhile tools that the Commission has created in its attempts to halt persistent and grave human rights violations around the world. They are particularly valuable in that they allow investigation, including on-site visits, and discussion of grave human rights violations in many countries, including those which the Commission has failed to put under full scrutiny under Item 12 [resolution 1235] of its agenda.

In the case of China, for example, Amnesty International has submitted information over the last year to the Special Rapporteurs on torture, extrajudicial, summary or arbitrary executions and religious intolerance, and the Working Group on arbitrary detention. . . . Amnesty International calls on the government to cooperate with the relevant theme mechanisms and enable them to visit the country.

In Peru, since the introduction of wide-ranging anti-terrorism legislation in May 1992, at least 2,000 people have been arbitrarily detained with the vast majority being kept incommunicado for at least the first 15 days of their detention. Until the legislation was amended in November 1993, the filing of *habeas corpus* petitions in favour of those detained was prohibited. These circumstances led to reports of scores, probably hundreds, of detainees being tortured, and to their "confessions" being used against them in cases heard *in camera* before civilian and military tribunals. The report [published in November 1992] of the UN Special Rapporteur on extrajudicial, summary or arbitrary executions, following his visit to Peru, documents the prevalence of extrajudicial executions in recent years. Amnesty International calls on the government to invite the Working Group on arbitrary detention and the Special Rapporteur on torture to visit to investigate this new pattern of human rights violations.

In other cases, the work of the thematic mechanisms can serve to inform the Commission more fully on situations that are considered elsewhere on this agenda, such as Zaire, which was the subject of a resolution under item 12 last year. . . . President Mobutu and those responsible for the security forces have neither condemned the horrific abuses nor responded to appeals for their end. In the absence of any investigation into these violations by the government, the Commission should call on the Zairean authorities to invite the appropriate thematic mechanisms to visit the country.

The point has repeatedly been made that the thematic mechanisms can only be effective if governments cooperate fully with them and, in particular, implement their recommendations. In the case of Sri Lanka, for example, the government's invitation to the Working Group on Enforced or Involuntary Disappearances to visit in 1991 and 1992 is to be welcomed. However, many of the Working Group's recommendations, particularly those dealing with the investigation of "disappearances" which occurred prior to 11 January 1991 and the prosecution of those responsible for "disappearances" and other human rights violations, have yet to be fully implemented. . . . In this year's reports, as previously, the mechanisms have identified those governments which have not replied as well as those, notably Indonesia, which have ignored proposals that they issue invitations for on-site visits.

NOTES AND QUESTIONS

1. Resolution 1503 calls for a review of its procedure "if any new organ entitled to deal with such communications should be established within the United Nations or by international agreement." On March 23, 1976, the Optional Protocol to the International Covenant on Civil and Political Rights entered into force authorizing the Human Rights Committee to consider communications from individuals who claim to be victims of violations by governments party to the Optional Protocol. In 1977 the Human Rights Committee began considering such communications. In 1979 the Secretary-General prepared an analysis comparing resolution 1503 procedures with the Optional Protocol and concluding that the two procedures were quite different. U.N. Doc. E/CN.4/1317, at 8-12 (1979). Resolution 1503 communications must reveal a consistent pattern of gross and reliably attested violations of human rights. Communications under the Optional Protocol can relate simply to a single individual. Also, 1503 communications may be filed against any government, but the Optional Protocol applies only to the 87 countries that are party to it. *See* U.N. CENTRE FOR HUMAN RIGHTS, HOW DO THE PROCEDURES DIFFER, COMMUNICATIONS PROCEDURES, FACT SHEET NO. 7, at 12-13 (1989); *see also* chapter 4, *supra*.

2. How do the Optional Protocol and the thematic mechanisms differ?

3. In addition to human rights actions taken by special rapporteurs, thematic rapporteurs, and working groups, the United Nations High Commissioner for Human Rights monitors and responds to human rights violations. The General Assembly created that position in 1993 because of shortcomings in the existing procedures. For example, they suffered from inadequate funding and understaffing, which resulted in incomprehensive reactions to situations. The High Commissioner has a great deal of discretion in his activities, but his mandate does direct him to take "an active role . . . in preventing the continuation of human rights violations around the world." U.N. Doc. E/CN.4/1995/98 (1995); *see also* Philip Alston, *The United Nations High Commissioner for Human Rights*, ASIL NEWSLETTER, at 1 (Sept.-Oct. 1995).

4. For further reading on ECOSOC resolutions 728F, 1235, and 1503, see:

MARIA BARTOLOMEI, GROSS AND MASSIVE VIOLATIONS OF HUMAN RIGHTS IN ARGENTINA, 1976-1983: AN ANALYSIS OF THE PROCEDURE UNDER ECOSOC RESOLUTION 1503 (1991);

Marc Bossuyt, *The Development of Special Procedures of the United Nations Commission on Human Rights*, 6 HUM. RTS. L.J. 179 (1985);

Reed Brody, Penny Parker, & David Weissbrodt, *Major Developments in 1990 at the UN Commission on Human Rights*, 12 HUM. RTS. Q. 559 (1990);

Karen Kenny, *Formal and Informal Innovations in the United Nations Protection of Human Rights: The Special Rapporteur on the Former Yugoslavia*, 48 AUSTRIAN JOURNAL OF PUBLIC AND INTERNATIONAL LAW 19 (1995).

Manfred Nowak, *Country-Oriented Human Rights Protection by the UN Commission on Human Rights and its Sub-Commission*, 22 NETHERLANDS Y.B. INT'L L. 39 (1991);

Penny Parker & David Weissbrodt, *Major Developments at the UN Commission on Human Rights in 1991*, 13 HUM. RTS. Q. 573 (1991);

Joe Pitts & David Weissbrodt, *Major Developments at the UN Commission on Human Rights in 1992*, 15 HUM. RTS. Q. 122 (1993);

B.G. RAMCHARAN, THE CONCEPT AND PRESENT STATUS OF THE INTERNATIONAL PROTECTION OF HUMAN RIGHTS 104-09 (public debate principally under 1235), 113-14 (written NGO statements), 136-41 (1503), 151-57 ("thorough study") (1989);

HOWARD TOLLEY, THE U.N. COMMISSION ON HUMAN RIGHTS 111-33 (1987);

Howard Tolley, *The Concealed Crack in the Citadel: The United Nations Commission on Human Rights' Response to Confidential Communications*, 6 HUM. RTS. Q. 420 (1984);

United Nations Action in the Field of Human Rights, U.N. Doc. ST/HR/2/Rev.3, at 314-26 (1988);

TON ZUIJDWIJK, PETITIONING THE UNITED NATIONS (1982).

5.   Freedom of Information Act (FOIA) and Confidentiality Under ECOSOC Resolution 1503 in Regard to the U.S.

The Freedom of Information Act (FOIA), 5 U.S.C. § 552, requires the U.S. government to make public government documents with certain specified exceptions. Complainants under ECOSOC resolution 1503 have used this statute to obtain copies of the U.S. government's response to their complaints. In June 1981 the President of the Black Law Student Association at the University of Minnesota filed a communication under ECOSOC resolution 1503 against the U.S. The communication alleged multiple violations of the human rights of black people in the U.S. The Working Group on Communications considered the communication but did not recommend it to the Sub-Commission. In October 1981 another student at the University of Minnesota requested, under the FOIA, a copy of the U.S. government's response to the 1503 communication. The U.S. government sent the material requested without protest.

Similarly, the Indian Law Resource Center submitted a 1503 communication in 1980 relating to human rights violations against the Six Nations Iroquois Confederacy. The communication was held for a year by the Sub-Commission and was then referred to the U.N. Working Group on Indigenous Populations. The Working Group on Indigenous Populations never considered the communication. The Indian Law Resource Center filed an FOIA request for the U.S. response to the 1503 communication. At first the State Department refused because the U.N. process was not clearly completed. After it became obvious that the Six Nations communication was no longer under consideration, the State Department released the U.S. response to the communication.

CHAPTER 6

COLLECTIVE AND UNILATERAL HUMANITARIAN INTERVENTION

A. INTRODUCTION   Page   217

B. QUESTIONS   217

C. U.N. MISSIONS TO MAINTAIN OR RESTORE INTERNATIONAL
    PEACE AND SECURITY   218
        United Nations, The Blue Helmets: A Review of United Nations
            Peace-keeping   219
        U.N. Secretary-General, An Agenda for Peace: Preventive Diplo-
            macy, Peacemaking and Peace-keeping   223
        Amnesty International, Peace-keeping and Human Rights   224
        Claire Palley, Sub-Commission on Prevention of Discrimination
            and Protection of Minorities, Implications of Humanitarian Ac-
            tivities for the Enjoyment of Human Rights   229
        Nancy D. Arnison, The Law of Humanitarian Intervention   234
        U.N. Secretary-General, Supplement to an Agenda for Peace   235

D. UNILATERAL ACTION   243
        Richard B. Lillich, A United States Policy of Humanitarian Inter-
            vention and Intercession   243
        Abraham D. Sofaer, International Law and the Use of Force   245
        Tom J. Farer & Christopher C. Joyner, The United States and
            the Use of Force: Looking Back to See Ahead   247

A. INTRODUCTION

The previous chapter examined procedures of the U.N. Commission on Human Rights and its Sub-Commission to use persuasion and scorn to respond to widespread and grave human rights violations. This chapter focuses on the role of the U.N. Security Council and General Assembly in authorizing armed and other collective intervention to protect human rights, and also looks at unilateral humanitarian intervention.

B. QUESTIONS

1. What roles does the U.N. play in maintaining or restoring international peace and security?

a. How have those roles evolved from the formation of the U.N. through today?

b. What are the legal bases for U.N. authority? Have they changed over the years?

2. What roles does the U.S. play in U.N. efforts to protect human rights?

a. What roles has the U.S. historically taken in U.N. human rights missions? What roles do you think the U.S. should take? How might you help convince skeptical members of Congress to adopt your views?

b. What obligations does the U.S. have as a U.N. member? As a member of the Security Council?

3. What unilateral actions can and should the U.S. take to protect human rights abroad?

a. What limits does international law impose on peaceful unilateral intervention? What additional rules apply if armed force is involved.

4. As you read this chapter, place yourself in the role of a foreign policy advisor to the President of the United States. You have been asked to propose a plan of action in light of the following hypothetical facts:

> Country Y is in northern Africa. For the past three years since its victory in Y's third-ever democratic elections, the majority party has struggled to retain popular support in the face of rampant poverty, a sudden increase in the spread of AIDs, rising crime rates, skyrocketing inflation, and charges that it is controlled by a drug cartel. Despite Y's problems, the U.S. government has continued its longstanding financial and diplomatic support of the majority.
>
> An opposition coalition had, until six months ago when its two leaders were assassinated, experienced great success in pushing for legislative and policy changes and mounting support for its candidates in elections to have been held this month. Speculation that the majority party leadership was behind the assassinations caused an outburst of violence and protest.
>
> The majority party responded by mobilizing military troops to maintain order and declaring a state of emergency. The international media has reported that troops ambushed and killed opposition leaders in most every township known to house strong opposition-support. Opposition supporters have flocked to neighboring countries out of fear for their safety. These countries have, however, begun to turn them back at the borders, claiming that their own fragile economies cannot support a refugee influx.
>
> Six weeks ago the majority party proposed and guided the passage of legislation to postpone the scheduled elections indefinitely. One week later, members of the most violent opposition faction raided an apartment complex and kidnapped 60 U.S. citizens, several of whom teach in Y's national music and theatre arts school. The captors demand U.S.-mediated negotiations of the majority's withdrawal from power—in exchange for release of the hostages. The majority refuses to step down, conduct elections, or negotiate with the opposition. The majority leader has asked the U.S. to refuse negotiations with the captors and to send troops to maintain security in Y.

C. U.N. MISSIONS TO MAINTAIN OR RESTORE INTERNATIONAL PEACE AND SECURITY

Before proceeding, students should read carefully Article 2(7) and Chapters VI and VII (particularly Articles 33, 39, and 41-42) of the U.N. Charter, reprinted in *Selected International Human Rights Instruments*. In recent years, U.N. peacekeeping efforts have increased dramatically and views as to appropriate U.N. roles have changed in response to the demands of new situations. As you read the following excerpts, focus on how the U.N. response to international emergencies has changed. Also note the variety of views as to U.N. successes and failures.

UNITED NATIONS, THE BLUE HELMETS: A REVIEW OF UNITED NATIONS PEACE-KEEPING xv-xvii, 3-8 (2d ed. 1990):

In 1988 and 1989 the United Nations Security Council set up five new peace-keeping operations. This doubled, in two years, the number of operations in the field, a striking increase when it is remembered that only thirteen such operations had been established during the previous 40 years. In September 1988, the Norwegian Nobel Committee awarded the Nobel Peace Prize to the peace-keeping forces of the United Nations.

These events have been hailed as a renaissance of peace-keeping, the innovative technique of conflict control and resolution which the United Nations has developed over the years. The late 1980s have certainly seen a much greater readiness on the part of Member States to make use of this technique. There has also been wider recognition of the contribution which it can make to the maintenance of international peace and security.

. . . [P]eace-keeping evolved as a technique for controlling dangerous regional conflicts at a time when relations between the most powerful nations were not such as to permit the Security Council to function fully in the manner envisaged in the Charter. Now, . . . the world has witnessed a dramatic improvement in the ability of the Council's members—both permanent and non-permanent—to work together to help control and resolve regional conflicts. Rather than leading to activation of the Charter provisions for the use of force by the Security Council, the new political climate has permitted greater and more effective use of the United Nations' armoury of non-violent means of controlling and resolving conflicts. . . .

An overview

The Charter . . .

Concrete measures to be taken by the United Nations Security Council, . . . [to maintain] international peace and security . . . are set out in Chapters VI and VII of the Charter. Chapter VI [Article 33] provides that international disputes "likely to endanger the maintenance of international peace and security" can be brought to the attention of the Security Council or the General Assembly. The Security Council is expressly mandated to call on the parties to settle their disputes by peaceful means, to recommend appropriate procedures or methods of adjustment and, in addition, to recommend actual terms of a settlement. The action of the Security Council in this context is limited to making recommendations; essentially, the peaceful settlement of international disputes must be achieved by the parties themselves, acting on a voluntary basis to carry out the decisions of the Council in accordance with the Charter.

If the Security Council determines that a threat to the peace, breach of the peace or act of aggression exists, the Council may use the broad powers given it in Chapter VII of the Charter. In order to prevent an aggravation of the situation, the Security Council may call upon the parties concerned to comply with such provisional measures as it deems necessary or desirable. Next, it may decide, under Article 41, what measures not involving the use of armed force are to be employed by the Members of the United Nations, including the complete or partial interruption of economic relations, communications, and the severance of diplomatic relations. Should the Security Council consider such measures inadequate, it may take, under Article 42, "such action by air, sea and land forces as may be necessary to maintain or restore international peace and security". For this purpose, all Members of the United Nations undertake to make available to the Security Council, on its call and in accordance with special agreements, the necessary armed forces, assistance and facilities. Plans for the application of armed force are to be made by the Security Council with the assistance of a Military Staff Committee.

The measures outlined in Articles 41 and 42 constitute the core of the system of collective security envisaged by the Charter. A basic feature of this system is the determining role assigned to China, France, the [Russian Federation], the United Kingdom of Great Britain and Northern Ireland and the United States of America. These Powers are permanent members of the Security Council and can block any of its substantive decisions by their veto. They also control the activities of the Military Staff Committee, which is made up exclusively of their military representatives. Consequently, the United Nations collective security system, and especially its key provision concerning the use of armed force, can work only if there is full agreement and co-operation among the [five] permanent members.

A holding action

During most of the United Nations' history this condition has not been met. The evolution of international relations after the Second World War quickly brought to the fore differences which existed among the Member States, and in particular the five permanent members of the Security Council, and these inevitably affected the functioning of the Organization. New conflicts arose, particularly during the process of decolonization, and many could not be resolved by peaceful means. A way had to be found to stop hostilities and to control conflicts so that they would not develop into broader conflagrations. Out of that need, United Nations peace-keeping operations evolved as, essentially, holding actions. . . .

As the United Nations practice has evolved over the years, a peace-keeping operation has come to be defined as an operation involving military personnel, but without enforcement powers, undertaken by the United Nations to help maintain or restore international peace and security in areas of conflict. These operations are voluntary and are based on consent and co-operation. While they involve the use of military personnel, they achieve their objectives not by force of arms, thus contrasting them with the "enforcement action" of the United Nations under Article 42.

Feace-keeping operations have been most commonly employed to supervise and help maintain cease-fires, to assist in troop withdrawals, and to provide a buffer between opposing forces. However, peace-keeping operations are flexible instruments of policy and have been adapted to a variety of uses, including helping to implement the final settlement of a conflict.

Peace-keeping operations are never purely military. They have also included civilian personnel to carry out essential political or administrative functions, sometimes of a very large scale. . . . In [several] operations, . . . civilian police have also played an important role. . . . [T]he expectation has developed that the peace-keeping operations of the future . . . may well be closely integrated civilian/military undertakings with overall responsibility in the field being entrusted to a civilian rather than a military officer.

It is difficult to subsume all these various operations under any one clause of the Charter. It is clear that they fall short of the provisions of Chapter VII described above, which deal with enforcement. At the same time they go beyond purely diplomatic means or those described in Chapter VI of the Charter. . . . Initially, questions were raised about the legality of the United Nations' use of military personnel in a manner not specifically provided for in the Charter. In recent years, however, something close to consensus has developed that these operations can be considered as having a basis, apart from the principle of consent, in the broad powers conferred by the Charter upon the United Nations and especially the Security Council.

Characteristics

In practice, there has evolved a broad degree of consensus on the essential characteristics of peace-keeping operations and on the conditions that must be met if they are to succeed.

The first of these essential characteristics is that peace-keeping operations are set up only with the consent of the parties to the conflict in question. Their consent is required not only for the operation's establishment but also, in broad terms, for the way in which it will carry out its mandate. The parties are also consulted about the countries which will contribute troops to the operation. It is a key principle that the operation must not interfere in the internal affairs of the host countries and must not in any way favour one party against another. This requirement of impartiality is fundamental, not only on grounds of principle but also to ensure that the operation is effective. A United Nations operation cannot take sides without becoming a part of the conflict which it has been set up to control or resolve. For their part, the parties to the conflict are expected to provide continuing support to the operation by allowing it the freedom of movement and other facilities which it needs to carry out its task. This co-operation is essential. . . .

In line with the Security Council's primary responsibility for the maintenance of international peace and security, peace-keeping operations have mainly been established by the Council (though two were, exceptionally, authorized by the General Assembly). This means that no operation can be established without a broad consensus within the international community that it is the right thing to do. It is the Security Council's responsibility to ensure that the operation is given a mandate which is clear, accepted by the parties concerned and practicable in the situation existing on the ground. Also essential is the continuing support of the Security Council, which may be asked by the Secretary-General to intervene if one or other of the parties fails to provide the necessary support and co-operation. If the mandate is unclear or ambiguous, the operation is likely to face recurrent difficulties and its activities may become controversial, with the consequent risk that it may lose the necessary support of the Security Council or the necessary agreement of one of the parties concerned. Nevertheless, there have been times when the mandate of a peace-keeping operation has not been as clear as could have been wished, e.g., when the Security Council has decided that the primary requirement of international peace and security requires the creation of an operation even if it is clear from the outset that the operation will not easily achieve the objectives given to it.

The military personnel who serve in peace-keeping operations are provided by Member States on a voluntary basis. Once so provided, they pass under the command of the Secretary-General in all operational matters, as the Secretary-General is responsible for the direction of the operation and is required to report thereon at regular intervals to the Security Council. Those who serve in military observer missions are almost invariably unarmed. Those who serve in peace-keeping forces are equipped with light defensive weapons but are not authorized to use force except in self-defence. . . .

Finally, it is essential that the operation should have a sound financial basis. The financing of peace-keeping has been one of its most controversial and least satisfactory aspects. Almost all operations are now financed by obligatory contributions levied on Member States. If the Member States do not pay their contributions promptly and in full, the Secretary-General lacks the financial resources needed to reimburse the troop-contributing Governments the sums due to them. This means, in effect, that those Governments have to pay an unfairly high share of the cost of the operation in question, in addition to sending their soldiers to serve in unpredictable and sometimes dangerous situations.

Peace-keeping and peace-making

Peace-keeping operations have usually been mounted only after hostilities have already broken out. However, the Charter of the United Nations aims at a system of international relations wherein the use of force as a means of foreign policy is eliminated altogether. Consequently, the Charter deals at length with the peaceful settlement of disputes. This may be achieved by various means, including multilateral diplomatic efforts within the framework of the Security Council, bilateral efforts of Member States, or through the good offices of the Secretary-General. These approaches to peace-making are by no means mutually exclusive. On the contrary, the Organization has been most successful when co-ordinated efforts were undertaken at all levels.

In recent years, there has been a marked increase in the demand for the Secretary-General's good offices, with a view to helping the parties to a conflict to compose their differences. In responding to these demands, the Secretary-General has usually been able to rely on a formal request of the Security Council or the General Assembly. In some cases, peace-keeping operations were established as a direct result of agreements reached through his and others' diplomatic efforts, and in some cases . . . as part of the complex arrangements for the final and, in the end, peaceful settlement of the conflict.

Peace-keeping operations are intended to be provisional and thus temporary measures. They can never, alone, resolve a conflict. Their tasks are essentially two: to stop or contain hostilities and thus help create conditions in which peace-making can prosper; or to supervise the implementation of an interim or final settlement which has been negotiated by the peace-makers. Ideally, peace-keeping should move in step with peace-making in a combined effort leading to the peaceful resolution of a conflict. In practice this ideal cannot always be attained. Sometimes it is less difficult to keep a cease-fire in being than to negotiate away the causes of the original conflict. In such cases it is right for the Security Council to ask itself from time to time whether the peace-keeping operation has "become part of the problem" by protecting the parties from the consequences of their negotiating stands. But it should not be assumed that longevity means that a peace-keeping operation has failed; on the contrary, longevity may be a measure of its success in preventing a recurrence of hostilities in spite of the intractability of the conflict between the parties.

*　*　*　*　*

U.N. Secretary-General, *An Agenda for Peace: Preventive Diplomacy, Peacemaking and Peace-keeping* 4-6, U.N. Doc. A/47/277 (1992):

Since the creation of the United Nations in 1945, over 100 major conflicts around the world have left some 20 million dead. The United Nations was rendered powerless to deal with many of these crises because of the vetoes—279 of them—cast in the Security Council, which were a vivid expression of the divisions of that period.

With the end of the cold war there have been no such vetoes since 31 May 1990, and demands on the United Nations have surged. Its security arm, once disabled by circumstances it was not created or equipped to control, has emerged as a central instrument for the prevention and resolution of conflicts and for the preservation of peace. Our aims must be:

- To seek to identify at the earliest possible stage situations that could produce conflict, and to try through diplomacy to remove the sources of danger before violence results;

- Where conflict erupts, to engage in peacemaking aimed at resolving the issues that have led to conflict;

- Through peace-keeping, to work to preserve peace, however fragile, where fighting has been halted and to assist in implementing agreements achieved by the peacemakers;

- To stand ready to assist in peace-building in its differing contexts: rebuilding the institutions and infrastructures of nations torn by civil war and strife; and building bonds of peaceful mutual benefit among nations formerly at war;

- And in the largest sense, to address the deepest causes of conflict: economic despair, social injustice and political oppression. . . .

This wider mission for the world Organization will demand the concerted attention and effort of individual States, of regional and non-governmental organizations and of all of the United Nations system, with each of the principal organs functioning in the balance and harmony that the Charter requires. . . .

The foundation-stone of this work is and must remain the State. Respect for its fundamental sovereignty and integrity are crucial to any common international progress. The time of absolute and exclusive sovereignty, however, has passed; its theory was never matched by reality. It is the task of leaders of States today to understand this and to find a balance between the needs of good internal governance and the requirements of an ever more interdependent world. . . .

The terms preventive diplomacy, peacemaking and peace-keeping are integrally related and. . .are defined as follows:

Preventive diplomacy is action to prevent disputes from arising between parties, to prevent existing disputes from escalating into conflicts and to limit the spread of the latter when they occur.

Peacemaking is action to bring hostile parties to agreement, essentially through such peaceful means as those foreseen in Chapter VI of the Charter of the United Nations.

Peace-keeping is the deployment of a United Nations presence in this field, hitherto with the consent of all the parties concerned, normally involving United

Nations military and/or police personnel and frequently civilians as well. Peace-keeping is a technique that expands the possibilities for both the prevention of conflict and the making of peace.

[An additional and] critically related concept [is] post conflict *peace-building*—action to identify and support structures which will tend to strengthen and solidify peace in order to avoid a relapse into conflict. Preventive diplomacy seeks to resolve disputes before violence breaks out; peacemaking and peace-keeping are required to halt conflicts and preserve peace once it is attained. If successful, they strengthen the opportunity for post-conflict peace-building, which can prevent the recurrence of violence among nations and peoples.

These four areas for action, taken together, and carried out with the backing of all Members, offer a coherent contribution towards securing peace in the spirit of the Charter. The United Nations has extensive experience not only in these fields, but in the wider realm of work for peace in which these four fields are set. Initiatives on decolonization, on the environment and sustainable development, on population, on the eradication of disease, on disarmament and on the growth of international law—these and many others have contributed immeasurably to the foundations for a peaceful world. The world has often been rent by conflict and plagued by massive human suffering and deprivation. Yet it would have been far more so without the continuing efforts of the United Nations. This wide experience must be taken into account in assessing the potential of the United Nations in maintaining international security not only in its traditional sense, but in the new dimensions presented by the era ahead.

*   *   *   *   *

Amnesty International, *Peace-keeping and human rights*, AI Index: IRO 40/01/94, at 2-6, 29-32 (1994) (footnotes omitted):

Human rights in United Nations field operations

Peace-keeping mushroomed during 1992 and 1993. Over one-third of all United Nations peace-keeping operations were established during the last three years. 1992 saw a fivefold increase in the United Nations personnel involved in peace-keeping activities. By October 1993, over 75,000 military personnel and civilian police were deployed in 18 separate peace-keeping missions. The troop strength of the UN operation in Somalia stood at 27,961 on 22 December 1993 representing one of the largest deployments ever. At the same time, the contours of what these operations are mandated to do have radically changed.

Amnesty International considers that attention to the promotion and protection of human rights has to be a central tenet of any type of peace-keeping operation. . . . With the end of the Cold War and East-West paralysis of UN decision-making, the United Nations has been presented with new opportunities for more comprehensive approaches to peace-keeping, including in some cases the formulation of specific UN mandates to address human rights issues. Some recent peace-keeping operations and civilian observer missions established in wartorn countries have been able to address human rights problems on the spot with the potential for taking immediate corrective measures and establishing programs for longer-term institution building. The fact that these are field-based missions, working over a relatively long period in the country concerned, is what makes these activities potentially very effective.

As yet, however, the United Nations has not really come to terms with this new role. While there are a growing number of precedents for human rights work being officially conducted in the context of UN peace-keeping, these measures have been elaborated in haphazard ways, illustrating a conceptual and political gap which needs to be bridged before the UN can be said to be adequately addressing the human rights aspects of conflict and post-conflict situations. Much of the thinking as well as the existing organizational structures in this area remain mired in the history of traditional peace-keeping, rather than in the future of peace-building. This has meant that many of the newer operations—or the UN Member States which collectively decide the parameters of their activities—are sometimes making up or adapting the rules to new situations as they go along, with mixed results. . . .

. . . [T]he cardinal rule of peace-keeping has traditionally been that operations are only deployed with the consent of all concerned parties. In recent years, the presumption of consent has started to become somewhat blurred as the UN has become more involved in conflicts of an internal nature. In these situations, the "consent" of the parties—whether governmental, non-governmental opposition groups, or military or paramilitary bodies—may be impossible to seek, verify or maintain. Where the absence of consent actually approaches hostility, even if only from a small sector of the population, then the UN's role begins to approach that of an active combatant and its overall role risks being coloured by this factor.

A.   Historical Overview

1.   *Traditional peace-keeping adapts to new situations*

Within the traditional conceptualization of peace-keeping, there are two main types: military observer groups and infantry-based parties. Military observer groups, which are usually unarmed, are intended to create the conditions for successful political negotiations to proceed. Essentially this means trying to maintain a cease-fire simply by virtue of the presence of an accepted impartial monitor. . . . Infantry-based forces, which carry arms, albeit usually light weapons, are generally mandated to establish and control demilitarized or buffer zones in order to physically separate parties to a conflict. This sometimes includes disengaging and supervising separation of forces. . . .

In the current proliferation of peace-keeping operations and the variety of situations and tasks to which such missions are assigned, traditional peace-keeping functions are now also being applied in more novel situations. . . .

The UN Observer Mission in Liberia (UNOMIL) represents a particularly interesting new development in the UN's "traditional" military observer role. In this case, the UN's mandate is mainly to oversee the actions of the regional peace-keepers, rather than the Liberian parties themselves. In view of the inability of the Economic Community of West African State's peace-keeping force in Liberia (ECOMOG) to keep the peace in accordance with a 1991 peace plan, the warring parties signed a new peace agreement in Cotonou in July 1993. The Cotonou agreement stipulated that the UN should deploy military observers to monitor the cease-fire verification and demobilization activities of the new ECOMOG. While some degree of peace enforcement powers are conferred upon the regional organization, the UN will be responsible for monitoring the prescribed actions of the regional peace-keeping force, including search, seizure and storage of weapons, demobilization of forces and the guarding of encampments. Among actions which, as defined in the Cotonou agreement, would constitute violations of the cease-fire are: obstruction, harassment and attacks on peace-keeping personnel. Although the United Nations is acting merely as an observer force in Liberia, the Cotonou agreement does provide for comprehensive traditional measures leading to elections. . . .

A new form of peace-keeping which is also traditional in terms of its basic function, but which has only become a viable political option since the end of the Cold War, is now called "preventive deployment". Sometimes called a "trip-wire" force, this refers to an international force deployed in a country not yet experiencing or involved in conflict but where conflict could occur. UN Secretary-General Dr. Boutros Boutros-Ghali has called for the increased use of preventive deployment in countries whose neighbours are at war and there is a fear of "spill-over". He has also suggested preventive deployment as an option for countries experiencing civil crises which could result in armed conflict. The country where the UN troops are based would normally request their deployment at a point when there is no actual conflict taking place. This type of operation has been used so far only in the former Yugoslav Republic of Macedonia where about 1,000 peace-keepers have been guarding the border with Serbia since June 1993.

2. *The new wave: implementation of comprehensive settlements (peace-keeping meets peace-building)*

The comprehensive 1978 settlement plan for the independence of Namibia, which was finally enabled to go forward in 1988, initiated the new wave of peace-keeping operations, characterized by the implementation of comprehensive peace settlements. . . . The most recent operation of this type is in Rwanda . . ., which was approved by the Security Council in October 1993. . . .

All of these operations have been based on broad peace agreements between parties to the conflict. In some cases the agreements have been brokered by the UN. . ., while other agreements. . .had little UN involvement during initial negotiations. In all cases, however, the parties have agreed that the UN should play a key role in verifying the implementation of the agreement. . . . These peace agreements are called comprehensive settlements because they have involved significant internal restructuring processes in the country concerned in military and civilian sectors. They have generally aimed to culminate in national elections.

In these operations UN personnel have been deployed in the country to oversee the restructuring process in accordance with an agreed timetable. This has involved a range of military and civilian tasks for the UN, including: monitoring cease-fires; overseeing demobilization of troops and weapons destruction; monitoring the integration or formation of and training new armed forces and national police forces; investigating human rights violations; resettling refugees and demobilized soldiers; providing humanitarian assistance; observing and verifying elections; conducting public information campaigns or technical assistance programs with legislative, judicial and administrative tasks; and working with or supporting the development of national institutions as well as local non-governmental organizations ('NGOs').

In the new vocabulary of the UN, therefore, such operations have not served just as a passive barrier between fighting forces (peace-keeping), but they have also established and actively monitored longer-term institution-building processes (peace-building). Various peace-building tasks have generally been allocated to separate specialized components within the UN operation, for example: military observers, civilian police monitors, civilian human rights observers, refugee protection officers, electoral monitors, judicial or legislative advisers, technical development and demining experts, and political and administrative personnel. Often specialized agencies, such as the UN High Commissioner for Refugees, have a major role in the peace process, but they have usually remained structurally outside of the peace-keeping operation itself. Regrettably, however, most of these operations and any human rights components they have included have been worked out in New York at UN headquarters with a marked lack of involvement, consultation or cooperation with the UN's own human rights bodies and experts or its Centre for Human Rights, based in Geneva, and with hardly any reference to other UN programs such as the Vienna-based crime prevention and criminal justice program. Amnesty International considers that these other programs, which have specialist experience to contribute, need to be much more closely integrated into the planning, design, implementation and follow-up of the relevant aspects of these operations, particularly the human rights components. . . .

Attacks on peace-keepers and indiscriminate use of force by peace-keepers

1. Attacks on UN peace-keepers: investigations and jurisdiction

With the massive expansion of UN military and civilian personnel deployed in the field in the last couple of years, peace-keepers have faced increasing attacks and higher numbers of casualties among their ranks, with over 170 killed in 1993 alone. . . . This has made UN Member States understandably increasingly reluctant to risk the safety and lives of their own soldiers in such operations, and the UN is now faced with a crisis of confidence in this regard.

It is now almost standard for Security Council resolutions authorizing peace-keeping operations to include statements that individuals found guilty of attacks on international peace-keeping and humanitarian personnel will be held individually accountable for these acts. . . .

In many cases where a UN presence has been secured without recourse to enforcement powers, it should be expected that the national authorities in the country where the peace- keepers are stationed would investigate and prosecute such attacks. . . . However, operations mandated under Chapter VII of the UN Charter, where peace-keepers are authorized to use force beyond what would be necessary purely for self-defense, present particularly complex problems in this regard. . . .

While it may be quite legitimate for the Security Council to authorize the investigation of attacks on the UN and the arrest of those suspected of being responsible, Amnesty International considers that it is necessary that the review of the grounds for detention, prosecution, judgment and any eventual punishment be handled by independent judicial bodies. At the moment, however, such bodies do not exist at the international level to adjudicate crimes of this nature, except in respect of the conflict in the former Yugoslavia. The February 1993 decision to establish the International Tribunal for Crimes in the Former Yugoslavia marks the first time such an international mechanism with a jurisdiction for trying individuals under international law has existed since the Nuremburg and Tokyo war crimes tribunals. . . . Amnesty International has urged that this tribunal be a first step towards setting up a *permanent* international court competent to try grave violations of humanitarian and human rights law, *wherever* these may occur. . . .

. . . Amnesty International considers it equally imperative, when drawing up any declaration or mechanism outlining the obligations on Member States and possible individual criminal responsibility in relation to attacks on UN forces and personnel, that similar obligations are attached to UN forces themselves, and the Member States which contribute troops to those forces. If UN forces are to be covered by special status and agreements, and privileges of diplomatic immunity and noncombatant status, the corollary is that their own rules of engagement have to restrain UN forces from resorting to excessive use of force . . ..

2. Disproportionate use of force and other abuses by UN peace-keeping troops

According to Security Council Resolution 794, the Secretary-General and Member States are authorized under Chapter VII of the Charter "to use all necessary means to establish as soon as possible a secure environment for humanitarian relief operations" in Somalia. . . . On occasion, peace-keeping forces are clearly involved in open combat situations, responding to armed attacks. But when launching operations to establish a secure environment, . . . forces cannot exceed the Council's authorization and pursue a course which is aimed at traditional military gains. It must be stressed that the word "necessary" has a legal meaning which implied that there are no alternative options which would be less harmful. In fact, applying the customary principle of proportionality in this context demands that, for any one attack, the civilian damage must be the minimum necessary to achieve the particular aim (in the Somalia example, establishing a secure environment for the delivery of humanitarian aid). If the civilian casualties and damage are disproportionate to the attempted gains by the international forces, then those forces and their commanders would be in breach of international humanitarian law and acting outside the authority mandated to them by the Security Council.

It is explicit in the UN Charter that the Security Council must "act in accordance with the Purposes and Principles of the United Nations," which include respect for justice and international law. However, Amnesty International believes that it must also be explicitly stated that UN personnel are bound by international humanitarian and human rights law in the carrying out of their tasks. In particular, the UN must ensure that troops under its command carrying out law enforcement functions, such as arrest, detention, search and seizure, crowd dispersal or ensuring public order, are trained in and abide by international human rights and criminal justice standards. . . . The fundamental principle of these standards is that force may be used only when strictly necessary and only to the minimum extent required under the circumstances. . . .

When actually responding to an armed attack it must similarly be made clear to all troops that, despite the humanitarian nature of their mission and the authorization of the Security Council, they still have to abide by international humanitarian law as set out in the Geneva Conventions and their Protocols as well as general principles of humanitarian law such as proportionality and the avoidance of indiscriminate attacks. Proportionality in this context means only using the force necessary to avert the immediate danger. It cannot relate to the mission's overall military objectives, as peace-keeping soldiers are not fighting a war with military aims. The principle is applicable whether or not the Geneva Conventions are legally binding. In fact, the report of the independent expert engaged to carry out an investigation into the 5 June 1993 attacks on UN forces in Somalia notes that, with regard to the principles embodied in the Conventions: "Plainly a part of contemporary international customary law, they are applicable wherever political ends are sought through military means. No principle is more central to the humanitarian law of war than the obligation to respect the distinction between combatants and noncombatants." Amnesty International considers that forces acting under UN authority are similarly bound by these principles.

According to Article 51(4) of Protocol I of the Geneva Conventions, indiscriminate attacks are those which cause incidental civilian losses and damage excessive in relation to the concrete and direct military advantage anticipated. Again, because the advantages are not military but merely what is necessary for self-defence or the protection of humanitarian assistance, or even exceptionally the arrest of someone wanted in connection with war crimes, the permissible use of force is likely to be even less that which might be justified in the event of all-out war. It has recently been pointed out that there is now increasing danger that UN forces operating in an enforcement capacity may perceive themselves to be fighting a just war and therefore believe those objectives would somehow warrant taking the risk of greater collateral civilian casualties than would normally be anticipated.

NOTES AND QUESTIONS

1.   The excerpts identify several forms of U.N. intervention. What are those different forms? How do they differ? When might the use of each be appropriate? Which might be a reasonable response to the crisis in Y; *see supra at 2*? What factors seem most supportive of an argument to deploy U.N. forces? What factors might contradict that position?

2.   Does the U.N. Charter authorize the Security Council to decide that a humanitarian emergency, absent any act of aggression or threat of international armed conflict, constitutes a threat to the peace?

3.   Did the Charter create a collective decision-making process, or do individual permanent Security Council members seem to control where, when, and how the U.N. will or will not intervene under Chapter VII?

4.   The Amnesty International excerpt above references the problem of U.N. troops committing violations of international human rights and their U.N. mandates. In 1994 nine soldiers from Canada's peacekeeping regiment in Somalia were court-martialed for the torture and death of a Somali teenager suspected of stealing. Investigations revealed also that members of white supremacist groups had developed a strong presence in a Canadian peacekeeping unit in Somalia and thus cast doubt on other incidents where Canadian peacekeepers killed Somali civilians. *See* Charles Trueheart, *Tapes Embarrass Canada Airborne Unit Shown as Violent, Racist*, WASH. POST, Jan. 21, 1995, at A17; Charles Trueheart, *Canadian Peace Keepers Accused: Cases of 2 Killings in Somalia Spark Criticism of Revered Forces*, WASH. POST, May 22, 1993, at A18.

5.   What steps may the U.N. and governments participating in U.N. peacekeeping efforts take to ensure that peacekeepers will abide by international humanitarian and human rights laws? Should the Security Council adopt a decision requiring all U.N. forces to follow the Geneva Conventions, other tenets of humanitarian law, and such human rights norms as the Convention Against Torture and Other Cruel, Inhuman or Degrading Treatment or Punishment?

Claire Palley, Sub-Commission on Prevention of Discrimination and Protection of Minorities, *Implications of Humanitarian Activities for the Enjoyment of Human Rights* 2-11, U.N. Doc. E/CN.4/Sub.2/1994/39 (1994) (footnotes and paragraph numbers omitted):

The expansion of classical peace-keeping (by way of verification by and neutral interposition of forces stationed by consent of the host State) into authorization of the use of force . . . into authorization of full-scale war against Iraq after the latter's invasion of Kuwait, and then into lesser but still considerable use of armed force in internal and international armed conflict in Somalia and in Bosnia and Herzegovina, has required alterations in the United Nations rules of engagement and raised questions about the applicability of humanitarian law to United Nations forces, in particular the permissible degree of force employable, the requirement of proportionality, the prohibition against indiscriminate use of force impacting on civilian populations, the applicability of humanitarian law to protect United Nations personnel in conflict or when captured, and the observance of human rights by members of United Nations forces or any United Nations administration.

It will be obvious that these issues raise potential difficulties of reconciliation between the Security Council's security-cum-political dispute settlement mandate and its duty under Article 24.2 of the Charter to act in accordance with the United Nations Purposes and Principles. Articles 1 and 2 of the Charter arguably require the Council to respect human rights, to act in conformity with international law (i.e. including humanitarian customary law) and to cooperate in solving problems of a humanitarian character. There will in practice always be difficult choices between values and their respective primacy when the Security Council authorizes peacekeeping—itself a humanitarian operation because armed conflict results in human rights violations and flows of displaced persons and refugees. The use of force has political effects, which may counteract the humanitarian objectives of the action. For example, force used to protect persons or in United Nations forces' self-defence involves direct confrontation with other armed forces or factions, such a protective role leading to rejection of the notion that United Nations forces are neutral and impartial. The threat or use of force to protect "safe areas" and besieged towns likewise means that the United Nations forces will not be perceived as neutral.

Similarly, United Nations reporting of alleged crimes against humanity, war crimes and genocide means that its political function of negotiating a settlement becomes more difficult. If the United Nations seeks a settlement, rather than seeing continuing or worsening violence, its negotiators will in practice have to deal with persons allegedly responsible for such crimes and they will be tempted to ignore the violations, effectively tolerating impunity, a violation itself of human rights. . . . Once the Secretary-General, or negotiators accepted by concerned parties, has proposed compromises to end particular conflicts, there is risk of having to choose between restoring peace and long-term observance of human rights. A settlement in Bosnia and Herzegovina or Croatia, which legitimated "ethnic cleansing," ethnic discrimination, grave violations of human rights and the fruits of covert aggression by any neighbouring State, would, were it endorsed by the Security Council, contravene the Purposes and Principles of the United Nations as well as the purposes pledged by Article 56 to be achieved by joint and separate State action in cooperation with the Organization. . . .

Another significant development occurred in a sphere where the Security Council's security and humanitarian mandates intersect with the Charter-confirmed authority of States to retain their sovereignty and normal incidents of that sovereignty. . .unless their has been modification by the procedures stipulated in the Charter, e.g., amendment or agreement. The Council determined that the commission of atrocities in the former Yugoslavia constituted a threat to the peace, and subsequently established machinery to prosecute and try in an international criminal tribunal individuals alleged to have committed crimes against humanity in armed conflict. The tribunal's establishment was considered by the Council to be a contribution to the restoration of peace, but it is arguable whether the Charter has given power to the Council to create judicial tribunals, and whether it may deal with matters of individual responsibility.

Anticipatory action, deterrence, counter-measures to restore or maintain peace and measures of reparation potentially conflict with other United Nations mandates, notably States' sovereign equality, self-determination (of their peoples) and legal rights preserved by Articles 1.2, 2.1 and 2.7 of the Charter and thus authorized in so far as not limited by the exception within Article 2.7. The Security Council, by Article 24.2, must in discharging its duties act in accordance with these mandates, as they form part of the United Nations Purposes and Principles. Arguably, the demarcation of the Iraq-Kuwait boundary . . . is contrary to the rule of international law that boundaries are demarcated by States, either in treaties or following arbitral awards made by agreement. More significant from a human rights perspective is Iraqi subjection. . .to a compensation mechanism, with a Compensation Commission composed of 15 Security Council members, and the sequestration of Iraq's major natural resource, with its allocation for compensation purposes to persons other than those determined by Iraq. This arguably contravenes the Iraqi peoples' right freely to dispose of their natural wealth. Furthermore, article 1.2 of the International Covenant on Economic, Social and Cultural Rights provides that "In no case may a people be deprived of its own means of subsistence."

There are also conflicts as between mandates or functions and duties of the same organ. Whereas the Security Council has authority by Article 41 to impose measures interrupting economic relations (sanctions or embargoes) it is also mandated by Article 1 of the Charter to promote respect for human rights (including the social and economic rights), to solve problems of a humanitarian character, and to settle international disputes in conformity with international law, this last comprehending humanitarian law. Sanctions imposed by the Council have indiscriminately impacted on civilian populations. . . .

There are no criteria, developed by the United Nations for guiding decision-making and choice in cases of conflict between duties, functions, rights and values. Practitioners with refugee and international relations expertise and experts in the human rights and moral fields have proposed operational guidelines, assisting the taking of difficult decisions. . . . Legal principles akin to these prudential criteria need to be enunciated to assist United Nations decision-making. Such principles are implicit in humanitarian law and in general international law, in particular the principle of humanity, which underlies both human rights and humanitarian law. Other implied legal principles are proportionality and necessity.

Minimum use of force has long been a principle recognized in the United Nations rules of engagement. Other principles include universality, impartiality and non-selectivity in the application of human rights standards. . . .

It should also be noted that there has been no legal argument produced as to a duty to take humanitarian enforcement action. The legal duty is to consider, in accordance with legal principles, whether such action is appropriate and is likely to be effective. If this is done, decisions to act may or may not be taken, depending upon the circumstances, but criticism that there have been apparently arbitrary exercises of discretion not overtly guided by recognized criteria will be more difficult to level. . . .

The rapidly evolving role of the Security Council in authorizing peace-keeping forces to meet pressing humanitarian needs by ensuring safe delivery of aid and by protecting threatened civilian populations, with such action culminating in collective use of force, has been the most controversial development. It began in 1991 with the determination. . .that Iraq's repression of the Kurds, Iraqi nationals in Iraq, threatened international peace and security in the region. Kurdish refugees were streaming towards the Turkish border, which gave colour to that characterization. However, without Iraq's consent, safe havens were established in the area, which assisted that area in subsequently becoming autonomous. The resolution also insisted that Iraq allow immediate access by international humanitarian organizations to all in need of assistance in all parts of Iraq.

Another development of acting without consent of a State concerned was the continued stationing of UNPROFOR [U.N. Protection Force] in Croatia. . ., initial consent not being renewed. Many mandatory resolutions, affecting various of the new States formed from the former Yugoslavia and engaged in conflict in its one-time territory, have since then been made under Chapter VII of the Charter—such developments, however, being within traditional concepts, because neighbouring States were covertly or overtly threatening the peace.

Finally, in Somalia, where the Government has collapsed in a civil war continued by armed factions, [the] Security Council . . ., expressing grave alarm at widespread violations of humanitarian law and dismay at the impeding of delivery of humanitarian supplies, authorized deployment of United States forces in order to secure a safe environment for relief operations. The Somalia precedent is a less weighty precedent for possible future humanitarian interventions, because of the absence of a functioning Government. Indeed, the argument has been put that there is a "collapsed State" incapable of manifesting consent or non-acquiescence. . . .

Recent Security Council practice abandoning the requirement for State consent or implied acquiescence to United Nations collective intervention under Security Council authority has reraised questions concerning the scope of Article 2.7 (the author[ization] . . . by the Charter for States to retain exclusive competence in matters essentially within their domestic jurisdiction other than in case of action under Chapter VII).

There has been an explosion of writing on the lawfulness of collective humanitarian intervention, and revival of argument that individual States or a group of States have not only the right to take coercive action by way of self-defence under Article 51 of the Charter, combined with a duty to notify the Council, but also individual rights as States to engage in humanitarian interventions.

The most radical approach to humanitarian intervention (or intervention following massive violation of human rights) has been put forward by American jurists. Professor Reisman reinterprets Article 2.4 of the Charter, which prohibits the threat or use of force against territorial integrity or political independence, so as not to preclude forcible assistance in pursuit of self-determination (a construction consistent with earlier assistance to overthrow colonialist regimes, something not contemplated by doctrine when the Charter was agreed, but later developed) or to maintain world order. Employing the concepts of political thought, he also sees "sovereignty" as "popular," and not as "State" sovereignty, in the context of the ongoing development of the concept of self-determination. On this basis, it would be lawful, assuming that refugee flows from the island of Haiti do not constitute a threat to the peace, for there to be intervention because the Haitian people's right to self-determination has been thwarted by a military *coup d'état*.

Conversely, an expansive concept of self-determination may have the effect of precluding or invalidating intervention. The right to self-determination arguably encompasses the right of a people to survive in their current State and territory and this requires the people and State to have the right to defend itself. Such a right, it can be asserted, is a matter apart from Article 51, which allows self-defence until the Council has taken measures "necessary to maintain international peace"—objective wording implying that the right of self-defence persists if inadequate measures are taken. It may be that the continued application of the arms embargo, which the Security Council imposed . . . on the former Yugoslavia, now extinct, can be characterized as being in breach of Bosnia and Herzegovina's right to self-determination. . . .

Another approach has tentatively been put forward by Mr. Deng, the Representative of the Secretary-General on internally displaced persons: he proposes an international standard stipulating that "any Government that fails to provide the most fundamental rights for major segments of its population can be said to have forfeited sovereignty and the international community can be said to have a duty in those instances to re-establish it." Sovereignty will have "collapsed" by virtue of the Government's incapacity to prevent gross violations. If the world community intervenes to restore democratic self-government, the question is, how far may it go? May it establish a temporary government, or may it establish a constitution? In Somalia the Security Council has thought it inappropriate to take such steps, encouraging the various factions themselves to agree on such matters. If agreement is not forthcoming, should the Council content itself with temporary restoration of order and then just remove the forces it has authorized, at which stage human rights violations and human suffering will recommence?

An equally radical view of the right of humanitarian intervention, but one excluding the use of force, has been proposed by French humanitarian thinkers. They claim that States have a right of unconditional free access to victims to safeguard life. Admittedly, the General Assembly, in a series of resolutions . . ., has declared its concern about the suffering of victims of natural disasters and of emergency situations and emphasized the importance of humanitarian assistance. It has recommended that States in proximity facilitate such aid and has called for cooperation. . . . This is not a recognition by the General Assembly of such a right. However, the Assembly has welcomed the establishment by concerted action of temporary relief corridors for distribution of emergency aid and subsequently indicated that State acquiescence would suffice to permit provision of aid, rather than treating such provision as requiring a formal request by the State whose population was to be aided.

In the longer term the duty of all Member States to cooperate in solving humanitarian problems (Charter, Article 1.3), the duty (under Articles 55 and 56) to promote solutions of economic, social, health and related problems and to achieve universal respect for human rights (including the economic and social rights) may come to be seen as imposing a responsibility on States to respect, as a minimum, the right to life of individuals and as creating a correlative right by State actors in a world constitutional system with a human regime to intervene when there are large-scale threats to life. . . .

An alternative approach, facilitating the right of States to provide assistance, would be recognition of an individual right to seek humanitarian assistance and protection.

Such a right is a necessary implication of the right to life. A parallel notion is the right to seek asylum, which permits an asylum-granting State to contend that it is not committing an unfriendly act towards the asylum-seeker's State of origin. The great conceptual leap, however, is from action outside another State's territorial jurisdiction (in the case of receiving an asylum-seeker) to action within another State's territory (provision of humanitarian assistance).

NOTES AND QUESTIONS

1. Both U.N. Secretary-General Boutros-Ghali (in "An Agenda for Peace") and Amnesty

International praised the Security Council's increased deployment of humanitarian intervention. Considering the report by Claire Palley, do you think the increase has come at the cost of excessive erosion of protection for the "sovereignty" and independence of smaller countries?

2.   Palley's report highlighted the conflict inherent in the multiple roles assigned to U.N. peacekeeping forces: peacekeeper, peacemaker, neutral party, and insurer of human rights protection. Can the conflicts be resolved while ensuring that each role is respected? Would doing so require a redistribution of authority within, or apart from, U.N. forces? How might roles come into conflict in the context of the Y crisis?

3.   The Palley report raised questions regarding the justification for and legality of humanitarian intervention. She and the U.N. Sub-Commission on Prevention of Discrimination and Protection of Minorities recommended further study of the issue, but the United States, in March 1995, persuaded the U.N. Commission on Human Rights to reject the proposal. C.H.R. dec. 1995/107, at 1-2, U.N. Doc. E/CN.4/1995/L.42 (1995). Why do you think the U.S. opposed further U.N. study and assessment of humanitarian intervention?

4.   The Palley report questioned whether the U.N. Charter authorizes the Security Council to create the international criminal tribunal for the former Yugoslavia and, by inference, Rwanda. Considering the material presented in chapter 7 and here in chapter 6, how do you assess that issue?

5.   The Palley report also expressed concern that the Security Council's demarcation of the Iraq-Kuwait boundary may have been contrary to international laws regarding state sovereignty. Do you agree?

*   *   *   *   *

Nancy D. Arnison, *The Law of Humanitarian Intervention*, in REFUGEES IN THE 1990s: NEW STRATEGIES FOR A RESTLESS WORLD, 37, 37-38, 40-42 (Harlan Cleveland ed., 1993):

Framing the Issue

The world community is often paralyzed when confronted with grave human suffering inside nations which block humanitarian aid from the outside world. National sovereignty has been revered as an almost sacred principle. Regrettably, it has been used to bar the international community from intervening to protect and assist internally displaced persons and other human rights victims. Some abusive governments still use the cloak of "state sovereignty" to repress, brutalize or starve their citizens, decrying outside intervention as interference with domestic affairs. The international community has failed to develop consistent policies and mechanisms for challenging the sovereignty of recalcitrant governments in order to provide aid across national boundaries or to assist victims of conflict when no government is in control. . . .

Recommendations

Sovereignty must yield to human suffering. The international community must increase its capacity and political will to reach the desperate, vulnerable populations trapped inside repressive and strife-ridden states. . . . A system of genuine humanitarian intervention will require firm legal underpinnings, consistent criteria, collective decision-making, and adequate institutional and financial resources. . . .

Forcible humanitarian intervention currently can be authorized under the collective security provisions of the UN Charter (Chapter VII) when the Security Council decides that a humanitarian crisis constitutes a threat to international peace and security. . . .

Situations undoubtedly will arise where the suffering alone is so severe as to warrant humanitarian intervention even though international peace is not apparently at risk. Is it morally defensible to allow the use of force to preserve peace and security, but not to alleviate massive human suffering? . . .

Despite its weaknesses, the "threats to international peace" justification for forcible humanitarian intervention is a necessary and valid tool for overriding sovereignty and should be further developed. Most cases of massive displacement and grave human rights violations will pose obvious threats to international peace and will thus fit directly within Charter principles. The legality of forcible relief, however, should not be denied solely because a particular human tragedy fails to put other countries at risk. International law should recognize massive human suffering, in its own right, as a legitimate challenge to sovereignty for purposes of both forcible and non-forcible humanitarian intervention. . . .

. . . The central principle of any process must be collective decision-making. There is new opportunity for collective action within the UN structure in light of renewed confidence in the ability of the United Nations to tackle global challenges. Collective action will decrease the ability of individual states to use humanitarian intervention as a pretext for interfering in another state's affairs.

*   *   *   *   *

U.N. Secretary-General, *Supplement to an Agenda for Peace: Position Paper of the Secretary-General on the Occasion of the Fiftieth Anniversary of the United Nations* 2-18, U.N. Doc. A/50/60 (1995) (paragraph numbers omitted):

I.   INTRODUCTION

. . . Most of the ideas in "An Agenda for Peace" have proved themselves. A few have not been taken up. The purpose of the present position paper, however, is not to revise "An Agenda for Peace" nor to call into question structures and procedures that have been tested by time. . . . Its purpose is, rather, to highlight selectively certain areas where unforeseen, or only partly foreseen, difficulties have arisen and where there is a need for the Member States to take the "hard decisions" I referred to two and a half years ago. . . .

II.   QUANTITATIVE AND QUALITATIVE CHANGES

It is indisputable that since the end of the cold war there has been a dramatic increase in the United Nations activities related to the maintenance of peace and security. [Boutros-Ghali then cites statistics showing that the number of military personnel deployed by the U.N. has increased from 9,570 in January 1988 to 73,393 in December 1994 and that the U.N.'s budget for peacekeeping operations increased almost 15-fold during the same period. The number of disputes and conflicts in which the U.N. was actively involved in preventive diplomacy or peacemaking increased from 11 to 28 during the 7-year period.]

This increased volume of activity would have strained the Organization even if the nature of the activity had remained unchanged. It has not remained unchanged, however: there have been qualitative changes even more significant than the quantitative ones.

One is the fact that so many of today's conflicts are within States rather than between States. The end of the cold war removed constraints that had inhibited conflict in the former Soviet Union and elsewhere. As a result there has been a rash of wars within newly independent States, often of a religious or ethnic character and often involving unusual violence and cruelty. The end of the cold war seems also to have contributed to an outbreak of such wars in Africa. In addition, some of the proxy wars fuelled by the cold war within States remain unresolved. Inter-state wars, by contrast, have become infrequent. . . .

The new breed of intra-state conflicts have certain characteristics that present United Nations peace-keepers with challenges not encountered since the Congo operation of the early 1960s. They are usually fought not only by regular armies but also by militias and armed civilians with little discipline and with ill-defined chains of command. They are often guerrilla wars without clear front lines. Civilians are the main victims and often the main targets. Humanitarian emergencies are commonplace and the combatant authorities, in so far as they can be called authorities, lack the capacity to cope with them. . . .

Another feature of such conflicts is the collapse of state institutions, especially the police and judiciary, with resulting paralysis of governance, a breakdown of law and order, and general banditry and chaos. . . . It means that international intervention must extend beyond military and humanitarian tasks and must include the promotion of national reconciliation and the re-establishment of effective government.

The latter are tasks that demand time and sensitivity. The United Nations is, for good reasons, reluctant to assume responsibility for maintaining law and order, nor can it impose a new political structure or new state institutions. It can only help the hostile factions to help themselves and begin to live together again. . . .

Peace-keeping in such contexts is far more complex and more expensive than when its tasks were mainly to monitor cease-fires and control buffer zones with the consent of the States involved in the conflict. . . .

A second qualitative change is the use of United Nations forces to protect humanitarian operations. Humanitarian agencies endeavour to provide succour to civilian victims of war wherever they may be. Too often the warring parties make it difficult or impossible for them to do so. . . . There is also a growing tendency for the combatants to divert relief supplies for their own purposes. Because the wars are intra-state conflicts, the humanitarian agencies often have to undertake their tasks in the chaotic and lawless conditions described above. . . .

A third change has been in the nature of United Nations operations in the field. During the cold war United Nations peace-keeping operations were largely military in character and were usually deployed after a cease-fire but before a settlement of the conflict in question had been negotiated. Indeed one of their main purposes was to create conditions in which negotiations for a settlement could take place. In the late 1980s a new kind of peace-keeping operation evolved. It was established after negotiations had succeeded, with the mandate of helping the parties implement the comprehensive settlement they had negotiated. . . .

The negotiated settlements involved not only military arrangements but also a wide range of civilian matters. As a result, the United Nations found itself asked to undertake an unprecedented variety of functions [enumerated *supra* at *13*].

Fourthly, these multifunctional peace-keeping operations have highlighted the role the United Nations can play after a negotiated settlement has been implemented. It is now recognized that implementation of the settlement in the time prescribed may not be enough to guarantee that the conflict will not revive. Coordinated programmes are required, over a number of years and in various fields, to ensure that the original causes of war are eradicated. This involves the building up of national institutions, the promotion of human rights, the creation of civilian police forces and other actions in the political field. . . . [O]nly sustained efforts to resolve underlying socio-economic, cultural and humanitarian problems can place an achieved peace on a durable foundation.

III.   INSTRUMENTS FOR PEACE AND SECURITY

The United Nations has developed a range of instruments for controlling and resolving conflicts between and within States. The most important of them are preventive diplomacy and peacemaking; peace-keeping; peace-building; disarmament; sanctions; and peace enforcement. The first three can be employed only with the consent of the parties to the conflict. Sanctions and enforcement, on the other hand, are coercive measures and thus, by definition, do not require the consent of the party concerned. Disarmament can take place on an agreed basis or in the context of coercive action . . . .

The United Nations does not have or claim a monopoly of any of these instruments. All can be, and most of them have been, employed by regional organizations, by ad hoc groups of States or by individual States, but the United Nations has unparalleled experience of them and it is to the United Nations that the international community has turned increasingly since the end of the cold war. . . .

Perceived shortcomings in the United Nations performance of the tasks entrusted to it have recently, however, seemed to incline Member States to look for other means, especially, but not exclusively, where the rapid deployment of large forces is required. It is thus necessary to find ways of enabling the United Nations to perform better the roles envisaged for it in the Charter.

A.   Preventive diplomacy and peacemaking

. . . The Security Council's declaration of 31 January 1992 . . . mandated me to give priority to preventive and peacemaking activities. I accordingly created a Department of Political Affairs to handle a range of political functions that had previously been performed in various parts of the Secretariat. That Department has since passed through successive phases of restructuring and is now organized to follow political developments worldwide, so that it can provide early warning of impending conflicts and analyse possibilities for preventive action by the United Nations, as well as for action to help resolve existing conflicts. . . .

B.   Peace-keeping. . .

There are three aspects of recent mandates that, in particular, have led peace-keeping operations to forfeit the consent of the parties, to behave in a way that was perceived to be partial and/or to use force other than in self-defence. These have been the tasks of protecting humanitarian operations during continuing warfare, protecting civilian populations in designated safe areas and pressing the parties to achieve national reconciliation at a pace faster than they were ready to accept. The cases of Somalia and Bosnia and Herzegovina are instructive in this respect. . . .

In peace-keeping, too, a number of practical difficulties have arisen during the last three years, especially relating to command and control, to the availability of troops and equipment, and to the information capacity of peace-keeping operations.

As regards command and control, it is useful to distinguish three levels of authority:

(a)   Overall political direction, which belongs to the Security Council;

(b)   Executive direction and command, for which the Secretary-General is responsible;

(c)   Command in the field, which is entrusted by the Secretary-General to the chief of mission (special representative or force commander/chief military observer).

The distinctions between these three levels must be kept constantly in mind in order to avoid any confusion of functions and responsibilities. . . .

There has been an increasing tendency in recent years for the Security Council to micro-manage peace-keeping operations. . . . To assist the Security Council in being informed about the latest developments I have appointed one of my Special Advisers as my personal representative to the Council. As regards information, however, it has to be recognized that, in the inevitable fog and confusion of the near-war conditions in which peace-keepers often find themselves, . . . time is required to verify the accuracy of initial reports. . . .

Troop-contributing Governments, who are responsible to their parliaments and electorates for the safety of their troops, are also understandably anxious to be kept fully informed, especially when the operation concerned is in difficulty. I have endeavoured to meet their concerns by providing them with regular briefings and by engaging them in dialogue about the conduct of the operation in question. Members of the Security Council have been included in such meetings and the Council has recently decided to formalize them. . . .

Another important principle is unity of command. . . . That necessity is all the more imperative when the mission is operating in dangerous conditions. There must be no opening for the parties to undermine its cohesion by singling out some contingents for favourable and others for unfavourable treatment. Nor must there be any attempt by troop-contributing Governments to provide guidance, let alone give orders, to their contingents on operational matters. To do so creates division within the force, adds to the difficulties already inherent in a multinational operation and increases the risk of casualties. It can also create the impression amongst the parties that the operation is serving the policy objectives of the contributing Governments rather than the collective will of the United Nations as formulated by the Security Council. Such impressions inevitably undermine an operation's legitimacy and effectiveness. . . .

As regards the availability of troops and equipment, problems have become steadily more serious. Availability has palpably declined as measured against the Organization's requirements. A considerable effort has been made to expand and refine stand-by arrangements, but these provide no guarantee that troops will be provided for a specific operation. . . .

In these circumstances, I have come to the conclusion that the United Nations does need to give serious thought to the idea of a rapid reaction force. Such a force would be the Security Council's strategic reserve for deployment when there was an emergency need for peace-keeping troops. It might comprise battalion-size units from a number of countries. These units would be trained to the same standards, use the same operating procedures, be equipped with integrated communications equipment and take part in joint exercises at regular intervals. They would be stationed in their home countries but maintained at a high state of readiness. The value of this arrangement would of course depend on how far the Security Council could be sure that the force would actually be available in an emergency. This will be a complicated and expensive arrangement, but I believe that the time has come to undertake it.

Equipment and adequate training is another area of growing concern. The principle is that contributing Governments are to ensure that their troops arrive with all the equipment needed to be fully operational. Increasingly, however, Member States offer troops without the necessary equipment and training. In the absence of alternatives, the United Nations, under pressure, has to procure equipment on the market or through voluntary contributions from other Member States. . . . A number of measures can be envisaged to address this problem, for example, the establishment by the United Nations of a reserve stock of standard peace-keeping equipment, as has been frequently proposed, and partnerships between Governments that need equipment and those ready to provide it.

An additional lesson from recent experience is that peace-keeping operations, especially those operating in difficult circumstances, need an effective information capacity. This is to enable them to explain their mandate to the population and, by providing a credible and impartial source of information, to counter misinformation disseminated about them, even by the parties themselves. . . . I have instructed that in the planning of future operations the possible need for an information capacity should be examined at an early stage and the necessary resources included in the proposed budget. . . .

[Boutros-Ghali went on to address economic sanctions and concluded by discussing the need for coordination among U.N. bodies and among the U.N. and various regional and non-governmental organizations. He also renewed his calls for Member States to remain current on their assessments and to provide in a timely manner promised troops and equipment.]

NOTES AND QUESTIONS

1.   Does Arnison's notion that "sovereignty must yield to human suffering" help to address concerns raised by the Palley study? If adopted by the Security Council, how might this dictum affect the frequency and type of U.N. efforts to maintain or restore international peace and security? What, if any, issues of sovereignty might affect the U.S. decision regarding a response to the crisis in Y?

For further reading on the conflict between traditional notions of sovereignty and the use of humanitarian intervention, see chapter *1, supra* at *13; see also* Jarat Chopra & Thomas G. Weiss, *Sovereignty is No Longer Sacrosanct: Codifying Humanitarian Intervention*, 6 ETHICS & INT'L AFF. 95 (1992); David J. Scheffer, *Toward a Modern Doctrine of Humanitarian Intervention*, 23 U. TOL. L. REV. 253 (1992).

2.   Boutros-Ghali's supplement to his 1992 "Agenda for Peace" builds in part on suggestions made after release of the Agenda. *See, e.g.*, Paul Lewis, *U.N. is Developing Control Center to Coordinate Growing Peacekeeping Role*, N.Y. TIMES, Mar. 28, 1993, Sec. 1, at 10. The supplement quickly generated negative reactions from some Member States, who expressed concern about his suggestion that the U.N. create a permanent U.N. force. *See* Julia Preston, *U.N. Aide Proposes Rapid-Reaction Unit; In Face of U.S. Congressional Opposition, Boutros-Ghali's Plan Appears to Have Little Chance*, WASH. POST, Jan. 6, 1995, at A23.

3.   Several commentators refer to the cost of U.N. peacekeeping operations. The total U.N. peacekeeping budget was estimated to exceed $3 billion for 1994. Barbara Crossette, *U.N. is Concerned Over Bill to Limit U.S. Peacekeeping Role*, N.Y. TIMES, Feb. 10, 1995, at A6. The U.S. paid 31.7% of those costs early in 1995, but President Clinton stated that U.S. contributions would drop to 25% later that year. Eric Schmitt, *House Votes Bill to Cut U.N. Funds for Peacekeeping*, N.Y. TIMES, Feb. 17, 1995, at A1. Because of voluntary U.S. contributions of in-kind payments for humanitarian relief and international peace, however, actual direct

and indirect expenditures greatly exceeded the assessed portion. One journalist estimated 1994 U.S. military costs for humanitarian and peacekeeping missions at $1.7 billion, most of which was not reimbursed. Dana Priest, *House Votes to Reduce Payments to U.N.*, WASH. POST, Feb. 17, 1995, at A1; *Id.*

4.   U.S. Congressional resistance to financing peacekeeping operations is nothing new. The U.S. for many years has been in arrears on payments to the U.N. for peacekeeping. In 1988, prior to the Persian Gulf Crisis, the U.S. owed $70 million. By September 1989, the amount had ballooned to more than $400 million. In January 1995, despite payments of over $1 billion the previous year, the U.S. still owed $290 million to the U.N. peacekeeping budget. *See* Julia Preston, *Massive World Body Resists Shaping: Up Reform Efforts at U.N. Meet Opposition*, WASH. POST, Jan. 3, 1995, at A1; Don Shannon, *U.N. to Tackle Drugs, Environment Issues*, L.A. TIMES, Sept. 20, 1989, at 7; *Shultz Calls U.S. Debt to U.N. "a Disgrace"*, L.A. TIMES, Aug. 17, 1988, at 1.

5.   In *Certain Expenses of the United Nations*, 1962 I.C.J. 151 (July 20), the International Court of Justice (World Court) issued an advisory opinion—at the request of the General Assembly—concerning obligations of member states to contribute to peacekeeping operations. The Soviet Union, France, and several other countries refused to pay their assessed contributions to the U.N. Emergency Force and the U.N. Operation in the Congo. The Soviet Union argued that the General Assembly, in authorizing the action, had acted beyond the scope of its authority; and it argued that only the Security Council could fund peacekeeping operations. France argued that only the states that voted for the operations were required to pay for them. The Court refused to intervene, and held that Article 17 of the U.N. Charter binds all member states to help fund peacekeeping operations. Richard W. Nelson, *International Law and U.S. Withholding of Payments to International Organizations*, 80 AM. J. INT'L L. 973, 978-79 (1986). *See also* RICHARD FALK, REVIVING THE WORLD COURT (1986); J. Patrick Kelly, *The Changing Process of International Law and the Role of the World Court*, 11 MICH. J. INT'L L. 129 (1989); Ebere Osieke, *The Legal Validity of Ultra Vires Decisions of International Organizations*, 77 AM. J. INT'L L. 239 (1983); Elisabeth Zoller, *The "Corporate Will" of the United Nations and the Rights of the Minority*, 81 AM. J. INT'L L. 610 (1987).

6.   The U.S. has duties as a U.N. member, particularly those prescribed in the U.N. Charter. Illustratively (in Articles 1(3) and 55-56), members pledge to promote and encourage respect for human rights and fundamental freedoms. Has the U.S. complied with those duties under the Charter and as defined in U.N. treaties? In answering that question, consider U.S. action at home as well as abroad.

For instance consider the work of U.S. troops in Somalia. The U.S. led a mission there in December 1992 that was intended to save the East African country from the ravages of war and famine. Some Somalis, as well as some members of Congress, were critical of troops' efforts to capture Somali warlord Mohamed Farah Aideed. The troops raided wrong sites, arrested innocent people, and killed Somali citizens in their search for Aideed. Impatience peaked in July 1993 after a U.S. helicopter assault missed Aideed but left as many as 54 dead. Italy, which also had sent troops, called the air strike "unjustifiable." Muslim groups warned of plans to launch a retaliatory attack on U.S. compounds. Both houses of Congress passed non-binding resolutions requesting that President Clinton seek congressional approval for extending military operations in Somalia beyond mid-November 1993. Some senators began calling for complete withdrawal of U.S. troops. *See* Keith Richburg, *Criticism Mounts Over Somali Raid; 'Pack Up, Go Home,' U.S. Troops Urged*, WASH. POST, July 15, 1993, at A21; John M. Goshko, *Clinton Seen Calming Hill on Peace Keeping*, WASH. POST, Oct. 2, 1993, at A16. U.S. troops did unilaterally withdraw by 1994, but returned in February 1995 to protect U.N. peacekeepers who then were withdrawing.

Do you think U.S. actions in Somalia were consistent with duties imposed by human rights or humanitarian laws? Is it juridically significant that the actions took place while the U.S. aided a U.N. peacekeeping mission?

7. In early 1994, partly in response to criticism over U.N. operations in Somalia and Bosnia, the Clinton Administration issued extensive new guidelines designed to make U.S. participation in U.N. peacekeeping operations more selective. The Presidential Decision Directive (PDD) addresses six major issues of reform: making disciplined and coherent choices about which peace operations to support; reducing U.S. costs for U.N. operations; defining clearly U.S. policy regarding the command and control of U.S. military forces; reforming and improving U.N. capability to manage peace operations; improving the way the U.S. manages and funds peace operations; and creating better forms of cooperation between the Executive, Congress, and the public on peace operations. The PDD lists criteria that the U.S. will consider in determining whether to support a U.N. mission; the criteria vary depending on the requested level of U.S. involvement. The directive also indicates that the President will place U.S. troops under operational control of the U.N. only if doing so serves U.S. security interests. *See Administration Policy on Reforming Multilateral Peace Operations, reprinted in* 33 I.L.M. 795 (1994); Ann Devroy, *Clinton Signs New Guidelines for U.N. Peacekeeping Operations,* WASH. POST, May 6, 1994, at A30.

In June 1995, the U.S. Army Southern Command issued Human Rights Standing Orders stating, "U.S. Armed Forces support the UN and OAS standards of human rights to protect the integrity and dignity of each individual. . . . Human rights include fundamental protections for individuals such as freedom from illegal killing or torture. However, *any* severe and degrading physical mistreatment of *any* individual by a government official, either civilian or military, may be a human rights violation. U.S. military personnel must never participate in any activity which is contrary to this human rights policy nor encourage others to do so. It is the duty of all U.S. military personnel to object to any possible human rights violation they observe, regardless of who is involved." These and similar orders were issued in the form of a small wallet-sized card: "This USSOUTHCOM card constitutes legal and binding orders on all U.S. military personnel . . . .." U.S. Army, SC FORM 165, June 16, 1995.

The United Nations Office of Peace Keeping Operations has also drafted, in consultation with the International Committee of the Red Cross and others, human rights and humanitarian law standards for military forces serving under U.N. auspices. These standards have not yet been issued.

8. In the Security Council, U.S. resistance to deployment of U.N. troops to Rwanda, despite ongoing human rights abuses in that country, was greatly influenced by the Bosnia and Somalia experiences and Clinton's PDD. *See* Alain Destexhe, *The Third Genocide,* FOREIGN POL'Y, Winter 1994-95, at 3, 9-11.

9. As part of the Republican "Contract With America" the House of Representatives, in February 1995, approved the National Security Revitalization Act of 1995, a bill designed to limit U.S. participation in and funding of peacekeeping activities. 1995 H.R. 7. The bill would prohibit U.S. troops from being placed under U.N. command for international peacekeeping or peace-enforcement purposes and would prohibit defense funds from being expended on those activities without congressional approval, unless the President certifies that such command or control is necessary to protect U.S. security interests. The bill also requires the U.S. to deduct from its U.N. peacekeeping dues its indirect costs incurred in supporting U.N. missions, unless the President certifies that the activity is so vital to the national security interest that the U.S. would take the action unilaterally even without Security Council authorization. *Id.* As of February 1996, the bill was still pending in the Senate.

10. For further reading on U.N. intervention and peacekeeping activities, see:

Philip Alston, *The Security Council and Human Rights: Lessons to be Learned from the Iraqi-Kuwait Crisis and its Aftermath,* 13 AUSTL. Y.B. INT'L L. 107 (1993);

THE ASPEN INSTITUTE, HONORING HUMAN RIGHTS AND KEEPING THE PEACE (1995);

P.R. Baehr, *The Security Council and Human Rights, in* THE DYNAMICS OF THE PROTECTION OF HUMAN RIGHTS IN EUROPE, VOLUME III (Rick Lawson & Matthijs de Blois eds., 1994);

SYDNEY D. BAILEY, THE U.N. SECURITY COUNCIL AND HUMAN RIGHTS (1994);

Lincoln P. Bloomfield et al., *Collective Security in a Changing World*, OCCASIONAL PAPER 10 (Inst. for Int'l Stud., Brown U., 1992) (sketching the issues implied in applying the collective security concept to contemporary world politics);

BOUTROS BOUTROS-GHALI, BUILDING PEACE AND DEVELOPMENT 1994: ANNUAL REPORT ON THE WORK OF THE ORGANIZATION (1994);

BOUTROS BOUTROS-GHALI, CONFRONTING NEW CHALLENGES: ANNUAL REPORT OF THE WORK OF THE ORGANIZATION (1995);

Byron F. Burmester, Comment, *On Humanitarian Intervention: the New World Order and Wars to Preserve Human Rights*, 1994 UTAH L. REV. 269 (1994).

Lori Fisler Damrosch, *The Role of the Great Powers in United Nations Peace-Keeping*, 18 YALE J. INT'L L. 429 (1993);

Lois E. Fielding, *Taking the Next Step in the Development of New Human Rights: the Emerging Right of Humanitarian Assistance to Restore Democracy*, 5 DUKE J. COMP. & INT'L L. 329 (1995);

TATHIANA FLORES ACUÑA, THE UNITED NATIONS MISSION IN EL SALVADOR: A HUMANITARIAN LAW PERSPECTIVE (1995);

Diego García-Sayán, *Human Rights and Peace-Keeping Operations*, 29 U. RICH. L. REV. 41 (1994);

STEPHEN GOLUB, STRENGTHENING HUMAN RIGHTS MONITORING MISSIONS: AN OPTIONS PAPER PREPARED FOR THE UNITED STATES AGENCY FOR INTERNATIONAL DEVELOPMENT (1995);

LOUIS HENKIN ET AL., RIGHT V. MIGHT: INTERNATIONAL LAW AND THE USE OF FORCE (1991);

HUMAN RIGHTS WATCH, THE LOST AGENDA: HUMAN RIGHTS AND U.N. FIELD OPERATIONS (1993);

Larry Minear et al., *Humanitarianism and War: Learning the Lessons from Recent Armed Conflicts*, OCCASIONAL PAPER 8 (Inst. for Int'l Stud., Brown U., 1991);

Sean D. Murphy, *The Security Council, Legitimacy, and the Concept of Collective Security After the Cold War*, 32 COLUM. J. TRANSNAT'L L. 201 (1994);

Ved P. Nanda, *Tragedies in Northern Iraq, Liberia, Yugoslavia, and Haiti—Revisiting the Validity of Humanitarian Intervention Under International Law—Part I*, 20 DENV. J. INT'L L. & POL'Y 305 (1992).

NEW DIMENSIONS OF PEACEKEEPING (Daniel Warner ed., 1995);

Kelly K. Pease & David P. Forsythe, *Human Rights, Humanitarian Intervention, and World Politics*, 15 HUM. RTS. Q. 290 (1993);

THE POLITICS OF HUMANITARIAN INTERVENTION (John Harriss ed., 1995);

W. Michael Reisman, *Peacemaking*, 18 YALE J. INT'L L. 415 (1993);

Theodore Sorenson, *United States Policy on United Nations Peace-Keeping Operations*, 18 YALE J. INT'L L. 429 (1993);

TO LOOSE THE BANDS OF WICKEDNESS: INTERNATIONAL INTERVENTION IN DEFENCE OF HUMAN RIGHTS (Nigel S. Rodley ed., 1992);

Sir Brian Urquhart & Robert S. McNamara, *Toward Collective Security: Two Views*, OCCASIONAL PAPER 5 (Inst. for Int'l Stud., Brown U., 1991) (analyzing the use of international institutions in the Gulf War);

THOMAS G. WEISS ET AL., THE UNITED NATIONS AND CHANGING WORLD POLITICS 17-100 (1994).

D.   UNILATERAL ACTION

Thus far, this chapter has focused on collective action through the U.N.. The remaining materials examine unilateral humanitarian intervention, a method that governments, including the U.S., can use to encourage other governments to respect human rights. Humanitarian intervention essentially involves a government's using physical force to stop another government from engaging in human rights violations. The following excerpts discuss the legality of humanitarian intervention in light of the U.N. Charter and highlight examples of past U.S. intervention.

Richard B. Lillich, *A United States Policy of Humanitarian Intervention and Intercession, in* HUMAN RIGHTS AND AMERICAN FOREIGN POLICY, 278, 287-90 (Donald P. Kommers & Gilburt D. Loescher eds. 1979) (footnotes omitted):

As far as humanitarian intervention's legality is concerned, the present writer concluded some years ago that "the doctrine appears to have been so clearly established under customary international law, that only its limits and not its existence is subject to debate." However, what has been the impact of the U.N. Charter upon this customary international law doctrine? Here two problems arise. The first is whether such interventions still are lawful or whether they now are precluded by the U.N. Charter. The second, assuming that such interventions remain lawful, is what criteria should be used to judge a particular intervention's legality.

Although Article 1(7) of the U.N. Charter enjoins the United Nations itself not "to intervene in matters which are essentially within the domestic jurisdiction of any state," Article 2(4), which applies to member states, contains no mention of intervention. Rather, it requires states to refrain from "the threat or use of force against the territorial integrity or political independence of any state." Although many commentators have concluded that this provision prohibits humanitarian intervention, among those international lawyers who believe such intervention still is legal, at least four different legal theories have been advanced.

The first approach is that of the Australian jurist Julius Stone, who advocates a literal reading of the language of Article 2(4). It "does *not* forbid 'the threat or use of force' *simpliciter*," he contends; "it forbids it only when directed 'against the territorial integrity or political independence of any State, or in any other manner inconsistent with the Purposes of the United Nations.'" In his opinion a humanitarian intervention would not be so directed and, hence, would not fall within the prohibition of Article 2(4). . . .

The second approach employed to justify the claim that humanitarian intervention has survived the adoption of the U.N. Charter is that of [W. Michael] Reisman. Adopting what some critics have labeled a "teleological" interpretation, Reisman views Article 2(4) as an important part of the document, but still only a part. Looking at the Preamble, Article 1, and Articles 55 and 56, all of which evidence great concern for the advancement of human rights, he concludes that

> [T]he cumulative effect of the Charter in regard to the customary institution of humanitarian intervention is to create a coordinate responsibility for the active protection of human rights: members may act jointly with the organization in what might be termed a new organized, explicitly statutory humanitarian intervention or singly or collectively in the customary or international common law humanitarian intervention. In the contemporary world there is no other way the most fundamental

purposes of the Charter in relation to human rights can be made effective.

Reisman's approach is distinguished from Stone's in that humanitarian intervention is not unaffected by the charter as Stone thinks but, rather, is a logical extension of concern for norms that are rooted firmly in the charter. One must look to the dominant purposes of the charter as a whole and not blindly allow a single general principle like Article 2(4)—admirable though that principle may be—to impede other major goals of the charter.

There is a third approach that stands apart from the first and perhaps from the second in that it does not necessarily accord a permanent status in international law to humanitarian intervention. Rather, this approach permits its substitution for the procedure contemplated by the charter, an emergency mechanism to be deactivated should the normal U.N. machinery in the Security Council ever begin to function smoothly. The problem with—and the virtue of—this approach is that it requires a rather sophisticated reinterpretation of the charter in light of events since 1945. Because the enforcement machinery of the Security Council has not worked out as planned or hoped, the argument goes, one is left with the undesirable choice of applying stopgap measures or doing nothing at all. Of these two choices, certainly the former requires adoption. As Richard Baxter, who has suggested this approach, puts it:

> Given the fact that we do live in an imperfect world, in which the United Nations is not operating as it should, it seems to me inevitable that there will be [humanitarian interventions]. It is almost as if we were thrown back on customary international law by a breakdown of the Charter system. . . .

A fourth approach by which humanitarian intervention might be condoned, if not actually justified, has been developed by Richard Falk and, to a lesser extent, by Ian Brownlie. Both scholars view the U.N. charter as prohibiting humanitarian intervention yet consider this broad prohibition potentially counterproductive. Thus, while not approving such interventions, Falk, by using a "second-order level of legal inquiry" which involves criteria similar to ones suggested by advocates of humanitarian intervention, nevertheless would not condemn them all. Brownlie, in a less sophisticated but nevertheless interesting analysis of the problem, compares humanitarian intervention to euthanasia. Both actions, he contends, are unlawful, but at the same time they are both moral actions which may find justification in higher considerations of public policy and moral choice. Brownlie's variant of the fourth approach has been criticized by John Norton Moore and the present writer for its failure "to perform the . . . intellectual task of trying to develop a set of criteria. You can't end it by saying it is illegal but also moral. We have to go beyond that and develop criteria for appraisal of the kinds of situations that we would recommend *ought* to be legal."

. . . In 1966 Ved Nanda advanced five criteria for judging the legality of humanitarian interventions. The following year the present writer recommended five of his own. Subsequently Moore synthesized the Nanda-Lillich criteria, with some additions and modifications. Moore's synthesis in turn has been summarized most recently by Tom Farer:

> That there be an immediate and extensive threat to fundamental human rights.

> That all other remedies for the protection of those rights have been exhausted to the extent possible within the time constraints posed by the threat.

> That an attempt has been made to secure the approval of appropriate authorities in the target state.

That there is a minimal effect on the extant structure of authority (e.g., that the intervention not be used to impose or preserve a preferred regime).

That the minimal requisite force b[e] employed and/or that the intervention is not likely to cause greater injury to innocent persons and their property than would result if the threatened violation actually occurred.

That the intervention be of limited duration.

That a report of the intervention be filed immediately with the Security Council and, where relevant, regional organizations.

*   *   *   *   *

Abraham D. Sofaer, *International Law and the Use of Force*, NAT'L INTEREST, Fall 1988, at 54-57 (footnotes omitted):

The United States Position

The Charter expressly reserves in Article 51 . . . the "inherent right of individual or collective self defense." That provision is written in terms of defense against "armed attack" but the right of self-defense is termed "inherent," thus conveying the sense that it includes the right to defend those fundamental interests customarily protected. The United States . . . has always assumed that Charter principles provide a workable set of rules to deal with the array of needs that potentially require the use of force, including such threats as state-supported terrorism and insurgencies, even if they are deemed not to amount to an "armed attack." General Assembly interpretive declarations make clear that "force" means physical violence, not other forms of coercion. But they also indicate that aggression includes both direct and indirect complicity in all forms of violence, not just conventional hostilities. Our position has been that the inherent right of self-defense potentially applies against any illegal use of force, and to the extent the term "armed attack" is relevant in use-of-force issues that it should be defined to include forms of aggression historically regarded as justifying resort to defensive measures. Furthermore, the U.S. has assumed that it may lawfully engage in collective self-defense in any situation in which the nation assisted is entitled to act, and to the same extent. On the other hand, we recognize that force may be used only to deter or prevent aggression, and only to the extent it is necessary and proportionate.

From Truman to Carter

The actions of presidents of the United States . . . have consistently demonstrated this principled but practical approach to the use-of-force rules. In his message to Congress requesting aid for Greece, President Truman announced the Truman Doctrine, which recognized the importance of the peaceful development of nations under the UN system, but called for the protection of free nations from "aggressive movements" seeking to impose totalitarian regimes. "This is no more than a frank recognition," he said, "that totalitarian regimes imposed upon free peoples, by direct or indirect aggression, undermine the foundations of international peace and hence the security of the United States."

When President Eisenhower sent U.S. forces into Lebanon in 1958 at President Chamoun's request, both the United States and Lebanon asserted a realistic definition of "armed attack." Secretary of State Dulles said: "[W]e do not think that the words 'armed attack' preclude treating as such an armed revolution which is fomented from abroad, aided and assisted from abroad." . . .

When President Johnson intervened in the Dominican Republic, no attack of any kind had occurred on the U.S. or its citizens. The danger to Americans there was serious, however, and a communist takeover was seen as a real possibility. Legal Adviser Leonard Meeker defended the intervention as justified to protect Americans "in imminent danger of life and limb from rioting mobs," and he argued that a continued U.S. presence was necessary to prevent anarchy. He rejected criticisms based on what he called "fundamentalist views about the nature of international law," as such views were "not very useful as a means to achieving practical and just solutions of difficult political, economic, and social problems." He called for a "practical idealism," in which international law could be read as consistent with efforts to prevent bloodshed and communist takeovers. He said that "an international law which cannot deal with facts such as these, and in a way that has some hope of setting a troubled nation on the path of peace and reconstruction, is not the kind of law I believe in." President Johnson added explicitly the justification of intervening to prevent revolutions by "evil persons who had been trained in overthrowing governments and establishing communist control."

The Vietnam conflict generated a great deal of legal debate about the use of force, and the legal adviser's office found the U.S. intervention to assist South Vietnam legally justified under the doctrine of collective self-defense. . . .

President Ford relied on Article 51 in ordering U.S. forces to attack Cambodian naval assets to secure release of the vessel *Mayaguez* and its crew. The seizure of a U.S. merchant vessel was deemed "a clear-cut illegal use of force" which UN Ambassador Scali asserted justified appropriate measures in self-defense. Similarly, President Carter used force in an attempt to rescue American hostages in Iran, arguing that the United States is entitled to seek to protect its citizens abroad "where the government of the territory in which they are located is unable or unwilling to protect them." . . . [T]he President was condemned by some international law experts, who argued that by no stretch of the imagination was the seizure of Americans as hostages an armed attack, and therefore that the U.S. was precluded from using force to secure their release.

The Reagan Years

The Reagan administration has continued to adhere to the practical but principled approach to use-of-force rules which has in general characterized United States policy since the UN Charter's adoption. The President has repeatedly made clear, moreover, that he will continue the policy of assisting nations in preventing nondemocratic takeovers conducted by outside forces (as in Afghanistan) or fomented or aided by them. The Grenada operation involved no armed attack on the U.S. but was justified as necessary to protect U.S. lives and to respond to invitations of the governor general and of members of the Organization of the Eastern Caribbean States. . . .

We relied on the same approach in exercising our rights of self-defense by attacking facilities in Libya used to support terrorists. Before December 1985, we had exhausted virtually every measure short of force to convince Libya to stop supporting terrorists in attacks on Americans. Then came the mindlessly cruel attacks at the Rome and Vienna airports in which seven Americans were killed, including 11-year old Natasha Simpson. Tunisian passports were found on the killers that were traced to Libyan officials, and Qadhafi praised the terrorists as heroes. Nevertheless, the President decided not to use force at that point, but instead to exhaust all remaining economic sanctions and to warn Libya one more time, explicitly invoking our view of the governing law. He said:

By providing material support to terrorist groups which attack U.S. citizens, Libya has engaged in armed aggression against the United States under established principles of international law, just as if it had used its own armed forces.

Secretary Shultz explained our position in greater detail in January 1986, at the National Defense University:

A nation attacked by terrorists is permitted to use force to prevent or preempt future attacks, to seize terrorists, or to rescue its citizens when no other means is available. The law requires that such actions be necessary and proportionate. But this nation has consistently affirmed the rights of states to use force in exercise of their right of individual or collective self-defense. The UN Charter is not a suicide pact.

Despite these warnings, Libya organized and supported additional attacks. . . . We reliably knew that Libya was planning several more attacks. The purpose of the limited air strike was to convince Libya to halt this support for terrorist operations.

* * * * *

Tom J. Farer & Christopher C. Joyner, *The United States and the Use of Force: Looking Back to See Ahead*, 1 TRANSNAT'L L. & CONTEMP. PROB. 15, 16, 19, 28-38 (1991) (footnotes omitted):

II.   International Law and the Use of Force

. . . Intervention usually involves a conflict between two fundamental principles of international law: the right of self-defense, habitually invoked by the intervening State, and the targeted State's right of independence and territorial integrity. U.N. Charter Articles 2(4) and 51 mediate their tense relationship. . . .

In conformity with the generally prevailing view of international law, the Charter unmistakably asserts that a State's breach of Article 2(4) through an act of intervention constitutes aggression, unless certain exceptional circumstances are convincingly demonstrated. . . .

III.   Permissible Exceptions to Nonintervention

The majority of active participants in the international legal process arguably have accepted a number of special exceptions to the prohibition against armed intervention. These special exceptions arise: (1) in certain circumstances during civil conflict; (2) in circumstances where only armed intervention can prevent awful violations of human rights; (3) in cases where the lives and safety of a State's nationals are imminently endangered; (4) in instances of *collective* self-defense; (5) in situations where an existing treaty permits such intervention; and (6) where internal disorder and the collapse of legitimate authority seriously threaten vital interests of other States. . . .

V.   Intervention and U.S. Practice: Contemporary Case Studies . . .

A.   Nicaragua (1980s)

Beginning no later than 1981, the United States furnished military aid to Nicaraguan insurgents who ultimately came to number roughly 15,000. Known as "contras," they were trained in Honduras with financial and material support from the Central Intelligence Agency. The United States' covert backing of the Contras took a dramatic turn in March 1984, when it was revealed that the CIA had assisted in mining three Nicaraguan ports, supposedly to interdict arms shipments from Nicaragua to an anti-governmental rebel movement in El Salvador.

On the basis of its own, frequently inflated and occasionally mendacious, claims about levels of human rights abuses, the United States might have invoked humanitarian intervention as a legal rationale for its campaign against Nicaragua. But in order to sustain a claim under this dubious exception to the prohibition on military intervention, support for the contras would have had to comply with the legal restrictions placed on such humanitarian actions, particularly that they not be guided primarily by an intention to overthrow the target State's authority structure.

The principal legal explanation that the United States actually advanced was self-defense. The Reagan administration contended that U.S. aid to the contras in 1981 was justified as a necessary and proportional response to the Nicaraguan government's complicity in the supply of weapons to anti-government insurgents in El Salvador. In the mind of the Reagan administration, such arms supplies were the legal equivalent of an armed attack by Nicaragua against El Salvador. In effect, Nicaragua was engaged in "indirect aggression" against El Salvador, which necessitated acts of self-defense against the Sandinista government. U.S. military assistance to El Salvador had been requested by the lawful government of that State. Hence, the argument ran, U.S. actions were lawfully undertaken in collective self-defense to aid a victim of Nicaraguan aggression.

Nettlesome problems cloud this legal reasoning. It is true that state practice since 1945 may have broadened the narrowly confined right to collective self-defense conceded by Charter Article 51. But in all events, self-defense must be necessary and proportionate to an alleged offense.

It is also true that an "armed attack" can occur under international law if a State sends armed bands, irregulars or mercenaries into another State on a sufficiently large scale. But mere provision of weapons, equipment, or logistical support by one State to rebels in another State does not perforce constitute an "armed attack" under international law that would justify use of force in self-defense. States do not possess a legal right of collective armed response to actions which do not qualify as an "armed attack" under the law. Whether the level of assistance by Nicaragua to El Salvadoran rebels after 1981 qualified as an "armed attack" within the U.N. Charter's definition is at best arguable. As a consequence, since no "armed attack" unequivocally occurred, or was occurring, automatic resort to collective self-defense would not be permissible, even if carried out within the bounds of necessity and proportionality. . . .[1]

B. Grenada (1983)

On October 25, 1983, U.S. armed forces invaded Grenada. Washington claimed that it had received an urgent appeal from the Organization of Eastern Caribbean States (OECS) for military assistance and participation in a collective security operation. The government of Maurice Bishop on Grenada had been overthrown two weeks previously. The resultant political turmoil and the possible triumph of a more doctrinaire Marxist faction of the minuscule party apparatus on the island

---

[1] Ed. note: Human rights violations by the contras provide an additional basis on which to question U.S. conduct. Abuses by the contras included torture, summary executions of both civilian and military prisoners, and large-scale abductions of civilians for the purpose of recruitment. AMNESTY INTERNATIONAL, NICARAGUA: THE HUMAN RIGHTS RECORD 1986-1989, AI Index: AMR 43/02/89, at 5 (1989).]

were viewed by Washington as threatening to the regions' stability and security. The invasion was carried out by some 2,000 U.S. Marines along with 300 troops representing Jamaica, Barbados, Dominica, St. Lucia, Antigua and Barbuda, and St. Vincent. By October 30, the island had been secured militarily and the political situation stabilized.[2]

The official explanation stressed a threat to the 1,100 American nationals on Grenada. . . . United States' participation in the invasion would also assist in restoring political stability to Grenada and permit the restoration of democratic institution there. Administration rhetoric also emphasized the importance of halting Marxist influence in the Caribbean Basin. In short, a successful invasion of Grenada would not only rescue U.S. nationals from harm's way; it would also help evict Soviet-Cuban influence from Grenada and deny the communists strategic opportunities that the island could afford them in the region.

Was the use of force by the United States against Grenada taken in self-defense against an armed attack? Obviously not. The strict test under international law that makes such action permissible is the presence of a real, immediate threat to a State. The territorial integrity and political independence of the United States was not militarily threatened by a 2,000-man army of Grenada, located 1,600 miles away. Nor could it be said that Grenada constituted a future direct threat to the United States that might legitimize use of force in anticipatory self-defense. To qualify as lawful preemptive intervention, the danger to the United States would have to be real and imminent, not merely hypothetical and potential.

Clearly, an important legal consideration in the case of Grenada concerned the protection of U.S. nationals on the island. Even so, caution must be exercised in reaching for these grounds to legitimize U.S. intervention in Grenada. To be lawful, the risk to the threatened nationals must be genuine, imminent, and substantial. That this was the situation for U.S. nationals on the island in October 1983 is dubious. Second, the military operation should be conducted as a limited-purpose rescue mission, not as a formidable attack against the authority structure of the internal government. The United States undoubtedly had this latter purpose in mind, as it intended to restore—actually create for the first time since independence—democratic institutions in Grenada after the invasion. . . .[3]

C. Libya (1986)

On April [14], 1986, the United States launched an attack against military and intelligence targets in and around the Libyan capital of Tripoli and the port of Benghasi. The Reagan administration ordered the use of force against Libya as retaliation for Libya's complicity in international terrorist activities. At least 29 U.S. aircraft participated in the air raid, which lasted only 12 minutes, but reportedly killed 37 civilians and injured nearly 100 others. One U.S. F-111 plane carrying two crewmen was lost in the mission.

The legal justification immediately announced by Secretary of State George

---

[2 Ed. note: The Grenada action was not without human rights consequences. 45 Grenadians were killed and 337 wounded, and 18 U.S. personnel were killed in action and 116 wounded. Additionally, 29 Cubans were killed and 59 wounded. Langhorne A. Motley, *The Decision to Assist Grenada*, DEPARTMENT OF STATE BULLETIN, Mar. 1984, at 70, 70.]

[3 [Ed. note: On November 2, 1983, the U.N. General Assembly adopted (108 in favor, 9 against) a resolution stating, *inter alia*, that it "deeply deplore[d] the armed intervention in Grenada, which constitutes a flagrant violation of international law and of the independence, sovereignty and territorial integrity of that State." G.A. res. 38/7, 38 U.N. GAOR (No. 47) at 19, U.N. Doc. A/38/47 (1984).]

[Shultz] was that the attack reflected the inherent right of self-defense as embodied in Article 51 of the U.N. Charter. The United States maintained that Libya had been involved in aiding and abetting several violent terrorist acts during the previous year, including the *Achille Lauro* seajacking in October 1985, attacks on the Rome and Vienna airports in December 1985, an unsuccessful attempt to destroy a TWA flight from Rome to Athens on April 2, 1986, and the bombing of a West Berlin nightclub on April 5, 1986, in which a U.S. serviceman was killed. As perceived by the Reagan administration, these incidents were acts of State-sponsored terrorism by Libya. And, by virtue of their being directed or facilitated by Libya as part of an ongoing strategic offensive against the United States, they qualified as an "armed attack" against the United States. Such a view pushes against the standard interpretation of "armed attack" contained in Article 51. Even granting Libya's implication in the terrorist incidents that culminated in the bombing of the West Berlin night-clubs, a matter that is now disputed, the characterization of those composite events as an "armed attack against the political independence or territorial integrity of the United States," is a little strained. The administration's decision not to present hard evidence linking Libya to these acts of terrorist violence, allegedly on ground of national security and protection of sources, added to the strain.

The pivotal question turns on whether the air raid was necessary and proportional to the collection of terrorist delicts believed to have been perpetrated in recent months with help from the Quaddafi government. Was the U.S. air raid on Libya actually necessary to defend the national security of the United States against the State-sponsored terrorism of the Quaddafi government? Suppose that the great majority of terrorist incidents directed against the United States during the mid-1980s were sponsored by Libya. A plausible case then might be made for declaring this aggregate of Libyan terrorism an ongoing attack on the United States and asserting the necessity to take some proportional action in self-defense. It remains uncertain whether such a conclusion was warranted.

Also relevant to assessment of the U.S. air raid on Libya as the doctrine of anticipatory self-defense. As Secretary of State Daniel Webster put it in 1837, the requirements for anticipatory self-defense involve a "necessity of self defense [which is] instant, overwhelming, and leaving no choice of means, and no moment for deliberation." If, as reported, the raid was intended specifically to head off Libyan-sponsored attacks against U.S. facilities and diplomatic missions around the world, then a preemptive strike against Libya would appear legally permissible, providing that clear and compelling evidence of the impending attacks were produced by the Reagan administration.

D.   Panama (1988)

On December 20, 1989, the United States launched a massive military operation in Panama aimed at ousting the government of Manuel Noriega. The operation included some 12,500 U.S. troops stationed in Panama, reinforced by another 12,000 soldiers airlifted from the United States. Military objectives were seized quickly and within a few days the fighting had ended. The reported casualties: 23 U.S. servicemen and 3 civilians dead, 300 wounded; 300 members of the Panamanian Defense Forces killed, and 125 wounded; 500 Panamanian civilians dead, thousands wounded, and massive destruction of property, with more that $1 billion in damage claimed in the commercial sector alone.

The objectives of the Panama incursion, dubbed "Operation Just Cause" by the Bush administration, were to: (1) "protect American lives"; (2) "support democracy" in Panama; (3) bring the indicted drug trafficker Manuel Noriega to justice; and (4) to "protect the integrity of the Panama Canal Treaties." Given these multiple and far-ranging goals, the action exceeded a mere rescue mission; it became a full-scale invasion of the small Central American State of 2 million inhabitants, having a defense force of 12,000.

Two avowed objectives were achieved almost immediately. First, the 35,000 U.S. citizens in Panama were unquestionably safer after the attack; and second, democracy now stood a much better chance of succeeding in Panama with the installation of President Guillermo Endara by the United States on an American base minutes before the armed assault was launched. The third objective of bringing General Noriega to justice was not met until January 3, 1990, when Noriega left the home of the papal nuncio where he had sought sanctuary and turned himself over to the U.S. officials.

The United States justified its military action primarily as an exercise of the inherent right to self-defense. The killing of an American military officer on December 16, the wounding of a second, and the beating of a third, accompanied by sexual harassment of his wife, prompted President Bush to conclude that U.S. military lives in Panama were at risk and that self-defense was warranted. Self-defense took the form of "Operation Just Cause."

Legal support for this action is found in Article 51 of the U.N. Charter, which recognizes the inherent right of self-defense. Also relevant was Article 21 of the O.A.S. Charter, which prohibits members from resorting to force "except in the case of self-defense in accordance with existing treaties." The legal authority of Article 21 is diluted by Article 18 in the same document, which denies to any State the right to intervene "directly or indirectly, for any reason whatever, in the internal or external affairs of any other State."

The Bush administration also cited as legal justification the need to guarantee security of the Panama Canal. Two principal treaty regimes control the U.S.-Panama relationship with respect to the Canal: the 1977 Panama Canal Treaty and the 1977 Permanent Neutrality Treat, along with their respective implementing agreements and ratification documents. . . .

Protection and defense of the Panama Canal are addressed in Article IV of the Canal Treaty, which declares that the United States "shall have primary responsibility to protect and defend the Panama Canal." Even so, this agreement was ratified with an appended joint communique of reservations and understandings that flatly renounced any U.S. right to intrude into the internal affairs of Panama. Were any U.S. action ever to occur, it would "be directed at insuring that the Canal will remain open, secure, and accessible," but would "never be directed against the territorial integrity or political independence of Panama."

Thus, contrary to the Bush administration's assertions, neither the Canal Treaty nor the Neutrality Treaty conferred any special right of intervention on the United States that compromised Panama's political independence or territorial and sovereign integrity. At best, the treaties permitted use of force in line with the U.N. Charter regime. Although the security of the canal itself was never at issue, international law could sanction reasonable use of force by the United States to safeguard the lives of its nationals, if they were indeed in danger. At worst, the Canal Treaty imposed a more stringent additional primary purpose test concerning the use of force by the United States. It is undeniable that U.S. nationals were under escalating threat evidenced by physical, political, and verbal abuse from members of the Panamanian Defense Force. To be lawful, however, the U.S. response should have been proportional to the threats encountered. One can not help but wonder whether the murder of a serviceman made it absolutely necessary for the United States to invade a sovereign country with 25,000 troops, install a new government, take captive the *de facto* head of the former government, and transport him back to the intervening State for arraignment on domestic drug-smuggling charges.

A nagging legal point about this instance of U.S. intervention concerns the declaration of war against the United States adopted by the Panamanian National government on December 15, 1989. In this resolution, the 510-member National Assembly declared that "the Republic of Panama was in a state of war for the duration of the aggression unleashed against the Panamanian people by the U.S. government." The reference to U.S. aggression apparently was to the economic sanctions imposed by the United States in April 1988—and tightened only weeks before to ban Panamanian ships from U.S. ports—as well as to military maneuvers conducted in Panama by the Southern Command and the constant rhetorical attacks being levied at Noriega by the Bush administration. The original Spanish text of the declaration implied that a state of war already existed, and it suggested that the Panamanian people must cope with domestic economic conditions like those in a state of war.

Admittedly, the significance of the National Assembly's resolution remains open to interpretation. The Bush administration at first downplayed the declaration's legal relevance and in fact dismissed it as merely "another hollow step" by Noriega and little more than "charade and nonsense." In the immediate aftermath of the invasion, however, President Bush cited the declaration as legal justification for U.S. military action. Whether intended to be rhetorical or not, the resolution by Panama's National Assembly at least marginally buttressed the legal credibility of the U.S. response. An official declaration of war, or one that leaves open the possibility of being considered as such, adopted by the municipal legislative body constitutionally empowered to issue such a proclamation, could reasonably be construed as a threat to escalate the prevailing level of violence.

NOTES AND QUESTIONS

1. In 1988 Fernando Tesón wrote a book that analyzed humanitarian intervention and concluded that it contravenes international law. He defines it as "the proportionate transboundary help, including forcible help, provided by governments to individuals in another state who are being denied basic human rights and who themselves would be rationally willing to revolt against their oppressive government." FERNANDO TESÓN, HUMANITARIAN INTERVENTION: AN INQUIRY INTO LAW AND MORALITY 5 (1988). He first establishes a moral and philosophical framework (*Id.* at 3-123) and then discusses legality under the U.N. Charter. *Id.* at 127- 244.

For other views, see FRANCIS A. BOYLE, THE FUTURE OF INTERNATIONAL LAW AND AMERICAN FOREIGN POLICY (1989); NATALINO RONZITTI, RESCUING NATIONALS ABROAD THROUGH MILITARY COERCION AND INTERVENTION ON GROUNDS OF HUMANITY (1985). For analyses of humanitarian intervention from an ethical and philosophical perspective, see J. Bryan Hehir, *Intervention: From Theories to Cases*, 9 ETHICS & INT'L AFF. 1 (1995); Pierre Laberge, *Humanitarian Intervention: Three Ethical Positions*, 9 ETHICS & INT'L AFF. 15 (1995).

2. In *Military and Paramilitary Activities in and Against Nicaragua* (Nicar. v.U.S.), 1986 I.C.J. 14 (June 27), the World Court held, *inter alia*, that U.S. mine-laying in Nicaraguan waters without notice to those engaged in international shipping breached principles of humanitarian law. *Id.* at 112. The Court also held that the U.S. had violated rules of customary international law by producing and disseminating a war manual, to the Contras, that advocated acts contrary to general principles of humanitarian law. *Id.* at 114-15, 129-30. *See* Keith Highet, *Evidence, the Court, and the Nicaragua Case*, 81 AM. J. INT'L L. 1 (1987).

For reading on the ICJ's role in dealing with humanitarian law problems, see Panel, *World Court Jurisdiction and U.S. Foreign Policy in Latin America*, 78 AM. SOC'Y INT'L L. PROC. 321 (1986); Stephen M. Schwebel, *Human Rights in the World Court*, 24 VAND. J. TRANSNAT'L L. 945 (1991); George K. Walker, *United States National Security Law and United Nations Peacekeeping or Peacemaking Operations*, 29 WAKE FOREST L. REV. 435, 468-70 (1994).

3.   Some human rights advocates argue that states have a *duty* to intervene to stop human rights abuses. *See, e.g.,* Bernard Kouchner, *A Call for Humanitarian Intervention*, REFUGEES, Dec. 1992, at 14.

4.   Has the government of Y committed violations that justify humanitarian intervention? Would human rights abuses by the opposition merit intervention?

5.   In September 1994, President Clinton ordered the U.S. military to intervene in Haiti to restore deposed President Jean-Bertrand Aristide to power. U.S. troops invaded the island and, with little bloodshed, ousted the military government that had overthrown Haiti's first democratically elected president. The intervention followed unsuccessful efforts to depose the military regime by way of economic embargo and diplomacy. On March 31, 1995, after more than 20,000 U.S. troops had already restored peace and returned Aristide to power, the U.N. assumed command over international security forces. *See* John F. Harris, *Clinton Cheers Haiti's "2nd Chance" President, on Visit, Puts U.S. Troops Under U.N. Command*, WASH. POST, Apr. 1, 1995, at A1. For a discussion of the U.N.'s role in the Haiti intervention, see Richard Falk, *The Haiti Intervention: A Dangerous World Order Precedent for the United Nations*, 36 HARV. INT'L L.J. 341 (1995).

6.   Is the situation in Y similar to that in Haiti? How do the two differ?

7.   When the Lillich article excerpted above was published, the U.N. Security Council had not often adjudged human rights violations as threats to peace so as to justify Article 39 intervention. During the Cold War the Council considered only five such cases. *See* chapter *1, supra*. After the Cold War, however, the Council began to find threats to the peace when grave human rights emergencies existed. Between 1989 and mid-1993, the Council authorized on-site activities in 12 countries. Do those developments change your view as to arguments for humanitarian intervention presented in the Lillich article?

8.   The U.S. often has participated in humanitarian interventions through U.N. peacekeeping operations. How does unilateral intervention differ from U.N. intervention? Do you believe that U.S. intervention may be justified even when alternative means are practicable?

9.   Do you agree that U.S. force was justified in each of the situations discussed in the Sofaer article? What are some of the dangers of unilateral intervention such as the U.S. undertook in the early 1990s when it invaded Panama? Would the U.S. be justified in using unilateral force in Y? Does the detention of U.S. citizens provide justification, or is it mere pretense for a politically motivated use of force?

10.   For a survey of U.S. use of or threat to use covert action against elected non-European governments during the cold war, see David P. Forsythe, *Democracy, War, and Covert Action*, 29 J. PEACE RES. 385 (1992).

11.   For further reading on U.S. support of the Nicaraguan Contras, see Frank G. Colella, Note: *Beyond Institutional Competence: Congressional Efforts to Legislate United States Foreign Policy toward Nicaragua— The Boland Amendments*, 54 BROOK. L. REV. 131 (1988); JASON COOKE, IRAN/CONTRA AFFAIR CHRONOLOGY (1987); Anthony D'Amato, *Comment: Nicaragua and International Law: the "Academic" and the "Real,"* 79 AM. J. INT'L L. 657 (1985); THEODORE DRAPER, A VERY THIN LINE: THE IRAN-CONTRA AFFAIR (1991); John Norton Moore, *The Secret War in Central America and Future of World Order*, 80 Am. J. Int'l L. 43 (1986); PRESIDENT'S SPECIAL REVIEW BOARD, REPORT (1987).

For additional reading on the Grenada invasion, see Christopher C. Joyner, *The U.S.*

Action in Grenada: Reflections on the Lawfulness of Invasion, 78 AM. J. INT'L L. 131 (1984); John Norton Moore, *The U.S. Action in Grenada: Grenada and the International Double Standard*, 78 AM. J. INT'L L. 145 (1984); Ronald M. Riggs, *The Grenada Intervention: A Legal Analysis*, 109 MIL. L. REV. (1985); Detlev F. Vagts, *The U.S. Action in Grenada: International Law under Time Pressure: Grading the Grenada Take-Home Exam*, 78 AM. J. INT'L L. 169 (1984).

For reading on the Libya attack, see BRIAN L. DAVIS, QADDAFI, TERRORISM, AND THE ORIGINS OF THE U.S. ATTACK ON LIBYA (1990); Gregory Francis Intoccia, *American Bombing of Libya: An International Legal Analysis*, 19 CASE W. RES. J. INT'L L. 177 (1987); Wallace F. Warriner, USMC, *The Unilateral Use of Coercion Under International Law: A Legal Analysis of the United States Raid on Libya on April 14, 1986*, 37 NAVAL L. REV. 49 (1988).

For reading on the Panama invasion, see KENNETH ANDERSON, THE LAWS OF WAR AND THE CONDUCT OF THE PANAMA INVASION (1990); Alan Berman, *In Mitigation of Illegality: The U.S. Invasion of Panama*, 79 KY. L.J. 735 (1991); Anthony D'Amato, *The Invasion of Panama Was a Lawful Response to Tyranny* 84 AM. J. INT'L L. 516 (1990); Tom J. Farer, *Panama: Beyond the Charter Paradigm*, 84 AM. J. INT'L L. 503 (1990); Ved P. Nanda, *The Validity of United States Intervention in Panama under International Law*, 84 AM. J. INT'L L. 494 (1990); John Embry Parkerson, Jr., *United States Compliance with Humanitarian Law Respecting Civilians During Operation Just Cause*, 133 MIL. L. REV. 31 (1991); PHYSICIANS FOR HUMAN RIGHTS, OPERATION "JUST CAUSE:" THE HUMAN COST OF MILITARY ACTION IN PANAMA (1991); David Scheffer, *Use of Force After the Cold War: Panama, Iraq, and the New World Order, in* RIGHT V. MIGHT: INTERNATIONAL LAW AND THE USE OF FORCE (Louis Henkin et al. eds., 1991).

CHAPTER 7

CAN HUMAN RIGHTS VIOLATIONS BE PUNISHED AND VICTIMS ASSURED REDRESS?

A. INTRODUCTION	Page	256
B. QUESTIONS		256
C. RESPONDING TO PAST HUMAN RIGHTS VIOLATIONS		259
Diane F. Orentlicher, Settling Accounts: The Duty to Prosecute Human Rights Violations of a Prior Regime		259
José Zalaquett, Balancing Ethical Imperatives and Political Constraints: The Dilemma of New Democracies Confronting Past Human Rights Violations		262
David Weissbrodt & Paul W. Fraser, Political Transitions and Commissions of Inquiry		264
Thomas Buergenthal, The United Nations Truth Commission for El Salvador		267
D. NUREMBERG PRINCIPLES		276
1. The Nuremberg and Tokyo Tribunals		276
2. Control Council Law No. 10 and "Minor" Tribunals		277
3. Nuremberg's Legacy		278
E. THE INTERNATIONAL TRIBUNAL FOR THE FORMER YUGOSLAVIA		280
1. Historical Background		280
2. U.N. Response: War Crimes Tribunal for the former Yugoslavia		281
Diane F. Orentlicher, Legal Basis of the Tribunal for the former Yugoslavia		283
Statute of the International Criminal Tribunal for the former Yugoslavia		284
3. Efficacy of the Tribunal for the Former Yugoslavia		288
Aryeh Neier, War Crimes Tribunal is an Imperative		288
Herman Schwartz, War Crimes Trials—Not a Good Idea		289
Françoise J. Hampson, Violation of Fundamental Rights in the Former Yugoslavia: The Case for a War Crimes Tribunal		291
David P. Forsythe, Politics and the International Tribunal for the Former Yugoslavia		292
F. CREATING A PERMANENT INTERNATIONAL CRIMINAL COURT		298

M. Cherif Bassiouni, The Time Has Come for an International
    Criminal Court   298
Michael P. Scharf, The Jury is Still Out on the Need for an Interna-
    tional Criminal Court   300

A. INTRODUCTION

This chapter examines national and international measures that can be taken
to respond to human rights violations. The chapter will first present some of the
issues that confront governments seeking to address violations committed by past
governments. Options include establishing a national or international Truth Commission to investigate violations, criminal prosecution by a national or international
court, and national or international administration of a system to help redress
victims. The chapter then proceeds to focus on benefits and disadvantages of establishing an international criminal court to prosecute human rights violators. It will
examine *ad hoc* efforts, beginning with the Nuremberg and Tokyo tribunals, and
leading to prosecution of less visible offenders under Control Council Law No. 10
or comparable laws and, most recently, to the establishment of tribunals to prosecute
war criminals in the former Yugoslavia and Rwanda. The chapter will conclude by
examining the concept of a permanent international criminal tribunal.

B. QUESTIONS

Media have increasingly been turning the world's attention to the situation in
the (hypothetical) Latin American nation of Laria. The government of Laria was,
from 1984 until six months ago, controlled by General Ramon Clonto and military
forces under his command. Local opposition groups had, for several decades, accused
the government of systematically committing severe human rights violations against
the nation's large Lawarii indigenous community. Though no reliable census has
ever been taken in Laria, the Lawarii community estimates that it constitutes 25%
of the population—largely located in rural and mountainous regions. Despite the
military's efforts to repress perceived insurgents, Lawarii leaders successfully have
recruited and trained a sizable armed resistance movement.

The resistors initially sought to establish a dialogue with the Clonto government
and staged peaceful demonstrations calling for reform and power sharing. The
military responded with violent attacks on Lawarii villages, aimed at deterring
citizens from participating in the resistance movement. When the resistance resorted
to armed attack on military installations, the military retaliated by wiping out entire
Lawarii villages. Several NGOs—including Amnesty International and Human
Rights Watch—have released reports detailing abductions, torture, rape, and summary executions perpetrated by the military. The reports, compiled from interviews
conducted with hundreds of Larian residents, estimate that several hundred officers
and at least five thousand soldiers were involved in carrying out human rights
violations. The military is credited with having killed 50,000 Lawarii over a ten-
year period.

Despite heavy losses on both sides, the armed conflict continued until six months ago, when the resistors forced Clonto to surrender and gained control of the government via a bi-lateral settlement agreement.

A majority of Lawarii have expressed a desire to attain "justice"—to punish the perpetrators of, and acquire retribution for, human rights violations and the loss of family members. Most Lawarii have, however, no confidence in the domestic courts, which the military government used to control and suppress the resistance movement. The NGO reports suggest that it will take years of judicial reform to train and organize a new judiciary. Furthermore, Lawarii leaders fear that prosecution of past violations would incite violence by military officers, many of whom still harbor loyalty to Clonto and other former government officials. Moreover, the settlement agreement contains a clause that grants immunity to the eight highest-ranking leaders of the former government "from any criminal prosecution (including before any international tribunal established in the future)," and several former officials have fled to London, New Delhi, and New York.

You have been selected by the U.N. Secretary-General to provide expert advisory services, *see infra* at , to Laria. You will be asked, *inter alia*, to help Laria determine whether national or international responses are appropriate; whether it should respond to all violations or only those committed by certain individuals or groups; what remedies are appropriate; and whether and how compensation should be assured.

1.   Who are potential subjects of punishment and sources of redress for past human rights violations?

    a.   The Government of Laria? *maybe S.o.r.*
    b.   Individual government officials? *p.*
    c.   Non-governmental groups? *maybe proof prob.*
    d.   Individuals not associated with the government?

2.   Who are the victims deserving of redress?

    a.   Governments of Laria or other countries?
    b.   Non-governmental groups?
    c.   Individuals?

3.   How does international human rights law help define who the violators and victims are?

4.   What sanctions might be imposed on violators?

    a.   Criminal sanctions:

        1.   If Larian statutes criminalize murder and rape? *wd work*
        2.   If Larian statutes incorporate international norms such as prohibition of genocide and torture? *would work in theory*
        3.   If Laria has no statutes incorporating international norms, what might be accomplished by proposing and enacting such legislation?

    b.   Civil sanctions: What types of civil provisions might enable the Larian government to punish violators?

5.   Is the Larian government likely to succeed in imposing criminal or civil sanctions? Which of the following might impede their doing so: limited resources; insufficient infrastructure; lack of trained personnel; provisions for immunity or amnesty?

6.   To what extent are the following national measures appropriate for addressing human rights violations committed by government officials?

a.   Establishment of a citizens' Truth Commission to conduct an investigation of past human rights violations:

1.   What benefits might be derived from establishment of a national Truth-Commission? What negative consequences can you foresee?
2.   How important is government acceptance of the Truth Commission's authority and conclusions?
3.   Whose actions should the Truth Commission investigate? High, middle, or low-level government officials?
4.   What might be accomplished by release of a Truth Commission report without criminal prosecution?

b.   Criminal prosecution of suspected perpetrators before national courts:

1.   Does the desirability of domestic prosecution change depending upon whether domestic courts can impose the death penalty?
2.   Considering the weak condition of the Larian judiciary and the fact that most victims are from the indigenous Lawarii community, might prosecution in indigenous community courts be appropriate? *See infra* at 25.

c.   Disqualification from office of government officials proved to have committed human rights violations?

d.   Administration of a system by which violators are required to compensate victims and their families? Should the new government also be responsible for compensating victims and their families?

e.   Grant, by the new government, of immunity from prosecution or amnesty for human rights violators?

7.   If Laria cannot ensure imposition of criminal or civil sanctions, are international bodies capable of doing so?

8.   To what extent are the following international measures appropriate for addressing human rights violations committed by government officials?

a.   Establishment of a U.N. Truth Commission, composed of international representatives, to conduct an authoritative investigation of past human rights violations?

b.   Criminal prosecution of suspects before an international criminal tribunal, in which the death penalty cannot be imposed?

1.   Is the Security Council authorized to create an international tribunal for criminal prosecution of officials' violations? What conditions must first be met?
2.   What goals might be accomplished by establishing an international tribunal?
3.   What are the drawbacks to establishing an international tribunal?
4.   If established, should the new tribunal be modeled after the U.N. Tribunal for the former Yugoslavia? What changes would you recommend?
5.   Would use of the Tribunal for the former Yugoslavia be more desirable than establishing a new international tribunal for Laria?
6.   Who would fund the establishment and operation of an international tribunal for Laria?

7.   What penalties would be most appropriate for persons convicted by an international criminal tribunal for Laria?

c.   Disqualification from office of government officials proved to have committed human rights violations?

d.   U.N. administration of a system by which former government officials and human rights violators are required to compensate victims and their families?

e.   Should the new government also be responsible for compensating victims and their families?

9.   If an international tribunal were established, are countries to which Larian officials accused of human rights violations have fled likely to agree to either prosecute or extradite the accused?

10.   How would you address the present government's concern that ambitious efforts to investigate and prosecute officials of the former government and the military might engender rivalry from political opponents in Laria and the military?

C.   RESPONDING TO PAST HUMAN RIGHTS VIOLATIONS

Diane F. Orentlicher, *Settling Accounts: The Duty to Prosecute Human Rights Violations of a Prior Regime*, 100 YALE L.J. 2537, 2539-53, 2562-69 (1991) (footnotes omitted):

Introduction

From Latin America to Asia, from Eastern Europe to Africa, long-entrenched dictatorships have given way to elected civilian governments. . . . The outcome of recent transitions cannot yet be known, but it is now clear that nations emerging from dictatorship face formidable challenges as they seek to establish or restore the rule of law.

Many of the new governments replaced regimes responsible for brutal crimes— forced "disappearances," political killings and torture-inflicted on a staggering scale and with wholesale impunity. Whether these crimes should be prosecuted has loomed as one of the most urgent, and agonizing, issues confronting the nascent democracies. In some instances, security forces responsible for the worst abuses retain substantial power, and make clear that they will not brook any legal accounting. In several countries, governments have responded by granting de facto impunity; in others, the military has insisted upon amnesties which are designed, as one writer has observed, "to enforce a total amnesia regarding [its] crimes." . . .

I. *Why Punish?* . . .

A. The Case for Prosecutions

The fulcrum of the case for criminal punishment is that it is the most effective insurance against future repression. By laying bare the truth about violations of the past and condemning them, prosecutions can deter potential lawbreakers and inoculate the public against future temptation to be complicit in state-sponsored violence. Trials may, as well, inspire societies that are reexamining their basic values to affirm the fundamental principles of respect for the rule of law and for the inherent dignity of individuals.

Above all, however, the case for prosecutions turns on the consequences of failing to punish atrocious crimes committed by a prior regime on a sweeping scale. If law is unavailable to punish widespread brutality of the recent past, what lesson can be offered for the future? A complete failure of enforcement vitiates the authority of law itself, sapping its power to deter proscribed conduct. This may be tolerable when the law or the crime is of marginal consequence, but there can be no scope for eviscerating wholesale laws that forbid violence and that have been violated on a massive scale. . . .

B. The Case Against Prosecutions

The chief argument against a general rule requiring prosecution is that fragile democracies may not be able to survive the destabilizing effects of politically charged trials. Many countries emerging from dictatorship are polarized and unstable, and may be further fractured by prosecutions of the prior regime's depredations. Under these circumstances, some urge, democratic consolidation can be furthered by implementing a policy of reconciliation embodied in an amnesty law covering past violations.

In countries where the military retains substantial power after relinquishing office, efforts to prosecute past violations may provoke rebellions or other confrontations that could weaken the authority of the civilian government. And in countries where security forces have retained modest power relative to an elected government, prosecutions may induce the military to "close ranks." In these circumstances, prosecutions could reinforce the military's propensity to challenge democratic institutions.

In light of these constraints, some analysts believe that democratic consolidation may be best served if a precarious government stays the hand of prosecution. Their argument rests, in large measure, on the claim that transitional societies may not yet possess the attributes of a viable democracy—in particular, the new governments may lack the power to bring the military to account—and holds that the international community should not press these governments to act as though they were fully consolidated when in fact the transition process has only begun. Stripped of its essence, their argument is one of lesser evils. Opponents of law requiring prosecutions concede that impunity erodes the rule of law. But, they argue, if a fragile democratic government institutes prosecutions, it may provoke its overthrow by sectors that are ill-disposed to respect human rights.

C. The Role of International Law

As thus framed, the policy debate has tended to view the imperatives of the rule of law as somehow fundamentally at odds with political reality. This approach is unwarranted. The law itself can accommodate the constraints surrounding transitional societies while securing crucially important values. Addressing the dilemma of tenuous democracies through law assures that an appropriate balance is struck between the demands of justice and potentially conflicting values, such as political stability. . . .

I am not, of course, suggesting that governments should press prosecutions to the point of provoking their own collapse. Rather, I am suggesting that, by generally requiring prosecutions, international law helps assure that governments do not forego trials simply because it seems politically expedient to do so. A critical distinction to be drawn here is between military insubordination and a challenge that poses a genuine and serious threat to national life. Because trials secure preeminent rights and values, governments should be expected to assume reasonable risks associated with prosecutions, including a risk of military discontent.

. . . International law requiring punishment of atrocious crimes—and, more to the point, international pressure for compliance—can provide a counterweight to pressure from groups seeking impunity. . . .

Further, when prosecutions are undertaken pursuant to international law, they are less likely to be perceived—and opposed—as political revanchism. It is easy to believe that prosecutions are politically motivated when the decision to institute them is a matter of unbridled discretion; justice is readily mistaken for vengeance. . . .

. . . The argument that amnesty laws may be necessary to mend social divisions falsely assumes that such laws are the only means of achieving reconciliation. There are other means. Further, amnesty laws can be used to promote national reconciliation, provided they do not cover atrocious crimes which international law requires states to punish. . . .

II. The Duty to Punish Under Current International Law

. . . International human rights law traditionally has allowed governments substantial discretion to determine the means they will use to ensure protected rights, while international penal law has often focused on the power—not duty—of governments to punish violations committed outside their territorial jurisdiction. When the law has required states to punish offenses committed in their territory, the duty traditionally has applied principally to crimes committed against foreign nationals.

Increasingly, however, international law has required states to punish certain human rights crimes committed in their territorial jurisdiction. Several human rights treaties require States Parties to criminalize particular abuses, such as genocide and torture, investigate violations and seek to punish the wrongdoers. On their face, the more comprehensive treaties, such as the International Covenant on Civil and Political Rights, are silent about a duty to punish violations of the rights they ensure. But authoritative interpretations of these treaties make clear that a State Party fails in its duty to ensure the cluster of rights protecting physical integrity if it does not investigate violations and seek to punish those who are responsible. Moreover a state's failure to punish repeated or notorious violations breaches the customary obligation to respect the same set of preeminent rights.

A. International Criminal Law

1. General Principles

. . . While definitions of "international crimes" vary, the term in its broadest sense comprises offenses which conventional or customary law either authorizes or requires states to criminalize, prosecute, and/or punish. Although international law generally establishes rights and duties between and among states, international criminal law imposes obligations on individuals, making them liable to criminal punishment. It also imposes duties on states with respect to matters usually left to their discretion. Thus, an amnesty law or an exercise of prosecutorial discretion that is valid under domestic law may nonetheless breach a state's international obligations. . . .

B. Human Rights Conventions Specifying a Duty to Prosecute

The most explicit obligations to punish human rights crimes that are likely to be relevant to societies emerging from dictatorship are established by the Convention on the Prevention and Punishment of the Crime of Genocide ("Genocide Convention") and the Convention Against Torture, and Other Cruel, Inhuman or Degrading Treatment or Punishment ("Convention Against Torture"). Although both require States Parties to prosecute the conduct they proscribe, the two conventions embody profoundly different visions of international human rights law. Drafted in the wake of World War II, the Genocide Convention reflects a paradigm, inspired by the Nuremberg prosecutions, of a world order in which internationally recognized rights are enforced by an international tribunal. . . . By the time the drafters' work was completed, support for an international penal tribunal had so dissipated that the convention's provision of jurisdiction by such a court was little more than an acknowledgement of a faded vision, and chief responsibility for prosecuting genocide fell to the state most responsible for the crimes. . . .

The Convention Against Torture, which the General Assembly adopted thirty-six years after it adopted the Genocide Convention, reflects a pragmatic acceptance of the limited role of international enforcement in securing protected rights. No mention is made of an international tribunal. And while the Convention establishes a form of universal jurisdiction over torturers, chief responsibility for punishing violators lies with the state in which the crime occurred. . . .

C. Comprehensive Human Rights Conventions

In contrast to the conventions on torture and genocide, three comprehensive human rights treaties—the International Covenant on Civil and Political Rights ("International Covenant"), the European Convention for the Protection of Human Rights and Fundamental Freedoms ("European Convention"), and the American Convention on Human Rights ("American Convention")—do not explicitly require States Parties to prosecute or punish violations of rights set forth in the conventions. Authoritative interpretations make clear, however, that these treaties require States Parties generally to investigate serious violations of physical integrity—in particular, torture, extra-legal executions, and forced disappearances—and to bring to justice those who are responsible. . . .

The duties derive from States Parties' affirmative obligation to ensure rights set forth in these conventions. Adherents to all three treaties pledge not only to respect enumerated rights, but also to ensure that persons subject to their jurisdiction enjoy the full exercise of those rights. The International Covenant and American Convention further require States Parties to adopt legislation or other measures necessary to give effect to the rights and freedoms recognized in the treaties, and all three conventions require Parties to ensure that individuals whose rights are violated have an effective remedy before a competent body, even if the violation was committed by someone acting in an official capacity. . . .

*   *   *   *   *

José Zalaquett, *Balancing Ethical Imperatives and Political Constraints: The Dilemma of New Democracies Confronting Past Human Rights Violations*, 43 HASTINGS L.J. 1425, 1429-32 (1992):

In ambiguous transitional situations, dealing with past human rights violations is indeed a wrenching ethical and political problem. But there are no hard and fast rules on how to proceed. Ethical principles provide guidance but not definite answer. Political leaders cannot afford to be moved only by their convictions, oblivious to real-life constraints, lest in the end the very ethical principles they wish to uphold suffer because of a political or military backlash. In the face of a disaster brought about by their own misguided actions, politicians cannot invoke as a justification that they never yielded on matters of conviction. That would be as haughty as it would be futile, and certainly would bring no comfort to the people who must live with the consequences of the politician's actions.

A variation of that position is often put forward by ideological purists of all stripes: it is preferable to suffer longer under tyranny, in the hope of a fully satisfactory political outcome, than to make progress through untidy compromises. Implicit in this position is the arrogant expectation that the future will comply with one's wishes and a disdain for the dreadful costs of such a cavalier gamble. However, it must also be firmly stated that a politician cannot invoke the need for prudence in an attempt to justify mere temporization and neglect. The ghosts of the past, if not exorcised to the fullest extent possible, will continue to haunt the nation tomorrow.

. . .

Let us examine, then, the two considerations that must be balanced—the ethical principles that ought to be pursued, and actual political opportunities and constraints that ought to be taken into account. By balancing these factors, ethical principles can be realized to the fullest possible extent.

No single international convention or set of norms exists where such principles can be found. These principles must be fashioned from existing international norms, from ethical postulates, and from judgment, taking into account all relevant experiences.

I submit that these principles should be the following:

a)   A policy to deal with past human rights abuses should have two overall objectives: Preventing the recurrence of such abuses and, to the extent possible, repairing the damage they have caused.

b)   For a policy to be legitimate it must, first, be adopted with full cognizance of past human rights violations. Second, it must be adopted through a body of democratically elected representatives or by other means clearly reflecting the sovereign will of the nation.

c)   Within the terms just stated, nations have ample discretion concerning the content of the policy. They may lean towards severity or clemency. But international law limits such sovereign discretion. The treatment of alleged perpetrators, including their prosecution and punishment, must not violate the perpetrator's rights. Measures of governmental magnanimity are also limited by international law inasmuch as it imposes the duty to prosecute those who have committed certain crimes.

[Examination of several emerging democracies reveals] several typical situations involving a balance of political opportunities and constraints that will allow us to put these principles into practice. At one extreme, if the perpetrators have been completely defeated, the new government has the greatest latitude of action. But past experience suggests that unfettered power to mete out punishment is itself a factor that may place justice at risk. At the other extreme, if the perpetrators are a cohesive and determined force enjoying a monopoly on military strength, the obstacles to justice are most severe. Yet political situations are far from static, and if the new government consistently follows the best possible approach, despite being limited by the circumstances it faces, new possibilities may open up along the way.

Many other factors combine in real life to make each situation unique. The following are some examples:

(a)   Those who committed the human rights abuses may have persuaded themselves and others that such acts, although not desirable, were required to avoid subversion or an impending civil war. While such justification is, of course, unacceptable, it may strengthen the perpetrators' resolve to oppose trials and punishment.

(b)   Peace may have been achieved after protracted civil war or a similar armed conflict, with neither side having been defeated and neither wishing to have its people subjected to prosecutions.

(c)   Some opponents of the deposed dictatorial regime may also have engaged in violence, sometimes against innocent targets, or otherwise transgressed basic rules of humane behavior. Their liability for past acts of resistance may be used by partisans of the previous regime to press for a general amnesty or for impunity for agents of the dictatorship.

(d)   Ethnic, religious, or nationalistic divisions may conspire against the possibility of adopting a policy that would be generally accepted as fair and impartial.

It is amidst such complex and changing circumstances that political leaders must obey the call to act responsibly. Since there is no blueprint to direct their actions, they must rely on good judgment. Responsibility also requires taking into account the accomplishments and failures of other countries that have faced similar challenges.

*   *   *   *   *

David Weissbrodt & Paul W. Fraser, Book Review, 14 HUM. RTS. Q. 601, 604-609 (1992) (reviewing National Commission on Truth and Reconciliation, Report of the Chilean National Commission on Truth and Reconciliation (1991)) (footnotes omitted):

Recent Political Transitions and Commissions of Inquiry

. . . [T]ransitions from repressive military dictatorships to democracy in Argentina (1983), Brazil (1985), Guatemala (1985), the Philippines (1986), and Uruguay (1984) offered valuable lessons within differing political circumstances. . . . Incoming governments in each of these countries initially had a popular mandate for a democratically elected president and a diminished role for the military. In all of these countries, the new government faced political constraints due to the continued influence of the military. Not all of these countries managed even to appoint a bona fide commission of inquiry. Those commissions of inquiry that were appointed offer many lessons in the pitfalls of overly narrow mandates, poor timing, faulty methodology, resistance from the military, and inadequate resources. . . .

A. The Case of Argentina

On 24 March 1976, a military coup overthrew the government of Isabel Mart[í]nez de Peron with the objective of stabilizing the economy and suppressing "leftist subversion."

Argentina underwent a grave human rights crisis during the period of military rule between 1976 and 1983 and emerged as a democracy in late 1983 with the election of President Raúl Alfonsoín. At the end of 1983, President Alfonsín appointed a commission of inquiry, headed by the prominent Argentine novelist Ernesto Sabato, to undertake a thorough accounting of the organization and methods the Argentine security forces used in carrying out their policy which resulted in thousands of disappearances. The Sabato Commission, as it became known, took advantage of the Argentine military's loss of power and prestige in their defeat during the War in the South Atlantic, to produce a detailed report of human rights violations and the related system of repression. . . .

The Sabato Commission forwarded its report to President Alfonsín in September 1984 along with documentation which included the names of over 1,300 military officers implicated by the testimony received and the research done by the Commission. President Alfonsín decided not to make public the names of the officers, on the ground that they should be accused of criminal acts only by means of formal charges brought against them. The names, however, were leaked to the press and published in the journal *El Periodista*. The detailed Sabato Commission report raised great hopes among Argentine victims, their families, and human rights organizations that the perpetrators would be brought to justice.

During five months in 1985, nine military leaders were tried for the specific offenses of the "dirty war." On 9 December 1985, the court issued its verdict. The tribunal sentenced General Jorge Videla and Admiral Emilio Massera, who commanded the Army and Navy, to life in prison. It sentenced two other participants to a term of years and acquitted the remaining defendants. Although hundreds of other prosecutions were initiated, [legislation] during Alfonsín's presidency ultimately prevented action against almost all of the more junior officers and the perpetrators of the most heinous abuses. . . .

A top advisor to President Alfonsín on human rights policy now admits that Argentina should have moved more rapidly in trying military officers. As time passed, officers became more inclined to protect their comrades, and they closed ranks and covered over distinctions between military personnel who had murdered and tortured and those who had committed less serious offenses. Also, once the euphoria of the new democracy had faded, economic and social problems weakened the administration. . . .

B. Other Transitional Situations in Latin America and the Philippines

Transitions in Latin America and elsewhere during the 1980s offered examples of the political constraints on governments in pursuing the imperatives of truth and justice. In Uruguay, President Julio Sanguinetti was elected in November 1984 on a platform that included bringing the military to justice for human rights violations under the dictatorship (1973-1984). The military that ruled Uruguay between 1973 and 1984 was responsible for the widespread use of torture and arbitrary imprisonment. . . . In September 1986, not long after the opening of hearings in several of the forty criminal cases pending against 180 military officers, Sanguinetti's Colorado Party proposed a blanket amnesty law for the military. The ruling party pushed a bill through the legislature which had the effect of precluding the state from seeking punishment for most of the military's human rights violations before 1985. . . .

Brazil underwent a period of repression between 1964 and 1985, and if not for the efforts of a nongovernmental group, much of the truth about human rights violations might not have been revealed. In Brazil, the transition was accomplished within a framework of consensus that there would be no need for trials of the perpetrators. . . . [T]he worst violations had occurred some fifteen years before the transition to democracy. The violence in Brazil had been aimed at a comparatively small sector of society, and the military managed to leave the government gradually over a period of years. The interests of truth were served by the efforts of a secret team that, working under the auspices of the Archbishop of Sao Paulo, produced the book *Brasil: Nunca Mais*.

In Guatemala, President Vinicio Cerezo was elected in 1985, but he refused to capitalize on an initial mandate to investigate and prosecute the military for the human rights violations under previous dictatorships.

In the Philippines, the military played a vital role in the revolution that overthrew President Ferdinand Marcos in 1986; hence, any attempt by the successor Aquino government to inquire into past abuses was tenuous from the start. The People's Power Revolution raised the hope that the military would revert to its role during the premartial days and that militarization would end. Nonetheless, because then Defense Minister Juan Ponce Enrile, Chief of Staff Fidel Ramos, and elements of the armed forces assisted in ousting Marcos, combatting the New People's Army, and stopping several attempted military coups, the military's role in society became an entrenched part of the administration of Corazon Aquino.

The opportunity to begin meaningful prosecutions probably only existed during the first few months after President Aquino took office, when Mrs. Aquino's popularity was at its height. After that, the military was too strong to permit an effective investigation or sanction. The government was engaged in an ongoing civil war which required the help of the military and also resulted in more human rights abuses.

Each transition brought hope among human rights organizations, survivors, relatives of the victims, and others that the true story about human rights violations would be revealed and that the perpetrators would be brought to justice. None of the transitional political situations in Argentina, Brazil, Guatemala, the Philippines, or Uruguay offered an ideal outcome. Each country still faced a formidable military presence and risked a return to military control if it pressed too hard for information about violations and convictions of military perpetrators.

[Ed. note: The summaries above served as background for the authors' assessment of the work of the Chilean National Commission on Truth and Reconciliation, which was created in 1990 by President Patricio Aylwin. Aylwin had taken office earlier that year, ending sixteen and one-half years of military dictatorship under General Augusto Pinochet. The Commission was charged with gathering information about human rights violations, including murder, arbitrary detentions, disappearances, and torture committed by the military during the Pinochet years.

The Commission sought to expose the truth, pursue justice, and achieve national reconciliation—repentance by the perpetrators and forgiveness by the victims. Despite several obstacles, the most formidable of which was the continued presence of Pinochet as Commander-in-Chief of the Chilean Army, the Commission submitted its final report to President Aylwin in February 1991. The Commission provided an officially sanctioned forum in which victims and relatives could give their testimony, and succeeded in establishing the "official truth" and in attaining government acknowledgement of responsibility for violations.

The second volume of the Commission's report identifies more than 2,000 victims. The Commission also succeeded in proposing reparations procedures, which were later implemented by the Chilean Congress. The Commission stopped short, however, of fully exposing the "truth" by avoiding explicit findings of individual responsibility. The Commission did not identify individuals and thus conducted no prosecutions.]

*   *   *   *   *

Thomas Buergenthal,[1] *The United Nations Truth Commission for El Salvador*, 27 VAND. J. TRANSNAT'L L. 497, 498-503, 513-22, 533-38 (1994) (footnotes omitted):

I. *Introduction*

. . . The Commission on the Truth for El Salvador (Truth Commission or Commission) was formally established on July 15, 1992, pursuant to the provisions of the Salvadoran Peace Accords (Peace Accords), a series of agreements negotiated between 1989 and 1992 under the auspices of the United Nations. The parties to these negotiations were the government of El Salvador and the Frente Farabundo Martí para la Liberacion Nacional (FMLN). . . . The negotiations were formally concluded with the signing on January 16, 1992, in Mexico City of a comprehensive peace agreement, named the "Chapultepec Agreement" . . .. This instrument incorporated by reference a series of earlier accords concluded by the Parties. The establishment of the Truth Commission is provided for in the so-called "Mexico Agreements," which were signed on April 27, 1991. These agreements, amplified by one provision of the Chapultepec Agreement, spell out the functions and powers or mandate of the Truth Commission.

. . . The overall task of the Commission was to investigate the "serious acts of violence" that occurred in El Salvador between 1980 and 1991 "and whose impact on society urgently requires that the public should know the truth." . . . [N]ot all serious acts of violence were necessarily to be investigated. The main focus was to be on acts that had a special or broader impact on society in general. Moreover, in ascertaining the truth, the Commission was not to lose sight of the fact that the promotion of national reconciliation was an overarching aim of the investigation.

In addition to these general powers, the Commission was assigned a specific task under Article 5 of the Chapultepec Agreement, which reads in part as follows:

> The parties recognize the need to clarify and put an end to any indication of impunity on the part of officers of the armed forces, particularly in cases where respect for human rights is jeopardized. To that end, the Parties refer this issue to the Commission of Truth for consideration and resolution. . . .

To understand the role and powers of the Truth Commission, it is important to note at the outset that in addition to investigating the serious acts of violence, the Commission was also charged with the task of "recommending the legal, political or administrative measures which can be inferred from the results of the investigation," including measures designed "to prevent the repetition of such acts." Moreover, the Parties undertook "to carry out the Commission's recommendations." In other words, by signing the Peace Accords, the FMLN and the government of El Salvador agreed to accept the recommendations as binding on them. . . .

The establishment of the Truth Commission marks the first time that the parties to an internal armed conflict, in negotiating a peace agreement, conferred on a commission composed of foreign nationals designated by the United Nations the power to investigate human rights violations committed during the conflict and to make binding recommendations. . . .

II. *The Context*

The twelve-year Salvadoran civil war . . . was played out in the context of the

---

[1] Thomas Buergenthal was one of three Commissioners of the U.N. Commission on the Truth for El Salvador.

Cold War, with the United States supporting the Salvadoran government. The FMLN, an alliance of five leftist insurgent groups, received substantial assistance . . . from Cuba, Sandinista Nicaragua, the Soviet Union, and other Soviet bloc countries. . . .

The war was particularly brutal in its impact on the civilian population. Not surprisingly, both sides to the struggle accused each other of bearing responsibility for the numerous atrocities that had been committed over the twelve-year period. . . .

As the peace negotiations advanced, the charges and countercharges relating to [human rights] atrocities threatened to become serious obstacles to any peaceful resolution of the conflict. It was soon recognized, therefore, that the hate and mistrust built up over the years required the inclusion in the peace agreements of various "confidence[-]building" arrangements, among them some mechanism permitting an honest accounting of these terrible deeds. The FMLN had no confidence in the Salvadoran judicial system, which had not been particularly eager or effective in solving any crimes attributed to the government side. . . .

[Ed. note: In part III, the author explains the process by which the Commission sought to gather information.]

IV. *Getting to the Truth*

A. The Obstacles

During the first two to three months of its stay in El Salvador, the Commission was able to gather very little useful information. Relatively few victims or their next of kin came forward to tell their stories, which was not all that surprising. The country had just come out of a brutal civil war and . . . fear and suspicion were pervasive. That segment of the population which had been victimized by government forces had reason to fear reprisals. Similarly, the victims of FMLN violence, particularly those living in areas still controlled by the FMLN or its sympathizers, could expect no better from that side.

It should also not be forgotten that the average Salvadoran had no reason to assume that the Commission would in fact carry out an honest and serious investigation. There had been many so-called "investigations" in the past, principally domestic ones, and they produced little information and even less truth. . . .

B. The Wall Begins to Crumble

Our investigation began to make progress some three months after we arrived in El Salvador. That is, towards the end of October and the beginning of November 1992, various people, including some military officers, began to talk. What happened? My own sense is that at least three interrelated factors played an important role. One was the report of the so-called Ad Hoc Commission. . . .

The Ad Hoc Commission, also a creature of the Peace Accords, was established to review the past performance of Salvadoran military officers by reference to their human rights record, their professional competence, and their capacity to function in democratic society. Composed of three distinguished Salvadoran civilians, with two retired Salvadoran generals assigned to it as advisers, this body was empowered to recommend the dismissal, demotion, or detention of officers. . . . The government, in turn, was under an obligation to comply with these recommendations within a period of two months. There is strong evidence to suggest that the government and the military only agreed to the establishment of the Ad Hoc Commission because they were convinced that it would not dare to discharge its responsibilities honestly.

At most, they thought the Commission would call for the dismissal of a few low-ranking officers. That is what had happened in the past with similar bodies, and there was little reason to assume that this one would act differently. But, to the great surprise of many in El Salvador, it did. The result was a secret report presented to the Secretary-General of the United Nations and to the President of El Salvador. The report, which was eventually leaked to the press, charged more than one hundred officers, including the Minister and Deputy Minister of Defense as well as the Chief of the General Staff, with serious violations of human rights and called for their dismissal from the service. The three members of the Ad Hoc Commission delivered their report in New York and, fearing for their lives, remained outside El Salvador for some time.

The report of the Ad Hoc Commission, coming some three months after the Truth Commission had begun its work, had a very perceptible impact on the work of the Truth Commission. It was the first clear indication—the first signal—received by the people of El Salvador that the days of "business as usual," of military impunity and cover-ups, might be over. Suddenly people no longer looked at the Truth Commission with their accustomed cynicism. If three Salvadorans had dared to undertake an honest investigation despite the risks this action exposed them to, it was certainly more likely that three distinguished foreigners working under UN auspices could do no less. Thus, some individuals implicated in serious acts of violence no longer felt sure that they would be protected. Because the Truth Commission had the power to make recommendations concerning criminal trials and amnesties, and might be able to help implicated parties get asylum abroad, a few of them began to provide the Commission with important information. That information in turn elicited testimony from others who then realized that the protective dike they had constructed was beginning to leak. . . . [M]any more ordinary citizens also came forward to provide evidence, still very fearful, but now with greater confidence in the integrity of the process.

V. *Naming Names . . .*

Until the issue became the subject of a heated debate in and outside of El Salvador towards the end of our investigation, it had certainly never occurred to me that the Report would not name names. . . .

. . . [A]ll three of us were unanimous on this subject and never doubted that, unless both Parties decided to amend our mandate, we were legally and morally obliged to identify those we found to be guilty of the serious abuses we had been investigating. In the Report, we explained our decision as follows:

In the peace agreements, the Parties made it quite clear that it was necessary that the "complete truth be made known," and that was why the Commission was established. Now, the whole truth cannot be told without naming names. After all, the Commission was not asked to write an academic report on El Salvador, it was asked to investigate and describe exceptionally important acts of violence and to recommend measures to prevent the repetition of such acts. This task cannot be performed in the abstract, suppressing information (for example, the names of person[s] responsible for such acts) where there is reliable testimony available, especially when the persons identified . . . occupy senior positions and perform official functions directly related to the violations or the cover-up of violations. Not to name names would be to reinforce the very impunity to which the Parties instructed the Commission to put an end. . . .

[Ed. note: The author explained the drafting process in Part VI of his article.]

VII. *The Report* . . .

C. The Recommendations . . .

The Commission could have recommended that the individuals identified as responsible for the serious acts of violence described in the Report be tried by Salvadoran courts. However, such a recommendation would have made sense only if the Commissioners believed that the justice system of that country was capable of doing justice, which we did not. Although the Peace Accords had ended the armed conflict and called for substantial reforms in the justice system, very few of these changes had been implemented or were likely to be implemented in the near future. . . .

Taking this reality into account, the Commission decided not to call for trials, nor for that matter to recommend amnesties. The former made no sense until the full implementation of the Peace Accords. The latter seemed worthwhile only, if at all, after a national consensus that an amnesty would promote the goal of reconciliation in El Salvador. Ultimately, the decision whether to grant amnesty was one for the people of El Salvador to make after appropriate dialogue on the subject.

At the same time, it was clear that the Commission's findings required some recommendations for immediate action. In the Commission's view, those identified as responsible for serious acts of violence had to be removed from the offices that had enabled them to commit these acts. To this end, the Commission made a series of recommendations. First, it called for the dismissal from the armed forces of those active military officers who had committed or covered up serious acts of violence. Second, the Commission recommended the dismissal from their positions of those civilian government officials and members of the judiciary who committed or covered up serious acts of violence or failed to investigate them. Third, the Commission declared that "under no circumstances would it be advisable to allow persons who committed acts of violence such as those which the Commission has investigated to participate in the running of the State." Therefore, we recommended that appropriate legislation be adopted to ensure that all individuals found by the Commission to have been implicated in serious acts of violence—whether active or retired military officers, civilian officials, FMLN members or military commanders, judges, or civilians—should be disqualified from holding any public office for a period of no less than ten years. . . .

The Commission made a series of recommendations designed to promote national reconciliation. It proposed, *inter alia*, the construction of a national monument listing the names of all victims of the Salvadoran conflict; a national holiday honoring them; and the creation of a Forum for Truth and Reconciliation, comprising representatives of all sectors of Salvadoran society, to address the conclusions and recommendations of the Truth Commission with a view to promoting their implementation. The Commission also recommended the establishment of a fund to compensate all victims of serious acts of violence. . . .

VIII. *Conclusions*

It will take years to fully assess the work and achievements of the United Nations Truth Commission for El Salvador. After all, its success and failure can only be meaningfully judged in the context of long-term developments in that country. At this point, therefore, it is not really possible to do more than offer some very tentative observations concerning its contribution to the Salvadoran peace process.

A. Follow-Up and Compliance

A few days after the publication of the Report, the government of President Cristiani and the national legislature controlled by his party granted an across-the-board amnesty to all individuals charged with serious acts of violence. This measure did not, however, nullify the Commission's work or have a serious effect on it. The amnesty merely prevented those identified by the Commission as responsible for acts of violence from being tried in Salvadoran courts and resulted in the release from prison of a few others who had been convicted earlier in that country on similar charges. Since the Commission did not recommend the trial of those it named, the amnesty cannot be said to violate its recommendations. However, while amnesties after a civil war may be a legitimate way to put an end to the conflict, the manner in which this amnesty was rushed through the Salvadoran legislature—a legislature in which the FMLN was not represented—with no time or opportunity for a full national debate on the subject, was unseemly at the very least, indicative of a lack of respect for democratic processes, and thus incompatible with the spirit of the Peace Accords. It should be emphasized, however, that the amnesty did not affect the Commission's recommendations or override those calling for the dismissal from their positions of individuals named in the Report. Particularly noteworthy in this connection is the fact that all military officers identified by the Commission were retired from the service not long after the Report was issued.

*   *   *   *   *

In 1955, the U.N. General Assembly approved Resolution 926 (X), which created a program to provide advisory services and technical assistance in the field of human rights.[2] G.A. res. 926 (X), 10 U.N. GAOR Supp. (No. 19), U.N. Doc. A/3116 (1955). Administered by the Centre for Human Rights, advisory services have primarily been deployed to assist governments in strengthening national infrastructures, such as the legal system, that are essential to the implementation of international human rights standards. Assistance is provided only on request by governments concerned, and the amount and conditions under which it is rendered are determined by the Secretary-General. Since the establishment of the Voluntary Fund for Advisory Services and Technical Assistance in the Field of Human Rights in 1987, voluntary contributions by several governments, intergovernmental organizations, and NGOs have helped fund supplementary advisory services activities. (The Voluntary Fund has been subsequently renamed the Voluntary Fund for Technical Cooperation in the Field of Human Rights.)

The General Assembly has authorized several types of assistance, including advisory services of experts, fellowships and scholarships, international and regional seminars, and regional and national training courses. In recent years, at the request of the U.N. Human Rights Commission, the Secretary-General has authorized expert advisory services to assist newly established governments seeking to address human rights violations of past regimes. Technical assistance has been provided to help the new governments modify their laws and practices to comply with international standards. Assistance has included provision of law books, training of police and prison officers regarding international human rights standards, rewriting of national

---

[2] Resolution 926 (X) consolidated several technical assistance programs previously created under General Assembly resolutions. *See* G.A. res. 729 (VIII), 8 U.N. GAOR Supp. (No. 17), U.N. Doc. A/2630 (1953) (authorizing assistance to states in promoting and safeguarding the rights of women); G.A. res. 730 (VIII), 8 U.N. GAOR Supp. (No. 17), U.N. Doc. A/2630 (1953) (authorizing assistance to states in eradicating discrimination and protecting minorities); G.A. res. 839 (IX), 9 GAOR Supp. (No. 21), U.N. Doc. A/2890 (1954) (authorizing assistance to states in promoting freedom of information).

constitutions to specify human rights protections, and translation of human rights texts into local languages.

Pursuant to the Human Rights Commission's resolution 1993/87, the Secretary-General appointed a board of trustees for the Voluntary Fund to advise "on the administration and operation of the Fund; . . . to assist . . . in streamlining and rationalizing the procedures of the Fund, . . . [and] to promote and solicit contributions to the Fund." Boutros Boutros-Ghali, *Report of the Board of Trustees of the Voluntary Fund for Technical Cooperation in the Field of Human Rights*, U.N. Doc. E/CN.4/1995/89/Add.1 (1995).

Ethiopia provides an example of U.N. use of advisory services. The Mengistu government, which ruled beginning in 1974, was forced from power in May 1991 by rebel forces of the Ethiopian People's Revolutionary Democratic Front and the Eritrean People's Liberation Front. Upon taking control, the new government detained thousands of former officials for alleged human rights violations. Despite the establishment of a Special Prosecutor's Office in 1992, investigation and trial of the alleged violators developed slowly. In 1994, the U.N. Centre for Human Rights responded to an Ethiopian government request for assistance by sending an expert mission to Ethiopia. The mission focused on the government's handling of the detainees in light of international human rights and humanitarian law and Ethiopia's obligations under treaties to which it is a party. The mission investigated and advised on impunity, retroactive application of penal laws, long-term detention without trial, and capital punishment. Trials began in December 1994 and were ongoing but subjected to seemingly endless recesses and adjournments. *See* John Ryle, *Letter From Ethiopia: An African Nuremberg*, NEW YORKER, Oct. 2, 1995, at 50; U.N. CENTRE FOR HUM. RTS., ADVISORY SERVICES, TECHNICAL ASSISTANCE AND PUBLICATIONS BRANCH, ETHIOPIA: REPORT OF THE EXPERT MISSION TO ADVISE THE SPECIAL PROSECUTOR'S OFFICE (1994); Alan Zarembo, *In Ethiopia, Time to Settle Accounts*, SAN FRANCISCO CHRONICLE, Apr. 29, 1995, at A1.

Other countries receiving assistance have included Bolivia, the Central African Republic, Equatorial Guinea, Guatemala, Haiti, Mongolia, the Palestinian Gaza Strip, and Uganda. For a summary of 1994 activities financed by the voluntary fund and the general U.N. budget, see Boutros Boutros-Ghali, *Advisory Services in the Field of Human Rights*, at 24-31, U.N. Doc. E/CN.4/1995/89 (1995). His report was submitted pursuant to the Human Rights Commission's 1994 request for an annual report concerning "progress made in the implementation of the programme and on the administration of the Voluntary Fund." *Id.* at 2.

For additional reading, see LAWYERS COMMITTEE FOR HUMAN RIGHTS, ABANDONING THE VICTIMS: THE U.N. ADVISORY SERVICES PROGRAM IN GUATEMALA (1990); U.N. CENTRE FOR HUM. RTS., UNITED NATIONS ACTION IN THE FIELD OF HUMAN RIGHTS at 345, U.N. Doc. ST/HR/2/Rev.4 (1994); U.N. CENTRE FOR HUM. RTS., ADVISORY SERVICES AND TECHNICAL ASSISTANCE IN THE FIELD OF HUMAN RIGHTS, Fact Sheet No. 3 (1988).

NOTES AND QUESTIONS

1.   If one accepts Orentlicher's duty to prosecute proposal, what criteria should be applied, and by whom, to determine whether human rights violations are sufficiently "massive" to require prosecution?

2.   The Weissbrodt & Fraser article suggested that the new governments in Argentina and the Philippines waited too long to begin prosection of military and government officials. What probably prevented the new governments from quick initiation of prosecutions? Would

prosecution in an international court have enhanced or further limited the possibility of more timely prosecutions?

3.   Unlike the settlement in El Salvador, the settlement in Laria did not contain provisions for a Truth Commission. Will the omission prevent the post-settlement creation of such a body? If established, would a Truth Commission be likely to receive more or less cooperation from witnesses than if its mandate had been written into the settlement?

4.   Do you agree with Buergenthal that the grant of mass amnesty that followed publication of the El Salvador Truth Commission's Report did not nullify or seriously affect the Commission's work? What results could the Commission realistically have hoped to achieve in the absence of prosecutions?

5.   Was it appropriate for the El Salvador Commission to identify individuals without guaranteeing that the accused be informed of charges and have an opportunity to respond? Compare the El Salvador Commission's action with that of the Kahan Commission in Israel. In 1982, Israeli troops failed to intervene while members of the Christian Phalange ransacked the Shatila and Sabra refugee camps and killed hundreds of civilians. The Israeli Government established the Kahan Commission to investigate and report on the massacres. The Commission's report condemned the Army's conduct and assigned responsibility to several individuals, including high ranking officials such as Defense Minister Ariel Sharon and Foreign Minister Yitzhak Shamir. Prior to finding individual responsibility, however, the Commission invited the accused to appear with lawyers to present testimony and respond to the accusations. *See* THE COMMISSION OF INQUIRY INTO THE EVENTS AT THE REFUGEE CAMPS IN BEIRUT—FINAL REPORT (1983) (authorized trans.), reprinted in JERUSALEM POST, Feb. 9, 1983, at 1.

6.   Critics of the El Salvador Commission's decision to identify individuals point out that it galvanized opposition to the Commission's report and led to the declaration of amnesty. Are you convinced that the Commission should have left the issue of assigning individual responsibility to the Salvadoran political process?

7.   Human rights organizations and scholars have begun to place greater emphasis on compensation for victims rather than focusing solely on prosecution of perpetrators. *See, e.g.,* Frank Newman, *Redress for Gulf War Violations of Human Rights,* 20 DENV. J. INT'L L. & POL'Y 213 (1992). The U.N. demonstrated a commitment to probing the issue by appointing Theo van Boven as Special Rapporteur to study legal and practical issues associated with compensation. *See* Theo van Boven, *Study Concerning the Right to Restitution, Compensation and Rehabilitation for Victims of Gross Violations of Human Rights and Fundamental Freedoms,* U.N. Doc. E/CN.4/Sub.2/1993/8 (1993).

In 1991, the U.N. Security Council adopted Resolution 687, establishing the U.N. Compensation Commission to process claims deriving from Iraq's invasion of Kuwait and administer a fund to satisfy successful claims. S.C. res. 687, 46 U.N. SCOR, U.N. Doc. S/RES/687 (1991), *reprinted in* 30 I.L.M. 846 (1991). Pursuant to Security Council Resolution 778, funds are composed of proceeds from Iraqi oil sales. S.C. res. 778, 47 U.N. SCOR, U.N. Doc. S/RES/778 (1992). As of November 1994, the Commission had received over 2.6 million claims worth more than $160 billion. Eric Schmitt, *Righting Wrongs of War: Billions in Claims Against Iraq,* N.Y. TIMES, Nov. 18, 1994, at B9. For further reading on the U.N. Compensation Commission, see Ronald J. Bettauer, *Current Development: The United Nations Compensation Commission—Developments Since October 1992,* 89 AM. J. INT'L L. 416 (1995); David D. Caron, *United Nations Compensation Commission: Report with Decisions of the Governing Council,* 31 I.L.M. 1009 (1992); John Crook, *The United Nations Compensation Commission—A New Structure to Enforce State Responsibility,* 87 AM. J. INT'L L. 144 (1993).

For additional reading on compensating victims of human rights violations, see Michael Garcia Bochenek, *Compensation for Human Rights Abuses in Zimbabwe,* 26 COLUM. HUM. RTS. L. REV. 483 (1995); Ellen L. Lutz, *The Marcos Human Rights Litigation: Can Justice be Achieved in U.S. Courts for Abuses that Occurred Abroad?,* 14 B.C. THIRD WORLD L.J. 43 (1994) and *After the Elections: Compensating Victims of Human Rights Abuses, in* NEW DIRECTIONS IN HUMAN RIGHTS 195 (Ellen L. Lutz, Hurst Hannum, & Kathryn J. Burke eds., 1989); Jordan Paust, *Suing Saddam: Private Remedies for War Crimes and Hostage-Taking,* 31 VA. J. INT'L L. 351 (1991); Beth Stephens, *The Civil Lawsuit as a Remedy for International Human Rights Violations Against Women,* 5 HASTINGS WOMEN'S L.J. 143 (1994).

Victims of human rights violations can also seek regional redress via litigation in the European Court of Human Rights, Inter-American Court for Human Rights, and United States courts. *See infra* chapters 11 and 12.

8. The indigenous character of the Lawarii community adds a unique dimension to be considered in addressing the violations committed in Laria. In 1982, the U.N. Sub-Commission on Prevention of Discrimination and Protection of Minorities created the Working Group on Indigenous Populations to draft a declaration of indigenous rights. For the next 12 years, the Working Group collected comments and suggestions from hundreds of indigenous groups, nongovernmental organizations, intergovernmental organizations, and governments. In August 1994, the Sub-Commission completed its draft Declaration on the Rights of Indigenous People and submitted it for approval to the Commission on Human Rights. Sub-Comm'n res. 1994/45, at 103, U.N. Doc. E/CN.4/1994/2 (1994).

The draft declaration provides for separate indigenous identities and direct access to international bodies, and asserts that indigenous peoples have the right to autonomy and self-government. Indigenous leaders have described the rights set forth in the articles as including freedom from economic and political domination, self-government, the right to their own independent government, and the right to participate in the international community at the same level as other governments. In 1995, the Human Rights Commission established an open-ended inter-sessional working group to consider the draft declaration. Comm'n res. 1995/32, U.N. Doc. E/CN.4/1995/L.62 (1995)

These are the draft declaration clauses that seem most relevant to violations committed against the Lawarii:

> *Article 6:* Indigenous peoples have the collective right to live in freedom, peace and security as distinct peoples and to full guarantees against genocide or any other act of violence. . . . In addition, they have the individual rights to life, physical and mental integrity, liberty and security of person.

> *Article 7:* Indigenous peoples have the collective and individual right not to be subjected to ethnocide and cultural genocide, including prevention of and redress for:

> (a) Any action which has the aim or effect of depriving them of their integrity as distinct peoples, or of their cultural values or ethnic identities;

> (b) Any action which has the aim or effect of dispossessing them of their lands, territories or resources;

> (c) Any form of population transfer which has the aim or effect of violating or undermining any of their rights;

> (d) Any form of assimilation or integration by other cultures or ways of life imposed on them by legislative, administrative or other measures;

> (e) Any form of propaganda directed against them. . . .

> *Article 33:* Indigenous peoples have the right to promote, develop and maintain their institutional structures and their distinctive juridical customs, traditions, procedures and practices, in accordance with internationally recognized human rights standards. Sub-Comm'n res. 1994/45, at 103, 107-08, 113, U.N. Doc. E/CN.4/1994/2 (1994).

9. Consider the hypothetical situation in Laria in light of recent events in Algeria. In 1991, Islamic fundamentalists represented by the Islamic Salvation Front appeared to take a

commanding lead in Algeria's first free parliamentary elections. Unwilling to relinquish power to the fundamentalists—who had announced their intention to end democratic rule— President Chadli Bendjedid resigned; and the military took control of the government, cancelling elections to "preserve" democracy and national unity. The military has been unable to eliminate the fundamentalists' drive for control, despite violent suppression of their efforts. In February 1994, the military appointed Lamine Zeroual to serve as president for a three-year "transition" term leading up to new elections. *See Algeria's President Takes Office with Vow of Firmness and Dialogue*, BOSTON GLOBE, Feb. 1, 1994, Nat'l/Foreign sec. at 11; Jonathan C. Randal, *Algerian Leader Quits, Imperiling Power Shift to Muslims*, WASH. POST, Jan. 12, 1992, at A23; Elaine Ganley, *Islamic Fundamentalists Seen Leading in Landmark Algerian Elections*, WASH. POST, Dec. 27, 1991, at A14. Do the events in Algeria inform your decision regarding an appropriate response to the situation in Laria?

10.   For additional reading on transitions to democracy, see:

Amnesty International, *Argentina: The Right to the Full Truth*, AI Index: AMR 13/03/95 (1995);

Amnesty International, *Chile: Transition at the Crossroads; Human Rights Violations Under Pinochet Rule Remain the Crux*, AI Index: AMR 22/01/96 (1996);

Amnesty International, *Ethiopia: Accountability Past and Present: Human Rights in Transition*, AI Index: AFR 25/06/95 (1995);

Lynn Berat, *Prosecuting Human Rights Violators from a Predecessor Regime: Guidelines for a Transformed South Africa*, 13 B.C. THIRD WORLD L.J. 199 (1993);

Kathryn Lee Crawford, *Due Obedience and the Rights of Victims: Argentina's Transition to Democracy*, 12 HUM. RTS. Q. 17 (1990);

Joan Fitzpatrick, *Nothing But the Truth? Transitional Regimes Confront the Past*, 16 MICH. J. INT'L L. 713 (1995) (book review of IMPUNITY AND HUMAN RIGHTS IN INTERNATIONAL LAW AND PRACTICE (Naomi Roht-Arriaza ed., 1995));

Luc Huyse, *Justice after Transition: On the Choices Successor Elites Make in Dealing with the Past*, 20 L. & SOCIAL INQUIRY 51 (1995);

IMPUNITY AND HUMAN RIGHTS IN INTERNATIONAL LAW AND PRACTICE (Naomi Roht-Arriaza ed., 1995);

Jamie Malamud-Goti, *Transitional Governments in the Breach: Why Punish State Criminals*, 12 HUM. RTS. Q. 1 (1990);

THEODOR MERON, HUMAN RIGHTS AND HUMANITARIAN NORMS AS CUSTOMARY LAW (1989);

Carlos S. Nino, *The Duty to Punish Past Abuses of Human Rights Put Into Context: The Case of Argentina*, 100 YALE L.J. 2619 (1991);

Mike Oquaye, *Human Rights and the Transition to Democracy Under the PNDC in Ghana*, 17 HUM. RTS. Q. 556 (1995);

Jo M. Pasqualucci, *The Whole Truth and Nothing But the Truth: Truth Commissions, Impunity and the Inter-American Human Rights System*, 12 B.U. INT'L L.J. 321 (1994);

HUMAN RIGHTS WATCH/AMERICAS, PERU: THE TWO FACES OF JUSTICE (1995);

Margaret Popkin & Naomi Roht-Arriaza, *Truth as Justice: Investigatory Commissions in Latin America*, 20 L. & SOCIAL INQUIRY 79 (1995);

Robert J. Quinn, Note, *Will the Rule of Law End? Challenging Grants of Amnesty for the Human Rights Violations of a Prior Regime: Chile's New Model*, 62 FORDHAM L. REV. 905 (1994);

George C. Rogers, *Argentina's Obligation to Prosecute Military Officials for Torture*, 20 COLUM. HUM. RTS. L. REV. 259 (1989);

Symposium, *Transitions to Democracy and the Rule of Law*, 5 AM. U. J. INT'L L. & POL'Y 965 (1990);

TRANSITION TO DEMOCRACY IN LATIN AMERICA: THE ROLE OF THE JUDICIARY (Irwin P. Stotzky ed., 1993);

TRANSITIONAL JUSTICE: HOW EMERGING DEMOCRACIES RECKON WITH FORMER REGIMES (vol. I-III) (Neil J. Kritz ed., 1995);

Jon M. Van Dyke & Gerald W. Berkley, *Redressing Human Rights Abuses*, 20 DENV. J. INT'L L. & POL'Y 243 (1992).

D. NUREMBERG PRINCIPLES

1. The Nuremberg and Tokyo Tribunals

During World War II and the immediate post-war period the victors, confronted with the task of responding dramatically to wartime human rights violations, laid the foundation for criminal prosecutions. From at least 1942 the Allied governments received innumerable reports of Nazi atrocities involving civilians. In response, the allies vowed to punish the perpetrators.

The International Military Tribunal that sat at Nuremberg was created on August 8, 1945, when representatives of the Soviet Union, the United Kingdom, the United States, and the provisional government of the French Republic signed the Agreement for the Prosecution and Punishment of the Major War Criminals of the European Axis, otherwise known as "The London Agreement." 58 Stat. 1544, E.A.S. No. 472, 82 U.N.T.S. 280. It set forth the Charter of the International Military Tribunal (IMT), which laid down the substantive and procedural rules to be applied by the Tribunal.

Article 6 of the Charter set forth crimes within the Tribunal's jurisdiction for which there was to be individual responsibility—crimes against peace, war crimes, and crimes against humanity:

> The following acts, or any of them, are crimes coming within the jurisdiction of the Tribunal for which there shall be individual responsibility:

> (a)   Crimes against Peace: namely, planning, preparation, initiation or waging of a war of aggression, or a war in violation of international treaties, agreements or assurances, or participation in a common plan or conspiracy for the accomplishment of any of the foregoing;

> (b)   War Crimes: namely, violations of the laws or customs of war. Such violations include, but not be limited to, murder, ill-treatment or deportation to slave labor or for any other purpose of civilian population of or in occupied territory, murder or ill-treatment of prisoners of war or persons on the seas, killing of hostages, plunder of public or private property, wanton destruction of cities, towns or villages, or devastation not justified by military necessity;

> (c)   Crimes against Humanity: namely, murder, extermination, enslavement,deportation, and other inhumane acts committed against any civilian population, before or during the war, or persecutions on political, racial or religious grounds in execution of or in connection with any crime within the

jurisdiction of the Tribunal, whether or not in violation of the domestic law of the country where perpetrated. . . .

The trials of the 22 Nazi military and political leaders indicted under Article 6 of the London Agreement began on November 20, 1945, and were monumental in scope and complexity. The IMT held 403 open-sessions, conducted in four languages simultaneously—English, German, Russian, and French. The prosecution presented 33 witnesses and placed over 4,000 documents in evidence. The defense presented 61 witnesses in addition to 19 defendants, and 143 witnesses supplied evidence for them by way of interrogatories. More than one hundred other witnesses testified and tens of thousands of affidavits were presented, regarding indictments of criminal organizations such as the S.S., S.A., and the Gestapo. The trial's reported evidence filled 24 printed volumes and 17 volumes of documents. ROBERT K. WOETZEL, THE NUREMBERG TRIALS IN INTERNATIONAL LAW 2-3 (1962).

Judgments were announced on September 30 and October 1, 1946. Nineteen of the accused were convicted; three were acquitted. Twelve of the convicted were sentenced to death; the remaining seven were sentenced to imprisonment for terms ranging from ten years to life.

* * * * *

The International Military Tribunal for the Far East (IMTFE) was established by Special Proclamation of the Allied Supreme Commander in the Pacific on January 19, 1946. Representatives from 11 states convened on May 3, 1946, to consider war crimes indictments against 25 defendants. Judgment was pronounced on November 12, 1948. All defendants were convicted, with 7 sentenced to death and the others sentenced to imprisonment for terms ranging from seven and one-half years to life. The procedural and substantive rules applied by the Tokyo Tribunal were modeled after those applied in Nuremberg.

2. Control Council Law No. 10 and "Minor" Tribunals

In addition to the trials conducted by the IMT and international panels at Tokyo, several national courts were established by the Allies to try those accused of "Nuremberg crimes." The U.S. conducted approximately 900 trials involving more than 3,000 defendants. About half the cases were tried in Germany and its occupied territories; the remainder in Japan, Austria, Italy, the Philippines, China, and the Pacific Islands.

The trials of "the less visible war criminals" were based on Control Council Law No. 10, promulgated by the four major Allied Powers on December 20, 1945. It authorized the Allies to arrest suspected war criminals and defined triable offenses for prosecution before courts other than the IMT.

Control Council Law No. 10, Punishment of Persons Guilty of War Crimes, Crimes Against Peace and Against Humanity, 3 Official Gazette Control Council for Germany 50-55 (1946), stated:

> In order to give effect to the terms of the . . . London Agreement of 8 August 1945, and the Charter issued pursuant thereto and in order to establish a uniform legal basis in Germany for the prosecution of war criminals and other similar offenders, other than those dealt with by the International Military Tribunal,

> the Control Council enacts as follows: . . .

Article II

1. Each of the following acts is recognized as a crime:

    (a) *Crimes against Peace*. Initiation of invasions of other countries and wars of aggression in violation of international laws and treaties, including but not limited to planning, preparation, initiation or waging a war of aggression, or a war in violation of international treaties, agreements, or assurances, or participation in a common plan or conspiracy for the accomplishment of any of the foregoing.

    (b) *War Crimes*. Atrocities or offences against persons or property, constituting violations of the laws or customs of war, including but not limited to, murder, ill treatment or deportation to slave labour or for any other purpose of civilian population from occupied territory, murder or ill treatment of prisoners of war or persons on the seas, killing of hostages, plunder of public or private property, wanton destruction of cities, towns or villages, or devastation not justified by military necessity.

    (c) *Crimes against Humanity*. Atrocities and offences, including but not limited to murder, extermination, enslavement, deportation, imprisonment, torture, rape, or other inhumane acts committed against any civilian population, or persecutions on political, racial or religious grounds whether or not in violation of the domestic laws of the country where perpetrated.

2. [Persons responsible for offenses.]

3. [Punishments.]

4. (a) The official position of any person, whether as Head of State or as a responsible official in a Government Department, does not free him from responsibility for a crime or entitle him to mitigation of punishment.

    (b) The fact that any person acted pursuant to the order of his government or of a superior does not free him from responsibility for a crime, but may be considered in mitigation. . . .

Does Law No. 10 define crimes against humanity more broadly than the London Agreement? Crimes against humanity were punished by the IMT only if they had a nexus to "a war." Law No. 10 courts could convict defendants on the basis of crimes committed before the war. *See, e.g., United States v. Ohlendorf, reprinted in* 4 TRIALS OF WAR CRIMINALS BEFORE THE NUREMBERG MILITARY TRIBUNALS UNDER CONTROL COUNCIL LAW NO. 10 (1949). *Cf. United States v. Flick, reprinted in* 6 TRIALS OF WAR CRIMINALS BEFORE THE NUREMBERG MILITARY TRIBUNALS UNDER CONTROL COUNCIL LAW No. 10 (1949). What words in the Nuremberg Charter and Law No. 10 guided courts' decisions on this issue? For further discussion, see *infra* at *42* and for the text of Control Council Law No. 10, see *Selected International Human Rights Instruments*.

3. Nuremberg's Legacy

In 1946, the U.N. General Assembly adopted a resolution affirming "the principles of international law recognised by the Charter of the Nuremberg Tribunal and the Judgment of the Tribunal." G.A. res. 95(I), 1 U.N. GAOR at 188, U.N. Doc. A/ 64/Add.1 (1946). Proscriptions detailed in the London Agreement have broadly been recognized as customary international law, which is one of the sources of international law identified by Article 38(b) and (c) of the Statute of the International Court of Justice. *Cf.* U.S. Army Field Manual 27-10, The Law of Land Warfare § 498 (1956).

One of the London Agreement's most important contributions was its affirming the principle of individual responsibility, that individuals—not only governments— are obliged to comply with international law. *See, e.g., U.S. v. Goering,* 6 F.R.D. 69, 110 (1946) ("individuals have international duties which transcend the national obligations of obedience"). In addition, the Agreement reaffirmed that national laws can be subordinate to international law. Hence, as Article 6(c) of the IMT Charter commands, "inhumane acts committed against any civilian population" are crimes against humanity "whether or not in violation of domestic law of the country where perpetrated."

In 1947, the U.N. General Assembly established the International Law Commission, charged with tasks of developing and codifying international law. On November 21, 1947, the Assembly directed the Commission to "[f]ormulate the principles of international law recognized by the Charter of the Nürnberg Tribunal and in the judgment of the Tribunal, and. . .[p]repare a draft code of offences against the peace and security of mankind, indicating clearly the place to be accorded to the principles. . . ." G.A. res. 177(II), 2 U.N. GAOR at 111-12, U.N. Doc. A/519 (1947). In 1950, the International Law Commission adopted a formulation of principles of international law including acknowledgement, as suggested by Control Council Law No. 10, that crimes against humanity may be committed during peacetime as well as during war. The International Law Commission submitted those principles, together with commentaries, to the General Assembly. 2 Y.B. INT'L L. COMM'N 374-78, U.N. Doc. A/CN.4/SER.A/1950/Add.1 (1950).

In 1954, the Commission submitted a Draft Code of Offences Against the Peace and Security of Mankind to the Assembly. The Assembly did not accept the draft code largely because of its inability to agree on what constituted an act of "aggression," which was criminalized by Article 2(1) of the Draft Code. Work on the Draft Code was tabled, and the General Assembly did not define aggression until 1974. Definition of Aggression, G.A. res. 3314 (XXIX) (Annex-Definition of Aggression), 29 U.N. GAOR Supp. (No. 31) at 142, U.N. Doc. A/9631 (1974). In 1981, the Assembly asked the Commission to resume its work on a renamed Draft Code of Crimes Against the Peace and Security of Mankind. Aside from repeated redrafting, however, no action has yet been taken. *See* Report Int'l L. Comm'n, 43 U.N. GAOR Supp. (No. 10) at 140, U.N. Doc. A/43/10 (1988); U.N. Doc. A/CN.4/L.436 (1989); U.N. Doc. A/ CN.4/L.482 (1993); U.N. Doc. A/CN.4/460 (1994). *See* M. CHERIF BASSIOUNI, COMMENTARIES ON THE INTERNATIONAL LAW COMMISSION'S 1991 DRAFT CODE OF CRIMES AGAINST THE PEACE AND SECURITY OF MANKIND; Timothy L.H. McCormack & Gerry J. Simpson, *The International Law Commission's Draft Code of Crimes Against the Peace and Security of Mankind: An Appraisal of the Substantive Provisions,* 5 CRIM. L.F. 1 (1994).

NOTES AND QUESTIONS

1. Although Nuremberg laid the foundations for prosecuting war criminals, war-crimes trials in one form or another date back at least as far as the Middle Ages. More recently, the

Allied Powers discussed and planned for international war crimes trials following World War I, but failed to create a working international tribunal. *See* Jules Deschênes, *Toward International Criminal Justice*, 5 CRIM. L.F. 249, 249-53 (1994); ROBERT K. WOETZEL, THE NUREMBERG TRIALS IN INTERNATIONAL LAW 17-40 (1962).

2.   Several scholars have criticized the Nuremberg trials as having violated the maxim *nullum crimen sine lege, nulla poena sine lege* (no punishment without a law). They emphasize that crimes against humanity had been neither defined nor codified prior to Nuremberg; and they argue that the principle of individual responsibility was absent from the law prior to Nuremberg. *See, e.g.*, David Luban, Remarks at the American Society of International Law Proceedings (Apr. 8-11, 1987), *in* 81 AM. SOC'Y INT'L L. PROC. 415, 423-424, 441.

The IMT did not directly address the issue of *ex post facto* adjudication, but instead emphasized that justice demanded prosecution. The judges, and many legal scholars, also argued that defendants must have been aware of treaties signed by Germany such as the Kellogg-Briand Pact of 1928, which bound them to peaceful settlements of disputes and criminalized aggressive war. *See, e.g.*, Steven Fogelson, Note, *The Nuremberg Legacy: An Unfulfilled Promise*, 63 S. Cal. L. Rev. 833, 866 (1990); Matthew Lippman, *Nuremberg: Forty Years Later*, 7 Conn. J. Int'l L. 1 (1991); HERBERT WECHSLER, *The Issues at the Nuremberg Trial, in* PRINCIPLES, POLITICS, AND FUNDAMENTAL LAW: SELECTED ESSAYS 138, 155 (1961). Which position do you find convincing? Does prosecution of war crimes call for an exception to the prohibition against *ex post facto* laws? What role, if any, should this issue play in prosecuting war crimes committed after the Nuremberg trials?

3.   For further reading on the minor tribunals, see Maximilian Koessler, *American War Crimes Trials in Europe*, 39 Geo. L.J. 18 (1950); TRIALS OF WAR CRIMINALS BEFORE THE NUERNBERG MILITARY TRIBUNALS UNDER CONTROL COUNCIL LAW No. 10, NUERNBERG, October 1946-April 1949 (1949-1953); Note, *United States Navy War Crimes Trials (1945-1949)*, 5 Washburn L.J. 89 (1965).

4.   Investigation and prosecution of persons accused of committing crimes against humanity during World War II did not end with trials in the 1950s. The Nuremberg principles have continued to guide lawyers and judges during succeeding decades. *See* Lisa J. Del Pizzo, Note, *Not Guilty—But Not Innocent: An Analysis of the Acquittal of John Demjanjuk and its Impact on the Future of Nazi War Crimes Trials*, 18 B.C. INT'L & COMP. L. REV. 137 (1995); Nicholas R. Doman, *Aftermath of Nuremberg: the Trial of Klaus Barbie*, 60 U. COLO. L. REV. 449 (1989); Matthew Lippman, *The Trial of Adolf Eichmann and the Protection of Universal Human Rights Under International Law*, 5 HOUS. J. INT'L L. 1 (1982); Leila Sadat Wexler, *The Interpretation of the Nuremberg Principles by the French Court of Cassation: From Touvier to Barbie and Back Again*, 32 COLUM. J. TRANSNAT'L L. 289 (1994).

E.   THE INTERNATIONAL TRIBUNAL FOR THE FORMER YUGOSLAVIA

1.   Historical Background

The territory formerly known as Yugoslavia has long been divided along ethnic lines. Cultural and religious differences among Serbs, Bosnians, Croats, Slovenians, and many other groups were the result of numerous divisions of the region by successive empires including the Romans, Turks, and Austro-Hungarians. Religious lines were drawn when Christians converted to Islam during Turkish rule. Further division emerged between Orthodox Christian Serbs and Catholic Croats. Dusan Cotic, *Introduction*, 5 CRIM. L.F. 223, 225-26 (1994).

The Kingdom of Serbs, Croats, and Slovenians was founded in 1918 and adopted the name Yugoslavia in 1930. The dictatorship of Josip Broz Tito suppressed much ethnic division, but after Tito's death in 1980 ultranationalist politicians exploited ethnic differences. Years of escalating intolerance and hostility erupted into armed conflict when Croatia declared its independence from Yugoslavia in 1991 and was recognized by Germany. The Serbs responded to the original Constitution of the new republic, which declared a state of only Croats, by declaring the formation of the Serb Republic of Krajina. Croatians, from the outset, treated the Serbs as rebels, terrorists, and aggressors against their new Croatian republic. The breakup also inspired the formation of independent republics in Slovenia and Macedonia. *Id.* at 225-27.

The most devastating armed conflict has occurred in Bosnia-Herzegovina. The magnitude of the crisis can be attributed to the fact that it differs from the other regions in that it has no overwhelming majority of one ethnic group. Prior to the conflict, Bosnia- Herzegovina was a "community" comprising three intermixed ethnic communities of Yugoslavia: Muslims—43.7 percent; Serbs—31.4 percent; Croats—17.3 percent; with the remainder of the population identifying themselves as Yugoslavian or other ethnicity. The Bosnian Serbs rejected a referendum to separate from Yugoslavia, and seized nearly 70% of Bosnian territory. On April 7, 1992, the Bosnian Serbs proclaimed the formation of an independent Bosnian Serb Republic. The Bosnian Croats sought to preclude political domination by Bosnian Muslims and to form ties to the Croatian republic. The large contingent of Bosnian Muslims, despite intermittent alliances with the Bosnian Croats, has struggled to gain a foothold in the power structure of the new republic. *Id.* at 228-29.

The armed conflict has been brutal and has resulted in massive violations of human rights and international humanitarian law. A Special Rapporteur of the U.N. Commission on Human Rights reported on rampant ethnic cleansing measures, including harassment, discrimination, beatings, torture, summary executions, expulsion, and forced work. He emphasized that Croats, Muslims, and Serbs have all been victims of widespread violations. *See* Tadeusz Mazowiecki, *Report on the Situation of Human Rights in the Territory of the Former Yugoslavia*, U.N. Doc. E/CN.4/1993/50 (1993); Tadeusz Mazowiecki, *Report of the Special Rapporteur to the Commission on Human Rights of 28 August 1992*, U.N. Doc. E/CN.4/1992/S-1/9 (1992).

2.   U.N. Response: War Crimes Tribunal for the former Yugoslavia

On October 6, 1992, largely in response to rising media and public outcry over violence in Bosnia, the Security Council adopted Resolution 780—establishing a Commission of Experts to investigate and document "grave breaches of the Geneva Conventions and other violations of international humanitarian law" committed in the former Yugoslavia. S.C. res. 780, 47 U.N. SCOR at 36, U.N. Doc. S/INF/48 (1992). Four months later, the Commission's initial report was submitted to the Security Council. *Letter Dated 9 February 1993 from the Secretary-General Addressed to the President of the Security Council*, U.N. Doc. S/25274 (1993) (transmitting "Interim Report of the Commission of Experts Established Pursuant to Security Council Resolution 780 (1992)"). It stated, *inter alia*, that "grave breaches and other violations of international humanitarian law have been committed." *Id.* at 12, ¶ 32. The report concluded that establishment of an *ad hoc* international tribunal "would be consistent with the direction of its work." *Id.* at 20, ¶ 74.

On February 22, 1993, the Security Council decided that "an international criminal tribunal shall be established for the prosecution of persons responsible for serious violations of international humanitarian law committed in the territory of the former Yugoslavia since 1991." S.C. res. 808, 48 U.N. SCOR at 1, U.N. Doc. S/RES/808 (1993). Pursuant to the resolution, the Secretary-General submitted a report on May 3, 1993, analyzing and supporting the establishment of an international tribunal. *Report of the Secretary-General Pursuant to Paragraph 2 of Security Council Resolution 808 (1993)*, U.N. Doc. S/25704 and Add.1 (1993). The proposed Statute of the International Tribunal was presented in an annex to the Secretary-General's report. *Id.* at 36.[3]

On 25 May 1993, the Security Council unanimously adopted Resolution 827, which stated:

The Security Council, . . .

Having considered the report of the Secretary-General (S/25704 and Add.1) pursuant to paragraph 2 of resolution 808 (1993),

Expressing once again its grave alarm at continuing reports of widespread and flagrant violations of international humanitarian law occurring within the territory of the former Yugoslavia, and especially in the Republic of Bosnia and Hercegovina, including reports of mass killings, massive, organized and systematic detention and rape of women, and the continuance of the practice of "ethnic cleansing", including for the acquisition and the holding of territory,

Determining that this situation continues to constitute a threat to international peace and security, . . .

Acting under Chapter VII of the Charter of the United Nations,

1.   Approves the report of the Secretary-General;
2.   Decides hereby to establish an international tribunal for the sole purpose of prosecuting persons responsible for serious violations of international humanitarian law committed in the territory of the former Yugoslavia between 1 January 1991 and a date to be determined by the Security Council upon the restoration of peace and to this end adopt the Statute of the International Tribunal annexed to the above-mentioned report[.]

S.C. res. 827, 48 U.N. SCOR at 2, U.N. Doc. S/RES/827 (1993). The Council also authorized the Commission of Experts to continue its evidence-gathering efforts. *Id.* The judges of the Tribunal were elected by the General Assembly on September

---

[3] The Security Council previously had reviewed several draft statutes for establishing the tribunal for the former Yugoslavia. See *Letter Dated 18 February 1993 from the Permanent Representative of Sweden to the United Nations Addressed to the Secretary-General*, U.N. Doc. S/25307 (1993) (transmitting "Proposal for an International War Crimes Tribunal for the Former Yugoslavia" by Rapporteurs under the Conference on Security and Cooperation in Europe (CSCE)); *Letter dated 16 February 1993 from the Permanent Representative of Italy to the United Nations Addressed to the Secretary-General*, U.N. Doc. S/25300 (1993) (transmitting a draft statute for a war crimes tribunal for the former Yugoslavia); *Letter dated 10 February 1993 from the Permanent Representative of France to the United Nations Addressed to the Secretary-General*, U.N. Doc. S/25266 (1993) (transmitting a report of the Committee of French Jurists on the establishment of an international tribunal).

17, 1993,[4] and the court first convened in the Hague on November 17, 1993.

* * * * *

DIANE F. ORENTLICHER, AMERICAN SOCIETY OF INTERNATIONAL LAW NEWS-LETTER, YUGOSLAVIA WAR CRIMES TRIBUNAL 1-2 (ASIL Focus Special Insert to the June-August 1993 issue):

Legal Basis of Tribunal

The first substantial issue raised by Resolution 808 was whether the *ad hoc* tribunal should be established by treaty or, instead, through a Security Council resolution. Following the recommendation of the Secretary-General, the Security Council established the IT [International Tribunal for the Prosecution of Persons Responsible for Serious Violations of International Humanitarian Law Committed in the Territory of the Former Yugoslavia since 1991] as an enforcement measure under Chapter VII of the UN Charter. As such, the decision had to be (and was) predicated on a Security Council determination that the situation giving rise to its action constituted a threat to the peace, breach of the peace, or an act of aggression.

Although the Council had previously determined that the situation in the former Yugoslavia constitutes a threat to international peace and security, its decision to establish a tribunal under Chapter VII was not without controversy. Some States, including China, feared that this represented an unwarranted intrusion on sovereignty. Others, such as Brazil, suggested that the establishment of an international tribunal might exceed the Security Council's competence, and took pains to insist that Resolution 827 and the Statute for the IT "are . . . not meant to establish new norms or precedents of international law," a "legislative act thought to be beyond the Council's competence. Instead, the IT would only apply "existing norms of international humanitarian law." . . .

The Secretary-General's report to the Security Council makes clear that, whatever theoretical issues the Security Council's action might raise, the decision was driven by pragmatic concerns. Noting that an international tribunal would ordinarily be established by treaty, the Secretary-General observed that this approach would require "considerable time," and "there could be no guarantee that ratifications will be received from those States which should be parties to the treaty if it is to be truly effective.

The most significant consequence of the Security Council's approach will likewise be practical: Member States of the United Nations are legally required to comply with the decision establishing the IT. (This, of course, is a key reason why some countries thought establishment of the IT by any route other than treaty an undue infringement of sovereignty.) This obligation may prove to be critical in addressing one of the most daunting challenges that the prosecution will face—obtaining jurisdiction over indicted suspects. Among the obligations that the IT Statute imposes

---

[4] The court consists of eleven judges, including three in each of two trial chambers and five in an appeals chamber. The eleven original judges, elected for four-year terms, were Georges Michel Abi-Saab (Egypt), Antonio Cassese (Italy), Jules Deschenes (Canada), Adolphus Godwin Karibi-Whyte (Nigeria), Germain Le Foyer De Costil (France), Li Haopei (China), Gabrielle Kirk McDonald (U.S.), Elizabeth Odio-Benito (Costa Rica), Rustam S. Sidhwa (Pakistan), Sir Ninian Stephen (Australia), and Lal Chand Vohrah (Malaysia). On 18 November 1993, the Tribunal elected Antonio Cassese as its first President. Peter Burns, *An International Criminal Tribunal: The Difficult Union of Principle and Politics*, 5 CRIM. L.F. 341, 349 n.21 (1994).

on Member States is a duty to comply with any orders of the Tribunal relating to the arrest or detention of persons. That obligation may help assure, at the very least, that suspected war criminals effectively become prisoners in their own countries, lest they risk arrest abroad. In this respect, the Security Council's action may help mitigate the risk that the IT will appear ineffectual by virtue of its inability to obtain personal jurisdiction over key defendants.

* * * * *

Establishing the Tribunal's competence *ratione materiae* (subject matter jurisdiction) was one of the most complicated matters before the Security Council. Article 1 of the Statute pronounces that the "Tribunal shall have the power to prosecute persons responsible for serious violations of international humanitarian law . . . ." *Report of the Secretary-General Pursuant to Paragraph 2 of Security Council Resolution 808 (1993)*, Annex: Statute of the International Criminal Tribunal, art. 1, U.N. Doc. S/25704 and Add.1 (1993). The Secretary-General elaborated on the Council's approach:

> [T]he application of the principle of *nullum crimen sine lege* requires that the international tribunal should apply rules of international humanitarian law which are beyond any doubt part of customary law so that the problem of adherence of some but not all States to specific conventions does not arise. . . .
>
> The part of conventional international humanitarian law which has beyond doubt become part of international customary law is the law applicable in armed conflict as embodied in: the Geneva Conventions of 12 August 1949 for the Protection of War Victims; the Hague Convention (IV) Respecting the Laws and Customs of War on Land and the Regulations annexed thereto of 18 October 1907; the Convention on the Prevention and Punishment of the Crime of Genocide of 9 December 1948; and the Charter of the International Military Tribunal of 8 August 1945.

Report of the Secretary-General Pursuant to Paragraph 2 of Security Council Resolution 808 (1993), at ¶¶ 34-35, U.N. Doc. S/25704 and Add.1 (1993). For discussion of *nullum crimen sine lege* as related to the Nuremberg trials, see *supra* at 32.

* * * * *

Articles 2-5 of the Statute detail the categories of crimes over which the Tribunal has jurisdiction.

Report of the Secretary-General Pursuant to Paragraph 2 of Security Council Resolution 808 (1993), Annex: Statute of the International Criminal Tribunal, art. 2-5, U.N. Doc. S/25704 and Add.1 (1993) [hereinafter Statute]:

Article 2

Grave breaches of the Geneva Conventions of 1949

The International Tribunal shall have the power to prosecute persons committing or ordering to be committed grave breaches of the Geneva Conventions of 12 August 1949, namely the following acts against persons or property protected under the provisions of the relevant Geneva Convention:

(a) wilful killing;

(b) torture or inhuman treatment, including biological experiments;

(c)   wilfully causing great suffering or serious injury to body or health;

(d)   extensive destruction and appropriation of property, not justified by military necessity and carried out unlawfully and wantonly;

(e)   compelling a prisoner of war or a civilian to serve in the forces of a hostile power;

(f)   wilfully depriving a prisoner of war or a civilian of the rights of fair and regular trial;

(g)   unlawful deportation or transfer or unlawful confinement of a civilian;

(h)   taking civilians as hostages.

Article 3

Violations of the laws or customs of war

The International Tribunal shall have the power to prosecute persons violating the laws or customs of war. Such violations shall include, but not be limited to:

(a)   employment of poisonous weapons or other weapons calculated to cause unnecessary suffering;

(b)   wanton destruction of cities, towns or villages, or devastation not justified by military necessity;

(c)   attack, or bombardment, by whatever means, of undefended towns, villages, dwellings, or buildings;

(d)   seizure of, destruction or wilful damage done to institutions dedicated to religion, charity and education, the arts and sciences, historic monuments and works of art and science;

(e)   plunder of public or private property.

Article 4

Genocide

1.   The International Tribunal shall have the power to prosecute persons committing genocide as defined in paragraph 2 of this article or of committing any of the other acts enumerated in paragraph 3 of this article.

2.   Genocide means any of the following acts committed with intent to destroy, in whole or in part, a national, ethnical, racial or religious group, as such:

(a)   killing members of the group;

(b)   causing serious bodily or mental harm to members of the group;

(c)   deliberately inflicting on the group conditions of life calculated to bring about its physical destruction in whole or in part;

(d)   imposing measures intended to prevent births within the group;

(e)   forcibly transferring children of the group to another group.

3.   The following acts shall be punishable:

(a)   genocide;

(b)   conspiracy to commit genocide;

(c)   direct and public incitement to commit genocide;

(d)   attempt to commit genocide;

(e)   complicity in genocide.

Article 5

Crimes against humanity

The International Tribunal shall have the power to prosecute persons responsible for the following crimes when committed in armed conflict, whether international or internal in character, and directed against any civilian population:

(a)   murder;

(b)   extermination;

(c)   enslavement;

(d)   deportation;

(e)   imprisonment;

(f)   torture;

(g)   rape;

(h)   persecutions on political, racial and religious grounds;

(i)   other inhumane acts.

*   *   *   *   *

Persons accused of planning, ordering, or committing the above crimes will be held individually responsible for their acts. *Id.* Art. 7(1). In addition, persons charged will not be relieved of criminal responsibility for acting pursuant to superior orders, but such a finding may be considered in mitigation of punishment if the Tribunal determines that justice so requires. *Id.* Art. 7(4). Penalties are limited to imprisonment, thus excluding the death penalty. *Id.* Art. 24(1). Unlike the Nuremberg trials, no defendant may be tried *in absentia. Id.* Art. 21(4)(d).

NOTES AND QUESTIONS

1.   Orentlicher emphasizes that the Security Council's decision to establish the Tribunal by resolution under Chapter VII was motivated by pragmatic concerns. Does she sufficiently consider the legality of the Council's decision? Does Chapter VII truly grant the Council authority to establish the Tribunal? *Cf.* Article 29 of the U.N. Charter, which states that the Council "may establish such subsidiary organs as it deems necessary for the performance of its functions?" For discussion of the legal basis for the Tribunal's establishment, see Herman von Hebel, *An International Tribunal for the Former Yugoslavia: An Act of Powerlessness or a New Challenge for the International Community,* 11 NETH. Q. HUM. RTS. 437, 442-47 (1993); Roman A. Kolodkin, *An Ad Hoc International Tribunal for the Prosecution of Serious Violations of International Humanitarian Law in the Former Yugoslavia,* 5 CRIM. L.F. 381, 385-95 (1994); *see also* Claire Palley, Sub-Commission on Prevention of Discrimination and Protection of Minorities, *Implications of Humanitarian Activities for the Enjoyment of Human*

Rights, at 6, ¶ 12, U.N. Doc. E/CN.4/Sub.2/1994/39 (1994) (questioning the Council's authority to create the Tribunal).

2.   Dusan Tadic, the first defendant to appear before the Tribunal, challenged its jurisdiction. His attorneys argued that the Tribunal was improperly established and violates the sovereignty of states. The Tribunal rejected that defense as without merit on August 10, 1995. *See* Peter Benesh, *War Crimes Tribunal Pledges to Protect Victims' Identities*, PITTSBURGH POST-GAZETTE, Aug. 11, 1995, at A10; Mike Corder, *Defense to Appeal Tribunal Jurisdiction Ruling*, AP, Aug. 15, 1995, *available in* LEXIS, News Library, APINTL File. On appeal, the Tribunal again ruled that it had jurisdiction. *The Prosecutor v. Dusko Tadic*, Case No. IT-94-1-AR72 (1995). For additional discussion of Dusan Tadic, see *infra* at 52.

3.   In establishing the Tribunal, the Security Council had to decide what substantive law the Tribunal would apply: the law of the former Yugoslavia or international law. The CSCE rapporteurs (*see supra* footnote 3 at 35) recommended adopting national law because provisions of the Penal Code of the former Yugoslavia were still in force in the new Republics. Most others, however, argued for international law. The French report (*see supra* footnote 3 at 35) stated that an international court trying international crimes must apply international law and asserted that holding defendants to this standard was justified by the fact that the former Yugoslavia was party to several instruments of international human rights and humanitarian law, including the Genocide Convention, the Covenant on Civil and Political Rights, and all 1949 Geneva Conventions and 1977 Additional Protocols. The Security Council selected the international law approach. *See* Herman von Hebel, *An International Tribunal for the Former Yugoslavia: An Act of Powerlessness or a New Challenge for the International Community*, 11 NETH. Q. HUM. RTS. 437, 447 (1993); Roman A. Kolodkin, *An Ad Hoc International Tribunal for the Prosecution of Serious Violations of International Humanitarian Law in the Former Yugoslavia*, 5 CRIM. L.F. 381, 395-99 (1994).

4.   Not all words contained in Common Article 3 of the Geneva Conventions (*see infra* chapter 12) are included in Article 2 of the Statute; nor are pertinent clauses of the two 1977 Protocols. Note also that *U.N. human rights treaty provisions* are mentioned in none of the articles of the Tribunal's Statute. Why do you think the Security Council omitted those proscriptions?

5.   Article 5 is a somewhat perplexing admixture of words from the Nuremberg Charter and Allied Control Council Law No. 10. For Nuremberg and Law No. 10 texts, see *supra* section D above.

   a.   Why do you think the Secretary-General followed the precedent of Law No. 10 by including imprisonment, torture, and rape among the Statute's enumerated crimes against humanity?

   b.   Conversely, the Statute's requirement that crimes be "committed in armed conflict" conceivably could reincorporate the section of the Nuremberg Charter that limits crimes to those committed "before or during the war." Law No. 10 contained no similar restriction. What might have led the Secretary-General to make that drafting decision? For discussion of the nexus between crimes against humanity and war, as provided for in the Nuremberg Charter, Law No. 10 and the Statute, see Theodor Meron, *Editorial Comment: War Crimes in Yugoslavia and the Development of International Law*, 88 AM. J. INT'L L. 78, 84-87 (1994); DIANE F. ORENTLICHER, AMERICAN SOCIETY OF INTERNATIONAL LAW NEWSLETTER, YUGOSLAVIA WAR CRIMES TRIBUNAL 2-3 (ASIL Focus Special Insert to the June-August 1993 issue). Would you recommend that the "committed in armed conflict" requirement be included in a Statute establishing a tribunal for Laria?

   c.   Why might the Secretary-General have selected the word "crimes" rather than "atrocities and offenses" found in Law No. 10?

   d.   Why delete "including but not limited to" (found in Law No. 10)?

   e.   What effect, if any, might the following choice of language have had on theTribunal's jurisdiction?

Statute of the Tribunal for the former Yugoslavia: "crimes . . . directed against any civilian population: . . . (g) rape; (h) persecutions on political, racial and religious grounds; (i) other inhumane acts."

Law No. 10: "rape, or other inhumane acts committed against any civilian population, or persecutions on political, racial or religious grounds"

6.   The court may impose only penalties of imprisonment. Might civil penalties be more effective? Options could include restrictions on international travel, expulsion from government service, disqualification from service as military officers, and redress for victims. For further discussion of remedies and compensation, see *supra* at *24*.

7.   Articles 20 and 21 of the Statute of the Tribunal for the former Yugoslavia provide several procedural protections. Important rules, absent from the Nuremberg and Tokyo trials, include prohibition of trials *in absentia* and the death penalty, and provisions for a right to appeal. Amnesty International, acknowledging the importance of these provisions, called for further protections of the accused during the pre-trial stage. *See* Theodor Meron, *Editorial Comment: War Crimes in Yugoslavia and the Development of International Law*, 88 Am. J. Int'l L. 78, 83-84 (1994); Amnesty International, *Moving Forward to Set Up the War Crimes Tribunal for the Former Yugoslavia*, AI Index: EUR 48/03/93 (1993).

---

3.   Efficacy of the Tribunal for the Former Yugoslavia

Aryeh Neier, *War Crimes Tribunal is an Imperative*, Hum. Rts. Brief (American University Center for Hum. Rts. & Humanitarian L., D.C.), Spring 1994, at 6, 8:

Sad to say, the enormity of the crimes that have been committed in the war in Bosnia-Herzegovina is not distinctive in our time. What is unprecedented, however, is the extent to which these crimes are known worldwide so soon after they are committed. In this respect, the war in Bosnia differs from World War II when few Western officials obtained information about Nazi concentration camps and other aspects of genocide, and most of the international public was not well informed. Moreover, because the international community's view of the war in Bosnia is not obscured by the fog of Cold War controversy, there is more clarity about the commission of crimes against humanity and less confusion about culpability than there was in such well-publicized conflicts as those of Vietnam and El Salvador.

Continuous press coverage has contributed to the prominence of the war in Bosnia. More remarkable, however, has been the on-the-scene presence of numerous international noncombatant observers, including UN troops. . . .

. . . [T]hough their numbers are not great, human rights investigators are making important contributions to the awareness of what is transpiring in Bosnia. . . .

There is no precedent for such a vast international noncombatant presence with such a close-up view of crimes against humanity as they are being committed. The consequence is that the world knows about the crimes, knows who the victims are, and knows the identity of arch-criminals. . . . Not only are there identities known, but there is no significant controversy about their culpability.

Because we know so much about Bosnia, the establishment of another United Nations (UN) commission to investigate crimes against humanity in Bosnia, but without punitive powers, would be a pointless exercise. There is a great need to fix responsibility for the crimes that have been committed. By and large, as far as the word is concerned, that has already been accomplished. In the Bosnian context, a "truth" commission would amount to a further wringing of the hands by the international community. Having refused to intervene to stop crimes that it knows about too well, the least that is required from the UN at this point is a good-faith effort to punish those with the highest level of responsibility for the most egregious crimes.

In pointing out these characteristics of Bosnia, it is important to distinguish them from the situation that prevailed in El Salvador, where a UN Truth Commission made an important contribution. Among the characteristic crimes of the Salvadoran war were death-squad killings and disappearances, perpetrated so that their authors could deny responsibility; that is, they were intended to deceive. . . .

In the Bosnian case, it is critical that the war crimes tribunal established by the UN function effectively. For now, it faces two serious obstacles: one is the tepid support it is getting from the UN Secretariat; the other is the difficulty in getting custody of those who will be indicted.

As to the first, pressure on the Secretary General, Mr. Boutros-Ghali, is required to make him comply with the directive of the UN Security Council. As to the second, U.S. [A]mbassador to the UN Madeleine Albright sounded the right note in January when she said that the UN should impose sanctions, or maintain economic and diplomatic sanctions, against countries refusing to turn over for trial those indicted. If that is done, it would be very difficult for defendants to evade trial. . . . Moreover, by itself, indicting someone as a war criminal would be a greater sanction than merely naming that person in a report. An indicted war criminal would never risk traveling beyond his country's borders; would be susceptible to political attacks within his own country that focus on his evasion of trial; and would always have to fear being turned over because of political changes in his country . . . .

There seems little question that the UN War Crimes Tribunal *will* succeed. Given the UN's inability, though, to take any other meaningful action to punish those responsible for crimes committed during this conflict, effective prosecution is the last available means for the UN to redeem its own reputation. The open question is whether the UN will overcome its own lassitude and its deference to the interests of a few very powerful states that worry that prosecutions will impede a peace settlement.

*   *   *   *   *

Herman Schwartz, *War Crimes Trials—Not a Good Idea*, HUM. RTS. BRIEF (The Center for Hum. Rts. & Humanitarian L., D.C.), Spring 1994, at 7-8:

The following is an excerpt from an article I wrote for the *New York Times* in April 1993:

> "Despite its superficial appeal, [the establishment of a war crimes tribunal] is not a good idea. The effort to hold such trials is almost certain to fail: instead of advancing the international rule of law, it is likely to set it back.

> "The need for formal condemnation of those who planned, ordered and carried out the outrages that fill our TV screens every night is indisputable . . .

> "But no one would expect [those charged with war crimes] to show up voluntarily. Serbia, the principal offender, is unlikely to turn them over, despite the obligation to do so . . .

"Nor are nations likely to impose meaningful sanctions on Serbia or any other country just because it refuses to turn people over to a tribunal. [. . .]

"[. . .]   If the charges cannot be tried because the defendants refuse to appear, the effort becomes another failure of the international community to advance the rule of law.

"How, then, can the world signal its outrage at the brutalities perpetrated in the Balkans? One possibility is to create a high-level U.N.-sponsored truth commission similar to the one that issued a report on atrocities in El Salvador . . .

"The commission on El Salvador was not limited to pursuing war crimes, nor was it bound by technical rules of evidence. It drew conclusions where testimony was corroborated or otherwise clear. It named names. And so far neither its findings nor methods have been challenged in any significant way.

"If such a commission, making no pretense that it was conducting a criminal trial, sought to carry out an investigation in the former Yugoslavia, Serbia and Croatia would be hard-pressed to refuse it access. [. . .]

"The Nuremberg trials were possible only because we had won World War II and had physical control of the accused . . .[.] Any Serbians or Croatians likely to be accused would be victors in the Balkan war. They would be anything but under our control.

"New mechanisms and institutions are necessary for the chaotic international arena. The El Salvador Truth Commission offers one useful model. It certainly seems better than trials that would probably be nothing more than another exercise in futility."

Since the publication of this article, a lot has happened. The UN did indeed establish a war crimes tribunal, and it is now in operation. Judges have been chosen . . . ; investigations are under way. A great deal of evidence has been amassed, and things seem to be moving along.

Not really. None of this deals with the fundamental question: How does the tribunal obtain the evidence and authority to bring to justice the real war criminals, those who planned, ordered, and oversaw the atrocities?

Perhaps it is useful to prosecute a few underlings who actually committed the rapes, executions, tortures, the ones who actually did the "ethnic cleansing." Most, as in Nazi Germany after World War II, will escape. And if post World War II behavior, not only in the former Yugoslavia, but throughout the world, is any indication, there will be little deterrence, if any.

The real perpetrators, today's version of the Hitlers, Himmlers, Goerings, and others, will escape. Yugoslavia's Slobodan Milosevic, who started the whole mess, is now a "statesman" and a "peacemaker." The U.S. Helsinki Commission. . . named seven Serbs whom it considered war criminals. These included Milosevic; Bosnian Serb political leader Radovan Karadzik, considered by the co-chairs of the Commission, . . ., as the person "most responsible for the atrocities and ethnic cleansing which have taken place in Bosnia"; Bosnian Serb military leader General Ratko Mladic, who has been called "the Ethnic Cleanser in Chief" . . .

Is it plausible that any of these individuals will be brought to justice? Any settlement (if there ever is any) will require their assent and a condition of this assent will almost certainly be immunity to prosecution. Europe and the United States have shown themselves too feeble to insist on anything else.

The process itself is in trouble. There have been numerous delays and despite the additional $24 million given by the United States, there is still not enough money. Furthermore, the Western European nations show little enthusiasm for the whole idea, making it even more unlikely that they will ever turn anyone over to be tried. . . .

. . . The South Slav tragedy is a catastrophe, not just for its immediate victims, the Muslims, Croats, and Serbs caught in these brutal and cynical political machinations, but also for the hopes of a world rule of law. The Bosnian people, in particular, have suffered too much to have to endure what is likely to be just another episode in a tragic farce.

*   *   *   *   *

Françoise J. Hampson, *Violation of Fundamental Rights in the Former Yugoslavia: The Case for a War Crimes Tribunal*, OCCASIONAL PAPER 3, at 1-5 (The David Davies Memorial Inst. of Int'l Stud., 1993) (footnotes omitted):

Desirability of war crimes trials . . .

There are at least five reasons which, taken together, make it imperative that the international community should indicate the unacceptability of certain types of conduct even, or particularly, in conflict situations. First, there is the particular nature of the offences and the context in which they take place.

War crimes, by definition, take place during an armed conflict. That represents a breakdown in the international legal order. The United Nations Charter envisages the primary aim of the organization as being the maintenance of international peace and security. The outbreak of an armed conflict represents not only a specific failure but a more general threat to the maintenance of minimal international legal order. It is therefore vital to the existence of the international community that the threat be contained. . . .

. . . In the case of 'Yugoslavia', the well-attested allegations point to a systematic practice of severe ill-treatment of prisoners, many of whom have died whilst in custody. They point to both arbitrary and intentional killings of civilians, who could by no stretch of the imagination be seen as posing a threat to the other side. The allegations go far beyond the breaches to which one has become accustomed in 'civil wars'. It seems that the arbitrary detention of civilians is not sufficient; their humiliation or degradation also appears to be being sought. . . .

The conflicts have been marked not only by individual acts in breach of every conceivable moral and legal norm but also by the institutionalization of unlawful practices. The practice of 'ethnic cleansing' or 'ethnic purification' seems to involve a combination of individually unlawful acts to achieve an unlawful object, one which if it is allowed to succeed endangers the peace throughout central and eastern Europe.

The first argument in favour of war crimes trials is, therefore, the nature of the acts alleged and the threat that anything less than legal condemnation poses to the maintenance of international peace in a much larger area.

The second argument for war crimes trials is the need for reconciliation. If by reconciliation is meant *real* peace and the ability of different groups to live alongside one another, then not only is that consistent with but it actually *requires* war crimes trials. It requires the assertion of individual, particularized responsibility by means of a *legal* condemnation in the name of the values of the international community. That condemnation must be legal and not merely political. The issue is not who wins, nor even the imposition of the victor's values. The issue is the respect for certain minimum values, necessary to the maintenance of international peace and security. . . .

A third reason for holding war crimes trials, one linked to the second, is that the victims need it. If they are not to blame whole groups, they need to be able to attach responsibility for a particular act to a particular individual. In a disconcerting number of cases, the victims of violations in the conflicts in former Yugoslavia are able to identify by name those allegedly responsible. That makes is all the more important that responsibility is attached to the individual. Otherwise the international community appears to condone the act. . . . The insistence on individual responsibility is particularly important if the victim and the perpetrator are expected to live in close proximity to one another in the future. . . .

A fourth reason is that not only the victims but also the perpetrators seem to need war crimes trials. Consider the case of Borislav Herak, currently awaiting trial in Sarajevo. The indictment lists twenty-nine murders, including eight rape-murders. The trial is based on his own confession. . . . He is reported to have told a journalist who interviewed him, 'All these things have tried my conscience.' His dreams are haunted by a captured Muslim soldier who pleaded for his life, saying that he had a wife and two small children, and by a little girl in a red dress who tried to hide behind her grandmother when Mr. Herak participated in the killing of ten civilians, including four children. What would it do to *that* man, showing as he does some signs of remorse, to say that, in the interests of peace and reconciliation, he should go back to his old life and everything will go back to what it was?

Finally, war crimes trials are necessary to protect those who, at some risk, have taken action to help or to protect potential victims from death or 'ethnic cleansing'. They will share in the blame attached to their group unless war crimes trials are held in which individual responsibility for atrocities is reaffirmed.

For all these reasons, there needs to be a legal condemnation, based on universal values, of the gross violation of fundamental norms of humanitarian law and human rights law.

* * * * *

David P. Forsythe, *Politics and the International Tribunal for the Former Yugoslavia*, 5 CRIM. L.F. 401, 403-07, 410-11, 413-17 (1994):

Covert and Cogent Policies

Like most enterprises, the Tribunal came into existence because of mixed motives. One set of motives must be inferred from circumstantial evidence, documentary evidence being lacking for the moment. But those motives are reasonably plain nevertheless.

A number of European states, most clearly the United Kingdom, felt the need to give the appearance of doing something about violations of humanitarian law in the former Yugoslavia. Lacking the political will to act decisively to curtail abuses of prisoners and civilians, they endorsed or went along with the creation of the Tribunal. They were also concerned that the Tribunal, seeking punitive judgments, would interfere with diplomatic efforts to terminate the fighting, efforts that depend on the cooperation of suspected war criminals. Since these states have never supported the Tribunal with significant personnel and financial contributions or important documentary evidence, it is clear that they do not regard the Tribunal as a serious venture. Their real political motives have remained covert: to placate opinion by formally supporting the court, but to give free reign to diplomacy.

Agreement that the Commission of Experts and the Tribunal have been underfunded, understaffed, and otherwise lacking in support indicates that many states do not regard this exercise of international criminal justice as a top priority. . . .

The British record is quite evident in this regard. In public, Britain went on record several times in support of war crimes proceedings. Behind the scenes, the British were a break on various proposals. They provided little money, scant personnel, and few documents to the Commission and Tribunal. British officials made known to the press that they had strong misgivings about the practicality of what they saw as a U.S. push for criminal proceedings. . . .

The . . . French and Italian record[s are] somewhat more ambivalent, as is the German. Both France and Italy participated actively in drafting the Tribunal's Statute. In other ways, France spoke out strongly against war crimes. . . . But neither France nor Italy offered much financial support to the Commission and Tribunal. Press reports periodically linked France with Britain in believing that the Tribunal complicated peacemaking in the Balkans. . . . France is also reported to have joined Britain and China in watering down various U.S. initiatives about the Commission and the Tribunal.

Germany, while not providing much support to the Commission and Tribunal, arrested approximately fifty suspected war criminals among refugees in its territory and appeared to be proceeding either toward holding national trials or turning the suspects over to the United Nations. . . .

Some UN officials were also less than enthusiastic about the Tribunal, although here the record is rather unclear. The first head of the Commission of Experts, the Dutch national Frits Kalshoven, was quoted as saying that an international criminal court could not effectively function in an ongoing armed conflict without a clear loser. . . . Kalshoven, however, was also quoted as laying blame for the Commission's early dismal performance on certain western European states that failed to provide the necessary financial and personnel support. . . .

Kalshoven . . . claimed he was told by high but unnamed UN officials not to go after top Serbian leaders. . . .

There were press reports that mediators David Owen (from the United Kingdom, on behalf of the European Union) and Cyrus Vance (from the United States, on behalf of the United Nations) saw the Tribunal as complicating their peacemaking mission, since it would be difficult to get leaders of fighting parties to make peace if after the peace they were to be make to stand trial for war crimes. Both Owen and Vance denied taking this position and went on record in support of war crimes trials. . . .

One or two states clearly did not like the idea of a court but were not prepared to block its creation. Most notable in this regard was China, which of course possessed the veto in the Security Council. . . . They wanted to elevate state sovereignty over international action to protect human rights. . . .

More enthusiastic about the Commission and Tribunal was another group of states led by the United States and including the Netherlands, Canada, Norway, New Zealand, Pakistan, and a few others. . . .

These supportive states appealed to cogent reasons for criminal prosecution . . . . First, since international humanitarian law existed on the books, it would undermine that law not to provide for criminal proceedings. Avoiding prosecution now would make legal protection more difficult in the future. Second, there was a need to build on the precedent of the Nuremberg and Tokyo war crimes trials. Not to do so would be a step backward. It was important not to engage simply in victors' justice; the International Tribunal for the former Yugoslavia should function even while the conflict was in progress, and not just against the losing party. Third, there was a need to promote healing among the combatants. Not to do so would leave group hostilities to fester and erupt again. Only by seeking individual justice through a criminal court could one get neighbors in the Balkans to put the past, with its group antagonisms, behind them.

These are indeed morally cogent reasons, especially to supporters of a legal approach to problem-solving.

Compelling Problems

What is morally cogent may not prove politically compelling. If in domestic court one presents a creative argument for the protection of human rights, but the timing is premature in terms of what the court will accept as controlling legal interpretation, one has actually set back the cause of human rights at least temporarily. A new and potentially promising theory of controlling law is discredited. Timing is a critical calculation.

Likewise in international law, if one creates a criminal court that basically fails in its efforts, one has set back the cause of human rights at least for a time. As Professor Diane F. Orentlicher was quoted as saying, if the Tribunal fails "its establishment will have done far more harm to fundamental principles of international law than if criminal accountability had never been attempted." . . . The obstacles to the success of an international criminal court for the former Yugoslavia are profound.

Almost every combatant in this theater of armed conflict is a war criminal. What armed partisan has not shot at civilians or attacked civilian areas or abused prisoners? It is generally agreed that serious violations of humanitarian law have widely occurred among Serbs, Croats, and Bosnians, even if Serbian partisans have committed a disproportionate share. . . .

The leaders of the various fighting parties . . . are unlikely ever to be prosecuted and convicted. Ending the fighting would eliminate the major cause of affronts to human dignity in the region, and these leaders are unlikely to cooperate fully with peacemakers without assurances of immunity or amnesty. . . .

Would leaders of states turn over their subordinates, those who actually ran the prison camps and were locally in charge of ethnic cleansing and other atrocities? Could trials be held of intermediate or field commanders? That is doubtful. . . .

Given these difficulties and others. . .it would have been preferable in the Balkans to deal with war crimes by an international truth commission along the lines of the model in El Salvador, combined with national criminal proceedings. Such an approach would not have overextended further the already overextended United Nations, which exists perpetually on the edge of financial ruin and which does not need a controversial judicial effort to complicate further its record in the Balkans. . . .

NOTES AND QUESTIONS

1.   The U.N.'s failure to prevent and halt violence in the former Yugoslavia severely under-

mined its credibility. Establishment of the Tribunal was viewed by many as an effort to restore lost credibility. Was it merely an act of symbolism or desperation?

2. As of the end of February 1996, the Tribunal had issued only 53 indictments, and had not yet completed its first trial. Dean E. Murphy, *Serb General Indicted by U.N. Tribunal*, L.A. TIMES, Mar. 2, 1996, at A1. Dragan Nikolic received the Tribunal's first indictment in November 1994. Commander of the Bosnian Serb detainment camp at Susica during the summer of 1992, he was charged with eight murders and the torture and/or serious physical assault of seven people, and was charged with being a superior responsible for the criminal acts of subordinates. He was believed to be at large in Bosnian Serb-controlled territory and was not apprehended for trial. In October 1995, the Tribunal heard testimony on which it based its decision to take the unprecedented step of issuing an international arrest warrant for Nikolic. *See* Peter S. Canellos, *UN Court Charges Bosnian Camp Leader; Indictment Alleges Murder, Torture of Civilians*, BOSTON GLOBE, Nov. 8, 1994, Nat'l/Foreign sec. at 2; Wilbur G. Landrey, *Justice Promised for Bosnia Victims*, ST. PETERSBURG TIMES, Oct. 22, 1995, at 1A; Ian Traynor, *Serb War Crime Hearing Makes Legal History*, GUARDIAN, Oct. 10, 1995, at 13.

In February 1995, Dusan Tadic and 20 others were indicted for crimes allegedly committed in 1992 at the Omarska concentration camp. He was the first individual to be arrested and brought to the Hague to face trial. He was charged with both genocide and crimes against humanity. All others indicted in connection with Omarska were at large as of the end of February 1996. On July 25, 1995, Bosnian Serb leader Radovan Karadzic, his top military commander, Ratko Mladic, and 22 other Serbs were indicted for war crimes. None of the 24, however, was in custody as of the end of February 1996. As of the end of February 1996, only two indicted suspects, Tadic and Serb General Djordje Djukic, were held in custody. *See* William Drozdiak, *Top Serbs Charged with War Crimes*, WASH. POST, July 26, 1995, at A1; William Drozdiak, *War Crimes Tribunal Arraigns 1st Suspect; Bosnian Serb Pleads Not Guilty to Charges that He Killed Muslims at Detention Camp*, WASH. POST, Apr. 27, 1995, at A31; *Serb is Indicted as War Criminal; Jailed General Spurned Court Request to Testify*, CHICAGO TRIB., Mar. 2, 1996, at 10. The Tribunal's November 1994 and February 1995 indictments are reprinted in 34 I.L.M. 996 (1995). For a summary of indictments handed down prior to December 18, 1995, see *The Accused, The Allegations*, WASH. POST, Dec. 18, 1995, at A17.

3. Neier states that "the least that is required from the UN at this point is a good-faith effort to punish those with the highest level of responsibility for the most egregious crimes." Considering the slow pace of indictments, and the views of Hampson, Schwartz, and Forsythe, do you believe that such an effort remains a possibility?

4. Neier also states that "an indicted war criminal . . . would be susceptible to political attacks within his own country." On the contrary, might penal procedures turn accused into martyrs for whom sympathies could arise in certain circles?

5. Armed conflicts continued long after the establishment of the Tribunal. Can the Tribunal still hope to accomplish aims of punishment, reconciliation, and deterrence? Do you think the Tribunal will be more or less effective after fighting is finally precluded?

6. On November 1, 1995, the Presidents of Bosnia, Croatia, and Serbia began to meet near Dayton, Ohio with the goal of reaching a peace agreement. Weeks of difficult negotiations concluded on November 21 with the initialing of the Dayton Peace Accords, which were officially signed in Paris on December 14, 1995. The Accords provide for recognition of a single unified Bosnia, containing one Serb-controlled state and one state shared by Muslims and Croats. They also call for one Bosnian currency and a common presidency, but each state is to have its own government and army. *See* Peter Slevin, *America Will Enter Bosnia with Eyes Open to Problems*, PORTLAND OREGONIAN, Nov. 23, 1995, at A4. The official texts of the Dayton Peace Agreement can be accessed through the U.S. State Department's World Wide Web site at http://dosfan.lib.uic.edu/WWW/current/bosnia/bosagree.html.

7. Some prosecutions have been in national courts. In March 1993, a Bosnian military court sentenced to death two Serbs accused of killing at least 40 people, most of them young women who were first raped as part of an ethnic cleansing campaign. A U.N. military commander, Lt. Gen. Philippe Morillon, appealed for pardon of two Serbs—Borislav Herak and Sretko Damjanovic—and stated that the Tribunal, not the Bosnian court, should have tried the case. *See* David Ottaway, *Bosnia Convicts 2 Serbs in War Crimes Trial; U.N. Officer Seeks Amnesty to Promote Peace*, WASH. POST, Mar. 31, 1993, at A21.

8. Prosecuting those responsible for systematic rapes of thousands of Muslim women and girls in Bosnia is one of the most important challenges facing the Tribunal. According to a European Community investigation team, Serb forces raped up to 20,000 women throughout the conflict. Investigators emphasized that rapes were not random occurrences, but rather a weapon of war to intimidate and drive Muslims from their homes. William Drozdiak, *Serbs Raped 20,000, EC Team Says*, WASH. POST, Jan. 8, 1993, at A12.

In 1993, the Center for Constitutional Rights (CCR) filed a class-action civil suit in New York on behalf of female victims in the former Yugoslavia. The suit charged Radovan Karadzic, commander of Bosnian-Serbian forces in Bosnia-Herzegovina, with directing his forces to commit "widespread and systematic human rights abuses" including rape and other sexual abuse, genocide, summary execution, torture, and cruel, inhuman, or degrading treatment. The U.S. government filed a strong brief on behalf of the plaintiffs. The court in *Doe v. Karadzic*, 866 F.Supp. 734, dismissed the case for lack of subject matter jurisdiction, but the U.S. Court of Appeals for the Second Circuit reversed and found jurisdiction, 70 F.3d 232 (2d Cir. 1995). See also *infra* chapter 12.

For further reading on the crime of rape under international law, see *infra* chapter 12; *see also* C.P.M. Cleiren & M.E.M. Tijssen, *Rape and Other Forms of Sexual Assault in the Armed Conflict in the Former Yugoslavia: Legal, Procedural, and Evidentiary Issues*, 5 CRIM. L.F., 471 (1994); Thedor Meron, *Rape as a Crime Under International Humanitarian Law*, 87 AM. J. INT'L L. 424 (1993); Amy Schwartz, *Brought Together by Bosnia*, WASH. POST, May 14, 1993, at A31.

9. Critics and supporters alike agree that funding is perhaps the overwhelming threat to successful prosecution of war criminals in the former Yugoslavia. The Secretary-General estimated that a U.N. appropriation of $39,158,600 would be required to operate the Tribunal in 1994-1995. The total estimate included $3,230,000 for salaries and allowances for judges, $76,800 for consultants and experts, and $9,440,600 for prosecution staff. Voluntary member-contributions as of October 31, 1994, totalled only $8,241,967. *Report of the Secretary General as Requested by the General Assembly in Resolution 48/251*, U.N. Doc. A/C.5/49/42 (1994). Can the U.N., in view of its increasingly severe financial crisis, amass the funds required to keep the Tribunal operative? Are the U.N.'s limited resources best spent in this manner?

10. On November 8, 1994, the Security Council adopted Resolution 955, establishing an *ad hoc* international tribunal "for the sole purpose of prosecuting persons responsible for genocide and other serious violations of international humanitarian law committed in the territory of Rwanda and Rwandan citizens responsible for genocide and other such violations committed in the territory of neighbouring States, between 1 January 1994 and 31 December 1994." S.C. res. 955, 49 U.N. SCOR at 1, U.N. Doc. S/RES/955 (1994). The Rwanda Tribunal Statute borrows heavily from the Statute of the former Yugoslavia Tribunal, and the two share the same prosecutor and appeals judges. Julia Preston, *Tribunal Set on Rwanda War Crimes; Kigali Votes No on U.N. Resolution*, WASH. POST, Nov. 9, 1994, at A44;

The Rwanda tribunal, like that for the former Yugoslavia, was an international response to armed conflict between rival ethnic groups. Rwanda's population at the beginning of 1994 was approximately 7,000,000, composed of 80% Hutu and 20% Tutsi. Though the two groups share their language and most cultural and religious traditions, they have been sharply divided across economic lines. German colonials created, and Belgian administrators maintained, the division by establishing the Tutsi as wealthy landowners over Hutu peasant farmers. Helen Signy, *Rwanda: It Was Planned This Way - News Review*, SYDNEY MORNING HERALD, June 4, 1994.

In 1959, three years prior to Rwandan independence, the Hutu majority ousted Tutsi leaders in a bloody rebellion. Tens of thousands of Tutsi fled to neighboring nations, the largest number to Uganda. In response to discrimination by the Hutu government of President Juvenal Habyarimana, exiled Tutsi refugees formed the rebel RPF, based in Uganda, and invaded Rwanda in 1990. The two sides engaged in peace talks and then signed an accord in August 1993 providing for power sharing and the return of Tutsi refugees. *Id.*

On April 6, 1994, however, massive violence followed the mysterious crash of a plane carrying President Habyarimana and Burundian President Cyprien Ntaryamira. Most observers believe that extremist Hutus were responsible for the two deaths, and soon they organized an effort to slaughter the opponents of Hutu dominance. Mass killings by the militia were directed at the whole Tutsi population and also at moderate Hutus opposed to the government. Human rights investigators believe that government extremists had been promoting anti-Tutsi paranoia and planning mass murders for almost two years. In the first two months of the conflict, approximately 500,000 people were killed and over 2,000,000 displaced to neighboring countries. *Id.*

The Rwanda Tribunal was established in Arusha, Tanzania, despite its facing even more serious financial difficulties than the Yugoslavia Tribunal. In December 1995, it handed down its first indictments in connection with mass killings in Kibuye. None of the eight indicted supects was, however, taken into custody. In February 1996, the Tribunal issued its first indictments against persons already in custody. Georges Rutaganda, a former vice president of the Hutu militia group Interahamwe, was accused of playing a significant role in planning and carrying out massacres in Kigali and Nyanza. Jean Paul Akayesu was charged with encouraging the murder of a Tutsi teacher, and was suspected of having ordered the torture and murders of several other Tutsi. In March 1996, the government of Cameroon arrested Theoneste Bagosora, a former Rwandan army colonel accused of being one of the prime architects of the 1994 massacre. He was also wanted by Belgium in connection with murders of ten Belgian peacekeepers in Rwanda. As of mid-March 1996, the Rwandan government was urging Cameroon to extradite Bagosora to Rwanda. James C. McKinley, Jr., *Rwanda War Crimes Tribunal Indicts Two Men in Jail in Zambia*, N.Y. TIMES, Feb. 20, 1996, at A9. Rwanda began its own genocide trials in April 1995, against a few military officers, but suspended additional trials because of lack of funding and scarcity of judges. *One Year Later, Rwandans on Trial*, WASH. POST, Apr. 7, 1995, at A33; *Rwanda Asks for Ex-officer's Return*, BOSTON GLOBE, Mar. 13, 1996, at 36; *Rwandan Army Puts 14 on Trial*, WASH. POST, May 3, 1995, at A24.

For additional reading on the armed conflict in Rwanda and the International Tribunal for Rwanda, see Amnesty International, *Rwanda and Burundi—The Return Home: Rumours and Realities*, AI Index: AFR 02/01/96 (1996); Melissa Gordon, Note and Comment, *Justice on Trial: The Efficacy of the International Criminal Tribunal for Rwanda*, 1 ILSA J. INT'L & COMP. L. 217 (1995); Raymond Bonner, *In Once-Peaceful Village, Roots of Rwanda Violence*, N.Y. TIMES, July 11, 1994, at A8; *see also* Chapter 8, *infra*.

11. For additional reading on the International Tribunal for the former Yugoslavia, see:

AMERICAN BAR ASSOCIATION, REPORT ON THE INTERNATIONAL TRIBUNAL TO ADJUDICATE WAR CRIMES COMMITTED IN THE FORMER YUGOSLAVIA (1993);

M. Cherif Bassiouni, *The Commission of Experts Established Pursuant to Security Council Resolution 780*, 5 CRIM. L.F. 279 (1994);

M. Cherif Bassiouni, *The Need for an International Criminal Court in the New International World Order*, 25 VAND. J. TRANS. L. 151 (1992);

Philip J. Cohen, *Ending the War and Securing Peace in Former Yugoslavia*, 6 PACE INT'L L. REV. 19 (1994);

Alfred de Zayas, *The Right to One's Homeland, Ethnic Cleansing, and the International Criminal Tribunal for the Former Yugoslavia*, 6 CRIM. L.F. 257 (1995);

W.J. Fenrick, *Some International Law Problems Related to Prosecutions before the International Criminal Tribunal for the Former Yugoslavia*, 6 DUKE J. COMP. & INT'L L. 103 (1995);

Richard J. Goldstone, *The International Tribunal for the Former Yugoslavia: A Case Study in Security Council Action*, 6 DUKE J. COMP. & INT'L L. 5 (1995);

Nicholas Howen, *From Nuremberg to the Balkans: The International War Crimes Tribunal for the Former Yugoslavia, in* MONITORING HUMAN RIGHTS IN EUROPE 261 (Arie Bloed et al. eds., 1993);

INTERNATIONAL CRIMINAL TRIBUNAL FOR THE FORMER YUGOSLAVIA, BASIC DOCUMENTS 1995 (1995);

LAWYERS COMMITTEE FOR HUM. RTS., THE INTERNATIONAL CRIMINAL TRIBUNAL FOR THE FORMER YUGOSLAVIA: ESTABLISHMENT, ORGANIZATION, JURISDICTION, AND PROCEEDINGS TO DATE (1995);

Theodor Meron, *The Case for War Crimes Trials in Yugoslavia*, FOREIGN AFF., Summer 1993, at 122;

VIRGINIA MORRIS & MICHAEL SCHARF, AN INSIDER'S GUIDE TO THE INTERNATIONAL CRIMINAL TRIBUNAL FOR THE FORMER YUGOSLAVIA: A DOCUMENTARY HISTORY AND ANALYSIS (1995);

Daniel D. Ntanda Nsereko, *Rules of Procedure and Evidence of the International Tribunal for the Former Yugoslavia*, 5 CRIM. L.F. 507 (1994);

Jordan J. Paust, *Applicability of International Criminal Laws to Events in the Former Yugoslavia*, 9 AM. U. J. INT'L L. & POL'Y, 499 (1994);

Alfred P. Rubin, *An International Criminal Tribunal for Former Yugoslavia?*, 6 PACE INT'L L. REV. 7 (1994);

UN Documents Establishing an International Tribunal for the Former Yugoslavia, 32 I.L.M. (1993);

Minna Schrag, *The Yugoslav Crimes Tribunal: A Prosecutor's Views*, 6 DUKE J. COMP. & INT'L L. 187 (1995).

F.   CREATING A PERMANENT INTERNATIONAL CRIMINAL COURT

M. Cherif Bassiouni, *The Time Has Come for an International Criminal Court*, 1 IND. INT'L & COMP. L. REV. 1, 1, 11-19, 33-34 (1991) (footnotes omitted):

Introduction

The end of the "Cold War" presents an historic opportunity to advance the international rule of law by establishing an international criminal court to preserve peace, advance the protection of human rights and reduce international and transnational criminality.

The idea for such a court is not new and the efforts to establish it have increased over the years. All of the precedents, however, have been *ad hoc* international tribunals which ceased to exist when the specific function or purpose for which they were designed ended. But the important legal fact is that they existed, albeit with all the weaknesses and shortcomings of having been hastily established, created for a single adjudicating purpose and temporary in nature. Nevertheless, these precedents are the backdrop of international experience which must now ripen into a permanent international adjudicating structure designed to apply international criminal law with consistency and objectivity, and by means of fair process.

[Ed. Note: The author next presented a historical summary of efforts to create international criminal courts, beginning with Breisach, Germany in 1474, continuing through the Nuremberg and Tokyo Tribunals, and culminating with the International Law Commission's consideration of draft statutes for a permanent court.]

Political, Practical and Technical Legal Considerations

The obstacles to the establishment of an international criminal court fall essentially into three categories: (1) political; (2) practical; and, (3) legal-technical. Of these three, the political factor is the most significant, followed by the practical one, while the legal-technical one does not pose any serious difficulties.

The political factor stems essentially from objections generated by those who adhere to rigid conceptions of sovereignty, even though such conceptions have been depassé in so many other areas of international law, particularly with respect to the international and regional protections of human rights embodied in conventional and customary international law. The real opposition, however, comes from government officials who fear two types of situations.

The first is the risk that they and other senior officials, especially heads of state, can be called to answer for their acts which may constitute international violations and which would be subject to the Court's jurisdiction. . . .

. . . Strange as it may seem, the efforts of public officials to shield themselves from accountability . . . has consistently been the same for as long as there is a record of these occurrences. They invariably argue that their action was necessary in order to protect or save the nation, or to advance its vital or national security interests.

Another argument advanced against such a court, as well as another risk perceived by public officials, is the apprehension that an international adjudication body can, for purely political reasons, embarrass governments and public officials. But surely sufficient safeguards could be developed to prevent such possibilities, much as certain mechanisms have been developed in domestic legal systems to avoid abuse of power through prosecutorial misconduct and abuse of prosecutorial discretion. Such issues as well as other legal-technical issues cannot be raised *a priori* to oppose the realization of the idea. They are valid concerns to be raised in the context of drafting the norms and provisions of an international criminal court system so as to develop appropriate safeguards. It is, therefore, more likely that this argument is raised in order to obfuscate the fact that the [desire to shield public officials is the true concern of those who oppose the establishment of a permanent court].

Practical questions are also raised with frequency and have a ring of authenticity to them, particularly to the non-initiated. Among these questions are: where to locate the Court; how to secure the presence of the accused to stand trial; how to select judges, etc. These and other practical questions are no different than those which faced the drafters of the 1899 Hague Convention establishing the Permanent Court of Arbitration, or those of the 1920 Permanent Court of International Justice and of the 1945 International Court of Justice, respectively part of the League of Nations and United Nations Charters. . . .

Legal-technical issues are easily resolvable and many thoughtful models have been developed by the League of Nations, the United Nations, non-governmental organizations and individual scholars. . . .

Recent Developments

In the last three years, the question of establishing an international criminal court has emerged at the highest levels in the world and renewed interest has been expressed by world leaders and by the United Nations. . . .

Current international interests, however, seem to focus only on drugs and terrorism. What is needed instead is an international criminal court with universal jurisdiction to prosecute all or most of the 22 categories of international crimes covered by conventional and customary international law, including, but not limited to: aggression (crimes against peace); war crimes; crimes against humanity; genocide; apartheid; slavery and slave-related practices; torture; unlawful human experimentation; piracy; hijacking and sabotaging of aircraft; kidnapping of diplomats and other internationally protected persons; taking of hostages; and criminal damage to the environment. . . .

[Ed. Note: The author next proposes a model for creating an international criminal court.]

Conclusion

We no longer live in a world where narrow conceptions of jurisdiction and sovereignty can stand in the way of an effective system of international cooperation for the prevention and control of international and transnational criminality. If the United States and the Soviet Union can accept mutual verification of nuclear arms controls, then surely they and other countries can accept a tribunal to prosecute not only drug traffickers and terrorists, but also those whose actions constitute such international crimes as aggression, war crimes, crimes against humanity and torture.

Many of the international crimes for which the Court would have jurisdiction are the logical extension of international protection of human rights. Without enforcement, these rights are violated with impunity. . . . We cannot rely on the sporadic episodes of the victorious prosecuting the defeated and then dismantle these *ad hoc* structures as we did with the Nuremberg and Tokyo tribunals. The permanency of an international criminal tribunal acting impartially and fairly irrespective of whom the accused may be is the best policy for the advancement of the international rule of law and for the prevention and control of international and transnational criminality.

*   *   *   *   *

Michael P. Scharf, *The Jury is Still Out on the Need for an International Criminal Court*, 1991 DUKE J. COMP. & INT'L L. 135, 135-36, 159, 164-67 (1991) (footnotes omitted):

I. Introduction

After languishing in the shadow of international ambivalence for some seventy years, the proposal for the creation of an international criminal court is enjoying a modern revival. Within the last year, the United Nations International Law Commission ("ILC"), the U.N. Crime Congress, a conference of international scholars in Italy, and the International Law Section of the American Bar Association ("ABA") all have endorsed the concept of an international criminal court. . . . While these developments have been accompanied by a torrent of commentary in favor of the concept, until now the proposal has not been publicly subjected to anything approaching critical scrutiny. . . .

III. Weighing the Benefits and Costs . . .

Problems Posed by the Creation of an International Criminal Court . . .

1. The Need for an Acceptable Jurisdictional Scheme

Perhaps the most difficult obstacle to the establishment of an international criminal court is the need to formulate a jurisdictional arrangement that would overcome states' general reluctance to submit themselves or their nationals to the jurisdiction of an international authority. . . .

2. The Danger of Disrupting the Existing System . . .

An initial concern is that the quest for the creation of an international court would "divert resources and attention away from more practical and readily achievable means for combatting international criminal activities." The international community's principal long term law enforcement objectives have been: (1) seeking acceptance by more countries of existing international conventions that contain the prosecute or extradite principle; (2) negotiating agreements to facilitate international legal assistance and cooperation; (3) ensuring adherence to the obligations of existing conventions by state parties; (4) refining the provisions of existing conventions to close gaps and loopholes where desirable; and (5) adopting new conventions to reach specific areas not already covered by existing international conventions. Continuing efforts to pursue the establishment of an international criminal court could preempt and obscure the progress already made in these five areas. . . .

A second concern is that trial of terrorists in an international criminal court would run counter to current efforts to "deglamorize" terrorism by treating terrorists as common criminals. While prosecution in domestic courts advances this goal, prosecution before an international criminal court would likely have the reverse effect. The possibility of being tried before an international court, with accompanying publicity and prestige, could become an objective for future terrorists. . . .

A final concern is that the international criminal court "could develop into a politicized body, . . . interpreting crimes in unhelpful ways and releasing criminals who might no longer be prosecutable." . . .

Extraordinary efforts would be necessary to ensure that the international criminal court would not be subject to political currents and that its judges would be free from the inevitable political influences which so often afflict other U.N. organs. . . . In order to ensure the neutrality of the bench, it has been suggested that each state appoint one judge to the court, that cases be tried before three-judge panels, and that the full court hear appeals *en banc*. Though a sound start, these measures alone probably would not be sufficient to dispel serious concerns about the integrity of an international criminal court and its effect on the existing system.

3. Other Practical Concerns

The creation of an in international criminal court would be an enormously complex matter, requiring consensus on a host of practical matters such as the court's composition, rules of procedure or evidence, standard of proof . . . . Most of these matters, although cumbersome, are neither insurmountable nor historically unique. . . .

To be a truly neutral body, an international criminal court would require its own independent prosecuting machinery. . . . In addition, the international criminal court's prosecuting arm would have to satisfy common law countries, where public prosecutors are responsible for criminal investigation and prosecution, and civil law countries, where prosecution is conducted by the judiciary.

The creation of an international court also might require the establishment of an international detention facility. . . . Others believe that so long as international law depends upon national institutions for its enforcement, sentences should be carried out in the penal facilities of national systems . . . .

There are no specific proposals for dealing with, or assessing the costs of creating these international prosecutions and penal mechanisms. Such issues, however, are not merely administrative details to be worked out at a later date. Rather, "[t]hey are fundamental, and must be answered before it is possible to decide whether the Court is worthwhile."

* * * * *

In 1993, a working group of the International Law Commission (ILC), at its 45th session, produced a preliminary draft-statute for a permanent international criminal court. *Report of the International Law Commission on the Work of its Forty-fifth Session*, 48 U.N. GAOR Supp. (No. 10), U.N. Doc. A/48/10 (1993). The text was divided into seven parts, focusing on such questions as jurisdiction and applicable law, investigation and prosecution, and cooperation and judicial assistance. The ILC reported to, and received feedback from, the General Assembly's 48th session later that year.

In 1994, the ILC, at is 46th session, completed a second draft. *Report of the International Law Commission on the Work of its Forty-sixth Session*, 49 U.N. GAOR Supp. (No. 10) at 382, U.N. Doc. A/49/10 (1994). Revisions were aimed at underscoring the extent to which the proposed court would supplement and not displace existing national jurisdiction and regimes for international cooperation. The ILC also replaced the first draft's general reference to customary international law with a list of widely recognized specific crimes and added clauses emphasizing the primacy of the Security Council's role in the maintenance of peace and security. Robert Rosenstock, *Current Development: The Forty-sixth Session of the International Law Commission*, 89 AM. J. INT'L L. 390, 390-91 (1995).

On December 9, 1994, the General Assembly adopted Resolution 49/53, in which it decided to establish a committee "to review the major substantive and administrative issues arising out of the draft statute prepared by the International Law Commission and, in the light of that review, to consider arrangements for the convening of an international conference of plenipotentiaries[.]" Establishment of an International Criminal Court, G.A. res. 49/53, 49 U.N. GAOR at ¶ 2, U.N. Doc. A/RES/49/53 (1994). The *Ad Hoc* Committee on the Establishment of an International Criminal Court met twice in 1995 and reported to the General Assembly. U.N. Doc. A/50/22 (1995). The General Assembly directed its Sixth Committee to debate the issue, and the Committee did so at several meetings. U.N. Doc. A/C.6/50/SR.25-31 and 46 (1995). The Committee proposed a draft resolution for the establishment of a Preparatory Committee to draft a statute based on the ILC's draft statute and taking into account the *Ad Hoc* Committee's report and written comments submitted by member states to the Secretary-General. *Establishment of an International Criminal Court: Report of the Sixth Committee*, at 3, U.N. Doc. A/50/639 (1995). The General Assembly adopted the resolution on December 11, 1995. U.N. Doc. A/RES/50/46 (1995).

NOTES AND QUESTIONS

1.   Note that both Bassiouni and Scharf wrote their articles prior to the establishment of the tribunals for the former Yugoslavia and Rwanda. How do the experiences of those two efforts affect the drive for creating a permanent court?

2.   Do you think that the existence of a permanent international criminal court prior to the crises in the former Yugoslavia and Rwanda would have prevented or alleviated human rights and humanitarian law violations?

3.   U.S. officials traditionally have opposed establishing an international criminal court. Timothy Evered summarized the primary concerns as "generally converg[ing] around the issues of due process, the need to ensure fair trials, threats to national sovereignty, the danger of judges from foreign and alien judicial systems convicting American citizens, and unresolved problems related to the court's structure." Timothy C. Evered, *An International Criminal Court: Recent Proposals and American Concerns*, 6 PACE INT'L L. REV. 121, 131 (1994).

In 1994, the Clinton Administration expressed cautious support for the ILC's draft statute, but presented the Secretary-General with a report enumerating several concerns. The report explained concerns regarding the expense associated with operating an international criminal court and emphasized that such a court must supplement, rather than displace, existing national and international law-enforcement processes. In addition, it stressed the U.S. position that only the Security Council should have authority to refer war crimes, crimes against humanity, and genocide cases to an international criminal court. U.S. DEP'T OF STATE, COMMENTS OF THE GOVERNMENT OF THE UNITED STATES OF AMERICA ON DRAFT ARTICLES FOR A STATUTE OF AN INTERNATIONAL CRIMINAL COURT, (1994); *see also* United States Mission to the United Nations, Press Release, *Statement by the Honorable Conrad K. Harper*, USUN 171-(93) (1993).

4.   In addition to its work on an International Criminal Court, the International Law Commission is also developing draft articles on the international law of state responsibility. The law of state responsibility addresses the conditions under which a state incurs liability to other states or to the international community as a whole, for its actions. Naomi Roht-Arriaza, *State Responsibility to Investigate and Prosecute Grave Human Rights Violations in International Law*, 78 CALIF. L. REV. 449, 500 (1990). Because they establish basic rules for holding states accountable for their actions, several provisions in the ILC's Draft Articles on State Responsibility have important implications for the international protection of human rights.

Part one of the Draft Articles addresses how international liability is imputed to a state. Article 10 of part one provides that a state is responsible for the conduct of its officials even when they act beyond the scope of their authority. 2 Y.B. INT'L L. COMM'N 1980 (pt. 2) 31, art. 10, U.N. Doc. A/CN.4/SER.A/1980/Add.1 (Part 2). The application of this principle to human rights law is particularly important because, in most cases, the most egregious violations of human rights also violate the laws or official policy of the states where they are committed. Under Article 10, a state could not escape liability by claiming that an official acted beyond the scope of his or her official duties. Theodore Meron, *State Responsibility for Violations of Human Rights*, 83 AM. SOC'Y INT'L L. PROC. 372, 375 (1989).

The most controversial provision of the Draft Articles is Article 19 of part one: "International Crimes and Delicts." This article states that any act by a state which violates an international obligation of that state is an "internationally wrongful act." 2 Y.B. INT'L L.COMM'N 1976 (pt. 2) 95, art. 19 (1), U.N. Doc. A/CN.4/SER.A/1976/Add.1 (Part 2). Under part two of the Draft Articles, any such act may be subject to sanctions by the state or states injured by the violation. U.N. Doc. A/CN.4/L.480 and Add.1, art. 6-11 (1993). But Article 19 also asserts that a state may commit certain acts which are so egregious that they constitute a "crime" against the international community. Article 19 (2) defines an international crime as a "breach by a State of an international obligation so essential for the protection of fundamental interests of the international community that its breach is recognized as a crime by that community as a whole." 2 Y.B. Int'l L.Comm'n 1976 (pt. 2) 95, art. 19, U.N. Doc. A/CN.4/SER.A/1976/ Add.1 (Part 2). Article 19 (3)(c) states that an international crime may result, *inter alia*, from "a serious breach on a widespread scale of an international obligation of essential importance for safeguarding the human being, such as those prohibiting slavery, genocide and *apartheid*." *Id.* An internationally wrongful act which rises to the level of an international crime may entail greater consequences for the offending state than would a lesser violation, 2 Y.B. Int'l L. Comm'n 1985 (pt. 2) 20-21, art. 14, U.N. Doc. A/CN.4/SER.A/1985/Add.1 (Part 2). But the ILC has yet to determine what these greater consequences might be. Menno T. Kamminga, Inter-State Accountability for Violations of Human Rights 160 (1992).

Part two of the draft articles concerns the legal consequences of an internationally wrongful act for both the offending state and the rest of the international community. It focuses particularly on the rights of states which have been "injured" by the wrongful act. Traditionally, a state could seek reparations or other satisfaction for another state's breach of its international obligations only if it suffered some material injury because of that violation. Kamminga, *supra* at 137. In the field of human rights, however, the mere fact of the violation of an international norm is increasingly accepted as a legal injury justifying a response, regardless of its material consequences for other states. *Id.*; Meron, *supra* at 383. Article 5 of part two, which codifies this principle, provides:

"(e)   if the right infringed by the act of a State arises from a multilateral treaty or from a rule of customary international law, any other State party to the multilateral treaty or bound by the relevant rule of customary international law [shall be considered an injured state], if it is established that:

(iii)   the right has been created or is established for the protection of human rights and fundamental freedoms."

2 Y.B. Int'l L.Comm'n 1985 (pt. 2) 25, U.N. Doc. A/CN.4/SER.A/1985/Add.1 (Part 2). Note that injury to other states inheres in the very violation of the norm. Under this definition, any state in the international community might bring a claim against a state for violating international human rights norms. Kamminga asserts that the ILC adopted this definition of "injured states" to codify the principle that international human rights obligations are obligations *erga omnes*. Kamminga, *supra* at 163. The International Court of Justice enunciated the principle of *erga omnes* obligations—obligations of a state to the international community as a whole—in the *Barcelona Traction* case. *Barcelona Traction, Light & Power Co., Ltd.*, (Belg. v. Spain), 1970 I.C.J. 3 (Feb. 5). In *Barcelona Traction*, the court asserted that *erga omnes* obligations arise, *inter alia*, from "the outlawing of acts of aggression, and of genocide, as also from the principles and rules concerning the basic rights of the human person, including protection from slavery and racial discrimination." *Id.* at 32. The ILC has interpreted *Barcelona Traction* to stand for the proposition that all states have a legal interest in the proper observance of *erga omnes* obligations, and any state may seek redress for their violation. Kamminga, *supra* at 156 (citing 2 Y.B. Int'l L.Comm'n 1976 (pt. 2) 99, U.N. Doc. A/CN.4/SER.A/ 1976/Add.1 (Part 2)).

As of this writing, the International Law Commission has not completed work on its Draft Articles on State Responsibility. For an excellent discussion of the evolution of the articles, see generally Ian Brownlie, System of the Law of Nations: State Responsibility, Part I (1987); The International Law Commission's Draft Articles on State Responsibility (Shibtai Rosenne ed., 1991); United Nations Codifications of State Responsibility (Marina Spinedi & Bruno Simma eds., 1987). For a discussion of the law of state responsibility as it relates to human rights, see generally Menno T. Kamminga, Inter-State Accountability for Violations of Human Rights (1992); Thomas Meron, Human Rights and Humanitarian Norms as Customary International Law (1989).

5.   Does the U.S. Government's desire to ensure the Security Council's extensive control over which cases go to a permanent court suggest underlying concerns not among those enumerated by Evered? Might U.S. officials fear that U.S. Government employees would be subject to prosecution for violations of international law? Would they reasonably fear that other countries might be particularly anxious to embarrass the U.S. via criminal prosecutions?

6.   Amnesty International, despite its support for an international criminal court, has warned that the ILC draft statute lacks sufficient procedural protections for defendants. Among AI's concerns are the omission of adequate safeguards to help ensure a fair trial, inadequate provision for judicial supervision over the provisional arrest of suspects, particularly during detention by national authorities, and insufficient provision for effective international judicial supervision over the rights of defendants during *all* stages of the proceedings. Amnesty International, *Establishing a Just, Fair and Effective International Criminal Court* 5, AI Index: IOR 40/05/94 (1994).

7.   For additional reading on the establishment of a permanent international criminal court, see:

American Bar Association Task Force on an International Criminal Court—Final Report, 28 INT'L LAW. 475 (1994);

M. CHERIF BASSIOUNI, DRAFT STATUTE: INTERNATIONAL TRIBUNAL (1993);

M. Cherif Bassiouni & Christopher Blakesley, *The Need for an International Criminal Court in the New International World Order*, 25 VAND. J. TRANSNAT'L L. 151 (1992);

Christopher L. Blakesley, *Obstacles to the Creation of a Permanent War Crimes Tribunal*, 18-Fall FLETCHER F. WORLD AFF. 77 (1994);

James Crawford, *The ILC Adopts a Statute for an International Criminal Court*, 89 AM. J. INT'L L. 404 (1995);

Robert F. Drinan, *Is a Permanent Nuremberg on the Horizon*, 18-Fall FLETCHER F. WORLD AFF. 103 (1994);

Benjamin B. Ferencz, *An International Criminal Code and Court: Where They Stand and Where They're Going*, 30 COLUM. J. TRANSNAT'L L. 375 (1992);

William N. Gianaris, *The New World Order and the Need for an International Criminal Court*, 16 FORDHAM INT'L L.J. 88 (1992);

INT'L COMMISSION OF JURISTS, *The Establishment of a Permanent International Penal Court*, *in* TOWARDS UNIVERSAL JUSTICE 11 (1993); Jelena Pejic, *The International Criminal Court: Issues of Law and Political Will*, 18 FORDHAM INT'L L.J. 1762 (1995).

CHAPTER 8

INTERNATIONAL HUMAN RIGHTS FACT-FINDING

A.	**Introduction**	Page 308
B.	**Questions**	308
C.	**Background on Rwanda**	311
	Rwanda, Human Rights Watch	313
	Andrew Clapham & Meg Henry, Peacekeeping and Human Rights in Africa and Europe	314
	Rwanda and Burundi, A Call for Action by the International Community	316
D.	**Fact-Finding Procedures**	319
	1. **Preparation for an On-Site Investigation**	320
	2. **Methods of On-Site Fact-Finding**	322
	3. **Analysis, Verification, Follow-up, and Reporting**	330
	4. **U.S. State Department Country Reports**	332
E.	**Experience of the Inter-American Commission on Human Rights**	334
	Inter-American Commission on Human Rights, Report on the Situation of Human Rights in Argentina	334
	Thomas Buergenthal, Robert Norris & Dinah Shelton, Protecting Human Rights in the Americas: Selected Problems	341
	Inter-American Commission, Case 9265	343
	Edmundo Vargas, Visits on the Spot: The Experience of the Inter-American Commission on Human Rights	348
F.	**Fact-Finding Without On-Site Observation: Democratic People's Republic of Korea**	351
G.	**Impact of Fact-Finding Investigations**	358
	1. **Americas Watch, Asia Watch & Helsinki Watch, Four Failures: A Report on the U.N. Special Rapporteurs on Human Rights in Chile, Guatemala, Iran, and Poland**	358
	2. **Assessing the Impact of Fact-Finding**	361
	Maria Bartolomei & David Weissbrodt, The Impact of Fact-Finding International Pressures on the Human Rights Situation in Argentina, 1976-1983	361
	3. **Fact-Finding for United States Violations of Human Rights**	371

A. INTRODUCTION

This chapter examines an issue that has arisen in earlier chapters—how organizations can ascertain the truth of allegations that governments are violating human rights norms. Fact-finding is a critical aspect of the U.N. on-site missions discussed in chapter 6 and international criminal tribunals examined in chapter 7. Also, when U.N. bodies such as the Human Rights Committee and the Committee Against Torture examine individuals' communications and state governments' reports, the process involves fact-finding—as does the work of country and thematic rapporteurs appointed by the U.N. Commission on Human Rights. *See* chapter 5 *supra*.

The Inter-American Commission on Human Rights, a regional intergovernmental organization, also has had extensive fact-finding experience. *See* chapter 10 *infra*. This chapter focuses on methods of fact-finding by intergovernmental and nongovernmental organizations that are concerned with situations in particular countries.

Human rights fact-finding includes (1) long-term, on-site operations to monitor situations in various countries as well as individual cases when they arise, (2) short-term visits for the purpose of gathering information on a specific theme or event, (3) information-gathering without on-site visits, and (4) adjudicative proceedings.

Fact-finding is undertaken by intergovernmental organizations (IGOs), nongovernmental organizations (NGOs), national governments, and, sometimes, individuals. Information comes from personal interviews and other contacts with victims and witnesses, trial observation, prison visits, election observation, discussions with authorities, and much more. There are analogous but differing procedures and methods for each type of organization and fact-finding operation.

Readers will be asked to play roles as members of the U.N. Human Rights Field Operation in Rwanda. The operation has had a continuing presence under the direction of the U.N. High Commissioner for Human Rights.[1] Readers will consider appropriate procedures for dealing with rights violations of the kind described below. The material requires readers to consider the effect their investigation could have on the situation in Rwanda and how to tailor procedures in order to have an optimum impact.

B. QUESTIONS

You are a member of the Human Rights Field Operation in Rwanda (HRFOR) under the aegis of the U.N. High Commissioner for Human Rights. It is being conducted "(a) to carry out investigations into violations of human rights and humanitarian law, (b) to monitor the ongoing human rights situation, essentially for the purposes of the mandate of the Special Rapporteur, (c) to cooperate with other international agencies in re-establishing confidence and thus facilitate the return of refugees and displaced persons and the rebuilding of civic society, (d) to implement programmes of technical cooperation in the field of human rights."

---

[1] The position of the High Commissioner for Human Rights was established in February 1994. The High Commissioner for Human Rights is responsible for implementing U.N. activities by attempting to secure respect for human rights through diplomacy and dialogue.

Report of the High Commissioner for Human Rights, U.N. Doc. E/CN.4/1995/98 (1995).

You have been informed of the recent killing of five people in Ruhengeri (in Northwestern Rwanda). You are to help design plans for an investigation of this situation, from the decision to begin investigating to the preparation and dissemination of a report on the results, keeping in mind the four objectives listed in the preceding paragraph. Read the materials in this chapter carefully and then consider these questions:

1.   In what circumstances should an organization decide to undertake a fact-finding visit? A long-term presence?

2.   Should the objectives be relatively narrow or open-ended? From what sources should U.N. human rights observers derive their overall mandate, objectives, and methods? Should there be limits on the kinds of human rights violations examined by U.N. observers? What about concerns relating to economic, social, and cultural rights? What should be done with information about violations reportedly occurring one year before the U.N. presence, two years, five years, etc.?

3.   What are potential advantages and disadvantages of conducting on-site fact-finding? Is information obtained on-site necessarily more reliable than that available from sources outside the country?

4.   Should the organization seek the permission of the government to visit or establish a presence in the area? What assurances should be requested from the government before the fact-finding commences? Does it make a difference whether the sending organization is an IGO or an NGO? What should be the relationship between U.N. human rights fact-finders and U.N. civilian police officers, U.N. military observers, other IGO delegates, and NGOs? How can there be coordination in regard to their efforts?

5.   Why might a government accept on-site observers? Can its willingness to receive a fact-finding visit be misused as, for instance, a public relations measure? What can the sending organization do to prevent misuse by the government of the fact that a visit has occurred or is occurring?

6.   What is the relation between fact-finding and human rights protection? Are there basic principles for fact-finders?

7.   What factors should be considered when choosing fact-finding delegates? What briefing or training should they receive before beginning work? In regard to fact-finding in Rwanda, what qualifications might be useful? Should there be a preference for or against observers from particular countries or regions?

8.   Are there U.N. human rights or humanitarian law standards which U.N. human rights observers should apply in doing their work? Are they bound by those standards in regard to their own conduct? What ethical standards apply to observers?

9.   What research should be done and contacts developed before a fact-finding delegation enters a country or visits a site where violations may have occurred? For example: What more information is required about the incident in Ruhengeri? How much information should be gathered before going to the location of the incident?

10.   Is it enough to wait passively for information about the incident or should delegates actively seek people to interview?

11.   What factors should be considered in deciding whom to interview and what to see?

a.   Will all victims and/or witnesses be interested in talking with U.N. fact-finders? Before contacting delegates, might they have concerns about their own security? Are there ways to mitigate such concerns? Should delegates offer to pay for information? What about a witness from a distance who needs funds to return home or even for food? What should be done for witnesses who seek redress the U.N. cannot provide or who proffer information falling outside the U.N.'s mandate?

b.   What location(s) should be used for interviews? In beginning an interview what can delegates do to make the interviewee feel comfortable?

c.   How should delegates introduce themselves and explain their mandate?

d.   What approach should fact-finders use during the interview and further investigation?

e.   Should the delegate explain how the information provided may be used and give the interviewee an opportunity to withhold? How can delegates avoid creating false expectations of prompt and immediate results?

f.   What sorts of information should U.N. delegates seek? A preliminary list might include: type of violation, identity and characteristics of the victim, reasons for the violation, context and circumstances of the violation, the perpetrators, and response, if any, of the authorities. Are there other sorts of information which should be sought?

g.   How should the delegate record the information received in the interview? Tape recording, photographs, or videotaping? Should witnesses be asked to sign statements or affidavits? Are there risks in using such techniques?

h.   How can the delegate determine if the information is accurate?

i.   How detailed should the information be?

j.   Should delegates expect to get all useful information in a single interview, or might repeated contacts be useful?

12.   What should an observer do after interviewing witnesses?

a.   What can be done to protect witnesses who provide information? Can the security of information be assured?

b.   When evaluating statements of witnesses, what can be done to help ensure that the information is reliable? Should the delegate try to verify information of one witness by saying to another witness: Mr. Smith told me this; can you verify it?

c.   How can a delegate avoid being misled by government-staged testimony, newly cleaned prisons, and other deceptive measures?

d.   What standards of proof should a fact-finding delegation use: beyond a reasonable doubt, preponderance of the evidence, or another standard taken from civil or criminal litigation? Are different standards of proof appropriate for different sorts of fact-finding?

e.   What should be done with the information collected? Are published reports the only option? Should fact-finders seek to improve directly the human rights situation in a country during a visit or should they only prepare a report? In what circumstances might prompt and direct efforts to seek corrective action be appropriate? Are there effective techniques for using information gathered during a visit other than publishing a report?

f.   Are there circumstances in which delegates should make statements to the media during the fact-finding process?

g. How should delegates or higher U.N. officials make interventions with responsible government officials?

h. What material should be found in a useful report? How important are timeliness, accuracy, and action-orientation? Should a delegation submit its report to the government for comment before publication? What are advantages and disadvantages of such an approach?

1) At what points in its visit to Argentina did the Inter-American Commission meet with the Argentine government? When should delegates meet with the authorities? At the beginning, when issues arise, at the end of the investigation, when the report is prepared, or at other times? What can be learned from the experience of the Inter-American Commission?

2) Note how the Inter-American Commission handled the problem of identifying government officials reportedly responsible for violations? Page *39, infra*. Do you agree with the Commission's approach? What are the risks of naming the perpetrators? Are there questions of fairness at stake?

3) What are potential disadvantages of issuing preliminary recommendations to the government? Should those recommendations, if made, be released to the media?

4) After the visit is completed, should fact-finders make recommendations to the government or should they leave that to the organization which sponsored the visit?

5) What are potential disadvantages of publishing accounts such as "Discovering Disappeared Persons: A Staff Member's Notes"?

13. What special considerations would be relevant to fact-finding in periods of armed conflict, prison visits, visiting refugee or displaced person camps, monitoring freedom of expression in the context of demonstrations, election observation, trial observation, etc.?

14. Can human rights fact-finding be used to assist in gathering evidence for later use in prosecuting violations of international humanitarian law either in Rwandan courts or in the International Criminal Tribunal for Rwanda? Are there potential conflicts of interest between investigators for the International Criminal Tribunal and human rights fact-finders?

15. How can the results of fact-finding by on-site U.N. observers be used in other U.N. procedures? *See* chapters 5 and 6, *supra*.

16. Is it feasible to develop a code of conduct or a set of procedures that human rights fact-finders should follow? What role should good judgment play in modifying such a code or set of procedures in the light of circumstances faced by fact-finders?

C. BACKGROUND ON RWANDA

On October 1, 1990, an armed force of several hundred former Rwanda residents entered Northern Rwanda from Uganda. The invading force (known as the RPF) was largely of the Tutsi ethnic community which sought refuge in Uganda after the Tutsi monarchy in Rwanda was overthrown in 1959 or after Rwanda became independent from Belgium in 1962, under control of the Hutu majority. It is estimated that 40,000 Tutsi refugees fled to Uganda in the late 1950s and early 1960s. The invaders were not initially opposed even while they took control of portions of the Northern and Northeast frontier regions of Rwanda.

Rwandan President Habyarimana immediately responded to the 1990 crisis by declaring a state of siege. For several days law enforcement officers arrested both Ugandan nationals in Rwanda and Rwandans of Tutsi origin who had been under surveillance or were considered to be sympathetic with the invaders.

On the night of October 4, 1990, gunshots were heard all over the capital city, Kigali, and a dusk-to-dawn curfew was imposed throughout the country. There are many versions of what happened that night. Some residents believe the Rwandan army was instructed to fire weapons in the hope of flushing out invaders who had infiltrated the city; others believe that a few infiltrators actually did surface in the early morning. Apparently the worst fighting occurred at the airport, where French paratroopers arrived to assist the government, but were thought by Rwandan soldiers to be invaders. In the resulting affray, several Rwandan soldiers died; and a number of civilians also were found dead. There apparently have been no official investigations of the deaths.

For two-or-three days and nights following the shootings, law enforcement and military personnel made a house-to-house search for invaders, for people sympathetic to the invaders, and for others who lacked authority to be where they were found. Searchers also examined papers and anything else which might indicate disloyalty of residents. The searchers were assisted by local counselors and members of sector committees who were expected to know whether each person in their area was authorized to be there or was an invader in disguise. Because Rwandan society is organized in sectors of 50 houses (sometimes even as few as 10), travel/residence permits are required for all, and identity papers indicate one's ethnic group (Hutu, Tutsi, or other), it is possible for authorities to identify intruders. Unfortunately some sector-committee members were motivated by personal prejudices in encouraging the arrest of people in their areas—particularly Tutsis. By October 8 about 3,000 arrested people had been taken to a stadium. Officials estimated that 5,265 were detained throughout the country, mostly in Kigali; and others estimated that throughout the country more than 8,000 were detained. Some in the stadium were kept without food or water for three to five days. Many were beaten at the time of arrest or in vehicles en route to the stadium. Also, some were taken to police barracks where they were beaten and then imprisoned. Others were hospitalized and treated for serious wounds. Apart from the Tutsis, Ugandans and others also were arrested, taken to prison, and, as they left the trucks, beaten.

By mid-October 1990, assisted by French and Belgian troops, the Rwandan army retook the northern areas and slowly removed the invaders. By the end of November most invaders had been forced back into Uganda. Armed opposition forces in Uganda, however, continued to enter frontier regions and engage in guerilla tactics—including killing civilians, destroying property, and stealing from residents. Following the recommendations of a government Commission de Triage (sorting commission) almost all of the 8,000 detainees were released from detention and returned home.

The conflict continued until August 1993, when a cease-fire and peace agreement (the "Arusha Accords") was signed by the Rwanda Patriotic Front (mostly Tutsi invaders) and the Rwandese army. It ended the struggle and established a transition government that divided power between government and opposition forces. It also integrated the forces into one army and provided for the repatriation of refugees. In June the U.N. established an observer mission and, in October, set up the United Nations Assistance Mission to Rwanda (UNAMIR), which consisted of peace-keeping forces to assist in the implementation of the peace agreement but which, unfortunately, ended neither the violence nor the violations of human rights.

Also in 1993 the U.N. Special Rapporteur on Summary or Arbitrary Executions, Bacre Waly Ndiaye, visited Rwanda and submitted a report to the U.N. Commission on Human Rights. The report included 12 specific recommendations for action in Rwanda, and warned of possible problems in the near future: "[T]he international community cannot remain indifferent to their situation and must therefore provide its assistance wherever that of the Rwandese State is inadequate or non-existent." Report by Mr. B.W. Ndiaye, Special Rapporteur, on his mission to Rwanda from 8 to 17 April 1993, U.N. Doc. E/CN.4/1994/7/Add.1 (1993). The Commission, however, took no action.

On April 6, 1994, an unexplained plane-crash killed the President of Rwanda and the President of Burundi. Massive killings by Hutu forces in Rwanda followed, claiming the lives of between a half million and a million people (mostly Tutsis) in four months. A group of observers is investigating past and continuing human rights violations under the mandate of the U.N. High Commissioner for Human Rights. The following excerpts describe the situation in early 1994 and the U.N.'s response.

Rwanda, HUMAN RIGHTS WATCH WORLD REPORT 41-42 (1995).

When the president's plane crashed on April 6, the armed forces command seized the opportunity to set in motion a plan of genocide that had developed over months. Within thirty minutes of the plane crash, military, police, and civilian militia set up roadblocks around the city, and the killing began. . . .

The presidential guard was soon joined by the party militias. Together, they killed an estimated 20,000 people in Kigali and its immediate environs within a week. Shortly after the crash and the beginning of the massacres, a group of politicians close to Habyarimana and backed by the military proclaimed themselves the new government. The RPF resumed the civil war on April 8, with an immediate objective the rescue of its troops in Kigali and in an attempt to stop the massacres. On April 12 Belgium announced its intent to withdraw its 400-person UNAMIR contingent. Emboldened by the evacuation of Belgian troops and the failure of the remaining UNAMIR forces to respond, the leaders of the genocide extended its scope outside the capital to the east and the southwest by April 15.

In communities where the killing was not proceeding rapidly or thoroughly, outside elements, usually militia members, were imported to spur the slaughter. In the southern prefecture of Butare, it was both militia and members of the presidential guard who were brought in to execute massive killings in a region in which local people had largely resisted carrying out the genocide of their Tutsi neighbors. In such cases, local people were often given the choice of kill or be killed. Faced with such a choice, most agreed to join in the slaughter.

In most communities, local government officials organized and personally directed the murders. Eyewitnesses in several places reported that the killers arrived under the direction of local officials to begin their "work" at 8 a.m. and to finish at 4 p.m. The assailants then returned home singing, to come back the next morning and begin the slaughter once more. In most communities the repeated attacks continued until all the Tutsi were killed: clearly the goal was complete elimination of the minority rather than its simple defeat.

Barriers on all roads and paths prevented victims from fleeing massacre sites. All Rwandans were required to carry identity cards which specify their ethnic group. Tutsi who sought to pass the barriers were selected on the basis of these identity cards and killed on the spot. When people sought shelter in neighborhood churches, hospitals, or schools, they were killed all the more efficiently, often through the use of grenades. Survivors were finished off with machetes, clubs, or guns. At such sites as Kubungo, Cyahinda, and Shangi, thousands of people were executed in a matter of hours.

By mid-May, militia leaders were calling upon their members to finish "cleaning up" Tutsi and members of the Hutu opposition who had escaped death up to that point. In the months that followed, militia backed by the military made nightly visits to other locations where people at risk had taken refuge and removed groups of people to be executed. Anyone who was educated or had shown capacity for leadership was targeted first to ensure that the mass of victims would be left disorganized and unresisting for later slaughter. A substantial number of Catholic clergy were among the victims. The RTLM radio urged attackers not to repeat the mistake of sparing children, as had been done in previous massacres. The killers, some of whom had a radio in one hand and a machete in the other, heeded the advice and slaughtered children as well as adults. . . .

Although representatives of the RPF and the Rwandan army reportedly agreed to a cease-fire on June 14, the agreement never took effect. In tandem with the genocide, but quite distinct from it, the active fighting continued throughout the month of June. On July 4 the RPF took control of Kigali, prompting a mass exodus of Hutu soldiers and civilians to Zaire, Burundi, and Tanzania. In late October there were an estimated 1.2 million Rwandan refugees in Zaire, 270,000 in Burundi, and over 500,000 in Tanzania.

By the end of 1994, soldiers of the former Rwandan army and members of the militia were terrorizing the refugee camps, particularly in Zaire. Unrestrained either by authorities of the former Rwandan government or by authorities of the local government, they were murdering, raping, and stealing at will. They systematically intimidated any refugees who might have wanted to return to Rwanda and in several cases killed those who appeared ready to leave the camps. One of the most serious incidents occurred in late August in Kibumba camp where several hundred refugees awaiting transport were attacked by militia members. Thirty Rwandan boy scouts in Katale camp, who had been charged with organizing security and helping with food distribution, vanished in late September, apparently murdered because they had represented an obstacle to full militia control of the camp. Militia members also threatened expatriate members of the relief community in late 1994.

Soldiers in Zaire continued to be paid by the former Rwandan government and, as the year ended, were preparing to resume the war against the new government of Rwanda. At the end of October, these soldiers were apparently the assailants responsible for killing thirty-six civilians in an early morning raid in the northwestern prefecture of Gisenyi.

* * * * *

Andrew Clapham & Meg Henry, *Peacekeeping and Human Rights in Africa and Europe, in* HONORING HUMAN RIGHTS AND KEEPING THE PEACE 152-56 (Alice Henkin ed., 1995).

On April 21, [1994,] the Security Council reduced the authorized strength of the force from over 2,000 to 270. The continuing horrific killings and mutilations were characterized as genocide by the Secretary-General, and estimates of the deaths reached several hundred thousand by the end of June. The ability of the United Nations to turn away when Rwandans were in their hour of need shocked humanitarian organizations in Rwanda and people around the world. The reality was that no one had the stomach for assertive peacekeeping, and the thought of UN enforcement powers, coming less than a year after the Somalia adventure, left the big powers feeling awkward but unmoved. . . .

The newly installed UN High Commissioner for Human Rights, Jose Ayala Lasso, issued a public statement on May 4, 1994, announcing that he would go to Burundi and Rwanda together with a number of UN officials and an independent expert, Louis Joinet. He said he hoped that the UN Human Rights Commission would meet in a special session and consider appointing a special rapporteur as well as a team of human rights monitors.

The Commission did indeed hold a special session on May 24 and 25 to hear the report of the High Commissioner, and passed a resolution on the 25th appointing a Special Rapporteur for Rwanda, Professor Rene Degni-Segui. It also called for the High Commissioner to arrange for a team of human rights field officers to assist the Special Rapporteur and the UN peacekeeping operation. The Special Rapporteur has issued a number of reports, as has the High Commissioner, who went back to Rwanda in mid-August 1994. Before leaving for Rwanda, the High Commissioner appealed for $2.1 million to fund an additional 20 human rights monitors to work in Rwanda. These monitors are, according to the Special Rapporteur, to perform a number of functions: persuasion, deterrence, prevention, and defense. The first task will be to persuade the refugees and displaced persons that they can return without fear of further massacres. The presence of the monitors will also act as a deterrent to reprisals by the new authorities and as prevention and defense against further violence. The Special Rapporteur has also called for a second phase, whereby 150-200 human rights experts would be deployed throughout the country to "monitor not only the return, but also the reconstruction of Rwanda, and to conduct the necessary inquiries to ascertain the facts regarding the massacres." . . .

* * * * *

By July 31, 1995, the U.N. High Commissioner for Human Rights had deployed 188 members of the Human Rights Field Operation in Rwanda (HRFOR). The delegation is comprised of fixed-term staff, volunteers, and observers contributed by the European Union. Together they operate in eleven field offices across Rwanda. The UNAMIR troops were removed from Rwanda in early 1996. The HRFOR has remained, but the U.N. may have to discontinue its work or decrease the number of observers due to a shortage of funds.

The first HRFOR emphasis was on investigation of past human rights violations for purposes of building a record and collecting evidence to be used by the criminal tribunal. The focus slowly changed to monitoring the current human rights situation and building confidence. The delegates have interviewed victims, witnesses, and government authorities and have visited prisons, detention centers, and refugee camps. They have submitted reports of their activities and observations to the U.N., but those reports have not been widely disseminated. *See, e.g., Human Rights Field Operation in Rwanda, Modus Operandi for the Human Rights Field Officers*, U.N. Doc. CER/MISC.16 (1994); *The Human Rights Field Operation in Rwanda, Operational Plan*, U.N. Doc. HR/FOR/Misc.1 (1994); *Update on the Activities of the HRFOR 13 July 1995-28 July 1995*.

The Legal Analysis and Coordination Unit (LACU), formerly the Special Investigations Unit, is a section of the HRFOR involved in investigating the genocide. It was created by the High Commissioner for Human Rights in October 1994. In November 1994 the Security Council passed Resolution 935, creating an international criminal tribunal for purposes of prosecuting the individuals responsible for violations in Rwanda. The establishment of the tribunal gave the LACU a legal framework. The LACU has worked with other international organizations to identify the perpetrators and with forensic experts to analyze the killings, and also has visited mass grave and massacre sites. *See Special Investigations Unit: Final Report on the Genocide Investigation*, Apr. 12, 1995.

Following the killings and other violations, the Rwandan government arrested nearly 50,000 individuals, largely of Hutu origin. The individuals are being held for trial or other disposition. The government has established a Commission de Triage (sorting commission) to determine who should be tried and who should be released. The system of government, however, essentially has not begun to function; and it is unclear how long these individuals will be held before disposition.

The following excerpt takes a critical look at HRFOR's work.

Amnesty International, *Rwanda and Burundi, A Call for Action by the International Community*, AI Index: AFR 02/24/95 (1995) (citations and footnotes omitted):

1.1 Investigation of the genocide

The Human Rights Field Operation was created in response to the genocide and other crimes against humanity committed in Rwanda, but the work of the Human Rights Field Operation in documenting the genocide has been hidden by excessive secrecy. Not even the operation's own field officers, let alone the Rwandese Government and people, have been adequately informed of the investigation work being carried out. There has also been damaging confusion about the operation's contribution to the process of bringing to justice those responsible for genocide, exacerbated by delays and shortfalls in the arrival of expert personnel such as police investigators, experienced prosecutors, lawyers and forensic pathologists. . . .

The distinction between documenting the massacres and criminal investigations was overlooked. There is a qualitative difference between documenting patterns of human rights violations where individual cases are used as representative examples of the pattern and gathering first-hand testimony and physical evidence, admissible in court, to prove that particular individuals committed particular crimes. Documenting the genocide is a massive descriptive exercise that continues to require the efforts of a large proportion of the Human Rights Field Operation staff, working in conjunction with Rwandese local officials and non-governmental organizations. However, criminal investigations should be carried out by expert criminal investigators in the Prosecutor's Office from the Tribunal. The Prosecutor's Office of the Tribunal asked the Special Investigations Unit within the Human Rights Field Operation not to prepare cases for prosecution or to conduct detailed field investigations. The Prosecutor asked for general information, particularly maps of massacre sites, and this was carried out by Human Rights Field Operation staff in early 1995. The Special Investigations Unit, with the teams of seconded personnel, collected numerous affidavits along with photographs, weapons, reports and other evidence which was turned over to the Tribunal in April 1995.

Unfortunately the final report of the Special Investigations Unit remains confidential, even though no witnesses or perpetrators are identified by name in the main part of the report. Nor has the Human Rights Field Operation issued any other report on its investigations into the genocide in Rwanda.

It is clear that the identities of witnesses and suspects must remain confidential until trial, and that evidence must be carefully safeguarded. But somehow these necessary measures came to mean that those who were involved in genocide investigations could not talk to anyone about what they were doing, even in the most general terms.

This secrecy led to a widespread perception that nothing was being done to investigate the genocide. But clearly this is not the case. . . .

1.2   Assisting in the administration of justice

The Human Rights Field Operation for Rwanda has been hindered in its efforts to assist in the rehabilitation of the judicial system by divisions and bureaucratic wrangling in the UN Centre for Human Rights in Geneva. As a result, it has not been able to carry out training programs or supply desperately needed basic materials to the Rwandese judicial system, undermining the credibility of the operation as a whole. . . .

Potential donors have come to doubt that aid can be delivered to Rwanda via the UN human rights programs. This failure to meet even the most basic of needs hinders the work of the field officers in the provinces, and is creating a further obstacle to progress in rebuilding the Rwandese judicial system. Every delay exacerbates the human rights problems in Rwanda, in particular the prolonged detention of over 50,000 people in seriously overcrowded prisons, awaiting charge and trial. Furthermore, it appears that in certain government circles, there may be a lack of political will to begin processing the cases of these tens of thousands of prisoners. The authorities appear to content themselves with turning long-term detention without trial into a substitute for justice. If the necessary foreign aid were promptly delivered, such absence of political will would be exposed and the absence of resources could no longer be presented as an obstacle to the full operation of the Rwandese judicial system.

1.3   Establishing an international human rights presence

The widely perceived need to establish a human rights presence in Rwanda led to considerable pressure to get human rights monitors into the country quickly. However, the UN Centre for Human Rights in Geneva lacked the experience and capacity to cope with a crisis of the magnitude being experienced by Rwanda. The process for recruiting human rights monitors fell below acceptable standards. There were also delays in logistical support, especially a lack of vehicles and communications equipment, which impeded the transfer of personnel from Kigali to the provinces.

Some staff were deployed who did not have the appropriate skills and experience. Others were frustrated by being held up in Kigali for weeks after their arrival in Rwanda. All the personnel suffered from inadequate orientation, training and guidelines in the first months of the operation. Many, recruited on short-term contracts, did not stay long in the country. In addition, staff were frequently rotated, often in response to various local crises. Many of these problems have now been addressed. Comprehensive training has been instituted and a Field Coordination Unit is now analyzing developments and coordinating the synthesis of reports from the field. . . .

1.4   Monitoring the current human rights situation

The remaining key component of the Human Rights Operation for Rwanda— monitoring and correcting human rights problems—has been left isolated and exposed. The Human Rights Field Operation's failure to report on its work in investigating the genocide and to provide material assistance to the judicial system has led to the perception that the human rights operation only monitors current violations, and that this activity is biased against the current Rwandese Government.

Human rights monitoring can enhance the accountability of the security forces and in many cases saves lives through sustained vigilance over the fate of detainees and returnees. But monitoring alone is insufficient: incidents of human rights violations must be reported publicly if progress is to be made. It is never the "perfect time" to publish human rights reports especially in a highly polarized situation such as that which prevails in Rwanda after the genocide. The only principled approach is to publish human rights information consistently. Other UN human rights field operations in countries such as Haiti, El Salvador, Cambodia and Guatemala have enhanced their preventive role by publishing detailed and useful human rights reports. These reports, as well as exceptional reports on specific incidents, were published every few months. They were published either as reports of the operation's Director of Human Rights or of the UN Secretary-General and were circulated as UN documents available in all official languages.

Confusion about the public reporting role of the High Commissioner for Human Rights has left the operation with no regular means of reporting publicly. Although recent information sheets have started to explain the work of the field operation, these are no substitute for more thorough UN reports on the investigations and the human rights situation.

Amnesty International believes that to guarantee the effectiveness and credibility of international human rights personnel, they must report their activities and finding frequently; these reports should be disseminated nationally as well as internationally. The information should be made available to the news media, to all parts of the UN system (especially its human rights mechanisms), and to relevant intergovernmental bodies and non-governmental organizations. Particular care should be taken to keep the local populations informed. . . .

The Human Rights Field Operation for Rwanda is now fulfilling a real protection role, thanks to the determination and dedication of some of the field officers. These positive achievements have received very little publicity amidst the criticism of the UN's overall failure to avert the human rights tragedy in Rwanda. Yet Amnesty International's delegates in Rwanda in 1995 noted that in prefectures such as Butare, field officers have played a life-saving role in protecting returnees under extremely difficult circumstances. Field officers throughout the country have identified places of detention, negotiated the release of certain detainees, and won better treatment for detainees. Their assistance to the prosecutor's office and judicial police is vital in making progress to bring people to justice and thus relieving the prison overcrowding.

On 7 June 1995, Amnesty International delegates visited Gitarama prison. They were shocked by the degree of overcrowding: 6,847 prisoners were held in a space intended originally for about 500. About four prisoners were reported to be dying in the prison every day, and the overcrowding together with the lack of sanitation is leading to serious health problems such as infected feet and gangrene (more than 10 amputations have been performed). The International Committee of the Red Cross (ICRC) and *Medicins Sans Frontieres* (MSF), Doctors Without Border, have appealed several times to the Rwandese authorities to resolve the severe overcrowding. In some prisons, several people are held per square metre. . . .

1.5 Conclusion

Amnesty International's representatives met a number of Human Rights Field

Operation teams in several provinces. Notwithstanding the problems cited in this report, it should be emphasized that Amnesty International's delegates encountered a number of highly qualified human rights professionals who were doing outstanding human rights protection work in Rwanda—exactly the sort of work that UN human rights field operations are intended to carry out.

The Human Rights Field Operation for Rwanda is now having a positive effect and its monitoring and reporting role is set to become more important as the size of UNAMIR is reduced in the coming months. The operation should be given greater support by the UN secretariats in Geneva and New York as well as by governments around the world.

*   *   *   *   *

For further reading on the situation in Rwanda and the role of the U.N. see AFRICAN RIGHTS, RWANDA: DEATH, DESPAIR AND DEFIANCE (rev. ed. 1995); *Report on the Situation of Human Rights in Rwanda*, U.N. Doc. E/CN.4/1996/68 (1996).

D.   FACT-FINDING PROCEDURES

There are many approaches to fact-finding, some of which have been or could be used by the observers in Rwanda. As you read the following materials, try to segregate procedures that might be useful in Rwanda from those that might not.

Human rights investigations generally involve related purposes: monitoring a government's human rights violations and related conduct, collecting information for the historical record, collecting information for a tribunal, providing relief to victims, publicizing human rights violations, and more. The methods can include on-site investigation for a limited period of time, on-site investigations for a longer period, research studies, assessments as to the need for international assistance, trial observation, prison visits, visits to refugee camps, election observation, and sessions with government officials. At times the purposes and functions overlap.

The observers sometimes represent intergovernmental organizations (IGOs), national governments, and/or nongovernmental organizations (NGOs). One of the main differences between an IGO and an NGO operation is that states often have consented in advance to cooperate with an IGO investigation, either by becoming a party to a treaty or simply by being a member of the organization, while international NGOs usually notify governments of their visits but must rely on other factors to gain cooperation of a government and sometimes must operate without cooperation. National NGOs resident in the country have greater access to facts but also face greater risks of reprisal. IGOs often insist on certain preconditions (such as assurance of protection for witnesses) before undertaking visits; NGOs often cannot obtain that assurance. Another difference is that IGOs sometimes have permanent bodies with fixed rules for conducting long-term fact-finding investigations while NGOs often utilize *ad hoc* procedures. Nonetheless, IGOs and NGOs face many of the same problems when conducting investigations.

This section looks at the on-site investigation as a fact-finding tool. Many organizations, however, engage in fact-finding without such investigation. Readers should keep the distinction between on-site and other investigations in mind as they read these materials, observing how procedural issues differ depending on the type of investigation. Readers should also note the advantages and disadvantages of conducting on-site investigations.

1. Preparation for an On-Site Investigation

TERMS OF REFERENCE

Before sending on-site observers, objectives for the visit ordinarily are determined and set out as terms of reference. The terms of reference include a general, impartial statement of the objectives, as well as more specific information on the length of time needed, the violations to be investigated, the territory to be included, and the standards to be used in analyzing and relaying the information.

Terms of reference are determined by the sponsoring organization. The process differs, however, depending on whether the organization is an IGO or NGO. IGOs receive the power to conduct on-site investigations in particular countries from multilateral agreements or instruments, and specific terms of reference are negotiated by the states parties or the sending institutions, such as the Security Council. The authority for NGO fact-finding is usually self-created. They define the scope of their study and legitimize their efforts mostly by the quality of their findings.

Terms of reference may induce governments to cooperate, and often may be subject to negotiation with governments. Though most NGO visits are not governed by formal agreement between the NGO and the state, there often are contacts with the government prior to the visit. Terms of reference also act as the fact-finders' letter of introduction and help not only the investigation itself but also a group's making contact with embassies and consulates. Terms of reference serve too as an aid to delegates when disputes arise as to the scope of their activities.

DELEGATES

Both IGOs and NGOs face the problem of finding qualified delegates. Most fact-finding is done by permanent employees and aided by distinguished individuals who participate at the request of the organization. Large-scale IGO operations sometimes experience particular difficulty in finding and training qualified human rights observers.

There is no standard method for ensuring expertise and objectivity. Since service on most fact-finding operations is voluntary and can involve some hardship, participants characteristically have a strong interest in and should be knowledgeable as to human rights. Organizations that regularly engage in fact-finding utilize previous experiences of individuals. Typically because of evidence as to violations of physical integrity, organizations often enlist physicians. Some visits have also included foreign scholars who are knowledgeable regarding the country visited. In addition to expertise, impartiality, objectivity, and planning for translation and interpretation is, of course, essential.

BACKGROUND FACT-FINDING

The bulk of fact-finding takes place in the offices of the organizations. At their offices IGOs and NGOs gather information from newspapers, magazines, professional journals, U.N. publications, government reports, letters, telegrams, phone calls, and visits. Sources include public officials, church officials, relatives of prisoners, former prisoners or refugees, tourists and other visitors, labor unions, opposition groups, expatriate groups, lawyers, journalists, and other international organizations. Church-sponsored organizations and other NGOs within a country often obtain information through webs of personal contact. Some organizations have clipping files and dossiers on human rights violations dating back many years. IGOs also obtain information from individual victims, or others on their behalf, in the form of communications that allege violations of human rights.

Both IGOs and NGOs seek background information before undertaking on-site operations. For example, one of the first actions of the U.N. *Ad Hoc* Working Group of Experts on South Africa in 1967 was to ask all U.N. member states for information—particularly for the names of possible witnesses—and to issue communiques through the U.N. Office of Public Information inviting contact with "all the persons who believe that they could provide specific and relevant information on this matter, in particular those who have been 'imprisoned or detained for opposing or violating the policies of apartheid.'" In inquiries about South Africa, the *Ad Hoc* Group of Experts solicited names of witnesses and information not only from member States and the general public, but from the Organization of African Unity and various private organizations, including some African liberation movements.

NOTES AND QUESTIONS

1. As we have noted, members of the Human Rights Field Operation in Rwanda have a broad mandate. *See supra* at 315. More-specific terms of reference governed the 1993 operation in Haiti. It prescribed the members' objectives as (a) informing themselves of the situation, (b) devoting attention to respect for the right to life, to the integrity and security of the person, to individual liberty, and to freedom of expression and association, and (c) taking all initiatives considered to be necessary for the recognition of and respect for human rights. *The Situation of Democracy and Human Rights in Haiti*, U.N. Doc. 1/47/908 (1993). What are the benefits and dangers of a narrow mandate? A broad one? What problems do you foresee in carrying out the Rwandan mandate?

2. Various sets of procedural rules exist to help guide fact-finders. The first international codification of fact-finding procedure was apparently the Hague Convention for the Pacific Settlement of Disputes of 1907, 36 Stat. 2199, T.S. No. 536. It provided for commissions of inquiry that would be constituted by agreement between disputing states and set out rules of procedure for the inquiry. Though the Hague Convention's inquiry mechanism received little use, the procedural rules still are of interest.

Many IGOs have formulated their own fact-finding procedures. This chapter in section E, at 334, *infra* describes one such procedure, that of the Inter-American Commission on Human Rights. More general standards can be found in the Declaration on Fact-finding by the U.N. in the Field of the Maintenance of International Peace and Security, U.N. Doc. A/ RES/46/59, Annex (1992), which provides in part:

1. In performing their functions in relation to the maintenance of international peace and security, the competent organs of the United Nations should endeavour to have full knowledge of all relevant facts. To this end they should consider undertaking fact-finding activities.

2. For the purpose of the present Declaration fact-finding means any activity designed to obtain detailed knowledge of the relevant facts of any dispute or situation which the competent United Nations organs need in order to exercise effectively their functions in relation to the maintenance of international peace and security. . . .

6. The sending of a United Nations fact-finding mission to the territory of any State requires the prior consent of that State, subject to relevant provisions of the Charter of the United Nations. . . .

16. In considering the possibility of undertaking a fact-finding mission, the competent United Nations organ should bear in mind other relevant fact-finding efforts, including those undertaken by the States concerned and in the framework of regional arrangements or agencies.

17. The decision by the competent United Nations organ to undertake fact-finding should

always contain a clear mandate for the fact-finding mission and precise requirements to be met by its report. The report should be limited to a presentation of findings of a factual nature. . . .

25.   Fact-finding missions have an obligation to act in strict conformity with their mandate and perform their task in an impartial way. Their members have an obligation not to seek or receive instructions from any Government or from any authority other than the competent United Nations organ. They should keep the information acquired in discharging their mandate confidential even after the mission has fulfilled its task.

26.   The States directly concerned should be given an opportunity, at all stages of the fact-finding process, to express their views in respect of the facts the fact-finding mission has been entrusted to obtain. When the results of fact-finding are to be made public, the views expressed by the States directly concerned should, if they so wish, also be made public. . . .

*   *   *   *   *

Another set of rules that deserves mention is one adopted by the International Law Association. *The Belgrade Minimum Rules of Procedure for International Human Rights Fact-finding Visits*, 75 Am. J. Int'l L. 163 (1981).

3.   Concerning the 1992 U.N. Declaration on Fact-finding excerpted above:
   a.   When should a U.N. body decide (or not decide) to sponsor a fact-finding operation?
   b.   Does the 1992 Declaration bar fact-finding visits not approved by the host state? May a State deny access to a fact-finding visit for any reason?
   c.   Should NGOs adopt or adapt the guidelines of the 1992 Declaration for their own fact-finding missions? What information acquired during a fact-finding visit should be kept confidential?
   d.   Does the 1992 Declaration apply to the U.N.'s fact-finding operation in Rwanda?

2.   Methods of On-Site Fact-Finding

On-site investigations supplement information obtained by "passive" fact-gathering. They are first-hand, lend credibility to fact-finding reports, and can sometimes afford relief because of the mere presence of outside observers. They can also produce information needed for prompt action.

To help inspire corrective efforts by governments and, sometimes, other groups, human rights organizations seek reliable factual conclusions from information gathered via generally accepted procedures. A reputation for fairness and impartiality can lend credibility to the organization's observations of human rights conditions in the countries investigated, proposals for action, and other work.

On-site research involves collecting both oral and written evidence. Oral testimony often is regarded as more reliable, because it affords the chance to question the witness about her or his story and to assess her or his character. Participants in fact-finding will want to interview as many knowledgeable persons as practicable, including government officials, victims and their families, witnesses, human rights and other activists, scholars, and local leaders. Documentary evidence such as relevant laws, trial records, government documents, and even press reports is usually an essential supplement.

Here are some observations based on experiences of several human rights fact-finders:

INTERVIEWING

Interviewers, when preparing for an interview, consider who should conduct the interview; who will, if necessary, translate into and from the relevant language; where it should be held; how it should be recorded; what the interviewer needs to know before the encounter; and how it will be initiated.

During the first contact with an apparent victim or informant about a situation, the observer introduces herself/himself, briefly explains the mandate of the fact-finding operation, emphasizes the confidentiality of information received, and stresses the importance of obtaining as many details as possible to establish that there have been rights violations. The interviewer should be sensitive to the suffering an individual may have experienced as well as to the need to take steps to protect the individual's security, at least by keeping in touch, but without guaranteeing the individual's safety.

In general, it helps to have two interviewers. One interviewer can maintain eye contact and ask questions. The other interviewer can take notes and suggest missed questions. It may, however, be practically impossible to have two interviewers present for all or even most interviews. Also, if an interpreter is necessary, three individuals may be too large a group of listeners. In general, people are willing to be more candid when there are fewer people present.

Delegates choose interpreters carefully, checking their background to assure that the interview is not infiltrated by informers from the government. Interpreters often need to be protected from reprisal as well, just like the interviewer and witnesses.

The interpreter is asked to relay questions word for word to the extent possible. If questions are unclear or the witness seems not to understand them, the interviewer asks the interpreter to let the interviewer know, so that questions can be rephrased. The interviewer speaks in concise sentences, so that they are easy to understand and translate.

Human rights delegates also try to preserve the confidentiality of all sensitive information. Respect for confidentiality is essential because any breach of this principle might jeopardize seriously the person interviewed, the victim, and the organization conducting the investigation. Witnesses have been arrested, tortured, and killed for giving information to human rights monitors.

Delegates try to choose a location for the interview that will present the least risk of eavesdropping and possible retaliation against the witness. Risk arises in places such as hotels where interviews may be overheard and there is often a likelihood of surveillance. Places are chosen to raise the least suspicion among others who see the participants enter or see them talking. An ideal location establishes the proper atmosphere for the interview, permitting frank discussion without undue interruptions.

If security conditions permit, interviewers may consider the use of a tape recorder, particularly when there is only one interviewer and note taking is difficult. Also, tape recorders are helpful where translation/interpretation is needed. A delegate will only use a tape recorder, however, where the witness has developed a considerable degree of trust in the interviewer. The tape recorder should be introduced after the interviewer has established her/his credibility and reassured the witness about the objectives of the interview, confidentiality, and the need to assist the interviewer in recalling the information. The tape should not disclose the name of the witness, whose identity is recorded in another place and in a manner which helps assure that no connection can be made between the taped interview and the name of the individual. After the tape has been made, the tape is carefully safeguarded, so that it cannot be confiscated or be related easily to the witness.

Interviewers are very careful not to communicate through body language, facial expressions, or other means that they do not believe what they are being told. Instead, the interviewer will politely cross-examine the witness, asking questions in a slightly different manner, or otherwise seeking to get a fuller picture of consistent and inconsistent elements in the testimony.

Interviewers try to be patient with circular and repetitive statements, which are not logically ordered. Psycholinguists have learned that recall strategies are different from strategies for communicating. The witness will be using a recall strategy. The witness is given prompts to help that recall and it is the task of the interviewer later to communicate the material recalled into a logical presentation.

Interviewers also try to avoid leading questions, because the witness may be tempted to give the questioner only the information they want—rather than the truth.

In the interview report the interviewer ordinarily explains why they did or did not believe a witness' account. In considering issues of credibility, the interviewer considers several general observations. First, a person would not ordinarily take the time and risk to give an interview unless something serious had happened.

Second, many fact-finders consider a person to be credible if they are assertive and clear. A credible witness may have been neither clear nor assertive, however, due to feelings of powerlessness and traumatization. There is normally a core of important information which the interviewer needs to identify.

Third, individuals who have been traumatized often have difficulties with their memory. This problem of memory loss applies to all traumatized individuals and not just torture victims.

Fourth, the interviewer needs to be patient with a witness who is not very clear about time sequence. Many witnesses may not refer regularly to the calendar in their daily lives. They may need to be assisted by tying the events of concern to holidays or other remarkable days which are clearly fixed.

Fifth, the interviewer tries to identify the information from the witness which is consistent with the information from entirely independent sources. Many fact-finders consider that a fact cannot be established unless at least two witnesses give concordant testimony. The reliability of the witnesses and the experience of the interviewer with that reliability may be an important factor in assessing the veracity of information. Also, some witnesses may have evident biases and those biases need to be factored into the assessment of veracity.

TRIAL OBSERVATION

Trial observation is one of many types of fact-finding. International trial observers have been sent by governments and nongovernmental organizations to trials of political or human rights interest at least since the end of the 19th Century, when Queen Victoria sent the Lord Chief Justice of England to the Dreyfus trial. Observers attended significant trials in Nazi Germany during the 1930s and the 1956 Poznan trials in Poland. Given the several hundred trials observed during the past thirty-five years, it is fair to conclude that an international practice of sending and receiving trial observers has developed. The work of trial observers is based on the internationally recognized right to an open trial and does not impermissibly interfere in the domestic affairs of states.

The presence of international observers at a trial involving human rights issues can have a substantial impact on the fair treatment of the defendant. A visit for the purpose of trial observation makes known to the court, the government officials, and the public the international interest and concern for the trial in question. The delegate influences the court by maintaining an authoritative, impartial, and visible presence during the trial. At the same time, the observer can collect information on the nature of the charges, the law pertaining to the trial, and the manner in which the court conducts the trial. The observation may induce a fairer trial for the accused. Previous experience and comments of defense advocates in many parts of the world attest to the change in atmosphere in the court and facilities available to the defense resulting from observation.

The purposes of an observer mission usually are: (a) to prepare an independent, impartial, and objective report on the fairness of the trial, taking into account its legal, economic, and political context; (b) to help assure the defendant a fair trial through the influence of the observer; (c) to give the defense counsel, the defendant, and the defendant's supporters a sense of international concern; and (d) to express the sponsor's concern about the fairness of the proceedings without prejudging whether the trial is fair.

The observer conducts himself or herself with dignity, impartiality, independence, and humanitarian concern, keeping in mind the sensitive nature of trials and the objectives of the sponsoring organization. The trial is assessed under (1) the law of the country concerned, (2) any relevant human rights treaties, and (3) customary international law.

International organizations select trials for observation in light of the purposes outlined above, as well as the political or human rights significance of the proceedings, the media attention given the trial, the possible role of unjust laws, the political or cultural importance of the defendant, the invitation of the government involved, and the financial resources of the sponsor.

The principal factors to consider in choosing a trial observer include the individual's (a) prestige and reputation for impartiality; (b) knowledge of the legal system in which the trial will occur; (c) knowledge of the language in which the trial will be held; (d) availability on short notice; (e) appropriate nationality and other personal characteristics given the country where the trial will occur; (f) ability to enter the country of trial without a visa; (g) distance from the trial in terms of expense and traveling difficulty; (h) trustworthiness in following directions and familiarity with the sponsoring organization; (i) experience as a trial observer; and (j) knowledge of international human rights standards.

The observer makes contact, before trial if possible, with the defense attorney, prosecutor, and judge. The observer attempts to maintain an appearance of impartiality in balancing contacts with the defense and prosecution. It is helpful for the observer to arrange for an impartial and respected attorney (or if not, a defense attorney) to introduce him or her to the judge before proceedings begin. At this initial meeting the observer exchanges the usual courtesies, explains the purpose of the mission if asked, and makes arrangements for entry to the courtroom and for seating.

Depending upon the sponsor's instructions and the nature of the case, the observer may contact not only individuals who can facilitate matters such as entry into the courtroom, but also the Minister of Justice and other government officials who can provide background information, or who should be contacted as a courtesy. The observer will explain that he or she has been sent by the sponsoring organization to observe the trial and prepare a report, but that he or she does not (absent specific instructions or an official position) represent the organization in a more general capacity.

Also, the observer attempts to interview the defendant in a location that would permit maximum confidentiality while allowing the observer to ascertain the defendant's mental and physical state and the conditions of confinement.

In the absence of guidance from the sponsor, the observer will not make any public statements before the conclusion of the case, except as may be necessary to confirm to the press that he or she is a representative of the sending organization, that he or she is not authorized to make public statements before or during the trial, and that he or she will, upon completion of the mission, submit a report to the organization, to which all inquiries may be directed. In the absence of instructions to the contrary, if at the end of the trial there is a significant matter which calls for immediate comment, the observer ordinarily has discretion to make a statement to the press—preferably after leaving the country.

PRISON VISITS

Visits to prisons constitute one of the most difficult and sensitive fact-finding tasks. The International Committee of the Red Cross has the greatest experience in regard to prison visits and it is helpful to consult them when a visit is planned.

Basic principles for prison visits (drawn largely from ICRC experience) include the need to make regular, repeated visits to all prisons; the need to visit all detainees (unless there is a more limited objective in visiting the prison); the ability to speak with detainees freely and without witnesses; and the need to visit all places of detention in the country.

The ICRC generally visits only prisoners of war and "political prisoners," but not common law prisoners. It focuses on prisoners of war and political prisoners because they are more at risk, since they are considered to be "enemies" of the government. Only in exceptional cases does the ICRC work for the release of prisoners. In the large majority of cases, it is only interested in improving the prison conditions to prevent unnecessary suffering.

Delegates may announce a planned visit in advance to give the authorities an opportunity to improve conditions as much as possible. It may seem at first glance that such warning would give the authorities enough time to cover up any poor conditions, but the ICRC generally considers this effort an advantage. The Government's improvements will help the prisoners. *E.g.*, the government painted the whole prison blue just before the ICRC visit. The ICRC delegate's coat was marked by blue paint after the visit. The visitors are careful, however, to look out for "temporary improvements." In the Philippines, all the prisoners were restricted to their cells and not allowed to use basketball courts and other exercise equipment for the whole day before the visit, so that the prisoners were actually harmed by the visit. Hence, one of the questions which delegates may ask is: How does this day and the treatment you received differ from other days at the prison? Such "temporary improvements" may also be the subject of discussions with the warden/prison director at the end of the visit, so that such problems will not happen on future visits. To avoid such problems, the ICRC and other organizations also sometimes make surprise visits to prisons.

Before going to a prison, it would be helpful if the human rights delegates collect the names of some individuals who are thought to be held in the prison, so that they have particular individuals about whom they have independent information.

The delegation ordinarily includes a doctor and other persons who can assess the health of the prisoners as well as prison conditions. Several delegates can help compare notes during the visit and can defend each other. For prisons where women are detained, delegates should include women.

It is helpful for delegates to wear clothing which clearly distinguishes them from prison employees, as well as a badge or other clear indication of the organization they represent. The ICRC recommends that delegates not bring cameras, tape recorders, or similar instruments into the prison as such technology may raise suspicions in the authorities about the desire to publicize the information gathered.

On entering the prison the human rights delegates ordinarily discuss the visit with the prison governor, director, or warden. The delegates explain that they expect to visit all parts of the prison and to meet with all prisoners in confidence. In some prisons the guards will be cooperative. In others, the guards may be uncooperative and possibly even threatening with their weapons. It may be useful to carry letters of introduction from the government to help assure cooperation. Nonetheless, the human rights observers conduct themselves with confidence and self-assurance. They make it clear that they expect cooperation and that cooperation is the standard process.

Delegates ask the prison officials for a list of all prisoners held in the facility. If no such list exists, they consider whether it would be feasible to expend the considerable effort necessary to develop one during their visit including date of birth, other personal details, the charges against each individual, the date of detention, the date of the next expected judicial procedure, health problems, etc. In any case, the delegates encourage the prison authorities to keep such a list.

The delegates ask the authorities a series of standardized questions. The same questions are asked to the prisoners, so that trouble spots and inconsistencies can be identified.

The visit is conducted by the visiting human rights observers and not by the authorities. The observers decide which doors should be opened. (People who have previously been in the prison will be useful in finding hidden cells.) Delegates press for as much access as possible. Refusal to cooperate is communicated immediately to the headquarters of the observer mission, for prompt follow-up with the highest levels of government. If a delegate knows that a prisoner is being held in a cell and is in grave danger, but the authorities refuse to allow access, the observers may determine that s/he will not leave the facility until the door is opened, so as to save the life of the individual who is behind the door.

The ICRC also interviews groups of prisoner in their cells to get a sense of generally recognized problems. Then the ICRC may choose certain prisoners for individual interviews. Interviews with detainees take place without witnesses and at a spot decided by the delegates. The delegates try to identify a place which appears to be most secure from eavesdropping. Often the prison authorities will have prepared a particular room for interviewing. The delegates generally will not accept such offers. (In some countries there will be a danger of electronic eavesdropping. It is more likely, however, that eavesdropping will be done by a guard at the door or in some more direct fashion.) Sometimes interviews can be done in an unoccupied cell. (In other countries, it may be possible to do the interview in a courtyard or in the prisoner's own cell, but such locations may be too unsecure and may make the prisoner too nervous.) It is important to gain the confidence of the prisoner. The prisoner is likely to think that the observers are fake and have been planted by the authorities.

In most countries the first ICRC interview with a prisoner lasts about 20 minutes. It is the ICRC view that if the first interview lasts longer, the prisoner may get very excited about being able to talk to an outsider who may be able to help him. (Interviews may take longer because of the greater need to develop a sense of confidence and rapport.) Human rights observers try to be very patient with the prisoner interviews. The prisoners may not have had any other opportunity to tell their stories. The delegates also are prepared to hear very similar stories from each prisoner. Nonetheless, the prisoners have a real need to tell their own experiences.

They are likely to get very depressed at the end of a visit. The human rights observer may be the first visitor the prisoner has seen in a number of years.

A prison visit ends with another meeting with the prison director. At that point the delegates may request clarification of discrepancies between the initial information provided by the director and the information collected during the visit from observation and interviewing the prisoners. It is the ICRC practice to make preliminary suggestions for improvements and to offer assistance where appropriate (*e.g.*, blankets, disinfection of cells, mail services, or training of prison officers—to the extent those services are available. These kinds of services are provided routinely by the ICRC.) The delegates may also explain relevant international standards for the treatment of prisoners.

The ICRC practice has been to submit its written reports only to the government concerned and not to publish them unless the government publishes selective parts of a report. Then the ICRC may publish the whole report, as it did, for example, about several reports relating to Greece and Iran. The human rights observers will consider how they want to handle the publication of their reports. They may wish to treat prison reports more discretely than some of the other material they receive in order to build a level of trust between prison officials and the observer group. The observers may also communicate the formal report to those ministers in the de facto government responsible for prisons. The reports may be the subject of demarches to improve prison conditions. Publication may be used if the authorities are not sufficiently cooperative.

ELECTION OBSERVATION

Increasingly, IGOs, NGOs, and national governments have sent observers to monitor elections and other important national events. Delegations established for the purpose of observing elections function much as in trial observation, maintaining a neutral presence and gathering as much information as possible on the conduct of the elections. Election observation can also assist in assuring a fair election and can lead to a report on whether the election was free and fair. In addition to their political effect, election observers can affect rights related to elections, such as freedom of opinion and expression. As on-site observers, the delegates can also gain information on the general human rights situation in the country.

Most international organizations inform the government that election observers will be sent to monitor an upcoming election. Once the delegates arrive, they announce their presence publicly, emphasizing their objectivity and willingness to receive any information. They meet with government officials, party leaders, candidates, and election administrators. They also travel throughout the country, visiting as many polling locations as possible, because the most "fair" elections generally take place in the capital cities. Some election observers have departed from a purely neutral approach as observers, but give on-site advice and assistance prior to elections to improve the fairness of the process. Election observers, however, do not interfere with the election process itself. They instead take careful notes and report on the fairness of the election.

INVESTIGATIONS FOR A CRIMINAL TRIBUNAL

Some fact-finding investigations have the purpose of collecting information to be used as evidence in an international criminal court. Those operations differ from other human rights fact-finding, because the operation focuses on the perpetrator instead of the victim. Victim testimony plays a much smaller role, as many victims cannot identify perpetrators of the violations or the responsible authorities. These investigations are also more confidential than other fact-finding procedures. Further, there is often a higher level of proof for the evidence collected than is required for other types of fact-finding. In gathering the evidence it is helpful for fact-finders to work with the prosecutors and with forensic experts. The experts can identify the approximate date and means of killing, which can then be compared with testimony from witnesses. They may also be helpful, however, in identifying the victims or their ethnicity.

CONTACTS WITH GOVERNMENT OFFICIALS AND OTHER PURPOSES

Human rights delegations visiting government officials seek either to discuss the human rights situation with the government of the country visited or to present a report on the findings of a previous inquiry. Presenting a report can be the first step in improving human rights through recommendations from previous fact-finding, or it can be part of ongoing monitoring of compliance with human rights standards. As a part of fact-finding, trial observation, or other visits, the delegate usually wants to interview relevant officials to learn the government position on the matter in question. Government contacts are least likely to result in a report, unless combined with an element of fact-finding.

The range of purposes for other visits may vary with the human rights concern addressed. Previous visits have observed political demonstrations, interviewed refugees and visitors from other nations, or provided technical assistance in implementing recommendations for improving human rights conditions. On some visits, medical personnel have accompanied human rights lawyers to examine victims of torture for evidence. In addition, on-site visits are being used increasingly in connection with peace-keeping, humanitarian assistance, monitoring of police, etc.

NOTES AND QUESTIONS

1.   Problems that fact-finders encounter while conducting on-site observations include restrictions in travel caused by government authorities or dangerous conditions, other threats to safety of fact-finders or informants, unreliable information, reluctance of witnesses, unreported violations, and a lack of adequate training and resources for the fact-finders. ASIAN FORUM FOR HUMAN RIGHTS AND DEVELOPMENT, HANDBOOK ON FACT-FINDING AND DOCUMENTATION OF HUMAN RIGHTS VIOLATIONS (1994). What measures would you take to minimize the impact of such problems in Rwanda?

2.   Should there be different procedures for (1) a short-term or a long-term presence? (2) fact-finding by an IGO or NGO? (3) visits to prisons or refugee camps?

3.   For further reading on fact-finding investigations, see:

Amnesty International, *Political Killings and Disappearances: Medicological Aspects*, AI Index: ACT 33/36/93 (1993);

Douglas G. Anglin, *International Monitoring of the Transition to Democracy in South Africa, 1992-1994*, 94 AFRICAN AFFAIRS 519 (1995);

ASIAN FORUM FOR HUMAN RIGHTS AND DEVELOPMENT, HANDBOOK ON FACT-FINDING AND DOCUMENTATION OF HUMAN RIGHTS VIOLATIONS (1994);

KATHRYN ENGLISH & ADAM STAPLETON, THE HUMAN RIGHTS HANDBOOK, A PRACTICAL GUIDE TO MONITORING HUMAN RIGHTS (1995);

GUY S. GOODWIN-GILL, FREE AND FAIR ELECTIONS: INTERNATIONAL LAW AND PRACTICE (1994);

THE INTERNATIONAL HUMAN RIGHTS LAW GROUP, GUIDELINES FOR INTERNATIONAL ELECTION OB-SERVING (1984);

INTERNATIONAL LAW AND FACT-FINDING IN THE FIELD OF HUMAN RIGHTS (B.G. Ramcharan ed., 1982);

Diane Orentlicher, *Bearing Witness: The Art and Science of Human Rights Fact-Finding*, 3 HARV. HUM. RTS. J. 83 (1990);

HANS THOOLEN & BERTH VERSTAPPEN, HUMAN RIGHTS MISSIONS: A STUDY OF THE FACT-FINDING PRACTICE OF NON-GOVERNMENTAL ORGANIZATIONS (1986);

BERTH VERSTAPPEN, HUMAN RIGHTS REPORTS: AN ANNOTATED BIBLIOGRAPHY OF FACT-FINDING MISSIONS (1987);

David Weissbrodt, *International Factfinding in Regard to Torture*, 57 NORDIC J. INT'L L. 151 (1988);

David Weissbrodt & James McCarthy, *Fact-Finding by International Nongovernmental Human Rights Organizations*, 22 VA. J. INT'L L. 1 (1981).

---

3.   Analysis, Verification, Follow-Up, and Reporting

After information is gathered, observers often followup on individual cases. The first kind of follow-up is really part of the investigation, that is, to verify the information received. It is considered essential to verify the accuracy of the reported human rights violations before taking any steps, such as interventions with the authorities. Information is verified with any human rights organization or person having knowledge of the matter. Careful observation of the general human rights conditions in the country supplies the context in which to interpret the information gathered.

Delegates use a variety of procedures to verify the accuracy of the information they collect. For example, after interviewing a victim or witness to an incident, they may interview background witnesses such as family members, friends, neighbors, local authorities who may know of occurrences in the region, clergy members, or doctors. The most common method of ensuring the reliability of information is corroboration. Observers look for patterns of information from several independent sources.

Standards of admissibility are considered when verifying information. Fact-finding bodies have traditionally taken a broad approach and avoided the sort of restrictions on the admissibility of evidence normally recognized by common law courts. The necessary level of proof may differ depending on the organization and the potential follow-up actions. For example, an urgent appeal to a government without publicity in regard to a specific violation will be verified at a lower standard than evidence to be used in a criminal tribunal.

In addition to verifying the information, the observer consults with colleagues from the sponsoring organization before taking any follow-up actions. Consultation with other human rights organizations having knowledge of the situation may also be helpful.

Follow-up may include publication of reports, intervention with different levels of authorities, or a decision by a court or international tribunal. Some cases may be urgent and require prompt follow-up. In general, local and prompt interventions are made by the individual who performed the investigation, because they will be best informed about the case. In making interventions, observers are polite, but firm. They pursue the matter until there has been a satisfactory response from the authorities. If local interventions are not successful, or if a matter raises broader concerns, the fact-finding delegates inform the sending organization, who can appoint someone to make a presentation to the authorities at the highest levels and to which the observers can provide information.

The last step in the monitoring process is reporting. The collection of information has very little use unless it is communicated in writing. IGOs and NGOs prefer reports which are detailed, complete, accurate, careful, unbiased, and prompt. The urgency and use of the information may affect both the form and the nature of the report. The report of a specific case includes as much information as possible about the victim, the perpetrator, and the violation. More general reports about the broad human rights situation may indicate any recent increase, decrease, or stabilization in the number of various kinds of violations—including arbitrary arrests, killings, ill-treatment, etc.. Reports also include information about contacts with the authorities and other follow-up action taken or recommended. In addition, they reflect the terms of reference, efforts to validate the information, the level of proof used, and efforts to obtain comments from the government.

Publication and dissemination of a report usually are handled by the sending organization. Some international organizations wait to publish reports or make them otherwise available until the government has had an opportunity to comment on the finished report. Sometimes permission to review the report is made a condition for permission to conduct an on-site observation.

NOTES AND QUESTIONS

1.   For examples of reports see *Special Rapporteur: Report on the Situation of Human Rights in Rwanda,* U.N. Doc. E/CN.4/1995/7 (1995); *Special Investigations Unit: Final Report on the Genocide Investigation,* Apr. 12, 1995; *Special Rapporteur: Report on the Situation of Human Rights in Haiti,* U.N. Doc. E/CN.4/1993/47 (1993); *Report of the Independent Expert on El Salvador,* U.N. Doc. E/CN.4/1993/11 (1993); *Special Rapporteur: Report on the Situation of Human Rights in Iraq,* U.N. Doc. E/CN.4/1993/45 (1993); *Report of the Mission Dispatched by the Secretary-General on the Situation of Prisoners of War in the Islamic Republic of Iran and Iraq,* U.N. Doc. S/20147 (1988).

2.   For reading on the U.N.'s new activism in promoting and protecting human rights through on-site monitoring, humanitarian assistance, and peacekeeping, see:

Nancy C. Arnison, *The Law of Humanitarian Intervention, in* NEW STRATEGIES FOR A RESTLESS WORLD 37 (Harlan Cleveland ed., 1993);

Jost Delbruck, *A Fresh Look at Humanitarian Intervention Under the Authority of the United Nations,* 67 IND. L.J. 887 (1992);

WILLIAM DURCH, THE EVOLUTION OF UN PEACEKEEPING: CASE STUDIES AND COMPARATIVE ANALYSIS (1993);

David Forsythe & Kelly Pease, *Human Rights, Humanitarian Intervention, and World Politics,* 15 HUM. RTS. Q. 290 (1993);

Gregory Fox, *The Right to Political Participation in International Law,* 17 YALE J. INT'L L. 539 (1992);

Thomas Franck & Faiza Patel, *UN Police Action in Lieu of War: "The Old Order Changeth",* 85 AM. J. INT'L L. 63 (1991);

Kim Holmes, *New World Disorder: A Critique of the United Nations*, 46 J. INT'L AFF. 323 (1993);

HONORING HUMAN RIGHTS AND KEEPING THE PEACE: LESSONS FROM EL SALVADOR, CAMBODIA, AND HAITI (Alice Henkin ed., 1995);

A New Guardian to Protect Humanitarian Law, 2 TORTURE 63 (1992);

Report of the Secretary-General: An Agenda for Peace, U.N. Doc. A/47/277, S/24111 (1992);

---

4.   State Department Country Reports

Each year the State Department issues reports on human rights practices in nearly all countries of the world. The reports are the result of an extensive fact-finding process within the U.S. Government concerning human rights in all countries which are members of the U.N. or receive U.S. aid.

The Country Reports were initiated by a 1976 amendment to Section 502B of the 1961 Foreign Assistance Act that required the State Department to prepare a "full and complete report . . . with respect to practices regarding the observance of and respect for internationally recognized human rights in each country proposed as a recipient of security assistance." 22 U.S.C. § 2304(b). The initial report was published in 1977. DEPARTMENT OF STATE, COUNTRY REPORTS ON HUMAN RIGHTS PRAC-TICES FOR 1977, REPORT SUBMITTED TO THE SENATE COMMITTEE ON FOREIGN RELATIONS, 95th Cong., 1st Sess. (1977). It dealt with 82 countries receiving military assistance but not all 139 countries which had received arms exports from the United States. The report was criticized as being "vague, extremely general, and 'tactfully' drafted to protect the countries discussed." *See* David Weissbrodt, *Human Rights Legislation and United States Foreign Policy*, 7 GA. J. INT'L L. 231, 264 n.11 (1977). The first report stressed general historical, structural, and legalistic descriptions rather than specific human rights "practices."

The reports have improved immensely over the years, in both quantity and quality. Congress broadened the requirements in 22 U.S.C. § 2151n to include all U.N. members and nations receiving economic assistance. The 1994 report covered 193 nations, including a few which neither receive aid nor are U.N. members. While some of the individual reports may be criticized for hewing too close to U.S. foreign policy objectives, the State Department has over the years "become decidedly better informed and sensitized to human rights violations as they occur around the globe." COUNTRY REPORTS FOR 1988 at 1. In 1994 the Department describes its process as follows:

DEPARTMENT OF STATE, COUNTRY REPORTS ON HUMAN RIGHTS PRACTICES FOR 1994, 104th Cong., 1st Sess. 1269-70 (1995).

We base the annual Country Reports on Human Rights Practices on information available from all sources, including American and foreign government officials, victims of human rights abuse, academic and congressional studies, and reports from the press, international organizations, and nongovernmental organizations (NGO's) concerned with human rights. We find particularly helpful, and make refer-ence in most reports to, the role of NGO's, ranging from groups in a single country to those that concern themselves with human rights worldwide. While much of the information we use is already public, information on particular abuses frequently cannot be attributed, for obvious reasons, to specific sources.

By law, we must submit the reports to Congress by January 31 [of each year]. To comply, we provide guidance to United States diplomatic missions in September for submission of draft reports in October, which we update by year's end as necessary. Other offices in the Department of State provide contributions and the Bureau of Democracy, Human Rights, and Labor prepares a final draft. Because of the preparation time required, it is possible that year-end developments may not be fully reflected. We make every effort to include reference to major events or significant changes in trends.

We have attempted to make these country reports as comprehensive as space will allow, while taking care to make them objective and as uniform as possible in both scope and quality of coverage. We have given particular attention to attaining a high standard of consistency despite the multiplicity of sources and the obvious problems related to varying degrees of access to information, structural differences in political and social systems, and trends in world opinion regarding human rights practices in specific countries.

It is often difficult to evaluate the credibility of reports of human rights abuses. With the exception of some terrorist groups, most opposition groups and certainly most governments deny that they commit human rights abuses and often go to great lengths to cover up any evidence of such acts. There are often few eyewitnesses to specific abuses, and they frequently are intimidated or otherwise prevented from reporting what they know. On the other hand, individuals and groups opposed to a particular government sometimes have powerful incentives to exaggerate or fabricate abuses, and some governments similarly distort or exaggerate abuses attributed to opposition groups. We have made every effort to identify those groups (*e.g.*, government forces, terrorists, etc.) that are believed, based on all the evidence available, to have committed human rights abuses. Where credible evidence is lacking, we have tried to indicate why. Many governments that profess to oppose human rights abuses in fact secretly order or tacitly condone them or simply lack the will or the ability to control those responsible for them. Consequently, in judging a government's policy, it is important to look beyond statements of policy or intent in order to examine what in fact a government has done to prevent human rights abuses, including the extent to which it investigates, tries, and effectively punishes those who commit such abuses. We continue to make every effort to do that in these reports.

To increase uniformity, the introductory section of each report contains a brief setting, indicating how the country is governed and providing the context for examining the country's human rights performance. A description of the political framework and the role of security and law enforcement agencies with respect to human rights is followed by a brief characterization of the economy. The setting concludes with an overview of human rights developments in the year under review, mentioning specific areas (*e.g.*, torture, freedom of speech and press) in which abuses occurred.

* * * * *

The Lawyers Committee for Human Rights regularly issues reviews of the State Department reports. *See, e.g.*, LAWYERS COMMITTEE FOR HUMAN RIGHTS, CRITIQUE: REVIEW OF THE U.S. DEPARTMENT OF STATE'S COUNTRY REPORTS ON HUMAN RIGHTS PRACTICES FOR 1994 (1995). *See also* chapter 9, *infra*, for discussion of the Reports in the context of overall foreign policy.

For histories and analyses of the reports see Judith Innes, *Human Rights Reporting as a Policy Tool: An Examination of the State Department Country Reports, in* HUMAN RIGHTS AND STATISTICS: GETTING THE RECORD STRAIGHT 235 (Thomas Jabine &

Richard Claude eds., 1992); Kathleen Pritchard, *Human Rights Reporting in Two Nations: A Comparison of the United States and Norway, id.* at 259. Innes observes that the reports have come to be widely known and respected. Pritchard compares the U.S. reports with the Norwegian YEARBOOK and concludes that the YEARBOOK, covering only ten countries, offers more in-depth coverage than do the U.S. reports. The YEARBOOK is careful too in documenting its sources; the U.S. reports sometimes fail to attribute information to specific sources, casting some doubt on the reliability of the data.

For a look at another regularly published report see, *e.g.*, HUMAN RIGHTS IN DEVELOPING COUNTRIES, YEARBOOK 1994 (Peter Baehr, Hilde Hey, Jacqueline Smith, Theresa Swinehart eds., 1994).

E.   EXPERIENCE OF THE INTER-AMERICAN COMMISSION ON HUMAN RIGHTS

The Inter-American Commission has one of the most well-developed and respected procedures for on-site fact-finding. It has sponsored numerous on-site observations in conjunction with the investigation of human rights in member states. The U.N. Commission on Human Rights, through its Special Rapporteurs and Working Groups, has also been active in on-site fact-finding. In contrast, many other human rights bodies, such as the Human Rights Committee and the European Commission on Human Rights, largely rely for factual information on materials submitted by governments and other interested organizations and persons. Even the Inter-American Commission often engages in that type of "passive" fact-finding when investigating individual petitions, as illustrated in the readings of chapter 10.

The first two readings in this section illustrate the Inter-American Commission's procedures for on-site fact-finding in connection with the Commission's visit to Argentina in 1980. The first reading is an excerpt from the report the Commission prepared based on the information it gathered during its visit. The second reading is a description of an incident which occurred during the visit.

Inter-American Commission on Human Rights (IACHR), Report on the Situation of Human Rights in Argentina at 1-12, 221-234, O.A.S. Doc. OEA/Ser.L/V/II.49, doc. 19 corr. 1 (1980) (footnotes omitted):

Introduction

A. *Background*

1.   In recent years, both before and after the March 1976 military takeover, the IACHR has received denunciations of serious violations of human rights in Argentina, which it has processed according to its regulations. In addition, on a number of occasions, it has informed representatives of the Argentine Government of its concern about the increase in the number of denunciations, and about information received from various sources that comprises a pattern of serious, generalized and systematic violations of basic human rights and freedoms.

2.   In light of this situation, the IACHR decided to prepare the present report, and when it informed the Argentine Government of this decision, the Commission also advised it of its interest in conduct[ing] an on-site observation in Argentina, in the belief that this is the most suitable method of determining precisely and

objectively the status of human rights in a particular country at a particular time in history.

3. In a Note dated December 18, 1978, the Argentine Government extended an invitation to the IACHR to conduct an on-site observation, pursuant to its regulations . . ..

B. *Activities of the Commission during its on-site observation* . . .

2. The on-site observation began on September 6, and was completed on September 20, 1979. The Commission's first step upon arrival in Buenos Aires was to [issue] a press release. . . .

a. *Interviews with public authorities*:

From September 7 through September 20, the Commission met with [various government authorities, including: the President, the members of the military junta, several government ministers, the President of the Supreme Court of Justice, the members of the Federal Chamber of Appeals, a federal judge, and selected governors and military officials.]

The members of the Commission explained the objectives of the mission to all these officials, and received offers of full cooperation from the authorities.

b. *Former Presidents of the Republic*

The Commission felt it advisable to visit all the former presidents of Argentina to discuss the status of human rights in the country. . . .

c. *Interviews with major religious figures . . .*
The Commission . . . had the opportunity to talk with representatives of various religious groups.

d. *Human rights organizations*
In the afternoon of Friday, September 7, the Commission held separate meetings with Argentine human rights organizations, including: the Permanent Assembly for Human Rights; the Argentine League for Human Rights; the Ecumenical Movement for Human Rights; the Mothers of the Plaza de Mayo, and the leaders of the group called Families of "the Disappeared" and Persons detained for Political Reasons (*Familiares de Desaparecidos y Detenidos por Razones Políticas*).
In the days following, the Commission received other groups and delegations from a number of cities in the interior of the country, who had traveled to meet it. . . .

e. *Representatives of political organizations*
[The Commission met with various representatives.]

f. *Professional associations*
The Commission exchanged views with the Argentine Federation of Bar Associations, and with the Buenos Aires Bar Association. These institutions received the Commission in their headquarters on September 8 and September 13, respectively.
The Commission discussed a number of aspects of the legal profession during a visit at its offices from a group of defense lawyers and trade union lawyers.
Meetings were also held with [professional associations of architects, physicians, engineers, and psychologists.]

g. *Trade-union organization[s] and syndicates*
[The Commission met with various representatives.]

h. *Commercial, industrial and business entities*
The Commission met with representatives . . .

i. *Other meetings held* . . .
[T]he Commission met with a number of other individuals whose testimony it was particularly interested in hearing. These included meetings with the author Ernesto Sábato; the trade union leader Lorenzo Miguel; the journalist Jacobo Timerman, and the trade union leader Professor Alfredo Brazo.

Lastly, on Tuesday, September 18, the Commission met with the director or representatives of the mass communications media to discuss the topic of freedom of the press.

j. *Investigation of certain cases*
In the cities of Buenos Aires, Córdoba, La Plata and Rosario, the Commission did some investigative work inherent in the on-site observation, and received individuals and groups interested in stating problems or filing denunciations about human rights violations.

k. *Detention centers*
The Commission visited [various prisons and police stations].

l. *Denunciations received*
In its initial press release, the Commission invited all persons who considered that any of their rights, as defined in the American Declaration, had been violated, to submit the corresponding denunciation.

Members of the public were received in Buenos Aires (in the offices on Avenida de Mayo 760) from Friday, September 7, to Saturday, September 15. In Córdoba, denunciations were received in the Hotel Crillón from September 10 through September 14, and in the city of Tucumán, in the Hotel Versailles, on April 14 and 15.
. . .

4. The Argentine Government cooperated with the Commission at all times, provided it with all the facilities it needed for its work, and repeated its commitment to take no reprisals against persons or institutions who provided the Commission with information, testimony, or evidence of whatever nature. . . .

5. On Thursday, September 20, the full Commission met for the second and last time with the President, Lieutenant General (Retired) Jorge Rafael Videla, who was accompanied by the Ministers of the Interior and of Foreign Affairs. In light of its importance, the Commission at that time delivered to the President a document containing preliminary recommendations, the text of which appears below:

RECOMMENDATIONS OF THE
INTER-AMERICAN COMMISSION ON HUMAN RIGHTS TO THE
GOVERNMENT OF ARGENTINA

The Inter-American Commission on Human Rights, on the occasion of its on-site observation to the Republic of Argentina, takes the liberty of making the following preliminary recommendations to the Government of Argentina:

I. *The Disappeared*:

The Commission believes that the problem of the disappeared is one of the most serious human rights problems that Argentina faces. The Commission thus recommends the following:

a) That detailed information be provided on the status [of] the disappeared persons, understood to mean those persons who have been apprehended in operations in which, because of the conditions in which they took place and because of their characteristics, it is presumed that the state authorities participated.

b) That the necessary instructions be given to the proper authorities that minors who have disappeared as a result of the detention of their parents and other relatives, and children born in detention centers, whose where-abouts are unknown, be handed over to their natural parents or other close family members.

c) That the relevant measures be adopted to discontinue the procedures that have led to the disappearance of persons. In this regard, the Commission notes that cases of this nature have occurred recently, and should be clarified as soon as possible, as should all the other cases.

II. *Persons detained under orders of the Executive ("PEN"), and the right to exercise one's option to leave the country*:

The Commission learned of the status of persons detained under orders of the Executive, and of the procedures for exercising the right of option to leave the country. The Commission recommends the following in this regard:

a) That the power granted to the Head of State under Article 23 of the Constitution, which authorizes the detention of persons during a State of Siege, be made subject to a test of reasonable cause, and that such detentions not be extended indefinitely.

b) That, as a result, the following persons, detained at the disposal of the Executive (PEN) be released:

i. Those who have been detained without reasonable cause for a prolonged period, in order that the preventive detention itself not become the pun-ishment, which may only be imposed by the Judiciary;

ii. Those who have been acquitted or who have already completed their sentences;

iii. Those who are eligible for parole, provided they have been sentenced.

c) That the exercise of the right of option to leave the country be completely restored, so that the processing of applications not be delayed in any way that might hinder the actual exercise of this right.

III. *Methods of Investigation*:

The Commission recommends the following with regard to methods of investigation:

That there be an in-depth investigation of denunciations concerning the use of torture and other illegal uses of force in the interrogation procedures used on detainees, that those responsible for such acts be punished with the full force of the law, and that the necessary measures be taken to prevent the use of such measures.

IV. *Prison System*:

The Commission recommends the following with respect to the prison system:

That the relevant measures be taken to ensure that detainees in some penitentiaries no longer be deprived of the conditions for their physical and mental health, such as sunlight, reading and physical exercise, that excessive time spent in cells be reduced, and that punishment not be imposed for trivial infractions.

V.   *Military Jurisdiction*:

The Commission recommends the following with respect to persons who are in the process of being tried and sentenced by military tribunals:

a)   That persons brought to trial before military tribunals be assured of due process guarantees particularly the right to a defense by an attorney of the defendant's choosing.

b)   That a Commission of qualified jurists be appointed to study the trials conducted by military tribunals during the state of siege, and which would be authorized to make pertinent recommendations in those cases where due process guarantees were lacking.

VI.   *Guarantees of due process and fair trials*:

The Commission recommends the following with regard to the due process guarantees and fair trials:

a)   That guarantees and facilities be provided to judges so that they may effectively investigate cases of persons detained under the security laws.

b)   That the guarantees essential for an effective defense by attorneys providing legal services to defendants be granted.

Buenos Aires, Federal Capitol
September 20, 1979

6.   On September 20, the Commission concluded its on-site observation in Argentina and issued its final press release.

C.   *Methodology*

1.   In preparing this report, the IACHR used information obtained through its own resources, both before, during, and after the on-site observation. Special consideration was given to denunciations, testimonies and information received by the IACHR or by the Special Commission that visited Argentina, which were used in preparing the present document, although the report is not merely an aggregate of these denunciations, testimonies and information.

Careful study also was given to the Argentine legal system, the body of laws handed down by domestic courts and the applicable international human rights instruments. The IACHR consulted various documents that directly or indirectly deal with the status of human rights in Argentina or in some way enable the Commission to increase its understanding of the recent history of that country, which included documents prepared by the Argentine Government and by various Argentine organizations.

2.   The IACHR also wishes to record that during its on-site observation, in addition to the information provided by governmental authorities, it received information and heard from officials of institutions representing all sectors of Argentine society, and also heard from all the individuals who wished to submit complaints or testimony on the Argentine human rights situation.

3.   The present report takes into consideration the Argentine Government's observations dated February 29, 1980, on the preliminary report, which had been

approved by the Commission, and delivered to the Argentine Government, on December 14, 1979.

The Commission considers it appropriate to make some general comments about those observations, particularly in relation to the individual case histories included in the present report.

In the judgment of the Commission, these case histories are used to illustrate various topics and situations discussed in the report, and an attempt was made to use them in order to present with greater objectivity the situation of human rights in Argentina.

The Commission wishes to point out that its presentation of these case histories does not necessarily entail any prejudgment of them, in those instances where the Commission has not yet taken a resolution. Each individual case mentioned in the present report has been or will be processed according to the Commission's Regulations. The end of the process in each case is a statement or resolution on the merits.

The IACHR has already adopted a resolution on some individual cases included in the present report. In cases where the Argentine Government has requested a reconsideration, careful study has been made of the cases in the light of new information supplied by the Government; if they are still included, it is because, in the opinion of the Commission, reconsideration of the case was not justified.

In cases where the Commission has decided to include a denunciation which has not yet been completely processed, it is because the Commission has decided, on the basis of the available evidence, that the charges are *prima facie* true, particularly in cases where the observations of the Argentine Government do not permit the denunciation to be refuted.

Moreover, the report contains not only individual cases, but also refers to information and documents received during the on-site observation, which was conducted precisely in order to collect such information.

With respect to the information collected during the on-site observation, the IACHR considered that the proper procedural moment to make it known to the Government, was, of course, in the preliminary report itself; this gave the Government the opportunity to make whatever observations it considered appropriate.

It should also be noted that in each of the case histories recorded—which are identified in this report by number—the IACHR informed the Argentine Government of the case prior to the Commission's approval of the report, and that in each case, the Government has had an opportunity to make such comments and observations as it considered appropriate.

4. Finally, the Commission wishes to note that in transcribing the pertinent parts of the denunciations contained in the report, it was decided to omit the names of those public officials or security agents who were accused of human rights violations, in cases where the Commission had no direct information. However, the Commission is confident that such an omission will not prevent the Argentine Government from taking the necessary measures, in accordance with its domestic laws, to investigate these denunciations, and in the event abuses or crimes are proven, to punish those responsible with the full force of the law.

[The following excerpt from the report illustrates how the Commission outlined the violations it investigated.]

. . . C. *Military Tribunals*

1. . . . The very day of the military takeover, Law 21.264 was promulgated. This

law creates Special Standing Military Tribunals throughout all of Argentina . . .. [T]hese special tribunals have the power to pass judgment on crimes covered in this law. . . .

On the same date, March 24, 1976, the Military Junta stated that as of 1:00 p.m. of that day, personnel of the security forces, police and penitentiary forces, both national and provincial, were under military jurisdiction. . . .

2.   During its on-site observation, the Commission confirmed the complaints submitted to it to the effect that a large number of persons detained for subversive activity had been judged and sentenced by military courts. The sentences were as high as 25 years in prison.

The alleged criminals were not allowed to choose their own defense attorneys but were assigned official military defenders who are not licensed lawyers. These circumstances and the fact that civilians were made subject to military jurisdiction under the prevailing legislation were serious infringements of the right to defense inherent in due process.

The Commission flagged its concern about this matter with the national authorities. It also heard the ideas of experts in this field. These experts all agreed that both the military courts and trials for which they assumed responsibility were unconstitutional; they said they did not know of any cases in which civil attorneys had been allowed to participate. These situations violate basic provisions of the Constitution. . . .

D.   *Guarantees of Administration of Justice*

1. . . . As will be explained further on, . . . fundamental guarantees of the administration of justice have been seriously violated in Argentina. Protection of these guarantees is taken up in the American Declaration of the Rights and Duties of Man and in the Argentine Constitution itself. Among these guarantees the following should be mentioned:

2.   a.   *Nullum crimen, nulla pena, sine lege* (no crime, no penalty, without law) is provided in Article No. XXV of the American Declaration and Article 18 of the Argentine Constitution. The latter reads as follows: "No inhabitant of the Nation may be punished without a prior judgment pursuant to a law which antedates the trial. . .".

Despite the express norms implementing this juridical principle, the Military Government, in the Act of Institutional Responsibility, expressly abrogated this principle, establishing explicit[l]y the retroactivity of these norms in referring to prior actions, and in establishing in Article 1, that: "The Military Junta assumes the function and responsibility of considering the conduct of those persons who have prejudiced the national interest by having committed. . .".

3.   b.   *Declaration of Presumption of Innocence*, is provided for in Article XXVI of the American Declaration. This principle was eliminated as a judicial guarantee by Law 21.460 which gave the Armed Forces and security personnel the power to detain persons suspected of crimes of subversion against which they have "half proof" of their guilt, and to institute against them the corresponding proceedings, whenever they have knowledge of that "half proof:" . . .

4.   c.   *Right to an impartial trial*. This elementary and basic principle, expressly recognized by Article XXVI of the American Declaration of the Rights and Duties of Man, has been the subject of much testimony and information received by the Commission. According to this information, the Military Courts composed of

officers involved in the repression of the same crimes they are judging, do not offer guarantees of sufficient impartiality. This is aggravated by the fact that in a military court, the defense is in the hands of a military officer, meaning, that the defense is taken over by a person who is also part of, and has strong disciplinary ties to, the same force responsible for investigation and repressing the acts with which the accused is charged.

5. d. *Right to be brought to trial within a reasonable time.* This guarantee, as stipulated in Article XVIII of the American Declaration of the Rights and Duties of Man, is not enforced in Argentina, because, as the great majority of the complaints involving detainees show, the corresponding appeals generally are not resolved opportunely. . . .

NOTES AND QUESTIONS

The Argentine government challenged the report, claiming that it exaggerated the overall problem and gave a false impression of conditions in Argentina. Nonetheless, Argentina at an OAS meeting in November 1980 reported actions taken to improve the situation. *See* DEPARTMENT OF STATE, COUNTRY REPORTS ON HUMAN RIGHTS PRACTICES FOR 1980, 97th Cong., 1st Sess., 337-38 (Joint Comm. Print 1981).

THOMAS BUERGENTHAL, ROBERT NORRIS, & DINAH SHELTON, PROTECTING HUMAN RIGHTS IN THE AMERICAS: SELECTED PROBLEMS, 179-81 (1986):

2. Discovering Disappeared Persons: A Staff Member's Notes [Ed.: written by a staff member of the Inter-American Commission.]

According to the Executive Secretary of the [Inter-American] Commission, the government of Argentina had declared that there were no political prisoners in Córdoba. Therefore, during the course of the [Commission's] visit, I was not to visit the Cárcel Penitenciaria in that city; however, I had requested my liaison with the Ministry of Foreign Affairs to provide me with a list of all the prisoners held in the provinces of Córdoba and Tucumán.

Upon arriving in Córdoba on September 7, I arranged to speak with the Minister of Government of that Province with regard to my mission and to the plans I would make for the visit of two Members of the Inter-American Commission scheduled to arrive several days later. I explained that we had no plans to visit the penitentiary, but that Commissioners often changed their minds and we should be aware of that possibility. On the basis of previous experience, I described very briefly our normal procedure for visiting jails and other detention centers. The Members would meet with the prison authorities for a briefing, prior to a tour of the locale. They would be interested in interviewing any prisoners who might have a case before the Commission, and they would probably select several prisoners at random for personal interviews with regard to prison conditions. Those interviews would take place in private, and the Members of the Commission might require a temporary office for the purpose. I reminded him that I had requested an alphabetized list of the prisoners in the Province of Córdoba and would need it as soon as possible.

As I conducted interviews with petitioners during the next few days, I was informed of the names of several persons who were allegedly being held in the Cárcel Penitenciaria for political reasons. Without mentioning this information, I called the Minister of Government to advise him that the Members would visit the prison and would need the list previously requested.

When the list finally arrived, I carefully went over the names, searching for the "political" cases reportedly detained at the penitentiary. One fact stood out; not one of those names was on the list! I then called a private individual who I knew could make contact with one of the prisoners and asked him to try to obtain a list of all the persons held in the same cellblock. He was only partially successful; he could not get all the names, but he did bring back several, along with the exact number of men and women being held there. Again I checked the list and none of those names were on it. It was an exciting moment; I had a "gut feeling" that some of those people were "disappeared," and the mission had yet to uncover any of the thousands of people who had been abducted and literally dropped from sight. I was afraid at the same time that someone might tip the authorities off and the prisoners would be moved before the visit of the Commissioners.

The prisoners sent word through my contact that they were worried about the confidentiality of the interviews. They were afraid of being overheard, and they were also afraid that the government might take advantage of the announced visit to send a "fake party", as it had allegedly done in that prison some months before under the guise of a Red Cross visit.

I replied, again through the contact, that I would bring plenty of paper and pens in my briefcase so they would not have to talk. They would be sure that it was an official visit by the Commission by asking "Are you Dr. . . ."? My only reply would be to take out my official OAS passport and show them. Any verbal reply should put them on guard.

When the Members of the Commission did arrive, I briefed them on the situation and provided them with a memorandum on how we should proceed if they wished to visit the penitentiary. They accepted and asked me to finalize the arrangements.

On September 13, I accompanied Professor Carlos Dunshee de Abranches (Brazil) and Dr. Luis Tinoco Castro (Costa Rica) to the penitentiary. In our preliminary briefing by the Director of the prison, Professor Abranches asked for a general explanation of prison rules affecting the inmates. When the Director had finished speaking about visiting rights, Professor Abranches inquired whether all prisoners had the same rights. The reply was affirmative. He then noted that, "according to Dr. . . . [the staff member] there is a sign in one part of the prison which refers to "special prisoners". "We have a complete list of the names of those prisoners, eleven women and thirty-one men, but it is an unofficial list, and we would like to have an official list before we visit that cellblock."

We had no such list, of course, but the fact we knew the exact number must have convinced them that we did. The Director turned to one of his assistants and asked: "Didn't you give them a list of the special prisoners"? "No sir." "Oh, I see. You didn't give them a list of the special prisoners!"

There followed a long moment of silence. Professor Abranches interrupted: "Since there are only a few names involved, we will simply wait here while the list is prepared." The Director then asked an assistant to bring a list. It only required a few minutes as a list was apparently brought from a file in another room. I could hardly believe my eyes. It was a bonanza, containing not only the names, but under whose disposition. Only seven had been presented before a court of law. Many of the others were at the orders of special councils of war, meaning they were being held indefinitely. Most were held by executive decree, but three were at the orders of the local military commandant. Those three had "disappeared" in the typical fashion just a month before!

When we reached the women's section, we asked to be allowed behind the bars into a large area which served as a dining hall. On the other side of the dining area was a long corridor with tiny cells on either side. We asked that the prisoners be released from their cells, and the Director complied. Not all of the women were accounted for. Professor Abranches shouted down the corridor: "Is anyone else there"? We heard a scream "We're here, we're here" and a hand emerged from a small opening in the door of the very last cell on the right. We had "found" two disappeared persons—Irma Cristina Guillen de Palazzesi and Stella Maria Palazzesi de Cavigliasso. The other women later told us that they had been warned not to mention the presence of the two prisoners being held incommunicado. They were not allowed to talk to them at all.

We left Dr. Tinoco to talk to the women and we continued with the Director to the men's section upstairs. There was another surprise in store. Professor Abranches told the prison officials, "Now that we are here, we'll just stay in the cellblock and interview the prisoners here." "But you can use my office; it's all prepared," blurted the Director. "Tell us who you want to see, and we'll take him to the office where you'll have all the facilities necessary." "No, thank you very much," said Professor Abranches, "we'll stop and see you on the way out!"

Again, we had the prisoners released from their cells, into the dining area, which was also behind bars. The guards withdrew, I brought out the paper and pens and explained what type of information we wanted. When everyone had finished, I took a small tape recorder from by briefcase, chose a cell at random, and interviewed a group of prisoners on general prison conditions. . . .

NOTES AND QUESTIONS

Was it a good idea for Commission members to reveal this incident to the public? What potential advantages and disadvantages might the revelation have created for future fact-finding missions?

Inter-American Commission on Human Rights, Case 9265 Inter-Am. C.H.R. 113, OEA/Ser.L/V/II.66, doc. 10 rev. 1 (1985):

[Ed.: The Commission ordinarily engages in "passive" fact-finding when it examines individual petitions. As this case illustrates, though, the Commission occasionally undertakes on-site fact-finding in connection with its consideration of individual petitions.]

BACKGROUND

1. On December 6, 1983, the Inter-American Commission on Human Rights received the following complaint and forwarded it to the Government of the Republic of Suriname for its observations:

> We have received the names of the following people reportedly arrested during the past two weeks and detained at Fort Zeelandia Military Police headquarters:

Iwan Rajwinderpersad Gobardhan, aged 27.
Omprakash (Oemperkash) Gobardhan, aged 24, Dutch citizen.
Krishnapersad Gobardhan, aged 21, reportedly badly beaten; present at the arrest of his brother-in-law (below).
Ramlall Bekaroe, aged 27, brother-in-law of above brothers.

Harden Kasi, aged 21.

Mrs. Ch. Doerga, aged 40 arrested on 27 November at Nickerie.

K. P. Doerga, aged 24, arrested on 27 November at Nickerie.

Parents of Mrs. Doerga, above; mother reported to suffer from diabetes and may die if she does not receive medication.

Mr. Alibux (not Prime Minister).

Radiksjoen (spelling uncertain).

Austen, businessman.

Linveld.

On 29 November 1983, the Suriname authorities announced that they had arrested ten people during the previous week on suspicion of plotting a coup against the Government. They are reportedly being held for questioning at Fort Zeelandia Military headquarters. Other reports alleged that up to 69 people, mainly from the Indian (Hindustani) community have been arrested during this period. We have received reports that some of those arrested have been beaten while in custody.

A further report was received from a refugee arriving in Holland that for the past 2-3 weeks four bodies were kept under military guard in the Paramaribo mortuary. Bodies rumoured to include Imro Themen and Henk Essed (leader of People's Militia, dismissed three weeks ago).

Two of those arrested—Omprakash Gobardhanand Linveld above—appeared on Suriname television on 29 November at a press conference given by the Deputy Commander of the Military Police, Sergeant Major Zeeuw. The two men 'confessed' to their involvement in the attempted coup. The Government has accused those involved of having distributed anti-government leaflets and of setting fire to Government buildings, reportedly in preparation for an invasion by mercenaries.

We are concerned for the safety of those in custody, in view of the past treatment of people arrested on suspicion of plotting coups in Suriname. We urge the Government to grant those detained protection of right to life and humane treatment.

2.   On March 20, 1984, the Commission received the following response from the Government of Suriname and forwarded it to the complainant for his observations:

According to information from the Attorney-General to the Court of Justice in Suriname, the accused persons referred to in the appendix were brought up before the Chief-Prosecutor, Mr. A.I. Ramnewash LI.D., by the Military Police on 10 December 1983. In respect of the accused I. Bissumbar and H. Kasie, an order for their release was issued when they were brought in for the second hearing on 20 December 1983. On January 3, 1984 the case was referred to the examining magistrate for a preliminary judicial examination.

In regard to the rumour that there would be bodies placed under military guard, in respect of which the names of Mssrs. Imro Themen and Henk Essed have been mentioned, we wish to comment as follows: Mr. Imro Themen is at present a civil servant employed at the Ministry of General Affairs, while Mr. Henk Essed was recently on vacation in the United States of America.

The Government of Suriname deplores the fact that your Commission is being supplied with incomplete and incorrect information, and cannot resist the impression that insinuations in this respect are made on purpose, evidently with the intention to discredit our country with your organization. We take the most definite exception to this. . . .

3.   Subsequently the following additional information was received and transmitted by the Government for its comments:

Arrest of Political Opponents on 24 November 1983:

Names:

1.   Gobardhan, Iwan Rajinderpersad

Born on 22 November 1956.
2. Gobardhan, Omprakash
Born on 5 August 1960.
3. Gobardhan, Krishnapersad
Born on 22 April 1962.
4. Bekaroe, Ramlall
Born on 16 December 1950.
5. Kasi, Harden
Born on 12 October 1962.
6. Doerga, Lila
7. Doerga, Krishna
8. Lindveld, Karel
9. Oudsten

On 24 November 1983 these Surinamese citizens were arrested and transported to Fort Zeelandia by armed men in civilian clothes. This was kept secret. Even when relatives went to the military police they denied having arrested the above-mentioned people.

In December 1983 Omprakash Gobardhan and Lindveld were interrogated on TV in the presence of the press including the Dutch media.

Only military Police Commander Liew Yen Tair put a few questions to the prisoners, who had to answer with a yes or no. The press was not allowed to ask questions. On the film the expression of fear and terror could be seen clearly on their faces. In this 'show' the Council was accused of destabilizing activities in Suriname and sending mercenaries to Suriname. However, all persons who had been arrested had Surinamese nationality.

Mrs. Lila Doerga is a diabetic but she could not take any medicine.

In February, the prisoners were put under custody of the civil police. It is reported that in the meantime Karsi, Lila Doerga, and Krishna Doerga have been released.

The others prisoners are still held. Most probably they will appear before the court on June 14, 1984.

4. On July 27, 1984 the Commission received the further observations of the Government of Suriname. The pertinent parts of the observations read as follows:

Referring to Your letter of July 5, 1984, Case 9265, I have the honour to inform You as follows: . . .

Mr. Harden Kasi, Mrs. Lila Doerga, Mr. Krishna Doerga, and Mr. R. Oudsten were not prosecuted and have been released.

Mr. Iwan R. Gobardhan was sentenced to 1 year and 6 months, with reduction of the time of his pre-trial detention.

Mr. O. Gobardhan was sentenced to 2 years with reduction of the time of his pre-trial detention.

Mr. Ramlall Bekaroe was sentenced to 1 year with reduction of the time of his pre-trial detention.

Mr. Karel Lindveld was sentenced by the judge in the first circuit (Kanton) to 1 year and by the judge in the third circuit (Kanton) to 2 years. In both cases his time was reduced with the time of his pre-trial detention.

In case Your Secretariat would like to receive a copy of the above-mentioned judiciary decisions, please feel free to notify us.

5. Subsequently, on November 5, 1984 the Government of Suriname sent photostatic copies of the sentences handed down by the Court on Mssrs. Krisnapersad Gobardhan, Iwan Gobardhan, and Karel Lindveld.

6. On January 9, 1985 a special commission of the IACHR interviewed certain

eyewitnesses to the detention of the subjects of this case and heard testimony to the effect that they were tortured at the outset of their incarceration, in some cases lasting several months, and effectively denied legal counsel until the day before their trials in July of 1984, more than seven months after their arrest. The tortures included severe beatings over their entire bodies including their sex organs. These usually took place at night either in Fort Zeelandia or Membre Boekoe Kazerne. Specific mistreatment also included the placing of a chair leg on the victims's outstretched hand while the torturer jumped on the chair. Another technique consisted of forcing the prisoner to drink a liquid that burned the drinker's throat. The torture also included punches, kicks and beatings with clubs and rifle butts. The Commission saw evidence on a number of the victims of broken teeth, noses, legs, collarbones and assorted scars. One had been tied to a car and dragged. Several had been forced to sign confessions.

Psychological torture included the firing of machine guns at the victims' feet. Threats were also made against the wives, mothers and other relatives of the victims. On one occasion several of the victims were forced to lie in freshly dug graves in a local cemetery and threatened with summary execution. One of the victims was subject to an attempted homosexual rape by a military policeman.

7. On January 16, 1985 the special commission of the IACHR visited Santo Boma Penitentiary outside of Paramaribo. There it interviewed a number of prisoners including four who are the subjects of this case.

8. The Commission has verified that most of the subjects of this case have been released.

9. From independent eyewitnesses the Commission received testimony that the torturers included [certain] Surinamese military personnel . . ..

10. The special commission of the IACHR met with certain military authorities during its on-site visit in Suriname and discussed these accusations of torture and denial of due process. Colonel Liew Yen Tair and Sgt. Major Zeeuw denied the allegations of torture and stated that the decree laws in force under the state of siege permit prolonged detention without judicial warrant and without benefit of counsel by the military police. As to the injuries reported by the victims, the officers indicated that these occurred because the subjects had resisted arrest.

CONSIDERING:

1. That the Government of Suriname has made no response to the Commission regarding the alleged beatings and torture of the subjects of this case.

2. That the decree laws currently in force in Suriname that deal with due process of law *prima facie* violate this non-derogable right.

3. That the American Declaration of the Rights and Duties of Man to which the Government of Suriname is bound as a member state of the Organization of American States, *inter alia*, provides:

Article I. Every human being has the right to life, liberty and the security of his person.

Article XVIII. Every person may resort to the courts to ensure respect for his legal rights. There should likewise be available to him a simple, brief procedure whereby the courts will protect him from acts of authority that, to his prejudice, violate any fundamental constitutional rights.

Article XXV.   No person may be deprived of his liberty except in the cases and according to the procedures established by pre-existing law.

Every individual who has been deprived of his liberty has the right to have the legality of his detention ascertained without delay by a court, and the right to be tried without undue delay or otherwise to be released. He also has the right to humane treatment during the time he is in custody.

Article XXVI.   Every accused person is presumed to be innocent until proved guilty.

Every person accused of an offense has the right to be given an impartial and public hearing, and to be tried by courts previously established in accordance with pre-existing laws, and not to receive cruel, infamous or unusual punishment.

4.   That the oral testimony of the various non-military eye-witnesses interviewed by the Commission regarding the torture of the subjects of this case and the denial of due process coincide in their essential aspects and corroborate the original complaint and are deemed to be credible by the Commission.

5.   That the physical evidence viewed by the Commission in Suriname and abroad bearing on the allegations under consideration tend to corroborate the original complaint insofar as torture and denial of due process are concerned.

6.   That the denial of said allegations by the military authorities cited above is deemed by the Commission to be unpersuasive.

THE INTER-AMERICAN COMMISSION ON HUMAN RIGHTS, RESOLVES:

1.   To declare that the Government of Suriname violated the human rights of the subjects of this case notwithstanding the fact that some were ultimately released from custody.

2.   To observe that the violations in question consist in the practice of torture and the denial of due process as provided for in Articles I, XVIII, XXV and XXVI of the American Declaration of the Rights and Duties of Man.

3.   To recommend to the Government of Suriname that it immediately commence an exhaustive investigation into the circumstances of this case and duly prosecute and punish those persons responsible for the human rights violations cited herein.

4.   To recommend that the Government of Suriname send said report to the IACHR within 60 days of the date of this Resolution.

5.   To publish this Resolution in its next Annual Report to the General Assembly of the Organization of American States in the event that the recommendations cited in this Resolution are not satisfactorily implemented.

NOTES AND QUESTIONS

1.   The government of Suriname requested reconsideration on September 11, 1985, approximately two months after the Commission decided the case. *See* Case 9265 (Decision on a Request for Reconsideration), Inter-Am. C.H.R. 119, OEA/Ser.L/V/II.66, doc. 10 rev. 1 (1985).

The government requested that, since it had cooperated with the Commission, had learned of the torture allegations only when it received the Commission's decision, and was currently investigating the allegations, the Commission reconsider its decision as premature. *Id*. at 120.

The Commission denied the request, noting that the original petition contained allegations of beatings which should have put the government on notice that the case involved torture; and the government had failed to show that the torture allegations, overwhelmingly corroborated by evidence collected during the Commission's visit, were false. *Id*. at 121.

2. In another complaint against Suriname the Commission referred the situation to the Inter-American Court. The Court awarded $453,102 to the families of seven men who had been beaten and killed by soldiers in 1987. *Aloeboetoe et al. Case*, Judgment of Sep. 10, 1993, Inter-Am. Ct. H.R. *See* chapter 11, *infra*.

Edmundo Vargas, *Visits on the Spot: The Experience of the Inter-American Commission on Human Rights, in* INTERNATIONAL LAW AND FACT-FINDING IN THE FIELD OF HUMAN RIGHTS 137-50 (Bertie G. Ramcharan ed., 1982):

The Decision to Undertake an On-site Observation

A visit of the Commission may arise from a spontaneous gesture from the government, inviting the Commission to carry out a visit, or, it may be the result of an express request on the part of the Commission for that government's consent. The latter situation generally arises when, in the judgement of the Commission, there is reason to believe that the situation of human rights in that country warrants investigation.

There is also an intermediate "diplomatic" situation, by which the Commission initiates negotiations with a government, affording it the opportunity to invite the Commission, before its consent is formally requested. This generally happens when the Commission takes the initiative by planning a study of human rights in a particular country. Upon communicating this decision to the government, the Commission suggests that, since a report is in preparation, its understanding would be enhanced if the Commission had the opportunity to visit that country. . . .

If the government does not decide to invite the Commission, the Commission makes a public request for consent to carry out an investigation. If there are still objections, the Commission notes the government's denial of consent in its country report as it did in the cases of Uruguay and Paraguay. . . .

On the other hand, in the cases of Panama, El Salvador, Haiti, Colombia and the second mission to Nicaragua, the initiative for the invitation came from the Governments themselves. These Governments were interested in having the Commission report on the human rights situation in their respective countries which they felt would constitute a reply to what they considered had been unjust criticism levelled against them. . . .

Regulations Governing On-Site Observations

. . . The present Statute of the Commission, approved at the General Assembly in La Paz, Bolivia in 1977, leaves without doubt the Commission's authority to conduct on-site observations even in States not party to the American Convention. The source for this authority is Article 18(g), which states that the Commission shall have powers with respect to all member states of the OAS:

g) to conduct on-site observations in a state, with the consent or at the invitation of the government in question. . . .

Chapter IV (Article 51 to 55) of the Commission's Regulations govern on-site observations.

These articles prescribe the creation of a Special Commission. If a member is a national or a resident of the State in question he is to be disqualified from participation in this Special Commission. In extending its invitation, or in the act of granting its consent to a visit, the government offers to furnish the Special Commission with all the facilities necessary for carrying out an on-site observation. And under the provision of "all necessary facilities" is understood that the government undertakes not to engage in any reprisals against those persons or organizations that provide information or testimony to the Commission. This guarantee is so crucial that it is set forth twice in the Regulations. . . .

Under 'all the necessary facilities' which the government undertakes to furnish the Commission during its on-site observation, the following are specifically singled out:

—freedom to interview anyone the Commission chooses in private, without fear of reprisal against the informant;

—freedom to travel freely throughout the national territory in available local means of transportation;

—access to prisons and other centers of detention in order to interview prisoners and detainees, in private;

—access to governmental documents required for the writing of the report;

—freedom to use whatever recording or reproducing devices the Commission chooses in collecting information;

—access to adequate security measures to ensure the safety of the Commission; and

—access to appropriate lodging.

Except for the provision of adequate security measures, the expenses of the Commission and support staff during the visit are borne by the Commission. Until now, the average duration of an on-site visit by the Commission has been between 6 and 16 days.

Upon arrival, the Special Commission meets to schedule its program of activities using as a working paper the provisional program prepared by the Secretariat.

Next, the Special Commission usually holds a press conference to publicize its program and to call upon the representative sectors of society to present their points of view. This communiqué also alerts persons, who feel that their human rights have been violated, to present their complaints at the local offices of the Commission, which are usually set up in the hotel where the Commission is staying.

The program undertaken by the Commission basically consists of interviews with government officials and with representatives of the different sectors of the national life. . . .

Immediate Importance and Results of the Visit

Whereas the principal objective of an on-site observation is to investigate the situation of human rights in a country in order to prepare a report, the very presence of the Commission in a country, in addition to facilitating the verification of certain facts, also brings about a certain improvement in the observance of human rights. The fact that a government invites or consents to a Commission visit, reveals, at a minimum, a desire to improve the observance of human rights.

The case of the Colombia visit in 1980 evidenced the Commission's utility in the resolution of a specific problem which the Government (as well as the militants) wished to see resolved.

When the Commission arrived in Bogotá on April 21, 1980, it was invited by the Colombian Government to participate in the negotiation process then being carried out between the Government and the captors of the Embassy of the Dominican Republic in that capital. The latter were members of an urban guerrilla organization known as M-19.

The Commission, in keeping with its humanitarian mandate, decided to intervene in that process but refused to act as either mediator or a formal negotiator. Rather, it limited its role to offering its good offices to both sides.

Based on an understanding between the M-19 guerrillas and the Government, the IACHR, by means of an exchange of letters between its President and the Minister of Foreign Relations, agreed to assure the guerrillas' safe-conduct out of the country by physically accompanying the captors and their hostages to the airport.

In addition the Commission committed itself to monitoring certain ongoing military trials in which members of M-19 and another guerrilla organization, known as the Fuerzas Armadas Revolucionarias Colombianas (FARC), were tried on charges of having committed crimes against the state. The Commission's task in this regard consists in assuring the fairness of the trials and respect for the human rights of the accused.

Even the most skeptical observers of the Commission acknowledge that its visits have an impact. A politician, known for his criticism of the OAS, expressed the following when the Commission arrived in his country: "I think that this visit will only serve to obtain the release of certain political prisoners and to have the walls of the jails painted." Certainly, this statement is an over-simplification, for the results of the visits have been much more important; but, even if such were the case, the judge of the utility of a Commission visit ought to be that of released political prisoners.

[Some] governments have responded to the Commission's recommendations [by] permitt[ing] gradual improvements. Moreover, as in the case of Panama, suggestions made by the Commission towards the end of its visit to the Head of State, General Omar Torrijos, brought about some changes in legislation. Three decrees, restrictive of freedom of assembly, freedom of expression, and the right to due process, were revoked just prior to the Special Commission's departure. In the course of the second visit to Nicaragua, the Minister of Interior, Commander Tomas Borge, during his visit with the members of the Commission, ordered the release of all the women prisoners (with the exception of two).

But the most important result obtained from an on-site observation is the confirmation of certain violations of which the government has been accused. In El Salvador, for example, the Special Commission was able to confirm the existence of secret cells by means of marks left by the former detainees who had subsequently disappeared, and in Nicaragua in 1978, it collected evidence of the acts of violence attributed to the National Guard, in particular, during September, 1978.

Drafting, Approval and Publication of the Report

Once the visit is completed, the staff of the Commission, in addition to processing the complaints received, compiles all available documentation and in some cases prepares a draft report on the on-site observation. . . .

The structure of each must follow that used in all of the country reports prepared by the IACHR. A report begins with an introduction, a description of the background history of the visit, and a summary of the program of activities carried out by the Special Commission. In Chapter One, there follows a study of the legal system of the country with respect to human rights, and in successive chapters, an analysis, the observance of each of the rights set forth in the American Declaration of the Rights and Duties of Man or the American Convention on Human Rights, when appropriate—the right to life, integrity of the person, physical liberty, justice, and due process, including *habeas corpus* and *amparo*,[2] the freedom of expression, of religion and conscience, and of assembly and association. Finally, in the last chapter, the Commission summarizes its conclusions and makes its recommendations. . . .

[A]fter [the report] is approved [by the Commission] it is sent to the government in question which is requested to present its observations and comments.

Usually the Commission requests the government to submit its reply within six weeks, but in special circumstances, that period is adjusted. In Nicaragua, because of the urgency of the human rights situation, the fact that the 17th Meeting of Consultation of Foreign Ministers had requested the Commission to accelerate the date for its trip, and the fact that the Commission was not scheduled to meet until some months later, motivated the Commission to request that the Government of Nicaragua respond within eight days, without prejudice to presenting further observations to the Meeting of Consultation at a later date.

The government's observations and comments are considered in a plenary session of the Commission, which may decide to modify the report as regards evident inaccuracies in the light of the reply. If the government makes no observations, but only comments, as was the case with Panama, the Commission does not change the original text but publishes the report together with the government's comments.

* * * * *

For critique of the work of the Inter-American Commission on Human Rights, see chapter 10, *infra*.

F.   FACT-FINDING WITHOUT ON-SITE OBSERVATION

Though on-site operations have been the main focus of this chapter, most fact-finding is done without visiting the country or establishing a local presence. Due to limited monetary and human resources, on-site operations are not always possible or practicable. In addition, many governments do not cooperate with requests regarding fact-finding in their countries.

On-site monitoring, however, is not always necessary for effective fact-finding. Reliable, first-hand information can be obtained from refugees and others who have lived in or visited the country; from legal documents; from government responses to allegations of abuse; by telephone, fax and electronic mail; and from other connections with people in the country. Fact-finding without on-site observations avoids potentially misleading information, which results from attempts by authorities to

---

[2] [Ed. note: *Amparo* is a Latin American writ whereby the claimant can seek protection from governmental infringement of rights. Like habeas corpus, *amparo* can be used to challenge illegal detention, but it also can be used against other illegal conduct.]

prevent access to important information, prisoners, and witnesses. On-site operations can also be dangerous for observers, witnesses, and victims.

The following reading is an excerpt from a study prepared by two NGOs on the human rights situation in the Democratic People's Republic of Korea. The study was prepared without a visit for reasons described in the report. As you read the report, note the fact-finding techniques the NGOs were able to utilize without a visit to the country and question how a visit, assuming one was feasible, might have aided or hindered the investigation. Consider (1) the usefulness of investigating a country like the Democratic People's Republic of Korea, about which sources of reliable information are extremely limited and (2) problems associated with such an investigation.

Asia Watch & Minnesota Lawyers International Human Rights Committee, *Human Rights in the Democratic People's Republic of Korea (North Korea)* 1-11 (1988) (footnotes omitted):

I. *Introduction*

A. *Objectives*

We undertook this study out of a desire to examine a society that had largely evaded international scrutiny of its human rights practices. Most human rights organizations, including our own, have devoted scant attention to the Democratic People's Republic of Korea because of the tremendous difficulty of acquiring information. We found this inattention troubling. Because the credibility of human rights organizations depends in large measure on their willingness to apply human rights standards to all countries of the world, we feared that the failure to address human rights conditions in countries like the DPRK, albeit for practical reasons, might call that credibility into question.

We began this study with an optimism that, even as to the DPRK, a sustained effort could overcome the many obstacles to human rights monitoring. Now that the study has been completed, we must concede that we have succeeded only in part. Although we believe that we have unearthed substantial evidence of a pattern of gross human rights violations in the DPRK, we at times have been required to state our conclusions in relatively tentative terms. For example, as explained more fully in the next section on methodology, we were denied access to the DPRK, and thus were forced to rely on accounts by former residents now outside the DPRK and foreign travelers. As a result, the information we managed to acquire was often less comprehensive, or more dated, than we would have liked, limiting our ability to make unequivocal assertions of fact.

We believe, nonetheless, that the conclusions we do reach are sound. There remains the possibility, however, that further research will require modification or updating of our findings. We welcome such research, and, indeed, hope that this study will serve as a springboard to further monitoring efforts. Only ongoing attention will reveal the full dimensions of the serious human rights violations plaguing the DPRK. In the meantime, we feel justified in assigning responsibility to the DPRK Government for any inaccuracies that its policies of enforced secrecy might have caused.

B. *Methodology*

1. *Obstacles*

We faced several obstacles in our research. The first, which we did not really expect, was a widespread indifference to human rights in the DPRK based on a sense that the problem was so overwhelming that efforts at change were futile. One very visible human rights leader told us that he was initially uninterested in our study because, he believed, everyone knows that "there are no human rights in North Korea; the people are so repressed that there is no dissent and no one in prison." But while human rights in the DPRK are, indeed, severely repressed, we believe that there is a distinct value in documenting that repression in order to illustrate the emptiness of the DPRK's professed respect for human rights, with the aim of encouraging greater respect for international human rights norms.

A second, and rather similar, unexpected obstacle came from some Asian scholars who believe the DPRK is so unique that comparing its human rights situation to that of any other country is useless. This study, like the rest of our work, does not engage in such comparisons, but assesses the record of the DPRK against established international standards to which the Government of the DPRK has agreed to be bound. On 14 September 1981 the DPRK acceded to the International Covenant on Civil and Political Rights and the International Covenant on Economic, Social and Cultural Rights. By this action, the Government indicated its willingness to be bound by the fundamental human rights guarantees protected by those two multilateral treaties and related international human rights instruments.

We also anticipated a number of barriers to our research which often plague human rights monitoring efforts. These included:

a.   A climate of fear that would prevent individuals from reporting violations because of an inordinate risk of reprisal. . . . [T]he DPRK Penal Code contains a number of provisions which effectively forbid the transmission of information about human rights violations abroad. The Penal Code and the policies of the DPRK Government have created a climate of fear which makes it almost impossible to obtain information directly from North Korean citizens currently living in the DPRK. Diplomats and many who have visited Pyongyang report being isolated from ordinary residents of the DPRK because of their extreme reluctance to talk to foreigners. At best, many DPRK residents simply repeat their Government's line that they live in the ideal society, even when faced with direct evidence to the contrary.

b.   A lack of popular awareness of human rights norms or expectation that basic rights should be respected. The DPRK Government has taken many measures . . . to prevent North Koreans from learning about their international human rights or receiving any information that the Government does not wish them to hear. Article 53 of the DPRK Constitution provides: "Citizens have freedom of speech, the press, assembly, association and of demonstration." In reality, however, these constitutional rights are not known to most North Koreans and are practiced only with specific permission of the DPRK authorities.

c.   The lack of an independent judiciary which could respond to reports of human rights violations from an independent bar. [T]here is very little evidence of an independent judiciary or an independent legal profession in the DPRK. Lawyers and judges are, in any case, too frightened to provide information to international human rights organizations or to challenge the Government in any way.

d.   The lack of domestic organizations which concern themselves with human rights. Because no such human rights organizations exist in the DPRK, there is no natural source of human rights information or publicity of human rights violations.. . .

e.   The inability of the local media to report human rights matters. We have monitored DPRK newspapers and radio for several years and have found no reporting on human rights matters, even though the media does provide some indirect information that gives an indication of human rights problems. The newspapers, radio, and all other forms of media are controlled completely by the Government. No foreign journalists are known to be accredited to Pyongyang, although a few have traveled to the DPRK for very brief and closely monitored visits. . . .

f.   The unreliability of human rights information that does become available. Because the Government is nearly the only source of information from within the DPRK, it emits a steady stream of self-congratulatory statements which almost certainly are unreliable. Indeed, visitors are frequently presented with obviously fraudulent statements, materials, and demonstrations. For example, a Latin American visitor to the 1987 meeting of the Non-aligned Movement in Pyongyang told of being taken past stores with fully stocked windows. When the meeting adjourned at an unscheduled hour, the delegate passed the same stores to find that the food had been removed before any North Korean shopper could have had access. Another visitor was shown a "typical" apartment with many electrical appliances. The visitor noted, however, that the apartment lacked electrical outlets to accommodate the appliances. A tall Scandinavian visitor was surprised to find that a Pyongyang newspaper photograph of Kim Il Sung and him had been cropped and altered to make it appear that the visitor was not much taller than Kim Il Sung. Many visitors have indicated that their guides made statements which the visitors thought to be absurd and unbelievable; the guides were apparently unwilling to retract these statements even if shown obvious evidence to the contrary.

The Republic of Korea (South Korea) has also engaged in a systematic pattern of issuing misinformation and inaccurate information about the DPRK, often providing inaccurate data to outsiders and then quoting their reports as if they were independent. As a result, any material which derives directly or indirectly from South Korean sources must be checked and rechecked against independent data.

g.   A language with which human rights researchers tend not to be familiar. Many human rights organizations do not employ Korean-speaking researchers to investigate abuses in the Korean peninsula. The language barrier has been overcome in the case of South Korea because the country is relatively open to foreign travel, journalists, and to human rights investigators. But since the flow of information from the DPRK is so limited, the lack of Korean-speaking human rights investigators can severely hamper research capacity.

h.   The lack of communication links (e.g., telephone, letters, business travel, etc.) with the outside world. . . . [T]he DPRK is almost completely isolated from the Western countries where most international human rights organizations and international media are located. The diplomats stationed in Pyongyang represent mainly socialist and Third World countries. Other visitors are often confined to highly regulated show tours which prevent them from seeing more than the Government wishes them to see. Some business travel into North Korea has begun to occur in recent years, but most business visitors are afraid to talk lest their business relations be severed by the Government. And it appears that correspondence with the DPRK is monitored by government censors.

i.   The difficulty of relying on a refugee or expatriate community. Much of the information about the DPRK comes from refugees who, because they must continually justify their decision to flee, may not always be the most trustworthy source of information. Since the end of the Korean Conflict in 1953, there have been somewhat less than 1,000 people who have escaped from North to South Korea. The Government of the Republic of Korea (South Korea) has developed a practice of isolating escaped North Koreans for a period varying from a few weeks to two years so as to debrief them thoroughly and ensure that they are not spies. Because these escaped North Koreans are often indoctrinated during this period, evidence gleaned from them must be carefully scrutinized and cross-checked. Some North Koreans, however, have escaped via Japan, Singapore, and other countries, so that they can provide somewhat more reliable information.

j.   The impossibility of sending a fact-finding mission to the country. As discussed above, no international human rights organization has been able to send a fact-finding mission to the DPRK. Asia Watch and the Minnesota Lawyers International Human Rights Committee sought on several occasions during the past two years to obtain permission to visit the DPRK. The DPRK did not answer any of the letters requesting visits and failed to respond substantively to oral requests tendered to DPRK diplomats at the United Nations. The DPRK Government has been willing to receive various visitors—many of whom we interviewed—including selected scholars, journalists, church leaders, and Korean-Americans. But these visits are strictly controlled, and visitors are encouraged to write adulatory comments about what they see. Scholars and others know that strongly negative portrayals of life in North Korea will jeopardize their future access to the country. Some visitors and Asian scholars also have political leanings which may limit the trustworthiness of their reports on the DPRK.

2.   Research Steps

These considerable obstacles make understandable the failure of international human rights organizations to undertake more fact-finding and reporting about the DPRK. We hoped to overcome these obstacles through a concentrated effort by a group of scholars who, unlike many human rights researchers, would work only on this single country.

First, the most important step in conducting this study was to recruit a Korean-speaking researcher. We were very fortunate to have a Korean-speaking lawyer who had no previous involvement or apparent bias on issues relating to the DPRK or the Republic of Korea.

Second, we undertook a very thorough survey of the available secondary information on the DPRK, of which we found a tremendous quantity. Although much of this information is in the English language, the most valuable material was in Korean and Japanese. There was additional material in German, Russian, Swedish, and other languages.

Third, we subscribed to the Foreign Broadcast Information Service (FBIS) and other journals that allowed some monitoring of recent information about events in the DPRK.

Fourth, we notified over one hundred scholars and other potential sources of information that we were undertaking the research. We received written responses and obtained documentary information from a large number of these scholars, and we interviewed many of them as well as other secondary informants.

Fifth, we gathered the reports which the DPRK Government has issued about its own human rights performance. For example, the Government has submitted reports to the Human Rights Committee and the Committee on Economic, Social and Cultural Rights, pursuant to the International Covenant on Civil and Political Rights and the International Covenant on Economic, Social and Cultural Rights.

Sixth, we traveled to and/or gathered relevant information from the People's Republic of China, Denmark, France, Japan, the Republic of Korea, Sweden, the Union of Soviet Socialist Republics, and other countries. For example, there are over 8,000 Koreans in Japan who have visited relatives in the DPRK. These Korean-Japanese are a substantial resource for information on the DPRK. Very few scholars and human rights organizations have systematically interviewed these refugees.

We visited Japan several times to gather information. There also exists a rather insular community of Koreans in Dong-bei, which is the region of the People's Republic of China adjoining the DPRK. We undertook some research in that area, but additional resources and time would yield far more information than we were able to obtain.

Seventh, we interviewed a number of North Koreans who had escaped from their country, as well as foreigners who had previously lived in North Korea but have now left. It would have been best primarily to have interviewed persons whose first place of residence outside the DPRK was not South Korea, as such persons might provide somewhat more reliable information. Unfortunately, we had only limited sources in this regard, as most of the ex-residents of North Korea whom we interviewed came first to live in the South. Nonetheless, we took measures to attempt to guard against bias. Rather than solicit generalities, the interviews concentrated on personal experiences and observations, daily life, and other concrete matters. These informants were politely cross-examined and the information provided was cross-checked with other sources. We undertook these interviews without the presence of any translator or other person who might have made the interviewed individual reluctant to speak freely. We have summarized several of the interviews in appendix 4, but we have omitted the names of the persons interviewed to protect them and their families from reprisals. The individuals were assured that their identities would be held in confidence. . . .

Eighth, we organized our analysis around the internationally accepted definition of human rights provided by the Universal Declaration of Human Rights. The Universal Declaration furnishes a simpler format for presenting the report than do the more detailed and complex provisions of the two International Covenants. The basic rights in the Universal Declaration are amplified by the provisions of the International Covenant on Civil and Political Rights and the International Covenant on Economic, Social and Cultural Rights, which have been ratified by the DPRK and which are cited where their provisions add substantially to the norms quoted from the Universal Declaration.

Ninth, we have generally begun each chapter of this report with pertinent provisions from the DPRK Constitution and other laws, as well as official statements of the rights that are afforded in the DPRK. These citations allow the reader to assess the degree to which these official pronouncements reflect the facts we present.

Tenth, we have followed the format of most international human rights fact-finding reports in omitting most footnotes and references to individuals who provided information—particularly if there is fear of retaliation against family members. We also have not disclosed the identity of other sources (such as academics, businesspeople, and diplomats) because their access to the DPRK might be jeopardized. In some contexts we have cited secondary sources because they provided significant supporting material. The bibliography provides a list of the most significant primary and secondary sources of published information. By providing only some references, however, the text may give the impression that we lacked sources for the other findings in the report. On the contrary, the findings in the report are supported by interviews, primary materials, or the secondary materials listed in the bibliography, as well as our analysis of the accuracy and consistency of the information that we gathered.

Eleventh, this report does not claim to give a completely up-to-date record of human rights violations in the DPRK, but rather represents a pattern of such violations documented over several years. This report reflects research which was completed up to January 1988, but some more recent information has been added up through October 1988. In some cases we have only been able to illustrate recent violations by reference to occurrences of the past. We believe these gaps reflect our lack of access to contemporary information rather than a fundamental change in current practices. Before incorporating such cases in our reports, we made certain that corroborative information suggested that the practices continued into the recent period. Such corroborative information has come from more recent documents, as well as from diplomats, visiting scholars, businesspeople, and other travelers. Indeed, as a general matter, we have reason to believe that the human rights situation in the DPRK has not changed significantly over the past fifteen years. For example, the information that we collected from multiple sources about the ill-treatment of prisoners shows a very consistent pattern over a wide span of years, through at least the mid-1980s. There is no information suggesting that prisoners at any time through the present have been treated humanely. Contributing to this continuity is the fact that, throughout its history, the Government of the DPRK has had one leader, whose role has been steadily consolidated. For all these reasons, we believe that we have painted an accurate picture despite the obvious difficulties we encountered in gathering information. Nonetheless, with respect to specific reports of abuses, the reader should take seriously the qualifying language that we use, as it has not been possible to confirm each and every report that we believe merited inclusion in this study. If errors emerge, we believe they will be due principally to the DPRK Government, which has sought to shroud its actions under a veil of secrecy. Within these constraints, however, we take responsibility for the conclusions drawn in this report.

Twelfth, we sent a draft of this study to the DPRK Government for its response and comments before publication. . . . The response charged that the draft report was "full of lies and falsifications," asserted that human rights violations in the DPRK are "unthinkable" because the country "is a most advanced one which places the highest value on the sovereignty and dignity of man," and threatened that if we printed the report, we would be "held fully responsible for all the consequences arising therefrom." The response failed, however, to address any of the specific concerns detailed in the report. A short time later, an assistant to the DPRK Ambassador telephoned to inquire whether his letter had been received and whether the report would be published. We told the assistant that the Ambassador's letter was inadequate because of its lack of specificity. The Ambassador then sent a second letter . . ., which repeated the general denials, again without reference to any specific point in the report. . . .

NOTES AND QUESTIONS

1.   For further reading see FACT-FINDING BEFORE INTERNATIONAL TRIBUNALS [Eleventh Sokol Colloquium] (Richard B. Lillich ed., 1991); Robert Norris, *Observations In Loco: Practice and Procedure of the Inter-American Commission on Human Rights*, 1979-1983, 19 TEX. INT'L L J. 285 (1984).

2.   The Democratic People's Republic of Korea (DPRK) allowed observers from Amnesty International (AI) to visit its territory in 1991. The AI delegates attended the Inter-Parliamentary Conference being held in Pyongyang. They also spoke with legal scholars and government representatives about the country's legal system. *See AI Newsletter* (July 1991).

Despite their being able to undertake the on-site visit, however, the delegates were not able to make comprehensive findings regarding the DPRK human rights record. Interviewees denied allegations of abuses; delegates obtained access to only one criminal trial and one public security station; the visitors mostly were unable to travel unescorted; and the visit was confined to the city of Pyongyang. Still, the delegation did receive texts of the most recent criminal and civil codes, which until then had been unobtainable. The visit did represent a positive step towards gaining access to the DPRK.

In April 1995, AI delegates made a second visit. Their discussions with Officials of the Ministry of Public Security resulted in information on recent amendments to the criminal code and some political prisoners and prisoners of conscience. In regard to many prisoners whose cases had been raised by the delegates, however, the officials said that "many of these people had never been detained and that in other cases, information provided by Amnesty International had been insufficient to identify the relevant individuals or to investigate their whereabouts." Amnesty International, *DPRK (North Korea): What Happened to Cho HO Pyong and His Family?*, AI Index: ASA 24/05/95 (1995); Amnesty International, *Amnesty International Delegation Visits North Korea, Discusses Legal Reforms and Prisoner Cases*, AI Index: ASA 23/07/95 (1995). Should international organizations undertake on-site investigations when they are given such limited access to information? Can the investigations really make a difference?

G.   IMPACT OF FACT-FINDING INVESTIGATIONS

1.   Americas Watch, Asia Watch, & Helsinki Watch, *Four Failures: A Report on the U.N. Special Rapporteurs on Human Rights in Chile, Guatemala, Iran and Poland* 15-21 (1986):

[Ed.: The following is an excerpt from a report criticizing the work of four U.N. special rapporteurs. As you will recall, chapter 5 introduced the Special Rapporteur process. You may want to review pages 183-85, 208-13, which describe that process.]

The Colville Report on Guatemala

Since 1979, at its annual sessions, the Commission on Human Rights has repeatedly expressed its concern about the human rights situation in *Guatemala*. In March 1982, in resolution 1982/31 the Commission requested its Chairman to appoint a Special Rapporteur to prepare a study of the situation of human rights in Guatemala to be presented to the Commission at its next session.

The government of Guatemala declared its willingness to cooperate with the Special Rapporteur, a fact acknowledged in resolution 37/184 of the General Assembly on December 17, 1982. As of that date, a Rapporteur had not yet been appointed. On December 31, 1982, the Chairman of the Commission appointed Mrs. Elizabeth Odio Benito to the post. The government of Guatemala, however, objected to this choice and requested that another candidate should be proposed before the next session of the Commission. . . .

In March 1983 the Chairman appointed Viscount Colville of Culross, former member of the Conservative government in Britain, as Special Rapporteur on human rights in Guatemala. Sources close to the Human Rights Commission have told Americas Watch that before Lord Colville was appointed, the Guatemalan government had made it clear that it would cooperate if he was designated.

A.   Methodology

Over the past three years, Lord Colville's reports have drawn criticism of methodology and substance from many quarters. The major concern over methodology is Colville's use of military escort and transportation during his site visits. Lord Colville continues to assert, however, that a stranger, flying by Army helicopter to remote Indian villages, accompanied by a member of a Guatemalan Army intelligence unit and a member of the Foreign Ministry, will receive candid accounts from victims in cases where it is alleged that the Army has been implicated in gross abuses of human rights. Lord Colville addressed these criticisms in his 1985 report, saying that it was the Guatemalan government's concern for his safety that required him to travel with a military escort.

In contrast to his previous reports, Lord Colville's 1985 report described cases where informants appeared frightened or unwilling to cooperate. In one case, Lord Colville indicated that one of his informants had been murdered. These difficulties in his fact-finding are not mentioned in the section of his report in which Lord Colville addresses criticisms of his methodology.

B. Reinterpretation of the Mandate

The 1985 Colville report differs from his previous reports in another respect. According to paragraph 15 of U.N. Human Rights Commission resolution 1985/36, the Special Rapporteur for Guatemala is asked "to assess in particular allegations of politically motivated killings, disappearances, acts of torture, extrajudicial executions and confinement in clandestine prisons." In his 1985 report, however, Colville asserted that the issue of disappearances fell under the purview of the U.N. Working Group on Enforced or Involuntary Disappearances. Having thus re-defined his task, Lord Colville eliminated from his mandate one of the major aspects of human rights abuse in Guatemala. The problem of disappearances has been an ongoing tragedy there for the past 20 years. Of some 90,000 disappearances reported throughout Latin America, an estimated 35,000 occurred in Guatemala where the practice originated in 1966. Colville did not decline to consider disappearances in 1983 and 1984. But, in 1985, the Special Rapporteur on Human Rights for Guatemala unilaterally altered the mandate given him by resolution of the U.N. Human Rights Commission.

C. Civil Patrols

There are other problems of continuity in Colville's reports. The 1985 report allots three paragraphs for discussion of civil patrols in which some 900,000 males perform onerous unpaid service. The Special Rapporteur fails to address the compulsory nature of service, although in a previous report he acknowledged that an army circular required all men between 18 and 50 to join, with refusal regarded as an indication of subversive tendencies. He also failed to address the complaint that service in civil patrols turns villagers into combatants, and therefore under the international laws of war, legitimate targets for the insurgents. Though Colville has compared service in the civil patrols to military service, he neglects any mention that patrollers are unpaid, while soldiers are paid. Instead, Colville indirectly justifies this distinction by noting that, though the patrols may disrupt a man's work, they are considered worthwhile for the sense of security they bring.

Guatemala's new Constitution includes a provision guaranteeing that no one may be required to join an organization for the purpose of self-defense. While not directly acknowledging the compulsory nature of civilian patrols, Colville does recognize that this provision would have to be amended for their continued operation.

D. Evidence of Official Responsibility for Abuses

Colville has consistently played down any evidence of official responsibility for killings and disappearances. He has done this by omission, denial, or by understated acknowledgment of evidence pointing to government culpability.

In 1985, for the first time, Colville took note of the statistics on politically-motivated killings provided by the Guatemalan Human Rights Commission, a group that is based in Mexico. Based on these statistics, Colville focused on seven incidents of allegations of major human rights abuses. In two cases, he found evidence that abuses did take place. In three cases, he did not have time to visit the site involved. In one case, he found no evidence of government involvement and chose not to make a site visit.

The final case involved a report published in the Guatemalan press that the bodies of two finca administrators were thrown from a helicopter into Mazate Stadium. Both bodies were recovered revealing evidence of torture including amputation of genital organs, stab wounds, and bullet holes.

Colville reported that the National Police knew of the case, but that they disputed the press account. According to the police, "The two men were not dead but wounded; they were picked up by a helicopter and lowered onto the football stadium at Mazatenango with ropes. It was the only site to ensure their transfer to hospital. Police records will be provided and the Special Rapporteur will report further."

In another case, one in which the Special Rapporteur visited Saquiya, he reports that he spoke with villagers who confirmed the disappearances of eleven people. He took this information to the *comandante* in Chimaltenango who reported that indeed, eleven people had been captured in army operations against a guerrilla band. Colville transmitted the list of eleven names to the Working Group on Enforced or Involuntary Disappearances. In the next paragraph, Colville reached the conclusion that "there was no easy answer available to the question of who was responsible," despite the admission of army involvement by the *comandante* himself.

As the Special Rapporteur's findings sharply contradict virtually every other report from international human rights organizations—such as the OAS Inter-American Commission on Human Rights, Amnesty International and Americas Watch—one is led to ask what accounts for such a drastic divergence. Lord Avebury, chairman of the British Parliamentary Human Rights Group and co-author of its report on Guatemala, *Bitter and Cruel*, who has discussed the differences in his findings with the Special Rapporteur, suggests a possible explanation. Colville takes the view, according to Avebury, that it is important to take all steps possible to further Guatemala's movement toward democracy. This goal is widely shared. However, is the furtherance of this goal intended by the United Nations to justify efforts to influence reporting on the level of human rights abuse?

In an interview with the *Wall Street Journal*, Colville made it clear that he does consider that his particular agenda—which may be laudable in and of itself—should affect his reporting:

> The question is, unless you're in favor of a communist victory, how do you persuade a military government to give up its power and go back to the barracks. You don't do that by writing a 100-page report of pure condemnation.

The Special Rapporteur has apparently taken on a political role that involves him at the center of current internal developments in Guatemala.

Lord Colville has stated that he has tried to produce a balanced report, in which the good can be weighed against the bad. Yet, how can political murder and disappearances be "weighed" against progress in electoral reform? Wedding the publication of a balanced report to an assessment of the actual human rights situation seriously compromises the mission of the Special Rapporteur and his findings must be evaluated accordingly.

NOTES AND QUESTIONS

What effects did perceived flaws in methodology have on the impact of the Special Rapporteur's fact-finding? Are his justifications for the procedures valid? What could he have done to avoid criticism and yet still protect his safety and expedite the fact-finding process? Did circumstances surrounding his appointment affect the impact of the process? Carefully consider the lessons learned regarding the need for fair and unbiased procedures as you formulate rules for your own (hypothetical) fact-finding operation in Rwanda.

2.   Assessing the Impact of Fact-Finding Investigations

It is often difficult to assess the impact of fact-finding. As the material on Argentina suggests, the focus of international attention on human rights violations in a country may lead to significant improvement. Human rights abuses often decrease after fact-finding inquiries, because of the government's embarrassment with disclosure of abuses and a desire to improve its repute in the world community. At the very least, confirming the allegations of violations makes denial difficult and typically forces governments to speak up in international forums regarding the allegations.

Apart from embarrassment ("the mobilization of shame"), to have alleged violations confirmed by fact-finding occasionally leads to sanctions directed at the violating country. The U.S., for example, sometimes hinges its foreign aid on human rights records of recipient countries. Though sanctions usually are bilateral, in a few egregious cases—such as South Africa—countries have been targeted by multilateral sanctions. Yet a too-common pairing of sanctions with fact-finding makes it difficult to assess fact-finding's impact without considering the sanction's impact on violators pursued as a result of the fact-finding.

In studying the excerpt below, readers should consider whether there is a connection between human rights fact-finding and other international pressures, on the one hand, and improvement in human rights situations on the other.

Maria Bartolomei & David Weissbrodt, The Impact of Factfinding and International Pressures on the Human Rights Situation in Argentina, 1976-1983:[3]

It is remarkable that there are almost no academics or activists who have even attempted to assess the effectiveness of human rights measures. It is, of course, very difficult to demonstrate effectiveness in many areas of human endeavor and particularly in international human rights work. Human rights activists investigate abuses and write letters to governments because they believe that speaking out is better than remaining silent in the face of repression. When challenged they can

---

[3] The article is an edited version of a more-detailed study with the same title. *See* MARIA BARTOLOMEI, GROSS AND MASSIVE VIOLATIONS OF HUMAN RIGHTS IN ARGENTINA, 1976-1983 (1994).

point to anecdotal evidence of prisoners released, torture stopped, and executions prevented. More formal proof of results is harder to find.

The case of Argentina during the period 1976-83 provides an opportunity to consider the effectiveness of human rights factfinding and pressure. There are at least two reasons for selecting the case for study: First, an historical record has been developed on what happened during the relevant period. The Argentine government made considerable efforts after 1983 to investigate what happened. A lot of evidence was adduced at the trials of some of the leaders who were responsible. Many victims have written accounts of their experiences. There is also an extensive scholarly literature about the period, even though this article is apparently the first to correlate human rights efforts with results. Second, there exist relatively reliable statistics about the most prevalent form of human rights abuse, that is, disappearances. Such statistics permit an analyst to track the prevalence of abuses against the human rights measures attempted.

The difficulties in this analysis are impressive. Unfortunately, no one has systematically interviewed high government officials or the less well-known perpetrators of human rights abuses to learn why they started killing people and why they stopped. There are also so many different influences which may affect a government's conduct. External pressures are often far less significant than internal events. In the case of Argentina, Ronald Dworkin has written, "The junta's power was finally broken, not by any domestic or international concern about human rights, but by its own economic and, in the end, military ineptitude."[4] Dworkin in some ways reflects the popular view that it was the 1982 war in the South Atlantic which brought down the Argentine military government. But he realized that the disappearances had ended far earlier, that is, in 1979. The question is why did they end? There is no simple answer.

1. *The Human Rights Situation in Argentina*

On March 24, 1976, a military coup overthrew the government of "Isabella" Peron to stabilize the economy and to get rid of "leftist threats" to public order. In a matter of days, the new Argentine military government dissolved the Congress and other legislative bodies; dismissed judges, including judges of the Supreme Court with life tenure; appointed new judges; authorized the military to arrest "subversives"; and suspended constitutional rights. At first, the military government focused their repressive measures against the members of "guerilla groups" and militant workers in factories. The "dirty war," as it was called even by the military, soon extended much further: During 1976 and 1977 thousands were arrested, were subjected to disappearance, were tortured, and were killed. The military government focused principally on younger people in that over 80% of those affected were aged 21 to 40. In addition to the disappeared, thousands of Argentine nationals were acknowledged by the government to be in detention. Many of those prisoners were tortured and/or killed. During the period 1976 through 1983 approximately 12-15,000 persons disappeared in Argentina.

2. *Human Rights Factfinding and Pressure*

There were at least five kinds of international human rights fact-finding and pressure brought to bear in the case of Argentina. The world got its *first* warning

---

[4] Dworkin, *Introduction*, in Argentine National Commission on the Disappeared, Nunca Más xv (1986).

of the horrors of the "dirty war" when families of victims were alerted. A *second* wave of information came from Argentine organizations—like the Mothers of the Plaza de Mayo. *Third*, international human rights organizations investigated and publicized the abuses. *Fourth*, the Inter-American Commission on Human Rights of the Organization of American States, together with the U.S. Government, played an important role. And *fifth*, the assistance of the United Nations was sought.

a. *Early Warning: Foreigners Caught in the Net*

The first warning of the government's "dirty war" came to the families of the many young people who were abducted. The families tried to discover what had happened to their relatives who had disappeared. The families sought explanations from the Argentine government and the authorities refused to acknowledge that they had custody of the disappeared individuals. For the outside world, the first indication of what was occurring in Argentina came when foreigners were abducted. For example, Gwen Loken Lopez—a Minnesota native who had married a young Argentine lawyer—was abducted in April 1976, tortured, and then released in September 1976 after Representative Donald Fraser of Minneapolis obtained the intercession of Alejandro Orfila, the Argentine Secretary-General of the Organization of American States. Father Patrick Rice, an Irish priest working in Argentina, was detained in October 1976 and was later released due to the efforts of the Irish government. Dagmar Hagelin, a seventeen year-old with joint Swedish and Argentine nationality, was shot, stuffed in the trunk of an automobile, and abducted by a group of men outside the home of one of her friends in January 1977. The Swedish government took up the case, but she was never found. The deteriorating situation was further publicized by the disappearance of two French nuns. The Argentine government's refusal to acknowledge their detention prompted the French government and the French media to seek information about the whereabouts of the two French nationals. While their fate is still unknown, there is some indication that they were killed by being thrown from an airplane into the sea.

After March 1976 a considerable number of refugees from other countries in Latin America, who had previously sought refuge in Argentina, were abducted; some were returned forcibly to their countries of origin where they suffered persecution; others were threatened with abduction or *refoulement*. The United Nations High Commissioner for Refugees sought to protect the refugees in Argentina, to seek their release, and/or to find new homes for them in other countries.

b. *The Role of Argentine Nongovernmental Organizations*

In addition to the publicity caused by the abduction of foreigners, a number of organizations in Argentina drew national and international attention to the human rights violations. For example, a number of women whose children had been abducted, began in April-May 1977 to hold vigils in the Plaza de Mayo directly across from the President's residence. The women received considerable attention from the international media and were called the Mothers of the Plaza de Mayo. In October-November 1977 another group of women organized themselves as the Grandmothers of the Plaza de Mayo. The two organizations became known for their continuing courageous vigils which provided a public witness to the plight of the thousands of disappeared and their families.

The Permanent Assembly for Human Rights was established in 1976 prior to the military coup. The Argentine League for the Rights of Man had been in existence since the 1930's. The Ecumenical Movement for Human Rights was composed of representatives of the various religious denominations. A number of other human rights organizations, including the Center of Legal and Social Studies (CELS), which was formed in 1979, and the Servicio Paz y Justicia also worked against the repression in Argentina. The Permanent Assembly for Human Rights, in cooperation with several other organizations, produced several lists of the thousands of individuals who had disappeared after 1975. The lists were submitted to the Argentine authorities, but the lists were confiscated. The offices of the organizations and their bank accounts were seized by the Argentine authorities.

Some Argentinians were also able to leave the country and attempted to inform world opinion about the situation in their homeland. For example, the Argentine Commission for Human Rights presented testimony during hearings in September 1976 before the House Subcommittee on International Organizations, chaired by Donald Fraser, and before the Senate Subcommittee on Foreign Assistance in April 1977. The Argentine Commission successfully sought the cut-off of U.S. military aid to the Argentine government, as discussed below.

c. *The Role of International Nongovernmental Organizations*

In addition to the efforts of Argentine groups, several international nongovernmental organizations received information about the abuses in Argentina. Some sent factfinding missions to the country and issued significant reports that drew the attention of the Inter-American Commission on Human Rights of the Organization of American States and the United Nations, as well as alerting the international media. The most visible nongovernmental organization was Amnesty International (AI).

Amnesty sent a factfinding mission to Argentina in November 1976. Amnesty selected prominent delegates who gave visibility to the mission. They included Lord Avebury, a member of the British House of Lords, and Father Robert Drinan, a member of the U.S. House of Representatives. They met with a number of high ranking officials but not with President Videla. They were followed by 20 plainclothed police officers wherever they went, who then questioned, intimidated, and even detained individuals with whom the delegates met. The mission received testimony from prisoners who were tortured. In addition, the AI delegates received personal testimony from the relatives of more than 100 individuals who had been abducted by government agents.

Amnesty International published its report based on the November 1976 mission in March 1977 describing the new repressive legislation and estimating that there were between 5,000 and 6,000 political prisoners. Amnesty also reported that the most commonly quoted figure for disappearances in Argentina at that time was 15,000.

Amnesty kept up the pressure with thousands of letters from AI members—principally from Europe, but also from other countries to the Argentine government as well as appeals to the Inter-American Commission of Human Rights and to the United Nations. Somewhat less visible, but similar missions to Argentina were undertaken by the International Federation of Human Rights in January 1978 and by the Lawyers Committee for Human Rights in April 1979. Other human rights organizations, including the International Commission of Jurists and Pax Christi, also publicized the abuses in Argentina and lobbied in the United Nations and the Inter-American Commission on Human Rights.

d. *Inter-American Commission on Human Rights*

Beginning in 1975 before the coup, the Inter-American Commission on Human Rights of the Organization of American States received an increasing number of complaints about human rights violations in Argentina. The Organization of American States is an intergovernmental organization comprised of almost all of the governments in the Western Hemisphere. The OAS is centered in Washington, D.C., and its principal human rights institution is comprised of seven independent experts who are elected to the Inter-American Commission on Human Rights. As early as 1977 the Commission asked for permission to conduct an on-site visit to Argentina to resolve the many complaints it was receiving as to human rights violations in Argentina. When the Commission did not receive permission to enter, the Commission informed the Argentine government of its decision to prepare a report anyway. In early 1978 the Argentine Government accepted a visit for the limited purpose of reviewing the legal situation. The Commission refused that limitation on their on-site visit. Finally, in late 1978 the Argentine government notified the Commission that it would accept a visit according to the standard conditions of the Commission which permitted the Commission to choose its own itinerary.

There is some question as to why the Argentine Government accepted the visit of the Commission. It may have been that the government believed that it had completed the killing of its principal opposition. Another possibility was that the United States placed pressure on Argentina that led to the visit by the Commission. After the coup the State Department began to make appeals on behalf of the U.S. citizens who were arrested or abducted. Soon after President Carter took office in January 1977, Secretary of State Vance announced that U.S. military aid to Argentina would be reduced from $48.4 million to $15 million. In July 1977 Congress cut off all military aid and sales to Argentina, effective as of September 1978. During 1977 and 1978 there were several visits to Argentina by State Department officials to discuss the human rights situation, culminating in the visit of Secretary Vance in November 1977, during which he submitted a list of thousands of disappeared to the Argentine government.

In July 1978 the State Department indicated that it could not recommend Export-Import (EXIM) Bank financing for the export of Allis Chalmers generators for the Yaciretá hydroelectric power project. During the same period the U.S. began to abstain when votes were taken on loans to Argentina in the Inter-American Development Bank. In September 1978, however, the State Department gave approval for the EXIM Bank financing—apparently in exchange for the agreement of the Argentine government to accept the Inter-American Commission visit.

Before the Inter-American Commission visited Argentina it received briefings from representatives of the Mothers of the Disappeared in Argentina, other Argentine human rights organizations, Amnesty International, and similar groups. These preliminary interviews provided the Commission with information and ideas for the agenda of their visit. Six members of the Commission (from Brazil, Colombia, Costa Rica, El Salvador, the United States, and Venezuela) and a staff of five visited Argentina from September 6-20, 1979. They met with President Videla, other government officials, political figures, representatives of Argentine human rights organizations, trade union officials, lawyers, victims, and their families. The Commission received over 5,500 complaints of which over 4,000 were new.

The most dramatic illustration of the immediate impact of a fact-finding visit occurred when the Commission announced that it would receive testimonies in person from victims and their families. In Buenos Aires thousands of individuals filled a street in front of the building where the Commission was hearing testimonies. That single outpouring of people who had suffered has been credited with giving confidence to many people to seek information concerning the whereabouts of their relatives, thus taking an important step toward the end of repression.

The report of the Commission was broadly disseminated outside of Argentina and was very influential in focusing world public opinion on the human rights abuses in Argentina. The report made it difficult for people outside Argentina to say they did not know what was happening in Argentina. When the report was initially released, newspapers in Argentina published the conclusions and recommendations together with a reply by the government. The report was not officially available in Argentina, but 500 copies were informally distributed and 2,000 photocopies of a clandestine edition were disseminated to journalists, judges, bishops, and others. Human rights organizations in Argentina were able to use the report as proof of the disappearances and other rights violations.

After the Commission's visit it appears that the disappearances in Argentina diminished. Indeed, the Commission was told that the government "had won the war" against subversion as of the time the Commission visited Argentina. The Commission noted that "compared with 1975, 1976, 1977, and 1978, there was a smaller number of disappeared detainees in 1979, and that since October 1979 [just after the Commission's visit of September 1979], the Commission has received no new claims of disappearances." Information submitted to the Argentine National Commission on the Disappeared and to the U.N. Working Group on Enforced or Involuntary Disappearances indicates that relatively few disappearances did occur after the visit. For example, the U.N. Working Group published a chart of the frequency of disappearances since 1971, based on the date of occurrence and based on information received by the Working Group. The data show that disappearances virtually ceased after the Inter-American Commission's visit in September 1979 and declined precipitously in September 1978—that is, a year before the Commission's visit and just when the Argentine government agreed under pressure from the U.S. government to accept the Commission's visit. That agreement apparently occurred when Vice President Mondale met with President Videla, the leader of the Argentine junta, while they were both in Rome attending the funeral of Pope John Paul I.

e.   *United Nations*

While arrangements for the visit of the Inter-American Commission and the actual visit played a very important role in the Argentine case, the same cannot generally be said of the United Nations activities. The U.N. Sub-Commission on Prevention of Discrimination and Protection of Minorities adopted a resolution in August 1976—only a few months after the coup—expressing deep concern about reports that basic human rights "are in jeopardy in Argentina" and referring particularly to the plight of refugees. During the period 1977-79 several nongovernmental organizations as well as the Austrian, French, Swedish, and U.S. delegates to the Commission on Human Rights also mentioned violations of human rights in Argentina. Despite those speeches and the prompt Sub-Commission resolution, the Commission neither established a working group to investigate the situation, as had been done in regard to Chile (1975-1979) and South Africa (1967-present), nor took any other action authorized by Economic and Social Council resolution 1235.

Instead of using the more expeditious and thus usually more effective approach available under resolution 1235, nongovernmental organizations and the U.N. generally pursued the more elaborate, slower, and confidential procedure delineated by ECOSOC resolution 1503. The first communications on Argentina under the 1503 procedure were submitted during 1976 and 1977. Those communications were not, however, found by the Sub-Commission's Working Group on Communications to merit transmission to higher U.N. bodies.

During 1978 three more 1503 communications were submitted by nongovernmental organizations. The Working Group on Communications, meeting in July 1978, decided that the communications did present a consistent pattern of gross and reliably attested violations of internationally recognized human rights. The Sub-Commission, however, under the influence of its Argentine member, Mario Amadeo, decided in August 1978 *not* to transmit them to the Commission on Human Rights.

After the Sub-Commission refused to act, three more communications were submitted by nongovernmental organizations. The Working Group on Communications again found a consistent pattern of gross and reliably attested violations in the three communications from 1979, plus the three held from 1978, and transmitted all six to the Sub-Commission. On September 5, 1979, during a closed session, the Sub-Commission voted—18 in favor, 1 (Argentina) against, and four abstaining—to refer the situation of Argentina to the Commission.

The Commission during confidential sessions in February 1980 discussed the situation on the basis of the communications referred by the Sub-Commission and the government's replies to the communications. The Commission decided to ask several searching questions of the government, in order to place some pressure on Argentina to improve the situation. It was at that same 1980 session that the Commission authorized the establishment of the Working Group on Enforced or Involuntary Disappearances. The Working Group was designed to consider the problem of disappearances in all parts of the world, but there was no doubt that the presence of Mothers of the Disappeared from Argentina in the meeting room gave the Commission a sense of the urgent need for action on the problem of the disappeared.

There were several more 1503 communications on Argentina during the period 1980-1983 with the most important coming from Amnesty and the Lawyers Committee for Human Rights. Each year from 1980 through 1983 the Working Group on Communications transmitted the communications to the Sub-Commission; the Sub-Commission by consensus found a situation warranting Commission attention; and the Commission kept the situation under consideration.

For several reasons, the U.N. encountered difficulty in achieving a consensus for action in the case of Argentina. *First*, the U.N. normally requires a substantial factual showing in order to pursue action. Hence, action by the U.N. was stalled until the Inter-American Commission, Amnesty International, and other human rights organizations had published persuasive reports. *Second*, under the 1503 procedure the U.N. needs to establish that there is a consistent pattern of reliably attested gross violations of human rights, which requires the sort of factual showing that was not available until about 1979. *Third*, Argentina was represented by an ambassador, Gabriel Martinez, who was an experienced and effective advocate in using U.N. procedures to block action by the Commission on Human Rights. *Fourth*, his work was reinforced by the influential role of Argentina in its own region and in the world. Governments were reluctant to take a stand against a Third World country which, unlike Chile, had important friends. Also, Argentina cared about its image in the world and worked hard to present a favorable case against U.N. action. Accordingly, it always answered complaints against it, so that no government could say Argentina was not cooperating. It realized that failure to cooperate would constitute an important reason for coercive U.N. action under the authority of ECOSOC resolution 1235. Another example can be found in Argentina's decision to retain an expensive public relations firm to present a good image in the world. *Fifth*, consensus for U.N. action was made more difficult by an unusual alliance of Argentina and the U.S.S.R. Trade relations between them grew substantially as early as 1974.

Those relations significantly increased after the U.S. imposed a grain embargo in 1979 against the U.S.S.R. The U.S.S.R. and its allies thus also supported Argentina in resisting U.N. action. . . .

5. *Conclusion*

a. *War in the South Atlantic*

The war in the South Atlantic between Argentina and the United Kingdom occurred in April-June 1982. As a consequence of their defeat, the Argentine military were forced to resign. Indeed, even before the war the military government was criticized and weakened by strikes and demonstrations—particularly related to human rights abuses under the military. Despite significant changes in the government of Argentina, the U.N. Commission on Human Rights in February 1983 kept Argentina under consideration in the 1503 process. Only after President Alfonsín was installed in office in December 1983 did the U.N. Commission on Human Rights end the consideration of the situation under the 1503 process.

b. *What factfinding and pressures were effective?*

The Inter-American Commission was much more effective in responding to the situation in Argentina than were U.N. bodies. The Commission was able to respond promptly in 1976-77 because its staff was able to collect information and initiate efforts to obtain an on-site visit. The Commission has a small membership of seven individuals who meet two or three times a year and thus can respond quickly to evolving human rights problems. It has developed a practice of visiting countries with human rights problems that may be unmatched in the human rights world. It need not seek a consistent pattern of gross violations in order to undertake a mission; it need find only that a mission might be useful to help resolve complaints it has received. Arranging the visit and then the visit itself played a crucial role in changing the climate for protection of rights in Argentina. The Commission's work also was facilitated by the pro-human rights policies of the U.S. Congress and the Carter Administration.

The Inter-American Commission has a relatively simple, staff-motivated, flexible, and, in important ways, independent process for responding to alleged violations. In contrast, several U.N. procedures, particularly under ECOSOC resolution 1503, are complex and require many steps vulnerable to political influence. U.N. discussions and decisions were almost entirely secret under ECOSOC resolution 1503; whereas the Inter-American Commission published a full, detailed, and influential report. Indeed, that report formed the factual foundation for later U.N. action under ECOSOC resolution 1503.

In the U.N. the process is controlled by the Commission on Human Rights and its Sub-Commission, which [had at that time] 43 and 26 members respectively. The two bodies meet separately, but only once per year; both require considerable efforts to obtain a consensus before action is possible. Visits to countries on behalf of U.N. bodies are exceptional. Ironically, it was the Argentine situation that prompted the establishment of the Working Group on Enforced or Involuntary Disappearances— one of the first U.N. bodies that has begun to develop a practice of visiting countries where there are problems, but too late to help stop disappearances in Argentina.

In the Argentine case the U.N. was slow to respond; but, once the Commission decided to consider the case under 1503, the consideration continued well beyond the point at which the worst violations were occurring. Indeed, most disappearances, arrests, and killings had ended before the 1503 procedure began. By 1982 and 1983 the principal issue was the need to account for what had happened to the disappeared from the 1976-79 period. So one can say that the Commission was slow to act, but also was slow to respond to improvements. And though the 1503 procedure ended in 1984 after the election that brought President Alfonsin to power, the Working Group on Enforced or Involuntary Disappearances is still pursuing Argentina for explanations about the disappeared.

In conclusion, the present account demonstrates how difficult it is to sort out actions that may cause improvements in a human rights situation. Despite the difficulties, the Argentine case provides one of the best opportunities to consider causation issues. One can state that a complex combination of multilateral and bilateral pressures on the Argentine government, combined with internal pressures, did have an effect in diminishing and ultimately ending the grave violations of human rights that were prevalent during the period 1976-79. Indeed, one can compare the frequency of disappearances during that period with the activities of nongovernmental organizations, governments, the Inter-American Commission on Human Rights, and U.N. bodies. Such a comparison suggests that the final cut-off of U.S. military aid at the end of September 1978 and the Mondale-Videla deal in the same month, which led to the Argentine acceptance of the Inter-American Commission on Human Rights visit, coincide with a significant decrease in the frequency of disappearances. Having accepted the Inter-American Commission's visit, the Argentine government apparently recognized that it had to end the most virulent of its human rights abuses.

If human rights factfinding and pressure apparently did work in the case of Argentina, the question arises as to why they have not yet succeeded in several other countries of the Western Hemisphere or in other places. That question requires further study.

Postscript

For five months in 1985 nine military leaders were tried for specific offenses during the "dirty war." On December 9, 1985, the court issued its verdict. Jorge Videla and Emilio Massera, who commanded the army and the navy, were sentenced to life in prison. Two were sentenced to a term of years, and the remaining defendants were acquitted. Although hundreds of other prosecutions were initiated, almost all of the junior officers and perpetrators of the most heinous abuses were ultimately exempted from prosecution by the Punto Final legislation and the Law of Due Obedience during the Presidency of Raul Alfonsin. Human rights organizations have continued to seek information about thousands of disappeared whose cases have not been resolved.

After President Alfonsin had served nearly six years, Carlos Menem, a candidate allied with the Peronist Party, was elected President on May 14, 1989. Carlos Menem took office as President in July 1989—several months ahead of schedule. On October 6, 1989, he issued a pardon of nearly all the remaining military officers and civilians who were subject to prosecution for their role in violating human rights and undermining democracy during the "dirty war," except for Guillermo Suarez-Mason and the high military officers who had already been convicted.

NOTES AND QUESTIONS

1. On December 29, 1990, President Menem pardoned and released all remaining perpetrators of "dirty war" crimes, including Suarez-Mason.

2.   For more information on the situation in Argentina, see MARIA BARTOLOMEI, GROSS AND MASSIVE VIOLATIONS OF HUMAN RIGHTS IN ARGENTINA, 1976-1983: AN ANALYSIS OF THE PROCEDURE UNDER ECOSOC RESOLUTION 1503 (1991); Alejandro M. Garro, *Nine Years of Transition to Democracy in Argentina: Partial Failure or Qualified Success?*, 31 COLUM. J. TRANSNATL L. 1 (1993); Carlos Nino, THE DUTY TO PUNISH PAST ABUSES OF HUMAN RIGHTS PUT INTO CONTEXT: THE CASE OF ARGENTINA, 100 YALE L.J. 2619 (1991).

3.   The situation in Argentina helped focus attention on the issue of how successor governments should deal with the human rights violations of the previous government. *See* chapter 7 *supra; see also*:

STATE CRIMES: PUNISHMENT OR PARDON (Alice Henkin ed., 1989); *see also* AMERICAS WATCH, CHILE: THE STRUGGLE FOR TRUTH AND JUSTICE FOR PAST HUMAN RIGHTS VIOLATIONS (1992);

RICHARD CARVER, ZIMBABWE: A BREAK WITH THE PAST? (1989);

Diane Orentlicher, *Settling Accounts: The Duty to Prosecute Human Rights Violations of a Prior Regime*, 100 YALE L.J. 2537 (1991);

Naomi Roht-Arriaza, *State Responsibility to Investigate and Prosecute Grave Human Rights Violations in International Law*, 78 CALIF. L. REV. 449 (1990);

Jon van Dyke & Gerald Berkley, *Redressing Human Rights Abuses*, 20 DEN. J. INT'L L. & POL'Y 243 (1992);

David Weissbrodt & Paul Fraser, *Report of the Chilean National Commission on Truth and Reconciliation*, 14 HUM. RTS. Q. 601 (1992) (book review).

4.   Scholars have begun to explore the impact of fact-finding and pressures on human rights abuses, with varying success. Reed Brody, executive director of the International Human Rights Law Group, spoke at a 1993 conference about the effect of fact-finding on rights violations. He stated, "This new, activist, operational approach can have a dramatic impact on human rights. In both El Salvador and Cambodia, the mere presence of the UN has had an important dissuasive effect on violations. . . ." Address by Reed Brody, *International Human Rights Agenda For the Post-Cold War World: Improving Current UN Human Rights Structures*, 1993 World Conference (June 1993).

5.   Another example of a positive result from a fact-finding investigation and report is the work of the special rapporteur to Equatorial Guinea. In a May 1995 report, he sought clemency for 26 individuals being held in government detention. In August 1995 he reported that all detainees had been released. *Report of the Special Rapporteur: The Situation in Equatorial Guinea*, U.N. Doc. HR/95/38 (1995).

6.   For more information on the U.N.'s increased on-site activities, see chapter 6 *infra*; see also:

Douglas Sanders, *The UN Working Group on Indigenous Populations*, 11 HUM. RTS. Q. 406, 422-27 (1989) (concerning Bangladesh);

A. SCHMID, RESEARCH ON GROSS HUMAN RIGHTS VIOLATIONS (1989);

Dinah Shelton, *Utilization of Fact-Finding Missions to Promote and Protect Human Rights: The Chile Case*, 2 HUM. RTS. L.J. 1 (1981);

Kathryn Sikkink, *Human Rights, Principled Issue-Networks and Sovereignty in Latin America*, 47 INT'L ORG. 411 (1993);

David Weissbrodt, *International Trial Observers*, 18 STAN. J. INT'L L. 1, 110-14 (1982).

3. Fact-Finding for United States Violations of Human Rights

Most fact-finding discussed in this chapter involved large-scale violations with physical elements such as torture, arbitrary arrest and detention, and summary execution. Those violations often can be confirmed via visits to prisons and examination of alleged victims.

In contrast, investigations involving the U.S. and many other countries typically focus on more subtle and complex violations; for instance, racial, religious, and ethnic discrimination. To establish government-tolerated discrimination in countries like the U.S. requires data on numerous situations involving both minorities and non-minorities, to show that non-minorities receive better treatment. In the U.S., ease of access to public records makes the endeavor possible but increases the bulk of materials through which a finder of fact must search in order to make an accurate analysis. The problems often require data-collection by national NGOs which regularly monitor U.S. actions in certain fields.

As the Inter-American Commission's visit to Argentina illustrates, fact-finders often consult with local human rights organizations. In situations like the Argentina visit, however, observers have an opportunity to verify the information they receive from NGOs while fact-finders in the U.S. might not find verification possible.

NOTES AND QUESTIONS

1. Complaints alleging racial discrimination have been filed against the U.S. in the U.N. Commission on Human Rights under the confidential Resolution 1503 procedure. *See* chapter 5 *supra*. To establish the consistent pattern of gross and reliably attested violations required, those petitions have often relied on illustrative cases and statistical data. *See, e.g.*:

(a) Communication to the U.N. Commission on Human Rights and Subcommission on Prevention of Discrimination and Protection of Minorities: Human Rights Violations by the Police Against Blacks in the U.S.A., submitted by A. Ray McCoy, Black American Law Student Ass'n, U. of Minn. Chapter, June 10, 1982 (detailing two situations of police brutality against blacks and alleging a pattern of police officers depriving blacks of life without procedural guarantees, coupled with exoneration of the officers);

(b) Communication to the U.N. Commission on Human Rights and Sub-Commission on Prevention of Discrimination and Protection of Minorities: Human Rights Violations of Black People in the U.S., submitted by Theophous Reagans, President, Black American Law School Association, U. of Minn. Law School Chapter, June 22, 1981 (alleging violation of numerous economic and social rights of blacks);

(c) Petition to the U.N. Commission on Human Rights and Sub-Commission on Prevention of Discrimination and Protection of Minorities: Human Rights Violations in the U.S., submitted by The National Conference of Black Lawyers, The National Alliance Against Racist and Political Repression, & United Church of Christ Commission for Racial Justice, Dec. 13, 1978 (presenting case histories of racial minority prisoners allegedly targeted and convicted for political beliefs).

It is interesting to note that the petitioners in that last communication organized their own fact-finding investigation to confirm that their allegations were sufficient to trigger an in-depth study by the U.N. The members of the on-site mission were jurists, invited by the petitioners to participate. The visit took place from August 3 to 20, 1979, and consisted mainly of interviewing prisoners whose cases were detailed in the petition. The jurists published a report explaining their findings and recommending that the U.N. investigate the allegations.

See Report of International Jurists Visit with Human Rights Petitioners in the United States, August 3-20, 1979.

The International Human Rights Association of American Minorities submitted a complaint against the U.S. under the 1503 procedure that focused on the beating of Los Angeles motorist Rodney King by police. The letter to the U.N. stated:

> The recent torture beating of an African-American motorist followed by the beatings, arrest and detention of hundreds of other African- and Spanish-American human rights protesters is only the tip of the proverbial iceberg, which is made up of a consistent pattern of past gross violations of the human rights of African-Americans (enslavement, torture, murder, lynching, forced cultural assimilation (ethnocide)) with neither apology nor compensation (reparations), past gross violations whose ramifications continue into the present.

Letter from the International Human Rights Association of American Minorities to United Nations Secretary General Boutros Boutros Ghali, 30 April 1992.

The Working Group on Communications in 1992 forwarded to the Sub-Commission complaints against 15 countries, including the above complaint against the U.S. The Sub-Commission decided in confidential session, by vote of 11-10, not to refer the complaint to the Commission on Human Rights. The Sub-Commission kept the complaint pending again in 1993 and 1994. *See* Adrien-Claude Zoller, *Analytical Report of the 44th Session of the Sub-Commission,* 17-18 HUM. RTS. MONITOR 6, 18 (1992); Alya Kayal, Penny Parker, & David Weissbrodt, *The Forty-Fourth Session of the UN Sub-Commission on Prevention of Discrimination and Protection of Minorities and the Special Session of the Commission on Human Rights on the Situation in the Former Yugoslavia,* 15 HUM. RTS. Q. 410, 428 (May 1993); INTERNATIONAL SERVICE FOR HUMAN RIGHTS, HUMAN RIGHTS MONITOR 25 (Sep. 1994).

Besides being the subject of a 1503 complaint to the U.N., the Rodney King beating was also the focus of an Amnesty International investigation. AI concluded that beating was part of a pattern of excessive force commonly used by the L.A. police. Amnesty International, *United States of America: Torture, Ill-Treatment and Excessive Force by Police in Los Angeles, California,* AI Index: AMR 51/76/92 (1992).

2.   Fact-finding in the U.S. also has been conducted by the U.N. Special Rapporteur on racism and xenophobia. He visited in 1994, studied the situation concerning racial minorities, and reported his findings at the 1995 session of the Commission on Human Rights. A resolution was introduced by Cuba which endorsed the report and expressed concern about persisting racial discrimination in the U.S. The resolution was rejected with only three countries voting in favor. *See Violation of Human Rights in the United States as a Result of Racism and Racial Discrimination Persisting in United States Society,* U.N. Doc. E/CN.4/1995/L.26/Rev.2 (1995); U.N. Doc. E/CN.4/1995/78; *see also* chapter 5 *supra.*

3.   The U.N. Human Rights Committee reviewed carefully the initial U.S. report on compliance with the Civil and Political Covenant. *See* chapter 3 *supra.*

4.   Amnesty International has conducted other fact-finding investigations in the U.S., based on both individual cases and statistical compilations. *See, e.g.,* Amnesty International, *United States of America: The Death Penalty,* AI INDEX: AMR 51/01/87 (1987); Amnesty International, *Proposal for a Commission of Inquiry into the Effect of Domestic Intelligence Activities on Criminal Trials in the United States of America,* AI Index: AMR 51/05/81 (1981).

CHAPTER 9

HOW CAN THE U.S. GOVERNMENT INFLUENCE RESPECT FOR HUMAN RIGHTS IN OTHER COUNTRIES?

A. **INTRODUCTION**   Page   374

B. **QUESTIONS**   374

C. **INTERNATIONAL DUTIES**   375

     1. **U.S. Duties as a U.N. Member-Nation**   375
         a. The U.N. Charter   375
         b. International Human Rights Treaties   376

     2. **President Clinton's Early View of U.N. Human Rights Obligations**   376
         Address to the 49th U.N. General Assembly   377

D. **INCORPORATING HUMAN RIGHTS GOALS INTO U.S. FOREIGN POLICY**   379
         Warren Christopher, Human Rights and the National Interest   379
         Department of State, Country Reports on Human Rights Practices for 1988   383
         James Baker, Hearing of the Senate Foreign Relations Committee   385
         Warren Christopher, Remarks at the World Conference on Human Rights   386

E. **DEFINING AND IMPLEMENTING U.S. HUMAN RIGHTS POLICY**   391

     1. **The Role of Congress**   391
         Donald M. Fraser, Congress's Role in the Making of International Human Rights Policy   392
         Olufunmilayo B. Arewa & Susan O'Rourke, Country-Specific Legislation and Human Rights: The Case of Peru   396

     2. **The Role of the Administration**   399
         Human Rights Watch & Lawyers Committee for Human Rights, Critique: A Review of the Department of State's Country Reports on Human Rights Practices for 1988   399
         Stephen B. Cohen, Conditioning U.S. Security Assistance on Human Rights Practices   403
         David D. Newsom, The Diplomacy of Human Rights: A Diplomat's View   411

     3. **Economic Sanctions**   415
         Barry E. Carter, International Economic Sanctions: Improving the Haphazard U.S. Legal Regime   415

A. INTRODUCTION

This chapter explores how the U.S. government has used bilateral—distinguished from multilateral—relations with other governments to affect human rights. Perspectives of recent presidential administrations have differed views on the role of human rights in foreign policy. Readers should begin to consider how the U.S. should balance human rights aims against security, economic, and other critical interests.

Several U.S. statutes, regulations, and other instruments link the granting of some types of foreign assistance to the human rights record of countries seeking assistance. Readers should think about the appropriate role of Congress in setting standards for assistance, and also varying methods executive officials have used to help promote and protect human rights in other countries.

This chapter focuses on one rather intrusive method of protecting human rights abroad—economic coercion—and discusses its propriety under international law. Chapter 6 discussed a different method of protecting human rights—physical intervention in other countries through U.N. peace-keeping and humanitarian intervention.

B. QUESTIONS

Assume you are a campaign assistant to a presidential candidate. You have been asked to help develop the candidate's platform concerning proper roles of the U.S. in the U.N. and foreign policy as to human rights. In formulating your draft, consider the following questions. In addition, consider policies the challenging candidate might formulate and how you would handle criticism of your own or the other candidate's platform.

1. Should U.S. foreign policy help promote and protect international human rights? What arguments can you make for and against such a policy? What are U.S. legal foundations for policies based on human rights? Do Sections 116 and 502B provide an answer?

2. Should international human rights get priority over other national interests in U.S. foreign policy? Commercial interests? Security interests?

3. What tools are available to an administration that wants to promote and protect international human rights? Which measures seem to have been most effective?

    a. When should an administration use quiet diplomacy?

    b. To what extent should the U.S. use multilateral rather than bilateral approaches?

    c. Are there legal limits, national or international, to action against human rights violators?

    d. What are arguments for and against linking military or economic aid to human rights?

4. How should an administration develop a foreign policy that favors international human rights?

    a. Consider the four previous administration's approaches to human rights.

Which, if any, would you recommend your candidate adopt? What problems do you see with each approach?

b.   What is the appropriate role of Congress? Can statutes help ensure greater consistency in policy among administrations?

c.   Is it feasible to treat all countries equally regarding their human rights performance? Or should a general platform be tailored to varying countries? Is it possible to avoid charges of a "double standard" if you adopt the latter approach? How should the U.S. treat human rights violations by its closest allies?

d.   What should the standards be for action against human rights violations? Is Section 502B adequate?

e.   What should be the role of (1) nongovernmental and (2) intergovernmental organizations in U.S. human rights policy?

5.   How can one measure the success or failure of an international human rights policy? What are the benefits? The costs? Should an administration reward human rights improvements?

6.   In an era of budget deficits, how might your candidate convince Congress that a foreign aid program is vital to strengthening the U.S. role in the world community? To the promotion and protection of human rights?

C.   INTERNATIONAL DUTIES

1.   U.S. Duties as a U.N. Member-Nation

a.   The U.N. Charter

The U.S. formally has obligated itself to comply with prescriptions of the U.N. Charter, which entered into force on October 24, 1945. According to Article 1(3), a major aim of the U.N. is "[t]o achieve international co-operation in solving international problems of an economic, social, cultural, or humanitarian character, and in promoting and encouraging respect for human rights and for fundamental freedoms for all without distinction as to race, sex, language, or religion . . .." In pursuit of those goals Article 2(2) requires that the U.N. and all member-nations shall "fulfill in good faith the obligations assumed by them in accordance with the present Charter."

Articles 55 and 56 specify several of these obligations. Article 55 reads:

With a view to the creation of conditions of stability and well-being which are necessary for peaceful and friendly relations among nations based on respect for the principle of equal rights and self-determination of peoples, the United Nations shall promote:

a.   higher standards of living, full employment, and conditions of economic and social progress and development;

b.   solutions of international economic, social, health, and related problems; and international cultural and educational co-operation; and

c.   universal respect for, and observance of human rights and fundamental freedoms for all without distinction as to race, sex, language, or religion.

Article 56 sets forth the members' pledge "to take joint and separate action in cooperation with the [U.N.] Organization for the achievement of the purposes set forth in Article 55."

Section 502B of the Foreign Assistance Act of 1961, as amended, prescribes U.S. policy with respect to human rights in accordance with the Charter:

> (a) (1) The United States shall, in accordance with its international obligations as set forth in the Charter of the United Nations and in keeping with the constitutional heritage and traditions of the United States, promote and encourage increased respect for human rights and fundamental freedoms throughout the world without distinction as to race, sex, language, or religion. Accordingly, a principal goal of the foreign policy of the United States shall be to promote the increased observance of internationally recognized human rights by all countries.

The text of Section 502B, reprinted in *Selected International Human Rights Instruments*, should now be read carefully.

b.   International Human Rights Treaties

The U.N. Charter is the world's supertreaty (see its Article 103), and the U.S. is of course bound also to comply with mandates of the other human rights treaties to which it is a party. The International Bill of Human Rights includes the two most important U.N. treaties, the Covenant on Economic, Social and Cultural Rights and the Covenant on Civil and Political Rights. Its other two documents are the Universal Declaration of Human Rights and an Optional Protocol to the Covenant on Civil and Political Rights. As noted in Chapter 2, *infra*, the U.S. is party to neither the Covenant on Economic, Social and Cultural Rights nor the Optional Protocol.

Article 2(1) of the Civil and Political Covenant requires each party "to respect and to ensure to all individuals within its territory and subject to its jurisdiction the rights recognized in the present Covenant . . .." In Article 2(2) each party further agrees, to the extent "not already provided for by existing legislative or other measures . . . to take the necessary steps, in accordance with its constitutional processes and with the provisions of the present Covenant, to adopt such legislative or other measures as may be necessary to give effect to the rights recognized in the present Covenant."

To supplement the International Bill of Human Rights, the U.N. has promulgated other treaties regarding such matters as slavery, genocide, torture, racial and gender discrimination, refugees, and children; and the U.S. has ratified many but not all of them. *See supra* chapter 2 for discussion of the ratification process and a list of treaties the U.S. has ratified. For detailed discussion of U.N. implementation and enforcement procedures regarding those treaties, see *supra* chapters 3 and 4.

In addition to the rights prescribed by the U.N. Charter and various treaties, the Constitution and other U.S. laws are of course used constantly to help protect human rights. For discussion of how U.S. courts and administrative agencies redress rights violations occurring outside the U.S., see *infra* chapter 12. For discussion of how international human rights law is used to protect human rights within the U.S., see *infra* chapter 13.

2.   President Clinton's Early View of U.N. Human Rights Obligations

The President's views do, indeed, affect the extent of U.S. cooperation with the

U.N. The White House influences priorities placed on human rights through the appointment of ambassadors and human rights leaders in the State Department, proposed human rights legislation, and seeking the Senate's advice and consent to treaties. As you read the following excerpt, focus on President Clinton's views of the U.N. and the U.S. role in international human rights efforts.[1]

Text of Address by President Clinton to the 49th U.N. General Assembly, September 26, 1994:

We meet today in a time of great hope and change. The end of the Cold War, the explosion of technology, and trade and enterprise have given people the world over new opportunities to live up to their dreams and their God-given potential. This is an age of hope. Yet in this new world we face a contest as old as history—a struggle between freedom and tyranny, between tolerance and bigotry, between knowledge and ignorance, between openness and isolation. It is a fight between those who would build free societies governed by laws and those who would impose their will by force. Our struggle today, in a world more high tech, more fast moving, more chaotically diverse than ever, is the age-old fight between hope and fear. . . .

Our generation has a difficult task. The Cold War is over. We must secure the peace. It falls to us to avoid the complacency that followed World War I without the spur of the imminent threat to our security that followed World War II. We must ensure that those who fought and found the courage to end the Cold War, those from both East and West who love freedom, did not labor in vain. Our sacred mission is to build a new world for our children, more democratic, more prosperous, more free of ancient hatreds and modern means of destruction.

That is no easy challenge, but we accept it with confidence; after all, the walls that once divided nations in this very chamber have come down. . . .

But while the ideals of democracy and free markets are ascendant, they are surely not the whole story. Terrible examples of chaos, repression and tyranny also mark our times. The 20th Century proved that the forces of freedom and democracy can endure against great odds. Our job is to see that in the 21st Century these forces triumph.

The dangers we face are less stark and more diffuse than those of the Cold War, but they are still formidable—the ethnic conflicts that drive millions from their homes; the despots ready to repress their own people or conquer their neighbors; the proliferation of weapons of mass destruction; the terrorists wielding their deadly arms—the criminal syndicates selling those arms or drugs and infiltrating the very institutions of fragile democracy; a global economy that offers great promise but also deep insecurity and, in many places, declining opportunity; diseases like AIDS that threaten to decimate nations; the combined dangers of population explosion and economic decline . . .; global and local environmental threats that demand that sustainable development becomes a part of the lives of people all around the world; and, finally, within many of our nations, high rates of drug abuse and crime and family breakdown, with all their terrible consequences.

These are the dangers we face today. We must address these threats to our future. Thankfully, the end of the Cold War gives us a chance to address them together. In our efforts, different nations may be active in different situations in

---

[1] [Keep in mind the discussion of "peacekeeping" in chapter 6.]

different ways, but their purposes must be consistent with freedom and their practices consistent with international law. Each nation will bring to our common task its own particular strengths—economic, political or military.

Of course, the first duty of every member of the United Nations is to its own citizens, to their security, their welfare, and their interests. . . . When our national security interests are threatened, we will act with others when we can, but alone if we must. We will use diplomacy when we can, but force if we must.

The United States recognizes that we also have a special responsibility in these common endeavors that we are taking, the responsibility that goes along with great power, and also with our long history of democracy and freedom. But we seek to fulfill that responsibility in cooperation with other nations. Working together increases the impact and the legitimacy of each of our actions, and sharing the burdens lessens everyone's load. We have no desire to be the world's policeman, but we will do what we can to help civil societies emerge from the ashes of repression, to sustain fragile democracies, and to add more free markets to the world and, of course, to restrain the destructive forces that threaten us all. . . .

A coalition for democracy—it's good for America. Democracies, after all, are more likely to be stable, less likely to wage war. They strengthen civil society. They can provide people with the economic and political opportunities to build their futures in their own homes, not to flee their borders. Our efforts to help build more democracies will make us all more secure, more prosperous and more successful as we try to make this era of terrific change our friend and not our enemy.

In my nation, as in all of your nations, there are many people who are understandably reluctant to undertake these efforts because, often, the distances are great or the cultures are different. There are good reasons for the caution that people feel. Often the chances of success, or the costs, are unclear. And, of course, in every common endeavor there is always the potential for failure and, often, the risk of loss of life. And yet, our people . . . genuinely want to help their neighbors around the world and want to make some effort in our common cause. We have seen that progress can be made as well.

The problem is deciding when we must respond, and how we shall overcome our reluctance. This will never be easy—there are no simple formulas. All of us will make these decisions, in part, based on the distance of the problem from our shores, or the interests of our nation, or the difference we think we can make, or the cost required or the threat to our own citizens in the endeavor.

Hard questions will remain and cannot be erased by some simple formula, but we should have the confidence that these efforts can succeed . . . .

The growth of cooperation between the United States and the Russian Federation also should give us all great cause for confidence. This is a partnership that is rooted in democracy, a partnership that is working, a partnership of not complete agreement but genuine mutual respect. After so many years of nuclear terror, our two nations are taking dramatic steps to ease tensions around the world. . . .

Our progress in the last year also provides confidence that, in the post-Cold War years, we can adapt and construct global institutions that will help to provide security and increase economic growth through the world. . . .

Here, at the United Nations, we must develop a concrete plan . . . to revitalize the U.N.'s obligations to address the security, economic and political challenges ahead—obligations we must all be willing to assume.

Our objectives should include ready, efficient and capable U.N. peacekeeping forces . . . . We must also pledge to keep U.N. reform moving forward so that we do more with less. And we must improve our ability to respond to urgent needs. Let me suggest that it is time for the members of this assembly to consider seriously President [of Argentina] Menem's suggestion for the creation of a civilian rapid response capability for humanitarian crises.

And let us not lose sight of the special role that development and democracy can play in preventing conflicts once peace has been established. Never before has the United Nations been in a better position to achieve the democratic goals of our founders. The end of the Cold War has freed us from decades of paralyzing divisions, and we all know that multilateral cooperation is not only necessary to address the new threats we face, but possible to succeed. . . .

[W]e must also think of our children and the world we will leave them in the 21st Century. History has given us a very rare opportunity—the chance to build on the greatest legacy of this century without reliving its darkest moments. And we have shown that we can carry forward humanity's ancient quest for freedom—to build a world where democracy knows no borders but where nations know their borders will always be secure, a world that gives all people the chance to realize their potential and to live out their dreams.

D. INCORPORATING HUMAN RIGHTS GOALS INTO U.S. FOREIGN POLICY

The varying policies of U.S. administrations illustrate widely differing views of foreign policy and the role of human rights in that policy. Excerpts here have been selected to reflect the Carter, Reagan, Bush, and Clinton administrations. The first is from a speech by Warren Christopher when he was Deputy Secretary of State in the Carter Administration. The second is the introduction to the State Department Country Reports for 1988, which reflects views of the Reagan Administration. The third is from a speech by James Baker, Secretary of State in the Bush Administration; and the fourth is an excerpt from a speech by Christopher, delivered as Secretary of State in the Clinton Administration. Examine each of the excerpts regarding (1) the place of moral and ethical concerns in U.S. foreign policy; (2) the definition of human rights; (3) the extent to which promotion of rights is in the national interest; and (4) effective policies to promote and protect human rights. As you read these excerpts think about how Clinton's 1994 address to the U.N. General Assembly echoes some visions of the preceding administrations.

Deputy Secretary Warren Christopher, *Human Rights and the National Interest*, Dep't of State, Bureau of Public Affairs, Current Policy No. 206 (1980):

Three and a half years ago, President Carter introduced into our foreign policy a theme both old and new: old, because it arose from our most basic national values; new in the sharp emphasis the President gave it. I am referring, of course, to human rights. "Because we are free," the President said in his inaugural address, "we can never be indifferent to the fate of freedom elsewhere."

From the beginning, the President was determined that American foreign policy should give active, explicit support to three categories of human rights:

— The right to be free from violations of personal integrity—torture, arbitrary arrest or imprisonment, and violations of due process;

—   The right to fulfill vital economic needs, such as food, shelter, health care and education; and

—   Civil and political rights—freedom of thought, expression, assembly, travel, and participation in government. . . .

[O]ur commitment to human rights rests upon a large and growing body of law. Domestically, human rights legislation enacted by our Congress makes clear that our commitment is truly a national commitment—and that it is here to stay. Internationally, the human rights conventions, the Universal Declaration of Human Rights, and other basic documents make clear that the values we are seeking to advance are truly global values. . . .

In the 3½ years since President Carter proclaimed his policy, we have made real progress. We have effectively institutionalized human rights as a major element of U.S. foreign policy. A Bureau of Human Rights and Humanitarian Affairs has been established by statute, headed by an Assistant Secretary of State. Every American Ambassador has been instructed to report regularly on human rights conditions in the country to which he or she is posted. And the State Department's annual country reports on human rights have become one of the most important and objective sources of information on human rights conditions around the world. . . .

[H]uman rights has been placed squarely on the diplomatic table. The subject has become an item of serious discussion between us and the nations with which we deal—a dramatic change from past diplomatic practice. We have worked to strengthen the human rights effort of international bodies like the United Nations and the Inter-American Human Rights Commission. And human rights performance has become one of the criteria we use in apportioning American aid to other nations.

This new emphasis in our foreign policy has not come without controversy. There has been rigorous criticism of our human rights policy on the ground that it smacks of fuzzy-headed liberalism, that it is unrelated to the pursuit of our basic national interests. Some critics have suggested that human rights are a millstone around the neck of U.S. foreign policy; that it has injected into our diplomacy an interventionist element that can only weaken our position in the world and even destabilize other governments.

. . . To abandon the pursuit of human rights would gravely damage not only the hopes of millions abroad but also the foreign policy and long-term security of the United States.

A firm emphasis on human rights is not an alternative to "realpolitik," nor is it simply a side issue in our foreign policy. It is, instead, a central part of a pragmatic, tough-minded policy. Our human rights policy serves not just the ideals but the interests of the United States.

Let me support that assertion by discussing four ways in which our stress on human rights serves important interests of our nation.

Peace and Stability

First, our human rights policy directly serves our long-term interest in peace and stability.

There is, perhaps, a natural temptation to equate stability with status quo. Yet experience has demonstrated that the opposite is often true. The silence of official repression may appear to be "stability"—but it is often far more fragile than it appears. The misleading quiet of repression has too often turned out to be the calm before a violent, revolutionary storm. In such storms of violence, American interests are often damaged—and targets of opportunity are created for the Soviet Union or other forces hostile to the United States.

Governments that respect the rights of their people, and which reflect the will of their people, are far less vulnerable to such disruptions. . . .

By advancing human rights, we help to alleviate the sources of tension and instability before they erupt into violence, before our interests are harmed.

Our human rights policy is, thus, a vital element of our effort to align the United States with support for peaceful, constructive change. We are not so naive as to equate all change with progress—for that equation makes no more sense than equating stability and the status quo. But we recognize that the suppression of peaceful change often makes violence and terror inevitable. . . .

There is, as I have said, an economic dimension to our support for human rights. Some of the most dangerous sources of instability in the world are economic. Such instability is bad for our security interests, and it is bad for American business, too. Respect for human rights creates an atmosphere of stability in which business and investment can flourish.

Foreign assistance is one of the most effective tools for coping with these economic sources of instability. Today, unfortunately, our foreign assistance is too meager to serve adequately our own humanitarian, economic, or security interests. But we try to target such aid as we can provide to narrow income disparities, to help people directly, and thus to ease social tensions in developing countries. We also channel our aid increasingly to countries that respect human rights, to countries that are trying to preserve representative government or to move from dictatorship to democracy.

This channeling of our aid is sometimes attacked as "intervention." We are admonished that other governments have a right to choose their own practices and forms of governments. Of course they do. But we have the right, and the obligation, to choose which governments and practices we will support with our scarce dollars.

Our resources and our powers are limited. But by working to ease grinding poverty, by supporting peaceful, constructive change, we believe we serve the cause of real peace and stability in the world. And this is very much in our national interest.

U.S. Security

The second point I wish to emphasize is that the United States will be more secure in a world where more governments respect the rights of their people—because countries that respect human rights make stronger allies and better friends.

This reality is illustrated by the democracies in Western Europe, in the Andean Pact in South America, in Japan and in the ASEAN [Association of South East Asian Nations] group in Southeast Asia. Their commitment to human rights gives them an inner strength and stability that enables them to stand steadfastly with us on the most difficult security issues of our time. By seeking to widen the circle of such countries, our human rights policy directly enhances our security interests.

Unfortunately, of course, not all our friends and allies can meet this high standard. One of the greatest challenges we will face in future years is the challenge of meshing our security assistance with human rights persuasion; combining military assistance to those who need it with strong encouragement to undertake the kind of internal reform necessary for long-term stability.

We face this challenge in our dealing with allies like South Korea and the Philippines—nations whose friendship is important to our security, nations whose governments we are trying to influence on human rights issues. Our security assistance to such countries supports a basic human right—the right of their people to live in safety from external attack. At the same time, by encouraging governments to undertake internal reforms that will improve life for their people, we serve their long term security interests and our own.

U.S. Influence

Third, support for human rights enhances the influence of the United States in important world arenas.

Too often in the past, the United States has allowed itself to be portrayed as a complacent, status quo power, insensitive to the quest of others for the freedoms we enjoy. And the result has often weakened the influence of the United States.

Our human rights policy counters that tendency. It identifies the United States with leaders around the world who are trying to improve the lot of their people.

We stand at a moment in history when widening literacy, mass communications, and urbanization have produced a global political awakening. This is a fundamental event in human history that expresses itself, above all, in the intensified demand for human rights. And our response to that demand has meant a new influence and good will for our country. . . .

In essence, our support for human rights gives us a way of emphasizing what we are for, not simply what we oppose. It gives us a way of taking the ideological initiative, instead of merely reacting. It gives us a rubric under which to organize our support for due process, economic progress, and democratic principles.

In the competition between the Soviet Union and ourselves, we benefit from the comparison between our values and political methods and those of the Soviets. We pursue human rights for their own sake and would do so even if there were no Soviet Union. But there can be no doubt that our human rights policy does confound our adversaries.

The Soviets fear our human rights policy because their own human rights record is so abysmal and because they sense the power that the ideas of freedom and human dignity exert. Georgi Vladimov, a Soviet author and dissident, recently commented on U.S. human rights policy, "I don't know if President Carter will enter American history," he said, "but he has already entered Russian history with his policy." . . .

The influence and goodwill we gain by standing up for human rights cannot always be tangibly measured, but it is real. Our embassy reports, our conversations with foreign diplomats, and the foreign press show that U.S. foreign policy is widely perceived as clearly and courageously supporting human rights. We need more, not less, of this positive policy.

Refugee Problem

Fourth, our support for human rights may offer the only long-term solution to one of the most pressing problems on the international agenda—the problem of refugees.. . .

[T]he solution lies not simply in arrangements to ease the plight of refugees; it lies in efforts to end the misery and repression that caused them to flee in the first place.

When a government respects the human rights of its citizens, refugees are a rare phenomenon. And we know that refugees are more likely to return home when the human rights situation has improved at home. . . .

Global Progress

As we look over the past three and a half years, we can see that the United States is identified more clearly than ever as a beacon of support for human rights. Worldwide publicity and concern for human rights have increased dramatically. . . .

Our efforts to express our deepest values through our human rights policy are working. They give us a glimpse of something we see all too seldom in the world; a happy situation in which American interests and American ideals converge.

*   *   *   *   *

DEP'T OF STATE, COUNTRY REPORTS ON HUMAN RIGHTS PRACTICES FOR 1988, REPORT SUBMITTED TO THE SENATE COMMITTEE ON FOREIGN RELATIONS AND THE HOUSE COMMITTEE ON FOREIGN AFFAIRS, 101st Cong., 1st Sess. 1 (1989):

This report is submitted to the Congress by the Department of State in compliance with Sections 116(d)(1) and 502B(b) of the Foreign Assistance Act of 1961, as amended. The legislation requires human rights reports on all countries that receive aid from the United States and all countries that are members of the United Nations. In the belief that the information would be useful to the Congress and other readers, we have also included reports on the few countries which do not fall into either of these categories and which are thus not covered by the Congressional requirement.

Congress amended the Foreign Assistance Act with the foregoing sections of law so as to be able to consult these reports when considering assistance programs for specific foreign countries. One of the very important consequences—perhaps unintended—of these legislative provisions is that they have made human rights concerns an integral part of the State Department's daily reporting and daily decisionmaking. A human rights officer in an Embassy overseas who wants to write a good annual human rights report on the country in which he or she works must carefully monitor and observe human rights developments throughout the year on a daily basis. As a consequence he or she will report on such developments whenever something of human rights significance happens in the country of assignment. In the past 12 years, the State Department has become decidedly better informed on and sensitized to human rights violations as they occur around the globe. . . .

Definition of Human Rights

Human rights, as defined in Section 116(a) of the Foreign Assistance Act, include freedom from torture or other cruel, inhuman, or degrading treatment or punishment; prolonged detention without charge; disappearance due to abduction or clandestine detention; and other flagrant denial of the rights to life, liberty, and the security of the person. Internationally recognized worker rights, as defined in Section 502(a) of the Trade Act, include (A) the right of association; (B) the right to organize and bargain collectively; (C) prohibition on the use of any form of forced or compulsory labor; (D) a minimum age for the employment of children; and (E) acceptable conditions of work with respect to minimum wages, hours of work, and occupational safety and health.

In addition to discussing the topics specified in the legislation, *our reports as in previous years, cover other internationally recognized political rights and civil liberties and describe the political system of each country.*

In applying these internationally recognized standards, we seek to be objective.

But the reports unashamedly reflect the U.S. view that the right of self-government is a basic political right, that government is legitimate only when grounded on the consent of the governed, and that government thus grounded should not be used to deny life, liberty, and the pursuit of happiness. Individuals in a society have the inalienable right to be free from governmental violations of the integrity of the person; to enjoy civil liberties such as freedom of expression, assembly, religion, and movement, without discrimination based on race, ancestry, or sex; and to change their government by peaceful means. The reports also take into account the fact that terrorists and guerrilla groups often kill, torture, or maim citizens or deprive them of their liberties; such violations are no less reprehensible if committed by violent opponents of the government than if committed by the government itself.

We have found that the concept of economic, social, and cultural rights is often confused sometimes willfully, by repressive governments claiming that, in order to promote these "rights," they may deny their citizens the right to integrity of the person as well as political and civil rights. There exists a profound connection between human rights and economic development. Experience demonstrates that it is individual freedom that sets the stage for economic and social development; it is repression that stifles it. Those who try to justify subordinating political and civil rights on the ground that they are concentrating on economic aspirations invariably deliver on neither. *That is why we consider it imperative to focus urgent attention on violations of basic political and civil rights. If these basic rights are not secured, experience has shown, the goals of economic development are not reached either.* This is a point which the Soviet Union's reformers seem to have recognized.

United States Human Rights Policy

From this premise, that basic human rights may not be abridged or denied, it follows that our human rights policy is concerned with the limitations on the powers of government that are required to protect the integrity and dignity of the individual. Further, it is in our national interest to promote democratic processes in order to help build a world environment more favorable to respect for human rights and hence more conducive to stability and peace. We have developed, therefore, a dual policy, reactive in the sense that we continue to oppose specific human rights violations wherever they occur, but at the same time active in working over the long term to strengthen democracy.

In much of the world, the United States has a variety of means at its disposal to respond to human rights violations. We engage in traditional diplomacy, particularly with friendly governments, where frank diplomatic exchanges are possible and productive. Where we find limited opportunities for the United States to exert significant influence through bilateral relations, we resort to public statements of our concerns, calling attention to countries where respect for human rights is lacking. In a number of instances, we employ a mixture of traditional diplomacy and public affirmation of American interest in the issue.

The United States also employs a variety of means to encourage greater respect for human rights over the long term. Since 1983 the National Endowment for Democracy has been carrying out programs designed to promote democratic practices abroad, involving the two major United States political parties, labor unions, business groups, and many private institutions. Also, through Section 116(3) of the Foreign Assistance Act, funds are disbursed by the Agency for International Development for *programs designed to promote civil and political rights abroad*. We also seek greater international commitment to the protection of human rights and respect for democracy through our efforts in the United Nations and other international

organizations, and in the process devised by the Conference on Security and Cooperation in Europe.

Preparation of these annual reports constitutes an important element of our
human rights policy. The process, since it involves continuous and well-publicized
attention to human rights, has contributed to the strengthening of an international
human rights agenda. Many countries that are strong supporters of human rights
are taking steps of their own to engage in human rights reporting and have established offices specifically responsible for international human rights policy. Even
among countries without strong human rights records, sensitivity to these reports
increasingly takes the form of constructive response, or at least a willingness to
engage in a discussion of human rights policy. In calling upon the Department of
State to prepare these reports, Congress has created a useful instrument for advancing the cause of human rights.

*   *   *   *   *

James Baker, Secretary of State, Hearing of the Senate Foreign Rela-
tions Committee, Feb. 2, 1990:

During my confirmation hearings before this committee a year ago I talked
about a world that was in transition and said that the only sure policy guide for us
in the midst of change like that is the compass of American values—the compass
of democracy, respect for human rights, fair play, market principles, and the peaceful
settlement of conflicts.

I also said we can advance our foreign policy objectives if we are resolved on
the necessity of continuing American leadership and the need for bipartisanship.
After one year on the job now . . . I am more than ever convinced that those statements
are correct and represent the formula on the basis of which we should proceed. . . .

[O]ur task is to consolidate the democratic revolution that is now transforming
the world. It can scarcely be otherwise, for our fundamental values—self-determination, human rights, the rule of law, political freedom, all push the United States of
America in this direction. We seek to promote democratic values abroad simply
because they reflect the best that is in the United States of America, and we do so
because championing democracy is in our interest. Where democratic values take
hold the United States has historically found friends. Where they don't sometimes
all too often we find enemies.

Democracies are more likely to open their economies to the world and legitimate
democratic governments are more likely to focus on the livelihood of their people
than they are on foreign conquest or aggression. Political freedom, economic growth
and global security are all interdependent and they are all, we think at least,
dependent upon American leadership, strengthened alliances and worldwide engagement.

So, as I see it, . . . we face five key foreign policy challenges in the course of this
next decade. The first, and the preeminent one is to consolidate democracy. When
the barriers to democratic values come down, as we have seen and are seeing, even
as we speak this morning, in Eastern Europe, prospects open wide for legitimate
government, for revitalized societies, for improved relations and, indeed, for lasting
security. . . .

Our goals are to institutionalize a new strategic relationship with the Soviet
Union through verifiable arms-control treaties and confidence-building measures.
We would like to forge a new global relationship with the Soviets, by pressing them

to help end regional conflicts peacefully, and we seek a more democratic Soviet Union, where human rights gains are made permanent—permanent through the rule of law and democratic processes. . . .

Our second challenge will be to foster global growth by promoting market principles bilaterally and multilaterally through the IMF, the World Bank, and the GATT. As we all know in this country political and economic liberty go hand-in-hand. Fragile democracies around the world are reinforced by strong economies, and open societies give scope to the creativity and entrepreneurship essential to economic success. . . .

Our third challenge . . . is to promote the secure global environment that is vital if democratic and market values are to flourish. We want to build a peace that will last. . . . Revolutionary changes in the communist world and increasingly cooperative US-Soviet relations are creating the political conditions which are necessary for enduring and strategically significant arms control.

I think we have an historic opportunity to transform East-West security competition. Uncertainty about the fate of reform in the Soviet Union is all the more reason, not less, to negotiate agreements that reduce threats and that constrain the military options that are available to the leaders in the Kremlin. United States' diplomacy has played a central and highly successful role in preemption and resolving regional conflicts. We will continue to support the constructive efforts of other states and of the United Nations and other organizations which are committed to those same goals. . . .

Our fourth challenge for the '90s is to work with all nations, allies, friends, and traditional adversaries alike, against new global dangers such as environmental degradation, narcotics trafficking, and terrorism. These threats can endanger lives and they can destroy the very fabric of our societies. Our non-renewable resources, human lives and the values of civilized society, are irreplaceable assets which we cannot fail to protect.

Our fifth challenge . . . is to reshape and renew our alliances and our other important ties. Meeting this last challenge is critical, I think, to meeting all the others. We need to adjust our Atlantic and Pacific partnerships and the international institutions to the already favorable conditions that those very partnerships and organizations have created.

* * * * *

Warren Christopher, *Democracy and Human Rights: Where America Stands*, Remarks at the World Conference on Human Rights (June 14, 1993):

America's identity as a nation derives from our dedication to the proposition "that all Men are created equal and endowed by their Creator with certain inalienable rights." Over the course of two centuries, Americans have found that advancing democratic values and human rights serves our deepest values as well as our practical interests.

That is why the United States stands with the men and women everywhere who are standing up for these principles. And that is why President Clinton has made reenforcing democracy and protecting human rights a pillar of our foreign policy—and a major focus of our foreign assistance programs.

Democracy is the moral and strategic imperative for the 1990s. Democracy will build safeguards for human rights in every nation. Democracy is the best way to advance lasting peace and prosperity in the world.

The cause of freedom is a fundamental commitment for any country. It is also a matter of deep personal conviction for me. I am proud to have headed the U.S. Government's first interagency group on human rights under President Carter... . President Carter will be remembered as the first American President to put human rights on the international agenda. He has helped to lift the lives of people in every part of the world. Today, we build upon his achievements—and those of the human rights movement since its inception. . . .

Beyond our support for multilateral efforts [to promote human rights], the United States recognizes that we have a solemn duty to take steps of our own.

In that spirit, I am pleased to announce that the United States will move promptly to obtain the consent of our Senate to ratify the International Convention on the Elimination of All Forms of Racial Discrimination.[2]

We strongly support the general goals of the other treaties that we have signed but not yet ratified. The Convention on the Elimination of All Forms of Discrimination Against Women; the American Convention on Human Rights; and the International Covenant on Economic, Social and Cultural Rights; each of these will constitute important advances. Our Administration will turn to them as soon as the Senate has acted on the racism Convention. And we expect soon to pass implementing legislation for the Convention Against Torture in furtherance of the worldwide goal of eliminating torture by the year 2000. To us, these far-reaching documents are not parchment promises to be made for propaganda effect, but solemn commitments to be enforced. [*See supra* chapter 2 for U.S. ratification of and reservations to human rights treaties.]

My country will pursue human rights in our bilateral relations with all governments—large and small, developed and developing. America's commitment to human rights is global, just as the UN Declaration is universal.

As we advance these goals, American foreign policy will both reflect our fundamental values and promote our national interests. It must take account of our national security and economic needs at the same time we pursue democracy and human rights. We will maintain our ties with our allies and friends. We will act to deter aggressors. And we will cooperate with like-minded nations to ensure the survival of freedom when it is threatened. . . .

We will insist that our diplomats continue to report accurately and fully on human rights conditions around the world. Respect for human rights and the commitment to democracy-building will be major considerations as we determine how to spend our resources on foreign assistance. And we will weigh human rights considerations in trade policy. . . .

We will help new democracies make a smooth transition to civilian control of the military. And we will assist militaries in finding constructive new rules in pursuit of peace and security—roles that respect human rights and contribute to international peace.

Working with the UN and other international organizations, we will help develop the public and private institutions essential to a working democracy and the rule of law. And we will continue to support America's own National Endowment for Democracy in its mission to help nourish democracy where it is struggling to grow.

---

[2] [Ed. note: The Senate gave its advice and consent to the Race Convention on June 24, 1994. The U.S. ratified the treaty in October 1994.]

NOTES AND QUESTIONS

1.   How central have human rights concerns been in each administration? Do our excerpts reflect shifts in emphasis regarding bilateral vs. multilateral efforts? Economic vs. civil and political rights? What plans did each administration advance for promoting and protecting rights?

2.   President Carter stressed international human rights as a central concern of foreign policy. Though his administration was not always able to put human rights on a par with other national interests affected by foreign affairs, his rhetoric placing human rights at the core of foreign policy proved popular with the U.S. public.

   That popularity helped force the Reagan Administration to include human rights improvement as one of its goals. At the beginning of President Reagan's first term, however, it was argued that human rights work was most effective as a weapon against communism. Ernest Lefever, Reagan's first nominee for head of the Human Rights Bureau, publicly opposed U.S. attempts to change policies of other countries by making human rights a foreign policy concern. He stated, for instance: "[w]e have no moral mandate to remake the world in our own image." AMERICAN ASSOCIATION FOR THE INTERNATIONAL COMMISSION OF JURISTS, HUMAN RIGHTS AND AMERICAN FOREIGN POLICY: THE FIRST DECADE 1973-1983, at 32 (1984) (quoting MORALITY AND FOREIGN POLICY, Ethics and Public Policy Center, Georgetown University, 1977). In his view, according too much significance to human rights could endanger primary goals of foreign policy; *i.e.*, U.S. security and economic interests. The Senate rebuffed his nomination, forcing Reagan to rethink his own position.

   Do you think U.S. foreign policy should include promotion and protection of human rights in other countries? What about the contention that the U.S. has no moral mandate to remake the world but should instead look to its own interests? Should the U.S. use promotion of human rights as an ideology, or as an organizing principle to justify some of its conduct in the global arena?

   If you believe that human rights do merit a role in foreign policy decisions, should human rights goals ever take precedence over security and economic goals when there is a clash? As you read the materials in this chapter consider whether in fact it is possible or desirable for a country to place promotion of human rights ahead of other goals.

3.   In her article *Dictatorships and Double Standards*, Commentary, Nov. 1979, at 34-45, Reagan's U.N. Ambassador Jeanne Kirkpatrick criticized the Carter Administration's human rights policy, arguing for instance that distinctions should be made between dictators friendly to the U.S. and Marxist dictators. She argued that rights violations by friendly dictators should be viewed with less hostility because their governments may be more subject to liberalization, and friendly relations are required by U.S. security interests. Marxist states, the argument continues, create situations in which the worst violations of rights occur. Do you agree? Do you think that violations have occurred more often in those states than in states governed by right-wing dictators? Does recent history help confirm or contradict Kirkpatrick's arguments?

   Cyrus Vance, Secretary of State under Carter, criticized the Reagan Administration's adoption of Kirkpatrick's distinction. According to Vance, the idea that the U.S. should turn a blind eye to, and perhaps even support, serious human rights abuses committed by any government makes U.S. foreign policy morally bankrupt. Individual victims, Vance observed, suffer regardless of the abuser's political orientation. Cyrus Vance, *The Human Rights Imperative*, 63 FOREIGN POL'Y 3, 9-12 (1986).

   In 1992, Kirkpatrick, praising transitions from totalitarianism to democracy that had taken place in Central and Eastern Europe, condemned countries that still repressed human rights such as China, Cuba, Iraq, Syria, and Haiti. She also stated that countries which do enjoy basic freedoms have a responsibility to support governments that seek to implement democracy. Are those views consistent with her earlier statements? *See* Jeanne Kirkpatrick, *A Revolution That Goes On*, WASH. POST, Feb. 10, 1992, at A11.

4. The theory for promoting democracy as part of foreign policy is that most democracies, compared with non-democratic countries, are more likely to respect human rights, adhere to international law, settle conflicts peacefully, declare war rarely and reluctantly, respect rights of minorities, and encourage free-market economies. Not all rights advocates agree, however, that merely promoting democracy will in fact protect rights. For criticism of the Reagan Administration's concentration on "democracy" over humanitarian concerns, see Larry Minear, *The Forgotten Human Agenda*, 73 FOREIGN POLICY 76 (1988-89). *Cf.* Thomas Carothers, *Democracy and Human Rights: Policy Allies or Rivals?*, 17 WASH. Q. 109 (1994) (rejecting the idea that democracy promotion and human rights policies are either inherently consistent or inconsistent and proposing a middle ground). For discussion of methods the U.S. could use in promoting democracy and the legality of proposed methods under international law, see Tom J. Farer, *The United States as Guarantor of Democracy in the Caribbean Basin: Is There a Legal Way?*, 10 HUM. RTS. Q. 157 (1988); *cf.* Henry J. Steiner, *Political Participation as a Human Right*, 1 HARV. HUM. RTS. Y.B. 77 (1988).

There is a developing literature on the right to democracy as a human right. For further reading, see HUMAN RIGHTS AND PLURALIST DEMOCRACY (Allan Rosas & Jan Helgesen eds., 1992); Michael J. Kane, *Promoting Political Rights to Protect the Environment*, 18 YALE J. INT'L L. 389 (1993).

In 1990, the Conference on Security and Cooperation in Europe adopted a document asserting

> (1) that the protection of human rights is one of the basic purposes of government, (2) that a freely elected representative government is *essential* for the protection of human rights and (3) that states have a responsibility to protect democratically elected governments—their own and other states'—if they are threatened by acts of violence of terrorism.

Malvina Halberstam, *The Copenhagen Document: Intervention in Support of Democracy*, 34 HARV. INT'L L.J. 163, 164 (1993). Is Reagan's concentration on "democracy" over human rights thus supported?

5. For analyses of the Carter and Reagan administrations' human rights policies, see:

AMERICAN ASSOCIATION FOR THE INTERNATIONAL COMMISSION OF JURISTS, HUMAN RIGHTS AND U.S. FOREIGN POLICY: THE FIRST DECADE 1973-1983, at 15-44 (1984);

David Carleton & Michael Stohl, *The Foreign Police of Human Rights: Rhetoric and Reality From Jimmy Carter to Ronald Reagan*, 7 HUM. RTS. Q. 205 (1985);

DAVID P. FORSYTHE, HUMAN RIGHTS AND WORLD POLITICS 88-124 (1983);

A. GLENN MOWER, HUMAN RIGHTS AND AMERICAN FOREIGN POLICY: THE CARTER AND REAGAN EXPERIENCES (1987);

JOSHUA MURVACHIK, THE UNCERTAIN CRUSADE: JIMMY CARTER AND THE DILEMMA OF HUMAN RIGHTS POLICY (1986);

Jacoby, *The Reagan Turnaround on Human Rights*, 64 FOREIGN AFFAIRS 1066 (1986);

Rossiter & Smith, *Human Rights: The Carter Record, The Reagan Reaction*, INT'L POL'Y REP., Sept. 1984;

Richard Schifter, *Building Firm Foundations: The Institutionalization of United States Human Rights Policy in the Reagan Years*, 2 HARV. HUM. RTS. Y.B. 3 (1989);

Jerome J. Shestack, *An Unsteady Focus: The Vulnerabilities of the Reagan Administration's Human Rights Policy*, 2 HARV. HUM. RTS. Y.B. 25 (1989).

For a disturbing look at U.S. policy in El Salvador, see Mark Danner, *A Reporter at Large: The Truth of El Mozote*, NEW YORKER, Dec. 6, 1993, at 50.

6.   On April 19, 1994, testifying before the Senate Appropriations Subcommittee on Foreign Operations, John Shattuck, Assistant Secretary of State for Democracy, Human Rights and Labor, outlined the Clinton Administration's nine objectives for U.S. democracy and human rights policy:

(1) "build new institutions of accountability that will hold violators to account";

(2) "link[] trade and economic relations to human rights";

(3) recognize "economic development, political development, human rights protection and democracy protection . . . as an integrated whole";

(4) "build new multilateral institutions to address racial, ethnic and religious conflict . . . to defuse conflicts before they lead to gross human rights violations";

(5) "integrat[e] . . . women's rights into all aspects of our human rights policy";

(6) "press[] for the enactment of implementing legislation on the Torture Convention";

(7) "strengthen the United Nations' human rights machinery";

(8) "strengthen[] our relationship with the NGOs working in many countries to promote democracy and human rights"; and

(9) "tighten[] the focus and coordination of our programs to promote democracy and human rights abroad."

He also argued that "the Clinton Administration is committed to strengthening multilateral instruments of democracy and human rights" and that "[t]oday, human rights promotion is equal to other factors in shaping our bilateral ties with foreign governments." Have the Clinton Administration's actions comported with those principles?

7.   For review of the Clinton Administration's human rights record, see

HUMAN RIGHTS AND U.S. FOREIGN POLICY: WHO CONTROLS THE AGENDA? (Stanley Foundation, Iowa) (reporting on the 35th Strategy for Peace, U.S. Foreign Policy Conference held on Oct. 27-29, 1994);

Harold Hongju Koh, *The "Haiti Paradigm" in United States Human Rights Policy*, 103 Yale L.J. 2391 (1994);

Robbyn Reichman-Coad, Note, *Human Rights Violations in China: A United States Response*, 15 N.Y.L. SCH. J. INT'L & COMP. L. 163 (1994);

Patricia L. Rengel, *Ratification of International Human Rights Treaties: Progress and Prospects in the Clinton Administration*, 1994 PROC. OF THE ANN. MEETING-AM. SOC'Y INT'L L. 363;

Alan Tonelson, *Jettison the Policy*, FOREIGN POL'Y, Dec. 1994, at 121.

8.   Other governments too have considered the role of human rights in their foreign policies. *See, e.g.,*

Marc J. Bossuyt, *Human rights as an element of foreign policy*, 89/1 BULL. HUM. RTS. 27 (1990);

JAN EGELAND, IMPOTENT SUPERPOWER, POTENT SMALL STATE: POTENTIALS AND LIMITATIONS OF HUMAN RIGHTS OBJECTIVES IN THE FOREIGN POLICIES OF THE UNITED STATES AND NORWAY (1988);

HUMAN RIGHTS IN DOMESTIC LAW AND DEVELOPMENT ASSISTANCE POLICIES OF THE NORDIC COUNTRIES (Lars A. Rehof & Claus Gulmann eds., 1989);

Kathryn Sikkink, *The Power of Principled Ideas: Human Rights Policies in the United States and Western Europe, in* IDEAS AND FOREIGN POLICY: BELIEFS, INSTITUTIONS AND POLITICAL CHANGE 139 (J. Goldstein & R. Keohane eds., 1993);

Sigrun I. Skogly, Human Rights in the New Europe: Problems and Progress (David P. Forsythe ed., 1994).

E. DEFINING AND IMPLEMENTING U.S. HUMAN RIGHTS POLICY

1. The Role of Congress

Prior to Carter's election, Congress in the 1970s passed statutes that required or permitted linking human rights aims with security assistance, economic assistance, and participation in international financial institutions. Two sections were notable amendments to the 1961 Foreign Assistance Act:

Section 502B consists of four major provisions. *First*, 502B(a)(1) mandates that promotion of human rights be a principal goal of U.S. foreign policy. *Second*, 502B(a)(3) directs the President to administer security assistance in a manner that promotes human rights and avoids identifying the U.S. with repressive governments. *Third*, 502B(a)(2) forbids security assistance to countries which engage "in a consistent pattern of gross violations of internationally recognized human rights." (Notwithstanding that clause, however, security assistance may be provided under 502B(a)(2) if the President certifies that extraordinary circumstances exist or, under §502B(e), if he finds that the rights situation in a proposed recipient-country has significantly improved.) *Fourth*, 502B(b) requires the State Department to prepare a report on the human rights practices of each proposed recipient of security assistance.

In language similar to 502B, Section 116 (the Harkin Amendment) prohibits granting economic aid to countries engaged "in a consistent pattern of gross violations of internationally recognized rights"; but it exempts situations in which assistance will directly benefit "needy people" in the country.

Supplementing those Foreign Assistance Act clauses, Section 701 of the International Financial Institutions Act requires the U.S. government, in connection with its vote in certain international financial institutions, to advance human rights "by seeking to channel assistance toward countries other than those whose governments engage in . . . a consistent pattern of gross violations of internationally recognized human rights."

The first two statutes, Sections 116 and 502B, are reproduced in *Selected International Human Rights Instruments.*

NOTES AND QUESTIONS

1. Sections 502B and 116 are sometimes labeled "general legislation" because they apply to all countries. General legislation often grants discretion to the administering officials, and that discretion has made it possible to avoid aims of the law when granting assistance. For discussion of situations where both the Carter and Reagan administrations thus avoided aims of human rights legislation, see David P. Forsythe, *Congress and Human Rights in U.S. Foreign Policy: The Fate of General Legislation*, 9 HUM. RTS. Q. 382, 382-95 (1987).

2. Decisions at multilateral-development banks and, in particular, the World Bank are supposed to be made solely on the basis of economic factors, without taking into account political considerations. That has led some commentators to argue that Section 701's mandate

that the U.S. use its vote in the banks to channel assistance toward countries with good rights records violates the apolitical nature of the banks. *See, e.g.*, Robert W. Kneller, *Human Rights, Politics, and the Multilateral Development Banks*, 6 YALE STUD. WORLD PUB. ORD. 361 (1980) (arguing that directors can consider human rights when voting on loans only to the extent that such considerations have economic implications relevant to the banks' basic purposes).

Others have argued that, though the banks' purposes were originally apolitical, certain decisions had become politicized in some areas. Consequently it would do no harm to recognize human rights as a relevant consideration in making loan decisions. *See, e.g.*, Elizabeth P. Spiro, *Front Door or Back Stair: U.S. Human Rights Policy in the International Financial Institution, in* HUMAN RIGHTS AND U.S. FOREIGN POLICY 133 (Barry M. Rubin & Elizabeth P. Spiro eds. 1979).

The International Monetary Fund (IMF) provides short-term credit to countries experiencing balance-of-payment difficulties and recommends measures to assist governments in improving their economic balance with the rest of the world. The recommendations may require austerity measures that could result in widespread suffering—including violations of economic, social, and cultural rights; and some governments have resorted to repression in order to sustain the austerity measures. Hence it may be difficult to show that decisions are truly apolitical and that rights-implications need not be considered. For further reading on the World Bank and its role in promoting democracy, see Daniel D. Bradlow & Claudio Grossman, *Limited Mandates and Intertwined Problems: A New Challenge for the World Bank and the IMF*, 17 HUM. RTS. Q. 411 (1995); Jonathan Cahn, *Challenging the New Imperial Authority: The World Bank and the Democratization of Development*, 6 HARV. HUM. RTS. J. 159 (1993); David Gillies, *Human Rights, Governance, and Democracy: The World Bank's Problem Frontiers*, 11 NETH. Q. HUM. RTS. 3 (1993); LAWYERS COMMITTEE FOR HUMAN RIGHTS, THE WORLD BANK: GOVERNANCE AND HUMAN RIGHTS (1995); Joe Oloka-Onyango, *Beyond the Rhetoric: Reinvigorating the Struggle for Economic and Social Rights in Africa*, 27 CAL. WEST. INTL L.J. 1 (1995).

3.   Congress has enacted other statutes with clauses designed to promote human rights, though the primary purposes of the statutes may not have been principally related to human rights. For example, the 1988 Omnibus Trade and Competitiveness Act authorizes the President to impose sanctions against countries that violate workers' rights. It authorizes presidential action when a country's labor practices constitute "a persistent pattern of conduct that: (I) denies workers the right of association, (II) denies workers the right to organize and bargain collectively, (III) permits any form of forced or compulsory labor, (IV) fails to provide a minimum age for the employment of children, or (V) fails to provide standards for minimum wages, hours of work, and occupational safety and health of workers." 19 U.S.C.A. §2411(d)(3)(B)(iii) (1988 & Supp. 1994). For further reading, see LAWYERS COMMITTEE FOR HUMAN RIGHTS, WORKER RIGHTS UNDER THE U.S. TRADE LAWS (1989). In March 1996, U.S. Trade Representative Mickey Kantor recommended that President Clinton suspend some of Pakistan's benefits under the Generalized System of Preferences (GSP) Program whereby the U.S. helps developing countries by permitting goods to be brought in duty-free. Kantor's decision was based on findings of persistent child and bonded labor throughout Pakistan and Pakistan's failure to take sufficient steps to conform to internationally recognized workers' rights.

4.   For an uncomplimentary assessment of U.S. human rights legislation and other approaches, see KATARINA TOMASHEVSKI, DEVELOPMENT AID AND HUMAN RIGHTS 50-59 (1989) and also her FOREIGN AID AND HUMAN RIGHTS: CASE STUDIES OF BANGLADESH AND KENYA (1988).

Donald M. Fraser, *Congress's Role in the Making of International Human Rights Policy, in* HUMAN RIGHTS AND AMERICAN FOREIGN POLICY 247, 247-54 (Donald P. Kommers & Gilburt D. Loescher eds. 1979):

This paper attempts to answer four questions. *First, what is Congress's role in monitoring the impact of American foreign policy on human rights abroad and developing legislative guidelines for such a policy?*

Congress has an important role to play in this matter. First, through public discussion of issues, particularly through hearings as well as on the floor of the House, Congress can very effectively draw attention to human rights problems abroad and thereby increase public concern and the receptivity of foreign governments to ameliorate their practices. Second, it establishes through law the standards upon which the Executive Branch uses the various assistance programs for leverage in the promotion of human rights.

Hearings have been a principal means by which the Congress has monitored foreign policy and sought to influence its direction. An important example of such a forum is the Fascell Commission—a joint Congressional-Executive Branch commission specifically designed to monitor compliance with the final act of the Helsinki Agreement. Over the last few years my own subcommittee has held more than 80 hearings on the subject of human rights and foreign policy. Nongovernmental witnesses have proved an invaluable resource in providing us with information with which to compare Department of State testimony. By listening to and questioning departmental testimony, we believe we have influenced the conduct of policy at least a little. If nothing else, the hearings have required the Department of State to place matters on the record that otherwise might not have been disclosed publicly. Also, from my own personal experience with respect to our subcommittee's hearings, I am certain that the hearings are taken very seriously by most foreign governments. They make every effort to indicate that their performance conforms with international human rights standards.

Congress also has enacted legislation in the field of human rights and foreign policy. Specific examples include Sections 502B (human rights and security assistance) and 116 (human rights and development assistance) of the Foreign Assistance Act as well as the human rights amendments aimed at the multilateral banks.

Both Sections 502B and 116 provide the Executive with a general framework within which the Administration is expected to shape its security and development assistance programs. However, neither law dictates specific decisions; rather, each allows flexibility for action in individual circumstances. For example, Section 502B prohibits, except under extraordinary circumstances, military aid or sale of military equipment to governments with a consistent pattern of gross violations of internationally recognized human rights. Congress has placed especially stringent standards on military aid because of the symbolic and sometimes practical importance of such assistance in carrying out repressive policy in numerous countries.

The relationship between human rights and development aid poses a more complicated question. Because we do not want to penalize the poor, Section 116 prohibits bilateral development aid to a repressive government only if that aid is not directly beneficial to needy people. Congress enacted this legislation under the Nixon and Ford administrations because of our belief that in certain nations, particularly Chile and South Korea, the Administration was using economic aid to prolong the staying power of regimes more than to provide help for needy people. . . .

Congress also has enacted legislation concerning specific countries. Such legislation was enacted during the Ford Administration and has continued during the Carter Administration. . . .

Ironically, during the Carter Administration, an even greater number of specific country legislative prohibitions or limitations on military aid were enacted as compared with the Ford Administration. Many members of Congress are not as patient as the Administration in terms of encouraging repressive regimes to change their practices. They believe that many of these regimes have had a long enough time to mend their practices. They do not favor compromising the legislative principle that repressive regimes, except in extraordinary circumstances, should be disqualified from receiving military assistance. They favor a policy of frankness, of public opprobrium, and of a straightforward disassociation of the United States with the repressive regime through termination of military aid. . . .

The second question is what tensions exist between Congress and the Executive? As the conflict over specific country legislation and legislation affecting the international institutions indicates, Congress has not accepted as fully bona fide the Administration's commitment to human rights. Tensions do exist; perhaps they are inevitable and desirable—even when the same party controls both the White House and Congress. Even if Congress had complete faith in the Administration's commitment, disagreement might remain over its implementation. There are many forces militating against a strong human rights element in foreign policy. The Executive Branch needs Congressional support, and in some instances this may mean that the Congress will take the lead on human rights initiatives or principles in human rights policy. Particularly since the Carter Administration took office, my preference has been for a "low-profile" Congressional policy giving the Executive an opportunity to work out a human rights policy and a reasonable period of time in which to achieve results. . . .

The promotion of human rights is a complicated and difficult task. National pride makes other governments extremely sensitive to foreign criticism. The Executive Branch, as compared with Congress, has more tools and instruments at its disposal for bringing its concern regarding human rights to the attention of other governments. It can act with greater subtlety. It can take firm measures, including sanctions, without introducing these sanctions into the public arena. Consequently, an Administration willing to exert itself can have more effectiveness in this field than can Congress. . . .

The third question is how effective is the Congressional role? Despite the confrontational relationship that has existed between the executive and legislative branches in recent years, the Congress has achieved some positive results, Congress has laid a basis for the new Administration's human rights policy. Congressional initiatives have included the following:

1. The establishment of the human rights performance of the recipient government has a basic factor in decisions regarding military and economic assistance.

2. The creation of the Office of Coordinator for Human Rights and Humanitarian Affairs in the State Department and the suggestion that human rights officers in the regional bureaus be appointed. This suggestion has been accepted, and the coordinator has been elevated to the rank of assistant secretary.

3. The establishment of human rights reporting as a regular function of the embassies and of public reporting on proposed recipients of security and development assistance.

4. Pressure on the State Department to make human rights representations to foreign governments.

5. Pressure on the State Department in public hearings to take positions on human rights situations in individual countries.

All these activities have had the effect of raising the consciousness of foreign service officers regarding the relevance of human rights to foreign policy. . . .

The fourth question is how can Congress play a more effective role? The Congressional role as a partner, rather than as an adversary, in the formulation of foreign policy will be enhanced if the Executive maintains a steady dialogue with the Congress. . . .

Congress needs to think creatively rather than to merely react belatedly to situations. Congress has often been reactive because it has lacked the resources—particularly information—upon which to foretell developments. Perhaps Congress needs its own independent source of information apart from the services already provided by the Congressional Research Service. . . .

Clearly, not enough is known of the initiatives taken by the foreign governments, parliaments, and political parties around the world with respect to human rights issues. Congress can encourage international parliamentary efforts in defense of human rights. Concerting international responses to human rights violations may be one of the effective means open to outsiders seeking to influence another government's actions. . . .

Congress, of course, must ratify more of the human rights conventions. The United States lags badly behind most countries in the numbers of such conventions it has ratified.[3]

*   *   *   *   *

In addition to the statutes discussed above, Congressman Fraser noted that Congress can pass country-specific legislation which places conditions on executive discretion in awarding assistance to a named country. Congress may exercise that power when it is displeased with the Executive's decisions regarding a certain country under general legislation. The general legislation may authorize a broad range of discretion in granting assistance; country-specific legislation narrows that discretion for a target country. Past country-specific statutes have taken several forms, including e.g., the prohibition of assistance to a target country or establishing conditions it must satisfy in order to receive assistance. The latter type attempts to improve the human rights situation in a target country through the promise of increased assistance. For discussion of country-specific legislation and its use with respect to El Salvador, see James Moeller, Comment, Human Rights and United States Security Assistance: El Salvador and the Case for Country-Specific Legislation, 24 HARV. INT'L L.J. 75 (1983).

One possible problem with the statute used in El Salvador, contrasted with legislation that prohibits assistance, is that the former gives the Executive more discretion. That discretion inheres in the Executive role in certifying whether a target country has or has not met legislative conditions for increased assistance. For discussion of the first two presidential certifications under the El Salvador legislation and congressional criticism of them, see Scott Horton & Randy Sellier, The Utility of Presidential Certifications of Compliance with United States Human Rights Policy: The Case of El Salvador, 1982 WIS. L. REV. 825.

Congress also has experimented with action-specific legislation that ties security assistance to achievement of particular human rights goals in a country. Action-

---

[3] [Ed. note: The U.S. ratified the International Covenant on Civil and Political Rights in 1992, and the Convention on the Elimination of All Forms of Racial Discrimination and the Convention Against Torture and Other Cruel, Inhuman or Degrading Treatment or Punishment in 1994.]

specific legislation interferes less drastically with bilateral relations by allowing the U.S. to reduce rather than eliminate assistance to the target country.

Here is an excerpt illustrating use of country-specific legislation in Peru:

Olufunmilayo B. Arewa & Susan O'Rourke, *Country-Specific Legislation and Human Rights: The Case of Peru*, 5 HARV. HUM. RTS. J. 183, 183-92 (1992):

In the late 1980s and early 1990s, the focus of United States foreign policy in Latin America gradually shifted from Central America to the Andean countries of Bolivia, Peru, and Columbia. . . . President Bush announced the Andean Strategy in 1989 as a central component of the National Drug Strategy. The goal of the Andean Strategy has been to attack the drug problem at its source by reducing the cocaine supply from Andean countries using a combination of resources from the United States and host governments. . . .

The Peruvian military is one of Latin America's leading human rights violators. . . . In 1990, Peru was the world leader in disappearances. Security forces, operating in zones under military command, were responsible for the overwhelming majority of the disappearances. . . . In addition, the military has resorted to extrajudicial executions and torture. . . . The disregard for human rights in Peru is compounded by an ineffective judicial system and inhumane penal conditions. . . .

The 1990 International Narcotics Control Act (INCA) supplemented 502B and existing narcotics control legislation by imposing specific conditions upon United States Foreign Assistance to the Andean region. At a minimum, INCA requires the United States executive to make a formal determination that the recipient government "has made significant progress in protecting internationally recognized human rights." Such progress is to be measured by the extent to which the foreign government ensures that (1) torture, incommunicado detention, disappearances, and other flagrant denials of the right to life, liberty, or security of the person are not practiced; (2) access is granted for international organizations, United Nations, and Organization of American States groups to places of detention; and (3) civilian institutions have effective control over police and military counternarcotics and counterinsurgency activities.

INCA also contains notification requirements which give Congress additional mechanisms to control executive foreign assistance disbursement. INCA requires that the President notify congressional appropriations committees "not less than 15 days" before funds to the Andean countries are committed to military or economic and development assistance. Four congressional committees have the authority to withhold aid under notification procedures: the House Foreign Affairs and Senate Foreign Relations committees, and the House Foreign Operations and Senate Foreign Operations subcommittees. . . .

On July 30, 1991, the Bush Administration issued a formal determination that Peru had met INCA human rights standards. The determination directly contradicted the findings of human rights organizations. . . . On July 31, 1991, . . . the Administration notified Congress of its intention to commit $94.9 million of the 1991 security assistance allocated for Peru.

Congress responded to the substance of the determination and the timing of the notification by temporarily withholding security assistance. . . . Congress withheld the aid and conditioned its release on Peru's fulfillment of several human rights standards.

Congress was primarily concerned about military aid. On September 24, 1991, Congress agreed to remove the holds on all of the $60 million in Economic Support Funds because of the serious economic crisis in Peru. However, obligation of the military aid was subject to some limitations: Congress cut $10.05 million in military aid for counter-insurgency training, weapons, and equipment but allowed $3.7 million for army civic action programs. The remaining $24.9 million in military aid was left subject to further consideration and could be released to the Peruvian government upon compliance with human rights and counternarcotics conditions. On September 27, 1991, . . ., the Administration agreed to congressional conditions on aid. Congress then released the military aid, dividing it into "tranches" (portions), and specified that no military aid could be delivered unless the Administration reported to Congress that Peru complied with a list of human rights conditions. . . .

Congressional conditions on aid to Peru, and its continued vigilance with regard to human rights progress, put significant pressure on President Fujimori. In response to congressional demands, Fujimori took limited steps to ensure the release of assistance. On August 14[, 1992,] Fujimori announced the creation of a register of army detainees. Two weeks later, on September 3, the Peruvian government issued a decree giving civilian prosecutors access to all military and police detention facilities. The government also allowed the International Committee of the Red Cross access for a six month period. . . .

Country-specific legislation aimed at Peru's human rights record has proved to be of limited effectiveness. INCA's design has allowed Congress to apply a measured and refined pressure aimed at specific reforms. Combined with sustained congressional interest in the fulfillment of mandated conditions, the legislation has focused attention on military abuses and forced President Fujimori to implement certain procedural safeguards. It remains to be seen whether these reforms will translate into substantive improvements in human rights. However, the pressure thus far exerted on Peru speaks well for the potential effectiveness of country-specific legislation.

NOTES AND QUESTIONS

1.   Note that Congressman Fraser wrote his piece during the Carter Administration. Despite Carter's goal of making human rights promotion an important part of U.S. foreign policy, Fraser opined that many members of Congress viewed progress on that goal as too slow. Do you think the Congressional majority and the Executive will hold different views on human rights in foreign policy? Why? *See* Stephen B. Cohen, *Conditioning U.S. Security Assistance on Human Rights Practices*, reprinted *infra* at 43.

2.   In a speech titled, "Human Rights and the Moral Dimension of U.S. Foreign Policy," one time Secretary of State George Shultz observed,

> The role of Congress is another question. There is no doubt that congressional concerns and pressures have played a very positive role in giving impetus and backing to our efforts to influence other governments' behavior. This congressional pressure can strengthen the hand of the executive branch in its efforts of diplomacy. At the same time, there can be complications if the legislative instrument is too inflexible or heavy-handed, or, even more, if Congress attempts to take on the administrative responsibility for executing policy. Legislation requires that we withhold aid in extreme circumstances. If narrowly interpreted, this can lead us rapidly to a "stop-go" policy of fits and starts, all or nothing—making it very difficult to structure incentives in a way that will really fulfill the law's own wider mandate: to "promote and encourage increased respect for human rights and fundamental freedoms. . . ."

DEPT OF STATE, BUREAU OF PUBLIC AFFAIRS, CURRENT POLICY NO. 551 (1984).

Contrast Fraser's view on the importance of congressional initiative with Shultz's remarks. Who do you think spoke more perceptively?

3.   What are advantages and disadvantages of a strong congressional role in the promotion and protection of human rights and U.S. foreign policy?

4.   Congress took action against Indonesia during the Clinton Administration. The most visible human rights problems there stem from troubled relations with the former Portuguese colony of East Timor, annexed by Indonesia in 1976. In 1991, an estimated 100 East Timorese were killed by army troops while taking part in a peaceful protest at a cemetery. In 1993, soldiers shot three people on the island of Medura because they were participants in a 500-person protest against a dam project. That year the U.S. had vetoed Jordan's sale of U.S.-made jetplanes to Indonesia. *See Indonesia Reduces Separatist's Prison Term*, N.Y. TIMES, Aug. 15, 1993, at 6.

In September, the Senate Foreign Relations Committee passed a resolution to condition further arms-sales on improvements in human rights, but the condition was not included in the final appropriations bill. *See* Lee Kim Chew, *Pragmatism Now Rules US-Jakarta Ties*, STRAITS TIMES, May 9, 1994, at 27; Merrill Goozner, *Indonesia Pays a Price for Rapid Turnaround*, CHIC. TRIB., Nov. 15, 1993 at C1; Charles P. Wallace, *Indonesia's Labor and Human Rights Practices Fray U.S. Ties*, L.A. TIMES, Sept. 24, 1993, at A5.

The Clinton Administration then began to loosen its stand that gave priority to economic harmony. In December 1993, Congress discovered that the U.S. was providing military training to Indonesians despite congressional action eliminating funds for such training. *Indonesia Military Allowed to Obtain Training in U.S.*, N.Y. TIMES, Dec. 8, 1993, at A14. During a November 1994 meeting of Asia-Pacific leaders and Clinton in Indonesia, U.S. officials warned Indonesian President Suharto to improve his country's rights record regarding East Timor, but the officials nonetheless witnessed the signing of 15 business deals between residents of the two countries totalling $40 billion.

The conflicting messages to Indonesia mirrored the administration's practice, since May 1994, when it discarded linking trade-benefits to China with human rights performance. Clinton argued that increasing trade through commercial diplomacy is the best way to spread democracy and encourage countries to improve their human rights performance. *See* Elaine Sciolino, *Clinton is Stern with Indonesia on Rights but Gleeful on Trade*, N.Y. TIMES, Nov. 17, 1994, at A1.

5.   Congress has used tax laws to discourage investment in certain countries, but those laws were not targeted directly at human rights abuses. Tax benefits have been denied to U.S. taxpayers for income earned in designated countries with governments the U.S. (1) does not recognize, (2) has severed or does not conduct diplomatic relations, or (3) has designated as repeated providers of support for acts of international terrorism. 26 U.S.C. § 901(j) (1988 & Supp. 1994). The list of designated countries published by the Internal Revenue Service in 1992 included Afghanistan, Angola, Cambodia, Cuba, Iran, Iraq, Libya, North Korea, Syria, and Vietnam. Rev. Rul. 92-63, 1992-2 C.B. 195. (South Africa and Albania had been removed in 1991.)

6.   The Senate also can affect human rights policy by using its power to accept or reject presidential nominations for executive positions with human rights responsibilities. Recall, for instance, the Senate's reaction to Reagan's nomination of Ernest Lefever for head of the Human Rights Bureau, discussed *supra* at 21.

7.   In a symposium on human rights planning for the administration, which was to take office in 1989, two commentators recommended that Congress strengthen its role by enacting more country-specific legislation, conducting closer review of diplomatic initiatives, cutting off aid to countries with serious and ongoing human rights violations, and forcing the Executive to report more frequently on particular countries' rights situations and U.S. assistance and trade policies toward those countries. Michael Posner & Cathy Zavis, *Human Rights Priorities for a New Administration and Congress*, 28 VA. J. INT'L L. 893, 897-98 (1988).

8.   For further reading on U.S. human rights legislation and the role of Congress in promoting human rights, see:

Hugo A. Bedau, *Human Rights and Foreign Assistance Programs, in* HUMAN RIGHTS AND U.S. FOREIGN POLICY: PRINCIPLES AND APPLICATIONS 29 (Peter G. Brown & Douglas MacLean eds. 1979);

DAVID P. FORSYTHE, HUMAN RIGHTS AND FOREIGN POLICY: CONGRESS RECONSIDERED (1988);

Margaret Galey, *Congress, Foreign Policy and Human Rights Ten Years After Helsinki,* 7 HUM. RTS. Q. 334, 343-67 (1985);

Tom Harkin, *Human Rights and Foreign Aid: Forging an Unbreakable Link, in* HUMAN RIGHTS AND U.S. FOREIGN POLICY: PRINCIPLES AND APPLICATIONS 15 (Peter G. Brown & Douglas MacLean eds. 1979);

Lisa L. Martin & Kathryn Sikkink, *U.S. Policy and Human Rights in Argentina and Guatemala, 1973-1980, in* DOUBLE-EDGED DIPLOMACY (Peter Evans et al. eds. 1993);

Steven Poe et al., *Human Rights and US Foreign Aid Revisited: The Latin American Region,* 16 HUM. RTS. Q. 539 (1994);

David Weissbrodt, *Human Rights Legislation and U.S. Foreign Policy,* 7 GA. J. INT'L & COMP. L. 231 (1977).

Concerning the Canadian Parliament's role in implementing human rights policy, see Cathal Nolan, *The Influence of Parliament on Human Rights in Canadian Foreign Policy,* 7 HUM. RTS. Q. 373 (1985).

---

2.   The Role of the Administration

A commitment to human rights by the White House is essential for effective implementation of U.S. rights policy. The Constitution grants the President significant authority in the area of foreign policy. Though Congress may legislate as to human rights concerns and wield great power via the appropriations process and the oversight function, the dynamic nature of foreign affairs and human rights situations requires that the President and State Department manage the rights policy on an almost month-to-month basis.

The following statements by Human Rights Watch and the Lawyers Committee for Human Rights analyze the Reagan and Bush administrations' preparation of the annual Country Reports on Human Rights Practices and also comment on the administrations' handling of human rights policy. Human Rights Watch and/or the Lawyers Committee annually prepare critiques of these reports and the administrations' human rights record in general.

While reading these excerpts, think about impacts a single administration or Congress can have on the development of long-range U.S. human rights policies:

HUMAN RIGHTS WATCH & LAWYERS COMMITTEE FOR HUMAN RIGHTS, CRITIQUE: A REVIEW OF THE DEPARTMENT OF STATE'S COUNTRY REPORTS ON HUMAN RIGHTS PRACTICES FOR 1988, at 1-8 (1989):

INTRODUCTION

The biases in the State Department's reporting shifted over the course of the Reagan Administration. In the initial years, the reports reflected East-West conflicts. Reports on human rights abuses in the Soviet Union, Eastern Europe and some other Communist-ruled countries, such as Cuba and Vietnam, were thorough and complete and in some cases exaggerated. Meanwhile, the reports on certain allies, Guatemala, Honduras, El Salvador, the Philippines, Chile and Pakistan, for example, often understated the extent of abuses or attempted to shift the blame from the governments of those countries.

As time passed, however, a more complex pattern emerged which reflected both the Reagan Administration's changing approach to the human rights cause and the evolution of East-West relations.

After an initial repudiation, the Reagan Administration publicly embraced the human rights cause. The Administration's new human rights policy soon focused on electoral democracy as the way to promote respect for human rights. A perceived transition from dictatorship to democracy through elections ensured favorable reporting on the human rights situation, as exemplified in reports on Turkey, Guatemala and the Philippines. Elsewhere, as in Chile, where a democratic transition has not yet occurred, the Reagan Administration shifted over time from outspoken friendship and support for the Pinochet dictatorship to criticism, and then to outright support for its replacement by a democratic government during the Administration's last year. This shift is reflected in the *Country Reports* by the welcome fact that the reporting on Chile and Paraguay is currently as comprehensive and as critical as the reporting on Bulgaria and Czechoslovakia.

Yet the emphasis on elections and "transitions to democracy" has led the State Department to overlook the influence of the military and paramilitary groups in numerous nominally democratic countries and to understate the extent of human rights abuses in these nations. The reports on El Salvador, Guatemala, Colombia and the Philippines illustrate the State Department's equating the emergence of elected civilian governments with the existence of civilian rule and respect for human rights. Though these countries have had elected civilian presidents who are not suspected by anyone of personal complicity in political violence, those presidents have not prevented their armed forces from committing many gross abuses of human rights. The State Department's reporting on these countries presents a misleading picture in which the extent of violence is understated and the government's responsibility for curbing the violence and punishing those responsible is almost entirely ignored.

. . . State Department reports . . . such as those on Chile, South Africa, the Sudan and Czechoslovakia are comprehensive and balanced and the methods of analysis employed in these reports should be used in all. These reports should serve as models for future reports, in part because they:

— include detailed accounts of specific cases;

— cite information and statistics from a variety of sources, especially from non-governmental groups and court records, where applicable;

— describe comprehensively the context surrounding an event or issue;

— assert the State Department's own views and conclusions unambiguously;

— distinguish between rights and freedoms theoretically guaranteed by law and the actual observance of such rights and freedoms.

In particular, close and sustained contact between an embassy and local human rights monitors and other groups spanning the political spectrum is a common characteristic of the better reports.

The roster of weak reports is depressingly familiar. The reports on Haiti, El Salvador, Guatemala, the Philippines, Indonesia, Singapore and Malaysia, for example, fail to convey the causes, extent and frequency of human rights violations. In addition to political and geopolitical considerations this weakness stems from the State Department's use of certain methods common to many of the poorer reports:

— Accepting a government's statements of intent, the passage of legislation or the launching of investigations as proof of improvement in human rights observance . . .;

— Excusing violations because of a lack of resources rather than stating that in many cases violations stem from a failure of will . . .;

— Failure to offer an independent analysis and a conclusion in the State Department's own voice . . .;

— Excusing human rights violations because of poor training of soldiers and police or ascribing violations to "irregular" forces . . .;

— Failing to see connections between facts . . .;

— Misleading use of words: in Kenya the report notes that Parliament voted "unanimously" for certain constitutional amendments, yet Kenya is a *de jure* one-party state and one party dominates Parliament; the Yugoslavia report states that Yugoslavia "extends temporary asylum to refugees" yet fails to explain that "asylum" often means a jail cell for Romanian refugees;

— Creating a misleading impression of the human rights situation by describing events or violations in one section while such events or violations should have been included in a different or additional section . . .;

— Criticizing human rights groups for failing to fulfill certain tasks . . .; the effect of these criticisms is to appear to excuse the governments . . .;

— Omitting important background information thereby creating a partial and often misleading context . . ..

In addition, the State Department sometimes treats the same issue differently depending on the country. The China report does not discuss the effects of the population transfers of ethnic Chinese to Tibet. The report on Vietnam, however, details the government's program to resettle ethnic Vietnamese in the central highlands and assimilate minorities. The Vietnam report also describes carefully circumscribed visits by outside delegations while remaining silent on similarly orchestrated visits to East Timor in the Indonesian report.

The El Salvador report notes that accounts of a resurgence of death squads "have not been substantiated." The Liberia report states there are "unconfirmed allegations" of deaths in prisons. In these cases independent and reliable information confirms increased death squad activity in El Salvador and deaths in Liberian prisons. Yet in the China report, the State Department relies without qualification on official estimates of deaths during demonstrations. This pattern of applying different standards to substantiate evidence appears in many reports.

The State Department adopts a passive and non-judgmental position regarding the accuracy of accounts of torture and beatings in the Israeli occupied territories. . . . The State Department sheds this passivity when discussing torture in Syria ("there have been numerous credible reports of torture") and Iraq ("reliable reports

make clear that both physical and psychological torture are used by the authorities").
. . .

One foreign service officer's account of his experiences in Guatemala as a human rights officer . . . identifies a number of chronic problems that contribute to the uneven quality of the reports and permit the injection of political concerns into the analysis. Some of these problems are of a managerial nature. . . . [H]uman rights officers "are usually chosen at random and receive no training for their jobs" and they do not debrief their predecessors. More important, we believe, is the lack of bureaucratic clout of the Bureau of Human Rights and Humanitarian Affairs within the State Department, resulting in the Bureau's inability to provide consistent support to human rights officers. Thus, . . . "the quality of human rights reporting depends on the demands made of the officer by his geographic bureau and his ambassador." This lends support to our view that the demands of the geographic bureaus at the State Department, and of particular ambassadors, have undermined the objectivity of certain reports.

Despite the criticisms set forth here, we believe that the *Country Reports* have continued to improve and that they serve as an ever more useful compendium of information on human rights practices worldwide. . . .

Yet just as well-trained police officers will not produce respect for human rights when the political leadership of a country is intent on repression, so well-trained foreign service officers will not produce a reliable volume of *Country Reports* unless the political leadership of the Department of State is committed to fair, objective and comprehensive reporting. We call on the Bush Administration in general, and on Secretary of State James Baker in particular, to send out the message that, regardless of political and geopolitical considerations, each of the reports should be a reliable record of human rights developments; that the United States should speak in its own voice in condemning abuses; and that efforts to excuse or cover up abuses by understanding them, exculpating those responsible, or pretending that culpability has not been established, have no place in the reports. . . .

NOTES AND QUESTIONS

1.   For analysis of the State Department Country Reports and their history and impact, see Judith I. de Neufville, *Human Rights Reporting as a Policy Tool: An Examination of the State Department Country Reports*, 8 HUM. RTS. Q. 681 (1986). She recommends that "participation of NGOs and academic experts in evaluating and improving the methods of gathering and analyzing the data should be formalized and regularized through task forces, advisory groups, or user groups." *Id.* at 699.

Do you think providing an official NGO role in compiling the reports would help alleviate administrations' biases? Is a formal requirement practicable?

Despite her recommendation, de Neufville concludes that the staff who prepare reports seem "increasingly willing and able to resist pressures to slant the *Reports* for political purposes." *Id.* at 690. Do you think those who have criticized the reports would agree? Is it ever possible for a branch of the Executive to resist all "political" pressures? See LAWYERS COMMITTEE FOR HUMAN RIGHTS, BUREAUCRACY AND DIPLOMACY (1989); *see also* Peter J. Spiro, *New Global Communities: Nongovernmental Organizations in International Decision-Making Institutions*, 18 WASHINGTON Q. 45 (1994).

2.   In its 1991 critique of the Country Reports, the Lawyers Committee suggested that the government focus more on human rights and its foreign policy generally. The Committee praised improvements in the country reports, but added that they have only highlighted the shortcomings of U.S. policy. Specifically:

Each year the introduction to the country reports repeats the incantation that the reports are "submitted to the Congress by the Department of State in compliance with Sections 116(d)(1) and 502B(b) of the Foreign Assistance Act of 1961, as amended." Section 502B prohibits giving aid to countries engaged in a "consistent pattern of gross violations of internationally recognized human rights." Yet since Section 502B(b) was enacted 14 years ago, it has never been formally invoked, despite the compelling evidence of gross human rights violations contained in many of the State Department reports.

Unfortunately, the reports' increased credibility has not been accompanied by increased use in policymaking; more than ever these reports seem to exist in a vacuum. The reports risk being regarded in splendid isolation as a commendable but academic exercise unless U.S. policy comes to reflect the information on human rights violations so comprehensively assembled. In this evolving and much more fluid era, accurate reporting alone is not enough.

LAWYERS COMMITTEE FOR HUMAN RIGHTS, CRITIQUE: REVIEW OF THE U.S. DEPARTMENT OF STATE'S COUNTRY REPORTS ON HUMAN RIGHTS PRACTICES 1991, at 4 (1992). *See also* LAWYERS COMMITTEE FOR HUMAN RIGHTS, HUMAN RIGHTS AND U.S. FOREIGN POLICY 1992: REPORT AND RECOMMENDATIONS (1992).

3.   In a 1988 symposium, W. Michael Reisman proposed a different way of insulating rights-reporting from political pressures. Under his proposal a statutory agency would be established, which would monitor all pertinent information obtained and release information about possible violations as soon as it becomes available. The agency would be independent, and thus relatively insulated from pressures that might influence the withholding of information when publication appears to conflict with other national interests. W. Michael Reisman, *American Human Rights Diplomacy: The Next Phase*, 28 VA. J. INT'L L. 899, 901-02 (1988).

What do you think of Professor Reisman's proposal? Would it solve problems of biased information? Is it realistic?

4.   For discussion of difficulties inherent in collecting and interpreting data for differing countries, see Stanley Heginbotham & Vita Bite, *Issues in Interpretation and Evaluation of Country Studies, in* HUMAN RIGHTS AND U.S. FOREIGN POLICY 195 (Barry M. Rubin & Elizabeth P. Spiro, eds. 1979). The Country Reports are also discussed briefly in chapter 8, *supra*, as a kind of fact-finding.

5.   For analysis of the long-observed tradition of judicial abdication in foreign affairs matters, see THOMAS M. FRANCK, DOES THE RULE OF LAW APPLY TO FOREIGN AFFAIRS (1992); Michael P. Scharf, *The Role of the Judiciary in Foreign Policy Litigation*, 86 AM. SOC'Y INT'L L. PROC. 211 (1992) (summarizing panel discussion).

Section 502B of the Foreign Assistance Act, discussed *supra* at 391, and reproduced in *Selected International Human Rights Instruments*, stresses the significance of human rights in U.S. foreign policy. Despite clauses in that section regarding security and economic assistance, discussed previously, experiences of the Carter and Reagan administrations expose many obstacles to implementing human rights policies. The following discusses implementation of Section 502B under the Carter Administration:

Stephen B. Cohen, *Conditioning U.S. Security Assistance on Human Rights Practices*, 76 AM. J. INT'L. L. 246, 246, 256-74 (1982) (footnotes omitted):

In the United States, with its government of separated powers and functions, it is the executive branch, and in particular the Department of State, that bears responsibility for implementing legislation on foreign relations. The success of implementation will depend on political decisions, involving competing national interests, as well as on institutional and personal considerations of the officials concerned. Inevitably, there is a gap between legislation and execution, especially when the Executive is not wholly sympathetic to the law. The gap may even devour legislated policies as the Executive refuses "to take Care that the Laws be faithfully executed," and bureaucratic and personal considerations distort judgments, exploit the generality and uncertainty of language, and lead to abuse of discretion. A notable instance of this problem has been executive implementation of legislation on international human rights. . . .

II. RESISTANCE OF THE CAREER BUREAUCRACY UNDER CARTER

The installation of the Carter administration in January 1977 produced a dramatic shift in attitudes of high political officials on the human rights issue. As a presidential candidate, Jimmy Carter had strongly advocated increased emphasis on human rights in American foreign policy and he reaffirmed this position in his inaugural address. Although he did not mention the specific issue of human rights and military ties or indicate his position on implementation of section 502B, his personal call for a human rights oriented foreign policy implied a promise to do considerably more than his predecessors to follow the legislation.

The executive branch, however, did not attempt to conform to the statute's requirements without a fierce internal struggle. Despite the change in attitudes at the highest political level (from opposition to section 502B to endorsement of its underlying principle), the Department of State's career bureaucracy remained implacably hostile and continued to resist implementation. The result was intense bureaucratic warfare between career officials, who resisted implementation, and the office of the newly established Assistant Secretary for Human Rights, which sought adherence to the law.

The Attitude of the Career Bureaucracy

The career bureaucracy of the Department of State is the Foreign Service, and the core of the Foreign Service serves in the five regional bureaus for Africa, East Asia, Europe, Latin America, and the Near East. Each bureau has responsibility for managing relations with countries within its region, including issues of military aid and arms sales.

The opposition of the Foreign Service to section 502B was a logical consequence of its conception of its special role or of (what one student of the bureaucracy has labeled) its "organizational essence." The Foreign Service views its primary role or essence as the maintenance of smooth and cordial relations with other governments. It believes that military aid and arms sales are an indispensable means to achieving this goal. When provided, the other government is grateful and more inclined to get along with the United States. When refused, a cordial relationship may be harder to maintain, especially if the other government suspects that the reason for refusal is a judgment that it has mistreated its own citizens.

Keeping other governments happy becomes an end in itself. This phenomenon is often referred to as "clientism" because the Foreign Service views other governments as "clients" with whose interests it identifies, rather than as parties to be dealt with at arm's length according to the national interest of the United States. . . .

The phenomenon of "clientism" has a number of causes. A Foreign Service officer is typically required to develop personal relations and spend substantial periods of time with high officials of other governments. He tends, therefore, to sympathize and identify with their point of view. If the other government is accused of human rights abuses, he deals with officials who either deny the accusations or explain the excesses as regrettable, but necessary to stem "terrorism" and avoid social chaos. He is much less likely to encounter the victims of repression and hear their point of view.

In addition, the tour of duty in the Foreign Service is usually of 2 to 3 years' duration, after which the officer is rotated to another post. . . . Thus, the short duration reduces the incentive to consider the longer run consequences of decisions.

. . . [T]he regional bureaus have continually opposed implementation of legislation conditioning security assistance on human rights concerns. . . . Even after the Carter administration entered office in 1977, the regional bureaus vigorously fought nearly all attempts to apply section 502B to specific cases. This resistance took a number of different forms. First, they tried to minimize the relevance of section 502B. During the first 2 years, they argued that it could be ignored because it was merely a statement of policy and not legally binding. After it was made legally binding, they argued that the statutory rule was only one of several factors to be weighed in decisions on security assistance.

Second, the career bureaucracy attempted to distort information about human rights conditions in particular countries. The extent of abusive practices was consistently underreported. . . .

As it minimized or concealed negative aspects of a "client's" human rights practices, the career bureaucracy exaggerated positive signs. Improvements were said to have occurred on the basis of insubstantial evidence or self-serving declarations of the government power. . . .

Third, the regional bureaus overstated the extent of U.S. interests at stake in particular cases and the damage that could possibly result from failure to approve proposed security assistance. . . .

The Human Rights Bureau

Given the resistance of the career bureaucracy, concentrated in the regional bureaus, implementation of section 502B during the Carter administration depended on the newly created Bureau of Human Rights, headed by an outsider who was personally committed to the policy of the statute and staffed, to a significant degree, by persons from outside the career bureaucracy. The new bureau began to serve as a counterweight to the "clientism" of the regional bureaus. It took the initiative in insisting that section 502B had to be satisfied before security assistance could be provided, notwithstanding the argument of the career bureaucracy that the statute could be ignored or treated merely as one of several factors. The bureau also developed independent sources of information about human rights conditions in particular countries, which enabled it to challenge the factual reporting of the career bureaucracy. Finally, it attempted to question the national security reasons offered to justify security assistance when the recipient appeared to "engage in gross [human rights] violations." . . .

This newly strengthened human rights office inserted itself into the established Department of State procedures with vigor. By virtue of section 502B, it was able to claim a right to participate in all decisions on security assistance. When it disagreed with the regional bureaus, which was quite frequent, it insisted that a decision paper—known formally as an action memorandum—be prepared and sent to the Secretary of State for resolution of the issue.

During the first 18 months of the Carter administration, individual proposals for both military aid and arms sales were continually at issue between the regional bureaus and the Bureau of Human Rights and therefore "litigated" through the action memorandum procedure. In some ways, this resembled a judicial process, for it was adversarial in nature, and the action memorandum can be viewed as containing briefs for the position of each side. . . . The Human Rights Bureau argued its position in the context of section 502B. The bureau cited the statute and emphasized that there were two basic issues for decision: first, whether the proposed recipient was engaged in gross abuses, and second, whether extraordinary circumstances nevertheless required such assistance. The Human Rights Bureau challenged security assistance proposals when it believed the intended recipient was engaged in serious human rights abuses. The concerned regional bureau virtually always disagreed.

The action memorandum process thus provided a formal mechanism by which the Human Rights Bureau could attempt to apply section 502B to specific cases. . . .

The Significance of Bureaucratic Resistance

A recurring theme in modern studies of American government is the unresponsiveness of the bureaucracy to presidential decisions and directives. . . .

The history of section 502B illustrates that the same basic point can be made about congressional directives. . . .

The bureaucracy is most likely to succeed in resisting legislation when high political officials are hostile to the congressional effort . . . . With the approval of its superiors, the bureaucracy can simply ignore the statute. . . .

III. INTERPRETATION AND APPLICATION OF THE STATUTE UNDER CARTER

The public generally identifies the Carter administration with aggressive pursuit of a human rights oriented foreign policy. Some foreign affairs specialists have charged that its "single-minded" approach seriously overemphasized human rights objectives and failed to consider or pursue other important foreign policy goals, to the detriment of U.S. interests. The general public's impression and the specialists' criticism are attributable, in large measure, to the rhetoric of high administration officials, particularly President Carter himself, who even 2 years into his term declared, "Human rights is the soul of our foreign policy." . . .

Yet a careful examination of actual decisions under section 502B leads to a very different conclusion: that the Carter administration exhibited a remarkable degree of tentativeness and caution, so that its pursuit of human rights goals was anything but "single-minded." Relatively few governments were considered to be "engaged in a consistent pattern of gross [human rights] violations." Security assistance was actually cut off to even fewer, because other U.S. interests were often found to outweigh human rights concerns under the exception for "extraordinary circumstances." Moreover, in some instances, the Carter administration adopted a highly strained reading of the statute which, although not contrary to its literal terms, produced a result contrary to congressional intent. In other cases, the language was simply disregarded, so that decisions violated even the letter of the law.

Fear of Finding

Perhaps the most remarkable evidence of the administration's conservative approach to section 502B was its policy never to determine formally, even in a classified decision, that a particular government was engaged in gross abuses. The primary reason for this policy was the belief that such a determination, even if classified, would inevitably be leaked to the press and become generally known. It was feared that each country named would then consider itself publicly insulted, with consequent damage to our bilateral relationship. In addition, there was concern that once such a finding was revealed, the freedom to alter it might be severely constrained by public political pressures. . . .

The Development of a Body of Precedents

Because of the administration's policy of not making explicit findings under section 502B, the legal basis for particular outcomes was rarely made clear to the contesting bureaus. It was often difficult to say in a particular case exactly why the Secretary of State believed that section 502B did or did not apply. . . .

Owing to this lack of clear direction and the persistence with which both the Human Rights Bureau and the regional bureaus pursued their respective objectives, a considerable volume of action memorandums on security assistance issues were produced during the first half of the Carter administration. After the initial period, however, when a body of precedents was created, the amount of "litigation" began to decrease as contesting bureaus inferred by the pattern of outcomes how the Secretary of State was interpreting section 502B. The major issues of interpretation are discussed below. The three key questions were:

(1)   When was a foreign government considered to be engaged "in a consistent pattern of gross violations of internationally recognized human rights"?

(2)   What U.S. interests constituted "extraordinary circumstances"?

(3)   What was encompassed by the category "security assistance"?

1.   *Gross Violations.* The threshold issue under section 502B is whether a particular government "engages in a consistent pattern of gross violations of internationally recognized human rights." . . .

A definition of internationally recognized human rights is contained in section 502B itself. According to subsection (d)(1), this term *"includes* torture or cruel, inhuman, or degrading treatment or punishment, prolonged detention without charges and trial, and other flagrant denial of the right to life, liberty, or the security of the person" (emphasis added). The use of the word "includes" suggests that the list of abusive practices in the statute is not meant to be all encompassing. . . . However, the . . . legislative history contains strong evidence that Congress wanted the quoted language to be interpreted narrowly rather than expansively. . . .

The Carter administration followed [the latter] interpretation. In its decisions on security assistance, it was careful to go no further than required by the abuses specifically listed in subsection (d)(1). . . .

The second element, that the violations must be "gross," was read to mean that they must be significant in their impact. For example, although arbitrary imprisonment is one of the listed violations, detention without charges for several days was not considered "gross" because of the relatively brief period of confinement.

Third, the element of a "consistent pattern" was held to mean that abuses had to be significant in number and recurrent. Isolated instances of torture or summary execution, while certainly gross abuses, would not trigger termination of security assistance under section 502B. . . .

Even when gross abuses were significant in number and recurrent, the "pattern" was occasionally held not to be "consistent," if steps were taken to stop some abuses. . . .

Ordinarily, the fourth element, that the government itself engage in or be responsible for the violations, was not an issue if the other criteria were already met. In most instances, governments did not deny responsibility but sought to justify the abuses to U.S. officials on grounds of national security, fighting terrorism, anticommunism, and the like. Absent such an admission, however, the word "engages" was read to require "approval" by the highest ranking officials of the government in question, even if they lacked effective control over the military forces committing the abuses. . . .

2. *Extraordinary Circumstances.* The Carter administration always gave considerable weight to arguments that other U.S. interests might require continuation of security assistance, even when the government in question was thought to be a "gross violator." Thus, the charge that its pursuit of human rights was "single-minded" and to the exclusion of other interests was far wide of the mark. If anything, the administration gave excessive credence to claims that some specific foreign policy objective would and could be promoted only if security assistance were provided, and often failed to subject such claims to rigorous analysis.

The administration did require some showing of a substantial and specific interest before the exception for extraordinary circumstances was available. A mere desire for cordial relations, without more, was never held sufficient to constitute "extraordinary circumstances." However, once a specific interest of some substantiality was cited, the exception was usually invoked. Because of the liberal use made of the exception for "extraordinary circumstances," the number of countries subject to a section 502B cutoff was quite modest. In the end, human rights concerns resulted in the termination of security assistance to only eight countries, all in Latin America . . ..

3. *Security Assistance.* Even when a government was considered to be a "gross violator" and there were no "extraordinary circumstances," the termination of security assistance by the Carter administration was at times less than complete. Special exceptions to the general rule of subsection (a)(2) were created, most notably for the sale of certain military items to "gross violators" when it was believed that approval might induce human rights progress. These exceptions were not set out in the statute and therefore went beyond the letter of the law. . . .

The Carter administration did not automatically terminate all sales of defense items when a government was considered to be engaged in "gross violations" and "extraordinary circumstances" were not found. It adopted instead a "flexible" approach and broke up the panoply of defense items subject to the Arms Export Control Act (and therefore section 502B) into a number of subcategories:

(1) New weapons: tanks, artillery, fighters and bombers, and naval warships;

(2) Spare parts for previously acquired weapons;

(3) Support equipment: trucks, unarmed aircraft and ships, radios, and radars; and

(4) Safety-related items: ambulance aircraft and air-sea rescue equipment.

New weapons were consistently withheld, whenever requested. On the other hand, safety-related items were almost never denied, and spare parts and support equipment were approved for sale on numerous occasions. These exceptions, of course, are contrary to the literal language of section 502B, and the regional bureaus advocating approval felt it necessary to construct a legal rationale for this position.

The exception for safety-related items was justified in terms of the underlying purpose of the statute, that is, the protection of basic human rights. To disapprove the sale of equipment devoted to rescuing lives, it was argued, would defeat the basic goals of the statute. Items in the two middle categories (spare parts for weapons and support equipment) were approved on the basis of a different, but related, consideration: that a sale of defense items was on occasion needed to encourage another government to improve human rights conditions, and that spare parts and support equipment (as contrasted with new weapons) were an acceptable means of providing an inducement. In effect, section 502B was read to mean that Congress was concerned most about actual weapons and would be willing to permit the sale of other items when it was reasonable to suppose that it would lead to human rights improvements.

While the exception for safety-related items appears reasonable because of the direct connection with saving lives, that for spare parts and support items is fraught with danger. Such items are as critical to military performance as weapons themselves. Moreover, spare parts and support equipment typically make up a large part of a military's total acquisitions. Thus, to continue to approve such items is to continue a significant military supply relationship between the United States and the recipient. This danger may be acceptable if there are definite advantages to be gained in terms of human rights improvements. The risk, however, is that exceptions will be granted on the basis of unrealistic hopes that improvements will follow. If that turns out to be the case, then making these exceptions could undermine the purposes of section 502B.

*   *   *   *   *

Difficulties governments face when implementing rights policies indeed did confront the Clinton Administration. Amnesty International, for example, criticized it for offering security assistance without demonstrated concern for rights violations occurring within recipient countries. *See* Amnesty International, *Human Rights and U.S. Security Assistance* (1993). In particular, AI criticized not condemning abuses in Turkey, Egypt, and Israel—major recipients of U.S. Foreign Military Financing (FMF).

For fiscal year 1994, Clinton requested $3 billion in FMF for Israel (the most sought for any nation), and $2.3 billion for Egypt. Clinton asked, however, for only $146.2 million for Turkey, compared with $203 million for fiscal year 1993. *See* John M. Goshko, *Clinton to Continue Foreign Aid Cuts*, WASH. POST, Aug. 14, 1993, at A13. In October 1995, House and Senate conferees voted to further cut foreign aid to Turkey—to $33.5 million—in response to concerns regarding Turkey's human rights record. *See* Thomas W. Lippman, *Conferees Loosen Ban on Arms to Pakistan, Soften Senate Language on Russia*, WASH. POST, Oct. 25, 1995, at A6.

Clinton has been much criticized for his human rights policy toward China. In 1993, he renewed the Most Favoured Nation (MFN) status for China, stating that further renewal was dependent on human rights improvements. Exec. Order No. 12,850, 58 Fed. Reg. 31,327 (1993). (MFN status allows China to export goods into the U.S. at reduced tariffs.) He cited areas where improvements were needed including the treatment of political prisoners, protection of Tibet's heritage, freedom of emigration, nuclear non-proliferation, and the use of prison labor. In 1994, he again renewed MFN status though China had done little to improve human rights. He also severed the link between trade and human rights, reasoning that the U.S. could more effectively advocate improving rights in China if the U.S. and China continued to have a trading relationship. He did, though, ban the import of some weapons and munitions that China seeks to sell in the U.S.. *See* Ann Devroy, *Clinton Reverses Course on China*, WASH. POST, May 27, 1994, at A1; Lyndsay Griffiths, *Clinton Ends Rights Link to Chinese Trade Status*, CHIC. SUN-TIMES, May 27, 1994, at 10; Robin Wright & Jim Mann, *Clinton Outlines Program Aimed at Human Rights in China*, L.A. TIMES, May 31, 1994, at A6. *See generally* Lim Soon Neo, *Clinton's new policy towards China working, says Brown*, BUSINESS TIMES, Sept. 3, 1994, at 4; Patrick E. Tyler, *Abuses of Rights Persist in China Despite U.S. Pleas*, N.Y. TIMES, Aug. 29, 1994, at A1.

Supporters of continuing China's MFN status argue that the U.S. will not be able to influence the Chinese if trade relations are not maintained. Supporters also argue that MFN status furthers the development of a market economy in China, which eventually will lead to more rights for China's citizens. Critics argue that Clinton should not intentionally put business interests ahead of human rights. *See* Timothy A. Gelatt, *Public Law, Private Actors: The Impact of Human Rights on Business Investors in China*, 14 J. INT'L L. BUS. 66 (1993); Howard Kleinberg, *Who changed? Not the Chinese, so it must have been Clinton*, STAR TRIB. (MINNEAPOLIS), June 8, 1993 at 13A; Daniel M. Kolkey, *Lousy Odds in Playing Trade Status Card; Bolstering China's Bustling Economy Would Better Achieve U.S. Goals in Both Nations*, L.A. TIMES, June 7, 1993 at B7; W. Gary Vause, *Article: Tibet to Tienanmen: Chinese Human Rights and United States Foreign Policy*, 42 VAND. L. REV. 1575 (1989).

In an address to the Asia Foundation's Center for Asian Pacific Affairs, Assistant Secretary of State for Democracy, Human Rights, and Labor John Shattuck emphasized that Clinton has favored policies that encouraged China and other Asian countries to adopt democratic forms of government. John Shattuck, *Human Rights and Democracy in Asia*, U.S. DEP'T OF STATE DISPATCH, July 18, 1994 (Vol. 5, No. 29). The Clinton Administration has, for example, pressed China at the U.N. Commission on Human Rights on its violations.

The Clinton Administration has not, of course, completely disregarded rights concerns when extending security assistance. Concerning the use of economic sanctions generally and by the Clinton Administration, see *infra* at 59.

NOTES AND QUESTIONS

1. According to one study, neither in the Carter years nor in early years of the Reagan Administration was the relation between foreign assistance and human rights statistically significant. David Carleton & Michael Stohl, *The Foreign Policy of Human Rights: Rhetoric and Reality from Jimmy Carter to Ronald Reagan*, 7 HUM. RTS. Q. 205, 211-227 (1985). The study suggests, as did the Cohen article excerpted above, that even an executive committed to promoting rights on a moral level may have difficulty putting that commitment into practice. Why has it seemed so difficult to implement a commitment to human rights in foreign policy? Must the competing interests almost always win out over human rights?

2. The Reagan and Bush administrations did not continue to implement Sections 116 and 502B in ways described by Professor Cohen. At a 1988 symposium several commentators suggested ways the Executive could carry out a declared commitment to human rights in foreign policy. *See Symposium on Human Rights: An Agenda For the New Administration*, 28 VA. J. INT'L L. 827 (1988) (various authors).

3. This chapter, partly because of the statutes, tends to focus on foreign aid, sanctions, and other country-specific concerns. Yet even as to concerns affecting the many governments charged with rights violations, U.S. officials are aware that action by members of the U.N.,

the OAS, European organizations, and other intergovernmental groups can have immense impact. Nonetheless the bulk of attention (in the media and by scholars and other observers) seems to have involved surprisingly little commentary on the U.S. stance in the multilateral contrasted with the bilateral sphere. To mention Afghanistan, Angola, Burma, Cuba, Iran, Iraq, Lebanon, Libya, Nicaragua, and the West Bank merely introduces a list of dozens of countries as to which the State Department annual reports disclose egregious violations of human rights. For many reasons—including, *e.g.*, the avoidance of apparent double standards—the U.S. might wisely seek more productive cooperation from multilateral organizations and less-frequent resort to questions such as: "Unilaterally shall we cut off military and/or economic aid and impose other sanctions too?"

An outstanding survey of many matters highlighted in this chapter is a paper titled "Bureaucracy and Diplomacy" published by the Lawyers Committee on Human Rights. This brief summary sets forth conclusions of the Lawyers Committee project:

LAWYERS COMMITTEE FOR HUMAN RIGHTS, HUMAN RIGHTS AND U.S. FOREIGN POLICY: BUREAUCRACY AND DIPLOMACY, 1988 PROJECT SERIES NO. 4, at 96 (1989):

> This study presents a critique of the administration of human rights policy by the U.S. government, focusing upon five areas of concern: 1) the bureaucracy of the State Department; 2) the Inter-Agency Group on Human Rights and Foreign Assistance; 3) the preparation of the annual country reports; 4) human rights training for foreign service officers; and 5) the bureaucracy of other federal departments as it relates to human rights. This study shows that there are weaknesses in the way the U.S. human rights policy is administered. Fortunately, the steps that must be taken to make necessary improvements are well within reach.

Readers may be enlightened also by several reports the project inspired: LAWYERS COMMITTEE FOR HUMAN RIGHTS, HUMAN RIGHTS AND U.S. FOREIGN POLICY: REPORT AND RECOMMENDATIONS (1988); LINKING SECURITY ASSISTANCE AND HUMAN RIGHTS (1989); UNITED STATES POLICY TOWARD SOUTH AFRICA (1989); WORKER RIGHTS UNDER THE U.S. TRADE LAWS (1989). The report quoted above was also published in Edwin S. Maynard, *The Bureaucracy and Implementation of US Human Rights Policy*, 11 HUM. RTS. Q. 175 (1989).

David D. Newsom, *The Diplomacy of Human Rights: A Diplomat's View, in* THE DIPLOMACY OF HUMAN RIGHTS 3, 5-9 (David D. Newsom, ed. 1986) (footnotes omitted):

The effectiveness of U.S. diplomacy in the field of human rights has been aided by the fact that most nations are sensitive to how the outside world looks at their internal practices. . . . Most nations respond to charges of mistreatment of their citizens either with genuine efforts to correct abuses or cosmetic actions to divert attention, or by defending what they are doing. International pressure helps focus attention on the abuses. Governments, however, will not readily submit to changes that may threaten their political power. Where improvements are possible without running this risk, the chances are likely that improvements can be made. Where the abuses are deemed essential for the retention of power, changes are less likely.
. . .

Effective diplomatic action in support of human rights in another country involves both the individual actions of the diplomat and those policies and measures of the diplomat's country that can provide leverage and inducements for change.

In an ideal world, the diplomat would like to see change result from such efforts. In many regimes . . . change may not be possible, at least in the short term. The diplomat must then consider whether it is in the interest of his or her country to recommend "distance" from the regime. Public statements and policy actions can lessen the degree to which the diplomat's country is publicly identified, both at home and abroad, with the policies of the offending regime. Distancing is not necessarily "walking away" from an issue. It may serve to make our policies and principles more credible with others. The pressure of the resulting isolation can sometimes influence an internal situation.

"Distancing"can also give a signal of the seriousness of U.S. intentions to other countries where similar violations exist.

Where a U.S. diplomat determines that influence is possible, there are a number of tools available:

1. *Access*. A diplomat cannot effectively influence the actions or decisions of another country without access to that country's leaders, decision makers and opinion molders. The diplomat of the United States often has the advantage that, even if the host country is not sympathetic with the efforts being made, high officials are available because relations with the United States are important for other reasons. The ability to meet with human rights organizations and the political opposition is also important, both to gain information on the circumstances in the country and to give a signal that the United States is not wholly committed to the position of the government in power.

The diplomat must weigh carefully the degree to which he presses for access either to government officials or private organizations. There are limits in both cases. There may be only limited time or opportunities for discussions with senior leaders; the agenda must be carefully constructed. Contacts with human rights organizations or opposition groups in authoritarian countries may be firmly opposed by the government—or, if carried out, can create serious barriers in relations with the authorities on other matters.

2. *Public Statements*. Depending on the objective of the diplomatic efforts, the diplomat abroad may wish to speak out on the human rights situation in the host country or encourage the home government back in the capital to do so. Herein lies the heart of the debate over "quiet diplomacy." The diplomat must weigh whether a statement will move a government to take action or will increase its sensitivity to outside pressures and make other diplomatic efforts more difficult. Generally, public statements are used in the diplomacy of human rights when it appears that quiet efforts may not bear fruit or when the objective is more to "distance" the United States from a foreign regime than it is to influence that regime. The impact of such statements is of course enhanced if they are made at the presidential level or cabinet level. Official statements can be given further strength by special efforts to make them known internationally through the Voice of America and the other media of USIA [U.S. Information Agency].

3. *Legislation*. For the United States diplomat the existence of legislation requiring annual reports on the human rights situations in individual countries and requiring a consideration of human rights and emigration in questions of foreign assistance and trade provides both a problem and an opportunity. The problem arises when foreign governments consider that the application of U.S. legislative sanctions or requirements (such as the annual reports to the Congress) constitutes an unacceptable intrusion into their internal affairs. U.S. laws may represent a genuine political problem for foreign leaders if actions are taken in the face of such pressures. It is possible, however, for the diplomat to use the existence of legislation as an indication of the general feeling of the American people on an issue. If this

is presented without the suggestion of a threat, it can assist in supporting diplomatic efforts to make progress on a human rights problem . . ..

U.S. laws can be more effective in abeyance than in application. It is difficult to find cases where the actual application of the laws has led to changes in another country's human rights practices. Knowledge of a U.S. law, however, can sometimes help a faction within a foreign government arguing for more liberal practices. . . .

4. *U.S. Programs.* The legislation enacted during the 1970s provided U.S. administrations with the authority and, in some cases, with a mandate to apply human rights criteria to programs of military assistance, military sales, police assistance, export credits, trade, and economic assistance programs that did not fall in the category of "basic human needs." These were obvious tools of pressure on foreign governments. The legislation in many instances, however, left the interpretation of given situations to the discretion of the administration. During the Carter administration, major interagency machinery was established to monitor and manage the application of human rights legislation and executive policies. Much of the diplomacy of the period was devoted to explaining the rationale for U.S. actions to affected countries and to other nations that had an interest in the U.S. programs. . . .

5. *Consultation with Like-minded Governments.* Many Western European democracies share the concern of the United States over human rights violations. . . . They are less inclined to use economic and military programs for pressure, but they are often prepared to support the United States with diplomatic efforts. Human rights issues have become in recent years an important part of our agenda of diplomatic consultation with allies, including Japan. Diplomats from such countries have often been helpful to United States diplomats in reinforcing the international concern in specific situations. . . .

6. *Multilateral Banks.* Another area of pressure created by the legislation in support of U.S. diplomacy relates to actions in the multilateral lending agencies—the World Bank, the Inter-American Development Bank, the Asian Development Bank, and the African Development Bank. It was the clear sense of Congress that the United States should not support any loans by these agencies to countries that were violators of human rights principles, except where it could clearly be shown that the loans would support projects related to "basic human needs." In practice, the only activity of these agencies over which the United States has a veto is the "soft loan" window of the Inter-American Bank. Actions in the other banks are limited to voting or abstaining. The United States has not ever been able to get sufficient support from other members of the banks to stop any loans. In some cases, the threat of U.S. opposition has led countries to withhold or withdraw applications.

To U.S. diplomats in developing countries, this "tool" has been, in many ways, the least effective. The use of the banks as instruments of pressure has been seen as "politicizing" the banks. Such actions are often resented particularly by those technocrats and managers in offending countries who are potential allies on many human rights issues. The task of bilateral diplomacy in this phase of the human rights policy has been to seek to explain and defend the action of the United States in taking action against a loan. . . .

[Ed. note: The author proceeded to discuss diplomatic efforts through international organizations, such as the U.N., and the work of nongovernmental organizations, such as the International Commission of Jurists and Amnesty International.]

NOTES AND QUESTIONS

1.   As the preceding excerpt suggests, quiet diplomacy usually is the initial approach of the executive in addressing violations in another country. If it fails, the Executive must decide whether to engage in public denunciation of a country for its violations. The Reagan Administration criticized the Carter Administration for seeking too much public pressure—open diplomacy—rather than first trying quiet diplomacy. Reagan officials, in turn, were then criticized for proceeding too quietly with friendly governments and refusing to denounce U.S. allies publicly. Not all but most of the Reagan open diplomacy on rights was aimed at communist governments. For further reading on the diplomacy of human rights in the Carter and Reagan administrations, see Warren Christopher, *The Diplomacy of Human Rights: The First Year, in* HUMAN RIGHTS AND U.S. FOREIGN POLICY 257 (Barry M. Rubin & Elizabeth P. Spiro eds. 1979); A. GLENN MOWER, HUMAN RIGHTS AND AMERICAN FOREIGN POLICY: THE CARTER AND REAGAN EXPERIENCES 89-100 (1987); John P. Salzberg, *The Carter Administration and Human Rights, in* THE DIPLOMACY OF HUMAN RIGHTS 61 (David Newsom ed. 1986).

2.   The Clinton Administration has been criticized for continued use of quiet diplomacy with Guatemala regarding the case of Efraín Bámaca Velásquez. Bámaca, a combatant with Unidad Revolucionaria Nacional Guatemalteca (URNG), a guerrilla group seeking to overthrow the government, disappeared in 1992 after a fight between the URNG and government soldiers. The evidence on whether Bámaca was killed at the scene or taken alive is conflicting. The government denied causing his death, but numerous prisoners reported seeing him alive in various detention camps. His spouse, a U.S. citizen, garnered international attention by staging a hunger strike in 1994 in front of the National Palace in Guatemala City. A November 1994 segment of CBS's "60 Minutes" reported that after she was advised he had been killed, the CIA was told by a Guatemalan army source that he was alive. That television report led to criticism of the Clinton Administration's handling of the disappearance and apparently compelled the State Department publicly to hold the Guatemalan army responsible for Bámaca's disappearance.

  Clinton officials had made early efforts to help the wife find her husband by raising her claim privately with Guatemalan officials. The efforts led only to superficial examination by Guatemalan officials. When it became apparent to rights advocates that quiet diplomacy had failed they began to pressure the administration to publicize the case. The administration, reluctant to criticize the Guatemalan government in light of the U.S. role in U.N.-mediated peace talks for Guatemala, refused until "60 Minutes" highlighted Bámaca's case. The administration also refused to impose sanctions on Guatemala. *See* Human Rights Watch/Americas, *Disappeared in Guatemala: The Case of Efraín Bámaca Velásquez* (Human Rights Watch/Americas, New York, N.Y.), Mar. 1995. Eventually, the publicity generated acknowledgment by the Guatemalan government of responsibility for Bámaca's death and information about U.S. complicity with the military officer who killed Bámaca.

3.   What are advantages and disadvantages of both quiet and open diplomacy? Should the Executive always proceed quietly before making public denouncements when the U.S. has diplomatic relations with the country? Should the Executive always make public denouncements when quiet diplomacy fails?

4.   James Thyden of the State Department's Office of Human Rights under the Reagan Administration defended the administration's use of diplomacy to effectuate human rights improvements. He noted that the Department had been fairly outspoken on rights issues, and he pointed out that the essence of quiet diplomacy is keeping quiet about not only diplomatic efforts but also resulting improvements. James Thyden, *An Inside View of United States Foreign Policy Under the Reagan Administration*, 7 WHITTIER L. REV. 705, 711-12 (1985).

5.   For illustrations of rights diplomacy as it has operated in eight countries —Argentina, Brazil, Indonesia, Iran, Korea, Romania, South Africa, and the Soviet Union—see THE DIPLOMACY OF HUMAN RIGHTS, 69-200 (David D. Newsom ed. 1986).

6.   As the Newsom book excerpted *supra* at 411 points out, the U.S. does not have veto power in most international banks; its vote is merely one of many. Consequently, even when the U.S. has complied with Section 701 and voted against loans to countries with violations, the banks nonetheless have approved the loans. To carry out Section 701's intent more effectively, a study by the Lawyers Committee for Human Rights argues that the U.S. "should launch diplomatic efforts both within the [banks] and bilaterally to secure negative votes on loans to—or investments in—countries with [egregious] violations." LAWYERS COMMITTEE FOR HUMAN RIGHTS, HUMAN RIGHTS AND U.S. FOREIGN POLICY: REPORT AND RECOMMENDATIONS 24-25 (1988). *See also* Daniel D. Bradlow, *International Organizations and Private Complaints: The Case of the World Bank Inspection Panel*, 34 VA. J. INT'L L. 553 (1994); Jonathan Earl Sanford, *U.S. Policy Toward the Multilateral Development Banks: The Role of Congress*, 22 GEORGE WASHINGTON J. INT'L L. & ECON. 1 (1988).

7.   For further reading, see

ERIC BIEL, LINKING SECURITY ASSISTANCE AND HUMAN RIGHTS (1989);

Daniel J.B. Hofrenning, *Human Rights and Foreign Aid: A Comparison of the Reagan and Carter Administrations,* 18 AMER. POLITICS Q. 514 (1990) (concluding that concern for human rights was more prevalent in foreign aid allocations of the Reagan Administration than in the Carter Administration);

Steven C. Poe, *Human Rights and Economic Aid Allocation under Ronald Reagan and Jimmy Carter*, 36 AMER. J. POLITICAL SCIENCE 147 (1992) (concluding that human rights considerations affected economic aid allocations worldwide as well as in the U.S. backyard under both the Reagan and Carter administrations);

Steven C. Poe, *Human Rights and the Allocation of U.S. Military Assistance*, 28 J. PEACE RESEARCH 205 (1991) (concluding that human rights abuses did affect allocation of military aid in Western hemisphere countries and a random sample of the other countries during both Carter and Reagan administrations);

George W. Shepherd, Jr., EFFECTIVE SANCTIONS ON SOUTH AFRICA: THE CUTTING EDGE OF ECONOMIC INTERVENTION (1991);

SOUTH AFRICA: THE SANCTIONS REPORT: DOCUMENTS AND STATISTICS (Joseph Hanlon ed., 1990).

---

3.   Economic Sanctions

The U.S., mostly in concert with the U.N., has increasingly resorted to economic sanctions against states that violate rights of their own citizens. In considering the following excerpt, readers should think about the advisability of imposing sanctions to achieve rights objectives. Humanitarian intervention—the use of armed force by one or more governments to stop other governments' violations—is a possible alternative to economic sanctions and is discussed in chapter 6, *supra.*

Barry E. Carter, *International Economic Sanctions: Improving the Haphazard U.S. Legal Regime*, 75 CAL. L. REV. 1159, 1170-82 (1987) (footnotes omitted):

THE PURPOSES AND EFFECTIVENESS OF ECONOMIC SANCTIONS . . .

A.   *The Purposes of Sanctions*

There are three broad rationales for imposing sanctions:

— seeking to influence a country to change its policies or even its government;

— punishing a country for its policies; and

— symbolically demonstrating opposition against the target country's policies to many possible audiences, including constituencies in the sender country as well as audiences in the target country, other potential target countries, or allied countries.

More than one rationale can be involved in the decision to employ a sanction or set of sanctions in a particular situation. For example, the widening U.S. sanctions against South Africa stem from a mix of all the above considerations. The sanctions involve an effort to influence South Africa to change its apartheid policy, a dose of punishment, and a symbolic statement of U.S. opposition to apartheid.

Besides these broad rationales, a sender country generally has more specific foreign policy motives for imposing sanctions. Hufbauer and Schott characterized these objectives as follows:

(1) "Change target country policies in a relatively modest way (modest in the scale of national goals, but often of burning importance to participants in the episode)." These goals include slowing nuclear proliferation, promoting human rights, fighting terrorism, and resolving expropriation claims;

(2) "Destabilize the target government," and thus change its policies;

(3) "Disrupt a minor military adventure," as illustrated by the United Kingdom's sanctions against Argentina over the Falkland Islands dispute;

(4) "Impair the military potential of the target country," as illustrated by sanctions against the Warsaw Pact by the United States and its allies; and

(5) "Change target country policies in a major way," as illustrated by U.S. efforts and those of other countries against South Africa's system of apartheid. . . .

B.   *Effectiveness of Sanctions*

It is difficult to measure the success of sanctions because of the frequent ambiguity of the rationales and objectives behind their use. Even if the real goal is discernible, it still may be difficult to determine the extent to which the sanctions contributed to the desired outcome.

. . . Target countries are perhaps becoming more immune to sanctions because of two factors. First, the recent targets have been less dependent on trade with the United States. Second, other countries, such as the Soviet Union, have stepped forward more often to assist the target states.

1.   *Effectiveness as a Function of Purpose*

The success rate varies according to the foreign policy objective being pursued. Sanctions designed to destabilize a government (objective 2) have been especially effective. Examples include the toppling of Haiti's Duvalier in February 1986, Uganda's Idi Amin in 1979, Chile's Allende in 1973, and the Dominican Republic's Trujillo in 1961. Indeed, it would appear that in the study's fourteen cases since 1954 where the United States applied economic sanctions for destabilization purposes, it was successful in ten episodes and unsuccessful in two. The outcome of two cases is still uncertain, as U.S. sanctions continue against Libya and Nicaragua. [Ed. note: In 1990, a U.S.-backed coalition won elections and took power in Nicaragua.]

U.S. sanctions designed to achieve *more narrow policy goals*—such as dealing with expropriation of U.S. corporations, nuclear proliferation, terrorism, or human rights abuses (objective 1)—have been effective about 40% of the time, though the rate varies according to the particular goal. . . .

In the area of human rights, sanctions such as cutting back on U.S. military and economic assistance usually have not been successful in stopping the target countries' gross violations of international recognized rights.

The United States has also used economic sanctions—such as restricting various financial assistance programs and imposing export controls—against countries designated as supporting terrorism. It does not appear, however, that these selective sanctions had much effect in the 1980s on the policies of two of the principal target countries—Syria and Libya. . . .

2. *Effectiveness of Sanctions by Type*

An analysis of the effectiveness of sanctions must also consider whether certain *types* of sanctions are more effective than others, in achieving their objectives. Relative effectiveness may, of course, also depend on the circumstances of particular situations.

For example, if the United States were to impose sanctions against South Korea for human rights violations, import controls might be more effective economically than export controls, given the importance of U.S. purchases to South Korean trade. The United States imports about 39% of all of South Korea's foreign sales. In contrast, U.S. exports total about 21% of South Korea's foreign purchases. Product breakdowns reveal more subtle differences. The amount and type of the principal U.S. imports from South Korea (manufactured articles and clothes) suggest that South Korea cannot easily change long-established business relationships and find willing buyers in other countries. At the same time, South Korea would probably have less trouble and incur fewer additional costs finding other suppliers for present U.S. exports to it, such as machinery, crude materials and chemical products. These are generally available in world markets.

Even for countries where the United States plays about the same role in percentage terms as an exporter and as an importer, import controls might, for similar reasons, still be more effective than export controls. For example, the United States imports about 40% of Guatemala's foreign sales and exports about 40% of its purchases. Guatemala, however, might have serious difficulty selling elsewhere, at comparable prices, the coffee, sugar, bananas, and other vegetables and fruits that constitute its principal U.S. sales, because trade barriers against agricultural products are widespread.

Similarly, the United States imports a large amount of Chile's copper production, an important revenue earner for that country. Chile would probably find it more difficult to change its long-established relationships with U.S. copper purchasers than to find new suppliers for the goods it buys from the United States. Thus, U.S. import controls would likely be more effective than export restrictions.

An analysis of the relative effectiveness of sanctions should also assess the possible contribution of controls on private financial transactions. For example, . . . U.S. banks now make a large share of the foreign loans to borrowers in certain countries, such as South Korea (26%), Guatemala (33%), and Chile (47%). Controls on financial transactions might be effective, but there are many potential problems . . ..

History provides several concrete examples of the effectiveness of controls on imports and private financial transactions. Increased U.S. duties on the Dominican

Republic's sugar imports in 1961-62 helped topple the Trujillo regime. U.S. threats to deny most-favored-nation (MFN) status to Romania seem to have encouraged it to relax its emigration restrictions. As for financial controls, the freeze on $12 billion in Iranian deposits in 1979-81 probably had the greatest impact among all the comprehensive sanctions. Similarly, the private decisions by several U.S. banks not to roll over South Africa's short-term loans helped create a financial crisis there in August-September 1985. The official U.S. sanctions later included a ban on new loans to that government, and then on new investment in that country. These financial controls have probably created more problems for South Africa than any of the other recently imposed sanctions.

In short, each use of sanctions should be rooted in a careful analysis of the vulnerabilities of the target country. In terms of effectiveness, export controls do not have any natural advantage over import controls or financial controls. Indeed, one of the most interesting conclusions of the Hufbauer and Schott study was that "[t]he multiple regression analysis suggests that financial controls are marginally more successful than export controls, but that import controls are the most successful of all types.". . .

3. Costs to the Sender Country

It is also important to recognize that economic sanctions usually involve some costs to the sender country. The type and amount of these costs depend, of course, on the particular situation and on the type of sanctions imposed. Many costs stem from the indirect effects of sanctions, such as the loss of sales by a supplier when the manufacturer is prevented from making an export sale to a target country. Other costs result from long-term changes in business patterns, which often occur when the target country seeks to minimize the financial effects of future sanctions.

These myriad domestic costs are rarely calculated in any detail or with much reliability. Cost calculations might not be important to U.S. policymakers, particularly when the United States is imposing sanctions against a country with a much smaller economy, like Nicaragua. Moreover, there may be considerable incentives for the government *not* to calculate domestic costs. Careful estimates might highlight those costs and exacerbate political problems with domestic constituencies hurt by the sanctions.

Despite the complexities, a few general observations about U.S. costs are worth mentioning. First, terminating or reducing bilateral programs, such as foreign assistance can initially *save* money. Such measures may, however, involve indirect costs, as in lost sales for U.S. companies. Foreign recipients of U.S. programs often spend much of their aid on U.S. goods and services, sometimes because U.S. laws require them to do so.

Second, restrictions on imports and private financial transactions often cost less than export controls, though all these sanctions have domestic costs. Export sanctions directly cause lost sales and lost jobs. The immediate impact might be reduced by finding other customers, but complete substitutability is not assured, and such alternative sales would presumably be on less favorable terms (or they would have occurred before the controls were imposed). Export restrictions also create long-term problems for U.S. sales abroad, as they jeopardize the reputation of U.S. businesses as reliable suppliers.

Import controls generally involve smaller costs. Since new foreign policy sanctions are usually applied against only one country or a few countries, alternative foreign supplies frequently exist. As a result, the U.S. purchaser does not have to do without a good, but faces only the increased costs that must be paid to a higher-priced supplier. While this increased cost might mean that the U.S. purchaser has to raise its prices and thus lose some sales of its own product, the cost differences are often so small that the resulting losses are marginal.

Moreover, the initial U.S. purchaser should be able to pass on much of the added costs to its customers by raising its own prices. While these customers will then bear some of the costs, their individual burden will probably be a small share of the total domestic costs of import sanctions, because the costs may be spread among many purchasers at different levels of the distribution process.

*   *   *   *   *

The United States, under the Bush and Clinton administrations, has been a leader in encouraging the United Nations Security Council to impose economic sanctions against countries with poor human rights records. Sanctions against Haiti, Iraq, Libya and the former Yugoslavia (Serbia and Montenegro) have achieved only limited success.

In response to the military coup that ousted Haitian President Jean-Bertrand Aristide's government, the Security Council imposed broad economic sanctions including a general embargo on trade with Haiti and a prohibition on the sale of oil to Haiti. Although Aristide was returned to power after more than three years in exile, he faced a Haitian economy that was devastated by years of international sanctions. *See* Douglas Farah, *Toughest Task in Haiti: Reviving Economy*, WASH. POST, Sept. 23, 1994, at A1; Ruth Marcus, *Clinton Lifts Most Economic Sanctions, Keeps Up Pressure on Military Leaders*, WASH. POST, Sept. 27, 1994, at A17. *See generally* Harold Hongju Koh, *Democracy and Human Rights in the United States Foreign Policy?: Lessons from the Haitian Crisis*, 48 SMU L. REV. 189 (1994); Douglas E. Matthews, *Economic Sanctions and Economic Strategies: Toward Haiti's Integration into the World Economy*, 6 ST. THOMAS L. REV. 281 (1994).

The Security Council imposed trade sanctions against Iraq following that country's 1990 invasion of Kuwait. The U.S. has been an adamant supporter of continued sanctions to force Iraq to return Kuwaiti prisoners of war, comply with certain U.N. resolutions, end persecution of Shiites in southern Iraq, and dismantle its weapons of mass destruction. The sanctions, many still in effect as of February 1996, have crippled the Iraqi economy but failed to ensure compliance with U.N. demands. *See* John M. Goshko, *Around the World—U.N., Iraq to Discuss Oil Sales*, WASH. POST, Feb. 28, 1996, at A22; Julia Preston, *U.N. Offers Plan to Ease Oil Embargo on Iraq for Humanitarian Reasons*, WASH. POST, Apr. 14, 1995, at A28; *Recognition of Kuwait Expected; But Iraq's Grudging Acknowledgment May Not Be Enough to Ease Sanctions*, S.F. EXAMINER, Oct. 20, 1994, at A17.

The Security Council in 1992 imposed sanctions on Libya for failing to surrender for trial, in Britain or the U.S., two Libyans accused of having in 1988 planted a bomb on Pan Am flight 103 which exploded in midair and killed 270 people. Sanctions included an air embargo, a ban on the sale or transfer of arms and certain oil equipment to Libya, and a ban on some Libyan assets abroad. The sanctions, having failed to achieve the surrender of the two alleged bombers, were still in place as of February 1996. *See* Jimmy Gurulé, *Terrorism, Territorial Sovereignty, and the Forcible Apprehension of International Criminals Abroad*, 17 HASTINGS INT'L & COMP. L. REV. 457, 478 n.102 (1994); *Sanctions on Libya Unchanged*, WASH. POST, Mar. 31, 1995, at A39.

In response to ethnically divided fighting that in 1992 erupted in the former Yugoslavia, the Security Council imposed sanctions against Serbia and Montenegro, the remaining members of the Yugoslav Federation. The Council's goal was to cut off the flow of supplies and support, from Serbia and Montenegro, to the Bosnian Serbs. Under the leadership of President Milosevic, Serbia resisted U.N. offers to ease the sanctions in exchange for Serb recognition of an independent Bosnia. Despite the heavy toll on the Serb economy, the sanctions remained in place for over two years. In November 1995, the Security Council suspended the sanctions in light of the Dayton peace talks. *See* Michael Dobbs, *Bosnian Serbs Test West's Will as Settlement Options Dissolve*, WASH. POST, June 12, 1995, at A1; Jeong Hwa Pires, *North Korean Time Bomb: Can Sanctions Defuse It? A Review of International Economic Sanctions as an Option*, 24 GA. J. INT'L & COMP. L. 307, 337-38 (1994); John Pomfret, *The Dayton Hurrahs vs. Bosnian Reality: Can Serbian Leader Deliver Peace?*, WASH. POST, Nov. 23, 1995, at A35. The conflict in the former Yugoslavia is discussed in detail in chapter 7, *supra*, and 12, *infra*.

NOTES AND QUESTIONS

1.   Some jurists and governments have maintained that sanctions violate Article 2(4) of the U.N. Charter. Documents such as the Charter of Economic Rights and Duties of States, G.A. res. 3171, 29 U.N. GAOR, Supp. (No. 31) at 50, 55, U.N. Doc. A/9631 (1974), which prohibits states from using economic sanctions to subordinate a state's sovereign rights, support this view. For further reading, see Derek W. Bowett, *International Law and Economic Coercion*, 16 VA. J. INT'L L. 245 (1976); Comment, *The Use of Nonviolent Coercion: A Study in Legality Under Article 2(4) of the Charter of the United Nations*, 122 U. PA. L. REV. 983 (1974).

2.   Professor Carter, who authored the excerpt above, expanded on his article in BARRY E. CARTER, INTERNATIONAL ECONOMIC SANCTIONS (1988).

3.   Does the fact that the U.S. is party to only some of the U.N. human rights treaties affect the legality of U.S. intervention (economic or otherwise) based on human rights conditions in other countries? *See* Paul Szasz, *The International Legal Aspects of the Human Rights Program of the United States*, 12 CORNELL INT'L L. J. 161, 164-67 (1979).

4.   For further reading on the use of economic sanctions, see Kenneth W. Abbott, *Coercion and Communication: Framework for Evaluation of Economic Sanctions*, 19 N.Y.U. J. INT'L L. & POL. 781 (1987); Kenneth W. Abbott, *Linking Trade to Political Goals: Foreign Policy Export Controls in the 1970s and 1980s*, 65 MINN. L. REV. 739 (1981); M.S. DAOUDI & M.S. DAJANI, ECONOMIC SANCTIONS, IDEALS AND EXPERIENCE (1983); GARY C. HUFBAUER & JEFFREY J. SCHOTT, ECONOMIC SANCTIONS RECONSIDERED: HISTORY AND CURRENT POLICY (rev. ed. 1990); Jeong Hwa Pires, *North Korean Time Bomb: Can Sanctions Defuse It? A Review of International Economic Sanctions as an Option*, 24 GA. J. INT'L & COMP. L. 307 (1994).

5.   Because of *apartheid* policies the U.S. successfully imposed trade and financial sanctions on South Africa. *See* Comprehensive Anti-Apartheid Act of 1986, 22 U.S.C. §§ 5001-16 (Supp. IV 1986). For reading on sanctions and other policy options in regard to South Africa, see LAWYERS COMMITTEE FOR HUMAN RIGHTS, UNITED STATES POLICY TOWARD SOUTH AFRICA (1989), *reprinted in* Lynda M. Clarizio, Bradley Clements & Erika Geeter, *United States Policy Toward South Africa*, 11 HUM. RTS. Q. 249 (1989); Wendell C. Maddrey, Note, *Economic Sanctions Against South Africa: Problems and Prospects for Enforcement of Human Rights Norms*, 22 VA. J. INT'L L. 345 (1982); Winston P. Nagan, *Economic Sanctions, U.S. Foreign Policy, International Law and the Anti-Apartheid Act of 1986*, 4 FLORIDA INT'L L.J. 85 (1988); Louis K. Rothberg, *Sections 402 and 403 of the Comprehensive Anti-Apartheid Act of 1986*, 22 GEORGE WASHINGTON J. INT'L L. & ECON. 117 (1988); David Weissbrodt & Georgina Mahoney, *International Legal Action Against Apartheid*, 4 LAW & INEQ. J. 485 (1986).

6.   Perhaps the most significant use of sanctions by the Clinton Administration was the

suspension of aid to Guatemala in response to a coup d'etat headed by former President Serrano in 1993. The U.S. cut off all economic aid, worth about $45.3 million for 1993. After imposition of the sanctions, constitutionally appointed President Ramiro de Leon Carpio took office and negotiated for resumption of aid. For three years before his appointment to the presidency he had served as Guatemala's Attorney General for Human Rights. Following his election, the Clinton Administration reinstated more than $60 million for Guatemala. *See* Peter Hakim, *Behind Guatemala's 'Miracle'*, CHRISTIAN SCI. MONITOR, June 23, 1993, at 18.

In August 1993, Congress and the administration sought to convince the International Olympic Committee to reject Beijing as host for the year 2000 Olympics because of China's human rights abuses. The efforts were successful and, in September 1993, the Olympic Committee selected Sydney, Australia as host. *See* Robert Greenberger, *U.S., Unhappy with Beijing's Abuse of Human Rights, Focuses on Olympics*, WALL ST. J., Aug. 23, 1993, at A7.

In response to losing its bid, the Chinese government apparently increased repression of some citizens. Roman Catholic and Buddhist clerics were arrested and pro-democracy protestors detained and tried secretly for setting up "counter-revolutionary organizations." *See Wave of Repression in Shanghai, Dissidents Say*, AGENCE FRANCE PRESSE, Oct. 19, 1993. The U.S. and European governments have criticized the Chinese government in the United Nations for its continuing violations, but the problems continue.

CHAPTER 10

HOW ARE PRONOUNCEMENTS OF HUMAN RIGHTS IN INTERNATIONAL INSTRUMENTS INTERPRETED?

The *Baby Boy* Case in the Inter-American Commission

		Page	
A.	**Introduction**		424
B.	**Questions**		424
C.	**Jurisprudence of the Inter-American Commission**		426
	1. **Case 2141 (the *Baby Boy* Opinion)**		426
	2. **Regulations of the Inter-American Commission**		436
	3. **Additional Cases Raising Difficult Interpretive Issues**		437
	4. **Typical Cases in the Inter-American Commission**		440
D.	**The Inter-American Commission on Human Rights**		444
	Juan Méndez & José Vivanco, Disappearances and the Inter-American Court: Reflections on a Litigation Experience		444
E.	**Treaty Interpretations and Reservations**		450
	The Vienna Convention on the Law of Treaties		450
	Four Treaties Pertaining to Human Rights: Message from the President of the United States		452
	Restatement (Third) of the Foreign Relations Law of the United States		453
F.	**Advisory Jurisdiction of the Inter-American Court of Human Rights**		454
	Thomas Buergenthal, The Inter-American Court of Human Rights		454
	Thomas Buergenthal, The Advisory Practice of the Inter-American Human Rights Court		457
	Restrictions to the Death Penalty, Advisory Opinion OC-3/83		459
G.	**Other Regional Systems**		463
	1. **The Organization of African Unity**		464
	2. **Human Rights in Asia**		466

A. INTRODUCTION

The previous chapters have introduced U.N. human rights instruments and procedures for their implementation. Future chapters will discuss additional U.N. instruments and procedures. The U.N. is not, however, the only international organization that promulgates human rights instruments and works to protect human rights. Regional systems in Africa, the Americas, and Europe function similarly for governments in their regions. The present chapter examines one of those systems—that of the Organization of American States (OAS).

Chapter 1 briefly introduced the individual petition process of the Inter-American Commission on Human Rights—the chief OAS body charged with promoting human rights in its member states. In chapter 8, the reader learned also about fact-finding visits undertaken by the Inter-American Commission. This chapter re-examines the petition process in the context of a complaint filed with the Commission on behalf of an aborted fetus referred to as *Baby Boy*. The petition alleged that the United States, by allowing the abortion, violated Baby Boy's right to life guaranteed by Article I of the American Declaration of the Rights and Duties of Man (American Declaration). The Commission's analysis and decision illustrate both its procedure in dealing with petitions and possible limitations of its decision-making power when it is confronted with a case requiring sophisticated interpretation of human rights instruments.

This chapter also will introduce readers to the principal aid used for interpreting treaties, the basic canons of interpretation codified in the Vienna Convention on the Law of Treaties (Treaty on Treaties). The questions require readers to consider whether these canons ought to apply to the American Declaration and whether the Commission correctly applied the canons in *Baby Boy*. The chapter examines also the Treaty on Treaties clauses on reservations, in the context of a proposed U.S. reservation to the right-to-life provision (Article 4) of the American Convention on Human Rights (American Convention). In addition, the chapter raises the question as to whether the American Declaration, with its relatively vague language, should be applied as a legally binding instrument.

Finally, the chapter discusses the advisory jurisdiction of the Inter-American Court of Human Rights and asks readers to consider whether the Commission—a body more accustomed to dealing with factual issues than with analyses of the scope of prescribed rights—should consider requesting an advisory opinion from the Court when it confronts difficult issues comparable to those raised in *Baby Boy*.

B. QUESTIONS

1. In regard to the *Baby Boy* case, what are the final legal conclusions (holdings) of the Commission?

2. Does the Commission consider whether there is a jurisdictional problem in this case?

a. Can you see a jurisdictional problem under Article 26 of the Commission's Regulations?

b. Why do you think the Commission does not discuss the jurisdictional problem?

3. Does the Commission follow the canons of interpretation set forth in the Treaty on Treaties?

a.   Do the dissenting and concurring opinions respect those rules?

b.   Since the United States has not ratified the Treaty on Treaties, are its rules relevant in this case?

c.   Is it significant that the American Declaration was not promulgated as a treaty? Should it be applied as a legally binding instrument?

4.   What is the Commission's conclusion from the *travaux préparatoires* [Ed. note: drafting history similar to legislative history] of the American Declaration?

a.   Is that conclusion correct?

b.   What difference do you see between the initial and the final versions?

c.   If the Commission is correct about the removal of the "moment of conception" language, what should be inferred from the removal of the other words from that same sentence?

d.   Are there other significant changes in the final version?

5.   What do you think of the Commission's observation that many member states permitted abortion at the time the Declaration was adopted? Is it appropriate to interpret a right by reference to state practice at the time of its adoption?

6.   Is the difference between the wording of Article 1 and all of the other articles of the American Declaration (*See* the accompanying handbook *Selected International Human Rights Instruments*) significant?

7.   What do you think of the way the Commission interpreted the wording of Article 4 of the American Convention on Human Rights? Do you think that the Commission will follow this approach consistently?

a.   Considering United Nations instruments, is there reason to interpret the Universal Declaration of Human Rights in light of the two Covenants? Focus on Article 29 of the Universal Declaration (*See Selected International Human Rights Instruments*) and Article 4 of the Civil and Political Covenant (*See Selected International Human Rights Instruments*) in formulating your answer.

b.   Since the U.S. has signed but not ratified the American Convention, would Article 18 of the Treaty on Treaties suggest how the American Convention ought to be viewed in the *Baby Boy* case? Should the American Convention have been applied in the *Baby Boy* case?

c.   What about the proposed U.S. reservation to Article 4? Is that reservation acceptable under American Convention Article 75 (*See Selected International Human Rights Instruments*) and Article 19 of the Treaty on Treaties?

d.   Suppose the American Convention does apply to the U.S. Would the proposed U.S. reservation violate Article 4?

e.   Is Article 32 of the American Convention (*See Selected International Human Rights Instruments*) relevant?

8.   Based on materials in this chapter, do you think the Commission is a reliable decision-making body when it considers cases involving complex legal issues? When it considers cases involving primarily factual issues? Should advocates advance creative legal arguments for expanding the meaning of the American Declaration? What sort of case would you bring before the Commission?

a.   Would it have been possible in 1981 for the Commission to seek an advisory opinion from the Court on the legal issues posed by the *Baby Boy* case? Could the Commission seek such an advisory opinion now?

b.   In view of the inadequate reasoning of the Commission's opinion, do you think it would be wise for the Commission to ask for an advisory opinion from the Court? If so, on which issues should the Commission seek advice?

c.   Would there be legal objections to the Court's acceptance of advisory opinion jurisdiction over some of the issues raised in the *Baby Boy* case?

d.   Do you believe the *Baby Boy* case will make it more or less likely that the United States will eventually ratify the American Convention?

e.   Is there reason for optimism that the Commission will improve the quality of its decision-making in the future?

C.   JURISPRUDENCE OF THE INTER-AMERICAN COMMISSION

1.   The *Baby Boy* Opinion

The *Baby Boy* Opinion, Case 2141, Inter-Am. C.H.R. 25, OEA.Ser.L/V/II.54, doc. 9 rev. 1 (1981) (citations omitted):

SUMMARY OF THE CASE:

1.   On January 19, 1977, Christian S. White and Gary K. Potter. . .filed with the Inter-American Commission on Human Rights a petition against the United States of America and the Commonwealth of Massachusetts for the purposes established in the Statute and Regulations of the Commission. . . .

2.   The pertinent parts of the petition are the following: Name of the person whose human rights have been violated: *"Baby Boy".* . . .

Description of the violation: *Victim was killed by abortion process (hysterectomy), by Dr. Kenneth Edelin, M.D., in violation of the right to life granted by the American Declaration of the Rights and Duties of Man, as clarified by the definition and description of "right to life" contained in the American Convention on Human Rights.* . . .

Final decision of the authority (if any) that acted in the matter: *The Supreme Judicial Court of Massachusetts, Boston, Massachusetts, acquitted Edelin [of manslaughter] on appeal, on December 17, 1976.* . . .

3.   In the "Amplificatory Document" attached to the petition, the petitioners add, *inter alia*, the following information and arguments: . . .

b)   This violation of the following rights granted by the American Declaration of the Rights and Duties of Man,[1] Chapter 1, Article I (". . . right to life. . ."), Article II ("All persons are equal before the law. . . without distinction as to race, sex, language, creed, or any other factor," here, age), Article VII ("All children have the

---

[1] [Ed. note: The American Declaration can be found in the accompanying handbook, *Selected International Human Rights Instruments*.]

right to special protection, care, and aid") and Article XI ("Every person has the right to the preservation of his health. . .") began on January 22, 1973, when the Supreme Court of the United States handed down its decisions in the cases of *Roe v. Wade*, 410 U.S. 113 and *Doe v. Bolton*, 410 U.S. 179.

c) The effect of the *Wade* and *Bolton* decisions, *supra*, in ending the legal protection of unborn children set the stage for the deprivation of "Baby Boy's" right to life. These decisions in and of themselves constitute a violation of his right to life, and the United States of America therefore stands accused of a violation of Chapter 1, Article I of the American Declaration of the Rights and Duties of Man.

The United States Government, through its Supreme Court, is guilty of that violation.

d) At trial, the jury found Dr. Edelin guilty of manslaughter, necessarily finding as fact that the child was such as to fit within a "protectable exception" (over six months past conception and/or alive outside the womb) to the Supreme Court of the United States' rubric in the *Wade* and *Bolton* cases. On appeal, the Supreme Judicial Court of Massachusetts reversed, on these grounds:

1) Insufficient evidence of "recklessness" and "belief in" [or concern about] "the viability of the fetus" (paraphrased). . . .

2) Insufficient evidence of life outside the womb.. . .

3) Procedural error. . . .

e) This decision came down on December 18, 1976, and, by preventing Dr. Edelin from being punished for his acts, put the State of Massachusetts in the posture of violating "Baby Boy's" right to life under the Declaration. . . .

WHEREAS:

1. The basic facts described in the petition as alleged violations of articles I, II, VII and [XI] of the American Declaration occurred on January 22, 1973 (date of the decisions of cases *Roe v. Wade* and *Doe v. Bolton* by U.S. Supreme Court), October 3, 1973 (date of abortion of Baby Boy performed at the Boston City Hospital) and December 17, 1976 (date of final decision of the Supreme Judicial Court of Massachusetts that acquitted Dr. Edelin, the performer of the abortion). The defendant, the U.S. Government[,] is not a state party to the American Convention on Human Rights. The petition was filed on January 19, 1977, before the Convention entered into force on July 18, 1978.

2. Consequently, the procedure applicable to this case is that established in articles 53 to 57 of Regulations of the Commission, approved in 1960 as amended, in accordance with Article 24 of the present Statute and Article 49 of the new Regulations. . . .

15. The international obligation of the United States of America, as a member of the Organization of American States (OAS), under the jurisdiction of the Inter-American Commission on Human Rights (IACHR) is governed by the Charter of OAS (Bogotá, 1948) as amended by the Protocol of Buenos Aires on February 27, 1967, ratified by United States on April 23, 1968.

16. As a consequence of articles 3 *j*, 16, 51 *e*, 112 and 150 of [the OAS Charter], the provisions of other instruments and resolutions of the OAS on human rights,

acquired binding force. Those instruments and resolutions approved with the vote of U.S. Government, are the following:

— American Declaration of the Rights and Duties of Man (Bogotá, 1948)

— Statute and Regulations of the IACHR 1960, as amended by resolution XXII of the Second Special Inter-American Conference (Rio de Janeiro, 1965)

— Statute and Regulations of IACHR of 1979-1980.

17.   Both Statutes provide that, for the purpose of such instruments, the IACHR is the organ of the OAS entrusted with the competence to promote the observance and respect of human rights. For the purpose of the Statutes, human rights are understood to be the rights set forth in the American Declaration in relation to States not parties to the American Convention on Human Rights (San José, 1969). (Articles 1 and 2 of 1960 Statute and article 1 of 1979 Statute).

18.   The first violation denounced in the petition concerns article I of the American Declaration of Rights and Duties of Man: "Every human being has the right to life. . .". The petitioners admitted that the Declaration does not [answer] "when life begins," "when a pregnancy product becomes a human being" or other such questions. However, they try to answer these fundamental questions with two different arguments:

a)   The *travaux préparatoires* [Ed. note: drafting history similar to legislative history], the discussion of the draft Declaration during the IX International Conference of American States at Bogotá and the final vote, demonstrate that the intention of the Conference was to protect the right to life "from the moment of conception."

b)   The American Convention on Human Rights, promulgated to advance the Declaration's high purposes and to be read as a corollary document, gives a definition of the right to life in article 4.1: "This right shall be protected by law from the moment of conception."

19.   A brief legislative history of the Declaration does not support the petitioner's argument, as may be concluded from the following information and documents:

a)   Pursuant to Resolution XL of the Inter-American Conference on Problems of War and Peace (Mexico, 1945), the Inter-American Juridical Committee of Rio de Janeiro formulated a preliminary draft of an International Declaration of the Rights and Duties of Man to be considered by the Ninth International Conference of American States (Bogotá, 1948). . . .

b)   Article I—Right to Life—of the draft submitted by the Juridical Committee reads: "Every person has the right to life. This right extends to the right to life from the moment of conception; to the right to life of incurables, imbeciles and the insane. Capital punishment may only be applied in cases in which it has been prescribed by pre-existing law for crimes of exceptional gravity."

c)   A Working Group was organized to consider the observations and amendments introduced by the Delegates and to prepare an acceptable document. As a result of its work, the Group submitted to the Sixth Committee a new draft entitled *American Declaration of the Fundamental Rights and Duties of Man*, article I of which reads: "Every human being has the right to life, liberty, security and integrity of his person."

d)   This completely new article I and some substantial changes introduced by the Working Group in other articles have been explained, in its Report of the Working Group to the Committee, as a compromise to resolve the problems raised by the Delegations of Argentina, Brazil, Cuba, United States of America, Mexico, Peru, Uruguay, and Venezuela, mainly as consequence of the conflict existing between the laws of those States and the draft of the Juridical Committee.

e)   In connection with the right to life, the definition given in the Juridical Committee's draft was incompatible with the laws governing the death penalty and abortion in the majority of the American States. In effect, the acceptance of this absolute concept—the right to life from the moment of conception—would imply the obligation to derogate the articles of the Penal Codes in force in 1948 in many countries because such articles excluded the penal sanction for the crime of abortion if performed in one or more of the following cases: A—when necessary to save the life of the mother; B—to interrupt the pregnancy of the victim of a rape; C—to protect the honor of an honest woman; D—to prevent the transmission to the fetus of a hereditary or contagious disease; E—for economic reasons (*angustia económica*).

f)   In 1948, the American States that permitted abortion in one of such cases and, consequently, would be affected by the adoption of article I of the Juridical Committee, were: Argentina . . .; Brazil . . .; Costa Rica . . .; Cuba . . .; Ecuador . . .; Mexico (Distrito y Territorios Federales) . . .; Nicaragua . . .; Paraguay . . .; Peru . . .; Uruguay . . .; Venezuela . . .; United States of America . . .; Puerto Rico . . ..

h)   Consequently, the defendant is correct in challenging the petitioners' assumption that article I of the Declaration has incorporated the notion that the right of life exists from the moment of conception. Indeed, the conference faced this question but chose not to adopt language which would clearly have stated that principle.

20.   The second argument of the petitioners, related to the possible use of the Convention as an element for the interpretation of the Declaration, requires also a study of the motives that prevailed at the San José Diplomatic Conference with the adoption of the definition of the right to life. . . .

25.   To accommodate the views that insisted on the concept "from the moment of conception," with the objection raised, since the Bogotá Conference, based on the legislation of American States that permitted abortion, *inter alia*, to save the mother's life, and in case of rape, the IACHR, redrafting article 2 [of the Convention] (Right to life), decided, by majority vote, to introduce the words "in general." This compromise was the origin of the new text of article 2: "1. Every person has the right to have his life respected. This right shall be protected by law, *in general*, from the moment of conception."

26.   The rapporteur of the *Opinion* proposed, at this second opportunity for discussion of the definition of the right [to] life, to delete the entire final phrase ". . .in general, from the moment of conception." He repeated the reasoning of his dissenting opinion in the Commission; based on the abortion laws in force in the majority of the American States, with an addition: "to avoid any possibility of conflict with article 6, paragraph 1, of the United Nations Covenant on Civil and Political Rights, which states this right in a general way only." . . .

27.   However, the majority of the Commission believed that, for reasons of principle, it was fundamental to state the provision on the protection of the right to life in the form recommended to the Council of the OAS in its *Opinion* (Part One). It was accordingly decided to keep the text of paragraph 1 without change. . . .

30.   In the light of this [drafting] history, it is clear that the petitioners' interpretation of the definition given by the American Convention on the right of life is incorrect. The addition of the phrase "in general, from the moment of conception" does not mean that the drafters of the Convention intended to modify the concept of the right to life that prevailed in Bogotá, when they approved the American Declaration. The legal implications of the clause "in general, from the moment of conception" are substantially different from the shorter clause "from the moment of conception" as appears repeatedly in the petitioners' briefs.

31.   However, accepting *gratia argumentandi* [for the sake of argument], that the American Convention had established the absolute concept of the right to life from the moment of conception—it would be impossible to impose upon the United States Government or that of any other State Member of the OAS, by means of "interpretation," an international obligation based upon a treaty that such State has not duly accepted or ratified.

32.   The question of what reservation to article I of the Convention should be admissible, as suggested by President Jimmy Carter in his Letter of Transmittal to the Senate on February 23, 1978, has no direct link with the objective of the petition. *This is not the appropriate place or opportunity for the consideration of this matter.* [Emphasis added.]

33.   The other rights which the petitioners contend were violated—Articles II, VII and XI of the American Declaration—have no direct relation to the facts set forth in the petition, including the decision[s] of the U.S. Supreme Court and the Supreme Judicial Court of Massachusetts which were challenged in this case.

THE INTER-AMERICAN COMMISSION ON HUMAN RIGHTS

RESOLVES:

1.   The decision[s] of the U.S. Supreme Court and the Supreme Judicial Court of Massachusetts and other facts stated in the petition do not constitute a violation of articles I, II, VII and XI of the American Declaration of Rights and Duties of Man. . . .

CONCURRING DECISION OF DR. ANDRES AGUILAR . . .

5.   In my view, the opinion of the majority, comes to the correct conclusion, that none of the rights set forth in said Declaration had been violated. In effect, it is clear from the *travaux préparatoires* that Article I of the Declaration, which is the fundamental legal provision in this case, sidesteps the very controversial question of determining at what moment human life begins.

The legislative history of this article permits one to conclude that the draft which was finally approved is a compromise formula, which even if it obviously protects life from the moment of birth, leaves to each State the power to determine, in its domestic law, whether life begins and warrants protection from the moment of conception or at any other point in time prior to birth. . . .

7.   The decision of the majority does not begin, and could not begin, to judge whether abortion is reprehensible from a religious, ethical, or scientific point of

view, and it correctly limits itself to deciding that the United States of America has not assumed the international obligation to protect the right to life from conception or from some other moment prior to birth and that, consequently, it could not be correctly affirmed that it had violated the right to life set forth in Article I of the American Declaration of the Rights and Duties of Man.

8.   For the reasons expressed, I dissent on this point, from the opinion of my distinguished colleagues Dr. Luis Demetrio Tinoco and Dr. Marco Gerardo Monroy Cabra. On the other hand, I completely share their judgment, based in the opinions of well-known men of science, that human life begins at the very moment of conception and ought to warrant complete protection from that moment, both in domestic law as well as international law. . . .

DISSENT OF DR. MARCO GERARDO MONROY CABRA

I dissent from the majority opinion of the Inter-American Commission on Human Rights in Case 2141 for the following reasons:

1.   Article I of the American Declaration of the Rights and Duties of Man reads: "Every human being has the right to life, liberty, and the security of his person." Since the text is not explicit, I think that the interpretation most in accord with the genuine protection of the right to life is that this protection begins at conception rather than at birth.

2.   The historical argument, upon which the majority opinion of the Commission is based, is unclear. Indeed, a review of the report and the minutes of the Working Group of the Sixth Committee shows that no conclusion was reached to permit the unequivocal inference that the intention of the drafters of the Declaration was to protect the right to life from the time of birth—much less to allow abortion, since this topic was not approached. . . .

5.   Since Article I does not define when life begins, one can resort to medical science which has concluded that life has its beginning in the union of two series of chromosomes. Most scientists agree that the fetus is a human being and is genetically complete.

6.   If international agreements are to be faithfully and literally interpreted, in keeping with the meaning that should be attributed to the terms of a treaty and read in context, taking into account the objective and purpose of that treaty, there is no doubt that the protection of the right to life should begin at the moment of conception. Since Article I is general, the protection should begin when life begins, and we have already seen that life begins at the time fertilization is completed in the union of two series of chromosomes. . . .

8.   The intentional and illegal interruption of the physiological process of pregnancy, resulting in the destruction of the embryo or death of the fetus, is unquestionably an offense against life and, consequently, a violation of Article I of the American Declaration of the Rights and Duties of Man. The maternal womb in which the flame of life is lighted is sacred and may not be profaned to extinguish what God has created in his image and in his likeness. It has been said repeatedly, that, from the biological standpoint, human life exists from the moment that the ovum is fertilized by the sperm and, more specifically, from the time the egg travels to the uterus. . . .

9.   Life is the primary right of every individual. It is the fundamental right

and the condition for the existence of all other rights. If human existence is not recognized, there is no subject upon which to predicate the other rights. It is a right that antecedes other rights and exists by the mere fact of being, with no need for the state to recognize it as such. It is not up to the state to decide whether that right shall be recognized in one case and not in another, since that would mean discrimination. The life of the unborn child, the infant, the young, the old, the mentally ill, the handicapped, and that of all human beings in general, must be recognized.

The foregoing means that if conception produces a human life, and this right is the primary and fundamental one, abortion is an attack on the right to life and, therefore, runs counter to Article I of the American Declaration of the Rights and Duties of Man. . . .

DISSENT OF DR. LUIS DEMETRIO TINOCO CASTRO . . .

I depart from the opinion of the majority when it affirms, in paragraph 19 of the Preamble of the Resolution, that "a brief legislative history of the Declaration does not support the petitioners' argument" and that may be concluded from the report presented by the Working Group that studied the draft wording of Article I of the Declaration, as well as from the fact that in that Group the concept contained in the draft of the Inter-American Juridical Committee had been eliminated, where it said, after stating every person has the right to life, "This right extends to the right to life from the moment of conception; to the right to life of incurables, imbeciles, and the insane." . . .

Study of the Minutes and Documents of the Working Group concerned, and of the Sixth Committee, which was responsible for consideration of these articles of the Draft Declaration, leads me to conclusions contrary to those established in the vote of the majority. . . .

The American Declaration of the Rights and Duties of Man, for its part, plainly and clearly states: "Every human being has the right to life."

Leaving aside the legal background that led to this simple wording of Article I of the Declaration, to decide this Case it is necessary first to answer the transcendental question of the nature of the unborn, the topic of most significant legal and moral consequences of stipulating whether what has been formed in the womb of a woman and is still therein is a "human being" with the right to life. Or whether it should be understood that the "right to life" that every human being has in accordance with the above-mentioned Article I of the Declaration of Bogotá should be understood to protect only those already living their own lives, outside the womb. In other words: at what moment in his long process of formation, development, decadence, and death is it considered that there exists a "human being" with the "right to life" and to the protection given him by the basic legal instruments of the new discipline of Human Rights? More specifically, as it affects the problem raised by Case 2141, to which I refer: when the woman's ovum is fertilized by action of the man, has a human being been constituted and does it have the right to life?

The question was put barely three years ago to the eminent Dean of the Teaching and Research Unit of the University of Paris, holder of the Chair of Fundamental Genetics, there, Professor Jerome Lejeune. . . . "Of course," he replied, adding, "It has been shown that all the genetic qualities of the individual are already present in that first cell, that the embryo, seven days after fertilization. . .emits a chemical message that stops the menstruation of his mother. . .that at twenty days after fertilization. . .his heart (as large as a grain of wheat) begins to beat. . .at two months. . .he already has human form completely: he has a head, he has arms, he has his fingers and toes. . .and even the lines on his hands drawn. . .and between the second and third months. . .the fingerprints are already indicated. . .and will not change to the end of his life. . .at three months he is already able to close his eyes, to clench his fists, and if at that moment his upper lip were caressed with a thread, he would make a face. . . . A human being exists. . .there is no doubt about that." And the same Professor, in a magazine article, stated: "The fetus is a human being. Genetically he is complete. This is not an appearance; it is a fact."

The opinion of the vast majority of scientists, not to say all of them, is the same as that of Professor Lejeune. . . . Dr. Ingelman-Sundberg and Dr. Cears Wirsen in their work *The Drama of Life Before Birth*, published in 1965. Dr. Bart Hefferman, in a book entitled *The Early Biography of Every Man*, published in 1972. . . .

The reasons stated leave no doubt in my mind that the American Declaration of the Rights and Duties of Man refers to the complete period of human life—from conception to death—when it states that "every human being has the right to life"; that, for that valuable instrument of international law, life does not begin at birth— the final phase of the process of gestation—but at the moment of conception, which is the moment at which a new human being, distinct from the father and from the mother, is formed; and that, in recognizing the right of the unborn to life, the Declaration rejects the legitimacy of any act that authorizes or considers acceptable acts or practices that will lead to its death.

NOTES AND QUESTIONS

1.   The O.A.S. Charter provisions mentioned in paragraphs 15-16 of the *Baby Boy* opinion are reproduced in the accompanying handbook, *Selected International Human Rights Instruments*.

2.   For commentary on *Baby Boy*, see Dinah Shelton, *Abortion and the Right to Life in the Inter-American System: The Case of "Baby Boy"*, 2 H.R.L.J. 309 (1981); David Weissbrodt, *Ethical Problems of an International Human Rights Law Practice*, 7 MICH. Y.B. INT'L LEGAL STUD. 217, 245-48 (1985).

3.   The opinion mentions *Roe v. Wade*, 410 U.S. 113 (1973), which recognized a woman's constitutional right to abortion. In *Roe* the Court first struck down a Texas statute which criminalized nontherapeutic abortions; and second set forth a trimester framework by which to judge abortion legislation generally.

Writing for the Court, Justice Blackmun used the trimester framework to balance the woman's right to privacy against the state's interest in protecting the health of both the mother and the fetus. Justice Blackmun concluded that women have a constitutional right to abortion during the first trimester of pregnancy. He stated also that, during the second trimester, states may regulate abortions only to the extent necessary to protect the health of the mother. States may, though, restrict access to abortion at the point of fetal viability, which usually coincides with the third trimester. At that point, the Court held, a state's interest in protecting the life of the fetus becomes compelling.

The Court's decision in *Roe* inspired much criticism. Before she became a Supreme Court Justice, for instance, Ruth Bader Ginsburg argued that the Court overstepped its bounds in prescribing the trimester framework. Ginsburg stated:

> *Roe* ventured too far in the change it ordered. The sweep and detail of the opinion stimulated the mobilization of a right-to-life movement and an attendant reaction in Congress and state legislatures. In place of the trend "toward liberalization of abortion statutes" noted in *Roe*, legislatures adopted measures aimed at minimizing the impact of the 1973 rulings, including notification and consent requirements, prescriptions for the protection of fetal life, and bans on public expenditures for poor women's abortions.

Ruth Bader Ginsburg, *Some Thoughts on Autonomy and Equality in Relation to* Roe v. Wade, 63 N.C. L. REV. 375, 381-82 (1985) (footnotes omitted). Ginsburg argued that the Court should have used an equal protection/sex discrimination analysis, rather than a substantive due process/personal autonomy analysis, in deciding *Roe*. She asserted that her analysis would have had a far less sweeping impact and would likely have generated less opposition. *Id*. at 376.

Statutes on abortion have been the focus of several post-*Roe* decisions by the Supreme Court. For example, the Court has rejected constitutional challenges against measures which prohibit the use of state employees and facilities in nontherapeutic abortions. *Webster v. Reproductive Health Services*, 492 U.S. 490 (1989). It also has upheld measures which prohibit medical facilities from using federal funding for abortion procedures, counseling, or referrals. *Rust v. Sullivan*, 500 U.S. 173 (1991). In those cases the Court stated that, while *Roe v. Wade* established a constitutional right to abortion, the Due Process Clause generally does not confer affirmative rights to governmental aid. *Webster,* at 510.

In *Webster* the Court also upheld provisions of a Missouri statute requiring physicians to perform viability tests for any fetus of at least twenty weeks gestational age. Chief Justice Rehnquist's opinion states that the *Roe v. Wade* trimester framework should no longer be used as a standard for evaluating the interests of the mother and the state. Justice O'Connor, concurring, also found the *Roe* trimester-framework problematic. She asserted, however, that viability testing did not conflict with past decisions and thus did not necessitate a re-examination of *Roe*. Justice Scalia argued that the entire *Roe* decision should be overruled in order to avoid the court's further involvement in an area where "the answers to most of the cruel questions posed are political and not juridical." *Id*.

In one of its most comprehensive opinions on abortion rights, the Court upheld provisions of a Pennsylvania statute which required, *inter alia*, the woman's informed consent to abortion. *Planned Parenthood of Southeastern Pennsylvania v. Casey*, 505 U.S. 833 (1992). The Court also upheld provisions requiring doctors to delay performing abortions until at least 24 hours after the woman has offered her informed consent and approved a parental-notification provision that required minor patients to obtain the consent of one parent or a court before seeking an abortion. The Court, however, struck down a provision that required married women to notify their husbands before seeking an abortion. *Id*.

More important than the Court's holding on that Pennsylvania statute, however, was its reaffirmation of *Roe v. Wade*. Justice O'Connor, announcing the judgment of the Court, wrote that the essential holding of *Roe v. Wade* should be retained despite various requests that the Court overrule it. Her opinion rejected *Roe*'s trimester framework but left intact the recognition of a woman's right to abortion before fetal viability.

4.   The United States is not the only country that has addressed the abortion issue. In *R. v. Morgentaler*, [1988] 1 S.C.R. 30, 44 D.L.R. (4th) 385 (Can.), the appellants challenged the constitutionality of section 251 of the Criminal Code of Canada which imposed criminal sanctions for all abortions unless they were performed for a "therapeutic purpose." To be "therapeutic" an abortion had to be found necessary to end a pregnancy which "would or would be likely to endanger [the woman's] life or health," by a "therapeutic abortion committee" composed of three or more physicians. The Canadian Supreme Court invalidated section 251 in a five to two decision with three distinct supporting decisions.

The Court relied on sections 1 and 7 of the Charter of Rights and Freedoms which was adopted in 1982 as an amendment to the Canadian Constitution. Section 1 applies strict scrutiny to government limitations on the rights contained in the Charter to ensure they can be "demonstrably justified in a free and democratic society." Section 7 guarantees everyone the right to, "life, liberty and security of the person and the right not to be deprived thereof except in accordance with the principles of fundamental justice."

Four justices found that section 251 violated the right to security of the person because it denied pregnant women the right to make their own decisions, caused delays which threatened their physical and mental health, and granted permission for a therapeutic abortion in a manner that was so arbitrary and unfair as to make this defense to criminal sanctions illusory. Two of these justices did not read section 7 as protecting a right to privacy and found both the pregnant woman's life and health and fetal life to be important government interests. The other two justices found section 7 to guarantee the right to abortion to protect the life and health of the pregnant woman and found that government interest to be more important than the interests in prohibiting abortions and protecting fetal life.

One justice opined that section 251 denied pregnant women their rights to security of the person and liberty which guarantee the substantive right to individual autonomy in making decisions of fundamental importance, such as the decision to terminate their pregnancies. The justice found this deprivation not to be in accordance with fundamental justice because it was in violation of section 2(a) of the Charter of Rights and Freedoms which guarantees freedom of conscience and religion. By making abortion a criminal offence, the government was enforcing a moral view against abortion. The justice stated that section 251 could not be justified under section 1 because it was not a limitation of a right, but a complete denial of the right to liberty and security of the person. Even though the justice stated abortions in the early stages of pregnancy should be solely the decision of the pregnant woman in consultation with her doctor, she did recognize the government's interest in fetal life and would allow restrictions on this autonomy in the later stages of pregnancy.

The two dissenting justices stated that the defense to section 251 was not illusory but simply narrowly tailored to cover those situations in which Parliament thought it was not criminal to have an abortion.

That case was not the last time Dr. Morgentaler appeared in a Canadian court defending abortion rights. In January 1989, Dr. Morgentaler was planning to open a free-standing abortion clinic in Nova Scotia. The province responded by enacting legislation which prohibited the performance of an abortion outside an approved hospital, denied medical services insurance coverage for abortions not performed in a hospital, and imposed substantial fines on persons who violated the act. Morgentaler opened his clinic and was subsequently charged with fourteen counts of unlawfully performing abortions. The Provincial Court of Nova Scotia, the Nova Scotia Supreme Court, Appeal Division, and the Supreme Court of Canada all found the act to be criminal in substance and therefore within the exclusive jurisdiction of the Canadian Parliament and beyond the jurisdiction of the government of Nova Scotia. Dr. Morgentaler was acquitted of all charges. *R. v. Morgentaler*, [1993] 3 S.C.R. 463, 107 D.L.R. (4th) 537 (Can.).

In April 1993, Dr. Morgentaler successfully applied for a declaration that the Hospital and Health Services Commission of Prince Edward Island policy, which states that the government will pay only for abortions which are medically necessary and performed in hospitals, is ultra vires. *Morgentaler v. Prince Edward Island (Minister of Health & Social Serv.)*, 112 D.L.R. (4th) 756 (P.E.I. Sp. Ct. 1994).

5.   The European Court of Human Rights has not yet decided whether a fetus has a right to life, but decisions of the European Commission do not recognize such a right. In *Brüggemann and Scheuten v. Federal Republic of Germany*, App. No. 6959/75, 10 Eur. Comm'n H.R. Dec. & Rep. 100 (1978), 3 Eur. H.R. Rep. 244 (1981), the Commission held that Germany was not in violation of Article 8 of the European Convention, which guarantees the right to respect for private and family life, because German women were not free to have an abortion in the case of an unwanted pregnancy. The Commission stated that the private life of the woman is closely connected with the developing fetus. The Commission did not, though, determine whether the fetus should be protected as "life" under Article 2 of the Convention or whether it could justify an interference with the right to private life "for the protection of others" under Article 8(2). The Commission found that fetuses have certain rights in all of the states parties to the Convention.

In *Paton v. United Kingdom*, App. No. 8416/78, 3 Eur. H.R. Rep. 408 (1981), the Commission had to decide whether a fetus' right to life and a father's right to private life had been violated when the father was denied an injunction to prevent his wife's abortion. The Commission decided that "everyone" (in Article 2) cannot apply to a fetus and, also, that a fetus does not have an absolute right to life because its "life" is so intimately connected with the pregnant woman. The Commission found that the interference with the husband's right to private life caused by his wife's abortion was justified under Article 8(2) since it was performed to protect her health.

In *Open Door and Dublin Well Woman v. Ireland*, 246 Eur. Ct. H.R. (ser. A) (1993), the European Court of Human Rights held that an injunction against the provision of information concerning abortion facilities abroad violated Article 10 of the European Convention, which protects the right to receive and impart information and ideas. For a similar case before the Court of Justice of the European Union see Case 159/90, *Society for the Protection of Unborn Children Ireland Ltd v. Grogan and Others*, 1991 E.C.R. 4733, 3 C.M.L.R. 849 (1991).

6.   In Ireland the right to life of a fetus is protected under the Constitution and by statute. The Attorney General had obtained an injunction prohibiting a fourteen-year-old rape victim from travelling to England for an abortion. In *Attorney General v. X*, [1992] 1 I.R. 1, 17, the Irish Supreme Court allowed her to have an abortion in Ireland because she was suicidal and therefore the abortion was justified in order to protect her life.

7.   For further readings on abortion rights see MAURO CAPPELLETTI & WILLIAM COHEN, COMPARATIVE CONSTITUTIONAL LAW (1979) (comparing the constitutional decisions on abortion from Austria, the European Commission on Human Rights, France, Germany, Italy, and the United States); PIETER VAN DIJK & G.J.H. VAN HOOF, THEORY AND PRACTICE OF THE EUROPEAN CONVENTION ON HUMAN RIGHTS 218-20, 375-76, 386, 447 (1990); PIETER SMITS, THE RIGHT TO LIFE OF THE UNBORN CHILD IN INTERNATIONAL DOCUMENTS, DECISIONS AND OPINIONS (1992); K. D. Ewing and C. A. Gearry, *Terminating Abortion Rights?*, 142 NEW L.J. 1696 (1990); Margherita Rendel, *Abortion and Human Rights*, 141 NEW L.J. 1270 (1991).

2.   Regulations of the Inter-American Commission

REGULATIONS OF THE INTER-AMERICAN COMMISSION ON HUMAN RIGHTS, in Basic Documents Pertaining to Human Rights in the Inter-American System, OAS Doc. OEA/SER.L.V/II.71, at 75, 84 (1988):

ARTICLE 26

Presentation of Petitions

1.   Any person or group of persons or nongovernmental entity legally recognized in one or more of the Member States of the Organization may submit petitions to the Commission, in accordance with these Regulations, on one's own behalf or on behalf of third persons, with regard to alleged violations of a human right recognized, as the case may be, in the American Convention on Human Rights or in the American Declaration of the Rights and Duties of Man.

2.   The Commission may also, *motu propio* [Ed. note: on its own motion], take into consideration any available information that it considers pertinent and which might include the necessary factors to begin processing a case which in its opinion fulfills the requirements for that purpose.

NOTES AND QUESTIONS

1.   Do you see a jurisdictional problem for the Commission's consideration of the *Baby Boy* case under Article 26 of the Commission's Regulations?

2.   Why, do you think, did the Commission not discuss the jurisdictional problem?

3.   The Commission's Regulations have not been changed since 1988. For a more current

reprinting of the Regulations, see Basic Documents Pertaining to Human Rights in the Inter-American System, OAS Doc. OEA/Serv.L.V/II.82, at 103, 112 (1992).

3.   Additional Cases Raising Difficult Interpretive Issues

Three other petitions filed with the Commission against the United States raise questions of interpretation comparable to those in *Baby Boy*.

In Case 9647 (*Roach*), U.S. lawyers brought a petition on behalf of James Roach and Jay Pinkerton, juveniles sentenced to death for separate crimes committed when they were 17-years-old. Case 9647, Inter-Am. C.H.R. 147, OEA/Ser.L/V/II.71, doc. 9 rev. 1 (1987). The petition alleged that execution of juveniles violated not only the right to life prescribed in Article I of the American Declaration, construed by the Commission in *Baby Boy*, but also the Article VII protection for children and the Article XXVI prohibition of cruel, infamous or unusual punishments.

Petitioners urged the Commission to find that customary international law proscribes execution of juveniles, pointing to the prohibition of juvenile executions in several treaties, including the American Convention, and widespread practice of governments in abolishing juvenile execution. Petitioners asked the Commission to use that norm in interpreting the American Declaration as prescribed by Article 31 of the Treaty on Treaties (Vienna Convention on the Law of Treaties, *supra*).

The U.S. denied the existence of a customary norm proscribing juvenile executions and claimed also that, even if a norm existed, the U.S. had dissented from it and thus was not bound. Moreover, the U.S. argued, capital punishment for juveniles did not constitute cruel, infamous or unusual punishment because many governments allowed such punishment at the time of the American Declaration's adoption. Finally the U.S. disagreed with petitioners' interpretation of children in Article VII to mean those under 18.

The Commission reaffirmed its holding in *Baby Boy* that the American Declaration is binding on the U.S. as a member of the OAS. *Id*. para. 48. It refused to find a customary norm prohibiting execution of juveniles under 18, although it did find that such a norm was emerging. *Id*. para. 60. The Commission commented that the U.S. had protested the emerging norm by proposing a reservation to Article 4 of the American Convention, designed to preserve current U.S. practice of capital punishment including the execution of juveniles. The Commission stated that, due to this protest, the U.S. could not be bound by the norm. *Id*. paras. 53-54. It noted that, if a norm attains the status of *jus cogens*,[2] it binds all states, even protesters. *Id*. para. 54. The Commission found that a *jus cogens* norm proscribing the execution of children exists among the OAS member states; yet the Commission itself could not agree on an age limit for the norm. *Id*. para. 56.

Instead of basing its decision on the right to life, the Commission found that by allowing its states to execute Roach and Pinkerton, the United States had violated Article II of the American Declaration which ensures the right to equality before the law. *Id*. para. 63. The Commission reasoned that the United States violated that right by not mandating a uniform minimum age for imposition of the death

---

[2] A "*jus cogens*" norm is a peremptory rule of international law that prevails over any conflicting rule or agreement. It permits no derogation and can be modified only by a subsequent international norm of the same character. 1 Restatement (Third) of the Foreign Relations Law of the United States § 102 comment k (1987).

penalty in all 50 states. *Id*. Thus the Commission avoided the issue of whether the Declaration prohibits juvenile execution.

Commentators have criticized the Commission for refusing to find a prohibition in customary international law and then announcing a *jus cogens* norm. The Commission's position appears anomalous because the existence of a *jus cogens* norm has been much more difficult to establish than a rule of customary law. The Commission has also been criticized for finding, without sufficient evidence, that the U.S. is a persistent objector to the customary norm, for partially basing its decision on different laws authorizing the execution of juveniles in the states of the U.S. federal system, and for basing its decision on an article of the American Declaration which neither party had raised or argued before the Commission.

Another case requiring a sophisticated interpretation of the right to life in Article I of the American Declaration is still pending before the Commission. Case 9213, Inter-Am. C.H.R., OAS Doc. OEA/ser.L./V/II.67, doc. 6 (1986), (decision on admissibility). Disabled Peoples International (DPI) filed a petition on behalf of patients in a Grenadan mental institution who were either killed or injured when the United States bombed the institution. Though controversy as to the factual circumstances surrounding the bombing exists, the chief issue is the applicability of Article I's right-to-life guarantee in armed conflict. In resolving this issue, DPI asked the Commission to construe Article I in conformity with international humanitarian law principles. (International humanitarian law governs armed conflict. *See supra* chapter 6.) Since Article I of the American Declaration does not indicate how governments are to observe the right to life in armed conflict, Article 31 of the Treaty on Treaties allows the Commission to consider humanitarian law obligations of the United States when interpreting the right to life. The Commission requested an on-site visit to Grenada but it has not been arranged. As of November 1994, the case has not been considered on the merits.

The third case (No. 10,031) involved the application of the death penalty. Unlike the petitioner in *Roach*, however, the petitioner in the third case—Willie Celestine—was not a juvenile. He was a black man sentenced to death in a Louisiana court for raping and murdering an elderly white woman. Celestine sought review of his sentence in state and federal courts, claiming violation of the 8th and 14th amendments to the U.S. Constitution. He based his claim on the racial prejudice admitted by one juror before trial, the elimination from the jury of any jurors who revealed reluctance to impose the death penalty, and statistical studies which demonstrated that Louisiana applied the death penalty in a racially discriminatory manner. All appeals were defeated, however, and a petition was then filed with the Commission. Unfortunately, despite urgent appeals from the Commission to the U.S. Secretary of State and the governor of Louisiana, Louisiana executed Celestine before the Commission could decide his case.

The petitioners alleged that the U.S. violated three clauses of the American Declaration. First, the petitioners claimed that the U.S. arbitrarily deprived Celestine of the right to life guaranteed by Article I, because Louisiana applies the death penalty in a racially discriminatory manner, a practice which also would violate Article II's guarantee of equal treatment before the law. Second, the U.S. denied Celestine the impartial hearing guaranteed by Article XXVI, because his jurors were selected because of their willingness to impose the death penalty, which violated Article II's guarantee of equal treatment before the law. Third, the death penalty violated Article XXVI's prohibition against cruel, infamous or unusual punishment, because it was imposed without an impartial hearing and equality before the law.

In 1989, the Commission decided against Celestine, finding that the petitioners failed to establish an adequate factual basis for the claim of discrimination. Case 10,031, Inter-Am. C.H.R. res. 23/89, OEA/Ser.L./V/II.76, doc. 44 (1989). Seemingly, the Commission was convinced as to the fairness of the proceedings by the fact that blacks were seated as jurors in the case.

NOTES AND QUESTIONS

1.   For commentary on *Roach*, see Christina Cerna & Wendy Young, *The Inter-American Commission on Human Rights and the Death Penalty*, 34 FED. B. NEWS & J. 398 (1987); *Inter-American Commission on Human Rights (IACHR), Washington: Application of Death Penalty on Juveniles in the U.S. / Violation of Human Rights Obligation Within the Inter-American System*, 8 H.R.L.J. 345 (1987) (including commentary by Dinah Shelton); David Weissbrodt, *Execution of Juvenile Offenders by the United States Violates International Human Rights Law*, 3 AM. U. J. INT'L L. & POL'Y 339 (1987); *see also* Christina Cerna, *US Death Penalty Tested Before the Inter-American Commission on Human Rights*, 10 NETH. Q. HUM. RTS. 155 (1992).
     For further reading on efforts within the United States to end the practice of executing juvenile offenders, see Joan Hartman, *"Unusual" Punishment: The Domestic Effects of International Norms Restricting the Application of the Death Penalty*, 52 CIN. L. REV. 655 (1983); Laura Dalton, Stanford v. Kentucky *and* Wilkins v. Missouri: *A Violation of an Emerging Rule of Customary International Law*, 32 WM AND MARY L. REV. 161 (1990). Hartman (now Joan Fitzpatrick) and Dalton argue that recognition of international law by the U.S. Supreme Court might persuade the Court to declare juvenile executions to be cruel and unusual.

2.   For suggestions on how the Commission could interpret the American Declaration in light of international humanitarian law, see David Weissbrodt & Beth Andrus, *The Right to Life During Armed Conflict:* Disabled Peoples' International v. United States, 29 HARV. INT'L L.J. 59 (1988).

3.   In chapter 11 the reader will become acquainted with the *Soering Case*, 161 Eur. Ct. Hum. Rts. (Ser. A) (1989). At that point the reader may consider whether the Inter-American decisions in *Baby Boy* and *Roach* were as well-reasoned as *Soering*.

4.   In 1992 the Commission received another complaint against the United States involving its application of the death penalty. It alleged racial bias in the execution of William Andrews. An all-white jury found Andrews guilty of murder in 1974. The judge refused the defense counsel's request for a mistrial and failed to conduct an investigation despite evidence that the jury foreman at trial had received a note reading "Hang the Niggers." Though the Commission requested delay until it could review the case, Andrews was executed in Utah on July 30, 1992.
     In 1993 the United States responded to the Commission by defending Andrews' sentence under international law, arguing that the petition was time-barred, and contending that the American Declaration and Commission Regulations are not binding international law.
     Andrews' attorneys believe they can meet the evidentiary burden of *Celestine*, which requires, "sufficient evidence that (petitioner's) sentence resulted from racial discrimination," which must include more than statistical data supporting discriminatory administration of the death penalty. Petitioner's attorneys also argued Mr. Andrews endured the "death row phenomenon" found by the European Court of Human Rights in *Soering, infra*, chapter 11.
     Another death penalty case pending before the Commission is that of Gary Graham, Case No. 11.193. Mr. Graham's attorneys argued the following:

     1.)   Habeas corpus limitations on introducing new evidence of Graham's innocence violate the American Declaration's rights to life, fair trial, and due process. (Articles I, XVIII, and XXVI).

2.) Execution of a seventeen year old was found to be a violation of the Declaration's right to equality before the law in *Roach, supra*.

3.) Representation by an attorney appointed by Texas denied Graham the right to representation by a competent attorney guaranteed by the Declaration's rights to a fair trial and due process.

Mr. Graham's attorneys also alleged his denial of an evidentiary hearing on his innocence violated the International Convention on Civil and Political Rights.

The Commission issued precautionary measures against the United States and called for a hearing before the Board of Pardons and Paroles in Texas and assurances that the sentence would not be executed.

In 1994 the United States government informed the Commission that the Texas Court of Criminal Appeals has decided to allow Graham to pursue a claim of actual innocence through a writ of habeas corpus and that he has not, therefore, exhausted all domestic remedies. For commentary on *Graham* and *Andrews* see Rick Wilson, *Race, Criminal Justice and the Death Penalty in the Inter-American Human Rights System*, 15 WHITTIER L. REV. 395 (1994).

---

4. Typical Cases in the Inter-American Commission

Cases requiring sophisticated interpretation in human rights instruments, such as *Baby Boy*, are not typical of the work pursued by the Commission. Generally it has focused its expertise on studying the human rights situation in member countries, often utilizing fact-finding missions rather than individual petitions. This book examines the Commission's experience with fact-finding studies in chapter 8.

Further, most individual petitions filed with the Commission allege conduct that applicable instruments clearly prohibit, such as torture or arbitrary arrest and imprisonment. In the typical case, the main issue is whether the alleged ill-treatment actually took place. If the Commission establishes the truth of the allegations it can easily find violations of human rights provisions. That approach contrasts with the situation in *Baby Boy*, where the parties did not dispute the facts but rather contested whether the facts constituted a violation of human rights norms.

The following case provides an example of a typical petition filed with the Commission. The case involves the situation where the government fails to give effective protection against the alleged violations.

Case 10.537, Inter-Am. C.H.R. 117, OEA/Ser.L/V/II.85, doc. 9 rev. (1994):

[On February 7, 1990 the Commission received a petition and eyewitness testimony alleging the arrest and disappearance of Olga Esther Bernal Dueñas from Buenaventura, Colombia, on January 7, 1988. A witness stated she was screaming for help as she was taken to the police station by four police agents including one known as "La Escoba." According to the witness, Bernal was taken to an inside office, and some five minutes later "La Escoba" appeared carrying women's underwear that he handed to Captain Cháves Ocaña. "La Escoba" was identified as an agent of the National Police. Olga has not been seen since January 7, 1988. The petition declared that Colombia violated articles IV (right to life), V (right to humane treatment), VII (right to personal liberty), and VIII (right to a fair trial) of the American Convention on Human Rights.]

. . .

2. Within the required time period, the Government of Colombia forwarded the following provisional response, which was sent to the petitioner on April 6, 1990:

I have the honor to address Your Excellency, on behalf of the Government of Colombia, in reference to your communication of April 6, 1990, in connection with Case 10,537, concerning Ms. OLGA ESTHER BERNAL DUEÑAS.

In this regard, I should inform Your Excellency that on September 5, 1989, the Office of the Special Prosecutor for the Defense of Human Rights commissioned the Section Chief of Buenaventura to investigate whether the police agents may have had a hand in the purported disappearance of the young woman OLGA ESTHER BERNAL DUEÑAS.

As soon as a response is received concerning the present status of the inquiries, both criminal and disciplinary, that information will be made available to the Inter-American Commission.

3.   On September 7, 1990, the petitioners sent additional information, which was also forwarded to the Colombian Government. It included the following testimony:

[Olga's sister, Melba Stella Bernal Dueñas, stated that she was notified on January 10, 1988 that Olga had been arrested and that her brother-in-law and sister left the next day for Buenaventura to make inquiries. Commandant Guillermo Cháves Ocaña, then police chief of Buenaventura, denied that Olga had been arrested. A woman who recognized Olga's photo said she saw two police officers carry Olga to the hospital early on the day after her arrest and that she had been beaten. She also stated that the police brought her out again about a half an hour later and said she had to be put in jail again. The doctor on duty said he would not risk saying anything about Olga. Melba also testified that Olga was a member of the Unión Patriótica. Another witness declared that the police put Olga in the cells where they torture people and that he and others could hear her screams when they hit her. He said that the "rule of silence prevails. No one knows anything, no one sees anything."]

4.   On October 22, 1990, the following reply was received from the Colombian Government, which was forwarded to the petitioner:

[The Government stated that the Chief of the Technical Corps of the Judicial Police of Buenaventura certified on February 15, 1990, to the Office of the Section Prosecutor for Buenaventura that he interviewed the supervisor and employees of the establishment from which Olga had disappeared and that they had not witnessed any of the alleged events. A detective for the Administrative Security Department (DAS) questioned some of the establishment's employees and neighbors of the police station, and no one had seen the alleged arrest.]

Nevertheless, for the sake of defending and protecting human rights, the Office of the Special Prosecutor for Human Rights is continuing its investigation and at the present time the inquiries that the Buenaventura Prosecutor was assigned to conduct are being evaluated by the Office of the Special Prosecutor for Human Rights.

As for the criminal investigation, at this time the case is with the Third Special Court of Buenaventura. On January 23, 1990, an order was given to take the statements from other witnesses. Likewise, the Investigative Unit of the Technical Corps of Buenaventura Judicial Police is cooperating in this investigation.

As Your Excellency can appreciate, the remedies under domestic law are fully under way. Any information that the investigations currently in progress produce will be made available to the Commission immediately.

[In a subsequent communication the petitioner expressed fear that the investigation would soon be suspended. The Colombian Government stated that they were unable to identify those responsible for the alleged disappearance but that investigations would continue and, therefore, domestic remedies had not been exhausted. The petitioner responded that almost four years had passed and the criminal justice system had still issued no ruling on Olga's case.]

8.   During its Eighty-third Session in March 1993, the Commission issued a Report 6/93, which was sent to the Government of Colombia so that the latter might issue any observations it deemed appropriate within a period of three months from the date of transmittal.

WHEREAS:

1.   As to admissibility:

a.   The Commission is competent to examine this case because it involves violations of rights recognized in the American Convention on Human Rights: Article 4, the right to life; Article 7, the right to personal liberty; and Article 25, the right to judicial protection, as provided in Article 44 of that Convention, to which Colombia is a State Party.

b.   The petition satisfies the formal requirements for admissibility as contained in the American Convention on Human Rights and in the Regulations of the Inter-American Commission on Human Rights.

c.   In the present case, it is obvious that the petitioners have been unable to obtain effective protection from the domestic jurisdictional organs.

d.   The petition is not pending settlement in another procedure under an international governmental organization and is not a duplication of a petition already examined by the Commission.

2.   As to the Colombian Government's investigation:
In spite of the testimony given by Euclides Mosquera del Castillo, no decision has been handed down in the proceedings concerning the arbitrary arrest and subsequent disappearance of Olga Ester Bernal.

3.   As for other aspects related to the Commission's processing of this case:

a.   By their nature, the facts that prompted the petition cannot be resolved through application of the friendly settlement procedure and the parties did not request the Commission to apply that procedure, which is provided for in Article 48.1.f of the Convention and in Article 45 of the Regulations of the Inter-American Commission on Human Rights.

b.   Since the friendly settlement procedure does not apply, the Commission must carry out the provisions of Article 50.1 of the Convention, by issuing its opinion and conclusions on the matter submitted to it for consideration.

c.   In prosecuting the present case, all of the legal and regulatory procedures established in the Convention and in the Commission's regulations have been exhausted.

4.   Other considerations:

a. To in any way allow the authors of a punishable act to go unpunished, is a violation of the rule of law and the principles of justice.

b. That the Government of Colombia, on July 8, 1993, presented its observations on Report 6/93 of March 11, 1993;

c. That, in the remarks contained in its reply note, the Government of Colombia does not provide any information that refutes the accusations made or that shows that appropriate measures have been taken to resolve the situation described in the complaint; and

d. That the Commission has no new evidence that would justify a modification of the original report,

THE INTER-AMERICAN COMMISSION ON HUMAN RIGHTS,

[handwritten: as close as gets to a judgment]

CONCLUDES:

1. That the Colombian Government has failed in its duty to respect and guarantee Article 4 (right to life), Article 13 (freedom of thought and expression), Article 25 (judicial protection), in respect of Article 11, recognized in the American Convention on Human Rights, of which Colombia is a State Party, in the arbitrary arrest and forced disappearance of Olga Ester Bernal.

2. To recommend to the Colombian Government that the investigations be continued until those responsible are identified and punished in accordance with criminal law, thereby avoiding the consummation of serious acts of impunity that strike at the very foundation of the legal system.

3. To recommend to the Colombian State that it pay compensatory damages to the victim's next of kin.

4. To request the Colombian Government to guarantee the safety of Mr. Euclides Mosquera del Castillo and Ms. Melba Stella Bernal Dueñas, and to provide them all with necessary protection.

5. To order the publication of this report in the Annual Report to the General Assembly, pursuant to Article 53.1 of the American Convention and Article 48 of the Commission's Regulations, because the Government of Colombia did not adopt measures to correct the situation denounced, within the time period stipulated in Reports Nº 6/93 of March 11, and Nº 24/93 of October 12, 1993, approved by the Commission in its 83º and 84º sessions.

NOTES AND QUESTIONS

1. In 1988 the Inter-American Court of Human Rights issued its decision on a complaint of disappearances in Honduras. *See Velasquez Rodriguez Case*, Judgment of July 29, 1988, Inter-Am. Ct. H.R. (Ser. C.) No. 4, 28 I.L.M. 294 (1989). In that case, Honduran armed forces had detained Angel Manfredo Velasquez Rodriguez, after which time he never reappeared. The Court found that the disappearance was the responsibility of the Government and ordered it to pay compensation to the family. For a discussion of this case from a litigation perspective, see Juan Méndez & José Vivanco, *Disappearances and the Inter-American Court: Reflections on a Litigation Experience*, 13 HAMLINE L. REV. 507, 542-57 (1990). For more information on disappearances in Honduras see Amnesty International, *"Disappearances" in Honduras: A Wall of Silence and Indifference*, AI Index: AMR: 37/02/92 (1992).

2.   The OAS adopted the Inter-American Convention on Forced Disappearance of Persons on June 9, 1994. As of November 1994, twelve countries have signed the Convention.

3.   The United Nations General Assembly adopted the Declaration on the Protection of All Persons from Enforced Disappearances on December 18, 1992. G.A. res. 47/133, 47 U.N. GAOR Supp. (No.49) at 207, U.N. Doc. A/47/49 (1992).

D. THE INTER-AMERICAN COMMISSION ON HUMAN RIGHTS

Juan Méndez & José Vivanco, *Disappearances and the Inter-American Court: Reflections on a Litigation Experience*, 13 HAMLINE L. REV. 507, 519-27 (1990) (footnotes omitted):

III.   OVERVIEW OF THE INTER-AMERICAN SYSTEM ON HUMAN RIGHTS PROTECTION

The bodies responsible for the protection of fundamental freedoms in the Inter-American system are the Inter-American Commission on Human Rights and the Inter-American Court of Human Rights. [Ed. note: *See* section F of this chapter, *infra*, for more information on the Inter-American Court of Human Rights.] Both bodies are empowered by the American Convention on Human Rights to protect and promote human rights. The Commission is also empowered to monitor human rights according to the American Declaration of the Rights and Duties of Man. This last instrument is technically a "recommendation," but has gained enforceability in practice and is applied by the Commission to OAS member states which have not ratified the Convention. Nevertheless, today the legal elements under both the Convention and the Declaration are basically the same. The Commission may seek a settlement in a case involving State Parties to the Convention or, in the alternative, refer a case to the Court if it involves a State that has recognized the Court's jurisdiction.

A.   The Commission

The Commission is an autonomous entity of the OAS whose principal function is to promote the observance and defense of human rights and to serve as an advisory body to the OAS. It is a quasi-judicial body with legal, diplomatic and political powers, established in 1959 by Resolution VI of the Fifth Meeting of Consultation of Ministers of Foreign Affairs in Santiago, Chile. Since its creation, the Commission has been the subject of reforms intended to broaden its powers.

The most important legal reform affecting the work of the Commission occurred in 1969 with the adoption of the Convention. Today, the majority of OAS member states have become State Parties to the Convention. The Convention, unlike the Declaration, is an international treaty. It established a sophisticated procedure for individual petitions, similar to its European counterpart and, more significantly, established the Court.

The Commission and the Court, according to the Convention, are each made up of seven experts in the human rights field, elected in their individual capacities and not as government representatives. Both organs include an Executive Secretariat whose function is to support members in the performance of their duties.

The Commission's members are elected by the General Assembly's member states, independent of their ratification of the Convention. Only State Parties to the Convention, however, may elect members of the Court. In contrast to Commission members, the Court's judges should be jurists and nationals of the member states of the OAS.

The Commission has three primary functions: processing individual complaints of alleged human rights violations; preparing reports on human rights situations in OAS member states; and proposing measures to be taken by the OAS to increase respect for human rights in the region.

1. Processing Individual Complaints

Individuals may petition the Commission directly or through representatives, with complaints based upon alleged violations of the Convention. Similarly, NGOs can file petitions on behalf of individuals for alleged violation of the Convention. By contrast, the European Convention only allows petitions from those individuals who claim to have had their fundamental rights violated. When the Commission receives a petition, it may solicit information from the State concerned, which has the obligation to cooperate with the proceeding. In serious and urgent cases, the Commission, with the consent of the State involved, may carry out an independent, on site, fact-finding investigation. In serious cases the Commission may also request the State to adopt precautionary measures, a type of preliminary injunction, to avoid irreparable harm to individuals. The Commission's request for such measures, however, is without prejudice to the State's interest in the final disposition of the case. As part of the precautionary measures, the Commission may contact the Ministry of Foreign Relations of the State asking for an urgent reply to the requested, pertinent information.

The Commission also has the power to turn to the Court and request the adoption of provisional measures when the State involved has ratified the Convention. The Commission can exercise this power even in matters not yet submitted to the Court, although so far it has never used this power. [As of March 1996, there have been 13 official requests for provisional measures. For example, on May 16, 1990, the Commission asked the Court to adopt provisional measures against Peru in the Bustos-Rojas case. The President of the Court enjoined the Government of Peru to "adopt without delay whatever measures are deemed necessary to protect the right to life and personal safety" of the witnesses in the case. On August 8, 1990, the Court ratified the Order of the President. Annual Report of the Inter-American Court of Human Rights 27, OEA/Ser.L/V/III.23, doc. 12 (1991). On January 17, 1991, the Court required the Government of Peru to implement additional protections in the Bustios-Rojas case. Annual Report of the Inter-American Court of Human Rights 15, OAS/Ser.L/V/III.25, doc. 7 (1992). On July 15, 1991, the Court required the Government of Guatemala to take all necessary measures to protect the right to life and the physical integrity of colleagues and relatives of murdered human rights activists in the village of Chunimá, witnesses to the crimes, and judges working on their cases. The Court adopted the provisional measures of the President of the Court on August 1, 1991. Annual Report of the Inter-American Court of Human Rights 46, OAS/Ser.L/V/III.25, doc. 7 (1992). On November 19, 1993, the Court adopted provisional measures against Argentina in the Reggiardo-Tolosa case. The President of the Court enjoined the Government of Argentina to adopt necessary measures to protect the mental integrity of two minors who were registered as the children of another couple after their parents were victims of forced disappearances. After these measures were taken the children were returned to their legitimate family. Annual Report of the Inter-American Court of Human Rights 95, OAS/Ser.L/

V/III.29, doc. 4 (1994).] This preliminary injunction requested by the Commission appears to be the final recourse available within the Inter-American system to prevent irreparable harm to individuals.

For the Commission to admit a petition, the request must satisfy certain minimal, formal requirements such as the identification of the person or NGO filing the complaint; a description of the facts surrounding the alleged violation(s); the State allegedly responsible; the specific rights of the Convention that were allegedly violated; and the exhaustion of domestic remedies. In situations where the State concerned does not afford due process, or the petitioner does not have access to, or is prevented from exhausting the applicable domestic remedies, or there is an unjustified delay in rendering a final judgment, the requirement that domestic remedies be exhausted is waived.

A petitioner must file his or her claim no more than six months after notification of the final disposition in a domestic case which represents the exhaustion of remedies. However, the Commission has the flexibility to accept or deny petitions, setting aside statutory limitations, by taking into account the particular circumstances of a case. . . .

Petition processing may be characterized as adversarial, since a bilateral discussion occurs between the petitioner (individual or NGO) and the accused State. In this investigative phase, the Commission plays a passive role, mediating the discussion [in writing] between the parties. It acts as carrier and investigator soliciting responses to the petitioner's claims from the State, and transmitting information between the parties. In overseeing the exchange, the Commission limits the response time available to each party.

The Commission is interested in promoting a fluid discussion between the parties concerned; the discussion will provide the Commission with the information required to adopt a resolution. In some cases, communication is only a formality. For example, a State may respond so generally to specific points in an individual's complaint that the Commission, *ex officio* or at the petitioner's request, may submit a separate questionnaire about controversial or confusing points in the complaint which have not been clarified by the State in its response. . . .

Where a State completely fails to cooperate, the Commission may issue a warning that it intends to apply Article 42 of its Regulations, which establishes a presumption of truth regarding pertinent facts in favor of the petitioner. This Article is an original creation of the Commission and represents the "last resort," intended to persuade the State to cooperate with the Commission. It has also been perceived as a sanction against a State's insensitivity or unwillingness to work with the Commission. The Commission, however, must use this provision prudently. . . .

The Commission has been extraordinarily flexible and informal with regard to rules of evidence. It has permitted the admission of affidavits, videotaped testimonies, personal documents, newspaper clippings, and technical expert testimony, viewing broadly what might serve as evidence.

During the initial investigative period, the petitioner plays a fundamental role. If the petitioner so chooses, he or she may appear in a private hearing during the Commission's sessions personally, or through a representative, to explain his or her version of the alleged facts and present relevant evidence.

During its annual meetings, the Commission, on its own initiative or at the request of either of the parties, may offer to mediate a friendly settlement of the case. This procedure may be used only if in the Commission's judgment the alleged facts are sufficiently precise and the nature of the case is susceptible to the use of the friendly settlement mechanism. In any case, all settlements must be based on the respect for human rights recognized in the Convention.

Finally, if the Commission believes that a State has violated any of the rights protected under the Convention or Declaration, it may approve a resolution condemning the State as well as make certain recommendations. If the State does not adopt the Commission's recommendations or provide new facts or invoke additional legal arguments within a ninety day period, the Commission may then publish the resolution in its Annual Report which is submitted to the [OAS] General Assembly. For State Parties to the Convention that have accepted the contentious jurisdiction of the Court, the Commission is empowered to submit a case to the Court. Yet the Commission [seldom exercises] this power. . . . [The Commission first submitted a case to the Court in 1986. *See Velasquez* Judgment, *supra.* The Commission also referred two companion cases with the *Velasquez* case. *See Godinez Cruz Case,* Judgment of Jan. 20, 1989, Inter-Am. Ct. H.R. (Ser. C.) No. 5; *Fairen Garbi and Solis Corrales Case,* Judgment of Mar. 15, 1989, Inter-Am. Ct. H.R. (Ser. C.) No. 6.] On two other occasions, the Commission unsuccessfully called upon State Parties to the Convention to recognize the Court's jurisdiction in resolving specific cases.

2. Preparing Reports on Human Rights

As a consequence of the Commission's own initiative or by invitation from a particular State, the Commission conducts on-site investigations from which it usually prepares reports on the situation of human rights in that specific State. The request for a mission by the Commission can also be made by a political body of the OAS, such as the Meeting of Consultation of Foreign Ministers. All visits conducted by the Commission for the purpose of reporting on human rights conditions in a country require the prior consent of the State concerned. . . .

The on-site investigations of the Commission and the special country reports which may follow have been extraordinarily effective in the defense of human rights, particularly during the 1970s and early 1980s when military regimes were numerous in Latin America.

The country reports, for example, have helped the Inter-American system of human rights protection to confront gross and massive human rights violations in the region, even in those countries where the Commission was denied government consent to conduct an on-site investigation. Country reports, however, are an indirect channel of protection against abuse. The reports are strongest in their capacity to expose and denounce human rights violations. Through the publication of its country reports, the Commission can alert the domestic and international community (particularly for debates during the General Assembly of the OAS) to the unacceptable behavior of States or to a particular phenomenon, such as the practice of disappearances or extrajudicial executions. These publications have the salutary effect of provoking strong reaction from democratic governments, the public, the media, NGOs and other political actors. [*See* the discussion of the Inter-American Commission's fact-finding work in chapter 8, *supra.*]

. . .

3. Proposing Measures for the OAS

Through the Annual Reports it submits to the OAS General Assembly, the Commission also focuses on the promotion of human rights and the steps necessary toward a full observance of the rights set forth in the Declaration and the Convention. These include the draft of the Inter-American Convention to Prevent and Punish

Torture (submitted in 1978 and signed in Colombia on December 9, 1985), the draft of the Additional Protocol to the American Convention on Human Rights Relevant to Economic, Social and Cultural Rights (submitted in 1986 and signed in El Salvador on November 17, 1988) and the draft of the Inter-American Convention on Forced Disappearance of Persons (submitted in 1988 [and adopted on June 9, 1994, in Brazil]). The Commission has also submitted specific proposals to the General Assembly on such issues as the independence of the judiciary, refugee rights, and the rights of indigenous populations.

[In 1990, the OAS General Assembly approved the Commission's draft of the Protocol to the American Convention on Human Rights to Abolish the Death Penalty. Ratifying nations agree "not to apply the death penalty in their territory to any person subject to their jurisdiction." Protocol to Abolish the Death Penalty, *approved* June 8, 1990, Art. 1, O.A.S.T.S. No. 73. Governments may not make any reservations except that they may reserve the right to apply the death penalty in wartime. Death Penalty Protocol, Art. 2, para. 1. As of March 1996, Costa Rica, Ecuador, Nicaragua, Panama, Uruguay, and Venezuela have signed the Protocol to the American Convention on Human Rights to Abolish Death Penalty; but only Panama, Uruguay, and Venezuela have ratified.]

NOTES AND QUESTIONS

1. For further reading, see:

THOMAS BUERGENTHAL, INTERNATIONAL HUMAN RIGHTS IN A NUTSHELL, 174-207 (1995);

SCOTT DAVIDSON, THE INTER-AMERICAN COURT OF HUMAN RIGHTS (1992);

Tom J. Farer, *The Inter-American Commission on Human Rights: Operations and Doctrine*, 9 INT'L J.L. LIBR. 251 (1981);

Claudio Grossman, *Proposals to Strengthen the Inter-American System of Protection of Human Rights*, 32 GERMAN Y.B. INT'L L. 264 (1990);

INTER-AMERICAN COMMISSION ON HUMAN RIGHTS, 25 YEARS OF STRUGGLE FOR HUMAN RIGHTS IN THE AMERICAS (1984);

LAWRENCE LEBLANC, THE OAS AND THE PROMOTION AND PROTECTION OF HUMAN RIGHTS (1977);

Juan E. Méndez, *The OAS and Human Rights* (1993) (presented as part of the Inter-American Dialogue, Dec. 2-3, 1993);

Robert Norris, *The Individual Petition Procedure of the Inter-American System for the Protection of Human Rights, in* GUIDE TO INTERNATIONAL HUMAN RIGHTS PRACTICE 108 (Hurst Hannum ed., 1984);

DANIEL O'DONNELL, PROTECCIÓN INTERNACIONAL DE LOS DERECHOS HUMANOS (2d ed. 1989);

Jo M. Pasqualucci, *The Inter-American Human Rights System: Establishing Precedents and Procedure in Human Rights Law*, 26 U. MIAMI INTER-AM. L. REV. 297 (Winter 1994-95);

C. MEDINA QUIROGA, THE BATTLE OF HUMAN RIGHTS: GROSS, SYSTEMATIC VIOLATIONS AND THE INTER-AMERICAN SYSTEM (1988);

Cesar Sepulveda, *The Inter-American Commission on Human Rights (1960-1981)*, 12 ISRAEL Y.B. HUM. RTS. 46 (1982);

Cesar Sepulveda, *The Inter-American Commission on Human Rights of the Organization of American States*, 28 GERMAN Y.B. INT'L L. 65 (1985);

Dinah Shelton, *The Inter-American Human Rights System, in* GUIDE TO INTERNATIONAL HUMAN RIGHTS PRACTICE 119 (Hurst Hannum 2d ed. 1992);

DANIEL ZOVATTO, LOS ESTADOS DE EXCEPCIÓN Y LOS DERECHOS HUMANOS EN AMERICA LATINA (1990).

2.   Professor Dinah Shelton has recommended measures that the Commission could take to improve its effectiveness. They include decreasing the response-time for urgent cases, emphasizing prevention, improving legal analysis, adopting a policy favoring published decisions, and appointing counsel for victims unable to afford counsel. Dinah Shelton, *Improving Human Rights Protections: Recommendations for Enhancing the Effectiveness of the Inter-American Commission and Inter-American Court of Human Rights*, 3 AM. U.J. INT'L L. & POL'Y 323 (1988).

3.   In 1993, the Association of the Bar of the City of New York released a report criticizing the Commission. In particular, the report questioned the Commission's ability to investigate and issue decisions on violations of human rights. *See* COMMITTEE ON INTERNATIONAL HUMAN RIGHTS OF THE ASSOCIATION OF THE BAR OF THE CITY OF NEW YORK, THE INTER-AMERICAN COMMISSION ON HUMAN RIGHTS: A PROMISE UNFULFILLED (1993).

In its report, the Association stated, "The Commission decides few cases, usually after long delay, and often its decisions are not drafted in a persuasive manner. The decisions receive very little notice, are not cited or relied on in other cases, and are often not obeyed." A PROMISE UNFULFILLED at 3. The Association concluded that inadequate budget and staffing, as well as politicization of cases, were to blame for the Commission's weaknesses. *Id.* It placed some of the blame on the United States, because of its failure "to put its influence and prestige behind the Commission,. . .in particular its failure to ratify the American Convention." *Id.* at 4.

Though the Association criticized the Inter-American Commission's inefficiency, it praised the work of the European Commission. (*See* chapter 11, *infra.*) A PROMISE UNFULFILLED at 12. The Association reported that the European Commission takes action on a continuous stream of cases, even though it operates under procedures similar to those of the Inter-American Commission. *Id.* Assuming the Association is correct, what do you suppose underlies the difference in output and effectiveness between the two commissions?

4.   As the Association of the Bar of the City of New York stated in its report, the United States has yet to ratify the American Convention on Human Rights. Do you think the United States should ratify the Convention? Would U.S. ratification fully address the criticisms of the Association as described in note 3? For further reading, *see* Brian Burns, *The Time for Full United States Participation in the Inter-American System for the Protection of Human Rights*, 24 COLUM. HUM. RTS. L. REV. 435 (1993) (reviewing SCOTT DAVIDSON, THE INTER-AMERICAN COURT OF HUMAN RIGHTS (1992)); Mark Kirk, *Should the United States Ratify the American Convention on Human Rights?*, 14 IIDH (Inter-American Institute of Human Rights) 65 (1991).

5.   A number of complaints against the United States have been brought before the Commission. The Indian Law Resource Center has filed a complaint with the Commission against the United States. That complaint, submitted on April 2, 1993, alleges that the United States denied two Western Shoshone women their constitutional rights when it extinguished their title to a Nevada ranch. The complaint is believed to be the first filed with the Commission on behalf of American Indians.

Citizens of the District of Columbia v. United States, Case No. 11.204, alleges violations of Articles II and XX of the American Declaration, because residents of Washington, D.C. fulfill their obligations as U.S. citizens, but do not have the right either to elect members of Congress or to enact local legislation without intrusion by Congress.

The Commission has found admissible a petition by Panamanians alleging claims of death, personal injury, and destruction of property as a result of the United States invasion of Panama. Case 10.573, Inter-Am. C.H.R. 312, OEA/Ser.L/V/II.85, doc. 9 rev. (1994). The

Commission has heard oral arguments on the merits, but no decision has yet been rendered on the Panama case, as of February 1996. It has declared admissible another petition contesting the legality of the U.S. policy of interdicting Haitians on the high seas. Case 10.675, Inter-Am. C.H.R. 334, OEA/Ser.L/V/II.85, doc. 9 rev. (1994). The Commission took precautionary measures in regard to this case in 1993. No decision on the merits has been rendered as of February 1996, and the situation has substantially changed since the filing of the case. There is also a petition before the Commission concerning human rights violations on the Mexican border by the Border Patrol and INS agents. *See* Rick Wilson, *Litigation at the Inter-American Human Rights Commission and Court*, ACLU INTERNATIONAL CIVIL LIBERTIES REPORT, July 1994, at 28. In addition, the Inter-American Commission has declared admissible and is considering a complaint on the merits as to racial discrimination in the execution of William Andrews in Utah.

E.   TREATY INTERPRETATIONS AND RESERVATIONS

THE VIENNA CONVENTION ON THE LAW OF TREATIES, 1155 U.N.T.S. 331, T.S. No. 58 (1980), 8 I.L.M. 679 (1969), *entered into force Jan. 27, 1980:*

Article 18

*Obligation not to defeat the object and purpose
of a treaty prior to its entry into force*

A State is obliged to refrain from acts which would defeat the object and purpose of a treaty when:

(a)   it has signed the treaty or has exchanged instruments constituting the treaty subject to ratification, acceptance or approval, until it shall have made its intention clear not to become a party to the treaty; or

(b)   it has expressed its consent to be bound by the treaty, pending the entry into force of the treaty and provided that such entry into force is not unduly delayed.

SECTION 2.   RESERVATIONS

Article 19

Formulation of reservations

A State may, when signing, ratifying, accepting, approving or acceding to a treaty, formulate a reservation unless:

(a)   the reservation is prohibited by the treaty;

(b)   the treaty provides that only specified reservations, which do not include the reservation in question, may be made; or

(c)   in cases not falling under sub-paragraphs (a. and b.), the reservation is incompatible with the object and purpose of the treaty.

SECTION 3. INTERPRETATION OF TREATIES

Article 31

General rule of interpretation

1.   A treaty shall be interpreted in good faith in accordance with the ordinary meaning to be given to the terms of the treaty in their context and in the light of its object and purpose.

2.   The context for the purpose of the interpretation of a treaty shall comprise, in addition to the text, including its preamble and annexes:

(a)   any agreement relating to the treaty which was made between all the parties in connection with the conclusion of the treaty;

(b)   any instrument which was made by one or more parties in connexion with the conclusion of the treaty and accepted by the other parties as an instrument related to the treaty.

3.   There shall be taken into account, together with the context:

(a)   any subsequent agreement between the parties regarding the interpretation of the treaty or the application of its provisions;

(b)   any subsequent practice in the application of the treaty which establishes the agreement of the parties regarding its interpretation;

(c)   any relevant rules of international law applicable in the relations between the parties. . ..

4.   A special meaning shall be given to a term if it is established that the parties so intended.

Article 32

Supplementary means of interpretation

Recourse may be had to supplementary means of interpretation, including the preparatory work of the treaty and the circumstances of its conclusion, in order to confirm the meaning resulting from the application of article 31, or to determine the meaning when the interpretation according to article 31:

(a)   leaves the meaning ambiguous or obscure; or

(b)   leads to a result which is manifestly absurd or unreasonable.

NOTES AND QUESTIONS

1.   The Vienna Convention on the Law of Treaties represents a consensus on how treaties should be construed. It entered into force on January 27, 1980, but has not yet been ratified by the United States. In its Letter of Submittal to the President, however, the Department of State reported that "the Convention is already generally recognized as the authoritative guide to current treaty law and practice." S. Exec. Doc., 92nd Cong., 1st Sess. 1 (1971). The Legal Advisor of the Department of State wrote:

> While the United States has not yet ratified the Vienna Convention on the Law of Treaties, [the United States has] consistently applied those of its terms which constitute a codification of customary international law. Most provisions of the Vienna Convention, including Articles 31 and 32 on matters of treaty interpretation, are declaratory of customary international law.

Marian Nash, *Contemporary Practice of the United States Relating to International Law*, 75 AM. J. INT'L L. 142, 147 (1981).

For possible differences between treaty interpretation in the U.S. and treaty interpretation under the Vienna Convention, see the Restatement (Third) of the Foreign Relations Law of the United States §325 and comments following this note.

2.   The Inter-American Court of Human Rights in several of its opinions seems to have used the rules of interpretation in the Vienna Convention as its sole guide for construing the American Convention. In its opinions the court has acknowledged that the Vienna Convention contains the principles of international law relevant to the interpretation of treaties.

Though the American Declaration on the Rights and Duties of Man was not initially promulgated as a treaty, it arguably has become incorporated by reference within the OAS Charter by the Protocol of Buenos Aires which revised the Charter and came into force in 1970. Even if the American Declaration is not considered to be incorporated in the OAS Charter, the Inter-American Commission arguably should still use the Vienna Convention approach to interpretation. *See* Ralf Wetzel, *Introduction*, THE VIENNA CONVENTION OF THE LAW OF TREATIES, TRAVAUX PRÉPARATOIRES 12-14 (1978).

3.   Dinah Shelton in an unpublished memorandum related to *Thompson v. Oklahoma*, 487 U.S. 815 (1988), has interpreted Article 18 of the Vienna Convention that forbids a government "from acts which would defeat the object and purpose of a treaty" it has signed, as follows:

The Inter-American Court of Human Rights has emphasized that "modern human rights treaties in general, and the American Convention in particular, are not multilateral treaties of the traditional type concluded to accomplish the reciprocal exchange of rights for the mutual benefit of the contracting States. Their object and purpose is the protection of the basic rights of individual human beings, irrespective of their nationality, both against the State of their nationality and all other contracting States." [The Effect of Reservations on the Entry into Force of the American Convention (Arts. 74 and 75), Advisory Opinion OC-2/82, Inter-Am. Ct. H.R. (Ser. A) (1982).]

Similarly, the character of human rights treaties has been recognized by the European Commission on Human Rights. It has said that the obligations of the European Convention are "designed rather to protect the fundamental rights of individual human beings from infringements by any of the High Contracting Parties than to create subjective and reciprocal rights for the High Contracting Parties themselves." [Austria v. Italy, 4 European Y.B. Hum. Rts. 116, at 140 (1961).]

Parallel views were voiced by the International Court of Justice in its *Advisory Opinion on Reservations to the Convention on the Prevention and Punishment of the Crime of Genocide*, 1951 I.C.J. 15, where the Court also noted that "the [human rights] principles underlying the Convention are principles which are recognized by civilized nations as binding on States, even without any conventional obligation."

4.   The acceptability of reservations tending to defeat the object and purpose of human rights treaties is also discussed in chapters 2, *supra* and 13, *infra*.

5.   Should the American Convention have been applied in the *Baby Boy* case since the U.S. has signed but not ratified it? Exactly what legal effect, if any, should have been given to the Convention? Should the Commission have discussed the proposed U.S. reservation to Article 4 of the American Convention, reproduced below?

Four Treaties Pertaining to Human Rights: Message From the President of the United States, 95th Cong., 2nd Sess. at xvii-xxiii (1978):

[Ed. note: After President Carter signed the American Convention on Human Rights and three other treaties on June 1, 1977, the State Department proposed a number of reservations, understandings, and declarations for the advice and consent of the Senate as to the ratification of the American Convention.]

The following is a summary of the provisions of the Convention, with the reservations, understandings and declarations to them recommended to the Senate by the Department of State [and transmitted to the Senate by President Carter]. . . .

Article 4 deals with the right to life generally, and includes provisions on capital punishment. Many of the provisions of Article 4 are not in accord with United States law and policy, or deal with matters in which the law is unsettled. The Senate may wish to enter a reservation as follows:

"United States adherence to Article 4 is subject to the Constitution and other law of the United States."

* * * * *

1 Restatement (Third) of the Foreign Relations Law of the U.S. §325 (1987):

Interpretation of International Agreement

(1) An international agreement is to be interpreted in good faith in accordance with the ordinary meaning to be given to its terms in their context and in the light of its object and purpose.

(2) Any subsequent agreement between the parties regarding the interpretation of the agreement, and subsequent practice between the parties in the application of the agreement, are to be taken into account in its interpretation. . . .

Comment . . .

e. *Recourse to travaux préparatoires.* The Vienna Convention, in Article 32, requires the interpreting body to conclude that the "ordinary meaning" of the text is either obscure or unreasonable before it can look to "supplementary means." Some interpreting bodies are more willing to come to that conclusion than others. (Compare, for example, the experience in the United States with the parol evidence rule in interpreting contracts.) Article 32 of the Vienna Convention reflects reluctance to permit the use of materials constituting the development and negotiation of an agreement (*travaux préparatoires*) as a guide to the interpretation of the agreement. The Convention's inhospitality to *travaux* is not wholly consistent with the attitude of the International Court of Justice and not at all with that of United States courts. *See* Comment g.

g. *Interpretation by United States courts.* This section suggests a mode of interpretation of international agreements somewhat different from that ordinarily applied by courts in the United States. Courts in the United States are generally more willing than those of other states to look outside the instrument to determine its meaning. In most cases, the United States approach would lead to the same result, but an international tribunal using the approach called for by this section might find the United States interpretation erroneous and United States action pursuant to that interpretation a violation of the agreement.

NOTES AND QUESTIONS

1. How does the Restatement approach to treaty interpretation compare to the approach taken by the Vienna Convention? What appears to be the principal difference between the two approaches? What are advantages and disadvantages of each approach?

2. In the *Baby Boy* case, did the Inter-American Commission follow the rules for interpretation set forth in the Vienna Convention?

3.   FRANK NEWMAN & STANLEY SURREY, LEGISLATION: CASES AND MATERIALS 645-59 (1955) discusses basic methods of statutory interpretation under U.S. law. There are many other scholarly discussions of statutory interpretation. *See generally* WILLIAM ESKRIDGE & PHILIP FRICKEY, CASES AND MATERIALS ON LEGISLATION: STATUTES AND THE CREATION OF PUBLIC POLICY 569-828 (1988). What are the similarities and differences between statutory interpretation and treaty interpretation? Are there differences between the two contexts that would justify different rules of interpretation?

4.   The method of treaty interpretation in the Vienna Convention represents the majority view, but different approaches do exist. One is suggested by Myres McDougal, Howard Lasswell, and James Miller, whose approach emphasizes giving effect to the parties' shared expectations to the fullest extent possible—using interpretive methods such as those found in the Vienna Convention to ascertain the expectations. When traditional methods are unable to clarify the parties' expectations, this approach supplements the more explicit expressions of the parties by analysis of basic constitutive policies of the larger community. Finally the interpreter must consider the parties' expectations in light of fundamental community policy, including policies of the world community, in order to determine whether the parties' goals conflict with community policy. Where such a conflict exists, community policy overrides the expectations of the parties. *See* MYRES MCDOUGAL, HOWARD LASSWELL, & JAMES MILLER, THE INTERPRETATION OF AGREEMENTS AND WORLD PUBLIC ORDER: PRINCIPLES OF CONTENT AND PROCEDURE 35-118 (1967).

5.   Frank Newman has suggested another, more constitutional approach to interpreting human rights clauses of the U.N. Charter. He argues that the primary source should be the words of the Charter as they are reflected in basic U.N. documents such as those comprising the International Bill of Human Rights. *See* Frank Newman, *Interpreting the Human Rights Clauses of the U.N. Charter*, 1972 REVUE DES DROITS DE L'HOMME 283; *cf.* Frank Newman, *How Courts Interpret Regulations*, 35 CALIF. L. REV. 509 (1947).

   For agonizingly detailed analysis of approaches to interpreting various rights-to-fair-hearing expressed (and implied) in the two U.N. Covenants, see Frank Newman, *Natural Justice, Due Process, and the New International Covenants on Human Rights: Prospectus*, 1967 PUB. L. 274 (1967).

6.   For still another approach to treaty interpretation—as in civil law and socialist law—see EDWARD YAMBRUSIC, TREATY INTERPRETATION: THEORY AND REALITY 9-54 (1987).

   The interpretation of treaties is also discussed in chapter 13, *infra.*

F.   ADVISORY JURISDICTION OF THE INTER-AMERICAN COURT OF HUMAN RIGHTS

Thomas Buergenthal, *The Inter-American Court of Human Rights*, 76 AM. J. INT'L L. 231, 231-36, 239-40 (1982) (footnotes omitted):

   The Court was established by the American Convention on Human Rights, which entered into force in 1978. . . . The Court consists of seven judges, nominated and elected by the states parties to the Convention. The judges must be nationals of an OAS member state, but they need not have the nationality of the states parties to the Convention. The regular term of the judges is 6 years; they may be reelected for one additional term. The judges constituting the first Court were elected in May 1979. . . .

   The Convention provides that "the Court shall have its seat at the place determined by the States Parties to the Convention in the General Assembly of the

Organization." A resolution adopted by the Assembly in 1978 located the permanent seat of the Court in Costa Rica. A two-thirds vote of the states parties would be required to change the permanent seat. But the Court is not required to meet only in Costa Rica, for "it may convene in the territory of any member state . . . when a majority of the Court consider it desirable, and with the prior consent of the state concerned." . . .

II. THE COURT AND ITS INSTITUTIONAL CONTEXT

The draft Statute presented to the OAS General Assembly by the Court in 1979 envisaged a permanent tribunal consisting of full-time judges. This proposal was motivated by the Court's concern that a part-time tribunal might give that body an ad hoc image, likely to diminish the prestige and legitimacy it might need to obtain compliance with and respect for its decisions in the Americas. But the General Assembly found this proposal unacceptable, ostensibly at least on the ground that a full-time court would be too expensive and was unjustified until the Court had a substantial case load. The Assembly opted instead for a tribunal composed of part-time judges. It adopted a Statute that leaves the judges free to exercise their respective professions and stipulates merely that certain types of employment, particularly active government service, are incompatible with their judicial functions. As a result, the judges are not on the OAS payroll; they are not required to live in Costa Rica; and they are free to practice law, to teach, and to engage in whatever other occupations they may have in their native countries. . . .

All judicial decisions of the Court must be adopted by the Plenary Court. It does not sit in smaller panels or chambers as does the European court of Human Rights, for example. Both its small size and the requirement under Article 56 of the Convention that "five judges shall constitute a quorum for the transaction of business by the Court" would seem to rule out the use of chambers. . . .

The Inter-American Court of Human Rights has adjudicatory or so-called contentious jurisdiction, that is, jurisdiction to decide disputes involving charges that a state party has violated the human rights guaranteed by the Convention. It also has advisory jurisdiction, which empowers the Court to interpret the Convention and other human rights instruments at the request of OAS member states and various OAS organs.

Adjudicatory Jurisdiction

The Submission of Cases.   The Court's power to decide a case referred to it for adjudication is conditioned on the acceptance of its jurisdiction by the states parties to the dispute. A state is not deemed to have accepted the jurisdiction of the Court merely by ratifying the Convention. Acceptance of its jurisdiction is optional under the Convention and requires a separate declaration or a special agreement. That "declaration may be made unconditionally, on condition of reciprocity, for a specific period, or for specific cases." . . . In addition, of course, all states parties to the Convention may permit the Court at any time, on an *ad hoc* basis, to adjudicate a specific dispute relating to the application of the Convention.

Article 62(3) of the Convention reads as follows:

> The jurisdiction of the Court shall comprise all cases concerning the interpretation and application of the provisions of this Convention that are submitted to it, provided that the States Parties to the case recognize or have recognized such jurisdiction, whether by special declaration pursuant to the preceding paragraphs, or by a special agreement.

This provision needs to be read together with Article 61(1), which declares that "only the States Parties and the Commission shall have the right to submit a case to the Court." Individuals have no standing to do so. Moreover, the states suing and those being sued have to have accepted the jurisdiction of the Court before it may hear the case. Of course, the Commission is free to invite a state that has not accepted the Court's jurisdiction to do so for a specific case, but the state is free to reject the request.

Before the Court may "hear a case, . . . the procedures set forth in Articles 48 to 50 shall have been completed." The procedures referred to are those that govern the disposition by the Commission of cases submitted to it by states or individuals charging violations of the Convention. . . .

Judgments and Preliminary Decisions.   The proceedings before the Court in a contentious case terminate with a judgment. By ratifying the Convention, the states parties assumed the obligation "to comply with the judgment of the Court in any case to which they are parties." The Court has the power to enter a declaratory judgment and to award damages. The basic provision on the subject is Article 63(1), which reads as follows:

> If the Court finds that there has been a violation of a right or freedom protected by this Convention, the Court shall rule that the injured party be ensured the enjoyment of his right or freedom that was violated. It shall also rule, if appropriate, that the consequences of the measure or situation that constituted the breach of such right or freedom be remedied and that fair compensation be paid to the injured party.

This provision requires the Court to determine not only whether in the specific case before it there has been a violation of the Convention and what rights the injured party is entitled to enjoy, but also what steps may have to be taken to remedy the violation. As for the power of the Court to award damages, Article 68(2) provides that that part of a "judgment that stipulates compensatory damages may be executed in the country concerned in accordance with domestic procedure governing the execution of judgments against the state." . . .

In addition, the Court has the power to grant an extraordinary remedy in the nature of a temporary injunction. This power is spelled out in Article 63(2) of the Convention, which reads as follows:

> In cases of extreme gravity and urgency, and when necessary to avoid irreparable damage to persons, the Court shall adopt such provisional measures as it deems pertinent in matters it has under consideration. With respect to a case not yet submitted to the Court, it may act at the request of the Commission.

As this provision indicates, the temporary injunction is available in two distinct circumstances: for cases already pending before the Court and for cases being dealt with by the Commission that have not yet been referred to the Court for adjudication. . . .

Enforcement of Judgments.   The Convention does not establish a formal procedure to enforce the rulings of the Court against recalcitrant states. One provision, however—Article 65—does bear on this subject. It reads:

> To each regular session of the General Assembly of the Organization of American States the Court shall submit, for the Assembly's consideration, a report on its work during the previous year. It shall specify, in particular, the cases in which a state has not complied with its judgments, making any pertinent recommendations.

This provision enables the Court to inform the OAS General Assembly of situations involving noncompliance with its decisions, and it permits the Assembly to discuss the matter and to adopt whatever political measures it deems appropriate.

NOTES AND QUESTIONS

1. As the preceding excerpt points out, individuals do not have the right to bring cases before the Inter-American Court of Human Rights. Rather, the proper forum for individual petitions is the Inter-American Commission on Human Rights. Nevertheless, an individual's case might come before the Court, for example, where the Commission refers to the Court a case involving a state that has accepted the Court's adjudicatory jurisdiction. For further suggestions as to how individuals can obtain access to the Court, see Edmundo Vargas, *Individual Access to the Inter-American Court of Human Rights*, 1 INT'L L. & POL. 601, 604-16 (1984).

2. As the preceding excerpt explained, the Inter-American Court of Human Rights has contentious jurisdiction only over those states which have recognized the Court's power to decide cases. As the excerpt also pointed out, the Court may request a State to recognize its jurisdiction in particular cases. State Parties, however, seldom honor such requests. *See* Juan Méndez & Josesmín Vivanco, *supra*, at 529. Furthermore, of the 35 OAS member states which have ratified the Convention, only 17 have recognized the contentious jurisdiction of the Court. *See* Basic Documents Pertaining to Human Rights in the Inter-American System, OAS Doc. OEA/Ser.L.V/II.82, at 53 (1992). This information about states which have ratified the Convention and recognized the contentious jurisdiction of the Court remained accurate as of November 1994.

3. The following contentious cases are currently pending in the Inter-American Court of Human Rights: *Neira Alegría et al. v. Peru*, Case No. 10.078 (disappearance of three men being held in detention by Peruvian authorities); *Isidoro Caballero Delgado and María del Carmen Santana v. Colombia*, Case No. 10.319 (disappearance after being seized by the military); *Juan Paul Genie v. Nicaragua*, Case No. 10.792 (alleged extra-judicial killing by bodyguards of General Humberto Ortega under consideration on preliminary objections); *José Indalecio Guerrero et al. (El Amparo) v. Venezuela*, Case No. 10.602 (failure to prosecute members of the Judicial Technical Police implicated in the killing of 14 people).

Thomas Buergenthal, *The Advisory Practice of the Inter-American Human Rights Court*, 79 AM. J. INT'L L. 1, 3-12 (1985) (footnotes omitted):

II. ADVISORY JURISDICTION: ITS ROLE AND SCOPE

The advisory power of the Court is spelled out in Article 64 of the Convention, which reads as follows:

1. The member states of the Organization may consult the Court regarding the interpretation of this Convention or of other treaties concerning the protection of human rights in the American states. Within their spheres of competence, the organs listed in Chapter X of the Charter of the Organization of American States, as amended by the Protocol of Buenos Aires, may in like manner consult the Court.

2. The Court, at the request of a member state of the Organization, may provide that state with opinions regarding the compatibility of any of its domestic laws with the aforesaid international instruments. . . .

Treaties Subject to Interpretation.   Article 64(1) extends the Court's advisory jurisdiction to the interpretation of the "Convention or. . .other treaties concerning the protection of human rights in the American states." While the reference to the "Convention" needs no explanation, the same is not true of the meaning of "other treaties." Some of the issues it raises were dealt with by the Court in its first advisory opinion. In that case, the Government of Peru asked the Court to decide "how. . .the phrase 'or of other treaties concerning the protection of human rights in the American states' [should] be interpreted." Without taking a position on the meaning of the phrase, Peru suggested that it might be interpreted to refer either to treaties adopted within the framework of the inter-American system, to treaties concluded solely among American states, or to treaties that included one or more American states as parties. The Court ruled that, in principle, the provision conferred on it "the power to interpret any treaty as long as it is directly related to the protection of human rights in a Member State of the inter-American system." In short, the treaty need not be one that was adopted within the inter-American system or a treaty to which only American states may be parties. It may be bilateral or multilateral, and it need not be a human rights treaty as such, provided the provisions to be interpreted relate to the protection of human rights.

This holding is probably narrower than it appears at first glance. After concluding that there was no valid reason, in principle, to distinguish between regional and international human rights treaties, the Court emphasized that its power to comply with a request to interpret these instruments was discretionary. Whether it would exercise the power depended upon various factors related to the purposes of its advisory jurisdiction. "This jurisdiction," the Court declared, "is intended to assist the American States in fulfilling their international human rights obligations and to assist the different organs of the inter-American system to carry out the functions assigned to them in this field." Consequently, "any request for an advisory opinion which has another purpose would weaken the system established by the Convention and would distort the advisory jurisdiction of the Court." . . .

Two other questions bearing on the meaning of the phrase "other treaties concerning the protection of human rights in the American states" suggest themselves. They have not as yet been dealt with by the Court. One has to do with the definition of "human rights." It has already been noted that the reference is not only to human rights treaties as such, and that it permits the Court to interpret the human rights provisions of bilateral or multilateral treaties, whether or not such treaties deal exclusively with human rights. Examples here might be the human rights provisions of an extradition treaty or of a bilateral commercial agreement. But, and this is a question that remains to be answered, what is a "human rights" provision? In dealing with this problem, the Court might look to the catalog of rights found in the principal international and regional human rights instruments and in the constitutions of the states constituting the inter-American system. The OAS Charter and the American Convention, it should be noted, refer expressly not only to civil and political rights, but also to economic, social and cultural ones. The same is true of many international human rights instruments, which suggests the pervasive scope of the Court's advisory jurisdiction.

The second question is more difficult. It concerns the Court's jurisdiction to interpret the American Declaration of the Rights and Duties of Man. The Declaration was adopted in 1948 in the form of an inter-American conference resolution. As such, it is clearly not a "treaty" within the meaning of Article 64(1) of the American Convention. It is generally recognized, however, that the Protocol of Buenos Aires, which amended the OAS Charter, changed the legal status of the Declaration to an instrument that, at the very least, constitutes an authoritative interpretation and definition of the human rights obligations binding on OAS member states under the Charter of the Organization. This view is reflected in the Statute of the Inter-American Commission on Human Rights, which was adopted by the OAS General Assembly in 1979 pursuant to Article 112 of the OAS Charter and Article 39 of the American Convention. Article 1 of the Statute, after declaring in paragraph 1 that the Commission is an OAS organ "created to promote the observance and defense of human rights and to serve as consultative organ of the Organization in this matter," reads as follows:

2.   For the purposes of the present Statute, human rights are understood to be:

a.   The rights set forth in the American Convention on Human Rights, in relation to the States Parties thereto;

b.   The rights set forth in the American Declaration of the Rights and Duties of Man, in relation to the other member states.

The Statute also relies on the Declaration in defining the powers of the Commission in relation to all OAS member states as well as with respect to states that have not ratified the Convention. Since the Commission's powers with regard to the latter states are derived from the OAS Charter, it can be argued that the General Assembly, in approving the Commission's Statute and the references to the Declaration, confirmed the normative status of the Declaration as an instrument giving specific meaning to the vague human rights provisions of the Charter. If these considerations justify the conclusion that the Charter incorporates the Declaration by reference or that the Declaration constitutes an authoritative interpretation of the human rights provisions of the Charter, the Court's power under Article 64(1) to interpret the Charter would embrace the power to interpret the Declaration as well. It remains to be seen whether the Court will adopt the approach just indicated or opt for a strict textual construction, concluding that since the Declaration is not a "treaty," it does not fall within the Court's jurisdiction under Article 64(1).

A related question concerning the status of the Universal Declaration of Human Rights, which raises similar issues, might be presented to the Court in the context of a request for an advisory opinion seeking an interpretation of the human rights provisions of the UN Charter. Here it is relevant to note that the Convention makes specific reference to the American Declaration and to the Universal Declaration of Human Rights. The reference to the American Declaration in Article 29(d) of the Convention is particularly significant, for it declares that no provision of the Convention shall be interpreted as "excluding or limiting the effect that the American Declaration of the Rights and Duties of Man and other international acts of the same nature may have." To the extent that the Court, in applying Article 29, may be called upon to interpret the American Declaration, it has the power to do so under Article 64(1); it would merely be interpreting the Convention.

Restrictions to the Death Penalty, Advisory Opinion OC-8/83, 3 Inter-Am. Ct. H.R. (Ser. A) 54-56, 65-75 (1983) (citations omitted):

STATEMENT OF THE ISSUES

8.   Invoking Article 64(1) of the [American] Convention [on Human Rights], the Commission requested the Court, in communications of April 15 and 25, 1983, to

render an advisory opinion on the following questions relating to the interpretation of Article 4 of the Convention:

> 1) May a government apply the death penalty for crimes for which the domestic legislation did not provide such punishment at the time the American Convention on Human Rights entered into force for said state?
>
> 2) May a government, on the basis of a reservation to Article 4(4) of the Convention made at the time of ratification, adopt subsequent to the entry into force of the Convention a law imposing the death penalty for crimes not subject to this sanction at the moment of ratification?. . .

10.   In its explanation of the considerations giving rise to the request, the Commission informed the Court of the existence of certain differences of opinion between it and the Government of Guatemala concerning the interpretation of the last sentence of Article 4(2) of the Convention as well as on the effect and scope of Guatemala's reservation to the fourth paragraph of that article. . . .

OBJECTIONS TO THE JURISDICTION OF THE COURT

30.   The Court can now turn to the jurisdictional objections advanced by the Government of Guatemala. It contends that, although Article 64(1) of the Convention and Article 19(d) of the Statute of the Commission authorize the latter to seek an advisory opinion from the Court regarding the interpretation of any article of the Convention, if that opinion were to concern a given State directly, as it does Guatemala in the present case, the Court could not render the opinion unless the State in question has accepted the tribunal's jurisdiction pursuant to Article 62(1) of the Convention [which Guatemala has not done]. The Government of Guatemala argues accordingly that because of the form in which the Commission submitted the present advisory opinion request, linking it to an existing dispute between Guatemala and the Commission regarding the meaning of certain provisions of Article 4 of the Convention, the Court should decline to exercise its jurisdiction.

31.   The Convention distinguishes very clearly between two types of proceedings: so-called adjudicatory or contentious cases and advisory opinions. The former are governed by the provisions of Articles 61, 62 and 63 of the Convention; the latter by Article 64. . . .

32.   In contentious proceedings, the Court must not only interpret the applicable norms, determine the truth of the acts denounced and decide whether they are a violation of the Convention imputable to a State Party; it may also rule "that the injured party be ensured the enjoyment of his right or freedom that was violated." [Convention, Art. 63(1).] The States Parties to such proceeding are, moreover, legally bound to comply with the decisions of the Court in contentious cases. [Convention Art. 68(1).] On the other hand, in advisory opinion proceedings the Court does not exercise any fact-finding functions; instead, it is called upon to render opinions interpreting legal norms. Here the Court fulfills a consultative function through opinions that "lack the same binding force that attaches to decisions in contentious cases."

33.   The provisions applicable to contentious cases differ very significantly from those of Article 64, which govern advisory opinions. Thus, for example, Article 61(2) speaks of "case" and declares that "in order for the Court to hear a *case*, it is necessary that the procedures set forth in Articles 48 to 50 shall have been completed (emphasis added)." These procedures apply exclusively to "a petition or communica-

tion alleging violation of any of the rights protected by this Convention." [Convention, Art. 48(1).] Here the word "case" is used in its technical sense to describe a contentious case within the meaning of the Convention, that is, a dispute arising as a result of a claim initiated by an individual (Art. 44) or State Party (Art. 45), charging that a State Party has violated the human rights guaranteed by the Convention.

34.   One encounters the same technical use of the word "case" in connection with the question as to who may initiate a contentious case before the Court, which contrasts with those provisions of the Convention that deal with the same issue in the consultative area. Article 61(1) provides that "only States Parties and the Commission shall have a right to submit a case to the Court." On the other hand, not only "States Parties and the Commission," but also all of the "Member States of the Organization" and the "organs listed in Chapter X of the Charter of the Organization of American States" may request advisory opinions from the Court. [Convention, Art. 64(1).] There is yet another difference with respect to the subject matter that the Court might consider. While Article 62(1) refers to "all matters relating to the interpretation and application of this Convention," Article 64 authorizes advisory opinions relating not only to the interpretation of the Convention but also to "other treaties concerning the protection of human rights in the American states." It is obvious, therefore, that what is involved here are very different matters, and that there is no reason in principle to apply the requirements contained in Articles 61, 62 and 63 to the consultative function of the Court, which is spelled out in Article 64.

35.   Article 62(3) of the Convention—the provision Guatemala claims governs the application of Article 64—reads as follows:

> The jurisdiction of the Court shall comprise all *cases* concerning the interpretation and application of the provisions of this Convention that are submitted to it, provided that the States Parties to the *case* recognize or have recognized such jurisdiction, whether by special declaration pursuant to the preceding paragraphs, or by a special agreement (emphasis added).

It is impossible to read this provision without concluding that it, as does Article 61, uses the words "case" and "cases" in their technical sense. . . .

38.   The powers conferred on the Commission require it to apply the Convention or other human rights treaties. In order to discharge fully its obligations, the Commission may find it necessary or appropriate to consult the Court regarding the meaning of certain provisions whether or not at the given moment in time there exists a difference between a government and the Commission concerning an interpretation, which might justify the request for an advisory opinion. If the Commission were to be barred from seeking an advisory opinion merely because one or more governments are involved in a controversy with the Commission over the interpretation of a disputed provision, the Commission would seldom, if ever, be able to avail itself of the Court's advisory jurisdiction. . . .

39.   The right to seek advisory opinions under Article 64 was conferred on OAS organs for requests falling "within their spheres of competence." This suggests that the right was also conferred to assist with the resolution of disputed legal issues arising in the context of the activities of an organ, be it the Assembly, the Commission, or any of the others referred to in Chapter X of the OAS Charter. It is clear, therefore, that the mere fact that there exists a dispute between the Commission and the Government of Guatemala regarding the meaning of Article 4 of the Conven-

tion does not justify the Court to decline to exercise its advisory jurisdiction in the instant proceeding. . . .

41.   The Commission, as an organ charged with the responsibility of recommending measures designed to promote the observance and protection of human rights . . ., has a legitimate institutional interest in the interpretation of Article 4 of the Convention. The mere fact that this provision may also have been invoked before the Commission in petitions and communications filed under Articles 44 and 45 of the Convention does not affect this conclusion. Given the nature of advisory opinions, the opinion of the Court in interpreting Article 4 cannot be deemed to be an adjudication of those petitions and communications.

42.   In The Effect of Reservations on the Entry into Force of the American Convention (Arts. 74 and 75) (I/A Court H.R., Advisory Opinion OC-2/82 of September 24, 1982. Series A No. 2), this Court examined in considerable detail the requirements applicable to OAS organs requesting advisory opinions under Article 64. The Court there explained that Article 64, in limiting the right of OAS organs to advisory opinions falling "within their spheres of competence," meant to restrict the opinions "to issues in which such entities have a legitimate institutional interest." (*Ibid.*, para. 14.) After examining Article 112 and Chapter X of the OAS Charter, as well as the relevant provisions of the Statute of the Commission and the Convention itself, the Court concluded that the Commission enjoys, in general, a pervasive legitimate institutional Interest in questions bearing on the promotion and protection of human rights in the Inter-American system, which could be deemed to confer on it, as a practical matter, "an absolute right to request advisory opinions within the framework of Article 64(1) of the Convention." (*Ibid.*, para. 16.) Viewed in this light, the instant request certainly concerns an issue in which the Commission has a legitimate institutional interest. . . .

44.   Article 49(2)(b) of the Rules of Procedure requires that each request for an advisory opinion by an OAS organ "shall indicate the provisions to be interpreted, how the consultation relates to its sphere of competence, the considerations giving rise to the consultation, and the name and address of its delegates." The requirement of a description of "the considerations giving rise to the consultation" is designed to provide the Court with an understanding of the factual and legal context which prompted the presentation of the question. Compliance with this requirement is of vital importance as a rule in enabling the Court to respond in a meaningful manner to the request. . . .

Thus, merely because the Commission, under the heading of "Considerations giving rise to the consultation," has described for the Court a set of circumstances indicating that there exist differences concerning the interpretation of some provisions of Article 4 of the Convention, it certainly does not follow that the Commission has violated the Rules of Procedure or that it has abused the powers conferred on it as an organ authorized to request advisory opinions. The same conclusion is even more valid when the issue presented calls for the interpretation of a reservation, considering how difficult it is to respond with precision to a question that relates to a reservation and which is formulated in the abstract.

45.   The fact that this legal dispute bears on the scope of a reservation made by a State Party in no way detracts from the preceding conclusions. Under the Vienna Convention on the Law of Treaties (hereinafter cited as Vienna Convention), incorporated by reference into the Convention by its Article 75, a reservation is defined as

any "unilateral statement, however phrased or named, made by a State when sign-ing, ratifying, accepting, approving or acceding to a treaty, whereby it purports to exclude or to modify the legal effect of certain provisions of the treaty in their application to that State." [Art. 2(d).] The effect of a reservation, according to the Vienna Convention, is to modify with regard to the State making it the provisions of the treaty to which the reservation refers to the extent of the reservation. [Art. 21(1)(a).] Although the provisions concerning reciprocity with respect to reservations are not fully applicable to a human rights treaty such as the Convention, it is clear that reservations become a part of the treaty itself. It is consequently impossible to interpret the treaty correctly, with respect to the reserving State, without interpre-ting the reservation itself. . . .

NOTES AND QUESTIONS

1.   In its Restrictions to the Death Penalty Advisory Opinion, *supra*, the Inter-American Court of Human Rights held that "a reservation which was designed to enable a State to suspend any of the non-derogable fundamental rights must be deemed to be incompatible with the object and purpose of the Convention and, consequently, not permitted by it."

The Court is considering the following related questions: What effect does a law have that is in violation of a party's obligations under the American Convention if it was enacted after ratification? To what extent are state actors who implement a law in contravention of the Convention responsible for the violation? For further information see Advisory Opinion OC-14, Inter-Am Ct. H.R. 101, OEA/Ser.L/V/III.29 doc. 4 (1994).

2.   In 1989, the Inter-American Court of Human Rights issued an advisory opinion on the legal effect to be given to the American Declaration of the Rights and Duties of Man. The government of Colombia had requested an advisory opinion as to whether the Inter-American Court of Human Rights has authority under the Inter-American Convention on Human Rights to render advisory opinions interpreting the American Declaration. The Inter-American Court decided that it possessed authority to interpret the American Declaration. The Court also stated that a government which has ratified the Convention is not thereby freed from its obligations deriving from the Declaration, because the government continues to be a member of the Organization of American States. The Court concluded that "the Declaration is not a treaty does not, then, lead to the conclusion that it does not have legal effect, nor that the Court lacks the power to interpret it. . . ." Interpretation of the American Declaration of the Rights and Duties of Man in the Context of Article 64 of the American Convention on Human Rights, Advisory Opinion OC-10/89, Inter-Am. Ct. H. R., 50 (1989).

At the Court's public hearing on this case, OAS member states asserted that the Court would have to address the legal effect of the Declaration. For example, the United States told the Court that the Declaration "was not drafted as a legal instrument" and therefore did not carry "a binding set of obligations." *Id.* at 36. The Court also recognized that in issuing its advisory opinion, it "might have to pass on the legal status of the American Declaration." *Id.* at 40. Despite such recognition, the Court avoided explicitly deciding this key issue.

G.   OTHER REGIONAL SYSTEMS

As mentioned previously, regional systems for the protection of human rights also exist in Africa and Europe. *See infra* chapter 11 for more information on the European system. No regional or sub-regional human rights system, however, has been established in Asia.

1. The Organization of African Unity

The Organization of African Unity (OAU) is a regional intergovernmental organization that brings together governments of the African continent and its surrounding islands. The Charter of the OAU was adopted in 1963 and reaffirms adherence to the principles of the U.N. Charter and the Universal Declaration of Human Rights. Charter of the Organization of African Unity, 479 U.N.T.S. 39, *entered into force* Sept. 13, 1963. When the OAU was established it did not focus on the protection of human rights. Instead, the governments were concerned with ending apartheid, decolonizing, promoting stability, preventing international interference, and increasing cooperation. The OAU adopted its human rights treaty, the African Charter on Human and Peoples' Rights, in 1981. African [Banjul] Charter on Human and Peoples' Rights, OAU Doc. CAB/LEG/67/3 rev. 5, 21 I.L.M. 58 (1982), *entered into force* Oct. 21, 1986. As of January 1995, 49 African governments had ratified the Charter.

The African Charter contains clauses roughly comparable to those in other human rights instruments—covering economic, social, and cultural as well as civil and political rights. Its distinctive features include the right to development, various duties of the individual to family, state, society, and recognized communities, and state duties such as the duty to strengthen the national independence and contribute to its defense. Unlike the Covenant on Civil and Political Rights, the Charter contains no clause permitting derogation in times of emergency. It also establishes no form of judicial review of its Commission on Human and Peoples' Rights, the body charged with supervising implementation of the Charter. The Commission can take measures to promote human rights such as researching specific situations, organizing seminars and conferences, giving recommendations to states, setting out human rights principles, and cooperating with other international organizations. The power to protect human rights is much weaker and consists only of receiving communications on human rights violations.

The Commission monitors states' behavior via two procedures: First, the Charter requires that states submit reports on implementation of human rights to the Commission every two years. The Commission reviews the report, conducts an oral examination with representatives of the state, and gives opinions and recommendations to the governments. In practice, the process has not been effective. As of December 1994, only 17 states had submitted reports; and only two, Senegal and The Gambia, had submitted more than one. Wolfgang Benedek, *Enforcement of Human and Peoples' Rights in Africa—The Communication System and State Reporting Under the African Charter*, 15 NETH. Q. HUM. RTS. 36 (1995). Results of the examinations have not been published, which makes follow-up by the Commission or other organizations difficult. If the states did comply with the reporting requirement the Commission would likely be overwhelmed and unable to examine them all. Measures are currently being taken to increase compliance with the report procedure.

The Commission also has power to receive and review communications from states and other sources. No interstate communications have yet been submitted. The individuals' procedure can be invoked by victims of violations or by anyone else on behalf of victims. Most complaints have been filed by NGOs on behalf of African citizens; but individuals, groups of individuals, and even non-African states could also file complaints. After receiving a communication, the Commission makes a decision first on admissibility and then on the merits. The decision is communicated to the applicant, the state, and the OAU Assembly of Heads of State and Governments. Remedies for violations are limited. When communications reveal a series of serious violations the OAU Assembly may request an in-depth study and a report from the Commission. Other possible but less formal remedies include publicity, fact-finding missions, and the use of special rapporteurs.

Some scholars have criticized the African system for its inadequate implementation of procedures. The Charter evidences a commitment to human rights but lacks the necessary mechanisms to disseminate and enforce. New procedures and the creation of a judicial body have been suggested, and in March 1995, the Commission passed a resolution for the establishment of an African Court on Human Rights. *See* Wolfgang Benedek, *Enforcement of Human and Peoples' Rights in Africa—The Communication System and State Reporting Under the African Charter*, 15 INTERNATIONAL PROTECTION OF HUMAN RIGHTS, NETHERLANDS INSTITUTE OF HUMAN RIGHTS 23 (1995); H.W.O. Okoth-Ogendo, *Human and Peoples' Rights: What Point is Africa Trying to Make?, in* HUMAN RIGHTS AND GOVERNANCE IN AFRICA 74-86 (Ronald Cohen et al. eds., 1993).

For further reading see:

JOHN AKPALU, ENFORCING THE AFRICAN CHARTER ON HUMAN AND PEOPLES' RIGHTS: AN ANALYSIS OF THE LEGAL AND INSTITUTIONAL FRAMEWORK (1991);

AMNESTY INTERNATIONAL, A GUIDE TO THE AFRICAN CHARTER ON HUMAN AND PEOPLES' RIGHTS (1991);

Amnesty International, *Observations on Possible Reform of the African Charter on Human and Peoples' Rights*, AI Index: IOR 63/03/93 (1993);

Wolfgang Benedek, *The African Charter and Commission on Human and Peoples' Rights; How to Make it More Effective*, 11 NETH. Q. HUM. RTS. 25 (1993);

THOMAS BUERGENTHAL, INTERNATIONAL HUMAN RIGHTS IN A NUTSHELL, 228 (1995);

Cees Flinterman & Evelyn Ankumah, *The African Charter on Human and Peoples' Rights, in* GUIDE TO INTERNATIONAL HUMAN RIGHTS PRACTICE 159 (Hurst Hannum ed., 2d ed. 1992);

MUNYONZWE HAMALENGWA ET AL., THE INTERNATIONAL LAW OF HUMAN RIGHTS IN AFRICA: BASIC DOCUMENTS AND ANNOTATED BIBLIOGRAPHY (1988);

HUMAN RIGHTS IN AFRICA: CROSS-CULTURAL PERSPECTIVES (Abdullahi Ahmed An-Na'im & Francis Deng eds., 1990);

Makau wa Mutua, *The Banjul Charter and the African Cultural Fingerprint: An Evaluation of the Language of Duties*, 35 VA. J. INT'L L. 339 (1995);

Anselm Chidi Odinkalu, *Proposals for Review of the Rules of Procedure of the African Commission on Human and Peoples' Rights*, 15 HUM. RTS. Q. 533 (1993);

THE ORGANIZATION OF AFRICAN UNITY AFTER THIRTY YEARS (Yassin El Ayouty ed., 1994);

ORGANIZATION OF AFRICAN UNITY, REVIEW OF THE AFRICAN COMMISSION ON HUMAN AND PEOPLES' RIGHTS (1991);

Claude Welch, *The African Commission on Human and Peoples' Rights: A Five-Year Report and Assessment*, 14 HUM. RTS. Q. 43 (1992).

2.   Other Regional Structures

Asian governments have not adopted regional treaties or created enforcement mechanisms like the Inter-American Court, the European Court of Human Rights, or the African Commission.[3] The failure in part may be due to the great variety of government systems, religions, philosophies, and cultural traditions of Asian countries. Governments in the Asian region for good reason may lack a sense of regional identity and cohesiveness necessary for the establishment of inclusive regional organizations and human rights machineries.

Varying sub-regional structures, such as the South Asia Association for Regional Cooperation (SAARC), the Association of Southeast Asian Nations (ASEAN), the South Pacific Forum, and the South Pacific Commission have been established. These organizations are based mostly on political, economic, and security concerns, however, and have taken little action regarding human rights. It is possible that they will help lead to establishing human rights structures in the future. The Pacific sub-region, for instance, has taken preliminary steps toward developing a human rights system, with proposals for a Pacific Charter on Human Rights and a commission to enforce it. Virginia Leary, *The Asian Region and the International Human Rights Movement, in* ASIAN PERSPECTIVES ON HUMAN RIGHTS 13 (Claude Welch & Virginia Leary eds., 1990); *cf Bangkok Declaration, in* OUR VOICE: BANGKOK NGO DECLARATION ON HUMAN RIGHTS 242 (1993); ASIAN PERSPECTIVES ON HUMAN RIGHTS (Virginia Leary & Claude Welch eds., 1990).

Human rights also have been addressed by Arab and Islamic states. The League of Arab States established a Human Rights Commission in 1968 and in 1994 adopted an Arab Charter on Human Rights. As of January 1995, there had been no ratifications.

The Arab Organization for Human Rights, established in 1983, was created to protect civil and political rights. In its Declaration of the Tunis Conference of 1983, members called for freedom of thought and expression, freedom from torture and violence, and acknowledgment of the U.N. Declaration of Human Rights. Jill Crystal, *The Human Rights Movement in the Arab World*, 16 HUM. RTS. Q. 435 (1994).

In 1990, the Organization of the Islamic Conference (OIC), to which Muslim governments belong, adopted the Cairo Declaration on Human Rights in Islam. It concerns a variety of rights such as those involving life, equality, property, travel, fair trial, health, and education. The Cairo Declaration offers a more limited range of rights, however, than does the International Bill of Human Rights, which the OIC has endorsed in other pronouncements. Its Article 6(b), for example, states "the husband is responsible for the support and welfare of the family." It is unclear how strictly the rights to equality and protection against discrimination will be interpreted. Ann Elizabeth Mayer, *Universal Versus Islamic Human Rights: A Clash of Cultures or a Clash with a Construct?*, 15 MICH. J. INT'L L. 307 (1994); *cf.* KEVIN DWYER, ARAB VOICES: THE HUMAN RIGHTS DEBATE IN THE MIDDLE EAST (1991).

---

[3] *See* van Dyke, *Prospects for the Development of Intergovernmental Human Rights Bodies in Asia and the Pacific, in* NEW DIRECTIONS IN HUMAN RIGHTS 51 (Ellen Lutz, Hurst Hannum, & Kathryn Burke, eds., 1989); Hiroko Yamane, *Approaches to Human Rights in Asia, in* INTERNATIONAL ENFORCEMENT OF HUMAN RIGHTS 99 (R. Bernhardt & J. Jolowicz, eds., 1987).

CHAPTER 11

WHAT CAN U.S. LAWYERS LEARN FROM THE EUROPEAN HUMAN RIGHTS SYSTEM?

A.	Introduction	Page 467
B.	Questions	468
C.	Areas of Protection in the European Court of Human Rights	470
	1. Homosexuality	470
	Dudgeon v. United Kingdom	470
	2. Death Penalty	476
	Soering v. United Kingdom	476
	3. Corporal Punishment	478
D.	Remedies in the European Court of Human Rights	478
	1. Bringing a Case	479
	2. Damage Awards	481
	Sporrong and Lönnroth v. Sweden	482
	3. Parallel Remedies Outside the European System	486
	Inter-American Court of Human Rights	486
	U.N. Compensation Commission	488
	U.S. Courts	488
E.	Interstate Human Rights Cases in the European System: The Greek Case	489
F.	Human Rights Law in Europe Apart From the European Convention	491
	1. European Union (EU)	491
	2. Organization for Security and Cooperation in Europe (OSCE)	494
	3. North Atlantic Treaty Organization (NATO)	496

A. INTRODUCTION

The preceding chapter examined regional systems for implementing and enforcing human rights law in Africa, the Americas, and Asia. This chapter examines the instruments and procedures of the European human rights systems.

The leading European organization for the promotion and protection of human rights is the Council of Europe, created in 1949. After Nazism, European governments concluded that international duties regarding human rights should not solely be those of the U.N. and its members. The original Council of Europe members, motivated too by a fear of Communism and hopes for a united Europe, saw the need for a treaty that would provide a mechanism for enforcing compliance with a limited set of human rights norms.

In 1950, the Council approved the European Human Rights Convention, which entered into force in 1953. [European] Convention for the Protection of Human Rights and Fundamental Freedoms, 213 U.N.T.S. 222 (1950), *entered into force* Sept. 3, 1953 (European Convention). As of March 1996, thirty-eight governments are parties to the Convention. The treaty established three organs for handling violations: the European Commission of Human Rights, the Committee of Ministers, and the European Court of Human Rights.

The European Convention emphasizes civil and political rights. It protects rights to life, liberty, and security of the person as well as privacy, freedom of conscience and religion, peaceful assembly, free association, and due process. It also proscribes servitude, forced labor, and discrimination based on race, gender, or national origin. Eleven protocols have been annexed that abolish the death penalty and codify rights to property, education, free elections, and travel.

The 11th Protocol, signed in 1994, will, when ratified, restructure the organization. For example, it will abolish the European Commission and focus enforcement work on the European Court of Human Rights. *See infra* at *16*. The Convention will, however, continue to apply to every individual within the jurisdiction of every ratifying government, whether or not she or he is a citizen.

In that respect, the European system is more developed than any of the other regional human rights systems. The Court has also helped create a more extensive jurisprudence than that of other regional systems, and also, under Article 50 of the European Convention, it has gone the farthest in providing judicial remedies for human rights violations.

U.S. legislators, administrators, courts, and lawyers may benefit from examining the European system. In several areas it has provided more protection to individuals than do U.S. courts and administrative agencies. Also, the U.S. has ratified several treaties, including the U.N. Covenant on Civil and Political Rights, which contain language similar to that in the European Convention and may be interpreted in the light of European experience. This chapter will look at cases involving the death penalty and rights of homosexuals in Europe, and will contrast achievements there with lesser progress made in the U.S. and elsewhere.

This chapter also will describe other European-based structures that play a role in protecting human rights, including the European Union (EU), Organization for Security and Cooperation in Europe (OSCE), and the North Atlantic Treaty Organization (NATO).

B. QUESTIONS

Homosexuals are subjected to discriminatory treatment in Europe, the U.S., and elsewhere. Legislatures, administrators, and courts have had to consider (1) whether freedom from discrimination based on sexual orientation should be a human right or (2) whether homosexuality should be criminalized. The U.S. Supreme Court analyzed issues of consensual, adult, homosexual activity in *Bowers v. Hardwick*, 478 U.S. 186 (1986):

One evening in 1982 a police officer entered the home of Michael Hardwick, a Georgia resident, under a warrant for drinking in public. The officer found him engaged in homosexual behavior and arrested him for violating Georgia's sodomy statute. The district attorney chose not to prosecute because he believed he had little chance of securing a favorable verdict if the case went to trial.

Hardwick filed a constitutional challenge against the statute. The U.S. district court dismissed the case for failure to state a claim on which relief could be granted. The appellate court reversed, finding error in the failure to recognize the right of homosexual privacy. In a 5 to 4 decision the U.S. Supreme Court upheld the sodomy statute because it furthered Georgia's interest in preserving morality, and the U.S. Constitution does not protect a right to engage in homosexual conduct. In a concurring opinion, Chief Justice Burger explained:

> Decisions of individuals relating to homosexual conduct have been subject to state intervention throughout the history of Western Civilization. Condemnation of those practices is firmly rooted in Judeao-Christian moral and ethical standards. Homosexual sodomy was a capital crime under Roman law and the Western Christian Tradition. During the English Reformation when powers of the ecclesiastical courts were transferred to the King's Courts, the first English statute criminalizing sodomy was passed. Blackstone described "the infamous crime against nature" as an offense of "deeper malignity" than rape, a heinous act "the very mention of which is a disgrace to human nature," and "a crime not fit to be named." The common law of England, including its prohibition of sodomy, became the received law of Georgia and other Colonies. In 1816 the Georgia Legislature passed the statute at issue here, and that statute has been continuously in force in one form or another since that time. To hold that the act of homosexual sodomy is somehow protected as a fundamental right would be to cast aside millennia of moral teaching.

Id. at 196-97 (citations omitted).

The European Court of Human Rights took a different approach toward consensual homosexual conduct and upheld it as a human right protected by the European Convention.

As you read this chapter, consider the following questions:

1. How might *Bowers* be decided by the European Court of Human Rights?

    a. What clauses of the European Convention are most relevant in deciding the case?

    b. Are there similar clauses in the U.S. Constitution or the U.N. Covenant on Civil and Political Rights that could be interpreted to reach the same result?

2. How does the European Court assess damages?

    a. In homosexuality cases, why has the Court awarded only costs and expenses and not damages?

    b. Does the pronouncement of a violation in itself really provide "just satisfaction" under Article 50 of the European Convention?

    c. How does the Court quantify non-pecuniary damages?

    d. How does the Court's assessment of remedies compare with that of other international courts? Of U.S. courts?

3.   How does the European system differ from the Inter-American system discussed in the previous chapter?

    a.   Which seems generally more effective?

    b.   Which seems more effective at handling individual cases?

    c.   Which seems more effective at ending gross and widespread violations?

4.   What roles do the OSCE and the EU seem to play in promoting and protecting human rights?

5.   Can the OSCE process be viewed as a means of integrating Eastern Europe into the Council of Europe and other European institutions? In other words, does the road to Brussels (center of the European Union) start at Helsinki (origin of the OSCE) and go through Strasbourg (center of the Council of Europe)?

    a.   If all European states join the Council of Europe what role might the U.S. play?

    b.   Would a human rights system in Europe be more protective if the U.S. did or did not participate?

    c.   Would human rights in the U.S. be improved if the Helsinki process were to become the focus of European economic, political, and human rights cooperation?

C.   AREAS OF PROTECTION IN THE EUROPEAN COURT OF HUMAN RIGHTS

1.   Homosexuality

***Dudgeon v. United Kingdom*, 45 Eur. Ct. H.R. (ser. A) (1982), 4 Eur. H.R. Rep. 149 (1981) (several paragraphs and citations omitted):**

13.   Mr. Jeffrey Dudgeon, who is 35 years of age, is a shipping clerk resident in Belfast, Northern Ireland.

    Mr. Dudgeon is a homosexual and his complaints are directed primarily against the existence in Northern Ireland of laws which have the effect of making certain homosexual acts between consenting adult males criminal offences. . . .

24.   On 27 July 1978, the Government published a proposal for a draft Homosexual Offences (Northern Ireland) Order 1978, the effect of which would have been to bring Northern Ireland law on the matter broadly into line with that of England and Wales. In particular, homosexual acts in private between two consenting male adults over the age of 21 would no longer have been punishable. . . .

25.   The numerous comments received by the Government in response to their invitation, during and after the formal period of consultation, revealed a substantial division of opinion. On a simple count of heads, there was a large majority of individuals and institutions against the proposal for a draft Order. . . .

[The Parliament decided in 1979 not to pursue the proposed reform.]

    E.   *Enforcement of the law in Northern Ireland*

30.   During the period from January 1972 to October 1980 there were 62 prosecu-

tions for homosexual offences in Northern Ireland. The majority of these cases involved minors, that is persons under 18; a few involved persons aged 18 to 21 or mental patients or prisoners. So far as the Government are aware from investigation of the records, no one was prosecuted in Northern Ireland during the period in question for an act which would clearly not have been an offence if committed in England or Wales. There is, however, no stated policy not to prosecute in respect of such acts . . . .

[In January 1976, police entered the applicant's home under a warrant to search for drugs. As a result, another person was charged with a violation of the Misuse of Drugs Act. The police also found and seized Mr. Dudgeon's personal papers, which included descriptions of his homosexual activities. He was questioned extensively by police about his sexuality. A year later he was informed that no proceedings would be brought against him and his papers were returned.]

DECISION:

I.   *THE ALLEGED BREACH OF ARTICLE 8*

   A.   *Introduction*

37.   The applicant complained that under the law in force in Northern Ireland he is liable to criminal prosecution on account of his homosexual conduct and that he has experienced fear, suffering and psychological distress directly caused by the very existence of the laws in question, including fear of harassment and blackmail. . . .

   He alleged that, in breach of Article 8 of the [European] Convention, he has hereby suffered, and continues to suffer, an unjustified interference with his right to respect for his private life.

38.   Article 8 provides as follows:

   1.   Everyone has the right to respect for his private and family life, his home and correspondence.

   2.   There shall be no interference by a public authority with the exercise of this right except such as is in accordance with the law and is necessary in a democratic society in the interests of national security, public safety or the economic well-being of the country, for the prevention of disorder or crime, for the protection of health or morals, or for the protection of the rights and freedoms of others.

39.   Although it is not homosexuality itself which is prohibited but the particular acts of gross indecency between males . . ., there can be no doubt but that male homosexual practices whose prohibition is the subject of the applicant's complaints come within the scope of the offences punishable under the impugned legislations; it is on that basis that the case has been argued by the Government, the applicant and the Commission. . . .

   B.   *The existence of an interference with an Article 8 right*

40.   The Commission saw no reason to doubt the general truth of the applicant's allegations concerning the fear and distress that he has suffered in consequence of the existence of the laws in question. The Commission unanimously concluded that "the legislation complained of interferes with the applicant's right to respect for his private life guaranteed by Article 8(1), in so far as it prohibits homosexual acts committed in private between consenting males". . . .

41.   The Court sees no reason to differ from the views of the Commission: the maintenance in force of the impugned legislation constitutes a continuing interference with the applicant's right to respect for his private life (which includes his sexual life) within the meaning of Article 8(1). In the personal circumstances of the applicant, the very existence of this legislation continuously and directly affects his private life. . . .

C.   *The existence of a justification for the interference found by the Court*

43.   An interference with the exercise of an Article 8 right will not be compatible with Article 8(2) unless it is 'in accordance with the law', has an aim or aims that is or are legitimate under that paragraph and is 'necessary in a democratic society' for the aforesaid aim or aims. . . .

45.   It next falls to be determined whether the interference is aimed at 'the protection of . . . morals' or 'the protection of the rights and freedoms of others', the two purposes relied on by the Government. . . .

49.   There can be no denial that some degree of regulation of male homosexual conduct, as indeed of other forms of sexual conduct, by means of the criminal law can be justified as 'necessary in a democratic society'. The overall function served by the criminal law in this field is, in the words of the Wolfenden report, 'to preserve public order and decency [and] to protect the citizen from what is offensive or injurious'. Furthermore, this necessity for some degree of control may even extend to consensual acts committed in private, notably where there is call to provide sufficient safeguards against exploitation and corruption of others, particularly those who are specially vulnerable because they are young, weak in body or mind, inexperienced, or in a state of special physical, official or economic dependence.

In practice there is legislation on the matter in all the member-States of the Council of Europe, but what distinguishes the law in Northern Ireland from that existing in the great majority of the member-States is that it prohibits generally gross indecency between males and buggery whatever the circumstances. It being accepted that some form of legislation is 'necessary' to protect particular sections of society as well as the moral ethos of society as a whole, the question in the present case is whether the contested provisions of the law of Northern Ireland and their enforcement remain within the bounds of what, in a democratic society, may be regarded as necessary in order to accomplish those aims.

50.   A number of principles relevant to the assessment of the 'necessity', 'in a democratic society', of a measure taken in furtherance of an aim that is legitimate under the Convention have been stated by the Court in previous judgments.

51.   First, 'necessary' in this context does not have the flexibility of such expressions as 'useful', 'reasonable', or 'desirable', but implies the existence of a 'pressing social need' for the interference in question.

52.   In the second place, it is for the national authorities to make the initial assessment of the pressing social need in each case; accordingly, a margin of appreciation is left to them. However, their decision remains subject to review by the Court. . . .

56.   . . . Northern Ireland society was said to be more conservative and to place greater emphasis on religious factors . . . .

Although the applicant qualified this account of the facts as grossly exaggerated, the Court acknowledges that such differences do exist to a certain extent and are a relevant factor. As the Government and the Commission both emphasised, in assessing the requirements of the protection of morals in Northern Ireland, the contested measure must be seen in the context of Northern Ireland society.

The fact that similar measures are not considered necessary in other parts of the United Kingdom or in other member-States of the Council of Europe does not mean that they cannot be necessary in Northern Ireland. . . .

59.   Without any doubt, faced with these various considerations, the United Kingdom Government acted carefully and in good faith; what is more, they made every effort to arrive at a balanced judgment between the differing viewpoints before reaching the conclusion that such a substantial body of opinion in Northern Ireland was opposed to a change in the law that no further action should be taken. Nevertheless, this cannot of itself be decisive as to the necessity for the interference with the applicant's private life resulting from the measures being challenged. Notwithstanding the margin of appreciation left to the national authorities, it is for the Court to make the final evaluation whether the reasons it has found to be relevant were sufficient in the circumstances, in particular whether the interference complained of was proportionate to the social need claimed for it.

60.   The Convention right affected by the impugned legislation protects an essentially private manifestation of the human personality.

As compared with the era when that legislation was enacted, there in now a better understanding, and in consequence an increased tolerance, of homosexual behaviour to the extent that in the great majority of the member-States of the Council of Europe it is no longer considered to be necessary or appropriate to treat homosexual practices of the kind now in question as in themselves a matter to which the sanctions of the criminal law should be applied; the Court cannot overlook the marked changes which have occurred in this regard in the domestic law of the member-States. In Northern Ireland itself, the authorities have refrained in recent years from enforcing the law in respect of private homosexual acts between consenting males over the age of 21 years capable of valid consent. No evidence has been adduced to show that this has been injurious to moral standards in Northern Ireland or that there has been any public demand for stricter enforcement of the law.

It cannot be maintained in these circumstances that there is a 'pressing social need' to make such acts criminal offences, there being no sufficient justification provided by the risk of harm to vulnerable sections of society requiring protection or by the effects on the public. On the issue of proportionality, the Court considers that such justifications as there are for retaining the law in force unamended are outweighed by the detrimental effects which the very existence of the legislative provisions in question can have on the life of a person of homosexual orientation like the applicant. Although members of the public who regard homosexuality as immoral may be shocked, this cannot on its own warrant the application of penal sanctions when it is consenting adults alone who are involved.

61.   Accordingly, the reasons given by the Government, although relevant, are not sufficient to justify the maintenance of force of the impugned legislation in so far as it has the general effect of criminalising private homosexual relations between adult males capable of valid consent. In particular, the moral attitudes toward male

homosexuality in Northern Ireland and the concern that any relaxation in the law would tend to erode existing moral standards cannot, without more, warrant interfering with the applicant's private life to such an extent. 'Decriminalisation' does not imply approval, and a fear that some sectors of the population might draw misguided conclusions in this respect from reform of the legislation does not afford a good ground for maintaining it in force with all its unjustifiable features.

     To sum up, the restriction imposed on Mr. Dudgeon under Northern Ireland law, by reason of its breadth and absolute character, is, quite apart from the severity of the possible penalties provided for, disproportionate to the aims sought to be achieved.

62. . . . The Court has already acknowledged the legitimate necessity in a democratic society for some degree of control over homosexual conduct notably in order to provide safeguards against the exploitation and corruption of those who are specially vulnerable by reason, for example, of their youth. However, it falls in the first instance to the national authorities to decide on the appropriate safeguards of this kind required for the defence of morals in their society and, in particular, to fix the age under which young people should have the protection of the criminal law.

     D. *Conclusion*

63. Mr. Dudgeon has suffered and continues to suffer an unjustified interference with his right to respect for his private life. There is accordingly a breach of Article 8. . . .

III. *THE APPLICATION OF ARTICLE 50* . . .

71. Counsel for the applicant stated that, should the Court find the Convention to have been violated, his client would seek just satisfaction under Article 50 in respect of three matters: first, the distress, suffering and anxiety resulting from the police investigation in January 1976; secondly, the general fear and distress suffered by Mr. Dudgeon since he was 17 years of age; and finally, legal and other expenses. . . .

     The Government, for their part, asked the Court to reserve the question.

72. Consequently, although it was raised under Rule 47 *bis* of the Rules of Court, this question is not ready for decision and must be reserved; in the circumstances of the case, the Court considers that the matter should be referred back to the Chamber in accordance with Rule 50(4) of the Rules of Court. . . .

NOTES AND QUESTIONS

1. The Court awarded 3,315 pounds sterling (at that time, $6000 in the U.S.) for costs and expenses. Though the Court acknowledged emotional suffering, neither pecuniary nor non-pecuniary damages were awarded.

2. Article 50 of the Convention empowers the Court to award "just satisfaction." What that means is addressed only after the Court determines that the complainant has proved a violation of the Convention. *See infra* at 20.

3. The European Court of Human Rights reaffirmed *Dudgeon* in *Norris v. Northern Ireland*, 142 Eur. Ct. H.R. (ser. A) (1988) and *Modinos v. Cyprus*, 259 Eur. Ct. H.R. (ser. A) (1993). In *Modinos*, the president of the Liberation Movement of Homosexuals in Cyprus complained

that he suffered from a fear of prosecution because a Cypriot statute criminalized homosexual activities. The government argued that though the statute existed, it was not in force. The Court held that mere existence of the legislation violated the applicant's right to privacy under Article 8.

The *Dudgeon* and *Norris* decisions led Northern Ireland in 1993 to pass the Criminal Law (Sexual Offences) Act, which decriminalized homosexual acts between consenting adults over the age of 17.

4.   In March 1994, the U.N. Human Rights Committee examined a Tasmanian statute which criminalized sexual intercourse between men. The communication was submitted by a member of the Tasmanian Gay Law Reform Group. *Toonen v. Australia* (No. 488/1992), U.N. Doc. CCPR/C/50/D/488/1992 (1994). The Committee mentioned the *Dudgeon* case in passing and reasoned that the statute infringed privacy, was neither reasonable nor necessary, and therefore violated the U.N. Covenant on Civil and Political Rights. *Id.* at 11.

5.   No words in the U.S. Constitution expressly protect family life. By five votes to four the Supreme Court upheld Georgia's sodomy statute in *Bowers v. Hardwick, see supra* at 469. Ten years after *Bowers*, the Supreme Court struck down an amendment to the Colorado Constitution which repealed and prohibited any legislative, executive, or judicial acts to protect homosexuals. In a 6-3 decision, the Court held that the amendment violated the Equal Protection clause of the Fourteenth Amendment by singling out a specific group and denying them a right to seek protection from the government. *Romer v. Evans*, 64 U.S.L.W. 4353 (1996).

The majority failed to use international jurisprudence in supporting its decision and did not even cite *Bowers*. *See also Hurley v. Irish-American Gay, Lesbian and Bisexual Group of Boston*, 115 S.Ct. 2338 (1995).

6.   In its paragraph 59, the *Dudgeon* Court left a "margin of appreciation" to governments. This doctrine says that governments may determine situations and measures to be taken, but only under international control. A "margin of appreciation" is necessary because international tribunals face the problem of how far to pursue factual and legal questions on a national level, while still respecting the sovereignty of individual states. *See* DAVID BEATTY, HUMAN RIGHTS AND JUDICIAL REVIEW 308 (1994); R. ST. J. MACDONALD, THE EUROPEAN SYSTEM FOR THE PROTECTION OF HUMAN RIGHTS (MacDonald et al. eds., 1993).

7.   The right to private life has also been invoked in a series of cases concerning transsexuals. The applicant in each case had undergone gender-conversion surgery and sued national officials for refusing to take account of her or his new status.

In *Rees v. United Kingdom*, 106 Eur. Ct. H.R. (ser. A) (1986), Rees complained that English law did not allow modification of birth certificates to reflect her changed gender. The Court stated that in determining whether to recognize changed gender a balance had to be struck between the interest of the community and the individual's interest. The Court ruled that the U.K. was entitled to a wide margin of appreciation because, with regard to transsexuals, there is little agreement among European states. The Court held that Article 8 had not been violated but noted that, as the Convention must be interpreted and applied in light of current circumstances, the government was required to keep appropriate legal measures under review. The decision was reaffirmed in *Cossey v. United Kingdom*, 184 Eur. Ct. H.R. (ser. A) (1990).

The European Court distinguished conditions in France from those in the U.K. by holding that not allowing a post-operative transsexual to change her birth certificate and other official documents violated Article 8. *B. v. France*, 232 Eur. Ct. H.R. (ser. A) (1992). In the U.K., birth certificates are treated as historic facts, while in France they are updated regularly. Also, France has more stringent laws against transsexuals that make civil status and name changes more difficult than in other countries.

8.   *See also* LOUKES LOUKAIDES, ESSAYS ON THE DEVELOPING LAW OF HUMAN RIGHTS, 94-5 (1995);

Brenda Sue Thornton, *The New International Jurisprudence on the Right to Privacy: A Head-On Collision with Bowers v. Hardwick*, 58 ALB. L. REV. 725 (1995); Pieter van Dijk, *The Treatment of Homosexuals under the European Convention on Human Rights, in* HOMOSEXUALITY: A EUROPEAN COMMUNITY ISSUE 179 (Kees Waaldijk & Andrew Clapham eds., 1993).

2. Death Penalty

The European approach to the death penalty is far more restrictive of the death penalty than is U.S. law. Nearly all parties to the European Convention have abolished the death penalty. Though the European Convention does not ban the death penalty *per se*, Article 3 prohibits inhuman or degrading treatment or punishment. Additionally, several governments have ratified Protocol 6, which explicitly abolishes the death penalty. By March 1996, twenty-four governments had ratified the protocol.

The United States allows its constituent states to decide whether or not to impose the death penalty. The European Court of Human Rights commented on that U.S. stance and Virginia's treatment of death row inmates in *Soering v. United Kingdom*, 161 Eur. Ct. H.R. (ser. A) (1989).

Jens Soering, a German national, brought a complaint alleging that the United Kingdom's agreement that he should be extradited to the U.S. violated Article 3 of the European Convention, which prohibits inhuman or degrading treatment or punishment. Soering had admitted that he killed two people in Virginia during 1985. He fled to England, where he was arrested for an unrelated offense in 1986.

U.S. officials requested that Soering be extradited to the U.S. The British embassy asked for assurance, as a condition of extradition, that the death penalty would not be carried out. The prosecutor in Virginia said he would seek the death penalty for Soering, but Virginia authorities assured the British embassy that they would explain the U.K.'s position on the death penalty to the sentencing judge. The U.K. agreed to extradite, and Soering challenged the decision, citing Article 3 of the European Convention.

The European Court of Human Rights set out a two-part test to determine if the extradition would violate Article 3. First the Court asked whether truly there was a risk that Soering would be sentenced to death. The Court found there was a substantial risk, based on Soering's confession and the prosecutor's statement that he would seek the death penalty. Second, the Court asked whether the treatment Soering would receive if sentenced to death constitutes inhuman or degrading treatment in violation of Article 3.

Article 3 does not, of course, proscribe the death penalty *per se*. The 6th Protocol to the Convention bans the penalty, but the U.K. has not ratified it. Imposition of the penalty without more, therefore, does not constitute a breach of the Convention.

To determine whether Soering would be subjected to inhuman or degrading treatment, the Court examined Soering's personal characteristics and the circumstances on death row. The Court noted that at the time of the homicides Soering was just eighteen years old and that his mental state was substantially impaired. The Court found that Soering would likely experience the "death row phenomenon," which it defined as the extreme mental anguish and psychological impacts experienced by inmates awaiting death. In Virginia the average inmate on death row waits six to eight years before execution. Medical evidence showed that Soering already had experienced extreme dread of physical violence and homosexual abuse which had severe psychiatric effects on him.

A unanimous Court concluded that, in the light of (1) the long wait on death row and the mental anguish already suffered by the applicant and typical of death row inmates, and (2) the applicant's young age and mental condition at the time of the killings, a risk of a breach of Article 3 had been proved. Because Soering had not been extradited, there was no actual violation of the Convention. Therefore, the Court awarded Soering only costs and expenses.

The U.S. government did not formally appear in the *Soering* case. It considered making an appearance, but instead, decided that the U.K. would adequately represent U.S. interests. After the decision, the prosecutor in Virginia amended the charges to remove the offense of capital murder. The United Kingdom then extradited Soering for trial in Virginia, where he was found guilty and received a life sentence.

Soering should be compared to extradition cases in other jurisdictions. In *Ahmad v. Wigen*, 910 F.2d 1063 (2d Cir. 1990), a U.S. circuit court denied the accused's petition for habeas corpus to prevent his extradition from the U.S. to Israel. He was charged with terrorist activity on a bus in Israeli-occupied territory. The court held that judges should not consider the risk to the life of the accused in determining whether extradition is appropriate. *Id.* at 1066.

In *Kindler v. Canada*, [1991] 2 S.C.R. 779, and *Reference re Ng Extradition v. Canada*, [1991] 2 S.C.R. 858, the Canadian Supreme Court approved the extradition of two prisoners to the United States despite the potential that they would face the death penalty. Petitioner Ng then filed a communication with the U.N. Human Rights Committee, arguing that as a result of extradition he faced a substantial risk of execution by gas asphyxiation in violation of his rights under the Covenant on Civil and Political Rights. The Committee decided that since Canada could reasonably foresee the imposition of death by gas asphyxiation and did not seek assurance from the U.S. that the penalty would not be imposed, the Covenant's requirement of the "least possible physical and mental suffering" had been violated. U.N. GAOR, Hum. Rts. Comm., 49th Sess., U.N. Doc. CCPR/C/49/D/469 at 21 (1991).

The authors of an amicus brief encouraged a U.S. appeals court to follow similar reasoning in affirming *Fierro v. Gomez*. Brief of Amici at 7. In *Fierro*, a California federal court held that execution by gas asphyxiation violates the eighth amendment to the U.S. Constitution, which protects against cruel and unusual punishment. *Fierro v. Gomez*, 865 F.Supp 1387 (N.D. Cal. 1994). In February 1996, the ninth circuit affirmed the district court's holding. *Fierro v. Gomez*, No. 94-16775, 1996 U.S. App. LEXIS 2867 (9th Cir. Feb. 21, 1996). The result suggests support for the Human Rights Committee position. In 1992, Canada refused to extradite Lee O'Bomsawin to Florida to stand trial for double murder unless Florida guaranteed that the death penalty would not be sought. *See* John Burns, *Canada Wins U.S. Extradition Deal*, N.Y. TIMES, Feb. 14, 1992, at A3.

NOTES AND QUESTIONS

1. *Forti v. Suarez-Mason*, 672 F. Supp. 1531 (N.D. Cal. 1988), held that the prohibition against torture is a customary norm enforceable in U.S. courts, but that the U.N. prohibition of cruel, inhuman or degrading treatment or punishment is not. Is *Forti* consistent with *Soering*?

2. Compare the reasoning in *Dudgeon* and *Soering*, on the one hand, with the *Baby Boy* and *Roach* cases discussed in chapter 10, on the other. Should the U.S. be more receptive to the decision-making process of the European Court or of the Inter-American Commission?

3. For further reading see Sandra Coliver, *European Court of Human Rights Condemns*

Conditions on Virginia's Death Row, 13 HUMAN RIGHTS ADVOCATES NEWSLETTER 23 (November 1989).

---

3.   Corporal Punishment

We have seen that the European Convention provides certain protection for homosexuals and for prisoners facing extradition. Corporal punishment exemplifies another area in which the European system protects individual human rights to a greater extent than do United States courts.

Florida students argued that corporal punishment violated their rights in *Ingraham v. Wright*, 430 U.S. 651 (1977). The Court held first, that the 8th Amendment prohibition of cruel and unusual punishment does not apply to discipline in public schools, and second, that the Due Process clause does not require notice and a hearing before corporal punishment is imposed.

In *Tyrer v. United Kingdom*, 26 Eur. Ct. H.R. (ser. A) (1978), the Court considered whether the birching of a 15-year-old boy, ordered by an Isle of Man court, contravened the prohibition of "torture and inhuman or degrading treatment or punishment" in Article 3 of the European Convention. The Court held that birching undermined the boy's dignity and physical integrity and thus did violate Article 3. The Court conceded that every punishment is somewhat degrading, and based its standard for "degrading punishment" on the degree of humiliation endured.

In *Campbell and Cosans v. United Kingdom*, 60 Eur. Ct. H.R. (ser. A) (1982), the two complainants attended schools that used leather straps on misdemeanant students. Mrs. Campbell requested assurance from her son's school that he would not be strapped, but the school refused her request. Jeffrey Cosans was to have received the punishment, but on his father's advice, refused to accept it and was then suspended from school. The Court held there was no violation of Article 3, because corporal punishment was only threatened and the boys in fact had not been struck. Article 2 of Protocol 1, however, was held to have been violated. That provision requires that public schools respect the religious and philosophical convictions of parents; and, further, the suspension of Cosans was also a violation of the right to education. The case led to a prohibition against corporal punishment in U.K. state schools.

The European Court addressed corporal punishment in private schools in *Costello-Roberts v. United Kingdom*, 247-C Eur. Ct. H.R. (1993). A seven-year-old boy had been hit three times on the buttocks with a rubber-soled shoe. The Court held that evidence of the punishment's effects had not been presented and, therefore, the minimum level of humiliation needed to establish a violation of Article 3 had not been met. See the discussion of corporal punishment in chapter 4, *supra*.

D.   REMEDIES IN THE EUROPEAN COURT OF HUMAN RIGHTS

Aside from developing a substantial body of human rights jurisprudence and enjoying a remarkable record of compliance with its decisions, the European Court has been a leader in providing compensatory remedies for individual victims. Article 50 of the Convention grants it the power to provide "just satisfaction" to injured parties. This section will introduce procedures for bringing a case through the European Court and discuss remedies that have been awarded. The Court's assessment of damages will be compared with damage awards in other international systems.

1. Bringing a Case

Article 25 of the European Convention allows governments to accept the competence of the Court to hear applications by individuals. In addition, under Article 24, any State Party to the Convention may allege violations by other states. Applications brought by one state against another, however, are rare. *See infra* at *31*. Most of the cases heard by the Court are brought against a state by or on behalf of individuals.

Originally a tripartite structure was established to enforce the Convention. The European Commission on Human Rights presided during the beginning stages of a case. The Commission determined admissibility, established facts, encouraged friendly settlement, and issued opinions on whether the alleged activity violated the Convention.

After the Commission decision, cases were referred for judgment to either the Committee of Ministers or the European Court. The Committee of Ministers is composed of the Foreign Ministers of member states or their representatives who, unlike members of the Commission and Court, serve as government representatives rather than in their individual capacities. The Committee of Ministers ruled on violations of the Convention if cases could not be, or were not, referred to the Court. The Committee also enforced the Court's judgments.

In recent years, the number of cases increased significantly. More applications have been referred to the Court by the Commission, and new states have joined the Council of Europe. To illustrate, 404 applications were filed with the Commission in 1981 compared with 2,944 filed in 1994. The average case takes five years to reach final judgment. To prevent an overlap of duties and to increase efficiency, the member states signed Protocol 11 to the Convention in 1994. This protocol will have the effect of amending the Convention when ratified by all member states. As of March 1, 1996, all thirty-eight states had signed the protocol; but only nineteen had ratified. Most significant among the changes is the creation of a single, permanent Human Rights Court in place of the current Commission and Court.

Cases will begin when an application is registered with the Court. A three-judge panel will then rule on admissibility, and complaints may be dismissed as inadmissible only by a unanimous decision. For a case to be admissible, the applicant must be a "victim"; the alleged violation must have been perpetrated by a government; the applicant must have exhausted all available national remedies; the application must not be anonymous; the issue must not be substantially the same as in any case previously rejected by the Commission or Court; the complaint must not be ill-founded; the violation must fit within the scope of protections provided in the Convention; and the application must be filed within six months of the national decision. The panel's determination of admissibility is final.

If at least one panel member finds the case admissible, the complaint will be communicated to the defendant government; and the case will be assigned for decision by a Court Chamber, comprised of seven judges. Written evaluations will be taken, and oral hearings may be held by the Chamber. Friendly settlement negotiations will be conducted; and, if unsuccessful, the Chamber will issue a judgment.

After judgment, applicants may apply for an appeal to a Grand Chamber consisting of 17 judges. Five members of the Grand Chamber will consider the request for appeal and determine whether the case merits re-examination. Only in exceptional cases will individuals' cases be referred to a Grand Chamber; interstate cases, however, will be assigned directly to it.

The Committee of Ministers will continue to supervise the execution of the Court's judgment. Though the Committee's supervision of compliance with judgments sometimes has been criticized as perfunctory, states adjudged to be in violation of the Convention generally have been prepared to take corrective action. If a state refuses to comply with a decision of the Court, the Committee of Ministers could suspend or expel the state from the Council of Europe. Such action has not so far been necessary, but from 1969 to 1974, Greece withdrew from the Convention to avoid being suspended. *See infra* at *32*.

The European system has compiled its jurisprudence patiently. Though the Commission received more than 2,700 applications in its first 13 years of operation, it referred only three cases to the Court. During the same period, the Committee of Ministers considered only 10 cases. The figures reflect narrow interpretations that the Commission initially gave to the Convention, finding admissible less than one half of one percent of the first 2,700 applications.

The European Court gradually compiled its jurisprudence and had received 620 cases from the Commission as of March 1, 1996. Its first decision, the *Lawless Case*, 1961 Y.B. Eur. Conv. on Human Rights 430 (Eur. Ct. H.R.), was issued in 1961. The Court's opinion described the kind of public emergency that would permit derogations from the Convention under Article 15.

The Court subsequently has addressed applications invoking the Convention's guarantees to a fair public trial, the presumption of innocence, and the right to counsel. Other claimants successfully have alleged violations of the Convention's prohibition against torture and inhuman or degrading treatment or punishment. The Court also has examined allegations that state criminal procedures have unreasonably deprived persons of liberty. Of particular interest to the U.S. is the *Soering Case*, 161 Eur. Ct. H.R. (ser. A) (1989) (*see supra* at *13*), in which the Court concluded that a German national could not be extradited to Virginia because he might face prolonged detention on death row.

The increased awareness by Europeans of the existence of the European Convention produced a steady rise in the number of applications the Commission received each year. The system clearly has been successful in implementing the human rights codified in the Convention. Its case by case approach has not, however, been an adequate response to massive and gross violations such as those arising in connection with migrant-labor crises, for example, or in the former Yugoslavia.

NOTES AND QUESTIONS

1. For further reading, see:

RALPH BEDDARD, HUMAN RIGHTS AND EUROPE (3d ed. 1993);

Kevin Boyle, *Europe: The Council of Europe, the CSCE, and the European Community*, in GUIDE TO INTERNATIONAL HUMAN RIGHTS PRACTICE 133 (Hurst Hannum ed., 2d ed. 1984);

THOMAS BUERGENTHAL, INTERNATIONAL HUMAN RIGHTS IN A NUTSHELL 102-59 (1995);

ANDREW CLAPHAM, HUMAN RIGHTS IN THE PRIVATE SPHERE (1993);

LUKE CLEMENTS, EUROPEAN HUMAN RIGHTS: TAKING A CASE UNDER THE CONVENTION (1994);

Andrew Drzemczewski, *The Role of NGOs in Human Rights Matters in the Council of Europe*, 8 H.R.L.J. 273 (1987);

Andrew Drzemczewski, *A Single Court of Human Rights in Strasbourg*, Directorate of Human Rights, Council of Europe (Dec. 31, 1995);

MARK JANIS & RICHARD KAY, EUROPEAN HUMAN RIGHTS LAW (2d ed. 1995);

DIGEST OF STRASBOURG CASE-LAW RELATING TO THE EUROPEAN CONVENTION ON HUMAN RIGHTS (Peter Leuprecht & Pieter van Dijk, eds., 1984);

JOHN MERRILLS, THE DEVELOPMENT OF INTERNATIONAL LAW BY THE EUROPEAN COURT OF HUMAN RIGHTS 34-41 (1988); A.H. ROBERTSON & JOHN MERRILLS, HUMAN RIGHTS IN EUROPE: A STUDY OF THE EUROPEAN CONVENTION ON HUMAN RIGHTS (3d ed. 1993);

MICHAEL SPENCER, STATES OF INJUSTICE, A GUIDE TO HUMAN RIGHTS AND CIVIL LIBERTIES IN THE EUROPEAN UNION (1995);

PIETER VAN DIJK & G.J.H. VAN HOOF, THEORY AND PRACTICE OF THE EUROPEAN CONVENTION OF HUMAN RIGHTS (2d ed. 1990);

Karel de Vey Mestdagh, *Reform of the European Convention on Human Rights in a Changing Europe, in* 3 THE DYNAMICS OF THE PROTECTION OF HUMAN RIGHTS IN EUROPE 337 (Rick Lawson & Matthijs de Blois eds., 1994);

TOM ZWART, THE ADMISSIBILITY OF HUMAN RIGHTS PETITIONS: THE CASE LAW OF THE EUROPEAN COMMISSION OF HUMAN RIGHTS AND THE HUMAN RIGHTS COMMITTEE (1994).

2. Damage Awards

The European Court is unique among international bodies because routinely it imposes sanctions on governments for violating the human rights of their nationals. Even though it has no power to grant equitable relief or to order revisions of national law, most governments willingly comply with its decisions. The Court's power goes beyond investigating violations and focussing public attention on them. Article 50 of the Convention states:

> If the Court finds that a decision or a measure taken by a legal authority or any other authority of a High Contracting Party is completely or partially in conflict with the obligations arising from the . . . Convention, and if the internal law of the said Party allows only partial reparation to be made for the consequences of this decision or measure, the decision of the Court shall, if necessary, afford just satisfaction to the injured party.

The European Court gradually developed its authority to grant pecuniary relief and did not grant relief under Article 50 until 1974. In *Neumeister v. Austria*, 17 Eur. Ct. H.R. (ser. A) (1974), the Court found a violation of Article 5 but awarded only legal fees of 30,000 Austrian schillings (at that time $1,800 in the U.S.). The Court first awarded more than costs and expenses in granting "token indemnity" of 100 Dutch guilders ($37) in *Engel and Others v. the Netherlands*, 22 Eur. Ct. H.R. (ser. A) (1976).

In 1980 the Court began a more active approach, awarding damages to five applicants in that year alone. Currently, the Court awards at least some damages in almost all cases where it finds a violation. The Court, however, devotes more attention to reimbursement of applicants' costs and expenses than it does to awarding compensation for harm.

The Court offers a variety of rationales for granting only costs and expenses. Most commonly it explains that a finding that the Convention has been breached itself is sufficient "just satisfaction" under Article 50. Often the Court finds too that the causal relation between the breach found and the harm alleged is not sufficiently evident to merit an award of either pecuniary or non-pecuniary damages.

The Court has developed three categories for awarding damages. First, pecuniary damages are awarded when a material or economic harm can be quantified. To receive pecuniary damages the applicant must prove actual harm and a causal connection to the alleged violation. For example, in *Campbell and Cosans v. United Kingdom*, 60 Eur. Ct. H.R. (ser. A) (1983), the Court found that the threat of corporal punishment breached the parents' rights but refused to award damages because of lack of evidence of the requisite degree of humiliation.

Second, non-pecuniary damages (also called moral damages) may be needed to address emotional suffering or interference with protected rights. Non-pecuniary damages are difficult to quantify. The practice of awarding non-pecuniary damages was established in *Artico v. Italy*, 37 Eur. Ct. H.R. (ser. A) (1980), where an alleged criminal was awarded damages for the anxiety and emotional suffering he endured while wrongfully detained and deprived of legal aid.

The third category is "costs and expenses," which includes legal fees and also expenses such as travel and accommodations. To receive costs and expenses, the applicant must establish that they were actually and necessarily incurred and that the amount is reasonable. In most cases where a breach of the Convention is found, the Court awards at least partial reimbursement of costs and expenses.

The greatest number of awards stems from violations of the Convention's Article 6, which guarantees a fair trial before an impartial tribunal within a reasonable time—in both civil and criminal cases. A case that primarily concerns other rights, such as the right to property, may be decided on fair-trial grounds alone. The Court may find no violation of the underlying right but still find a violation of Article 6.

The primary concern in awarding damages for violating the right to trial within a "reasonable time" seems to be the length of time spent in the national adjudicative proceedings. Anxiety and uncertainty have also provided a basis for large awards. In *H. v. France*, 162 Eur. Ct. H.R. (ser. A) (1989), a mental patient was given massive amphetamine injections without permission in 1961. A process ensued that lasted from 1971 to 1989. The Court awarded 50,000 French francs (at that time worth $8,013) for "anxiety and uncertainty" and "frustration and helplessness." The complainant also received 40,000 French francs ($6,410) for costs and expenses.

In roughly half of the criminal cases where the Court found violations of the "fair hearing" and "impartial tribunal" mandates, it has awarded pecuniary or non-pecuniary damages along with costs and expenses; in the remainder of cases, the Court gave only costs and expenses.

Article 6 protections often arise in relation to the right to property prescribed by Article 1 of Protocol 1. One of the largest damage awards by the Court was in *Sporrong and Lönnroth v. Sweden*, 88 Eur. Ct. H.R. (ser. A) (1985). The applicants alleged pecuniary and non-pecuniary damage, in addition to costs and expenses, for harm to the value of their real estate holdings, Riddaren No. 8 and Barnhuset No. 6. The Swedish government had threatened imminent expropriation of the property for more than ten years and also prohibited construction on building sites:

I. *EXISTENCE OF DAMAGE*

19.   In its above-mentioned judgement, the Court left open the question of the existence of damage (Series A no. 52, p. 28, section 73). . . . In the Court's view, the length of the validity of the expropriation permits affecting Riddaren No. 8 and Barnhuset No. 6 had had "prejudicial effects", which had been accentuated even further by the prohibitions on construction. As was alleged before and found by the

Court, the reduction of the possibility of disposing of the properties concerned had had several effects, namely difficulties of selling and normal market prices and of obtaining loans secured by way of mortgage, and additional risks involved in the event of expenditure being incurred; there was also the prohibition on any "new construction". The Court further noted that the applicants were left in complete uncertainty as to the fate of their properties and were not entitled to have any difficulties which they might have encountered taken into account by the Swedish Government.

20.   In order to decide whether or not the applicants have been prejudiced, the Court has to determine during which periods the continuation of the measures complained of was in violation of Protocol No. 1 (the "periods of damage") and then which constituent elements of damage warrant examination.

(a) Duration

21.   The expropriation permits remained in force for twenty-three years as regards Riddaren No. 8 and for eight years as regards Barnhuset No. 6. . . .

22.   The Court finds it reasonable that a municipality should, after obtaining an expropriation permit, require some time to undertake and complete the planning needed to prepare the final decision on the expropriation contemplated.

In the present case, four years should, in the Court's view, have been sufficient for the Stockholm City Council to arrive at decisions. The periods of damage should therefore be taken to be nineteen years for Riddaren No. 8 and four years for Barnhuset No. 6.

(b) Constituent elements

23.   . . . [T]he information before the Court does not prove that the return from the properties in question diminished on account of the excessive duration of the expropriation permits. . . .

25.   Whilst a comparison between the beginning and the end of the periods of damage thus does not show that the applicants were prejudiced in financial terms, the Court nevertheless does not conclude that there was no loss within that period.

There are, in fact, other factors which also warrant attention. Firstly, there are the limitations on the utilisation of the properties: the applicants could not erect any "new construction" on their own land and they would have exposed themselves to serious risks if, even with permission, they had had work carried out since they would have been obliged to undertake not to claim—in the event of expropriation - any indemnity for the resultant capital appreciation. To this were added the difficulties encountered in obtaining loans secured by way of mortgage; thus, Mrs. Lönnroth failed to obtain a loan for the renovation of the facade of Barnhuset No. 6.

In addition, it cannot be forgotten that during the periods of damage the value of the properties in question naturally fell; it is evident that a property which is subject to an expropriation permit and may thus be taken away from its owner at any moment will not continuously retain its former value, even though in the present case the applicants' properties were, after the said periods, once again worth no less in real terms than they were when the measures in question were adopted. Furthermore, any scheme for the redevelopment of the properties which the applicants may have contemplated was impracticable at the time. In this respect, they may be said to have suffered a loss of opportunities of which account must taken, notwithstanding the fact that the prospects of realisation would have been questionable.

Above all, the applicants were left in prolonged uncertainty. . . .

27.   The assessment of the damage suffered presents particular difficulties on this occasion and is thus very problematical. The difficulties turn in part on the technical nature of real-estate matters, the complexity of the calculations made by the experts acting for the applicants and for the Government and the intervening changes in the claims put forward by the injured parties; they arise above all from the virtual impossibility of quantifying, even approximately, the loss of opportunities. . . .

31.   . . . [T]he circumstances of the case prompt the Court to confine itself to, and make an overall assessment of, the factors which it has found to be relevant (duration and constituent elements of damage; see paragraphs 22 and 25 above).

32.   In conclusion, the violations of Article 1 of Protocol No. 1 [the right to property] and of Article 6 section 1 [the right to a fair hearing] of the Convention did cause prejudice to the applicants. The damage suffered is made up of a number of elements which cannot be severed and none of which lends itself to a process of precise calculation. The Court has taken these elements together on an equitable basis, as is required by Article 50. For this purpose, it has had regard, firstly, to the differences in value between Riddaren No. 8 and Barnhuset No. 6 and, secondly, to the difference between the two periods of damage.

The Court thus finds that the applicants should be afforded satisfaction assessed at 800,000 SEK [\$7,064,000] for the Sporrong Estate and at 200,000 SEK [\$1,766,000] for Mrs. Lönnroth.

II.   *COSTS AND EXPENSES* . . .

39.   The Court will apply the criteria which emerge from its case-law in the matter. . . . It has no reason to doubt that the applicants' expenses were actually incurred since it is in possession of the corresponding vouchers. As to whether they were necessarily incurred and were reasonable as to quantum, the Court finds that the amount of the costs and fees is high. However, it notes that this can be explained by at least two factors. In the first place, there is the length of the proceedings, nearly ten years having elapsed since the applications were lodged with the Commission. In the second place, there is the complexity of the case: it was not unreasonable to have recourse to the services of experts for the submission of the claims for just satisfaction, and the Agent of the Government also consulted specialists in real-estate matters.

The Court cannot, however, retain certain expenses which it is not persuaded were necessarily incurred: fees of Mr. Tullberg and Mr. Ahrenby for preparing documents which the Court has not taken into account, estimated at 50,000 SEK; sums paid to jurists for consultations and a legal course (149,512.54 SEK); tax on translation services and research work (14,797.60 SEK); costs for which bills have not yet been received (25,000 SEK).

In these circumstances, the applicants are entitled to be reimbursed in respect of costs and expenses, the sum of 723,865.75 SEK [\$6,391,734.50], less the 24,103 FF [\$227,773] received by Mrs. Lönnroth by way of legal aid.

FOR THESE REASONS, THE COURT

1.   *Holds* by twelve votes to five that the Kingdom of Sweden is to pay, for damage,

eight hundred thousand Swedish crowns (800,000 SEK) to the Sporrong Estate and two hundred thousand Swedish crowns (200,000 SEK) to Mrs. Lönnroth;

2.   *Holds* by thirteen votes to four that the Kingdom of Sweden is to pay, for costs and expenses, seven hundred and twenty-three thousand eight hundred and sixty-five Swedish crowns and seventy-five ore (723,865.75 SEK), less twenty-four thousand one hundred and three French francs (24,103 FF), to the Sporrong Estate and Mrs. Lönnroth jointly.

* * * * *

It is unusual for the European Court of Human Rights to grant such a large award or to take into account hypothetical possibilities. *Sporrong and Lönnroth* drew the Court into an unusual degree of speculation in calculating an award based on economic fruits of a hypothetical situation—sale or development under market conditions at a time which was past.

In December 1994, the Court granted another large award for a violation of Article 6. The case was against Greece for costs resulting from early termination of a contract. The Court granted pecuniary damages of over $16,000,000 plus costs and expenses. *Stran Greek Refineries and Stratis Andreadis v. Greece*, 15 H.R.L.J. 432 (1994).

Though most damage awards have been granted in Article 6 cases the Court has given relief for violations of other clauses as well. Damages have been granted for violations of Article 3 (prohibition of torture), Article 5 (right to liberty and security), Article 8 (right to respect for private and family life), Article 10 (freedom of expression), Article 11 (right to assembly and association), Article 12 (right to marry), Article 14 (prohibition of discrimination), Article 1 of Protocol 1 (protection of property), and Article 2 of Protocol 1 (right to education).

Sometimes the severity or lack of severity of the harm seems to provide a rationale for the award. Often, however, awards seem to be based primarily on the effectiveness of an applicant's pleading and proof of damages. In particular, proving a causal relation between the breach and the harm alleged is critical.

The Court often holds that its finding of a violation is sufficient "just satisfaction" under Article 50 in cases similar to cases where damages had been awarded. Possibly the Court is now examining the facts of cases and dispensing justice on a case-by-case basis. The equities governing particular awards are not always readily apparent.

It bears noting that some of the Court's most memorable and influential cases resulted in no or small awards. Numerous dissents regarding damages in *Marckx v. Belgium*, 31 Eur. Ct. H.R. (ser. A) (1979), stemmed partly from the difficulty of estimating the economic value of the harm to "family life." Belgian law required a formal act of recognition by a mother to establish her parentage of a child born out of marriage and also penalized the recognized children by restricting their rights of inheritance more than the rights of an unrecognized child or a stranger. Harm unquestionably was great in terms of the self-esteem and personality development of "illegitimate" children. The Court found discrimination in violation of Article 14, but ultimately refused even token damages.

In the homosexuality cases, *Dudgeon* and *Norris*, only costs and expenses were awarded even though the applicants had suffered emotional and mental harm. Other awards for violations of Article 8's right to respect for private and family life, however, have included non-pecuniary damages. For example, in *Erickson v. Sweden*, 156 Eur. Ct. H.R. (ser. A) (1989), a mother prevented from removing her daughter from foster care after public care had ended was awarded non-pecuniary damages.

In *Keegan v. Ireland*, 15 H.R.L.J. 193(1994), the Court granted separate awards for pecuniary damages, non-pecuniary damages, and costs and expenses in an Article 8 case. Keegan's girlfriend had given birth to a daughter of whom he was the father on September 29, 1988. During pregnancy, the relationship between Keegan and his girlfriend ended. Keegan saw the child when she was one-day old, but was refused access when he tried to visit her two weeks later. The mother had the child placed with adoptive parents on November 17, 1988, and informed Keegan of the adoption on November 22. The applicant complained that his right to family life had been breached, because the adoption proceedings had taken place without his knowledge or consent. He did not attempt to reverse the adoption.

The Court held that Irish law permitting the secret adoption had interfered with the applicant's family life in violation of Article 8. It awarded pecuniary damages for his expenses during the custody proceedings, non-pecuniary damages for his trauma and anxiety, plus costs and expenses.

Emotional harm certainly existed in each of these Article 8 cases. The homosexual's right to "family life" or personal relations under Article 8 would appear to have been less-highly valued than the rights of conventional families. Not surprisingly, the pattern of actual awards may reflect judges' subjective views of which harms are more painful or more important.

NOTES AND QUESTIONS

1. Why does the Court seem reluctant to grant monetary damages in some situations and not others?

2. Does the Court place more value on violations of property rights than on violations of other rights?

3. What does an applicant gain from a favorable decision on the merits but no monetary damages?

4. For further reading, see LUKE CLEMENTS, EUROPEAN HUMAN RIGHTS: TAKING A CASE UNDER THE CONVENTION 82-93 (1994).

3. Parallel Remedies Outside the European System

The Inter-American Court of Human Rights, a few other international tribunals, and U.S. courts also have awarded damages to individuals for human rights violations by governments. They have not yet granted remedies as extensively and compliance has not yet been as successful, however, as under the European Court of Human Rights.

The Inter-American Court of Human Rights, discussed in chapter 10, *supra*, has power to award damages similar to that of the European Court. Article 63(1) of the American Convention on Human Rights states:

> If the Court finds that there has been a violation of a right or freedom protected by this Convention, the Court shall rule that the party be ensured the enjoyment of his right or freedom that was violated. It shall also rule, if appropriate, that the consequences of the measure or situation that constituted breach of such right or freedom be remedied and that fair compensation be paid to the injured party.

American Convention on Human rights, O.A.S. Off. Rec. OEA/Ser.L./V/II.23, doc. 21, rev. 6 (1979), *entered into force* July 18, 1978.

That provision, however, is based on acceptance by governments of the contentious jurisdiction of the Inter-American Court. Of 25 states that have ratified the American Convention, only 16 have recognized that jurisdiction. A state may accept contentious jurisdiction at any time or for a specific case, but this limited acceptance rarely occurs in practice. The contentious function of the Court allows it to adjudicate disputes that challenge a member state based on an alleged violation of the American Convention on Human Rights. The Court also performs an advisory function, which allows it to interpret the American Convention on Human Rights and other treaties of governments in the Western Hemisphere.

Damages have been awarded less frequently by the Inter-American Court than by the European Court. Some complainants, however, have received substantial monetary awards.

In a series of cases against Honduras, damages were awarded for loss of income and moral harm. The Court held Honduran officials liable in each case for designing and implementing a plan to cause disappearances of citizens that resulted in death. *Velasquez Judgment*, Inter-Am. Ct. H.R. (ser. C) No. 4 (1988); *Godinez Judgment*, Inter-Am. Ct. H.R. (ser. C) No. 5 (1989); *Fairen and Solis Judgment*, Inter-Am. Ct. H.R. (ser. C) No. 6 (1989). The Court noted that out-of-pocket expenses, similar to costs and expenses in the European system, could be awarded, but had not been substantially proven. Compensation awarded is equal to a combination of the pecuniary and non-pecuniary damages in the European system. The families of the victims also requested punitive damages, but the Court held that Article 63(1) is only compensatory in nature. *See* Juan Mendez & Jose Vivanco, *Disappearances and the Inter-American Court: Reflections on a Litigation Experience*, 13 HAMLINE L. REV. 507 (1990).

Enforcement of damage awards in the Inter-American system generally is not as successful as in the European system. The European Convention sets up a procedure under which the Council of Ministers oversees compliance with decisions of the European Court and can suspend or expel con-complying states from the Council of Europe. The American Convention has no such formal enforcement mechanism. The only action the Court takes against non-complying states is to identify them in its annual report to the OAS General Assembly. Voluntary compliance, without the need for formal enforcement measures, is also not as successful in the Inter-American system. Most parties to the European Convention pay damages willingly and amend their laws to comply with European Court interpretations of the Convention. Also, complainants in the Inter-American system have had difficulty collecting damages and have received delayed payments—often diminished by inflation.

The Inter-American Court awarded damages in two cases against the state of Suriname, which has recognized the contentious jurisdiction of the Court since 1987. One case concerned the responsibility of Suriname for the detention, torture, and death of Gangaram Panday. *Gangaram Panday Case*, Judgment of January 21, 1994, Inter-Am. Ct. H.R. The Court found that detention by military police was a violation of Article 7(2) of the Convention, the right to physical liberty. The Court did not find a violation based on torture or wrongful death, due to a lack of conclusive evidence. The Court ordered Suriname to pay $10,000 to the victim's family within six months of the January 1994 judgment. Suriname has not yet complied, but the Court requested the General Assembly of the OAS to urge Suriname to pay the damages in its annual report for 1994.

The other case against Suriname, decided in September 1993, arose after seven men were detained, beaten, and killed by soldiers. The Court granted reparations, to be paid by Suriname, to the injured parties and an established Foundation. Of the

$453,102 granted to the complainants, Suriname has made only a partial payment of $134,990. *Aloeboetoe et al. Case*, Judgment of September 10, 1993, Inter-Am. Ct. H.R. The Court also reported on that judgment to the OAS General Assembly. *See Annual Report of the Inter-American Court of Human Rights,* ORGANIZATION OF AMERICAN STATES 17-18 (1994); *see also* David J. Padilla, *Reparations in Aloeboetoe v. Suriname,* 17 HUM. RTS. Q. 541 (1995).

The United Nations too has granted damage awards for human rights violations. On April 3, 1991, the Security Council passed resolution 687 creating the United Nations Compensation Commission (UNCC). It was designed to manage the compensation due thousands, perhaps millions, of victims of the 1990-91 Iraqi occupation of Kuwait. During the occupation, civilians were tortured, raped, and killed; were used as human shields; were taken as hostages; and were compelled to serve in Iraq's armed forces. Support for war-crimes trials quickly arose. The size and scope of the project are broader than any war tribunal in history. Resolution 687 prescribes that Iraq is liable for damages caused by the unlawful invasion of Kuwait. The resolution sets up a Governing Council, a Secretariat, groups of Commissioners to administer compensation, and a fund from which to draw compensation.

Damage claims are divided into six categories: (1) claims of non-Iraqis who left Iraq or Kuwait as a result of the invasion; (2) claims for personal injury or death, including physical and mental suffering; (3) claims for personal loss, such as business loss, amounting to less than $100,000; (4) claims of individuals amounting to more than $100,000; (5) claims of corporations; and (6) claims of governments and international organizations.

Commissioners have awarded damages for an initial group of complaints under the first three categories, and some small awards have been paid. Awards are set, for example, at $4,000 for victims under the first category—departure from Iraq or Kuwait—and $2,500 under the second category for personal injury or death. Complainants need provide only simple documentation to prove the harms they allege. The UNCC is continuing to issue damage awards in response to the more-than 2,000,000 complaints submitted. It is now facing the problem of securing funding for the awards, which could reach $100 billion. *See* Commission on Human Rights, *Study Concerning the Right to Restitution, Compensation, and Rehabilitation for Victims of Gross Violations of Human Rights and Fundamental Freedoms,* U.N. Doc. E/CN.4/Sub.2/1993/8 (1993); David Bederman, *The United Nations Compensation Commission and the Tradition of International Claims Settlement,* 27 N.Y.U. J. INT'L L. & POL. 1 (1994); Ronald Bettauer, *The United Nations Compensation Commission Developments Since October 1992,* 89 AM. J. INT'L L. 417 (1995); John Crook, *The United Nations Compensation Commission—A New Structure to Enforce State Responsibility,* 87 AM. J. INT'L L. 144 (1993); Gregory DiMeglio, *Claims Against Iraq: The UN Compensation Commission and Other Remedies,* 86 AM. SOC. INT'L L. PROC. 477 (1992); Frank Newman, *Redress for Gulf War Violations of Human Rights,* 28 DENVER J. INT'L L. S. POL'Y 213 (1992).

U.S. courts too have awarded damages against states for violations of international human rights standards. The cases are described in chapter 12, *infra*. In *Filartiga v. Peña-Irala,* 630 F.2d 876 (2d Cir. 1980), for example, Joel and Dolly Filartiga filed a suit against the Paraguayan Inspector General of Police for wrongful death and torture. The court awarded $375,000 in compensatory damages and $10 million in punitive damages. Punitive damages are awarded in U.S. courts to punish the defendant and to deter the defendant and others from behaving similarly in the future. The European Court has never awarded punitive damages. Efforts to recover the damages from Peña have proven unsuccessful.

In *Letelier v. Chile*, 502 F.Supp. 259 (D.C. 1980), the court approved large damage awards to two victims' families who asserted several tort claims including wrongful death for the bombing deaths of a Chilean ambassador, Orlando Letelier, and his passenger, Ronni Moffitt. The two were killed as a result of an explosion in Letelier's automobile while they were driving through Washington, D.C., on September 21, 1976. The family of Letelier recovered $30,000 for pain and suffering, $1,000,000 in punitive damages, and $1,526,479 for wrongful death, for a total of $2,556,479. The family of Moffitt received $80,000 for pain and suffering, $1,000,000 in punitive damages, and $916,096 for wrongful death, totaling $1,176,096. Michael Moffitt also was awarded $400,000 for his pain and suffering as the only surviving passenger of the car. In addition, the plaintiffs were awarded $110,220 jointly for costs and expenses. *Id* at 267-68.

The U.S. attempted for several years to secure the damage award on behalf of the Letelier and Moffitt families. In 1990 the government of Chile agreed to make an *ex gratia* payment, without admitting liability, in an amount determined by the Commission established under the 1914 Treaty for the Settlement of Disputes that May Occur Between the United States and Chile. The Commission awarded $1,696,400 to Letelier's family and $915,492 to Moffitt's. The figures were based on lost wages, moral damages, and direct medical expenses. *Contemporary Practice of the United States Relating to International Law*, 86 AM. J. INT'L L. 346 (1992).

Another large award was granted to over 9,000 plaintiffs in *Marcos, Human Rights Litigation*, a group of cases brought against the former Philippine leader for torture and wrongful deaths. In February 1994, a jury awarded $1.2 billion in punitive damages; and in January 1995 the same jury awarded more than $800 million in compensatory damages. The case currently is on appeal. *See* Joan Fitzpatrick & Paul Hoffman, *Human Rights Litigation Update Report*, ACLU INTERNATIONAL CIVIL LIBERTIES REPORT 30 (Mar. 1995).

NOTES AND QUESTIONS

1. Why does the European Court of Human Rights receive so much compliance as compared with the Inter-American Court?

2. Why are damage awards for international human rights violations so much larger in the U.S. courts than in the European or Inter-American courts?

3. For further reading, see Burns Weston et al., *Regional Human Rights Regimes: A Comparison and Appraisal*, 20 VAND. J. TRANSNAT'L L. 585 (1987); *see also* Michael Bochenek, *Compensation for Human Rights Abuses in Zimbabwe*, 26 COLUM. HUM. RTS. L. REV. 483 (1995).

E. INTERSTATE HUMAN RIGHTS CASES IN THE EUROPEAN SYSTEM

Another characteristic of the European human rights system has been the use of intergovernmental procedures. While the individual-petition procedure of Article 25 of the Convention is optional, all states parties have in Article 24 agreed to intergovernmental complaints of violations. Though these procedures exist in some other systems, they rarely have been invoked. Even under the European Convention there have been only 18 intergovernmental applications, relating to only six situations:

(a)   *Greece v. United Kingdom*, 2 Y.B. European Conv. Hum. Rts. 182-99 (1958-59); 18 Y.B. European Conv. Hum. Rts. 94 (1975)(two applications by Greece against the United Kingdom relating to Cyprus during 1956-57);

(b)   *Austria v. Italy*, 4 Y.B. European Conv. Hum. Rts. 116-82 (1961); 6 Y.B. European Conv. Hum. Rts. 740-800 (1963)(six youths contended that they had not received a fair trial for murder of a customs official);

(c)   *Denmark, Netherlands, Norway, & Sweden v. Greece; Denmark, Norway, & Sweden v. Greece*, 12 Y.B. Eur. Conv. Hum. Rts. (1969)(four applications relating to torture by the Greek colonels)(see note below);

(d)   *Cyprus v. Turkey*, 18 Y.B. European Conv. Hum. Rts. 82-126 (1975); 21 Y.B. European Conv. Hum. Rts. 100-246 (1978); 22 Y.B. European Conv. Hum. Rts. 440 (1979)(two applications by Cyprus relating to violations of the rights of Greek Cypriots after Turkey invaded Cyprus);

(e)   *Ireland v. United Kingdom*, 19 Y.B. European Conv. Hum. Rts. 516 (1976); 20 Y.B. Eur. Conv. Hum. Rts. 602 (1978)(12 suspected I.R.A. members were subjected to five interrogation techniques that constituted inhuman or degrading treatment);

(f)   *Denmark, France, Netherlands, Norway, & Sweden v. Turkey*, 35 Eur. Comm. Hum. Rts. 143-70 (1984)(five applications concerning torture, resolved by friendly settlement in 1985, including Turkey's agreement to accept individual petitions under Article 25).

*   *   *   *   *

The Greek case probably is the most dramatic use of state versus state complaints under the European Convention. It arose out of the April 1967 military coup in Greece. Immediately after taking power, the new government imposed martial law and suspended certain rights under that law and also under Article 15 of the Convention. Reports of mass arrests, torture, and other violations filtered out of Greece. The reports prompted four countries—Norway, Sweden, Denmark, and the Netherlands—to file applications to the Commission charging multiple violations of human rights.

The Commission considered the case for two years. It received submissions from the parties as to admissibility and then held hearings on the merits. The Greek government protested the intrusion and imposed economic sanctions against the four countries but continued to participate in the proceedings. The turning point came when a subcommission, formed to examine the merits, visited Greece. The government allowed some witnesses to appear but refused access to others and forbade on-site visits to notorious prisons. After its visit the subcommission refused to grant further extensions of time and began negotiations seeking a friendly settlement. No settlement was reached because the Greek government refused to establish a timetable for elections. On November 5, 1969, the Commission adopted its report and sent it to the Committee of Ministers. On December 11, 1969, the Committee independently was preparing to vote on a proposed suspension of Greece from the Council of Europe. It had to wait three months, but the contents of the report doubtless were influential at the final December meeting. Greek representatives walked out of the meeting when it became clear the vote would go against Greece. The government then withdrew from both the Council of Europe and the Convention. *See* Becket, *The Greek Case Before the European Human Rights Commission*, 1 HUM. RTS. 91 (1970); *The Greek Case*, 12 Y.B. Eur. Conv. on Hum. Rts. (1969) (Eur. Comm'n on Hum. Rts.); *The Greek Case*, Council of Europe (Committee of Ministers) (1970).

The U.N. Commission on Human Rights and its Sub-Commission on Prevention of Discrimination and Protection of Minorities also considered the issue of violations of human rights in Greece, under ECOSOC resolution 1503. *See* chapter 5, *supra*. For further reading on the treatment of Greece at the U.N., see RICHARD LILLICH & FRANK NEWMAN, INTERNATIONAL HUMAN RIGHTS: PROBLEMS OF LAW AND POLICY 340-71 (1979).

After Greece left the Council of Europe, European banks denied financing to Greece. The military government continued, however, bolstered by apparent support from the U.S. and elsewhere. In 1973, a coup established new leadership, but the military remained in power until it invaded Cyprus. The U.S. supported Turkey in the ensuing struggle, and a new coup overthrew the government in July 1974. The new government convicted accused torturers under Greek law. For more information, see AMNESTY INTERNATIONAL, TORTURE IN GREECE: THE FIRST TORTURERS' TRIAL 1975 (1977).

NOTES AND QUESTIONS

1.   Why do governments seem reluctant to bring actions against other governments? Might the same considerations apply to inter-state complaints against Eastern European governments that have now ratified the European Convention?

2.   Why have some governments overcome reluctance in certain cases?

3.   In view of the paucity of intergovernmental complaints, can they be considered an effective implementation-approach for the European Convention?

4.   For further reading, see Iain Cameron, *Turkey and Article 25 of the European Convention on Human Rights*, 37 INT'L & COMP. L. Q. 887 (1988); Scott Leckie, *The Inter-State Complaint Procedure in International Human Rights Law: Hopeful Prospects or Wishful Thinking?*, 10 HUMAN RIGHTS Q. 249 (1988).

F.   HUMAN RIGHTS LAW IN EUROPE APART FROM THE EUROPEAN CONVENTION

1.   European Union

The European Union (EU) consists of 15 member states: Austria, Belgium, Denmark, Finland, France, Germany, Greece, Ireland, Italy, Luxembourg, Netherlands, Portugal, Spain, Sweden, and the United Kingdom. (Austria, Finland, and Sweden finally joined in January 1995, and the EU may continue to expand in years ahead.) The European Community ("Common Market"), established in 1967, was restructured and renamed The European Union by the 1993 Maastricht Treaty.

Though the EU primarily deals with economic and social issues, it has issued directives and developed policies pertinent to human rights, particularly concerning employment discrimination, equality, migrant workers, freedom of association, education, fair application of the law, and related concerns. Human rights have become more important as the EC/EU has developed. For example, the Maastricht Treaty expands the rights of free movement, transportation, and residence for all individuals under the jurisdiction of EU member states. Two branches of the European Union, the European Court of Justice and the European Parliament, have dealt with human rights.

The European Court of Justice interprets and applies EU law. It also has a law-making function and has played an important role in shaping the EU law and that of its member states. The Court follows general principles of national and international law. Though no EU treaty contains a bill of rights, general principles of law have offered related human rights protections. Through its decisions, the Court has established human rights doctrines including, for example, protection against gender and other discrimination, the right to be heard, and the right to a fair hearing.

The European Court of Justice first referred to the protection of human rights in the *Stauder Case*, Case 29/69, E.C.R. 419 (1969). In *Stauder*, a German national challenged a Commission decision that required elderly welfare recipients to reveal their names in order to purchase butter at a reduced price. The complainant found this practice degrading and cited the German constitutional provisions prohibiting discrimination and ensuring the principle of proportionality. Because no treaty was relevant to this case, the ECJ found there was no conflict between the Commission decision and Community law. Significantly, however, it referred to protection of human rights as part of Community law when it observed that "human rights are enshrined in the general principles of Community law and protected by the Court." *Id.* at 425.

In the *Internationale Handelgesellschaft Case*, Case 11/70, E.C.R. 1125 (1970), the German constitutional court asked the ECJ for an advisory opinion on the validity of a common agricultural policy requirement held unconstitutional in Germany. The ECJ stated explicitly that respect for fundamental rights forms an integral part of the general principles of European Community law.

In 1974 France became the last member of the European Community to ratify the European Convention on Human Rights. During that same year the Court began to cite the European Convention as a guideline to be followed within the framework of European Community law. In *Nold v. Commission*, Case 4/73, E.C.R. 491 (1974), the Court decided that human rights protections are based on "constitutional traditions of Member States and on acts of public international law, such as the Convention for the Protection of Human Rights and Fundamental Freedoms." *Id.* at 503. The Convention has been cited in nearly all ECJ cases since 1975. For example, *Pecastaing v. Belgium*, Case 98/79, E.C.R. 691 (1980), dealt with a challenge to a Community directive as not compatible with fair trial clauses in the European Convention. The ECJ found that the directive "fulfills the requirement of fair hearing set out in Article 6 of the Convention."

The Single European Act (SEA) of 1986, which primarily establishes a free internal market, apparently was the first legally binding EC instrument to mention human rights. Single European Act, O.J. (L 169/1) (1987), [1987] 2 C.M.L.R. 741. In the preamble, EC member states pledge "to work together and promote democracy on the basis of the fundamental rights recognized in the Constitutions and laws of the member states, in the Convention for the Protection of Human Rights and Fundamental Freedoms and the European Social Charter."

The Maastricht Treaty on European Union provides further support for ECJ efforts to incorporate human rights as part of European law and to give prominence to the European Convention. Treaty on European Union, Feb. 7, 1992, O.J. (C 224/1) (1992), [1992] 1 C.M.L.R. 791, reprinted in 1 I.L.M. 247. For example, Article F in Title I (Common Provisions) of the Maastricht Treaty preamble states:

> The Union shall respect human rights, as guaranteed by the European Convention for the Protection of Human Rights and Fundamental Freedoms signed on 4 Novem-

ber 1950 and as they result from the constitutional traditions common to the Member States, as general principles of Community law.

The role of the ECJ in the European Union must be distinguished from the role of the Court of Human Rights under the European Convention. The ECJ, sitting in Luxembourg, deals with human rights only insofar as issues arise under the Treaty of Rome, the Maastricht Treaty, and related provisions of European law. The Court of Human Rights, sitting in Strasbourg, has authority to consider the compatibility of national laws with the European Convention on Human Rights.

The European Parliament, the legislative branch created under the European Community, has also addressed human rights. It discusses issues of global human rights abuse, prepares reports on specific situations as well as comprehensive annual reports, and has adopted a number of resolutions on human rights issues. In 1989, for example, the EP adopted a non-binding Declaration of Fundamental Rights for EC/EU citizens, covering a wide range of rights. Declaration of Fundamental Rights and Freedoms, European Communities, O.J. (C 120/52) Doc. A 2-3/89 (May 16, 1989). Since 1989, the EP has passed additional resolutions addressing a variety of issues. Some are enacted each year regarding individual cases of human rights violations or widespread situations within particular countries. Those resolutions urge governments to cease the human rights abuses. Other resolutions concern subjects of violations within the EU and the member-states. The subjects, for example, have included asylum; conditions of detention; conscientious objection; the death penalty; double jeopardy; legal assistance; length of proceedings; poverty; protection of personal integrity; racism, xenophobia, and discrimination; respect for privacy; and terrorism. *See e.g., Human Rights in the World and Community Human Rights Policy for the Years 1991-1992*, 14 H.R.L.J. 284 (1993).

Following the 1984 elections, a Human Rights Sub-Committee was established under the European Parliament to monitor global human rights concerns. The Sub-Committee serves as an important channel for collecting information from NGOs and others and communicating it to the European Parliament.

NOTES AND QUESTIONS

For further reading see:

Kevin Boyle, *Europe: The Council of Europe, the CSCE, and the European Community, in* GUIDE TO INTERNATIONAL HUMAN RIGHTS PRACTICE 133 (Hurst Hannum ed., 2d ed. 1992);

L. NEVILLE BROWN & TOM KENNEDY, THE COURT OF JUSTICE OF THE EUROPEAN COMMUNITIES (4th ed. 1994);

ANGELA BYRE, LEADING CASES AND MATERIALS ON THE SOCIAL POLICY OF THE EEC (1989);

Mark Janis, *Fashioning a Mechanism for Judicial Cooperation on European Human Rights Law among Europe's Regional Courts, in* 3 THE DYNAMICS OF THE PROTECTION OF HUMAN RIGHTS IN EUROPE 211 (Rick Lawson & Matthijs de Blois eds., 1994);

PAUL KAPTEYN & PIETER VAN THEMAAT, INTRODUCTION TO THE LAW OF THE EUROPEAN COMMUNITIES (Laurence Gormley ed., 2d ed. 1989);

NEILL NUGENT, THE GOVERNMENT AND POLITICS OF THE EUROPEAN UNION (3d ed. 1994);

Vincent Power, *Human Rights and the EEC, in* HUMAN RIGHTS A EUROPEAN PERSPECTIVE, 81 (Liz Heffernan ed., 1994);

MICHAEL SPENCER, STATES OF INJUSTICE, A GUIDE TO HUMAN RIGHTS AND CIVIL LIBERTIES IN THE
EUROPEAN UNION (1995);

Alain Van Hamme, *Human Rights and the Treaty of Rome, in* HUMAN RIGHTS A EUROPEAN
PERSPECTIVE 70 (Liz Heffernan ed., 1994).

---

2.   Organization for Security and Cooperation in Europe

All European states, the United States, and Canada were participants in the
Conference on Security and Cooperation in Europe (CSCE), established in 1973.
The thirty-four governments that created the CSCE were motivated by various Cold
War concerns. Eastern European governments sought confirmation of territorial
status quo and development of economic relations, while Western governments
hoped to build confidence and achieve security, as well as advance humanitarian
issues.

The CSCE operated during the Cold War as a forum for dialogue and a process
for governments to discuss timely issues. It gave context to bilateral discussions
and provided a platform for criticism. The CSCE consisted of follow-up meetings and
ad hoc conferences on specific subjects. At the meetings, participating governments
discussed political and military security matters, human rights, economic and environmental issues, information, technology, and culture.

The CSCE first convened on July 3, 1973, in Helsinki, and concluded two years
later. The Final Act, known as The Helsinki Accords, was signed in August 1975.
Neither a treaty nor an institution, it is rather a statement of principles of behavior
for governments, toward individuals and other governments. The Final Act includes
three categories known as baskets. Basket I outlines ten principles of behavior
involving relations among governments, security, and confidence building. Basket
II addresses cooperation in economics, technology, and the environment. Basket III
applies to cooperation in humanitarian and other fields. A less well-known Basket
IV provides for continuation of the CSCE process in the form of follow-up sessions.

In accordance with Basket IV, a first follow-up meeting was held in Belgrade
from October 1977 to March 1978. It was characterized by confrontation between
Eastern and Western states. The governments did not reach agreement on any
substantive issue. The Concluding Document was brief, containing a schedule for
more meetings and admitting disagreements among participants.

The Madrid follow-up meeting lasted from 1980 to 1983, and was also characterized by East-West clashes. The Madrid Concluding Document stressed security and
included an agreement to hold further meetings. It also included provisions for
protection of human rights such as trade union freedoms, religious freedom, free
flow of information, protection against terrorism, and family reunification.

The third follow-up meeting, in Vienna from 1986-1989, resulted in significant
achievements. The governments agreed to develop laws protecting rights and to
ensure that remedies were available in the event of violations. The Concluding
Document introduced the human dimension of the CSCE, which it described as
"undertakings entered into in the Final Act and in other CSCE documents concerning
respect for all human rights and fundamental freedoms, human contacts and other
issues of a related humanitarian character." The Vienna Human Dimension Mechanism provides for exchanges of information, encourages bilateral meetings to discuss
human rights questions or specific situations, and allows every government to bring
rights issues to the attention of the CSCE. The Moscow Human Dimension Mecha-

nism was then added in 1991. It allows investigations of human rights violations through independent experts and rapporteurs.

With the end of the Cold War, the CSCE struggled to find a place in the new Europe. Its confrontational approach was replaced by a more cooperative one. Part of its new role is as tutelage for Central and Eastern European states to integrate into Western Europe. The process provides a method of acculturation which may lead governments to ratify the European Convention on Human Rights and, eventually, to achieve some status in the European Union. From the end of the Cold War through 1995, ten countries joined the Council of Europe: Andorra, Bulgaria, Czech Republic, Estonia, Hungary, Lithuania, Poland, Romania, Slovakia, and Slovenia. Russia was permitted to join the Council in early 1996, though there remained doubt as to its capacity to protect human rights and respect the rights of its minority groups. To respond to current ethnic and national problems, for example, in the former Yugoslavia, the CSCE sees the need to take on more substantive tasks than those undertaken during the Cold War period. They include conflict- prevention, -management, and -resolution as well as post-conflict rehabilitation.

In 1990, government leaders convened for a CSCE summit meeting in Paris. They set future directions in the "Charter of Paris for a New Europe." That document created three permanent administrative organs: a Secretariat, a Conflict Prevention Center, and an Office for Free Elections (later replaced by the Office for Democratic Institutions and Human Rights), and also two decision-making bodies: the Council of Ministers for Foreign Affairs and the Committee of Senior Officials. It also provided for ad hoc meetings and reflected an intent of the participants to create a parliamentary body. The governments agreed to hold follow-up meetings, which they re-named review conferences, every two years beginning in 1992.

In 1992, the first post-Cold War review conference was held in Helsinki. The participants adopted a document comprised of the "Helsinki Summit Declaration" and "Helsinki Decisions." The document emphasized substantive issues of conflict prevention and management and described possible peacekeeping activities. It also established new institutions including a Chairman in Office, a CSCE Secretary-General, the CSCE Forum for Security Cooperation, the CSCE Economic Forum, and a High Commissioner on National Minorities. A new institutional structure for "the human dimension" was also created, which includes seminars and biennial implementation meetings.

In 1994, the CSCE changed its name to the Organization for Security and Cooperation in Europe (OSCE). The new name was chosen at the Budapest review conference and reflects the enlistment of personnel and an administrative structure.

The OSCE will continue to provide security and stability in Europe, with an emphasis on conflict prevention and crisis management. An example of the OSCE's continuing role is the Dayton Peace Agreement, signed on December 14, 1995, in Dayton, Ohio. The Agreement calls for peace in the former Yugoslavia. It places responsibility on the OSCE to supervise confidence-building, arms negotiations, and elections, and to monitor the human rights situation. For more information on the Dayton Peace Agreement, see chapter 7, *supra*.

The OSCE also recognizes the need to work with other international organizations. Though the European Court of Human Rights addresses individual human rights violations, the OSCE sees the need for continuing dialogue as to human rights among member states, giving advice and criticism to states in a non-confrontational manner. H.E. Laszlo Kovacs, Opening Statement of the Budapest Conference of the Conference for Security and Cooperation in Europe (October 10, 1994), *in* 3 OSCE BULLETIN 1 (1994-1995). Another review conference will meet in Lisbon during 1996.

NOTES AND QUESTIONS

1.   Will organizations like the OSCE continue to be needed even when EU membership has expanded?

2.   Is the U.S. ready to agree with Europe on human rights principles? If all European states join the EU, will the U.S. need to rely on the OSCE as the only joint human rights forum in the Atlantic/European region? Is that enough justification for the continued existence of the OSCE?

3.   Why has the Helsinki process seemingly been so important even though the Final Act is not a legally binding treaty?

4.   Are the highly-structured adjudicative procedures of the Strasbourg system more effective for implementing human rights than the more political and consensus-oriented Helsinki process?

5.   Is case-by-case adjudication—the principal approach of the Strasbourg system—an appropriate technique for discouraging gross and consistent violations of human rights? Is the open-ended and flexible nature of the Helsinki process better than the relatively rigid Strasbourg system?

6.   For further reading, see THOMAS BUERGENTHAL, INTERNATIONAL HUMAN RIGHTS IN A NUTSHELL 159-73 (1995); THE CONFERENCE ON SECURITY AND COOPERATION IN EUROPE: ANALYSIS AND BASIC DOCUMENTS (Arie Bloed ed., 1993); *CSCE High Commissioner on National Minorities*, 2 INTERNATIONAL JOURNAL ON GROUP RIGHTS (K. Huber & R. Zaagman eds. 1994); THE HUMAN DIMENSION OF THE HELSINKI PROCESS: THE VIENNA FOLLOW-UP MEETING AND ITS AFTERMATH (Arie Bloed and Pieter van Dijk eds. 1991); WILLIAM KOREY, THE PROMISES WE KEEP: HUMAN RIGHTS, THE HELSINKI PROCESS, AND AMERICAN FOREIGN POLICY (1993).

3.   North Atlantic Treaty Organization

The North Atlantic Treaty Organization (NATO) was established in 1949 as a military and political alliance under Article 51 of the U.N. Charter, which affirms the right of collective self-defense. There are 16 NATO countries: Belgium, Canada, Denmark, France, Germany, Greece, Iceland, Italy, Luxembourg, Netherlands, Norway, Portugal, Spain, Turkey, the United Kingdom, and the United States. The headquarters are in Brussels.

With the end of the Cold War, NATO leaders advocated a redefining of the alliance's role, now reflected both in the 1990 London Declaration on a Transformed North Atlantic Alliance and the 1991 Rome Declaration on Peace and Cooperation. The declarations called for changes in NATO's approach to security, outlining reductions in conventional and nuclear forces. The declarations also invited a partnership with former Warsaw Pact countries. Minimum preconditions, requiring commitments to democracy and a market economy, are being prepared by NATO. In addition, the Rome Declaration created the North Atlantic Co-operation Council (NACC).

Representatives from the sixteen NATO countries, six Central and East European countries, and the three new Baltic states (Estonia, Latvia, and Lithuania) convened at the NACC's inaugural meeting in December 1991. The newly independent states of the former Soviet Union joined the NACC in 1992, as did Albania. NACC members have focused on security issues such as arms control and defense conversion. NACC members also have discussed violence in the former Yugoslavia, the Nagorno-Karabakh region of Azerbaijan, and the Baltics.

Though both NATO and NACC have discussed reducing NATO's forces, NATO has not abandoned its military role. For example, in October 1992 NATO launched a rapid-reaction force fielding thousands of soldiers for use in the former Yugoslavia. In November 1992, NATO warships helped enforce a UN embargo of Yugoslavia. In August 1993 NATO and the U.S. deployed troops to Bosnia. NATO troops have also been deployed in Bosnia to implement the 1995 Dayton Agreements. NATO's military presence in Europe, however, is not entirely secure. Some countries, particularly France, have in the past favored a security force that does not include the United States. In addition, the Western European Union (WEU), which is considered to be the defense arm of the European Union, awakened recently from a long dormancy. In 1986, it joined the region's efforts to deal with conflict in the Persian Gulf. In 1993, it sent patrol boats to help NATO vessels enforce the U.N. trade ban on Yugoslavia, and later, to coordinate humanitarian assistance to Kurdish refugees.

CHAPTER 12

U.S. ADJUDICATIVE REMEDIES FOR VIOLATIONS OCCURRING OUTSIDE THE U.S.

Filartiga and its Progeny

		Page	
A.	**Introduction**		500
B.	**Questions**		500
C.	**Alien Tort Litigation**		504
	1. **Jurisdiction**		504
	Filartiga v. Peña-Irala (1980)		505
	Forti v. Suarez-Mason (Forti I)		510
	Forti v. Suarez-Mason (Forti II)		515
	Joan Fitzpatrick, The Future of the ATCA		521
	2. **International Rules Governing Rape**		523
	Geneva Conventions of 1949		523
	Protocol I		525
	Protocol II		525
	Covenant on Civil and Political Rights		526
	Convention on the Elimination of All Forms of Discrimination Against Women		527
	Declaration on the Elimination of Violence Against Women		528
	Theodor Meron, Rape as a Crime Under International Humanitarian Law		528
D.	**Obstacles to Adjudication Under the Alien Tort Claims Act**		533
	1. **Foreign Sovereign Immunities Act**		534
	2. **Acts of State and of Heads of State**		541
	Liu v. Republic of China		542
	3. **Statute of Limitations, Damages, and Choice of Law**		547
	Filartiga v. Peña-Irala (1984)		547
E.	**Torture Victim Protection Act Litigation**		550
	28 U.S.C. § 1350		550

A. INTRODUCTION

Chapter 9 focused on bilateral measures available principally through actions of the U.S. Congress and executive to protect human rights. Chapters 10 and 11 looked at adjudicative procedures principally in multilateral institutions. In this chapter we discuss how courts in the U.S. may be used by both citizens and aliens to encourage other countries to comply with international human rights norms and to redress violations of the norms. Chapter 13 discusses how and when resort may be had in U.S. courts, legislatures, and administrative agencies to help promote U.S. compliance with international norms.

On a global scale, by no means is it easy to persuade governments to cease human rights violations. Pressures from the United Nations, other governments, and various NGOs, including, for example, the International Committee of the Red Cross and Amnesty International, sometimes succeed in curbing abuses. Still too often, however, do the perpetrators ignore pleas of the international community; and thus other mechanisms are needed to prevent and help provide redress for violations.

One mechanism for enforcing compliance is a civil suit, filed by victims of human rights abuses against the perpetrators. Suits may be filed in U.S. federal and state courts. Since the early 1980s the filing of alien tort suits in U.S. courts has increased significantly. There are, though, complex legal and political issues surrounding the litigation.

Civil suits also may be filed in courts of the country in which atrocities occur. Those suits may not, however, adequately protect or compensate victims. For instance, repressive governments may refuse to enforce or even permit the legal actions. Also, when there is armed conflict, normal judicial processes may be disrupted and judgments not enforced.

Criminal sanctions may deter human rights violations and are discussed in chapter 7, *supra*. Another mechanism might be a case in the International Court of Justice. ICJ jurisdiction, however, is limited to suits between governments and judgments are not enforceable by individuals.[1] Victims' injuries, therefore, hardly ever are redressed.

This chapter will explore U.S. jurisdiction in suits by U.S. aliens and citizens against perpetrators of human rights abuse. We will explore the issue in the context of a suit filed in a Minnesota federal court by a Muslim woman, against Bosnian Serb defendants.

B. QUESTIONS

Bosnia-Herzegovina is one of six republics comprising the former Yugoslavia. The others are Croatia, Macedonia, Montenegro, Slovenia, and Serbia. A federal government existed through 1990, but efforts to conduct elections and promote reform failed when several regions adopted laws giving supremacy to republics rather than to a federal sovereign. In 1991, after Serbia blocked a proposal by Croatia and Slovenia to restructure Yugoslavia as a loose federation, Croatia and Slovenia each declared independence. The federal government responded by sending

---

[1] *See Committee of U.S. Citizens Living in Nicaragua v. Reagan*, 859 F.2d 929 (D.C. Cir. 1988), excerpted *infra* chapter 13.

troops to those areas, and fierce fighting followed. Fighting spread to Bosnia when federal forces mounted a full-scale offensive in support of Serb guerrillas in Croatia.

At the end of 1991, Bosnia sought recognition as an independent state, and in early 1992, 63% of its voters endorsed independence. On May 22, 1992, the U.N. admitted Bosnia-Herzegovina, Croatia, and Slovenia into membership. In April 1992, Serbia and Montenegro proclaimed themselves to be the new Federal Republic of Yugoslavia, but the U.N. General Assembly and Security Council rejected the claim to succession. *See, e.g.*, UNITED NATIONS, INTERNATIONAL COVENANT ON CIVIL AND POLITICAL RIGHTS; AIDE-MÉMOIRE Dated 15 March 1994 from the Permanent Mission of Croatia to the United Nations, Annex, at 2 (1994). The U.S., Canada, and members of the European Community also refused to recognize the new Federal Republic.

After declaring its independence, Bosnia-Herzegovina fell quickly into armed conflict. In 1990 elections, three nationalist parties—the Muslim Party of Democratic Action (SDA), the Croatian Democratic Union (HDZ), and the Serbian Democratic Party (SDS)—had formed a governing partnership under a Muslim president. The SDA and the HDZ wanted independence while the SDS wanted to remain part of Yugoslavia. In January 1992, before independence was declared, SDS leaders proclaimed their own Serbian entity within Bosnia. After the voters endorsed Bosnia's independence, paramilitary supporters of the SDS began a campaign of violence with the goal of combining Serbian-controlled areas of Bosnia, Croatia, and Serbia/Montenegro into an ethnically-pure "greater Serbia." The Bosnian Serb effort was supported by Serbs from Serbia/Montenegro and by former Yugoslav Army units which had organized themselves into a Bosnian Serb armed militia (BSA).

Sena is a Muslim woman aged 35.[2] In August 1992, she lived with her family in Doboj, a town situated in the Serb-controlled area of Bosnia-Herzegovina. One afternoon while she was gathering food in a field outside her home, a group of Serbian men in camouflaged uniforms approached her. She recognized one as Radovan Herak, a neighbor. She was aware that he was a member of the Serbian paramilitary forces.

The men took Sena into her home, where she was brutally raped by Herak. She became pregnant and gave birth to a boy nine months later. Because of the rape and forced pregnancy, her husband has ostracized her, and the Muslim community refuses to acknowledge her.

The abuse is part of a pattern of rapes, forced pregnancies, and other human rights abuses often called "ethnic cleansing"[3] committed by military, paramilitary, and police forces in the former Yugoslavia. The "ethnic cleansing" is intended to intimidate, terrorize, and force Muslims to flee their homes out of fear, and eventu-

---

[2] The facts of this case are hypothetical, but details reflect several cases reported to authorities. *See* Amnesty International, *Bosnia-Herzegovina: Rape and Sexual Abuse by Armed Forces*, AI Index: EUR 63/01/93 (1993); Amnesty International, *Bosnia-Herzegovina: Gross Abuses of Human Rights*, AI Index: EUR 63/01/92 (1992); Tom Post et al., *Crimes of War: A Pattern of Rape in Bosnia*, NEWSWEEK, Jan. 4, 1993, at 32; *see also Kadic v. Karadzic, Doe v. Karadzic*, 70 F.3d 232 (2nd Cir. 1995).

[3] "'[E]thnic cleansing' means rendering an area ethnically homogenous by using force or intimidation to remove persons of given groups from the area." COMMISSION OF EXPERTS ESTABLISHED PURSUANT TO SECURITY COUNCIL RESOLUTION 780 (1992), FINAL REPORT, U.N. Doc. S/1994/674, at 33 (1994). U.N. experts concluded that the Bosnian government had engaged in "ethnic cleansing":

ally to destroy the Muslim population of Bosnia.[4] Authorities rarely, if ever, seek to punish the abuses, though in fact they probably are aware of and generally condone them.

Sena now lives in the U.S. and receives medical and psychological treatment for her injuries. She is suing Herak, Zeljko Raznatovic (leader of the Serbian paramilitary forces), and the Bosnian government in a Minnesota federal court. Her complaint states that Herak committed the abuses under the direction and control of Raznatovic, and that the government failed to prevent or punish the abuses.

You are working with the Center for Constitutional Rights, which has been asked to represent Sena in her suit. Herak and Raznatovic were duly served while they were in Minnesota addressing the Minneapolis Business Bureau.

After reading the remainder of the chapter, you should be able to answer these questions:

1. Why would Sena want to sue the defendants in a U.S. court?

    a. What types of damages might she seek? Can she sue for punitive damages as well as compensatory damages?

    b. What benefits might there be to her suit if any damages awarded prove uncollectible?

    c. Will the adverse publicity of the trial serve as an effective deterrent to the defendants even if her suit is dismissed?

    d. How does her suit fit within the overall strategy for curbing human rights abuses in the former Yugoslavia and for seeking peace and justice in that region?

2. Can the Alien Tort Claims Act ("ATCA") provide federal courts with jurisdiction over Sena's claims?

    a. Is rape a tort?

    b. Is Sena an individual who may sue under the ATCA?

    c. Is rape a violation of a treaty of the U.S.?

        1) Does Common Article 3 of the Geneva Conventions apply to Herak's conduct?

            a) Is the conflict in Bosnia an internal armed conflict to which Article 3 applies?

On the basis of the information gathered, examined and analysed, the Commission [of Experts] has concluded that grave breaches of the Geneva Conventions and other violations of international humanitarian law have been committed in the territory of the former Yugoslavia on a large scale, and were particularly brutal and ferocious in their execution. The practice of so-called "ethnic cleansing" and rape and sexual assault, in particular, have been carried out by some of the parties so systematically that they strongly appear to be the product of a policy, which may also be inferred from the consistent failure to prevent the commission of such crimes and to prosecute and punish their perpetrators.

BOUTROS BOUTROS-GHALI, LETTER DATED 24 MAY 1994 FROM THE SECRETARY-GENERAL TO THE PRESIDENT OF THE SECURITY COUNCIL, U.N. Doc. S/1994/674 (1994).

[4] See generally Tadeusz Mazowiecki, Report on the Situation of Human Rights in the Territory of the Former Yugoslavia, U.N. Doc. A/48/92-S/25341, Annex, at 20, 57 (1993); Post, supra note 2, at 32.

b)   How would you argue the paramilitary forces are obligated to comply with Common Article 3?

c)   Is Sena a person protected by Article 3?

2)   Does Protocol II apply to Herak's conduct?

3)   Do the remaining articles of the Geneva Conventions and Protocol I apply to Herak's conduct?

4)   Do any other controlling treaties proscribe rape? Note the dates of ratification for the various countries in relation to the date the rape occurred.

5)   Could you argue that rape is a form of official torture? Is there any support for this position?

6)   Does any obligation on the part of the paramilitary leaders or the Bosnian government to "ensure respect" for the provisions of the Geneva Conventions apply to private acts of rape occurring during war?

d.   Alternatively, is rape a violation of the law of nations?

1)   What arguments would you make to support the existence of a customary international norm against rape, absent a controlling treaty provision? What sources would you cite?

2)   Is there a universally accepted norm proscribing rape?

3)   If there is a universally accepted norm, is it universally enforced as a matter of legal obligation?

3.   What prerequisites must be met in order for federal courts to accept jurisdiction under the ATCA?

a.   If there is not consensus among the circuits, how would you convince a district court in the Eighth Circuit to interpret the statute to provide the broadest jurisdiction possible?

b.   If Sena were a citizen of the U.S., could she sue under the ATCA?

c.   Would Sena have been able to sue under the ATCA if she was not living in the U.S. at the time the suit was filed?

4.   Are there any obstacles to suing the defendants in federal courts?

a.   Might Herak be able to argue his conduct was a private act and thus not a part of government-sponsored ethnic cleansing, such that treaty law or customary international norms do not apply?

b.   Does the Foreign Sovereign Immunities Act ("FSIA") insulate the Bosnian government from jurisdiction in the U.S.?

c.   Does the FSIA insulate Herak or Raznatovic from jurisdiction in the U.S.?

d.   Can the Bosnian government benefit from act of state immunity? What problems will it have in raising this argument?

e.   Can either Herak or Raznatovic benefit from head of state immunity? What prerequisites must be met before either man can successfully raise the defense?

5. Does the Torture Victim Protection Act ("TVPA") provide federal courts with jurisdiction?

a. Do the activities described in Sena's complaint constitute torture or extrajudicial killing under the Act?

b. Does the TVPA apply to the activities in light of the date of adoption versus the date the activities took place?

c. Is it necessary for any government to have ratified a treaty in order for the TVPA to apply to conduct in that country?

d. Does the TVPA provide jurisdiction over the Bosnian government?

e. Does the TVPA require Sena to attempt first to sue the defendants in Bosnian courts? Does the ATCA? Under what circumstances might you be able to argue such efforts are unnecessary even under the TVPA?

f. If the acts which form the basis of Sena's suit had taken place in August 1982, instead of August 1992, would her ability to sue under the TVPA be limited?

6. What are the alternatives to a suit in U.S. courts?

a. What alternatives are available through the U.N.? Would the International Tribunal for the Prosecution of Persons Responsible for Serious Violations of International Humanitarian Law Committed in the Territory of the Former Yugoslavia since 1991 provide a better approach? Does the Dayton Peace Agreement provide a viable alternative?

b. What are the advantages and disadvantages of using U.S. courts as compared with the use of international procedures?

1) for preventing harm to the victims?

2) for getting relief to the victims?

3) for fact-finding (*e.g.*, with respect to subpoena powers, depositions, and other access to relevant information)?

4) for punishing the perpetrators?

5) for publicity about human rights violations?

6) for access to the procedures?

7) for building international human rights structures possessing legitimacy?

c. Do all the steps required to bring a suit in U.S. courts obscure the initial objective?

d. How does the impact of using U.S. courts differ from using U.S. foreign policy objectives?

C. ALIEN TORT LITIGATION

1. Jurisdiction

U.S. federal courts have jurisdiction to hear suits by aliens for torts committed in violation of international law. The Alien [Tort] Claims Act ("ATCA"), 28 U.S.C. § 1350, provides:

> The district courts shall have original jurisdiction of any civil action by an alien for a tort only, committed in violation of the law of nations or a treaty of the United States.

The ATCA originally was included in the Judiciary Act of 1789, but the reasons for its inclusion are unclear. Joan Fitzpatrick, *The Future of the Alien Tort Claims Act of 1789: Lessons from* In Re Marcos Human Rights Litigation, 67 ST. JOHN'S L. REV. 491, 492 (1993). The Supreme Court has suggested that Congress wanted federal courts to adjudicate the claims to promote uniformity in application of international norms, *Banco Nacional de Cuba v. Sabbatino*, 376 U.S. 398, 427 n.25 (1964); but some commentators posit that Congress may have believed that providing such a remedy was part of the nation's responsibilities as a member of the world community, Anne-Marie Burley, *The Alien Tort Statute and the Judiciary Act of 1789: A Badge of Honor*, 83 AM. J. INT'L L. 461, 475-80 (1989).

The ATCA was not widely used until the 1980s, when a growing interest in protecting human rights and an increase in the number of lawyers familiar with international law heralded a resurgence in use of the statute. Fitzpatrick, *supra*, at 493. The Second Circuit's decision in *Filartiga v. Peña-Irala*, excerpted here, paved the way for many subsequent suits to compensate victims for violations of international law.

*   *   *   *   *

Filartiga v. Peña-Irala, 630 F.2d 876 (2d Cir. 1980) (footnotes and several citations omitted):

IRVING R. KAUFMAN, Circuit Judge . . .

I

[Plaintiffs appealed the district court's decision dismissing their wrongful death action for lack of subject matter jurisdiction. The plaintiffs, Dr. Joel Filartiga and his daughter Dolly, are citizens of Paraguay, as is the defendant, Americo Norberto Peña-Irala. Dolly is present in the U.S. under a visitor's visa, and has applied for political asylum. Peña also entered the U.S. under a visitor's visa, but stayed beyond the term of his visa.

Dr. Filartiga opposed the government of the President of Paraguay. Appellants contend on March 29, 1976, Dr. Filartiga's seventeen-year-old son, Joelito, was kidnapped and tortured to death by Peña, then Inspector General of Police in Asuncion, Paraguay, in Peña's home. Dolly was later forced to view the body of her severely tortured brother and was told, "Here you have what you have been looking for for so long and what you deserve. Now shut up," as she fled. Appellants believe Joelito was killed in retaliation for his father's political activities and beliefs.

Dr. Filartiga filed a criminal action against Peña and the police in Paraguayan courts. In response, Dr. Filartiga's attorney was arrested, shackled to a wall, threatened to death by Peña, and disbarred without just cause. When Dolly learned Peña was in the U.S., she and her father filed a civil suit against him in federal court, asking for $10,000,000 of compensatory and punitive damages.]

The cause of action is stated as arising under "wrongful death statutes; the

U.N. Charter; the Universal Declaration on Human Rights; the U.N. Declaration Against Torture; the American Declaration of the Rights and Duties of Man; and other pertinent declarations, documents and practices constituting the customary international law of human rights and the law of nations," as well as 28 U.S.C. § 1350, Article II, sec. 2 and the Supremacy Clause of the U.S. Constitution. Jurisdiction is claimed under the general federal question provision, 28 U.S.C. § 1331, and, principally on this appeal, under the Alien Tort Statute, 28 U.S.C. § 1350.

[The district court judge] . . . dismissed the complaint on jurisdictional grounds. [He] recognized the strength of appellants' argument that official torture violates an emerging norm of customary international law. Nonetheless, he felt constrained by dicta contained in two recent opinions of this Court . . . to construe narrowly "the law of nations," as employed in § 1350, as excluding that law which governs a state's treatment of its own citizens. . . .

II

Appellants rest their principal argument in support of federal jurisdiction upon the Alien Tort Statute, 28 U.S.C. § 1350, [excerpted *supra*]. . . . Since appellants do not contend that their action arises directly under a treaty of the United States, a threshold question on the jurisdictional issue is whether the conduct alleged violates the law of nations. In light of the universal condemnation of torture in numerous international agreements, and the renunciation of torture as an instrument of official policy by virtually all of the nations of the world (in principle if not in practice), we find that an act of torture committed by a state official against one held in detention violates established norms of the international law of human rights, and hence the law of nations.

The Supreme Court has enumerated the appropriate sources of international law. The law of nations "may be ascertained by consulting the works of jurists, writing professedly on public law; or by the general usage and practice of nations; or by judicial decisions recognizing and enforcing that law." . . .

The Paquete Habana, 175 U.S. 677 . . . (1900), reaffirmed that

> where there is no treaty, and no controlling executive or legislative act or judicial decision, resort must be had to the customs and usages of civilized nations; and, as evidence of these, to the works of jurists and commentators, who by years of labor, research and experience, have made themselves peculiarly well acquainted with the subjects of which they treat. Such works are resorted to by judicial tribunals, not for the speculations of their authors concerning what the law ought to be, but for trustworthy evidence of what the law really is.

Modern international sources confirm the propriety of this approach.

Habana is particularly instructive for present purposes, for it held that the traditional prohibition against seizure of an enemy's coastal fishing vessels during wartime, a standard that began as one of comity only, had ripened over the preceding century into "a settled rule of international law" by "the general assent of civilized nations." Thus it is clear that courts must interpret international law not as it was in 1789, but as it has evolved and exists among the nations of the world today.

. . .

The requirement that a rule command the "general assent of civilized nations" to become binding upon them all is a stringent one. Were this not so, the courts of one nation might feel free to impose idiosyncratic legal rules upon others, in the name of applying international law. . . .

The United Nations Charter (a treaty of the United States, *see* 49 Stat. 1033 (1945)) makes it clear that in this modern age a state's treatment of its own citizens is a matter of international concern. It provides:

> With a view to the creation of conditions of stability and well-being which are necessary for peaceful and friendly relations among nations . . . the United Nations shall promote . . . universal respect for, and observance of, human rights and fundamental freedoms for all without distinctions as to race, sex, language or religion.

Id. Art. 55. And further:

> All members pledge themselves to take joint and separate action in cooperation with the Organization for the achievement of the purposes set forth in Article 55.

Id. Art. 56.

While this broad mandate has been held not to be wholly self-executing, this observation alone does not end our inquiry. For although there is no universal agreement as to the precise extent of the "human rights and fundamental freedoms" guaranteed to all by the Charter, there is at present no dissent from the view that the guaranties include, at a bare minimum, the right to be free from torture. This prohibition has become part of customary international law, as evidenced and defined by the Universal Declaration of Human Rights, General Assembly Resolution 217 (III)(A) (Dec. 10, 1948), which states in the plainest of terms, "no one shall be subjected to torture." The General Assembly has declared that the Charter precepts embodied in this Universal Declaration "constitute basic principles of international law." G.A. Res. 2625 (XXV) (Oct. 24, 1970).

Particularly relevant is the Declaration on the Protection of All Persons from Being Subjected to Torture, General Assembly Resolution 3452, 30 U.N. GAOR Supp. (No. 34) 91, U.N. Doc. A/1034 (1975) . . .. The Declaration expressly prohibits any state from permitting the dastardly and totally inhuman act of torture. . . .

Turning to the act of torture, we have little difficulty discerning its universal renunciation in the modern usage and practice of nations. . . . The international consensus surrounding torture has found expression in numerous international treaties and accords. . . . The substance of these international agreements is reflected in modern municipal—*i.e.* national—law as well. Although torture was once a routine concomitant of criminal interrogations in many nations, during the modern and hopefully more enlightened era it has been universally renounced. According to one survey, torture is prohibited, expressly or implicitly, by the constitutions of over fifty-five nations, including both the United States and Paraguay. . . .[5] Having examined the sources from which customary international law is derived—the usage of nations, judicial opinions and the works of jurists—we conclude that official torture is now prohibited by the law of nations. The prohibition is clear and unambiguous, and admits of no distinction between treatment of aliens and citizens. . . . The treaties and accords cited above, as well as the express foreign policy of our own government, all make it clear that international law confers fundamental rights

---

[5] The fact that the prohibition of torture is often honored in the breach does not diminish its binding effect as a norm of international law. As one commentator has put it, "The best evidence for the existence of international law is that every actual State recognizes that it does exist and that it is itself under an obligation to observe it. States often violate international law, just as individuals often violate municipal law; but no more than individuals do States defend their violations by claiming that they are above the law." James Brierly, *The Outlook for International Law* 4-5 (Oxford 1944).

upon all people vis-a-vis their own governments. While the ultimate scope of those rights will be a subject for continuing refinement and elaboration, we hold that the right to be free from torture is now among them. . . .

III

Appellee submits that even if the tort alleged is a violation of modern international law, federal jurisdiction may not be exercised consistent with the dictates of Article III of the Constitution. The claim is without merit. Common law courts of general jurisdiction regularly adjudicate transitory tort claims between individuals over whom they exercise personal jurisdiction, wherever the tort occurred. Moreover, as part of an articulated scheme of federal control over external affairs, Congress provided, in the first Judiciary Act, § 9(b), 1 Stat. 73, 77 (1789), for federal jurisdiction over suits by aliens where principles of international law are in issue. The constitutional basis for the Alien Tort Statute is the law of nations, which has always been part of the federal common law.

It is not extraordinary for a court to adjudicate a tort claim arising outside of its territorial jurisdiction. A state or nation has a legitimate interest in the orderly resolution of disputes among those within its borders, and where the *lex loci delicti commissi* is applied, it is an expression of comity to give effect to the laws of the state where the wrong occurred.

. . . A case properly "aris[es] under the . . . laws of the United States" for Article III purposes if grounded upon statutes enacted by Congress or upon the common law of the United States. . . .

As ratified, the judiciary article contained no express reference to cases arising under the law of nations. Indeed, the only express reference to that body of law is contained in Article I, sec. 8, cl. 10, which grants to the Congress the power to "define and punish . . . offenses against the law of nations." Appellees seize upon this circumstance and advance the proposition that the law of nations forms a part of the laws of the United States only to the extent that Congress has acted to define it. This extravagant claim is amply refuted by the numerous decisions applying rules of international law uncodified in any act of Congress. . . .

Thus, it was hardly a radical initiative for Chief Justice Marshall to state in *The Nereide*, 13 U.S. (9 Cranch) 388, 422 . . . (1815), that in the absence of a congressional enactment,[6] United States courts are "bound by the law of nations, which is a part of the law of the land.". . .

Although the Alien Tort Statute has rarely been the basis for jurisdiction during its long history, in light of the foregoing discussion, there can be little doubt that this action is properly brought in federal court.[7] . . .

Since federal jurisdiction may properly be exercised over the Filartigas' claim, the action must be remanded for further proceedings. . . .

---

[6] The plainest evidence that international law has an existence in the federal courts independent of acts of Congress is the long-standing rule of construction first enunciated by Chief Justice Marshall: "an act of Congress ought never to be construed to violate the law of nations, if any other possible construction remains. . . ." [*Murray v. Schooner] Charming Betsy*, 6 U.S. (2 Cranch), 34, 67 . . . (1804), quoted in *Lauritzen v. Larsen*, 345 U.S. 571, 578 (1953).

[7] We recognize that our reasoning might also sustain jurisdiction under the general federal question provision, 28 U.S.C. §1331. We prefer, however, to rest our decision upon the Alien Tort Statute, in light of that provision's close coincidence with the jurisdictional facts presented in this case.

NOTES AND QUESTIONS

The lead lawyers for plaintiffs in *Filartiga* were associated with the Center for Constitutional Rights, which has since then been involved in many ATCA cases. On remand the plaintiffs won a default judgment awarding them compensatory damages of $375,000 and punitive damages of $10 million. They have been unable to collect; and for discussion of additional issues on remand see *Filartiga v. Peña-Irala*, 577 F. Supp. 860 (E.D.N.Y. 1984), excerpted *infra*, at 67.

The *Filartiga* opinion was widely publicized, and its author, Judge Kaufman, even penned an article advocating use of the ATCA to redress torture. Irving R. Kaufman, *A Legal Remedy for International Torture?*, N.Y. TIMES MAG., Nov. 9, 1980, at 44. The publicity focused not only on the novelty of *Filartiga* and its precedential value for future suits, but also on the human rights situation in Paraguay. Articles described the brutality of kidnappings, tortures, and murders under the dictatorship of President Stroessner and the widespread abuses perpetrated by his repressive government. Commentators praised the courage of the Filartigas in judicially protesting the treatment and drawing international attention to the situation, when most prior reaction had been to bury the victim quietly and deny abuse.

Under *Filartiga*, federal courts have ATCA jurisdiction only if international law proscribes the tortious conduct. The proscription may be contained in a treaty to which the U.S. and the country where the tort occurred are parties. When no U.S.-ratified treaty controls, § 1350 requires that "the law of nations" prohibit the acts giving rise to the lawsuit.

Article 38 of the Statute of the International Court of Justice, which because of Article 92 of the U.N. Charter forms an integral part of the Charter, prescribes the sources of non-treaty "law of nations" as follows: . . .

 b. international custom, as evidence of a general practice accepted as law;

 c. the general principles of law recognized by civilized nations;

 d. . . . judicial decisions and the teachings of the most highly qualified publicists of the various nations, as subsidiary means for the determination of rules of law.

Customary international law is thus a supplementary segment of "the law of nations." Customary norms reflect a general practice of governments accepted as law. *See* Deborah Perluss & Joan F. Hartman, *Temporary Refuge: Emergence of a Customary Norm*, 26 VA. J. INT'L L. 551, 554-58 (1986). Only widespread, rather than unanimous, acquiescence is needed, and acquiescence may occur in a short period of time. IAN BROWNLIE, PRINCIPLES OF PUBLIC INTERNATIONAL LAW 6-7 (3d ed. 1979); 1 RESTATEMENT (THIRD) OF THE FOREIGN RELATIONS LAW OF THE UNITED STATES § 102, comment b (1987).

A customary norm binds all governments, including those that have not recognized it, so long as they have not expressly and persistently objected to its development. 1 RESTATEMENT (THIRD) OF THE FOREIGN RELATIONS LAW OF THE UNITED STATES § 102, comment d (1987); *North Sea Continental Shelf Cases, supra*, 1969 I.C.J. at 41-44. Therefore, a state which is not a party to a treaty may nonetheless be bound by it if the rules of the treaty have become a norm of customary international law. MARK W. JANIS, AN INTRODUCTION TO INTERNATIONAL LAW 19 (1988); *see also United*

States v. Schiffer, 836 F. Supp. 1164, 1171 (E.D. Pa. 1993). Customary norms thus differ from treaty clauses, which bind only the parties to the treaties.

One of the most important principles is that new norms must be applied as they emerge. Hence, a conclusion that a rule has not achieved the status of a customary international norm should not discourage lawyers from relitigating the issue after a period of time, assuming subsequent state practice or other evidence of the norm's development.

As you read the next two opinions note the sources Judge Jensen used to identify customary international norms. Also think about why the treaties and customary norms were or were not sufficient to support the plaintiffs' claims.

* * * * *

Forti v. Suarez-Mason, 672 F. Supp. 1531 (N.D. Cal. 1987) (*Forti I*) (footnotes and some citations omitted):

JENSEN, District Judge.

I

FACTS

This is a civil action brought against a former Argentine general by two Argentine citizens currently residing in the United States. Plaintiffs Forti and Benchoam . . . [are] seeking damages from defendant Suarez-Mason for actions which include, *inter alia*, torture, murder, and prolonged arbitrary detention, allegedly committed by military and police personnel under defendant's authority and control. . . .

A. *Background*
Plaintiffs' action arises out of events alleged to have occurred in the mid-to late 1970s during Argentina's so-called "dirty war" against suspected subversives. In 1975, the activities of terrorists representing the extremes of both ends of the political spectrum induced the constitutional government of President Peron to declare a "state of siege" under Article 23 of the Argentine Constitution. President Peron also decreed that the Argentine Armed Forces should assume responsibility for suppressing terrorism. . . . [Defendant Suarez-Mason was commander of the army in the region in which plaintiffs resided.]

On March 24, 1976, the commanding officers of the Armed Forces seized the government from President Peron. The ruling military junta continued the "state of siege" and caused the enactment of legislation providing that civilians accused of crimes of subversion would be judged by military law. In the period from 1976 to 1979, tens of thousands of persons were detained without charges by the military, and it is estimated that more than 12,000 were "disappeared," never to be seen again. *See generally, Nunca Mas: The Report of the Argentine National Commission on the Disappeared* (1986).

In January 1984, the constitutionally elected government of President Raul Alfonsín assumed power. The Alfonsín government commenced investigations of alleged human rights abuses by the military, and the criminal prosecution of certain former military authorities followed. . . . [Suarez-Mason fled to the U.S. to avoid such prosecution. He was served with this civil suit while in custody awaiting extradition.]

B. *Allegations of the Complaint*

The Complaint alleges claims for damages based on acts allegedly committed by personnel. . .under General Suarez-Mason's command. According to the Complaint, police and military officials seized plaintiff Alfredo Forti, along with his mother and four brothers, from an airplane at Buenos Aires' Ezeiza International Airport on February 18, 1977. The entire family was held at . . . [a] detention center . . . in a suburb of Buenos Aires. . . . No charges were ever filed against the Fortis. After six days the five sons were released, dropped blindfolded on a street in the capital. The mother . . . was not released, and remains "disappeared" to this day . . ..

An Argentine court . . . attributed direct responsibility for the seizure to [military personnel under defendant's control].

As to plaintiff Debora Benchoam, the Complaint alleges that Benchoam and her brother were abducted from their Buenos Aires bedroom before dawn on July 25, 1977, by military authorities in plain clothes. At the time Benchoam was sixteen years old, and her brother, seventeen.

Benchoam was blindfolded and taken first to an unidentified house and later to a police station in Buenos Aires, where she was held incommunicado for a month. For the first week of detention Benchoam was kept blindfolded with her hands handcuffed behind her back, and was provided neither food nor clothing. A guard attempted to rape her.

On August 28, 1977, allegedly at the direction of defendant Suarez-Mason, Benchoam was transferred [to a prison where] she was imprisoned, without charge, for more than four years. . . . Finally, as a result of international and domestic appeals, plaintiff was granted the "right of option" and allowed to leave the country. She was released from prison on November 5, 1981, and came to the United States as a refugee.

The military personnel also abducted plaintiff's seventeen-year-old brother on July 25, 1977. The brother's body was returned to the Benchoam family the following day. He had died of internal bleeding from bullet wounds, and his face was "severely disfigured" from blows. . . .

Based on these above allegations, plaintiffs seek compensatory and punitive damages for violations of customary international law and laws of the United States, Argentina, and California. They press eleven causes of action. Both alleged claims for torture; prolonged arbitrary detention without trial; cruel, inhuman and degrading treatment; false imprisonment; assault and battery; intentional infliction of emotional distress; and conversion. Additionally Forti claims damages for "causing the disappearance of individuals," and Benchoam asserts claims for "murder and summary execution," wrongful death, and a survival action.

In response to these allegations, defendant moves to dismiss the entire Complaint [for] lack[] [of] subject matter jurisdiction . . . and, alternatively, [because] not all of the torts alleged constitute violations of the law of nations. . . .

II.

SUBJECT MATTER JURISDICTION

As a threshold matter, defendant argues that the Court lacks subject matter jurisdiction under 28 U.S.C. §1350, the "Alien Tort Statute." Defendant urges the Court to follow the interpretation of §1350 as a purely jurisdictional statute which requires that plaintiffs invoking it establish the existence of an independent, private right of action in international law. Defendant argues that the law of nations provides no tort cause of action for the acts of "politically motivated terrorism" challenged by plaintiffs' Complaint. Alternatively, defendant argues that even if §1350 provides a cause of action for violations of the law of nations, not all of the torts alleged by plaintiffs qualify as violations of the law of nations. For the reasons set out below, the Court rejects defendant's construction of §1350 and finds that plaintiffs allege sufficient facts to establish subject matter jurisdiction under the Alien Tort Statute and 28 U.S.C. §1331. . . .

A.   The Alien Tort Statute

. . . The district courts' jurisdiction [under the ATCA, excerpted *supra*,] is concurrent with that of state courts. As the cases and commentaries recognize, the history of the Alien Tort Statute is obscure. Nonetheless, the proper interpretation of the statute has been discussed at some length in the principal decisions upon which the parties rely: The unanimous decision in *Filartiga v. Peña-Irala*, 630 F.2d 876 (2d Cir. 1980), and the three concurring opinions in *Tel-Oren v. Libyan Arab Republic*, 726 F.2d 774 (D.C. Cir. 1984), *cert. denied*, 470 U.S. 1003 . . . (1985).

Defendant urges the Court to adopt the reasoning of Judges Bork and Robb in *Tel-Oren, supra*, where the court affirmed the dismissal of a §1350 tort action against various defendants based on a terrorist attack in Israel by members of the Palestine Liberation Organization. While the three judges concurred in the result, they were unable to agree on the rationale. Judge Bork found that §1350 constitutes no more than a grant of jurisdiction; that plaintiffs seeking to invoke it must establish a private right of action under either a treaty or the law of nations; and that in the latter category the statute can support jurisdiction at most over only three international crimes recognized in 1789—violation of safe-conducts, infringement of ambassadorial rights, and piracy. Judge Robb, on the other hand found that the dispute involved international political violence and so was "nonjusticiable" within the meaning of the political question doctrine.

The Court is persuaded, however, that the interpretation of §1350 forwarded by the Second Circuit in *Filartiga, supra*, and largely adopted by Judge Edwards in *Tel-Oren*, is better reasoned and more consistent with principles of international law. There appears to be a growing consensus that §1350 provides a cause of action for certain "international common law torts." It is unnecessary that plaintiffs establish the existence of an independent, express right of action, since the law of nations clearly does not create or define civil actions, and to require such an explicit grant under international law would effectively nullify that portion of the statute which confers jurisdiction over tort suits involving the law of nations. Rather, a plaintiff seeking to predicate jurisdiction on the Alien Tort Statute need only plead a "tort . . . in violation of the law of nations."

The contours of this requirement have been delineated by the *Filartiga* court and by Judge Edwards in *Tel-Oren*. Plaintiffs must plead a violation of the law of nations as it has evolved and exists in its contemporary form. This "international tort" must be one which is definable, obligatory (rather than hortatory), and universally condemned. The requirement of international consensus is of paramount importance, for it is that consensus which evinces the willingness of nations to be bound by the particular legal principle, and so can justify the court's exercise of jurisdiction over the international tort claim. . . .

The Court thus interprets 28 U.S.C. §1350 to provide not merely jurisdiction but a cause of action, with the federal cause of action arising by recognition of certain "international torts" through the vehicle of §1350. These international torts, violations of current customary international law, are characterized by universal consensus in the international community as to their binding status and their content. That is, they are universal, definable, and obligatory international norms. The Court now examines the allegations of the Complaint to determine whether plaintiffs have stated cognizable international torts for purposes of jurisdiction under §1350.

B.   *Analysis Under 28 U.S.C. § 1350*

In determining whether plaintiffs have stated cognizable claims under Section 1350, the Court has recourse to "the works of jurists, writing professedly on public law;. . . the general usage and practice of nations; [and] judicial decisions recognizing and enforcing that law." For purposes of defendant's motion to dismiss, the Court must accept as true all of plaintiffs' allegations, construing them in the light most favorable to plaintiffs. . . .

1.   *Official Torture*

In Count One, plaintiffs both allege torture conducted by military and police personnel under defendant's command. The Court has no doubt that official torture constitutes a cognizable violation of the law of nations. . . . [Citing *Filartiga v. Peña-Irala, supra*, the court noted "the law of nations contains a 'clear and unambiguous' prohibition of official torture" which is "universal, obligatory, and definable."] Of course, purely private torture will not normally implicate the law of nations, since there is currently no international consensus regarding torture practiced by non-state actors. Here, however, plaintiffs allege torture by . . . *state officials*. . . .

Plaintiffs allege official torture in conclusory terms. . . . Accordingly, the Court orders plaintiffs to amend Count One to state the specific acts on which they base their claim of official torture.

2.   *Prolonged Arbitrary Detention*

In Count Four plaintiffs both allege a claim for prolonged arbitrary detention, stating that defendant "arbitrarily and without justification, cause or privilege, forcibly confined both plaintiff Benchoam and [Forti's mother] for a prolonged period." Elsewhere plaintiffs allege that Benchoam was imprisoned for more than four years without ever being charged, while Forti's mother was arrested in 1977 but was never charged or released.

There is case law finding sufficient consensus to evince a customary international human rights norm against arbitrary detention. *Rodriguez-Fernandez v. Wilkinson,* 505 F. Supp. 787, 795-98 (D. Kan. 1980) (citing international treaties, cases, and commentaries), *aff'd,* 654 F.2d 1382 (10th Cir. 1981); *see also De Sanchez [v. Banco Central De Nicaragua,* 770 F.2d 1385, 1397 (5th Cir. 1985)] (right "not to be arbitrarily detained" incorporated into law of nations); *Nguyen Da Yen v. Kissinger,* 528 F.2d 1194, 1201 n. 13 (9th Cir. 1975) (illegal detention may constitute international tort); *but see Jean v. Nelson,* 727 F.2d 957, 964 & n. 4 (11th Cir. 1984) (disagreed with *Rodriguez-Fernandez* in holding that detention of uninvited aliens under national sovereign's exclusion power is no violation of customary international law), *aff'd,* 472 U.S. 846 . . . (1985). The consensus is even clearer in the case of a state's *prolonged* arbitrary detention of its own citizens. The norm is obligatory, and is readily definable in terms of the arbitrary character of the detention. The Court finds that plaintiffs have alleged international tort claims for prolonged arbitrary detention.

3.   *Summary Execution*

[The court then summarized various international treaties, court decisions, and provisions of the Tentative Draft of the Restatement (Revised) of the Foreign Relations Law of the United States that proscribe summary execution.]

The proscription of summary execution or murder by the state appears to be universal, is readily definable, and is of course obligatory. The Court emphasizes that plaintiff's allegations raise no issue as to whether or not the execution was within the lawful exercise of state power; rather, she alleges murder by state officials with neither authorization nor recourse to any process of law. Under these circumstances, the Court finds that plaintiff Benchoam has stated a cognizable claim. . . .

4. *Causing Disappearance*

[With respect to Forti's claim for "causing the disappearance" of his mother, the court noted that, while disappearance was common, such a tort was not universally recognized. Plaintiffs cited only a 1978 United Nations resolution, a 1980 congressional resolution, and a provision of the Tentative Draft of the Restatement (Revised) of the Foreign Relations Law of the United States in support of their claimed tort.]

Before this Court may adjudicate a tort claim under §1350, it must be satisfied that the legal standard it is to apply is one with universal acceptance and definition; on no other basis may the Court exercise jurisdiction over a claimed violation of the law of nations. Unfortunately, the Court cannot say, on the basis of the evidence submitted, that there yet exists the requisite degree of international consensus which demonstrates a customary international norm. Even if there were greater evidence of universality, there remain definitional problems. It is not clear precisely what conduct falls within the proposed norm, or how this proscription would differ from that of summary execution. The other torts condemned by the international community and discussed above—official torture, prolonged arbitrary detention, and summary execution—involve two types of conduct by the official actor: (1) taking the individual into custody; and (2) committing a wrongful, tortious act in excess of his authority over that person. In the case of "causing disappearance," only the first of these two actions can be proven—the taking into custody. However, the sole act of taking an individual into custody does not suffice to prove conduct which the international community proscribes. The Court recognizes the very real problems of proof presented by the disappearance of an individual following such custody. Yet there is no apparent international consensus as to the additional elements needed to make out a claim for causing the disappearance of an individual. For instance, plaintiffs have not shown that customary international law creates a presumption of causing disappearance upon a showing of prolonged absence after initial custody.

For these reasons the Court must dismiss Count Three for failure to state a claim upon which relief may be grounded.

5. *Cruel, Inhuman and Degrading Treatment*

Finally, in Count Five plaintiffs both allege a claim for "cruel, inhuman and degrading treatment" based on the general allegations of the Complaint and consisting specifically of the alleged torture, murder, forcible disappearance and prolonged arbitrary detention.

This claim suffers the same defects as Count Three [with respect to lack of evidence of universal recognition of the tort and definability]. The difficulties for a district court in adjudicating such a claim are manifest. Because this right lacks readily ascertainable parameters, it is unclear what behavior falls within the proscription—beyond such obvious torts as are already encompassed by the proscriptions of torture, summary execution and prolonged arbitrary detention. Lacking the requisite elements of universality and definability, this proposed tort cannot qualify as a violation of the law of nations. Accordingly, the Court dismisses Count Five of the Complaint for failure to state a claim upon which relief may be granted. . . .

*   *   *   *   *

Forti v. Suarez-Mason, 694 F. Supp. 707 (N.D. Cal. 1988) (*Forti II*) (footnotes and some citations omitted):

[The Court's previous Order had dismissed plaintiffs' claims (for causing disappearance and for cruel, inhuman, or degrading treatment) due to lack of evidence of universal consensus regarding recognition of the tort and problems with definability.]

. . . Plaintiffs subsequently filed this Motion, supported by numerous international legal authorities, as well as affidavits from eight renowned international law scholars. The Court has reviewed these materials and concludes that plaintiffs have met their burden of showing an international consensus as to the status and content of the international tort of "causing disappearance. . . ." The Court also concludes that plaintiffs have again failed to establish that there is any international consensus as to what conduct falls within the category of "cruel, inhuman or degrading treatment." Absent such consensus as to the content of this alleged tort, it is not cognizable under the Alien Tort Statute. . . .

II.

. . . The plaintiff's burden in stating a claim [under the Alien Tort Statute] is to establish the existence of a "universal, definable, and obligatory international norm[]." To meet this burden plaintiffs need not establish unanimity among nations. Rather, they must show a general recognition among states that a specific practice is prohibited. It is with this standard in mind that the Court examines the evidence presented by plaintiffs.

A. . . .

The legal scholars . . . are in agreement that there is universal consensus as to the two essential elements of a claim for "disappearance." In Professor Franck's words:

> The international community has also reached a consensus on the definition of a "disappearance." It has two essential elements; (a) abduction by a state official or by persons acting under state approval or authority; and (b) refusal by the state to acknowledge the abduction and detention.

Plaintiffs cite numerous international legal authorities which support the assertion that "disappearance" is a universally recognized wrong under the law of nations. For example, United Nations General Assembly Resolution 33/173 recognizes "disappearance" as violative of many of the rights recognized in the Universal Declaration of Human Rights, G.A. Res. 217 A (III), adopted by the U.N. Doc. A/810 (1948) . . . . These rights include: (1) the right to life; (2) the right to liberty and security of the person; (3) the right to freedom from torture; (4) the right to freedom from arbitrary arrest and detention; and (5) the right to a fair and public trial. *Id.*, articles 3, 5, 9, 10, 11. *See also* International Covenant on Political and Civil Rights, G.A.

Res. 2200 (XXI), adopted by the United Nations General Assembly, December 16, 1966, U.N. Doc. A/6316 (1966), articles 6, 7, 9, 10, 14, 15, 17.

Other documents support this characterization of "disappearance" as violative of universally recognized human rights. The United States Congress has denounced "prolonged detention without charges and trial" along with other "flagrant denial[s] of the right to life, liberty, or the security of person." 22 U.S.C. §2304(d)(1). The recently published Restatement (Third) of the Foreign Relations Law of the United States §702 includes "disappearance" as a violation of the international law of human rights. The Organization of American States has also denounced "disappearance" as "an affront to the conscience of the hemisphere and . . . a crime against humanity." Organization of American States, Inter-American Commission on Human Rights, General Assembly Resolution 666 (November 18, 1983).

Of equal importance, plaintiffs' submissions support their assertion that there is a universally recognized legal definition of what constitutes the tort of "causing disappearance." The Court's earlier order expressed concern that "the sole act of taking an individual into custody does not suffice to prove conduct which the international community proscribes." Plaintiffs' submissions on this Motion, however, establish recognition of a second essential element—official refusal to acknowledge that the individual has been taken into custody. For example, the United Nations General Assembly has expressed concern

> at the difficulties in obtaining reliable information from competent authorities as to the circumstances of such persons, including reports of the persistent refusal of such authorities or organizations to acknowledge that they hold such persons in custody or otherwise to account for them.

U.N. General Assembly Resolution 33/173 (December 20, 1978).

Likewise, the Organization of American States has recognized the importance of this element, commenting on the

> numerous cases wherein the government systematically denies the detention of individuals, despite the convincing evidence that the claimants provide to verify their allegations that such persons have been detained by police or military authorities and, in some cases, that those persons are, or have been, confined in specified detention centers.

Organization of American States, Inter-American Commission on Human Rights, 1977 Annual Report, at 26.

In the Court's view, the submitted materials are sufficient to establish the existence of a universal and obligatory international proscription of the tort of "causing disappearance." This tort is characterized by the following two essential elements: (1) abduction by state officials or their agents; followed by (2) official refusals to acknowledge the abduction or to disclose the detainee's fate. Upon review of the Second Amended Complaint it is clear that plaintiff Forti has sufficiently pled both these elements. . . .

B.

In its [previous] Order the Court found that plaintiffs had stated claims under the Alien Tort Statute for "official torture," but had failed to state claims for "cruel, inhuman and degrading treatment." Plaintiffs have now combined their two previous claims to allege "torture or other cruel, inhuman or degrading treatment or punishment." The Second Amended Complaint does not state precisely what alleged actions constitute the proposed tort. Rather, it merely incorporates *all* the factual allegations and alleges that these acts constitute ". . . [a] violation of customary international law."

In dismissing plaintiffs' earlier "cruel, inhuman or degrading treatment" claim this Court found that the proposed tort lacked "the requisite elements of universality and definability." Plaintiffs now submit the aforementioned declarations and several international legal authorities in support of their argument that "[t]he definition of cruel, inhuman or degrading treatment or punishment is inextricably related to that for torture." Specifically, plaintiffs argue that the two are properly viewed on a continuum, and that "torture and cruel, inhuman or degrading treatment differ essentially in the degree of ill treatment suffered." Thus while the latter treatment is not torture it is an analytically distinct tort which in plaintiffs' view, is actionable under the Alien Tort Statute.

Plaintiffs emphasize that virtually all international legal authorities which prohibit torture also prohibit cruel, inhuman or degrading treatment. For example, §702 of the Restatement (Third) of the Foreign Relations Law of the United States: "A state violates international law if, as a matter of state policy, it practices, encourages, or condones . . . torture or other cruel inhuman or degrading treatment or punishment." Likewise, 22 U.S.C. §2304(d)(1) lists "torture or cruel, inhuman or degrading treatment or punishment," among "gross violations of internationally recognized human rights." Article 5 of the Universal Declaration of Human Rights, *supra*, states that "[n]o one shall be subjected to torture or to cruel, inhuman or degrading treatment." *See also De Sanchez v. Banco Central De Nicaragua,* 770 F.2d 1385, 1397 (5th Cir. 1985) (recognizing "right not to be . . . tortured, or otherwise subjected to cruel, inhuman or degrading treatment").

While these and other materials establish a recognized proscription of "cruel, inhuman or degrading treatment," they offer no guidance as to what constitutes such treatment. The Restatement does not define the term. The cited statute (22 U.S.C. §2304) and the Universal Declaration of Human rights also both fail to offer a definition. The scholars whose declarations have been submitted likewise decline to offer any definition of the proposed tort. In fact, one of the declarations appears to concede the lack of a universally recognized definition. *See Lillich Declaration,* at 8 ("only the contours of the prohibition, not its existence as a norm of customary international law, are the subject of legitimate debate").

This problem of definability is evidenced by the Second Amended Complaint. Plaintiffs simply incorporate all the factual allegations and without elaboration, allege that these constitute the alleged cruel, inhuman or degrading treatment. However, the complaint alleges a wide range of discrete acts associated with the detentions. Some of the acts result in physical injury, some do not. Does the proposed tort require physical injury? If purely psychological harm is cognizable, as it would appear to be, is it actionable when caused by purely verbal conduct? . . . Absent some definition of what constitutes "cruel, inhuman or degrading treatment" this Court has no way of determining what alleged treatment is actionable, and what is not.

Plaintiffs cite *The Greek Case,* 12 Y.B. Eur. Conv. on Human Rights 186 (1969), for a definition of "degrading treatment" as that which "grossly humiliates [the victim] before others or drives him to act against his will or conscience." But this definitional gloss is of no help. From our necessarily global perspective, conduct, particularly verbal conduct, which is humiliating or even grossly humiliating in one cultural context is of no moment in another. An international tort which appears and disappears as one travels around the world is clearly lacking in that level of common understanding necessary to create universal consensus. Likewise, the term "against his will or conscience" is too abstract to be of help. For example, a pacifist who is conscripted to serve in his country's military has arguably been forced to act "against his will or conscience." Would he thus have a claim for degrading treatment?

. . . Plaintiffs' submissions fail to establish that there is anything even remotely approaching universal consensus as to what constitutes "cruel, inhuman or degrading treatment." Absent this consensus in the international community as to the tort's content it is not actionable under the Alien Tort Statute. . . .

NOTES AND QUESTIONS

1. For discussion of issues involved in Suarez-Mason's efforts to avoid extradition, see *Matter of the Requested Extradition of Suarez-Mason*, 694 F. Supp. 707 (N.D. Cal. 1988).

2. What sources of international law were used in *Filartiga*? How did the court use the treaties it cited?

3. What persuaded Judge Jensen in *Forti II* to change his decision regarding an international proscription of "causing disappearance"?

4. What were the considerations in Jensen's decision not to find the proscription of "cruel, inhuman or degrading treatment" to be a customary norm? The Senate has ratified the Convention Against Torture and Other Cruel, Inhuman or Degrading Treatment or Punishment and passed implementing legislation, and it entered into force in 1994. (*See* discussion in chapter 2, *supra*) Which of the *Forti* court's concerns would be addressed by ratification and which would not?

5. Now that the U.S. is party to the Covenant on Civil and Political Rights, has the approach of *Filartiga*, *Forti I*, and *Forti II* been changed?

6. Note that Jensen in *Forti I* declares that to support a tort action a customary norm must be "universal, definable, and obligatory." 672 F. Supp. 1531, 1540 (N.D. Cal. 1987). In *Forti II*, however, he explained that "plaintiffs need not establish unanimity among nations . . . [but only] a general recognition among states that a specific practice is prohibited." 694 F. Supp. 707, 709 (N.D. Cal. 1988). What persuaded him to add that clarification? Compare this footnote in an amicus brief submitted by Frank Newman in a related case, *Matter of the Requested Extradition of Suarez-Mason*, 694 F. Supp. 676 (N.D. Cal. 1988):

> This court in *Forti* [*I*] uses "universal" . . . to describe the requisite degree of consensus. "Universal" conceivably could create confusion if it suggests "unanimous". Less ambiguous terms include "international consensus", "internationally recognized", and "widely accepted". *See* U.S. Government's Filartiga memorandum, 19 I.L.M. at 604 (1980) (requiring "a consensus in the international community that there is a widely shared understanding of the scope of this protection"). *See also* Foreign Assistance Act of 1961, sections 116 and 502B (providing for termination of assistance to governments that engage in consistent patterns of "gross violations of internationally recognized human rights").

That paragraph underscores the need for correct adjectives and the danger of using words like "universal," that may have a connotation in international discourse different from U.S. usage.

7. In 1995, a Massachusetts federal court found that though the definition of cruel, inhuman, and degrading treatment is unclear, it should at least be interpreted to cover behavior that would be governed by the U.S. Constitution. The court stated:

> It is not necessary that every aspect of what might comprise a standard such as "cruel, inhuman or degrading treatment" be fully defined and universally agreed upon before a given action meriting the label is clearly proscribed under international law, any more

than it is necessary to define all acts that may constitute "torture" or "arbitrary detention" in order to recognize certain conduct as actionable misconduct under that rubric. Accordingly, any act by the defendant which is proscribed by the Constitution of the United States and by a cognizable principle of international law plainly falls within the rubric of "cruel, inhuman or degrading treatment" and is actionable before this court under § 1350.

Xuncax v. Gramajo, 1995 WL 254818 at *19 (D. Mass. Apr. 12, 1995).

International law experts in an amicus curiae brief encouraged the Ninth Circuit to follow *Xuncax* in *In re Ferdinand Marcos Human Rights Litigation*, discussed *infra*. Amici argued that the norm against cruel, inhuman, and degrading treatment has been recognized by all branches of the United States government and is specific enough to be actionable under the Alien Tort Claims Act—at least as narrowly construed by *Xuncax* and by the U.S. reservations to the Treaty against Torture and the Civil and Political Covenant. *See* chapter 2, *supra*.

8. Assume you are the lawyer assigned to brief and argue, on appeal, the segment of *Forti II* concerning "cruel, inhuman or degrading treatment." Federal Rule of Evidence 44.1 provides that foreign law presents a question of law, not fact, and has been construed to permit appellate courts to consider sources of law not presented to the trial court. *United States v. Peterson*, 812 F.2d 486 (9th Cir. 1987). Would you move to submit a supplemental affidavit by Professor Lillich, pursuant to Rule 44.1? If he asked you to prepare the draft, what points would you make? What facts might present the most persuasive claim for proscribing cruel, inhuman, or degrading treatment? Would you follow the limiting approach of *Xuncax*?

9. Many courts have adopted *Filartiga* as the governing interpretation of §1350. *See, e.g., In re Estate of Ferdinand E. Marcos Human Rights Litigation*, 978 F.2d 493, 499-500 (9th Cir. 1992) (allowing alien mother to sue former head of Philippine police and military for kidnapping, torture, and death of her son and rejecting argument that ATCA exceeded the bounds of the U.S. constitution); *Paul v. Avril*, 812 F. Supp. 207, 211-12 (S.D. Fla. 1993) (allowing Haitians to sue former head of Haitian military for torts in Haiti that defendant supervised and approved); *Negewo v. Abebe-Jira*, 72 F.3d 844 (11th Cir. 1996) (allowing Ethiopian women to sue a police official for detention and cruel, inhuman, and degrading treatment and punishment in Ethiopia).

10. One federal district judge found that jurisdiction was proper under the ATCA. In a default judgment, the five plaintiffs, who were related to victims of torture and killings in Rwanda, were awarded over $100 million. The defendant, Rwandan military leader Jean Bosco Barauagwiza, played a role in the massacre of thousands.

11. Judge Jensen in *Forti I* addressed the source of a cause of action necessary to invoke customary norms. Debate flared in the mid-1980s following issuance of three concurring opinions, including the oft-argued one by Judge Bork, in *Tel-Oren v. Libyan Arab Republic*, 726 F.2d 774, 798-823 (D.C. Cir. 1984). Debate was fanned by the Justice Department's endorsement of Bork's view in an amicus brief in *Trajano v. Marcos*, 878 F.2d 1439 (9th Cir. 1989).

Jensen in *Forti I* rejected the reasoning endorsed by Bork in *Tel-Oren* and held that the ATCA did provide a right of action. He noted that "since the law of nations clearly does not create or define civil actions, . . . to require such an explicit grant under international law would effectively nullify that portion of the statute which confers jurisdiction over tort suits involving the law of nations." 672 F. Supp. at 1539. One could also argue the ATCA was intended to provide a remedy rarely provided in international law.

Courts of other countries have recognized that international law does include the right to an effective remedy. For example, in *Borovsky v. Commissioner of Immigration*, 90 Phil. Rpts. 107 (1951), the Philippine Supreme Court, whose jurisprudence draws heavily on that of the U.S., ordered an excludable alien released from indefinite detention on the ground that his detention violated the customary law reflected in the Universal Declaration of Human

Rights. Similarly the German Constitutional Court has declared that though "contemporary generally recognized principles of international law included only a few legal rules that directly create rights and duties of private individuals by virtue of the international law itself," they do create rights and duties in "the sphere of the minimum standards for the protection of human rights." *In the Matter of Republic of the Philippines*, 46 BVerfGE 342, 362 (2BvM 1/76 December 13, 1977).

12.   A slight variant of Jensen's view—that international law may, but need not, supply a cause of action—was endorsed by international law experts in an amicus brief submitted in *Trajano v. Marcos, supra* note 9.[8] In the brief, drafted by the Center for Constitutional Rights, the experts argued that plaintiffs do not necessarily lack an enforceable cause of action even if the ATCA were construed not to provide one. "As the United States itself established in its Memorandum in *Filartiga*, a right of action can be located *in international law itself* for certain egregious customary international law violations." Brief on Behalf of International Experts, citing Memorandum of the United States as amicus curiae submitted in *Filartiga v. Peña-Irala, reprinted in* 19 I.L.M. 585, 601-06 (1980).

The experts also argued, consistently with the Government's position in its *Filartiga* brief, that:

> [M]odern international law recognizes that individuals may invoke domestic reme-dies for violations of certain fundamental norms of international human rights law, such as torture. [Article 8 of] [t]he Universal Declaration of Human Rights, which is widely acknowledged as reflecting binding norms of customary international law, guarantees the . . . right . . . to an effective remedy by the competent national tribunals for acts violating the fundamental rights granted him by the constitution or by law. . . . [Article 2(3) of] [t]he International Covenant on Civil and Political Rights, also cited. . .by the *Filartiga* court as evidence of customary international law, . . . similarly obligates states to provide individuals with "an effective remedy" for violations of human rights.

The experts concluded "where, as here, there is no effective remedy other than the domestic judicial remedy, customary law requires that that judicial remedy be made avail-able." This conclusion has been "well-accepted in United States jurisprudence," because courts have routinely allowed individuals to enforce customary international law in domestic courts.

13.   In an alternative holding in *Forti I*, Judge Jensen ruled that 28 U.S.C. § 1331, which confers jurisdiction over federal questions, creates a right of action for international torts because their prohibition is part of federal common law. That ruling is significant because it grants U.S. citizens, in addition to aliens, a right to sue and thus eliminates a distinction which led to the anomalous result that aliens, but not citizens, could sue in U.S. courts for international torts. Does the holding render the ATCA redundant? In other words, if violations of international law represent violations of federal common law, is § 1350 necessary to confer jurisdiction on federal courts?

14.   Exactly what arguments support the conclusion that international law includes the right to an effective remedy? If a government were party to the Covenant on Civil and Political Rights and its Optional Protocol, which provides a procedure whereby the Human Rights Committee hears complaints from victims of a state's violation of the Covenant, do you think

---

[8] On the brief were D'Amato, Days, Falk, Glennon, Grossman, Hartman (Fitzpatrick), Koh, Lich-tenstein, Lillich, Lobel, McDougal, Newman, Schachter, Steiner, Weissbrodt, Weston, and Lake. It was published in David Cole et al., *Interpreting the Alien Tort Statute: Amicus Curiae Memorandum of International Law Scholars and Practitioners in* Trajano v. Marcos, 12 HASTINGS INT'L & COMP. L. REV. 1 (1988). For discussion of juridical underpinnings of the right to an effective remedy, see Jordan J. Paust, *On Human Rights: the Use of Human Rights Precepts in U.S. History and the Right to an Effective Remedy in Domestic Courts*, 10 MICH. J. INT'L L. 543 (1989).

the availability of the Protocol procedure would satisfy the Covenant's requirement of an effective national remedy? Or would the government in addition be obliged to recognize a right to seek redress before a judicial or administrative body?

15. For recent readings, see:

Anne-Marie Burley, *The Alien Tort Statute and the Judiciary Act of 1789: A Badge of Honor*, 83 AM. J. INT'L L. 461 (1989);

Jorge Cicero, *The Alien Tort Statute of 1789 as a Remedy for Injuries to Foreign Nationals Hosted by the United States*, 23 COLUM. HUM. RTS. L. REV. 315 (1992);

Joan Fitzpatrick, *The Future of the Alien Tort Claims Act of 1789: Lessons from* In Re Marcos Human Rights Litigation, 67 ST. JOHN'S L. REV. 491 (1993);

Kenneth C. Randall, *Federal Jurisdiction Over International Law Claims: Inquiries into the Alien Tort Claims Statute*, 18 N.Y.U. J. INT'L L. & POL. 1 (1985);

Kenneth C. Randall, *Federal Questions and the Human Rights Paradigm*, 73 MINN. L. REV. 349 (1988);

Jean-Marie Simon, *The Alien Tort Claims Act: Justice or Show Trials?*, 11 B.U. INT'L L.J. 1(1993);

Ralph G. Steinhardt, *Fulfilling the Promise of* Filartiga: *Litigating Human Rights Claims Against the Estate of Ferdinand Marcos*, 20 YALE J. INT'L L. 65 (1995);

Joseph M. Sweeney, *A Tort Only in Violation of the Law of Nations*, 18 HASTINGS INT'L & COMP. L. REV. 445 (1995).

   See also Beth Stephens et al., SUING FOR TORTURE AND OTHER HUMAN RIGHTS ABUSES IN FEDERAL COURT: A LITIGATION MANUAL (1993) (discussing the Alien Tort Claims Act, the Torture Victim Protection Act, who may sue in U.S. courts, who may be sued, and what human rights violations give rise to suit); GARY B. BORN & DAVID WESTIN, INTERNATIONAL CIVIL LITIGATION IN UNITED STATES COURTS, COMMENTARY & MATERIALS (2d ed. 1992) (discussing the procedural aspects of international litigation); Jonathan Pratter & Joseph R. Profaizer, *A Practitioner's Research Guide and Bibliography to International Civil Litigation*, 28 TEX. INT'L L.J. 633 (1993).
   For an early article recommending suits by alien human rights victims in U.S. courts see David Weissbrodt, *Domestic Legal Activity in Furtherance of International Human Rights Goals, in* IMPLEMENTING INTERNATIONAL HUMAN RIGHTS THROUGH THE DOMESTIC LEGAL PROCESS 10, 17-18 (John Bassett Moore Soc'y of Int'l Law, 1975).

Despite benefits to alien plaintiffs, the widespread acceptance of *Filartiga*, and the rejection of the Bork views, federal courts are still criticized for accepting jurisdiction. In a recent article Joan Fitzpatrick summarized several of the objections.

   First, the competence of the federal courts to determine the substantive scope of international human rights law has been doubted, sometimes reflecting deeper doubt whether any such law exists. Second, skepticism has been voiced whether those norms may be legally enforced in the context of domestic litigation, in the absence of specific implementing legislation. Third, the hypothetical danger of retaliation by means of suits in foreign countries against United States officials has been cited as a reason for the courts to decline jurisdiction until more clearly commanded by Congress to act. Fourth, the constitutionality of conferring jurisdiction over suits between aliens for violations of the law of nations has been questioned. Finally, the dominance by the political branches over foreign policy has been deemed responsible for an exceedingly cautious approach by the courts to ATCA suits, especially those

brought against an exiled dictator or other leading figure whose presence in the
United States is explained by a policy objective of the Executive.

The Future of the Alien Tort Claims Act of 1789: Lessons from In Re Marcos Human
Rights Litigation, 67 St. John's L. Rev. 491, 494 (1993) (footnotes omitted).

She also discussed goals and benefits of the ATCA suits, only some of which
relate to compensating victims:

> [A]lthough transnational public law plaintiffs routinely request retrospective dam-
> ages or even prospective injunctive relief, their broader strategic goals are often
> served by a declaratory or default judgment announcing that a transnational norm
> has been violated. Even a judgment that the plaintiff cannot enforce against the
> defendant in the rendering forum empowers the plaintiff by creating a bargaining
> chip for use in other political fora.
>
> [A]ll tort judgments, whether domestic or transnational, serve several ends:
> compensation for victims; denial of safe haven to the defendant in the judgment-
> rendering forum; deterrence of others who might contemplate similar conduct; and
> enunciation of legal norms opposing the conduct for which the defendant has been
> found liable. . . . [N]orm-enunciation, deterrence, and denial of safe haven assume
> greater prominence in a transnational setting, where highly mobile defendants and
> the absence of full faith and credit impair the collectability of judgments.

Id. at 500-01 (quoting Harold H. Koh, *Transnational Public Law Litigation*, 100
Yale L.J. 2347, 2349 n. 11 (1991)).

NOTES AND QUESTIONS

1.   If only some goals or benefits of ATCA lawsuits can be satisfied by an uncollectible default
judgment, why bother with lawsuits? Are there other ways of achieving those objectives that
do not involve courts? How does a single ATCA suit fit the pattern of strategies available for
pursuing human rights objectives?

2.   The ATCA confers jurisdiction only over suits by aliens and is inapplicable to suits by
U.S. citizens. *Linder v. Calero Portocarrero*, 747 F. Supp. 1452, 1460-61 (S.D. Fla. 1990),
rev'd on other grounds, 963 F.2d 332 (1992). The Torture Victim Protection Act ("TVPA"),
codified at 28 U.S.C. § 1350 and 1331, however, open federal courts to suits by citizens for
certain human rights violations. *See* Part E, *infra* page 550, for further discussion of the
TVPA.

   The ATCA also does not apply when the Foreign Sovereign Immunities Act ("FSIA")
applies because it confers the sole method of obtaining jurisdiction over a foreign sovereign.
Argentine Republic v. Amerada Hess Shipping Corp., 488 U.S. 428 (1989). *See* Part D, *infra*,
at 533, for further discussion.

3.   Other U.S. statutes also provide broad jurisdiction over acts committed outside the U.S.
The Hostage Taking Act, 18 U.S.C. § 1203, for example, criminalizes the taking of hostages
inside or outside the U.S. If the hostage-taking occurred outside the U.S., the statute requires
that the offender either be a U.S. citizen or be found in the U.S., that the hostage be a U.S.
citizen, or that the hostage-taking be designed to compel the U.S. to do or abstain from any
act. *Id.* The provisions also parallel the ATCA in that they authorize federal courts to adjudicate claims arising from actions occurring outside the U.S. between aliens, provided the alien
defendant is in the U.S. at the time he is served.

   United States v. Yunis, 924 F.2d 1086 (D.C. Cir. 1991) upheld the constitutionality of
the Hostage Taking Act. The court rejected arguments that international law had not yet
recognized hostage-taking as a crime and, therefore, that international law precluded personal
jurisdiction under the Act. *Id.* at 1091. The court stated that international law cannot invali-

date federal statutes and thus affirmed an alien's conviction for hijacking a Jordanian flight departing from Lebanon on the ground that two of the hostages were U.S. citizens. *Id.* at 1090-91. The court did not rule on the claim that the defendant was not "found" in the U.S. because he was seized in international waters and then brought forcibly to the U.S. *Id.* at *1090.* That action may be considered acceptable, however, under *United States v. Alvarez-Machain*, 504 U.S. 655, which upheld federal court jurisdiction over a Mexican doctor who was kidnapped and forcibly brought to the U.S. for trial. *Alvarez-Machain* is discussed further in chapter 13, *infra.*

See also Kenneth C. Randall, *Universal Jurisdiction Under International Law*, 66 TEX. L. REV. 785, 815-34 (1988) (discussing universal jurisdiction for human rights violations).

4. Can you justify using international law in U.S. courts to compensate victims of actions legal in countries where they occur? The ATCA does not require plaintiffs to sue in such a country before suing in the U.S.

5. ATCA jurisdiction is effective in large part because the U.S. uses a "presence is power" theory of personal jurisdiction. In other words, service of process may be made on anyone physically present within the jurisdiction. Therefore aliens may sue even those alien defendants who are present in the U.S. illegally, as was the *Filartiga* defendant.

Article 2(3) of the Covenant on Civil and Political Rights provides:

Each State Party to the present Covenant undertakes:

(a)   To ensure that any person whose rights or freedoms as herein recognized are violated shall have an effective remedy, notwithstanding that the violation has been committed by persons acting in an official capacity. . . .

Does that increase the likelihood of legislation similar to the ATCA in other countries? *See also* Article 3(b) & (c).

---

2.   International Rules Governing Rape

In seeking law that applies to the hypothetical rape case presented at the beginning of this chapter, it will be helpful to determine whether wrongdoings in Bosnia-Herzegovina have been part of an international or internal armed conflict. Generally the four Geneva Conventions and their first Protocol are applicable to conflicts of an international character. In contrast, Common Article 3 of the Conventions and the second Protocol apply to internal conflicts.

In insurgency situations covered by Common Article 3 and Protocol II, several criteria determine when an insurgent force is obligated to abide by the provisions. Generally the party in revolt against the government must "possess[] an organized military force [and] an authority responsible for its acts" and must be "acting within a determinate territory and have the means of respect and ensuring respect" for the Conventions and the Protocol. COMMENTARY ON THE GENEVA CONVENTIONS OF 12 AUGUST 1949 49-50 (Jean Pictet ed. 1952).

Geneva Conventions of 1949, Conventions I-IV, *adopted* Aug. 12, 1949, 6 U.S.T. 3114, 3217, 3316, 3516; T.I.A.S. No. 3362-3365; 75 U.N.T.S. 31, 85, 135, 287, *entered into force* Oct. 21, 1950:

Common Article 1

The High Contracting Parties undertake to respect and to ensure respect for the present Convention in all circumstances.

Common Article 2

... [T]he present Convention shall apply to all cases of declared war or of any other armed conflict which may arise between two or more of the High Contracting Parties, even if the state of war is not recognized by one of them. ...

Common Article 3

In the case of armed conflict not of an international character occurring in the territory of one of the High Contracting Parties, each Party to the conflict shall be bound to apply, as a minimum, the following provisions:

(1)   Persons taking no active part in the hostilities ... shall in all circumstances be treated humanely, without any adverse distinction founded on race, colour, religion or faith, sex, birth or wealth, or any other similar criteria.

To this end, the following acts are and shall remain prohibited at any time and in any place whatsoever with respect to the above-mentioned persons:

(a)   violence to life and person, in particular murder of all kinds, mutilation, cruel treatment and torture; [and] ...

(c)   outrages upon personal dignity, in particular humiliating and degrading treatment . . ..

*   *   *   *   *

Geneva Convention for the Protection of Civilian Persons in Time of War, 6 U.S.T. 3516, T.I.A.S. No. 3365, 75 U.N.T.S. 287, *entered into force* Oct. 21, 1950:

Article 27 ...

Women shall be especially protected against any attack on their honour, in particular against rape, enforced prostitution, or any form of indecent assault. ...

Article 32

The High Contracting Parties specifically agree that each of them is prohibited from taking any measure of such a character as to cause the physical suffering or extermination of protected persons in their hands. This prohibition applies not only to murder [or] torture, . . . but also to any other measures of brutality whether applied by civilian or military agents.

Article 147

Grave breaches [of this Convention] shall be those involving any of the following acts, if committed against persons or property protected by the present Convention: wilful killing, torture or inhuman treatment, . . . wilfully causing great suffering or serious injury to body or health. . . .

[The Commission of Experts appointed to study the situation in the former Yugoslavia concluded that the 1949 Geneva Conventions "prohibit, *inter alia*, . . . torture, rape or inhuman treatment of protected persons. . . ." Commission of Experts Established Pursuant to Security Council Resolution 780 (1992), *Final Report*, U.N. Doc. S/1994/674, at 14. Article 5 of the Statute of the International Tribunal established to prosecute persons responsible for serious violations of international humanitarian law committed in the territory of the former Yugoslavia since 1991 declared that, during armed conflict, rape directed against any civilian population constituted a crime against humanity. U.N. Security Council, *Report of the Secretary-General Pursuant to Paragraph 2 of Security Council Resolution 808 (1993)*, U.N. Doc. S/25704, Annex (1993).]

* * * * *

Protocol Additional to the Geneva Conventions of 12 August 1949, and Relating to the Protection of Victims of International Armed Conflicts (Protocol I), U.N. Doc. A/32/144, Annex I, 16 I.L.M. 1391 (1977), *entered into force* Dec. 7, 1978:

Article 1—General principles and scope of application

1. The High Contracting Parties undertake to respect and to ensure respect for this Protocol in all circumstances. . . .

3. This Protocol, which supplements the Geneva Conventions of 12 August 1949 for the protection of war victims, shall apply in the situations referred to in Article 2 common to those Conventions.

4. The situations referred to in the preceding paragraph include armed conflicts in which peoples are fighting against colonial domination and alien occupation and against racist régimes in the exercise of their right of self-determination. . . .

Article 51—Protection of the civilian population

2. The civilian population as such, as well as individual civilians, shall not be the object of attack. Acts or threats of violence the primary purpose of which is to spread terror among the civilian population are prohibited.

Article 75—Fundamental guarantees

2. The following acts are and shall remain prohibited at any time and in any place whatsoever, whether committed by civilian or by military agents:

(a) violence to the life, health, or physical or mental well-being of persons, in particular:

  (i)   murder;
  (ii) torture of all kinds, whether physical or mental;
  (iii) corporal punishment; and
  (iv) mutilation;

(b) outrages upon personal dignity, in particular humiliating and degrading treatment, enforced prostitution and any form of indecent assault. . . .

Article 76—Protection of women

1. Women shall be the object of special respect and shall be protected in particular against rape, forced prostitution and any other form of indecent assault.

* * * * *

Protocol Additional to the Geneva Conventions of 12 August 1949, and Relating to the Protection of Victims of Non-International

Armed Conflicts (Protocol II), U.N. Doc. A/32/144, Annex II, 16 I.L.M. 1442 (1977), *entered into force* **Dec. 7, 1978:**

Article 1—Material field of application

1.   This Protocol, which develops and supplements Article 3 common to the Geneva Conventions of 12 August 1949 without modifying its existing conditions of application, shall apply to all armed conflicts which are not covered by Article 1 of . . .Protocol I and which take place in the territory of a High Contracting Party between its armed forces and dissident armed forces or other organized armed groups which, under responsible command, exercise such control over a part of its territory as to enable them to carry out sustained and concerted military operations and to implement this Protocol.

2.   This Protocol shall not apply to situations of internal disturbances and tensions, such as riots, isolated and sporadic acts of violence and other acts of a similar nature, as not being armed conflicts.

Article 4—Fundamental guarantees

2.   . . . [T]he following acts against [persons who do not take a direct part or who have ceased to take part in hostilities] are and shall remain prohibited at any time and in any place whatsoever:

(a)   violence to life, health and physical or mental well-being of persons, in particular murder as well as cruel treatment such as torture, mutilation or any form of corporal punishment; . . .

(e)   outrages upon personal dignity, in particular humiliating and degrading treatment, rape, enforced prostitution and any form of indecent assault. . . .

*   *   *   *   *

Control Council Law No. 10, Punishment of Persons Guilty of War Crimes, Crimes Against Peace and Against Humanity, 3 Official Gazette Control Council for Germany 50-55 (1946):

Article II

1.   Each of the following Acts is recognized as a crime: . . .

c)   *Crimes against Humanity.* Atrocities and offenses, including but not limited to murder, extermination, enslavement, deportation, imprisonment, torture, rape, or other inhumane acts committed against any civilian population, or persecutions on political, racial or religious grounds whether or not in violation of the domestic laws of the country where perpetrated.

*   *   *   *   *

Covenant on Civil and Political Rights, G.A. res 2200A (XXI), 21 U.N. GAOR Supp. (No. 16) at 52, U.N. Doc. A/6316 (1966), *entered into force* **Mar. 23, 1976:**

Article 2

Each State Party to the present Covenant undertakes to respect and to ensure to all individuals within its territory and subject to its jurisdiction the rights recognized in the present Covenant, without distinction of any kind, such as race, colour, sex, language, religion, political or other opinion, national or social origin, property, birth or other status.

Article 7

No one shall be subjected to torture or to cruel, inhuman or degrading treatment or punishment. . . .

Article 9

Everyone has the right to liberty and security of person. No one shall be subjected to arbitrary arrest or detention. . . .

Article 17

1.   No one shall be subjected to arbitrary or unlawful interference with his privacy, family, [or] home. . ., nor to unlawful attacks on his honour and reputation.

2.   Everyone has the right to protection of the law against such interference or attacks.

*   *   *   *   *

Convention on the Elimination of All Forms of Discrimination against Women, G.A. Res. 34/180, U.N. GAOR, 34th Sess., Supp. No. 46, at 193, U.N. Doc. A/34/46 (1980), *reprinted in* 19 I.L.M. 33 (1980), *entered into force* Sept. 8, 1981:

Article 1

For the purposes of the present Convention, the term "discrimination against women" shall mean any distinction, exclusion or restriction made on the basis of sex which has the effect or purpose of impairing or nullifying the recognition, enjoyment or exercise by women, irrespective of their marital status, on a basis of equality of men and women, of human rights and fundamental freedoms in the political, economic, social, cultural, civil or any other field.

Article 2

States Parties condemn discrimination against women in all its forms [and] agree[:] . . .

(d)   To refrain from engaging in any act or practice of discrimination against women and to ensure that public authorities and institutions shall act in conformity with this obligation. . . .

Article 6

States Parties shall take all appropriate measures, including legislation, to suppress all forms of traffic in women and exploitation of prostitution of women.

*   *   *   *

The Committee on the Elimination of Discrimination against Women has issued an interpretation of those provisions in General Recommendation No. 19, HRI/GEN/ 1 (1992), at p. 74 (Eleventh session, 1992): "The definition of discrimination includes gender-based violence, that is, violence that is directed against a women because she is a woman or that affects women disproportionately. It includes acts that inflict physical, mental or sexual harm or suffering, threats of such acts, coercion or other deprivations of liberty. . . ."

In a general comment on Article 6, *id.* at 76, the Committee noted, "[w]ars, armed conflicts and the occupation of territories often lead to increased prostitution, trafficking in women and sexual assault of women, which require specific protective and punitive measures."

*   *   *   *   *

Declaration on the Elimination of Violence Against Women, G.A. Res. 104, U.N. GAOR, 48th Sess, U.N. Doc. A/48/629 (1993):

Article 1

For the purposes of this Declaration, the term "violence against women" means any act of gender-based violence that results in, or is likely to result in, physical, sexual or psychological harm or suffering to women, including threats of such acts, coercion or arbitrary deprivation of liberty, whether occurring in public or in private life.

Article 2

Violence against women shall be understood to encompass, but not be limited to, the following: . . .

(b)   Physical, sexual and psychological violence occurring within the general community, including rape [and] sexual abuse . . .;

(c)   Physical, sexual and psychological violence perpetrated or condoned by the State, wherever it occurs.

*   *   *   *   *

Theodor Meron, *Rape as a Crime Under International Humanitarian Law*, 87 Am. J. Int'l L. 424, 425-27 (1993) (several footnotes omitted):

That the practice of rape has been deliberate, massive and egregious, particularly in Bosnia-Herzegovina, is amply demonstrated in reports of the United Nations, the European Community, the Conference on Security and Co-operation in Europe and various nongovernmental organizations. The special rapporteur appointed by the UN Commission on Human Rights, Tadeusz Mazowiecki, highlighted the role of rape both as an attack on the individual victim and as a method of "ethnic cleansing" "intended to humiliate, shame, degrade and terrify the entire ethnic group." Indescribable abuse of thousands of women in the territory of former Yugoslavia was needed to shock the international community into rethinking the prohibition of rape as a crime under the laws of war. . . . [But] what . . . is the current status of rape as a crime under international humanitarian law?

Rape by soldiers has of course been prohibited by the law of war for centuries, and violators have been subjected to capital punishment under national military codes . . . . Of more immediate influence on the modern law of war was the prohibition of rape as a capital crime by the Lieber Instructions (1863). Indeed, rape committed on an individual soldier's initiative has frequently been prosecuted in national courts.

In many cases, however, rape has been given license, either as an encouragement for soldiers or as an instrument of policy. Nazi and Japanese practices of forced prostitution and rape on a large scale are among the egregious examples of such policies.

. . . Rape was neither mentioned in the Nuremberg Charter nor prosecuted in Nuremberg as a war crime under customary international law. But it was prosecuted in Tokyo as a war crime.

. . . [Though] both the fourth Geneva Convention and the Additional Protocols explicitly and categorically prohibit rape, . . . [they] do not list rape among the grave breaches subject to universal jurisdiction.

It is time for a change. Indeed, under the weight of the events in former Yugoslavia, the hesitation to recognize that rape can be a war crime or a grave breach has already begun to dissipate. The International Committee of the Red Cross (ICRC) and various states aided this development by adopting a broad construction of existing law. The ICRC declared that the grave breach of "wilfully causing great suffering or serious injury to body or health" (Article 147 of the fourth Geneva Convention) covers rape. If so, surely rape—in certain circumstances—can also rise to the level of such other grave breaches as torture or inhuman treatment. Moreover, the massive and systematic practice of rape and its use as a "national" instrument of "ethnic cleansing" qualify it to be defined and prosecuted as a crime against humanity.

Independently of the ICRC aide-mémoire and soon after it was issued, the U.S. Department of State unequivocally stated that rape already was a war crime or a grave breach under customary international law and the Geneva Conventions and could be prosecuted as such.[9]

NOTES AND QUESTIONS

1. The following list shows which nations concerned with the hypothetical case described at the beginning of this chapter have ratified the treaties excerpted above. The date in parentheses represents the date of ratification or succession.

United States

Geneva Conventions I-IV (August 2, 1955)
Covenant on Civil and Political Rights (June 8, 1992)
Convention against Torture and Other Cruel, Inhuman or Degrading Treatment or Punishment (October 21, 1994)

---

[9] The Department stated:

We believe that . . . the legal basis for prosecuting troops for rape is well established under the Geneva Conventions and customary international law. As stated in the authoritative Department of the Army Law of War Manual, any violation of the Geneva Conventions is a war crime (FM 27-10, para. 499.). Article 27 of the Geneva Convention Relative to the Protection of Civilian Persons in Time of War provides that women shall be "especially protected . . . against rape." Article 13 of the Geneva Convention Relative to the Treatment of Prisoners of War provides that prisoners "must at all times be protected, particularly against acts of violence"; article 14 requires that women "be treated with all the regard due to their sex." Both Conventions list grave breaches, including willful killing, torture or inhuman treatment, and (with regard to civilians) willfully causing great suffering or serious injury to body or health. . . .

Letter from Robert A. Bradtke, Acting Assistant Secretary for Legislative Affairs, to Senator Arlen Specter (Jan. 27, 1993).

Bosnia-Herzegovina

Geneva Conventions I-IV (December 31, 1992)
Protocol I & II (December 31, 1992)
Covenant on Civil and Political Rights (September 1, 1993)
Convention on the Elimination of All Forms of Discrimination Against Women (September 1, 1993)
Convention against Torture and Other Cruel, Inhuman or Degrading Treatment or Punishment (September 1, 1993)

Croatia

Geneva Conventions I-IV (May 11, 1992)
Protocol I & II (May 11, 1992)
Covenant on Civil and Political Rights (October 12, 1992)
Convention on the Elimination of All Forms of Discrimination Against Women (September 2, 1992)
Convention against Torture and Other Cruel, Inhuman or Degrading Treatment or Punishment (October 12, 1992)

Yugoslavia

Geneva Conventions I-IV (April 21, 1950)
Protocol I & II (June 11, 1979)
Covenant on Civil and Political Rights (June 2, 1971)
Convention on the Elimination of All Forms of Discrimination Against Women (February 26, 1982)
Convention against Torture and Other Cruel, Inhuman or Degrading Treatment or Punishment (September 10, 1991)

On May 22, 1992,

> [R]epresentatives of four parties in Bosnia-Herzegovina—the Presidency of the Republic of Bosnia-Herzegovina, [the SDS, the SDA, and the HDZ]—signed an agreement . . . at the invitation of the International Committee of the Red Cross (ICRC) in which they committed themselves to "respect and ensure respect for" provisions in the Geneva Conventions including those for the protection of civilians. . . . In particular, the parties agreed to be bound by Common Article 3 of the Geneva Conventions.

Amnesty International, *Bosnia-Herzegovina: Gross Abuses of Human Rights*, AI Index: EUR 63/01/92, at 2-3 (1992). *See also* Yves Sandoz, *A Consideration of the Implementation of International Humanitarian Law and the Role of the International Committee of the Red Cross in the Former Yugoslavia* (Geneva, Sept. 28, 1993) (discussing agreements entered into by the warring factions within Yugoslavia, the implementation of those agreements, and the role of the United Nations and the International Committee of the Red Cross in that region).

2. The Commission of Experts appointed to study the situation in the former Yugoslavia concluded "[r]ape constitutes a crime under international humanitarian law." Commission of Experts Established Pursuant to Security Council Resolution 780 (1992), *Final Report*, U.N. Doc. S/1994/674, at 27 (1994). James O'Brien, an attorney in the Office of the Legal Adviser, U.S. Department of State, agrees that rape is a crime against humanity, genocide, and a war crime. James C. O'Brien, *The International Tribunal for Violations of International Humanitarian Law in the Former Yugoslavia*, 87 Am. J. Int'l L. 639, 645-51 (1993).

Professor MacKinnon emphasizes, however, that though rape has been recognized as a war crime, mass rapes are not recognized as human rights abuses. Catharine A. MacKinnon, *Crimes of War, Crimes of Peace*, 4 UCLA Women's L.J. 59 (1993). She argues rape is often treated as merely a byproduct of war, such that it goes largely unpunished. In addition, she notes,

> Formally illegal or not, as policy or merely as what is systematically done, practices

of sexual and reproductive abuse occur not only in wartime but also on a daily basis in one form or another in every country in the world. Under domestic and international law, whether or not prohibited on their face, these practices are widely permitted as the liberties of their perpetrators, understood as excesses of passion or spoils of victory, legally rationalized or officially winked at or formally condoned.

Id. at 62. (That article originally was published in ON HUMAN RIGHTS: THE OXFORD AMNESTY LECTURES 1993 at 83 (Stephen Shute & Susan Hurley eds., 1993)). *See also* Danise Aydelott, Comment, *Mass Rape During War: Prosecuting Bosnian Rapists Under International Law*, 7 EMORY INT'L L. REV. 585 (1993); Arden B. Levy, *International Prosecution of Rape in Warfare: Nondiscriminatory Recognition and Enforcement*, 4 UCLA WOMEN'S L.J. 255 (1994).

3.   The U.N. Commission on Human Rights adopted a resolution in 1995 expressing concern over violations of humanitarian standards during armed conflict. The resolution refers to a working paper that had been submitted to the Commission in 1991. U.N. Res. 1995/29 (1995). The working paper specifically lists rape as a violation of minimum humanitarian standards. U.N. Doc. E/CN.4/Sub.2/1991/55 (1991).

4.   Rape, particularly rape of the magnitude found in Bosnia-Herzegovina, also may be construed as a form of torture. Article 1 of the Convention against Torture and Other Cruel, Inhuman or Degrading Treatment or Punishment, G.A. res. 39/46, U.N. GAOR, 39th Sess., Supp. No. 51, at 179, U.N. Doc. A/39/51 (1984), defines torture as:

> any act by which severe pain or suffering, whether physical or mental, is intentionally inflicted on a person for such purposes as obtaining from him or a third person information or a confession, punishing him for an act he or a third person has committed or is suspected of having committed, or intimidating or coercing him or a third person, or for any reason based on discrimination of any kind, when such pain or suffering is inflicted by or at the instigation of or with the consent or acquiescence of a public official or other person acting in an official capacity.

If rape is construed as torture, are the norms recognized in *Filartiga* and *Forti I* and *II* applicable to our hypothetical case?

5.   When may systematic rape and forced pregnancy be construed as genocide? All countries listed *supra* note 1 have ratified the Genocide Convention—the United States on November 25, 1988; Bosnia-Herzegovina on December 29, 1992; Croatia on October 12, 1992; and Yugoslavia on August 29, 1950.

6.   The egregious and widespread nature of acts occurring in the former Yugoslavia prompted the U.N. Security Council to establish the first international war crimes tribunal since Nuremberg and Tokyo. S.C. Res. 808, U.N. Doc. S/RES/808 (1993). The tribunal is charged with prosecuting persons responsible for serious violations of international humanitarian law committed in the territory of the former Yugoslavia since 1991. The Statute of the Tribunal specifically includes rape as a crime against humanity over which the tribunal has jurisdiction. The Statute also includes within genocide "imposing measure intended to prevent births within the group." Security Council; *Report of the Secretary-General Pursuant to Paragraph 2 of Security Council Resolution 808 (1993)*, U.N. Doc. S/25704, Annex, at 37-38 (1993). In one judgment, the international tribunal found crimes against humanity to be a violation of common Article 3. U.N. Doc., Case No. IT-94-1-AR72 (1995). For discussion of the prosecution of war crimes in the former Yugoslavia, see chapter 7, *supra*. The Dayton Peace Agreement, calling for peace in that region was another step taken by the international community. The agreement was signed in Dayton, Ohio in 1995. For information on the agreement, see chapter 7, *supra*.

7.   Two class action suits in New York federal court raised whether rape is a tort for which aliens can sue. In *Doe v. Karadzic*, No. 93 Civ. 0878 (S.D.N.Y. filed Feb. 11, 1993) and *Kadic v. Karadzic*, No. 93 Civ. 1163 (S.D.N.Y. filed March 2, 1993), Muslim women sued a Serbian military leader, Radovan Karadzic, for rape and other crimes in Bosnia-Herzegovina, based

on the Alien Tort Claims Act and the Torture Victim Protection Act. Karadzic is President of the self-proclaimed Bosnian-Serb republic of "Srpska." Professor Fitzpatrick has emphasized the importance of these cases as a chance to deter continuing conduct. Joan Fitzpatrick, *The Karadzic Cases: Establishing Accountability for On-Going Gross Human Rights Violations through Litigation in U.S. Courts* (May 20, 1995). Most ATCA cases involve decisions regarding behavior by officials who are already out of power. The *Karadzic* cases, however, confront violations while they are being committed. *Id.*

In September 1994, the district court granted Karadzic's motion to dismiss both actions on the grounds that he did not act under the color of any recognized state law and, thus, his acts did not constitute official state action required by the ATCA and TVPA. *Doe v. Karadzic*, 866 F.Supp. 734, 741 (S.D.N.Y. 1994); *S.K. v. Karadzic*, 866 F.Supp 734, 741 (S.D.N.Y. Sept. 7, 1994).

In October 1995, however, the Court of Appeals for the Second Circuit reversed the dismissal. *Kadic v. Karadzic, Doe v. Karadzic*, 70 F.3d 232 (2nd Cir. 1995). The court of appeals considered (1) whether violations of the law of nations may be remedied when committed by a non-state actor, (2) whether Karadzic, present in the United States as an invitee of the United Nations, is immune from service of process, and (3) whether the political question doctrine makes the case nonjusticiable. *Id.* at 236.

The court of appeals held that subject matter jurisdiction exists because Karadzic may be found liable for genocide and war crimes in his private capacity and for other violations if he were acting as a government official, that he is not immune from service of process, and that the issues do not present nonjusticiable political questions. *Id.*

The court first addressed subject matter jurisdiction in the context of the Alien Tort Claims Act. The appellate court decided that the district court erred when it dismissed the cases based on a state action requirement. "We do not agree that the law of nations, as understood in the modern era, confines its reach to state action. Instead, we hold that certain forms of conduct violated the law on nations whether undertaken by those acting under the auspices of a state or only as private individuals." *Id.* at 239. The court noted, however, that a limited category of violations may be remedied when committed by private individuals, including such violations as piracy and slave trade.

The court then considered whether the specific violations alleged by the appellants—genocide, war crimes, and other instances of death, torture and degrading treatment—may be remedied based on individual action.

The Genocide Convention prohibits the infliction of serious bodily or mental harm. The court decided that "appellants' allegations that Karadzic personally planned and ordered a campaign of murder, rape, forced impregnation, and other forms of torture designed to destroy the religious and ethnic groups of Bosnian Muslims and Bosnian Croats clearly state a violation of the international law norm proscribing genocide." *Id.* at 242. In addition, the "proscription of genocide has applied equally to state and non-state actors." *Id.* Since the appellants asserted violations of the law of nations, which could be remedied whether committed by a state actor or an individual, the district court has subject matter jurisdiction over the genocide claims.

The appellate court used similar reasoning in concluding that the district court has subject matter jurisdiction over the allegations of war crimes. The court cited the Geneva Conventions and concluded that "the offenses alleged by the appellants, if proved, would violate the most fundamental norms of the law of war embodied in common article 3." *Id.* at 243. The court also found that individuals have been held liable for war claims and thus state action is not a requirement.

The court found that many of the acts claimed under the category of torture and summary execution could be remedied under genocide and war crimes. To the extent they do not fit under those headings, the violations could only be remedied if the district court found the defendant to be acting under color of law. These violations "when not perpetrated in the course of genocide or war crimes—are proscribed by international law only when committed by state officials or under color of law." *Id.*

The court then addressed the state-action requirement, concluding that international laws apply to governments, whether or not they are recognized as such by the international community. Appellants are entitled to prove Srpska is a state and that Karadzic acted under color of law by acting in concert with the former Yugoslavia. *Id.* at 244-45.

In its discussion of the Torture Victim Protection Act, the court noted "by its plain language, the Torture Victim Act renders liable only those individuals who have committed torture or extrajudicial killing 'under actual or apparent authority, or color of law, of any foreign nation.'" *Id.* at 245. The appellants may pursue their TVPA claims based on the jurisdiction conferred under the ATCA. The district court therefore has subject matter jurisdiction.

The court also found personal jurisdiction, based on service of process. "[I]f appellants personally served Karadzic with the summons and complaint while he was in New York but outside of the U.N. headquarters district, as they are prepared to prove, he is subject to the personal jurisdiction of the District Court." *Id.* at 248.

For discussion of issues raised in the complaints, see Yolanda S. Wu, Note, *Genocidal Rape in Bosnia: Redress in United States Courts Under the Alien Tort Claims Act*, 4 UCLA WOMEN'S L.J. 101 (1993); Michele Brandt, Comment, *Doe v. Karadzic: Redressing Non-State Acts of Gender-Specific Abuse Under the Alien Tort Statute*, 79 MINN. L. REV. 1413 (1995).

8.   How might lawsuits affect the situation in Bosnia? Do you think the impact would differ depending on whether a judgment for plaintiffs is actually paid? What other use might be made of such lawsuits?

9.   The U.N. Commission on Human Rights has studied violence toward women during wartime. For example, it directed a study on contemporary forms of slavery against women and established a Special Rapporteur on Violence Against Women. The Special Rapporteur on Violence Against Women has researched issues such as sexual slavery and rape during wartime. *See Report on the Situation of Systematic Rape, Sexual Slavery, and Slavery-like Practices During Wartime, Including Internal Armed Conflict*, U.N. Doc. E/CN.4/Sub.2/1995/ 38 (1995); *Report on the Mission to the Democratic People's Republic of Korea, the Republic of Korea and Japan on the Issue of Military Sexual Slavery in Wartime*, U.N. Doc. E/CN.4/ 1996/53/Add.1 (1996).

10.   For comments generally on using international law to help protect women from domestic violence, see Declaration on the Elimination of Violence Against Women, G.A. res. 104, U.N. GAOR, 48th Sess., U.N. Doc. A/48/629 (1993), excerpted *supra* at 528; CENTRE FOR SOCIAL DEVELOPMENT AND HUMANITARIAN AFFAIRS, UNITED NATIONS, STRATEGIES FOR CONFRONTING DOMESTIC VIOLENCE: A RESOURCE MANUAL (1993); Katherine M. Culliton, *Finding a Mechanism to Enforce Women's Right to State Protection from Domestic Violence in the Americas*, 34 HARV. INT'L L.J. 507 (1993); *Report of the Special Rapporteur on Violence Against Women, its Causes and Consequences*, U.N. Doc. E/CN.4/1996/53 (1996); Dorothy Q. Thomas & Michele E. Beasley, *Domestic Violence as a Human Rights Issue*, 15 HUM. RTS. Q. 36 (1993). *See also* ANDREW CLAPHAM, HUMAN RIGHTS IN THE PRIVATE SPHERE (1993); Rebecca J. Cook, *State Responsibility for Violations of Women's Human Rights*, 7 HARV. HUM. RTS. J. 125 (1994); Anthony Ewing, *Establishing State Responsibility for Private Acts of Violence Against Women under the American Convention on Human Rights*, 26 COLUM. HUM. RTS. L. REV. 751 (1995).

D.   OBSTACLES TO ADJUDICATION UNDER THE ALIEN TORT CLAIMS ACT

In addition to determining whether it has jurisdiction and whether plaintiff has a cause of action, the court must decide whether any rules preclude adjudication of the claim. For example, if defendant is a current or former foreign official, the court must decide whether protection is accorded by sovereign immunity or the act of state doctrine. If the claim is against a foreign sovereign, the court must decide whether the Foreign Sovereign Immunities Act ("FSIA") is a bar. If the FSIA applies, the ATCA no longer applies.

Immunities law in general is driven by a concern for international comity. As you read the discussion and excerpts that follow, note how this concern impacts courts' decisions.

1.   Foreign Sovereign Immunities Act

Prior to enactment of the FSIA, the validity of claims of foreign sovereigns was determined primarily by the Executive Branch, whose recommendations generally were followed by courts without much question. *See Siderman v. Republic of Argentina*, 965 F.2d 699, 705-06 (9th Cir. 1992), *cert. denied*, 507 U.S. 1017 (1993). The FSIA codified a restrictive theory of sovereign immunity, the prevailing view at the time of its passage. Under that theory immunity is recognized for a state's public acts but not for its private acts. *Id.*

Section 1330 of the FSIA allows federal courts to decide civil suits against foreign state governments that are not immune; section 1604 provides that they are presumptively immune unless any of the exceptions contained in §§ 1605-1607 apply.

Some of the important exceptions to immunity are the waiver exception, 28 U.S.C. § 1605(a)(1), the commercial activity exception, 28 U.S.C. § 1605(a)(2), the international taking exception, 28 U.S.C. § 1605(a)(3), and the noncommercial torts exception, 28 U.S.C. § 1605(a)(5). These provisions are excerpted below.

28 U.S.C. § 1605. General exceptions to the jurisdictional immunity of a foreign state:

(a)   A foreign state shall not be immune from the jurisdiction of courts of the United States or of the States in any case —

(1)   in which the foreign state has waived its immunity either explicitly or by implication. . .;

(2)   in which the action is based upon a commercial activity carried on in the United States by the foreign state; or upon an act performed in the United States in connection with a commercial activity of the foreign state elsewhere; or upon an act outside the territory of the United States in connection with a commercial activity of the foreign state elsewhere and that act causes a direct effect in the United States;

(3)   in which rights in property taken in violation of international law are in issue and that property or any property exchanged for such property is present in the United States in connection with a commercial activity carried on in the United States by the foreign state; or that property or any property exchanged for such property is owned or operated by an agency or instrumentality of the foreign state and that agency or instrumentality is engaged in a commercial activity in the United States;. . .

(5)   not otherwise encompassed in paragraph (2) above, in which money damages are sought against a foreign state for personal injury or death, or damage to or loss of property, occurring in the United States and caused by the tortious act or omission of that foreign state or of any official or employee of that foreign state while acting within the scope of his office or employment; except this paragraph shall not apply to —

(A)   any claim based upon the exercise or performance or the failure to exercise or perform a discretionary function regardless of whether the discretion be abused, or

(B)   any claim arising out of malicious prosecution, abuse of process, libel, slander, misrepresentation, deceit, or interference with contract rights. . . .

The Supreme Court construed the FSIA in *Argentine Republic v. Amerada Hess Shipping Corp.*, 488 U.S. 428 (1989), and *Saudi Arabia v. Nelson*, 507 U.S. 349 (1993). *Amerada Hess* involved a Liberian oil tanker which was attacked in international waters by the Argentine military during the war in the South Atlantic between Great Britain and Argentina. 488 U.S. at 431-32. *Nelson* involved a U.S. employee of a government-owned hospital in Saudi Arabia who was detained and tortured by the Saudi Arabian government at the hospital's request after he reported safety defects that endangered patient safety and posed fire hazards. 507 U.S. 352-54.

In *Amerada Hess*, the Supreme Court first concluded the FSIA was the sole means of obtaining jurisdiction over a foreign sovereign. The ATCA thus does not provide an additional avenue for obtaining jurisdiction in these cases. 488 U.S. at 434-40. After reaching that conclusion, the Court analyzed whether any exceptions to the FSIA applied so that jurisdiction was proper.

The plaintiffs in *Amerada Hess* relied on the noncommercial tort exception, 28 U.S.C. § 1605(a)(5), to provide jurisdiction. The Supreme Court rejected their argument by construing the exception to apply only to suits for damages to or loss of property occurring within the territorial United States. Since the attack on the plaintiff's ship occurred off the coast of Argentina, the FSIA exception did not apply. *Id.* at 440-42.

In *Nelson*, the Court construed the FSIA's commercial activity exception. The plaintiff based his commercial activity argument on the following facts: (1) the hospital recruited him in the U.S. through an advertisement in a U.S. magazine; (2) Nelson signed his employment contract with the hospital in the U.S.; and (3) the hospital designated its U.S. purchasing agent as the point of contact for Nelson's family in case of emergency. 507 U.S. 351-54. The Supreme Court rejected Nelson's argument and held that the claim was not "based on" these activities since the acts did not constitute the elements which, "if proven, would entitle [the] plaintiff to relief under his theory of the case." *Id.* at 356-57. Moreover, the activities on which the claim was based did not have sufficient nexus with the U.S. to fall under the commercial torts exception. *Id.* at 357-59. The Court then contrasted this suit with one based on breach of contract, which presumably would be sufficiently related to Saudi Arabia's contacts in the U.S. to constitute a commercial activity in the U.S. *Id.*

The Court next held that the tortious conduct itself—the detention and torture of Nelson—was not a commercial activity. *Id.* at 357-61. Analyzing the tortious conduct under the restrictive theory of sovereign immunity, which the FSIA codified, the Court concluded:

[A] state engages in commercial activity under the restrictive theory where it exercises only those powers that can also be exercised by private citizens, as distinct from those powers peculiar to sovereigns. Put differently, a foreign state engages in commercial activity for purposes of the restrictive theory only where it acts in the manner of a private player within the market.

. . . [W]hether a state acts "in the manner of" a private party is a question of behavior, not motivation. . . . We [do] not ignore the difficulty of distinguishing purpose (*i.e.*, the reason why the foreign state engages in the activity) from nature (*i.e.*, the outward form of the conduct that the foreign state performs or agrees to perform), but recognize[] that the Act unmistakably commands us to observe the distinction. . . .

. . . The conduct [in this case] boils down to abuse of the power of its police by the Saudi Government, and however monstrous such abuse undoubtedly may be, a foreign state's exercise of the power of its police has long been understood for purposes of the restrictive theory as peculiarly sovereign in nature. Exercise of the powers of police and penal officers is not the sort of action by which private parties can engage in commerce. Such acts as legislation, or the expulsion of an alien, or a denial of justice, cannot be performed by an individual acting in his own name. They can be performed only by the state acting as such.

Id. at 359-61 (footnotes, citations, and internal quotations omitted). The Court's reasoning suggests that wrongful arrest, imprisonment, and torture are particularly sovereign in nature and thus are likely to be immune under the FSIA. The Court also rejected Nelson's argument that the conduct was commercial because it was inflicted on him in retaliation for his reporting of safety violations. The Court found that argument went to the purpose of the acts, which the FSIA "renders irrelevant to the question of an activity's commercial character." *Id.* at 361.

In a concurring opinion Justice White chastised the majority for basing its decision on the status of the individuals used by the hospital to retaliate for Nelson's whistleblowing.

. . . As countless cases attest, retaliation for whistleblowing is not a practice foreign to the marketplace. . . .

Therefore, had the hospital retaliated against Nelson by hiring thugs to do the job, I assume the majority—no longer able to describe this conduct as "a foreign state's exercise of the power of its police"—would consent to calling it "commercial." For, in such circumstances, the state-run hospital would be operating as any private participant in the marketplace and respondents' action would be based on the operation by Saudi Arabia's agents of a commercial business.

Id. at 364 (White, J., concurring) (citation omitted). He concluded that the defendants' operation of the hospital and their employment practices and disciplinary procedures were commercial activities. He nonetheless reached the same conclusion as the majority because defendants' tortious conduct did not have substantial contact with the United States. *Id.* at 366.

Between the two Supreme Court decisions, the Ninth Circuit construed exceptions to the FSIA in *Siderman v. Republic of Argentina*, 965 F.2d 699 (9th Cir. 1992), *cert. denied*, 507 U.S. 1017 (1993). *Siderman* involved claims by four family members, one of whom was a U.S. citizen and three of whom were Argentine citizens, against Argentina. Plaintiffs stated that Argentine military officials detained and tortured one of the plaintiffs and expropriated property belonging to all family members because of their Jewish faith. They argued that two of the FSIA exceptions applied to their expropriation claims—the commercial activity exception and the international takings exception, excerpted *supra* at 534; 965 F.2d at 704-05.

The court concluded that all three clauses of the commercial activity exception applied. Part of the property expropriated by Argentina was an Argentine corporation whose largest asset was an Argentine hotel. The hotel advertised in and solicited guests from the U.S. through its U.S. agent and accepted American credit cards from its numerous American guests. The court concluded these facts were sufficient to demonstrate that Argentina was engaging in a commercial activity, and that Argentina's operation of this hotel had substantial contact with the U.S. *Id.* at 708-09. Even if the Sidermans' claims weren't based on a commercial activity carried on in the U.S., however, jurisdiction was proper, because Argentina's activities were materially connected to the operation of the commercial activity in Argentina. The court reached this conclusion, because plaintiffs were claiming profits from the hotel which partially were derived from American guests. Argentina's advertising and credit reimbursement activities in the U.S. thus contributed to the profit resulting from a commercial activity conducted outside of the U.S. *Id.* at 709-10.

With respect to the third clause of the commercial activity exception, the court emphasized that the Sidermans' claims must be based on an act occurring outside the U.S. which had a direct effect in the U.S. "Under the direct effect requirement, the 'foreign sovereign's activities must cause an effect in the United States that is substantial and foreseeable in order to abrogate sovereign immunity.'" *Id.* at 710. Although "mere financial loss" in the U.S. is not sufficient, the direct effect requirement was met here since the dividends from the expropriated corporation were to have been paid at the shareholders' places of residence in the U.S. *Id.* at 710-11.

The court next construed the international takings exception and concluded that it, too, provided jurisdiction, but only for the claims of the plaintiff who was a U.S. citizen. The exception is not applicable where the plaintiff is a citizen of defendant country at the time of the taking, "because '[e]xpropriation by a sovereign state of the property of its own nationals does not implicate settled principles of international law.'" *Id.* at 711, (quoting *Chuidian v. Philippine Nat'l Bank*, 912 F.2d 1095, 1105 (9th Cir.1990)). In order for the clause to apply, "the property at issue must have been taken in violation of international law." *Id.* at 712. The court concluded here that Argentina's taking of property discriminatorily based on ethnicity, without payment of just compensation, violated the international law of expropriation.

The court then turned to the Sidermans' torture claims. The Sidermans argued that Argentina should not enjoy sovereign immunity as to torture since there is a customary international norm against torture which has risen to the level of a *jus cogens* norm. *Id.* at 714. *Jus cogens* norms, also called peremptory norms, are customary international norms "accepted and recognized by the international community of states as a whole as a norm from which no derogation is permitted and which can be modified only by a subsequent norm of general international law having the same character." Vienna Convention on the Law of Treaties, art. 53, 1155 U.N.T.S. 332, 8 I.L.M. 679, *entered into force* May 23, 1969. Though the court concluded that the prohibition against official torture had attained the status of a *jus cogens* norm, based on *Filartiga* and *Forti* and the authorities cited therein, *Id.* at 716-17, the court found *Amerada Hess* precluded the adoption of plaintiffs' argument. *See* chapter 13 *infra* for further discussion of *jus cogens*.

The court agreed plaintiffs' argument had merit. Sovereign immunity itself is a principle of international law which is trumped, however, by *jus cogens*. Thus international law does not recognize an act that violates *jus cogens* as a sovereign act. Therefore, a state's violation of the *jus cogens* norm prohibiting official torture would not be entitled to the immunity afforded by international law. In enacting the FSIA, however, the court concluded that Congress intended to occupy the field of sovereign immunity. Based on the inclusive nature of the language of the Act and the Supreme Court's declaration in *Amerada Hess* that jurisdiction was improper unless one of the exceptions to the FSIA applied, the court concluded "a violation of a *jus cogens* norm does not confer jurisdiction under the FSIA." *Id.* at 718.

In establishing the FSIA, Congress provided the rules were "[s]ubject to existing international agreements to which the United States [was] a party at the time of enactment of" the FSIA. 28 U.S.C. § 1604. In *Amerada Hess*, the plaintiffs had argued that the Geneva Convention on the High Seas and the Pan American Maritime Neutrality Convention created an exception to FSIA immunity under section 1604. The *Amerada Hess* Court rejected the argument, adopting a narrow view of section 1604:

> This exception applies when international agreements expressly conflict with the immunity provisions of the FSIA, hardly the circumstances in this case. [The Geneva and Pan American Conventions] only set forth substantive rules of conduct and state that compensation shall be paid for certain wrongs. They do not create private rights of action for foreign corporations to recover compensation from foreign states in United States courts.

488 U.S. at 442-43. Similarly, in *Siderman*, the plaintiffs argued Argentina's immunity under the FSIA was subject to the Universal Declaration of Human Rights and the U.N. Charter. The court, following *Amerada Hess*, rejected those arguments. Because the Universal Declaration of Human Rights is only a resolution of the General Assembly, the court concluded that it was not an "international agreement" within the meaning of section 1604. Though the U.N. Charter is a treaty, its language is not sufficiently specific regarding individual remedies to fall within the mandate of § 1604. *Siderman, supra,* 965 F.2d at 719-20.

The court lastly construed the FSIA's waiver exception, and noted that it is to be narrowly construed.

> The House Report accompanying the passage of the FSIA gives three examples of an implied waiver:
>
> With respect to implicit waivers, the courts have found such waivers in cases where a foreign state has agreed to arbitration in another country or where a foreign state has agreed that the law of a particular country should govern a contract. An implicit waiver would also include a situation where a foreign state has filed a responsive pleading in an action without raising the defense of sovereign immunity.

Id. at 721 (citation omitted). Yet as a general proposition, however, "where a written agreement entered into by a foreign sovereign 'contemplates adjudication of a dispute by the United States courts,' we will find the sovereign to have waived its immunity." *Id.,* (quoting *Joseph v. Office of Consulate General of Nigeria*, 830 F.2d 1018, 1023 (9th Cir.1987), *cert. denied*, 485 U.S. 905 (1988)).

On the facts before it, the court concluded that Argentina had waived its immunity from suit. After the Sidermans fled to the U.S. to avoid persecution, Argentina requested U.S. assistance in extraditing one member of the family. The Sidermans suggested that extradition was a part of the plan to torture, and perhaps kill, that individual. Such request for assistance, the court concluded, constituted an implied waiver of sovereign immunity with respect to the torture claims. "The evidence indicates that Argentina deliberately involved United States courts in its efforts to persecute [the Sidermans]. If Argentina has engaged our courts in the very course of activity for which the Sidermans seek redress, it has waived its immunity as to that redress." *Id.* at 722.

NOTES AND QUESTIONS

1.   Is *Siderman* still valid after *Nelson*? For example, the court in *Siderman* concluded that

soliciting U.S. guests for an Argentine hotel and accepting U.S. credit cards in payment constituted a commercial activity based in the U.S. Moreover, the court concluded those activities formed the basis of the Sidermans' expropriation claims. Would the Supreme Court agree?

2.   Courts have followed *Nelson* in holding that kidnapping is not a commercial activity. For example, two victims of kidnapping and torture brought a suit against the Islamic Republic of Iran. *Cicippio v. Islamic Republic of Iran*, 30 F.3d 164 (D.C. Cir. 1994), *cert. denied*, 115 S.Ct. 726 (1995). In dismissing their claim, the court based its decision on the FSIA as analysed in *Nelson*. How does the Court's holding in *Nelson* that the tortious activity itself was not a commercial activity limit the liability of some defendants in the hypothetical situation presented at the beginning of this chapter?

3.   The Court's decision in *Nelson* spurred a bill in Congress to amend the FSIA to allow U.S. citizens to sue foreign states for torture or extrajudicial execution. H.R. 934, 103d Cong., 1st Sess. (1993). The amendment, still pending, would add an exception to 28 U.S.C. § 1605(a) allowing plaintiffs to seek damages from a foreign state for personal injury or death occurring in that country. The amendment would require, however, that claimants exhaust all "adequate and available" remedies in the country in which the conduct occurred before suing in U.S. courts. *Id.* at Sec. 1(3).

4.   For criticism of *Nelson*, see Keith Highet et al., *Foreign Sovereign Immunities Act— Commercial Activity Exception—Nature and Purpose Tests—Police Power as Sovereign Power*, 87 AM. J. INT'L L. 442 (1993); Harvard Law Review Ass'n, Leading Cases, *Foreign Sovereign Immunity: Commercial Activities*, 107 HARV. L. REV. 264 (1993).

    For further reading on the commercial activity exception to the FSIA, see Joan E. Donoghue, *Taking the "Sovereign" out of the Foreign Sovereign Immunities Act: A Functional Approach to the Commercial Activity Exception*, 17 YALE J. INT'L L. 489 (1992); Margot C. Wuebbels, Note, *Commercial Terrorism: A Commercial Activity Exception Under § 1605(a)(2) of the Foreign Sovereign Immunities Act*, 35 ARIZ. L. REV. 1123 (1993) (arguing some Iranian terrorism should be considered a commercial activity); Richard Wydeven, Note, *The Foreign Sovereign Immunities Act of 1976: A Contemporary Look at Jurisdiction Under the Commercial Activity Exception*, 13 REV. LITIG. 143 (1993).

5.   In *Coleman v. Alcolac, Inc.*, 888 F. Supp. 1388 (S.D. Tex. 1995), a suit brought by veterans of the Persian Gulf War against various chemical component manufacturers, including some foreign companies, the issue of foreign sovereign immunity arose. The court addressed the Foreign Sovereign Immunities Act commercial activity exception and the direct effects in the United States provision, as well as the non-commercial tort exception. Neither exception was held to be applicable.

6.   One court refused to follow the Supreme Court's strict construction of FSIA exceptions in a case involving a renegade government. In *Princz v. Federal Republic of Germany*, 813 F. Supp. 22 (D.D.C. 1992), the court allowed a Jew who was interred by Nazis during World War II to sue Germany for damages. The court rejected Germany's claim that the court lacked jurisdiction because the suit did not fit within one of the exceptions under the FSIA, noting "in enacting the [FSIA], Congress [cannot have] . . . intended to bar a U.S. citizen from seeking redress against a nation standing in the shoes of his or her would-be-butcher in U.S. courts in a case such as this." *Id.* at 25-26. The court noted the FSIA was simply inapplicable to suits involving "a one-time outlaw nation . . . which at the time [the] barbaric acts were committed neither recognized nor respected U.S. or international law." *Id.* Therefore, Germany could not now "assert[] U.S. law to evade its responsibilities. . . . To allow otherwise would create a severe imbalance in the reciprocity and mutual respect which must exist between nations, and would work an intolerable injustice against the plaintiff and the principles for which this country stands." *Id.*

    On appeal, the Court of Appeals reversed. It first considered, but did not decide, whether the FSIA even applied to events occurring before enactment. *Princz v. Federal Republic of*

Germany, 26 F.3d 1166, 1169-71 (D.C. Cir. 1994). The court then concluded that, even if the FSIA did control, none of the statutory exceptions applied to grant jurisdiction. *Id.* at 1171-75. In reaching that result, the court applied a strict statutory analysis rather than the purposive analysis used by the district court.

7.   A significant issue in FSIA litigation involves determining whether the party asserting immunity is an "agency or instrumentality of a foreign state." The definition in 28 U.S.C. § 1603(a) provides that "foreign state" includes an "agency or instrumentality" of the state. 28 U.S.C. § 1603(b) then defines "agency or instrumentality" as "a separate legal person, corporate or otherwise, . . . which is an organ of a foreign state or political subdivision thereof" or in which the state owns a majority interest.

In *Chuidian v. Philippine Nat'l Bank*, 912 F.2d 1095, 1101 (9th Cir. 1990), the court held that "agency or instrumentality" includes an individual government employee acting in his official capacity. The court reasoned that "a suit against an individual acting in his official capacity is the practical equivalent of a suit against the sovereign directly." *Id.* Though language from the legislative history could support a conclusion that "Congress was primarily concerned with organizations . . . and may not have expressly contemplated the case of individuals acting as sovereign instrumentalities," the Act did not expressly exclude individuals from the definition. *Id.* Since the FSIA primarily codified the existing law of sovereign immunity as of 1976, which "expressly extended immunity to individual officials acting in their official capacity," the court determined individuals can fall within the definition of foreign state for purposes of the FSIA. *Id.*

In a human rights context the Ninth Circuit later reaffirmed the holding in *In re Estate of Ferdinand E. Marcos Human Rights Litigation*, 978 F.2d 493 (9th Cir. 1992). In *In re Estate of Marcos*, an alien mother sued Imee Marcos-Manotoc, former head of military intelligence, for the torture and wrongful death of her son in the Philippines. *Id.* at 495. The court cited *Chuidian* for the proposition that "an official is not entitled to immunity for acts which are not committed in an official capacity (such as selling personal property), and for acts beyond the scope of her authority (for example, doing something the sovereign has not empowered the official to do)." *Id.* at 497. Since Marcos-Manotoc conceded she was acting solely on her own authority by defaulting, her acts did not fall within the immunity granted by the FSIA. *Id.* at 498. A jury later awarded $1,200,000,000 in punitive damages and over $800,000,000 in compensatory damages to the plaintiffs in the action. *In Re Estate of Ferdinand E. Marcos Human Rights Litigation*, MDL No. 840 (D. Haw. 1994).

Chuidian followed many earlier courts in reaching its conclusion. *See, e.g., Kline v. Kaneko*, 685 F. Supp. 386, 389 (S.D.N.Y. 1988); *American Bonded Warehouse Co. v. Compagnie Nationale Air France*, 653 F. Supp. 861, 863 (N.D. Ill. 1987). *See also Intercontinental Dictionary Series v. DeGruyter*, 822 F. Supp. 662, 674 (C.D. Cal. 1993) (holding individuals sued in their official capacities as university employees were "agencies or instrumentalities" under the FSIA). At least one earlier court reached a different conclusion. In *Republic of the Philippines v. Marcos*, 665 F. Supp. 793, 797 (N.D. Cal. 1987), the court concluded that "[t]he terminology of [28 U.S.C. § 1603(b)]—'agency,' 'instrumentality,' 'entity,' 'organ'—makes it clear that the statute is not intended to apply to natural persons."

8.   Does the FSIA shield government officials from liability for acts that affect human rights which are within the scope of their official duties? Professor Joan Fitzpatrick argues, "[b]ecause 'color of law' requirements are essential to make out many violations of human rights norms, including protections against summary execution, torture, and arbitrary detention, a broad *Chuidian* approach would render the ATCA a dead letter for all but piracy-type cases." Joan Fitzpatrick, *The Future of the Alien Tort Claims Act of 1789: Lessons from* In Re Marcos Human Rights Litigation, 67 St. John's L. Rev. 491, 507 (1993). "If *Chuidian*'s reading of section 1603(b) of the FSIA is correct, all ATCA defendants sued for human rights torts that require proof that the violator acted under color of foreign law will be immune, having been able to commit the torts in question only by exercising power delegated to them by the sovereign." *Id.* at 511. She urges courts to reject these precedents or, at a minimum, construe an exception to the inclusion of individuals as agencies or instrumentalities where

the foreign officials violate international law. *Id.* at 515. *See also* Tom Lininger, Recent Development, *Overcoming Immunity Defenses to Human Rights Suits in U.S. Courts*, 7 HARV. HUM. RTS. J. 177, 186-88 (1994) (citing legislative history and Restatement sections in support of the conclusion that the FSIA is not applicable to individuals).

9.   A foreign state may waive its sovereign immunity as well as the immunity enjoyed by a current or former government official. In fact, it implicitly waives immunity by participating in litigation; for example, by filing a responsive pleading without raising the sovereignty defense. *Drexel Burnham Lambert Group, Inc. v. Committee of Receivers for A.W. Galadari*, 810 F. Supp. 1375, 1383 (S.D.N.Y. 1993).

One court held that the following waiver by Haiti constituted a waiver of any and all immunity enjoyed by a former official of its military:

> [Defendant], ex-Lieutenant-General of the Armed Forces of Haiti and former President of the Military Government of the Republic of Haiti, enjoys absolutely no form of immunity, whether it be of a sovereign, a chief of state, a former chief of state; whether it be diplomatic, consular, or testimonial immunity, or all other immunity, including immunity against judgment, or process, immunity against enforcement of judgments and immunity against appearing before court before and after judgment.

Paul v. Avril, 812 F. Supp. 207, 210 (S.D. Fla. 1993). In rejecting Avril's head of state defense, the court also rejected his argument that according weight to the waiver "would encourage countries to disavow those former leaders who do not curry favor with the new government." *Id.* at 210-11. In 1994, the judge entered a default judgment for $41 million.

Another court noted that waivers must be explicit, presumably to prevent "inadvertent, implied or constructive waiver in cases where the intent of the foreign state is equivocal or ambiguous." *Lafontant v. Aristide*, 844 F. Supp. 128, 134 (E.D.N.Y. 1994) (quoting *Libra Bank Ltd. v. Banco Nacional de Costa Rica*, 676 F.2d 47, 49 (2d Cir. 1982)). The court also implied that the waiver must be accepted as such by the U.S. government. *Id.*

10.   Does the FSIA apply to criminal cases? In *United States v. Hendron*, the court held that the FSIA did not preclude a conviction for conspiracy and armed-weapons charges against a director of a state-owned Polish corporation. 813 F. Supp. 973 (E.D.N.Y. 1993). The court reasoned that both the words of the Act and the legislative history implied an intent to limit it to civil actions. *Id.* at 974-76.

In *Gould, Inc. v. Mitsui Mining & Smelting Co.*, however, a different court held that the FSIA granted immunity to a foreign company acting as an agent of the French government. 750 F. Supp. 838, 843-44 (N.D. Ohio 1990). The court reasoned that the FSIA was "the only method of obtaining jurisdiction over foreign sovereigns." *Id.* Since "[t]he [*Amerada Hess*] Court did not limit its conclusion concerning the FSIA to civil cases," the court held that the U.S. had no jurisdiction to prosecute a French corporation for mail or wire fraud or for violations of the Racketeer Influenced and Corrupt Organizations Act. *Id.* at 844.

---

2.   Acts of State and Heads of State

The Supreme Court delineated the boundaries of the act of state doctrine as follows in *Underhill v. Hernandez*, 168 U.S. 250, 252 (1897):

> Every sovereign State is bound to respect the independence of every other sovereign State, and the courts of one country will not sit in judgment on the acts of the government of another done within its own territory. Redress of grievance by reason of such acts must be obtained through the means open to be availed of by sovereign powers as between themselves.

A century ago the purpose for the rule thus was to show respect for co-equal sovereigns. More recently, the Supreme Court noted that the doctrine is "a consequence of domestic separation of powers, reflecting 'the strong sense of the Judicial Branch that its engagement in the task of passing on the validity of foreign acts of state may hinder' the conduct of foreign affairs. *W.S. Kirkpatrick & Co. v. Environmental Tectonics Corp., Int'l*, 493 U.S. 400, 404 (1990) (citing *Banco Nacional de Cuba v. Sabbatino*, 376 U.S. 398, 423 (1964)).

As the Court reiterated in *Kirkpatrick*, those purposes are relevant only to determining "whether, despite the doctrine's technical availability, it should nonetheless not be invoked." 493 U.S. at 409. The policies cannot be used to "expan[d] the act of state doctrine . . . into new and uncharted fields." *Id.* The policies may be useful, however, in formulating arguments regarding application of the doctrine and in predicting how a court may rule. *See generally* DAVID EPSTEIN & JEFFREY L. SNYDER, INTERNATIONAL LITIGATION: A GUIDE TO JURISDICTION, PRACTICE AND STRATEGY § 8.02[2] (1993).

As you read the following excerpt note the court's discussion of the interplay between the FSIA and the act of state doctrine. In addition, think about how the policies underlying the act of state doctrine influenced the court's decision.

Liu v. Republic of China, 892 F.2d 1419 (9th Cir. 1989) (footnotes and several citations omitted), *cert. dismissed*, 497 U.S. 1058 (1990):

[Helen Liu brought an action against the Republic of China (ROC) and Admiral Wong, its Director of the Defense Intelligence Bureau, for ordering two gunmen to kill her husband in California.]

. . . THE ACT OF STATE DOCTRINE . . .

First, we address whether Liu's suit against the ROC for damages for the assassination of her husband is barred by the doctrine. Although the ROC did not raise this argument, we are concerned with the potential for embarrassing the Executive Branch, and raise the issue *sua sponte*.

In *Letelier*, 488 F. Supp. [665,] 673-74 [(D.D.C. 1989)], Chile argued that even if its officials ordered the assassination of Letelier, those acts would be immune from review under this doctrine because they occurred within Chile, although the assassination occurred in the United States. The court rejected this argument because:

> To hold otherwise would totally emasculate the purpose and effectiveness of the Foreign Sovereign Immunities Act by permitting a foreign state to reimpose the so recently supplanted framework of sovereign immunity as defined prior to the Act "'through the back door, under the guise of the act of state.'" *Id.* at 674.

. . .

In *International Ass'n of Machinists & Aerospace Workers v. OPEC*, this court held that the OPEC nations' price fixing activities, although not entitled to sovereign immunity under the FSIA, were acts of state. We held that the FSIA did not supersede the act of state doctrine because the doctrine addressed different concerns than the doctrine of sovereign immunity. "While the FSIA ignores the underlying purpose of a state's action, the act of state doctrine does not." Consequently, the mere fact that the FSIA confers jurisdiction on this court to hear this type of case does not end our inquiry. We must still determine whether the act of state doctrine mandates abstention in cases alleging that a foreign government ordered the assassination of an American citizen in the United States. We conclude that it does not.

One factor we must consider is whether the foreign state was acting in the public interest. "When the state *qua state* acts in the public interest, its sovereignty is asserted. The courts must proceed cautiously to avoid an affront to that sovereignty." Thus, any injunctive relief "instructing a foreign sovereign to alter its chosen means of allocating and profiting from its own valuable natural resources" would affront the sovereignty of a state. Ordinarily, this type of concern will be generated only when courts are asked to judge the legality or propriety of public acts committed within a foreign state's own borders. *See Banco Nacional de Cuba v. Sabbatino*, 376 U.S. 398, 400-01 [1964] (act of state involved the Cuban government's act of expropriating the property of aliens located within Cuba); *see also Republic of Iraq v. First Nat'l City Bank*, 353 F.2d 47, 51 (2d Cir. 1965), *cert. denied*, 382 U.S. 1027. . .(1966) ("when property confiscated is within the United States at the time of the attempted confiscation, our courts will give effect to acts of state 'only if they are consistent with the policy and law of the United States.'". . .). In this case, however, we are asked to judge the legality and propriety of an act that occurred within the borders of the United States. Such an inquiry would hardly affront the sovereignty of a foreign nation.

Another factor to be considered is the degree of international consensus regarding an activity. In *Sabbatino*, the Supreme Court stated:

> It should be apparent that the greater the degree of codification or consensus concerning a particular area of international law, the more appropriate it is for the judiciary to render decisions regarding it, since the courts can then focus on the application of an agreed principle to circumstances of facts rather than on the sensitive task of establishing a principle not inconsistent with the national interest or with international justice.

Last, this is not the sort of case that is likely to hinder the Executive Branch in its formulation of foreign policy, or result in differing pronouncements on the same subject. Rather, this court would more likely embarrass the Executive Branch if we summarily invoked the act of state doctrine to bar an American citizen from litigating a wrongful death suit for a murder that occurred in the United States. "The decision to deny access to judicial relief is not one we make lightly." We conclude that none of the factors present in *OPEC* that warranted the invocation of the act of state doctrine is present in this case. . . .

To the credit of the ROC, rather than attempting to hide the sordid circumstances involved in Liu's assassination, it made an investigation and publicly brought to trial individuals involved, even including one in . . . a high position . . . . Our decision merely applies California law to the facts as ascertained by the ROC courts. While the result may involve the financial responsibility of the ROC, it does not affront its sovereignty and can cause no more embarrassment than the exposures already made by the ROC courts. . . . Under these circumstances the act of state doctrine is not a bar to Liu's suit.

CONCLUSION

We hold that the act of state doctrine does not automatically bar a suit against a foreign nation when it is alleged that the nation ordered the assassination of an American citizen within the United States. We reverse the district court's decision dismissing the ROC as a party defendant. . . .

REVERSED and REMANDED.

*   *   *   *   *

Like sovereign immunity the act of state doctrine bars U.S. courts from hearing certain claims. In *W.S. Kirkpatrick & Co. v. Environmental Tectonics Corp., Int'l,* 493 U.S. 400, 401 (1990), the Supreme Court held that the doctrine did not bar courts from adjudicating disputes that did not "rest upon the asserted invalidity of an official act of a foreign sovereign, but . . . require[d] imputing to foreign officials an unlawful motivation (the obtaining of bribes) in the performance of such an official act." The case involved a U.S. company accused of offering a bribe to the Nigerian government in exchange for a construction contract—an act which violates both U.S. and Nigerian law. An unsuccessful bidder for the contract sued the company and the Nigerian government for damages. The defendants claimed the action was barred by the act of state doctrine. *Id.* at 401-02.

Justice Scalia, writing for a unanimous Court, concluded the doctrine was inapplicable to this case:

> The parties have argued at length about the applicability of . . . possible exceptions, and, more generally, about whether the purpose of the act of state doctrine would be furthered by its application in this case. We find it unnecessary, however, to pursue those inquiries, since the factual predicate for application of the act of state doctrine does not exist. Nothing in the present suit requires the Court to declare invalid, and thus ineffective as "a rule of decision for the courts of this country," the official act of a foreign sovereign.
>
> In every case in which we have held the act of state doctrine applicable, the relief sought or the defense interposed would have required a court in the United States to declare invalid the official act of a foreign sovereign performed within its own territory. In *Underhill v. Hernandez,* 168 U.S. 250, 254 . . . (1897), holding the defendant's detention of the plaintiff to be tortious would have required denying legal effect to "acts of a military commander representing the authority of the revolutionary party as government, which afterwards succeeded and was recognized by the United States." In *Oetjen v. Central Leather Co.,* [246 U.S. 297, 304 (1918)], and in *Ricaud v. American Metal Co.,* [246 U.S. 304, 310 (1918)], denying title to the party who claimed through purchase from Mexico would have required declaring that government's prior seizure of the property, within its own territory, legally ineffective. In *Sabbatino,* upholding the defendant's claim to the funds would have required a holding that Cuba's expropriation of goods located in Havana was null and void. In the present case, by contrast, neither the claim nor any asserted defense requires a determination that Nigeria's contract with Kirkpatrick [the U.S. company] . . . was, or was not, effective.

Id. at 405-06.

The Court then concluded,

> The short of the matter is this: Courts in the United States have the power, and ordinarily the obligation, to decide cases and controversies properly presented to them. The act of state doctrine does not establish an exception for cases and controversies that may embarrass foreign governments, but merely requires that, in the process of deciding, the acts of foreign sovereigns taken within their own jurisdictions shall be deemed valid. That doctrine has no application to the present case because the validity of no foreign sovereign act is at issue.

Id. at 409-10.

The act of state doctrine thus should be understood as a rule limiting the scope of a foreign court's inquiry into certain acts of a sovereign. As stated in *Kirkpatrick,* the doctrine does not result in dismissal for lack of jurisdiction, but precludes a court from questioning the validity of certain actions.

Similar to act of state immunity, but jurisdictional in nature, is head of state immunity. Under this doctrine, the head of state is immune from the jurisdiction of foreign courts for acts within the scope of his or her duties. Unlike the act of state doctrine, which has been justified by separation of powers concerns, head of state immunity is still based on customary international law. The rationale behind both doctrines, however, is similar: they are intended to "promote international comity and respect among sovereign nations by ensuring that leaders are free to perform their governmental duties without being subject to detention, arrest, or embarrassment in a foreign country's legal system." *United States v. Noriega*, 746 F. Supp. 1506, 1519 (1990).

The contours of both act of state and head of state immunity are a product of federal common law. Several limitations were highlighted in the criminal prosecution of Manuel Noriega, former leader of the Panamanian armed forces, for various narcotics-related crimes. *United States v. Noriega*, 746 F. Supp. 1506 (S.D. Fla. 1990). The court first noted that, '[i]n order to assert head of state immunity, a government official must be recognized as a head of state." *Id.* at 1519. Since Noriega was never recognized by the United States or the Panamanian constitution as the leader of Panama, he was not entitled to assert the defense. *Id.*

The court further noted that "the grant of immunity is a privilege which the United States may withhold from any claimant." *Id.* at 1520, citing *The Schooner Exchange v. M'Faddon*, 11 U.S. (7 Cranch) 116 (1812). The court therefore found irrelevant Noriega's claim that he was the *de facto* ruler of Panama. *Id.* In general, courts tend to defer to the Executive Branch's decisions regarding matters of foreign relations, including head of state immunity. As a result, the doctrine is more flexible than foreign sovereign immunity and potentially could be applied inconsistently.

The *Noriega* court noted that "[a]lthough stated in terms of acts of the 'State' or 'sovereign,' the [act of state] doctrine also extends to governmental acts of State officials vested with sovereign authority." *Id.* at 1521. Unlike head of state immunity, however, it is not clear whether such state officials and their governments must be officially recognized. *Compare Underhill v. Hernandez*, 168 U.S. 250, 252 (1897) (stating the act of state doctrine "[cannot] be confined to lawful or recognized governments") *with Banco Nacional de Cuba v. Sabbatino*, 376 U.S. 398, 428 (1964) (implying that courts would only extend the act of state doctrine to a "sovereign foreign government, extant and recognized by this country at the time of suit.").

In any case, as stated briefly in *Liu*, act of state immunity applies only to public acts performed on behalf of the state, not to private acts performed on behalf of the actor. *Alfred Dunhill of London, Inc. v. Republic of Cuba*, 425 U.S. 682, 694 (1976). In *Noriega*, the court rejected Noriega's assertion that his narcotics-related actions were public acts performed on behalf of Panama. The acts instead benefitted him personally. Whether Noriega's status as leader of Panama aided his criminal activities was irrelevant in determining whether the acts were performed on behalf of Panama. *Id.* at 1522.

NOTES AND QUESTIONS

1.   Think about the interplay between foreign sovereign immunity, act of state immunity, and head of state immunity. What are the differences and similarities? In what different situations is each one applicable? Why do three doctrines still exist?

2.   Is there a relation between proving the existence of an international tort and determining

whether the act of state doctrine bars adjudication? Remember that to prove most international torts, plaintiff must show the defendant was acting under color of law.

3.   Significant precedential rules have emerged as a result of suits against Ferdinand Marcos, former leader of the Philippines. In *Republic of the Philippines v. Marcos*, 806 F.2d 344 (2d Cir. 1986) (*Marcos I*), the Philippines sued Marcos to recover property he embezzled while in power. The Philippines was successful in obtaining a preliminary injunction limiting Marcos' power to transfer the property while the trial was pending. *Id.* at 346. Upholding the injunction, the court rejected the argument that the act of state doctrine shielded the embezzlement from judicial review. The court concluded that embezzling property was not a public act, and, thus, that the act of state doctrine did not apply. *Id.* at 358. The court noted, however, that even acts illegal in the country in which they occur can be considered acts of state if there is a public purpose. Marcos' embezzlement, which contravened Philippine law, could have been covered by act of state immunity if it had not been merely a private act. *Id.* at 359.

In *Marcos I*, the court questioned whether foreign sovereign immunity extended to its head of state. The court noted "[t]he rationale underlying sovereign immunity—avoiding embarrassment to our government and showing respect for a foreign state—may well be absent when the individual is no longer head of state and the current government is suing him." The court did not reach a conclusion, however, because it determined the appellants lacked standing to raise the claim. *Id.*

In *Republic of the Philippines v. Marcos*, 862 F.2d 1355 (9th Cir. 1988) (en banc), *cert. denied*, 490 U.S. 1035 (1989) (*Marcos II*), the court reached a conclusion similar to that in *Marcos I*. In *Marcos II*, The Philippines again sued Marcos, this time under the Racketeer Influenced and Corrupt Organizations Act, for mail fraud, wire fraud, and transporting stolen property in foreign or interstate commerce. *Id.* at 1358. In affirming a preliminary injunction enjoining Marcos from disposing of any assets which were not needed to pay attorney fees or "normal" living expenses, the court rejected Marcos' act of state defense. It noted that the doctrine was not to be used to protect a deposed head of state who was now being sued by his former country. Instead, it should only apply to heads of state currently in power. *Id.* at 1360-61. The court reasoned, "the [act of state] doctrine is meant to facilitate the foreign relations of the United States, not to furnish the equivalent of sovereign immunity to a deposed leader." *Id.* at 1361.

In his concurring and dissenting opinion, Judge Schroeder expanded on that idea. After concluding that the act of state doctrine is not jurisdictional but rather a self-imposed limitation on the judiciary, he argued that the rationale behind the doctrine does not apply when the defendant is a government no longer in power. *Id.* at 1368-69. Showing respect for an independent sovereign and maintaining a balance in the separation of powers between the executive and judicial branches are less important when the defendant no longer enjoys a preferred position as leader of a foreign state. *Id.*

4.   In *Liu*, the court concluded that the degree of judicial self-restraint varies depending on the level of international consensus condemning the acts in question. Does that conclusion suggest that courts would be more likely to utilize the act of state defense to avoid adjudicating the rape case outlined in the hypothetical fact situation at the beginning of the chapter, assuming that rape has not yet been adjudicated as an international tort?

5.   *Filartiga*, excerpted *supra* at 8, did not address the act of state issue because the defense was raised for the first time on appeal. The court noted that it doubted "whether action by a state official in violation of the Constitution and laws of the Republic of Paraguay, and wholly unratified by the nation's government, could properly be characterized as an act of state." 630 F.2d at 889. May an act violating laws of an official's country nonetheless be an act of state? *See Marcos I*, discussed *supra* note 3. If a government asserts that wrongdoing was not part of an official's duties, is that assertion dispositive of the act of state doctrine's applicability? Or relevant to determining whether the doctrine bars adjudication? Would the answer differ if the official were part of a government that had been deposed but would have ratified the action had it remained in power?

6.   One further immunity that may apply in alien tort litigation is diplomatic immunity. In general, diplomatic immunity exempts diplomats from civil and criminal jurisdiction in states to which they are sent. Diplomatic immunity is therefore best understood as immunity from suit rather than immunity from legal liability. Stephen L. Wright, Note, *Diplomatic Immunity: A Proposal for Amending the Vienna Convention to Deter Violent Criminal Acts*, 5 B.U. INT'L L.J. 177, 177 (1987). The international law of diplomatic immunity is codified in the Vienna Convention on Diplomatic Relations, 23 U.S.T. 3227, T.I.A.S. No. 7502, 500 U.N.T.S. 95, *entered into force* April 18, 1961, *entered into force for the U.S.* Dec. 13, 1972.

Like head of state immunity, diplomatic immunity is contingent upon official recognition by the receiving state. *United States v. Lumumba*, 741 F.2d 12, 15 (2d Cir. 1984) (denying immunity to defendant claiming to be Vice President and Minister of Justice of the Provisional Government of the Republic of New Afrika, a "[n]ation of Afrikans born in North America as a consequence of . . . slavery" encompassing Alabama, Georgia, Louisiana, Mississippi, and South Carolina, because the nation had not been recognized by the Executive Branch). In addition, like other immunities, diplomatic immunity may be waived. RESTATEMENT (THIRD) OF THE FOREIGN RELATIONS LAW OF THE UNITED STATES § 464 comment j (1986).

In the context of the hypothetical case presented at the beginning of this chapter, how might diplomatic immunity limit the ability of the court to adjudicate Sena's claims? Would the answer be different if Herak and Raznatovic had been in the U.S. to attend a U.S.-government-sponsored meeting on the political situation in Bosnia? What if the U.S. had not yet recognized Bosnia as a sovereign state? Or Herak and Raznatovic as officials of the Bosnian government? How would those hypothetical situations affect the defendants' ability to raise head of state and act of state immunities?

7.   For further reading, see:

Frederic L. Kirgis, *Editorial Comment: Understanding the Act of State Doctrine's Effect*, 82 AM. J. INT'L L. 58 (1988);

Tom Lininger, Recent Development, *Overcoming Immunity Defenses to Human Rights Suits in U.S. Courts*, 7 HARV. HUM. RTS. J. 177, 191-96 (1994) (discussing strategies for suing individuals under the ATCA and TVPA);

Jerrold L. Mallory, Note, *Resolving the Confusion Over Head of State Immunity: The Defined Rights of Kings*, 86 COLUM. L. REV. 169 (1986).

---

3.   Statute of Limitations, Damages, and Choice of Law

Filartiga v. Peña-Irala, 577 F. Supp. 860 (E.D.N.Y. 1984) (several citations omitted):

[This opinion was issued on remand from *Filartiga v. Peña-Irala*, 630 F.2d 876 (2d Cir. 1980), excerpted *supra* at 505.]

NICKERSON, District Judge. . . .

III

Following remand Peña took no further part in the action. This court granted a default and referred the question of damages to [a] Magistrate. . . . The Magistrate. . .recommended damages of $200,000 for Dr. Joel Filartiga and $175,000 for Dolly Filartiga. Plaintiffs filed objections to the report, and the matter is now here for determination. . . .

The common law of the United States includes, of course, the principles collected under the rubric of conflict of laws. For the most part in international matters those principles have been concerned with the relevant policies of the interested national states, and with "the needs" of the "international systems." Restatement (Second) of Conflict of Laws (1971) §6(2). The chief function of international choice-of-law rules has been said to be to further harmonious relations and commercial intercourse between states. *Id.*, comment d.

However, where the nations of the world have adopted a norm in terms so formal and unambiguous as to make it international "law," the interests of the global community transcend those of any one state. That does not mean that traditional choice-of-law principles are irrelevant. Clearly the court should consider the interests of Paraguay to the extent they do not inhibit the appropriate enforcement of the applicable international law or conflict with the public policy of the United States.

In this case the torture and death of Joelito occurred in Paraguay. The plaintiffs and Peña are Paraguayan and lived in Paraguay when the torture took place. . . . It was in Paraguay that plaintiffs suffered the claimed injuries, with the exception of the emotional trauma which followed Dolly Filartiga to this country. The parties' relationships with each other and with Joelito were centered in Paraguay.

Moreover, the written Paraguayan law prohibits torture. The Constitution of Paraguay, art. 50. The Paraguayan Penal Code, art. 337, provides that homicide by torture is punishable by a imprisonment for 15 to 20 years. Paraguay is a signatory to the American Convention on Human Rights, which proscribes the use of torture. Paraguayan law purports to allow recovery for wrongful death, including specific pecuniary damages, "moral damage," and court costs and attorney's fees. Thus, the pertinent formal Paraguayan law is ascertainable.

All these factors make it appropriate to look first to Paraguayan law in determining the remedy for the violation of international law. It might be objected that, despite Paraguay's official ban on torture, the "law" of that country is what it does in fact, and torture persists throughout the country.

Where a nation's pronouncements form part of the consensus establishing an international law, however, it does not lie in the mouth of a citizen of that nation, though it professes one thing and does another, to claim that his country did not mean what it said. In concert with the other nations of the world Paraguay prohibited torture and thereby reaped the benefits the condemnation brought with it. Paraguayan citizens may not pretend that no such condemnation exists. . . .

To the extent that Peña might have expected that Paraguay would not hold him responsible for his official acts, that was not a "justified" expectation, Restatement (Second) of Conflict of Laws (1971) §6(2)(d) and comment g, so as to make unfair the application to him of the written law of Paraguay.

IV

Plaintiffs claim punitive damages, and the Magistrate recommended they be denied on the ground that they are not recoverable under the Paraguayan Civil Code. While compensable "moral" injuries under that code include emotional pain and suffering, loss of companionship and disruption of family life, plaintiffs' expert agrees that the code does not provide for what United States courts would call punitive damages. Paraguayan law, in determining the intensity and duration of the suffering and the consequent "moral" damages, takes into account the heinous nature of the tort. However, such damages are not justified by the desire to punish the defendant. They are designed to compensate for the greater pain caused by the atrocious nature of the act.

Yet because, as the record establishes, Paraguay will not undertake to prosecute

Peña for his acts, the objective of the international law making torture punishable as a crime can only be vindicated by imposing punitive damages. . . .

Moreover, there is some precedent for the award of punitive damages in tort even against a national government. . . .

Where the defendant is an individual, the same diplomatic considerations that prompt reluctance to impose punitive damages are not present. . . .

This court concludes that it is essential and proper to grant the remedy of punitive damages in order to give effect to the manifest objectives of the international prohibition against torture.

V

In concluding that the plaintiffs were entitled only to damages recoverable under Paraguayan law, the Magistrate recommended . . . against an award of punitive damages and of $10,364 in expenses incurred in connection with this action. Plaintiffs object only to these . . . recommendations. . . .

Chief among the considerations the court must weigh is the fact that this case concerns not a local tort but a wrong as to which the world has seen fit to speak. Punitive damages are designed not merely to teach a defendant not to repeat his conduct but to deter others from following his example. . . .

There are no binding precedents to guide the court in determining what amount lies within those respectable bounds that hedge the judiciary and yet may serve to come to the attention of those who think to practice torture . . ..

The record in this case shows that torture and death are bound to recur unless deterred. This court concludes that an award of punitive damages of no less that $5,000,000 to each plaintiff is appropriate to reflect adherence to the world community's proscription of torture and to attempt to deter its practice.

NOTES AND QUESTIONS

1.   The *Filartiga* plaintiffs have been unable to collect the award of $10.4 million. Peña did not have assets in the United States; efforts to recover in Paraguay have been unsuccessful. Nonetheless, what other benefits may have come from the litigation? Recall the discussion in part C, *supra* at 521, regarding the various purposes of ATCA litigation.

2.   Another example of a large damage award is *Mushikiwabo v. Barayagwiza*, 94 Civ. 3627 (1996). In that case the five plaintiffs, relatives of victims tortured and killed in Rwanda, were awarded over $100 million in a default judgment. The defendant, Rwandan military leader Jean Bosco Barayagwiza, played a significant role in the massacre of thousands of Tutsi minority members. The judge found jurisdiction under the ATCA and the TVPA. *See* chapter 8, *supra* for a discussion of the Rwandan massacre.

3.   In *Forti I*, excerpted in part C, *supra* at 516, the court held that the statute of limitations could be borrowed from the forum state, California, and that defendant's hiding tolled the statute of limitations.

4.   For a discussion of the political question doctrine, which may arguably bar adjudication of certain claims, see chapter 13, *infra*.

5.   For a discussion of the various doctrines limiting the justiciability of international human rights violations in U.S. courts, see American Soc'y Int'l Law, *Foreign Governments in United States Courts*, 85 AM. SOC'Y INT'L L. PROC. 251 (1991).

E. TORTURE VICTIM PROTECTION ACT LITIGATION

On March 12, 1992, presumably to codify the result in *Filartiga* (at least with respect to torture and extrajudicial killing) and to make that result available to U.S. citizens, Congress passed the Torture Victim Protection Act ("TVPA"), excerpted now as follows:

28 U.S.C. § 1350

Sec. 2. Establishment of civil action.

(a) Liability.—An individual who, under actual or apparent authority, or color of law, of any foreign nation—

(1) subjects an individual to torture shall, in a civil action, be liable for damages to that individual; or

(2) subjects an individual to extrajudicial killing shall, in a civil action, be liable for damages to the individual's legal representative, or to any person who may be a claimant in an action for wrongful death.

(b) Exhaustion of remedies.—A court shall decline to hear a claim under this section if the claimant has not exhausted adequate and available remedies in the place in which the conduct giving rise to the claim occurred.

(c) Statute of limitations.—No action shall be maintained under this section unless it is commenced within 10 years after the cause of action arose.

Sec. 3. Definitions.

(a) Extrajudicial killing.—For the purposes of this Act, the term "extrajudicial killing" means a deliberated killing not authorized by a previous judgment pronounced by a regularly constituted court affording all the judicial guarantees which are recognized as indispensable by civilized peoples. Such term, however, does not include any such killing that, under international law, is lawfully carried out under the authority of a foreign nation.

(b) Torture.—For the purposes of this Act—

(1) the term "torture" means any act, directed against an individual in the offender's custody or physical control, by which severe pain or suffering (other than pain or suffering arising only from or inherent in, or incidental to, lawful sanctions), whether physical or mental, is intentionally inflicted on that individual for such purposes as obtaining from that individual or a third person information or a confession, punishing that individual for an act that individual or a third person has committed or is suspected of having committed, intimidating or coercing that individual or a third person, or for any reason based on discrimination of any kind; and

(2) mental pain or suffering refers to prolonged mental harm caused by or resulting from—

A) the intentional infliction or threatened infliction of severe physical pain or suffering;

(B) the administration or application, or threatened administration or application, of mind altering substances or other procedures calculated to disrupt profoundly the senses or the personality;

(C)   the threat of imminent death; or

(D)   the threat that another individual will imminently be subjected to death, severe physical pain or suffering, or the administration or application of mind altering substances or other procedures calculated to disrupt profoundly the senses or personality.

NOTES AND QUESTIONS

1.   Like the ATCA, the TVPA opens U.S. courts to suits between aliens for violations of international law. There are differences, however. The TVPA applies to "an individual" and litigation thus is not restricted to aliens but may involve U.S. citizens too. In addition, the TVPA provides a cause of action for described torts and thus eliminates the need to find a customary international norm. The TVPA is limited, however, by a ten year statute of limitations. Further, it requires litigants to "exhaust[] adequate and available remedies in the place in which the conduct giving rise to the claim occurred." Does that clause avoid some of the problems leading to criticism of the ATCA? What are the implications for plaintiffs? Does the exhaustion requirement unnecessarily restrict the reach of the statute?

2.   How would you construe the requirement that remedies be "adequate and available"? Would a court waive the requirement if courts in the country wherein torture or extrajudicial killing occurred were not functioning? If the ruling government refuses to enforce judgments for torture? If otherwise it seems futile to pursue national remedies there?

3.   How does the TVPA's definition of torture compare with the definition contained in the Convention against Torture? *See supra* at 531.

4.   One issue in TVPA litigation is retroactivity. In *Xuncax v. Gramajo*, 886 F. Supp. 162 (D. Mass. 1995), an American nun claimed that Hector Gramajo, Minister of Defense for Guatemala from 1987 to 1990, was responsible for the acts of torture she experienced while working in Guatemala as a missionary. The U.S. District Court for Massachusetts ruled that the TVPA applies retroactively to grant jurisdiction over pre-TVPA torture and awarded $3,000,000 in compensatory damages. The court declined, however, to award punitive damages retroactively. *See* Joan Fitzpatrick et al., *Recent Developments in International Human Rights Litigation and Legislation*, ACLU INTERNATIONAL CIVIL LIBERTIES REPORT 37 (1993).

Retroactivity did not present a problem for the 11th Circuit in *Abebe-Jira v. Negewo*, 72 F.3d 844 (11th Cir. 1996). In that case an Ethiopian official appealed a decision awarding three Ethiopian women $1,500,000 for arbitrary detention, torture, and cruel, inhuman, and degrading treatment. Though the lower court did not address the TVPA, defendant-appellant argued on appeal that it did not apply. He argued in part that, since the plaintiffs' complaint was filed before the TVPA was enacted, it could not provide jurisdiction. Brief of Defendant-Appellant, at 10. In an amici brief, international law experts argued that the issue was not retroactivity.[10] Brief of Amici, at 21. Pursuant to the Supreme Court's decision in *Bradley v. School Bd. of City of Richmond*, 416 U.S. 696, 711 (1974), a "court should 'apply the law in effect at the time it renders its decision.'" *Id.* In effect, since the TVPA did not create new legal consequences but merely codified *Filartiga*, it should apply to all actions decided after

---

[10] Parties to the brief include the International Human Rights Law Group, Allard K. Lowenstein International Human Rights Clinic, Lawyers Committee for Human Rights, Minnesota Advocates for Human Rights, Deborah Anker, David Bederman, Ann-Marie Slaughter Burley, Abram Chayes, Anthony D'Amato, Lori Damrosch, Richard Falk, Joan Fitzpatrick, Michael Glennon, Cynthia Lichtenstein, Richard B. Lillich, Jules Lobel, Oscar Schachter, Henry Steiner, and David Weissbrodt.

its enactment. *Id.* at 22. The 11th Circuit affirmed the decision of the lower court based on the ATCA and agreed with the amici stating "we find support for our holding in the recently enacted Torture Victim Protection Act of 1991." The court did not discuss retroactivity with respect to the TVPA.

One federal district court, however, dismissed a TVPA claim based on retroactivity in a suit by a Mexican physician against Mexican and U.S. officials responsible for his abduction in 1990. *Alvarez-Machain v. Berellez*, Civil No. CV-93-4072-JGD, (C.D. Cal. Jan. 23, 1995). The court granted a motion to dismiss his TVPA claim because the TVPA does not apply to events which occurred before it was enacted in 1992. In a brief to the 9th Circuit, where the case is pending, amici argued that the court should follow *Xuncax*, and find the TVPA to be retroactive. Brief of Amici, at 21.[11] Urging reversal, they argued "Defendants possessed no 'right' to torture with impunity before 1992. They were fully liable for such conduct and had legal duties to refrain from committing such acts. Hence, they remain fully subject to the District Court's jurisdiction under the codification of those duties in the TVPA." *Id.* at 22. *See* Joan Fitzpatrick et al., *Human Rights Litigation Update Report*, ACLU INTERNATIONAL CIVIL LIBERTIES REPORT 30 (1995).

5.   One court has concluded that neither the FSIA nor the TVPA eliminated act of state immunity. In *Lafontant v. Aristide*, 844 F. Supp. 128, 137 (E.D.N.Y. 1994), the judge reasoned that both the history and the underlying policy of comity compel a conclusion that the FSIA did not affect the existing head of state immunity doctrine. Similarly, the legislative history supports the conclusion that it was "not intended to trump diplomatic and head of state immunities." *Id.* at 138. Both act of state and head of state doctrines therefore may remain as additional defenses to human rights claims in U.S. courts. The court dismissed plaintiff's claims against President Aristide of Haiti on grounds of head of state immunity, despite its concluding that "[t]he TVPA on its face does give federal courts jurisdiction over some suits against foreign officials who kill illegally on foreign territory." *Id.*

For actions brought under the TVPA, however, Congress may have intended to make the act of state defense inapplicable. Statements in the legislative history imply that the defense should not be used to avoid liability under the TVPA. *See, e.g.*, 138 *Cong. Rec.* S2668 (daily ed. Mar. 3, 1992) (statement of Senator Specter) (arguing that torture cannot be committed as a matter of official policy and therefore cannot be considered an act of state).

6.   Re-read note 5, *supra* at 523. Though the remedies that must be ensured pursuant to Article 2(3) of the Covenant on Civil and Political Rights appear to be national remedies to redress violations of the Covenant by a nation's government, might the words be construed to authorize legislation such as the TVPA? Under other nations' statutes similar to the TVPA, might the U.S. be sued for its violations of the Covenant occurring in the U.S.? Would such a construction validate the hypothetical danger of retaliatory suits?

7.   For additional reading, see Robert F. Drinan, S.J. & Teresa T. Kuo, *Putting the World's Oppressors on Trial: The Torture Victim Protection Act*, 15 HUM. RTS. Q. 605 (1993).

---

[11] Parties to the Brief include the Lawyers Committee for Human Rights, The Allard K. Lowenstein International Human Rights Clinic, The Center for Constitutional Rights, Minnesota Advocates for Human Rights, International Human Rights Law Group, and several law professors.

CHAPTER 13

U.S. REMEDIES FOR HUMAN RIGHTS VIOLATIONS WITHIN THE U.S.

Alien Children in Detention

		Page	
A.	**Introduction**		554
	Justice Harry Blackmun, Comments		555
B.	**Questions**		557
C.	**U.S. Law**		560
	1. **Constitution**		560
	Article VI, § 2		560
	Amendment V		560
	Amendment VIII		560
	2. **Federal Statutes and Regulations**		560
	8 U.S.C. § 1252		560
	8 U.S.C. § 1357		561
	8 C.F.R. § 242.24		561
	3. **Judicial Interpretation**		562
	Reno v. Flores		562
D.	**International Standards**		568
	1. **U.S.-Ratified Treaties**		568
	Covenant on Civil and Political Rights		568
	2. **Treaties Which the U.S. Has Not Ratified**		572
	Convention on the Rights of the Child		572
E.	**Approaches to Using International Human Rights Law**		574
	Judge Hans Linde, Comments		576
F.	**Treaties**		580
	Vienna Convention on the Law of Treaties		580
	1. **Treaties in U.S. Law**		581
	United States v. Palestine Liberation Organization		581
	2. **Treaties Which the U.S. Has Not Ratified**		585
	3. **The Doctrine of Self-Executing Treaties**		585
	Kathryn Burke, et al., Application of Human Rights Law		586
	Matter of Medina, Board of Immigration Appeals		589
	Matter of Medina, ACLU Amicus Brief		591
	4. **Reservations**		594
	5. **Implementing Legislation: The U.S. Refugee Act of 1980**		597

G. **Customary International Law**   598

    1. **Proving a Customary Norm**   599

    2. **General Principles of Law Recognized by the Community of Nations**   601

    3. **Peremptory Norms**   601

H. **Using International Law to Guide Interpretation of U.S. Law**   602

    1. **Prison Conditions**   602
        Lareau v. Manson   602

    2. **U.S. Supreme Court Opinions**   607

    3. **Protesting International Crimes**   608
        Declaration of Frank Newman, in *People v. Wylie*   608

    4. **Rights of Aliens**   610

    5. **Other Rights**   611

I. **Incorporating International Law in U.S. Statutes**   612
        Sandra Coliver & Frank Newman, Using International Human Rights Law   612

J. **Obstacles to Application of International Law**   613

    1. **Challenges to U.S. Foreign Policy: Political Questions, Sovereign Immunity, Standing, and Failure to State a Cause of Action**   614
        Committee of U.S. Citizens in Nicaragua v. Reagan 614

    2. **Challenges to U.S. Policies: Customary Norms and Executive, Legislative, and Judicial Acts**   622

K. **Strategy Issues: When to Invoke International Law in U.S. Courts; When to Seek Relief Through Administrative Processes; When to Seek Incorporation of International Law in U.S. Statutes?**   624
        Conference Report: Human Rights in American Courts   624

A. INTRODUCTION

In chapter 3 we discussed U.S. compliance with international treaty obligations. In chapter 12 we discussed the use of international law in federal courts in civil suits to remedy human rights violations occurring outside the United States. In this chapter we discuss the related issue of how international law may be applied in both federal and state courts to influence domestic enforcement of international human rights norms. This chapter thus discusses enforcing U.S., rather than foreign, compliance with international human rights law.

Innumerable statutes in the U.S. help protect civil liberties and civil rights. Several treaties to which the U.S. is a party contain clauses that seem analogous, but international and U.S. law often reflect different systems. Sometimes, though by no means always, U.S. law is more protective of human rights than are international laws. Yet U.S. citizens and others indeed can benefit by raising the pertinent international norms in U.S. legislatures, administrative agencies, courts, and elsewhere.

A century and more ago a U.S. Supreme Court dictum suggested, in words seemingly applicable to all sources of international law, that a treaty

> depends for the enforcement of its provisions on the interest and the honor of the governments which are parties to it. If these fail, its infraction becomes the subject of international negotiations and reclamations . . . [but] with all this the judicial courts have nothing to do and can give no redress.

Head Money Cases, 112 U.S. 580, 598 (1884). That dictum has been proved inaccurate. Courts here can and have done much with international norms. When a U.S. court refuses to enforce an international duty, its refusal says nothing about the existence or importance of the duty. The *Head Money* dictum rather suggests that the U.S. government (1) remains bound, (2) may in fact even be in default, and (3) may be subject to international sanctions such as diplomatic, political, economic, and even military measures. (For discussion of sanctions, see chapters 5 and 9, *supra*.)

While judges in the U.S. often seem reluctant to compel officials to comply with international obligations, they often have done so. Under the Supremacy Clause of Article VI, § 2 of the U.S. Constitution (*see* Part C, *infra* at 560), they have required state governments to comply with international duties assumed by the U.S. government. International law also has been used to convince courts to interpret U.S. laws in the light of international law, to command administrative decision-makers, and to convince legislators to adjust statutes which are inconsistent with international standards.

This chapter discusses using treaties in courts, legislatures, and administrative agencies. It also describes the use of customary international law in forums where there is no controlling U.S.-ratified treaty. We discuss the issues in the context of a situation arising in the U.S. where international standards might aid the intended beneficiaries of international human rights norms. The illustrative situation, discussed in Part B, concerns detention of alien children by U.S. officials pending deportation hearings.

As you read, keep in mind that courts in the U.S. are not infallible, as is highlighted in these comments by Justice Blackmun to the American Society of International Law in April 1994.

Justice Harry A. Blackmun, *The Supreme Court and the Law of Nations: Owing a Decent Respect to the Opinions of Mankind*, ASIL NEWSL. (American Soc'y of Int'l Law, Wash., D.C.), Mar.-May 1994, at 1, 1, 6-9 (several citations omitted) (material in brackets added by the editors):

I am here tonight to speak about the Supreme Court, the law of nations, and the place in American jurisprudence for what the drafters of the Declaration of Independence termed "a decent respect to the opinions of mankind."

The early architects of our nation were experienced diplomats who appreciated that the law of nations was binding on the United States. John Jay, the first Chief Justice of the United States, observed, in a case called *Chisolm v. Georgia*, 2 Dall. 419 (1793), that the United States "had, by taking a place among the nations of the earth, become amenable to the laws of nations." Although the Constitution, by Art. I, § 8, cl. 10, gives Congress the power to "define and punish . . . Offenses against the Law of Nations," and by Art. VI, cl. 2, identifies treaties as part of "the supreme Law of the Land," the task of further defining the role of international law in the nation's legal fabric has fallen to the courts.

Several first principles have been established. As early as 1804, the Supreme Court recognized that "an act of congress ought never to be construed to violate the law of nations if any other possible construction remains." In a trilogy of cases in the 1880s, the Court established that treaties are on equal footing with federal statutes and that, where a treaty and statute cannot be reconciled, the later in time is controlling.

Finally, in the case of *The Paquete Habana*, 175 U.S. 677, decided in 1900, the Supreme Court addressed the power of courts to enforce customary international law. In invalidating the wartime seizure of fishing vessels as contrary to the law of nations, the Court observed: "International law is part of our law, and must be ascertained and administered by the courts." Where no treaty or other legal authority is controlling, resort must be had to the customs of nations.

These early principles established during the Supreme Court's first century continue to define the relationship between the law of nations and domestic American law. Tonight I consider the Supreme Court's application of these principles in four of the Court's recent cases. The first two, *United States v. Alvarez-Machain* and *Haitian Centers Council v. McNary*, required the Court to examine the validity of executive action in light of binding international treaties. The last two, *Thompson v. Oklahoma* and *Stanford v. Kentucky*, addressed the implications of international law for Eighth Amendment death-penalty jurisprudence. I conclude from these cases that, unfortunately, the Supreme Court has shown something less than "a decent respect to the opinions of mankind."

[Justice Blackmun criticized both *Alvarez-Machain*, discussed *infra* Part F at 580, and *Haitian Control Centers*, where the Court upheld the U.S. policy of intercepting Haitian refugees on the high seas and summarily returning them to Haiti without any consideration of their asylum claims. He noted that in both cases, the Court ignored the spirit of international treaties in favor of formalistic interpretations of the treaties in the context of U.S. domestic law. In doing so, the Court construed treaties contrary to their plain meaning, spirit, and purpose.]

Do not the decisions in the *Alvarez* and *Haitian Centers Council* cases reflect a disturbing disregard for the Supreme Court's obligations when construing international law? Treaties are contracts among nations and thus must be interpreted with sensitivity toward the customs of the world community. In each of those cases, however, the Court ignored its first principles and construed the challenged treaty directly contrary to the opinions of mankind.

[Justice Blackmun then discussed the juvenile death penalty cases, *Thompson v. Oklahoma* and *Stanford v. Kentucky*. These cases are discussed *infra*, Part H at 607-08. Despite earlier precedents incorporating international norms into the Eighth Amendment definition of cruel and unusual punishment, the Supreme Court ultimately concluded that international standards had no place in Eighth Amendment analysis.]

Professor Henkin poignantly has observed that "almost all nations observe almost all principles of international law and almost all of their obligations almost all of the time." [Louis Henkin, *How Nations Behave* 47 (2d ed., 1979).] Unfortunately, as the cases I have cited illustrate, the Supreme Court's own recent record in the area is somewhat more qualified. I would say that, at best, the Supreme Court enforces *some* principles of international law and *some* of its obligations *some* of the time.

The reasons for the Court's failures in this area are not very clear. Concerns about separation of powers and judicial competence make courts reluctant to second-guess the Legislature and Executive in areas involving international affairs. Modern jurists also are notably lacking in the diplomatic experience of early Justices such as John Jay and John Marshall, who were familiar with the law of nations and felt comfortable navigating by it. Today's jurists, furthermore, are relatively unfamiliar with interpreting instruments of international law.

I have been serving on the federal bench for 34 years. During that time, the United States has become economically and politically intertwined with the rest of the world as never before. International human rights conventions—still a relatively new idea when I came to the bench in 1959—have created for nations mutual obligations that are accepted throughout the world. As we approach the 100th anniversary of *The Paquete Habana*, then, it perhaps is appropriate to remind ourselves that now, more than ever, "international law is part of our law" and is entitled to the respect of our domestic courts. Although the recent decisions of the Supreme Court do not offer much hope for the immediate future, I look forward to the day when the Supreme Court, too, will inform its opinions almost all the time with a decent respect to the opinions of mankind.

B. QUESTIONS

Assume that in 1985 eleven-year-old Jenny Lopez emigrated from Guatemala to the U.S. to escape violence in her home country.[1] She hoped to join family members living in Los Angeles. Instead she was arrested at the border by Immigration and Naturalization Service (INS) employees, handcuffed, strip-searched, and placed in a juvenile-detention facility. Though she was neither a flight risk nor a threat to herself or the community, she could not be released into the temporary custody of her twenty-three-year-old cousin, a U.S. citizen, because her cousin did not fit within the definition of relatives to whom automatic release was authorized under governing regulations. (*See* 8 C.F.R. § 242.24, *infra* Part *C*.) Her mother was in the U.S. illegally and because of fear of being arrested and deported, did not come forward to claim her daughter.

Jenny was detained in one of the many detention facilities along the Mexican border.[2] The facilities are often shacks, tents, or other make-shift shelters surrounded by barbed wire. Detained children have virtually no access to health care and personal counseling, or to attorneys, telephones, or other means to prepare

---

[1] The facts are analogous to the situation in *Reno v. Flores, infra* Part *C*, at 13. They are summarized generally in Thomas A. Bockhorst, Note, *The Constitutionality of INS Pre-Hearing Detention of Alien Children:* Flores v. Meese, *942 F.2d 1352 (9th Cir. 1991) (En Banc), cert. granted sub nom.* Barr v. Flores, *60 U.S.L.W. 3598 (U.S. Mar. 2, 1992),* 62 U. CIN. L. REV. 217, 217-19 (1993); Erin E. Gorman, Comment, *Reno v. Flores: The INS' Automatic Detention Policy for Alien Children,* 7 GEO. IMMIGR. L.J. 435, 435-36 (1993); Pamela Theodoredis, Comment, *Detention of Alien Juveniles: Reno v. Flores,* 12 N.Y.L. SCH. J. HUM. RTS. 393 (1995).

[2] The conditions of confinement are summarized in Michael A. Olivas, *Unaccompanied Refugee Children: Detention, Due Process, and Disgrace,* 2 STAN. L. & POL'Y REV. 159, 160 (1990). *See also* Jay Mathews, *Group Says INS Uses Children as Lures for Illegal Alien Parents; Salvadoran Youths Ordered Released,* WASH. POST, July 20, 1985, at A8; David G. Savage, *INS Detention of Children Upheld,* L.A. TIMES, Mar. 24, 1993, at A3. Detention facilities are concentrated in rural California and Texas. Additional facilities are found in rural Arizona, Florida, and Louisiana. The conditions in most of the facilities are similar.

their asylum cases. They generally are not provided with educational facilities as required by state law for other minors. They often do not receive the special protection required for minors in other contexts. In some cases they are confined with adults, creating a potential for abuse. Illustrative of problems faced by detained children was a case during the spring of 1989 in which an INS guard was convicted of sexually assaulting detained children.

The problems are growing. INS figures show over 800 children detained in Texas and 1,200 in California during 1990-1991. Olivas, *supra*, at 160. Other estimates have placed the number at more than 5,000. Claudia Weinstein, *The Children San Diego Forgot*, AMERICAN LAWYER, Sept. 1987, at 102. At one San Diego facility almost 10% of the detained aliens (20 of 230) were juveniles. *Flores v. Meese*, 681 F.Supp. 665, 666 (C.D. Cal. 1988). Some INS authorities have disputed these figures, claiming only about 200 children are detained at any one time nationwide. David Holley & Elizabeth Lu, *Judge Orders INS to Free 2 Children; Advocates Say Ruling Could Aid Hundreds of Illegals*, L.A. TIMES, July 20, 1985, at 21.

INS officials also dispute the length of time unaccompanied minors are detained. The Western Regional Commissioner estimated the average length of detention at 28 days. *Id.* Lawyers estimate the length in terms of months, noting cases where detention has lasted almost a year. Weinstein, *supra*, at 102. By statute, however, detention can be almost indefinite.

* * * * *

In developing a strategy to help secure the release of Lopez, consider the following questions:

1. Does U.S. constitutional or statutory law protect Lopez?

    a. Does federal substantive and procedural law permit Lopez to challenge the INS decision not to allow her release into the custody of her adult cousin?

    b. Does federal substantive and procedural law permit Lopez to challenge the conditions of the facility in which she is detained?

2. Why do you think the INS detention policy was changed to allow automatic release only to close family members? Is that a good policy?

    a. Does the policy achieve the INS' stated purpose?

    b. What is the impact of the INS policy and the *Flores* decision on alien children and their families?

    c. Does that impact seem appropriate? Justifiable?

    d. Are there any domestic avenues of relief available to protect Lopez?

    e. How might you convince the INS to issue new administrative regulations governing the detention of alien children?

    f. Might you effectively lobby Congress to pass new legislation to protect Lopez? Who would you expect to support such legislation? What opposition might you expect?

3. Do international standards provide more protection for Lopez?

    a. Does the Civil and Political Covenant forbid the detention of unaccompanied alien minors awaiting deportation hearings? What provision(s) of that Covenant would you cite on her behalf?

b. Might customary international norms be used to protect Lopez?

    1) Are there any customary international norms potentially relevant to this case?

    2) Where do you find those norms?

    3) What provision(s) of the Convention on the Rights of the Child might be relevant? How could you argue those provisions constitute customary international norms?

    4) How most effectively might you argue for their application in federal court? Should those arguments be made even though the U.S. has ratified the Civil and Political Covenant?

    5) Are there tests for determining whether a customary international norm may be invoked by an individual in federal court? Do the potentially relevant norms meet that test?

4. How might the international standards identified in question 3 be used to protect Lopez?

    a. What are the three ways in which international standards may be invoked?

    b. Which would you now consider most effective: advocacy based on (1) treaties, (2) customary law, or (3) the use of international law to interpret relevant federal laws? Why?

    c. If treaties are the supreme law of the land, why didn't the international standards influence the Court in *Flores*? Does the subsequent ratification by the U.S. of the Covenant on Civil and Political Rights suggest *Flores* may not be followed in the future?

    d. What are the legal and practical impediments to U.S. application of the Civil and Political Covenant?

        1) Are there any federal statutes in conflict with the Covenant?

        2) Are the statutes later in time?

        3) Are the relevant provisions of the Covenant self-executing?

        4) What is the impact of the U.S. declaration that the Covenant is not self-executing? Of the reservation limiting the definition of "cruel, inhuman or degrading treatment or punishment" to that definition encompassed in the U.S. Constitution?

    e. What is the impact of a federal statute or regulation on a customary norm concerning the issue? What did *The Paquete Habana* say in dicta about that question? Should we pay attention to that ancient dicta?

    f. How could you argue Lopez should receive the benefit of the most protective laws available?

5. How might the international standards identified in question 4 be used to convince a judge to interpret domestic law to protect Lopez?

    a. Which federal laws—constitutional or statutory—might be construed in light of international norms to protect Lopez?

b.   How likely would judges be to use these international instruments to inform the interpretation of these laws? What arguments would you use to convince judges they ought to use international instruments in this manner?

c.   What obstacles stand in the way of using international human rights law in U.S. courts to deal with human rights violations in the U.S.?

6.   What are the advantages and disadvantages of using U.S. courts, legislatures, and administrative officials, as compared with the use of international procedures:

a.   for preventing harm to the victim?

b.   for getting relief to the victims?

c.   for fact-finding (*e.g.*, with respect to subpoena powers, depositions, and other access to relevant information)?

d.   for publicity about human rights violations?

e.   for access to the procedures?

f.   for helping to build international human rights structures and norms possessing legitimacy?

C.   U.S. LAW

1.   Constitution

Article VI, § 2:

> This Constitution, and the Laws of the United States which shall be made in Pursuance thereof; and all Treaties made, or which shall be made, under the Authority of the United States, shall be the supreme Law of the Land; and the Judges in every State shall be bound thereby, any Thing in the Constitution or Laws of any State to the Contrary notwithstanding.

Amendment V:

> No person shall . . . be deprived of life, liberty, or property, without due process of law. . . .

Amendment VIII:

> Excessive bail shall not be required, nor excessive fines imposed, nor cruel and unusual punishment inflicted.

2.   Federal Statutes and Regulations

8 U.S.C. § 1252 (1952): Apprehension and deportation of aliens

(a)   Arrest and custody; review of determination by court.

(1)   Pending a determination of deportability . . ., [a detained] alien may, upon warrant of the Attorney General, be arrested and taken into custody. Except [for aliens suspected of committing aggravated felonies], any such alien taken into custody may, in the discretion of the Attorney General and pending such final determination of deportability, (A) be continued in custody; or (B) be

released under bond in the amount of not less than $500 with security approved by the Attorney General, containing such conditions as the Attorney General may prescribe; or (C) be released on conditional parole. But such bond or parole, whether heretofore or hereafter authorized, may be revoked at any time by the Attorney General, in his discretion. . . . Any court of competent jurisdiction shall have authority to review or revise any determination of the Attorney General concerning detention, release on bond, or parole pending final decision of deportability upon a conclusive showing in habeas corpus proceedings that the Attorney General is not proceeding with such reasonable dispatch as may be warranted by the particular facts and circumstances in the case of any alien to determine deportability.

8 U.S.C. § 1357 (1952): Powers of immigration officers and employees

(a) Powers without warrant. Any officer or employee of the Service authorized under regulations prescribed by the Attorney General shall have power without warrant . . .

(2) to arrest any alien who in his presence or view is entering or attempting to enter the United States in violation of any law or regulation made in pursuance of law regulating the admission, exclusion, or expulsion of aliens, or to arrest any alien in the United States, if he has reason to believe that the alien so arrested is in the United States in violation of any such law or regulation and is likely to escape before a warrant can be obtained for his arrest, but the alien arrested shall be taken without unnecessary delay for examination before an officer of the Service having authority to examine aliens as to their right to enter or remain in the United States. . . .

8 C.F.R. § 242.24 (1988):

(a) Juveniles. A juvenile is defined as an alien under the age of eighteen (18) years.

(b) Release. Juveniles for whom bond has been posted, for whom parole has been authorized, or who have been ordered released on recognizance, shall be released pursuant to the following guidelines:

(1) Juveniles shall be released, in order of preference, to: (i) a parent; (ii) legal guardian; or (iii) adult relative (brother, sister, aunt, uncle, grandparent) who [is] not presently in INS detention, unless a determination is made that the detention of such juvenile is required to secure his timely appearance before the Service or the immigration court or to ensure the juvenile's safety or that of others. . . .

(3) In cases where the parent or legal guardian is in INS detention or outside the United States, the juvenile may be released to such person as designated by the parent or legal guardian in a sworn affidavit, executed before an immigration officer or consular officer, as capable and willing to care for the juvenile's well-being. Such person must execute an agreement to care for the juvenile and to ensure the juvenile's presence at all future proceedings before the Service or an immigration judge.

(4) In unusual and compelling circumstances and in the discretion of the district director or chief patrol agent, a juvenile may be released to an adult,

other than those identified in paragraph (b)(1) of this section, who executes an agreement to care for the juvenile's well-being and to ensure the juvenile's presence at all future proceedings before the INS or an immigration judge.

(c)   The case of a juvenile for whom detention is determined to be necessary should be referred to the Juvenile Coordinator, whose responsibilities should include, but not be limited to, finding suitable placement of the juvenile in a facility designated for the occupancy of juveniles. . . .

NOTES AND QUESTIONS

1.   Do the laws quoted above—8 U.S.C. § 1252 and § 1357 and 8 C.F.R. § 242.24—permit Lopez to *ever* be released into the custody of her adult cousin? If yes, under what circumstances?

2.   If her cousin is willing to care for her, can he compel the INS to release her?

3.   Judicial Interpretation

There have been many complaints regarding the asserted desirability of detaining unaccompanied alien children, their separation from the family, and the unsatisfactory conditions of detention. This decision by the U.S. Supreme Court is illuminating:

Reno v. Flores, 507 U.S. 292 (1993) (footnotes and several citations omitted; material in brackets added by this book's editors):

JUSTICE SCALIA delivered the opinion of the Court.

Over the past decade, the Immigration and Naturalization Service (INS) has arrested increasing numbers of alien juveniles who are not accompanied by their parents or other related adults. Respondents, a class of alien juveniles so arrested and held in INS custody pending their deportation hearings, contend that the Constitution and immigration laws require them to be released into the custody of "responsible adults."

I

Congress has given the Attorney General broad discretion to determine whether and on what terms an alien arrested on suspicion of being deportable should be released pending the deportation hearing [8 U.S.C. § 1252(a)(1)]. The Board of Immigration Appeals has stated that "an alien generally . . . should not be detained or required to post bond except on a finding that he is a threat to the national security. . .or that he is a poor bail risk." In the case of arrested alien juveniles, however, the INS cannot simply send them off into the night on bond or recognizance. The parties to the present suit agree that the Service must assure itself that someone will care for those minors pending resolution of their deportation proceedings. That is easily done when the juvenile's parents have also been detained and the family can be released together; it becomes complicated when the juveniles are arrested alone, *i.e.* unaccompanied by a parent, guardian, or other related adult. This problem is a serious one, since the INS arrests thousands of alien juveniles each year (more than 8,500 in 1990 alone)—as many as 70% of them unaccompanied. Most of these minors are boys in their mid-teens, but perhaps 15% are girls and the same percentage 14 years of age or younger.

For a number of years the problem was apparently dealt with on a regional and *ad hoc* basis, with some INS offices releasing unaccompanied alien juveniles not only to their parents but also to a range of other adults and organizations. In 1984, responding to the increased flow of unaccompanied juvenile aliens into California, the INS Western Regional Office adopted a policy of limiting the release of detained minors to "a parent or lawful guardian," except in "unusual and extraordinary cases," when the juvenile could be released to "a responsible individual who agrees to provide care and be responsible for the welfare and well being of the child." [The INS later codified a national policy in 8 C.F.R. § 242.24, *supra*, which provides for release to an expanded group of individuals and designates the procedure for placement of the detained juvenile in a proper facility.]

. . . [R]espondents filed an action . . . on behalf of a class . . . consisting of all aliens under the age of 18 who are detained by the INS Western Region because "a parent or legal guardian fails to personally appear to take custody of them." [The suit was continued as a challenge to 8 C.F.R. § 242.24 after that regulation was released.] The complaint raised seven claims, the first two challenging the Western Region release policy (on constitutional, statutory, and international law[3] grounds), and the final five challenging the conditions of the juveniles' detention.

[The District Court approved a consent decree (Juvenile Care Agreement) settling the claims regarding the detention conditions.]

Juveniles placed in these facilities are deemed to be in INS detention. . . . "Legal custody" rather than "detention" more accurately describes the reality of the arrangement, however, since these are not correctional institutions but facilities that meet "state licensing requirements for the provision of shelter care, foster care, group care, and related services to dependent children," and are operated "in an open type of setting without a need for extraordinary security measures." The facilities must provide, in accordance with "applicable child welfare statutes and generally accepted child welfare standards, practices, principles and procedures," an extensive list of services, including physical care and maintenance, individual and group counseling, education, recreation and leisure-time activities, family reunification services, and access to religious services, visitors, and legal assistance. . . .

II

Respondents make three principal attacks upon INS regulation 242.24. First, they assert that alien juveniles suspected of being deportable have a "fundamental" right to "freedom from physical restraint," and it is therefore a denial of "substantive due process" to detain them, since the Service cannot prove that it is pursuing an important governmental interest in a manner narrowly tailored to minimize the restraint on liberty. Secondly, respondents argue that the regulation violates "procedural due process," because it does not require the Service to determine, with regard to each individual detained juvenile who lacks an approved custodian, whether his best interests lie in remaining in INS custody or in release to some other "responsible adult." Finally, respondents contend that even if the INS regulation infringes no constitutional rights, it exceeds the Attorney General's authority under 8 U.S.C. § 1252(a)(1). . . .

---

[3] Ed. note: The Court of Appeals did not rule on international law issues, but based its decision solely on constitutional grounds. The parties did not raise international arguments in their briefs before the Supreme Court, and the Court discussed none.

[The Court noted that the burden of proof on respondents was high: on a facial challenge they must establish there is no set of circumstances under which the regulation would be valid. The court further noted that, although not an issue on appeal, respondents and amici spent much time condemning the conditions of detention. These allegedly severe conditions implied that the retention of custody was an unconstitutional infliction of punishment without trial. The court disposed of these allegations by noting that respondents could enforce the Juvenile Care Agreement in District Court but had not yet done so, and proceeded on the arguably inaccurate assumption that the conditions were in compliance with governing standards.]

III

Respondents' "substantive due process" claim relies upon our line of cases which interprets the Fifth and Fourteenth Amendments' guarantee of "due process of law" to include a substantive component, which forbids the government to infringe certain "fundamental" liberty interests at all, no matter what process is provided, unless the infringement is narrowly tailored to serve a compelling state interest. . . . The "freedom from physical restraint" invoked by respondents is not at issue in this case. Surely not in the sense of shackles, chains, or barred cells, given the Juvenile Care Agreement. Nor even in the sense of a right to come and go at will, since, as we have said elsewhere, "juveniles, unlike adults, are always in some form of custody," and where the custody of the parent or legal guardian fails, the government may (indeed, we have said must) either exercise custody itself or appoint someone else to do so. Nor is the right asserted the right of a child to be released from all other custody into the custody of its parents, legal guardian, or even close relatives: the challenged regulation requires such release when it is sought. Rather, the right at issue is the alleged right of a child who has no available parent, close relative, or legal guardian, and for whom the government is responsible, to be placed in the custody of a willing-and-able private custodian rather than of a government-operated or government-selected child-care institution.

[The Court refused to find the fundamental right it defined, noting that, when the conditions of detention are decent and humane, custody is not equivalent to punishment. The custody is rationally related to legitimate governmental interests in "preserving and promoting the welfare of the child" and therefore passes a rational basis test. The Court similarly refused to find a more limited fundamental right to an individualized hearing on whether private placement would be in the child's best interests. Institutional custody, in itself constitutional, is not made unconstitutional when some other arrangement can be shown to be more desirable. The "best interests of the child" cannot be the sole criterion for determining custody because of the government's conflicting responsibilities, particularly when institutionalized custody is "good enough."]

. . . Minimum standards must be met, and the child's fundamental rights must not be impaired; but the decision to go beyond those requirements—to give one or another of the child's additional interests priority over other concerns that compete for public funds and administrative attention—is a policy judgment rather than a constitutional imperative. . . .

If we harbored any doubts as to the constitutionality of institutional custody over unaccompanied juveniles, they would surely be eliminated as to those juveniles (concededly the overwhelming majority of all involved here) who are aliens. "For reasons long recognized as valid, the responsibility for regulating the relationship between the United States and our alien visitors has been committed to the political branches of the Federal Government." *Mathews v. Diaz*, 426 U.S. 67, 81 . . . (1976). "'Over no conceivable subject is the legislative power of Congress more complete.'" *Fiallo v. Bell*, 430 U.S. 787, 792 . . . (1977) (quoting *Oceanic Steam Navigation Co. v. Stranahan*, 214 U.S. 320, 339 . . . (1909)). Thus, "in the exercise of its broad power over immigration and naturalization, 'Congress regularly makes rules that would be unacceptable if applied to citizens.'" 430 U.S., at 792 . . . (quoting *Mathews v. Diaz*, supra, at 79-80 . . .). Respondents do not dispute that Congress has the authority to detain aliens suspected of entering the country illegally pending their deportation hearings. And in enacting the precursor to 8 U.S.C. § 1252(a), Congress eliminated any presumption of release pending deportation, committing that determination to the discretion of the Attorney General. Of course, the INS regulation must still meet the (unexacting) standard of rationally advancing some legitimate governmental purpose—which it does. . . .

Respondents also argue, in a footnote, that the INS release policy violates the "equal protection guarantee" of the Fifth Amendment because of the disparate treatment evident in (1) releasing alien juveniles with close relatives or legal guardians but detaining those without, and (2) releasing to unrelated adults juveniles detained pending federal delinquency proceedings, but detaining unaccompanied alien juveniles pending deportation proceedings. The tradition of reposing custody in close relatives and legal guardians is in our view sufficient to support the former distinction; and the difference between citizens and aliens is adequate to support the latter.

IV

We turn now from the claim that the INS cannot deprive respondents of their asserted liberty interest *at all*, to the "procedural due process" claim that the Service cannot do so on the basis of the procedures it provides. It is well established that the Fifth Amendment entitles aliens to due process of law in deportation proceedings. *See The Japanese Immigrant Case*, 189 U.S. 86, 100-101 . . . (1903). To determine whether these alien juveniles have received it here, we must first review in some detail the procedures the INS has employed.

[The Court reviewed the deportation process and rejected, for the same reasons it rejected the similar substantive due process argument, respondents' contention that procedural due process requires an individualized assessment to determine whether detention is in the best interest of the child. Procedural due process is also satisfied by giving aliens the right to request a judicial review of any adverse determination by an immigration judge; automatic judicial review of every decision is not required.]

V

Respondents contend that the regulation goes beyond the scope of the Attorney General's discretion to continue custody over arrested aliens under 8 U.S.C. § 1252(a)(1). That contention must be rejected if the regulation has a "reasonable foundation," that is, if it rationally pursues a purpose that it is lawful for the INS to seek. We think that it does.

[The Court deferred to INS discretion and to the stated purpose for the policy—ensuring child welfare. The means chosen to achieve this purpose, adopting a blanket detention policy, are justified because the INS has neither the expertise nor the resources to conduct individualized placement studies. Administrative convenience justifies the choice of means if not the underlying purpose. Parents, close blood-relatives, and legal guardians have traditionally enjoyed preferential status in custody law. Therefore the regulation incorporates reasonable classifications. Finally, the Court rejected respondents' argument that the regulation constituted an abuse of discretion by allowing indefinite detention because § 1252(a)(1) authorizes habeas corpus proceedings if the deportation hearings are not conducted in a timely manner.]

We think the INS policy now in place is a reasonable response to the difficult problems presented when the Service arrests unaccompanied alien juveniles. It may well be that other policies would be even better, but "we are [not] a legislature charged with formulating public policy." On its face, INS regulation 242.24 accords with both the Constitution and the relevant statute.

The judgment of the Court of Appeals [holding the detention policy unconstitutional] is reversed . . ..

JUSTICE O'CONNOR, with whom JUSTICE SOUTER joins, concurring.

[Justice O'Connor stressed that both children and adults have a fundamental right to freedom from bodily restraint and institutional confinement, but argued that the majority opinion was not inconsistent with that interest. She countered the assertion that children are always in some form of custody and its implication that children are, therefore, less entitled to freedom from bodily restraint by noting that institutionalization is "a decisive and unusual event" with potentially tragic consequences. Nonetheless, she found the regulation narrowly tailored to further the government's compelling interest in protecting the welfare of alien children because it only applies when normal forms of custody have failed.]

. . .Because this is a facial challenge, . . . [i]t is proper to presume that the conditions of confinement are no longer "most disturbing," and that the purposes of confinement are no longer the troublesome ones of lack of resources and expertise published in the Federal Register, but rather the plainly legitimate purposes associated with the government's concern for the welfare of the minors. With those presumptions in place, "the terms and conditions of confinement . . . are in fact compatible with [legitimate] purposes," and the Court finds that the INS program conforms with the Due Process Clause. On this understanding, I join the opinion of the Court.

JUSTICE STEVENS, with whom JUSTICE BLACKMUN joins, dissenting.

[Justice Stevens disagreed with the majority's use of administrative convenience to justify the policy of detaining "harmless children, even when the conditions of detention are 'good enough,'" particularly since the INS denied administrative convenience as a motivation. He emphasized that the children posed no risk of flight or threat of harm to themselves or the community, and that they had responsible adults willing and able to care for them. Also, many never will be deported. The fact that juveniles are always in some form of custody is irrelevant because institutional detention is "vastly different" from custody in the form of release to a responsible person. A different liberty interest is implicated, one not affected by the conditions of the detention.]

[He also noted a lack of evidence of either harm to juveniles or undue administrative burdens under prior policy to support the Western Region policy change or § 242.24. Further, at the time the preference for detention over release was adopted confinement conditions were "deplorable." Children were commingled with adults of the opposite sex, detention centers were protected by barbed-wire fences, children were not provided with education, recreation, or visitation and were subject to arbitrary strip searches. Those conditions undermine the conclusion that confinement was in the best interest of children. Evidence also showed that undocumented parents who came to claim their children detained in the Western Region were immediately arrested and deportation proceedings were instituted against them.

Finally, he found telling the lack of theoretical or practical justification for § 242.24 in light of the criticism of Western Region policy.]

[He also concluded that the preference for government detention over release for alien juveniles is contrary to Congress' expressed intent, and that the Due Process Clause requires an individualized determination of suitability for custody in light of diverse circumstances facing children and the significance of the consequences. By defining the constitutionally protected interest narrowly as the right to be released to a responsible adult rather than as the right to be free from confinement, the majority were able to define and reject a novel right rather than uphold one encompassed within precedent. He then concluded the regulation failed strict scrutiny. Though the U.S. has a substantial interest in protecting the welfare of juveniles that come into its custody, the uniform presumption that detention is more appropriate than release to responsible adults is not narrowly focused on serving that interest.]

Ultimately, the Court is simply wrong when it asserts that "freedom from physical restraint" is not at issue in this case. That is precisely what is at issue. The Court's assumption that the detention facilities used by the INS conform to the [Juvenile Care Agreement] has nothing to do with the fact that the juveniles who are not released to relatives or responsible adults are held in detention facilities. They do not have the "freedom from physical restraint" that those who are released do have. That is what this case is all about. That is why the respondent class continues to litigate. These juveniles do not want to be committed to institutions that the INS and the Court believe are "good enough" for aliens simply because they conform to standards that are adequate for the incarceration of juvenile delinquents. They want the same kind of liberty that the Constitution guarantees similarly situated citizens. And as I read our precedents, the omission of any provision for individualized consideration of the best interests of the juvenile in a rule authorizing an indefinite period of detention of presumptively innocent and harmless children denies them precisely that liberty.

I respectfully dissent.

NOTES AND QUESTIONS

1. The majority seem to have foreclosed all constitutional challenge to the detention policy, leaving administrative or legislative action as the remedy. They were, however, operating under an assumption that the conditions of confinement were in compliance with governing standards. Though respondents could enforce those standards in the Western District, through the Juvenile Care Agreement, no such relief is available to detainees in other regions. Does that suggest a different result in other regions? Or may detainees there still seek judicial action to improve the conditions?

2. As suggested in the dissent the conditions of confinement—even in the Western District—are often not, as the majority presumed, "good enough." The majority, however, rejected arguments that the constitutionality of confinement depends on such conditions.

Does due process in fact guarantee minimal standards for conditions of confinement? For instance, *Haitian Centers Council, Inc. v. Sale*, 823 F.Supp. 1028, 1043 (E.D.N.Y. 1993), held that Haitian refugees who had tested positive for HIV and were detained on Guantanamo Bay Naval Base in Cuba were entitled to adequate medical care and safe conditions while in U.S. government custody, even before entering the U.S. *See also Youngberg v. Romeo*, 457 U.S. 307, 315-16 (1983) (holding that a mentally retarded man involuntarily committed to a hospital had a liberty interest to "reasonably safe conditions of confinement" that must be balanced against relevant State interests); *Bell v. Wolfish*, 421 U.S. 520, 535 (1979) (holding that conditions of confinement for pretrial detainees may be so severe as to rise to the level of punishment).

3.   Several critics agree with the dissent in *Flores* that the true purpose of the detention policy is not to protect children's welfare. They argue that detention is intended to deter other aliens from illegal entry and that the INS uses juveniles to "bait" illegal aliens into revealing their whereabouts by restricting the class of family members who may claim the detained children. Olivas, *supra* note at 160, *citing* LAWYERS COMMITTEE FOR HUMAN RIGHTS, THE DETENTION OF ASYLUM SEEKERS IN THE UNITED STATES: A CRUEL AND QUESTIONABLE POLICY 20 (1989). Is using children to promote deterrence or as "bait" justifiable? *See infra* Part *D*, for international arguments on that question.

4.   Underlying the Scalia opinion in *Flores* is a strong tradition of judicial deference to Congress in immigration matters. The deference has a long history. *See, e.g.*, T. Alexander Aleinikoff, *Federal Regulation of Aliens and the Constitution*, 83 AM. J. INT'L L. 862 (1989); Louis Henkin, *The Constitution and United States Sovereignty: A Century of Chinese Exclusion and Its Progeny*, 100 HARV. L. REV. 853 (1987); Peter H. Schuck, *The Transformation of Immigration Law*, 84 COLUM. L. REV. 1, 14-18 (1984); *see also United States v. Valenzuela-Bernal*, 458 U.S. 858, 876 n.1 (1982); *United States v. Restrepo*, 999 F.2d 640, 644 (2nd Cir. 1993); *Price v. INS*, 962 F.2d 836, 841 n.4 (9th Cir. 1992).

   The Court also has rejected requests for a more-searching inquiry when discretionary acts of administrators involve other constitutional rights of aliens. *Fiallo v. Bell*, 430 U.S. 787, 794-95 (1977) (family relations); *Kleindienst v. Mandel*, 408 U.S. 753 (1972) (First Amendment). For a discussion of judicial deference in the area of immigration law see STEPHEN LEGOMSKY, IMMIGRATION AND THE JUDICIARY: LAW AND POLITICS IN BRITAIN AND AMERICA (1987).

5.   For more information on alien detention see Angela M. Elsperger, *Florida's Battle With the Federal Government Over Immigration Policy Holds Children Hostage: They Are Not Our Children?*, 13 LAW AND INEQUALITY 141 (1994); Margaret H. Taylor, *Detained Aliens Challenging Conditions of Confinement and the Porous Border of the Plenary Power Doctrine*, 22 Hastings Const L.Q. 1087 (1995); Pamela Theodoredis, Comment, *Detention of Alien Juveniles: Reno v. Flores*, 12 N.Y.L. SCH. J. HUM. RTS. 393 (1995).

D.   INTERNATIONAL STANDARDS

1.   U.S.-Ratified Treaties

The U.S. has ratified (or acceded to) many treaties that create binding rules. The most important human rights treaties to which the U.S. is a party include the U.N. Charter, the Covenant on Civil and Political Rights, the Protocol Relating to the Status of Refugees, and the Genocide and Slavery Conventions. The most pertinent here are the Charter and the Covenant. Complete texts are found in the accompanying handbook *Selected International Human Rights Instruments*, and the especially relevant clauses are these:

International Covenant on Civil and Political Rights, G.A. res. 2200A, (XXI), December 16, 1966, 21 U.N. GAOR Supp. (No. 16) at 52, U.N. Doc. A/6316 (1966), 999 U.N.T.S. 171, *entered into force* March 23, 1976, *entered into force in the U.S.* September 8, 1992: . . .

Article 2(1)

Each State Party to the present Covenant undertakes to respect and to ensure to all individuals within its territory and subject to its jurisdiction the rights recognized in the present Covenant, without distinction of any kind, such as race, colour, sex, language, religion, political or other opinion, national or social origin, property, birth or other status. . . .

Article 9

1.   Everyone has the right to liberty and security of person. No one shall be subjected to arbitrary arrest or detention. No one shall be deprived of his liberty except on such grounds and in accordance with such procedure as are established by law. . . .

3.   . . . It shall not be the general rule that persons awaiting [criminal] trial shall be detained in custody, but release may be subject to guarantees. . . .

[The Human Rights Committee has issued an authoritative interpretation of this provision in its General Comment on Article 9, HRI/GEN/1 (1992), at 7 (16th Session, 1982): "Article 9 . . . is applicable to all deprivations of liberty, [including] immigration control. . . ."]

Article 10

1.   All persons deprived of their liberty shall be treated with humanity and with respect for the inherent dignity of the human person. . . .

[General Comment on Article 10, HRI/GEN/1 (1992), at p. 32 reads in part:

2.   Article 10, paragraph 1 . . . applies to any one deprived of liberty under the laws and authority of the State who is held in . . . detention camps. . . .

4.   Treating all persons deprived of their liberty with humanity and with respect for their dignity is a fundamental and universally applicable rule. Consequently, the application of this rule, as a minimum, cannot be dependent on the material resources available in the State party. This rule must be applied without distinction of any kind, such as race, colour, sex, language, religion, political or other opinion, national or social origin, property, birth or other status.]

Article 17

1.   No one shall be subjected to arbitrary or unlawful interference with his privacy, family, home or correspondence, nor to unlawful attacks on his honour and reputation. . . .

Article 23(1)

The family is the natural and fundamental group unit of society and is entitled to protection by society and the State.

[General Comment on Article 23, Adopted by the Human Rights Committee, HRI/GEN/1 (1992), at p. 28-29 (39th session, 1990): "The right to found a family implies, in principle, the possibility to . . . live together. . . . [T]he possibility to live together implies the adoption of appropriate measures . . . to ensure the unity or reunification of families, particularly when their members are separated for political, economic or similar reasons."

Article 24(1)

Every child shall have, without discrimination as to race, colour, sex, language, religion, national or social origin, property or birth, the right to such measures of protection as are required by his status as a minor, on the part of his family, society and the State.

[General Comment on Article 24, Adopted by the Human Rights Committee, HRI/GEN/1 (1992), at p. 22 (Thirty-fifth session, 1989): "[T]he rights provided in article 24 are not the only ones that the Covenant recognizes for children and . . ., as individuals, children benefit from all of the civil rights enunciated in the Covenant."]

Article 26

All persons are equal before the law and are entitled without any discrimination to the equal protection of the law. In this respect, the law shall prohibit any discrimination and guarantee to all persons equal and effective protection against discrimination on any ground such as race, colour, sex, language, religion, political or other opinion, national or social origin, property, birth or other status.

*   *   *   *   *

In its General Comment applicable to the whole Covenant, General Comment, Adopted by the Human Rights Committee, HRI/GEN/1 (1992), at p. 18 (27th session, 1986), the Committee opined:

2.   . . . [T]he general rule is that each one of the rights of the Covenant must be guaranteed without discrimination between citizens and aliens. . . .

5.   The Covenant does not recognize the right of aliens to enter or reside in the territory of a State party. It is in principle a matter for the State to decide who it will admit to its territory. However, in certain circumstances an alien may enjoy the protection of the Covenant even in relation to entry or residence, for example, when considerations of non-discrimination, prohibition of inhuman treatment and respect for family life arise.

NOTES AND QUESTIONS

1.   If the Supreme Court had considered clauses of the Covenant in *Reno v. Flores*, might the result have been different? Which clauses would you have used to convince the Court that illegal aliens should be permitted to live with their families?

2.   The Executive Committee of the U.N. High Commissioner for Refugees concluded that in light of the hardship it involves, detention of aliens seeking refuge or asylum should be used only if necessary, and then only for a limited period of time. The Executive Committee enumerated the situations in which temporary detention is permissible—to verify identity, to investigate a claim to refugee or asylum status, to review the case of an alien whose travel documents are fraudulent or missing, and to protect national security or public order. Detention of Refugees and Asylum-Seekers, UNHCR Ex. Comm. Conclusion 44, 37th Sess., *reprinted in Conclusions on the International Protection of Refugees adopted by the Executive Committee of the UNHCR Programme* 96 (1980). Although the Executive Committee's conclusion governs only a subset of the alien population, does it nonetheless support an argument that international law, in general, disfavors the detention of aliens not accused of crime?

3.   As of February 1996, 132 governments had ratified or acceded to the Covenant on Civil and Political Rights, including the United States. The United States ratified the Covenant on June 8, 1992; the treaty entered into force for the United States on September 8, 1992. *Article 7* of the Covenant, which declares "[n]o one shall be subjected to torture or to

cruel, inhuman or degrading treatment or punishment," would in most countries be pertinent to protests against the detention of unaccompanied minor aliens. In fact, *Article 4* makes this provision non-derogable, even in times of public emergency. General Comment on Article 7, Adopted by the Human Rights Committee, HRI/GEN/1 (1992), at 6 (Sixteenth session, 1982). In ratifying the Covenant, however, the U.S. attached five reservations, five under-standings, and four declarations to its ratification. The full text of the limitations is found in *Selected International Human Rights Instruments* at *264*. Those limitations most relevant to this chapter, including a significant limitation on Article 7, are reproduced below:

102 Cong. Rec. S4781-4784 (daily ed., April 2, 1992):

I.   The Senate's advice and consent is subject to the following reservations: . . .

(3)   That the United States considers itself bound by Article 7 to the extent that "cruel, inhuman or degrading treatment or punishment" means the cruel and unusual treatment or punishment prohibited by the Fifth, Eighth and/or Fourteenth Amendments to the Constitution of the United States. . . .

III.   The Senate's advice and consent is subject to the following declarations:

(1)   That the United States declares that the provisions of Articles 1 through 27 of the Covenant are not self-executing. . . .

*   *   *   *   *

To what extent do the above reservations limit the application of the Covenant to alien juvenile detention cases?

4.   Some commentators have criticized the U.S. package of limitations, calling it unnecessary and excessive. *See* Lawyers Committee for Human Rights, *Statements on U.S. Ratification of the CCPR*, 14 HUM. RTS. L.J. 125, (1993). For more on reactions to the U.S. limitations, see chapter 2, *supra*.

The Lawyers Committee responded to the reservations by drafting an International Human Rights Conformity Act. *See* chapter 3, *supra*. The Act would prohibit the execution of juvenile offenders; adopt international standards of cruel, inhuman or degrading treatment and punishment; and require segregation of juvenile and adult offenders, as well as the convicted and the accused.

5.   The Human Rights Committee noted several negative aspects of U.S. behavior in a recent comment on the implementation of the Covenant. The behavior included expansions of the death penalty, ill-treatment by police, detention of aliens, overcrowding of prisons, abuses to women in prisons, research on minors or mentally-ill patients, and lack of respect for private life by criminalizing homosexual behavior between consenting male adults. The Human Rights Committee, *Consideration of Reports Submitted by States Parties Under Article 40: Comments of the Human Rights Committee*, U.N. Doc. CCPR/C/79/Add.50 (1995).

6.   The U.S. reservation limiting "cruel, inhuman or degrading treatment or punishment" to the cruel and unusual treatment or punishment prohibited by the Eighth Amendment has, as indicated above, drawn criticism from those commentators who think the U.S. should adopt a universal standard. The application of an international standard may have yielded a different result in cases such as *Ingraham v. Wright*, 430 U.S. 651 (1977). In *Ingraham*, the Supreme Court held the Eighth Amendment was inapplicable to corporal punishment used to discipline junior high school students in Florida public schools. *Id.* at 670-71. In the Court's reasoning, "[t]he openness of the public school and its supervision by the community afford significant safeguards against the kind of abuses from which the Eighth Amendment protects the prisoner." *Id.* at 670. *Ingraham* thus implies the Eighth Amendment's protections are limited to prisoners and cannot be applied to minors detained pending deportation hear-ings, although the reasoning for this conclusion in *Ingraham* is not persuasive in the latter case. *Cf. Cramer v. Tyars*, 588 P.2d 793, 805 (Cal. 1979) (Newman, J., dissenting) (requiring a mentally retarded man to admit and act out alleged assaultive behavior in civil commitment

proceedings was cruel and degrading in violation of the California Constitution, citing the Universal Declaration of Human Rights).

7.   While reading limitations the U.S. placed on ratification of the Covenant on Civil and Political Rights, bear in mind the Vienna Convention on the Law of Treaties, discussed *infra* Part *F* at 580, which prohibits parties from defeating "the object and purpose of a treaty" when formulating reservations. Do any of the U.S. limitations on the Covenant's mandates violate the Vienna Convention?

8.   The Human Rights Committee, ruling on claims brought under the Optional Protocol to the International Covenant on Civil and Political Rights, has found violations of the Covenant when persons accused of criminal conduct have been held in custody, prior to trial, for periods in excess of nine months. Communication No. R.1/6 (Sequeira v. Uruguay), U.N. GAOR, Hum. Rts. Comm., 35th Sess., Supp. No. 40, at 127, U.N. Doc. A/35/40 (1980), *reprinted in* HUMAN RIGHTS COMMITTEE, SELECTED DECISIONS UNDER THE OPTIONAL PROTOCOL (SECOND TO SIXTEENTH SESSIONS), vol. 1 at 52, U.N. Doc. CCPR/C/OP/1, (1985) [hereinafter SELECTED DECISIONS] (holding that a detention in excess of nine months violated Article 14 of the Covenant, which enumerates fair procedures for criminal trials). In some instances, pre-trial detentions of as little as four months have been held to violate an accused's right under Article 9(3) of the Covenant to be brought before a judge within a reasonable time. Communication No. R.8/33 (Carballal v. Uruguay), U.N. GAOR, Hum. Rts. Comm, 36th Sess., Supp. No. 40, at 125, U.N. Doc. A/35/40 (1981), *reprinted in* SELECTED DECISIONS, *supra*, vol. 1 at 63. Should a *minor* held for *no* criminal conduct be entitled to at least the same rights as an accused?

---

2.   Treaties Which the U.S. Has Not Ratified

There are numerous U.N. treaties that the U.S. has not ratified. They thus are not binding on the U.S. as treaties. They may, however, bind the U.S. to the extent their clauses constitute customary international norms, discussed *infra* Part *G* at *599* and *supra* chapter 12.

In 1989 the General Assembly adopted the Convention on the Rights of the Child and opened it for ratification. 166, U.N. Doc. A/RES/44/49, 28 I.L.M. 1448 (1989), *entered into force* Sept. 2, 1990. The full text of the convention is found in the *Selected International Human Rights Instruments* at *80*. As of February 1996, 187 governments had ratified. The United States signed on February 16, 1995, but has not yet ratified. *See infra* Part *F* at 585 for a discussion of U.S. treaties which have been signed but not ratified.

Article 3

1.   In all actions concerning children. . .the best interests of the child shall be a primary consideration. . . .

3.   States Parties shall ensure that the institutions, services and facilities responsible for the care or protection of children shall conform with the standards established by competent authorities. . . .

Article 16

1.   No child shall be subjected to arbitrary or unlawful interference with his or her privacy, family, home or correspondence . . . .

Article 19

1.   States Parties shall take all appropriate legislative, administrative, social and educational measures to protect the child from all forms of physical or mental

violence, injury or abuse, neglect or negligent treatment, maltreatment or exploitation, including sexual abuse, while in the care of parent(s), legal guardian(s) or any other person who has the care of the child.

Article 20

1.   A child temporarily or permanently deprived of his or her family environment, or in whose best interests cannot be allowed to remain in that environment, shall be entitled to special protection and assistance provided by the State.

Article 22

1.   States Parties shall take appropriate measures to ensure that a child who is seeking refugee status or who is considered a refugee in accordance with applicable international or domestic law and procedures shall, whether unaccompanied or accompanied by his or her parents or by any other person, receive appropriate protection and humanitarian assistance in the enjoyment of applicable rights set forth in the present Convention and in other international human rights or humanitarian instruments to which the said States are Parties.

2.   For this purpose, States Parties shall provide, as they consider appropriate, co-operation in any efforts by the United Nations and other competent intergovernmental organizations or non-governmental organizations co-operating with the United Nations to protect and assist such a child and to trace the parents or other members of the family of any refugee child in order to obtain information necessary for reunification with his or her family. In cases where no parents or other members of the family can be found, the child shall be accorded the same protection as any other child permanently or temporarily deprived of his or her family environment for any reason, as set forth in the present Convention.

Article 28

1.   States Parties recognize the right of the child to education, and with a view to achieving this right progressively and on the basis of equal opportunity, they shall, in particular:

(a)   Make primary education compulsory and available free to all. . . .

Article 37

States Parties shall ensure that:

(a)   No child shall be subjected to torture or other cruel, inhuman or degrading treatment or punishment. . . .

(b)   Every child deprived of liberty shall be treated with humanity and respect for the inherent dignity of the human person, and in a manner which takes into account the needs of persons of his or her age. . . . [D]etention or imprisonment of a child shall be used only as a measure of last resort and for the shortest appropriate period of time.

Article 41

Nothing in the present Convention shall affect any provisions which are more conducive to the realization of the rights of the child and which may be contained in:

(a)   The law of a State Party; or

(b)   International law in force for that state.

NOTES AND QUESTIONS

1.   In its concluding observations of June 1995, the Committee on the Rights of the Child criticized a Canadian practice, which is similar to the United States' practice of alien child detention. The Committee stated:

13.   The Committee recognizes the efforts made by Canada for many years in accepting a large number of refugees and immigrants. Nevertheless, the Committee regrets that the principles of non-discrimination, of the best interests of the child and of the respect for the views of the child have not always been given adequate weight by administrative bodies dealing with the situation of refugees or immigrants children. It is particularly worried by the resort by immigration officials to measures of deprivation of liberty of children for security or other related purposes and by the insufficient measures aimed at family reunification with a view to ensure that it is dealt in a positive, humane and expeditious manner. . . .

24.   The Committee recommends that the State party pay particular attention to the. . .best interests of the child and respect for his or her views, in all matters relating to the protection of refugees and immigrant children, including in deportation proceedings. . . . Deprivation of liberty of children, particularly unaccompanied children, for security or other purposes should only be used as a measure of last resort in accordance with article 37(b) of the Convention.

Committee on the Rights of the Child, *Concluding Observations of the Committee on the Rights of the Child: Canada*, at 4-5, 8, U.N. Doc. CRC/C/15/Add.37 (1995).

2.   Article 37 of the treaty provides that detention of children should be used only as a last resort. Article 9(3) of the Covenant on Civil and Political Rights suggests that adults not be detained, as a general rule. By creating an even more exacting standard for children the Convention on the Rights of the Child seeks to minimize the negative consequences that result from separating families and loss of liberty during early stages of development. GERALDINE VAN BUEREN, THE INTERNATIONAL LAW ON THE RIGHTS OF THE CHILD 210 (1995).

3.   Article 41 of the children's treaty suggests a policy of applying the most protective law available, regardless of its source. A similar view is utilized in relating the protections of federal and state law in the U.S. *See, e.g., Pruneyard Shopping Center v. Robins*, 447 U.S. 74, 81 (1980); Harvard Law Review Ass'n, *State Constitutional Rights in the Federal System*, 95 HARV. L. REV. 1331 (1982). The Covenant on Civil and Political Rights, excerpted *supra* at *21*, does not contain a similar provision. Should the principle be applied to the Covenant and all later human rights treaties? How would you argue for such application?

4.   International standards also prohibit the taking of hostages in times of armed conflict. For example, Common Article 3(1)(b) of the Geneva Conventions of 1949, Conventions I-IV, *adopted* Aug. 12, 1949, 6 U.S.T. 3114, 3217, 3316, 3516; T.I.A.S. No. 3362-3365; 75 U.N.T.S. 31, 85, 135, 287, *entered into force* Oct. 21, 1950, provides the taking of hostages "[is] and shall remain prohibited at any time and in any place whatsoever. . . ." Does this suggest any additional arguments to protest the detention of alien children?

E.   APPROACHES TO USING INTERNATIONAL HUMAN RIGHTS LAW

In seeking to apply "better" international standards in U.S. forums, there are several ways in which international law is sometimes incorporated into national law. A few commentators have characterized U.S. law as evidencing elements of both "dualist" and "monist" approaches. *See Committee of U.S. Citizens Living in Nicaragua v. Reagan*, 859 F.2d 927, 937 (D.C. Cir. 1988), excerpted in part *J, infra* at 85; *cf. Introductory Note*, 1 RESTATEMENT (THIRD) OF THE FOREIGN RELATIONS LAW OF THE UNITED STATES 40-42 (1987); IAN BROWNLIE, PRINCIPLES OF PUBLIC INTERNATIONAL LAW 32-35 (4th ed. 1990).

Countries that appear to adopt the monist view, such as Austria and Belgium, treat international law as an integral part of national law with status equal to or sometimes even supreme over national law. A few countries, such as the Netherlands, view international law as supreme even over its national constitution. In contrast, dualist countries such as Britain more generally do not consider treaties to be judicially enforceable unless there is implementing legislation. BROWNLIE, *supra*, at 48; ANDREW Z. DRZEMCZEWSKI, THE EUROPEAN CONVENTION IN DOMESTIC LAW 177-87 (1983). International customary norms are usually judicially enforceable to the extent there is no conflicting legislative act or judicial decision. BROWNLIE, *supra*, at 43-47. Even the countries mentioned above as "monist" or "dualist", however, are not always consistent. In addition, many countries have not fit international law into this simplistic dichotomy. There is tremendous diversity among countries as to how international law gets incorporated into national law.

A country's adoption of a particular approach may be due partially to that country's attitude toward nationalism and international cooperation and partially to historical background. Under a monist system, international standards supplant domestic ones and partially delegate the country's power to define its domestic laws. In contrast, under a dualist approach, countries retain the power to define national law and choose which elements of international law to incorporate. *But see* Covenant on Civil and Political Rights, Article 2 (requiring that states provide an effective remedy for violations of the Covenant). Historically there has been a tendency for civil law countries to adopt a monist approach and for common law countries to adopt a dualist approach. The U.S. system, described in detail below, is essentially a compromise between the competing theories.

Federal and state courts, as well as administrative agencies in the U.S., have applied international law pursuant to three theories. First, if the right sought to be advanced is confirmed by a self-executing treaty clause, courts and agencies may apply the clause directly. Second, if the right is protected by a customary international norm, adjudicators may enforce it. Third, courts and agencies may find clauses of international instruments, whether or not they have attained the status of customary law, persuasive in construing open-ended provisions of national law.

"Direct incorporation" of international law pursuant to the first two of those theories results in law that binds courts. For that reason direct incorporation may appear more powerful than the third theory—"indirect incorporation"—which leaves application of international law to the discretion of judges. But various rules of interpretation and application create obstacles to direct incorporation. Moreover, direct incorporation—a bolder step—gives rise to resistance among judges who seem reluctant to be compelled to apply international law. Also, litigators in state courts may have a special interest in urging indirect incorporation of international law into state law in order to develop independent state grounds and thus avoid creation of federal issues. *See* Paul L. Hoffman, *The Application of International Human Rights in State Courts: A View from California*, 18 INT'L LAWYER 61, 63 (1984). Therefore, in most cases, lawyers are better advised to pursue indirect incorporation.

Efforts to persuade courts and agencies to apply international law pursuant to any of the three theories are assisted by incorporation of, or at least reference to, international standards in federal and state statutes and regulations. For that reason, activists committed to advancing internationally recognized rights are well-advised to consider legislative as well as judicial and administrative strategies.

In the following comments Judge Linde of the Oregon Supreme Court offers advice to lawyers on how most effectively to use international human rights law in federal and state courts, concluding with a reminder to work with the legislative and executive branches as well.[4]

Hans A. Linde, *Comments*, 18 INT'L LAWYER 77 (1984) (footnotes omitted):

I am here today not because I am an expert in international human rights law, but because I am a judge who has written an opinion which refers to that source of law. . . . You can take what I say as illustrative of what you may face in actually talking to a domestic court about international human rights law. . . .

. . . [I]t is largely taken as an article of faith that the United States provides the best protection for human rights in the world. If there are any rights recognized in international law that are not recognized in U.S. law, people may assume that there is a good reason for that nonrecognition. On the other hand, whether or not our protection of human rights is the best, there is a strong urge to agree that it *should* be the best. These ingrained perspectives give you both an opportunity and a challenge.

You may as well assume, simply as a matter of probability, that these views also are likely to prevail among the judges you will face. If we judges have not yet decided to recognize a certain right under one of the numerous, elastic clauses that are available to courts in this country, we probably believe that there is a good reason why we haven't. A lawyer who comes to tell us that we should follow some principle because it is part of an evolving body of international human rights law has a lot of explaining to do. But we also take pride in American law as being in the lead on individual human rights. These attitudes, I think, are important in understanding what role international human rights materials can play in domestic courts.

It is potentially a powerful argument to say to a court that a right which is guaranteed by an American constitutional provision, state or federal, surely does not fall short of a standard adopted by other civilized nations.

It is a much more difficult, and riskier, argument to tell a court that it must displace some law of a state, or of the United States, with an external international standard.

A lawyer considering the use of international human rights law in a national court, state or federal, must consider carefully whether he or she means to claim the international document as a source of standards for the proper application of the nation's own law, or as a source of legally binding obligations. A lawyer must tell a court clearly whether he or she is asserting a claim under international law, or presenting an international norm in support of a desired interpretation of our domestic law.

To point to the international standard as a goal or an achievement to be matched

---

[4] Judge Linde authored the majority opinion in *Sterling v. Cupp*, 290 Or. 611, 625 P.2d 123 (1981) (construing a state constitutional provision prohibiting "unnecessarily rigorous treatment" of inmates in light of the International Bill of Human Rights and other international instruments).

may prove very successful. To point to it as an external law to be obeyed may backfire. It may backfire because, unless the legally binding nature of the international source is clear and strong, opposing counsel and the court may give more time and attention to refuting the claim that the international source has binding force than to looking at the substance of the human rights in question.

The use of human rights norms as customary international law. . .is undeniably appealing. Here we have documents full of more or less eloquent and powerful language, adopted in many cases by unanimous vote in the United Nations, the Organization of American States, or the European Commission on Human Rights. Eminent authorities, including Frank Newman, Louis Sohn, Louis Henkin, and Anthony D'Amato, have devoted a great deal of very able effort to showing (1) that the "pledge" made by U.N. members under article 56 of the charter to take separate as well as joint action in cooperation with the organization to promote human rights created an obligation binding on the United States, and (2) that the aggregate international bill of human rights offers an authoritative, or at least persuasive, interpretation of the article 56 obligation.

I have little problem with those separate conclusions. Assuming they are correct, nevertheless, they are insufficient to establish the direct applicability of international documents in domestic courts. Incantation of the classic formula that the law of nations is part of the law of the United States, . . . by itself is not enough to establish that even the most widely accepted norms of human rights law displace American law in American courts.

The U.N. Charter, of course, is a treaty and part of the "supreme law of the land." But the Universal Declaration on Human Rights was deliberately drafted not to be a treaty. Other human rights documents that were drafted to be treaties or covenants have not been ratified by the United States. These have been deliberate governmental decisions not to undertake certain legal obligations, made with full attention to the choices among instruments that are designed to create one or the other legal effect.

The problem in establishing that a provision of an international document binds our courts as domestic law is that you must show a decision on the part of our government to be so bound. And you cannot show such an intention regarding any instrument other than treaties or similar formal agreements. Other declarations and draft conventions are entered into simply by presidential instruction to ambassadors. They reflect no more than a presidential decision that a certain stance in one of the international forums, or a particular speech, or a vote for a specific declaration advances the foreign policy interests of the United States. Presidents generally do not mean to make domestic law by these means. Ordinarily they take great care to reassure everyone, including the Congress, that they are not making any law binding on this country by voting for or even signing international human rights documents. Even when a President has signed a draft convention that is intended to be a proposed treaty, he or his successor often has decided not to submit the convention for the advice and consent of the Senate, or perhaps to submit it with the explicit reservation that the ratified treaty would have no domestic effect.

For instance, Dean Rusk, who worked with Eleanor Roosevelt in her efforts to have the Universal Declaration of Human Rights unanimously adopted, wrote in a recent article that it was perfectly well understood at the time that the declaration would have no legal consequences within the United States. . . .

Human rights enthusiasts understandably welcome any theory that promises to promote human rights without too much scrutiny of its implications. But the trouble with theory is that it always extends beyond the immediate case. We have learned to be cautious about unilateral executive power to act in domestic affairs, say, to settle a labor dispute by seizing the steel industry. Why should the executive have more domestic power by agreeing with other governments, say, to assure equal employment rights in the steel industry? If the president can make human rights law for the United States by having an ambassador make a speech, negotiate a declaration, or cast a vote in the General Assembly, can he make other kinds of American law by the same means? Could he, for instance, act on his own to override the property law of the states and transfer property from one claimant to another?

. . . I have no doubt that the United States could commit itself to expend money by ratification of a treaty. But this is far from empowering a court to mandate a state to spend money in order to help the United States achieve some general treaty goal, even at the wish of the national executive. . . .

In short, if you are to succeed with your argument that a provision of human rights law is law in a domestic court, you must be able to show that the national lawmakers, by treaty or otherwise, intended this effect. This, at least, is the kind of skeptical reaction that a lawyer is likely to meet if he or she tries to convince a court to apply purely declaratory international human rights documents as legally binding on the court. But often there is no need to take on that burden.

If instead, you argue that a court should look to international instruments to assist it in interpreting a domestic statute or constitution, then you are asking the court to do what it is empowered to do and using international law in the process. Moreover, an advocate wishing to invoke international human rights norms reasonably could argue that an applicable domestic law already contains the protections that the claimant contends, but that, if the court were not to accept this view, then the court might well find itself running afoul of national policy as expressed by the United States government through its participation in international human rights activities and declarations.

. . . So if the court is persuaded of the merits of a particular human rights claim, the court almost certainly can recognize that claim under a clause of a state constitution or of the federal constitution without venturing onto the thin ice of making doubtful precedents about the domestic effect of executive declarations in international forums.

I venture a guess that arguments invoking international human rights standards would have the greatest chance of success in matters where the claim invokes an issue of international interest, or where other countries and international agencies have had greater experience than has the United States. Examples may include linguistic, religious and nationality groups, and the treatment of detained persons.

In conclusion, I want to leave you with a theme that for twenty years has been a favorite of Frank Newman's and mine and that Paul Hoffman also mentioned, namely, that it is a grave mistake to think that courts are the only forums in which human rights law is made or developed. The harder, less immediately rewarding, but more important pursuit of international human rights, as of other policies, occurs not in the courts, but in persuading those responsible for policy-making, in the Congress, the State Department, and the White House that Americans care about human rights abroad as well as at home. . . .

NOTES AND QUESTIONS

For discussion of theories of incorporation of international law in U.S. law, see:

Richard B. Bilder, *Integrating International Human Rights Law into Domestic Law—U.S. Experience*, 4 Hous. J. Int'l L. 1 (1981);

Lea Brilmayer, *International Human Rights Law in American Courts: A Modest Proposal*, 100 Yale L.J. 2277 (1991);

Kathryn Burke et al., *Application of International Human Rights Law in State and Federal Courts*, 18 Tex. Int'l L.J. 291 (1983);

Gordon A. Christenson, *The Uses of Human Rights Norms to Inform Constitutional Interpretation*, 4 Hous. J. Int'l L. 39 (1981);

Lori Fisler Damrosch, *International Human Rights Law in Soviet and American Courts*, 100 Yale L.J. 2315 (1991);

Joan F. Hartman, *"Unusual" Punishment: The Domestic Effects of International Norms Restricting the Application of the Death Penalty*, 52 U. Cin. L. Rev. 655 (1983);

Arthur C. Helton, *The Mandate of U.S. Courts to Protect Aliens and Refugees Under International Human Rights Law*, 100 Yale L.J. 2335 (1991);

Paul L. Hoffman & Nadine Strossen, *Enforcing International Human Rights Law in the United States, in* Human Rights: An Agenda for the Next Century 477 (Louis Henkin & John L. Hargrove eds., 1994);

Richard B. Lillich, *Invoking International Human Rights Law in Domestic Courts*, 54 U. Cin. L. Rev. 367 (1985);

Richard B. Lillich, *The United States Constitution and International Human Rights Law*, 3 Harv. Hum. Rts. J. 53 (1990);

Harold G. Maier, *The Authoritative Sources of Customary International Law in the United States*, 10 Mich. J. Int'l L. 450 (1989);

Covey T. Oliver, *Problems of Cognition and Interpretation in Applying Norms of Customary International Law of Human Rights in United States Courts*, 4 Hous. J. Int'l L. 59 (1981);

Kenneth C. Randall, Federal Courts and the International Human Rights Paradigm (1990);

Eric G. Reeves, Note, *United States v. Javino: Reconsidering the Relationship of Customary International Law to Domestic Law*, 50 Wash. & Lee L. Rev. 877 (1993);

Jordan J. Paust, *Litigating Human Rights: A Commentary on the Comments*, 4 Hous. J. Int'l L. 81 (1981);

Steven M. Schneebaum, *International Law as a Guarantor of Judicially-Enforceable Rights: A Reply to Professor Oliver*, 4 Hous. J. Int'l L. 65 (1981);

Barbara Stark, *Economic Rights in the United States and International Human Rights Law; Toward an "Entirely New Strategy,"* 44 Hastings L.J. 79 (1992);

Ralph G. Steinhardt, *The Role of International Law as a Canon of Domestic Statutory Construction*, 43 Vand. L. Rev. 1103 (1990);

Connie de la Vega, *Civil Rights During the 90's—New Treaty Law Could Help Immensely* (1996) (manuscript, on file with the author);

Lawrence Wood, Alone Among its Peers: The United States Refusal to Join the International Movement to Abolish Capital Punishment (1991);

World Justice?: U.S. Courts and International Human Rights (Mark Gibney ed., 1991).

For a comparative perspective, see Anne F. Bayefsky, International Human Rights Law: Use

IN CANADIAN CHARTER OF RIGHTS AND FREEDOMS LITIGATION (1992) (discussing the enforcement of international law in Canadian courts).

F. TREATIES

Article 38(1) of the Statute of the International Court of Justice (which, because of the U.N. Charter's Article 92, is "an integral part of the present Charter") specifies the sources of international law as (a) treaties, (b) "international custom, as evidence of a general practice accepted as law," (c) "general principles of law recognized by civilized nations," and (d) "judicial decisions and the teachings of the most highly qualified publicists."

Most treaties to which the U.S. is party are bilateral or involve small numbers of states. They generally are interpreted pursuant to rules analogous to canons for interpreting contracts, and the parties' intent is deemed paramount.

In contrast, the human rights treaties are multilateral, drafted not by the parties but by governments acting under the auspices of an intergovernmental organization (e.g., the U.N., O.A.S., Council of Europe, and Organization of African Unity) or a nongovernmental organization (e.g., the International Committee of the Red Cross). Once drafted the treaties are adopted by general assemblies or other plenary bodies of the organizations and then are opened for ratification or other form of acceptance by governments, often including many not involved in the drafting process.[5]

Treaties thus drafted are interpreted pursuant to rules similar to those used in construing legislation. The most authoritative collection of rules concerning the interpretation of treaties is the Vienna Convention on the Law of Treaties, 1155 U.N.T.S. 331, T.S. No. 58 (1980), 8 I.L.M. 679 (1979), entered into force January 27, 1980. The Vienna Convention has not been ratified by the U.S., but the State Department has acknowledged that "the Convention already is generally recognized as the authoritative guide to current treaty law and practice." Vienna Convention on the Law of Treaties S. Exec. Doc., 92nd Cong., 1st Sess. 1 (1971); see excerpts and discussion in chapters 2 and 10, supra.

The Vienna Convention sets a hierarchy of interpretive sources. First, the "ordinary meaning [is] to be given to the terms of the treaty in their context and in the light of their object and purpose." The "context" includes the treaty itself, agreements among the parties in connection with the treaty, subsequent practice that evidences the parties' agreement regarding the treaty's interpretation, any instrument issued by one or more parties accepted by the others as an instrument related to the treaty, and relevant rules of international law. Second, if the meaning so construed remains obscure or leads to a manifestly unreasonable result, supplementary means of interpretation, including preparatory work (travaux préparatoires) and circumstances of the treaty's conclusion, may be consulted. The expressed intent of a party is relevant only when it appears to have been accepted by the other parties. See 1 RESTATEMENT (THIRD) OF THE FOREIGN RELATIONS OF THE UNITED STATES § 131, comment h, at 58 (1987).

A government may express consent to be bound by a treaty by any means agreed

---

[5] For instance, Switzerland is not a member of the U.N. and did not participate in drafting the Convention Against Torture and Other Cruel, Inhuman or Degrading Treatment or Punishment, G.A. res. 39/46, 39 U.N. GAOR Supp. (No.51) at 197, U.N. Doc. A/39/51 (1984), entered into force June 26, 1987. Nonetheless, it was one of the first countries to become a party to the treaty.

by the parties, including ratification, signature, approval, and accession. Vienna Convention, Art. 11.

The U.S. is party to only a few of the scores of multilateral treaties that contain human rights provisions. The most important treaties to which the U.S. is party are the U.N. Charter, the Charter of the Organization of American States as amended by the Protocol of Buenos Aires, the four Geneva Conventions of 1949, the U.N. Protocol Relating to the Status of Refugees, the Genocide Convention, the Covenant on Civil and Political Rights, the Convention on the Elimination of All Forms of Racial Discrimination, and the Convention Against Torture and Other Cruel, Inhuman or Degrading Treatment or Punishment. The U.S. is also party to three treaties on slavery and the Convention on the Political Rights of Women. U.S. ratification of human rights treaties and the process of ratification are discussed in chapter 2, *supra*.

1. Treaties in U.S. Law

A treaty accepted by the U.S. is part of the supreme law of the land, equal in dignity to federal statutes. U.S. CONST. art. VI, cl. 2. Conflicts between treaty clauses and existing law are resolved according to three rules. First, a treaty may not infringe on certain clauses of the U.S. Constitution. *Reid v. Covert*, 354 U.S. 1, 16-17 (1957). Second, if a treaty and a federal statute conflict, the more recent prevails. *Id.* at 18 n. 34. Third, if a treaty and state law conflict, the treaty controls. *Zschernig v. Miller*, 389 U.S. 429, 440-41 (1968); *Clark v. Allen*, 331 U.S. 503, 508 (1947); *see also Missouri v. Holland*, 252 U.S. 416, 433-35 (1920) (validity of treaty not undermined by possible infringement on states' rights under Tenth Amendment).

A well-settled rule is that courts should endeavor to construe a treaty and a statute on the same subject so as to give effect to both. *Whitney v. Robertson*, 124 U.S. 190, 194 (1888). Courts generally should construe a treaty "in a broad and liberal spirit, and when two constructions are possible, one restrictive of rights that may be claimed under it and the other favorable to them, the latter is to be preferred." *Asakura v. City of Seattle*, 265 U.S. 332, 342 (1924).

The following excerpt shows the lengths to which a court may go in order to construe a statute to be consistent with a treaty, even one ratified before enactment of the statute. The court held that the PLO could maintain its U.N. observer-mission in New York, as authorized by the U.N. Headquarters Agreement (a treaty in force between the U.S. and the U.N.) even though the Anti-Terrorism Act (ATA) of 1988 appeared to require the mission's closure. By its terms the ATA prohibited maintaining "an office, headquarters, premises, or other facilities or establishments within the jurisdiction of the United States at the behest or direction of, or with funds provided by" the PLO, if the aim is to further PLO interests. 22 U.S.C. § 5202(3). *U.S. v. Palestine Liberation Org.*, 695 F. Supp. 1456, 1468-71 (S.D.N.Y. 1988): . . .

The lengths to which our courts have sometimes gone in construing domestic statutes so as to avoid conflict with international agreements are suggested by a passage from Justice Field's dissent in *Chew Heong* . . . 112 U.S. at . . . 560-61 . . . (1884), [which] concerned the interplay of legislation regarding Chinese laborers with treaties on the same subject. During the passage of the statute at issue in *Chew Heong*, "it was objected to the legislation sought that the treaty of 1868 stood in the way, and that while it remained unmodified, such legislation would be a breach of faith to China. . . ." *Id.* at 569 . . .. In spite of that, and over Justice Field's dissent, the Court, in Justice Field's words, "narrow[ed] the meaning of the act so as measurably to frustrate its intended operation." Four years after the decision in *Chew Heong*, Congress amended the act in question to nullify that decision. . . . With the amended statute, there could be no question as to Congress' intent to supersede the treaties, and it was the later enacted statute which took precedence. *The Chinese Exclusion Case*, . . . 130 U.S. at 598-99 . . . (1889).

The principles enunciated and applied in *Chew Heong* and its progeny . . . require the clearest of expressions on the part of Congress. We are constrained by these decisions to stress the lack of clarity in Congress' action in this instance. Congress' failure to speak with one clear voice on this subject requires us to interpret the ATA as inapplicable to the Headquarters Agreement. This is so, in short, for the reasons which follow:

First, neither the Mission nor the Headquarters Agreement is mentioned in the ATA itself. Such an inclusion would have left no doubt as to Congress' intent on a matter which had been raised repeatedly with respect to this act, and its absence here reflects equivocation and avoidance, leaving the court without clear interpretive guidance in the language of the act. Second, while the section of the ATA prohibiting the maintenance of an office applies "notwithstanding any provision of law to the contrary," 22 U.S.C. §5202(3), it does not purport to apply notwithstanding any *treaty*. The absence of that interpretive instruction is especially relevant because elsewhere in the same legislation Congress expressly referred to "United States law (including any treaty)." 101 Stat. 1343. Thus Congress failed, in the text of the ATA, to provide guidance for the interpretation of the act, where it became repeatedly apparent before its passage that the prospect of an interpretive problem was inevitable. Third, no member of Congress expressed a clear and unequivocal intent to supersede the Headquarters Agreement by passage of the ATA. In contrast, most who addressed the subject of conflict denied that there would be a conflict: in their view, the Headquarters Agreement did not provide the PLO with any right to maintain an office. Here again, Congress provided no guidance for the interpretation of the ATA in the event of a conflict which was clearly foreseeable. . . .

. . . The proponents of the ATA were, at an early stage and throughout its consideration, forewarned that the ATA would present a potential conflict with the Headquarters Agreement. It was especially important in those circumstances for Congress to give clear, indeed unequivocal guidance, as to how an interpreter of the ATA was to resolve the conflict. Yet there was no reference to the Mission in the text of the ATA, despite extensive discussion of the Mission in the floor debates. Nor was there reference to the Headquarters Agreement, or to any treaty, in the ATA or in its "notwithstanding" clause, despite the textual expression of intent to supersede treaty obligations in other sections of the Foreign Relations Authorization Act, of which the ATA formed a part. Thus Congress failed to provide unequivocal interpretive guidance in the text of the ATA, leaving open the possibility that the ATA could be viewed as a law of general application and enforced as such, without encroaching on the position of the Mission at the United Nations.

That interpretation would present no inconsistency with what little legislative history exists. There were conflicting voices both in Congress and in the executive branch before the enactment of the ATA. Indeed, there is only one matter with respect to which there was unanimity—the condemnation of terrorism. This, however, is extraneous to the legal issues involved here. At oral argument, the United States Attorney conceded that there was no evidence before the court that the Mission had misused its position at the United Nations or engaged in any covert actions in furtherance of terrorism. If the PLO is benefiting from operating in the United States, as the ATA implies, the enforcement of its provisions outside the context of the United Nations can effectively curtail that benefit.

The record contains voices of Congressmen and Senators forceful in their condemnation of terrorism and of the PLO and supporting the notion that the legislation would close the mission. There are other voices, less certain of the validity of the proposed congressional action and preoccupied by problems of constitutional dimension. And there are voices of Congressmen uncertain of the legal issues presented but desirous nonetheless of making a "political statement." During the discussions which preceded and followed the passage of the ATA, the Secretary of State and the Legal Adviser to the Department of State, a former member of this Court, voiced their opinions to the effect that the ATA presented a conflict with the Headquarters Agreement.

Yet no member of Congress, at any point, explicitly stated that the ATA was intended to override any international obligation of the United States. . . .

In sum, the language of the Headquarters Agreement, the longstanding practice under it, and the interpretation given it by the parties to it leave no doubt that it places an obligation upon the United States to refrain from impairing the function of the PLO Observer Mission to the United Nations. The ATA and its legislative history do not manifest Congress' intent to abrogate this obligation. We are therefore constrained to interpret the ATA as failing to supersede the Headquarters Agreement and inapplicable to the Mission.

NOTES AND QUESTIONS

1.   What words added to the Anti-Terrorism Act might supersede the Headquarters Agreement?

2.   The text of 22 U.S.C. § 5202(3) remained unaltered as of March 1996, even after the U.S. had begun to work with the PLO on a comprehensive peace settlement in the Middle East. Does the lack of congressional response support or undermine the court's opinion?

3.   For other opinions construing a statute to be consistent with, rather than to supersede, a treaty clause, see: *Trans World Airlines, Inc. v. Franklin Mint Corp.*, 466 U.S. 243, 252 (1984); *Weinberger v. Rossi*, 456 U.S. 25, 32 (1982); *Washington v. Washington State Commercial Passenger Fishing Vessel Ass'n*, 443 U.S. 658, 690, *modified*, 444 U.S. 816 (1979); *Menominee Tribe of Indians v. United States*, 391 U.S. 404, 412-13 (1968); *Cook v. United States*, 288 U.S. 102 (1933).

For holdings that a statute did supersede a treaty clause, see: *The Chinese Exclusion Case*, 130 U.S. 581, 599-602 (1889); *The Head Money Cases*, 112 U.S. 580, 597-99 (1884); *South African Airways v. Dole*, 817 F.2d 119, 121 (D.C.Cir. 1987) (Anti-Apartheid Act of 1986, requiring termination of treaty between U.S. and South Africa, held irreconcilable with that treaty), *cert. denied*, 484 U.S. 896 (1987).

4.   For a survey of post-World War II civil rights cases invoking the human rights clauses of the U.N. Charter, see Bert B. Lockwood, Jr., *The U.N. Charter and United Nations Civil Rights Litigation: 1946-1955*, 69 IOWA L. REV. 901 (1984).

5.   Professor Hannum has urged that courts should show greater deference to treaty clauses when the inconsistent law is a state, rather than a federal, statute. HURST HANNUM, MATERIALS ON INTERNATIONAL HUMAN RIGHTS AND U.S. CRIMINAL LAW AND PROCEDURE 10-11 (1989).

6.   In *United States v. Alvarez-Machain*, 504 U.S. 655 (1992), the Court narrowly construed an extradition treaty between the U.S. and Mexico to avoid conflict with an executive action.

In *Alvarez-Machain*, U.S. Drug Enforcement Administration agents arranged for the kidnapping of a Mexican doctor suspected of assisting in the murder of a DEA agent in Mexico. The kidnappers forcibly brought Alvarez-Machain to the U.S. to stand trial for murder. A California district court dismissed the suit for lack of subject matter jurisdiction, stating that the kidnapping violated the U.S.-Mexico extradition treaty.

The Supreme Court reversed. It held that the kidnapping did not violate national law, and stated that the treaty did not explicitly forbid such kidnapping. The Court refused to interpret the treaty in light of customary international law, stating that such an approach would conflict with the treaty:

> Respondent would have us find that the Treaty acts as a prohibition against a violation of the general principle of international law that one government may not "exercise its police power in the territory of another state." There are many actions which could be taken by a nation that would violate this principle, including waging war, but it cannot seriously be contended an invasion of the United States by Mexico would violate the terms of the extradition between the two nations.

Id. at 2195-96 (citation omitted). The Court acknowledged that its conclusion "may be in violation of general international law principles." *Id.* at 2196.

On remand the Court of Appeals refused to consider whether customary international law alone, absent a treaty, supported Alvarez-Machain's repatriation to Mexico. 971 F.2d 310, 311 (9th Cir. 1992). Customary law could not support the repatriation as an exception to U.S. domestic law because the district court had originally found the government's conduct here was not "outrageous." *Id.*

Alvarez-Machain finally escaped prosecution when the district court dismissed his case for lack of sufficient evidence against him. He has since filed suit under 28 U.S.C. § 1350, discussed in chapter 12, against persons responsible for his kidnapping. His complaint alleged that the kidnappers' actions were "torts in violation of the law of nations, including state sponsored kidnapping; prolonged arbitrary detention; disappearance; torture; cruel, inhuman and degrading treatment or punishment; violations of the Fourth, Fifth and Eighth Amendments of the United States Constitution; and common law torts under California and Mexican law." Plaintiff's Complaint, *Alvarez-Machain v. Berellez*, at 1 (C.D. Cal., filed July 9, 1993). In January 1995 the court granted a motion to dismiss the claims based on the Fourth and Fifth Amendments and the TVPA. The case has been appealed and the claims are pending. In a brief to the Ninth Circuit, amici argued that aliens have a Due Process right against physical abuse while in custody of United States agents, and that the TVPA applies to the case. *See* Joan Fitzpatrick et al., *Human Rights Litigation Update Report,* ACLU INTERNATIONAL CIVIL LIBERTIES REPORT 30 (1995).

For critical analyses see Betsy B. Baker & Volker Röben, *To Abduct or to Extradite: Does a Treaty Beg the Question? The Alvarez-Machain Decision in U.S. Domestic Law and International Law,* 53 ZEITSCHRIFT FÜR AUSLÄNDISCHES ÖFFENTLICHES RECHT UND VÖLKERRECHT 657 (1993); Keith Highet & George Kahale III, *International Decisions (United States v. Alvarez-Machain),* 86 AM. J. INT'L L. 811 (1992); Michael J. Glennon, *State-Sponsored Abduction: A Comment on United States v. Alvarez-Machain,* 86 AM. J. INT'L L. 746 (1992); Malvina Halberstam, *In Defense of the Supreme Court Decision in Alvarez-Machain,* 86 AM. J. INT'L L. 736 (1992). *Cf.* Eyal Benvenisti, *Judicial Misgivings Regarding the Application of International Law: An Analysis of Attitudes of National Courts,* 4 EJIL 159 (1993).

7.   A bill to forbid arrests and abductions in foreign countries was introduced in the Senate on January 21, 1993. S. 72, 103d Cong., 1st Sess. (1993). The bill states that the abduction of Alvarez-Machain and the subsequent Supreme Court endorsement of the abduction "threaten to disrupt cooperation between the United States and Mexico, Canada, and the 101 other nations with which the United States has extradition treaties. . . ." *Id.* § 1(D). The bill was referred to the Senate Foreign Relations Committee, which did not act upon it.

8.   In *Sale v. Haitian Centers Council, Inc.,* 509 U.S. 155, 113 S.Ct. 2549 (1993), the Court again took a restrictive approach to treaty interpretation, upholding an executive order that

authorized summary return to Haiti of boat people intercepted on the high seas without considering asylum claims. The Court stated that the order violated neither Article 33 of the U.N. Protocol Relating to the Status of Refugees nor section 243(h) of the U.S. Immigration Act. (Both prohibit returning refugees to territories where their lives or freedom would be threatened.) The Court reasoned that neither the treaty nor U.S. law applies to actions of the U.S. committed outside its territorial waters.

---

2.   Treaties Which the U.S. Has Not Ratified

The U.S. has signed but not ratified four treaties that form much of the core of human rights law: the Covenant on Economic, Social and Cultural Rights; the Convention on the Elimination of All Forms of Discrimination Against Women; the American Convention on Human Rights: and the Convention on the Rights of the Child, excerpted *supra* at 27. The U.S. has not signed the Optional Protocol to the Covenant on Civil and Political Rights, which provides a procedure for hearing claims of a state's violation of the Covenant.

Article 18 of the Vienna Convention on Treaties requires a government that has signed but not ratified "to refrain from acts which would defeat the object and purpose of [the] treaty . . . until it shall have made its intention clear not to become a party. . . ." 1155 U.N.T.S. 331, *entered into force* January 27, 1980. *See* chapter 10, *supra*, for a discussion of a country's international obligations under Article 18. U.S. courts have not applied Article 18 to treaties the U.S. has signed but not ratified. Rather, to the extent they have relied on those instruments, they have looked to them as evidence of customary law or as aids in interpreting provisions of U.S. law. Nonetheless, Article 18 does support an argument for the application of signed, but unratified treaties.

3.   The Doctrine of Self-Executing Treaties

Though the Constitution states that treaties are supreme law of the land, courts have developed a doctrine that only self-executing clauses are judicially enforceable. Sometimes the rule is phrased in the alternative: treaty clauses are enforceable if they are either self-executing or have been implemented by legislation. In the latter case it is the legislation and not the treaty that becomes judicially enforceable.

The Supreme Court introduced the requirement of self-execution in *Foster v. Neilson*, 27 U.S. (2 Pet.) 253, 254 (1829). It declared that a treaty clause is self-executing and hence "equivalent to an act of the legislature, whenever it operates by itself without the aid of any legislative provision." Subsequent cases have focused on the intent of the parties. *See, e.g., Cook v. United States*, 288 U.S. 102, 119 (1933). In *Frolova v. U.S.S.R.*, 761 F.2d 370, 373 (7th Cir. 1985) (structure altered), the court compiled this list of factors to be consulted in determining whether a treaty provision is self-executing:

(1)   the language and purposes of the agreement as a whole;

(2)   the circumstance surrounding its execution;

(3)   the nature of the obligations imposed by the agreement;

(4)   the availability and feasibility of alternative enforcement mechanisms;

(5)   the implications of permitting a private right of action; and

(6)   the capability of the judiciary to resolve the dispute.

For a similar list, see *People of Saipan v. U.S. Dep't of Interior*, 502 F.2d 90, 97 (9th Cir. 1974), *cert. denied*, 420 U.S. 1003 (1975).

The Restatement (Third) suggests that "the intention of the United States determines whether an agreement is to be self-executing in the United States or should await implementing legislation." 1 RESTATEMENT (THIRD) OF THE FOREIGN RELATIONS OF THE UNITED STATES § 131, comment h, at 58 (1987). If the intent is unclear, courts should look to "any statement by the President in concluding the agreement or in submitting it to the Senate for consent or to the Congress as a whole for approval, and of any expression by the Senate or by Congress in dealing with the agreement." *Id.*

In multilateral treaties, however, parties rarely make clear the process by which they are expected to incorporate the treaty into national law. Countries have different methods of fulfilling international obligations, and few have incorporated treaties directly into national law or selectively incorporated them through the doctrine of self-execution.[6] Hence, the intent of the parties is neither a fruitful nor an appropriate inquiry.

The test that appears most relevant to multilateral human rights treaties is the three-step inquiry proposed by Professor Riesenfeld. Under this theory, a treaty ought to be deemed self-executing if it "(a) involves the rights and duties of individuals; (b) does not cover a subject for which legislative action is required by the Constitution; and (c) does not leave discretion to the parties in the application of the particular provision." Stefan A. Riesenfeld, *The Doctrine of Self-Executing Treaties and GATT: A Notable German Judgment*, 65 AM. J. INT'L L. 548, 550 (1970); *see also* Stefan A. Riesenfeld, *The Doctrine of Self-Executing Treaties and U.S. v. Postal: Win at Any Price?*, 74 AM. J. INT'L L. 892, 896 (1980). That approach is amplified in the following excerpt.

Kathryn Burke et al., *Application of International Human Rights Law in State and Federal Courts*, 18 TEX. INT'L L.J. 291, 302 (1983) (footnotes omitted):

> Whether or not a clause is self-executing depends, therefore, on what obligations the clause creates. If the obligation is merely to negotiate a supplementary contract or to seek legislative action, the clause is not self-executing. Examples of clauses that are not self-executing include articles 43(3) and 45 of the United Nations Charter, which create duties to negotiate supplementary contracts and seek legislative action. Simply because a provision requires future negotiation or legislative action does not, however, render it non-self-executing if the provision also creates specific obligations or proscribes certain acts. For example, articles 25, 100, and 105 of the United Nations Charter have been interpreted as self-executing because they require governments to perform or to refrain from certain acts, even though the same articles also require governments to negotiate supplementary contracts and seek legislative action. *See Keeney v. United States*, 218 F.2d 843 (D.C. Cir. 1954).

---

[6] Countries that have a self-execution doctrine include Argentina, Austria, Belgium, Cyprus, Egypt, France, Germany, Greece, Italy, Japan, Luxembourg, Malta, Mexico, the Netherlands, Spain, Switzerland, Turkey, and the European Communities. Richard B. Lillich, *Invoking International Human Rights Law in Domestic Courts*, 54 U. CIN. L. REV. 367, 373 n. 31 (1985).

Like Articles 43(3) and 45 of the U.N. Charter, Article 47 of the OAS Charter has been held to be non-self-executing. It reads, in part:

> The Member States will exert the greatest efforts, in accordance with their constitutional processes, to ensure the effective exercise of the right to education, on the following bases:
>
> (a)   Elementary education, compulsory for children of school age, shall also be offered to all others who can benefit from it. When provided by the State it shall be without charge. . . .

That language, a trial court explained, was

> [n]ot the kind of promissory language which confers rights in the absence of implementing legislation. The parties have engaged to perform a particular act, that is, to exert the greatest efforts to advance the cause of education. They have not contracted to provide free public education to all children of school age within the country.[7]

Nonetheless, the court opined that, in the absence of the introductory paragraph, part (a) would "no doubt [be] sufficiently direct to imply the intention to create affirmative and judicially enforceable rights." 501 F. Supp. at 590.

Article 13 of the International Covenant on Economic, Social and Cultural Rights, G.A. res. 2200A (XXI), Dec. 16, 1966, 21 U.N. GAOR Supp. (No. 16) at 49; U.N. Doc. A/6316 (1966), 993 U.N.T.S. 3, *entered into force* Jan. 3, 1976, contains language similar to Article 47 of the OAS Charter. It reads, in part:

> 1.   The States Parties to the present Covenant recognize the right of everyone to education. . . .
>
> 2.   The States Parties to the present Covenant recognize that, with a view to achieving the full realization of this right:
>
> (a)   Primary education shall be compulsory and available free to all;
>
> (b)   Secondary education in its different forms, including technical and vocational secondary education, shall be made generally available and accessible to all by every appropriate means, and in particular by the progressive introduction of free education; . . .
>
> (e)   The development of a system of schools at all levels shall be actively pursued . . ..

No federal court has had an opportunity to review this language to determine whether it is self-executing. Do you think a court would be more likely to construe this clause to be self-executing than the analogous clause in the OAS Charter?

Article 25 of the U.N. Charter, unlike Articles 43(3) and 45, has been held to be self-executing. In *Diggs v. Schultz*,[8] the court held that U.S. citizens who were

---

[7] *In re Alien Children Litigation*, 501 F. Supp. 544, 590 (S.D. Tex. 1980), *aff'd unreported mem.* (5th Cir. 1981), *aff'd* 457 U.S. 202 (1982). The issue was the legality of a Texas statute which denied free elementary education to children of undocumented aliens. 501 F. Supp. at 549. Both the Supreme Court and the district court found the statute violated equal protection. 457 U.S. at 210-30; *Id.* at 583-84. The Supreme Court, however, did not discuss the international law arguments.

[8] 470 F.2d 461 (D.C. Cir. 1972), *cert. denied*, 411 U.S. 931 (1973); *but see Diggs v. Richardson*, 555 F.2d 848, 850 (D.C. Cir. 1976), holding that a Security Council resolution prohibiting commerce with Namibia did not confer rights upon citizens.

denied entry into Rhodesia because of their race or who had suffered economic harm as a result of the government's racist policies were the intended beneficiaries of a Security Council resolution directing all U.N. members to impose an embargo on trade with Rhodesia. Accordingly, they had standing to sue to enforce that resolution pursuant to Article 25 of the U.N. Charter, which reads: "The Members of the United Nations agree to accept and carry out the decisions of the Security Council."[9]

Just as the U.N. resolution at issue in *Diggs* rendered Article 25 judicially enforceable, growing international recognition of various human rights should render relevant articles of the U.N. and OAS Charters self-executing. But are courts likely to hold clauses of the U.N. and OAS Charters to be self-executing? In *Sei Fujii v. California*, 38 Cal.2d 718, 722, 242 P.2d 617, 621 (1952), the California Supreme Court declared that Articles 55(c) and 56 of the U.N. Charter are not self-executing. Several commentators have urged that *Sei Fujii*'s analysis be rejected, and some courts have echoed that view.[10] Nonetheless, most federal and state courts continue to accept the *Sei Fujii* dictum uncritically. In particular, they have often stated that Articles 55 and 56 are phrased in general terms that are merely hortatory, not mandatory, and create obligations enforceable through political and diplomatic processes rather than by judicial intervention. *See Frolova, supra*, 761 F.2d at 374-75 and cases cited there.

These past decisions imply U.S. courts are unlikely to find Articles 55 and 56 of the U.N. Charter to be self-executing. If courts did so rule, it would likely be on the theory that various U.N. instruments, in particular the International Bill of Human Rights (the Universal Declaration of Human Rights, the Covenant on Civil and Political Rights, and the Covenant on Economic, Social and Cultural Rights), have become authoritative interpretations of Articles 55 and 56 and, accordingly, lend sufficient specificity to render those articles self-executing.[11]

Judge Tanaka of the International Court of Justice endorsed this idea when he stated "the Universal Declaration of Human Rights . . . although not binding in

---

[9] Ultimately, the court dismissed the claims on the separate ground that they presented a non-justiciable political question. Dismissal was based on the fact that, after adoption of the Security Council resolution, Congress passed legislation permitting importation of certain metals from Rhodesia under certain circumstances. The court decided that Congress intended to abrogate the U.S. treaty obligation and, accordingly, that plaintiffs' dispute was with Congress, not the Executive. 470 F.2d at 466.

[10] *See, e.g.*, RICHARD B. LILLICH & FRANK C. NEWMAN, INTERNATIONAL HUMAN RIGHTS: PROBLEMS OF LAW AND POLICY 76 (1979):

> [I]t would be most difficult to conclude that the Charter provisions on human rights cannot legitimately be given effect by the courts in appropriate cases. Indeed, it would be contrary to the letter and the spirit of the supremacy clause of the Constitution if the courts did not attempt to carry out a treaty provision to the fullest extent possible. *quoted in Von Dardel v. U.S.S.R.*, 623 F. Supp. 246, 256 (D.D.C. 1985), *vacated on other grounds*, 736 F.Supp. 1 (D.D.C. 1990); *see also People v. Mirmirani*, 30 Cal. 3d 375, 388 n. 1, 636 P.2d 1130, 1138 n. 1 (1981) (Newman J., concurring) (arguing the statements in *Sei Fujii* concerning the non-self-executing character of U.N. Charter articles were dicta and thus of dubious precedential value even in California); Bernhard Schlüter, *The Domestic Status of the Human Rights Clauses of the United Nations Charter*, 61 CALIF. L. REV. 110, 162 n.291 (1973). *But see People v. Ghent*, 43 Cal. 3d 739, 739 P.2d 1250, 1276 (1987) (affirming *Sei Fujii* in dictum, without analysis).

[11] The position, nicknamed the Newman-Berkeley thesis, has been urged by several human rights groups in amicus briefs. *See* Frank C. Newman, *Interpreting the Human Rights Clauses of the U.N. Charter*, 1972 REVUE DES DROITS DE L'HOMME 283; *see also* Kathryn Burke et al., *Application of International Human Rights Law in State and Federal Courts*, 18 TEX. INT'L L.J. 291, 309-10 (1983); Richard B. Lillich, *Invoking International Human Rights Law in Domestic Courts*, 54 U. CIN. L. REV. 367, 373 n. 54 (1985).

itself, constitutes evidence of the interpretation and application of the relevant Charter provisions. . . ." *South West Africa* (Ethiopia v. South Africa, Liberia v. South Africa), 1966 I.C.J. 6, 293 (Tanaka, J., dissenting). The majority later adopted this opinion in another case when it held that South Africa had an obligation under the Charter of the United Nations "to observe and respect . . . human rights and fundamental freedoms for all without distinction as to race." *Advisory Opinion on the Legal Consequences for States of the Continued Presence of South Africa in Namibia*, 1971 I.C.J. 16, 57. Establishing and enforcing contrary policies, "is a flagrant violation of the purposes and principles of the Charter." *Id. See* Egon Schwelb, *The International Court of Justice and the Human Rights Clauses of the Charter*, 66 AM. J. INTL L. 337 (1972). Later, the International Court of Justice observed "[w]rongfully to deprive human beings of their freedom and to subject them to physical constraint of hardship" was contrary to both the U.N. Charter and the Universal Declaration of Human Rights. *United States Diplomatic and Consular Staff in Tehran* (United States v. Iran), 1980 I.C.J. 3, 42; *see also* Memorial of the Government of the United States of America, *Case Concerning United States Diplomatic and Consular Staff in Tehran* (Jan. 1980), 1982 I.C.J. 121, 182 (Memorials, Pleadings, Documents). Hence, the International Court of Justice recognized that the human rights provisions in the U.N. Charter establish binding obligations on all U.N. member states.

Whether Articles 55 and 56 should be found to be self-executing as to a particular right depends on whether language in the interpreting documents is sufficiently precise and generally accepted. No U.S. court has apparently accepted the argument that the human rights clauses of the U.N. or OAS Charters are self-executing. In contrast, non-human-rights clauses of the U.N. Charter are more likely to be held to be self-executing. For example, in *U.S. v. Toscanino*, 500 F.2d 267, 277 (2d Cir. 1974), the court found that U.N. Charter Article 2(4), which obliges all U.N. members to "refrain . . . from the threat or use of force against the territorial integrity . . . of any State," would be violated and dismissal of the indictment required if U.S. agents participated in the seizure of an alien from Uruguay (with which the U.S. had an extradition treaty) in order to bring him to the U.S. for prosecution. The court found Article 2(4) to be sufficiently precise to impose judicially enforceable obligations in light of a Security Council resolution condemning as a violation of Article 2(4) the kidnapping in 1960 of Adolf Eichmann from Argentina by Israeli "volunteers." *Id.*

Provisions of the Geneva Convention Relative to the Protection of Civilian Persons in Time of War (Fourth Geneva Convention) of 1949 have also been found non-self-executing in several cases. *See, e.g., Tel-Oren v. Libyan Arab Republic*, 726 F.2d 774, 809 (D.C. Cir. 1984)(Bork, J. concurring); *Huynh Thi Anh v. Levi*, 586 F.2d 625, 629 (9th Cir. 1978). Below are excerpts from a much-cited decision of the U.S. Board of Immigration Appeals rejecting the contention that aliens may not be deported to countries whose governments are unable or unwilling to safeguard rights guaranteed by the Geneva Conventions and from an amicus brief urging that relevant treaty clauses be ruled self-executing.

* * * * *

Matter of Medina, **Interim Decision No. 3078 (Board of Immigration Appeals 1988):**

BY: Milhollan, Chairman; Dunne, Morris, and Vacca, Board Members

. . . [T]he immigration judge entered a decision that found the respondent deportable as charged, denied her applications for asylum and withholding of deportation and for relief under the Geneva Conventions of 1949, but granted her the privilege of voluntary departure. The immigration judge certified his decision in this case to the Board . . . in view of his findings regarding "unusually complex and novel questions of law." Along with the briefs of respondent and the Immigration and Naturalization Service on certification, the American Civil Liberties Union, the Lawyer's Committee for International Human Rights, and the Department of State submitted amicus curiae briefs. The decision of the immigration judge will be affirmed in part and reversed in part.

The respondent is a 26-year-old single female, a native and citizen of El Salvador, who entered the United States without inspection in November 1980, at Hidalgo, Texas. . . .

At her deportation hearing, the respondent applied for asylum and withholding of deportation [under U.S. immigration statutes]. She also sought relief from deportation under the provisions of the Geneva Convention Relative to the Protection of Civilian Persons in Time of War ("the Fourth Convention" or "the Convention"). . . .

. . . For the reasons set forth below, we find that the immigration judge erred in holding that the Fourth Convention creates a basis for relief from deportation that can be advanced by a respondent in deportation proceedings before an immigration judge.

I.   *The Fourth Convention*

(a) *Scope of Articles 1 and 3*

The Fourth Convention was the first Geneva convention to address the protection of civilians in time of war. . . .

Article 3 provides:

In the case of armed conflict not of an international character occurring in the territory of one of the High Contracting Parties, each Party to the conflict shall be bound to apply, as a minimum, the following provisions:

(1)   Persons taking no active part in the hostilities, including members of armed forces who have laid down their arms and those placed *hors de combat* by sickness, wounds, detention, or any other cause, shall in all circumstances be treated humanely, without any adverse distinction founded on race, colour, religion or faith, sex, birth or wealth, or any other similar criteria.

To this end, the following acts are and shall remain prohibited at any time and in any place whatsoever with respect to the above-mentioned persons:

(a)   violence to life and person, in particular murder of all kinds, mutilation, cruel treatment and torture;

(b)   taking of hostages;

(c)   outrages upon personal dignity, in particular humiliating and degrading treatment;

(d)   the passing of sentences and carrying out of executions without previous judgment pronounced by a regularly constituted court, affording all the judicial guarantees which are recognized as indispensable by civilized peoples. . . .

From its plain language, it is apparent that Article 3, which does not refer to the repatriation of displaced persons, applies only to *each party* to a non-international conflict. Since it binds only the parties to the conflict (in this case the Government of El Salvador and the guerrillas), by its terms it does not apply to the United States, which the respondent does not assert is a party to the conflict. . . .

. . . Article 1, one of the shortest articles of the Convention, provides:

> The High Contracting Parties undertake to respect and ensure respect for the present Convention in all circumstances. . . .

. . . [W]ithin the context of the Convention itself, it is doubtful whether Article 1 was intended to impose an affirmative duty on States of the nature argued by the respondent with regard to possible violations of Article 3 by other States, particularly those not under their control.

(b) *"Self-Execution" of Article 1*

In any event, however, we cannot conclude that Article 1 of the Convention is "self-executing," as that term has been used to refer to the creation by treaty of rights that are privately enforceable by individuals in the absence of implementing legislation. We agree with the Government that the language of Article 1 (*i.e.*, that parties "undertake to respect and ensure respect" for the Convention) does not evince an intent to create judicially enforceable rights in private persons. The Article addresses itself to the political rather than the judicial branch of government and uses language suggesting declarations of principle, rather than a code of privately enforceable legal rights. The language is akin to that in various provisions of the United Nations Charter long held not to be self-executing. . . . Moreover, the nature of the requirement to "ensure respect" for the Convention raises foreign policy issues committed to the political branch of government and not delegated to the immigration judges or this Board. It is "essentially the kind of standard that is rooted in diplomacy and its incidents, rather than in conventional adjudication." *Diggs v. Richardson*, 555 F.2d 848, 851 (D.C. Cir. 1976).

We further note that the Convention sets forth a specific mechanism for inquiries to be instituted into alleged violations of its provisions (Article 149) and reflects that signatory states will take measures through their own laws to enforce its provisions (Articles 145 and 146). Treaties that call for implementing legislation have been found by federal courts not to be "self-executing." *See In re Demjanjuk v. Meese*, 784 F.2d 1114, 1116 (D.C. Cir. 1986). . . .

* * * * *

The amicus brief submitted by the American Civil Liberties Union in *Medina* asserted the treaty provisions of the Geneva Convention IV were self-executing. Pertinent arguments follow:

Immigration Judges Must Refuse to Deport Salvadorans to El Salvador to Ensure Respect for Geneva Convention.

1. *The Applicable Treaty Norms.*

Respondent's treaty-based arguments are founded upon Article 1 of Geneva Convention IV . . ..

Common Article 3 of the Convention prescribes the protections which must be provided to civilians during non-international armed conflict . . ..

Article 147 of the Convention further provides:

> Grave breaches to which the preceding Article relates shall be those involving any of the following acts, if committed against persons or property protected by the present Convention: . . . unlawful deportation or transfer or unlawful confinement of a protected person, compelling a protected person to serve in the forces of a hostile power . . ..

The United States has acknowledged that norms protected by Common Article 3 of the Geneva Conventions are not being respected in El Salvador. . . .

The United States' forcible repatriation of civilians fleeing internal armed conflict in El Salvador contributes to additional violations and violates the treaty obligation to "ensure respect" for humanitarian law. . . .

> 2. *Treaties Are Self-Executing When They Contain a Rule by Which the Rights of Individuals Can be Determined, Unless There is a Clear Intent to the Contrary.*

The United States Constitution proclaims treaties to be the "supreme law of the Land," U.S. CONST. Art. VI §2, and it has long been recognized that private parties can enforce the provisions of a treaty to which the United States is a party. In 1884 the Supreme Court stated:

> A treaty may . . . contain provisions which confer certain rights upon the citizens or subjects of one of the Nations residing in the territorial limits of the other, which partake of the nature of municipal law, and which are capable of enforcement as between private parties in the courts of the country.

The Head Money Cases, 112 U.S. 580, 598 (1884).

The issue for the courts is one of intent. *Foster v. Neilson*, 27 U.S. (2 Pet.) 253, 314 (1829). Moreover, the issue is one of intent as reflected in the specific treaty provisions at issue. Certain provisions in a treaty can be self-executing while others in the same treaty are not. Compare, *Sei Fujii v. State, supra* (Arts. 55 and 56 of the United Nations Charter are not self-executing) *and Curran v. City of New York*, 191 Misc. 229, 77 N.Y.S.2d 206 (1947) (Arts. 104 and 105 of the Charter are self-executing). . . .

In determining whether the provisions of a treaty are intended to be self-executing, courts look first to the language of the treaty. If the treaty provisions establish rights and duties of individuals, then they should be held to be self-executing, unless the treaty expresses a clear intent to the contrary. As the Supreme Court has stated,

> A treaty . . . is a law of the land as an Act of Congress is, whenever its provisions prescribe a rule by which the rights of the private citizen or subject may be determined.

The Head Money Cases, [112 U.S. at 598-99]. The RESTATEMENT (REVISED) FOREIGN RELATIONS LAW OF UNITED STATES, §131, Reporters Vol. 5 (1980) expresses this same rule in a slightly more general fashion:

> In general, agreements which can be readily given effect by executive or judicial bodies, federal or state, without further federal legislation, are deemed self-executing, unless a contrary intention is manifest. . . . This has been true from early in our history. . . .

In some cases it may be difficult to determine that a treaty provision has "the mandatory quality and definiteness that would indicate the States' intent to create judiciable rights in private persons immediately upon ratification." *Sei Fujii, supra*, 242 P.2d at 622. Nevertheless, usually treaties are "self-executing." *Amaya v. Stanolind Oil & Gas*, 158 F.2d 554, 556 (5th Cir. 1946), *cert. denied*, 331 U.S. 808 (1947). For example, in *People of Saipan v. United States Department of Interior*, 502 F.2d 90 (9th Cir. 1974), [the U.S. Court of Appeals] considered whether Article VI of the Trusteeship Agreement for the Pacific Islands, 61 Stat. 3301, was self-executing. Article VI requires the United States to "promote the economic advancement and self-sufficiency of the inhabitants, and to this end . . . regulate the use of natural resources" and to "protect the inhabitants against the loss of their lands and resources. . . ." The plaintiffs in *Saipan* had brought an action to enjoin the construction and operation of a hotel on public land . . . until the environmental impact had been studied and evaluated. In holding the treaty to be self-executing, [the] court enunciated the following test for self-execution:

> The extent to which an international agreement established affirmative and judicially enforceable obligations without implementing legislation must be determined in each case by reference to any contextual factors: the purposes of the treaty and the objectives of its creators, the existence of domestic procedures and institutions appropriate for direct implementation, the availability and feasibility of alternative enforcement methods, and the immediate and long-range social consequences of self or non-self execution.

Saipan, supra, 502 F.2d at 97. [The Court of Appeals] held that though the substantive rights guaranteed through the Trusteeship Agreement were not precisely defined, the Agreement was capable of judicial enforcement.

> Its language is no more general than such terms as "due process of law," "seaworthiness," "equal protection of the law," "good faith," or "restraint," which courts interpret every day.

Thus, it is only in the exceptional case that a treaty provision will be found to be non-self executing. . . .

Amicus submits that the obligation not to return people to countries in which "grave breaches" of the Geneva Convention IV are occurring is so clear and so central to the overwhelming purpose of the Convention that the treaty provisions must be found to be "self-executing," unless congressional intent to the contrary is clear.

3. *There is no Clear Intent that Article 1, 3 and 147 of Geneva Convention IV Are "Non-Self-Executing".*

The Government has adduced no clear evidence that Congress intended Geneva Convention IV to be entirely "non-self-executing." Instead the Government argues that the Refugee Act of 1980 provides the exclusive avenue for the rights of refugees in the United States. However, the Government has cited to no passage in the legislative history of the Refugee Act of 1980 in which Geneva Convention IV is considered. . . .

NOTES AND QUESTIONS

1. The Board of Immigration Appeal's conclusion that Article 1 of the Fourth Geneva Convention is not self-executing was endorsed by the district court for the Northern District of

California in *American Baptist Churches v. Meese*, 712 F. Supp. 756 (N.D. Cal. 1989). The court further agreed that Article 3 did not apply to the U.S. in deportation cases regarding Salvadorans because it restrains only parties to non-international armed conflicts.

2. What factual circumstances would strengthen a Salvadoran's claim to asylum under Articles 1 and 3 of the Fourth Geneva Convention? *See* chapter 14, *infra*.

3. The following cases ruled human rights clauses of treaties to be self-executing: *Clark v. Allen*, 331 U.S. 503 (1947) (treaty gave aliens rights relating to inheritance of property in U.S.); *Asakura v. Seattle*, 225 U.S. 332 (1924) (treaty granted alien equal right to engage in trade); *People of Saipan v. U.S. Dep't of Interior*, 502 F.2d 90, 97 (9th Cir. 1974), *cert. denied*, 420 U.S. 1003 (1975); *Von Dardel v. U.S.S.R.*, 623 F. Supp. 246, 255 (D.D.C. 1985) (Vienna Convention and 1973 Convention allowed a diplomat's brother to sue the U.S.S.R. for his disappearance, although the U.S.S.R. was later held to be immune from suit under the Sovereign Immunities Act); *Curran v. City of New York*, 191 Misc. 229, 77 N.Y.S.2d 206 (1947) (U.N. Charter Arts. 104 and 105).

Cases that have found human rights clauses of treaties to be non-self-executing include the following: *Demjanjuk v. Meese*, 784 F.2d 1114, 1116 (D.C. Cir. 1986) (Genocide Convention is non-self-executing because Senate ratification was conditioned on Congress passing implementing legislation); *Frolova v. U.S.S.R.*, 761 F.2d 370, 374-76 (7th Cir. 1985) (U.N. Charter Arts. 55 and 56); *Filartiga v. Peña-Irala*, 630 F.2d 876, 881-82 n. 9 (2d Cir. 1980) (U.N. Charter Arts. 55 and 56 "not wholly self-executing," but prohibition of torture is self-executing); *Anh v. Levi*, 586 F.2d 625, 629 (6th Cir. 1978) (treaty language relied on was "very general . . .and does not answer the custody question presented by this case"); *United States v. Postal*, 589 F.2d 862, 876-77 (5th Cir. 1979) (Convention on the High Seas is generally declaratory), *cert. denied*, 444 U.S. 832 (1979); *Handel v. Artukovic*, 601 F. Supp. 1421, 1425 (C.D. Cal. 1985) (Geneva Conventions and Hague Convention); *Haitian Refugee Center v. Gracey*, 600 F. Supp. 1396, 1406 (D.D.C. 1985) (U.N. Protocol Relating to the Status of Refugees), *aff'd on other grounds*, 809 F.2d 794 (D.C. Cir. 1987); *see also Tel-Oren v. Libyan Arab Republic*, 726 F.2d 774, 809 (D.C. Cir. 1984) (Bork, J. concurring) (Fourth Geneva Convention not "self-executing"); *Bertrand v. Sava*, 684 F.2d 204, 218-19 (2d Cir. 1982).

4. *See* Peter Westen, *The Place of Foreign Treaties in the Courts of the United States: A Reply to Louis Henkin*, 101 HARV. L. REV. 511 (1987), and Louis Henkin, *Lexical Priority or "Political Question": A Response*, 101 HARV. L. REV. 524 (1987), for different views regarding the relation between treaties and U.S. law. *See also* Yuji Iwasawa, *The Doctrine of Self-Executing Treaties in the United States: A Critical Analysis*, 26 VA. J. INT'L L. 627 (1986); Jordan J. Paust, *Self-Executing Treaties*, 82 AM. J. INT'L L. 760 (1983).

5. For arguments that Articles 1 and 3 of the Fourth Geneva Convention are self-executing, see Kravitz, *Beyond Asylum and Withholding of Deportation: A Framework for Relief Under Geneva Convention IV of 1949*, 1 TEMPLE INT'L & COMP. L.J. 263 (1987).

---

4. Reservations

Chapter 2, *supra*, discusses the reservations, understandings, and declarations which the Senate put on its ratification of the Covenant on Civil and Political Rights. Several of these limitations may be relevant to the case of the detention of unaccompanied alien youths pending deportation hearings, as discussed *supra* Part D at 576.

In assessing these limitations, the Vienna Convention on the Law of Treaties, Art. 2(1)(d), 1155 U.N.T.S. 331, T.S. No. 58 (1980), 8 I.L.M. 679 (1979), *entered into force* January 27, 1980, defines a reservation as a "unilateral statement, however phrased or named, made by a state, when signing, ratifying, accepting, approving or acceding to a treaty, whereby it purports to exclude or to modify the legal effect of certain provisions of the treaty in their application to that state . . .." 14 MARJORIE M. WHITEMAN, DIGEST OF INTERNATIONAL LAW § 17, at 137-38 (1970), provides basic definitions of the terms "understanding," "declaration," and "statement":

> The term "understanding" is often used to designate a statement when it is not intended to modify or limit any of the provisions of the treaty in its international operation but is intended merely to clarify or explain or to deal with some matter incidental to the operation of the treaty in a manner other than as a substantive reservation. . . .

> The terms "declaration" and "statement" are used most often when it is considered essential or desirable to give notice of certain matters of policy or principle, without an intention of derogating from the substantive rights or obligations stipulated in the treaty.

The International Court of Justice delineated an authoritative standard for the assertion of reservations to a multilateral human rights treaty:

> Object and purpose of the Convention limit both the freedom of making reservations and that of objecting to them. It follows that it is the compatibility of a reservation with the object and purpose of the Convention that must furnish the criterion for the attitude of a State in making the reservation or accession as well as for the appraisal by a State in objecting to the reservation.

Advisory Opinion on Reservations to the Genocide Convention, 1951 I.C.J. 16, 24. Article 19 of the Vienna Convention on the Law of Treaties has codified this principle in providing that "A state may, when signing, ratifying, accepting, approving or acceding to a treaty, formulate a reservation unless . . . the reservation is incompatible with the object and purpose of the treaty."

Article 20 of the Vienna Convention establishes the process for governments to make objections to reservations to treaties. Articles 20 and 21 indicate that objections by other governments to particular reservations will not preclude the entry into force of the treaty. Unless an objecting government otherwise specifies, the treaty can go into force between the two governments but the provisions to which the reservation relates do not apply as between those governments.

The use of extensive limitations to minimize the effect of a treaty on domestic practices of parties may contravene established principles of international law. The Vienna Convention on the Law of Treaties restates in Article 27 the fundamental relationship between domestic and treaty law: "A party may not invoke the provisions of its domestic law as justification for its failure to perform a treaty." Although the U.S. government could formally evade this rule by incorporating domestic law into the treaty by way of reservation or other limitations, such an attempt would violate the spirit of Article 27.

Broad general reservations are disfavored. In the *Belilos Case*, 132 Eur. Ct. H.R. (ser. A)(1988), the European Court of Human Rights held an "interpretive declaration" to the European Convention on Human Rights to constitute a reservation and then held that reservation invalid as a reservation of a "general character" not permitted by Article 64 of the European Convention. *See* Henry J. Bourguignon, *The Belilos Case: New Light on Reservations to Multilateral Treaties*, 29 VA. J. INT'L L. 347 (1989).

In 1994, the U.N. Human Rights Committee issued General Comment 24, expressing disfavor over the number of reservations adopted by countries before ratifying treaties. The Comment states that broad reservations tend to weaken the authority of international treaties in protecting rights. The Comment also says that reservations conflicting with the purpose of a treaty will not be accepted. *General Comment No. 24*, U.N. Doc. CCPR/C/21/Rev.1/Add.6 (1994).

The United States responded to General Comment 24, stating that the Comment went too far and making a number of observations on it. Letter from Conrad Harper to Francisco José Aguilar-Urbina, Chairman, U.N. Human Rights Committee (Mar. 28-29, 1995). In May 1995, a bill was passed by the U.S. Senate declaring that the General Comment threatens United States power under the Constitution, and that by denying effectiveness of reservations, the Human Rights Committee imposes "legal obligations on the United States never accepted by the United States." The Bill suggests that the Human Rights Committee "should revoke its General Comment No. 24." H.R. 1561, 104th Cong., 1st Sess. (1995). A more detailed discussion of General Comment 24 and the United States response is included in chapter 2.

NOTES AND QUESTIONS

In considering the U.S. declaration that the provisions of the Covenant on Civil and Political Rights are not self-executing, bear in mind that the courts, not the Senate, ordinarily decide when treaty provisions are self-executing. *See* Anne Bayefsky & Joan Fitzpatrick, *International Human Rights Law in United States Courts: A Comparative Perspective*, 14 MICH. J. INT'L L. 1, 42-47 (1992); Lori Fisler Damrosch, *The Role of the United States Senate Concerning "Self-Executing" and "Non Self-Executing" Treaties*, 67 CHI.-KENT L. REV. 515, 526 (1991) ("[T]he decision whether a treaty is self-executing is ordinarily made by the courts on the basis of criteria elaborated in court decisions."); David Weissbrodt, *United States Ratification of the Human Rights Covenants*, 63 MINN. L. REV. 35, 67 (1978) (criticizing a similar provision in limitations proposed by the Carter administration at the time the Covenant was submitted to the Senate for ratification as "depriv[ing] American courts of their most potent technique for contributing meaningfully to the interpretation of the Human Rights Covenants.").

Other commentators have said a U.S. limitation that declares a treaty to be non-self-executing should not be given effect when it runs counter to the object and purpose of the treaty. *See* Stefan A. Riesenfeld & Frederick M. Abbott, *The Scope of U.S. Senate Control Over the Conclusion and Operation of Treaties*, 67 CHI.-KENT L. REV. 571 (1991). Riesenfeld and Abbott observe that treaties are self-executing not by legislative declaration but by their terms. A declaration that a treaty is non self-executing when its terms indicate otherwise, then, is not binding on the courts. "Whether a treaty requires municipal implementing legislation and is intended to confer rights directly on individuals is a question of the mutual intent of the parties to the treaty, to be determined by the language of the treaty and other indicia of intent." *Id.* at 608.

Even if the courts do give effect to a declaration that a treaty is not self-executing, one could argue administrative or executive agencies are not bound to do the same. One could also assert that even if federal courts give effect to such a declaration, state courts need not do the same.

If judges do choose to give effect to the Senate's declaration that the Covenant on Civil and Political Rights is not self-executing, they must still determine what the Senate meant by the phrase. The most recent and arguably determinative comments were made at the "Full Committee/OPEN" session on May 11, 1994, of the Senate Committee on Foreign Relations. Conrad Harper, Legal Adviser of the State Department, testified as follows (regarding the proposed ratification of the Convention on the Elimination of All Forms of Racial Discrimination):

> [W]e have submitted a proposed declaration indicating that the [Racial Discrimination] Convention's provisions are not self-executing. . . . By making clear that

this convention is not self-executing, we ensure that it does not create a new or independently enforceable private cause of action in U.S. courts. We have proposed and the Senate has concurred in the same approach to previous human rights treaties, such as . . . the International Covenant on Civil and Political Rights (1992).

As was the case with the earlier treaties, existing U.S. law provides extensive protection and remedies against racial discrimination sufficient to satisfy the requirements of the present convention. In addition, federal, state and local laws already provide a comprehensive basis for challenging discriminatory statutes, regulations and other governmental actions in court, as well as certain forms of discriminatory conduct by private actors. *There is thus no need for the establishment of additional causes of action* to enforce the requirements of the convention.

If the case arises in the context of an administrative adjudication, the Senate's declaration would apparently be inapplicable. Moreover, the equivalent of a private cause of action is often available in administrative settings. In any case, providing a remedy is required by Article 2(3)(b) of the U.N. Covenant, which commands the U.S. Government to "ensure that any person claiming [an effective remedy] shall have his right thereto determined by competent judicial, administrative or legislative authorities, or by any other competent authority provided for by the legal system. . . ." Further, the word "private" is critical. A federal agency should not be precluded from seeking judicial action regarding actions of state officials that allegedly violate the Covenant—and vice versa.

---

5. Implementing Legislation: The U.S. Refugee Act of 1980

The Protocol Relating to the Status of Refugees, 606 U.N.T.S. 267, 19 U.S.T. 6223, T.I.A.S. No. 6577, *entered into force* Oct. 4, 1967, is a human rights treaty which the Supreme Court held did include a self-executing clause. In *INS v. Cardoza-Fonseca*, 480 U.S. 421 (1987), the Court discussed Article 33.1 of the Convention Relating to the Status of Refugees, which is binding on the U.S. because of its incorporation in the U.N. Protocol. The Court noted that Article 33.1 precluded the Attorney General, between 1968 when the U.S. ratified the Protocol and 1980 when Congress passed implementing legislation, from deporting people who met the definition of "refugee" set forth in the Refugee Convention. *Id.* at 429.

An important lesson of *Cardoza-Fonseca* is that when implementing legislation has been passed it is the statute, and not the treaty, that will be applied. Moreover, though the Refugee Act of 1980 was adopted to bring the U.S. into compliance with its obligations under the Protocol, in construing the Refugee Act courts have looked to the content of the Protocol as recognized internationally in 1980 rather than as recognized at the time of litigation. *Id.* at 436-41. Limiting the Refugee Act to the meaning of the Protocol in 1980 may fly in the face of the principle that courts should interpret international law not as it was understood at the time it was incorporated into U.S. law but "as it has evolved and exists among the nations of the world today." *Filartiga v. Peña-Irala*, 630 F.2d 876, 881 (2d Cir. 1980), discussed *supra* chapter 12.

NOTES AND QUESTIONS

1. Basing its decision on the Refugee Act, one court upheld a very significant cause of action. It agreed to allow aliens to try to establish at trial that their right to equal protection had been violated by the Attorney General's practice of considering nationality when making

decisions as to the withholding of deportation and asylum. To establish wrongful discrimination the refugees have to show that: (1) Congress has not authorized the Attorney General to consider nationality in applying withholding of deportation and asylum provisions, and (2) the Attorney General did, in fact, apply statutes in a manner that discriminated on the basis of nationality. The court rejected the aliens' argument that in applying Fifth Amendment protections it should be guided by international law principles. *American Baptist Churches v. Meese*, 712 F.Supp. 756, 774 n. 12 (N.D.Cal. 1989). Rather, the court looks primarily at what Congress intended in enacting the Refugee Act.

In 1991 the court accepted a stipulation between the U.S. government and plaintiff aliens that defined members of the class eligible for *de novo* asylum adjudication and also set forth standards for adjudication. *American Baptist Churches v. Thornburgh*, 760 F.Supp. 796 (N.D.Cal. 1991).

2.   The courts in *INS v. Cardoza-Fonseca*, 480 U.S. 421 (1987), and *American Baptist Churches v. Meese*, 712 F. Supp. 756 (N.D. Cal. 1989), assumed they were to construe the Refugee Act in light of the international interpretation of the Protocol in 1980. Do you think courts are compelled to do so? Do you think they should do so?

3.   In *Canas-Segovia v. INS*, 902 F.2d 717 (9th Cir. 1990), the Ninth Circuit relied principally on the UNHCR Handbook on Procedures and Criteria for Determining Refugee Status (1979) in interpreting both the U.N. Protocol Relating to the Status of Refugees, *supra*, which entered into force in 1967 and to which the U.S. acceded in 1968, and the Refugee Act of 1980. *Canas-Segovia* considered whether El Salvador's forcible conscription policy amounted to persecution under the Immigration and Nationality Act when applied to conscientious objectors. The plaintiffs, both Jehovah's Witnesses, had fled El Salvador as teens because they feared persecution under the conscription policy. Their petitions for asylum asserted that forcible conscription amounted to religious persecution. The petitions also alleged refusal to serve in the armed forces would likely cause them to be viewed as political enemies of the government. *Id.* at 720. The court held that the plaintiffs had asserted viable grounds for asylum.

The Supreme Court vacated the judgment and remanded. 112 S.Ct. 1152 (1992). On remand, the court rejected the plaintiffs' claim of religious persecution as too broad. The court also stated, however, that the plaintiffs' petition alleging an "imputed political opinion" remained an alternative ground for relief. 970 F.2d 599 (9th Cir. 1992).

4.   In *United States v. Aguilar*, 871 F.2d 1436 (9th Cir. 1989), amended August 14, 1989, a panel of the Ninth Circuit, relying on a Supreme Court footnote, pronounced that "[t]he Protocol was not intended to be self-executing." *Id.* at 1454. The panel continued: "As the Protocol is not a self-executing treaty having the force of law, it is only helpful as a guide to Congress's statutory intent in enacting the 1980 Refugee Act." The footnote on which the panel relied states merely that "the language of Article 34 was precatory and not self-executing." *INS v. Stevic*, 467 U.S. 407, 428 n. 22 (1984). Did the *Aguilar* panel properly conclude that therefore "[t]he Protocol was not intended to be self-executing"?

G.   CUSTOMARY INTERNATIONAL LAW

Article 38 of the Statute of the International Court of Justice includes within the sources of international law not only treaties, but also customary international norms and general principles of law recognized by the community of nations. Therefore, U.S. courts are bound to apply customary international law domestically, subject to restrictions created by statute and judicial precedent.

The Supreme Court has declared that customary law is "part of our law, and must be ascertained and administered by the courts of justice of appropriate jurisdiction, as often as questions of right depending upon it are duly presented for their determination." *The Paquete Habana*, 175 U.S. 677, 700 (1900). The Court limited this principle, however, to situations where no other controlling law exists, and expanded on the sources of customary law:

> Where there is no treaty, and no controlling executive or legislative act or judicial decision, resort must be had to the customs and usages of civilized nations; and, as evidence of these, to the works of jurists and commentators, who by years of labor, research and experience, have made themselves peculiarly well acquainted with the subjects of which they treat. Such works are resorted to by judicial tribunals, not for the speculations of their authors concerning what the law ought to be, but for trustworthy evidence of what the law really is.

Id. More recently the Court acknowledged the "frequently reiterated" principle that federal common law is necessarily informed by international law. *First National City Bank v. Banco Para el Comercio Exterior de Cuba*, 462 U.S. 611, 623 (1983).

1. Proving a Customary Norm

Customary international norms were discussed in chapter 12 in connection with civil suits under the Alien Tort Statute. By way of review, a court faces several issues when confronted with the argument that it should apply a customary norm. It must decide first whether the asserted rule has indeed ripened into a customary norm. Second, it must determine whether the norm is judicially enforceable.

Although treaty and customary law are accorded the same status under international law, see 1 RESTATEMENT (THIRD) OF THE FOREIGN RELATIONS LAW OF THE UNITED STATES § 111 (1987), U.S. courts have treated them differently in certain important respects. Courts have upheld norms, as they have treaty clauses, in the face of inconsistent state and local laws, and have tried to construe customary norms and federal statutes so as to give effect to both. Nonetheless, when courts have found that a customary norm conflicts with a federal statute or executive act, they generally have given effect to the legislative or executive act even when the norm arguably crystallized after the act's adoption. *See Garcia-Mir v. Meese*, 788 F.2d 1446, 1453 (11th Cir. 1986), *cert. denied sub nom. Ferrer-Mazorra v. Meese*, 479 U.S. 889 (1986); *United States v. Aguilar*, 871 F.2d 1436, 1454 (9th Cir. 1989), amended August 14, 1989; *American Baptist Churches v. Meese*, 712 F.Supp. 756, 771-73 (N.D. Cal. 1989). Commentators have criticized those decisions on the ground that judicially enforceable norms should be accorded the same status as self-executing treaty clauses, that the later-in-time rule should prevail, and that executive acts should preempt customary norms only when the President exercises foreign affairs powers, *i.e.*, as commander-in-chief or chief diplomat. *See* Frederic L. Kirgis, Jr., *Federal Statutes, Executive Orders and "Self-Executing Custom"*, 81 AM. J. INT'L L. 371, 371-75 (1987).

Recall the cases excerpted in chapter 12 analyzing whether prohibitions against torture and prolonged arbitrary detention, among other things, had ripened into customary international norms for purposes of the Alien Tort Statute. In *Forti v. Suarez-Mason*, 672 F. Supp. 1531, 1539 (N.D. Cal. 1987) (*Forti I*), the court concluded:

> There is case law finding sufficient consensus to evince a customary international human rights norm against arbitrary detention. The consensus is even clearer in the case of a state's *prolonged* arbitrary detention of its own citizens. The norm is obligatory, and is readily definable in terms of the arbitrary character of the detention.

The court therefore agreed the prohibition against arbitrary detention had ripened into a customary norm, and that the norm was judicially enforceable. It decided, however, that the prohibition of cruel, inhuman and degrading treatment was not recognized as a customary norm, and would not grant relief on that ground.

NOTES AND QUESTIONS

1.   Do you think the holding of the *Forti* court will encompass alien juveniles detained pending deportation hearings? Recall that the detention in such cases is not limited by any statutory time constraints.

2.   In *Filartiga v. Peña-Irala, supra*, excerpted in chapter 12, the court states that "courts must interpret international law as it has evolved and exists among the nations of the world today." Do you think that statement does, could, or should apply to treaty as well as customary law? Should courts construe treaty clauses to impose duties based on understandings at the time of drafting, at the time the U.S. became a party, at the time that the court is applying the treaty, or at the time that the relevant events occurred? In *Filartiga*, by relying on a treaty adopted the year before the torture and murder of Dr. Filartiga's son occurred, the court implicitly accepted the proposition that certain international instruments may be declarative of custom at the time of adoption. Does such an approach seem appropriate?

3.   The Bush administration apparently was so concerned about the *Soering* decision of the European Court of Human Rights (chapter 11, *supra*) that it proposed and the Senate accepted a reservation to Article 7 of the Covenant on Civil and Political Rights stating that the prohibition of "cruel, inhuman or degrading treatment" would provide no more protection than afforded by the Fifth, Eighth, and Fourteenth Amendments of the U.S. Constitution. Would the proposed reservation have an impact on a U.S. judge who might be considering whether the proscription of "cruel, inhuman or degrading treatment" qualifies as a customary norm?

     The court in *Xuncax v. Gramajo* held that any act "which is proscribed by the Constitution of the United States and by a cognizable principle of international law plainly falls within the rubric of 'cruel, inhuman or degrading treatment' and is actionable before this Court under § 1350." *Xuncax v. Gramajo*, 1995 WL 254818 (D. Mass. Apr. 12, 1995). Could a consideration of cruel, inhuman, or degrading treatment be useful for alien children in detention?

4.   In *Jaffe v. Snow*, a Florida court refused to recognize a Canadian judgment awarding a Canadian citizen damages for unlawful extradition. 610 So.2d 482 (Fla. Dist. Ct. App. 1992), *reh'g denied*, 621 So.2d 482 (Fla. 1993). Plaintiff was the wife of a Canadian man who had been arrested and charged with violating the Florida Uniform Land Sales Practices Law. He posted bond, then went to Canada and failed to return for his trial. The prosecutor charged Jaffe with failure to appear. The prosecutor also sought to extradite Jaffe from Canada, but the crimes for which he was charged are not among the extraditable offenses listed in the U.S.-Canada treaty. *Id.* at 483.

     Jaffe's bondsman hired professional bail recovery agents to apprehend and return him to Florida. On return he was convicted for failure to appear and for unlawful land sales practice. The second conviction was later reversed. While on parole from his sentence for failure to appear, Jaffe again posted bond, this time to secure his return for trial on other charges. He again fled and did not return to Florida to stand trial. *Id.* at 484.

     Upon his return to Canada, Jaffe and his wife sued in Canadian court for tortious abduction. The Canadian court decided in Mrs. Jaffe's favor and awarded her damages, which judgment she sought to enforce in Florida. *Id.* The Florida court refused, citing the "fugitive from justice" doctrine. *Id.* at 485. The court stated, "Claimant has taken advantage of the rights accorded litigants—but wants to avoid the associated duties. He is trying to use this Court's processes as a sword while attempting to simultaneously shield himself from the same type of judicial process. This type of conduct is, simply stated, unfair." *Id.* at 486. The court concluded, "Although his eventual forceful return by [defendant] was wrongful in Canada's eyes, he, too was at fault for not honoring his bond. Two wrongs do not make a right, and neither wrongdoer should profit." *Id.* at 487.

5.   For an interesting discussion of the Hong Kong practice of indefinitely detaining Vietnamese asylum seekers to deter others from attempting to flee Vietnam (a government policy ironically called "humane deterrence"), see Eve B. Burton & David B. Goldstein, *Vietnamese Women and Children Refugees in Hong Kong: An Argument Against Arbitrary Detention*, 4 DUKE J. COMP. & INT'L L. 71 (1993). The authors argue that Hong Kong's policy contravenes both treaty law and customary norms, in part because Hong Kong does not conduct individualized hearings before continuing the detention. In addition, there is no effective mechanism to challenge the legality of the detention.

---

2.   General Principles of Law Recognized by the Community of Nations

In addition to treaties and customary norms, a third source of international law identified by Article 38(1) of the Statute of the International Court of Justice is "general principles of law recognized by civilized nations" (also called the "community of nations" in contemporary writings). *See, e.g.*, Covenant on Civil and Political Rights, Art. 15; *see also* Sandra Coliver & Frank Newman, *Using International Human Rights Law to Influence United States Foreign Population Policy: Resort to Courts or Congress?*, 20 N.Y.U. J. INT'L. L. & POL. 53, 65 (1987). Courts in the U.S. apparently have not addressed the status of general principles in U.S. law. A compelling argument may be made that general principles, like practice, are part of customary law. *See* RICHARD B. LILLICH & FRANK C. NEWMAN, INTERNATIONAL HUMAN RIGHTS: PROBLEMS OF LAW AND POLICY 54 (1979).

General principles may be "drawn from private law principles common to the world's major legal systems and have been invoked primarily to develop international law interstitially, to resolve issues not adequately addressed by treaty or practice." Coliver & Newman, *supra*, at 65. General principles may also be derived from the resolutions, decisions, and other instruments of intergovernmental organizations. Some commentators view general principles "as derived from natural law: they exist regardless of whether or not they are followed in fact by states." LILLICH & NEWMAN, *supra* at 54; *see also* Theodor C. van Boven, *Survey of the Positive International Law of Human Rights, in* 1 THE INTERNATIONAL DIMENSIONS OF HUMAN RIGHTS 107 (Karel Vasak, ed. 1982).

U.S. courts have neither accepted nor rejected the view that general principles are part of customary law. A few have, however, discussed general principles in the course of discussing customary law. *See, e.g., United States v. Arlington, Va.*, 702 F.2d 485, 487-88 (4th Cir. 1983) (foreign government-owned property used for public non-commercial purposes is exempt from local real estate taxation); *Jeanneret v. Vichey*, 693 F.2d 259 (2d Cir. 1982) (illegal export of an art object does not render a good-faith importer liable for reduction in value of object); *Von Dardel v. U.S.S.R.*, 623 F. Supp. 246 (D.D.C. 1985) (unlawful imprisonment of a foreign diplomat), *vacated on other grounds*, 736 F.Supp. 1 (D.D.C. 1990); *Chiriboga v. International Bank for Reconstruction & Dev.*, 616 F. Supp. 963 (D.D.C. 1985) (international organizations are immune from suits by employees arising out of the employment relationship).

3.   Peremptory Norms

Vienna Convention on the Law of Treaties, 115 U.N.T.S. 331, T.S. No. 58 (1980), 8 I.L.M. 679 (1979), *entered into force* January 27, 1980:

Article 53

Treaties conflicting with a peremptory norm
of general international law (jus cogens)

A treaty is void if, at the time of its conclusion, it conflicts with a peremptory norm of general international law. For the purposes of the present Convention, a peremptory norm of general international law is a norm accepted and recognized by the international community of States as a whole as a norm from which no derogation is permitted and which can be modified only by a subsequent norm of general international law having the same character.

Article 64

Emergence of a new peremptory norm
of general international law (jus cogens)

If a new peremptory norm of general international law emerges, any existing treaty which is in conflict with that norm becomes void and terminates.

1 Restatement (Third) of the Foreign Relations Law of the United States §102, reporter's note 6 (1987):

> . . . The Vienna Convention requires that the norm (and its peremptory character) must be "accepted and recognized by the international community of States as a whole" . . ., which apparently means by "a very large majority" of states, even if over dissent by "a very small number" of states. . . .
>
> Although the concept of *jus cogens* is accepted, its content is not agreed. There is general agreement that the principles of the UN Charter prohibiting the use of force are *jus cogens*. . . . It has been suggested that norms that create "international crimes" and obligate all states to proceed against violations are also peremptory. . . . This might include rules prohibiting genocide, slave-trading and slavery, *apartheid* and other gross violations of human rights, and perhaps attacks on diplomats. . . .

H.   USING INTERNATIONAL LAW TO GUIDE INTERPRETATION OF U.S. LAW

1.   Prison Conditions

Lareau v. Manson, 507 F. Supp. 1177 (D. Conn. 1980):

JOSE\CABRANES, Judge.

The plaintiffs . . . are the class of inmates at the Hartford Community Correctional Center ("HCCC"), including both persons being detained pending trials on criminal charges and convicted inmates serving sentences of imprisonment. They challenge a number of the conditions of their confinement—principally, the overcrowding of the HCCC, but also other conditions, including allegedly inadequate health care, sanitation, food and heating—on constitutional grounds. . . .

Summary of Facts . . .

The HCCC was designed to hold 390 inmates—one in each cell. . . . Since January 7, 1980, the institution has had no fewer than 500 inmates on any night; the number of inmates incarcerated there—which fluctuates from day to day—was expected to reach the range of 580 to 630 to December 1980. . . .

In an effort to accommodate the increasing number of inmates assigned to the HCCC, the defendants have converted 120 cells which were designed for one inmate into "double-bunked" cells. . . . On occasion, the defendants have assigned two inmates to one cell in which there is no double bunk-bed; in such a cell, one inmate must sleep on a mattress on the floor, placed between the desk (at one end of the cell) and the toilet (at the other). Inmates so confined have no room at all to move about their cell. . . .

The overcrowding at the HCCC is manifested not only in its housing conditions, but in other aspects of life at the institution. Particularly noteworthy is the overcrowding of the "dayrooms.". . . There are regularly 15 to 20 inmates (and occasionally as many as 24) in the "dayrooms"; while eating meals, inmates have had to sit on the floor, a radiator or even the single toilet in the "dayroom." The crowding of the "dayrooms" increases the level of tensions, and the incidence of fighting, among inmates at the HCCC. More generally, the overcrowded conditions at the HCCC have had an adverse psychological impact—above and beyond that which is inevitably caused by incarceration—on the inmates, particularly the young inmates who make up much of the facility's population. . . .

Finally, overcrowding has jeopardized security at the HCCC. Tensions and fights among inmates have increased; correctional officers, each of whom is responsible for 48 to 60 inmates, have found it more difficult to police the institution. . . .

THE CONSTITUTIONAL ISSUES

A. *Bell v. Wolfish*

The starting point for the court's analysis of the plaintiffs' claims must be the decision of the Supreme Court in *Bell v. Wolfish*, 441 U.S. 520 [1979] . . . .

Wolfish was a class action challenging the conditions of confinement at . . . "a federally operated short-term custodial facility in New York City designed primarily to house pretrial detainees." . . .

. . . In the absence of a claim that a more specific constitutional right has been infringed—*i.e.*, where the detainee alleges only that he has been denied "the protection against deprivation of liberty without due process of law"—the Court [in *Wolfish*] held that "the proper inquiry is whether [the] conditions [of detention] amount to punishment of the detainee." The rationale for this standard, the Court noted, was that "under the Due Process Clause, a detainee may not be punished prior to an adjudication of guilt in accordance with due process of law."

. . . The Court gave the following guidance to lower courts faced with the task of distinguishing impermissible "punishment" from constitutionally acceptable "regulatory restraints":

A court must decide whether the disability is imposed for the purpose of punishment or whether it is but an incident of some other legitimate governmental purpose. Absent a showing of an expressed intent to punish on the part of detention facility officials, that determination generally will turn on "whether an alternative purpose to which [the restriction] may rationally be connected is assignable for it, and whether it appears excessive in relation to the alternative purpose assigned [to it]." Thus, if a particular condition or restriction of pretrial detention is reasonably related to a legitimate governmental objective, it does not, without more, amount to "punishment." . . .

In *Wolfish*, the Court . . . noted that the rights of prisoners are "subject to restrictions and limitations" imposed not only by the fact that they are confined, but also by "the legitimate goals and policies of the penal institution." [In addition], "maintaining institutional security and preserving internal order and discipline are essential goals that may require limitation or retraction of the retained constitutional rights of convicted prisoners and pretrial detainees." Finally, prison officials "should be accorded wide-ranging deference in the adoption and execution of policies and practices that in their judgment are needed to preserve internal order and discipline and to maintain institutional security." . . .

B.   *The Application of Bell v. Wolfish to Conditions at the HCCC*

Under *Bell v. Wolfish*, the court must determine: (1) whether the overcrowded living conditions of pretrial detainees at the HCCC constitute impermissible "punishment," as defined in *Wolfish*, and thus violate the Due Process Clause; (2) whether the overcrowded conditions in which "double-bunked" convicted prisoners live violate a specific constitutional provision—here, the prohibition of cruel and unusual punishment in the Eighth Amendment; and (3) whether conditions to which both pretrial detainees and convicted inmates are subjected, without regard to their status, violate the due process standard of *Wolfish*.

(1)   *Overcrowding of Pretrial Detainees* . . .

[Comparing overcrowding at HCCC to the overcrowding present in the facility in *Wolfish*, the court concluded conditions at HCCC imposed a greater hardship on detainees than in *Wolfish*. The court concluded the purpose of overcrowding was punishment, which cannot constitutionally be inflicted upon detainees, rather than any legitimate penological purpose.]

. . . Many of the pretrial detainees in the plaintiff class are forced to live in cells and dormitory accommodations which leave them with approximately one-half as much space as is described, as minimally acceptable, by experts (including administrators of correctional facilities) concerned with the architecture of jails and prisons and the establishment of generally recognized correctional standards.[12]. . .

(2)   *Overcrowding of Sentenced Inmates*

A different constitutional standard applies to the defendants' treatment of sen-

---

[12] As noted above, a "double-bunked" inmate at the HCCC has approximately 30 to 32½ square feet of space (including space occupied by fixtures and furniture), while an inmate assigned to the "fishtank" has less than 23 square feet of space (calculated the same way, on the assumption of 9 inmates in the "fishtank"). By way of contrast the plaintiffs have called the court's attention to the following standards:

>   (a)   The United Nations Standard Minimum Rules for the Treatment of Prisoners, adopted by the First United Nations Congress on the Prevention of Crime and Treatment of Offenders in 1955, and approved by the Economic and Social Council of the United Nations by its Resolutions 663C (LLIV) on July 31, 1957 and 2076 (LXII) on May 13, 1977. The Standard Minimum Rules—which were explicitly adopted as the "preamble to the Administrative Directives of the Connecticut Department of Correction" by the Connecticut Department of Correction on November 8, 1974, . . .—prohibit double-bunking. In adopting the Standard Minimum Rules, the Department acted in accordance with Conn. Gen. Stat. §18-81, which provides that the Commissioner of Correction "shall establish rules for the administrative practices . . . of [state correctional] institutions and facilities *in accordance with recognized correctional standards*." (emphasis supplied).

tenced inmates. For sentenced inmates the question posed . . . is whether [over-crowded] conditions contravene the Eighth Amendment's prohibition of "cruel and unusual punishment." . . .

. . . The "evolving standards of decency" with which the overcrowding of inmates at the HCCC are incompatible include the Standard Minimum Rules for the Treatment of Prisoners, which have been adopted by the United Nations Economic and Social Council (the members of which include some nations whose standards of decency and human rights are far less stringent than our own) and thus form part of the body of international human rights principles establishing standards for decent and humane conduct by all nations.[13]. . .

Article 9(1) of the Standard Minimum Rules provides that "each prisoner shall occupy by night a cell or room by himself." . . . Article 86 of the Standard Minimum Rules provides that pretrial detainees "shall sleep singly in separate rooms, with the reservation of different local custom in respect of the climate." The Department made no observation that, as of 1974, it was not in compliance with this rule. . . .

Apart from Connecticut's administrative adoption of the United Nations Standard Minimum Rules for the Treatment of Prisoners, those standards may be significant as expressions of the obligations to the international community of the member states of the United Nations, cf. Filartiga v. Peña-Irala, 630 F.2d 875, 883 (2d Cir. 1980), and as part of the body of international law (including customary international law) concerning human rights which has been built upon the foundation of the United Nations Charter. . . . It is well established that customary international law is part of the law of the United States. . . . The United Nations Charter is, of course, a treaty ratified by the United States. Although not self-executing, the Charter's provisions on human rights are evidence of principles of customary international law recognized as part of the law of the United States. . . . [The court then summarized the provisions of Articles 55, and 56. See supra Part G.] . . . Article 62(2) of the Charter authorizes the Economic and Social Council of the United Nations to "make recommendations for the purpose of promoting respect for, and observance of, human rights and fundamental freedoms for all."

In adopting the Standard Minimum Rules for the Treatment of Prisoners, the Economic and Social Council acted in furtherance of this mandate to set international standards promoting the observance of human rights. . . .

The adoption of the Standard Minimum Rules by the First United Nations Congress on the Prevention of Crime and Treatment of Offenders and its subsequent approval by the Economic and Social Council does not necessarily render them applicable here. However, these actions constitute an authoritative international statement of basic norms of human dignity and of certain practices which are repugnant to the conscience of mankind. The standards embodied in this statement are relevant to the "canons of decency and fairness which express the notions of justice" embodied in the Due Process Clause. . . . The due process guarantees in our Constitution are based on a concept which "is not final and fixed," but evolves on the basis of judgments "reconciling the needs both of continuity and of change in a progressive society." . . . Cf. . . . Rudolph v. Alabama, 375 U.S. 889, 890 & n.1, . . . (1963) (Goldberg, J., dissenting from denial of certiorari) (citing Economic and Social Council resolution as relevant to question whether Eighth Amendment has been violated). In this regard, it is significant that federal courts—including the Supreme Court and the Court of Appeals for the Second Circuit—have invoked the Standard Minimum Rules for guidance in particular cases. See, e.g., Estelle v. Gamble, 429 U.S. [97,] 103-104 & n.8 . . . (citing the Standard Minimum Rules as evidence of "contemporary standards of decency" for purposes of the Eighth Amendment); Detainees of Brooklyn House of Detention for Men v. Malcolm, 520 F.2d 392, 396 (2d Cir. 1975) (referring to the single cell provision of the Standard Minimum Rules).

[13] . . . The relevance of international norms such as the Standard Minimum Rules to the determination of the "evolving standards of decency" which are basic to our Eighth Amendment jurisprudence is underscored by Article 7 of the International Covenant on Civil and Political Rights, which prohibits "cruel, inhuman or degrading treatment or punishment" of individuals. The Covenant (which, in Article 7, parallels the Eighth Amendment to the United States Constitution) is an international treaty; although it has not been ratified by the United States Senate [Ed: The treaty was ratified in 1992.], it is not necessarily without significance for this country (which signed it on October 5, 1977), since "multilateral agreements designed for adherence by states generally . . . may come to be law for non-parties by virtue of state practice and opinio juris resulting in customary law." Comment f to Restatement of the Foreign Relations Law of the United States (Revised) § 102 (Tent. Draft No. 1, 1980). Similarly, Article 5 of the Universal Declaration of Human Rights prohibits "cruel, inhuman or degrading treatment or punishment." . . .

The defendants themselves have embraced these international standards. In 1974, the defendants adopted the Standard Minimum Rules as the preamble to the Administrative Directives of the Connecticut Department of Correction. This action was apparently taken pursuant to Commissioner Manson's statutory mandate to promulgate "rules for administrative practices . . . *in accordance with recognized correctional standards.*" Conn. Gen. Stat. §18-81 (emphasis added). . . .

. . . In these circumstances, the court cannot avoid holding that the defendants have violated their duty under the Eighth Amendment to provide adequate housing for convicted inmates at the HCCC. . . .

(3) *Other Conditions of Confinement.* . .

There is, however, one practice of the defendants which, standing alone, violates the Due Process Clause of the Constitution. The defendants have failed adequately to screen newly arrived inmates in order to identify and segregate from other inmates persons carrying communicable diseases. . . .

NOTES AND QUESTIONS

1. The court of appeals affirmed the trial court's findings of liability but remanded the case for reconsideration of the remedy. It stated that duration of confinement must also be considered under some of the challenged conditions, and remanded because the trial court did not allow for that item in its remedy. The court also vacated the imposition of an absolute population-ceiling as not feasible. *Lareau v. Manson*, 651 F.2d 96 (2nd Cir. 1981).

2. In *Sterling v. Cupp*, 625 P.2d 123, 130-32 (1981), the court discussed international law, not cited by the parties, in construing the Oregon Constitution's guarantee against "unnecessary rigor" to prohibit full patdowns of male prisoners by female guards.

3. In *Conservatorship of Hofferber*, 616 P.2d 836, 844 (1980), the court cited international law in support of the conclusion that the state has compelling interests in preventing inhumane treatment of the mentally disturbed.

4. Physicians for Human Rights, an organization of health professionals, has investigated restraint techniques used at the Onondaga County Public Safety Building in New York. PHYSICIANS FOR HUMAN RIGHTS, CRUEL AND INHUMAN TREATMENT: THE USE OF FOUR-POINT RESTRAINT IN THE ONONDAGA COUNTY PUBLIC SAFETY BUILDING SYRACUSE, NEW YORK (May, 1993). Medical evidence suggests that use of four-point restraints violates international standards, because it constitutes punishment and can have long-lasting psychological and physical effects. *Id.* at 7.

5. Consider the following remarks of Professor Philip Frickey regarding the use of international norms in cases involving indigenous peoples:

> Even if the courts will not look to those rights to inform every question of domestic law involving human rights, such as free speech or inhumane punishment, in federal Indian law cases the courts are compelled to consider international law. The reason is simple: the backdrop of international law provides the only satisfactory basis for sorting out the existence of an inherent federal power over Indian affairs. Accordingly, the backdrop of international law should likewise be relevant in considering limitations upon that power. The difference between my theory and the broader theory by which international norms may inform domestic law is that in my theory, international law has a direct—indeed, essential—linkage to the area of domestic law in question.
>
> Under this approach, international norms about the treatment of indigenous persons would not be directly enforceable in American courts, but instead would provide a relevant and worthwhile backdrop against which to consider constitutional

and quasi-constitutional claims. Thus, an international norm that does not link up with a constitutional provision limiting governmental power would presumably have less persuasive force than one that is closely connected to a constitutional limitation. Moreover, even those norms that have a close connection to constitutional limitations would not compel a constitutional interpretation equivalent to the international norm. Instead, the international norm should be treated as roughly equivalent to domestic norms that inform constitutional adjudication.

Philip P. Frickey, *Domesticating Federal Indian Law* 37-38 (1996) (manuscript, on file with the author) (footnotes and citations omitted).

---

2. U.S. Supreme Court Opinions

The U.S. Supreme Court has issued two important rulings concerning the execution of juveniles, an area in which U.S. standards are less protective than international standards. In *Thompson v. Oklahoma*, 487 U.S. 815, 838, (1988), a four-judge plurality ruled that the death sentence for an offender who was 15 at the time of the crime constituted cruel and unusual punishment proscribed by the Eighth Amendment. In the opinion Justice Stevens cited international authorities in reasoning that the death penalty would "offend civilized standards of decency." *Id.* at 830-31. He noted that Western European countries, as well as the Soviet Union, prohibit juvenile executions. *Id.* at 831. In addition he cited three treaties ratified or signed by the U.S. that explicitly prohibit juvenile death penalties: the Covenant on Civil and Political Rights, the American Convention on Human Rights, and the Geneva Convention Relative to the Protection of Civilian Persons in Time of War. *Id.* at 831 n.34.

Justice O'Connor, concurring, also referred to U.S. ratification of the Fourth Geneva Convention. *Id.* at 851. In providing the fifth vote, however, she chose not to decide the broad constitutional issue but concluded that a 15 year-old could not be executed pursuant to a statute that did not expressly specify a minimum execution age of 15 years or less. *Id.* at 857-58. Justice Scalia argued in dissent that international standards should never be imposed via the U.S. Constitution. *Id.* at 868-69 n.4.

One year after *Thompson*, the Supreme Court concluded that the death penalty for a crime committed at 16 or 17 years of age does not constitute cruel and unusual punishment. *Stanford v. Kentucky*, 492 U.S. 361, 380 (1989). Writing for the five-judge majority, Justice Scalia rejected the relevance of international law and practices of other countries as a guide to construing the Eighth Amendment. In a footnote, Scalia noted:

> We emphasize that it is *American* conceptions of decency that are dispositive, rejecting the contention of petitioners and their various *amici* (accepted by the dissent . . .) that the sentencing practices of other countries are relevant. While "the practices of other nations, particularly other democracies, can be relevant to determining whether a practice uniform among our people is not merely an historical accident but rather so 'implicit in the concept of ordered liberty' that it occupies a place not merely in our mores, but, text permitting, in our Constitution as well," they cannot serve to establish the first Eighth Amendment prerequisite, that the practice is accepted among our people.

Id. at 369 n. 1 (citations omitted).

In a dissent Justice Brennan, joined by Justices Marshall, Blackmun, and Stevens, disagreed and outlined the international consensus:

> Our cases recognize that objective indicators of contemporary standards of decency in the form of legislation in other countries is also of relevance to Eighth Amendment analysis. Many countries of course—over 50, including nearly all in Western Europe—have formally abolished the death penalty, or have limited its use to exceptional crimes such as treason. Twenty-seven others do not in practice impose the penalty. Of the nations that retain capital punishment, a majority—65—prohibit the execution of juveniles. Sixty-one countries retain capital punishment and have no statutory provision exempting juveniles, though some of these nations are ratifiers of international treaties that do prohibit the execution of juveniles. Since 1979, Amnesty International has recorded only eight executions of offenders under 18 throughout the world, three of these in the United States. The other five executions were carried out in Pakistan, Bangladesh, Rwanda, and Barbados. In addition to national laws, three leading human rights treaties ratified or signed by the United States explicitly prohibit juvenile death penalties. Within the world community, the imposition of the death penalty for juvenile crimes appears to be overwhelmingly disapproved.

Id. at 389 (citations omitted).

NOTES AND QUESTIONS

1.   The U.S. is one of the few countries that still execute juveniles. A March 1995 Human Rights Watch report noted that the U.S. had executed at least nine juvenile offenders between 1976 and 1993, four of those during the last half of 1993. HUMAN RIGHTS WATCH CHILDREN'S RIGHTS PROJECT, UNITED STATES: A WORLD LEADER IN EXECUTING JUVENILES 2 (Mar. 1995). "In addition, more juvenile offenders sit on death row in the United States than in any other country." U.N. reports show that eight other countries executed juvenile offenders between 1978 and 1993, including: Bangladesh (1, though the minimum age was later raised to 18); Barbados (1); Iran (number unknown); Iraq (number unknown but at least 13 were executed during November and December 1987); Nigeria (1); Pakistan (4); Saudi Arabia (1), and Yemen (1). *Id.* Contrastingly, "the execution of minors is prohibited by treaty or legislation" in 112 countries. *Id.*

2.   For further discussion see Joan Fitzpatrick & Alice Miller, *International Standards on the Death Penalty: Shifting Discourse*, 19 BROOK. J. INT'L LAW 273 (1993).

---

3.   Protesting International Crimes

Declaration of Frank C. Newman in Support of Defendants, filed June 12, 1989, in *People v. Wylie, et al.*, Santa Clara Municipal Court, California, No. E8849052 (some citations omitted):

[Defendants were charged with trespass for participating in a nonviolent protest at a Lockheed Missile and Space Company facility. The protestors opposed Lockheed's role in the production of U.S. nuclear weapons.]
   . . . [I]n their brief, defendants argue the reasonableness of their belief that current U.S. nuclear-weapons policy is unlawful under international law. This declaration augments that brief in two ways: 1) it highlights the Nuremberg prohibition of crimes against humanity, and 2) it sets forth judicially manageable standards

for lawful protest of threatened crimes against humanity proscribed by international law. . . .

In construing California statutory and constitutional law, international human rights law provides an accepted source of guidance. Relevant provisions are found in the Universal Declaration of Human Rights. That Declaration is now widely accepted as an authoritative interpretation of the human rights clauses of the United Nations Charter, a treaty to which the United States is a party. In addition the Universal Declaration evidences customary international law.

Preambular paragraph three of the Universal Declaration states:

> [I]t is essential, if man is not to be compelled to have recourse, as a last resort, to rebellion against tyranny and oppression, that human rights should be protected by the rule of law. . . .

Preambular paragraph eight states:

> [E]very individual and every organ of society . . . shall strive by teaching and education to promote respect for these rights and freedoms and by progressive measures, national and international, to secure their universal and effective recognition and observance, both among the peoples of Member States themselves and among the people of territories under their jurisdiction.

Art. 28 states:

> Everyone is entitled to a social and international order in which the rights and freedoms set forth in this Declaration can be full realized.

Those provisions support a right of protest under the circumstances of this case; namely, peaceful protest of threatened crimes against humanity. Destruction of civilian populations is inconsistent with the principle that "human rights should be protected by the rule of law. . . ." Peaceful protest of threatened destruction vindicates the rule of law while avoiding the extreme step of "recourse . . . to rebellion against tyranny and oppression." Peaceful protest fulfills also the responsibility to strive for the "recognition and observance" of human rights and promotes the attainment of a "social and international order in which rights and freedoms set forth in this Declaration can be fully realized."

The Nuremberg rules supply an additional source of guidance . . . to interpret California law in cases involving conduct reasonably believed necessary to help prevent Nuremberg offenses. Those rules reaffirm the principle of individual responsibility, that individuals—not only governments—are obliged to comply with international law. *See, e.g., U.S. v. Goering*, 6 F.R.D. 69, 110 (1946) ("individuals have international duties which transcend the national obligations of obedience").

It would go too far at present to say that law *requires* individuals to protest threatened crimes against humanity. But such protest—an assumption of individual responsibility to help promote compliance with law—is certainly consistent with Nuremberg rules.

Those rules also reaffirm that national and state laws are subordinate to the proscriptions of international law. Thus "inhumane acts committed against any civilian population" are crimes against humanity "whether or not in violation of domestic law of the country where perpetrated." [Nuremberg Charter, Art. 6(c), 58 Stat. at 1547.] That suggests a balancing of the relative evils of any threatened violation of international law and the alleged violation of state law (here, trespass).

. . .

NOTES AND QUESTIONS

1.   In *State of Vermont v. McCann*, No. 2857-7-86CnCr (D. Ct. Vt., Chittenden Cir. 1987), the defendant alleged his nonviolent obstruction of traffic at a General Electric plant was aimed at preventing the use of a rapid-fire cannon in random attacks against civilian populations in El Salvador. The court allowed him to present evidence at trial that his actions were privileged under international law as developed by Nuremberg tribunals. He cited *In Re Yamashita*, 327 U.S. 1, 16 (1945), for the proposition that individuals may be required to take appropriate measures to prevent international crimes.

2.   In *State of Hawaii v. Marley*, 500 P.2d 1095 (Hawaii 1973), nonviolent protesters had entered the premises of Honeywell Corporation to publicize what they believed to be the war crimes of Honeywell in supplying weapons for the Vietnam War. The trial court, upheld by the Hawaii Supreme Court, instructed the jury as follows:

> The United States has entered into treaties which prohibit as war crimes the use of weapons which cause unnecessary and indiscriminate injuries or death to non-combatant civilians, whether done by persons singly or in cooperation with others. . . . [A]n individual citizen or citizens may use reasonable means to prevent, or seek the prevention of, the commission of a crime only if such crime is being committed, or is about to be committed in such citizen or citizens' presence.

Id. at 1105-06, 1108. The jury convicted despite the instruction; on appeal, defendants argued against the "presence" requirement, but lost.

3.   *See also United States v. Montgomery*, 772 F.2d 733 (11th Cir. 1985); *United States v. May*, 622 F.2d 1000 (9th Cir. 1980); FRANCIS A. BOYLE, DEFENDING CIVIL RESISTANCE UNDER INTERNATIONAL LAW (1988).

---

4.   Rights of Aliens

Several courts of appeal have ruled on the constitutionality of the U.S. policy of detaining certain Marielito Cubans who came to the U.S. via the so-called Freedom Flotilla in the early 1980s. Under this policy, refugees who admitted to having been convicted of certain crimes in Cuba were automatically detained in federal penitentiaries rather than being paroled into the U.S.

In *Rodriquez-Fernandez v. Wilkinson*, 654 F.2d 1382 (10th Cir. 1981), the court interpreted the Due Process clause to prohibit prolonged arbitrary detention. In doing so, the court noted

> [I]n upholding the plenary power of Congress over exclusion and deportation of aliens, the Supreme Court has sought support in international law principles. It seems proper then to consider international law principles for notions of fairness as to propriety of holding aliens in detention. No principle of international law is more fundamental than the concept that human beings should be free from arbitrary imprisonment. *See* Universal Declaration of Human Rights, Arts. 3 and 9, U.N. Doc. A/801 (1948); The American Convention on Human Rights, Part I, ch. II, Art. 7, 77 Dept. of State Bull. 28 (July 4, 1977).

Id. at 1388 (citation omitted). Later the court concluded

> [W]e hold that detention is permissible during proceedings to determine eligibility to enter and, thereafter, during a reasonable period of negotiations for their return to the country of origin or to the transporter that brought them here. After such a time, upon application of the incarcerated alien willing to risk the possible alternatives to continued detention, the alien would be entitled to release. This construction is

consistent with accepted international law principles that individuals are entitled to be free of arbitrary imprisonment. . . .

Id. at 1389-90.

The U.S. Court of Appeals for the Eleventh Circuit disagreed. In *Fernandez-Roque v. Smith*, 734 F.2d 576, 582 (11th Cir. 1984), the court, without referencing *Rodriquez-Fernandez* or international standards, held that aliens have no constitutional right to be paroled into the U.S. *See also Garcia-Mir v. Meese*, 781 F.2d 1450 (11th Cir. 1986).

The Eleventh Circuit also rejected international standards as a source for interpreting the U.S. Constitution in *Jean v. Nelson*, 727 F.2d 957 (11th Cir. 1984), *modified* on other grounds 472 U.S. 846 (1985). In *Jean v. Nelson*, Haitian asylum seekers challenged the INS policy of "detaining aliens who could not establish a prima facie claim of admission to this country, rather than paroling them pending a hearing on their petitions." *Id.* at 961. In a footnote the court noted there was insufficient evidence to support the argument that the detention of uninvited aliens contravenes customary international law. *Id.* at 964 n. 4. The court then specifically rejected the reasoning of the Tenth Circuit in *Rodriquez-Fernandez*, partly because of the need for the flexibility needed by the political branches in immigration matters. *Id.* at 974-75. *See also Garcia-Mir v. Meese*, 788 F.2d 1446 (11th Cir. 1986), cert denied sub. nom.; *Ferrer-Mazorra v. Meese*, 479 U.S. 889 (1986); *Alvarez-Mendez v. Stock*, 941 F.2d 956 (9th Cir. 1991), cert. denied 113 S.Ct. 127 (1992); *Barrera-Echavarria v. Rison*, 44 F.3d 1441 (9th Cir. 1995).

NOTES AND QUESTIONS

1. In *Cerillo-Perez v. INS*, 809 F.2d 1419, 1423 (9th Cir. 1987), the court cited international law in support of its holding that the immigration judge erred in failing to consider the impact of the deportation of a Mexican couple on their U.S. citizen children.

2. *See* the discussion of *INS v. Cardoza-Fonseca*, 480 U.S. 421 (1986), *supra* Part F at 597, for a decision in which the Supreme Court interpreted language in a federal statute by reference to an international treaty.

---

5. Other Rights

In *Lipscomb v. Simmons*, 884 F.2d 1242 (9th Cir. 1989) (per curiam) the court discussed international law, even though not cited by the parties, in concluding that the right to live with one's family is fundamental and, accordingly, that Oregon violated due process rights by denying foster care funding to children who live with close relatives.

In *Santa Barbara v. Adamson*, 610 P.2d 436, 439 (1980), an ordinance prohibiting unrelated persons from living together in a family-residence zone violated the right of privacy under the California Constitution. The court cited international law in support of its conclusion that the right of privacy exists in one's home as well as within the family. *Cf., People v. Privatera*, 591 P.2d 919, 946 (1980) (Newman, J. dissenting).

In *Boehm v. Superior Court*, 223 Cal. Rptr. 716 (1986), the court cited international law in concluding that a county was required to include clothing, transportation, and medical care when dispensing minimum subsistence grants.

Further, in *Pauley v. Kelly*, 255 S.E.2d 859 (W. Va. 1979), the West Virginia Supreme Court cited the Universal Declaration of Human Rights in holding education to be a fundamental right under the West Virginia Constitution. Other state courts, however, have found that education is not a fundamental right. These courts relied on a Supreme Court case holding education is not a fundamental right protected by the Constitution, *San Antonio Ind. School Dist. v. Rodriguez*, 411 U.S. 1 (1973), rather than international standards. *See* Connie de la Vega, *The Right to Equal Education: Merely a Guiding Principle or Customary International Legal Right*, 11 HARV. BLACKLETTER J. 37, 55 (1994).

I. INCORPORATING INTERNATIONAL LAW IN U.S. STATUTES

Courts apparently have been most receptive to arguments that they should apply international law when a reference to that law appears in a relevant statute or regulation or, at a minimum, in the legislative history. In the following excerpt the authors suggest, illustratively, how reference to international law in the Foreign Assistance Act would strengthen arguments that the Administration may not cut off funds to foreign, nongovernmental family-planning agencies solely on the ground that they provide abortion information or use non-U.S. funds to perform abortions.

Sandra Coliver & Frank Newman, *Using International Human Rights Law to Influence United States Foreign Population Policy: Resort to Courts or Congress?*, 20 N.Y.U. J. INT'L L. & POL. 53, 85-90 (1987) (footnotes omitted): . . .

DIRECT INCORPORATION OF INTERNATIONAL LAW INTO U.S. LEGISLATION

International law can be used most effectively to promote U.S. policies consistent with that law when it is expressly incorporated into U.S. law. Thus a law that allows aliens to sue for torts "in violation of the law of nations" sustained a judgment by two Paraguayans against a Paraguayan official for the torture and killing of a family member in Paraguay. [*See Filartiga v. Peña-Irala*, chapter 12.] A clause of the Immigration and Nationality Act (INA) that requires consideration of "the provisions of this chapter or any other law or treaty" in deportation decisions provided the basis for a sanctuary worker's belief that a Salvadoran was lawfully in the United States even though he had entered without papers. [*United States v. Merkt*, 764 F.2d 266 (5th Cir. 1985).] Because the definition of refugee that Congress adopted in the Refugee Act of 1980 "is virtually identical" to the one in the U.N. Protocol Relating to the Status of Refugees, the Supreme Court interpreted the clause in accord with that treaty. [*See INS v. Cardoza-Fonseca*, discussed *supra* Part *F* at 597.] Adoption by the Connecticut Department of Correction of the U.N. Standard Minimum Rules for the Treatment of Prisoners as the preamble to its "Administrative Directives" persuaded a federal court to accord precedence to those rules in adjudicating inmates' claims of substandard prison conditions. [*See Lareau v. Mason, supra* Part *H* at 602.]

Incorporation in foreign assistance and policy legislation of international human rights language has had a notable impact on statutory programs and has nurtured U.S. attention to human rights generally. For example, the Foreign Assistance Act of

1961, [22 U.S.C. §2151,] precludes the provision of economic and security assistance, except under specified circumstances, "to any country the government of which engages in a consistent pattern of gross violations of internationally recognized human rights." Section 502B declares that "a principal goal of the foreign policy of the United States shall be to promote the increased observance of internationally recognized human rights by all countries, in accordance with its obligations as set forth in the Charter of the United Nations." To assist Congress in evaluating the human rights records of proposed aid recipients the Secretary of State must submit annually "a full and complete report . . . with respect to practices regarding the observance of and respect for internationally recognized human rights in each country." . . .

Similarly, incorporation of international human rights language into statutes that affect funding of foreign family planning activities seems desirable. . . .

. . . Inclusion of those and other instruments in the amendment's legislative history, though certainly not uncontroversial might be a more realistic lobbying goal. Similarly desirable would be legislative gloss suggesting that prohibited funding policies should not be limited to those that violate judicially enforceable international norms but in addition should reach those that are "inconsistent with" widely accepted international principles that may not yet have achieved customary status.

NOTES AND QUESTIONS

1.   The Clinton administration reversed the policy adopted by the Reagan administration which cut off funds to foreign agencies that provide abortion information. Early in his term Clinton restored the availability of resources to international programs that fund abortions. In a related context he has urged other nations to promote the use of family planning as a means of population control. He has reiterated, however, that he does not view abortion as a method of family planning. In 1995 Congress compelled the Clinton administration to reduce substantially funding for international family planning programs.

2.   For further reading about human rights legislation that relates to foreign assistance, see chapter 9, *supra*.

3.   Questions have been raised in Congress about an "exit tax," proposed by the Clinton administration, that would tax wealthy persons who renounce citizenship to avoid paying taxes. Opponents have argued that the tax affects individuals' right to travel or leave their country. Many scholars, however, support the proposal, finding it to be consistent with the International Covenant on Civil and Political Rights and General Comments of the Human Rights Committee.

J.   OBSTACLES TO APPLICATION OF INTERNATIONAL HUMAN RIGHTS LAW

The first part of this chapter may suggest that it is not easy to find a basis for litigating international human rights law in U.S. courts. There are, unfortunately, numerous other doctrines that further limit a plaintiff's ability to redress violations of international law. These doctrines include political question, sovereign immunity, standing, failure to state a claim, national policies that contradict customary norms, forum non conveniens, acts of state, foreign sovereign immunity, statute of limitations, damages, and choice of law. Some of the issues—such as foreign sovereign immunity, acts of state, damages, statute of limitations, and choice of law—were discussed in chapter 12 in connection with suits by aliens against foreign sovereigns in U.S. courts. Other issues may be presented by the hypothetical situation presented at the beginning of this chapter regarding detained alien youth awaiting deportation hearings. As you read the following excerpts, think about which doctrines the defense could raise successfully to defeat litigation by the alien children.

1. Challenges to U.S. Foreign Policy: Political Questions, Sovereign Immunity, Standing, and Failure to State a Cause of Action

Committee of U.S. Citizens Living in Nicaragua v. Reagan, 859 F.2d 929 (D.C. Cir. 1988) (several citations omitted):

Judge MIKVA. . . .

[Plaintiffs sought to bar the U.S. from continuing to provide assistance to the Nicaraguan Democratic Resistance Forces (the Contras), an armed force opposing the government of Nicaragua. The plaintiffs relied on the judgment of the International Council of Justice (ICJ) in the *Case Concerning Military and Paramilitary Activities in and Against Nicaragua* (Nicaragua v. United States), 1986 I.C.J. 14, which found the U.S. support of the Contras to be violative of its international law obligations.]

A. The Political Question Doctrine

"No branch of the law of justiciability is in such disarray as the doctrine of the 'political question.'" C. Wright, *The Law of Federal Courts* 74 (4th ed. 1983). Professor Wright concludes that "there is no workable definition of characteristics that distinguish political questions from justiciable questions, and. . .the category of political questions is 'more amenable to description by infinite itemization than by generalization.'" The Supreme Court has voiced a similar sentiment, warning us that "it is error to suppose that every case or controversy which touches foreign relations lies beyond judicial cognizance." *Baker v. Carr*, 369 U.S. 186, 211 . . . (1962). Given the care with which the political question doctrine should be applied and given the variety of claims encompassed by the present case, we find the trial court's blanket invocation of the political question doctrine to be inappropriate.

To the extent that political question cases contain factors that make them genuinely nonjusticiable, some of those elements can be found here. For example, judicial refusal to resolve political questions "is founded primarily on the doctrine of separation of powers." Courts often underscore this factor by pointing to "a textually demonstrable constitutional commitment of the issue to a coordinate branch of government." *Baker v. Carr*, 369 U.S. at 217 . . .; *see also* L. Tribe, *American Constitutional Law* 96 (2d ed. 1988) (distinguishing the textual commitment rationale as the "classical" version of the political question doctrine). As the trial court noted in this case, foreign policy decisions are the subject of just such a textual commitment. "The conduct of the foreign relations of our Government is committed by the Constitution to the Executive and Legislative—'the political'—Departments." Together, those departments possess the sole power to enter into treaties and subsequently to alter them. Similarly, only the political departments can submit our nation to an international court's jurisdiction or thereafter rescind that commitment.

This facet of the political question doctrine may well bar consideration of some appellants' claims. The first two groups of appellants comprise organizations seeking to strengthen the United Nations and to help the citizens of Nicaragua. These organizations' claims seem especially vulnerable to dismissal under a doctrine that "excludes from judicial review those controversies which revolve around policy choices and value determinations constitutionally committed for resolution to the [political branches]." Indeed, to the extent that the organizational appellants in this case allege "purely ideological interests in the agency's action," they may even lack standing. . . .

. . . Neither individuals nor organizations have a cause of action in an American court to enforce ICJ judgments. The ICJ is a creation of national governments working through the U.N.; its decisions operate between and among such governments and are not enforceable by individuals having no relation to the claim that the ICJ has adjudicated—in this case, a claim brought by the government of Nicaragua. Appellants try to sidestep this difficulty by alleging that our government has violated international law rather than styling their suit as an enforcement action in support of the ICJ judgment. The United States' contravention of an ICJ judgment may well violate principles of international law. But, as we demonstrate below, those violations are no more subject to challenge by private parties in this court than is the underlying contravention of the ICJ judgment. For these reasons, we do not rest on the political question doctrine in rejecting the claims brought by these first two groups of appellants. Rather, we dismiss these claims on the ground that private parties have no cause of action in this court to enforce an ICJ decision.

The third and final group of claims in this case is brought by those appellants who allege infringement of their personal liberty and property rights. The trial court's determination that these claims raise political questions is troubling. This court's recent warning about the political question doctrine applies to the case before us with special force: the doctrine's "shifting contours and uncertain underpinnings" make it "susceptible to indiscriminate and overbroad application to claims properly before the federal courts."

To be sure, even those appellants who advance claims based on personal rights persist in mingling those claims with an attempt to enforce the ICJ judgment. Nonetheless, the core of this third set of claims lies in the fifth amendment. Appellants contend that funding of the Contras deprives them of liberty and property "without due process of law" not only because they are generally threatened by the war in Nicaragua but also because they are intended targets of the Contra "resistance." These are serious allegations and not ones to be dismissed as nonjusticiable. As our court declared in rejecting a political question defense to a fifth amendment takings claim, "[t]he Executive's power to conduct foreign relations free from the unwarranted supervision of the Judiciary cannot give the Executive *carte blanche* to trample the most fundamental liberty and property rights of this country's citizenry." As appellants point out, the Supreme Court has repeatedly found that claims based on such rights are justiciable, even if they implicate foreign policy decisions.

Notwithstanding the fact that appellants' claims of infringed rights are justiciable, however, we find the claims themselves to be insufficient as a matter of law. Examining the factual pleadings closely, we find no allegation that the United States itself has participated in or in any way sought to encourage injuries to Americans in Nicaragua. We therefore conclude that appellants' fifth amendment cause of action fails to state a claim on which relief can be granted. On that basis, we dismiss this final group of appellants' claims.

B.   Appellants Have No Basis in Domestic Law for Enforcing the ICJ Judgment

1.   *The status of international law in the United States' domestic legal order*

Appellants argue that the United States' decision to disregard the ICJ judgment and to continue funding the Contras violates three types of international law. First, contravention of the ICJ judgment is said to violate part of a United States treaty, namely Article 94 of the U.N. Charter. That article provides that "[e]ach Member of the United Nations undertakes to comply with the decision of the International Court of Justice in any case to which it is a party." U.N. Charter art. 94. Second, disregard of the ICJ judgment allegedly violates principles of customary international law. One such principle holds that treaties in force shall be observed. Appellants contend that another such principle requires parties to ICJ decisions to adhere to those decisions. Third, the United States may have violated peremptory norms of international law. Such norms, often referred to as *jus cogens* (or "compelling law"), enjoy the highest status in international law and prevail over both customary international law and treaties. Appellants' contention that the United States has violated *jus cogens* forms their primary argument before this court. They contend that the obligation of parties to an ICJ judgment to obey that judgment is not merely a customary rule but actually a peremptory norm of international law.

For purposes of the present lawsuit, the key question is not simply whether the United States has violated any of these three legal norms but whether such violations can be remedied by an American court or whether they can only be redressed on an international level. In short, do violations of international law have domestic legal consequences? The answer largely depends on what form the "violation" takes. Here, the alleged violation is the law that Congress enacted and that the President signed, appropriating funds for the Contras. When our government's two political branches, acting together, contravene an international legal norm, does this court have any authority to remedy the violation? The answer is "no" if the type of international obligation that Congress and the President violate is either a treaty or a rule of customary international law. If, on the other hand, Congress and the President violate a peremptory norm (or *jus cogens*), the domestic legal consequences are unclear. We need not resolve this uncertainty, however, for we find that the principles appellants characterize as peremptory norms of international law are not recognized as such by the community of nations. Thus, as we explain below in greater detail, none of the claims that appellants derive from violations of international law can succeed in this court.

2.   *The effect of subsequent statutes upon prior inconsistent treaties*

. . . [As stated by the Supreme Court:]

> [S]o far as a treaty made by the United States with any foreign nation can become the subject of judicial cognizance in the courts of this country, it is subject to such acts as Congress may pass for its enforcement, modification or appeal.

[*Head Money Cases*, 112 U.S. 580,] at 598-99 [1884] . . .. No American court has wavered from this view in the subsequent century. Indeed, in a comparatively recent case, our court reaffirmed the principle that treaties and statutes enjoy equal status and therefore that inconsistencies between the two must be resolved in favor of the *lex posterior*. In *Diggs v. Shultz*, 470 F.2d 461 (D.C. Cir. 1972), *cert. denied*, 411 U.S. 931 . . . (1973), this court reviewed a claim by citizens of what was then Southern Rhodesia, assailing the United States' failure to abide by U.N. Security Council

Resolution 232. That resolution directed U.N. members to impose a trade embargo against Rhodesia. The court found that America's contravention of Resolution 232 was required by Congress' adoption of the so-called Byrd Amendment "whose purpose and effect . . . was to detach this country from the U.N. boycott of Southern Rhodesia in blatant disregard of our treaty undertakings." "Under our constitutional scheme," the court concluded, "Congress can denounce treaties if it sees fit to do so, and there is nothing the other branches of government can do about it . . . [; thus] the complaint [states] no tenable claim in law."

These precedents dispose of any claim by appellants that the United States has violated its treaty obligation under Article 94. It is true, of course, that the facts here differ somewhat from the situation in *Diggs*. Congress has not clearly repudiated the requirement in Article 94 that every nation comply with an ICJ decision "in any case to which it is a party." U.N. Charter, art. 94. Rather, our government asserts that it never consented to ICJ jurisdiction in cases like the Nicaragua dispute. Thus Congress may well believe that its support for the Contras, while contravening the ICJ judgment, does not violate its treaty obligation under Article 94. And, unless Congress makes clear its intent to abrogate a treaty, a court will not lightly infer such intent but will strive to harmonize the conflicting enactments.

At this stage of the present case, however, the key question is not whether Congress intended to abrogate Article 94. Since appellants *allege* that Congress has breached Article 94, we must determine whether such a claim could ever prevail. The claim could succeed only if appellants could prove that a prior treaty—the U.N. Charter—preempts a subsequent statute, namely the legislation that funds the Contras. It is precisely that argument that the precedents of the Supreme Court and of this court foreclose. We therefore hold that appellants' claims based on treaty violations must fail.

Our conclusion, of course, speaks not at all to whether the United States has upheld its treaty obligations under international law. As the Supreme Court said in the *Head Money Cases*, a treaty "depends for the enforcement of its provisions on the interest and honor of the governments which are parties to it. If these fail, its infraction becomes the subject of international negotiations and reclamations . . . [but] with all this the judicial courts have nothing to do and can give no redress." This conclusion reflects the United States' adoption of a partly "dualist"—rather than strictly "monist"—view of international and domestic law. "[D]ualists view international law as a discrete legal system [which] . . . operates wholly on an inter-nation plane." . . .

. . . Given that dualist jurisprudence, we cannot find—as a matter of domestic law—that congressional enactments violate prior treaties.

Finally, we note that even if Congress's breach of a treaty were cognizable in domestic court, appellants would lack standing to rectify the particular breach that they allege here. Article 94 of the U.N. Charter simply does not confer rights on private individuals. Treaty clauses must confer such rights in order for individuals to assert a claim "arising under" them. *See* U.S. Const. art. III, §2, cl. 1; 28 U.S.C. §1331 (1982). Whether a treaty clause does create such enforcement rights is often described as part of the larger question of whether that clause is "self-executing."

. . . We conclude that appellants' attempt to enjoin funding of the Contras based on a violation of Article 94 would fail even if Congress' abrogation of treaties were cognizable in domestic courts.

3. *Customary international law and subsequent inconsistent statutes*

In addition to relying on Article 94 to challenge continued funding of the Contras, appellants also invoke the rule "of customary international law that nations must obey the rulings of an international court to whose jurisdiction they submit." . . . We accept that some version of this rule describes a norm of customary international law. Even so, it is far from clear that this rule governs situations like the present one, in which a nation that has consented in advance to the Court's jurisdiction disputes whether the terms of that consent extend to a particular case. *Cf.* ICJ Statute art. 36, para. 6 ("dispute as to whether the [ICJ] has jurisdiction . . . shall be settled by decision of the Court"). . . . For the moment, we assume *arguendo* that Congress' decision to disregard the ICJ judgment violates customary international law.

The question is whether such a violation is cognizable by domestic courts. Once again, the United States' rejection of a purely "monist" view of the international and domestic legal orders shapes our analysis. Statutes inconsistent with principles of customary international law may well lead to international law violations. But within the domestic legal realm, that inconsistent statute simply modifies or supersedes customary international law to the extent of the inconsistency. Although the Supreme Court has never articulated this principle as a firm holding, the Court's persuasive dictum in an important early case established the principle that this and other courts follow.

In *The Paquete Habana*, 175 U.S. 677. . .(1900), the owner of fishing vessels captured and condemned as prize during the Spanish-American War sought compensation from the United States on the ground that customary international law prohibited such seizures. After canvassing prior state practice and the opinions of commentators, the Court concluded that the prohibition against seizure of boats engaged in coastal fishing, which arose at first from considerations of comity between nations, had ripened into "an established rule of international law." *Id.* at 708 . . . . The Court therefore held that the condemnation was improper because "international law is part of our law, and must be ascertained and administered by the courts of justice of appropriate jurisdiction." *Id.* at 700. . . .

Justice Gray, writing for the Court, qualified this famous statement about the domestic effect of international law with dictum of no less significance: "[W]here there is no treaty, and no controlling executive *or legislative act* or judicial decision, resort must be had to the customs and usages of nations." *Id.* (emphasis added) . . . . Thus, so far as concerned domestic law, the rule was laid down that subsequently enacted statutes would preempt existing principles of customary international law— just as they displaced prior inconsistent treaties. . . .

Few other courts have had occasion to consider the principle that, under domestic law, statutes supersede customary international law. But the principle is implicit in decisions that uphold the statutory abrogation of treaties, "since violation of a treaty is essentially a violation of the principle of customary international law requiring that treaties be observed."

As with their refusal to take notice of statutory abrogation of treaties, the courts' disregard of statutory breaches of customary international law is not necessarily required by the Constitution. . . . Nonetheless, the law in this court remains clear: no enactment of Congress can be challenged on the ground that it violates customary international law. Those of appellants' claims that are predicated on this theory of illegality cannot succeed. . . .

4. *Peremptory norms of international law (jus cogens)*

. . . [I]n order for . . . a customary norm of international law to become a peremptory norm, there must be a further recognition by "the international community . . . *as a whole* [that this is] a norm from which no derogation is permitted." Vienna Convention, art. 53[14]. . .

Such basic norms of international law as the proscription against murder and slavery may well have the domestic legal effect that appellants suggest. That is, they may well restrain our government in the same way that the Constitution restrains it. If Congress adopted a foreign policy that resulted in the enslavement of our citizens or other individuals, that policy might well be subject to challenge in domestic court under international law. . . .

We think it clear, however, that the harm that results when a government disregards or contravenes an ICJ judgement does not generate the level of universal disapprobation aroused by torture, slavery, summary execution, or genocide. Appellants try to bootstrap the ICJ's judgment against the United States into a form of *jus cogens* by pointing out that the judgment *relies* on a peremptory norm of international law—that is, that the ICJ invoked the norm proscribing aggressive use of force between nations when it rendered its decision in the Nicaragua case. This argument, however, confuses the judgment itself with the ICJ's rationale for that judgment. The gravamen of appellant's complaint is that compliance with an ICJ judgment is a nonderogable norm of international law, not that a particular judgment constitutes collateral estoppel against the United States as to its violation of a nonderogable norm. Were appellants to advance the latter contention, they would be applying nonmutual, offensive collateral estoppel against the federal government, which generally is not permitted even in domestic law cases . . . much less in international law cases where our government disputes the prior court's jurisdiction. In sum, appellants' attempt to enjoin funding of the Contras on the ground that it violates a peremptory norm of international law by contravening an ICJ judgment is unavailing. The ICJ judgment does not represent such a peremptory norm.

[Case dismissed.]

NOTES AND QUESTIONS

1. Appellants here alleged that Congress breached Article 94 of the U.N. Charter by appropriating money for the Contras in violation of the ICJ judgment. The court therefore found the question of whether Congress intended to breach Article 94 irrelevant. If appellants instead had alleged that Congress had not intended to breach Article 94, would they have had a stronger case? Compare the court's conclusion in the *PLO* case, *supra* part F, that Congress did not intend to breach the U.N. Headquarters Agreement in passing a statute requiring closure of the PLO observer mission.

2. The court notes that whether a treaty clause "confers rights on private individuals" is but one "part of the larger question of whether that clause is self-executing." What other issues must be analyzed in order to determine whether a treaty clause is self-executing?

In *Goldstar (Panama) S.A. v. United States*, Panamanian property owners sued to recover damages caused by rioting in the wake of the U.S. invasion of Panama City in 1989. 967 F.2d 965 (4th Cir. 1992). During the invasion U.S. forces had effectively eliminated Panama's

---

[14] Vienna Convention, Article 53 is reproduced *supra* Part G.

police force; and the owners asserted that U.S. forces failed to maintain order, thus violating the Hague Convention Respecting the Laws and Customs of War on Land. Oct. 18, 1907, 36 Stat. 2277. The Hague Convention imposes a duty to protect residents of occupied territories. It states, in Article 43, "The authority of the legitimate power having in fact passed into the hands of the occupant, the latter shall take all the measures in his power to restore, and ensure . . . public order and safety. . . ." It further states, in Article 3: "A belligerent party which violates the provisions of the said regulations shall, if the case demands, be liable to pay compensation." Goldstar argued that the U.S. violated Article 43, thus giving rise to liability under Article 3.

The Fourth Circuit affirmed the district court's dismissal of the claim, stating that the U.S. had not waived its sovereign immunity and thus was not subject to suit. The court stated that (1) the U.S. would have waived its sovereign immunity only if the Hague Convention were self-executing, and (2) a treaty is self-executing only when it shows intent to provide a private right of action. The Hague Convention, according to the court, did not explicitly show such intent; it created "substantive rules of conduct," not "private rights of action."

3.   The ICJ in the Nicaraguan case concluded that, even if Congress' breach of the U.N. Charter were cognizable in U.S. courts, plaintiffs' claims would fail because Article 94 does not confer rights on individuals. Putting aside other jurisdictional concerns, do you think Nicaragua would have a cause of action in a U.S. court to enforce the ICJ judgment? If Nicaragua did sue, what allegations should it make regarding continued funding of the Contras?

4.   The D.C. Circuit concluded no challenge can be made to a statute on the ground that it conflicts with a customary norm. 859 F.2d at 939. The court made no effort, however, to construe the customary norm and the statute consistently. If you were assigned to draft the issue in a petition for rehearing, what arguments would you make? Assume the statute appropriated a lump sum to aid the Contras but neither (1) designated how much had to be applied to purely humanitarian uses, nor (2) attached comparable limitations.

5.   The D.C. Circuit discussion of peremptory norms is intriguing, in particular its statement that "they may well restrain our government in the same way that the Constitution restrains it." Can you think of a case in which an argument could be strengthened by invocation of one of the peremptory norms listed in the opinion? In most cases, perhaps, the challenged conduct would be proscribed by the U.S. Constitution. Yet might there be good reasons for making a peremptory-norm argument as well?

Consider for instance a case in which indigenous peoples in the Amazon Region seek your help in stopping a U.S.-supported venture from constructing oil wells in, and a road into, their territory. They have statements from anthropologists showing that the construction would result in the death within 20 years of 50% of the indigenous people over five and 90% of those under five. The U.S. does not challenge that projection but asserts its right to proceed based on the contractor's having obtained a license from the Latin American government in whose territory the development is planned. If a lawsuit were filed in the Second Circuit, do you think the trial judge might find a cause of action based on genocide or other international rules that constrain the U.S. "in the same way that the [U.S.] Constitution" does? For a decision outlining the actual facts of this case and ordering the oil company to allow discovery of certain documents, see *Aguinda v. Texaco, Inc.*, 1994 WL 142006 (S.D.N.Y. 1994), *aff'd on reh'g* 1994 WL 160535 (S.D.N.Y. 1994).

6.   Courts continue to struggle with the political question doctrine. In *Klinghoffer v. S.N.C. Achille Lauro*, for example, the court refused to dismiss a wrongful-death case alleged to raise nonjusticiable foreign policy questions. 739 F. Supp. 854 (S.D.N.Y. 1990). In *Klinghoffer*, plaintiff's husband had been a passenger on the Italian liner Achille Lauro. According to the plaintiff, the PLO had seized the ship and, during the seizure, shot plaintiff's husband and threw his body overboard. *Id.* at 856.

The PLO moved to dismiss, contending *inter alia* that the suit raised a political question.

The PLO argued liability for terrorist attacks presents foreign policy questions not properly decided in court. *Id.* at 859. The court rejected the argument because, in its opinion, the PLO seizure was an act of piracy. "These are tort claims. They do not involve 'policy choices and value determinations constitutionally committed for resolution to the halls of Congress or the confines of the Executive Branch,' but familiar questions of responsibility for personal and property injuries." *Id.* at 860 (citation omitted).

Linder v. Portocarrero, 747 F. Supp. 1452 (S.D. Fla. 1990), reached a different conclusion. The family of a U.S. citizen killed by Nicaraguan Contra rebels sued three anti-government groups and four individuals for wrongful death, battery, intentional infliction of emotional distress, violation of customary law, and civil conspiracy. *Id.* at 1453. The court stated that the suit presented a nonjusticiable political question because neither customary international law, *id.* at 1462, nor the Geneva Conventions, *id.* at 1463, contained judicially manageable criteria by which to adjudicate the merits of plaintiffs' claims. The court also noted that precedent reflected the belief that "domestic tort actions are not appropriate remedies for injuries occurring outside the United States during conflicts between belligerents." *Id.* Finally the court noted that adjudication on the merits could lead to interference with the conduct of foreign policy by U.S. political branches. "For a court to involve itself in the adjudication of civil war in Nicaragua . . . would simply place too many actors on the diplomatic stage." *Id.* at 1468-69.

The Eleventh Circuit affirmed with respect to actions against the anti-government groups. 963 F.2d 332 (11th Cir. 1992), but reinstated the claims against individuals. As to the Contras the court stated it would "be required to measure and carefully assess the use of tools of violence and warfare in the midst of a foreign civil war" and inquire into "the relationship between United States policy and the actions of the contras." With respect to the individual defendants, however, "there is no foreign civil war exception to the right to sue for tortious conduct that violates the fundamental norms of the customary laws of war." *Id.* at 336.

More recently, in *Wang Zong Xiao v. Reno*, the court rejected the government's attempt to use the political question doctrine to defeat jurisdiction over a case involving a Chinese citizen who had been paroled to the U.S. (to testify at a heroin conspiracy trial) who challenged his treatment and impending deportation by U.S. officials. 837 F.Supp 1506, 1547 (N.D.Cal. 1993). The court held the political question doctrine was inapplicable because he challenged only the manner in which the government treated him, not the government's immigration policies in general. *Id.* The case is currently on appeal to the Ninth Circuit.

7.   Though standing may be an obstacle to successfully suing a government entity, "absence of standing [does not provide the government] with lawful authority to engage in such action." Michael S. Paulsen, *Is Lloyd Bentsen Unconstitutional?*, 46 STAN. L. REV. 907, 916 (1994). Paulsen further notes, "A constitutional violation is no less a constitutional violation simply because of the absence of a judicial ruling to that effect." *Id.* Does the same rationale hold true for violations of treaties and customary international law?

8.   Federal statutes delineate situations in which the government's immunity from suit is waived. For example, 28 U.S.C. § 1346(b) provides that the United States may be sued for money damages

> for injury or loss of property, or personal injury or death caused by the negligent or wrongful act or omission of any employee of the Government while acting within the scope of his office or employment, under circumstances where the United States, if a private person, would be liable to the claimant. . . .

The Federal Torts Claims Act, 28 U.S.C. § 2674, however, limits plaintiffs' rights to recover punitive damages. Another statute, 5 U.S.C. § 702, implicitly waives sovereign immunity by providing for judicial review of claims for injunctive relief against the United States.

For a discussion of the legal relationship between the U.S. and American citizens taken hostage abroad, see Kevin D. Hughes, *Hostages' Rights: The Unhappy Legal Predicament of an American Held in Foreign Captivity*, 26 COLUM. J.L. & SOC. PROBS. 555 (1993) (advocating that the Federal Tort Claims Act be amended to cover claims arising in foreign territory).

9.   The Supreme Court held in *United States v. Stanley*, 483 U.S. 669 (1987), that a service-man's claim against the United States for injuries sustained as a result of the Army secretly administering doses of lysergic acid diethylamide (LSD) to him in the 1950s must be dismissed because claims for injuries arising in the course of activity "incident to service" are disallowed under both the Federal Tort Claims Act (FTCA) and the Constitution. As a result of the LSD exposure, Stanley suffered from hallucinations, periods of incoherence and memory loss, was impaired in his military performance, and saw his marriage end because of the personality changes wrought by the LSD. *Id.* at 671.

---

2.   Challenges to U.S. Policies: Customary Norms and Executive, Legislative, and Judicial Acts

In *Matter of Medina*, Interim Decision No. 3078 (BIA 1988), the Bureau of Immigration Appeals not only rejected Medina's claim that her deportation was barred by the Fourth Geneva Convention of 1949 (*see* excerpts in part *F, supra* at 51); it also rejected her claim that she was entitled to temporary refuge in the U.S. under customary law. The BIA concluded that the right to temporary refuge had not ripened into a norm and that, in any event, Congress had preempted the operation of any such norm by failing to include the relief in the 1980 Refugee Act. Those conclusions were accepted specifically in *American Baptist Churches v. Meese*, 712 F. Supp. 756 (N.D. Cal. 1989), also discussed in part *F, supra* at 598.

At the time of this writing no appellate court has squarely addressed whether a statute may preempt international law that does not directly conflict with it. The Supreme Court, however, did express a willingness to interpret acts of Congress to occupy the field and thereby preempt international law. In *Argentine Republic v. Amerada Hess Shipping Corp.*, 488 U.S. 428, 434 (1989), the Supreme Court held the Foreign Sovereign Immunities Act (FSIA) was the sole basis for obtaining jurisdiction over foreign sovereigns. The Court's conclusion was based on the text, legislative history, and comprehensive nature of the Act. The Court thus interpreted the FSIA to preempt analogous provisions in the Alien Tort Statutes and the principle of universal jurisdiction recognized in customary international law, even when alternative interpretations are feasible. *See also Siderman de Blake v. Republic of Argentina*, 965 F.2d 699 (9th Cir. 1992) (holding that the peremptory norm against official torture did not provide a U.S. court with jurisdiction over a claim against a foreign sovereign for torture because the Foreign Sovereign Immunities Act did not so provide, even though sovereign immunity too is a matter of international law), *cert. denied*, 507 U.S. 1017 (1993).

That interpretation may be supported by a literal construction of the Supreme Court's statement in *The Paquete Habana* that "where there is no treaty and no controlling executive or legislative act or judicial decision, resort must be had to the customs and usages of civilized nations . . . ," 175 U.S. 677, 700 (1900). The Board of Immigration Appeals in *Matter of Medina* may have construed the dictum to mean that *any* executive, legislative, or judicial action preempts a contrary customary international norm, even when the two could be interpreted consistently with each other.

The conclusion that statutes preempt existing customary international norms is not inevitable. Rules of construction require courts to harmonize statutes with international norms unless Congress has clearly indicated its intent to renounce them. That interpretive mandate was stressed early in the Supreme Court's history, when Chief Justice Marshall proclaimed that "an Act of Congress ought never to be construed to violate the law of nations, if any other possible construction remains. . . ." *Murray v. Schooner Charming Betsy*, 6 U.S. (2 Cranch) 64, 118 (1804). That mandate has been reaffirmed in many opinions and was adopted in § 115(1)(a) of the Restatement (Third) of the Foreign Relations Law of the United States, which declares,

> An act of Congress supersedes an earlier rule of international law or a provision of an international agreement as law of the United States [only] if the purpose of the act to supersede the earlier rule or provision is clear or if the act and the earlier rule or provision cannot be fairly reconciled.

REFERENCES

GUY S. GOODWIN-GILL, THE REFUGEE IN INTERNATIONAL LAW (1983);

ATLE GRAHL-MADSEN, THE STATUS OF REFUGEES IN INTERNATIONAL LAW (1966, 1972);

Deborah Perluss & Joan F. Hartman, *Temporary Refuge: Emergence of a Customary Norm*, 26 VA. J. INT'L L. 551 (1986);

Ralph G. Steinhardt, *The United Nations and Refugees: 1945-1988*, AIUSA LEGAL SUPPORT NETWORK NEWSL., Fall 1988, at 103.

If legislative action may supersede contrary customary international law, what about executive action? In *Agora: May the President Violate Customary International Law?*, 81 AM. J. INT'L L. 371 (1987), Frederic L. Kirgis offers an overview of others' arguments and then proposes that only self-executing custom should be treated as part of national law. He further argues that executive actions should not automatically prevail over self-executing customary international norms. Instead, executive actions should be controlling only where the President has been given domestic lawmaking authority by Congress or where a domestic legislative effect is a necessary byproduct of the President's exercise of his constitutional powers. Kirgis applies this rule regardless of whether the executive action was taken before or after the rule at issue crystallized into a customary international norm. Therefore, when executive action that has domestic legislative effect is not within the scope of executive authority, a contrary customary international norm supersedes it. In essence he seems to conclude that the executive does not have the power to take legislative action which violates international law.

NOTES AND QUESTIONS

In an amici brief submitted by Human Rights Advocates, Frank Newman, and the ACLU of Southern California in *Echeverria v. INS*, No. 89-70236 (accepted for filing, December 11, 1989), amici argued that the Immigration and Nationality Act (INA) is not only consistent with the customary norm of temporary refuge but in fact directly incorporates that and other widely accepted norms of customary law. That argument is based on the Act's direction to the U.S. Attorney General to consider "all laws, conventions, and treaties of the United States" in making deportation decisions. "All laws" include customary norms, amici argued, given that those norms unquestionably are part of U.S. law. The court, however, rejected that argument. *Echeverria-Hernandez v. INS*, 923 F.2d 688 (9th Cir. 1991). A similar argument was rejected by the same court in *United States v. Aguilar*, 871 F.2d 1436, 1454 (9th Cir. 1989), amended August 14, 1989, and held that the failure of the INA expressly to include customary norms in its definition of "all laws," particularly in light of its reference to treaties, reflects congressional intent to exclude customary norms. Can you make arguments to counter that holding? Do you think *Aguilar* is fatal to amici's argument that the INA should be read to be consistent with customary norms even if it does not expressly incorporate them?

K. STRATEGY ISSUES: WHEN TO INVOKE INTERNATIONAL LAW IN U.S. COURTS; WHEN TO SEEK RELIEF THROUGH ADMINISTRATIVE PROCESSES; WHEN TO SEEK INCORPORATION OF INTERNATIONAL LAW IN U.S. STATUTES?

Deborah R. Gerstel & Adam G. Segall, *Conference Report: Human Rights in American Courts,* 1 AM. U. J. INT'L L. & POL'Y 137, 142-65 (1986):

[P]articipants . . . debate[d] . . . the propriety and effectiveness of bringing actions where the probability of a positive legal determination is doubtful. A wide range of views existed on this issue. One perspective was that a strategy of prolific litigation raises public awareness, forces recognition of international law, and serves to educate the judiciary. The competing viewpoint advocates a more selective strategy. Under this latter formulation, careful selection among cases would help weed out frivolous suits and concentrate limited legal resources.

There were several comments on the question of whether doubtful suits should be used to achieve effective publicity. One participant argued that the goal of introducing and establishing human rights norms in United States courts must be paramount. "Where the President is aiding in the torture of others, we want the judiciary to be able to come in against the President. The purpose of continuing lawsuits which may be frivolous, therefore, is to attempt to bring the action into a legal context. It is necessary to create a means for dialogue even if you know you are going to lose." As an example, this participant cited the *Greenham Women* case,[15] in which "it was understood that the case [seeking an injunction against the deployment of cruise missiles in a town in England] was unwinnable." Although held by the district court to present a non-justiciable political question, *Greenham Women* proved effective in focusing media attention in Europe and the United States on NATO's cruise missile deployment policy.

There were many responses to this line of reasoning. One participant stressed the need to adhere to Rule 11 of the Federal Rules of Civil Procedure, which bars attorneys from initiating proceedings with knowledge that the case is frivolous. A distinction was raised, however, between cases which lack a sufficient legal basis and those which merely appear "unwinnable" even though warranted by law. Another participant contended that there is often little or no time to decide whether to initiate an action. Therefore, consistent with ethical obligations, a practicing attorney has a duty to bring the suit if she holds the conviction that the case is not frivolous in the first instance.

Several individuals feared that the law ultimately produced by the initiation of

---

[15] Greenham Women Against Cruise Missiles v. Reagan, 591 F. Supp. 1332 (S.D.N.Y. 1984). . . .

doubtful cases could produce bad precedent. Confronted with borderline cases, judges may create new barriers resulting in "bad law" under which every human rights lawyer will then be obliged to work. Despite the positive benefits of increased legal awareness, many participants suggested that such "bad law" has a ripple effect extending to cases of all kinds brought before all adjudicatory bodies. Query, how successful is a highly publicized case if the legal result presents a new hurdle for future litigants? Under the *Sanchez*[16] analysis, for example, a broad range of questions formerly open for adjudication might now be considered non-justiciable under the broad "political question" doctrine. If the primary goal of those who brought the suit was simply to direct public and media attention to the situation in Nicaragua, one participant argued that Congressional trips to Nicaragua could have produced a positive dramatic effect without creating bad legal precedent.

Another participant recounted a discussion he had with attorneys for the plaintiffs in a suit which had yielded a significant set back for human rights case law. Most human rights activists regarded the particular case, *Tel-Oren v. Libyan Arab Republic*,[17] as a disaster from the outset. When asked why they intended to file for *certiorari* with the Supreme Court in light of the damaging opinion they had received below, the attorneys stated that their sole duty was to their clients. Had the petition been granted, negative review by the Supreme Court could have increased substantially the damage done. Upon reflection, this participant asserted that the ethical obligations of attorneys extend beyond their clients; they also owe a duty to the proper development of the law. If the possibility arises that a case may create a negative result in the body of law, participants suggested that attorneys should at least inform their clients of that consideration.

Discussion shifted next to a consideration of appropriate legal, political, administrative, and educational strategies to be employed in the future. Participants deemed publicity of human rights issues to be essential, but not at any cost. There was a general consensus that attorneys must consider the most efficient use of limited resources in deciding whether to litigate. . . . Participants noted that in the 1940's and 1950's the National Association for the Advancement of Colored People was the "only show in town" deeply involved in civil rights litigation. As a consequence, the NAACP could carefully select cases to be litigated, with a coordinated long-term strategy in mind. By contrast, many groups and individual practitioners involved in human rights cases today simply do not agree on strategy. They respond to different constituencies and different concepts of legal ethics and moral obligations. It is essential, participants stressed, that these groups and individuals meet on a more regular basis to coordinate their legal efforts and to consider how their respective suits may affect one another. . . .

To facilitate the proper selection and coordination of cases, many conference participants agreed on the need to establish operative criteria to distinguish between "hard" cases—those having a strong statutory jurisdictional basis, a meritorious claim, and solid popular support—and "soft" cases—those which are not necessarily frivolous but which have little chance of success and a high probability of an adverse ruling. In selecting such hard cases, one must look to the degree to which human rights practitioners can mobilize public opinion.

Participants discussed political options to expand access to the courts in human rights cases throughout the session. They generally agreed that an effective political

---

[16] Ed. note: *Sanchez-Espinoza v. Reagan*, 770 F.2d 202 (D.C. 1985).
[17] Ed. note: 726 F.2d 774 (D.C. Cir. 1984), *cert. denied*, 470 U.S. 1003 (1985).

strategy should take advantage of every public outcry against terrorism. One proposal called for legislation to facilitate action on behalf of the family of Leon Klinghoffer, victim of the *Achille Lauro* tragedy. The suggested legislation would create district court jurisdiction and provide tort remedies for victims of foreign terrorist acts to sue their perpetrators, but would likely be broad enough to encompass a wide range of human rights violations.[18]. . .

As an alternative to court actions, various participants urged greater concentration on administrative hearings as an effective means to influence foreign policy. They noted that customs and trade statutes have provided a particularly significant basis for successful administrative proceedings. In the *South African Coal Case*,[19] for example, petitioners attacked a South African law that effectively obliged black miners to work under contracts enforceable by penal sanctions. Petitioners argued that the importation of coal mined under these circumstances violated a statute that prohibits importing goods produced by indentured labor into the United States.

Although the Commissioner of Customs Services dismissed this complaint on the grounds that the plaintiffs did not satisfy a statutory proviso fixing a domestic consumptive demand, the South African government subsequently repealed all of its penal servitude laws. . . . [T]he hearing . . . create[d] favorable press, helped to define such terms as indentured labor, and may actually have induced South Africa to change its policy vis-á-vis the rights of workers.

The conference produced similar comments with respect to a case pending before the United States Court of International Trade, in which the plaintiffs were seeking to exclude various Soviet products from the United States under the Tariff Act of 1930.[20] Both Customs and Treasury Department officials have argued before the International Trade Commission that it is impossible to tell whether the U.S.S.R. uses forced labor to manufacture specific products imported into the United States. For that reason, it was suggested, the proceeding before the United States Court of International Trade will highlight the need for more effective enforcement of congressionally-mandated trade sanctions against countries that do not respect labor and workers' rights.

Beyond the customs and trade statutes, one participant suggested that attorneys in the human rights field should examine a broad array of administrative provisions and procedures. As an example, she noted one case in which an administrative action brought under the Marine Mammals Protection Act[21] reinforced United States policy towards Namibia. The conference participants concluded that increased concentration on administrative hearings is a significant means by which to influence national policy. This approach, they generally agreed, may also lay the foundation for later successful litigation. . . .

---

[18] Ed. note: This suggestion refers to the Torture Victim Protection Act of 1991, 28 U.S.C. § 1350 (1992), discussed *supra* Chapter 12. This statute provides a cause of action for redress of torture and extrajudicial killing, regardless of the nationality of the parties or the site of the action.

[19] Importation of Coal from The Republic of South Africa Case, Treasury Dep't, U.S. Cust. Serv., Res. 3-R:E:R 703971 T (1975). This was a 1975 proceeding brought by the United Mine Workers and the State of Alabama under § 307 of the Tariff Act of 1930, 19 U.S.C. § 1307 (1982), before the Commissioner of Customs to prevent the release of South African coal being imported by Gulf Power, a utility company. Butcher, *Southern African Issues in United States Courts*, 26 How. L.J. 601, 616 n.50 (1983).

[20] Tariff Act of 1930, 19 U.S.C. §1307 (1982). . . .

[21] In re Fouke Co. to Waive the Moratorium on the Importation of Cape Fur Seal Skins, Doc. MMPAH No. 1, National Marine Fisheries Serv., Dept. of Commerce (1975). . . .

B. LITIGATION STRATEGIES

Conference participants attempted to look behind the restrictive judicial attitude vis-á-vis international law often encountered in immigration cases. In so doing, certain participants laid the blame for this situation not with the judiciary, but with the faulty strategy of practitioners who come before it. Attorneys involved in immigration cases, it was remarked, often refrain from citing international law in their arguments. Attorneys are often concerned that judges will not be familiar with international standards and will therefore be confused by and uncomfortable with their invocation. For that reason, attorneys frequently raise international norms almost as an afterthought, thereby contributing to a denigrating judicial attitude toward this body of law. Particularly when cases raise questions as to the self-executing nature of treaties, many attorneys automatically assume that arguments based on international law will fail. In essence, they engage in a self-censoring process before the arguments are even raised. One participant argued that by not forcefully asserting claims based on international law where applicable, these immigration lawyers may in fact be guilty of malpractice in the representation of their clients.

It was also noted, however, that some attorneys in immigration cases "throw in international law" on too casual a basis. These practitioners use references to international law simply as boilerplate language to supplement their other arguments without careful consideration of the substance of the asserted international claims and their relative merits in each individual case. These practitioners may be equally culpable in providing the basis for a skeptical judicial approach to international law claims in immigration and asylum cases.

C. ADMINISTRATIVE HEARINGS

Conference participants noted that questions of immigration law are commonly raised not before the courts, but before those administrative tribunals designated by Congress as having exclusive original jurisdiction over deportation and asylum cases. This fact has yielded both positive and negative consequences. To the detriment of practitioners and their clients, one participant reiterated, domestic administrative law offers no relief to those refugees who fear returning to face an armed conflict, but only to those who will confront individualized persecution. In addition, several participants pointed out that administrative law judges in immigration cases are given only narrow authority and are reluctant to look beyond the relevant statute and regulations to broader questions of international law. On the positive side, proceedings before an administrative tribunal generally offer the opportunity to raise issues from a defensive posture, easing the burden a petitioner would encounter in an affirmative suit. . . .

D. THE NEED FOR JUDICIAL EDUCATION

Conference participants generally perceived domestic courts to be reluctant to rule on customary international law questions because of their tendency toward judicial restraint reinforced by judicial concern over deciding issues relatively alien to the domestic jurisprudential experience. Consequently, participants focused on the need to educate judges as to the existence of and the vital role to be played by customary international law. It was agreed that practitioners must take the initiative to show judges where and how to define international customary norms. They must also support these arguments with substantial and convincing evidence. Despite general agreement on the scope and nature of the challenge, participants' views varied widely on the means to be employed to accomplish this task.

One participant suggested that decisions of various European courts should be invoked to define terms and demarcate specific customary norms.[22] Decisions of international courts may also help to demonstrate the contours of customary norms. It was noted, however, that attorneys must proceed cautiously with this approach, because certain European countries take a rather restrictive view with regard to issues affecting human rights.

Other conference participants recommended increased use of briefs *amicus curiae* to educate the judiciary. This strategy makes efficient and effective use of legal resources while providing a broader base of support for the preferred outcome. One participant also suggested that *amicus* briefs present an opportunity to advocate broad developments in the law rather than limiting the focus to the specific grievances of one party. Alternatively, attorneys can use *amicus* briefs to concentrate judicial attention on certain narrowly targeted issues. A practical problem with increased use of *amicus* briefs, it was observed, is the difficulty of locating appropriate litigation in progress in order to submit a brief in a timely fashion.

Conference participants concluded with a brief review of certain evolving customary norms, and focused particularly on the question of basing claims in domestic suits on developing international norms in the area of economic and social rights. *Price v. Cohen*,[23] which raised the question of whether a right to subsistence existed under the Fourteenth Amendment, was cited as an example of a case in which evidence of such customary norms might have proven useful. In cases such as *Price*, it was urged, attorneys could use proof of international norms to persuade judges to employ higher standards of review, or to encourage an affirmative finding that the particular right is of a fundamental and absolute nature.

Some participants cautioned, however, that economic and social rights are not as clearly recognized as civil and political rights. Very little customary international law on economic and social rights exists. . . .

NOTES AND QUESTIONS

1.   There are many contexts in which international human rights law might be used. For example, prisoners sentenced to death in the U.S. are separated from the general prison population and held for years in cells known as death row. Research shows that prolonged waiting on death row can cause severe mental suffering, often coupled with physical deterioration. *See* ROBERT JOHNSON, CONDEMNED TO DIE—LIFE UNDER SENTENCE OF DEATH (1981). In *Trop v. Dulles*, 356 U.S. 86 (1958), the Supreme Court implied that imposing a condition on an individual, in which severe mental suffering is inherent, violates the Eighth Amendment's prohibition of cruel and unusual punishment. U.S. courts, however, consistently have disregarded the issue of mental suffering on death row by either refusing to consider whether suffering has reached unconstitutional proportions or by failing to separate the issue of mental suffering from the issue of the death penalty per se. *See* Note, *Mental Suffering Under Sentence of Death: A Cruel and Unusual Punishment*, 57 IOWA L. REV. 814, 821 (1972). Some courts have justified the time spent on death row as necessary in order to guarantee a careful review of the issues in the case. *Richmond v. Ricketts*, 640 F. Supp. 767, 803 (D.Ariz. 1986). The *Richmond* court also declared that the time spent on death row was not entirely harmful

---

[22] The Lawless Case, 1960 Y.B. EUR. CONV. ON HUMAN RIGHTS, 474 (Eur. Comm'n on Human Rights), *reprinted in* 31 I.L.R. 290; R. v. Commissioner of Police, (1983) Q.B. Div'l Ct., *reported in* THE TIMES (London), May 28, 1983, CO/565/83 (available June 26, 1986, on LEXIS, Enggen library, Cases file).
[23] . . . 715 F.2d 87 (3d Cir. 1983). . . .

because the prisoner developed "better skills in communicating with others" as well as "religious beliefs that he did not have before he went to prison." *Id.*

Though U.S. courts generally have failed to recognize the mental anxiety suffered on death row, that suffering did influence a decision by the European Court of Human Rights. In the *Soering Case*, 161 E.C.H.R. (ser. A) (1989), discussed in chapter 11, *supra*, the European Court considered "the ever present and mounting anguish of awaiting execution of the death penalty" and concluded that, if the United Kingdom were to extradite Soering (a national of the Federal Republic of Germany) to the U.S. to face trial for murder, the United Kingdom would violate its obligation under Article 3 of the European Convention on Human Rights: "No one shall be subjected to torture or to inhuman or degrading treatment or punishment." In arriving at that conclusion the Court considered the severity of the conditions on death row, Soering's age at the time of the offense (eighteen), and his impaired mental responsibility. Could *Soering* be influential in challenging the prolonged waiting on death row by U.S. prisoners?

2.   Another area in which international norms may be more protective than U.S. standards relates to conditions of confinement for mentally handicapped persons living in non-criminal state facilities. In *Youngberg v. Romeo*, 457 U.S. 307 (1982), the Supreme Court held that the Due Process Clause of the Fourteenth Amendment provides persons with mental retardation, who have been involuntarily committed, with certain substantive rights, including reasonable safety, freedom from unnecessary bodily restraint, and adequate training to ensure safety and freedom from bodily restraint. *Id.* at 324. In determining whether a state has met its obligations under those standards the Court declared that "decision[s], if made by a professional, [are] presumptively valid; liability may be imposed only when the decision by the professional is such a substantive departure from accepted professional judgment, practice, or standards as to demonstrate that the person responsible actually did not base the decision on such a judgment." *Id.* at 323. Federal intervention, therefore, is allowed only when the government has reason to question the presumption.

The First Circuit Court in *Doe v. Gaughan*, 808 F.2d 871 (1st Cir. 1986) used *Youngberg* in reasoning that conditions in a state hospital for the mentally ill did not violate the patients' due process rights. The trial court in *Gaughan* found that overcrowding and understaffing decreased the hospital's ability to deliver services and caused some patients to become even more ill. Despite the findings, however, the court held that the conditions did not violate patients' rights. The court of appeals affirmed, reasoning that, under *Youngberg*, "[t]he Constitution does not require a state to provide an ideal environment for each person in its mental institution. Rather, it must provide an environment in which professional judgment may be exercised. Because Bridgewater's facilities are not so lacking as to prevent this exercise of professional judgment, these shortcomings do not rise to the level of a constitutional deprivation." *Id.* at 886.

U.N. Principle 9(1) of Principles for the Protection of Persons with Mental Illness and the Improvement of Mental Health Care, G.A. res. 119, U.N. GAOR, 46th Sess., Supp. No. 49, at 189, U.N. Doc. A/46/49 (1991), provides "[e]very patient shall have the right to be treated in the least restrictive environment and with the least restrictive or intrusive treatment appropriate to the patient's needs." Principle 9(2) states "[t]he treatment and care of every patient shall be based on an individually prescribed plan, discussed with the patient, reviewed regularly, revised as necessary and provided by qualified professional staff." Might those norms influence a federal or state court in a lawsuit challenging conditions of detention for the mentally handicapped in a state institution?

3.   International norms were influential in encouraging Ohio to change its policy of commingling pre- and post-adjudicated juveniles in detention centers. Ohio had been committing youths found to have violated criminal laws to facilities designed for short-term, pre-trial custody. The facilities were overcrowded, poorly maintained, and understaffed. As a result of overcrowding in the entire state system, authorities were sometimes forced to detain youths awaiting trial in quarters with youths awaiting transfer to more secure facilities. The pre-adjudicated youth then were subject to violence and sexual abuse and were challenged by adjudicated youth to pursue further criminal behavior.

Various international norms prohibit detaining unconvicted persons with convicted persons. Other norms proscribe detaining youth with adults and civil offenders with more-violent criminal offenders. Using these international standards as well as similar U.S. standards, critics of the policy were able to persuade Ohio that its practices contravened international law.

4.   HURST HANNUM, MATERIALS ON INTERNATIONAL HUMAN RIGHTS AND U.S. CRIMINAL LAW AND PROCEDURE (1989) has identified other areas where international norms might be useful in U.S. courts; for example:

a.   The European Commission has found that a government must replace an appointed lawyer when the accused demonstrates that the interests of justice thus would be served. The Commission does not require the accused to demonstrate that actual prejudice resulted. The Supreme Court, however, requires an accused to "show how specific errors undermined the reliability of the finding of guilt." *Id.* at 88-89.

b.   The European Court of Human Rights held that pressure brought on an accused to pay a small fine rather than face the closure of his business violated the right to a fair trial. Plea bargaining is an essential element of the U.S. criminal justice system. *Id.* at 95.

5.   Professor Lillich has observed that counsel in *Bowers v. Hardwick*, 478 U.S. 186 (1986) (upholding Georgia's sodomy statute), could have used *Dudgeon v. United Kingdom*, 45 Eur. Ct. H.R. (ser. A) (1982) (adult male homosexuals have right to privacy). Richard B. Lillich, *The Constitution and International Human Rights*, 83 AM. J. INT'L L. 851, 861 (1989). *See* James D. Wilets, *Using International Law to Vindicate the Civil Rights of Gays and Lesbians in United States Courts*, 27 COLUM. HUM. RTS. L. REV. 33 (1995).

6.   Another area that may generate discussion regarding the use of international norms relate to radiation experiments conducted by the U.S. government during the Cold War. The Clinton administration released records detailing various types of human radiation experiments conducted by the government on civilian populations. The records show that children and the mentally or terminally ill were among those subject to tests. In most cases the individuals on whom experiments were conducted had not consented and were not aware of their exposure to radiation. Various international treaties, such as Article 7 of the Covenant on Civil and Political Rights, explicitly prohibit subjecting individuals to medical or scientific experimentation without their free consent.

7.   For further reading see chapter 12, *supra*, and:

Mark Gibney, *Human Rights and Human Consequences: A Critical Analysis of Sanchez-Espinoza v. Reagan*, 10 LOY. L.A. INT'L & COMP. L.J. 299 (1988);

Gregory D. Gisvold, Note, *Strangers in a Strange Land: Assessing the Fate of Foreign Nationals Arrested in the United States by State and Local Authorities*, 78 MINN. L. REV. 771 (1994) (discussing international standards regarding the involvement of consular representatives in cases of foreign nationals accused of committing crimes in the U.S.);

NADINE STROSSEN, RECENT U.S. AND INTERNATIONAL JUDICIAL PROTECTION OF INDIVIDUAL RIGHTS: A COMPARATIVE LEGAL PROCESS ANALYSIS AND PROPOSED SYNTHESIS (1989);

Howard Tolley, *International Human Rights Law in U.S. Courts, Public Interest Groups and Private Attorneys*, 1987 Annual Meeting, American Political Science Association;

David Weissbrodt, *Ethical Problems of an International Human Rights Law Practice*, 7 MICH. Y.B. INT'L L. STUD. 217 (1985);

David Weissbrodt, *Strategies for Selection and Pursuit of International Human Rights Objectives*, 8 YALE J. WORLD PUB. ORD. 62 (1981);

Linda A. Whisman, *Selected Bibliography: Articles and Cases on International Human Rights Law in Domestic Courts*, 18 INT'L LAW. 83 (1984).

CHAPTER 14

REFUGEE AND ASYLUM LAW; JURISPRUDENCE OF HUMAN RIGHTS; CULTURAL RELATIVISM

		Page	
A.	**Introduction**		632
B.	**Questions**		632
C.	**Introduction to Refugee Law**		636
	1. **Procedural Issues: Claiming Refugee Status**		636
	Deborah Anker, The Law of Asylum in the U.S.		636
	2. **Definition of Refugee**		640
	3. **Interpreting the Refugee Definition: Exactly What is a Well-Founded Fear of Persecution?**		642
	UNHCR Handbook		643
D.	**The Role of the UNHCR**		646
	1. **Purpose, Function, and Responsibility**		646
	Statute of the Office of the UNHCR		646
	Lawyers Committee, The UNHCR at 40		646
	2. **Participation in U.S. Asylum Proceedings**		649
	Letter from UNHCR Associate Legal Counselor		649
E.	**Gender-Based Refugee Claims**		650
	1. **Gender as a Social Group**		650
	Fatin v. INS		651
	UNHCR Guidelines on the Protection of Refugee Women		656
	Women Refugees Project Guidelines		657
	INS Guidelines for Consideration of Gender-Related Asylum Claims		658
	2. **Are FGM and Spousal Abuse Persecution?**		666
	UNHCR Position on FGM		668
	3. **Internal Flight**		675
	INS Basic Law Manual		675
F.	**Obstacles to FGM- and Spousal Violence-Based Asylum Claims**		677
	1. **Cultural Relativism**		677
	Katherine Brennan, The Influence of Cultural Relativism		677
	Jack Donnelly, Cultural Relativism and Universal Human Rights		678
	2. **Theoretical Foundations of Human Rights**		683

Hilary Charlesworth et al., Feminist Approaches to International
   Law   683
Nigel Purvis, Critical Legal Studies in Public International Law   687
Anthony D'Amato, Is International Law Really "Law"?   694

A. INTRODUCTION

According to 1994 estimates, between 19 and 23 million people sought refuge, more than double the number in 1984 and almost 10 times as many as in 1974. An additional 26 million were internally displaced—forced from homes but still within their home country.[1] *See* John Darnton, *U.N. Faces Refugee Crisis That Never Ends,* N.Y. TIMES, Aug. 8, 1994, at A1. Nearly half were children. *Report of the United Nations High Commissioner for Refugees,* at 19, U.N. Doc. E/1994/41 (1994). Because most refugee flows are caused by human rights abuses, continuing conflicts in Africa, the Middle East, central and eastern Europe, and elsewhere compel the conclusion that "the refugee crisis" will not end soon.

The problems as well as the machineries for dealing with them are complex. There are three durable solutions to the international refugee problem—repatriation to the country of origin, settlement in the country of first asylum, or resettlement in a third country. Repatriation is the favored solution, and most refugees are in fact repatriated. This chapter, however, focuses on people who seek refuge in the U.S. and discusses the applicable U.S. and international law. U.S. law is discussed in the context of a Ghanian woman seeking relief from her own and her daughter's deportation.

B. QUESTIONS

Awata is a 25-year old woman from Ghana, in West Africa.[2] She recently graduated from the University of Minnesota, after four years of study focused on agriculture. She entered the U.S. under a student visa, but it expired two months after her graduation; and now she is in the U.S. illegally. She has not returned home because of fear that her five-year-old daughter, born in Ghana shortly before they came to the U.S., would be subjected to female genital mutilation (FGM).

FGM encompasses three operations on female genitalia: (1) circumcision or *sunna* (Muslim for "tradition"), which entails cutting the hood of the clitoris; (2)

---

[1] It is difficult to estimate the number of refugees. Estimates issued by the U.N. High Commissioner for Refugees are considered the most reliable.

[2] Ghana in 1993 elected the President of a new government and thus ended 11 years of military rule. The Constitution called for an executive branch, a unicameral Parliament, and an independent judiciary. It also established a Commission for Human Rights and Administrative Justice, charged with investigating and remedying human rights violations.

See STATE DEPARTMENT, COUNTRY REPORTS ON HUMAN RIGHTS PRACTICES FOR 1993, 112-13 (1994).

The facts in this hypothetical reflect varying traditions in Africa. The details regarding female genital mutilation (FGM) represent a generalization of the practice in central Africa. *Lobola* (brideprice), in contrast, is more prevalent in southern Africa. The *lobola* laws set forth here hypothetically are in fact found in Zimbabwe. To facilitate presentation of fact patterns we have assumed that both FGM and *lobola* occur in Ghana.

excision, removing the entire clitoris and the inner vaginal lips; and (3) infibulation, sewing together the outer lips with thread or thorns after removing the clitoris and the inner lips. After that third procedure the girl's legs are bound from ankle to hip (sometimes for up to 40 days) to allow scar tissue to form. EFUA DORKENOO & SCILLA ELWORTHY, FEMALE GENITAL MUTILATION: PROPOSALS FOR CHANGE 7, 7 (1992).

Various forms of FGM are practiced in more than 40 countries. The concentration is in central Africa, Southeast Asia, and the Middle East; but it also occurs among indigenous people in parts of South America and Australia. Katherine Brennan, *The Influence of Cultural Relativism on International Human Rights Law: Female Circumcision as a Case Study*, 7 LAW & INEQ. J. 367, 373 n.26 (1989). It also has been reported among immigrant populations in the U.S. and Europe. Estimates of the number of women and girls affected range from 80 to more than 114 million. *Compare* Berhane Ras-Work, *Traditional Practices That Inflict Disability, in* WOMEN AND DISABILITY 23, 23 (Esther Boylan ed., 1991) *with* Randy Furst, *A Child is Spared*, STAR TRIB. (Minneapolis), Mar. 25, 1994, at 1B, 2B.

Operations are performed on approximately 2,000,000 girls each year by older women in rural villages who use crude instruments and no anaesthesia. They mostly have not been trained in medical or sterilization procedures, and as a result there can be numerous complications. For example, girls may in the short-term suffer from hemorrhaging, post-operative shock, damage to other organs, or infection. Long-term complications include chronic infection, cysts, extremely painful menstruation, infertility, AIDS, and difficulties associated with intercourse and childbirth. Both short-term and long-term complications may lead to death. DORKENOO & ELWORTHY, *supra*, at 8-10.

Though many opposed to the practice question its scientific and other bases, proponents advance several arguments to support it. *See* DORKENOO & ELWORTHY, *supra*, at 13-14; OLAYINKA KOSO-THOMAS, THE CIRCUMCISION OF WOMEN: A STRATEGY FOR ERADICATION 5-9 (1987). *First*, men and women in countries where FGM is practiced argue that it increases male pleasure (still of primary importance in patriarchal societies) while decreasing the likelihood that women (because of decreased pleasure for them) will engage in premarital or extramarital sex. It also increases a woman's matrimonial opportunities because female virginity, and often FGM itself, is a prerequisite to marriage.

Second, the practice frequently is justified as a religious ritual. FGM occurs primarily in Muslim-dominated areas, but also is practiced by Christians and others. Though theologians disavow the claim that their respective faiths require FGM, women frequently consent to the operation under a genuine but erroneous belief that it is required by religion.

Third, proponents stress sociological implications because FGM may mark identification with a cultural or ethnic group wherein membership hinges on participation in cultural rituals. Traditionally it was deemed a rite of passage into adulthood, an occasion often marked by elaborate ceremonies. The strength of that justification is diminished, however, by the trend toward performing the surgery at younger ages. In some countries FGM is performed on babies.

Fourth, FGM is justified by its purported hygienic and aesthetic benefits. Female genitalia are often considered "dirty," and removal is believed to promote cleanliness. There is evidence of a superstition that, unless destroyed, female genitalia will grow to resemble male genitalia. Furthermore, legend erroneously suggests that FGM promotes women's fertility. Some people believe that women who have not been subjected cannot get pregnant.

FGM has been condemned by several African and European countries and by the U.S., but has been outlawed in only a few countries. DORKENOO & ELWORTHY, *supra*, at 11. Statistics from 1992 show that some form of FGM is performed on approximately 30% (approximately 2.25 million) of the females in Ghana. FRAN P. HOSKEN, THE HOSKEN REPORT—GENITAL AND SEXUAL MUTILATION OF FEMALES (1992). The practice has become less popular in urban areas, where some men will marry women who have not been excised or infibulated. DORKENOO & ELWORTHY, *supra*, at 12. In addition, the government of Ghana has discouraged the practice via educational campaigns. U.S. DEP'T OF STATE, COUNTRY REPORTS ON HUMAN RIGHTS PRACTICES FOR 1993 at 116 (1994). As in other countries, however, a girl's relatives sometimes force her to submit to the procedure without the mother's knowledge or consent.

In addition to fearing that her daughter would in Ghana be subjected to FGM, Awata fears she will be abused by her husband, Johannes. They were married under traditional law when she was seventeen. Johannes, who remained in Ghana while Awata was studying in the U.S., physically abused her before she left Ghana, and she expects the abuse to continue when she returns. She has never asked police or other authorities to intervene. She did ask her family for assistance, but they refused to help or shelter her. Johannes and his family paid *lobola* in exchange for Awata, and her family fears he will demand that it be refunded if Awata leaves him. Awata's family used the *lobola* and has no funds with which to repay Johannes.

Lobola, or brideprice, is a traditional practice. *See generally* ADAM KUPER, WIVES FOR CATTLE: BRIDEWEALTH AND MARRIAGE IN SOUTHERN AFRICA 26-27 (1982); MARK MATHABANE, AFRICAN WOMEN: THREE GENERATIONS (1994). A prospective groom and his family will ask the prospective bride's family for permission to marry. Her family will request the *lobola*, which varies depending on the bride's age, appearance, education, and work skills. If the two families agree on a price the wedding may proceed. Pursuant to the traditional practice of *kuzvarira*—the giving of girls for marriage without their permission—the bride's consent is not required, and objections she may have are largely ignored. U.S. DEP'T OF STATE, COUNTRY REPORTS ON HUMAN RIGHTS PRACTICES FOR 1992 at 314 (1993).

Cash has generally replaced cattle as the form of payment. Regardless of form, however, *lobola* entitles the husband to numerous benefits. *First*, it legitimizes the marriage in the community and binds the wife to her husband. Most weddings evidenced by *lobola* are not, however, recognized in civil law, and thus give the wife few, if any, rights. *Second*, the arrangement subjugates her rights to her husband. For example, he or his family may demand all money she earns. Also, she has no right to question him regarding his activities. Because the arrangement is not recognized in civil law she has no right to "divorce" and often no right to the children. *Third*, by accepting *lobola* the bride's family guarantees she will produce children. If she is infertile or deserts her husband before having children, her family must refund *lobola* or provide him with another wife. If she divorces after having children neither she nor her family has any right to the children. *Fourth*, *lobola* entitles the husband to obedience. If the wife is not submissive, or rebels, he may request a refund of the *lobola*. He also may demand one if she objects to his taking an additional wife.

Lobola is widely practiced even where declared illegal. Through Ghana's Legal Age of Majority Act, and also the Matrimonial Causes Act, women were given equal rights with prospective husbands to decide when and whom to marry. Women also were given the right to own property independently. The acts later were reaffirmed in two judicial opinions in a case where a court held that the father of the prospective bride had no standing to object to the marriage of his daughter without the payment of *lobola*. Despite those laws, however, there is a strong tradition favoring *lobola*.

Though the new Constitution prohibits gender discrimination, Ghanaian women remain subject to extensive but covert societal discrimination. Violence against women, including rape and spousal abuse, is also a significant problem though laws prohibit such abuse. Despite participating in an educational campaign supporting women's rights, the government seldom intervenes in domestic disputes to protect the female. Also, criminal cases rarely are prosecuted. *See* U.S. DEP'T OF STATE, COUNTRY REPORTS ON HUMAN RIGHTS PRACTICES FOR 1993 at 112-16 (1993).

Awata recently was apprehended by the U.S. Immigration and Naturalization Service (INS) for residing in the U.S. without a valid visa. An immigration judge issued an order to show cause why she should not be deported. Assume you are her lawyer at a hearing before that judge. You have filed a claim for asylum and also withholding-of-deportation on the ground that she and her daughter have a well-founded fear of persecution if they are returned to Ghana.

You are to prepare for final arguments in which the preceding facts are raised. As you prepare be sure to anticipate arguments your adversary may make and be ready to counter them. Keep in mind the following questions. Your answers should address first, all facts presented above. Then proceed by assuming Awata does not have a daughter but fears that she herself will be subject to abuse by her husband if she is deported.

*   *   *   *   *

1. Do Awata and her daughter qualify for relief from deportation?

    a. Why might the daughter qualify for asylum or withholding of deportation? Why might Awata herself qualify for asylum or withholding of deportation?

    b. Do Awata and her daughter have a well-founded fear of persecution?

    c. Is the persecution on account of any one or more of the five permissible criteria?

    d. Do Awata and her daughter fear persecution because they are members of a social group?

    e. Is persecution from the government expected? If not, is it useful to argue that both still will be "persecuted" under the statutory definition of that term?

    f. Is it relevant that spousal abuse occurs frequently in the U.S. and women here are often without adequate protection?

    g. Can Awata divorce her husband to avoid abuse?

    h. As to withholding of deportation, is there a "clear probability" that Awata will be persecuted if she is deported to Ghana? That her daughter will be persecuted?

    i. As to asylum, what further showing must Awata make?

    j. If Awata qualifies for both asylum and withholding of deportation, which alternative is preferable? Which provides Awata and her daughter with the most protection?

    k. How might you counter the argument that FGM is not persecution because it is not a country-wide practice? Should Awata and her daughter have to relocate in Ghana? Should either have to be separated from family and community?

2. What procedural alternatives are available to Awata if the judge denies her claims for asylum and withholding of deportation?

3. How might the UNHCR assist you in the case before the judge and during appeals?

4. What obstacles confront your argument that FGM and spousal abuse are persecution?

  a. How does human rights law affect your need to show that Awata and her daughter fear persecution?

  b. There are several bases for explaining how human rights norms constitute law; *e.g.*, the cultural relativist view, Chinese view, natural law view, positivist view, feminist view, and the critical-legal view. Which might be most helpful in convincing the judge that Ghana has a responsibility to prohibit FGM and to enforce the prohibition against spousal violence?

  c. Is anything distinctive about the source of authority on which rights-theories are based that will assist or hinder you in persuading a judge that Ghana should comply with international norms relating to protection of women and children?

  d. What generally is the source of human rights in U.N. instruments, and what influence might that source have on Ghana's responsibilities for protection?

  e. Should the international community expect countries with varying civil, political, economic, social, and cultural traditions to respect human rights standards in the same ways? Is there room for diversity?

  f. Is the problem of cultural relativism in chapter 4, *supra*, distinguishable from the situation presented in this chapter?

C. INTRODUCTION TO REFUGEE LAW

1. Procedural Issues: Claiming Refugee Status

DEBORAH E. ANKER, THE LAW OF ASYLUM IN THE UNITED STATES: A GUIDE TO ADMINISTRATIVE PRACTICE AND CASE LAW 1-2, 24-25, 31-60 (2nd ed. 1991) (modified text) (several footnotes and section headings omitted) (emphases altered or omitted):

"Asylum" often is used imprecisely to describe three distinct categories in immigration law that allow persons fleeing persecution to enter or remain in the United States: (1) refugee status, (2) asylum status, and (3) withholding of deportation or return. The three categories allow an alien to enter or remain in the United States based upon a persecution claim, but each has distinct eligibility requirements and application procedures, so it is important not to confuse them.

Refugee status is available to persons outside United States territory or jurisdiction. It is conferred upon persons who are determined to meet the definition of "refugee," and to be "of special humanitarian concern to the United States" by the President, in special consultations with Congress. . . . Status is determined in third countries or in the country of origin, before entry to the United States. . . .

Asylum status and withholding of deportation generally are available to persons who are seeking direct protection from the United States, usually through applying within the United States or at its border. . . .

The time and place an alien applies for asylum will affect her procedural and appeal rights. The statutory and regulatory scheme provides two basic avenues for an alien seeking asylum. First, she can apply affirmatively by submitting an application for asylum (Form I- 589) *before* being apprehended and referred to formal deportation or exclusion proceedings to bring about her departure from the United States. . . . Second, after apprehension—or after denial or "referral" of her affirmative claim (see below)—she can raise asylum as a *defense* to exclusion or deportation proceedings. Current regulations maintain this two tier system, each of which is administered by a different agency within the Department of Justice, although 1994 regulatory changes have made the two processes more integrated. The affirmative process is administered by the I.N.S.; exclusion and deportation hearings are under the jurisdiction of the E.O.I.R. [Executive Office of Immigration Review], of which the Board of Immigration Appeals (BIA) and the immigration judges are a part.

1. Applying Affirmatively to the I.N.S. Asylum Office

Aliens apprehended at the border are referred to exclusion proceedings pursuant to I.N.A. § 236. Aliens apprehended within the United States are referred to deportation proceedings pursuant to I.N.A. §242(b).

[Affirmative asylum applications will be] adjudicated by an "asylum officer" in a specially constituted Asylum Branch within the I.N.S., *not* as in the case of most other I.N.S. benefits, by the I.N.S. district director. 8 C.F.R. § 208.2 (a).

Although many asylum applications are made at ports of entry, most affirmative applications are made from within the United States. Unlike other contexts, where encounters with immigration officials may precipitate the institution of proceedings and the asylum application process, asylum claimants within the United States in a more meaningful sense may make a choice to apply affirmatively. The statute makes clear that an alien may apply for asylum irrespective of immigration status, i.e. how she entered and whether or not she has any legal immigration status at the time she applies.

. . . By applying affirmatively, an alien effectively turns herself in to the I.N.S. thus hoping to avoid future apprehension and all the attendant consequences. . . . If she is without lawful status, applying for asylum affirmatively begins a process which, at least in the case of failure to grant, results in the institution of deportation or exclusion proceedings. However, the possible benefits to be obtained by applying affirmatively are:

1) Even if she subsequently is placed in deportation proceedings, the I.N.S. may be more likely to waive bond or set low bond for an alien who initially presented herself voluntarily.

2) . . . [The] earlier an alien applies, the sooner she may be able to work legally. (see below).

3) By waiting until apprehended to apply, an alien may appear to have purposefully violated United States immigration laws. Such a consideration generally should not be relevant. However, in the past, immigration examiners and immigration judges who, in addition to determining persecution claims, had other responsibilities related to enforcement and issuing deportation orders, may have considered immigration violations as a factor in the exercise of discretion, or in the evaluation of the credibility of the applicant's testimony.

4) The act of applying affirmatively may buttress an argument that an alien came to the United States to seek asylum, instead of for economic or other reasons, not related to persecution. Again, although in most cases such considera-

tions should not be relevant, applying affirmatively may be viewed as evidence of the bona fides of the alien's claim.

[Aliens] applying at . . . ports of entry who are not placed in exclusion proceedings, generally will file at the I.N.S. office with jurisdiction over that port of entry. Those within the United States may affirmatively request asylum by filing an application with one of eight asylum offices in different cities throughout the country.

Applications may be filed by mail to an I.N.S. Regional Service Center, which will forward the application to the appropriate asylum office. . . . 8 C.F.R. § 208.2 (a) and § 208.4 (a).

[The asylum application is made on Form I-589.] The application is forwarded to the State Department, which has the option to comment on it or provide relevant information, but under the 1994 changes, the asylum officer does not have to wait for a response for any period of time before issuing a decision.

The asylum officer will schedule a non-adversarial, private interview with the applicant. The expectation under the 1994 regulations is that this interview will take place within 60 days of filing. The applicant's attorney may be present at the interview but there is no right to representation and counsel does not formally present the applicant's case. Instead, the asylum officer questions the applicant and generally controls the course of the interview, although the applicant or her attorney have the right to make a statement or comment on the evidence at the end of the interview. 8 C.F.R. § 208.9 (b) and (d). The interview is not recorded.

The applicant will be told to appear in person to receive the decision on the claim. If the asylum claim is approved the applicant will be notified at that time and asylum will be granted for an indefinite period. If the claim is not approved, generally it will be "referred" to an immigration judge for a hearing.[3] When the applicant appears to receive the decision, she will be served with the referral, an official charging document and a specific date for a deportation or exclusion hearing. 8 C.F.R. §208.9 (d). The "referral" is not considered a denial for purposes of subsequent immigration judge adjudication. The same claim will be forwarded to the immigration judge, who is expected to adjudicate it de novo and without prejudice. . . .

2.   Applying in a Deportation or Exclusion Proceeding

When an asylum officer does not grant but "refers" a case, or when the I.N.S. institutes exclusion or deportation proceedings before the alien has had an opportunity to file affirmatively, an immigration judge can adjudicate a claim for asylum made in the course of those proceedings.

Deportation hearings are formal proceedings to determine whether an alien will be returned to her country . . . .. Immigration judge jurisdiction over deportation proceedings begins with the filing of the "Order to Show Cause" (OSC) with the immigration court and the service of the OSC on the alien. The Order names the alien as a respondent, and alleges the factual and legal basis for deportability. . . .

Unlike the affirmative interview, deportation and exclusion hearings are formally adversarial, with the government separately represented by counsel, an I.N.S. trial attorney. The applicant also has the right to representation by counsel, at no

---

[3] In some cases over which the Asylum Office has special jurisdiction—crewmen, stowaways, certain security risks—an asylum officer may issue a denial. Also, an applicant who is in valid non-immigrant status may be denied asylum by the officer who will restore her previous status; she will not be placed in [deportation] proceedings. 8 C.F.R. § 208.14 (b) (3) and (4).

expense to the government. The proceedings are record[ed] and the applicant is entitled to a decision based on the record.

Although courts have recognized the severity of the sanction of deportation, deportation hearings are considered civil in nature, so persons subject to deportation are not afforded the rights of criminal defendants. Claimants may remain incarcerated in I.N.S. detention facilities during the pendency of deportation proceedings. When an alien is finally deported, the I.N.S. will usually make travel arrangements and place her on an airplane bound for her country. Deported aliens . . . may not reenter the United States for five (5) years without prior permission from the Attorney General.

That an alien is denied asylum does not mean that she automatically will be deported. The immigration judge may grant the alien the right to voluntarily depart from the United States within a specified time, avoiding disabilities resulting from a final order of deportation.

The immigration judge will automatically consider an asylum request as a request for withholding of deportation. . . .

When filed for in deportation proceedings, asylum and withholding of deportation are forms of relief from deportation. Once the I.N.S. has proven the deportability of an alien, the alien may request these as two of several means of avoiding forcible departure from the United States. . . . Many aliens may have difficulty successfully opposing substantive deportability allegations. Although deportability must be proven by the I.N.S., the Service need only establish that the alien is a foreign national for the burden to shift to the alien to show that she is lawfully in the United States by proving the time, place and manner of her entry. The circumstances under which many asylum applicants flee to and enter the United States—without inspection or with false documents—constitute grounds of deportation. . . . Challenges to deportability are possible, but where a person has previously applied for asylum to the I.N.S., the information in that application may be used to establish deportability in a subsequent deportation hearing. In many cases, asylum and withholding, like other claims for relief from deportation, may be the most critical issue in the deportation proceeding.

An alien requesting asylum or withholding of deportation must prove she is statutorily eligible for either form of relief. Thus, the alien bears the burden of persuading the immigration judge that she is entitled to asylum and withholding. Asylum, unlike withholding of deportation, is discretionary, so the alien must also prove that she warrants a favorable exercise of discretion.

Denial of both asylum and withholding of deportation by the immigration judge can result in a final order of deportation (or exclusion) being lodged against the alien, or in an order requiring the alien to leave voluntarily by a specified date. The alien may appeal this decision to the BIA within ten (10) days of the immigration judge's order. . . . An alien may appeal the Board's decision to the federal courts . . ..

3. Employment Authorization

It is critical for most asylum applicants to be able to work legally in the United States. The 1994 regulations attempt to "decouple" employment authorization from the application for asylum in order to discourage the filing of non-genuine claims simply for the purpose of obtaining a work permit. With the 1994 regulations and increased resources, the Justice Department anticipates that most cases will be adjudicated through the immigration judge stage within 180 days. Therefore, the 1994 regulations make it impossible to receive interim employment authorization before at least 180 days have elapsed since initial filing of the asylum claim. . . . If the case is adjudicated by the immigration judge within 180 days, an applicant cannot receive employment authorization while she pursues administrative and judicial appeals. If the I.N.S. and immigration court do not complete the adjudication within 180 days, she may receive interim employment authorization. . . .

NOTES AND QUESTIONS

1. What are advantages and disadvantages of affirmatively applying for asylum? Of waiting and then later raising asylum or withholding of deportation as a defense to deportation?

2. On December 5, 1994, the INS issued new regulations governing (1) asylum and (2) withholding of deportation claims and applications for work authorizations. 59 Fed. Reg. 62,284 (1995) (codified at 8 C.F.R. § 208, 236, 242, 274a, and 299). The new regulations apply to all applications for asylum or withholding of deportation, whether before an asylum officer or immigration judge, that are filed on or after January 4, 1995, or pending as of that date. The regulations were promulgated primarily to expedite "deserving" applications and more promptly to identify and deny "meritless and abusive applications." 59 Fed. Reg. 14,779 (proposed Mar. 30, 1994). The clauses pertinent to the preceding excerpt include the following:

- Asylum officers may no longer deny an affirmative application made by an excludable or deportable alien, but may refer that application to an immigration judge to initiate exclusion or deportation proceedings. Accordingly, the Notice of Intent to Deny has been replaced by a referral letter. Asylum officers, previously required to provide justification for denials, need not justify referrals.
- A case referred to an immigration judge no longer receives a review based on a completely new review. The asylum application, and all other materials (*i.e.* affidavits, exhibits, etc.) in the applicant's file, become part of the record on referral.
- Applicants may request work authorization no earlier than 150 days after the INS receives their complete asylum application. Once the work authorization application is filed, the INS has 30 days to process it. If the INS fails to do so, the applicant will be given interim work authorization unless asylum is denied during the 30 day period. If asylum has been denied by the officer or judge during the 150 days, work authorization will be denied.
- Asylum officers and immigration judges may deny an otherwise approvable claim on the ground that the alien can be deported or returned to a country in which he or she will not face persecution and will have access to a full and fair procedure for determining his or her asylum claim, in accordance with an international agreement to which the U.S. is a party.

8 C.F.R. § 103, 208, 236, 242, 274a. Do the changes for 1995 alter your answers to Question 1?

3. For further reading on asylum reform, see: Jeanne A. Butterfield, *The New Asylum Regulations: A Practitioner's Guide*, IMMIGR. BRIEFINGS, Jan. 1995, at 1; KENNETH Y. GEMAN, PRACTISING LAW INSTITUTE, IMPORTANT NEW ASYLUM REGULATIONS (1995); Sarah Ignatius, *Restricting the Rights of Asylum Seekers: The New Legislative and Administrative Proposals*, 7 HARV. HUM. RTS. J. 225 (1994).

2.   Definition of Refugee

The word "refugee" is defined in both U.S. and international law. The U.S. defines a refugee as:

any person who is outside any country of such person's nationality or, in the case of a person having no nationality, is outside any country in which such person last habitually resided, and who is unable or unwilling to return to, and is unable or unwilling to avail himself or herself of the protection of, that country because of persecution or a well-founded fear of persecution on account of race, religion, nationality, membership in a particular social group, or political opinion. . . .

8 U.S.C. § 1101(a)(42). That definition appears in the Refugee Act of 1980, which was enacted to bring the U.S. into compliance with the U.N. Protocol of 1967 Relating to the Status of Refugees, 606 U.N.T.S. 267 [hereinafter 1967 Refugee Protocol]. The U.S. ratified it on November 1, 1968. As of February 1996, 127 countries had ratified the Protocol.

INS v. Cardoza-Fonseca, 480 U.S. 421, 437 (1987), held that the statutory definition should be interpreted by reference to corresponding U.N. instruments. Those instruments originally defined "refugee" narrowly, to cover primarily the persons displaced because of World War II. Article 1(a)(2) of the Convention Relating to the Status of Refugees, 189 U.N.T.S. 137 [hereinafter Refugee Convention], defines a "refugee" as any person who:

> As a result of events occurring before 1 January 1951 and owing to well-founded fear of being persecuted for reasons of race, religion, nationality, membership of a particular social group or political opinion, is outside the country of his nationality and is unable or, owing to such fear, is unwilling to avail himself of the protection of that country; or who, not having a nationality and being outside the country of his former habitual residence as a result of such events, is unable or, owing to such fear, is unwilling to return to it.

The 1967 Refugee Protocol expanded that definition by removing all reference to events occurring before January 1, 1951. Therefore, "refugee" as defined by both international and U.S. law now includes everyone who has a well-founded fear of persecution because of specified characteristics.

Though the Supreme Court in *Cardoza-Fonseca* concluded that the definition should be interpreted by reference to international instruments, it concluded that an applicant for asylum must demonstrate "a well-founded fear of persecution." *Cardoza-Fonseca*, 480 U.S. at 430, 449. In contrast, to prove a claim for withholding of deportation, an applicant must demonstrate a "clear probability of persecution" after deportation. *Id.* at 430. The Court summarized the distinctions between the procedures:

> First, as we have mentioned, there is no entitlement to asylum, it is only granted to eligible refugees pursuant to the Attorney General's discretion. Once granted, however, asylum affords broader benefits. As the [Board of Immigration Appeals] explained in the context of an applicant from Afghanistan who was granted § 243(h) relief [(*i.e.* withholding of deportation)] but was denied asylum: "Section 243(h) relief is 'country specific' and accordingly, the applicant here would be presently protected from deportation to Afghanistan pursuant to section 243(h). But that section would not prevent his exclusion and deportation to Pakistan or any other hospitable country . . . if that country will accept him. In contrast, asylum is a greater form of relief. When granted asylum the alien may be eligible for adjustment of status to that of a lawful permanent resident . . . after residing here one year, subject to numerical limitations and the applicable regulations."

Id. at 428-29 n.6 (structure altered).

NOTES AND QUESTIONS

1. Think about the different standards of eligibility for asylum and for withholding of

deportation. Which is more difficult to prove? Which status affords greater protection? Does your conclusion seem anomalous? Does the fact that granting asylum is discretionary explain the anomaly?

2.   For additional reading, see:

ASYLUM LAW AND PRACTICE IN EUROPE AND NORTH AMERICA (Jacqueline Bhabha & Geoffrey Coll eds., 1992);

Jacqueline Bhabha, *European Union Asylum and Refugee Policy*, INT'L PRACTITIONER'S NOTE-BOOK, Oct. 1995, at 29;

GUY S. GOODWIN-GILL, THE REFUGEE IN INTERNATIONAL LAW (1983);

ATLE GRAHL-MADSEN, THE STATUS OF REFUGEES IN INTERNATIONAL LAW (1966);

JAMES C. HATHAWAY, THE LAW OF REFUGEE STATUS (1991);

Patricia Hyndman, *The 1951 Convention and its Implications for Procedural Questions*, 6 INT'L J. REFUGEE LAW 245 (1994);

HÉLÈNE LAMBERT, SEEKING ASYLUM: COMPARATIVE LAW AND PRACTICE IN SELECTED EUROPEAN COUNTRIES (1995);

ALAN NICHOLS & PAUL WHITE, REFUGEE DILEMMAS: REVIEWING THE COMPREHENSIVE PLAN OF ACTION FOR VIETNAMESE ASYLUM SEEKERS (1993);

NEHEMIAH ROBINSON, CONVENTION RELATING TO THE STATUS OF REFUGEES: ITS HISTORY, CONTENTS AND INTERPRETATION (1953);

UNHCR, COLLECTION OF INTERNATIONAL INSTRUMENTS CONCERNING REFUGEES (1990);

UNHCR, HANDBOOK ON PROCEDURES AND CRITERIA FOR DETERMINING REFUGEE STATUS, U.N. Doc. HCR/IP/4/Eng. Rev.1 (1988);

PAUL WEIS, COMMENTARY ON THE CONVENTION RELATING TO THE STATUS OF REFUGEES (1992).

The following bibliographies may also serve as useful resource guides:

DISPLACED PEOPLES AND REFUGEE STUDIES (Julian Davies ed., 1990);

DONATELLA LUCA, THE 1951 CONVENTION RELATING TO THE STATUS OF REFUGEES: A SELECTED BIBLIOGRAPHY (1991);

REFUGEE STUDIES PROGRAMME, DIRECTORY OF RESEARCH ON REFUGEES AND OTHER FORCED MI-GRANTS (1993);

UNESCO, ACCESS TO HUMAN RIGHTS DOCUMENTATION: DOCUMENTATION, DATABASES AND BIBLI-OGRAPHIES ON HUMAN RIGHTS (1991).

---

3.   Interpreting the Refugee Definition: Exactly What is a Well-Founded Fear of Persecution?

In its Handbook on Procedures and Criteria for Determining Refugee Status, the Office of the U.N. High Commissioner for Refugees (UNHCR) interprets the phrase "well founded fear of being persecuted"; and interpretations "provide[] signifi-cant guidance in construing the [Refugee] Protocol, to which Congress sought to conform" when it enacted the Refugee Act of 1980. *Cardoza-Fonseca*, 480 U.S. at 439 n.22. Relevant excerpts include the following:

UNHCR, HANDBOOK ON PROCEDURES AND CRITERIA FOR DETERMINING REF-UGEE STATUS 11-17, U.N. Doc. HCR/IP/4/Eng. Rev.1 (1988) [hereinafter UNHCR HANDBOOK] (paragraph numbers omitted):

(a) General analysis

The phrase "well-founded fear of being persecuted" is the key phrase of the definition. It reflects the views of its authors as to the main elements of refugee character. . . .

To the element of fear—a state of mind and a subjective condition—is added the qualification "well-founded." This implies that it is not only the frame of mind of the person concerned that determines his refugee status, but that this frame of mind must be supported by an objective situation. The term "well-founded fear" therefore contains a subjective and an objective element, and in determining whether well-founded fear exists, both elements must be taken into consideration. . . .

An evaluation of the *subjective element* is inseparable from an assessment of the personality of the applicant, since psychological reactions of different individuals may not be the same in identical conditions. One person may have strong political or religious convictions, the disregard of which would make his life intolerable; another may have no such strong convictions. One person may make an impulsive decision to escape; another may carefully plan his departure.

Due to the importance that the definition attaches to the subjective element, an assessment of credibility is indispensable where the case is not sufficiently clear from the facts on record. It will be necessary to take into account the personal and family background of the applicant, his membership of a particular racial, religious, national, social or political group, his own interpretation of his situation, and his personal experiences—in other words, everything that may serve to indicate that the predominant motive for his application is fear. Fear must be reasonable. Exaggerated fear, however, may be well-founded if, in all the circumstances of the case, such a state of mind can be regarded as justified.

As regards the objective element, it is necessary to evaluate the statements made by the applicant. The competent authorities that are called upon to determine refugee status are not required to pass judgement on conditions in the applicant's country of origin. The applicant's statements cannot, however, be considered in the abstract, and must be viewed in the context of the relevant background situation. A knowledge of conditions in the applicant's country of origin—while not a primary objective—is an important element in assessing the applicant's credibility. In general, the applicant's fear should be considered well-founded if he can establish, to a reasonable degree, that his continued stay in his country of origin has become intolerable to him for the reasons stated in the definition, or would for the same reasons be intolerable if he returned there.

These considerations need not necessarily be based on the applicant's own personal experience. What, for example, happened to his friends and relatives and other members of the same racial or social group may well show that his fear that sooner or later he also will become a victim of persecution is well-founded. The laws of the country of origin, and particularly the manner in which they are applied, will be relevant. The situation of each person must, however, be assessed on its own merits. . . .

(b) Persecution

There is no universally accepted definition of "persecution," and various attempts to formulate such a definition have met with little success. From Article 33 of the 1951 Convention, it may be inferred that a threat to life or freedom on account of race, religion, nationality, political opinion or membership of a particular social group is always persecution. Other serious violations of human rights—for the same reasons—would also constitute persecution. . . .

In addition, an applicant may have been subjected to various measures not in themselves amounting to persecution (e.g. discrimination in different forms), in some cases combined with other adverse factors (e.g. general atmosphere of insecurity in the country of origin). In such situations, the various elements involved may, if taken together, produce an effect on the mind of the applicant that can reasonably justify a claim to well-founded fear of persecution on "cumulative grounds." Needless to say, it is not possible to lay down a general rule as to what cumulative reasons can give rise to a valid claim to refugee status. This will necessarily depend on all the circumstances, including the particular geographical, historical and ethnological context. . . .

(g) Agents of persecution

Persecution is normally related to action by the authorities of a country. It may also emanate from sections of the population that do not respect the standards established by the laws of the country concerned. . . . Where serious discriminatory or other offensive acts are committed by the local populace, they can be considered as persecution if they are knowingly tolerated by the authorities, or if the authorities refuse, or prove unable, to offer effective protection.

*   *   *   *   *

An issue often arising is whether an individual is "subject to persecution"—defined in neither the Immigration and Nationalization Act nor treaties to which the U.S. is party. Courts, therefore, have used guides ranging from dictionaries to the UNHCR Handbook to aid their decisions.

In *Kovac v. INS*, relying on Webster's Third New International, the court ruled that persecution includes "the infliction of suffering or harm upon those who differ . . . in a way regarded as offensive" and noted that while "minor disadvantage or trivial inconvenience" is insufficient, "substantial economic disadvantage" constitutes persecution. 407 F.2d 102, 107 (9th Cir. 1969). *See also Berdo v. INS*, 432 F.2d 824, 846 (6th Cir. 1970) (imposition of substantial economic disadvantage is persecution). *But see Zalaga v. INS*, 916 F.2d 1257, 1260 (9th Cir. 1990) (termination from employment and difficulty in obtaining additional farmland not sufficiently substantial harm to qualify alien for asylum); *Minwalla v. INS*, 706 F.2d 831, 835 (8th Cir. 1983) (mere economic detriment is insufficient to establish a well-founded fear of persecution).

In every case, persecution is "a seemingly broader concept than threats to 'life or freedom.'" *INS v. Stevic*, 467 U.S. 407, 428 n.22 (1984). *See also Cardoza-Fonseca v. INS*, 767 F.2d 1448, 1452 (9th Cir. 1985) (quoting *Stevic*), *aff'd*, 480 U.S. 421 (1987). It is important to remember, however, that "persecution" generally implies some difference of opinion or status between persecutor and victim. *Desir v. Ilchert*, 840 F.2d 723, 727 (9th Cir. 1988); *Hernandez-Ortiz v. INS*, 777 F.2d 509, 516 (9th Cir. 1985).

Another issue is whether the individual seeking asylum or withholding of deportation is subject to official persecution or merely private acts of violence. Actions by officials acting within the scope of their duties may clearly constitute a human rights violation. Yet as the final paragraphs of the UNHCR Handbook excerpted above indicate, actions by private individuals also may be considered persecution for purposes of defining "refugee."

For a discussion of the public/private dichotomy, see Part E, *infra* at 666.

NOTES AND QUESTIONS

1.   In 1990, the INS issued certain interpretive regulations regarding the Immigration and Naturalization Act. Pursuant to one of them, 8 C.F.R. § 208.13(b)(2), an asylum applicant may prove a well-founded fear of persecution if she or he (1) establishes that there exists a pattern or practice of persecution on account of race, religion, nationality, membership in a particular social group, or political opinion, and (2) if he or she proves inclusion in, or identification with, one such group. It is not necessary to show that one was personally subject to persecution in the past if evidence establishes a well-founded fear of *future* persecution in the country of nationality.

2.   In *INS v. Elias-Zacarias*, 502 U.S. 478 (1992), the Court held that a guerrilla organization's attempts to coerce an alien to join did not necessarily constitute persecution on account of political opinion. Elias-Zacarias testified that armed guerrillas had come to his home and requested that he join their organization. He refused because he feared that the Guatemalan government would retaliate, and he fled Guatemala because of fear that guerrillas would return. *Id.* at 479-80.

Justice Scalia for the majority began by noting that an applicant must produce enough evidence to show that a reasonable factfinder would conclude that the applicant has a genuine fear of persecution. On facts in the record Scalia concluded that Elias-Zacarias failed to sustain that burden. He concluded too that Elias-Zacarias' rejection of recruitment was not necessarily motivated by political opinion and noted a variety of non-political reasons that might have been motivating. "The ordinary meaning of the phrase 'persecution on account of . . . political opinion' . . . is persecution on account of the victim's political opinion . . . ." *Id.* at 480-82.

The attorneys had argued that the failure to join the guerrillas constituted an affirmative expression of a political opinion. The Court disagreed and held that he had not presented sufficient evidence to show that the fear he had was "well-founded." *Id.* at 483. Discussing the evidence necessary to prove the "on account of" part of the refugee definition, the majority concluded that applicants must present some evidence, either direct or circumstantial, regarding the persecutors' motives. The Court reasoned that, since the statute explicitly requires that persecution be *on account of* one of five factors, motive was critical. *Id.* at 483-84.

Dissenting, Justice Stevens disagreed with the conclusion that failure to act does not express a political opinion:

> A political opinion can be expressed negatively as well as affirmatively. A refusal to support a cause—by staying home on election day, by refusing to take an oath of allegiance, or by refusing to step forward at an induction center—can express a political opinion as effectively as an affirmative statement or affirmative conduct. Even if the refusal is motivated by nothing more than a simple desire to continue living an ordinary life with one's family, it is the kind of political expression that the asylum provisions of the statute were intended to protect. *Id.* at 486.

3.   Though *Elias-Zacarias* concerned only persecution on account of political opinion, its language regarding proof of motive might be construed to apply more broadly to all five grounds for refugee status. *Canas-Segovia v. INS*, for example, extended the reasoning to persecution on account of religion and required an alien to present either direct or circumstantial evidence of his persecutors' motives. 970 F.2d 599, 601 (9th Cir. 1992). The court held, however, that even after *Elias-Zacarias* imputed political opinion may be a valid basis for relief. By proving that persecution is based on a belief which persecutors assume an alien holds, he or she establishes motive. Hence, persecution based on political opinions falsely

attributed to the victim can be a basis for relief. *Id.* at 601-02. Though *Canas-Segovia* covered only political opinion, its conclusion presumably reaches as broadly as does the similar language in *Elias-Zacarias*.

4.   Might you successfully argue that Awata's refusal to subject her daughter to FGM expresses a political opinion? What problems of proof do you foresee in making that argument?

5.   Paragraph 51 of the UNHCR HANDBOOK declares that "serious violations of human rights . . . constitute persecution." No U.S. courts have directly addressed the issue of whether the violation of a human rights treaty constitutes persecution. In *Matter of Chang*, Interim Dec. No. 3107 (BIA 1989), however, the BIA suggested such an approach (in dicta):

> [E]ven if involuntary sterilization was demonstrated to be a violation of internationally recognized human rights, that fact in itself would not establish that an individual subjected to such an act was a victim of persecution "on account of race, religion, nationality, membership in a particular social group, or political opinion." We are satisfied that if an individual demonstrated a well-founded fear that such an act would occur "on account of" [one of the above reasons], the "refugee" definition . . . would be met.

Id. If U.S. courts adopted that approach, would violation of *any* treaty constitute persecution? Recall the discussion of the Covenant on Economic, Social and Cultural Rights in chapter 2. Would violation of a right guaranteed in that Covenant constitute persecution? What about case law holding that economic disadvantage must be substantial? Does the UNHCR Handbook's limiting persecution to "serious" violations adequately address that concern?

D.   THE ROLE OF THE UNHCR

1.   Purpose, Function, & Responsibility

Statute of the Office of the United Nations High Commissioner for Refugees, G.A. res. 428 (V), 5 U.N. GAOR Supp. (No. 20) at 46, U.N. Doc. A/1775 (1950):

CHAPTER 1

General Provisions

1.   The United Nations High Commissioner for Refugees, acting under the authority of the General Assembly, shall assume the function of providing international protection, under the auspices of the United Nations, to refugees who fall within the scope of the present Statute and of seeking permanent solutions for the problem of refugees by assisting Governments and, subject to the approval of the Governments concerned, private organizations to facilitate the voluntary repatriation of such refugees, or their assimilation within new national communities. . . .

*   *   *   *   *

LAWYERS COMMITTEE FOR HUMAN RIGHTS, THE UNHCR AT 40: REFUGEE PROTECTION AT THE CROSSROADS 13-30 (1991):

One of this century's most harrowing images is that of people in flight. The Russian famine victim in 1919; the family stumbling from ruins during the Spanish

Civil War; refugees fleeing Nazi persecution during World War II; desperate faces on a sinking Vietnamese boat in the Gulf of Thailand. . . .

If this century has produced unprecedented numbers of refugees, it has also been the century when the international community recognized that refugees are uniquely vulnerable, and began to develop an internationally-coordinated system of protection. The League of Nations laid the institutional foundation in 1921. . . . The legal base was laid in 1933, with the adoption of the first international refugee convention, which established a uniform set of obligations for governments.

These efforts, institutional and legal, have been consolidated and expanded under the United Nations. . . .

The creation of the UNHCR . . . was part of a broad move by the United Nations system to promote human rights. At the same time, however, East-West tensions ensured that the UNHCR's mandate would be subjected to a highly partisan, political interpretation. . . .

As a result, several key concepts ended up as compromises in the UNHCR mandate. Protection was one. The mandate asked UNHCR to provide "international protection" to refugees, without specifying what protection meant. To the U.S., protection was a narrow, legal function, like providing legal assistance. To the Europeans, it was all-encompassing. The term "international protection" was a compromise between these two positions. But the compromise was a recipe for disagreement that still exists: some feel protection begins in the country of origin; others that it is most urgent during flight; and others at the country of asylum.

The adoption of the Convention relating to the Status of Refugees . . . refined the UNHCR's mandate. It implied that the grant of asylum was a sovereign matter for governments, not a human right; it restricted coverage [to World War II refugees] and it endorsed the subjective definition of a refugee. . . . It was left to governments, not the UNHCR, to determine who qualified. "Persecution" was not defined. This ensured different rates of acceptance for people fleeing the same conflict. . . .

A major contradiction lay in the fact that while the UNHCR's task was "humanitarian," the mandate clearly implied a political role by asking the High Commissioner to promote repatriation and other "durable solutions." . . .

There were other notable gaps and limitations. One was that the mandate only covered people who were "outside their country of nationality." This excluded the so-called "internally displaced"—people who might flee for the same motives as a refugee, but find themselves unable to leave the country. . . .

The High Commissioner was to be kept under tight control. The High Commissioner was to report to an advisory committee of governments, which emerged in 1957 as the Executive Committee. . . . [T]he High Commissioner is partially independent while answering to the General Assembly. . . .

This mandate provided for great flexibility, but also was restrictive.

NOTES AND QUESTIONS

1.   What is the purpose of having the UNHCR report to and receive directives from only two U.N. bodies: the General Assembly and the Economic and Social Council? See UNHCR, AN INTRODUCTION TO THE INTERNATIONAL PROTECTION OF REFUGEES 6-7 (1992) (training module for UNHCR staff).

2.   One basic UNHCR function UNHCR is coordinating assistance to large groups of refugees. Created as a response to World War II and the Cold War, the UNHCR originally did not envision that type of assistance as one of its primary duties; the demographics of modern

refugee populations demand that it assume such a role. Civil wars in Africa and Yugoslavia, for example, displaced millions of people. Because most of today's refugees flow from less-developed countries, ensuring adequate food, shelter, and medical supplies is critical to the UNHCR's mandate. And the UNHCR must coordinate its efforts with those of organizations such as the World Health Organization, the U.N. International Children's Emergency Fund, the International Committee of the Red Cross, the American Refugee Committee, Doctors Without Borders, the International Rescue Committee, and Save the Children.

3.   Another highly visible UNHCR function is repatriation. Paragraph 8(c) of the U.N. Statute provides that one duty is to "assist[] governmental and private efforts to promote voluntary repatriation" once the conditions which caused displacement have been rectified. In 1993, for example, the UNHCR negotiated and monitored the return of thousands of Guatemalan refugees, displaced since the early 1980s. In 1992, the UNHCR supervised the return of over 1.5 million persons to Afghanistan. The early 1990s also saw repatriation programs implemented for countries such as Cambodia, Mozambique, and South Africa.

4.   The UNHCR also has begun to focus on prevention. "Refugee flows are a symptom of failure to prevent, respond to or resolve crises at home. . . ." Executive Committee of the High Commissioner's Programme, *Note on International Protection*, at 2, U.N. Doc. A/AC.96/ 815 (1993). The UNHCR interprets its mandate to "seek[] permanent solutions" to include prevention-initiatives. The UNHCR thus emphasizes the importance of removing or mitigating underlying causes of refugee flows and is supporting efforts by the international community to alleviate situations that threaten to cause refugee flows. *Id.* at 2-3.

5.   Since the 1970s, the UNHCR role has expanded to include persons who do not fall within traditional definitions of "refugee." The new class of protected persons includes those who flee their homes due to armed conflict and internal turmoil rather than persecution on account of one of the five factors. Though there is neither a precise definition of the new class nor consensus about forms of protection to which they are entitled, those persons generally are considered to be "of concern" to the UNHCR. That concern is reflected by efforts to ensure temporary protection. *See Note on International Protection*, at 3, U.N. Doc. A/AC.96/660 (1985), *Annual Report of the UNHCR*, para. 23, U.N. Doc. E/1985/62 (1985).

The emergence of a temporary protected status is paralleled in several regional organizations:

> The Organization of African Unity has enlarged the refugee definition to include those persons who are compelled to leave their homelands on account of "external aggression, occupation, foreign domination, or events seriously disturbing public order." Similarly, in the 1984 Cartagena Declaration on Refugees, Central American states recommended that the term "refugee" apply to "persons who have fled their country because their lives, safety, or freedom have been threatened by generalized violence, foreign aggression, internal conflicts, massive violation of human rights, or other circumstances which have seriously disturbed public order."
>
> It is, perhaps, not premature to conclude as a matter of customary law that those displaced for reasons other than a well-founded fear of persecution are entitled to some measure of "refugee-like" protection—though precisely how much and in what form is unclear. Although states are generally reluctant to give full conventional treatment to these "new" refugees, the language of the General Assembly resolutions and Executive Committee pronouncements suggests that these people deserve at a minimum both protection against [expulsion or return] and permission to remain in the territory until an appropriate solution is found for them.

Ralph G. Steinhardt, *The United Nations and Refugees: 1945-1988, in* THE UNIVERSAL DECLARATION OF HUMAN RIGHTS 1948-1988: HUMAN RIGHTS, THE UNITED NATIONS AND AMNESTY INTERNATIONAL 77, 86-87 (1988) (footnotes omitted).

The U.S. has recognized Temporary Protected Status. 8 U.S.C. § 1254(a) (enacted as part of the Immigration Act of 1990, Pub. L. No. 101-649, § 302(b)). *See generally:*

Peter C. Diamond, Comment, *Temporary Protected Status Under the Immigration Act of 1990*, 28 WILLIAMETTE L. REV. 857 (1992);

Joan Fitzpatrick, *Flight from Asylum: Trends Toward Temporary "Refuge" and Local Responses to Forced Migrations*, 35 VA. J. INT'L L. 13 (1994);

Donatella Luca, *Questioning Temporary Protection, together with a Selected Bibliography on Temporary Refuge/Temporary Protection*, 6 INT'L J. REFUGEE LAW 535 (1994);

Pamela M. Martin, Note, *Temporary Protected Status and the Legacy of Santos-Gomez*, 25 GEO. WASH. J. INT'L L. & ECON. 227 (1992);

Art Weitzhandler, Comment, *Temporary Protected Status: The Congressional Response to the Plight of Salvadoran Aliens*, 64 U. COLO. L. REV. 249 (1993);

RUTH E. WASEM, ASYLUM AND TEMPORARY PROTECTED STATUS UNDER U.S. IMMIGRATION LAW (1991).

The new U.S. status has benefited persons from Kuwait, Liberia, El Salvador, Somalia, and Bosnia. 14 REFUGEE REPORTS (U.S. Comm. on Refugees, Washington, D.C.), Apr. 23, 1993, at 16.

6.   For further discussion of the contemporary role of the UNHCR, see:

Report of the United Nations High Commissioner for Refugees, U.N. Doc. E/1994/41 (1994);

UNHCR, THE STATE OF THE WORLD'S REFUGEES 1995: THE CHALLENGE OF PROTECTION (1993) (discussing current refugee problems, the plight of 14.5 million refugees in 1995, the current agenda of protection, and policy alternatives);

UNHCR, HANDBOOK FOR EMERGENCIES (1982) (a guide to implementing and managing emergency refugee operations).

---

2.   Participation in U.S. Asylum Proceedings

The UNHCR has interpreted its mandate to encompass a broad range of functions and has engaged in numerous activities not specified in its Statute. Reproduced below is the standard response letter to submission of an asylum claim, discussing the varied services the UNHCR can provide to advocates in asylum cases.

*   *   *   *   *

Dear [Attorney or Representative],

I am writing in response to your recent mailing to our office regarding [your client's] applica[tion] for asylum in the United States. We will keep these materials on file in case we decide to take further action on this case.

Unlike the situation in some countries, the Office of the United Nations High Commissioner for Refugees (UNHCR) does not have any formal role in the decision-making process on asylum claims in the United States. Nor do we recognize persons as refugees in the United States; we perform such a function only in countries that are not [parties] to the 1951 Convention or 1967 Protocol relating to the Status of Refugees or that do not have refugee status determination procedures of their own. Nevertheless, we may be able to help you in making your client's asylum claim in the following ways:

(1)   We may file an advisory opinion in support of your client's claim. Such an

advisory opinion evaluates the merits of a person's claim according to UNHCR's standards and principles on refugee status determination. However, due to the large number of requests we receive, our policy is to comment on the merits of individual cases on an exceptional basis, in particular, only when the facts of the case are especially compelling (*e.g.* the applicant is in detention or is subject to immediate exclusion or deportation) or when the case presents issues the resolution of which will have a significant impact on U.S. law. In order to decide whether or not we will intervene in a specific case, we ask that you provide us with a copy of your client's Request for Asylum (Form I-589) and any other supporting documents relevant to your client's claim or to the decision by the U.S. authorities. We also need to know the date of any hearing on the merits of your client's claim and any other relevant deadlines for submission of additional materials in your client's case. We should emphasize that UNHCR opinions are not legally binding on the U.S. authorities in their determination of refugee status;

(2)   We may be able to provide you and your client with general UNHCR information and/or documentation to support or clarify your client's asylum claim;

(3)   If your client has been granted asylum or refugee status in another country, we can try to verify this information. In order to do so, we must have your client's complete name and age as well as the dates of his or her stay in that country;

(4)   If there is an issue as to whether your client enjoyed or may have sought protection in another country prior to coming to the United States, we may be able to provide relevant information about the laws, procedures and conditions pertaining to refugees and asylum seekers in such country.

If you would like our help in any of these ways, please communicate your request to us in writing and specify the type of help you desire. We would also appreciate it if you could let us know by letter the outcome of your client's asylum application when it is decided.

I am sending you a copy of a list of organizations that provide documentation on human rights conditions in various countries. You may wish to contact them to request further documentation to support your client's claim.

If you have any further questions, please feel free to contact us, preferably in writing.

Sincerely,

. . .

Associate Legal Counselor, UNHCR

E.   GENDER-BASED REFUGEE CLAIMS

1.   Gender as a Social Group

Though the definition of refugee and implications of being within it appear straightforward, determining whether an individual qualifies as refugee can be complex.

Jurisprudence regarding the contours of the "particular social group" category has been especially sparse. As you read the following, note how the court construes national and international instruments in deciding whether gender constitutes a social group.

*   *   *   *   *

Fatin v. INS, 12 F.3d 1233 (3rd Cir. 1993) (several footnotes and citations omitted) (commentary in brackets added by editors):

ALITO, Circuit Judge

Parastoo Fatin has petitioned for review of an order of the Board of Immigration Appeals (the "Board" or "BIA") requiring her to depart or be deported from the United States. [She] [a]rgu[es] that she has a well-founded fear of persecution and that she is likely to be persecuted if she returns to her native country of Iran . . . . Based on the administrative record before us, however, we are constrained to deny the petition for review.

I.

[Fatin, a native and citizen of Iran, entered the United States in 1978 approximately two weeks before the Shah left Iran. She attended high school and college in the U.S. and affirmatively applied for asylum in May 1984. On her application, she noted that she and certain family members had publicly supported the Shah, and that she refused to wear a veil, a sign of support for Khomeni. She asserted the Iranian government was suspicious of families with education and wealth. If deported, she believed she would be interrogated, forced to attend religious services against her will, and possibly jailed. As evidence, she stated that her father, a physician, had temporarily been harassed by "religious fanatics," and two cousins had been jailed for one year each.]

[The INS denied Fatin's claim for asylum and began deportation proceedings.] At a hearing . . . , she conceded deportability, but she renewed her application for asylum and also applied for withholding of deportation. . . .

At a later hearing . . . she . . . [stated] that one of her cousins had . . . been killed in a demonstration and that her brother was in hiding in order to avoid the draft. She also . . . stat[ed] that [prior to coming to the U.S.] she had been involved with a student political group and with a women's rights group associated with the Shah's sister.

When her attorney asked her why she feared going back to Iran, she responded: "Because of the government that is ruling the country. It is a strange government to me. It has different rules and regulation[s] th[a]n I have been used to." She stated that "anybody who [had] been a Moslem" was required "to practice that religion" or "be punished in public or be jailed," and she added that she had been "raised in a way that you don't have to practice if you don't want to." She subsequently stated that she would be required "to do things that [she] never had to do," such as wear a veil. When asked by her attorney [about the punishment for refusing to wear a veil], she replied:

> . . . I would be jailed or punished in public. Public mean[s] by whipped or thrown stones and I would be going back to barbaric years.

Later, when the immigration judge asked her whether she would wear a veil or submit to arrest and punishment, she stated:

> If I go back, I would try personally to avoid it as much as I could do. . . . I will start
> trying to avoid it as much as I could.

The petitioner also testified that she considered herself a "feminist" and explained:

> As a feminist I mean that I believe in equal rights for women. I believe a woman as
> a human being can do and should be able to do what they want to do. And over there
> in . . . Iran at the time being a woman is a second class citizen, doesn't have any
> right to herself. . . .

After the hearing, the immigration judge denied the petitioner's applications
for withholding of deportation [and] asylum. . . . Addressing her request for withholding of deportation, the immigration judge stated that, although she would be subject
to the same discriminatory treatment as all other women in Iran, there was "no
indication that there is a likelihood that the Iranian government would be particularly interested in this individual and that they would persecute her." Similarly,
with respect to her renewed request for asylum, the judge stated:

> Respondent has offered no objective indic[i]a which would lead the Court to believe
> that there is a possibility that she would be persecuted upon return to Iran. Respon-
> dent has not been political[ly] active in the United States nor openly opposed to the
> Khomeni Government. It would appear that her fear of return to Iran while indeed
> understandable is based upon uncertainty and the unknown. In addition, it would
> appear that the respondent's fear upon return to Iran is her apparent dislike for the
> system and her belief that she as a woman would be subject to the severe restrictions
> presently imparted on Iranian[s] in that country. Respondent therefore contends
> that her beliefs as a "feminist" would be compromised. While the Court is very much
> sympathetic to the respondent's desire not to return to Iran, nonetheless, in applying
> the law to include case law, the Court is compelled to find that the respondent has
> failed to sustain her burden of proof necessary to be accorded asylum in the United
> States. . . .

Petitioner then appealed to the Board of Immigration Appeals. In her brief, she
argued that she feared persecution "on account of her membership of a particular
social group, and on the basis of her political opinion." Her brief identified her
"particular social group" as "the social group of the upper class of Iranian women
who supported the Shah of Iran, a group of educated Westernized free-thinking
individuals." Her brief also stated that she had a "deep[ly] rooted belief in feminism"
and in "equal rights for women, and the right to free choice of any expression and
development of abilities, in the fields of education, work, home and family, and all
other arenas of development." In addition, her brief observed that she would be
forced upon return to Iran "to practice the Moslem religion." Her brief stated that
"she would try to avoid practicing a religion as much as she could." Her brief added
that she had "the personal desire to avoid as much practice as she could," but that
she feared that "through religious ignorance and inexperience she would be unable
to play the role of a religious Shi'ite woman." Her brief contained one passage
concerning the requirement that women in Iran wear a veil in public:

> In April 1983, the government adopted a law imposing one year's imprisonment on
> any women caught in public without the traditional Islamic veil, the Chador. How-
> ever, from reports, it is clear that in many instances the revolutionary guards . . .
> take the law into their own hands and abuse the transgressing women. . . .

Her brief did not discuss the question whether she would comply with the law regarding the wearing of a chador. Nor did her brief explain what effect submitting to that requirement would have upon her.

In the section of her brief devoted to political opinion, she mentioned her political activities while in Iran, as well as her current "deep-rooted beliefs in freedom of choice, freedom of expression [and] equality of opportunity for both sexes."

The Board of Immigration Appeals dismissed the petitioner's appeal. The Board . . . stated that there was no evidence that she would be "singled out" for persecution. Instead, the Board observed that she would be "subject to the same restrictions and requirements" as the rest of the population. The Board also noted that there had been "a considerable passage of time since [she] was in high school and participated in political activities."

In addition, the Board stated that her claims were based on circumstances that had arisen since her entry into this country and that "[s]uch claims are dimly viewed."

After the Board issued its order requiring her voluntary departure or deportation, the petitioner filed the current petition for review.

II. . . .

The petitioner in this case contends that she is entitled to withholding of deportation and is eligible for asylum based on her "membership in a particular social group" and based on her "political opinion." We will discuss each of these grounds separately.

. . . Both courts and commentators have struggled to define "particular social group." Read in its broadest literal sense, the phrase is almost completely open-ended. Virtually any set including more than one person could be described as a "particular social group." Thus, the statutory language standing alone is not very instructive.

Nor is there any clear evidence of legislative intent. The phrase "particular social group" was first placed in the INA when Congress enacted the Refugee Act of 1980. . . . [T]he legislative history of this act does not reveal what, if any, specific meaning the members of Congress attached to the phrase "particular social group." . . .

Article I of the [Refugee] Protocol generally adopted the definition of a "refugee" contained in Article I of United Nations Convention Relating to the Status of Refugees. . . . This latter provision defined a "refugee" using terms—i.e., "race, religion, nationality, membership of a particular social group or political opinion"—virtually identical to those now incorporated in the INA. When the Conference of Plenipotentiaries was considering the Convention in 1951, the phrase "membership of a particular social group" was added to this definition as an "afterthought." The Swedish representative proposed this language, explaining only that it was needed because "experience had shown that certain refugees had been persecuted because they belonged to particular social groups," and the proposal was adopted. Thus, neither the legislative history of the relevant United States statutes nor the negotiating history of the pertinent international agreements sheds much light on the meaning of the phrase "particular social group."

Our role in the process of interpreting this phrase, however, is quite limited. As the Supreme Court has explained, the Board of Immigration Appeals' interpretation of a provision of the Refugee Act is entitled to deference. . . . Thus, in considering an interpretation adopted by the Board, we must ask "whether Congress has directly spoken to the precise question at issue." If it has not, we may not "simply impose [our] own construction on the statute." "Rather, if the statute is silent or ambiguous with respect to the specific issue, the question for the court is whether the agency's answer is based on a permissible construction of the statute."

Here, the Board has interpreted the phrase "particular social group." In *Matter of*

Acosta, 19 I. & N. Dec. 211, 233 (BIA 1985), the Board noted that the United Nations Protocol refers to race, religion, nationality, and political opinion, as well as membership in a particular social group. Employing the doctrine of *ejusdem generis*, the Board then reasoned that a particular social group refers to "a group of persons all of whom share a common, immutable characteristic." The Board explained:

> The shared characteristic might be an innate one such as sex, color, or kinship ties, or in some circumstances it might be a shared past experience such as former military leadership or land ownership. The particular kind of group characteristic that will qualify under this construction remains to be determined on a case-by-case basis. However, whatever the common characteristic that defines the group, it must be one that the members of the group either cannot change, or should not be required to change because it is fundamental to their individual identities or consciences.

We have no doubt that this is a permissible construction of the relevant statutes, and we are consequently bound to accept it.

With this understanding of the phrase "particular social group" in mind, we turn to the elements that an alien must establish in order to qualify for withholding of deportation or asylum based on membership in such a group. We believe that there are three such elements. The alien must (1) identify a group that constitutes a "particular social group" within the interpretation just discussed, (2) establish that he or she is a member of that group, and (3) show that he or she would be persecuted or has a well-founded fear of persecution based on that membership.

In the excerpt from *Acosta* quoted above, the Board specifically mentioned "sex" as an innate characteristic that could link the members of a "particular social group." Thus, to the extent that the petitioner in this case suggests that she would be persecuted or has a well-founded fear that she would be persecuted in Iran simply because she is a woman, she has satisfied the first of the three elements that we have noted. She has not, however, satisfied the third element; that is, she has not shown that she would suffer or that she has a well-founded fear of suffering "persecution" based solely on her gender.

In *Acosta*, the BIA . . . interpreted "persecution" to include threats to life, confinement, torture, and economic restrictions so severe that they constitute a threat to life or freedom. By contrast, the BIA suggested that "[g]enerally harsh conditions shared by many other persons" do not amount to persecution. Among the . . . cases on which the BIA relied was *Blazina v. Bouchard*, 286 F.2d 507, 511 (3d Cir.), *cert. denied*, 366 U.S. 950 . . . (1961), where our court noted that the mere "repugnance of . . . a governmental policy to our own concepts of . . . freedom" was not sufficient to justify labelling that policy as persecution. Thus, we interpret *Acosta* as recognizing that the concept of persecution does not encompass all treatment that our society regards as unfair, unjust, or even unlawful or unconstitutional. If persecution were defined that expansively, a significant percentage of the world's population would qualify for asylum in this country—and it seems most unlikely that Congress intended such a result.[4]

---

[4] We are convinced that the BIA's interpretation of "persecution," like its interpretation of "particular social group," is permissible and thus must be followed. In ordinary usage, the term "persecution" denotes extreme conduct. . . . We are aware of nothing indicating that Congress intended to depart from the ordinary meaning of the term "persecution." Moreover, authoritative interpretations of the United Nations Convention and Protocol also recognize that the concept of persecution refers to extreme conduct. *See, e.g.*, United Nations High Commissioner for Refugees, Handbook of Procedures . . . §§ 51, 54, 55.

In this case, the evidence in the administrative record regarding the way in which women in Iran are generally treated is quite sparse. We certainly cannot say that "a reasonable factfinder would have to conclude," based on that record, that the petitioner, if returned to Iran, would face treatment amounting to "persecution" simply because she is a woman. . . .

The petitioner's primary argument, in any event, is not that she faces persecution simply because she is a woman. Rather, she maintains that she faces persecution because she is a member of "a very visible and specific subgroup: Iranian women who *refuse to conform* to the government's gender-specific laws and social norms." This definition merits close consideration. It does not include all Iranian women who hold feminist views. Nor does it include all Iranian women who find the Iranian government's "gender-specific laws and repressive social norms" objectionable or offensive. Instead, it is limited to those Iranian women who find those laws so abhorrent that they "refuse to conform"—even though, according to the petitioner's brief, "the routine penalty" for noncompliance is "74 lashes, a year's imprisonment, and in many cases brutal rapes and death."

Limited in this way, the "particular social group" identified by the petitioner may well satisfy the BIA's definition of that concept, for if a woman's opposition to the Iranian laws in question is so profound that she would choose to suffer the severe consequences of noncompliance, her beliefs may well be characterized as "so fundamental to [her] identity or conscience that [they] ought not be required to be changed." The petitioner's difficulty, however, is that the administrative record does not establish that she is a member of this tightly defined group, for there is no evidence in that record showing that her opposition to the Iranian laws at issue is of the depth and importance required.

[The court noted Fatin had never stated that she would refuse to comply with Iran's gender-specific laws or norms, merely that she would find the requirements "objectionable" and that she would seek to avoid compliance if possible.] Nor did she testify that wearing the chador or complying with any of the other restrictions was so deeply abhorrent to her that it would be tantamount to persecution. . . . This testimony does not bring her within the particular social group that she has defined—Iranian women who *refuse to conform* with those requirements even if the consequences may be severe.

The "particular social group" that her testimony places her within is, instead, the presumably larger group consisting of Iranian women who find their country's gender-specific laws offensive and do not wish to comply with them. But if the petitioner's "particular social group" is defined in this way, she cannot prevail because the administrative record does not satisfy the third element described above, i.e., it does not show that the consequences that would befall her as a member of that group would constitute "persecution." According to the petitioner, she would have two options if she returned to Iran: comply with the Iranian laws or suffer severe consequences. Thus, while we agree with the petitioner that the indicated consequences of noncompliance would constitute persecution, we must still inquire whether her other option—compliance—would also constitute persecution.

In considering whether the petitioner established that this option would constitute persecution, we will assume for the sake of argument that the concept of persecution is broad enough to include governmental measures that compel an individual to engage in conduct that is not physically painful or harmful but is abhorrent to that individual's deepest beliefs. . . .

Here, while we assume for the sake of argument that requiring some women to wear chadors may be so abhorrent to them that it would be tantamount to persecution, this requirement clearly does not constitute persecution for *all* women. Presumably, there are devout Shiite women in Iran who find this requirement entirely appropriate. Presumably, there are other women in Iran who find it either inconvenient, irritating, mildly objectionable, or highly offensive, but for whom it falls short of constituting persecution. As we have previously noted, the petitioner's testimony in this case simply does not show that for her the requirement of wearing the chador or complying with Iran's other gender-specific laws would be so profoundly abhorrent that it could aptly be called persecution. Accordingly, we cannot hold that she is entitled to withholding of deportation or asylum based on her membership in a "particular social group."

[The court rejected Fatin's argument that she was entitled to withholding of deportation or asylum based on her well-founded fear of persecution on account of her political opinion for similar reasons. Although the court accepted "feminism" as a political opinion which the petitioner did hold, the record did not support a conclusion that feminists in Iran were persecuted because of their beliefs. The court therefore denied Fatin's petition for review.]

*   *   *   *   *

Several organizations have issued guidelines related to protecting refugee women. The guidelines advocate treating gender as a "social group" for purposes of determining status. Though the guidelines are not binding on U.S. courts, their reasoning may help persuade judges to interpret "social group" broadly enough to encompass gender.

UNHCR, GUIDELINES ON THE PROTECTION OF REFUGEE WOMEN 7-8, 36 (1991) (paragraph numbers omitted):

I. Introduction

. . .Women share the protection problems experienced by all refugees. . . .

In addition . . . , refugee women and girls have special protection needs that reflect their gender: they need, for example, protection against manipulation, sexual and physical abuse and exploitation, and protection against sexual discrimination in the delivery of goods and services. These guidelines . . . recognize that special efforts may be needed to resolve problems faced specifically by refugee women. . . .

Ensuring the protection of refugee women requires adherence not only to the 1951 Convention [Relating to the Status of Refugees] and its 1967 Protocol but also to other relevant international instruments such as the Universal Declaration of Human Rights; the 1949 Geneva Conventions and the two Additional Protocols of 1977; the 1966 Human Rights Covenants [(the Covenant on Economic, Social and Cultural Rights and the Covenant on Civil and Political Rights)]; the Convention on the Elimination of All Forms of Discrimination Against Women; the Declaration on the Protection of Women and Children in Emergency and Armed Conflict; the Convention on Consent to Marriage, Minimum Age for Marriage and Registration of Marriages; the Convention on the Nationality of Married Women; and the Convention on the Rights of the Child. While individual States may not be parties to all of these instruments, they do provide a framework of international human rights standards for carrying out protection and assistance activities related to refugee women. . . .

III.   Protection Needs and Responses . . .

. . .The claim to refugee status by women fearing harsh or inhumane treatment because of having transgressed their society's laws or customs regarding the role of women presents difficulties under [the 1951 Convention definition of refugee]. As a UNHCR legal adviser has noted, *transgressing social mores is not reflected in the universal refugee definition.* Yet, examples can be found of violence against women who are accused of violating social mores in a number of countries. The offence can range from adultery to wearing of lipstick. The penalty can be death. The Executive Committee of UNHCR has encouraged States to consider women so persecuted as a *social group* to ensure their coverage, but it is left to the discretion of countries to follow this recommendation.

Women may also flee their country because of severe sexual discrimination either by official bodies or in local communities. Protection from sexual discrimination is a basic right of all women . . ., and discrimination can constitute persecution under certain circumstances, [although] the dividing line between discrimination and persecution is not a clear one.

*   *   *   *   *

NANCY KELLY, WOMEN REFUGEES PROJECT OF CAMBRIDGE AND SOMERVILLE LEGAL SERVICES AND HARVARD IMMIGRATION AND REFUGEE PROGRAM, GUIDELINES FOR WOMEN'S ASYLUM CLAIMS 2-5 (1994) (footnotes omitted):

Women asylum applicants may apply for protection based on grounds that are particular to their gender. The gender-related bases of their claims fall into two broad categories. First, the persecution may constitute a *type* of harm that is particular to the applicant's gender (*e.g.*, rape, sexual abuse, genital mutilation, bride burning, infanticide, forced marriage, forced sterilization, domestic violence or forced abortion). Second, the persecution may be imposed *because of* the applicant's gender (*e.g.*, persecution for violations of societal norms requiring women to live with male relatives or persecution for refusal to conform to norms severely restricting the rights and activities of women).

. . . The gender-related claims of women asylum applicants usually can be established based on the "political opinion" or "particular social group" categories of the refugee definition. In many cases, these grounds will overlap with each other or with other grounds enumerated in the definition. For example, a woman may have been persecuted or fear persecution based both on her membership within a particular social group and on a political opinion she holds or which is imputed to her. . . .

In evaluating gender-related claims to determine whether a particular form of treatment constitutes persecution, the adjudicator should consider the following:

1.   Women often face physical harm or abuses which are specific to their gender. . . . Most cases in which the meaning of persecution has been considered have been those of men. Therefore, persecution has not been widely interpreted to include these generally female-specific experiences.

2.   The fact that violence against women, including domestic violence, is widespread does not detract from the claim of an individual woman. The relevant issue is whether the woman applying for asylum was subjected to or reasonably fears being subjected to the violence with no recourse to state protection. This

lack of recourse to state protection may be because the state is unable or unwilling to provide such protection, or because the state willfully interferes with efforts of other groups to provide protection. . . .

4. Country-Wide Persecution: An asylum applicant does not have to establish that the persecution she fears exists nationwide if, under all the circumstances, it would have been unreasonable for her to seek refuge in another part of the country. In considering whether such an internal flight alternative is reasonable, the adjudicator should consider the ability of the persecutor to act nationwide, whether the woman could genuinely access protection in another part of her country and whether the protection would have been meaningful. Relevant factors to consider are financial, logistical and other barriers that may prevent the woman from reaching internal safety and whether the quality of internal protection meets basic norms of civil, political and socio-economic human rights. . . .

* * * * *

On May 26, 1995, the INS issued a memorandum containing guidelines to be followed by asylum officers adjudicating gender-based claims by women. The INS guidelines were largely modeled after those recommended by the Women Refugees Project of the Harvard Immigration and Refugee Program, Cambridge and Somerville Legal Services, which are excerpted above.

PHYLLIS COVEN, OFFICE OF INT'L AFFAIRS (INS), MEMORANDUM: CONSIDERATIONS FOR ASYLUM OFFICERS ADJUDICATING ASYLUM CLAIMS FROM WOMEN 1-19 (1995) (several footnotes and citations omitted):

This memorandum is written to provide the INS Asylum Officer Corps (AOC) with guidance and background on adjudicating cases of women having asylum claims based wholly or in part on their gender. . . .

I. *Background and International Guidance* . . .

The evaluation of gender-based claims must be viewed within the framework provided by existing international human rights instruments and the interpretation of these instruments by international organizations. The following international instruments and documents contain gender-related provisions that recognize and promote the principle that women's rights are human rights, and that women's rights are universal:

* CEDAW: The 1979 *Convention on the Elimination of All Forms of Discrimination Against Women* . . . prohibits actions by States which are discriminatory and requires States to take affirmative steps to eradicate discriminatory treatment of women.

* UN Declaration: . . . The 1993 *Declaration [on the Elimination of Violence Against Women]* recognizes violence against women as both a per se violation of human rights and as an impediment to the enjoyment by women of other human rights.

* UNHCR Conclusions/Guidelines: . . . *Conclusion* No. 39 . . . recognized that States are free to adopt the interpretation that women asylum-seekers who face harsh or inhuman treatment due to their having transgressed the social mores of the society in which they live may be considered a "particular social group." . . .

* *Conclusion* No. 73 . . . recognizes that asylum seekers who have suffered sexual violence should be treated with particular sensitivity. . . . The 1991 UNHCR guidelines [on the Protection of Refugee Women] . . . address gender-related persecution and recommend procedures to make the refugee adjudication process more accessible to women.

* Canadian Guidelines: . . . [T]he Canadian Immigration and Refugee Board (IRB). . . . "Guidelines on Women Refugee Claimants Fearing Gender-Related Persecution" . . . [were] the first national guidelines to . . . recognize [formally] that women fleeing persecution because of their gender can be found to be refugees. . . .

II.   Procedural Considerations for U.S. Asylum Officers

(a)   Purpose and Overview

The purpose of this section is to emphasize the importance of creating a "customer-friendly interview environment that allows women claimants to discuss freely the elements and details of their claims.

Asylum Officers should bear in mind the context of these human rights and cross-cultural considerations when dealing with women claimants:

* The laws and customs of some countries contain gender-discriminatory provisions. . . .

* . . . A woman may present a claim that may be analyzed and approved under one or more grounds. For example, rape . . . sexual abuse and domestic violence, infanticide and genital mutilation are forms of mistreatment primarily directed at girls and women and they may serve as evidence of past persecution on account of one or more of the five grounds. . . .

(d)   Interview Considerations. . .

. . . It should not be necessary to ask for precise details of the sexual abuse; the important thing is establishing whether it has occurred and the apparent motive of the perpetrator. . . .

(e)   Demeanor/Credibility Issues . . .

Women who have been subject to domestic or sexual abuse may be psychologically traumatized. Trauma . . . may have a significant impact on the ability to present testimony. . . .

III.   Legal Analysis of Claims . . .

. . . In order to qualify as a refugee under our laws, female applicants must—like any applicant—show that they cannot return home and cannot avail themselves of the protection of their country because of "persecution or a well-founded fear of persecution on account of race, religion, nationality, membership in a particular social group, or political opinion." Often, of course, the asylum claim of a female applicant will have nothing to do with her gender. In other cases, though, the applicant's gender may bear on the claim in significant ways to which the adjudicator should be attentive. . . .

Persecution: How Serious is the Harm?

As in all asylum cases, the asylum officer must assess whether the harm that the applicant fears or has suffered is serious enough to be regarded as "persecution" as that term is understood under the relevant international and domestic law. The Board of Immigration Appeals has interpreted persecution to include threats to life, confinement, torture, and economic restrictions so severe that they constitute a threat to life or freedom. *Matter of Acosta*, 19 I&N Dec. 211 (BIA 1985), *overruled on other grounds by Matter of Mogharrabi*, 19 I&N Dec. 439 (BIA 1987). "Generally harsh conditions shared by many other persons" do not amount to persecution. *Id.* . . .

. . . Asylum adjudicators should assess whether an instance of harm amounts to persecution on the basis of the general principles set out above.

A.   Rape and Other Forms of Sexual Violence as Persecution

Serious physical harm consistently has been held to constitute persecution. Rape and other forms of sexual violence clearly fall within this rule. . . . As in all cases, the determination that sexual abuse may be serious enough to amount to persecution does not by itself make out a claim to asylum. The applicant must still demonstrate that the fear of persecution is well-founded and that the persecution was threatened or inflicted on account of a protected ground.

B.   Violation of Fundamental Beliefs as Persecution . . .

. . . Citing *Fatin* [*v. INS*, 12 F.3d 1233 (3d Cir. 1993)], the court [in *Fisher v. INS*, 37 F.3d 1371 (9th Cir. 1994)] stated that "when a person with religious views different from those espoused by a religious regime is required to conform to, or is punished for failing to comply with laws that fundamentally are abhorrent to that persons's deeply held religious convictions, the resulting anguish should be considered in determining whether the authorities have engaged in 'extreme conduct' that is 'tantamount to persecution." 37 F.3d at 1381.

Nexus: the "On Account of" Requirement

Some of the most difficult issues in asylum law arise over whether a gender-based asylum claim involves persecution "on account of" one of the five statutory grounds. This is a critical part of the analysis under U.S. law. . . .

A.   Actual or Imputed Political Opinion . . .

. . . [*Fatin*] does make clear that an applicant who could demonstrate a well-founded fear of persecution on account of her (or his) beliefs about the role and status of women in society could be eligible for refugee status on account of political opinion. . . .

B.   Membership in a Particular Social Group . . .

(1)   General

"Membership in a particular social group" is perhaps the least clearly defined ground for eligibility as a refugee. . . .

(2)   Social Group Defined by Gender

An increasing number of asylum applicants claim that gender, alone or along with other characteristics, can define a "particular social group." . . .

. . . [W]hile some courts have concluded as a legal matter that gender can define a particular social group, no court has concluded as a factual matter that an applicant has demonstrated that the government (or a persecutor the government could not or would not control) would seek to harm her solely on account of her gender. The courts have then considered whether gender might be one characteristic that combines with others to define the particular social group.

In *Fatin*, for example . . . [the applicant] argued that she risked harm as a member of a "'very visible and specific subgroup: Iranian women who *refuse to conform* to the government's gender-specific laws and social norms.'" 12 F.3d at 1241. . . . The subgroup that the applicant asserted therefore could be seen as a particular social group. . . . The applicant was not a refugee, though, because she had not shown that she was a member of such a group.

(3)   Social Group Defined by Family Membership . . .

. . . [T]here is . . . Board and federal court support for the principle that family membership could define a "particular social group" under the asylum laws. Obviously all other elements of the definition must be satisfied for this to be the basis of eligibility as a refugee.

Public versus Private Acts

(1)   Is the Persecutor the Government or Someone the Government is Unable or Unwilling to Control?

After the adjudicator has examined the degree of harm and whether it has been threatened or inflicted on account of one or more of the five grounds, it is still necessary to inquire about the availability of protection within the country of claimed persecution.
This is based on the notion that international protection becomes appropriate where national protection is unavailable. . . .
. . . If the applicant asserts a threat of harm from a non-government source, the applicant must show that the government is unwilling or unable to protect its citizens. . . .

(2)   Is State Protection Possible Elsewhere in the Country? . . .

. . . [A]n applicant must generally demonstrate that the danger of persecution exists nationwide. If there is evidence that the applicant can avoid the threat by relocating to a different part of the country or that a government would offer protection from otherwise private acts of harm elsewhere in the country than the locality where those acts take place, the applicant will not qualify for asylum. . . .
. . . The adjudicator must consider whether protection was available as a factual matter as well as in the law of the country and whether, under all the circumstances, it would be reasonable to expect a woman to seek residency elsewhere in her country.
. . .

IV.   *Conclusions: Training & Monitoring / Follow-up*

(a)   Training

This guidance is ***required reading*** for all interviewing and supervising Asylum Officers. . . .

NOTES AND QUESTIONS

1.   *Fatin* was one of the first cases to recognize gender as a social group. The earlier *Sanchez-Trujillo v. INS* defined "particular social group" as:

a collection of people closely affiliated with each other, who are actuated by some common impulse or interest. Of central concern is the existence of a voluntary associational relationship among the purported members, which imparts some common characteristic that is fundamental to their identity as a member of that discrete social group.

801 F.2d 1571, 1576 (9th Cir. 1986) (rejecting a claim that the category of young, working-class, urban males of military age constituted a social group). The Second Circuit refined that definition by requiring that group members have a fundamental characteristic in common which is both "recognizable and discrete" and which "serves to distinguish them in the eyes of a persecutor—or in the eyes of the outside world in general." *Gomez v. INS*, 947 F.2d 660, 664 (2nd Cir. 1991). The court rejected "broadly-based characteristics such as youth and gender" and refused to find that women who had been sexually abused by Salvadoran guerrillas possessed any common, identifying characteristic. *Id.* Why do you think the *Fatin* court rejected the limiting language of *Sanchez-Trujillo* and *Gomez*? Which reasoning is persuasive?

2.   Recall the discussion of persecution in *Fatin*. Would FGM and spousal abuse be considered persecution? What about (1) a woman's inability to marry in her own ethnic group because of not yet being subjected to FGM or (2) being ostracized from her group and/or family? Would you argue that those two items impose a significant economic hardship? Might the 1995 INS guidelines alter your analysis? For further discussion of whether FGM and spousal abuse are persecution, see *infra* at 666.

3.   *Safaie v. INS*, 25 F.3d 636 (8th Cir. 1994) affirmed a BIA decision upholding an immigration judge's denial of both asylum and withholding of deportation to Safaie, who was punished in Iran because she refused to wear traditional clothing or accept Islamic rules regarding women's role. She was discharged from her job and later, while attending the University of Teheran, was detained for eight hours and interrogated. Afterwards she was issued a visa authorizing travel outside Iran. She had worn Islamic dress when it became mandatory and was not subjected to further persecution for wearing makeup or smoking. *Id.* at 638-39. On that evidence an immigration judge found that, though subjectively Safaie may have feared persecution if she were deported to Iran, there was insufficient evidence to prove that her fear of persecution was well-founded. The BIA affirmed.

   On appeal the court adopted *Fatin*'s three-factor definition of "social group," but held that "women" was too broad. The court stated that "no factfinder could reasonably conclude that all Iranian women had a well-founded fear of persecution based solely on gender." *Id.* at 640. The court agreed that "Iranian women who advocate women's rights or who oppose Iranian customs relating to dress and behavior . . . may well satisfy the definition" of social group but concluded that Safaie's eight-hour detention did not constitute persecution. *Id.* Moreover, as in *Fatin*, Safaie failed to prove that her "opposition" was of such depth and intensity that having to avoid further demonstrations against Islamic laws would constitute persecution, since she had complied previously with other Islamic traditions. *Id.* at 640-41.

4.   On June 16, 1994, the Attorney General designated, as a precedent-decision, *Matter of Toboso-Alfonso*, Interim Dec. No. 3222 (BIA 1990). It upheld the immigration judge's grant of withholding of deportation to an applicant who asserted that he had been persecuted by the Cuban government on account of homosexuality. *Id.* The BIA upheld the judge's conclusions that the applicant had been persecuted in Cuba, had a well-founded fear of continued persecution in that country, and that "this persecution resulted from the applicant's membership in a particular social group, namely homosexuals." *Id.* Might this precedent be applied to support the argument that gender should be recognized as a "particular social group"?

5.   In *Guo Chun Di v. Carroll* a district court held that aliens who have a well-founded fear of being sterilized because they oppose and disobey coercive population policies of the People's Republic of China (PRC) may be granted asylum on the ground of "persecution on account of . . . political opinion." 842 F. Supp. 858, 861 (E.D. Va. 1994). Under PRC law, Guo Chun Di and his wife were to be sterilized following the birth of their first child. He fled to the U.S. after being ordered by officials to report for sterilization procedures. Upholding his eligibility for asylum the court reasoned that his views regarding procreation, expressed by refusal to comply with the sterilization order, were analogous to publicly expressed feminism

and thus constituted a political opinion. *Id.* at 873. Reaching that conclusion, however, the court carefully noted that it was not passing judgment on whether mere compliance with PRC law would constitute persecution. *Id.*

The same court distinguished *Guo Chun Di* and denied asylum and withholding of deportation to a PRC citizen who fled to the U.S. after his wife was forcibly sterilized. *Yang Cheng Huan v. Carroll*, 852 F. Supp. 460. After the birth of their second child, Yang Cheng Huan and his wife were ordered under PRC law to pay a fine. They first refused, claiming they lacked funds, but eventually raised money and paid the fine. In addition the wife was involuntarily sterilized. Angered over the brutal treatment, Yang Cheng Huan assaulted a local family-planning official at the hospital. He was threatened with arrest and imprisonment for the assault and left the PRC out of fear that he would be imprisoned if he remained. *Id.* at 463-64.

The court agreed with the immigration judge and the BIA that Yang Cheng Huan fled the PRC out of fear of prosecution, not persecution. *Id.* at 466. His initial refusal to pay the fine was based on economics rather than politics, and his assault was motivated not by political opinion but by anger. Because "punishment for violation of a generally applicable criminal law is not persecution" the court could not grant asylum on the basis of his threatened imprisonment. *Id.* at 467. Therefore, though concluding that his opposition to PRC family-planning policies constituted a political opinion, the court held he was not subject to persecution *because of* that opinion.

The court also refused to grant asylum based on his membership in a "social group consisting of PRC families having more than one child":

> First, it appears that couples in the PRC who have more than one child are simply not a homogenous and discrete group. Different population control policies are in effect in different regions of the PRC. And the PRC government imposes different population control policies on different ethnic groups in the country. Further, not all families in the PRC who have more than one child do so for political reasons . . . .. Finally, accepting petitioner's interpretation of "social group" would require courts to become involved in foreign and social policy debates that are properly the province of the political branches of government.

Id. at 470-71 (citations omitted). *See also Matter of Chang*, Interim Dec. 3107 (BIA 1989) (holding that PRC's one-child policy is not on its face persecutive and that persons opposed to that policy do not constitute a particular social group).

Recall the discussion of *Elias-Zacarias, supra* at 20. Is the court's conclusion, in *Guo Chun Di* and *Yang Cheng Huan*, that a refusal to submit to sterilization constitutes the expression of a political opinion, consistent with *Elias-Zacarias*?

6.   Canada seems to adopt an even broader interpretation of "particular social group" than that adopted by *Fatin* and its progeny. In *Canada (Attorney-General) v. Ward*, 2 S.C.R. 689, 103 D.L.R.4th 1 (Can. 1993), the Supreme Court of Canada discussed "social group" in the context of adjudicating the asylum claim of a member of the Irish National Liberation Army (INLA) who defected from that organization and fled out of fear that Irish authorities would not protect him from INLA reprisals. The court began by summarizing various approaches to interpreting "social group" that have been advocated by Canadian and other contestants:

> (1)   a very wide definition . . . pursuant to which the class serves as a safety net to prevent any possible gap in the other four categories [of the refugee definition];
> (2)   a narrower definition that confines its scope by means of some appropriate limiting mechanism, recognizing that this class if not meant to encompass all groups; and
> (3)   an even narrower definition . . . that responds to concerns about morality and criminality by excluding terrorists, criminals and the like.

103 D.L.R.4th at 25-26.

Advocates of the first approach argue that the intent of the framers of the refugee treaty was to create a comprehensive category to encompass bases of persecution that may evolve. The court exemplified the first approach with several "relevant uniting characteristics": "ethnic, cultural and linguistic origin, education and family background, . . . economic activity, shared values, outlook and aspirations." *Id.* at 26 (citing GUY S. GOODWIN-GILL, THE REFUGEE IN INTERNATIONAL LAW 30 (1983)). But the court rejected that interpretation of "social group":

> Although the drafters of the [Refugee] Convention inserted the social group category in order to cover any possible *lacuna* left by the other four groups, this does not necessarily lead to the conclusion that any association bound by some common thread is included. If this were the case, the enumeration of these [other four] bases would have been superfluous; the definition of "refugee" could have been limited to individuals who have a well-founded fear of persecution without more. The drafters' decision to list these bases was intended to function as another built-in limitation to the obligations of signatory states. The issue that arises, therefore, is the demarcation of this limit.

Id. at 28-29.

The court also rejected the narrow definition of the third approach. It refused to accept a definition that explicitly excludes "undesirable claimants" because concerns as to them are addressed in other parts of refugee law. For example, treaties defining the term "refugee" specifically exclude from that definition members of certain groups and persons who have committed serious human rights violations. *Id.* at 34-36.

The court chose the second approach as the appropriate interpretation. The theme underlying the Refugee Convention was ensuring basic human rights without discrimination. That focus thus informs the interpretation of "refugee"; and the enumeration of five bases for claiming refugee status parallels international anti-discrimination law, which is concerned with an institutional imbalance in nations' power structures. Therefore, the court concluded that "the manner in which groups are distinguished for the purposes of discrimination law can thus appropriately be imported into this area of refugee law." *Id.* at 29-30. The court summarized:

> Canada's obligation to offer a haven to those fleeing their homelands is not unlimited. . . . Canada should not overstep its role in the international sphere by having its responsibility engaged whenever any group is targeted. Surely there are some groups, the affiliation in which is not so important to the individual that it would be more appropriate to have the person dissociate him- or herself from it before Canada's responsibility should be engaged. Perhaps the most simplified way to draw the distinction is by opposing that which one *is* against that which one *does*, at a particular time. . . .
>
> The meaning assigned to "particular social group" in the Act should take into account the general underlying themes of the defence of human rights and anti-discrimination that form the basis for the international refugee protection initiative. The tests proposed in [several Canadian and U.S. cases, and by James Hathaway in his book, The Law of Refugee Status,] provide a good working rule to achieve this result. They identify three possible categories:
>
> (1) groups defined by an innate or unchangeable characteristic;
> (2) groups whose members voluntarily associate for reasons so fundamental to their human dignity that they should not be forced to forsake the association; and
> (3) groups associated by a former voluntary status, unalterable due to its historical permanence.
>
> The first category would embrace individuals fearing persecution on such bases as gender, linguistic background and sexual orientation, while the second would encompass, for example, human rights activists. The third branch is included more because of historical intentions, although it is also relevant to the anti-discrimination influences, in that one's past is an immutable part of the person.

Id. at 33-34.

In 1993, Canada granted permanent residence to a Saudi Arabian woman who argued that, because of her sex, she would not be able to dress, travel, study, or work as she pleased in her homeland. The woman claimed she had been stoned and beaten for refusing to wear a chador. Based on that decision and on *Ward*, what conclusion do you think a Canadian immigration official would have reached in *Fatin*?

7.   In 1993, the lowest Canadian immigration court recognized *lobola* and *kuzvarira* as grounds for asylum. In *W. (Z.D.) (Re)*, Convention Refugee Determination Decisions C.R.D.D. No. 3, No. U92-06668 (Feb. 19, 1993), the Immigration and Refugee Board of Canada granted asylum to a 24-year-old Christian Zimbabwean woman. She had been forced into a polygamous marriage with a middle-aged businessman when she was 14. During the marriage, her husband physically, sexually, and emotionally abused her. Neither her family nor the police responded to her requests for protection and assistance.

The Board recognized the persistent abuses as persecution under applicable human rights treaties and the Refugee Protocol. Forcing the woman into a marital relation without her consent while she was a minor also violated her human rights. The Board concluded that the marriage, entered into against her will and under non-Christian rites, contravened her religious beliefs. Alternatively, they concluded that she was subject to persecution as a member of two particular social groups: (1) Zimbabwean females forced to marry according to the customary laws of *kuzvarira* and *lobola*, and (2) unprotected Zimbabwean females subject to spousal abuse. The Board thus concluded that she was eligible for asylum.

Would the *Fatin* court have reached the same conclusion? Should an Asylum Officer reach the same conclusion under the 1995 guidelines?

8.   Canada's liberal approach to interpreting "social group" is reflected in the Canadian Immigration and Refugee Board's (IRB) guidelines on gender-related persecution. IMMIGRATION AND REFUGEE BOARD, GUIDELINES ISSUED BY THE CHAIRPERSON PURSUANT TO SECTION 65(3) OF THE IMMIGRATION ACT: Women Refugee Claimants Fearing Gender-Related Persecution 1 (1993).

In the guidelines, the IRB concluded that gender-related claims are covered by one or a combination of the five enumerated grounds for refugee status. It recommended recognizing both the family and gender as social groups. *Id.* at 2-5. It finds irrelevant the suggestion in *Gomez, supra* at 662, that gender is too broad a category because race, religion, nationality, and political opinion are characteristics shared by similarly large numbers of people. *Id.* at 6.

9.   In May 1995, the BIA issued as a precedent-decision *Matter of D-V-,* ___, InterimDec. No. 3252 (BIA 1993), which overturned the immigration judge's denial of asylum to a Haitian woman who asserted that she had been gang-raped by military attachés in retaliation for her political activism and religious beliefs. It was the first binding BIA decision to recognize rape as persecution. *Harvard Clinic's Efforts Lead to U.S. Recognition of Politically Motivated Sexual Violence in Asylum Claims of Women Refugees*, HARVARD L. SCHOOL NEWS (Harvard Law School, Cambridge, MA) May 26, 1995, at 1-2, 4.

10.   The 1995 INS guidelines seek to raise awareness of, and sensitivity to, types of abuse and discrimination uniquely experienced by women. The guidelines also, however, stress the need to consider women's claims in the context of the statutory definition of refugee, traditional asylum analysis, and caselaw. What impact are the guidelines likely to have on the number of women granted asylum on the basis of gender-related persecution? Are those women more likely to have difficulty satisfying the definition of persecution or establishing the nexus between the persecution and one of the five grounds? Do the guidelines go far enough to protect refugee women? How do the guidelines differ from those proposed by the Women Refugees Project? *See supra* at 666.

11.   INS guidelines and memoranda, though not official regulations, have generally been held to bind INS officials but not immigration judges or the BIA. *See Zhang v. Slattery*, 840

F.Supp. 292, 292-95 (S.D. N.Y. 1994) (holding that the INS must adhere to internal directives that are not promulgated as Federal Regulations; *Matter of Chang*, Interim Dec. 3107 (BIA 1989) (holding that guidelines issued by the Attorney General were directed to the INS rather than to immigration judges and the BIA).

12.   For further reading on gender-based discrimination and asylum claims and the problems faced by refugee women, see:

Amnesty International, *"Inalienable, Integral and Indivisible"—Women's Rights are Human Rights: Discussion Paper on the 1995 Theme Campaign on Women and Human Rights*, AI Index: ACT 77/03/94 (1994);

Karen Bower, Note, *Recognizing Violence Against Women as Persecution on the Basis of Membership in a Particular Social Group*, 7 GEO. IMMIGR. L.J. 173 (1993);

Linda Cipriani, *Gender and Persecution: Protecting Women Under International Refugee Law*, 7 GEO. IMMIGR. L.J. 511 (1993);

Ivana Filice et al., *Women Refugees from Bosnia-Herzegovina: Developing a Culturally Sensitive Counselling Framework*, 6 INT'L J. REFUGEE LAW 207 (1994);

Maryellen Fullerton, *A Comparative Look at Refugee Status Based on Persecution Due to Membership in a Particular Social Group*, 26 CORNELL INT'L L.J. 505 (1993);

Pamela Goldberg, *Anyplace but Home: Asylum in the United States for Women Fleeing Intimate Violence*, 26 CORNELL INT'L L.J. 565 (1993);

Nancy Kelly, *Guidelines for Women's Asylum Claims*, 6 INT'L J. REFUGEE L. 517 (1994);

Nancy Kelly, *Gender-Related Persecution: Assessing the Asylum Claims of Women*, 26 CORNELL INT'L L.J. 625 (1993);

M. Jane Kronenberger, *Refugee Women: Establishing a Prima Facie Case Under the Refugee Convention*, 15 ILSA J. INT'L L. 61 (1992);

David L. Neal, Note, *Women as a Social Group: Recognizing Sex-Based Persecution as Grounds for Asylum*, 20 COLUM. HUM. RTS. L. REV. 203 (1988);

Todd Stewart Schenk, Note, *A Proposal to Improve the Treatment of Women in Asylum Law: Adding a "Gender" Category to the International Definition of "Refugee,"* 2 IND. J. GLOBAL LEGAL. STUD. 301 (1994);

Mattie L. Stevens, Note, *Recognizing Gender-Specific Persecution: A Proposal to Add Gender as a Sixth Refugee Category*, 3 CORNELL J.L. & PUB. POL'Y 179 (1993).

2.   Are FGM and Spousal Abuse Persecution?

Recall the discussion of "well-founded fear of persecution" in Part C, *supra* at 643. One issue is whether an individual is subject to private as well as public acts of violence. "Persecution" for purposes of the refugee definition generally does not encompass actions taken by private individuals absent a governmental duty to prevent such actions.

Various treaties require governments to protect individuals from the conduct of private actors. Article 2 of the Convention on the Elimination of All Forms of Discrimination Against Women provides that states must "take all appropriate measures to eliminate discrimination against women by any person, organization or enterprise." G.A. res. 34/180, 34 U.N. GAOR Supp. (No. 46) at 195, U.N. Doc. A/Res/34/180 (1981), *entered into force* Sept. 3, 1981. The U.N. Declaration on the

Elimination of Violence Against Women similarly includes all public and private acts of abuse within the definition of "violence against women," which the declaration requires states to prevent or adequately punish. G.A. res. 48/104, 48 U.N. GAOR, U.N. Doc. A/48/629 (1993). The committee overseeing implementation of the Women's Convention has noted that "[s]tates [which have ratified] may . . . be responsible for private acts if they fail to act with due diligence to prevent violations of rights, or to investigate and punish acts of violence." Committee on the Elimination of Discrimination Against Women, *Violence Against Women*, General Recommendation No. 19, at 1, U.N. Doc. CEDAW/C/1992/L.1/Add.15 (1992). The U.N. Convention on the Rights of the Child also requires states to "ensure the child such protection and care as is necessary for his or her well-being. . . ." G.A. res. 44/25, 44 U.N. GAOR Supp. (No. 49) at 166, U.N. Doc. A/44/49 (1989), *entered into force* Sept. 2, 1990.

U.S. law parallels international law. "Acts of persecution or feared persecution must have been committed by the government or by groups or individuals that the government either cannot or will not control." Pamela Goldberg, *Anyplace but Home: Asylum in the United States for Women Fleeing Intimate Violence*, 26 CORNELL INT'L L.J. 565, 571 (1993) (citing ASYLUM BRANCH, OFFICE OF GENERAL COUNSEL, IMMIGRATION & NATURALIZATION SERV., BASIC LAW MANUAL: ASYLUM, SUMMARY AND OVERVIEW CONCERNING ASYLUM LAW 25 (1991) [hereinafter INS MANUAL]).

The INS Manual explicitly states that an individual may have a "well-founded fear of persecution . . . because he or she is not adequately protected by his or her government." INS MANUAL, *supra*, at 25. *See also Sotelo-Aquije v. Slattery*, 17 F.3d 33, 37 (2nd Cir. 1994) (persecution includes violence perpetrated by Shining Path guerrillas if the government cannot control them); *McMullen v. INS*, 658 F.2d 1312, 1315 n.2 (9th Cir. 1981) ("The government concedes that persecution . . . includes persecution by non-governmental groups such as the [Provisional Irish Republican Army], where it is shown that the government . . . is unwilling or unable to control that group.").

In guidelines suggested by the Women Refugees Project, Nancy Kelly recommends the following to help an adjudicator determine whether a government is unable or unwilling to protect an applicant from harm perpetrated by a person not directly related to the government:

1. whether the applicant sought and was denied protection by the government,

2. whether governing institutions and/or governmental agents were aware of the harm to the applicant and did nothing to protect her, or

3. whether the applicant has other reasons to believe that it would be futile to seek the protection of the government (for example, if the government has denied protection to similarly situated women, or if the government has systematically failed to apply existing laws).

NANCY KELLY, WOMEN REFUGEES PROJECT OF CAMBRIDGE AND SOMERVILLE LEGAL SERVICES AND HARVARD IMMIGRATION AND REFUGEE PROGRAM, GUIDELINES FOR WOMEN'S ASYLUM CLAIMS 4 (1994).

*   *   *   *   *

In the following excerpt the UNHCR concludes that FGM is "persecution" even when performed by private actors:

UNHCR, UNHCR Position on Female Genital Mutilation (May 10, 1994) (unpublished memorandum):

1.   The United Nations High Commissioner for Refugees (UNHCR) takes the position that Female Genital Mutilation (FGM), an act which causes severe pain as well as permanent physical harm, amounts to a violation of human rights and of the rights of the child, and as such can be regarded as persecution. The toleration of these acts by the authorities, or the unwillingness of the authorities to provide protection against them, amounts to official acquiescence. Therefore, a woman can be considered as a refugee if she or her daughters/dependents fear being compelled to undergo FGM against their will; or, she fears persecution for refusing to undergo or to allow her daughters to undergo the practice.

2.   This position derives from earlier UNHCR analysis of gender-related claims and "particular social group." The Executive Committee of the UNHCR has acknowledged that gender can be a *factor* in persecution on the basis of one of the five listed categories, and, moreover, that women can in certain circumstances be considered to constitute a "particular social group." The Executive Committee, in Conclusion No. 30 on Refugee Women and International Protection (1985), recognized that States, in the exercise of their sovereignty, are free to adopt the interpretation that women asylum-seekers who face harsh or inhumane treatment due to their having transgressed the social mores of the society in which they live may be considered a "particular social group" within the meaning of Article 1A(2) of the [Refugee] Convention. In 1984, the European Parliament called upon States to consider women in certain situations as constituting a "particular social group" within the meaning of the Convention.

3.   The UNHCR Guidelines on the Protection of Refugee Women (1991) encourage the use of the "particular social group" category to encompass the circumstances of certain women—circumstances which may form the basis of an asylum claim. The guidelines state that a woman's claim to refugee status can be based on severe discrimination, on the grounds of sex, that rises to the level of "persecution for transgressing social mores," (para. 56). In cases where female genital mutilation (FGM) is an accepted and compulsory practice, women who refuse to undergo it or to have their children undergo it may be considered to have transgressed social mores and, depending on the particular circumstances, their treatment as a result may amount to persecution.

4.   There are no international conventions which explicitly prohibit FGM, although the Convention on the Rights of the Child comes close, in requiring States to take measures to abolish "traditional practices prejudicial to the health of children." In addition, FGM has been condemned by the World Health Organization (WHO) annual assembly several times, and WHO has appealed for an end to the practice. The relevant sections of international instruments include the following:

- *The Universal Declaration of Human Rights*: Article 3, providing for the right to "security of person," and Article 5, prohibiting "cruel, inhuman or degrading treatment."

- *The UN Convention Against Torture and Other Cruel, Inhumane and Degrading Treatment and Punishment*: Article 16 requires, inter alia, that the State "prevent . . . acts of cruel, inhuman or degrading treatment . . . , when such acts are committed by or with the consent or acquiescence of a public official."

- *The Convention on the Rights of the Child*: Article 9 provides that States take measures to protect the child from "all forms of physical violence (and) injury. . . ." Article 24(3) of the CRC requires that, "State Parties shall take all effective and appropriate measures with a view to abolishing traditional practices prejudicial to the health of children."

5.   Based on the foregoing analysis, we must conclude that a fear of forced FGM, which could be imposed on daughters upon their return to their country of origin, and/or a fear of the treatment that mothers might receive as a result of refusal to allow their daughters to undergo FGM, combined with the absence of state protection, can be considered persecution owing to membership of a particular social group under the 1951 Convention.

*   *   *   *   *

In its guidelines on assessing gender-related asylum claims of females, Canada too recommends recognizing domestic violence against women as persecution.

> The fact that violence, including sexual and domestic violence, against women is universal is irrelevant when determining whether rape, and other gender-specific crimes constitute forms of persecution. The real issues are whether the violence—experienced or feared—is a serious violation of a fundamental human right for a Convention ground and in what circumstances can the risk of that violence be said to result from a failure of state protection.

IMMIGRATION AND REFUGEE BOARD, GUIDELINES ISSUED BY THE CHAIRPERSON PURSUANT TO SECTION 65(3) OF THE IMMIGRATION ACT: WOMEN REFUGEE CLAIMANTS FEARING GENDER-RELATED PERSECUTION 7 (1993) (footnotes omitted).

Despite the long history of violence against women and the fact that it has been repeatedly condemned, few treaties specifically address it as a human rights violation. The Women's Convention, *supra* at 666, does not, for example, expressly refer to violence against women as a form of discrimination. Article 2 of the U.N. Declaration on the Elimination of Violence Against Women, *supra*, at 666, however, defines "violence against women" to involve:

> [p]hysical, sexual and psychological violence occurring in the family, including battering, . . . marital rape, female genital mutilation and other traditional practices harmful to women . . . .

In preambulatory remarks the General Assembly "affirm[ed] that violence against women both violates and impairs or nullifies the enjoyment by women of human rights and fundamental freedoms."

NOTES AND QUESTIONS

1.   Which of the following clauses of the Civil and Political Covenant may be relevant in determining whether FGM and spousal abuse are persecution:

Article 7

No one shall be subjected to torture or to cruel, inhuman or degrading treatment or punishment. . . .

Article 23 . . .

3.   No marriage shall be entered into without the free and full consent of the intending spouses.

4.   States Parties . . . shall take appropriate steps to ensure equality of rights and responsibilities of spouses as to marriage, during marriage and at its dissolution. . . .

Article 24

1.   Every child shall have . . . the right to such measures of protection as are required by his status as a minor, on the part of his family, society and the State. . . .

*   *   *   *   *

Article 1(1) of the U.N. Treaty Against Torture, excerpted in the UNHCR Position Paper on FGM *supra* at 668, includes within the definition of torture "any act by which severe pain or suffering . . . is intentionally inflicted . . . by or at the instigation of or with the consent or acquiescence of a public official or other person acting in an official capacity."

How might you use those provisions to argue that FGM is persecutory? That spousal abuse is persecutory in the absence of state protection? To address the argument that FGM and spousal abuse are merely private acts of violence?

2.   Ghana ratified the U.N. Convention on the Rights of the Child on February 5, 1990, and the Women's Convention on January 2, 1986. It has not ratified the Civil and Political Covenant or the Treaty Against Torture. How might ratification or non-ratification affect your arguments?

3.   Experts agree FGM is both a woman's and a children's issue. "Female genital mutilation is an extreme example of the general subjugation of women. . . ." EFUA DORKENOO & SCILLA ELWORTHY, FEMALE GENITAL MUTILATION: PROPOSALS FOR CHANGE 16 (1992). It is another vivid reminder of cultures in which the woman's role is defined by a male hierarchy. FGM, however, is performed mostly on unconsenting children with only their parents' permission. It compromises the child's opportunity to develop physically and mentally. Recall the short- and long-term complications associated with the procedures discussed in Part B, *supra* at 632.

4.   The U.N. Centre for Social Development and Humanitarian Affairs studied the social and economic effects of violence against women:

Violence against women in the home has both short-term and long-term effects for the individual woman, her children and society in general. It is a conduct that frequently results in severe physical injury, at time culminating in death. Moreover, the syndrome leads to multiple medical and psychological sequelae for her. Studies suggest that battered women are far more likely to have unsuccessful pregnancies, often being attacked while pregnant. Battered women are overrepresented among female alcoholics, drug abusers and women who have mental illness. Suicide is 12 times as likely to have been attempted by a woman who is subject to abuse than by one who has not.

Beyond the short term physical and mental effects that abuse has on the individual woman, such abuse has serious consequences for her self-image and that of her abuser. The woman is offered limited chances for progress and development, which in turn has a profound impact on the development of society as a whole as its female members are prevented from exercising their fundamental rights and creative potential.

Wife battery, furthermore, has negative implications for the stability of marriage, the quality of family life, and the health and socialization of children. Indeed, evidence exists which suggests that child abuse is more common in families where wife battery is present, delinquency and criminality in children in such families may be more frequent and that children of violent marriages are more likely to establish violent families of their own.

U.N. Office at Vienna, Centre for Social Dev. & Humanitarian Affairs, *Violence Against Women in the Family, 1989*, at 21, U.N. Doc. ST/CSDHA/2 (1989).

During the second U.N. Regional Seminar on Traditional Practices Affecting the Health of Woman and Children, held in 1994, participants, including representatives of countries in the regions affected, U.N. bodies, specialized agencies, and NGOs concluded:

> Violence against women [is] a manifestation of historically unequal power relationships between men and women, which ha[s] led to domination over and discrimination by men against women and to prevention of their full advancement. It [is] due primarily to the inferior social and economic status accorded to women and reflected in inequalities and discriminatory practices in all aspects and all stages of their lives.
>
> Through the socialization process, the girl child [is] made to accept her subordinate status and even violence. The image of women projected in the media ha[s] reinforced the image of women in a subordinate role and encouraged violent attitudes. Violence against women [is] one of the crucial social mechanisms by which women [are] forced into a subordinate position to men. It [is] essentially a violation of the human rights of women.
>
> Marriage ha[s] rendered women even more vulnerable to violence, in this instance from their own husbands. Since wives [a]re often considered to be the husband's property, husbands assume[] that the subordinate status of their wives carrie[s] with it the implicit right to abuse them. Domestic violence [is] a regular feature of marriage but [is] considered to be a private affair. In a number of countries, violence against women [is] on the rise, despite a large number of laws covering domestic violence. . . . Violence against women [is] generally under-reported for fear of public shame.

Sub-Commission on Prevention of Discrimination and Protection of Minorities, *Review of Further Developments in Fields with Which the Sub-Commission Has Been Concerned*, at 15, U.N. Doc. E/CN.4/Sub.2/1994/10 (1994).

Does the implication in those excerpts that FGM and spousal violence constitute gender discrimination suggest additional ways to argue that the practices constitute persecution? Is discrimination a human rights violation? How might you counter an INS argument that an applicant should be denied asylum because she did not seek protection from her own government? If a woman is seeking asylum, is she, as the preceding excerpt suggests, "accept[ing] her subordinate status and even violence?"

5.   Though not addressing spousal violence, the Executive Committee of the U.N. High Commissioners Programme concluded:

> There can be no doubt that when rape or other forms of sexual violence committed for reasons of race, religion, nationality, political opinion or membership of a particular social group is condoned by the authorities, it may be considered persecution under the definition of the term "refugee" in the 1951 Convention relating to the Status of Refugees . . ..

Executive Committee of the High Commissioner's Programme, *Note on Certain Aspects of Sexual Violence Against Refugee Women*, at 12, U.N. Doc. A/AC.96/822 (1993). How might you use that conclusion to support an argument that acts of domestic violence which are tolerated by the authorities constitute persecution?

6.   For a discussion of a Canadian Immigration and Refugee Board decision granting asylum to a Zimbabwean woman partly based on a repeated pattern of spousal abuse, see note 7, *supra* at 665. In that decision, the Board recognized that the persecution was carried out by the husband and not the state. Nonetheless, because the government was unable to protect her from her husband's abusive and persecutory acts, the Board concluded that she was subject to persecution.

7. Refugees were a concern in Western Europe and other non-communist countries after World War II and during the Cold War. Relatively minimal numbers of refugees enabled the West to adopt liberal policies without overburdening the capacity of the "system." Moreover, citizens of the U.S. and Western Europe could appreciate the reasons for flight during this era and could sympathize with persons subject to persecution. Contemporary attitudes, however, are less welcoming of refugees. An increase in racism, the end of the Cold War, and ethnic strife, as well as a decline in the power of governments over their nationals, have increased the perceived burden of receiving refugees. In addition, many citizens of the U.S. and Western Europe believe the system is abused by people who seek to flee economic hardship and by temporary residents seeking benefits while asylum claims are processed. Moreover, magnitudes of refugee flows may make governments less likely to liberalize their interpretation of "refugee," and more likely to restrict refugees' rights.

Might hostility toward refugees affect a judge's approach to "persecution" in the context of FGM and spousal abuse? Remember the number of women and girls who are subjected to FGM each year. How might conscientious officials resolve the conflict between justice and the fear of overburdening the U.S. with an increased influx of refugees?

8. In a widely-publicized decision in March 1994, an immigration judge in Oregon suspended deportation of a Nigerian woman because of her fear that two U.S.-born daughters would be forced to submit to FGM if the three returned to Nigeria. *See* Dimitra Kessenides, *Finding the Right Strategy to Stop a Deportation*, AM. LAW., June 1994, at 35; Jill Lawrence, *Gender Persecution New Reason for Asylum; Human Rights: Women Face Bride-Burning, Genital Mutilation, Forced Abortions and Politically Motivated Rape, But Nations Have Been Slow to Grant Refuge*, L.A. TIMES, Mar. 27, 1994, at A14; *Nigerians Spared Deportation*, N.Y. TIMES, Mar. 24, 1994, at A19; Colleen O'Connor, *Mutilation Custom*, CHI. TRIB., Jun. 27, 1994, at C7. That case apparently represented the first time FGM had been raised as a ground for suspension of deportation from the U.S. To be eligible for a discretionary suspension of deportation, an alien must prove she has resided in the U.S. for seven years, would experience extreme hardship if deported, and that she has shown good moral character. 8 U.S.C. § 1254(a)(1).

Lydia Oluloro, age four herself when relatives submitted her to FGM, testified that relatives had already told her they would force her daughters to submit to FGM if the three of them returned to Nigeria. Relatives claimed too that the two girls would be ostracized.

Her only alternative if she were deported was to leave the girls with their Nigerian father, a permanent U.S. resident. She argued, however, that he had abused her while they were married and expressed fear that he would abuse the girls or force them to submit to FGM. Immigration Judge Warren, relying on a U.N. study indicating that nearly all women in parts of Nigeria were subject to the practice, called FGM "cruel, painful and dangerous" and held that deporting Ms. Oluloro would result in "extreme hardship" to her and her family. Hence, he allowed her to stay in the U.S. Do you think he would have reached a different decision if the girls had been aliens? If FGM was not practiced on nearly all women in parts of Nigeria?

Though the decision was praised by many in the legal and international community, it was denounced by others. The Nigerian Ambassador to the U.S. argued that FGM is voluntary and done only with the consent of girls and their parents in accordance with Nigerian law. He believed that the claim that the daughters would be circumcised against the mother's will was false and an attempt to mislead the INS. Zubair M. Kazaure, *Forced Circumcision is Alien to Nigeria*, N.Y. TIMES, Apr. 9, 1994, at A20. Other critics of the decision argue that granting asylum will undermine attempts within African nations to eradicate the practice (*e.g.*, Timothy Egan, *An Ancient Ritual and a Mother's Asylum Plea*, N.Y. TIMES, Mar. 4, 1994, at A25) and warned that, though the judge's decision is not binding on other courts, it sets a dangerous precedent given the large number of aliens potentially affected.

Despite the criticism, a Minnesota immigration judge reached a similar decision in the case of a Palestinian couple and their daughter. As in the Oluloro case, a Saudi Arabian couple argued that their deportation should be suspended because their U.S.-born daughter would be subject to FGM if they were returned to Saudi Arabia. Randy Furst, *A Child is Spared: Family Escapes Deportation, Their Daughter's Ritual Mutilation*, STAR TRIB. (Minneapolis), Mar. 25, 1994, at 1B.

On June 13, 1996, the Board of Immigration Appeals held that fear of being subjected to female genital mutilation could qualify a woman for political asylum. Their ruling occurred in the case of Fauziya Kasinga from Togo. The Board failed to determine whether a woman could qualify if she had already been subjected to FGM.

9. In 1994, the Minnesota legislature enacted a bill that criminalized performance of FGM procedures on minors. The act imposes felony penalties on persons who perform FGM even if the victim or her parents consent. It also directs the Commissioner of Health to implement education, prevention, and outreach activities to communicate the risks associated with FGM. Genital Mutilation Bill, 1994 Minn. Laws Ch. 636, Art. 2, § (criminal penalty) (codified at MINN. STAT. § 609.2245); Ch. 636, Art. 9, § 9 (education and outreach component) (codified at MINN. STAT. § 144.3872). The North Dakota legislature then enacted a similar bill. 1995 ND S.B. 2454 (codified at N.D. CENT. CODE § 12.1-36-01). Similar legislation was proposed in seven states in early 1996. As of February, all of the bills were still under consideration.

In 1993, Representatives Patricia Schroeder and Barbara Rose Collins introduced a bill to outlaw FGM in the U.S., but were unable to obtain passage. H.R. 3247, 103d Cong., 1st Sess. (1993). The preamble noted that it was intended "to carry out certain obligations of the United States under the International Covenant on Civil and Political Rights by prohibiting the practice of female circumcision." *Id.* The bill sought to criminalize FGM operations under age 18 and to establish educational and other outreach programs within communities that traditionally have practiced FGM to inform persons of physical and emotional risks associated with the practice. In 1995, Representatives Schroeder and Collins, as well as Senator Harry Reid, introduced similar bills. H.R. 941, 104th Cong., 1st Sess. (1995); S. 1030, 104th Cong., 1st Sess. (1995). As of February 1996, the bills were still under consideration.

What effect might such laws have on a claim for asylum based on FGM?

10. In 1994, Canada became the first country in the world to accord refugee status based on the threat of FGM when its Immigration and Refugee Board (IRB) granted asylum to a Somali woman and her two children. The woman, whose husband resided in Somalia, argued that she could not protect her ten-year-old daughter from being subjected to FGM if returned to Somalia. The woman argued that she would be trapped in an abusive marriage were she deported. She refused to divorce her husband because, under Somali law, fathers automatically receive custody of children; and being separated from the children would destroy her. She also argued that separation would be difficult on the children because they had developed an emotional bond with her, and not their father.

The IRB concluded that Somali law did discriminate against women in giving automatic custody to the father after divorce. Because of emotional harm that would befall the mother if she lost custody, the serious repercussions she faced if she opposed the law, and physical violence to which she would be subject if she returned, the IRB concluded that she had a well-founded fear of persecution on account of membership in the social group of women. With respect to the minor daughter, the IRB concluded that the likelihood of her being subjected to FGM, which the Board found to be persecution, justified her fear and thus brought her within the definition of refugee. With respect to the seven-year-old son the IRB found that forcibly removing him from custody of the only parent he has ever known would not be in his best interests. Further, his best interests, which the U.N. Children's Convention makes the overriding consideration in human rights law, would not be considered in Somalia. Therefore, the IRB concluded, the boy had a well-founded fear of persecution on account of membership in the social group of minors and granted his claim for asylum.

11. France was the first country to recognize that FGM is persecution and that threats of it are sufficient grounds on which to grant refugee status. In 1991, a Mali woman who feared mutilation if she were sent home sought asylum. The French authorities denied her claim

but recognized FGM as persecution and later allowed her to remain in France on humanitarian grounds.

France also leads the world in prosecuting FGM cases. It has prosecuted mothers and fathers for subjecting their daughters to the procedure and has also prosecuted women who perform the operations. Though suspended sentences were the ordinary punishment for convicted parents, the recent trend has been to impose prison sentences for them as well as operators. *See* Rone Tempest, *Ancient Traditions vs. The Law*, L.A. TIMES, Feb. 18, 1993, at A1.

12.   For additional reading on the practice of FGM and human rights efforts to eradicate the practice, see:

Sub-Commission on Prevention of Discrimination and Protection of Minorities, *Plan of Action for the Elimination of Harmful Traditional Practices Affecting the Health of Woman and Children*, U.N. Doc. E/CN.4/Sub.2/1994/10/Add.1 (1994) (discussing suggested U.N. action to eradicate son preference, early marriages, and violence against woman and girl children);

ASMA EL DAREER, WOMEN, WHY DO YOU WEEP? (1982);

SEBLE DAWIT, FEMALE GENITAL MUTILATION: VIOLENCE & WOMEN'S HUMAN RIGHTS (1993);

EFUA DORKENOO, CUTTING THE ROSE; FEMALE GENITAL MUTILATION: THE PRACTICE AND ITS PREVENTION (1994);

Karen Engle, *Female Subjects of Public International Law: Human Rights and the Exotic Other Female*, 26 NEW ENGL. L. REV. 1509 (1992);

Isabelle R. Gunning, *Arrogant Perception, World-Travelling and Multicultural Feminism: The Case of Female Genital Surgeries*, 23 COLUM. HUM. RTS. L. REV. 189 (1992);

HANNY LIGHTFOOT-KLEIN, PRISONERS OF RITUAL: AN ODYSSEY INTO FEMALE GENITAL MUTILATION IN AFRICA (1989);

Hope Lewis, *Between "Irua" and "Female Genital Mutilation": Feminist Human Rights Discourse and the Cultural Divide*, 8 HARV. HUM. RTS. J. 1 (1995);

Note, *What's Culture Got to Do With It? Excising the Harmful Tradition of Female Circumcision*, 106 HARV. L. REV. 1944 (1993);

Alison T. Slack, *Female Circumcision: A Critical Appraisal*, 10 HUM. RTS. Q. 437 (1988);

Robyn C. Smith, Note, *Female Circumcision: Bringing Women's Perspectives into the International Debate*, 65 S. CAL. L. REV. 2449 (1992);

AWA THIAM, BLACK SISTERS, SPEAK OUT: FEMINISM AND OPPRESSION IN BLACK AFRICA (1986);

NAHID TOUBIA, FEMALE GENITAL MUTILATION: A CALL TO ACTION (1993);

ALICE WALKER, POSSESSING THE SECRET OF JOY (1992);

ALICE WALKER & PRATIBHA PARMAR, WARRIOR MARKS: FEMALE GENITAL MUTILATION & THE SEXUAL BLINDING OF WOMEN (1993).

13.   For additional information on campaigns to combat violence against women, see:

Charlotte Bunch et al., *Women's Rights as Human Rights*, 12 HUM. RTS. Q. 486 (1990);

Rebecca J. Cook, *International Human Rights Law Concerning Women: Case Notes and Comments*, 23 VAND. J. TRANSNAT'L L. 779 (1990);

Katherine M. Culliton, *Finding a Mechanism to Enforce Women's Right to State Protection from Domestic Violence in the Americas*, 34 HARV. INT'L L.J. 507 (1993);

FREEDOM FROM VIOLENCE: WOMEN'S STRATEGIES FROM AROUND THE WORLD (Margaret Schuler ed., 1992);

HUMAN RIGHTS OF WOMEN: NATIONAL AND INTERNATIONAL PERSPECTIVES (Rebecca J. Cook ed., 1994);

INTERNATIONAL LEAGUE FOR HUMAN RIGHTS, COMBATTING VIOLENCE AGAINST WOMEN (1993) (report of a conference sponsored by the League in collaboration with International Women's Rights Action Watch);

OURS BY RIGHT: WOMEN'S RIGHTS AS HUMAN RIGHTS (Joanna Kerr ed., 1993);

JULIE STONE PETERS, WOMEN'S RIGHTS, HUMAN RIGHTS: INTERNATIONAL FEMINIST PERSPECTIVES (1994);

U.N. OFFICE AT VIENNA, CTR. FOR SOCIAL DEV. AND HUMANITARIAN AFFAIRS; STRATEGIES FOR CONFRONTING DOMESTIC VIOLENCE: A RESOURCE MANUAL (1993).

14.   For further discussion of the public/private dichotomy, see:

Gordon Christenson, *Attributing Acts of Omission to the State*, 12 MICH. J. INT'L L. 312 (1991);

ANDREW CLAPHAM, HUMAN RIGHTS IN THE PRIVATE SPHERE (1993) (discussing "the application of human rights law to the actions of private bodies");

Theodor Meron, *Acts of State, Imputability, Private Acts, in* HUMAN RIGHTS AND HUMANITARIAN NORMS AS CUSTOMARY LAW 155 (1989);

Celina Romany, *Women as Aliens: A Feminist Critique of the Public/Private Distinction in International Human Rights Law*, 6 HARV. HUM. RTS. J. 87 (1993);

Dinah Shelton, *Private Violence, Public Wrongs, and the Responsibility of States*, 13 FORDHAM INT'L L.J. 1 (1989-90).

---

3.   Internal Flight

ASYLUM BRANCH, OFFICE OF GENERAL COUNSEL, IMMIGRATION & NATURALIZATION SERV., BASIC LAW MANUAL: ASYLUM SUPPLEMENT 8 (1993) (emphases omitted):

To establish an asylum claim the applicant has the burden of showing that the threat of persecution exists country-wide. *Matter of Acosta*, Int. Dec. 2986, (BIA 1985), slip opinion at 33; *Matter of Fuentes*, Inc. Dec. 3065 (BIA 1988), slip opinion at 7; *Quintanilla-Ticas v. I.N.S.*, 783 F.2d 955, 957 (9th Cir. 1986); *Cuadras v. INS*, 910 F.2d 567, 571, n.2 (9th Cir. 1990); *Etugh v. INS*, 921 F.2d 36, 39 (3rd Cir. 1991). Hence, if there is evidence that the applicant is able to safely avoid the threat by relocating to a different part of the country, it may serve to undercut the applicant's claim to asylum. In determining whether the threat of persecution is country-wide, the ninth circuit has suggested that one should determine whether the persecutor has the will and ability to enforce its will on a country-wide basis. *See Beltran-Zavala v. INS*, 912 F.2d 1027, 1030 (9th Cir. 1990); *Blanco-Lopez v. INS*, 858 F.2d 531, 534 (9th Cir. 1988). Additionally, the UNHCR Handbook provides that when persecution occurs in only one part of a country "a person will not be excluded from refugee status merely because he could have sought refuge in another part of the same country, if under all the circumstances it would not have been reasonable to expect him to do so." UNHCR HANDBOOK, para. 91; *see also*, G. GOODWIN-GILL, THE REFUGEE IN INTERNATIONAL LAW, 42 (1983).

The principal importance of inquiring whether the threat of persecution exists country-wide is in cases where an applicant's fear has to do with, for instance, a renegade local official or a regional guerrilla organization. In cases where the persecution the applicant fears is inflicted pursuant to national policy, or where it otherwise appears unlikely that national authorities would be inclined to protect the applicant from the persecution, a claim will not be defeated by the possibility that inefficiency or lethargy on the part of those in power might have helped the applicant avoid persecution by means of internal flight.

NOTES AND QUESTIONS

1.   The absence of country-wide persecution has on occasion been used by courts as a reason for denying asylum. Illustratively in *Cuadras v. INS*, 910 F.2d 567 (9th Cir. 1990), the court upheld a BIA determination that a Salvadoran's fear of persecution resulting from recruitment by guerrilla forces was not well-founded, in part because he could have relocated to other areas of El Salvador to avoid the violence. *Id.* at 571, n.2.

That decision followed two others upholding denial of asylum in part because of an internal-flight alternative. *Quintanilla-Ticas v. INS*, 783 F.2d 955 (9th Cir. 1986), upheld denial of asylum to three Salvadorans. The court noted that the "threat" was by an unknown party and directed against a group of people, and the only association with that group was that one petitioner was a former member. The court noted too that the applicants could avoid danger in their home town by relocating elsewhere. *Id.* at 957. Similarly *Diaz-Escobar v. INS*, 782 F.2d 1488 (9th Cir. 1986), upheld denial of asylum for a Guatemalan who feared persecution by guerrillas in his country. The court concluded that the fear was not objectively reasonable because it was based solely on an anonymous note left on his car. The court noted that any fear he had of returning to his home town was unreasonable because he could relocate safely to another part of Guatemala.

Might Awata be expected to relocate in Ghana to avoid the application of FGM and *lobola*?

2.   In granting asylum to a Zimbabwean woman on the basis of a repeated pattern of spousal abuse, see note 7, *supra* at 665, and note 6, *supra* at 671, the Canadian Immigration and Refugee Board concluded that she could not avoid persecution by internal flight. On several occasions, her parents returned her to her husband when she sought refuge with them. Her relatives in South Africa and Malawi similarly refused to shelter her. Moreover, because of her husband's wealth and influence she feared he would find her anywhere in Zimbabwe and subject her to even more serious abuse for trying to leave him. Therefore, the Board concluded that she should not be returned to Zimbabwe.

3.   Related to the issue of internal flight is the issue of internally displaced persons. The U.N. Secretary-General has used the term to describe "persons who have been forced to flee their homes suddenly or unexpectedly in large numbers; as a result of armed conflict, internal strife, systematic violations of human rights or natural or man-made disasters; and who are within the territory of their own country." *Analytical Report of the Secretary-General on Internally Displaced Persons*, U.N. ESCOR, 48th Sess., 23d mtg., at 5, U.N. Doc. E/CN.4/23 (1992). Commentators use the term to refer both to those who have been forced to flee from their homes but remain within the borders of their country of nationality, and to those who have been forcibly relocated to another part of their home country. According to a 1991 U.N. report, the number of internally displaced persons then exceeded the number of persons officially classified as refugees. Jacques Cuenod, *Report on Refugees, Displaced Persons and Returnees*, U.N. Doc. E/109/Add.1 (1991).

Because they have not crossed an international border, the internally displaced do not fit within traditional definitions of refugee; and no treaties adequately address problems of the internally displaced. As a result the international community has responded in an *ad hoc* fashion. Nonetheless, their problems often are similar to and as acute as those faced by traditional refugees. Most importantly, like traditional refugees internally displaced persons lack the protection of their own government.

4. Concerning the debate regarding protection of internally displaced persons, see:

ROBERTA COHEN & JACQUES CUENOD, THE BROOKINGS INSTITUTION—REFUGEE POLICY GROUP PROJECT ON INTERNAL DISPLACEMENT, IMPROVING INSTITUTIONAL ARRANGEMENTS FOR THE INTERNALLY DISPLACED (1995);

ROBERTA COHEN, REFUGEE POLICY GROUP, HUMAN RIGHTS PROTECTION FOR INTERNALLY DISPLACED PERSONS: AN INTERNATIONAL CONFERENCE (1991);

Corinne E. Lewis, *Dealing with the Problem of Internally Displaced Persons*, 6 GEO. IMMIGR. L.J. 693 (1992);

Richard Plender, *The Legal Basis of International Jurisdiction to Act with Regard to the Internally Displaced*, 6 INT'L J. REFUGEE LAW 345 (1994);

Analytical Report of the Secretary-General on Internally Displaced Persons, U.N. Doc. E/CN.4/1992/23 (1992).

F. OBSTACLES TO FGM- AND SPOUSAL VIOLENCE-BASED ASYLUM CLAIMS

1. Cultural Relativism

Katherine Brennan, Note, *The Influence of Cultural Relativism on International Human Rights Law: Female Circumcision as a Case Study*, 7 LAW & INEQ. J. 367, 368-73 (1991) (footnotes omitted):

. . . Cultural relativists criticize the current international human rights system because, in its search for potential human rights violations, it looks at cultural practices which have been condoned for centuries by the societies which engage in them. These critics assert that cultural practices have a legitimate function indigenous to the culture and that judging these practices according to international norms imposes outside values upon the society. Human rights proponents respond that their evaluation of cultural practices is based on universally accepted norms and, therefore, does not impose the views of outsiders.

. . . [C]ultural relativists often mention female circumcision as an example of traditional practices that should not be evaluated by outsiders. . . .

Cultural relativism can be described, in its simplest form, as the theory that there is infinite cultural diversity and that all cultural practices are equally valid. There are no absolutes upon which to judge one practice against another because, in the words of one scholar, "the principles that we may use for judging behavior or anything else are relative to the culture in which we are raised." This view of cultural practices calls into question the legitimacy of human rights theory, which purports to establish principles for judging the conduct of all cultures.

. . . Some proponents of human rights theory assert that [the] increased acceptance of cultural relativism [during the twentieth century] offers a growing threat to the validity of the current international human rights system.

That threat arises out of the relativists' belief that cultures have varied values and methods of protecting those values. Relativists generally agree with human rights proponents that all cultures value human dignity, but assert that non-Western societies do not use an individual rights approach to protect that dignity. Instead, in some non-Western societies the dignity of the individual is preserved through his or her membership in the community, while in others it is preserved through fulfillment of prescribed duties. If societies have adequate internal systems for protecting their own members, human rights instruments are unnecessary and irrelevant. In fact, judging cultural practices against international norms would be inappropriate according to cultural relativists because it imposes external values on those cultures. . . .

The application of cultural relativism to human rights theory has naturally prompted replies by proponents of the current international human rights system. Two major arguments are used to refute the claims of cultural relativists. One is the universalists' reply and the other is the approach of positivism.

Universalism, which draws from the natural law tradition in Western jurisprudence, is the theory that there exists some set of standards which all cultures espouse. These universal principles transcend cultural differences and serve as the authority for adopting international human rights. This theory assumes that all cultures value the protection of individual human dignity and that they would establish similar minimum standards for protecting their individual members. The official doctrine underlying the current international human rights systems is that the instruments which make up developing international human rights law enumerates these universal minimum standards. If at least some of the rights enumerated by the U.N. human rights instruments are universal, that core of rights would provide a standard against which cultural practices could legitimately be judged. Consequently, there has been a rather urgent search by some human rights scholars for this set of universal rights.

The postitivist response to cultural relativism is that, regardless of the conflicting ideologies and cultural values to which nations adhere, the U.N.-promulgated norms represent agreements by these participating nations to work toward a common goal. Whether or not particular member states have a tradition of valuing individual dignity is irrelevant. If they have ratified human rights instruments based on this theory of individual rights, these states have participated voluntarily in the U.N. process and have obligated themselves to protecting these rights. Just as the theory of positivism in Western jurisprudence asserts that law derives its authority from the consent of those governed, adherents of positivism in international human rights law assert that the authority for these rights is derived from the consent of the participant countries. Scholars who follow this approach respond to the criticism of cultural relativists by pointing out that countries that participate willingly in the U.N. process and that ratify the human rights treaties cannot claim to be exempt from the standards to which they voluntarily subject themselves.

*   *   *   *   *

Jack Donnelly, *Cultural Relativism and Universal Human Rights*, 6 HUM. RTS. Q. 400, 410-19 (1984) (footnotes omitted):

CULTURE AND RELATIVISM . . .

In the Third World today, more often than not we see dual societies and patchwork practices that seek to accommodate seemingly irreconcilable old and new ways. Rather than the persistence of traditional culture in the face of modern intrusions, or even the development of syncretic cultures and values, we usually see instead a disruptive and incomplete westernization, cultural confusion, or the enthusiastic embrace of "modern" practices and values. In other words, the traditional culture advanced to justify cultural relativism far too often no longer exists.

Therefore, while recognizing the legitimate claims of self-determination and cultural relativism, we must be alert to cynical manipulations of a dying, lost, or even mythical cultural past. We must not be misled by complaints of the inappropriateness of "western" human rights made by repressive regimes whose practices have at best only the most tenuous connection to the indigenous culture. . . .

In traditional cultures—at least the sorts of traditional cultures that would readily justify cultural deviations from international human rights standards—people are not victims of the arbitrary decisions of rulers whose principal claim to power is their control of modern instruments of force and administration. In traditional cultures, communal customs and practices usually provide each person with a place in society and a certain amount of dignity and protection. Furthermore, there usually are well-established reciprocal bonds between rulers and ruled, and between rich and poor. . . .

[In addition,] there are substantive human rights limits on even well-established cultural practices, however difficult it may be to specify and defend a particular account of what those practices are. For example, while slavery has been customary in numerous societies, today it is a practice that no custom can justify. Likewise, sexual, racial, ethnic, and religious discrimination have been widely practiced, but are indefensible today; the depth of the tradition of anti-Semitism in the West, for example, simply is no defense for the maintenance of the practice. . . .

RESOLVING THE CLAIMS OF RELATIVISM AND UNIVERSALISM

Despite striking and profound international differences in ideology, levels and styles of economic development, and patterns of political evolution, virtually all states today have embraced—in speech if not in deed—the human rights standards enunciated in the Universal Declaration of Human Rights and the International Human Rights Covenants. . . .

While human rights—inalienable entitlements of individuals held in relation to state and society—have not been a part of most cultural traditions, or even the western tradition until rather recently, there is a striking similarity in many of the basic values that today we seek to protect through human rights. This is particularly true when these values are expressed in relatively general terms. Life, social order, protection from arbitrary rule, prohibition of inhuman and degrading treatment, the guarantee of a place in the life of the community, and access to an equitable share of the means of subsistence are central moral aspirations in nearly all cultures.

This fundamental unity in the midst of otherwise bewildering diversity suggests a certain core of "human nature"—for all its undeniable variability, and despite our inability to express that core in the language of science. And if human nature is relatively universal, then basic human rights must at least initially be assumed to be similarly universal. . . .

ASSESSING CLAIMS OF CULTURAL RELATIVISM

Rights are formulated with certain basic violations, or threats to human dignity, in mind. Therefore, the easiest way to overcome the presumption of universality for a widely recognized human right is to demonstrate either that the anticipated violation is not standard in that society, that the value is (justifiably) not considered basic in that society, or that it is protected by an alternative mechanism. . . . I would argue that such a test can be met only rarely today, and that permissible exceptions usually are relatively minor and generally consistent with the basic thrust of the Universal Declaration.

For example, it is hard to imagine cultural arguments against recognition of the basic personal rights of Articles 3 through 11 [of the Universal Declaration of Human Rights]. . . . In fact, I am tempted to say that conceptions of human nature or society incompatible with such rights would be almost by definition indefensible; at the very least, such rights come very close to being fully universal.

Civil rights such as freedom of conscience, speech, and association would be a bit more relative; as they assume the existence and a positive evaluation of relatively autonomous individuals, they are of questionable applicability in strong traditional communities. In such communities, however, they would rarely be at issue. If traditional practices truly are based on and protect culturally accepted conceptions of human dignity, then members of such a community simply will not have the desire or need to claim such civil rights. But in the more typical contemporary case, in which the relatively autonomous individual faces the modern state, they would seem to be close to universal rights; it is hard to imagine a defensible modern conception of human dignity that did not include at least most of these rights. . . .

The Declaration does list some rights that are best viewed as "interpretations," subject to much greater cultural relativity. For example, the already mentioned right of free and full consent of intending spouses not only reflects a specific cultural interpretation of marriage, but an interpretation that is of relatively recent origin and by no means universal today even in the West. Notice, however, that the right, as Section 2 of Article 16, is subordinate to the basic right to marry and found a family. Furthermore, some traditional customs, such as bride price, provide alternative protections for women, and a sort of indirect conditionality to marriage that addresses at least some of the underlying concerns of Article 16(2). Such factors make it much easier to accept cultural relativity with regard to this right. . . .

Such cases, however, are the exception rather than the rule. And if my arguments above are correct, we can justifiably insist on some form of weak cultural relativism; that is, on a fundamental universality of basic human rights, tempered by a recognition of the possible need for limited cultural variations. Basic human rights are, to use an appropriately paradoxical phrase, relatively universal.

NOTES AND QUESTIONS

1. Do you agree with Donnelly that the content of some human rights may vary with the cultural context? Compare his view with some early interpretations of the U.S. 14th Amendment, under which the content of rights to racial equality varied from state to state and allowed substantial discrimination in some states. Do you think that permitting cultural relativism in international human rights law would achieve parallel results?

2. FGM has been both rationalized and condemned by various African governments. Several African organizations have joined international efforts to eradicate the practice on their continent. The Inter-African Committee on Traditional Practices Affecting the Health of Woman and Children, formed in 1984, uses informational campaigns and lobbying of officials to increase awareness about dangers of FGM. It also has developed groups in several countries, including Ghana, to address the practice.

3. In testimony before the Sub-Committee on International Security, International Organizations and Human Rights of the House Committee on Foreign Affairs, Dr. Nahid Toubia, a Sudanese-born obstetrician working in New York, stated:

> I stand here today to testify on behalf of many girls and women who had no choice when parts of their bodies were removed in the name of culture and social conformity. I testify for all the women and all the cultures, east and west, who undergo the physical pain and psychological agony of bodily manipulations to conform to the

prevailing forms of acceptable womanhood, the social prescriptions of femininity that keep women bound to maintain control over their lives, reproduction, and sexuality. In my society, that means cutting essential parts of genitals of girls and women. In America . . . it takes the form of the beauty cut which drives teenage girls and women to mutilate their bodies with plastic surgery, breast implants, bulimia and such procedures.

Women are never allowed to feel holistic, the way they are created. They have to be reshaped by society to please men. Because as women, we are made economically and socially powerless. Most of us have little chance to say no to stop the injustice imposed on us by society.

Most African women have very little power to say no, because as women their only means of survival is to marry, give their husbands sexual pleasure and give birth to many children while suffering in silence.

Today in Africa many of us have found our voice and are speaking out against the custom that abuses and humiliates. We are often silenced in the name of preserving culture and tradition. . . .

Today . . . I would like the world and the people here in this room and the United States to listen to the voices of many brave African women who are doing great work in their own communities but are rarely heard when the issue of female genital mutilation is discussed internationally. It is always seen that outsiders are going to come and save African woman, and very little credence is given to the actual work, very brave work that African women are doing, sometimes at risk to their own lives and health.

Do those comments suggest arguments against using cultural relativism to discount the persecutive nature of FGM?

4. Punishments prescribed by the Penal Code of Iran have raised concerns because it condones use of stoning, crucifixion, amputation of limbs and of other body parts, and flogging as penalties for crimes such as adultery, drinking alcohol, fornication, lesbianism, malicious accusation, prostitution, sodomy, and theft. Iran argues that its practices are based on tenets of Islam. The human rights situation in Iran is discussed in great detail in chapter 4. For a survey of other countries that allow some such punishments, see Tom Kuntz, *Beyond Singapore: Corporal Punishment, A to Z*, N.Y. TIMES, June 26, 1994, § 4, at 5.

5. China has followed a variation of cultural relativism with emphasis on state sovereignty:

[T]he evolution of the situation in regard to human rights is circumscribed by the historical, social, economic and cultural conditions of various nations, and involves a process of historical development. Owing to tremendous differences in historical background, social system, cultural tradition and economic development, countries differ in their understanding and practice of human rights. From their different situations, they have taken different attitudes towards the relevant UN conventions. Despite its international aspect, the issue of human rights falls by and large within the sovereignty of each country. Therefore, a country's human rights situation should not be judged in total disregard of this history and national conditions, nor can it be evaluated according to a preconceived model or the conditions of another country or region.

INFORMATION OFFICE OF THE STATE COUNCIL, HUMAN RIGHTS IN CHINA, at ii (1991). These views became more visible surrounding the 1995 Beijing Conference.

While the government advocates participation in U.N. human rights activities, it asserts that the ultimate responsibility lies with individual governments. "China advocates mutual respect for state sovereignty and . . . is opposed to interfering in other countries' internal affairs on the pretext of human rights. . . ." *Id.* at 79.

Unlike cultural relativists, Chinese officials do not advocate lessening international standards in accordance with a country's culture. Instead, their view holds that the international community should take a country's history and culture into account when judging its human rights record. In theory the Chinese and cultural relativist views seem similar; but in practice they differ. According to the cultural relativist view countries should be allowed flexibility in implementing human rights standards. The Chinese view advocates implementation of standards but on a less demanding timeline:

As a developing country, China has suffered from setbacks while safeguarding and developing human rights. Although much has been achieved in this regard, there is still much room for improvement. It remains a long-term historical task for the Chinese people and government to continue to promote human rights and strive for the noble goal of full implementation of human rights as required by China's socialism. *Id.* at iii.

For further reading, see Robert Drinan & Teresa Kuo, *The 1991 Battle for Human Rights in China*, 14 HUM. RTS. Q. 21 (1992); Winston Pan, *The Confucian Tradition and its Implications for Human Rights in China*, 3 GLOBAL JUST. 9 (1993).

6.   Cultural relativism and universalism were central issues at the 1993 World Conference on Human Rights in Vienna.

The Conference adopted the U.N. Vienna Declaration and Programme of Action. The first paragraph reaffirms universality of human rights. Paragraph 3 asserts that national, regional, cultural, and religious experiences are important but that it is still the duty of each government to "promote and protect all human rights and fundamental freedoms." Paragraph 19, however, reaffirms the importance of "universality, objectivity and non-selectivity." The notion of universality rejects the assertion of relativism, but "non-selectivity" may imply that U.N. human rights bodies should not single out countries on the basis of their human rights record.

The Vienna Conference thus to a great extent reaffirmed universality despite an articulate appeal for relativism delivered by Singapore's Foreign Minister. He stressed the need for a realistic approach:

Universal recognition of the ideal of human rights can be harmful if universalism is used to deny or mask the reality of diversity. The gap between different points of view will not be bridged if this is ignored. We deceive only ourselves if we pretend this is not so. . . .

Of course, there is a risk that tolerance for diversity will be used as a shield for dictators. This is unacceptable. But pragmatism and realism do not mean abdication. We need not, indeed we should not, cease to speak out against wanton cruelty or injustice. We can strike a realistic balance between the ideal of universality and the reality of diversity if we adopt a clinical approach.

Our aim should be to promote humane standards of behaviour without at the same time claiming special truths or seeking to impose any particular political pattern or societal arrangement.

. . . All cultures aspire to promote human dignity in their own ways. But the hard core of rights that are truly universal is perhaps smaller than we sometimes like to pretend.

Wong Kan Seng, The Real World of Human Rights, Statement at the World Conference on Human Rights, Vienna (16 June 1993).

7.   For further reading on cultural relativism and human rights, and its particular applications, see:

DONALD BROWN, HUMAN UNIVERSALS (1991);

Josiah A.M. Cobbah, *African Values and the Human Rights Debate: An Africa Perspective*, 9 HUM. RTS. Q. 309 (1987);

JACK DONNELLY, UNIVERSAL HUMAN RIGHTS IN THEORY AND PRACTICE (1989);

Asbjorn Eide, *Making Human Rights Universal: Unfinished Business*, 6 NORDIC J. HUM. RTS. 51 (No. 4, 1988);

Evan Gottesman, *The Reemergence of Quisas and Diyats in Pakistan*, 23 COLUM. HUM. RTS. L. REV. 433 (1992);

Sharon K. Hom, *Female Infanticide in China: The Human Rights Specter and Thoughts Toward An(other) Vision*, 23 COLUM. HUM. RTS. L. REV. 249 (1992);

RHODA E. HOWARD, HUMAN RIGHTS AND THE SEARCH FOR COMMUNITY (1995);

HUMAN RIGHTS AND CHINESE VALUES: LEGAL, PHILOSOPHICAL, AND POLITICAL PERSPECTIVES (Michael C. Davis ed. 1995);

HUMAN RIGHTS IN CROSS-CULTURAL PERSPECTIVES: A QUEST FOR CONSENSUS (Abdullahi Ahmed An-Na'im ed. 1991);

TORE LINDHOLM, THE CROSS-CULTURAL LEGITIMACY OF HUMAN RIGHTS: PROSPECTS FOR RESEARCH (1990);

Winston Nagan, *African Human Rights Process: A Contextual Policy-Oriented Approach*, 21 SW. U. L. REV. 63 (1992);

JAMES W. NICKEL, MAKING SENSE OF HUMAN RIGHTS: PHILOSOPHICAL REFLECTIONS ON THE UNIVERSAL DECLARATION OF HUMAN RIGHTS (1987);

ALISON D. RENTELN, INTERNATIONAL HUMAN RIGHTS: UNIVERSALISM VERSUS RELATIVISM (1990);

Alison D. Renteln, *The Unanswered Challenge of Relativism and the Consequences for Human Rights*, 7 HUM. RTS. Q. 514 (1985);

Fernando R. Tesón, *International Human Rights and Cultural Relativism*, 25 VA. J. INT'L L. 869 (1985).

---

2.   Theoretical Foundations of Human Rights

To determine whether FGM and spousal abuse constitute violations one must consider theoretical bases of human rights law. Several competing theories have been advanced to justify international norms. The theory a country embraces dictates whether it must comply with all norms or only those the state agrees to follow. Despite much debate, no dominant theory has emerged.

Recall the discussion of the natural law approach and positivism in the Brennan excerpt, *supra* at 677; and the materials in chapter 4 concerning the natural law approach and the Islamic conceptions of human rights. The following excerpts detail additional approaches. As you read, consider the implications of his theory on the recognition of FGM and spousal abuse as persecution.

*   *   *   *   *

Hilary Charlesworth, Christine Chinkin & Shelley Wright, *Feminist Approaches to International Law*, 85 AM. J. INT'L L. 613, 616-34 (1991) (footnotes omitted):

Feminist and Third World Challenges to International Law

[As a consequence of decolonization, Third World countries] challenged both substantive norms of international law and the traditional lawmaking processes as either disadvantageous to them or inadequate to their needs. The impact of this challenge to assumptions about the objective neutrality of norms by showing them to support western values and interests has been substantial. Developing states have also emphasized decision making through negotiation and consensus, and through the use of nontraditional methods of lawmaking such as the "soft law" of General Assembly resolutions. These techniques find some parallel in the types of dispute resolution sometimes associated with the "different voice" of women. . . . [One commentator compared feminine jurisprudence to] the "African world view" . . .. This world view is characterized by "a conception of the self as intrinsically connected with, as part of, both the community and nature." The attribution to women and Africans of "a concept of the self as dependent on others, as defined through relationships to others, as perceiving self-interest to lie in the welfare of the relational complex," permits the ascription to these groups of an ethic based on preservation of relationships and an epistemology uniting "hand, brain and heart." These perceptions contrast with the "European" and male view of the self as autonomous, separate from nature and from others, and with its associated ethics of "rule-governed adjudication of competing rights between self-interested, autonomous others" and its view of knowledge as an entity with a separate, "objective" existence. . . .

More general analogies have been drawn between the position of Third World states and that of women. Both groups are said to encounter the paternalist attitude that they must be properly trained to fit into the world of developed countries and men, respectively. Both feminists and developing nations have also resisted assimilation to prevailing standards and have argued for radical change, emphasizing cooperation rather than individual self-advancement. Both groups have identified unilinear structures that allow their systematic domination and the development of apparently generally applicable theories from very narrow perspectives.

Thus far, however, the "different voice" of developing nations in international law has shown little concern for feminist perspectives. The power structures and decision-making processes in these societies are every bit as exclusive of women as in western societies and the rhetoric of domination and subjugation has not encompassed women, who remain the poorest and least privileged. . . . Although the developing nations' challenge to international law has been fundamental, it has focused on disparities in economic position and has not questioned the silence of half the world's population in the creation of international law or the unequal impact of rules of international law on women. Indeed, this challenge to the European origins of international law and many of its assumptions may have had an adverse effect on the development of a gender-based analysis of international law precisely because of the further level of confrontation it is assumed such an analysis would cause. . . .

. . . THE MASCULINE WORLD OF INTERNATIONAL LAW . . .

The Organizational Structure of International Law

The structure of the international legal order reflects a male perspective and ensures its continued dominance. The primary subjects of international law are states and, increasingly, international organizations. In both states and international organizations the invisibility of women is striking. Power structures within governments are overwhelmingly masculine: women have significant positions of power in very few states, and in those where they do, their numbers are minuscule. Women are either unrepresented or underrepresented in the national and global decision-making processes.

States are patriarchal structures not only because they exclude women from elite positions and decision-making roles, but also because they are based on the concentration of power in, and control by, an elite and the domestic legitimation of a monopoly over the use of force to maintain that control. This foundation is reinforced by international legal principles of sovereign equality, political independence and territorial integrity and the legitimation of force to defend those attributes.

International organizations are functional extensions of states that allow them to act collectively to achieve their objectives. Not surprisingly, their structures replicate those of states, restricting women to insignificant and subordinate roles. Thus, in the United Nations itself, where the achievement of nearly universal membership is regarded as a major success of the international community, this universality does not apply to women. . . .

The silence and invisibility of women also characterizes those bodies with special functions regarding the creation and progressive development of international law. Only one woman has sat as a judge on the International Court of Justice and no woman has ever been a member of the International Law Commission. . . .

Despite the common acceptance of human rights as an area in which attention can be directed toward women, they are still vastly underrepresented on UN human rights bodies. The one committee that has all women members, the Committee on the Elimination of Discrimination against Women (CEDAW Committee), the monitoring body for the Convention on the Elimination of All Forms of Discrimination against Women (Women's Convention), has been criticized for its "disproportionate" representation of women by the United Nations Economic and Social Council (ECOSOC). . . .

Why is it significant that all the major institutions of the international legal order are peopled by men? Long-term domination of all bodies wielding political power nationally and internationally means that issues traditionally of concern to men become seen as general human concerns, while "women's concerns" are relegated to a special, limited category. . . .

The Normative Structure of International Law

Since the primary subjects of international law are states, it is sometimes assumed that the impact of international law falls on the state and not directly on individuals. In fact, the application of international law does affect individuals . . . . International jurisprudence assumes that international law norms directed at individuals within states are universally applicable and neutral. It is not recognized, however, that such principles may impinge differently on men and women; consequently, women's experiences of the operation of these laws tend to be silenced or discounted.

The normative structure of international law has allowed issues of particular concern to women to be either ignored or undermined. For example, modern international law rests on and reproduces various dichotomies between the public and private spheres, and the "public" sphere is regarded as the province of international law. One such distinction . . . is the distinction between matters of international "public" concern and matters "private" to states that are considered within their domestic jurisdiction, in which the international community has no recognized legal interest. . . .

At a deeper level one finds a public/private dichotomy based on gender. . . . The public realm of the work place, the law, economics, politics and intellectual and cultural life, where power and authority are exercised, is regarded as the natural province of men; while the private world of the home, the hearth and children is seen as the appropriate domain of women. The public/private distinction has a normative, as well as a descriptive, dimension. Traditionally, the two spheres are accorded asymmetrical value: greater significance is attached to the public, male world than to the private, female one. The distinction drawn between the public and the private thus vindicates and makes natural the division of labor and allocation of rewards between the sexes. Its reproduction and acceptance in all areas of knowledge have conferred primacy on the male world and supported the dominance of men. . . .

How is the western liberal version of the public/private distinction maintained? Its naturalness rests on deeply held beliefs about gender. . . .

Although the scientific basis of the public/private distinction has been thoroughly attacked and exposed as a culturally constructed ideology, it continues to have a strong grip on legal thinking. The language of the public/private distinction is built into the language of the law itself: law lays claim to rationality, culture, power, objectivity—all terms associated with the public or male realm. It is defined in opposition to the attributes associated with the domestic, private, female sphere: feeling, emotion, passivity, subjectivity. Moreover, the law has always operated primarily within the public domain; it is considered appropriate to regulate the work place, the economy and the distribution of political power, while direct state intervention in the family and the home has long been regarded as inappropriate. Violence within the home, for example, has generally been given different legal significance from violence outside it; the injuries recognized as legally compensable are those which occur outside the home. Damages in civil actions are typically assessed in terms of ability to participate in the public sphere.

Women have difficulty convincing law enforcement officials that violent acts within the home are criminal. . . .

What force does the feminist critique of the public/private dichotomy in the foundation of domestic legal systems have for the international legal order? Traditionally, of course, international law was regarded as operating only in the most public of public spheres: the relations between nation-states. We argue, however, that the definition of certain principles of international law rests on and reproduces the public/private distinction. It thus privileges the male world view and supports male dominance in the international legal order.

[The authors cite as an example the international proscription against torture. The Treaty against Torture is dominated by masculine references. The focus on intentional infliction which fulfills a purpose ignores the torture inflicted during random terror campaigns aimed at women and children. The requirement that torture be placed in the public realm excludes much of the torture inflicted on women within the home or by private persons.]

States are held responsible for torture only when their designated agents have direct responsibility for such acts and that responsibility is imputed to the state. States are not considered responsible if they have maintained a legal and social system in which violations of physical and mental integrity are endemic. In its draft articles on state responsibility, the International Law Commission did not widen the concept of imputability to incorporate such acts. A feminist perspective on human rights would require a rethinking of the notions of imputability and state responsibility and in this sense would challenge the most basic assumptions of international law. If violence against women were considered by the international legal system to be as shocking as violence against people for their political ideas, women would have considerable support in their struggle.

The assumption that underlies all law, including international human rights law, is that the public/private distinction is real: human society, human lives can be separated into two distinct spheres. This division, however, is an ideological construct rationalizing the exclusion of women from the sources of power. It also makes it possible to maintain repressive systems of control over women without interference from human rights guarantees, which operate in the public sphere. By extending our vision beyond the public/private ideologies that rationalize limiting our analysis of power, human rights language as it currently exists can be used to describe serious forms of repression that go far beyond the juridically narrow vision of international law. For example, coercive population control techniques, such as forced sterilization, may amount to punishment or coercion by the state to achieve national goals. . . .

. . . TOWARD A FEMINIST ANALYSIS OF INTERNATIONAL LAW

How can feminist accounts of law be applied in international law? Feminist legal theory can promote a variety of activities. The term signifies an interest (gender as an issue of primary importance); a focus of attention (women as individuals and as members of groups); a political agenda (real social, political, economic and cultural equality regardless of gender); a critical stance (an analysis of "masculinism" and male hierarchical power or "patriarchy"); a means of reinterpreting and reformulating substantive law so that it more adequately reflects the experiences of all people; and an alternative method of practicing, talking about and learning the law. Feminist method must be concerned with examining the fundamentals of the legal persuasion: the language it uses; the organization of legal materials in predetermined, watertight categories; the acceptance of abstract concepts as somehow valid or "pure"; the reliance in practice on confrontational, adversarial techniques; and the commitment to male, hierarchical structures in all legal and political organizations.

* * * * *

Nigel Purvis, *Critical Legal Studies in Public International Law*, 32 HARV. INT'L L.J. 81, 88-110, 113-14 (1991) (footnotes omitted):

Over the last decade, a "New Stream" of international legal scholarship has emerged. One of its most distinguishing features has been its hostility toward conceptual pragmatism. . . .

. . . [T]he New Stream has imported into international law tremendously diverse methodological approaches. These contemporary international legal theorists have incorporated insights from normative philosophy, critical theory, structuralism, anthropology, prepositional logic, literature, sociology, politics, and psychiatry. . . . The New Stream in international legal theory stands as part of a broader movement in contemporary legal theory commonly known as Critical Legal Studies (CLS) or critical jurisprudence.

The CLS movement has brought the radical insights of modernism into law. . . . . - Critical jurisprudence has sought to expose political choice, discredit the "rights" discourse of liberal legalism, demonstrate the indeterminacy of law, and reveal the bias of liberal ideology. It has aimed to demonstrate how law, through its capacity for "reification," "mystification," "legitimation," and "obfuscation," reinforces social injustice. To the extent that they have been articulated, CLS's visions about the ideal condition of law require a transformation of law that would eliminate all forms of "alienation," "domination," and "subjugation" from social life. . . .

. . . CLS ANALYSIS OF INTERNATIONAL LAW

According to its own adherents, the insights of New Stream scholarship have been directed against "the tragic voice of post-war public law liberalism." . . .

The critical attack on liberalism has advanced on four principal fronts. Contemporary international law scholars have maintained (1) that the logic of liberalism in international law is internally incoherent; (2) that international legal discourse operates within a constrained structure; (3) that international legal analysis is indeterminate; and (4) that whatever authority international law may have is self-validated. These criticisms parallel claims made by CLS scholars outside the area of international law, but only rarely have they been systematically discussed as a unified theory of international legal analysis. . . .

A.   The Logic of Liberal Ethics and International Law

1.   The Incoherence of Liberalism in International Law

Critical jurisprudence in international law has sought to demonstrate that the dominant conception of international social life—based on liberal ethics—is internally incoherent. . . .

Liberalism . . . conceives of sovereignty as being the foundation of international life. . . . Sovereigns are both the subjects and objects of international life. No "natural" world order pre-exists the sovereigns' appearance. Social ends are merely objectives that sovereigns hold in common, and world order represents nothing more than a social contract among sovereigns. Sovereignty also assumes an indivisible quality. Put another way, sovereignty is atomistic; it is international life's unencumbered basic unit. Liberalism's metaphoric expression of this concept equates sovereigns to individuals. In sum, the liberal psychology about our world portrays sovereignty as being all there is to international life. Sovereignty claims for itself a transcendent quality, as would an objective truth or an unexamined first principle.

The second premise of liberalism is the principle of subjective value. This radical epistemology emphasizes that moral truth and moral worth are subjective, because as an epistemological matter universal morality is unknowable. . . .

The two primary assumptions of liberalism inevitably lead to a few additional propositions. In particular, liberalism must claim that decisions about morality can only be made by . . . sovereigns. Subjectivity requires that, at the level of the sovereign, all moral choice is equally valid. . . . States must be equal in the moral sense, because no pre-existing objective morality can judge their conduct. . . .

Together, these fundamental assumptions of liberalism compel a particular vision of politics and law. As for politics, the atomistic existence of sovereigns and the principle of subjective value require liberals to believe that the only legitimate system of governance is one based on liberty and with liberty as its only substantive commitment. A world order based on liberty is said to free sovereigns to determine value in the market place of ideas. In fact, the pursuit of a world order (or lack thereof) that maximizes sovereign liberty is the only legitimate goal of international relations: a substantive notion of justice would introduce objective value and deny the primacy of sovereignty.

At a sufficiently elevated level of abstraction, liberal political theory seems logical. But as one makes concrete the meaning of liberty, liberalism risks incoherence. In concrete terms, liberty must include not only the freedom of sovereigns to act, individually or collectively based on consent, but also the freedom of other sovereigns to act in a manner entirely at odds with the first sovereign or sovereigns. . . .

Liberalism leaves the challenge of defining spheres of sovereign liberty to international law, with liberal legality being based on the rule of law. In international relations the rule of law is a set of prescriptive rules governing sovereign conduct. Its principal commitment is formal equality, meaning equal treatment with respect to rules. . . . International legal principles are said to enforce those rights neutrally and objectively. International law's claimed objectivity comes then from a purported ability to apply abstract principles to concrete problems, creating legal solutions that reflect only the legitimate normative bias of international law. . . . [T]he neutrality of legal solutions relates to the purported detachment of the process from some substantive outcome other than the preservation of sovereign liberty.

. . . Herein lies the contradiction that has been the object of the critical attack on the internal logic of liberalism: liberalism cannot deny the existence of objective value and at the same time claim to resolve international conflicts through an appeal to rules of objective neutrality. . . .

[A] common method of giving liberty meaning involves following rules built on distinctions between domestic jurisdiction and international concerns. Liberalism describes the world in dichotomies between sovereignty and world order, the domestic and the international, the private and the public. The priority of competing rights switches as one passes from one realm of the distinction to another. Yet what is it about international life that makes these distinctions natural, objective, or intelligible? The answer is simply nothing. The principle of subjective value precludes the existence of natural and objective distinctions. . . . [N]either rules nor distinctions can resolve disputes between conflicting sources of liberty in international life. . . .

2. Liberalism in International Law and Justice

The CLS analysis of international law has relied on a critique of the internal logic of international law to suggest the inadequacy of liberalism's explanation of international life. In a culture dominated by liberalism, rational argument cannot lead to moral consensus about what constitutes a just order. The principle of subjective value precludes the possibility of an objective truth from which a theory of justice can be derived. Moral consensus, to the degree it exists, is only the sum of moral decisions made by sovereigns. Given moral disagreement between them, logic cannot reconcile their positions.

International society cannot come to have a theory of justice by creating a democratic or pluralist theory of justice from the competing theories because we possess no rational way of weighing the claims of one against another. . . . Any system of deciding or acting must rest on a political theory, like majority rule, which by itself embodies a substantive commitment of the type subjective value precludes. Any program for action must accept some first principle as essential to the correct method of proceeding. The validity of that principle conflicts with liberalism's fundamental belief in the lack of intelligible essences. Liberalism itself makes no room for a theory of material justice in the world because it imagines the pursuit of liberty as the only legitimate substantive objective. And yet, as we have seen, liberty itself cannot stand as the liberal theory of justice because the commitment to liberty itself conflicts with the principle of subjective value.

The impossibility of sustaining a compelling vision of world justice consistent with liberalism has led New Stream scholars to characterize liberalism as an inadequate explanatory theory of international social life. . . .

B. The Structure of International Law

In their second critique of liberalism, CLS scholars contend that traditional international legal reasoning operates within a restricted intellectual structure. This structure makes international law narrowminded. International law accepts only some goals and values. Some arguments qualify as international legal arguments but others do not, and international law rules out some conceptions of international life altogether. The implications New Stream scholars have derived from the exposure of international law's structure have been threefold. They have maintained that: (1) the presence of structure reveals the existence of political choice within international law, (2) the existence of structure demonstrates the bias of international law, while simultaneously denying its claims of objectivity and neutrality, and (3) international law's denial or ignorance of its own structure serves to obscure the existence of that structure, which seems intolerable in light of the first two points. Critical scholars . . . maintain that legal reasoning in international law is constrained by the ideological underpinnings and patterns of legal argument inherent in liberalism. . . .

C. The Indeterminacy of International Legalism

1. Determinacy Under the Rule of Law

The third claim of critical jurisprudence in international law is that traditional international legal discourse is indeterminate. . . .

Liberalism conceives of the rule of law as a process that relates neutral principles to concrete occurrences. . . . [A]s a general matter most traditional academics would agree that liberal legality requires legal decisionmakers to resolve concrete issues by applying the theory of the law that they have before them. . . . When the correct theory is applied to the facts, the theory should determine a particular substantive outcome.

To be determinate, therefore, the rule of law must be capable of two processes. Because it needs to construct some grander abstraction or higher-level theory before it can resolve a case, liberal legality must allow for determinate theorizing. Because it must apply abstractions to concrete factual materials in such a way as to produce legal outcomes, liberal legality must achieve determinate application. . . .

2.   The Indeterminacy of Theorizing: Fundamental Contradictions

New Stream scholars have denied the possibility of determinate theorizing. Their basic claim is that the abstractions of liberalism are contradictory. As one moves to higher levels of abstraction in search of a controlling principle, liberalism constantly offers inconsistent theories about the nature of international law. . . .

. . . Perhaps some higher-level abstraction or lower-level application could reconcile these dilemmas. . . . To answer this challenge, New Stream scholars have argued that international legal doctrines have inherited liberalism's contradictions. . . . Given the presence of competing theories at all levels of abstraction, the selection of one theory over the others involves political choice. Legal reasoning as it relates to theorizing is correctly described as the process of choosing between theories, rather than a process of logical determinacy.

3.   The Indeterminacy of Application: The Reversibility of International Legal Argument

The indeterminacy of public international law is also illustrated by the drive for the concrete application of doctrines. Understood in this manner, the indeterminacy thesis reveals itself as a radical claim about the reversibility of international legal argument. By reversibility, New Stream scholars mean that any international legal doctrine can justify multiple and competing outcomes in any legal debate. . . .

For the rule of law to determine the result of a dispute, legal doctrines must justify one outcome above others. But when legal analysts try to descend from a conceptual abstraction, they find that for each pro argument there is a con argument about why one result is desirable instead of another. Each result is equally valid as a logical matter. So, it becomes impossible to deduce implications from concepts and consequently, abstractions cannot "compel" any decision. . . .

D. International Law's Self-Validation . . .

CLS's analysis of international law has concluded that international law is ethically incoherent, intellectually constrained, and logically indeterminate. Nevertheless, quite importantly, international law seems to have some experiential authority. Its authority operates on two levels. On the most basic level, sovereigns seem to take for granted the propriety of engaging in international legal discourse (instead of some other type of discourse) when they seek to resolve international issues. Moreover, international law operates as though it makes a difference. Sovereigns seem to debate international legal principles as though they were determinate and coherent. On occasion, states seem to act as if they actually were "complying" with international law. Sovereign acceptance of the rule of law as the appropriate mechanism for structuring intentional state life represents the second source of international law's authority. . . .

E. Summary of CLS Analysis . . .

A common theme emerges from these insights. Both focus on the normative and political choices in international legal reasoning. The selection of values, ideologies, arguments, and applications provide points of political choice from which no neutral and objective decision can emerge. These political decisions permeate the legal texts of international organization—its ideology, rules, and doctrine. Under the assumptions of liberalism, international law must collapse into political choice, for no neutral system can exist in a sovereign-centric world of subjective value.

NOTES AND QUESTIONS

1.   Human rights theorists often attempt now to address liberty-equality tensions and create a system of rights. Their theories borrow concepts from earlier theories to achieve synthesis. For further reading, see:

ANTONIO CASSESSE, HUMAN RIGHTS IN A CHANGING WORLD (1990);

RONALD M. DWORKIN, TAKING RIGHTS SERIOUSLY (1977);

Tom J. Farer, *Human Rights in Law's Empire: The Jurisprudence War*, 85 AM. J. INT'L L. 117 (1991);

Michael Freeman, *The Philosophical Foundations of Human Rights*, 16 HUM. RTS. Q. 491 (1994);

LOUIS HENKIN, THE AGE OF RIGHTS (1990);

KEVIN T. JACKSON, CHARTING GLOBAL RESPONSIBILITIES: LEGAL PHILOSOPHY AND HUMAN RIGHTS (1994);

David Kennedy, *A New Stream of International Law Scholarship*, 7 WIS. INT'L L.J. 1, 28-39 (1988);

Winston P. Nagan, *African Human Rights Process: A Contextual Policy-Oriented Approach*, 21 Sw. U. L. Rev. 63 (1992);

Robert Nozick, Anarchy, State, and Utopia (1974);

John Rawls, *The Law of Peoples, in* On Human Rights: The Oxford Amnesty Lectures 1993 41 (Stephen Shute & Susan Hurley eds., 1993);

John Rawls, A Theory of Justice (1971);

Morton Winston, The Philosophy of Human Rights (1989).

For a brief overview of both traditional and modern theories, see Jerome J. Shestack, *The Jurisprudence of Human Rights, in* Human Rights in International Law: Legal and Policy Issues 70 (Theodor Meron ed., 1984).

2.   Some theorists assert a "natural rights" formulation of human rights, and point to several Universal Declaration provisions as reflecting their approach. The preamble uses phrases such as "inherent dignity" and "equal and inalienable rights", and Article 1 asserts that "[a]ll human beings are born free and equal in dignity and rights." *See* Johannes Morsink, *The Philosophy of the Universal Declaration*, 6 Hum. Rts. Q. 309 (1984).

3.   One noted theorist—Hans Kelsen—developed a theory of law based on a hierarchy of legal norms. According to his view, legal systems are founded on one basic norm from which further norms are created and validated. *See* Albert A. Ehrenzweig, Law: A Personal View 27- 67 (1977); Hans Kelsen, General Theory of Law and State 3-161 (Anders Wedberg trans. 1945).

4.   H.L.A. Hart, a leading jurisprudential theorist in the area of positivism, developed a theory based on primary and secondary rules. Primary rules are those that create obligations. Secondary rules govern recognition of primary rules and create power to modify, adjudge, create, or destroy primary rules. *See* Herbert L.A. Hart, The Concept of Law (1981).

5.   The Critical Legal Studies ("CLS") movement came into existence at the first conference on Critical Legal Studies in 1977. As with any new movement, its jurisprudence has yet to be codified, and there is no unified CLS theory of rights. The thrust of CLS rights-analysis seems to be criticizing the legitimacy of labeling as rights what are in fact concepts. One underlying tenet is that rights are bestowed by ruling powers to disguise and legitimate their control without providing entitlements. *See* Michael Freeman, *Racism, Rights and the Quest for Equality of Opportunity: A Critical Legal Essay*, 23 Harv. C.R.-C.L. L. Rev. 295 (1988); *cf.* Katherine Van Wenzel Stone, *The Post-War Paradigm in American Labor Law*, 90 Yale L.J. 1509 (1981) (critiquing the ideology which underlies the current structure of collective bargaining).

   Freeman mentions two critiques focused by CLS scholars on the concept of rights—the indeterminacy critique and the contradiction critique. Freeman, *supra*, at 316. Another CLS critique is that calling a concept a right divorces it from human experience and "reifies" it into an abstract concept. One scholar has argued, building on reification and indeterminacy critiques, that a system of rights leads to individual alienation by substituting the passive possibility of possessing rights for active exercise of those rights, in concert with others, for a common good. Peter Gabel, *The Phenomenology of Rights-Consciousness and the Pact of the Withdrawn Selves*, 62 Tex. L. Rev. 1563 (1984).

6.   For further reading on the CLS rights critique, see:

Adeno Addis, *Critical Legal Studies and the Issue of Constructive Alternatives*, 34 Loy. L. Rev. 277 (1988);

Andrew Altman, Critical Legal Studies: A Liberal Critique (1990);

Leslie Espinoza, *Masks and Other Disguises: Exposing Legal Academia*, 103 Harv. L. Rev. 1878 (1990);

Ed Sparer, *Fundamental Human Rights, Legal Entitlements, and the Social Struggle: A Friendly Critique of the Critical Legal Studies Movement*, 36 STAN. L. REV. 509 (1984);

David M. Trubek, *Where the Action Is: Critical Legal Studies and Empiricism*, 36 STAN. L. REV. 575 (1984);

Mark Tushnet, *An Essay on Rights*, 62 TEX. L. REV. 1363 (1984);

PATRICIA WILLIAMS, THE ALCHEMY OF RACE AND RIGHTS (1991).

7.   Consider whether an example of what Hilary Charlesworth et al. describe as "the masculine world of international law" is found in the contrast among measures that human rights instruments require or permit governments to take in order to eliminate different types of discrimination. Professor Stephanie Farrior, in *Molding the Matrix: The Theoretical and Historical Foundations of International Law Concerning Hate Speech* (1995) (draft on file with editors), points out that although several treaties suggest that prohibition of hate speech can be an effective mechanism to prevent racial discrimination no corresponding clause appears in provisions designed to end gender discrimination:

> The Civil and Political Rights Covenant and the American Convention on Human Rights require governments to prohibit certain advocacy of national, racial or religious hatred or discrimination; the International Convention on the Elimination of All Forms of Racial Discrimination contains a similar provision with reference to discrimination on the basis of race, colour or ethnic origin. Civil and [Political] Rights Covenant, Article 20(2); American Convention, Article 13(5); Convention on Racial Discrimination, Article 4.
>
> Gender is not mentioned in the hate speech provisions of any of these instruments, even though equality of the sexes appears as a fundamental principle in the Charter of the United Nations, and non-discrimination on the basis of sex is a requirement in the International Bill of Human Rights. During the drafting of Article 20(2) of the Civil and Political Rights Covenant, the Philippines proposed an amendment adding several categories, including "sex," to the prohibited bases for advocating hatred and discrimination, but the proposal was not adopted. U.N. Doc. E/CN.4/365 (1950).
>
> Among the central provisions of the Convention on the Elimination of All Forms of Racial Discrimination is the requirement in Article 4 that governments prohibit speech that incites racial discrimination. In striking contrast, the Convention on the Elimination of All Forms of Discrimination Against Women contains no similar provision regarding statements that incite discrimination against women. A strong argument exists, however, that the limitations clauses of the Civil and Political Rights Covenant, American Convention and European Convention allow governments to prohibit certain statements which denigrate women, just as a limitations clause in the European Commission on Human Rights in interpreting a limitations clause in the European Convention, Article 17, has been interpreted by the European Commission on Human Rights to allow governments to prohibit statements that denigrate racial and ethnic groups. *See, e.g., Glimmerveen and Hagenbeek v. Netherlands*, [1980] 23 Y.B. Eur. Conv. on H.R. 366.

8.   For more on feminist jurisprudence, see:

BEVERLY BALOS & MARY LOUISE FELLOWS, LAW AND VIOLENCE AGAINST WOMEN (1994);

Gayle Binion, *Human Rights: A Feminist Perspective*, 17 HUM. RTS. Q. 509 (1995);

Ustinia Dolgopol, *Women's Voices, Women's Pain*, 17 HUM. Rts. Q. 127 (1995);

Feminist Jurisprudence Symposium, 24 GA. L. REV. 759 (1990);

Angela Harris, *Race and Essentialism in Feminist Legal Theory*, 32 STAN. L. REV. 581 (1990);

JOAN HOFF, LAW, GENDER, AND INJUSTICE: A LEGAL HISTORY OF U.S. WOMEN (1990);

Pamela Karlan & Daniel Ortiz, *In a Diffident Voice: Relational Feminism, Abortion Rights, and the Feminist Legal Agenda*, 87 Nw. U. L. Rev. 858 (1993);

Nancy Kim, *Toward a Feminist Theory of Human Rights: Straddling the Fence Between Western Imperialism and Uncritical Absolutism*, 25 Colum. Hum. Rts. L. Rev. 49 (1993);

Judith Resnik, *On the Bias: Feminist Reconsiderations of the Aspirations for Our Judges*, 61 S. Cal. L. Rev. 1877 (1988);

Barbara Stark, *Nurturing Rights: An Essay on Women, Peace, and International Human Rights*, 13 Mich. J. Int'l L. 144 (1991).

Anthony D'Amato, *Is International Law Really "Law"?*, 79 Nw. U. L. Rev. 1293, 1293-95, 1299, 1303-04, 1308-13 (1985)[5]:

Many serious students of the law react with a sort of indulgence when they encounter the term "international law," as if to say, "well, we know it isn't *really* law, but we know that international lawyers and scholars have a vested professional interest in calling it 'law.'" Or they may agree to talk about international law as *if* it were law, a sort of quasi-law or near-law. But it cannot be true law, they maintain, because it cannot be enforced: How do you enforce a rule of law against an entire nation, especially a superpower such as the United States or the Soviet Union? . . .

One intriguing answer to these serious students of the law is to attempt to persuade them that enforcement is not, after all, the hallmark of what is meant, or what should be meant, by the term "law." As Roger Fisher observed, much of what we call "law" in the domestic context is also unenforceable. For example, where the defendant is the United States, such as in a case involving constitutional law, how would the winning private party enforce his or her judgment against the United States? Upon reflection, we see that the United States, whenever it loses a case . . . only complies with the court's judgment because it wants to. . . . In terms of power, there is nothing to stop the United States from disregarding adverse judgments of its own courts. In this sense, therefore, a great deal of what we normally call "law" in the United States is unenforceable by private parties arrayed against the state. . . .

Let us then consider a second line of reasoning against the proposition that enforcement is the hallmark of law. This argument is not associated with any particular writer, because it relies on early conceptions of law and also on the philosophy of law itself. If we consider what law is not, we soon realize that it is not a rationale for the application of force. It is not a system of "might makes right" in the sense that the state constantly has to compel people, at gunpoint, to behave in a certain way. . . . Most of "law" concerns itself with the interpretation and enforcement of private contracts, the redress of intentional and negligent harms, rules regarding sales of goods and sales of securities, rules relating to the family and the rights of members thereof, and other such rules, norms, and cases. The rules are obeyed not out of fear of the state's power, but because the rules by and large are perceived to be right, just, or appropriate. . . .

Yet the serious student of law may not be satisfied with the preceding argument

---

[5] The article, by Professor D'Amato, from which the above material was excerpted also appears in Anthony D'Amato, International Law: Process and Prospect (2d ed. 1995).

in its entirety. We want to ask what happens if the need for physical coercion should arise. In the international system, at least, we have states which occasionally break the rules of international law and which seem not to be deterred by expressions of social disapproval from the other states. This is a reality of international life. . . .

I believe that a conclusive argument can be fashioned that international law is really law, by showing that international law is enforceable in the same way that domestic law is enforceable. . . .

[National law] typically provides for deprivations, for disabilities. When a person disobeys the law, the law "punishes" him in some way. The possibility of punishment, in turn is supposed to deter a rational person from violating the law in the first place. . . .

. . . As a construct of international law, a nation is nothing more nor less than a bundle of entitlements, of which the most important ones define and secure its boundaries on a map, while others define its jurisdictional competency and the rights of its citizens when they travel outside its borders. . . .

[A]s a matter of its very identity, a state should act in such a manner as to preserve its entitlements. Yet, its identity as a state, its "bundle of entitlements," is dependent upon the acquiescence of all the other states in the system. Since every state has the same bundle of entitlements—otherwise there would be legal inequality among states, a proposition that has never seriously been advanced—the other states in the system have an obvious interest in acquiescing in the entitlements of any given state. In this manner, a new state starts out . . . with its full complement of entitlements.

But just as all the states in the international legal system have a collective interest in acquiescing to all the entitlements for any given state in the system, they also have an interest in preserving the entitlements per se. For ease of illustration, let us consider the . . . entitlement of diplomatic immunity. . . .

To preserve this entitlement, the states in the system collectively will allow certain actions to be taken against any given state which violates the entitlement of diplomatic immunity. Prior to 1979, it would have been difficult to come up with a single example of a state which directly violated that entitlement. . . . But in 1979, after some radical students occupied the American Embassy in Teheran, the government of Iran took the unprecedented step of ratifying the action and holding the American diplomatic personnel hostage. This was a case of a deliberate violation of international law, the violation of the entitlement of diplomatic immunity. To allow it to go unremedied would constitute a threat to the existence of that entitlement in the international legal system.

What legal recourse did states have to prevent the erosion of such an entitlement? An obvious move would be to allow the United States to violate Iran's similar entitlement by arresting diplomatic and consular officials of Iran who were physically present in the United States at the time of the takeover of the American embassy in Iran. While this tit-for-tat strategy is generally regarded as legal under international law, . . . it nevertheless could operate to erode rather than to preserve the entitlement in question. For instance, if the United States had jailed all Iranian diplomatic and consular officials, such an action at least in theory could be interpreted not as an attempt to punish Iran for its initial act but rather as a recognition that Iran's act was correct and that in fact diplomats are not entitled to immunity. . . .

The United States, in fact, did not retaliate by jailing Iranian consular and diplomatic officials. . . . Instead, the United States took steps that were also justified under international law and which constitute a more sophisticated . . . method of enforcement. The United States "froze" approximately thirteen billion dollars of Iranian deposits in American banks and in various European banks where the United States, through American corporations, had the power to act. If it were not for the initial Iranian act of holding the American diplomats hostage, the United States would be unjustified under international law in violating the Iranian entitlement to the use of its own bank deposits abroad. Indeed by freezing the Iranian assets, the United States was effectively confiscating the interest those assets would have earned. This was a direct deprivation of Iranian property by the United States. Yet there was no condemnation of the American action by the international community; instead, the American action in violating a different Iranian entitlement from the one that Iran violated in the first place (diplomatic immunity) was tolerated by general silence, whereas governments from all over the world expressly condemned Iran's seizure of the American embassy. The workings of international law are rarely as explicit as scholars might like them to be, but I believe we are entitled to infer from the reaction of the community of nations that they did not perceive a threat to the shared entitlement of keeping state-owned deposits in foreign banks as a result of the American action, but rather regarded the U.S. action as a temporary infringement of an Iranian entitlement for the limited purpose of enforcing the original entitlement of diplomatic immunity. . . .

Of course, I am not attempting here to support my theory of a reciprocal-violation-of-a-different-entitlement by the single case of the American hostages in Teheran. The pattern is a general one and can be substantiated by numerous examples. Moreover, the tit-for-a-different-tat pattern "makes sense" in a legal system that does not have a central court of compulsory jurisdiction, a world legislature, and a world police force. The absence of these institutions does not mean that international law isn't really law; rather, it simply means that international law is enforced in a different way.

There is a danger in relying on the enforcement of international law by allowing a retaliatory deprivation of the offending nation's entitlement. The danger is the potential escalation of entitlement violations, ultimately leading to international anarchy. . . . But the fact that law can become ineffective doesn't mean that it isn't law in the first place. . . . [W]hile international law could destroy itself through a runaway series of violations of entitlements, until then it polices itself by the meta-rule I have described: that it is legal to deter the violation of an entitlement by threatening a counter-violation of the same or a different entitlement. This latter enforcement action is the "physical sanction" provided by the international legal system, just as the rules regulating police, prison officials, sheriffs, etc., are its domestic legal equivalents.

NOTES AND QUESTIONS

1.   Commentator J. Shand Watson has a different view on the binding nature of international human rights norms. He argues that under the current system international is not superior to national law. Rather, states create norms through interaction with each other and must *consent* to either treaties or customary law before being bound. States will not, the argument continues, consent to be bound by norms with which they do not agree. Moreover, the principal enforcement mechanisms of international law constitute (1) sanctions by other states, or (2) compliance—in order to receive the benefit of reciprocal compliance. Neither enforcement mechanism works well in the context of human rights law, argues Watson; states will be unwilling to sanction other states for violations because future situations may arise in which they will want to invoke their sovereignty against criticism of behavior that arguably violates

their citizens' rights. In addition, states receive no reciprocal benefit from protecting their citizens' rights under human rights law. Hence, he concludes that international norms are valuable only as goals towards which states may strive, not as binding law. *See* J. Shand Watson, *Normativity and Reality in International Human Rights Law*, 13 STETSON L. REV. 221 (1984).

2.   For further discussion of the binding character of international law, addressing and challenging the validity of arguments made by skeptics such as Watson, see Oscar Schachter, *International Law in Theory and Practice: General Course in Public International Law*, 178 COLLECTED COURSES OF THE HAGUE ACAD. OF INT'L LAW 1, 21-39 (1982).

CHAPTER 15

WHAT SEEM TO BE THE CAUSES OF HUMAN RIGHTS VIOLATIONS AND HOW MIGHT KNOWLEDGE AS TO CAUSATION BE USED?

		Page	
A.	Introduction		700
B.	Questions		701
C.	Political and Economic Factors		705
	1. Political and Economic Theories and Research		705
	Neil Mitchell & James McCormick, Economic and Political Explanations of Human Rights Violations		705
	Reinhard Heinisch, Political Explanations of Basic Human Rights Performance		712
	Steven Poe & C. Neal Tate, Repression of Human Rights to Personal Integrity in the 1980s: A Global Analysis		715
	2. Military Expansion and Conflict		721
D.	Sociological Aspects of Power		723
	James Scott, The Value and Cost of the Public Transcript		723
E.	Psychological Factors		729
	Robert Jay Lifton, Socialization to Killing		732
F.	Sociocultural Factors		738
	1. Group Identity and Scapegoating		738
	Philip Mayer, Witches		739
	Robert Jay Lifton, Genocide		742
	2. Change, Uncertainty, and Political Manipulation		743
	J.R. Crawford, The Consequences of Allegation		743
	H.R. Trevor-Roper, The European Witch-Craze		743
	Joyce Bednarski, The Salem Witch-Scare Viewed Sociologically		745
	A. Rebecca Cardozo, A Modern American Witch-Craze		747
G.	Additional Readings		749
	1. General research on human rights violations		749
	2. Economic & Political Factors		749
	a. Economic Development		749
	b. Political Theories		750
	c. Military Expansion & Conflict		750
	d. U.S. Foreign Policy		751

3. **Sociocultural & Psychological Factors**   752
    a. Ingrouping & Outgrouping   752
    b. Obedience & Group Conformity   752
    c. Sociological Aspects of Political Power   752
    d. Socialization to Violence & War   752
    e. Torture—Effects on Victims   752

4. **Violations of Human Rights in Latin America**   753

A. INTRODUCTION

Earlier chapters have dealt with various techniques for dealing with human rights violations. Most of the techniques were developed with very little attention to the underlying causes of violations. Indeed, only in the past decade have there been concerted efforts to explore the causes of international violations and explain why they occur. Consequently, the strategies employed to address violations have not had the benefit of a body of research that might shed light on sources of the problems. Yet one may ask whether increased understanding of causes would contribute to efforts to prevent or stop violations. How might such knowledge be used, and with what aims?

One can hardly pin the occurrence of violations down to a single cause or set of causes. Factors which may relate to poor human rights compliance in some countries may seem to have no consequence in others. Are there really "causes" or merely innumerable contributing factors? Social scientist James Scott faced a similar problem in his study of "resistance" in settings of political and social domination. He observed that, even after all factors that might shed light on the matter had been considered, it remained impossible to predict with any precision when or how collective acts of resistance will occur. He concluded nonetheless that there is "a role for social analysis in understanding this phenomenon. A public health physician may not be able to predict whether a particular individual will fall ill, but he or she may be able to say something useful about the conditions that may promote an epidemic.[1] In thinking about the materials in this chapter, readers might consider whether the same diagnostic analogy might apply to the phenomenon of rights violations. Is it possible to draw some conclusions about the factors and conditions that may provide fertile ground for an outbreak?

As will become apparent, much work remains to be done in developing more thorough understandings of rights violations. To date only a few theories have been proposed and subjected to empirical research, most of which examine political or economic factors. The first section in this chapter presents an overview of some studies and their findings. The remaining sections present materials from other fields of study which, while they do not directly address human rights as such, offer readers an opportunity to consider further paths to the exploration and understanding of human rights violations.

---

[1] James C. Scott, *The Value and Cost of the Public Transcript, in* JAMES C. SCOTT, DOMINATION AND THE ARTS OF RESISTANCE: HIDDEN TRANSCRIPTS 219 (1990).

B. QUESTIONS

1. What causes violations? What theories have been proposed to explain differences in the human rights performance of nations? What theories attempt to explain changes in human rights conditions over time within a given country?

a. What is the reasoning behind each of the explanations? Which explanations seem most plausible?

b. Can any explanations be applied to all countries, or are there additional considerations which make broad or universal application impracticable?

c. Do any causes or explanations seem to work alone or do they rather seem to work in combination with others? Can a proposed explanation do more than describe violations after the fact?

d. To what extent are explanations of human rights violations shaped by the ideological biases or the researchers?

e. What theory best explains human rights violations?

2. Consider the above questions with regard to each of the following propositions:

a. Economic Explanations

1) The poorer the country, the greater the probability of human rights violations; the wealthier or more developed the country, the better its human rights conditions.

2) Modernization or rapid economic development contributes to higher levels of human rights violations.

3) Involvement with foreign capitalist interests contributes to worsening human rights conditions.

4) Trade and foreign investment will improve human rights.

5) Unequal distribution of wealth increases the risk of violations.

b. Population Explanations

1) The larger a population, the higher will be the level of human rights violations.

2) Rapid population growth contributes to worsening human rights conditions.

c. Political Explanations

1) Human rights conditions vary according to type of regime; democracies do a better job of respecting human rights than authoritarian or totalitarian states.

2) Countries that were colonized by Great Britain tend to have better human rights records; the longer a British presence in a country, the better its human rights conditions.

3) The longer a country has been independent, the better will be its human rights conditions.

4) Countries with greater political participation and economic competition

have better human rights conditions than countries with little or no participation or competition.

d.   Military Explanations

1)   Military engagement or threat of engagement increases human rights violations.

2)   Expansion of the military's role into political and civilian spheres contributes to worsening human rights conditions.

3)   Foreign involvement in or support of a country's military raises the likelihood of human rights violations in that country.

e.   Sociological Theories on Political Power

1)   Poor human rights conditions are related to government control over public expression.

2)   Governments which invoke scientific or other rationalizations to justify violations of human rights are more likely to commit them.

f.   Psychological Factors

1)   Human rights violations are made possible, in part, by a widespread human tendency toward group conformity and obedience to authority.

2)   Certain cultural values, child-rearing practices, and/or socialization techniques may strengthen the tendency toward unquestioned obedience to authority.

3)   A human propensity for rational thought enables individuals to perform actions which violate their sense of "rightness" when such actions are explained and justified within a rational ideology.

g.   Sociocultural Factors

1)   Human rights violations occur, in part, as a result of a human tendency to identify groups of persons who are different than, and inferior to, one's own group.

2)   Human rights violations are more likely to occur in times of turbulent social or cultural change, natural disaster, deteriorating economic conditions, or some other fear-generating hardship.

3)   Certain cultural views or socio-economic stratification may make some groups more vulnerable than others to human rights violations.

3.   Assuming that some of the above explanations are consistently supported by empirical research, how might they be put to practical use?

a.   Is it possible to design a checklist to predict the likelihood or verify reports of violations in a given country? What should be put on such a checklist? In what order of importance?

b.   Can any theory be used to predict or analyze human rights conditions in particular countries, or only to reflect broad tendencies?

c.   Once a pattern of violations has become a reality is it necessary, or even helpful, to know its causes in order to develop solutions? Could knowledge of causes be used to prevent or reduce the occurrence of violations?

d.   To what extent could a government's or NGO's adoption of particular economic or political theories jeopardize its efforts to promote and protect human rights?

    1)   Would the use of economic or political factors as a basis for deciding whether to investigate allegations in a given country undermine the government's willingness to cooperate?

    2)   How important is it to maintain impartiality in human rights work? For governments? For IGOs? For NGOs?

e.   What policy implications can be drawn from the material in this chapter?

4.   Does democracy generate better human rights conditions?

a.   Is there a difference between the effects of democracy on the security of its own citizens and citizens of non-democratic states?

b.   From a global perspective, does the development of democracy and a market economy diminish human rights violations, or merely displace them onto foreign soil?

c.   Do poorer, non-democratic regimes serve as "scapegoats" on which democratic/market economy states may place the responsibility for human rights violations and thus avoid confronting their own role in global patterns of abuse?

5.   What kinds of connections can be found between military readiness or engagement and human rights abuses?

a.   Is there anything inherent or inevitable in the way citizens are prepared for military service which predisposes them to acts of violence beyond that involved in actual combat, e.g., rape, brutality, torture? If so, how might those predispositions be held in check? If not, how might training and service be restructured to inspire the humanity of its military personnel?

b.   Are military governments, as a rule, more likely than civilian governments to violate their citizens' human rights?

6.   Are there specific government practices which seem to be associated with poor human rights conditions? What are they?

a.   Could such factors, either singly or in combination, serve as reliable indicators of the likelihood of violations? Can government actions alone be taken as symptomatic of poor human rights conditions?

b.   What other conditions, if known, would be useful in supporting allegations of human rights abuses?

7.   Are there particular social conditions, trends, or types of events which could serve as warning signs of deteriorating human rights conditions? How are they linked to civil, political, economic, or cultural factors?

a.   What lessons can be learned about early signs of serious human rights violations?

b.   Do racial, ethnic, cultural, or other kinds of diversity improve or worsen human rights conditions?

c.   In what ways may governments capitalize on existing social realities, *e.g.*, tendencies toward group conformity, faith in science or other authoritative discourse, or class/ethnic divisions, as means of carrying out human rights violations?

8.   What can psychology contribute to an understanding of human rights violations?

a.   Is the ability to harm others a universal human potential? Does this factor have any relevance in understanding human rights violations?

b.   How important are values such as conformity, obedience, or loyalty in causing individuals to participate in or comply with government violations?

c.   Is it necessary for large numbers of persons to acquiesce in order for a government to carry out large-scale violations? If so, how does such acquiescence occur? If not, how does a repressive government remain in power or persist in violations without its citizens' consent?

d.   How do voices of dissent or opposition influence the compliance of would-be participants in cruelty? The passivity of bystanders? A government's ability to implement repressive tactics?

e.   What analogies can be drawn between the role of bystanders and the role of human rights organizations or human rights movements in general?

f.   What implications for the development of human rights education and training can be drawn from the psychological factors underlying violations?

9.   What role does culture play in contributing to human rights conditions?

a.   Is it necessary for a country to have a history of racism, ethnocentrism, or some other form of prejudice in order for its government to commit violations against a particular group?

b.   Are there historical, social, or cultural factors which seem to make some groups more vulnerable than others to violations? What are they, and to what extent can they serve to predict or verify the occurrence of violations?

c.   Is the singling out of some groups as "different" or "inferior" a universal or merely a widespread human tendency?

1)   Are there common forces or factors which might explain the occurrence of violations aimed at particular groups in diverse cultural and historical settings?

2)   Are there social practices or political institutions which seem to prevent hostilities toward a vulnerable group from erupting into violations of their rights? Could such safety mechanisms be promoted or enforced without infringing on a country's style of government, economic structure, or cultural heritage?

10.   Is enough known about the causes of human rights violations to permit the development of more effective strategies?

a.   What explanations and theories are best supported by empirical research? What other research should be done? What other questions should be asked?

b.   Based on the readings, what other factors seem to be related to human rights violations but have not yet been researched? What questions would you ask? How might such questions be translated into research designs?

11.   What lessons can be learned from the materials in this chapter about the education that should be given to young people to make human rights violations less likely?

C.   POLITICAL AND ECONOMIC FACTORS

1.   Political and Economic Theories and Research

Neil J. Mitchell & James M. McCormick, *Economic and Political Explanations of Human Rights Violations*, WORLD POLITICS 476, 476-82, 484-85, 488-98 (July 1988) (citations omitted):

Governments organize police forces and armies to protect their citizens, build schools and hospitals to educate and care for them, and provide financial assistance for the old and unemployed. But governments also kill, torture, and imprison their citizens. This dark side of government knows no geographic, economic, ideological, or political boundary. . . . There is, however, a substantial variation between nations in the degree of these human rights violations. . . . [Nonetheless], relatively little empirical research has been done to account for these differences. [What research has been done has instead] tended to concentrate on the influence of a country's human rights record on U.S. foreign policy, primarily on decisions concerning American aid. . . . Beyond these analyses—and a considerable dialogue on what exactly constitutes human rights—little work has proceeded to the next important step: the characteristics of countries that are most likely to violate human rights. . . . [In the end], few efforts have been made to theorize on a global level about the kinds of governments that are likely to engage in human rights violations.

Where, then, do we look for some theoretical guidance? Our point of departure, some writing on democracy and political instability, does not always address human rights violations directly; it does, however, carry important implications for the relative propensity of states to violate the rights of their citizens. Moreover, it allows us to develop several plausible economic and political hypotheses about states and human rights violations that can be tested empirically.

ECONOMIC CONDITIONS AND HUMAN RIGHTS VIOLATIONS

Economic modernization, it is sometimes argued, leads to political stability and, in turn, to increased respect for human rights. The poorest countries, with substantial social and political tensions created by economic scarcity, would be most unstable and thus most apt to use repression in order to maintain control. Robert McNamara has succinctly summarized this view: "There can . . . be no question but that there is an irrefutable relationship between violence and economic backwardness." The implication of McNamara's analysis is that the poorer the country, the greater the probability of human rights violations as the government seeks to maintain some semblance of order. Empirically, then, a first proposition for testing would be a simple one: an inverse relationship would exist between the wealth of a society and its human rights violations.

Samuel Huntington, in his classic investigation of political stability . . . has sought to refute this "simple poverty thesis." Although human rights violations are not the focus of his work, he does suggest some likely correlates: he argues that it is not the poorest countries that will be the most unstable "because people who are really poor are too poor for politics and too poor for protest.". . . As social and economic change broadens, [however], political participation increases, and the demands on government are greater. According to Huntington, traditional sources of political authority are thus challenged, and new political institutions (particularly political parties) are necessary to moderate and channel the demands of the newly mobilized citizenry. If such institutions are not developed, instability and disorder will result. Such a situation is ripe for political repression. The inference from Huntington's analysis, unlike that from McNamara's, is that the "modernizing" states would be most susceptible to a high level of human rights violations. Put differently, a curvilinear relationship should exist between the relative wealth of a nation and human rights violations: the very poor and the very rich countries would be less likely to have substantial levels of human rights violations, while those who are in the process of modernization would be more likely to exhibit such a pattern.

A third economic explanation is largely Marxist in orientation and has less to do with poverty *per se* and more with the external economic relationships of a country. [Chomsky and Herman], for example, argue that "the balance of [human rights violations] appears to have shifted to the West and its clients, with the United States setting the pace as sponsor and supplier." This shift is systematically linked to the economic interests of the United States and other advanced capitalist countries, and to their efforts to maintain favorable conditions for investment in the third world. Such efforts include the containment of reform (*e.g.*, the formation of trade unions) and the prevention of revolution. Consequently, there is an increase in human rights violations by countries that are more involved with external capitalist interests. In other words, the greater the economic association with the United States or other advanced capitalist countries, the greater the degree of human rights violations.

POLITICAL CONDITIONS AND HUMAN RIGHTS VIOLATIONS

While poverty, levels of development, and dependence represent the principal economic conditions that may be associated with human rights violations, political culture and regime type seem to be the principal political conditions. The dominant attitudes and beliefs of a society are considered to be of great importance in the choice of methods of political control and the relative propensity of governments to violate human rights. . . .

One important factor that is thought to have shaped political culture for most states in the world is the colonial experience. Since most are relatively new (over 90 newly independent states have been created since 1945), the political culture derived from the colonial experience may be a useful starting point for understanding variations in respect for human rights. British colonial rule, for instance, is commonly thought to be strongly associated with the postcolonial development of democracy. . . . By contrast, other colonial experiences (Spanish, for instance) are generally assumed to have introduced a greater degree of hierarchy and authoritarianism. The legacy here may well involve higher levels of human rights violations.

The thesis based upon political culture may be affected by the length of colonial rule and, alternatively, by the "newness" of the state. For example, 18th-century British colonies such as India are thought to have a better record in terms of democracy than 19th-century British colonies such as those in Africa. Presumably, "democratic" culture—insofar as any colonizing culture can be democratic—is more or less influential depending on the time it has had to permeate the colonized society. It is also possible that politics in countries that achieved independence relatively recently, regardless of colonial rule, may be more unsettled than in those that have had a considerable time to unify their states. Because ethnic and religious divisions may be more important than the sense of belonging to one nation, human rights violations may be particularly pronounced in the newest states as they attempt to "build" a new nation.

Other political explanations of differences in human rights focus on the kind of political regime in power. . . . Kirkpatrick maintains that . . . left-wing, totalitarian regimes are the greatest offenders against human rights. These regimes render the individual virtually defenseless in relation to the state and offer little prospect of evolutionary or revolutionary change. Authoritarian regimes, though hardly innocent of human rights violations, are based upon traditional social patterns with less complete control; in time, they are thus subject to evolutionary change. Because governmental control in authoritarian regimes is less complete and more subject to change than in totalitarian regimes, human rights violations in the former are likely to be less extensive than in the latter. . . . To our knowledge, this regime explanation for human rights violations has not been systematically tested.

Howard and Donnelly cast a wider net than Kirkpatrick by grouping regimes into two general categories: liberal or communitarian. They maintain that only governments that operate within the liberal tradition are likely to observe their citizens' human rights. . . . Their contention is based on the premise that only "liberal" regimes have the requisite "substantive conception of human dignity" to make the observance of internationally recognized human rights possible. "Communitarian" societies, by contrast, in which the community or the state has priority over the individual, will not be receptive to the observance of human rights. Howard and Donnelly do not extend their argument to the identification of regimes that are to be considered liberal; our database, however, permits a rough comparison, suggested by their work, of presumed liberal states—that is, first-world nations—with the rest of the world.

DEFINING AND MEASURING HUMAN RIGHTS VIOLATIONS

Our analysis is based on the latest available human rights survey (at the time) by Amnesty International (*Amnesty International Report* 1985); we developed a two-dimensional scale of human rights violations for each of the countries included in the 1985 *Report*. . . . First, one of the authors surveyed the *Report* to identify the categories of human rights violations recorded in order to develop a coding format that is comparable across all nations. The coding categories ranged from the holding of "prisoners of conscience" (those imprisoned for their beliefs, color, religion, and so forth, and who are nonviolent) and other political prisoners detained without a trial conforming to internationally recognized standards, to disappearances, executions, and the torture of prisoners. . . . Each of the authors then read and coded all 123 countries listed in the *Report*. . . . The next task was to construct a summary measure for comparing countries. A two-dimensional measure of human rights violations was developed—one dimension based upon the degree of arbitrary imprisonment, the other based upon the systematic use of killings and torture of prisoners. The conceptual justification for this dichotomy was based upon the view that, although arbitrary imprisonment was certainly reprehensible, resort to torture and killing was a distinct, and qualitatively worse, activity. . . . Furthermore, we noted that . . . there is a considerable gulf between states with political prisoners and those that use torture and killing. . . . Finally, in order to provide greater sensitivity to these dimensions, a five-point ordinal scale was developed for each. A country could be scored as (0) never having such violations, (1) rarely, (2) sometimes, (3) often, or (4) very often. . . .

FINDINGS

. . . .

ECONOMIC CONDITIONS AS EXPLANATIONS

Economic conditions can help us understand and begin to account for variations in human rights violations, but their impact is less potent than might be expected. . . . For the political prisoner analysis, McNamara's "simple poverty thesis" seems to have more support than Huntington's curvilinear explanation. That is, the wealthier the country, the less likely it is to hold a large number of political prisoners.

Yet even this assertion should not be pushed too far, for at least two reasons. First, the relationship is modest at best. . . . Second, [the results suggest] that only in countries that never or rarely hold political prisoners do we approach a linear relationship with the level of economic development. . . . When we look at countries that hold political prisoners sometimes or often, the pattern changes. The differences on the political prisoner dimension between the countries in the two lowest income categories are small, but the difference between these two categories and the highest income category is substantial. In effect, there is a threshold effect in the relationship between relative wealth and the holding of political prisoners.

On the torture dimension, the simple poverty thesis receives some support as well. Once again, those countries that have a relatively low per capita income are more likely to have higher levels of torture. But caution is in order to an even greater degree. . . . While the . . . relationship is somewhat stronger . . . than for the political prisoner analysis, the tabular results plainly show the threshold effect. Only 3 of the high-income countries . . . have torture records in the "often" or "very often" categories, while 25 have torture records that place them in the "rarely" or "sometimes" rankings. The low- and middle-income countries in our data set do not have that great a gap between those with relatively good records . . . and those with bad records. . . . Thus, in this case too, only countries with very high incomes do well on this dimension of human rights.

Our third economic hypothesis—capitalist involvement—is more difficult to test; it requires some discussion of how best to measure economic involvement with the United States and capitalist countries generally. As the hypothesis is essentially directed at third-world nations, first- and second-world countries were excluded from our analysis. We decided to operationalize capitalist involvement in two ways: first, by measuring the amount of trade between capitalist and third-world countries; and second, by measuring the total investment tie between capitalist and other countries. . . . Our hypothesis is that the greater the economic involvement with the capitalist countries, the greater the human rights violations, rather than the greater the relative weight of capitalist economic involvement in the domestic economy, the greater the human rights violations. . . .

Countries in the high trade category are, as expected, more likely to be in the "often" and "very often" imprisonment categories. . . . [The data reveals] a total of 65 percent in these categories, as compared to 38 percent in low trade countries. . . . Using the direct measure of investment, the high investment category again has the largest

share of countries that imprison citizens often or very often. . . . Investment is significantly associated with imprisonment. . . . When we control for size of population,
however, any significant associations between trade and imprisonment and investment
and imprisonment disappear.

Those countries that use torture often or very often tend to fall in the medium
and high trade categories; the low trade category has the largest share of countries
that make infrequent or no use of torture. . . . The medium and high investment
categories also contain most of the countries that use torture often or very often. . . . But
. . . the relationship between investment and torture is not significant, and the trade/
torture association disappears when population is held constant. So, while a substantial
number of countries that have very bad human rights records are economically heavily
involved with advanced capitalist countries, a third factor—population—appears to
account for some of the observed association.

POLITICAL CONDITIONS AS EXPLANATIONS

. . . .

The classic assertion that British colonial experience is associated with the
development of democracy and, by extension, with greater respect for human rights,
finds some support in our data. [C]ountries that were British colonies are less likely
to imprison political dissidents than countries that had other colonial experiences.
. . . About 58 percent of the countries that were British colonies are classified as
"rarely" or "sometimes" holding political prisoners. By contrast, 55 percent of the
countries with other colonial experiences fall into the "often" or "very often" categories. . . . When we control for both population and income, however, . . . the association
between former British colonies and lower levels of imprisonment is no longer statistically significant. A closer examination of the data suggests that the original relationship between these two variables was largely attributable to some small former
British colonies with medium (and, to some extent, high) per capita incomes and
good human rights records, as compared to similar states with other colonial experiences and poor human rights records. Put differently, and generally consistent with
our earlier results, low- and high-income countries—with or without British colonial
experience—do not have significantly different human rights records. Some caution
is still warranted in interpreting these results, however, because of the limited cases
in our data cells when these controls are built in.

Colonial background is even less important in differentiating nations on the
torture scale, although the results are in the predicted direction. While most countries with any colonial experience are classified as torturing "rarely" or "sometimes,"
those with a British colonial background are less likely to be in the "often" or "very
often" category than those with a non-British colonial background. The statistical
analysis indicates that the propensity to torture or kill is not significantly associated
with a British colonial experience. [When we control for population and income, we
find that], again, any relationship that does exist [seems to be] based on medium-
income former British colonies that have considerably better records on the torture
dimensions than do medium-income countries with other colonial experiences.

Taking our colonial analysis one step further, we found few differences in human
rights performance, both on our political prisoner scale and on our torture scale,
between the 21 countries in our dataset that had been British colonies for less than
a hundred years and the 19 countries that had been British colonies for more than

a hundred years. Thus, the sheer fact of British colonization seems to have somewhat more impact on human rights performance than length of colonization.

A second way to examine political conditions and human rights violations is to look at the relationship between the length of a state's independence and the treatment of its citizens. Are older nations more respectful of human rights than newer ones? To answer this question, we divided the states in our dataset into two categories: those that had gained independence before 1944, and those that had gained independence after that year. On our two dimensions of human rights violations, we found virtually no difference between these two classifications. The newness of the state appears to be unrelated to the observance of human rights.

[Turning to regime type theory advanced by Kirkpatrick], [i]n one sense [her] argument is confirmed by our data. All second-world nations fall into the "often" or "very often" political prisoner categories. . . . The strong and statistically significant relationship . . . between imprisonment and the second world survives our controlling for population differences and levels of income. On the torture dimension, however, we found no significant difference between the two types of regimes. Contrary to Kirkpatrick's argument, more authoritarian regimes (52 percent) than totalitarian regimes (40 percent) are in the "often" or "very often" category on the torture dimension. . . . For second-world governments, imprisonment is the preferred method of political control. Thus, only if "repression" is restricted to imprisonment is there evidence that confirms Kirkpatrick's thesis. If repression is defined as torture and killing, then the results, though not statistically significant, are contrary to her expectation. . . . And if repression is defined as both imprisonment *and* torturing and killing, our aggregate human rights measure, there is no statistically significant difference between the two types of regimes.

A reformulated and weaker version of Howard and Donnelly's argument—that liberal regimes are more attentive to human rights than are communitarian regimes—is borne out by our analysis. [W]e operationalized their thesis by comparing the degree of violations in first-world nations (advanced capitalist democracies) with that of the rest of the world. . . . In the course of our analysis, we found, not unexpectedly, that the "liberal" regimes have a superior human rights record on both the political prisoner and the torture dimensions. Almost all of the liberal states fall into either the "rarely" or "sometimes" categories on both dimensions; the lowest-scale category ("rarely") is the most prominent one. By contrast, the rest of the nations are spread across the scale, with over half in the "often" and "very often" ranks on the political prisoner dimension, and just under half in the same categories for the torture dimension.

CONCLUSION

. . . .

Although we tested several plausible explanations that might account for variations in human rights violations throughout the world, our results indicate that none of them is complete. Support for various hypotheses was generally weak-to-modest and not always consistent, especially when various controls for the size of a nation's population and its level of income were introduced into the analysis. In that sense, this study has begun to specify, and possibly to eliminate, several explanations for differences in human rights compliance around the world, but it has not found a wholly satisfactory one. Further work will need to be undertaken to complete the picture that we have begun to outline.

Nonetheless, the major themes of our results are worth emphasizing. We generally found that the economic hypotheses were better supported than the political ones. For instance, countries that enjoyed higher levels of economic well-being had somewhat consistently—albeit modestly so—better human rights records than those that did not. Extensive ties with capitalist states did not in themselves detract from or contribute to the level of human rights violations in the nations of our data set; the actual level of development—as measured by domestic income levels—seems to be a more important factor. . . . For the political explanations, the results are more mixed. While former British colonies are somewhat less likely to imprison their citizens than are countries with other colonial backgrounds, both were about equally likely to torture their citizens. The relative "newness" of a state turned out to be unrelated to both dimensions of human rights violations, and support was mixed for Kirkpatrick's thesis on authoritarian and totalitarian regimes. A weak version of Howard and Donnelly's thesis on liberal and communitarian regimes was generally borne out by our data, but their stronger version was not.

Where do we go from here? First, we need to introduce other political and social conditions within these nations that may help us sort out the relationships. Two factors immediately come to mind: the amount of warfare (both internal and foreign), and the magnitude of ethnic divisions within a state. Both of these factors can be expected to influence human rights violations; they should be incorporated into future analyses. Second, where possible, we need to move to greater precision in our data, and to more multivariate analyses of various alternate explanations. Our examination thus far has relied primarily on, at best, ordinal-level data with only a few limited controls. More sophisticated analyses are necessary, even though we are constrained by the limitations of our data (and of human rights data in general). Third, we should search for and examine additional explanations for human rights violations. By moving in all these directions, we may come closer to a position in which we can understand and work for change in human rights conditions. . . .

We began this article with some examples of violations of human rights in particular countries. In the course of our analysis, and with the unavoidable abstractions that accompany statistical discussion and the necessary attention given to methodological issues, we lose some sensitivity toward the phenomenon that we are trying to understand. It is important to end by reminding ourselves of the real terror and suffering contained in our concepts and percentages.

NOTES AND QUESTIONS

1. The "classical" study on stability to which Mitchell and McCormick refer is SAMUEL HUNTINGTON, POLITICAL ORDER IN CHANGING SOCIETIES (New Haven: Yale University Press, 1968). The Marxist theory that posits involvement with foreign capitalist countries as a contributor to poor human rights comes from NOAM CHOMSKY & EDWARD S. HERMAN, THE POLITICAL ECONOMY OF HUMAN RIGHTS: THE WASHINGTON CONNECTION AND THIRD WORLD FASCISM (Boston: South End Press, 1979).

2. For a discussion of impacts of British colonialism on democracy and human rights in colonized countries, see Samuel Huntington, *Will More Countries Become Democratic?*, POL. SCI. Q. 99 (Summer 1984). An earlier study summarized the difference between British and Iberian colonialism as follows:

> The Spanish and Portuguese colonies were founded on a set of institutions that were absolutist, authoritarian, hierarchical, Catholic, feudal or semifeudal, two-class, corporat-

ist, patrimonialist, orthodox, and scholastic to their core. By contrast the British colonies . . . derived from a set of institutions and practices that were fundamentally different.

LATIN AMERICAN POLITICS AND DEVELOPMENT 21-22 (Howard J. Wiarda & Harvey F. Kline eds., 1979).

3. The political theories tested by Mitchell & McCormick derive from Jeane Kirkpatrick, *Dictatorships and Double Standards*, 68 COMMENTARY 34-45 (November 1979); Rhoda E. Howard & Jack Donnelly, *Human Dignity, Human Rights, and Political Regimes*, 80 AM. POL. SCI. REV. 801-18 (1986).

Reinhard Heinisch, *Political Explanations of Basic Human Rights Performance*, Paper Prepared for the Annual American Political Science Association Meeting, New York City (1994) (citations omitted):

Given the difficulties encountered by comparative researchers trying to test the relationship between regime type and human rights practices, I believe we need to take a new and different route. . . . [Toward this end] I found it useful to return to a classic work on regime type literature. In his seminal piece *Polyarchy* Robert Dahl (1971) defines two theoretical dimensions of democratization. He argued that regimes vary along the dimensions of public contestation and electoral participation/inclusiveness. . . . Karen Remmer (1986) develops Dahl's regime type model further [by] operationalizing its key variables. . . . Depending on how participatory and competitive a nation's political system is, countries are classified as exclusionary authoritarian (not/little competitive; not/little inclusionary), exclusionary democratic (competitive; not/little inclusionary), inclusionary democratic (competitive; inclusionary) or inclusionary authoritarian (not/little competitive; inclusionary). . . .

Based on the literature on democracy and human rights surveyed above, . . . we can actually hypothesize about what to expect. If democracies . . . do a much better job in securing human rights than any other regime, we would expect the most competitive and most participatory regimes to deliver the best BHR-performance [Basic Human Rights]. By contrast, nations which are neither participatory nor competitive should do relatively wors[e]. Regimes with no or little electoral contestation, but with claims to having popular support, such as one-party regimes with large electoral turnouts, would attempt to make a great number of people happy by providing at least economic essentials without jeopardizing the party's hold on power. . . . We would therefore expect such a regime type to perform poorly on basic political rights, but considerably better in terms of guaranteeing some measure of economic and social security. In the reversed scenario, . . . exclusionary democracy, we would expect the opposite to happen. Contestation may be intense, but limited to a relatively exclusive strata of the population. That is, political rights and civil liberties may be provided to some segments in society, while others in the population, mostly those who would pose a threat [to] the ruling elites, are disenfranchised and alienated. Under conditions of exclusionary democracy, social cleavages are exacerbated and we would, therefore, expect these regimes to perform poorly in terms of basic economic and social rights. . . .

HYPOTHESES TESTING

. . . .

A bivariate correlation analysis between regime type and all three BHR-indices

finds a substantial association between regime conditions and human rights practices. . . . Good human rights performance continues to be significantly correlated
with more participatory and more competitive regimes. . . . When analyzing the
impact of our regime type variable on each of the two dimensions of human rights
separately we notice that its effect on [political] and subsistence rights performance
is about equal. . . . By breaking down regime type into its two components, competitiveness and participation, each showed a markedly different relationship with
human rights performance. [O]verall, participation appeared to be less associated
with either dimension of human rights than competitiveness, [but] it was, as hypoth-
esized, relatively more strongly correlated with subsistence rights performance than
with [political and] security rights performance. By comparison, more competitive
regimes were clearly more likely to guarantee [political and] security rights than
subsistence rights. . . .

The findings change somewhat when we focus on a sub-sample of developing
countries only. . . . [O]ther factors, notably economic components become, at this
level, more important predictors of BHR-performance. . . . [T]he relationship between
competitiveness and [political and] security rights performance remains. . .moder-
ately strong. . . . In turn, the relationship between participation and [political and]
security rights performance is notably weaker. . . . [Still more interesting] is that
for developing countries there appears to be *no statistically significant relationship*
between political competitiveness and subsistence rights, while there is *at least a*
moderate and statistically significant association between participation and both
BHR-dimensions. . . . [emphasis in original]

[An additional set of statistics] compares each of the four regime [categories]
in terms of [political and] security rights performance. As expected exclusionary
authoritarian and inclusionary democratic regimes show diametrically opposite results. While most of the former (95%) scored either low or medium on security rights,
some 87.5% of participatory and competitive regimes indicated good security rights
practices. While this does not come as a surprise, we are more interested in the mixed
regime types. In comparing inclusionary authoritarian regimes and exclusionary
democratic regimes in terms [of political and] security rights performance, it becomes
immediately evident that the former is considerably more repressive (35.8% have
low security rights performance) than the latter (11.3%). Conversely, almost twice
as many exclusionary democracies (13.2%) placed in the high security rights category
than did inclusionary authoritarian regimes (7.9%). The largest percentage of exclusionary democracies (42.1%) placed in the medium performance range. . . .

[T]he above regime clusters [are next compared] according to subsistence rights.
Once again exclusionary authoritarian and inclusionary democratic regimes form
polar opposites [in the expected directions]. . . . Among the mixed types inclusionary
authoritarian regimes performed somewhat better in guaranteeing basic economic
rights rather than security rights. In fact, overall, a smaller proportion of inclusionary authoritarian (69%) regimes placed in the low subsistence category, than
did exclusionary democracies (84.2%). Inclusionary authoritarian regimes were also
more likely (27.6%) to achieve a minimum subsistence rights performance when
compared with exclusionary democracies (10.5%). Given that of all regime types
exclusionary democracies have the largest percentage in the lowest subsistence
performance category we may conclude that the exclusionary democratic regimes
perform poorly [in this] respect . . . and are frequently outperformed by inclusionary
authoritarian regimes. . . . The case for authoritarian regimes as better providers
[of the] basic economic and social needs of their populations remains weak, however.
Authoritarian regimes with no or little popular participation tend to exhibit utter

disregard for any kind of human rights. Inclusionary authoritarian regimes may edge out exclusionary democracies to some extent in terms of subsistence rights performance, but the difference is often marginal and usually outweighed by the dramatically higher levels of political repression. . . .

From the perspective of human rights a clear order of preference emerges. Overall both [types of] authoritarian regimes log a dismal performance in either BHR-dimension, although the latter one does clearly better in securing subsistence rights and even outperforms, in that particular category, exclusionary democracies. . . . It should be remembered, though, that [the difference is only marginal]. . . . [Those small] economic benefits . . . often come at the expense of high levels of repression, suggesting an undesirable tradeoff. . . .

MULTIVARIATE MODELS OF BASIC HUMAN RIGHTS PERFORMANCE

[A second set of multivariate models were designed to] attempt to explain government performance in guaranteeing security rights, subsistence rights and overall basic human rights by drawing upon three "political" variables—regime type, British colonial heritage and length of independence. . . . As expected, . . . the most important predictor of human rights performance was regime type . . . suggesting that the higher the voter turnout and the lower party dominance the better the performance in both human rights dimensions. . . . [A second set of models combined] regime type and a number of economic variables . . ..

[A]ll other factors being equal, human rights are generally most likely guaranteed under the following conditions. Good human rights practices require a highly participatory and competitive political regime, a high level of development and a relatively equitable distribution of wealth. For less developed countries the same set of factors applies, [although] foreign trade may become more important (the effect of the latter being negative, however). Since the findings point squarely to the regime type as principal precondition for good human rights practices, we may have a cause for optimism. [Since] regime conditions are less immutable than economic conditions . . . change in favor of greater competitiveness and participation seems more achievable . . . than dramatic increases in GNP per capita.

CONCLUSION

. . . .

In pointing to . . . competitiveness and participation as the two most important factors in explaining cross-national variation in basic human rights performance I am not suggesting economic factors are unimportant or irrelevant. The latter have certainly an important place in human rights research, as economic constraints will arguably exacerbate social and political problems in society. The primary causes for the violations of basic human rights lie, in my view, with the political dimension, such as the regime arrangements, colonial heritage, institutional development and institutional capacity as well as political effort, political will, skill and commitment by political leaders and numerous other factors to be explored in future research. . . .

Answers to these issues have also important policy-consequences. . . . If, as suggested here, the primary causes of human rights violations are political rather than economic—something which is also indicated by the fact that over the recent decade the most significant improvements in human rights performance have occurred not in booming South East Asia but in two regions with major political reforms, but little economic betterment . . . —political pressure and economic sanctions may be more effective in undermining existing regime arrangements than . . . economic engagement. . . .

In conclusion, the most important result of this research is, therefore, the fact that human rights remain an eminently "political" phenomenon. . . . Much of the respect for human rights exhibited by governments is rooted in the philosophical commitment and in the political will of government leaders as well as in the institutions that make up the political regime. International support for economic development must be complemented by specific and well-targeted international efforts to support the expansion of political, social and economic rights. Relying simply on the "invisible hand" of market and the power of rising per capita GNP's to bolster magically the government performance in securing human rights is not only [not] warranted, but may also prove counter productive in the long run.

*   *   *   *   *

Steven C. Poe & C. Neal Tate, *Repression of Human Rights to Personal Integrity in the 1980s: A Global Analysis*, 88 AM. POL. SCI. REV. 853, 866-67 (1994) (citations and footnotes omitted):

We seek to build upon the strengths of existing empirical studies on [human rights violations], while improving upon them in several respects. We therefore construct a model of the most dramatic form of repression—repression of personal integrity rights—that tests several hypotheses suggested by previous studies, but goes on to test hypotheses suggested by theories not considered in previous empirical work on repression. The data set we employ clearly represents the most comprehensive yet analyzed in a global study of national human rights practices in terms of the number of countries and years it covers, as it includes relevant characteristics and behaviors for a pooled cross-sectional time-series sample of 153 countries for the eight years 1980-87. . . .

We shall focus on the subset of human rights categorized as dealing with the "integrity of the person." We also refer to violations of these rights as instances of *state terrorism*, which . . . we consider to be a category of coercive activities on the part of the government designed to induce compliance in others. Examples of such activities include murder, torture, forced disappearance, and imprisonment of persons for their political views. . . . [O]ur data includes two five-point ordinal human rights indices generated through analyses of the contents of both the State Department and Amnesty International reports. These five-point scales of human rights abuse range from 1 for a country with a healthy record of respect for personal integrity (Canada, the United States) to 5 for a human rights disaster (Iran during several years in the 1980s). . . .

BUILDING A MODEL OF HUMAN RIGHTS ABUSE

Democracy

That democracy ought to decrease governmental resort to terrorism is strongly argued by Henderson: "The democratic process, with its emphasis on bargaining and compromise, offer a meaningful alternative for handling conflict. . . ." Henderson goes on to note that democracy "cannot be based on pseudoparticipation. There must be legitimate channels, such as political parties and elections, that can carry interests forcefully into government." . . . The dampening effect of democracy on conflict surely does not represent the only way in which it inhibits repression.

Effective democracy also provides citizens (at least those with political resources) the tools to oust potentially abusive leaders from office before they are able to become a serious threat. In addition, the freedoms that are essential to procedural democracy may make it easier for citizens and opposition leaders to publicize attempts at repression, thereby bringing down on would-be abusive leaders the weight of majority or world opinion. . . .

Population Size and Growth

A large population may increase the occurrence of state terrorism in at least two ways. First, a large number of people increases the number of occasions on which such coercive acts can occur. As a matter of simple probability, such an increase should lead to the occurrence of more instances of coercion. Second, a large population places stress on national resources and bring the threat of environmental deterioration, further reducing available resources.

Arguments made by Henderson indicate that rapid population growth may also promote resource stress, perhaps even more than population size: ". . . in the more hard-pressed countries, burgeoning demands will keep governments off-balance and will incline them to resort to repression. Growing populations absorb any economic growth rate that may occur, thus frustrating governments' efforts." Rapid population growth also increases the proportion of the population falling into the youngest age categories that require the constant creation of new jobs, new housing, and many other government services, as well as posing the greatest tendency to engage in criminal activities and other threats to public order. . . .

Level of Development and Economic Growth

[T]he research we have summarized uniformly found a negative relationship between level of economic development or wealth and repression. . . . The presumed effect[s] of economic growth are more problematic. On the one hand, it is logical to assume that rapid economic growth, since it expands the resource base, should reduce the economic and social stresses that lead governments to use terrorism as a policy tool. But there has also been a strong argument that rapid economic growth is most likely to be a destabilizing force that will, in fact, increase instability and a regime's temptation to resort to coercive means to maintain control. The destabilizing effect of rapid growth may occur because it can rarely be rapid enough to outstrip the growth in expectations that is simultaneously occurring; because it increases the number of declassé individuals and groups most prone to promote instability; or because rapid growth inevitably occurs unevenly, possibly even creating growth by decreasing the well-being of the nonelite. . . .

Leftist Regimes

[C]ritics of U.S. foreign policy have taken Kirkpatrick and the State Department to task for what the critics see as their efforts unfairly to paint all socialist regimes with the tar of repression. We test the hypothesis that leftist regimes will be more coercive than other regimes, where leftist regimes are defined quite precisely as those governed by a socialist party or coalition that does not allow effective electoral competition with nonsocialist opposition.

Military Regimes

That we expect military regimes to be more coercive than others probably surprises no one. . . . Military juntas are based on force, and force is the key to coercion. Yet, in many of the nations in which soldiers forcibly take power, they do so alleging that the leaders they are replacing were themselves violating the constitution and, possibly, engaging in repression of the rights of the citizens. In addition, since military rule is by definition antithetical to democracy, it might be that any apparent relationship between military rule and state terrorism is spurious, a result of a failure to control for the democratic/nondemocratic nature of the regime. . . .

British Cultural Influence

This is certainly not the place to review the efficacy of political cultural explanations of national political behavior. At their best, they connote that certain attitudes inculcated by the culture, but not directly measured, are partially responsible for differences in the dependent behaviors of interest. That is the direct implication of Mitchell and McCormick's argument, and, following their lead, we include "British cultural influence" in our models of state terrorism. . . .

International War Experience

[A recent study has used] game theory to illustrate that when regime leaders ascend to power, they face the prospect of playing simultaneously in two distinct but nevertheless interrelated games: one is played in the domestic political arena, [where] the primary purpose is to keep power, whether through election or the use of terror; the other takes place in the international realm, with the other major players being the leaders of other countries, their representatives, and relevant international governmental and nongovernmental organizations. We believe that this analogy is also useful to researchers interested in explaining human rights abuse. The fact that these two games are intimately intertwined suggests that leaders' actions in the domestic political realm will likely be affected when their nations are a direct participant in an international crisis situation. In fact, . . . the results of some systematic empirical studies tend to point to the conclusion that there is a positive linkage between participation in international war and the levels of domestic political violence in participant countries. . . .

Civil War Experience

Just as governments may employ repression when threatened on the international front, it is also a tool commonly used by governments that are faced with internal problems. The most serious of threats in the domestic arena is posed by a condition of civil war, in which the authority of the regime in power is being challenged by an armed and organized resistance controlled by a shadow government. Therefore we shall propose a hypothesis that to our surprise had not yet been tested in quantitative studies of human rights and state terrorism—that regimes are more coercive when they are involved in civil conflict. . . .

SUMMARY AND CONCLUSIONS

As expected, democracy was shown to be associated with a decreased incidence in repression. . . . As a result of the cumulation of findings on this linkage, then, it would now seem difficult to deny that democratization decreases governments' use of coercion to abuse the human rights of private citizens. . . . With regard to the logged population size variable, the results were stable and quite clear, and we can therefore conclude that population size does have a positive impact on human rights abuse, with more populated countries having a greater propensity to abuse personal integrity rights. . . .

Our findings regarding several other variables thought to be related to state terror were negative. None of our results supported the conclusion that military control or British cultural influence affects levels of repression. Results for the effects of population growth . . . indicat[ed] no statistically significant or substantively important impact on repression. . . . However, here we should note that we dealt with only a seven-year time frame and that the population increase variable utilized in this study was an average of the population gain over this seven-year period . . ..

Rather mixed results were yielded by the variable identifying leftist governments. Leftist regimes appeared to violate personal integrity rights more seriously than others when such rights were [measured] using information gathered from U.S. State Department sources. When our analysis focused on the measure derived from Amnesty International information, however, no such relationship appeared. Here we are inclined to give less weight to the results obtained with the index derived from State Department reports, because our findings are consistent with those that would be expected if allegations regarding the biases of the State Department . . . against . . . some leftist regimes are valid. Thus we cannot conclude that, ceteris paribus, doctrinaire socialism is a cause of coercion that abuses human rights; but the results do perhaps provide limited empirical evidence of the different "pictures" of human rights realities painted by these two sources of human rights behavior during the 1980s.

Our study does provide very firm support for the hypotheses linking national experience of international and domestic threats . . . to an increased tendency to abuse personal integrity rights. Variables identifying countries that were participants in both kinds of wars were found to have statistically significant and substantively important impacts on national respect for the personal integrity of citizens . . ., with civil war participation having a somewhat larger impact than participation in international war. . . .

Finally, with regard to economic explanations of human rights abuse, we found . . . that economic standing is negatively, but only rather weakly, related to regimes' propensities to abuse of personal integrity rights.

Having now nearly finished this investigation of the conditions that lead to the most serious forms of human rights abuse, we believe we would be remiss if we failed to consider the vitally important question of what we have learned that might be helpful to scholars and practitioners hoping to decrease abuses of personal integrity worldwide. [O]ne way for these actors to make headway toward this goal is, not surprisingly, to promote democracy. Promoting democracy is clearly not the entire answer, however. . . . Neither should economic development be viewed as the panacea. . . . Neither would population control efforts be likely to have a substantively important impact on repression of these rights. . . . Our findings do, however, reveal another course toward greater respect of personal integrity, one that would have an impact of about the same magnitude as converting autocratic regimes to democratic ones. We have shown that these basic rights can be enhanced by actors who would encourage countries to solve their political conflicts short of war, and use whatever means are at their disposal to assist them in doing so.

NOTES AND QUESTIONS

1. Heinisch's regime-classification system was based on Karin L. Remmer, *Exclusionary Democracy*, 20 COMP. INT'L DEMOCRACY 64-83 (Winter 1985-86).

2. The theories formulated and tested by Poe & Tate derive, in part, from the following works:

Conway Henderson, *Conditions Affecting the Use of Political Repression*, 35 J. CONFLICT RESOL. 120-42 (1991) (reporting statistical evidence that levels of repression were affected negatively by democracy, positively by income inequality, and negatively by economic growth but were not significantly affected by level of economic development);

Conway Henderson, *Population Pressures and Political Repression*, 74 SOC. SCI. Q. 322-33 (1993) (finding statistical relationship between political repression and population growth, but no relationship between repression and population density);

R.D. McKinlay & A.S. Cohan, *A Comparative Analysis of the Political and Economic Performance of Military and Civilian Regimes*, 8 COMP. POL. 1-30 (1975);

R.D. McKinlay & A.S. Cohan, *Performance and Instability in Military and Nonmilitary Regimes*, 70 AMER. POL. SCI. REV. 850-64 (1976) (finding statistical support for hypothesis that poor countries and military regimes were more likely than wealthier countries and civilian regimes to ban constitutions, restrict freedom of assembly, and limit or ban political parties);

Han S. Park, *Correlates of Human Rights: Global Tendencies*, 9 HUM. RTS. Q. 405-13 (1987) (reporting statistically significant relationship between better human rights conditions and degree of urbanism, quality of life index, presence and amount of welfare expenditures, ethnic diversity, and the percentage of Christians in the population);

Karen Rasler, *War, Accommodation, and Violence in the United States, 1890-1970*, 80 AMER. POL. SCI. REV. 921-45 (1986) (reporting that in the U.S. since the turn of the century, political repression increased during periods of U.S. engagement in international military conflicts).

3.   Assume for a moment that there was a classification system which, according to its proponents, could accurately predict the likelihood and intensity of a country's rights violations based on measurable economic or political variables. How might such information be used? By whom? Consider that the U.N. Charter expresses the commitment of all member nations to respect the principle of "equal rights" and "self-determination" for all peoples. Could one or more countries, or the U.N. itself, pressure or require another country to change certain aspects of its economy or political structure which were "known" to cause or be associated with high levels of human rights abuse? Would a country be likely to continue friendly relations with governments or international bodies which had labeled it as a likely violator? Because of those and related concerns, many IGOs and NGOs attempt to deflect ideological controversy by focusing on specific rights or violations and excluding discussion of broader economic or political issues. Amnesty International, for example, has sought to refrain from adopting principles or practices which might subject it to criticisms of ideological bias:

> The notion of political impartiality has always been stressed, in the sense that the nature of the political or economic system under which violations of human rights occur is of no concern to the organization. This approach has had important consequences for its method of work. . . . [Amnesty International's statutory mandate focuses] on the fate of the victims of human rights violations, regardless of political systems.
>   Political impartiality is seen as contributing to Amnesty's credibility and thus to its effectiveness. The need for maintaining its political impartiality as well as the wish to avoid even the *appearance* of such partiality, was the main reason why Amnesty has not found it possible to condemn the best known legally based system of human rights violations in the world: Apartheid in South Africa. It wanted to avoid having to take up all kinds of discriminatory legislation in other parts of the world as well and limited itself to? . . . condemning and opposing those laws and practices of Apartheid which permit the imprisonment of people on grounds of conscience or race; the denial of fair trial to political prisoners; torture; or the death penalty. . . .
>   The wish for impartiality is also the main reason why Amnesty has included a non-violence clause with regard to the notion of prisoners of conscience in its mandate. It wants to avoid getting involved to a point where it would have to state, whether or not

a particular situation would justify the use of violence. As is the case with political impartiality, *consistency* is also seen as contributing to the credibility of the organization. Consistency means that similar cases are dealt with in a similar fashion. However, the problem is usually that cases are only similar up to a point and it is often rather difficult to decide what sort of action the principle of consistency requires in a given case. . . .

Peter R. Baehr, *Amnesty International and its Self-Imposed Limited Mandate*, NATL Q. HUM. RTS. 5, 9-10 (1994).

4.   Before comparative research on human rights performance can proceed, some determination must be made as to which violations will be measured. The studies presented so far illustrate three possible approaches. Mitchell & McCormick and Poe & Tate do not address economic or subsistence rights but focus instead on government violations of political and personal integrity rights. Mitchell & McCormick measure two kinds of violations, political imprisonment on the one hand, torture and execution on the other, and justify the distinction on the grounds, first, that torture and killing constitute a "distinct" and "qualitatively worse" kind of activity, and second, that governments are, in fact, statistically "quite distinct" on those two measures. Poe & Tate, in contrast, reject that dichotomy and urge that torture, execution, forced disappearance, and political imprisonment all manifest a single dimension: the willingness of a regime to harm citizens it sees as a threat. Heinisch, in turn, rejects the privileging of political over economic rights on the ground that "the provision of either of the two rights would be meaningless without the provision of the other." Rather, he sees both kinds of rights as "two dimensions of the same concept, like two sides of a coin," and thus measures the quality of political and economic rights both separately and together.

What are the advantages and limitations of each approach? Are there underlying assumptions or values which seem to influence the researchers' choice of measurement? What other values, if imbedded in a research design, might predispose a study toward particular findings? Are there classes of human rights that consistently seem to be overlooked in the studies? Note, for example, that the studies which examined human rights conditions in terms of modernization failed to address the impact of rapid economic development on indigenous peoples. Who else may be left out when violations are narrowly defined? For an anthology of studies which address the effects of modernization on indigenous peoples from colonialism to the present, see TRIBAL PEOPLES AND DEVELOPMENT ISSUES: A GLOBAL OVERVIEW (John H. Bodley ed., 1988).

5.   Heinisch identifies another way in which research might be skewed toward certain results. He challenges studies based on regime type *per se* and points out that they easily lend themselves to circular reasoning and self-fulfilling predictions. For instance, he observes the tendency of studies on the effects of democracy to begin by defining "democracy" as a form of government based on an ideology or having practices which reflect values of human dignity, personal liberty, and limited government, and then to hypothesize that such governments will do a better job of respecting human rights, which themselves may be defined in terms of personal liberty. His solution to this potential flaw was to classify countries based on the presence and degree of specific mechanisms, namely electoral participation and party competition.

What other factors might be used to compare human rights performance by varying forms of government? Should ideological preferences of the researcher be considered when evaluating research results?

Some scholars have adduced empirical evidence that democratic countries tend not to go to war with each other. They do, however, participate in wars against non-democratic countries. Wars between two or more non-democratic countries occur even more frequently. Of the 353 conflicts from 1816 to 1965, none occurred between two democratic countries, 155 were democratic countries against non-democratic countries, and 190 involved two or more non-democratic countries. One explanation is that in democratic countries many different organizations work for their own interests at the same time, so that loyalties are divided across the society. Such differences usually prevent any one powerful force from dominating. Also, democratic culture necessarily includes debate and negotiation, both within democratic countries and between them. R.J. Rummel, *Democide in Totalitarian States: Mortacracies and Megamurderers in* THE WIDENING CIRCLE OF GENOCIDE 3 (Israel W. Charny, ed., 1994) (Vol. 3 inGENOCIDE: A CRITICAL BIBLIOGRAPHIC REVIEW).

NOTES AND QUESTIONS

1. Do you agree with the proposition that democracy improves human rights conditions? What explanations have been offered for this argument? Which do you find compelling? Consider these findings in the above studies:

a. (Mitchell & McCormick) Advanced capitalist democracies had superior human rights records compared to other governments both in terms of both torture and political imprisonment; authoritarian states had higher incidents of torture than totalitarian regimes but similar incidents of political imprisonment.

b. (Heinisch)Regimes with high levels of political participation and competition showed better overall human rights performance than those with low levels of political participation and competition.

c. (Poe & Tate) The leftist and non-leftist distinction is not explanatory, partially because leftist includes socialist countries, such as France under Mitterand. Democracy is more predictive of human rights performance.

d. (Rummel) Democracies are involved in military conflicts less often than non-democracies.

2. Is the theory that democracy furthers respect for human rights supported by evidence? Why or why not? Are there other "regime type" theories that appear more consistent with the evidence? Are there non-governmental factors which play a significant role in influencing human rights?

2. Military Expansion and Conflict

Alfred Stepan has found that non-democracies tend to experience internal conflicts as well as the international wars discussed in the previous section. Latin American countries in particular experienced internal conflict during the 1950s and 1960s. The governments relied upon a national security theory, which combined notions of national development and strong internal security and legitimated military power and repression. Alfred Stepan, *The New Professionalism of Internal Warfare and Military Role Expansion, in* ARMIES AND POLITICS IN LATIN AMERICA 134-37, 139-43 (Abraham Lowenthal & J. Samuel Fitch eds., 1989).

Another explanation for repression in Latin American countries in the 1950s through 1970s is U.S. military aid. Fearing possible insurrectionary movements, the United States provided support in the form of military equipment and training. The training was administered through institutions such as the U.S. Army School of the Americas, the Inter-American Defense College, and the Office of Public Safety, which trained police in Latin American countries. U.S. authorities hoped that their support would allow the current Latin American governments to maintain control, and would allow economic development and facilitate democracy. Some scholars say, however, that the U.S. support actually fueled the systems of repression. Michael T. Klare & Cynthia Arnson, *Exporting Repression: U.S. Support for Authoritarianism in Latin America, in* CAPITALISM AND THE STATE IN U.S.-LATIN AMERICAN RELATIONS 138, 139-43, 145, 149, 152-58 (Richard R. Fagen ed., 1979).

NOTES AND QUESTIONS

1.   Does democracy reduce human rights violations or merely export them to foreign soil? Consider Rummel's argument that, because democracies are less likely to engage in war and more likely to exercise "limited, responsible" power, they foster better human rights conditions. Is that argument undermined or supported by U.S. relations with Brazil?

2.   Poe & Tate found that human rights conditions in countries under military governments were not significantly different from those in other countries, but that military engagement, especially against an internal threat, was a significant factor in increasing violations. Note too Heinisch's finding that income inequality and degree of international trade, but not foreign investment, were somewhat associated with violations in poorer, developing countries.

What factors best explain the case of Brazil? The indigenous population of Brazil paid a high price for an expanding and developing society. Many killings took place, along with the taking of land and property by the military government in power during the late 1960s and 1970s. Before colonization in the 1500s, approximately five million Indians lived in Brazil, and now less than 500,000 remain. Consider the following:

> Brazil did experience phenomenal [economic] growth once the [military government] had dampened resistance to their technocrats' policies . . ., but the Brazilian Miracle, as it came to be called, benefitted only the richest 10 percent of the population. Everyone else got much poorer. According to the Brazilian government's own statistics, the richest 10 percent, who in 1960 controlled almost 40 percent of the country's wealth, had by 1976 increased their share to almost 60 percent. The share of the poorest 10 percent went from 17.4 percent to 13.5 percent during the same period—a decline of almost a quarter in their already meager share of the pie. (In 1980, the bottom 25 percent of the population registered no income at all, and the next 25 percent earned below the minimum wage.)

LAWRENCE WESCHLER, A MIRACLE, A UNIVERSE 64-65 (1990).

3.   For a discussion of the impact of Brazil's economic development on the human rights of Amazonian indigenous peoples, see Christian Bay, *Human Rights on the Periphery: No Room in the Ark for the Yanomami?, in* TRIBAL PEOPLES AND DEVELOPMENT ISSUES: A GLOBAL OVERVIEW 258 (John H. Bodley ed., 1988). For more on the nexus between Brazil's economic and indigenous policies, see SHELTON H. DAVIS, VICTIMS OF THE MIRACLE: DEVELOPMENT AND THE INDIANS OF BRAZIL (1977).

The readings here present a diverse but by no means exhaustive survey of ways that human rights violations might be explored. Researchers in other areas of the social sciences have long been interested in issues which, though not directly related to human rights violations, may provide additional insights.

As you continue reading in this chapter, keep in mind questions the preceding studies illuminated but did not adequately answer. Does any of the following readings provide clues as to how such questions might be researched? What other questions should be asked?

It would be useful to review techniques of human rights work already explored in this book and to evaluate some of them in light of materials in this chapter.

Do the "legal" approaches, for instance, take into account the apparent causes of violations? Is it possible to prevent or reduce violations without addressing forces which apparently cause them? How might existing strategies be modified? Should other strategies be developed?

D. SOCIOLOGICAL ASPECTS OF POWER

As this book has shown, governments play a key role both in protecting and in violating the human rights of their citizens. Yet, as sociologists point out, government does not exist in a vacuum. The form a government takes both reflects and transforms the society in which it evolves. The previous section examined ways in which government policies and practices may impact on human rights conditions. The following readings broaden the inquiry and consider why a government may choose to act in certain ways and how government institutions and official ideology may capitalize upon as well as influence tensions, perceptions, and values in the society.

JAMES C. SCOTT, *The Value and Cost of the Public Transcript, in* DOMINATION AND THE ARTS OF RESISTANCE: HIDDEN TRANSCRIPTS 45, 48-53, 55-58, 61-63, 65-66, 205-06 (1990) (citations and footnotes omitted):

Relations of domination are, at the same time, relations of resistance. Once established, domination does not persist of its own momentum. [Power, when wielded] against the will of the dominated, . . . generates considerable friction and can be sustained only by continuous efforts at reinforcement, maintenance, and adjustment. A good part of the maintenance work consists of the symbolization of domination by demonstrations and enactments of power. Every visible, outward use of power—each command, each act of deference, each list and ranking, each ceremonial order, each public punishment, each use of an honorific or a term of derogation—is a symbolic gesture of domination that serves to manifest and reinforce a hierarchical order. The persistence of any pattern of domination is always problematic, and one may well ask what, given the resistances to it, is required to keep it in place . . ..

The successful communication of power and authority is freighted with consequences insofar as it contributes to something like a self-fulfilling prophecy. If subordinates believe their superior to be powerful, the impression will help him impose himself and, in turn, contribute to his actual power. Appearances do matter. Adolf Hitler has provided us with the most chilling version of this insight: "One cannot rule by force alone. True, force is decisive, but it is equally important to have this psychological something which the animal trainer also needs to be master of his beast." . . . [Quoting Gene Sharpe, *The Politics of Nonviolent Action, in* POWER AND STRUGGLE 43 (1973) (Boston: Porter Sargent).]

Concealment

By controlling the public stage, the dominant can create an appearance that approximates what, ideally, they would want subordinates to see. The deception—or propaganda—they devise may add padding to their stature but it will also hide whatever might detract from their grandeur and authority. . . . In extreme cases, certain facts, though widely known, may never be mentioned in public contexts—for example, forced labor camps in the Soviet Union, until Gorbachev's glasnost. Here it is a question of effacing from the public discourse facts that almost all know.

What may develop under such circumstances is virtually a dual culture: the official culture filled with bright euphemisms, silences, and platitudes and an unofficial culture that has its own history, its own literature and poetry, its own biting slang, . . . its own knowledge of shortages, corruption, and inequalities that may, once again, be widely known but that may not be introduced into public discourse. . . .

Euphemisms and Stigmas

The imposition of euphemisms on the public transcript plays a similar role [to concealment] in masking the many nasty facts of domination and giving them a harmless or sanitized aspect. In particular, they are designed to obscure the use of coercion. . . .

[T]he power to call a cabbage a rose and to make it stick in the public sphere implies the power to do the opposite, to stigmatize activities or persons that seem to call into question official realities. There is a pattern to much of this stigmatization. Rebels or revolutionaries are labeled bandits, criminals, hooligans in a way that attempts to divert attention from their political claims. Religious practices that meet with disapproval might similarly be termed heresy, satanism, or witchcraft. . . . [W]ith the rise of the modern state, this process is increasingly medicalized and made impersonal. Terms like *deviance, delinquency*, and *mental illness* appear to remove much of the personal stigma from the labels but they can succeed, simultaneously, in marginalizing resistance in the name of science.

Unanimity

[While a] great deal of communication—especially in contemporary societies—does not materially affect power relations[, it] is nonetheless true that under nearly any form of domination, those in power make a remarkably assiduous effort to keep disputes that touch on their claim to power out of the public eye. Their control is further enhanced if the impression of unanimity extends beyond themselves to subordinates as well. . . . The importance of *avoiding any public display of insubordination* is not simply derived from a strategy of divide and rule; open insubordination represents a dramatic contradiction of the smooth surface of euphemized power.

The question of whether a clear act of insubordination has occurred is not a simple matter, for the meaning of a given action is not given but is socially constructed. . . . When it suits them, the dominant may elect to ignore a symbolic challenge, pretend that they did not hear it or see it, or perhaps define the challenger as deranged, thus depriving his act of the significance it would otherwise have. Refusing to recognize a challenge may also be a strategy intended to afford the challenger an opportunity to reconsider his action . . . By the same token, the dominant may also choose to construe an ambiguous act as a direct symbolic challenge in order to make a public example of someone. . . . How an act . . . is construed is not merely a question of the mood, temper, and perceptiveness of the dominant; it is also very much a matter of politics. It is, for example, often in the interest of ruling elites to treat guerrillas or insurgents as bandits. By denying rebels the status in public discourse they seek, the authorities choose to assimilate their acts to a category that minimizes its political challenge to the state. . . . The political struggle to impose a definition on an action and to make it stick is frequently at least as important as the action per se.

Patterns of domination can, in fact, accommodate a reasonably high level of practical resistance so long as that resistance is not publicly and unambiguously acknowledged. Once it is, however, it requires a public reply if the symbolic status quo is to be restored. . . . The symbolic restoration of power relations may be seen in the importance accorded to public apologies. . . . The point has little to do with the sincerity of the retraction and disavowal, since what the apology repairs is the public transcript of apparent compliance. . . . Accounts of slavery in the antebellum South emphasize how much attention was paid to ritual requests for forgiveness by slaves about to be punished for insubordination. . . . In the twentieth century, perhaps the most extensive use of public apologies and confessions—followed typically by execution—was made in the late 1930s in the Stalinist purges and show trials. Doctrinal unanimity was so highly valued it was not enough for the party to crush dissent; the victims had to make a public display of their acceptance of the party's judgment. Those who were unwilling to make an open confession, thereby repairing the symbolic fabric before sentencing, simply disappeared.

[In all such public events], it is the show of compliance that is important and that is insisted on. Remorse, apologies, asking forgiveness, and generally, making symbolic amends are a more vital element in almost any process of domination than punishment itself. A criminal who expresses remorse at his crime typically earns, in exchange for his petty contribution to the repair of the symbolic order, a reduction in punishment. Similarly, of course, with the "misbehaving" child who says he is sorry and promises never to do it again. What all these actors offer is a *show of discursive affirmation from below*, which is all the more valuable since it contributes to the impression that the symbolic order is willingly accepted by its least advantaged members. . . .

Parades vs. Crowds: Authorized and Unauthorized Gatherings

Nothing conveys the public transcript more as the dominant would like it to seem than the formal ceremonies they organize to celebrate and dramatize their rule. Parades, inaugurations, processions, coronations, funerals provide ruling groups with the occasion to make a spectacle of themselves in a manner largely of their own choosing. . . . [Such public assemblies] are the ultimate in *authorized* gatherings of subordinates. . . . The political symbolism of most forms of personal domination carries with it the implicit assumption that subordinates gather only when they are authorized to do so from above. . . . The point of [this symbolism] is simply that [it] assume[s] . . . that there are no horizontal links among subordinates and that, therefore, if they are to be assembled at all it must be by the lord, patron or master, *who represents the only link joining them*. Without the hierarchy and authority that knits them into a unit, they are mere atoms with no social existence. . . .

Since no unauthorized *public* gathering of subordinates is imagined or legitimized by the official account, it follows that any such activity is . . . commonly seen as an implicit threat to domination. . . . The neutral terms *assembly* and *gathering* . . . are, on such occasions, likely to be replaced by charged terms such as *mob* by those who implicitly feel threatened. . . . In this respect, the petition to the ruler or lord—usually for redress of grievances—no matter how respectfully worded was implicitly a sign of autonomous collective action from below and, hence, troubling. . . . In Tokugawa Japan, [for example], the presentation of a petition to the ruler for redress of peasant grievances, implying autonomous organization among subordinates, was itself a capital crime. . . .

The implicit threat the dominant see in autonomous assemblies of their inferiors is not a form of ideologically induced paranoia. There is every reason to believe that such gatherings are, in fact, an incitement to boldness by subordinates. . . . First, there is the visual impact of collective power that a vast assembly of subordinates conveys both to its own number and to its adversaries. Second, such an assembly provides each participant with a measure of anonymity or disguise, thereby lowering the risk of being identified personally for any action or word that comes from the group. Finally, if something is said or done that is the open expression of [dissent], the collective exhilaration of finally declaring oneself in the face of power will compound the drama of the moment. . . .

*   *   *   *   *

Sociological aspects of power also can be considered in the form of symbolic power, created and held by a society's officials. Symbolic power consists of naming and classifying things, and therefore creating divisions, through words. Struggles for symbolic power arise out of uncertainty.

> Objective relations of power tend to reproduce themselves in relations of symbolic power. In the symbolic struggle for. . .the monopoly over legitimate naming, agents put into action the symbolic capital that they have acquired in previous struggles and which may be juridically guaranteed. Thus titles of nobility, like educational credentials, represent true titles of symbolic property which give one a right to share in the profits of recognition. . . . [N]ot all judgements have the same weight, and holders of large amounts of symbolic capital. . .are in a position to impose the scale of values most favourable to their [positions]. . . .

Pierre Bourdieu, *Social Space and Symbolic Power, in* In Other Words 123, 135 (1990). Symbolic power is created through increasing authority over a period time, and by creating classifications which are reflected in reality, since symbolic power is the power to reveal things which already exist. Symbolic power has the effect of changing the objective principles of a society. For example, class distinctions only exist through the imposition of division. Officials with symbolic power advance their ideas through public discourse, and therefore transform the principles of society. Bourdieu, *supra* at 137-38.

NOTES AND QUESTIONS

1.   What are some of the ways governments legitimize their existence and their exercise of power? Do the ways governments legitimize their authority vary according to (1) regime type or (2) other social or cultural factors? Does democracy, for example, rest upon certain ideological terminology and symbols wherever it occurs? Scott suggests that the trappings of democracy may at times be more a matter of symbolic form than a practical function:

> An election, assuming it is not purely ritualistic, may both provide an occasion for an electorate to choose their leaders while, at the same time, serving as a symbolic affirmation of the legitimacy of democratic forms embodying popular sovereignty. When an opposition movement calls for a boycott of what it believes to be a fraudulent or meaningless election, it presumably does this precisely to undercut the value of the election as a symbolic affirmation.

James C. Scott, *The Value and Cost of the Public Transcript, in* Domination and the Arts of Resistance: Hidden Transcripts 46 n.1 (1990). Is there a relation between the ways a government represents itself "symbolically" and the likelihood that it will repress its citizens' rights?

2.   Issues of legitimacy and public perception are of particular concern to new governments, especially those governments whose arrival in power was never fully accepted by influential sectors of the population, such as the military or leaders of a prior regime. A common dilemma

facing many such governments is whether or not, and to what extent, to prosecute officials of the prior government for human rights violations.

The potential for abuse of the prosecution power—underscored by the summary trial and execution of former Romanian leader Nicolae Ceausescu and his wife in December 1989—is cause for concern even for those who generally favor prosecutions.

Above all, however, the case for prosecutions turns on the consequences of failing to punish atrocious crimes committed by a prior regime on a sweeping scale. If law is unavailable to punish widespread brutality of the recent past, what lesson can be offered for the future? A complete failure of enforcement vitiates the authority of law itself, sapping its power to deter proscribed conduct. . . .

Some proponents believe that governments should prosecute their predecessors' atrocious crimes because the trials can advance a nation's transition to democracy. By demonstrating that no sector is above the law, prosecutions of state crimes can foster respect for democratic institutions and thereby deepen a society's democratic culture. Conversely, . . . failure to enforce the law may undermine the legitimacy of a new government and breed cynicism toward civilian institutions. . . .

By drawing a bright line between crimes that must be punished and those for which amnesties are permissible, international law helps answer an agonizing question confronting many transitional societies: How is it possible to seek accountability without setting off an endless chain of divisive recriminations? Writing of a proposal to purge Communist collaborators from formerly state-run enterprises, Polish Solidarity activist Adam Michnik evokes the dilemma confronting his nation in the wake of the prior regime's collapse:

> The struggle for freedom is beautiful. Anyone who has taken part in this struggle has felt, almost physically, how everything that is best and most precious within him was awakened. Revenge has a different psychology. Its logic is implacable. First, there is a purge of yesterday's adversaries, the partisans of the old regime. Then comes the purge of yesterday's fellow-oppositionists, who now oppose the idea of revenge. Finally, there is a purge of those who defend them. A psychology of vengeance and hatred develops. The mechanics of retaliation become unappeasable. . . .

Diane F. Orentlicher, *Settling Accounts: The Duty To Prosecute Human Rights Violations of a Prior Regime*, 100 YALE L. J. 2537, 2541 n.8, 2542-43, 2550 (1991) (quoting Weschler, *A Reporter at Large*, THE NEW YORKER, Dec. 10, 1990, at 127). Are new governments which follow in the wake of repressive regimes at a higher risk of perpetuating patterns of abuse? How can a government balance the need to bring human rights violators to justice against the need to break a historical pattern of political upheaval?

Some scholars suggest that science responds passively to political repression. Others, however, argue that science plays an active, and even leading, role. As an example, Robert Proctor has described the relation doctors had to the German Nazi government during the 1930s and 1940s. The Nazi ideology, which involved notions of biology and racial hygiene, attracted physicians to the Nazi movement from its inception. The combination of doctors and strong state control facilitated the government programs. A series of laws passed in the mid-1930s expanded doctors' participation in Nazi leadership. For example, the Sterilization Laws permitted sterilization of anyone with genetic diseases; the Nuremberg Laws prohibited intimate relationships between Jews and non-Jews; and the Marital Health Laws required couples to obtain a medical examination before they got married in order to prevent "racial pollution."

Beginning in 1939, the Nazis turned to killing biologically undesirable people.

Physicians continued to play an important role in Nazi activities. Victims of the first killings included terminally ill patients, psychiatric patients, handicapped children, and the elderly. These killings led to the "Final Solution" of gassing Jews, which employed many of the same medical personnel and equipment as had been used in the previous killings.

Proctor describes the relationship between doctors and the Nazi leaders as mutually beneficial. Physicians were attracted to the idea of a link between science and politics. They also received greater funding and support from the Nazis than they had under past governments. The Nazi leaders not only used doctors to carry out their programs, but exploited the trust patients put in doctors and disguised many killings as medical experiments. The doctors provided the Nazi leaders with a symbolic affirmation of the scientific justification for their killings, but many doctors also participated in choosing who would die and how they would die. Robert N. Proctor, *Nazi Doctors, Racial Medicine, and Human Experimentation, in* THE NAZI DOCTORS AND THE NUREMBERG CODE: HUMAN RIGHTS IN HUMAN EXPERIMENTATION 17 (George J. Annas & Michael A. Grodin eds., 1992).

NOTES AND QUESTIONS

1. In relations between the medical profession and Nazi leaders, who benefitted from whom? Could one have achieved the status it did without the other? In what other ways have governments capitalized on the authority and rationalization of science to bolster their agendas? Robert Lifton, a long-time student of government oppression from the Nazi period to China's Cultural Revolution, draws compelling parallels between Nazi exploitation of medical science and U.S. use of nuclear science during the Cold War. *See* ROBERT J. LIFTON & ERIC MARKUSEN, GENOCIDAL MENTALITY: NAZI HOLOCAUST AND NUCLEAR THREAT (1990). In both situations, he urges, the government's mobilization of science served not only to translate an otherwise dubious set of propositions into a more rational and cohesive world-view, it also made possible the recruitment of large numbers of persons to engage in activities which would otherwise have been repudiated as immoral or irrational. This subject will be taken up again in the next section, on psychological explanations.

2. German scientists were not unique in their use of both eugenics and racial hygiene. Such topics were subfields in the much-broader area of genetic research which was receiving a great deal of attention in the early twentieth century. Nor was the German government alone in its eagerness to use such research as a basis for addressing issues of public health and social welfare. All over the Western world, governments were confronting the negative byproducts of massive industrialization, urbanization, and population growth. Escalating crime rates and the breakdown of traditional social networks led to a growing need for government institutions and public services to address problems once relegated to the private sector. In the United States, for example, the number of persons in mental institutions grew from 45,000 in 1870 to 566,000 in 1936. JEFFREY L. GELLER & MAXINE HARRIS, WOMEN OF THE ASYLUM: VOICES FROM BEHIND THE WALLS, 1840-1945, at 256 (1994). Because a great majority of mental hospitals and prisons were state-run, the financial burden of maintaining and expanding the institutions to keep up with demands made the possibility of "genetic" solutions increasingly attractive. In 1927 the U.S. Supreme Court upheld a state law permitting the forced sterilization of mental patients and by 1945 twenty-four states had introduced such policies. *See Buck v. Bell*, 274 U.S. 200; C.J. Gamble, *State Sterilization Programs for the Prophylactic Control of Mental Disease and Mental Deficiency*, 102 AMER. J. PSYCHIATRY 289-93 (1945). So, when the Nazi party began implementing its biological vision of the world the United States already was a decade ahead. The Nazi sterilization laws followed American practices of sterilizing individuals, primarily prisoners and patients in mental institutions. Nazi leaders also envied the

United States for other racial policies, such as prohibition of marriage between people of different races.

> Sadly, there is yet another area where Nazi physicians were able to draw support from their American colleagues. In 1939, Germany's leading racial hygiene journal reported the refusal of the American Medical Association to admit black physicians to its membership. . . . German physicians only one year before . . . had barred Jews from practicing medicine (except on other Jews); Nazi racial theorists were thereby able to argue that Germany was "not alone" in its efforts to preserve racial purity.

> [Nor did the] idea of ending "lives not worth living" . . . begin with the Nazis. . . . In 1935 . . . the French-American Nobel Prize winner Alexis Carrel suggested . . . that the criminal and the mentally ill should be "humanely and economically disposed of. . . ." Six years later, as German psychiatrists were sending the last of their patients into the gas chambers, an article appeared in the *Journal of the American Psychiatric Association* calling for the killing of retarded children, "nature's mistakes."

Proctor, *supra*, at 21-24; *see also* Foster Kennedy, *The Problem of Social Control of the Congenitally Defective: Education, Sterilization, Euthanasia*, 99 AMER. J. PSYCHIATRY 13-16, 141-43 (1942). Given the widespread acceptance of genetic solutions to social problems, what perhaps prevented their escalation into genocide in countries outside of Germany?

3.   It has been suggested that totalitarian governments can more easily induce citizens to become violent than other regime types. Important factors include the rejection of opposition opinions and the participation of all members of society in government programs:

> In totalitarian systems, the whole society is induced to participate. [In Nazi Germany] and in the Soviet Union, all members of society were called upon to contribute to the building of a "new" society. . . . Everyone was expected to take steps against those who deviated or who were designated for mistreatment. But *participation* results in psychological changes. Human beings learn by doing, by actual participation, perhaps more than by any other way. . . . People learn to become perpetrators of violence by engaging in violent acts or in acts that are not directly violent but are in the service of such violence and contribute to others' suffering or eventual murder. In the process they learn to overcome the initial resistance they may have to directly or indirectly harm others. . . .

Ervin Staub, *The Psychology of Perpetrators and Bystanders*, POL. PSYCHOL. 61 (1985).

E.   PSYCHOLOGICAL FACTORS

Terms like "nation state" or "government" make it easy to forget that each violation of a human right is at bottom a very personal event, not only to the individual victim, but to the many persons whose individual actions, working in concert, form the substance and texture of the larger pattern. By shifting one's focus to the human beings who are the component parts of a government and its society, new kinds of questions emerge. Is it possible that a country's entire population, or at least a sufficient majority, may at times consist of innately "cruel" or sadistic human beings? If not, then how do governments obtain the compliance of enough "normal" people to make possible large projects of repression?

Sociologist Max Weber once wrote that individuals conduct their social affairs and relationships according to their perception of "legitimate authority"—an authority which organizes their social world and equips them with a "sense of duty" as to their appropriate role.[2] The individual's acceptance of an authority's legitimacy may be based on an "emotional surrender" and personal identification, on a "rational belief" in the values and assumptions expressed by the authority, or on a "religious" attitude where "salvation" or some other transcendent goal "depends on obedience to authority." Alternatively, where individuals are neither emotionally inspired nor intellectually persuaded of an authority's vision of the world, they may nevertheless subscribe to its dictates out of "self-interest," either for protection or personal betterment.[3]

This section examines some of the psychological forces which may come into play to transform ordinarily empathetic and gentle individuals into willing or even enthusiastic participants in actions they would ordinarily repudiate as cruel or immoral. As will be seen, authority plays a pivotal role in this transformation, although not merely in the conventional sense of government officials or physical coercion. As Weber's observation suggests, authority has a psychological aspect as well which, once its patterns and expectations are internalized, can mold human conduct even without the force of arms or sanctions.

In *Some Conditions of Obedience and Disobedience to Authority*, 10 HUM. REL. 57 (1965), social psychologist Stanley Milgram describes an experimental program conducted at Yale University in 1961. The experiments involved male subjects, between the ages of 20 and 50, from a variety of occupations. The subjects believed that the purpose was to study the effect of physical punishment on memory. Each test involved an experimenter, one subject, and an accomplice, who the subject thought was another subject. In a rigged drawing the subject was assigned to play the role of teacher and the accomplice was given the role of learner. The learner was then strapped in an electric chair. The subject was instructed to administer memory tests to the learner, and to punish the learner with increasingly strong electric shocks whenever he made an error. The shocks were administered by the subject through an electric generator. For each error the subject was directed to increase the shock intensity by one step.

The experiments were conducted with the subjects and victims at various distances. In one type of experiment, the victim was in the next room and could not be seen or heard by the subject. The victim pounded on the wall at a certain level of shock intensity, and then became silent at another, higher level. In the second situation, the victim remained in the next room, but the subject could hear his verbal protests to the shock treatment. The third type of experiment placed the victim and subject in the same room, only a few feet apart. Finally, experiments were conducted in which the victim would not receive a shock unless the subject physically forced his hand onto a shockplate, as ordered by the experimenter.

Obedience to the experimenter's demands was lower when the victim and subject were closer together. Milgram suggested several possible reasons for this result. For example, when the two are at a greater distance, the subject knows he is inflicting pain, but is not affected by it, so is not compelled to stop the behavior. Another explanation could be denial. A more distant victim allows the subject to disassociate his behavior and the harm to the victim, but when the two are in closer proximity, he can no longer deny the effect. Also, the subject may feel less shame and guilt about his action when he can not see the victim. Intimacy between the victim and experimenter is another possible factor in the results. Because those two remain in

---

[2] MAX WEBER, BASIC CONCEPTS IN SOCIOLOGY 71 (H. P. Secher trans., 1962).
[3] *Id.* at 75.

the same room, they may share an alliance in which the victim does not participate.

The spatial relationship between the experimenter and the subject was also important, because the subject naturally wanted to make a good impression. The proximity of the experimenter varied between remaining in the room with the subject, communicating with the subject over the telephone, and only leaving a tape recording in the room for the subject to play. Experimenters observed a sharp decline in compliance from the first to third type of test. For instance, obedience in the first situation was nearly three times greater than in the second situation. Also, some subjects in the second situation told the experimenter over the phone that they were following his orders, but they actually administered only the lowest shock level on the dial. If the experimenter entered the room at that point, he could usually force obedience.

In other experiments, extra actors participated and administered shocks along with the subject. If the actors refused to give the shocks, ninety percent of the subjects would also refuse. If the actors complied, the results did not differ significantly from experiments in which the actors were not included.

Throughout the tests, subjects showed physical signs of tension such as sweat, trembling, and stuttering. Also, many of them verbally rejected the behaviors or called them "senseless" and "stupid." Their protests, however, often did not affect their compliance with the demands of the experimenter.

The experimenters' purpose was to study under what conditions ordinarily good people will submit to authority, even under protest, and what conditions make disobedience probable. Milgram considered the importance of the fact that the experiments were conducted at Yale University, a highly regarded and respected institution. A similar experiment, conducted at a less prestigious university, however, resulted in similar findings. Milgram concluded that while an institutional structure is probably necessary, it need not be particularly well respected. He emphasized that context is connected to behavior and must always be considered when behavior is assessed. Milgram asked the question "if in this study an anonymous experimenter could successfully command adults to subdue a fifty-year-old man, and force on him painful electric shocks against his protests, one can only wonder what government, with its vastly greater authority and prestige, can command of its subjects." *Id.* at 75.

Other scholars have also discussed the point at which authority can make otherwise decent people commit cruel or violent acts. In studying how military training creates torturers, Janice Gibson and Mika Haritos-Fatouros show that torture does not come naturally, but is taught through forced obedience to authority and desensitization of violence.

For instance, Gibson and Haritos-Fatouros interviewed torturers from the Greek military government which was in power from 1967-74. The men had no record of violence before they were drafted into the military. To encourage obedience, the men were physically beaten, verbally abused, and forced to swear loyalty to the military. When orders were followed, or torture was carried out, rules would be relaxed, to reinforce the behavior. Disobedience, however, would result in harassment, punishment, and intimidation. Sensitivity to violence was reduced gradually, beginning with brutality toward the recruits themselves. Next, the men were forced to have contact with prisoners, and to watch while they were tortured. Finally, they participated in and administered beatings and other methods of torture. Gibson and Haritos-Fatouros interviewed many U.S. soldiers and found that similar training methods are used in the U.S. Marines and Green Berets as well.

Gibson and Haritos-Fatouros also describe an experiment conducted at Stanford

University in which students were randomly assigned roles of prisoners and guards. Over the course of the week-long experiment the guards developed strong feelings of group unity, and became violent and aggressive. The authors do not think that torture comes naturally to people, but rather anyone could be trained to be a torturer. Janice T. Gibson & Mika Haritos-Fatouros, *The Education of a Torturer*, PSYCHOL. TODAY 50, 52, 56-58 (1986).

*   *   *   *   *

ROBERT JAY LIFTON, *Socialization to Killing, in* THE NAZI DOCTORS: MEDICAL KILLING AND THE PSYCHOLOGY OF GENOCIDE 195-99, 211, 422, 425-27, 442, 445-47, 450, 453, 458, 460-61, 479-80, 493-96 (1986):

[During their initial months on duty at Auschwitz], most SS doctors underwent . . . an extraordinary individual-psychological shift from revulsion to acceptance. . . . This shift involved a *socialization* to Auschwitz, including the important transition from outsider to insider. . . . Alcohol was crucial to this transition. Drinking together, often quite heavily, evenings in the officers' club, doctors "spoke very freely" and "expressed the most intimate objections." . . . Such inebriated protests brought about no repercussions—indeed, may even have been encouraged—and was unrelated to commitment or action. . . .

[The] language of initiation is appropriate [to describe ramp selection duty, where physicians examined arriving train loads of prisoners and selected who would live and who would die;] selections were the specific "ordeal" the initiate had to undergo in order to emerge as a functioning Auschwitz "adult." And by exposing and combating doubts, the drinking sessions helped suppress moral aspects of the prior self in favor of a new Auschwitz self. . . . [As one former doctor] explained, doctors inwardly *wanted* to make that [psychological] transition because of the great urge to become an insider. For in so extraordinary a situation, . . . personal isolation would be intolerable, and one would become desperate to "establish contact somehow" with others. Newcomers would seek out men with whom they could identify— because of relatively similar backgrounds and outlooks. . . . Sometimes experienced Auschwitz doctors were assigned as mentors to arriving neophytes . . ., which suggests that the authorities were aware of the pattern of conflict during the early transition experience. . . . [At the same time, a] doctor could, if sufficiently determined, avoid performing selections without repercussions—though only if he expressed his reluctance as inability rather than defiance. . . .

The socialization of SS doctors to Auschwitz killing was enhanced by the camp's isolation from the world outside. . . . Doctors assigned there . . . had limited contact with anything but Auschwitz reality. They became preoccupied with adapting themselves to that reality, and moral revulsion could be converted into feelings of discomfort, unhappiness, anxiety, and despair. [Personal] struggles could replace moral questions. They became concerned not with the evil of the environment but with how to come to some terms with the place. . . .

Doubling

[One] way Nazi doctors coped with Auschwitz was to lead a double life that both reflected and enhanced their psychological doubling. Thus, they spent most of their time in the camp . . . but went on leave for a few days every other month or so to spend time, usually in Germany, with their wives and children. They remained extremely aware of the separateness of the two worlds. One's wife, children, and parents came to stand for purity, as opposed to an inner sense of Auschwitz filth. . . . [Consequently, an] SS doctor could call forth two radically different psychological constellations within the self: one based on "values generally accepted" and the education and background of a "normal person"; the other based on "[Nazi-Auschwitz] ideology with values quite different from those generally accepted." . . .

Doubling is an active psychological process, a means of *adaptation to extremity*. . . . In Auschwitz, the pattern was established under the duress of the individual doctor's transition period. . . . He needed a functional Auschwitz self to still his anxiety. . . . Nor did most Nazi doctors resist that usurpation [of their prior self] as long as they remained in the camps. Rather they welcomed it as the only means of psychological function. If an environment is sufficiently extreme, and one chooses to remain in it, one may be able to do so *only* by means of doubling. . . .

Indeed, Auschwitz as an *institution* . . . ran on doubling. . . . In an institution as powerful as Auschwitz, the external environment could set the tone for much of an individual doctor's "internal environment." The demand for doubling was part of the environmental message immediately perceived by Nazi doctors, the implicit command to bring forth a self that could adapt to killing without one's feeling oneself a murderer. Doubling became not just an individual enterprise but a shared psychological process, the group norm. . . . Doctors as a group may be more susceptible to doubling than others. . . . One feels it necessary to develop a "medical self," which enables one not only to be relatively inured to death but to function reasonably efficiently in relation to the many-sided demands of the work. . . .

Numbing and Derealization

The Auschwitz self depended upon radically diminished feeling, upon one's not experiencing psychologically what one was doing. . . . The Auschwitz self also called upon the related mechanism of "derealization," of divesting oneself from the actuality of what one is part of, not experiencing it as "real." . . .

The language of the Auschwitz self, and of the Nazis in general, was crucial to the numbing. A leading scholar of the Holocaust told of examining "tens of thousands" of Nazi documents without once encountering the word "killing," until, after many years he finally did discover the word—in reference to an edict concerning dogs. . . . For what was being done to the Jews, there were different words, words that perpetuated the numbing of the Auschwitz self by rendering murder nonmurderous. For the doctors specifically, these words suggested responsible military-medical behavior. . . . The Nazi doctor did not literally believe these euphemisms. Even a well-developed Auschwitz self was aware that Jews were not being resettled but killed, and that the "Final Solution" meant killing all of them. But at the same time the language used gave Nazi doctors a discourse in which killing was no longer killing; and need not be experienced, or even perceived, as killing. As they lived increasingly within that language—and they used it with each other—Nazi doctors became imaginatively bound to a psychic realm of derealization, disavowal, and nonfeeling. . . .

Nazi doctors discussing Auschwitz . . . describ[ed] a realm of experience so extreme, so removed from the imagination of anyone who had not been there, that it was literally a separate reality. That quality—that absolute removal from ordinary experience—provided the Auschwitz self with still another dimension of numbing. Even as part of itself was absorbed in routine, another part could feel the environment to be so distinct from the ordinary that *anything* that happened there simply did not count. One could not believe what one was doing, even as one was doing it. . . .

[T]he Auschwitz self quickly sought [a] stance of powerlessness . . . as a way of renouncing responsibility. . . . This emotional and moral surrender to the environment had great psychological advantages. The Auschwitz self could feel: "*I* am not responsible for selections. *I* am not responsible for phenol injections. *I* am a victim of the environment no less than the inmates." . . . The Auschwitz self could than become an absolute creature of context, and there is no better way to abnegate moral responsibility of any kind. . . .

Perhaps the single greatest key to the medical function of the Auschwitz self was the technicizing of everything. That self could divest itself from immediate ethical concerns by concentrating only on the "purely technical" or "purely professional". . . . For the Auschwitz self there is a logical sequence: a doctor's task is to alleviate suffering and to exert a humane influence in any setting. When the setting is one of mass murder, that means calling forth medical and technical skills to diminish the pain of victims. . . .

The Construction of Meaning

Finally, the Auschwitz self takes on a larger sense of meaning. Its activities take on a logic and purpose and come to seem appropriate to the environment and its overall ethos. . . . [The] proclivity toward constructing good motives while participating in evil behavior . . . is one of the remarkable dimensions of human adaptability. . . . For no reality is directly or fully given us as human beings. Rather we must inwardly "construct" that reality on the basis of what we inwardly bring to what is "out there." [W]e are meaning-hungry creatures; we live on images of meaning. Auschwitz makes all too clear the principle that the human psyche can create meaning out of anything. . . .

The meaning derives partly from *routine* as such. The daily happenings . . . became . . . a *route* or path, a direction of the inner as well as the outer being. To report to an office, to speak to colleagues, to make one's rounds on the medical block, to spend a bit of time at one's research, to confer with camp officials and prisoner functionaries on diet and sanitary procedures, to issue medical and disciplinary orders, to here and there exchange an amusing anecdote or tell a little joke, to conduct selections for an arriving transport, to have meals and evening entertainment with fellow officers—all these came together as a life form, within which the mind could build coherence and significance. . . .

The meaning structure of the Auschwitz self depended greatly upon the pattern of "blaming the victim." . . . [The] insistence that the Gypsies were genetically responsible for their fatal noma tumors, [the] disgust with the Gypsies for not distributing their food equitably among themselves, the repeated blame placed on prisoner doctors for the terrible condition of their patients and the frequent deaths among them—all these were psychologically of a piece. . . . [Similarly], Hitler's position was that, because Jews were, biologically and existentially, a permanent locus of evil and a permanent threat, it was *they* who must be blamed for anything done to overcome that threat and extirpate that evil. . . .

The Genocidal Threshold

There is a threshold in genocide—the step from image to act. The Nazi evidence suggests no single cause or trigger so much as a sequence of events and attitudes and problem solving . . . within an increasingly murderous atmosphere. . . . From early 1941, a series of [orders] came from high Nazi authorities that increasingly articulated a policy to kill not just Jews but *all* Jews. . . . [I]t is significant that scholars are uncertain about whether a single order bringing about the Final Solution can be identified[; but however it comes about] a point is reached at which a collective understanding takes shape that the designated group is to be annihilated. Collective understanding quickly becomes collective will as perpetrators join in the process on the basis of perceptions of what is expected of them. . . . With the Nazis, that genocidal process was probably well under way before the introduction of a systematic plan for the genocide. . . . [The] genocidal threshold requires extensive prior ideological imagery of imperative. One has to do this thing, see it through to the end, for the sake of a utopian vision of national harmony, unity, wholeness. . . . That vision was more fundamental for the Nazis than was any single myth about the Jews. . . .

One cannot say that any particular level of technology is required for genocide: the Turks killed about one million Armenians by means of shooting, clubbing, beating, slave labor, starvation, and other forms of torture. The Nazis killed millions of Jews by the same crude methods, even without benefit of gas chambers. . . . Higher technologies render the killing more efficient, in time and numbers, and in easing the psychological burden of the perpetrators. A clear example is the Nazi sequence from face-to-face shooting to fatal injections and carbon monoxide gas chambers to cyanide gas. . . . The sequence helps eliminate the impediment of empathy, of experiencing one's victim's as fellow human beings. . . .

In the process of being improved, the technology itself comes increasingly to dominate the perpetrators' field of attention. . . . And that preoccupation takes on a sense of everydayness, of normality. . . . The rationalized search for a "final solution of the Jewish question" involved the idea of solving a problem in the most conclusive or "final" manner. From top to bottom, each perpetrator's part in solving the problem can thus be looked upon as essentially technical. . . . Technological distancing and altering of the moral mind-set was illuminatingly demonstrated by the striking correlation between attitude and altitude among American pilots and air crews in Vietnam and Cambodia. B-52 pilots and crews, who bombed at such high altitudes that they saw nothing of their victims, tended to speak exclusively of professional skill and performance; those on fighter-bomber missions had glimpses of people below and tended to have at least a slight inclination to explain or rationalize what they did; those who flew helicopter gunships saw everything and could experience the fear, horror, questioning, and guilt that was felt by ground personnel. . . .

Bureaucracy [also] helps render genocide unreal. It further diffuses the impact of murderous events that, to begin with, are difficult to believe. In this sense we may say that the bureaucracy *deamplifies* genocide: diminishes the emotional and intellectual tones associated with the killing, primarily for perpetrators but also for bystanders and victims. Central to the process is the dampening of language, the use not only of euphemisms . . . but also of certain code terms. . . . The genocidal bureaucracy contributes also to collective feelings of inevitability. The elaborateness of the bureaucracy's organization conveys a sense of the inexorable—that one might as well . . . go along because nothing can be done. . . .

NOTES AND QUESTIONS

1. What does the Milgram study show about the role of bystanders? What lessons can be learned about the important role of human rights organizations in relation to the bystanders?

2. What facts does Lifton identify as leading to and making possible the Nazi "Final Solution"? Consider the sterilization, miscegenation, and segregation laws existing in the United States prior to World War II. Could something like the "Final Solution" have happened here? Why didn't it? In what other ways, besides "genocide" in the classic sense, do analogous

human rights violations occur in the United States? How are they rationalized or disguised to prevent wide scale public opposition?

3.   Several earlier readings explored the ways a government may draw support from science or some other rational discourse in order to justify state-sponsored violations of human rights and attain public support. James Scott poses an alternative explanation for a government's use of rational discourse:

> Any argument claiming that the ideological efforts of ruling elites are directed at *convincing* subordinates that their subordination is just must confront a good deal of evidence suggesting that it often fails to achieve its purpose. Catholicism, for example, is the logical candidate for the hegemonic ideology of feudalism. But it is abundantly clear that the folk Catholicism of the European peasants, far from serving ruling interests, was practiced and interpreted in ways that often defended peasant property rights. . .and even provided something of a millennial ideology with revolutionary import. . . . For this reason, [a number of researchers] have persuasively argued that the ideological effect of Catholicism was rather to help unify the feudal ruling class, define its purpose, and create a [system] that would hold property together. . . . This perspective on religious ideology is very much in keeping with Max Weber's analysis of doctrinal religion generally:
>
>> This universal phenomenon [the belief by the privileged that their good fortune is just] is rooted in certain psychological patterns. When a man who is happy compares his position with that of one who is unhappy, he is not content with the fact of his happiness, but desires something more, namely *the right to his happiness*, the consciousness that he has earned his good fortune, in contrast to the unfortunate one who must equally have earned his misfortune. . . . What the privileged classes require of religion, if anything at all, is this psychological reassurance of legitimacy.
>
> [quoting MAX WEBER, THE SOCIOLOGY OF RELIGION 107 (1963).]
>
> If Weber's assessment is a plausible interpretation of elite religious doctrine it might be applicable to more secular doctrines as well that purport to explain fundamental inequalities in status and conditions.

JAMES C. SCOTT, *Who is the Audience for the Performance?, in* DOMINATION AND THE ARTS OF RESISTANCE: HIDDEN TRANSCRIPTS 68-69 (1990) (footnotes and citations omitted). A similar argument has been made with regard to the ideological aspects of capitalism. *See* NICHOLAS ABERCROMBIE, STEPHEN HILL & BRYAN S. TURNER, THE DOMINANT IDEOLOGY THESIS (1980). Abercrombie urges that there is little evidence that the working class has ever been fully indoctrinated into the values and ideals of capitalism, and much evidence that capitalist ideology is rather a force for strengthening the cohesion and self-confidence of the upper classes which have the most direct interest in embracing it. *Id.* at 3-5. Is it necessary that a substantial portion of a country's citizenry be convinced of the appropriateness of government actions in order for them to be pursued? Who must be convinced? Who need not be convinced?

4.   Consider the French government's use of torture in its attempt to suppress Algeria's move toward political independence:

> It was necessary to make a barbaric act doable; to cloak with respectability an act that few [could accept] in the face of France's venerable democratic principles. It was necessary in fact to establish a premise of such extreme danger to the Republic that the derogation of nonderogable rights would appear the sole recourse. [Toward this end, the] ideology of the civilizing mission was pressed into service. . . . When the French soldier was charged to commit [torture], the banner of the civilizing mission helped bury his conscience. . . .
>
>   Ideology keeps the individual who commits an institutionally accredited atrocity from recognizing the destructive nature of the act . . . . France was "crusading for the defense of Western values against the barbarians from the East" and . . . France's decline would by that reasoning be "synonymous with the decline of Christian civilization." . . .

During this war, for example, a French Armed Forces Message said: "In effect, the fate of the West and of Christianity is what is being played out in Algeria today." . . . [In addition, most French officers agreed that revolutionary war] was a type of war in which normal rules of war were suspended. Defining this war as exempt from the rules of war provided the necessary rationale for numerous other violations besides torture: summary executions, displacement of populations, detention without trial . . ..

[A characteristic typical among torturers is] the instinctive reliance on a learned rationalization and the need for some justification for an act known to be in some way "wrong"—whether immoral, unkind, un-Christian, or illegal. Ideology functions as a reservoir from which the sought-after justification can be drawn. . . .

Locating the problem [of torture] within a country with a strong human rights tradition makes clear that reliance on governments' built-in and nominally benevolent traditions of rights may prove insufficient to protect individuals against state-directed violence.

RITA MARAN, TORTURE: THE ROLE OF IDEOLOGY IN THE FRENCH-ALGERIAN WAR 16-17, 110, 155, 188 (1989) (footnotes and citations omitted). Note that native Algerians, although recognized as French citizens, were at the same time a colonized people. Would the French military have succeeded in perpetrating similar human rights violations against persons native to and resident in France?

5.   Ervin Staub has detailed several factors which prompt ordinary people to commit acts of violence. Aggressive behavior depends partly on personal characteristics, but several less personal factors are also important. Whether a person becomes a perpetrator of violence may depend on the role the person plays in society. People in power can be convinced to view those with less power as non-human. Leaders will often degrade victims, so that they seem to belong to a lower class of people or things.

Staub finds that a desire to obey authority is another factor leading to aggression. Children learn to submit to authority from their families, schools, and communities. A lack of affection toward children, along with strict discipline and punishment for disobedience, leads to compliance with demands of authority figures as adults. Research has shown that serious threats and punishment were common in German schools during the Nazi period.

Reduced feelings of responsibility also contribute to the willingness to commit violent acts. People naturally feel a responsibility for helping each other. When certain groups are classified as sub-human, however, the feelings disappear. Also, in Nazi Germany, military recruits were told that government leaders would take responsibility for all of their acts of violence.

Further, Staub explains that bystanders influence perpetrators of violence, and can be effective in preventing human rights abuses. For example, the Nazis did not persist when large groups protested and refused to cooperate in Italy and Bulgaria. Despite potential effectiveness, however, bystanders rarely do more than oppose violence passively. The reluctance to act may stem from fear, a desire to believe that the government is always correct, and the tendency to conform with others. The last explanation is especially true in a repressive society, where people are exposed to only one point of view. The lack of any negative reaction from bystanders increases perpetrators' confidence in their activities, and thus encourages them to continue. Ervin Staub, *The Psychology of Perpetrators and Bystanders*, POL. PSYCHOL. 61 (1985).

6.   Compare Staub's view of "resistance" with that presented by Scott. Staub asserts that, although "bystanders" often remain passive in the face of oppression, public expressions of dissent to government violations can have a "tremendous influence" by raising doubts "in the minds of perpetrators." By the same token, he suggests that a diversity of views within a society increases the likelihood of resistance. Scott, however, urges that the ideology of a "dominating elite" is frequently rejected by the "dominated," and that diverse views persist beneath the surface of the official discourse. In addition, Scott outlines numerous ways governments may control, suppress, or discredit public expressions of dissent. Are these views

on the impact of resistance compatible? Under what circumstances can public opposition force a change in government practices?

7.   The complex relationships between ideology, social pressures, and the individual "conscience" are recurring themes in Hannah Arendt's coverage of the 1961 trial of Nazi leader Otto Eichmann. "As Eichmann told it," she writes, "the most potent factor in the soothing of his own conscience was the simple fact that he could see no one, no one at all, who actually was against the Final Solution." HANNAH ARENDT, EICHMANN IN JERUSALEM: A REPORT ON THE BANALITY OF EVIL 116 (1963). Was the lack of dissent among Eichmann's colleagues a result of unanimous complicity? What other factors might have caused the silence? Is it possible that some dissenting voices were simply not "heard" by government officials?

F.   SOCIOCULTURAL FACTORS

1.   Group Identity and Scapegoating

While the tendency toward aggression and violence may be partly genetic, it also stems from socialization. People naturally tend to divide the world into groups, based on even very minimal similarities. Ervin Staub has studied this tendency and its effects. He refers to the idea of preferring similar people as "ingrouping." People see others as similar and part of their "ingroup" or as a member of an "outgroup." For example, in one experiment subjects were told that they preferred one of two artists over the other. Subjects tended to admire others who favored the same artist more than those that favored the other.

Socialization contributes to the differentiation between groups, and further to the devaluation of individuals belonging to "outgroups." When the devaluation is then paired with certain conditions, such as derogatory labels by authority figures, it can cause people to commit acts of brutality. Devaluation leads to aggression, because groups of people are made to seem sub-human. Another sociological factor is the tendency to think of the world as fair, and therefore, that victims of brutality deserve to suffer. This idea of blameworthiness of victims further contributes to their devaluation.

Difficult life conditions can also lead to violent behavior. When people experience hard conditions, they tend to rely on ideologies for hope, or a belief in how the world should be. Hard times also lead to scapegoating, which means placing the blame for problems on a particular person or group. Normally, already devalued groups become scapegoats. Scapegoating provides an explanation for difficult conditions and reduces feelings of responsibility for problems. Difficult life conditions and ideologies can lead to massive violence against groups of people.

Staub uses Germany after World War I as an example of the devaluation of a particular outgroup. Jews had been devalued in German society for hundreds of years, and antisemitism was fostered in part because of conditions after World War I. Difficult conditions that existed for Germany then included political instability, poor economic conditions, and humiliation over the loss of the war. Hence, the conditions in Germany and the history of cultural and political antisemitism allowed Hitler's ideas to find support. Ervin Staub, *The Psychology of Perpetrators and Bystanders*, POL. PSYCHOL. 61 (1985).

In studies of the connection between religious beliefs and genocide, scholars have found that religious claims to exclusive truth have had a tendency to cause genocide, and have found many instances where massive killings have been perpetrated in the name of religious faith. Universalist religions, such as Christianity and Islam, declare that they are opposed to violence, yet their adherents have committed violent acts against some individuals opposed to their beliefs. For example, in the First Crusade of the 11th Century, Christians carried out massive killings against the Jews. Also, massacres have resulted from Christian proselytizing, which has nearly always accompanied colonization. Christians have also been the subjects of genocide, such as the Turkish attacks on the Christian Armenians in 1915-17. Those two groups had differences other than religion, but religion was definitely a factor in the conflict. Leonard B. Glick, *Religion and Genocide, in* THE WIDENING CIRCLE OF GENOCIDE 43-50, 52-56, 61 (Israel W. Charny ed., 1994) (Vol. 3 *in* GENOCIDE: A CRITICAL BIBLIOGRAPHIC REVIEW).

* * * * *

Philip Mayer, *Witches, in* WITCHCRAFT AND SORCERY 45-50, 53-58, 60-64 (Max Marwick ed., 1970) (footnotes omitted):

The idea of witchcraft . . . is not confined to any one set of peoples, but is distributed through many different races, cultures, and environments. It occurs among primitive peoples from Africa to the South Seas and from Asia to America. Its record among civilized peoples is only a little shorter. Everyone knows that Joan of Arc was a convicted witch. However, it is not always recalled that witches were still being burnt in Europe down to the age of the French Revolution. The last occasion was in 1782 in Switzerland. . . .

When one starts to think about witchcraft, common sense suggests the first question how it is that ideas so absurd, fantastic and often horrible have been so widely distributed in place and time. At the same time, since witchcraft ideas are widespread without being universal, one wants to account for their absence too. . . . One thing is clear: the witchcraft idea must be related to something real in human experience. Occurring at so many different times and places and cultural levels it cannot be lightly dismissed as a frill on the edge of human fantasy. . . . The kind of reality we are searching for is social and psychological. The witchcraft belief, and the persecution of witches, are a response to social and psychological strains. The more exactly we can identify those strains, the better we can hope to understand the response.

. . . I would suggest that the essence of the witchcraft idea is simply: People believe that the blame for some of their sufferings rests upon a peculiar evil power, embodied in certain individuals in their midst; although no material connexion can be empirically demonstrated between those individuals and the ills they are supposed to have caused. . . . The witch then is held to be a person in whom dwells a distinctive evilness, whereby he harms his own fellows in mysteriously secret ways. To this central mystical idea each society adds its own embellishments. . . .

[W]itchcraft myths nearly everywhere [consist of the following common elements]: First, the myth defines a category of persons who may be witches, and states how they can be recognized by particular signs. . . . Secondly, the myth tells what sorts of misfortune can be caused by witches. Often these include natural calamities such as death, sickness, drought or plague. . . . Thirdly, the myth states that witches turn against their own neighbours and kinsmen; they do not harm strangers or people from far away. . . . Fourthly, they work from envy, malice or spite, against individuals, rather than in pursuit of material gain as such. . . . Fifthly, witches always work in secret, and especially at night. . . . Sixthly, witches are not entirely human. Their evil power is . . . quite unlike ordinary ways of dealing injury such as force or poison. . . . Seventhly, witches reverse all normal standards. They particularly delight in 'unnatural' practices. . . . Lastly, witchcraft is always immoral. At best it is disapproved; at worst it inspires horror like other so-called unnatural practices. Witchcraft properly so-called cannot be justified. . . .

Even if some individuals do try to be witches, the witchcraft power itself is surely imaginary, but the power of the idea regularly inspires people to defence or counter-attack. . . . Let us start by distinguishing two broad categories of action against witches. These categories correspond to the two elements in the nature of the witch, who is non-human and yet human. In so far as the witchcraft power is non-human, one may try to nullify it by antidotes as mystical as itself. One may recite spells or wear amulets or put down medicines. This is a kind of duelling in the realm of fantasy, a duel between two equally imaginary forces. . . . But because the wielder of witch-power is also a human being, one may also try to evade or control him as a human being. . . .

When we consider all the activity that is directed against supposed witches, the question must be asked when or why people start going to all this trouble: what events or situations give them the impulse to start fighting this imaginary menace. . . . After all, many events and many situations regularly create anxiety, but not all of them bring the witchcraft idea into operation. Death and sickness, for instance, always create anxiety, but the emotion can often be dealt with by the ordinary responses. . . . The idea of witchcraft is invoked on occasions when these routine responses alone do not give emotional satisfaction. . . . [In addition, the] witch system can save other belief systems from being deluged with the blame which might otherwise often deservedly fall upon them. It gives a channel into which the blame can be turned more conveniently. [T]his helps one to assume that, but for witchcraft, all the wheels would always be turning smoothly. . . .

So far I have been discussing the witchcraft idea as a cosmological device, accounting for sufferings that people cannot or will not explain otherwise, and providing a pattern of action that the sufferer may follow when his misfortune makes him particularly uneasy. But the witchcraft idea has of course quite a different kind of social importance as well as this. It is a force in social relations; it is something that can break up a friendship or a marriage or a community; it is a banner under which people hate, denounce, and even kill one another. . . .

When we speak loosely of witches being tried or condemned we mean of course that individuals are being tried or condemned as witches. The witch does not exist in his own right; it is the judgement of society that creates him. Society creates the image of the witch, and pins this image down onto particular individuals. . . . Our question then is: In a given society, who is most likely to accuse whom?

. . . Two general rules seem to emerge from the literature. The first is that witches and their accusers are nearly always people close together, belonging to one neighbourhood community or even to one household. . . . The second rule is that a witchcraft accusation nearly always grows out of some personal antipathy or hostile emotion. . . .

When someone starts to argue that someone else is bewitching him, this notion may serve to bring to a head the tensions and strains of their relationship. . . . There is no law under which you can denounce a person for being personally distasteful to you, but you can denounce him on grounds of witchcraft. The witch idea then is a device that enables people to dress up their animosities in an actionable guise. . . .

It has been observed . . . that people accuse one another of witchcraft when they are prohibited from expressing their aggression in other ways such as physical brawling or going to law. . . . I would qualify this by adding that people who have both possibilities may still prefer to accuse each other of witchcraft . . . because the witchcraft case has a different objective. Legal cases . . . are usually meant to smooth out relationships by patching up quarrels over specific issues. However, . . . the parties to a witchcraft case probably do not want to be reconciled. What they want is an excuse for rupture. In a witchcraft case the thing at stake is not a specific legal issue but the whole tone of the relationship.

It is an extremely important question what kinds of sanction are used against a witch: when will the suspect be only pursued as a private enemy by his self-styled victim, and when will he be hounded down as a public enemy by community or state? For this largely determines the degree of danger to life and liberty. . . . Since the accusation of witchcraft can be such a dangerous weapon, we have to enquire what safeguards there are against its being used too freely. We all feel that a society that gives excessive prominence to witchcraft must be a sick society. . . . This is confirmed by anthropological studies which in several cases have shown an increase of witchcraft phenomena in communities undergoing social breakdown. . . .

The figure of the witch . . . embodies those characteristics that society specially disapproves. . . . The witch myth then recognizes an opposition of moral values. . . . However, I think that another or a more particular kind of opposition is also vitally involved. I mean the opposition between 'us' and 'them', between in-group and out-group, between allies and foes. The witch is the figure of a person who has turned traitor to his own group. . . . As we have seen, the witch is conceived as a person within one's own local community. . . . All human societies require a basic loyalty between members. . . . Injury to one should be felt as injury to all. But the witch is conceived as a person who withholds this elementary loyalty and secretly pursues opposed interests. . . . [Nor does he] come from outside like a raider; he dwells within the group and destroys by stealth. The witch is the hidden enemy within the gate. . . .

In the light of this principle we understand why the witch is regarded as not altogether human. . . . The person who denies those basic loyalties to family and community outrages the sentiments, on which all social life must rest. . . . Further, we understand why witchcraft is always secret, and always associated with the night. The witch is essentially a hidden enemy but an apparent friend. . . . Above all, we understand why witchcraft is treated as a criminal offence, even in those primitive societies where criminal sanctions otherwise hardly exist. By his treason the witch has forfeited his rights as a member of the in-group; he has outlawed himself; he has pursued the interests of an enemy; then let him be treated like an enemy, killed or put to flight. . . . I think that the same principle helps to some extent to explain how society chooses the individuals who fill the role of witches. The disloyal person will be sought among those who have failed to give public demonstrations of their loyalty. . . .

What I have been saying relates to the witches of primitive society, but I think it applies equally well to certain phenomena of the civilized world. For we too are often found in situations where our basic values and basic loyalties seem threatened; and we too are apt to seek out the enemies within our gates. . . . In civilized societies other demands for over-riding loyalties have been added to those of the family and community. We are divided not only into groups but also into parties. . . . Civilization still has its witches, but it is more apt to call them traitors to a cause, or an idea, or a way of life. . . .

A society in order to feel secure must feel that not only its material interests but also its way of life, its fundamental values, are safe. Witch-hunting may increase whenever either of these elements seems gravely threatened. Among primitive peoples, as we have seen, an increase in witch-hunting is apt to occur both when natural disasters threaten their material interests, and when culture contact threatens their way of life. If witch-hunting is a reaction to a society's feeling of insecurity, it seems unlikely to disappear from the civilized world at present, unless we can remove the radical feeling of insecurity which haunts our nations today.

*   *   *   *   *

ROBERT JAY LIFTON, *Genocide, in* THE NAZI DOCTORS: MEDICAL KILLING AND THE PSYCHOLOGY OF GENOCIDE 476-80 (1986):

Genocide requires both a specific victim group and certain relationships to that group. While their biological focus enabled the Nazis to extend their genocidal efforts to Gypsies, Russians, and Poles, the Jews remained the central target and the most specific psychological victim of the Nazi genocidal dynamic.

Nazi perpetrators had to see their victims as posing absolute danger, as "infecting" the "German national body," and as (in the last three words of Hitler's testament) "deadly Jewish poison." Similarly, *"Kultur*-poisoning Jews" were infiltrating the art world, and the general danger of "inner Judaization" and "racial pollution" was perceived as a fundamental threat to German biological and biosocial continuity and immortality. . . . Where the threat is so absolute and so ultimate— where the struggle becomes "fighting between humans and subhumans," in Himmler's phrase—genocide becomes not only appropriate but an urgent necessity. . . . Once that genocidal necessity is established, perpetrators can take the more casual tone of Himmler's suggestion that "anti-Semitism is exactly the same as delousing." . . .

The situation begins with Jews having not just integrated themselves into modern German culture but having helped to shape it, so that as . . . Jews gained intellectual respect . . ., they were viewed in another corner of the German mind as "upstarts . . . sons and grandsons of the ghetto," as a fundamentally alien people all the more threatening because of the depth of the their apparent cultural integration. . . .

Martin Luther . . . was first a defender of the Jews whom he wished to become "of one heart with us." But when they failed to convert and become part of the Christian-Protestant-German spiritual and biological community, he denounced them as "children of the Devil" who "being foreigners, should possess nothing," and were, moreover, profoundly dangerous. . . . To be sure, Luther stood for much else, including the internalization of conscience. . . . But that very achievement deepened the psychological power of his anti-Semitic message. . . . Thus perceived as an absolute threat to the continuous life of one's own people, the victimized group is seen as the bearer of death and therefore the embodiment of evil. More than merely nonhuman or heathen, it is dangerously anti-man and anti-God. . . .

NOTES AND QUESTIONS

Numerous ethnographic studies of witchcraft accusations in pre-industrialized societies have found that the class of persons defined as "witches" often represents an "outside" group which has moved into the community at some point in the past. Similarly, in many societies accusations of witchcraft are most frequently made against one's in-laws. Here, too, the persons most likely to be singled out are members of an "outside" group who have become connected to one's own kin through marriage. In both situations, tensions between groups may be exacerbated if the "out-group" is perceived as having gained some political or economic advantage over one's own group. *See* JOEL. C. KUIPERS, POWER IN PERFORMANCE: THE CREATION OF TEXTUAL AUTHORITY IN WEYEWA RITUAL SPEECH 53 (1990). What role did the "success" of Germany's Jews play in their eventual persecution? Would history have turned out any differently had the Jews occupied a lower position in social, economic, and cultural life? Do human rights violations which target a particular group vary in degree or kind depending on that group's status in the society?

---

2. Change, Uncertainty and Political Manipulation

J.R. CRAWFORD, WITCHCRAFT AND SORCERY IN RHODESIA 280-81, 290 (1967) (citations omitted):

[T]here can be no doubt that [wizardry accusations] can be used as a means of manipulating public opinion. . . . Malice can be expressed as an allegation of wizardry and will find credence if the person against whom hostility is expressed is unpopular, particularly if he has also acted in an unusual manner. It is thus easy to marshal public opinion against the social non-conformist. . . . Whether or not one's friends will believe what they are told will depend in part on whether other people want to believe the accusation and whether reasonable grounds for suspicion exist. . . . A person is most likely to dislike persons who are sexually, economically or politically in competition with him and the accusation of wizardry affords a technique for marshalling public opinion against the rival. . . . An allegation of wizardry is, therefore, an appeal to the moral feelings of the community in an attempt to involve the community emotionally in a certain state of affairs. The reasons for making the appeal depend on the person making it and the events of the moment. . . .

The use of the allegation of wizardry as a device for directing public opinion against a person is particularly obvious in a struggle for political power within a community in which each contestant tries to involve as many persons as possible in the dispute and get them on his side. The weapon is, of course, a two-edged weapon and is as useful in securing the retention of power in the face of a challenge as in securing the advantage of a person seeking to challenge the established power. . . .

* * * * *

H. R. Trevor-Roper, *The European Witch-Craze, in* WITCHCRAFT AND SORCERY 121, 131-33, 141-44 (Max Marwick ed., 1970) (footnotes and citations omitted):

[I]f we look at the revival of the witch-craze in the 1560s in its context, we see that it is not the product either of Protestantism or of Catholicism, but of both: or rather, of their conflict. Just as the medieval [Catholic] Dominican evangelist had ascribed witch-beliefs to the whole society which resisted them, so both the Protestant and Catholic evangelists of the mid-sixteenth century ascribed the same beliefs to the societies which opposed them. The [reemergence] of the absurd demonology . . . was not the logical consequence of any religious idea: it was the social consequence of renewed ideological war and the accompanying climate of fear. . . . The frontal opposition of Catholics and Protestants, representing two forms of society incompatible with each other, sent men back to the old dualism of God and the Devil and the hideous reservoir of hatred, which seemed to be drying up, was suddenly refilled. . . .

[That] the witch-craze in the 1560s was directly connected with the return of religious war is clear. It can be shown from geography: every major outbreak is in the frontier-area where religious strife is not intellectual, a dissent of opinion, but social, the dissidence of a society. . . . The persecution in England was sharpest in Essex and in Lancashire—two counties where Catholicism was strong and the Puritan evangelists particularly energetic. The Scottish Calvinists, when they obtained their witch-law, were similarly declaring war on Catholic society. Germany and Switzerland were also countries where the two religions faced each other in sharp social opposition: in Germany the persecution remained most persistent in Westphalia, the seat of medieval heresy and sixteenth-century Anabaptism, while in Switzerland the Calvinist cities made war on the obstinate peasantry of the country. In France the geographical antithesis was no less clear. [In] the Wars of Religion the Protestant south opposed the Catholic north. . . .

The same connection can be shown from chronology. The [persecutions of] the 1560s marks the period of Protestant evangelism. Thereafter almost every local outbreak can be related to the aggression of one religion upon the other. The Wars of Religion introduce the worst period of witch-persecution in French history. The outbreak in the Basque country in 1609 heralds the Catholic reconquest . . .. The terrible outbreaks in Germany, in Flanders and the Rhineland in the 1590s, and again in 1627-9, mark the stages of Catholic reconquest. . . .

[T]he witch-craze was created out of a social situation. In its expansive period, in the thirteenth century, the 'feudal' society of Christian Europe came into conflict with social groups which it could not assimilate, and whose defence of their own identity was seen, at first, as 'heresy'. . . . The medieval Church, as the spiritual organ of 'feudal' society, declared war on these 'heresies', and the friars, who waged that war, defined both orthodoxy and heresy in the process. . . .

Such, it seems, was the origin of the system. It was perfected in the course of a local struggle and it had, at first, a local application. . . . And in the fourteenth century, . . . among the miseries of the Black Death and the Hundred Years War in France, its application was made general. . . . The weapon forged for use against nonconformist societies was taken up to destroy nonconformist individuals. . . . Like the Jew, the witch became the stereotype of the incurable nonconformist; and in the declining Middle Ages, the two were joined as scapegoats for the ills of society. The founding of the Spanish Inquisition, which empowered the 'Catholic Kings' to destroy 'judaism' in Spain, and the issue of the Witch Bull, which urged cities and princes to destroy witches in Germany, can be seen as two stages in one campaign. . . .

The Reformation is sometimes seen as a progressive movement. No doubt it began as such: for it began in humanism. But in the years of struggle, of ideological wars, humanism was soon crushed out. . . . With the Catholic reconquest a generation later, the same pattern repeats itself. The Catholic missionaries too discover obstinate resistance. They too find it social as well as individual. . . . They too describe it now as Protestant heresy, now as witchcraft. . . .

Such, it seems, is the progress of the witch-craze as a social movement. But it is not only a social movement. From its social basis it also has its individual extension. It can be extended deliberately, in times of political crisis, as a political device, to destroy powerful enemies or dangerous persons. . . . It can also be extended blindly, in times of panic, by its own momentum. When a 'great fear' takes hold of a society, that society looks naturally to the stereotype of the enemy in its midst;

and once the witch had become the stereotype, witchcraft would be the universal accusation. . . .

* * * * *

Joyce Bednarski, *The Salem Witch-Scare Viewed Sociologically,* in WITCHCRAFT AND SORCERY 151, 153-60 (Max Marwick ed., 1970) (citations omitted):

The Salem witch-scare began quietly and gradually in the home of the Reverend Samuel Parris, minister in the local church. Several of the young girls of the village had taken a liking to listening to Parris's colored domestic servant, Tituba, tell stories of the supernatural which she had learned in the Barbados. They were enthralled by the excitement of her tales of witches, curses and spells, and began to spend more and more time at her feet listening to these accounts. . . .

By the end of the winter, several of the children began to suffer from a strange malady. They would, for no apparent reason, fall into convulsions, scream inhumanly, and engage in other extraordinary behavior. As their malady became public knowledge, more and more of the village children succumbed to it. . . . [Eventually] Dr. Griggs, the town physician, was called in. He tried all his remedies; he reread all of his medical books, but to no avail. Finally he admitted that the affliction of these children was outside the realm of medicine; his considered opinion was that they were bewitched. Given the stage of medical knowledge at that time, this was not an unreasonable assumption.

The problem was passed on to the spiritual mentors of the community. [Reverend] Parris. . .called together ministers from the neighboring area to decide what should be done. After witnessing the girls' contortions, the clergy agreed that Satan had come to Salem; and the only recourse was immediate action; the children would have to identify the witches who were harassing them. . . .

The character and background of those they named are significant. The first was Tituba, an obvious choice because of her vast knowledge of the 'art' and her cultural alienation from the community. The second, Sarah Good, was the town hag; a pipe-smoking tramp who wandered over the countryside begging from everyone and cursing those who refused her. Hated and disdained by all the upright Salemites, she was a prime target. The third, Sarah Osbourne, was of high status, but her reputation was tainted by the scandal that she had lived with a man nearly a year before marrying him. To the Puritan mind, this was among the worst of sins. Besides, she had not attended church in fourteen months, and that was judged as a further sign of her degeneracy and involvement with the forces of evil.

[I]t was the hearings at which the three accused women were examined that produced the snowballing effect which was to follow. . . . The children were in attendance at the hearings, where they made their presence known by crying out and rolling on the floor in agony. Everyone assumed that the women on trial were responsible for their suffering. . . . [After the hearing,] people began to look around for . . . additional witches . . .; the girls' status was elevated. . . . Indeed, once one had become one of the 'diviners', there was virtually no way out. This fact is exemplified by the case of Mary Warren who tried to renounce her accusations. . . . Not only would no one listen to her, but several of the girls intimated that Mary had finally succumbed to the power of the Devil and was trying to undermine the forces of good working against him. So, within a short time, Mary 'repented' and returned to the fold.

After the initial hearings, accusations fell like raindrops. . . . Barely a week had passed when another accusation was made, this time . . . of an upstanding and pious member of the community—Martha Cory. Hers was followed by Dorcas Good, the five-year-old daughter of Sarah Good, and of Rebecca Nurse and her two sisters, . . . three of the most saintly and respected members of the Church. And so it went [with the naming of still others]—most of whom had previously been considered fine, God-fearing members of the community. The county jail was bursting at its seams, and the list of upcoming trials grew to an unprecedented length. . . . The hysteria had run wild. By spring, it no longer confined itself to Salem, but spread to Andover and other surrounding towns. . . .

It was over less than a year after it began, but in the course of that time nineteen persons had been hanged, two had died in prison, and [another], who had adopted the course of standing mute at his trial, had been crushed under a pile of rocks (a persuasive procedure used by the magistrates to induce confession)—a grand total of twenty-two lives sacrificed. . . .

What were the conditions which caused the Salem witch-scare? Broadly speaking, most writers will agree that scares and crazes arise during a time of struggle, upheaval and change. In an era of uncertainty men will act and react in extraordinary ways. . . . At best, the political situation [in the Bay Colony] in 1690 could be described as uncertain. . . . In 1676, Charles II began to review property claims; in 1679, he ordered Massachusetts to allow the establishment of an Anglican Church (hitherto outlawed by the colonists). [I]n 1686 James revoked the [Colony's] Charter and sent a Royal Governor named Andros (both an Anglican and a disdainer of colonial self-assertion) to govern the Colony. In 1689, Bostonians revolted and imprisoned Andros. . . .

Meanwhile, Increase Mather had gone to England in 1688 to negotiate for the reinstitution of the Charter. He returned home in 1692 with a new charter instead, some of the provisions of which would make the colonists very unhappy. Indeed, they had already gotten wind of the bad news, for two of Mather's fellow delegates had refused to accept the new charter and had sailed home early to warn the populace and denounce Mather. The change which incensed them stated that the electorate was no longer to be limited to [Puritans], but broadened to include propertied members of every Christian sect except Catholics. This provision was a considerable blow to the Puritan political theocracy: previously, law had ensured that the elect [the Puritans] would remain in power, regardless of their numbers. With the new ruling, there was a strong possibility that the damned would rule. . . . Furthermore, William [of Orange, who had overthrown King James,] insisted that he name the governors of the Commonwealth, a bitter pill for the colonists to swallow, since they had been electing their own governors since the founding of the Colony more than fifty years before. . . .

The crisis in the political sphere was paralleled by one in the religious-moral realm. . . . The 'Puritan ethic' was undergoing a metamorphosis, too. But its upheaval was not the action of an outside force, as was the political change; its destruction came from within. . . . After fifty years in the New World, the Colonial Puritans had lost most of their meaningful contacts with the outside world, and no longer looked forward to a worldwide communion of the elect. The sense of mission which had sustained the sect in its infancy was gone. . . . Furthermore, the Puritan[s] had learned to accept tragedy and failure as God's will. However, by the 1690s, they saw all around them nothing but progress. Man had worked, and what he had produced was good. Where effort was put forth, progress had been made. . . . And so the people began to move from a reliance on fate to a confidence in man's ability.

This idea was not congruent with the original Puritan belief in predestination and was thus another rent in the fabric of the Puritan ethic.

Still another factor which undermined the stability of the society . . .. When the settlers landed in America, they were a body united against the evil world. . . . Now these adversaries had been overcome. The Indians and the wild beasts had retreated with the frontier—and Massachusetts was no longer the frontier. Even their righteous opposition to those who did not profess the 'True Faith' was taken away from them when the decree of 1679 ordered religious toleration (at least for Anglicans) in the Bay Colony. [T]here seemed to be no purpose for unity among the Puritans by 1690. And so the people grew away from their neighbors. Feelings of distrust and suspicion built up within the community because there was no effective avenue for channeling them toward an outside enemy.

*   *   *   *   *

A. Rebecca Cardozo, *A Modern American Witch-Craze, in* WITCHCRAFT AND SORCERY 369-70, 373-76 (Max Marwick ed., 1970) (Abridged version of A. Rebecca Cardozo, *Witches: Old and New*, 1968, original MS.) (footnotes and citations omitted):

Common Features of Crazes

In an atmosphere of confusion and uncertainty, people become intolerant toward change; and it is primarily social, political and religious intolerance that provides the initial impetus for a [witch] craze. . . . [Anthropologist] Malinowski describes this tendency as universally human and persistent. It permits the concentration of blame and hatred to fall 'on certain clearly defined groups suspected of causing evils for which one otherwise would have to blame all the members of the community, its government, the decrees of destiny, or other elements against which immediate reaction is not possible.' . . . The perpetuation of the hysteria associated with a craze can be accounted for in a number of ways. The mythological 'truths' stating the nature of the threatening enemy are disseminated throughout society and passed to succeeding generations in the language of local folklore. In modern times, the Press serves a similar purpose. However, it is fear itself that is primarily responsible for perpetuating a craze. Fear suppresses open dissent and resistance in the midst of widespread hysteria. Skeptics, in speaking out against the persecutors, risk their own persecution. . . . Resistance easily leads to guilt-by-association. . . .

McCarthyism: 1950-1954

The United States in 1950 was hardly Europe in the late Middle Ages. But the causes, development, consequences and decline of McCarthyism closely resemble those of the European witch-craze. Political intolerance provided the initial impetus for the movement. To America and her allies in the 1950s, the threat of Communist infiltration was a mysterious but very real threat. At the time, very little was understood about the Communist movement, its tactics and its direction, and fear of it was considerable.

McCarthyism was possible because of this fear and ignorance of Communism. However, Joe McCarthy's initial reason for seeking out the 'Communists in government' was hardly as patriotic as it sounded. Actually, his own political ambitions prompted his first accusations. . . . His first attack on these 'enemies of the people' came on 9 February 1950, when, in a speech in Wheeling, West Virginia, he told the people: 'I have here in my hand a list of 205 names that were made known to the Secretary of State . . . as being members of the Communist Party and who nevertheless are still working and shaping policy in the State Department.' He made similar accusations on the floor of the Senate a few days later. . . .

A Senate committee was appointed in February of 1950 to investigate the charges being made by McCarthy. . . . The 'Tydings Committee' called in the State Department to testify to the validity of the charges against its employees. Out of approximately eighty-one cases investigated, not one of the accused was proved to be a Communist. In effect, the members of the Committee were disgusted with McCarthy and his unfounded accusations. . . .

But McCarthy continued his search for Communists in government. And he was given the chance again to have the charges investigated by another Senate Committee. This time the chairman of the Sub-Committee on Internal Security was Pat McCarran, friend and supporter of McCarthy. . . . The McCarran hearings also failed to prove the existence of card-carrying Communists in the government. Yet, in spite of the findings of the Committee, McCarthyism endured. [Other Senators] believed McCarthy could in some way determine their political futures, particularly if they openly criticized his tactics. Tydings had spoken out against McCarthy; and, in the 1952 election campaign, McCarthy set out to discredit Tydings and ensure his defeat. Tydings, who had been in the Senate for many terms, was defeated; and many other Senators attributed his defeat to McCarthy. Even by 1954, McCarthy was still considered powerful. . . .

. . . It is now thought that McCarthy's influence on the electorate was considerably less than believed at the time; and that the defeat of several of McCarthy's enemies can be attributed as easily to the Eisenhower landslide as to McCarthy. But the Senators' fears nevertheless greatly suppressed open opposition to McCarthy, and their timid behavior, as well as that of influential members of society, directly aided in perpetuating McCarthyism.

The Press was also a vital force in helping McCarthyism to endure. Newspapers played up McCarthy's accusations in big headlines. . . . More importantly, newsmen and editors also feared the Senator. A news article critical of McCarthy's efforts could leave the author wide open to accusation. . . . Thus, what could have been a vital force against McCarthyism turned out as a force in his favor. . . . Of course many people did believe that the Senator was doing the ultimate good for America; and, following news reports of his campaign against traitors, money poured into his office. Indirectly, the Press was indeed an agent in McCarthy's favor, that is, until some newspapers regained their courage and openly condemned 'the hunt'.

Finally, in 1952, some Senators took a forceful stand against McCarthy. Senator Hubert Humphrey was one of these. After declaring that accusing people and demanding that they prove their innocence was 'Anglo-Saxon jurisprudence upside down', he added: 'I think it is time we stated that we are not going to let people be ruined, their reputations destroyed, and their names defiled because we happen to be in the great game of American politics.' . . . The United States Senate had regained its courage. For many [Americans], their renewed courage was too late in coming. . . .

But the final assault against McCarthy was testimony to Americans' faith in the due process of law. In July 1954, Senator Flanders introduced a resolution to censure Senator Joseph McCarthy. Hearings followed to investigate the charges against him; and, on 22 December 1954, following recommendations by the Investigating Committee, McCarthy was censured by the Senate on two of the original five charges, one, for 'contempt of the Senate or Senatorial Committee, and two, for

ridiculing a witness in a hearing and for violating certain rules of that committee.'
. . . Censure destroyed McCarthy, and with him the era of McCarthyism. He became
a thoroughly dejected man and died three years later. . . .

<hr>

NOTES AND QUESTIONS

Based on material in chapter 8, *supra*, were there similar factors underlying the genocide
in Rwanda? Did those factors also play a role in the former Yugoslavia, chapter 12, *supra*?

<hr>

G. ADDITIONAL READINGS

1. General Research on Human Rights Violations

CONTEMPORARY GENOCIDES, CAUSES, CASES, CONSEQUENCES (A.J. Jongman ed.,
1996).

HUMAN RIGHTS AND STATISTICS: GETTING THE RECORD STRAIGHT (Thomas B. Jabine & Richard P. Claude eds.) (Philadelphia: University of Pennsylvania, 1992).

John F. McCamant, *A Critique of Present Measures of Human Rights Develop-
ment and an Alternative, in* GLOBAL HUMAN RIGHTS: PUBLIC POLICIES, COMPARATIVE
MEASURES, AND NGO STRATEGIES (Ved P. Nanda, James R. Scarrit, & George W.
Shepard eds., 1981) (Boulder, CO: Westview).

POPULATION CRISIS COMMITTEE, INTERNATIONAL HUMAN SUFFERING INDEX (Washington: PCC, 1987).

ALEX P. SCHMID, RESEARCH ON GROSS HUMAN RIGHTS VIOLATIONS: A PROGRAMME
(2d ed. 1989); WHITHER REFUGEE? HUMAN RIGHTS VIOLATIONS AND REFUGEES: CAUSES
AND CONSEQUENCES, PROCEEDINGS OF PIOOM SYMPOSIUM OF JUNE 17, 1994 (1996).

Michael Stohl, David Carleton, George Lopez & Stephen Samuels, *State Violations of Human Rights: Issues and Problems of Measurement*, 8 HUM. RTS. Q. 592-
606 (1986).

2. Economic & Political Factors

a) Economic Development

DEPENDENCE, DEVELOPMENT, AND STATE REPRESSION (GeorgeA. Lopez & Michael
Stohl eds.) (New York: Greenwood Press, 1989).

Albert O. Hirschman, *The On-and-Off Connection Between Political and Economic Progress*, AMER. ECON. REV. 343-49 (May 1994).

Evelyn Hubner, Dietrich Ruessemeyer & John D. Stephens, *The Impact of Economic Development on Democracy*, 7(3) J. ECON. PERSPECTIVES 71-86 (Summer 1993).

Edward N. Muller, *Income Inequality, Regime Repressiveness, and Political Violence*, 50 AMER. SOC. REV. 47-61 (1985).

Mancur Olson, *Rapid Growth as a Destabilizing Force*, 23 J. ECON. HIST. 529-52
(1963).

Zehra F. Arat, *Some Characteristics of Modernization, in* THE POLITICS OF MODERNIZATION (1965) (Chicago: Chicago University Press); *Democracy and Economic Development—Modernization Theory Revisited*, COMPARATIVE POLITICS 21-36 (October 1988); DEMOCRACY AND HUMAN RIGHTS IN DEVELOPING COUNTRIES (Boulder & London: Lynne Rienner, 1991).

b) Political Theories

Kenneth A. Bollen, *Issues in the Comparative Measurement of Political Democracy*, 45 AMER. SOC. REV. 370-90 (1980); *Political Rights and Political Liberties in Nations: An Evaluation of Human Rights Measures, 1950-1984, in* 8 HUM. RTS. Q. 576-91 (1986); *Liberal Democracy: Validity and Method Factors in Cross-National Measures*, 37 AMER. J. POL. SCI. 1207-30 (1993).

DEMOCRACY: A WORLDWIDE SURVEY (Robert Wesson ed.) (New York: Praeger, 1987).

LARRY DIAMOND, JUAN J. LINZ & SEYMOUR MARTIN LIPSET, POLITICS IN DEVELOPING COUNTRIES: COMPARING EXPERIENCES WITH DEMOCRACY (Boulder, CO: Lynne Rienner Publishers, 1990).

Raymond Gastil, *The Comparative Survey of Freedom: Experiences and Suggestions*, 25 STUD. COMP. INT'L DEV. 25-50 (1990).

Ted Robert Gurr, *The Political Origins of State Violence and Terror: A Theoretical Analysis, in* GOVERNMENT VIOLENCE AND REPRESSION: AN AGENDA FOR RESEARCH (Michael Stohl & George A. Lopez eds.) (Westport, CT: Greenwood, 1986).

DOUGLAS A. HIBBS, JR., MASS POLITICAL VIOLENCE: A CROSS-NATIONAL CAUSAL ANALYSIS (New York: Wiley, 1973).

Seymour Martin Lipset, *Some Social Requisites of Democracy: Economic Development and Political Legitimacy*, 53 AMER. POL. SCI. REV. 69-105 (1959).

HAROLD. L. NIEBURG, POLITICAL VIOLENCE: THE BEHAVIORAL PROCESS (NewYork: St. Martin's Press, 1969).

ABBAS POULGERAMI, DEVELOPMENT AND DEMOCRACY IN THE THIRD WORLD (Boulder, CO: Westview Press, 1991).

Rudolph. J. Rummel, *Libertarianism and International Violence*, 27 J. CONFLICT RESOL. 27-71 (1983).

TATU VANHANEN, THE PROCESS OF DEMOCRATIZATION: A COMPARATIVE STUDY OF 147 STATES, 1980-88 (New York: Crane Russak, 1990).

EDUARD A. ZIEGENHAGEN, THE REGULATION OF POLITICAL CONFLICT (New York: Praeger, 1986).

c) Military Expansion & Conflict

PATRICK BROGAN, THE FIGHTING NEVER STOPPED: A COMPREHENSIVE GUIDE TO WORLD CONFLICT SINCE 1945 (New York: Vintage Books, 1990).

SAMUEL P. HUNTINGTON, THE SOLDIER AND THE STATE: THE THEORY AND POLITICS OF CIVIL-MILITARY RELATIONS (New York: Vintage Books, 1964); *Civilian Control of the Military: A Theoretical Statement, in* POLITICAL BEHAVIOR: A READER IN THEORY AND RESEARCH (H. Eulau, S. Eldersveld & M. Janowitz eds.) (New York: Free Press, 1956).

ROSEMARY H.T. O'KANE, THE LIKELIHOOD OF COUPS (Brookfield, VT: Gower, 1987).

GUY J. PAUKER, THE INDONESIAN DOCTRINE OF TERRITORIAL WARFARE AND TERRITO-RIAL MANAGEMENT (Santa Monica: RAND Corporation, RM-3312-PR, November 1963).

MELVIN SMALL & J. DAVID SINGER, RESORT TO ARMS: INTERNATIONAL AND CIVIL WARS, 1816-1980 (Beverly Hills: Sage, 1982).

ALFRED STEPAN, THE MILITARY IN POLITICS: CHANGING PATTERNS IN BRAZIL (Princeton: Princeton University Press, 1971).

JOHN. G. STOESSINGER, WHY NATIONS GO TO WAR (New York: St. Martin's Press, 1982).

Michael Stohl, *War and Domestic Violence: The Case of the United States, 1890-1970*, 19 J. CONFLICT RESOL. 379-416 (1975); WAR AND DOMESTIC POLITICAL VIOLENCE: THE AMERICAN CAPACITY FOR REPRESSION AND REACTION (Beverly Hills: Sage, 1976); *The Nexus of Civil and International Conflict*, in THE HANDBOOK OF POLITICAL CON-FLICT: THEORY AND RESEARCH (Ted Robert Gurr ed.) (New York: Free Press, 1980).

d)   U.S. Foreign Policy

David Carleton & Michael Stohl, *The Role of Human Rights in U.S. ForeignAssis-tance Policy*, 31 AMER. J. POL. SCI. 1002-18 (1987).

David L. Cingranelli & Thomas Pasquarello, *Human Rights Practices and the U.S. Distribution of Foreign Aid to Latin American Countries*, 29 AMER. J. POL. SCI. 539-63 (1985).

MICHAEL T. KLARE, WAR WITHOUT END: AMERICAN PLANNING FOR THE NEXT VIET-NAMS (1972).

JAMES M. MCCORMICK, AMERICAN FOREIGN POLICY AND AMERICAN VALUES (Itasca, IL: F.E. Peacock Publishers, 1985).

Edward N. Muller, *Dependent Economic Development, Aid Dependence on the United States, and Democratic Breakdown in the Third World*, INT'L STUD. Q. 29 (1985).

Steven C. Poe, *Human Rights and Foreign Aid: A Review of Quantitative Re-search and Prescriptions for Future Research*, 12 HUM. RTS. Q. 499-512 (1990); *Human Rights and the Allocation of U.S. Military Assistance*, 28 J. PEACE RES. 205-16 (1991).

Steven C. Poe & Rangsima Sirirangsi, *Human Rights and U.S. Economic Aid to Africa*, 18(4) INT'L INTERACTIONS 1-14 (1993).

Lars Schoultz, *U.S. Foreign Policy and Human Rights*, 13 COMP. POL. 149-70 (1980).

Kathryn Sikkink, *The Power of Principled Ideas: Human Rights Policies in the United States and Western Europe*, in IDEAS AND FOREIGN POLICY 139 (Ithaca: Cornell University Press, 1993).

Michael Stohl & David Carleton, *The Foreign Policy of Human Rights: Rhetoric and Reality from Jimmy Carter to Ronald Reagan*, 7 HUM. RTS. Q. 205-29 (1985).

Michael Stohl, David Carleton & Steven E. Johnson, *Human Rights and U.S. Foreign Assistance: From Nixon to Carter*, 21 J. PEACE RES. 215-26 (1984).

3. Sociocultural & psychological factors

a) Ingrouping & Outgrouping

J. Mack, *Nationalism and the Self*, 2 PSYCHOANALYTIC REV. 47-69 (1983). C. A. Pinderhughes, *Differential Bonding: Toward a Psychophysiological Theory of Stereotyping*, 136 AMER. J. PSYCHIATRY 33-37 (1979).

b) Obedience & Group Conformity

Stanley Milgram, *Behavioral Study of Obedience*, 67 J. ABNORMAL SOC. PSYCHOL. 371-78 (1963).

S. Davidson, *Group Formation and its Significance in the Nazi Concentration Camps*, 22 ISRAELI J. PSYCHIATRY & RELATED SCI. 41-50 (1985).

c) Sociological Aspects of Political Power

SAMUEL P. HUNTINGTON, POLITICAL ORDER IN CHANGING SOCIETIES (1968).

GERHARD LENSKI, POWER AND PRIVILEGE: A THEORY OF SOCIAL STRATIFICATION (New York: McGraw Hill, 1966).

THEDA SKOCPOL, STATES AND SOCIAL REVOLUTIONS: A COMPARATIVE ANALYSIS OF FRANCE, RUSSIA, AND CHINA (London: Cambridge University Press, 1979).

CHARLES TILLY, FROM MOBILIZATION TO REVOLUTION (Reading, MA: Addison-Wesley, 1978).

d) Socialization to Violence & War

CRIMES OF WAR: A LEGAL, POLITICAL-DOCUMENTARY, AND PSYCHOLOGICAL INQUIRY INTO THE RESPONSIBILITY OF LEADERS, CITIZENS, AND SOLDIERS FOR CRIMINAL ACTS IN WARS (Richard A. Falk et al. eds., 1971).

M. Deutsch, *The Prevention of World War III: A PsychologicalPerspective*, 4 POL. PSYCHOL. 3-31 (1983).

ROBERT J. LIFTON, HOME FROM THE WAR: LEARNING FROM VIETNAM VETERANS (1991).

PSYCHOLOGY AND THE PREVENTION OF NUCLEAR WAR: A BOOK OF READINGS (R. K. White ed.) (New York: New York University Press, 1986).

Kenneth Quinn, *Explaining the Terror, in* CAMBODIA 1975-1978: RENDEZVOUS WITH DEATH (Karl Jackson ed.) (Princeton: Princeton University Press, 1989).

Ervin Staub, *The Learning and Unlearning of Aggression: The Role of Anxiety, Empathy, Efficacy and Prosocial Values, in* THE CONTROL OF AGGRESSION AND VIOLENCE: COGNITIVE AND PHYSIOLOGICAL FACTORS (J. Singer ed.) (New York: Academic Press, 1971).

RALPH K. WHITE, FEARFUL WARRIORS: A PSYCHOLOGICAL PROFILE OF U.S.–SOVIET RELATIONS (New York: Free Press, 1984).

e) Torture—Effects on Victims

SIDNEY BLOCH & PETER REDDEWAY, SOVIET PSYCHIATRIC ABUSE: THE SHADOW OVER WORLD PSYCHIATRY (London: Victor Gollancz, 1984).

THE POLITICS OF PAIN, TORTURERS AND THEIR MASTERS (Ronald D. Crelinsten & Alex P. Schmid eds.) (Boulder: Westview Press, 1994).

PSYCHOLOGY AND TORTURE (Peter Suedfeld ed. 1990).

ERIC STOVER & ELEANOR O. NIGHTINGALE, THE BREAKING OF BODIES AND MINDS: TORTURE, PSYCHIATRIC ABUSE AND THE HEALTH PROFESSIONS (New York: W.H. Freeman, 1985).

4. Violations of Human Rights in Latin America

AUTHORITARIAN BRAZIL (A. Stepan ed.) (New Haven, CT: Yale UniversityPress, 1973).

FERNANDO CARDOSO AND ENZO FELETTO, DEPENDENCY AND DEVELOPMENT IN LATIN AMERICA (Berkeley: University of California Press, 1979).

David Cingranelli & Thomas Pasquarello, *Human Rights Practices and the Distribution of U.S. Foreign Aid to Latin American Countries* 27(3) AMER. J. POL. SCI. 539-63 (1985).

Dennis Davis & Michael D. Ward, *They Dance Alone: Deaths and the Disappeared in Contemporary Chile*, 34 J. CONFLICT RESOL. 449-75 (1990).

GEOFFREY KEMP, SOME RELATIONSHIPS BETWEEN U.S. MILITARY TRAINING IN LATIN AMERICA AND WEAPONS ACQUISITION PATTERNS: 1959-1969 (1970).

LATIN AMERICA AND THE UNITED STATES: THE CHANGING POLITICAL REALITIES (Julio Cotler and Richard Fagen eds., 1974).

James M. McCormick & Neil J. Mitchell, *Is U.S. Aid Really Linked to Human Rights in Latin America?*, 32 AMER. J. POL. SCI. 231-39 (1988); *Human Rights and Foreign Assistance: An Update*, 70 SOC. SCI. Q. 969-79 (1989).

TABLE OF AUTHORITIES

CASES

Abebe-Jira v. Negewo, 72 F.3d 844 (11th Cir. 1996), 551

Aguinda v. Texaco, Inc., 1994 WL 142006 (S.D.N.Y. 1994), *aff'd on reh'g*, 1994 WL 160535 (S.D.N.Y. 1994), 620

Ahmad v. Wigen, 910 F.2d 1063 (2d Cir. 1990), 477

Alfred Dunhill of London, Inc. v. Republic of Cuba, 425 U.S. 682, 694 (1976), 545

Aloeboetoe et al. Case, Judgment of September 10, 1993, Inter-Am. C.H.R., 488

Alvarez-Machain v. Berellez, Civil No. CV-93-4072-JGD, (C.D. Cal. Jan. 23, 1995), 552, 584

Alvarez-Mendez v. Stock, 941 F.2d 956 (9th Cir. 1991), *cert. denied*, 113 S. Ct. 127 (1992), 611

American Baptist Churches v. Meese, 712 F. Supp. 756 (N.D. Cal. 1989), 594, 598, 599, 622

American Baptist Churches v. Thornburgh, 760 F. Supp. 796 (N.D. Cal. 1991), 598

American Bonded Warehouse Co. v. Compagnie Nationale Air France, 653 F. Supp. 861 (N.D. Ill. 1987), 540

Anh v. Levi, 586 F.2d 625 (6th Cir. 1978), 594

Argentine Republic v. Amerada Hess Shipping Corp., 488 U.S. 428 (1989), 522, 535, 538, 622

Artico v. Italy, 37 Eur. Ct. H.R. (ser. A) (1980), 482

Asakura v. City of Seattle, 265 U.S. 332 (1924), 581

Asakura v. Seattle, 225 U.S. 332 (1924), 594

Attorney General v. X, [1992] 1 I.R. 1, 436

Austria v. Italy, 4 Y.B. European Conv. Hum. Rts. 116 (1961); 6 Y.B. European Conv. Hum. Rts. 740 (1963), 490

B. v. France, 232 Eur. Ct. H.R. (ser. A) (1992), 475

The *Baby Boy* Opinion, Case 2141, Inter-Am. C.H.R. 25, OEA/Ser.L/V/II.54, doc. 9 rev. 1 (1981), **426-433**

Banco Nacional de Cuba v. Sabbatino, 376 U.S. 398 (1964), 505, 545

Barcelona Traction, Light & Power Co., Ltd., (Belg. v. Spain), 1970 I.C.J. 3 (Feb. 5), 304

Barrera-Echavarria v. Rison, 44 F.3d 1441 (9th Cir. 1995), 611

Belilos Case, 132 Eur. Ct. H.R. (ser. A)(1988), 595

Bell v. Wolfish, 421 U.S. 520 (1979), 568

Bertrand v. Sava, 684 F.2d 204 (2d Cir. 1982), 594

Boehm v. Superior Court, 223 Cal. Rptr. 716 (1986), 611

Borovsky v. Commissioner of Immigration, 90 Phil. Rpts. 107 (1951), 519

Bowers v. Hardwick, 478 U.S. 186 (1986), 469, 475, 630

Bradley v. School Bd. of City of Richmond, 416 U.S. 696, 711 (1974), 551, 552

Brown v. Board of Education, 349 U.S. 483 (1954), preface n.1

Brüggemann and Scheuten v. Federal Republic of Germany, App. No. 6959/75, 10 Eur. Comm'n H.R. Dec. & Rep. 100 (1978), 3 Eur. H.R. Rep. 244 (1981), 435

Buck v. Bell, 274 U.S. 200, 728

Campbell and Cosans v. United Kingdom, 60 Eur. Ct. H.R. (ser. A) (1982), 478, 482

Canada (Attorney-General) v. Ward, 2 S.C.R. 689, 103 D.L.R.4th 1 (Can. 1993), 663, 664

Canas-Segovia v. INS, 970 F.2d 1436 (9th Cir. 1989), 598, 645, 646

Case 159/90, *Society for the Protection of Unborn Children Ireland Ltd v. Grogan and Others*, 1991 E.C.R. 4733, 3 C.M.L.R. 849 (1991), 436

Case 9213, Inter-Am. C.H.R., OAS Doc. OEA/Ser.L/V/II.67, doc. 6 (1986), 438

Case 9265 (Decision on a Request for Reconsideration), Inter-Am. C.H.R. 119, OEA/Ser.L/V/II.66, doc. 10 rev. 1 (1985), **343-347**

Case 9647, Inter-Am. C.H.R. 147, OEA/Ser.L/V/II.71, doc. 9 rev. 1 (1987), 437

Case 10,031, Inter-Am. C.H.R. res. 23/89, OEA/Ser.L/V/II.76, doc. 44 (1989), 438, 439

Case 10,537, Inter-Am. C.H.R. 117, OEA/Ser.L/V/II.85, doc. 9 rev. (1994), **440-443**

Case 10,573, Inter-Am. C.H.R. 312, OEA/Ser.L/V/II.85, doc. 9 rev. (1994), 449

Case 10,675, Inter-Am. C.H.R. 334, OEA/Ser.L/V/II.85, doc. 9 rev. (1994), 450

Cavalcarti Araujo-Jongen v. The Netherlands, No. 418/1990, U.N. Doc. A/49/40 (1994), 113 n.1

Cerillo-Perez v. INS, 809 F.2d 1419 (9th Cir. 1987), 611

The Chinese Exclusion Case, 130 U.S. 581 (1889), 582, 583

Chiriboga v. International Bank for Reconstruction & Dev., 616 F. Supp. 963 (D.D.C. 1985), 601

Chuidian v. Philippine Nat'l Bank, 912 F.2d 1095, 1105 (9th Cir. 1990), 537, 540

Cicippio v. Islamic Republic of Iran, 30 F.3d 164 (D.C. Cir. 1994), *cert. denied*, 1995 U.S. LEXIS 122, 539

Citizens of the District of Columbia v. United States, Case No. 11.204, 449

Clark v. Allen, 331 U.S. 503 (1947), 581, 594

Coleman v. Alcolac, Inc., 888 F. Supp. 1388 (S.D. Tex. June 6, 1995), 539

Committee of U.S. Citizens Living in Nicaragua v. Reagan, 859 F.2d 927 (D.C. Cir. 1988), 575, **614-619**

Conservatorship of Hofferber, 616 P.2d 836 (1980), 606

Cook v. United States, 288 U.S. 102 (1933), 583, 585

Cossey v. United Kingdom, 184 Eur. Ct. H.R. (ser. A) (1990), 475

Costello-Roberts v. United Kingdom, 247-C Eur. Ct. H.R. (ser. A), No. 89/1991/341/414 (1993), 164, 165, 478

Cramer v. Tyars, 588 P.2d 793 (Cal. 1979), 571

Cuadras v. INS, 910 F.2d 567 (9th Cir. 1990), 676

Curran v. City of New York, 191 Misc. 229, 77 N.Y.S.2d 206 (1947), 594

Cyprus v. Turkey, 18 Y.B. European Conv. Hum. Rts. 82 (1975); 21 Y.B. European Conv. Hum. Rts. 100 (1978); 22 Y.B. European Conv. Hum. Rts. 440 (1979), 490

De Sanchez v. Banco Central De Nicaragua, 770 F.2d 1385, 1397 (5th Cir. 1985), 20, 25

Demjanjuk v. Meese, 784 F.2d 1114 (D.C. Cir. 1986), 594

Denmark, France, Netherlands, Norway, & Sweden v. Turkey, 35 Eur. Comm'n H.R. 143 (1984), 490

Denmark, Netherlands, Norway, & Sweden v. Greece; Denmark, Norway, & Sweden v. Greece, 12 Y.B. European Conv. Hum. Rts. (1969), 490

Diaz-Escobar v. INS, 782 F.2d 1488 (9th Cir. 1986), 676

Doe v. Gaughan, 808 F.2d 871 (1st Cir. 1986), 629

Doe v. Karadzic, 70 F.3d 232 (2d Cir. 1995), 296

Doe v. Karadzic, 866 F. Supp. 734, 296

Doe v. Karadzic, No. 93 Civ. 0878 (S.D.N.Y. filed Feb. 11, 1993), 531

Drexel Burnham Lambert Group, Inc. v. Committee of Receivers for A.W. Galadari, 810 F. Supp. 1375, 1383 (S.D.N.Y. 1993), 541

Dudgeon v. United Kingdom, 45 Eur. Ct. H.R. (ser. A) (1982), 4 Eur. H.R. Rep. 149 (1981), **470-474, 630**

Echeverria v. INS, No. 89-70236 (accepted for filing, December 11, 1989), 623

Echeverria-Hernandez v. INS, 923 F.2d 688 (9th Cir. 1991), 623

Engel and Others v. The Netherlands, 22 Eur. C.H.R. (ser. A) (1976), 481

Fairen Garbi and Solis Corrales Case, Judgment of Mar. 15, 1989, Inter-Am. C.H.R. (Ser. C.) No. 6, 487

Fatin v. INS, 12 F.3d 1233 (3rd Cir. 1993), **651-656**

Fernandez-Roque v. Smith, 734 F.2d 576 (11th Cir. 1984), 611

Ferrer-Mazorra v. Meese, 479 U.S. 889 (1986), 599, 611

Fiallo v. Bell, 430 U.S. 787 (1977), 568

Fierro v. Gomez, 865 F. Supp 1387 (N.D. Cal. 1994), 477

Fierro v. Gomez, No. 94-16775, 1996 U.S. App. LEXIS 2867 (9th Cir. Feb. 21, 1996), 477

Filartiga v. Peña-Irala, 577 F. Supp. 860 (E.D.N.Y. 1984), **509**, 547

Filartiga v. Peña-Irala, 630 F.2d 876 (2d. Cir. 1980), 18, 23, 488, **505-508**, 546, 594, 597

Filartiga v. Peña-Irala, reprinted in 19 I.L.M. 585 (1980), 520

First National City Bank v. Banco Para el Comercio Exterior de Cuba, 462 U.S. 611 (1983), 599

Flores v. Meese, 681 F. Supp. 665 (C.D. Cal. 1988), 558

Forti v. Suarez-Mason, 672 F. Supp. 1531 (N.D. Cal. 1987), 477, 510-518, 599

Forti v. Suarez-Mason, 694 F. Supp. 707 (N.D. Cal. 1988), 518

Foster v. Neilson, 27 U.S. 253 (2 Pet.) (1829), 22, 585

Frolova v. U.S.S.R., 761 F.2d 370 (7th Cir. 1985) 585, 594

Furman v. Georgia, 408 U.S. 238 (1972), 43 n.8

Gangaram Panday Case, Judgment of January 21, 1994, Inter-Am. Ct. H.R., 486

Godinez Judgment, Inter-Am. Ct. H.R. (ser. C) No. 5 (1989), 487

Goldstar (Panama) S.A. v. United States, 967 F.2d 965 (4th Cir. 1992), 619

Gomez v. INS, 947 F.2d 660, 664 (2nd Cir. 1991), 662

Gould, Inc. v. Mitsui Mining & Smelting Co., 750 F. Supp. 838 (N.D. Ohio 1990), 541

Greece v. United Kingdom, 2 Y.B. European Conv. Hum. Rts. (1958-59); 18 Y.B. European Conv. Hum. Rts. 94 (1975), 490

The Greek Case, 12 Y.B. European Conv. Hum. Rts. (1969) (Eur. Comm'n H.R.), 490

The Greek Case, Council of Europe (Committee of Ministers) (1970), 490

Guo Chun Di v. Carroll, 842 F. Supp. 858 (E.D. Va. 1994), 662

H. v. France, 162 Eur. Ct. H.R. (ser. A) (1989), 482

Haitian Centers Council, Inc. v. Sale, 823 F. Supp. 1028 (E.D.N.Y. 1993), 567

Haitian Refugee Center v. Gracey, 600 F. Supp. 1396 (D.D.C. 1985), *aff'd on other grounds*, 809 F.2d 794 (D.C. Cir. 1987), 594

Handel v. Artukovic, 601 F. Supp. 1421 (C.D. Cal. 1985), 594

The Head Money Cases, 112 U.S. 580 (1884), 555, 583

Hurley v. Irish-American Gay, Lesbian and Bisexual Group of Boston, 115 S. Ct. 2338 (1995), 475

In *INS v. Elias-Zacarias*, ___ U.S. ___, 112 S. Ct. 812 (1992), 645

In re Estate of *Ferdinand E. Marcos Human Rights Litigation*, 978 F.2d 493 (9th Cir. 1992), 519, 540

In re Estate of *Ferdinand E. Marcos Human Rights Litigation*, MDL No. 840 (D. Haw. 1994), 540

In Re *Yamashita*, 327 U.S. 1 (1945), 610

In the Matter of *Republic of the Philippines*, 46 BVerfGE 342 (2BvM 1/76 December 13, 1977), 29, 520

Ingraham v. Wright, 430 U.S. 651, 97 S. Ct. 1401 (1977), 478, 571

INS v. Cardoza-Fonseca, 480 U.S. 421 (1986), 21, 597, 598, 611, 641

INS v. Stevic, 467 U.S. 407 (1984), 598

Intercontinental Dictionary Series v. DeGruyter, 822 F. Supp. 662 (C.D. Cal. 1993), 540

Internationale Handelgesellschaft Case, Case 11/70, E.C.R. 1125 (1970), 492

Ireland v. United Kingdom, 19 Y.B. European Conv. Hum. Rts. 516 (1976), 490, 512, **159-161**

Ireland v. United Kingdom, 20 Y.B. European Conv. Hum. Rts. 602 (1978); 25 Eur. Ct. H.R. (ser. A) (1978), **161-162**, 490

Isidoro Caballero Delgado and María del Carmen Santana v. Colombia, Case No. 10.319, 457

Jaffe v. Snow, 610 So. 2d 482 (Fla. Dist. Ct. App. 1992), *reh'g denied*, 621 So. 2d 482 (Fla. 1993), 600, 601

Jean v. Nelson, 727 F.2d 957 (11th Cir. 1984), *modified on other grounds*, 472 U.S. 846 (1985), 611

Jeanneret v. Vichey, 693 F.2d 259 (2d Cir. 1982), 601

José Indalecio Guerrero et al. (El Amparo) v. Venezuela, Case No. 10.602, 457

Joseph v. Office of Consulate General of Nigeria, 830 F.2d 1018 (9th Cir. 1987), *cert. denied*, 485 U.S. 905 (1988), 538

Juan Paul Genie v. Nicaragua, Case No. 10.792, 457

Kadic v. Karadzic, Doe v. Karadzic, 70 F.3d 232 (2nd Cir. 1995), 23

Kadic v. Karadzic, No. 93 Civ. 1163 (S.D.N.Y. filed March 2, 1993), 501 n. 2, 531

Kindler v. Canada, [1991] 2 S.C.R. 779, 477

Kleindienst v. Mandel, 408 U.S. 753 (1972), 568

Kline v. Kaneko, 685 F. Supp. 386 (S.D.N.Y. 1988), 540

Klinghoffer v. S.N.C. Achille Lauro, 739 F. Supp. 854 (S.D.N.Y. 1990), 620

Lafontant v. Aristide, 844 F. Supp. 128 (E.D.N.Y. 1994), 541, 552

Lareau v. Manson, 507 F. Supp. 1177 (D. Conn. 1980), **602-606**

Lareau v. Manson, 651 F.2d 96 (2nd Cir. 1981), 606

Lawless Case, 1961 Y.B. European Conv. Hum. Rts. 430 (Eur. Ct. H.R.), 480

Letelier v. Chile, 502 F. Supp. 259 (D.C. 1980), 489

Libra Bank Ltd. v. Banco Nacional de Costa Rica, 676 F.2d 47 (2d Cir. 1982), 541

Linder v. Calero Portocarrero, 747 F. Supp. 1452 (S.D. Fla. 1990), *rev'd on other grounds*, 963 F.2d 332 (1992), 621

Linder v. Portocarrero, 747 F. Supp. 1452 (S.D. Fla. 1990), 621

Lipscomb v. Simmons, 884 F.2d 1242 (9th Cir. 1989), 611

Liu v. Republic of China, 892 F.2d 1419 (9th Cir. 1989), 542

Matter of D-V-, Interim Dec. No. 3252 (BIA 1993), 665

Matter of Medina, Interim Dec. No. 3078 (BIA 1988), 589, 633

Matter of the Requested Extradition of Suarez-Mason, 694 F. Supp. 707 (N.D. Cal. 1988), 518

Matter of Toboso-Alfonso, Interim Dec. No. 3222 (BIA 1990), 662

McMullen v. INS, 658 F.2d 1312, 1315 n.2 (9th Cir. 1981), 667

Menominee Tribe of Indians v. United States, 391 U.S. 404 (1968), 583

Military and Paramilitary Activities in and Against Nicaragua (Nicar. v. U.S.), 1986 I.C.J. 14 (Judgment of June 27), 18, 252

Missouri v. Holland, 252 U.S. 416 (1920), 581

Modinos v. Cyprus, 259 Eur. Ct. H.R. (ser. A) (1993), 474

Morgentaler v. Prince Edward Island (Minister of Health & Social Serv.), 112 D.L.R. (4th) 756 (P.E.I. Sp. Ct. 1994), 435

Murray v. Schooner Charming Betsy, 6 U.S. (2 Cranch) 64 (1804), 623

Mushikiwabo v. Barayagwiza, 94 Civ. 3627 (1996), 549

Negewo v. Abebe-Jira, 72 F.3d 844 (11th Cir. 1996), 519

Neira Alegría et al. v. Peru, Case No. 10.078, 457

Neumeister v. Austria, 17 Eur. Ct. H.R. (ser. A) (1974), 481

Nold v. Commission, Case 4/73, E.C.R. 491 (1974), 492

Norris v. Northern Ireland, 142 Eur. Ct. H.R. (ser. A) (1988), 474

North Sea Continental Shelf Cases (W. Ger. v. Den.; W. Ger. v. Neth.), 1969 I.C.J. 3 (1969), 18, 509

Open Door and Dublin Well Woman v. Ireland, 246 Eur. Ct. H.R. (ser. A) (1993), 436

The Paquete Habana, 175 U.S. 677 (1900), 599, 622

Paton v. United Kingdom, App. No. 8416/78, 3 Eur. H.R. Rep. 408 (1981), 435

Paul v. Avril, 812 F. Supp. 207 (S.D. Fla. 1993), 519, 541

Pauley v. Kelly, 255 S.E.2d 859 (W. Va. 1979), 612

Pecastaing v. Belgium, Case 98/79, E.C.R. 691 (1980), 492

People of Saipan v. U.S. Dep't of Interior, 502 F.2d 90 (9th Cir. 1974), *cert. denied*, 420 U.S. 1003 (1975), 586, 594

Planned Parenthood of Southeastern Pennsylvania v. Casey, 505 U.S. 833, 112 S. Ct. 2791 (1992), 434

Princz v. Federal Republic of Germany, 813 F. Supp. 22 (D.D.C. 1992), 539

Princz v. Federal Republic of Germany, 26 F.3d 1166, 1169-71 (D.C. Cir. 1994), 539, 540

The Prosecutor v. Dusko Tadic, Case No. IT-94-1-AR72 (1995), 287

Pruneyard Shopping Center v. Robins, 447 U.S. 74 (1980), 574

Quintanilla-Ticas v. INS, 783 F.2d 955 (9th Cir. 1986), 676

R. v. Morgentaler, [1988] 1 S.C.R. 30, 44 D.L.R. (4th) 385 (Can.), 175, 434

R. v. Morgentaler, [1993] 3 S.C.R. 463, 107 D.L.R. (4th) 537 (Can.), 435

Rees v. United Kingdom, 106 Eur. Ct. H.R. (ser. A) (1986), 475

Reid v. Covert, 354 U.S. 1 (1957), 581

Reno v. Flores, 507 U.S. 292, 113 S. Ct. 1439 (1993), 557, 562

Republic of the Philippines v. Marcos, 665 F. Supp. 793 (N.D. Cal. 1987), 540

Republic of the Philippines v. Marcos, 806 F.2d 344 (2d Cir. 1986), 546

Republic of the Philippines v. Marcos, 862 F.2d 1355 (9th Cir. 1988) (en banc), *cert. denied*, 490 U.S. 1035 (1989), 546

Richmond v. Ricketts, 640 F. Supp. 767 (D. Ariz. 1986), 628

Rodriquez-Fernandez v. Wilkinson, 654 F.2d 1382 (10th Cir. 1981), 610, 611

Roe v. Wade, 410 U.S. 113 (1973), 433, 434

Romer v. Evans, 64 U.S.L.W. 4353 (1996), 475

Rust v. Sullivan, 500 U.S. 173 (1991), 434

S.K. v. Karadzic, 866 F. Supp 734 (S.D.N.Y. Sept. 7, 1994), 532

Safaie v. INS, 25 F.3d 636 (8th Cir. 1994), 662

Sale v. Haitian Centers Council, Inc., 509 U.S. 155, 113 S. Ct. 2549 (1993), 584

San Antonio Ind. School Dist. v. Rodriguez, 411 U.S. 1 (1973), 612

Santa Barbara v. Adamson, 610 P.2d 436 (1980), 611

Saudi Arabia v. Nelson, 507 U.S. 1017, 113 S. Ct. 1471 (1993), 535, 536

The Schooner Exchange v. M'Faddon, 11 U.S. (7 Cranch) 116 (1812), 545

Siderman de Blake v. Republic of Argentina, 965 F.2d 699 (9th Cir. 1992), *cert. denied*, 507 U.S. 1017, 113 S. Ct. 1812 (1993), 534, 536, 537, 538 , 622

Soering v. United Kingdom, 161 Eur. Ct. H.R. (ser. A) (1989), 231, 236, 439, 476, 480, 629

Sotelo-Aquije v. Slattery, 17 F.3d 33, 37 (2nd Cir. 1994), 667

South African Airways v. Dole, 817 F.2d 119, 121 (D.C. Cir. 1987) (Anti-Apartheid Act of 1986, requiring termination of treaty between U.S. and South Africa, held irreconcilable with that treaty), *cert. denied*, 484 U.S. 896 (1987), 583

Sporrong and Lönnroth v. Sweden, 88 Eur. Ct. H.R. (ser. A) (1985), **482-486**

Stanford v. Kentucky, 492 U.S. 361 (1989), **607-608**

State of Hawaii v. Marley, 500 P.2d 1095 (Hawaii 1973), 610

State of Vermont v. McCann, No. 2857-7-86CnCr (D. Ct. Vt., Chittenden Cir. 1987), 610

Stauder Case, Case 29/69, E.C.R. 419 (1969), 492

Sterling v. Cupp, 625 P.2d 123 (1981), 576 n.4, 606

Tel-Oren v. Libyan Arab Republic, 726 F.2d 774 (D.C. Cir. 1984), 519, 594

Thompson v. Oklahoma, 487 U.S. 815 (1988), 452, 607

Toonen v. Australia, (No. 488/1992), U.N. Doc. CCPR/C/50/D/488/1992 (1994), 475

Trajano v. Marcos, 878 F.2d 1439 (9th Cir. 1989), 519

Trans World Airlines, Inc. v. Franklin Mint Corp., 466 U.S. 243 (1984), 583

Tyrer v. United Kingdom, 26 Eur. Ct. H.R. (ser. A) (1978), **162-164, 165**, 478

U.N. Doc., Case No. IT-94-1-AR72 (1995), 531

U.S. v. Goering, 6 F.R.D. 69, 110 (1946), 279

Underhill v. Hernandez, 168 U.S. 250 (1897) 541, 545

United States v. Aguilar, 871 F.2d 1436 (9th Cir. 1989), 598, 599, 623

United States v. Alvarez-Machain, 504 U.S. 655, 112 S. Ct. 2188 (1992), 523, 583, 584

United States v. Arlington, Va., 702 F.2d 485 (4th Cir. 1983), 601

United States v. Flick, *reprinted in* 6 Trials of War Criminals Before the Nuremberg Military Tribunals Under Control Council Law No. 10 (1949), 278

United States v. Hendron, 813 F. Supp. 973 (E.D.N.Y. 1993), 541

United States v. Lumumba, 741 F.2d 12, 15 (2d Cir. 1984), 547

United States v. May, 622 F.2d 1000 (9th Cir. 1980), 610

United States v. Merkt, 764 F.2d 266 (5th Cir. 1985), 147

United States v. Montgomery, 772 F.2d 733 (11th Cir. 1985), 610

United States v. Noriega, 746 F. Supp. 1506, 1519 (1990), 545

United States v. Ohlendorf, reprinted in 4 TRIALS OF WAR CRIMINALS BEFORE THE NUREMBERG MILITARY TRIBUNALS UNDER CONTROL COUNCIL LAW NO. 10 (1949), 278

United States v. Percheman, 32 U.S. (7 Pet.) (1833), 22

United States v. Peterson, 812 F.2d 486 (9th Cir. 1987), 519

United States v. Postal, 589 F.2d 862 (5th Cir. 1979), *cert. denied*, 444 U.S. 832 (1979), 594

United States v. Restrepo, 999 F.2d 640 (2nd Cir. 1993), 568

United States v. Schiffer, 836 F. Supp. 1164 (E.D. Pa. 1993), 509

United States v. Stanley, 483 U.S. 669 (1987), 621

United States v. Valenzuela-Bernal, 458 U.S. 858 (1982), 568

United States v. Yunis, 924 F.2d 1086 (D.C. Cir. 1991), 522, 523

Velasquez Rodriguez Case, Judgment of July 29, 1988, Inter-Am. Ct. H.R. (Ser. C.) No. 4, 28 I.L.M. 294 (1989), 443, 487

Von Dardel v. U.S.S.R., 623 F. Supp. 246 (D.D.C. 1985), *vacated on other grounds*, 736 F.Supp. 1 (D.D.C. 1990), 594, 601

W.S. Kirkpatrick & Co. v. Environmental Tectonics Corp., Int'l, 493 U.S. 400 (1990), 542, 544

W. (Z.D.) (Re), Convention Refugee Determination Decisions C.R.D.D. No. 3, No. U92-06668 (Feb. 19, 1993), 665

Wang Zong Xiao v. Reno, 837 F. Supp 1506 (N.D. Cal. 1993), 621

Washington v. Washington State Commercial Passenger Fishing Vessel Ass'n, 443 U.S. 658, *modified*, 444 U.S. 816 (1979), 583

Webster v. Reproductive Health Services, 492 U.S. 490 (1989), 434

Weinberger v. Rossi, 456 U.S. 25 (1982), 583

Whitney v. Robertson, 124 U.S. 190 (1888), 581

Xuncax v. Gramajo, 886 F. Supp. 162 (D. Mass. 1995), 519, 551, 600

Yang Cheng Huan v. Carroll, 852 F. Supp. 460, 663

Youngberg v. Romeo, 457 U.S. 307 (1983), 567, 629

Zhang v. Slattery, 840 F. Supp. 292, 292-95 (S.D.N.Y. 1994), 665

Zschernig v. Miller, 389 U.S. 429 (1968), 581

BOOKS AND ARTICLES

A New Guardian to Protect Humanitarian Law, 2 TORTURE 63 (1992), 332

Kenneth W. Abbott, *Linking Trade to Political Goals: Foreign Policy Export Controls in the 1970s and 1980s*, 65 MINN. L. REV. 739 (1981), 420

Kenneth W. Abbott, *Coercion and Communication: Framework for Evaluation of Economic Sanctions*, 19 N.Y.U. J. INT'L L. & POL. 781 (1987), 420

NICHOLAS ABERCROMBIE, STEPHEN HILL & BRYAN S. TURNER, THE DOMINANT IDEOLOGY THESIS (1980), 146

The Accused, The Allegations, WASH. POST, Dec. 18, 1995, at A17, 295

TATHIANA FLORES ACUÑA, THE UNITED NATIONS MISSION IN EL SALVADOR: A HUMANITARIAN LAW PERSPECTIVE (1995), 242

Adeno Addis, *Critical Legal Studies and the Issue of Constructive Alternatives*, 34 LOY. L. REV. 277 (1988), 692

Administration Policy on Reforming Multilateral Peace Operations, reprinted in 33 I.L.M. 795 (1994), 241

Advisory Committee on Hum. Rts. and Foreign Pol'y, Economic, Social and Cultural Human Rights, *Advisory Report No. 18* (1994), 57

AFRICAN RIGHTS, RWANDA: DEATH, DESPAIR AND DEFIANCE *(rev. ed.* 1995), 319

Agora: What Obligation Does Our Generation Owe to the Next? An Approach to Global Environmental Responsibility, 84 AM. J. INT'L L. 190 (1990) (articles by Anthony D'Amato, Edith Brown Weiss, Lothar Gundling), 84

ABDULLAHI AHMED AN-NA'IM, TOWARD AN ISLAMIC REFORMATION: CIVIL LIBERTIES, HUMAN RIGHTS, AND INTERNATIONAL LAW (1990), 170

AI Newsletter (July 1991), 357

JOHN AKPALU, ENFORCING THE AFRICAN CHARTER ON HUMAN AND PEOPLES' RIGHTS: AN ANALYSIS OF THE LEGAL AND INSTITUTIONAL FRAMEWORK (1991), 465

T. Alexander Aleinikoff, *Federal Regulation of Aliens and the Constitution*, 83 AM. J. INT'L L. 862 (1989), 568

Algeria's President Takes Office with Vow of Firmness and Dialogue, BOSTON GLOBE, Feb. 1, 1994, Nat'l/Foreign sec. at 11, 275

Philip Alston & Bruno Simma, *First Session of the UN Committee on Economic, Social and Cultural Rights*, 81 AM. J. INT'L L. 747 (1987), 79

Philip Alston & Gerard Quinn, *The Nature and Scope of States Parties' Obligations Under the International Covenant on Economic, Social and Cultural Rights*, 9 HUM. RTS. Q. 156 (1987), **51-57**

Philip Alston & Bruno Simma, *Second Session of the UN Committee on Economic, Social and Cultural Rights*, 82 AM. J. INT'L L. 603 (1988), 79

Philip Alston, *A Third Generation of Solidarity Rights: Progressive Development or Obfuscation of International Human Rights Law?*, 29 NETH. INT'L L. REV. 367 (1982), 83

Philip Alston, *Conjuring Up New Human Rights: A Proposal for Quality Control*, 78 AM. J. INT'L L. 607 (1984), 83

PHILIP ALSTON, HUMAN RIGHTS IN 1993: HOW FAR HAS THE UNITED NATIONS COME AND WHERE SHOULD IT GO FROM HERE? (memorandum distributed at the Vienna Conference on Human Rights, June 1993), 66, 78

Philip Alston, *Making Space for New Human Rights: The Case of the Right to Development*, 1 HARV. HUM. RTS. Y.B. 3 (1988), 84

Philip Alston, *Out of the Abyss: The Challenges Confronting the New U.N. Committee on Economic, Social and Cultural Rights*, 9 HUM. RTS. Q. 332 (1987), **72-75**

Philip Alston, *The Committee on Economic, Social and Cultural Rights*, in THE UNITED NATIONS AND HUMAN RIGHTS: A CRITICAL APPRAISAL (Philip Alston ed., 1992), 79

Philip Alston, *The United Nations High Commissioner for Human Rights*, ASIL NEWSLETTER (Sept.-Oct. 1995), 215

Philip Alston, *The Security Council and Human Rights: Lessons to be Learned from the Iraqi-Kuwait Crisis and its Aftermath*, 13 AUSTL. Y.B. INT'L L. 107 (1993), 241

Philip Alston, *U.S. Ratfication of the Covenant on Economic, Social and Cultural Rights: The Need for an Entirely New Strategy*, 84 AM. J. INT'L L. 365 (1990), **58-65**

ANDREW ALTMAN, CRITICAL LEGAL STUDIES: A LIBERAL CRITIQUE (1990), 692

American Bar Association Task Force on an International Criminal Court—Final Report, 28 INT'L LAW. 475 (1994), 305

AMERICAN FOREIGN POLICY: THE FIRST DECADE 1973-1983, (1984), 388, 389

American Society of International Law, Foreign Governments in United States Courts, 85 AM. SOC'Y INT'L L. PROC. 251 (1991), 501 n.2, 530

Americas Watch, Asia Watch & Helsinki Watch, *Four Failures: A Report on the U.N. Special Rapporteurs on Human Rights in Chile, Guatemala, Iran and Poland* (1986), **358-361**

Amnesty International, *A Guide to the African Charter on Human and Peoples' Rights* (1991), 465

Amnesty International, *Amnesty International Report 1985*, 106

Amnesty International, *Amnesty International Delegation Visits North Korea, Discusses Legal Reforms and Prisoner Cases*, AI Index: ASA 23/07/95 (1995), 358

Amnesty International, *Amputation Sentences* (1987) AI Index: AFR 54/01/87, 166

Amnesty International, *Argentina: The Right to the Full Truth*, AI Index: AMR 13/03/95 (1995), 275

Amnesty International, *Bosnia-Herzegovina: Rape and Sexual Abuse by Armed Forces*, AI Index: EUR 63/01/93 (1993), 501, n.2

Amnesty International, *Bosnia-Herzegovina: Gross Abuses of Human Rights*, AI Index: EUR 63/01/92, at 2 (1992), 501, n.2, 530

Amnesty International, *Chile: Transition at the Crossroads; Human Rights Violations Under Pinochet Rule Remain the Crux*, AI Index: AMR 22/01/96 (1996), 275

Amnesty International, *"Disappearances" in Honduras: A Wall of Silence and Indifference*, AI Index: AMR: 37/02/92 (1992), 443

Amnesty International, DPRK (North Korea): What Happened to Cho Ho Pyong and His Family?, AI Index: ASA 24/05/95 (1995), 358

Amnesty International, *Establishing a Just, Fair and Effective International Criminal Court 5*, AI Index: IOR 40/05/94 (1994), 305

Amnesty International, *Ethiopia: Accountability Past and Present: Human Rights in Transition*, AI Index: AFR 25/06/95 (1995), 275

Amnesty International, *Human Rights and U.S. Security Assistance* (1993), 142

Amnesty International, *Iran: Violations of Human Rights: Documents Sent by Amnesty International to the Government of the Islamic Republic of Iran*, AI Index: MDE 13/09/87 (1987), **131-134**

Amnesty International, *Moving Forward to Set Up the War Crimes Tribunal for the Former Yugoslavia*, AI Index: EUR 48/03/93 (1993), 288

Amnesty International, *Myanmar, Conditions in Prisons and Labour Camps*, AI Index: ASA 16/22/95 (1995), 181

Amnesty International, *Nicaragua: The Human Rights Record 1986-1989*, AI Index: AMR/43/02/89 (1989), 248, n.1

Amnesty International, *Observations on Possible Reform of the African Charter on Human and Peoples' Rights*, AI Index: IOR 63/03/93 (1993), 465

Amnesty International, *Peace-Keeping and Human Rights*, AI Index: IRO 40/01/94 (1994), **224-229**

Amnesty International, *Political Killings and Disappearances: Medicological Aspects*, AI Index: ACT 33/36/93 (1993), 329

Amnesty International, *Proposal for a Commission of Inquiry into the Effect of Domestic Intelligence Activities on Criminal Trials in the United States of America*, AI Index: AMR 51/05/81 (1981), 372

Amnesty International, *Report 1993*, 181

Amnesty International, *Rwanda and Burundi—The Return Home: Rumours and Realities*, AI Index: AFR 02/01/96 (1996), 297

Amnesty International, *Rwanda and Burundi, A Call for Action by the International Community*, AI Index: AFR 02/24/95 (1995), 316-319

Amnesty International, *Suggested Further Action on Myanmar and Daw Aung San Suu Kyi*, AI Index: ASA 16/21/95 (1995), 181

Amnesty International, *Torture in Greece: The First Torturers' Trial 1975* (1977), 491

Amnesty International, *Union of Myanmar (Burma), Human Rights Violations Against Muslims in the Rakhine (Arakan) State*, AI Index: ASA 16/06/92 (1992), 181

Amnesty International, *United States of America: Torture, Ill-Treatment and Excessive Force by Police in Los Angeles, California*, AI Index: AMR 51/76/92 (1992), 372

Amnesty International, *United Nations: Oral Statement on Thematic Mechanisms*, AI Index: IOR 41/WU 02/1994 (Feb. 17, 1994), **214-215**

Amnesty International, *United States of America—Human Rights Violations: A Summary of Amnesty International's Concerns*, AI Index: AMR 51/25/95 (1995), 126

Amnesty International, *United States of America: The Death Penalty,* AI Index: AMR 51/01/87 (1987), 372

KENNETH ANDERSON, THE LAWS OF WAR AND THE CONDUCT OF THE PANAMA INVASION (1990), 25

DEBORAH E. ANKER, THE LAW OF ASYLUM IN THE UNITED STATES: A GUIDE TO ADMINISTRATIVE PRACTICE AND CASE LAW 1-2, 24-25, 31-60 (2nd ed. 1991), **636-640**

Zehra F. Arat, *Democracy and Economic Development—Modernization Theory Revisited,* COMPARATIVE POLITICS 21 (October 1988), 750

ZEHRA F. ARAT, DEMOCRACY AND HUMAN RIGHTS IN DEVELOPING COUNTRIES (Boulder & London: Lynne Rienner, 1991), 750

Zehra F. Arat, *Some Characteristics of Modernization, in* THE POLITICS OF MODERNIZATION (1965) (Chicago: Chicago University Press), 750

HANNAH ARENDT, EICHMANN IN JERUSALEM: A REPORT ON THE BANALITY OF EVIL 116 (1963), 738

Nancy C. Arnison, *The Law of Humanitarian Intervention, in* NEW STRATEGIES FOR A RESTLESS WORLD 37 (Harlan Cleveland ed., 1993), 331

Nancy D. Arnison, *The Law of Humanitarian Intervention, in* REFUGEES IN THE 1990s: NEW STRATEGIES FOR A RESTLESS WORLD (Harlan Cleveland ed., 1993), **234-235**

Olufunmilayo B. Arewa & Susan O'Rourke, *Country-Specific Legislation and Human Rights: The Case of Peru,* 5 HARV. HUM. RTS. J. 183 (1992), **396-397**

ARTICLE 19, STATE OF FEAR: CENSORSHIP IN BURMA (1991), 181

Asia Watch & Minnesota Lawyers International Human Rights Committee, *Human Rights in the Democratic People's Republic of Korea (North Korea)* 1 (1988), **352-357**

Asia Watch, *Burma (Myanmar): Worsening Repression* (1990), 181

Asian Forum for Human Rights and Development, *Handbook on Fact-Finding and Documentation of Human Rights Violations* (1994), 329

ASIAN PERSPECTIVES ON HUMAN RIGHTS (Virginia Leary & Claude Welch eds., 1990), 466

THE ASPEN INSTITUTE, HONORING HUMAN RIGHTS AND KEEPING THE PEACE (1995), 241

ASYLUM LAW AND PRACTICE IN EUROPE AND NORTH AMERICA (Jacqueline Bhabha & Geoffrey Coll eds., 1992), 642

AUTHORITARIAN BRAZIL (A. Stepan ed.) (New Haven, CT: Yale University Press, 1973), 168

Sir Brian Urquhart & Robert S. McNamara, *Toward Collective Security: Two Views, Occasional Paper* 5 (Inst. for Int'l Stud., Brown U., 1991), 242

Danise Aydelott, *Comment, Mass Rape During War: Prosecuting Bosnian Rapists Under International Law,* 7 EMORY INT'L L. REV. 585 (1993), 531

Peter R. Baehr, *Amnesty International and its Self-Imposed Limited Mandate,* NAT'L Q. HUM. RTS. 5 (1994), 720

Betsy B. Baker & Volker Röben, *To Abduct or to Extradite: Does a Treaty Beg the Question? The Alvarez-Machain Decision in U.S. Domestic Law and International Law,* 53 ZEITSCRIFT FÜR AUSLÄNDISCHES ÖFFENTLICHES RECHT UND VÖLKERRECHT 657 (1993), 584

L. Bachman, *Women Lessen Impact of Muslim Conservatives,* NEW ORLEANS TIMES-PICAYUNE, July 30, 1995, at A38, 171

P.R. Baehr, *The Security Council and Human Rights, in* THE DYNAMICS OF THE PROTECTION OF HUMAN RIGHTS IN EUROPE, VOLUME III (Rick Lawson & Matthijs de Blois eds., 1994), 241

Yasmine Bahrani, *The Rushdie Specter: For Muslim Intellectuals the Danger Deepens,* WASH. POST, Aug. 14, 1994, at C1, 171

BEVERLY BALOS & MARY LOUISE FELLOWS, LAW AND VIOLENCE AGAINST WOMEN (1994), 693

Russel Barsh, *Democratization and Development,* 14 HUM. RTS. Q. 120 (1992), 87

MARIA BARTOLOMEI & DAVID WEISSBRODT, THE IMPACT OF FACTFINDING AND INTERNATIONAL PRESSURES ON THE HUMAN RIGHTS SITUATION IN ARGENTINA, 1976-1983, **361-369**

MARIA BARTOLOMEI, GROSS AND MASSIVE VIOLATIONS OF HUMAN RIGHTS IN ARGENTINA, 1976-1983: AN ANALYSIS OF THE PROCEDURE UNDER ECOSOC RESOLUTION 1503 (1991), 215, 361, 370

M. Cherif Bassiouni & Christopher Blakesley, *The Need for an International Criminal Court in the New International World Order*, 25 VAND. J. TRANSNAT'L L. 151 (1992), 297, 305

M. CHERIF BASSIOUNI, COMMENTARIES ON THE INTERNATIONAL LAW COMMISSION'S 1991 DRAFT CODE OF CRIMES AGAINST THE PEACE AND SECURITY OF MANKIND, 279

M. Cherif Bassiouni, *The Commission of Experts Established Pursuant to Security Council Resolution 780*, 5 CRIM. L.F. 279 (1994), 297

M. Cherif Bassiouni, *The Time Has Come for an International Criminal Court*, 1 IND. INT'L & COMP. L. REV. 1 (1991), 298

M. CHERIF BASSIOUNI, DRAFT STATUTE: INTERNATIONAL TRIBUNAL (1993), 305

Christian Bay, *Human Rights on the Periphery: No Room in the Ark for the Yanomami?*, in TRIBAL PEOPLES AND DEVELOPMENT ISSUES: A GLOBAL OVERVIEW 258 (John H. Bodley ed., 1988), 722

ANNE F. BAYEFSKY, INTERNATIONAL HUMAN RIGHTS LAW: USE IN CANADIAN CHARTER OF RIGHTS AND FREEDOMS LITIGATION (1992), 579

Anne Bayefsky & Joan Fitzpatrick, *International Human Rights Law in United States Courts: A Comparative Perspective*, 14 MICH. J. INT'L L. 1 (1992), 579

Justice Harry A. Blackmun, *The Supreme Court and the Law of Nations: Owing a Decent Respect to the Opinions of Mankind*, ASIL NEWSL. (American Soc'y of Int'l Law, Wash., D.C.), Mar.-May 1994, at 1, **555**

DAVID BEATTY, HUMAN RIGHTS AND JUDICIAL REVIEW 308 (1994), 475

James Becket, *The Greek Case Before the European Human Rights Commission*, 1 HUM. RTS. 91 (1970), 490

Hugo A. Bedau, *Human Rights and Foreign Assistance Programs*, in HUMAN RIGHTS AND U.S. FOREIGN POLICY: PRINCIPLES AND APPLICATIONS 29 (Peter G. Brown & Douglas MacLean eds. 1979), **399-402**

RALPH BEDDARD, HUMAN RIGHTS AND EUROPE (3d ed. 1993), 480

David Bederman, *The United Nations Compensation Commission and the Tradition of International Claims Settlement*, 27 N.Y.U. J. INT'L L. & POL. 1 (1994), 488

Joyce Bednarski, *The Salem Witch-Scare Viewed Sociologically*, in WITCHCRAFT AND SORCERY 151 (Max Marwick ed., 1970), **745-747**

Wolfgang Benedek, *Enforcement of Human and Peoples' Rights in Africa—The Communication System and State Reporting Under the African Charter*, 15 NETH. Q. HUM. RTS. 36 (1995), 464, 465

Wolfgang Benedek, *The African Charter and Commission on Human and Peoples' Rights; How to Make it More Effective*, 11 NETH. Q. HUM. RTS. 25 (1993), 465

Peter Benesh, *War Crimes Tribunal Pledges to Protect Victims' Identities*, PITTSBURGH POST-GAZETTE, Aug. 11, 1995, at A10, 287

Karima Bennoune, *As-Salamu 'Alaykum?—Humanitarian Law in Islamic Jurisprudence*, 15 MICH J. INT'L L. 605 (1994), 170

Eyal Benvenisti, *Judicial Misgivings Regarding the Application of International Law: An Analysis of Attitudes of National Courts*, 4 EJIL 159 (1993), 584

Lynn Berat, *Prosecuting Human Rights Violators from a Predecessor Regime: Guidelines for a Transformed South Africa*, 13 B.C. THIRD WORLD L.J. 199 (1993), 275

Alan Berman, *In Mitigation of Illegality: The U.S. Invasion of Panama*, 79 KY. L.J. 735 (1991), 254

Ronald Bettauer, *The United Nations Compensation Commission Developments Since October 1992*, 89 AM. J. INT'L L. 417 (1995), 273, 488

Jacqueline Bhabha, *European Union Asylum and Refugee Policy*, INT'L PRACTITIONER'S NOTEBOOK, Oct. 1995, at 29, 642

ERIC BIEL, LINKING SECURITY ASSISTANCE AND HUMAN RIGHTS (1989), 415

Richard B. Bilder, *Integrating International Human Rights Law into Domestic Law—U.S. Experience*, 4 HOUS. J. INT'L L. 1 (1981), 579

Gayle Binion, *Human Rights: A Feminist Perspective*, 17 HUM. RTS. Q. 509 (1995), 693

J. Kenneth Blackwell & Howard Tolley, Jr., *The U.N. Commission on Human Rights*, 14 HUM. RTS. Q. 485 (1992) (book review), 66

Christopher L. Blakesley, *Obstacles to the Creation of a Permanent War Crimes Tribunal*, 18-FALL FLETCHER F. WORLD AFF. 77 (1994), 305

SIDNEY BLOCH & PETER REDDEWAY, SOVIET PSYCHIATRIC ABUSE: THE SHADOW OVER WORLD PSYCHIATRY (London: Victor Gollancz, 1984), 168

Lincoln P. Bloomfield et al., *Collective Security in a Changing World*, OCCASIONAL PAPER #10 (Inst. for Int'l Stud., Brown U., 1992), 242

Michael Bochenek, *Compensation for Human Rights Abuses in Zimbabwe*, 26 COLUM. HUM. RTS. L. REV. 483 (1995), 489

Thomas A. Bockhorst, *Note, The Constitutionality of INS Pre-Hearing Detention of Alien Children: Flores v. Meese, 942 F.2d 1352 (9th Cir. 1991) (En Banc), cert. granted sub nom., Barr v. Flores, 60 U.S.L.W. 3598 (U.S. Mar. 2, 1992)*, 62 U. CIN. L. REV. 217 (1993), 557, n.1

Ineke Boerfijn, *Towards a Strong System of Supervision: The Human Rights Committee's Role in Reforming the Reporting Procedure under Article 40 of the Covenant on Civil and Political Rights*, 17 HUM. RTS. Q. 766 (1995), 99

Kenneth A. Bollen, *Liberal Democracy: Validity and Method Factors in Cross-National Measures*, 37 AMER. J. POL. SCI. 1207-30 (1993), 750

Kenneth A. Bollen, *Political Rights and Political Liberties in Nations: An Evaluation of Human Rights Measures, 1950-1984*, 8 HUM. RTS. Q. 576-91 (1986), 750

Kenneth A. Bollen, *Issues in the Comparative Measurement of Political Democracy*, 45 AMER. SOC. REV. 370 (1980), 750

Raymond Bonner, *In Once-Peaceful Village, Roots of Rwanda Violence*, N.Y. TIMES, July 11, 1994, at A8, 297

GARY B. BORN & DAVID WESTIN, INTERNATIONAL CIVIL LITIGATION IN UNITED STATES COURTS, COMMENTARY & MATERIALS (2d ed. 1992), 521

Marc J. Bossuyt, *Human Rights as an Element of Foreign Policy*, 89/1 BULL. HUM. RTS. 27 (1990), 390

Marc Bossuyt, *The Development of Special Procedures of the United Nations Commission on Human Rights*, 6 HUM. RTS. L.J. 179 (1985), 143, 201, **211-213**, 215

Henry J. Bourguignon, *The Belilos Case: New Light on Reservations to Multilateral Treaties*, 29 VA. J. INT'L L. 347 (1989), 595

Pierre Bourdieu, *Social Space and Symbolic Power, in* IN OTHER WORDS 123 (1990), 726

BOUTROS BOUTROS-GHALI, BUILDING PEACE AND DEVELOPMENT 1994: ANNUAL REPORT ON THE WORK OF THE ORGANIZATION (1994), 242

BOUTROS BOUTROS-GHALI, CONFRONTING NEW CHALLENGES: ANNUAL REPORT OF THE WORK OF THE ORGANIZATION (1995), 242

Boutros Boutros-Ghali, *Letter Dated 24 May 1994 from the Secretary-General to the President of the Security Council*, U.N. Doc. S/1994/674 (1994), 502, n.3

Karen Bower, *Note, Recognizing Violence Against Women as Persecution on the Basis of Membership in a Particular Social Group*, 7 GEO. IMMIGR. L.J. 173 (1993), 666

Derek W. Bowett, *International Law and Economic Coercion*, 16 VA. J. INT'L L. 245 (1976), 420

FRANCIS A. BOYLE, DEFENDING CIVIL RESISTANCE UNDER INTERNATIONAL LAW (1988), 610

FRANCIS A. BOYLE, THE FUTURE OF INTERNATIONAL LAW AND AMERICAN FOREIGN POLICY (1989), 252

Daniel D. Bradlow, *International Organizations and Private Complaints: The Case of the World Bank Inspection Panel*, 34 VA. J. INT'L L. 553 (1994), 392, 415

Kevin Boyle, *Europe: The Council of Europe, the CSCE, and the European Community, in* GUIDE TO INTERNATIONAL HUMAN RIGHTS PRACTICE 133 (Hurst Hannum ed., 2d ed. 1984), 480, 493

Michele Brandt, *Comment, Doe v. Karadzic: Redressing Non-State Acts of Gender-Specific Abuse Under the Alien Tort Statute*, 79 MINN. L. REV. 1413 (1995), 533

Katherine Brennan, *Note, The Influence of Cultural Relativism on International Human Rights Law: Female Circumcision as a Case Study*, 7 LAW & INEQ. J. 367, 368-73 n.26 (1991), 633, **677-78**

Lea Brilmayer, *International Human Rights Law in American Courts: A Modest Proposal*, 100 YALE L.J. 2277 (1991), 579

Reed Brody, *International Human Rights Agenda For the Post-Cold War World: Improving Current UN Human Rights Structures*, 1993 World Conference (June 1993), 370

Reed Brody, Penny Parker & David Weissbrodt, *Major Developments in 1990 at the UN Commission on Human Rights*, 12 HUM. RTS. Q. 559 (1990), 215

PATRICK BROGAN, THE FIGHTING NEVER STOPPED: A COMPREHENSIVE GUIDE TO WORLD CONFLICT SINCE 1945 (New York: Vintage Books, 1990), 750

DONALD BROWN, HUMAN UNIVERSALS (1991), 682

L. NEVILLE BROWN & TOM KENNEDY, THE COURT OF JUSTICE OF THE EUROPEAN COMMUNITIES (4th ed. 1994), 493

IAN BROWNLIE, PRINCIPLES OF PUBLIC INTERNATIONAL LAW (3d ed. 1979), 18, 19

IAN BROWNLIE, PRINCIPLES OF PUBLIC INTERNATIONAL LAW 6-7 (3d ed. 1979), 509

IAN BROWNLIE, PRINCIPLES OF PUBLIC INTERNATIONAL LAW 32 (4th ed. 1990), 575

IAN BROWNLIE, SYSTEM OF THE LAW OF NATIONS: STATE RESPONSIBILITY, PART I (1987), 304

THOMAS BUERGENTHAL, INTERNATIONAL HUMAN RIGHTS IN A NUTSHELL, 174 (1995), 193, 258

THOMAS BUERGENTHAL, INTERNATIONAL HUMAN RIGHTS IN A NUTSHELL (1995), 448, 465, 480, 496

THOMAS BUERGENTHAL, ROBERT NORRIS & DINAH SHELTON, PROTECTING HUMAN RIGHTS IN THE AMERICAS: SELECTED PROBLEMS 179 (1986), **341-343**

Thomas Buergenthal, *The Advisory Practice of the Inter-American Human Rights Court*, 79 AM. J. INT'L L. 1 (1985), **457-458**

Thomas Buergenthal, *The United Nations Truth Commission for El Salvador*, 27 VAND. J. TRANSNAT'L L. 497 (1994), **267-271**

Thomas Buergenthal, *The Inter-American Court of Human Rights*, 76 AM. J. INT'L L. 231 (1982), 76

Charlotte Bunch et al., *Women's Rights as Human Rights*, 12 HUM. RTS. Q. 486 (1990), 674

Bureau of the Census, U.S. Dep't of Commerce, *1990 Census of Population: General Population Characteristics New York* (May 1992), 120, n.10

Bureau of the Census, U.S. Dep't of Commerce, *1990 Census of Population: General Population Characteristics United States* (Nov. 1992), 120, n.9, n.10

Bureau of the Census, U.S. Dep't of Commerce, *Statistical Abstract of the United States 1992*, 115, n.2

Bureau of the Census, U.S. Dep't of Commerce, *1990 Census of Population: General Population Characteristics Ohio* (June 1992), 120, n.9

Jan Herman Burgers, *The Road to San Francisco: The Revival of the Human Rights Idea in the Twentieth Century*, 14 HUM. RTS. Q. 447 (1992), **3-4**, 33

Kathryn Burke et al., *Application of International Human Rights Law in State and Federal Courts*, 18 TEX. INT'L L.J. 291 (1983), **579, 586**

Byron F. Burmester, *Comment, On Humanitarian Intervention: the New World Order and Wars to Preserve Human Rights*, 1994 UTAH L. REV. 269 (1994), 242

Anne-Marie Burley, *The Alien Tort Statute and the Judiciary Act of 1789: A Badge of Honor*, 83 AM. J. INT'L L. 461 (1989), 505, 521

Burma (Myanmar), *Human Rights Watch World Report* 132 (1995), **180-181**

Brian Burns, *The Time for Full United States Participation in the Inter-American System for the Protection of Human Rights*, 24 COLUM. HUM. RTS. L. REV. 435 (1993) (reviewing SCOTT DAVIDSON, THE INTER-AMERICAN COURT OF HUMAN RIGHTS (1992)), 449

John Burns, *Canada Wins U.S. Extradition Deal*, N.Y. TIMES, Feb. 14, 1992, at A3, 477

Peter Burns, *An International Criminal Tribunal: The Difficult Union of Principle and Politics*, 5 CRIM. L.F. 341 (1994), 282, n.4

Eve B. Burton & David B. Goldstein, *Vietnamese Women and Children Refugees in Hong Kong: An Argument Against Arbitrary Detention*, 4 DUKE J. COMP. & INT'L L. 71 (1993), 601

Jeanne A. Butterfield, *The New Asylum Regulations: A Practitioner's Guide*, IMMIGR. BRIEFINGS, Jan. 1995, at 1, 640

ANGELA BYRE, LEADING CASES AND MATERIALS ON THE SOCIAL POLICY OF THE EEC (1989), 493

Jonathan Cahn, *Challenging the New Imperial Authority: The World Bank and the Democratization of Development*, 6 HARV. HUM. RTS. J. 159 (1993), 392

Iain Cameron, *Turkey and Article 25 of the European Convention on Human Rights*, 37 INT'L & COMP. L.Q. 887 (1988),491

Peter S. Canellos, *UN Court Charges Bosnian Camp Leader; Indictment Alleges Murder, Torture of Civilians*, BOSTON GLOBE, Nov. 8, 1994, Nat'l/Foreign sec. at 2, 295

MAURO CAPPELLETTI & WILLIAM COHEN, COMPARATIVE CONSTITUTIONAL LAW (1979), 436

FERNANDO CARDOSO & ENZO FELETTO, DEPENDENCY AND DEVELOPMENT IN LATIN AMERICA (Berkeley: University of California Press, 1979), 168

David Carleton & Michael Stohl, *The Foreign Policy of Human Rights: Rhetoric and Reality From Jimmy Carter to Ronald Reagan*, 7 HUM. RTS. Q. 205 (1985), 389, 410

David Carleton & Michael Stohl, *The Role of Human Rights in U.S. Foreign Assistance Policy*, 31 AMER. J. POL. SCI. 1002 (1987), 751

Thomas Carothers, *Democracy and Human Rights: Policy Allies or Rivals?*, 17 WASH. Q. 109 (1994), 389

BARRY E. CARTER, INTERNATIONAL ECONOMIC SANCTIONS (1988), 420

Barry E. Carter, *International Economic Sanctions: Improving the Haphazard U.S. Legal Regime*, 75 CAL. L. REV. 1159 (1987), **415-419**

RICHARD CARVER, ZIMBABWE: A BREAK WITH THE PAST? (1989), 370

ANTONIO CASSESSE, HUMAN RIGHTS IN A CHANGING WORLD (1990), 691

Centre for Social Development and Humanitarian Affairs, *United Nations, Strategies for Confronting Domestic Violence: A Resource Manual* (1993), 533

Centre on Housing Rights and Evictions, *Forced Evictions & Human Rights: A Manual for Action* (1993), 79

Centre on Housing Rights and Evictions, *Forced Evictions: Violations of Human Rights* (6th compilation, 1994), 74, 75, 79

Christina Cerna & Wendy Young, *The Inter-American Commission on Human Rights and the Death Penalty*, 34 FED. B. NEWS & J. 398 (1987), 439

Christina Cerna, *US Death Penalty Tested Before the Inter-American Commission on Human Rights*, 10 NETH. Q. HUM. RTS. 155 (1992), 439

Hilary Charlesworth, Christine Chinkin & Shelley Wright, *Feminist Approaches to International Law*, 85 AM. J. INT'L L. 613, 616-34 (1991), **683-687**

NOAM CHOMSKY & EDWARD S. HERMAN, THE POLITICAL ECONOMY OF HUMAN RIGHTS: THE WASHINGTON CONNECTION AND THIRD WORLD FASCISM (Boston: South End Press, 1979), 711

Jarat Chopra & Thomas G. Weiss, *Sovereignty is No Longer Sacrosanct: Codifying Humanitarian Intervention*, 6 ETHICS & INT'L AFF. 95 (1992), 239

Gordon Christenson, *Attributing Acts of Omission to the State*, 12 MICH. J. INT'L L. 312 (1991), 675

Gordon A. Christenson, *The Uses of Human Rights Norms to Inform Constitutional Interpretation*, 4 HOUS. J. INT'L L. 39 (1981), 579

Warren Christopher, *Democracy and Human Rights: Where America Stands, Remarks at the World Conference on Human Rights* (June 14, 1993), **386-387**

WARREN CHRISTOPHER, THE DIPLOMACY OF HUMAN RIGHTS: THE FIRST YEAR, IN HUMAN RIGHTS AND U.S. FOREIGN POLICY 257 (Barry M. Rubin & Elizabeth P. Spiro eds. 1979), 414

Jorge Cicero, *The Alien Tort Statute of 1789 as a Remedy for Injuries to Foreign Nationals Hosted by the United States*, 23 COLUM. HUM. RTS. L. REV. 315 (1992), 521

David Cingranelli & Thomas Pasquarello, *Human Rights Practices and the Distribution of U.S. Foreign Aid to Latin American Countries*, 27(3) AMER. J. POL. SCI. 539 (1985), 168, 751

Linda Cipriani, *Gender and Persecution: Protecting Women Under International Refugee Law*, 7 GEO. IMMIGR. L.J. 511 (1993), 666

Andrew Clapham & Meg Henry, *Peacekeeping and Human Rights in Africa and Europe, in* HONORING HUMAN RIGHTS AND KEEPING THE PEACE 152 (Alice Henkin ed., 1995), 480

ANDREW CLAPHAM, HUMAN RIGHTS IN THE PRIVATE SPHERE (1993), 314, 533, 675

LUKE CLEMENTS, EUROPEAN HUMAN RIGHTS: TAKING A CASE UNDER THE CONVENTION (1994), 480

Josiah A.M. Cobbah, *African Values and the Human Rights Debate: An Africa Perspective*, 9 HUM. RTS. Q. 309 (1987), 682

Philip J. Cohen, *Ending the War and Securing Peace in Former Yugoslavia*, 6 PACE INT'L L. REV. 19 (1994), 297

ROBERTA COHEN & JACQUES CUENOD, THE BROOKINGS INSTITUTION—REFUGEE POLICY GROUP PROJECT ON INTERNAL DISPLACEMENT, IMPROVING INSTITUTIONAL ARRANGEMENTS FOR THE INTERNALLY DISPLACED (1995), 677

ROBERTA COHEN, REFUGEE POLICY GROUP, HUMAN RIGHTS PROTECTION FOR INTERNALLY DISPLACED PERSONS: AN INTERNATIONAL CONFERENCE (1991), 677

David Cole et al., *Interpreting the Alien Tort Statute: Amicus Curiae Memorandum of International Law Scholars and Practitioners in* Trajano v. Marcos, 12 HASTINGS INT'L & COMP. L. REV. 1 (1988), 520, n.8

Frank G. Colella, *Note: Beyond Institutional Competence: Congressional Efforts to Legislate United States Foreign Policy toward Nicaragua—The Boland Amendments*, 54 BROOK. L. REV. 131 (1988), 253

Sandra Coliver & Frank Newman, *Using International Human Rights Law to Influence United States Foreign Population Policy: Resort to Courts or Congress?*, 20 N.Y.U. J. INT'L. L. & POL. 53 (1987), 601, **612-613**

Sandra Coliver, *European Court of Human Rights Condemns Conditions on Virginia's Death Row*, 13 HUMAN RIGHTS ADVOCATES NEWSLETTER 23 (November 1989), 477

SANDRA COLIVER, INTERNATIONAL REPORTING PROCEDURES, IN GUIDE TO INTERNATIONAL HUMAN RIGHTS PRACTICE 245 (Hurst Hannum ed., 2d ed. 1992), 99, 141

Sandra Coliver, *United Nations Machineries on Women's Rights: How Might They Better Help Women Whose Rights are Being Violated?* in NEW DIRECTIONS IN HUMAN RIGHTS 25 (Ellen Lutz, Hurst Hannum & Kathryn Burke 1989), **214**

Comment, *International Convention on the Prevention and Punishment of the Crime of Genocide: United States Senate Grant of Advice and Consent to Ratification*, 1 HARV. HUM. RTS. Y.B. 227 (1988), 39

Comment, *The Use of Nonviolent Coercion: A Study in Legality Under Article 2(4) of the Charter of the United Nations*, 122 U. PA. L. REV. 983 (1974), 420

COMMENTARY ON THE GENEVA CONVENTIONS OF 12 AUGUST 1949, 49 (Jean Pictet ed. 1952), 523

The Commission of Inquiry into the Events at the Refugee Camps in Beirut—Final Report (1983) (authorized trans.), *reprinted in* JERUSALEM POST, Feb. 9, 1983, at 1, 273

Committee on International Human Rights of the Association of the Bar of the City of New York, *The Inter-American Commission on Human Rights: A Promise Unfulfilled* (1993), 449

CONFERENCES ON MOSLEM DOCTRINE AND HUMAN RIGHTS IN ISLAM (1974), 170

THE CONFERENCE ON SECURITY AND COOPERATION IN EUROPE: ANALYSIS AND BASIC DOCUMENTS (Arie Bloed ed., 1993), 496

CONTEMPORARY GENOCIDES, CAUSES, CASES, CONSEQUENCES (A.J. Jongman ed., 1996), 749

Contemporary Practice of the United States Relating to International Law, 86 AM. J. INT'L L. 346 (1992), 489

JASON COOKE, IRAN/CONTRA AFFAIR CHRONOLOGY (1987), 253

Rebecca J. Cook, *State Responsibility for Violations of Women's Human Rights*, 7 HARV. HUM. RTS. J. 125 (1994), 533

Rebecca J. Cook, *International Human Rights Law Concerning Women: Case Notes and Comments*, 23 VAND. J. TRANSNAT'L L. 779 (1990), 674

Fons Coomans, *Netherlands Inst. Hum. Rts., Economic, Social and Cultural Rights*, Netherlands Inst. Hum. Rts. SIM Special No. 16 (1995) (report commissioned by the Advisory Committee on Hum. Rts. and Foreign Pol'y of the Netherlands), 57

Mike Corder, *Defense to Appeal Tribunal Jurisdiction Ruling*, AP, Aug. 15, 1995, *available in* LEXIS, News Library, APINTL File, 287

Dusan Cotic, *Introduction*, 5 CRIM. L.F. 223, 225-26 (1994), 280

MATTHEW C.R. CRAVEN, THE INTERNATIONAL COVENANT ON ECONOMIC, SOCIAL, AND CULTURAL RIGHTS: A PERSPECTIVE ON ITS DEVELOPMENT (1995), 578

J.R. CRAWFORD, WITCHCRAFT AND SORCERY IN RHODESIA 280 (1967), **743**

James Crawford, *The ILC Adopts a Statute for an International Criminal Court*, 89 AM. J. INT'L L. 404 (1995), 305

Kathryn Lee Crawford, *Due Obedience and the Rights of Victims: Argentina's Transition to Democracy*, 12 HUM. RTS. Q. 17 (1990), 275

CRIMES OF WAR: A LEGAL, POLITICAL-DOCUMENTARY, AND PSYCHOLOGICAL INQUIRY INTO THE RESPONSIBILITY OF LEADERS, CITIZENS, AND SOLDIERS FOR CRIMINAL ACTS IN WARS (Richard A. Falk et al. eds., 1971), 167

John Crook, *The Fiftieth Session of the UN Commission on Human Rights*, 88 AM. J. INT'L L. 806 (1994), 202

John Crook, *The United Nations Compensation Commission—A New Structure to Enforce State Responsibility*, 87 AM. J. INT'L L. 144 (1993), 273, 488

Barbara Crossette, *U.N. is Concerned Over Bill to limit U.S. Peacekeeping Role*, N.Y. TIMES, Feb. 10, 1995, at A6, 239

CSCE High Commissioner on National Minorities, 2 INTERNATIONAL JOURNAL ON GROUP RIGHTS (K. Huber & R. Zaagman eds. 1994), 496

Jill Crystal, *The Human Rights Movement in the Arab World*, 16 HUM. RTS. Q. 435 (1994), 218

Katherine M. Culliton, *Finding a Mechanism to Enforce Women's Right to State Protection from Domestic Violence in the Americas*, 34 HARV. INT'L L.J. 507 (1993), 533, 674

Anthony D'Amato, *Comment: Nicaragua and International Law: the "Academic" and the "Real,"* 79 AM. J. INT'L L. 657 (1985), 253

Anthony D'Amato, *Is International Law Really "Law"?*, 79 NW. U. L. REV. 1293, 1293-95, 1299, 1303-04, 1308-13 (1985), **694-96**

Anthony D'Amato, *The Invasion of Panama Was a Lawful Response to Tyranny*, 84 AM. J. INT'L L. 516 (1990), 254

Laura Dalton, *Stanford v. Kentucky and Wilkins v. Missouri: A Violation of an Emerging Rule of Customary International Law*, 32 WM. AND MARY L. REV. 161 (1990), 439

Lori Fisler Damrosch, *International Human Rights Law in Soviet and American Courts*, 100 YALE L.J. 2315 (1991), 579

Lori Fisler Damrosch, *The Role of the Great Powers in United Nations Peace-Keeping*, 18 YALE J. INT'L L. 429 (1993), 242

Lori Fisler Damrosch, *The Role of the United States Senate Concerning "Self-Executing" and "Non Self-Executing" Treaties*, 67 CHI.-KENT L. REV. 515 (1991), 596

Mark Danner, *A Reporter at Large: The Truth of El Mozote*, NEW YORKER, Dec. 6, 1993, at 50, 390

M.S. DAOUDI & M.S. DAJANI, ECONOMIC SANCTIONS, IDEALS AND EXPERIENCE (1983), 420

Koen Davidse, *The 48th Session of the UN Commission on Human Rights and UN Monitoring of Violations of Civil and Political Rights*, 10 NETH. Q. HUM. RTS. 283 (1992), **211**

S. Davidson, *Group Formation and its Significance in the Nazi Concentration Camps*, 22 ISRAELI J. PSYCHIATRY & RELATED SCI. 41 (1985), 167

SCOTT DAVIDSON, THE INTER-AMERICAN COURT OF HUMAN RIGHTS (1992), 448

BRIAN L. DAVIS, QADDAFI, TERRORISM, AND THE ORIGINS OF THE U.S. ATTACK ON LIBYA (1990), 254

Dennis Davis & Michael D. Ward, *They Dance Alone: Deaths and the Disappeared in Contemporary Chile*, 34 J. CONFLICT RESOL. 449 (1990), 168

SHELTON H. DAVIS, VICTIMS OF THE MIRACLE: DEVELOPMENT AND THE INDIANS OF BRAZIL (1977), 722

SEBLE DAWIT, FEMALE GENITAL MUTILATION: VIOLENCE & WOMEN'S HUMAN RIGHTS (1993), 674

Alfred de Zayas, Jacob Th. Möller & Torkel Opsahl, *U.N. Centre for Human Rights Geneva, Application of the International Covenant on Civil and Political Rights under the Optional Protocol by the Human Rights Committee* (1990 ed.), 159

Alfred de Zayas, *The Right to One's Homeland, Ethnic Cleansing, and the International Criminal Tribunal for the Former Yugoslavia*, 6 CRIM. L.F. 257 (1995), 298

Connie de la Vega, *Protecting Economic, Social and Cultural Rights*, 15 WHITTIER L. REV. 471 (1994), 57

CONNIE DE LA VEGA, CIVIL RIGHTS DURING THE 90's—NEW TREATY LAW COULD HELP IMMENSELY (1996), 579, 612

Judith I. de Neufville, *Human Rights Reporting as a Policy Tool: An Examination of the State Department Country Reports*, 8 HUM. RTS. Q. 681 (1986), 402

Karel de Vey Mestdagh, *Reform of the European Convention on Human Rights in a Changing Europe, in* 3 THE DYNAMICS OF THE PROTECTION OF HUMAN RIGHTS IN EUROPE 337 (Rick Lawson & Matthijs de Blois eds., 1994), 481

Lisa J. Del Pizzo, *Note, Not Guilty—But Not Innocent: An Analysis of the Acquittal of John Demjanjuk and its Impact on the Future of Nazi War Crimes Trials*, 18 B.C. INT'L & COMP. L. REV. 137 (1995), 280

Jost Delbruck, *A Fresh Look at Humanitarian Intervention Under the Authority of the United Nations*, 67 IND. L.J. 887 (1992), 331

DEMOCRACY: A WORLDWIDE SURVEY (Robert Wesson ed.) (New York: Praeger, 1987), 750

Department of State, *Country Reports on Human Rights Practices for 1994*, 104TH CONG., 1ST SESS. (1995), 181

Deputy Secretary Warren Christopher, *Human Rights and the National Interest, Dep't of State, Bureau of Public Affairs, Current Policy No. 206* (1980), **379-383**

Jules Deschênes, *Toward International Criminal Justice*, 5 CRIM. L.F. 249 (1994), 280

Alain Destexhe, *The Third Genocide*, FOREIGN POL'Y, Winter 1994-95, 241

Detention of Refugees and Asylum-Seekers, UNHCR Ex. Comm. Conclusion 44, 37th Sess., *reprinted in Conclusions on the International Protection of Refugees adopted by the Executive Committee of the UNHCR Programme 96* (1980), 570

M. Deutsch, *The Prevention of World War III: A Psychological Perspective*, 4 POL. PSYCHOL. 3 (1983), 167

DEPENDENCE, DEVELOPMENT, AND STATE REPRESSION (George A. Lopez & Michael Stohl eds.) (New York: Greenwood Press, 1989), 749

Ann Devroy, *Clinton Reverses Course on China*, WASH. POST, May 27, 1994, at A1, 410

Ann Devroy, *Clinton Signs New Guidelines for U.N. Peacekeeping Operations*, WASH. POST, May 6, 1994, at A30, 241

LARRY DIAMOND, JUAN J. LINZ & SEYMOUR MARTIN LIPSET, POLITICS IN DEVELOPING COUNTRIES: COMPARING EXPERIENCES WITH DEMOCRACY (Boulder, CO: Lynne Rienner Publishers, 1990), 750

Peter C. Diamond, *Comment, Temporary Protected Status Under the Immigration Act of 1990*, 28 WILLIAMETTE L. REV. 857 (1992), 649

DIGEST OF STRASBOURG CASE-LAW RELATING TO THE EUROPEAN CONVENTION ON HUMAN RIGHTS (Peter Leuprecht & Pieter van Dijk, eds., 1984), 481

Gregory DiMeglio, *Claims Against Iraq: The UN Compensation Commission and Other Remedies*, 86 AM. SOC. INT'L L. PROC. 477 (1992), 488

THE DIPLOMACY OF HUMAN RIGHTS, 69-200 (David D. Newsom ed., 1986), 414

DISPLACED PEOPLES AND REFUGEE STUDIES (Julian Davies ed., 1990), 642

Michael Dobbs, *Bosnian Serbs Test West's Will as Settlement Options Dissolve*, Wash. Post, June 12, 1995, at A1, 420

Documentation, Information and Research Branch, Immigration and Refugee Board of Canada, *Human Rights Briefs: Women in the Islamic Republic of Iran* (1994), 147

Ustinia Dolgopol, *Women's Voices, Women's Pain*, 17 Hum. Rts. Q. 127 (1995), 693

Nicholas R. Doman, *Aftermath of Nuremberg: The Trial of Klaus Barbie*, 60 U. Colo. L. Rev. 449 (1989), 280

Jack Donnelly, *Cultural Relativism and Universal Human Rights*, 6 Hum. Rts. Q. 400, 410-19 (1984), **678-680**

Jack Donnelly, Universal Human Rights in Theory and Practice (1989), 682

Efua Dorkenoo & Scilla Elworthy, Female Genital Mutilation: Proposals for Change 7, (1992), 633, 670

Efua Dorkenoo, Cutting the Rose; Female Genital Mutilation: The Practice and its Prevention (1994), 674

Theodore Draper, A Very Thin Line: The Iran-Contra Affair (1991), 253

Robert F. Drinan, *Is a Permanent Nuremberg on the Horizon*, 18-Fall Fletcher F. World Aff. 103 (1994), 305

Robert F. Drinan, S.J. & Teresa T. Kuo, *Putting the World's Oppressors on Trial: The Torture Victim Protection Act*, 15 Hum. Rts. Q. 605 (1993), 552

Robert Drinan & Teresa Kuo, *The 1991 Battle for Human Rights in China*, 14 Hum. Rts. Q. 21 (1992), 682

William Drozdiak, *Serbs Raped 20,000, EC Team Says*, Wash. Post, Jan. 8, 1993, at A12, 296

William Drozdiak, *Top Serbs Charged with War Crimes*, Wash. Post, July 26, 1995, at A1, 295

William Drozdiak, *War Crimes Tribunal Arraigns 1st Suspect; Bosnian Serb Pleads Not Guilty to Charges that He Killed Muslims at Detention Camp*, Wash. Post, Apr. 27, 1995, at A31, 295

Andrew Drzemczewski, A Single Court of Human Rights in Strasbourg, Directorate of Human Rights, Council of Europe (Dec. 31, 1995), 481

Andrew Z. Drzemczewski, The European Convention in Domestic Law 177 (1983), 575

Andrew Drzemczewski, *The Role of NGOs in Human Rights Matters in the Council of Europe*, 8 H.R.L.J. 273 (1987), 480

P.J. Duffy, *Article 3 of the European Convention on Human Rights*, 32 Int'l & Comp. L.Q. 316 (1983), 159

William Durch, The Evolution of UN Peacekeeping: Case Studies and Comparative Analysis (1993), 496

Ronald M. Dworkin, Taking Rights Seriously (1977), 691

Kevin Dwyer, Arab Voices: The Human Rights Debate in the Middle East (1991), 170, 218

Economic, Social and Cultural Rights: A Textbook (Asbjorn Eide, Catarina Krause & Allan Rosas eds., 1995), 58

Timothy Egan, *An Ancient Ritual and a Mother's Asylum Plea*, N.Y. Times, Mar. 4, 1994, at A25, 672

Jan Egeland, Impotent Superpower, Potent Small State: Potentials and Limitations of Human Rights Objectives in the Foreign Policies of the United States and Norway (1988), 390

Asbjorn Eide, *Making Human Rights Universal: Unfinished Business*, 6 Nordic J. Hum. Rts. 51 (No. 4, 1988), 683

Albert A. Ehrenzweig, Law: A Personal View 27-67 (1977), 692

Asma El Dareer, Woman, Why Do You Weep? (1982), 674

Angela M. Elsperger, *Florida's Battle With the Federal Government Over Immigration Policy Holds Children Hostage: They Are Not Our Children?*, 13 Law and Inequality 141 (1994), 568

Karen Engle, *Female Subjects of Public International Law: Human Rights and the Exotic Other Female*, 26 New Engl. L. Rev. 1509 (1992), 674

Kathryn English & Adam Stapleton, The Human Rights Handbook, A Practical Guide to Monitoring Human Rights (1995), 329

David Epstein & Jeffrey L. Snyder, International Litigation: A Guide to Jurisdiction, Practice and Strategy § 8.02[2] (1993), 542

Leslie Espinoza, *Masks and Other Disguises: Exposing Legal Academia*, 103 Harv. L. Rev. 1878 (1990), 692

William Eskridge & Philip Frickey, Cases and Materials on Legislation: Statutes and the Creation of Public Policy 569 (1988), 454

Anthony Ewing, *Establishing State Responsibility for Private Acts of Violence Against Women under the American Convention on Human Rights*, 26 Colum. Hum. Rts. L. Rev. 751 (1995), 533

K. D. Ewing & C. A. Gearry, *Terminating Abortion Rights?*, 142 New L.J. 1696 (1992), 436

Fact-Finding Before International Tribunals [Eleventh Sokol Colloquium] (Richard B. Lillich ed., 1991), 357

Richard Falk, Reviving the World Court (1986), 240

Richard Falk, *The Haiti Intervention: A Dangerous World Order Precedent for the United Nations*, 36 Harv. Int'l L.J. 341 (1995), 253

Douglas Farah, *Toughest Task in Haiti: Reviving Economy*, Wash. Post, Sept. 23, 1994, at A1, 419

Daniel A. Farber, *Poverty and Discrimination: Notes on American Apartheid*, 11 Const. Comment. 455 (1994-95), 112

Daniel A. Farber, *Book Review: Black Races, Black Interests: The Representation of African Americans in Congress. By Carol M. Swain*, 11 Const. Comment. 613 (1994-95), 112

Tom J. Farer, *Panama: Beyond the Charter Paradigm*, 84 Am. J. Int'l L. 503 (1990), 254

Tom J. Farer & Christopher C. Joyner, *The United States and the Use of Force: Looking Back to See Ahead*, 1 Transnat'l L. & Contemp. Prob. 15 (1991), **247-252**

Tom J. Farer, *Human Rights in Law's Empire: The Jurisprudence War*, 85 Am. J. Int'l L. 117 (1991), 691

Tom J. Farer, *The Inter-American Commission on Human Rights: Operations and Doctrine*, 9 Int'l J.L. Libr. (1981), 389, 448

Ahmad Farrag, *Human Rights and Liberties in Islam, in* Human Rights in a Pluralist World (J. Berting et al. eds., 1990), 170

Stephanie Farrior, in Molding the Matrix: The Theoretical and Historical Foundations of International Law Concerning Hate Speech (1995), 693

Feminist Jurisprudence Symposium, 24 Ga. L. Rev. 759 (1990), 693

W.J. Fenrick, *Some International Law Problems Related to Prosecutions before the International Criminal Tribunal for the Former Yugoslavia*, 6 Duke J. Comp. & Int'l L. 103 (1995), 298

Benjamin B. Ferencz, *An International Criminal Code and Court: Where They Stand and Where They're Going*, 30 Colum. J. Transnat'l L. 375 (1992), 305

Lois E. Fielding, *Taking the Next Step in the Development of New Human Rights: the Emerging Right of Humanitarian Assistance to Restore Democracy*, 5 Duke J. Comp. & Int'l L. 329 (1995), 242

Ivana Filice et al., *Women Refugees from Bosnia-Herzegovina: Developing a Culturally Sensitive Counselling Framework*, 6 Int'l J. Refugee Law 207 (1994), 666

Dana D. Fischer, *Reporting Under the Covenant on Civil and Political Rights: The First Five Years of the Women Rights Committee*, 76 Am. J. Int'l L. 142 (1982), 99, 141

Joan Fitzpatrick & Paul Hoffman, *Human Rights Litigation Update Report*, ACLU International Civil Liberties Report 30 (Mar. 1995), 489

Joan Fitzpatrick & Alice Miller, *International Standards on the Death Penalty: Shifting Discourse*, 19 Brook. J. Int'l Law 273 (1993), 608

Joan Fitzpatrick et al., *Human Rights Litigation Update Report*, ACLU International Civil Liberties Report 30 (1995), 552, 584

Joan Fitzpatrick et al., *Recent Developments in International Human Rights Litigation and Legislation*, ACLU International Civil Liberties Report 37 (1993), 551

Joan Fitzpatrick, *Flight from Asylum: Trends Toward Temporary "Refuge" and Local Responses to Forced Migrations*, 35 Va. J. Int'l L. 13 (1994), 649

Joan Fitzpatrick, *Nothing But the Truth? Transitional Regimes Confront the Past,* 16 MICH. J. INT'L L. 713 (1995) (book review of IMPUNITY AND HUMAN RIGHTS IN INTERNATIONAL LAW AND PRACTICE (Naomi Roht-Arriaza ed., 1995)), 275

Joan Fitzpatrick, *The Future of the Alien Tort Claims Act of 1789: Lessons from* In Re Marcos Human Rights Litigation, 67 ST. JOHN'S L. REV. 491 (1993), 136, 505, 521, 522, 540, 541

Joan Fitzpatrick, *The* Karadzic *Cases: Establishing Accountability for On-Going Gross Human Rights Violations through Litigation in U.S. Courts,* (May 20, 1995), 532

Joan Fitzpatrick, *UN Action With Respect to "Disappearances" and Summary or Arbitrary Executions,* 5 AIUSA LEGAL SUPPORT NETWORK NEWSLETTER 35 (Fall 1988), 202

Cees Flinterman & Evelyn Ankumah, *The African Charter on Human and Peoples' Rights, in* GUIDE TO INTERNATIONAL HUMAN RIGHTS PRACTICE 159 (Hurst Hannum ed., 2d ed. 1992), 465

Steven Fogelson, *Note, The Nuremberg Legacy: An Unfulfilled Promise,* 63 S. CAL. L. REV. 833 (1990), 280

Steven Fogelson, *Note, United States Navy War Crimes Trials (1945-1949),* 5 WASHBURN L.J. 89 (1965), 280

David Forsythe & Kelly Pease, *Human Rights, Humanitarian Intervention, and World Politics,* 15 HUM. RTS. Q. 290 (1993), 331

DAVID P. FORSYTHE, HUMAN RIGHTS AND FOREIGN POLICY: CONGRESS RECONSIDERED (1988), 399

David P. Forsythe, *Democracy, War, and Covert Action,* 29 J. PEACE RES. 385 (1992), 253

David P. Forsythe, *Congress and Human Rights in U.S. Foreign Policy: The Fate of General Legislation,* 9 HUM. RTS. Q. 382 (1987), 391

David P. Forsythe, *Politics and the International Tribunal for the Former Yugoslavia,* 5 CRIM. L.F. 401 (1994), **292-294**

DAVID P. FORSYTHE, HUMAN RIGHTS AND WORLD POLITICS 88 (1983), 389

Gregory Fox, *The Right to Political Participation in International Law,* 17 YALE J. INT'L L. 539 (1992), 331

Thomas Franck & Faiza Patel, *UN Police Action in Lieu of War: "The Old Order Changeth",* 85 AM. J. INT'L L. 63 (1991), 331

THOMAS M. FRANCK, DOES THE RULE OF LAW APPLY TO FOREIGN AFFAIRS (1992), 403

THOMAS M. FRANCK, NATION AGAINST NATION (1985), 7

Donald M. Fraser, *Congress's Role in the Making of International Human Rights Policy, in* HUMAN RIGHTS AND AMERICAN FOREIGN POLICY 247 (Donald P. Kommers & Gilburt D. Loescher eds., 1979), **392-395**

Michael Freeman, *Racism, Rights and the Quest for Equality of Opportunity: A Critical Legal Essay,* 23 HARV. C.R.-C.L. L. REV. 295 (1988), 692

Michael Freeman, *The Philosophical Foundations of Human Rights,* 16 HUM. RTS. Q. 491 (1994), 691

FREEDOM FROM VIOLENCE: WOMEN'S STRATEGIES FROM AROUND THE WORLD (Margaret Schuler ed., 1992), 674

Friends World Committee for Consultation, Society of Friends, *Report on the 1995 UN Commission on Human Rights* (1995), 200

PHILIP P. FRICKEY, DOMESTICATING FEDERAL INDIAN LAW 37 (1996), 607

Maryellen Fullerton, *A Comparative Look at Refugee Status Based on Persecution Due to Membership in a Particular Social Group,* 26 CORNELL INT'L L.J. 505 (1993), 666

Randy Furst, *A Child is Spared: Family Escapes Deportation, Their Daughter's Ritual Mutilation,* STAR TRIB. (Minneapolis), Mar. 25, 1994, at 1B, 633, 673

Peter Gabel, *The Phenomenology of Rights-Consciousness and the Pact of the Withdrawn Selves,* 62 TEX. L. REV. 1563 (1984), 692

Margaret Galey, *Congress, Foreign Policy and Human Rights Ten Years After Helsinki,* 7 HUM. RTS. Q. 334 (1985), 399

C.J. Gamble, *State Sterilization Programs for the Prophylactic Control of Mental Disease and Mental Deficiency,* 102 AMER. J. PSYCHIATRY 289 (1945), 728

Elaine Ganley, *Islamic Fundamentalists Seen Leading in Landmark Algerian Elections*, WASH. POST, Dec. 27, 1991, at A14, 275

Michael Garcia Bochenek, *Compensation for Human Rights Abuses in Zimbabwe*, 26 COLUM. HUM. RTS. L. REV. 483 (1995), 273

Diego García-Sayán, *Human Rights and Peace-Keeping Operations*, 29 U. RICH. L. REV. 41 (1994), 242

Alejandro M. Garro, *Nine Years of Transition to Democracy in Argentina: Partial Failure or Qualified Success?*, 31 COLUM. J. TRANSNAT'L L. 1 (1993), 370

Raymond Gastil, *The Comparative Survey of Freedom: Experiences and Suggestions*, 25 STUD. COMP. INT'L DEV. 25 (1990), 750

Timothy A. Gelatt, *Public Law, Private Actors: The Impact of Human Rights on Business Investors in China*, 14 J. INT'L L. BUS. 66 (1993), 410

Jeffrey L. Geller & Maxine Harris, *Women of the Asylum: Voices from Behind the Walls*, 1840-1945, at 256 (1994), 728

KENNETH Y. GEMAN, PRACTISING LAW INSTITUTE, IMPORTANT NEW ASYLUM REGULATIONS (1995), 640

Deborah R. Gerstel & Adam G. Segall, *Conference Report: Human Rights in American Courts*, 1 AM. U. J. INT'L L. & POL'Y 137 (1986), **624-628**

William N. Gianaris, *The New World Order and the Need for an International Criminal Court*, 16 FORDHAM INT'L L.J. 88 (1992), 305

Mark Gibney, *Human Rights and Human Consequences: A Critical Analysis of* Sanchez-Espinoza v. Reagan, 10 LOY. L.A. INT'L & COMP. L.J. 299 (1988), 630

Janice T. Gibson & Mika Haritos-Fatouros, *The Education of a Torturer*, PSYCHOL. TODAY 50 (1986), 139

David Gillies, *Human Rights, Governance, and Democracy: The World Bank's Problem Frontiers*, 11 NETH. Q. HUM. RTS. 3 (1993), 392

Gregory D. Gisvold, *Note, Strangers in a Strange Land: Assessing the Fate of Foreign Nationals Arrested in the United States by State and Local Authorities*, 78 MINN. L. REV. 771 (1994), 630

Michael J. Glennon, *State-Sponsored Abduction: A Comment on* United States v. Alvarez-Machain, 86 AM. J. INT'L L. 746 (1992), 584

Leonard B. Glick, *Religion and Genocide, in* THE WIDENING CIRCLE OF GENOCIDE 43 (Israel W. Charny ed., 1994) (Vol. 3 in GENOCIDE: A CRITICAL BIBLIOGRAPHIC REVIEW), 739

Pamela Goldberg, *Anyplace but Home: Asylum in the United States for Women Fleeing Intimate Violence*, 26 CORNELL INT'L L.J. 565 (1993), 666, 667

Richard J. Goldstone, *The International Tribunal for the Former Yugoslavia: A Case Study in Security Council Action*, 6 DUKE J. COMP. & INT'L L. 5 (1995), 298

Stephen Golub, *Strengthening Human Rights Monitoring Missions: An Options Paper prepared for the United States Agency for International Development* (1995), 242

Jose L. Gomez del Prado, *United Nations Conventions on Human Rights: The Practice of the Human Rights Committee and the Committee on the Elimination of Racial Discrimination in Dealing with Reporting Obligations of States Parties*, 7 HUM. RTS. Q. 492 (1985), 99, 141

Mario Gomez, *Social Economic Rights and Human Rights Commissions*, 17 HUM. RTS. Q. 155 (1995), 81

GUY S. GOODWIN-GILL, THE REFUGEE IN INTERNATIONAL LAW (1983), 623, 642, 664

GUY S. GOODWIN-GILL, FREE AND FAIR ELECTIONS: INTERNATIONAL LAW AND PRACTICE (1994), 329

Merrill Goozner, *Indonesia Pays a Price for Rapid Turnaround*, CHIC. TRIB., Nov. 15, 1993 at C1, 398

Melissa Gordon, *Note and Comment, Justice on Trial: The Efficacy of the International Criminal Tribunal for Rwanda*, 1 ILSA J. INT'L & COMP. L. 217 (1995), 297

Erin E. Gorman, *Comment,* Reno v. Flores: *The INS' Automatic Detention Policy for Alien Children*, 7 GEO. IMMIGR. L.J. 435 (1993), 557, n.1

W. Paul Gormley, *Human Rights and Environment: The Need for International Cooperation* (1976), 84

John M. Goshko, *Clinton Seen Calming Hill on Peace Keeping*, WASH. POST, Oct. 2, 1993, at A16, 240

John M. Goshko, *Around the World—U.N., Iraq to Discuss Oil Sales,* WASH. POST, Feb. 28, 1996, at A22, 419

John M. Goshko, *Clinton to Continue Foreign Aid Cuts,* WASH. POST, Aug. 14, 1993, at A13, 409

Evan Gottesman, *The Reemergence of Quisas and Diyats in Pakistan,* 23 COLUM. HUM. RTS. L. REV. 433 (1992), 683

ATLE GRAHL-MADSEN, THE STATUS OF REFUGEES IN INTERNATIONAL LAW (1966), 642

ATLE GRAHL-MADSEN, THE STATUS OF REFUGEES IN INTERNATIONAL LAW (1966, 1972), 623

M. Christian Green, *The 'Matrioshka' Strategy: U.S. Evasion of the International Covenant on Civil and Political Rights,* 10 SO. AFR. J. HUM. RTS. 357 (1994), 41

Robert Greenberger, *U.S., Unhappy with Beijing's Abuse of Human Rights, Focuses on Olympics,* WALL ST. J., Aug. 23, 1993, at A7, 421

Stan R. Gregory, *Note, Capital Punishment and Equal Protection: Constitutional Problems, Race and the Death Penalty,* 5 ST. THOMAS L. REV. 257 (1992), **121**

Lyndsay Griffiths, *Clinton Ends Rights Link to Chinese Trade Status,* CHIC. SUN-TIMES, May 27, 1994, at 10, 410

Claudio Grossman, *Proposals to Strengthen the Inter-American System of Protection of Human Rights,* 32 GERMAN Y.B. INT'L L. 264 (1990), 448

Isabelle R. Gunning, *Arrogant Perception, World-Travelling and Multicultural Feminism: The Case of Female Genital Surgeries,* 23 COLUM. HUM. RTS. L. REV. 189 (1992), 674

TED ROBERT GURR, THE POLITICAL ORIGINS OF STATE VIOLENCE AND TERROR: A THEORETICAL ANALYSIS, IN GOVERNMENT VIOLENCE AND REPRESSION: AN AGENDA FOR RESEARCH (Michael Stohl & George A. Lopez eds.) (Westport, CT: Greenwood, 1986), 750

Jimmy Gurulé, *Terrorism, Territorial Sovereignty, and the Forcible Apprehension of International Criminals Abroad,* 17 HASTINGS INT'L & COMP. L. REV. 457 (1994), 419

Peter Hakim, *Behind Guatemala's 'Miracle',* CHRISTIAN SCI. MONITOR, June 23, 1993, at 18, 421

Malvina Halberstam, *In Defense of the Supreme Court Decision in* Alvarez-Machain, 86 AM. J. INT'L L. 736 (1992), 584

Malvina Halberstam, *The Copenhagen Document: Intervention in Support of Democracy,* 34 HARV. INT'L L.J. 163 (1993), 389

MUNYONZWE HAMALENGWA ET AL., THE INTERNATIONAL LAW OF HUMAN RIGHTS IN AFRICA: BASIC DOCU-MENTS AND ANNOTATED BIBLIOGRAPHY (1988), 465

Françoise J. Hampson, *Violation of Fundamental Rights in the Former Yugoslavia: The Case for a War Crimes Tribunal, Occasional Paper 3,* at 1 (The David Davies Memorial Inst. of Int'l Stud., 1993), **291-292**

HURST HANNUM, MATERIALS ON INTERNATIONAL HUMAN RIGHTS AND U.S. CRIMINAL LAW AND PROCEDURE 10 (1989), 583, 630

Tom Harkin, *Human Rights and Foreign Aid: Forging an Unbreakable Link, in* HUMAN RIGHTS AND U.S. FOREIGN POLICY: PRINCIPLES AND APPLICATIONS 15 (Peter G. Brown & Douglas MacLean eds., 1979), 399

Angela Harris, *Race and Essentialism in Feminist Legal Theory,* 32 STAN. L. REV. 581 (1990), 90

John F. Harris, *Clinton Cheers Haiti's "2nd Chance" President, on Visit, Puts U.S. Troops Under U.N. Command,* WASH. POST, Apr. 1, 1995, at A1, 253

HERBERT L.A. HART, THE CONCEPT OF LAW (1981), 692

Joan Hartman, *"Unusual" Punishment: The Domestic Effects of International Norms Restricting the Application of the Death Penalty,* 52 CIN. L. REV. 655 (1983), 439, 579

Joan Hartman, *Derogations from Human Rights Treaties in Public Emergencies,* 22 HARV. INT'L L.J. 1 (1981), 17

Harvard Clinic's Efforts Lead to U.S. Recognition of Politically Motivated Sexual Violence in Asylum Claims of Women Refugees, HARVARD L. SCHOOL NEWS (Harvard Law School, Cambridge, MA) May 26, 1995, at 1-2, 4, 665

Harvard Law Review Ass'n, *Leading Cases, Foreign Sovereign Immunity: Commercial Activities,* 107 HARV. L. REV. 264 (1993), 539

Harvard Law Review Ass'n, *State Constitutional Rights in the Federal System,* 95 HARV. L. REV. 1331 (1982), 574

Harvard Law School Human Rights Program, *Applying Rights Rhetoric to Economic and Social Claims, in* ECONOMIC AND SOCIAL RIGHTS AND THE RIGHT TO HEALTH 1 (An Interdisciplinary Discussion Held at Harvard Law School in September 1993) (1995), 65

Harvard Law School Human Rights Program, *Institutionalizing Economic and Social Rights, in* ECONOMIC AND SOCIAL RIGHTS AND THE RIGHT TO HEALTH 35 (An Interdisciplinary Discussion Held at Harvard Law School in September 1993) (1995), 65

Harvard Law School Human Rights Program, *Defining the Right to Adequate Health, in* ECONOMIC AND SOCIAL RIGHTS AND THE RIGHT TO HEALTH 17 (An Interdisciplinary Discussion Held at Harvard Law School in September 1993) (1995), 84

Suhail Hashmi, *Is There an Islamic Ethic of Humanitarian Intervention?,* 7 ETHICS & INT'L AFF. 55 (1993), 170

Riffat Hassan, *On Human Rights and the Qur'anic Perspective,* 19 J. ECUMENICAL STUD. 51 (Summer 1982), 170

S. FAROOQ A. HASSAN, THE ISLAMIC REPUBLIC: POLITICS, LAW AND ECONOMY (1984), **168-170**

JAMES C. HATHAWAY, THE LAW OF REFUGEE STATUS (1991), 6

Stanley Heginbotham & Vita Bite, *Issues in Interpretation and Evaluation of Country Studies, in* HUMAN RIGHTS AND U.S. FOREIGN POLICY 195 (Barry M. Rubin & Elizabeth P. Spiro, eds. 1979), 403

J. Bryan Hehir, *Intervention: From Theories to Cases,* 9 ETHICS & INT'L AFF. 1 (1995), 252

Reinhard Heinisch, *Political Explanations of Basic Human Rights Performance,* Paper Prepared for the Annual American Political Science Association Meeting, New York City (1994), **712-715**

Arthur C. Helton, *The Mandate of U.S. Courts to Protect Aliens and Refugees Under International Human Rights Law,* 100 YALE L.J. 2335 (1991), 579

Conway Henderson, *Conditions Affecting the Use of Political Repression,* 35 J. CONFLICT RESOL. 120 (1991), 719

Conway Henderson, *Population Pressures and Political Repression,* 74 SOC. SCI. Q. 322 (1993), 719

LOUIS HENKIN ET AL., RIGHT V. MIGHT: INTERNATIONAL LAW AND THE USE OF FORCE (1991), 242

Louis Henkin, *Lexical Priority or "Political Question": A Response,* 101 HARV. L. REV. 524 (1987), 594

Louis Henkin, *The Constitution and United States Sovereignty: A Century of Chinese Exclusion and Its Progeny,* 100 HARV. L. REV. 853 (1987), 568

LOUIS HENKIN, THE AGE OF RIGHTS (1990), 691

DOUGLAS A. HIBBS, JR., MASS POLITICAL VIOLENCE: A CROSS-NATIONAL CAUSAL ANALYSIS (New York: Wiley, 1973), 750

Keith Highet & George Kahale III, *International Decisions* (United States v. Alvarez-Machain), 86 AM. J. INT'L L. 811 (1992), 533

Keith Highet et al., *Foreign Sovereign Immunities Act Commercial Activity Exception Nature and Purpose Tests Police Power as Sovereign Power,* 87 AM. J. INT'L L. 442 (1993), 539

Keith Highet, *Evidence, the Court, and the Nicaragua Case,* 81 AM. J. INT'L L. 1 (1987), 252

DILYS HILL, DEVELOPMENT ASSISTANCE AND HUMAN RIGHTS: PRINCIPLES, CRITERIA AND PROCEDURES (1991), 87

Albert O. Hirschman, *The On-and-Off Connection Between Political and Economic Progress,* AMER. ECON. REV. 343 (May 1994), 749

Paul L. Hoffman, *The Application of International Human Rights in State Courts: A View from California,* 18 INT'L LAWYER 61 (1984), 575

Paul L. Hoffman & Nadine Strossen, *Enforcing International Human Rights Law in the United States, in* HUMAN RIGHTS: AN AGENDA FOR THE NEXT CENTURY 477 (Louis Henkin & John L. Hargrove eds., 1994), 579

Daniel J.B. Hofrenning, *Human Rights and Foreign Aid: A Comparison of the Reagan and Carter Administrations*, 18 AMER. POLITICS Q. 514 (1990), 415

David Holley & Elizabeth Lu, *Judge Orders INS to Free 2 Children; Advocates Say Ruling Could Aid Hundreds of Illegals*, L.A. TIMES, July 20, 1985, at 21, 558

Kim Holmes, *New World Disorder: A Critique of the United Nations*, 46 J. INT'L AFF. 323 (1993), 332

Sharon K. Hom, *Female Infanticide in China: The Human Rights Specter and Thoughts Toward A(nother) Vision*, 23 COLUM. HUM. RTS. L. REV. 249 (1992), 683

Harold Hongju Koh, *Democracy and Human Rights in the United States Foreign Policy?: Lessons from the Haitian Crisis*, 48 SMU L. REV. 189 (1994), 419

Harold Hongju Koh, *The "Haiti Paradigm" in United States Human Rights Policy*, 103 YALE L.J. 2391 (1994), 390

HONORING HUMAN RIGHTS AND KEEPING THE PEACE: LESSONS FROM EL SALVADOR, CAMBODIA, AND HAITI (Alice Henkin ed., 1995), 332

Scott Horton & Randy Sellier, *The Utility of Presidential Certifications of Compliance with United States Human Rights Policy: The Case of El Salvador*, 1982 WIS. L. REV. 825, 395

FRAN P. HOSKEN, THE HOSKEN REPORT—GENITAL AND SEXUAL MUTILATION OF FEMALES (1992), 634

Seyyed Hossein Nasr, *The Concept and Reality of Freedom in Islam and Islamic Civilization*, in THE PHILOSOPHY OF HUMAN RIGHTS: INTERNATIONAL PERSPECTIVES (Rosenbaum ed., 1980), 171

RHODA E. HOWARD, HUMAN RIGHTS AND THE SEARCH FOR COMMUNITY (1995), 683

Rhoda E. Howard & Jack Donnelly, *Human Dignity, Human Rights, and Political Regimes*, 80 AM. POL. SCI. REV. 801 (1986), 112

Rhoda Howard, *The Full Belly Thesis: Should Economic Rights Take Priority Over Civil and Political Rights*, 5 HUM. RTS. Q. 467 (1983), 65

Nicholas Howen, *From Nuremberg to the Balkans: The International War Crimes Tribunal for the Former Yugoslavia*, in MONITORING HUMAN RIGHTS IN EUROPE 261 (Arie Bloed et al. eds., 1993), 298

Evelyn Hubner, Dietrich Ruessemeyer & John D. Stephens, *The Impact of Economic Development on Democracy*, 7(3) J. ECON. PERSPECTIVES 71 (Summer 1993), 749

GARY C. HUFBAUER & JEFFREY J. SCHOTT, ECONOMIC SANCTIONS RECONSIDERED: HISTORY AND CURRENT POLICY (rev. ed. 1990), 420

Kevin D. Hughes, *Hostages' Rights: The Unhappy Legal Predicament of an American Held in Foreign Captivity*, 26 COLUM. J.L. & SOC. PROBS. 555 (1993), 621

THE HUMAN DIMENSION OF THE HELSINKI PROCESS: THE VIENNA FOLLOW-UP MEETING AND ITS AFTERMATH (Arie Bloed and Pieter van Dijk eds., 1991), 496

HUMAN RIGHTS AND CHINESE VALUES: LEGAL, PHILOSOPHICAL, AND POLITICAL PERSPECTIVES (Michael C. Davis ed., 1995), 683

HUMAN RIGHTS AND PLURALIST DEMOCRACY (Allan Rosas & Jan Helgesen eds., 1992), 389

HUMAN RIGHTS AND STATISTICS: GETTING THE RECORD STRAIGHT (Thomas B. Jabine & Richard P. Claude eds.) (Philadelphia: University of Pennsylvania, 1992), 749

HUMAN RIGHTS AND U.S. FOREIGN POLICY: WHO CONTROLS THE AGENDA? (Stanley Foundation, Iowa) (reporting on the 35th Strategy for Peace, U.S. Foreign Policy Conference held on Oct. 27-29, 1994), 390

HUMAN RIGHTS IN CROSS-CULTURAL PERSPECTIVES: A QUEST FOR CONSENSUS (Abdullahi Ahmed An-Na'im ed. 1991), 683

HUMAN RIGHTS IN AFRICA: CROSS-CULTURAL PERSPECTIVES (Abdullahi Ahmed An-Na'im & Francis Deng eds., 1990), 465

HUMAN RIGHTS IN ISLAM: REPORT OF A SEMINAR HELD IN KUWAIT, DECEMBER 1980 (1982), 170

HUMAN RIGHTS IN DOMESTIC LAW AND DEVELOPMENT ASSISTANCE POLICIES OF THE NORDIC COUNTRIES (Lars A. Rehof & Claus Gulmann eds., 1989), 390

Human Rights in the World and Community Human Rights Policy for the Years 1991-1992, 14 H.R.L.J. 284 (1993), 493

Human Rights in Developing Countries, YEARBOOK 1994 (Peter Baehr, Hilde Hey, Jacqueline Smith, Theresa Swinehart eds., 1994), 334

HUMAN RIGHTS OF WOMEN: NATIONAL AND INTERNATIONAL PERSPECTIVES (Rebecca J. Cook ed., 1994), 675

Human Rights Watch/Americas, *Disappeared in Guatemala: The Case of Efraín Bámaca Velásquez* (Human Rights Watch/Americas, New York, N.Y.), Mar. 1995, 399, 414

Human Rights Watch & American Civil Liberties Union, *Human Rights Violations in the United States: A Report on U.S. Compliance with The International Covenant on Civil and Political Rights* (1993), **115-118**

Human Rights Watch Children's Rights Project, *United States: A World Leader in Executing Juveniles,* Vol. 7, No., 2 (1995), 126

Human Rights Watch/Americas, *Peru: The Two Faces of Justice* (1995), 275

Human Rights Watch & Lawyers Committee for Human Rights, *Critique: A Review of the Department of State's Country Reports on Human Rights Practices for 1988,* at 1 (1989), 129

Human Rights Watch, *The Lost Agenda: Human Rights and U.N. Field Operations* (1993), 242

Human Rights Watch Children's Rights Project, *United States: A World Leader in Executing Juveniles* 2 (Mar. 1995), 608

SAMUEL HUNTINGTON, POLITICAL ORDER IN CHANGING SOCIETIES (New Haven: Yale University Press, 1968), 711

Samuel Huntington, *Will More Countries Become Democratic?,* POL. SCI. Q. 99 (Summer 1984), 711

SAMUEL P. HUNTINGTON, CIVILIAN CONTROL OF THE MILITARY: A THEORETICAL STATEMENT, IN POLITICAL BEHAVIOR: A READER IN THEORY AND RESEARCH (H. Eulau, S. Eldersveld & M. Janowitz eds.) (New York: Free Press, 1956), 750

SAMUEL P. HUNTINGTON, THE SOLDIER AND THE STATE: THE THEORY AND POLITICS OF CIVIL-MILITARY RELATIONS (New York: Vintage Books, 1964), 750

SAMUEL P. HUNTINGTON, POLITICAL ORDER IN CHANGING SOCIETIES (1968), 167

Luc Huyse, *Justice after Transition: On the Choices Successor Elites Make in Dealing with the Past,* 20 L. & SOCIAL INQUIRY 51 (1995), 275

Patricia Hyndman, *The 1951 Convention and its Implications for Procedural Questions,* 6 INT'L J. REFUGEE LAW 245 (1994), 642

Sarah Ignatius, *Restricting the Rights of Asylum Seekers: The New Legislative and Administrative Proposals,* 7 HARV. HUM. RTS. J. 225 (1994), 640

IMPUNITY AND HUMAN RIGHTS IN INTERNATIONAL LAW AND PRACTICE (Naomi Roht-Arriaza ed., 1995), 275

"INALIENABLE, INTEGRAL AND INDIVISIBLE"—WOMEN'S RIGHTS ARE HUMAN RIGHTS: DISCUSSION PAPER ON THE 1995 THEME CAMPAIGN ON WOMEN AND HUMAN RIGHTS, AI Index: ACT 77/03/94 (1994), 666

Indonesia Military Allowed to Obtain Training in U.S., N.Y. TIMES, Dec. 8, 1993, at A14, 398

Indonesia Reduces Separatist's Prison Term, N.Y. TIMES, Aug. 15, 1993, at 6, 398

Int'l Commission of Jurists, *The Establishment of a Permanent International Penal Court, in* TOWARDS UNIVERSAL JUSTICE 11 (1993), 305

Int'l Labor Rights Education and Research Fund, *Briefing Paper, U.S. Compliance with Labor Rights Provisoins of Article 22 of the ICCPR* (1994), 126

Inter-American Commission on Human Rights, *25 Years of Struggle for Human Rights in the Americas* (1984), 448

Inter-American Commission on Human Rights (IACHR), *Washington: Application of Death Penalty on Juveniles in the U.S./Violation of Human Rights Obligation Within the Inter-American System,* 8 H.R.L.J. 345 (1987), 180

INTERNATIONAL DIMENSIONS OF HUMAN RIGHTS 107 (Karel Vasak ed., 1982), 601

Timothy C. Evered, *An International Criminal Court: Recent Proposals and American Concerns,* 6 PACE INT'L L. REV. 121 (1994), 303

INTERNATIONAL HUMAN RIGHTS INSTRUMENTS (Richard Lillich ed., 1986), 39

THE INTERNATIONAL HUMAN RIGHTS LAW GROUP, GUIDELINES FOR INTERNATIONAL ELECTION OBSERVING (1984), 330

International Institute of Higher Studies in Criminal Sciences, *Draft Charter of Human and People's Rights in the Arab World* (1987), 170

International Institute of Human Rights, *Pour une Commission d'etude sur la protection des droits de l'homme dans le context musulman* (1971), 170

International Institute of Human Rights, *Sélection bibliographique des ouvrages concernant de droit en général et les droits de l'homme dans les pays islamiques* (1971), 170

INTERNATIONAL LAW AND FACT-FINDING IN THE FIELD OF HUMAN RIGHTS (Bertie G. Ramcharan ed., 1982), 330

THE INTERNATIONAL LAW COMMISSION'S DRAFT ARTICLES ON STATE RESPONSIBILITY (Shibtai Rosenne ed., 1991), 304

International League for Human Rights, *Combatting Violence Against Women* (1993) (report of a conference sponsored by the League in collaboration with International Women's Rights Action Watch), 675

International Service for Human Rights, HUMAN RIGHTS MONITOR 25 (Sep. 1994), 372

Gregory Francis Intoccia, *American Bombing of Libya: An International Legal Analysis*, 19 CASE W. RES. J. INT'L L. 177 (1987), 254

Judith Innes, *Human Rights Reporting as a Policy Tool: An Examination of the State Department Country Reports, in* HUMAN RIGHTS AND STATISTICS: GETTING THE RECORD STRAIGHT 235 (Thomas Jabine & Richard Claude eds., 1992), 338

Yuji Iwasawa, *The Doctrine of Self-Executing Treaties in the United States: A Critical Analysis*, 26 VA. J. INT'L L. 627 (1986), 594

Jacoby, *The Reagan Turnaround on Human Rights*, 64 FOREIGN AFFAIRS 1066 (1986), 389

KEVIN T. JACKSON, CHARTING GLOBAL RESPONSIBILITIES: LEGAL PHILOSOPHY AND HUMAN RIGHTS (1994), 691

MARK W. JANIS, AN INTRODUCTION TO INTERNATIONAL LAW 19 (1988), 509

MARK JANIS & RICHARD KAY, EUROPEAN HUMAN RIGHTS LAW (2d ed. 1995), 493

Mark Janis, *Fashioning a Mechanism for Judicial Cooperation on European Human Rights Law among Europe's Regional Courts, in* 3 THE DYNAMICS OF THE PROTECTION OF HUMAN RIGHTS IN EUROPE 211 (Rick Lawson & Matthijs de Blois eds., 1994), 493

Farrakh Jhabvala, *The Practice of the Covenant's Human Rights Committee, 1976-82: Review of State Party Reports*, 6 HUM. RTS. Q. 81 (1984), 100, 141

ROBERT JOHNSON, CONDEMNED TO DIE—LIFE UNDER SENTENCE OF DEATH (1981), 628

Sarah Joseph, *New Procedures Concerning the Human Rights Committee's Examination of State Reports*, 12 NETH. Q. HUM. RTS. 5 (1995), 100

Christopher C. Joyner, *The U.S. Action in Grenada: Reflections on the Lawfulness of Invasion*, 78 AM. J. INT'L L. 131 (1984), 253

Menno Kamminga, *The Thematic Procedures of the U.N. Commission on Human Rights*, 34 NETHER-LANDS INT'L L. REV. 299 (1987), 202, **208**

MENNO T. KAMMINGA, INTER-STATE ACCOUNTABILITY FOR VIOLATIONS OF HUMAN RIGHTS (1992), 304

MENNO T. KAMMINGA, INTER-STATE ACCOUNTABILITY FOR VIOLATIONS OF HUMAN RIGHTS (1990), 10

MENNO T. KAMMINGA, INTER-STATE ACCOUNTABILITY FOR VIOLATIONS OF HUMAN RIGHTS 160 (1992), 304

Wong Kan Seng, *The Real World of Human Rights*, Statement at the World Conference on Human Rights, Vienna (16 June 1993), 682

Michael J. Kane, *Promoting Political Rights to Protect the Environment*, 18 YALE J. INT'L L. 389 (1993), 389

Dietrich Kappeler, *Human Rights and Development: International Views*, 85 AM. J. INT'L L. 735 (1991) (book review), 87

PAUL KAPTEYN & PIETER VAN THEMAAT, INTRODUCTION TO THE LAW OF THE EUROPEAN COMMUNITIES (Laurence Gormley ed., 2d ed. 1989), 493

Pamela Karlan & Daniel Ortiz, *In a Diffident Voice: Relational Feminism, Abortion Rights, and the Feminist Legal Agenda*, 87 Nw. U. L. REV. 858 (1993), 694

Vladimir A. Kartashkin, *Economic, Social and Cultural Rights, in* INTERNATIONAL DIMENSIONS OF HUMAN RIGHTS 111 (Karel Vasak & Philip Alston eds., 1982), 58

Irving R. Kaufman, *A Legal Remedy for International Torture?*, N.Y. TIMES MAG., Nov. 9, 1980, at 44, 509

Natalie Hevener Kaufman & David Whiteman, *Opposition to Human Rights Treaties in the United States: The Legacy of the Bricker Amendment*, 10 HUM. RTS. Q. 309 (1988), 37, 66

Alya Kayal, Penny Parker & David Weissbrodt, *The Forty-Fourth Session of the UN Sub-Commission on Prevention of Discrimination and Protection of Minorities and the Special Session of the Commission on Human Rights on the Situation in the Former Yugoslavia*, 15 HUM. RTS. Q. 410 (May 1993), 370

Zubair M. Kazaure, *Forced Circumcision is Alien to Nigeria*, N.Y. TIMES, Apr. 9, 1994, at A20, 672

J. Patrick Kelly, *The Changing Process of International Law and the Role of the World Court*, 11 MICH. J. INT'L L. 129 (1989), 240

Nancy Kelly, *Gender-Related Persecution: Assessing the Asylum Claims of Women*, 26 CORNELL INT'L L.J. 625 (1993), 666

Nancy Kelly, *Guidelines for Women's Asylum Claims*, 6 INT'L J. REFUGEE L. 517 (1994), **657-658**, 666

NANCY KELLY, WOMEN REFUGEES PROJECT OF CAMBRIDGE AND SOMERVILLE LEGAL SERVICES AND HARVARD IMMIGRATION AND REFUGEE PROGRAM, GUIDELINES FOR WOMEN'S ASYLUM CLAIMS 2 (1994), 37, 52

HANS KELSEN, GENERAL THEORY OF LAW AND STATE 3-161 (Anders Wedberg trans., 1945), 692

GEOFFREY KEMP, SOME RELATIONSHIPS BETWEEN U.S. MILITARY TRAINING IN LATIN AMERICA AND WEAPONS ACQUISITION PATTERNS: 1959-1969 (1970), 168

David Kennedy, *A New Stream of International Law Scholarship*, 7 WIS. INT'L L.J. 1, 28-39 (1988), 666

Foster Kennedy, *The Problem of Social Control of the Congenitally Defective: Education, Sterilization, Euthanasia*, 99 AMER. J. PSYCHIATRY 13 (1942), **729**

Karen Kenny, *Formal and Informal Innovations in the United Nations Protection of Human Rights: The Special Rapporteur on the Former Yugoslavia*, 48 AUSTRIAN J. PUBLIC AND INT'L L. 19 (1995), 216

Dimitra Kessenides, *Finding the Right Strategy to Stop a Deportation*, AM. LAW., June 1994, at 35, 672

Lee Kim Chew, *Pragmatism now rules US-Jakarta ties*, STRAITS TIMES, May 9, 1994, at 27, 398

Nancy Kim, *Toward a Feminist Theory of Human Rights: Straddling the Fence Between Western Imperialism and Uncritical Absolutism*, 25 COLUM. HUM. RTS. L. REV. 49 (1993), 694

Frederic L. Kirgis, AGORA: MAY THE PRESIDENT VIOLATE CUSTOMARY INTERNATIONAL LAW?, 81 AM. J. INT'L L. 371 (1987), 623

Frederic L. Kirgis, *Editorial Comment: Understanding the Act of State Doctrine's Effect*, 82 AM. J. INT'L L. 58 (1988), 547

Frederic L. Kirgis, Jr., *Federal Statutes, Executive Orders and "Self-Executing Custom"*, 81 AM. J. INT'L L. 371 (1987), 599

Mark Kirk, *Should the United States Ratify the American Convention on Human Rights?*, 14 IIDH (Inter-American Institute of Human Rights) 65 (1991), 449

Jeanne Kirkpatrick, *A Revolution That Goes On*, WASH. POST, Feb. 10, 1992, at A11, 389

Jeanne Kirkpatrick, *Dictatorships and Double Standards*, COMMENTARY, Nov. 1979, at 34, 388

MICHAEL T. KLARE, WAR WITHOUT END: AMERICAN PLANNING FOR THE NEXT VIETNAMS (1972), 751

Michael T. Klare & Cynthia Arnson, *Exporting Repression: U.S. Support for Authoritarianism in Latin America, in* CAPITALISM AND THE STATE IN U.S.-LATIN AMERICAN RELATIONS 138 (Richard R. Fagen ed., 1979), 722

Howard Kleinberg, *Who changed? Not the Chinese, so it must have been Clinton*, STAR TRIB. (Minneapolis), June 8, 1993, at 13A, 410

Robert W. Kneller, *Human Rights, Politics, and the Multilateral Development Banks*, 6 YALE STUD. WORLD PUB. ORD. 361 (1980), 392

Maximilian Koessler, *American War Crimes Trials in Europe*, 39 GEO. L.J. 18 (1950), 280

Harold H. Koh, *Transnational Public Law Litigation*, 100 YALE L.J. 2347 (1991), 522

Daniel M. Kolkey, *Lousy Odds in Playing Trade Status Card; Bolstering China's Bustling Economy Would Better Achieve U.S. Goals in Both Nations*, L.A. TIMES, June 7, 1993 at B7, 410

Roman A. Kolodkin, *An Ad Hoc International Tribunal for the Prosecution of Serious Violations of International Humanitarian Law in the Former Yugoslavia*, 5 CRIM. L.F. 381 (1994), 287

WILLIAM KOREY, THE PROMISES WE KEEP: HUMAN RIGHTS, THE HELSINKI PROCESS, AND AMERICAN FOREIGN POLICY (1993), 496

OLAYINKA KOSO-THOMAS, THE CIRCUMCISION OF WOMEN: A STRATEGY FOR ERADICATION 5-9 (1987), 633

Bernard Kouchner, *A Call for Humanitarian Intervention*, REFUGEES, Dec. 1992, at 14, 253

Kravitz, *Beyond Asylum and Withholding of Deportation: A Framework for Relief Under Geneva Convention IV of 1949*, 1 TEMPLE INT'L & COMP. L.J. 263 (1987), 594

M. Jane Kronenberger, *Refugee Women: Establishing a Prima Facie Case Under the Refugee Convention*, 15 ILSA J. INT'L L. 61 (1992), 666

Tom Kuntz, *Beyond Singapore: Corporal Punishment, A to Z*, N.Y. TIMES, June 26, 1994, § 4, at 5, 681

La Commission arabe des droits de l'homme, 3 HUM. RTS. J. 101 (1970), 171

Pierre Laberge, *Humanitarian Intervention: Three Ethical Positions*, 9 ETHICS & INT'L AFF. 15 (1995), 252

HÉLÈNE LAMBERT, SEEKING ASYLUM: COMPARATIVE LAW AND PRACTICE IN SELECTED EUROPEAN COUNTRIES (1995), 642

Wilbur G. Landrey, *Justice Promised for Bosnia Victims*, ST. PETERSBURG TIMES, Oct. 22, 1995, at 1A, 295

LATIN AMERICAN POLITICS AND DEVELOPMENT 21 (Howard J. Wiarda & Harvey F. Kline eds., 1979), 711

Jill Lawrence, *Gender Persecution New Reason for Asylum; Human Rights: Women Face Bride-Burning, Genital Mutilation, Forced Abortions and Politically Motivated Rape, But Nations Have Been Slow to Grant Refuge*, L.A. TIMES, Mar. 27, 1994, at A14, 672

Virginia Leary, *Lessons from the Experience of the International Labour Organisation*, in THE UNITED NATIONS AND HUMAN RIGHTS: A CRITICAL APPRAISAL (Philip Alston ed., 1992), 97

Virginia Leary, *The Asian Region and the International Human Rights Movement*, in ASIAN PERSPECTIVES ON HUMAN RIGHTS 13 (Claude Welch & Virginia Leary eds., 1990), 466

Virginia A. Leary, *The Right to Health in International Human Rights Law*, 1 HEALTH & HUM. RTS. 25 (1994), 84

LAWRENCE LEBLANC, THE OAS AND THE PROMOTION AND PROTECTION OF HUMAN RIGHTS (1977), 448

Lawrence J. LeBlanc, *The Intent to Destroy Groups in the Genocide Convention: The Proposed U.S. Understanding*, 78 AM. J. INT'L L. 369 (1984), 39

Lawrence J. LeBlanc, *The ICJ, the Genocide Convention, and the United States*, 6 WISC. INT'L L.J. 43 (1987), 39

Lawyers Committee for Human Rights, *Worker Rights under the U.S. Trade Laws* (1989), 411

Lawyers Committee for Human Rights, *Abandoning the Victims: the U.N. Advisory Services Program in Guatemala* (1990), 272

Lawyers Committee for Human Rights, *Bureaucracy and Diplomacy* (1989), 402

Lawyers Committee for Human Rights, *Critique: Review of the U.S. Department of State's Country Reports on Human Rights Practices* 1991, at 4 (1992), 333, 403

Lawyers Committee for Human Rights, *Human Rights and U.S. Foreign Policy: Bureaucracy and Diplomacy*, 1988 Project Series No. 4 (1989), **411**

Lawyers Committee for Human Rights, *Human Rights and U.S. Foreign Policy: Report and Recommendations* 24 (1988), 415

Lawyers Committee for Human Rights, *The World Bank: Governance and Human Rights* (1995), 392

Lawyers Committee for Human Rights, *United States Policy Toward South Africa* (1989), *reprinted in* Lynda M. Clarizio, Bradley Clements & Erika Geeter, *United States Policy Toward South Africa*, 11 HUM. RTS. Q. 249 (1989), 420

Lawyers Committee for Human Rights, *Linking Security Assistance and Human Rights* (1989), 410

Lawyers Committee for Human Rights, *The International Criminal Tribunal for the Former Yugoslavia: Establishment, Organization, Jurisdiction, and Proceedings to Date* (1995), 298

Lawyers Committee for Human Rights, *The Detention of Asylum Seekers in the United States: A Cruel and Questionable Policy* 20 (1989), 568

Lawyers Committee for Human Rights, *Statements on U.S. Ratification of the CCPR*, 14 HUM. RTS. L.J. 125 (1993), 41, 571

Lawyers Committee for Human Rights, *The UNHCR at 40: Refugee Protection at the Crossroads* 13-30 (1991), **646-47**

Scott Leckie, *The Inter-State Complaint Procedure in International Human Rights Law: Hopeful Prospects or Wishful Thinking?*, 10 HUMAN RIGHTS Q. 249 (1988), 491

Scott Leckie, *The UN Committee on Economic, Social and Cultural Rights and the Right to Adequate Housing: Towards an Appropriate Approach*, 11 HUM. RTS. Q. 522 (1989), 79

STEPHEN LEGOMSKY, IMMIGRATION AND THE JUDICIARY: LAW AND POLITICS IN BRITAIN AND AMERICA (1987), 568

GERHARD LENSKI, POWER AND PRIVILEGE: A THEORY OF SOCIAL STRATIFICATION (New York: McGraw Hill, 1966), 167

Arden B. Levy, *International Prosecution of Rape in Warfare: Nondiscriminatory Recognition and Enforcement*, 4 UCLA WOMEN'S L.J. 255 (1994), 531

Corinne E. Lewis, *Dealing with the Problem of Internally Displaced Persons*, 6 GEO. IMMIGR. L.J. 693 (1992), 677

Hope Lewis, *Between "Irua" and "Female Genital Mutilation": Feminist Human Rights Discourse and the Cultural Divide*, 8 HARV. HUM. RTS. J. 1 (1995), 674

Paul Lewis, *U.N. is Developing Control Center to Coordinate Growing Peacekeeping Role*, N.Y. TIMES, Mar. 28, 1993, Sec. 1, at 10, 239

HANNY LIGHTFOOT-KLEIN, PRISONERS OF RITUAL: AN ODYSSEY INTO FEMALE GENITAL MUTILATION IN AFRICA (1989), 674

ROBERT J. LIFTON & ERIC MARKUSEN, GENOCIDAL MENTALITY: NAZI HOLOCAUST AND NUCLEAR THREAT (1990), 728

Robert Jay Lifton, *Socialization to Killing, in* THE NAZI DOCTORS: MEDICAL KILLING AND THE PSYCHOLOGY OF GENOCIDE 195 (1986), **732-735**

Robert Jay Lifton, *Genocide, in* THE NAZI DOCTORS: MEDICAL KILLING AND THE PSYCHOLOGY OF GENOCIDE 476 (1986), 742

Richard B. Lillich, *The Constitution and International Human Rights*, 83 AM. J. INT'L L. 851 (1989), 630

Richard B. Lillich, *Invoking International Human Rights Law in Domestic Courts*, 54 U. CIN. L. REV. 367 (1985), 579, 586

Richard B. Lillich, *The United States Constitution and International Human Rights Law*, 3 HARV. HUM. RTS. J. 53 (1990), 57

Richard B. Lillich, *A United States Policy of Humanitarian Intervention and Intercession, in* HUMAN RIGHTS AND AMERICAN FOREIGN POLICY, 278 (Donald P. Kommers & Gilburt D. Loescher eds., 1979), **243-245**

RICHARD LILLICH & FRANK NEWMAN, INTERNATIONAL HUMAN RIGHTS: PROBLEMS OF LAW AND POLICY 340 (1979), 491, 601

Hans A. Linde, *Comments*, 18 INT'L LAWYER 77 (1984), **576-578**

Tore Lindholm & Kari Vogt, Islamic Law Reform and Human Rights: Challenges and Rejoinders (1993), 171

Tore Lindholm, The Cross-Cultural Legitimacy of Human Rights: Prospects for Research (1990), 683

Tom Lininger, *Recent Development, Overcoming Immunity Defenses to Human Rights Suits in U.S. Courts,* 7 Harv. Hum. Rts. J. 177 (1994), 541, 547

Matthew Lippman, *Nuremberg: Forty Years Later,* 7 Conn. J. Int'l L. 1 (1991), 280

Matthew Lippman, *The Trial of Adolf Eichmann and the Protection of Universal Human Rights Under International Law,* 5 Hous. J. Int'l L. 1 (1982), 280

Thomas W. Lippman, *Conferees Loosen Ban on Arms to Pakistan, Soften Senate Language on Russia,* Wash. Post, Oct. 25, 1995, at A6, 409

Bert B. Lockwood, Jr., *The U.N. Charter and United Nations Civil Rights Litigation: 1946-1955,* 69 Iowa L. Rev. 901 (1984), 521

Elli Louka, The Transnational Management of Hazardous and Radioactive Wastes (1992), 84

Loukes Loukaides, Essays on the Developing Law of Human Rights (1995), 475

David Luban, *Remarks at the American Society of International Law Proceedings* (Apr. 8-11, 1987), in 81 Am. Soc'y Int'l L. Proc. 415, 280

Donatella Luca, *Questioning Temporary Protection, Together with a Selected Bibliography on Temporary Refuge/Temporary Protection,* 6 Int'l J. Refugee Law 535 (1994), 642, 649

Ellen L. Lutz, *The Marcos Human Rights Litigation: Can Justice be Achieved in U.S. Courts for Abuses that Occurred Abroad?,* 14 B.C. Third World L.J. 43 (1994), 273

Ellen L. Lutz, *After the Elections: Compensating Victims of Human Rights Abuses, in* New Directions in Human Rights 195 (Ellen L. Lutz, Hurst Hannum & Kathryn J. Burke eds., 1989), 274

R. St. J. MacDonald, The European System for the Protection of Human Rights (MacDonald et al. eds., 1993), 230

Catharine A. MacKinnon, *Crimes of War, Crimes of Peace,* 4 UCLA Women's L.J. 59 (1993), 530, 531

J. Mack, *Nationalism and the Self,* 2 Psychoanalytic Rev. 47 (1983), 167

Wendell C. Maddrey, *Note, Economic Sanctions Against South Africa: Problems and Prospects for Enforcement of Human Rights Norms,* 22 Va. J. Int'l L. 345 (1982), 320

Harold G. Maier, *The Authoritative Sources of Customary International Law in the United States,* 10 Mich. J. Int'l L. 450 (1989), 579

Jamie Malamud-Goti, *Transitional Governments in the Breach: Why Punish State Criminals,* 12 Hum. Rts. Q. 1 (1990), 275

Sally Mallison & William Mallison, Armed Conflict in Lebanon 1982: Humanitarian Law in a Real World Setting (1983), 17

Jerrold L. Mallory, *Note, Resolving the Confusion Over Head of State Immunity: The Defined Rights of Kings,* 86 Colum. L. Rev. 169 (1986), 547

Rita Maran, Torture: The Role of Ideology in the French-Algerian War 16 (1989), **736-737**

Ruth Marcus, *Clinton Lifts Most Economic Sanctions, Keeps Up Pressure on Military Leaders,* Wash. Post, Sept. 27, 1994, at A17, 419

Stephen P. Marks, *Emerging Human Rights: A New Generation for the 1980s?,* 33 Rutgers L. Rev. 435 (1981), **81-82**

Lisa L. Martin & Kathryn Sikkink, *U.S. Policy and Human Rights in Argentina and Guatemala, 1973-1980, in* Double-Edged Diplomacy (Peter Evans et al. eds., 1993), 399

Pamela M. Martin, *Note, Temporary Protected Status and the Legacy of* Santos-Gomez, 25 Geo. Wash. J. Int'l L. & Econ. 227 (1992), 649

Seymour Martin Lipset, *Some Social Requisites of Democracy: Economic Development and Political Legitimacy,* 53 Amer. Pol. Sci. Rev. 69 (1959), 750

Nunca Mas: The Report of the Argentine National Commission on the Disappeared (1986), 96

Douglas Massey & Nancy Denton, American Apartheid: Segregation and the Making of the Underclass (1993), 112

Jay Mathews, *Group Says INS Uses Children as Lures for Illegal Alien Parents; Salvadoran Youths Ordered Released*, WASH. POST, July 20, 1985, at A8, 557, n.2

Douglas E. Matthews, *Economic Sanctions and Economic Strategies: Toward Haiti's Integration into the World Economy*, 6 ST. THOMAS L. REV. 281 (1994), 419

Ann Elizabeth Mayer, *Universal Versus Islamic Human Rights: A Clash of Cultures or a Clash with a Construct?*, 15 MICH. J. INT'L L. 307 (1994), 171, 466

PHILIP MAYER, *Witches, in* WITCHCRAFT AND SORCERY 45 (Max Marwick ed., 1970), **739-742**

Tadeusz Mazowiecki, *Report on the Situation of Human Rights in the Territory of the Former Yugoslavia*, U.N. Doc. A/48/92-S/25341, Annex, at 20 (1993), 502, n.4

Edwin S. Maynard, *The Bureaucracy and Implementation of US Human Rights Policy*, 11 HUM. RTS. Q. 175 (1989), 411

John F. McCamant, *A Critique of Present Measures of Human Rights Development and an Alternative, in* GLOBAL HUMAN RIGHTS: PUBLIC POLICIES, COMPARATIVE MEASURES, AND NGO STRATEGIES (Ved P. Nanda, James R. Scarrit & George W. Shepard eds., 1981) (Boulder, CO: Westview), 163

Timothy L.H. McCormack & Gerry J. Simpson, *The International Law Commission's Draft Code of Crimes Against the Peace and Security of Mankind: An Appraisal of the Substantive Provisions*, 5 CRIM. L.F. 1 (1994), 279

JAMES M. MCCORMICK, AMERICAN FOREIGN POLICY AND AMERICAN VALUES (Itasca, IL: F.E. Peacock Publishers, 1985), 751

James M. McCormick & Neil J. Mitchell, *Human Rights and Foreign Assistance: An Update*, 70 SOC. SCI. Q. 969 (1989), 168

James M. McCormick & Neil J. Mitchell, *Is U.S. Aid Really Linked to Human Rights in Latin America?*, 32 AMER. J. POL. SCI. 231 (1988), 168

MYRES S. MCDOUGAL, HAROLD D. LASSWELL & LUNG-CHU CHEN, HUMAN RIGHTS AND WORLD PUBLIC ORDER: THE BASIC POLICIES OF AN INTERNATIONAL LAW OF HUMAN DIGNITY (1980), **166-168**

MYRES MCDOUGAL, HOWARD LASSWELL & JAMES MILLER, THE INTERPRETATION OF AGREEMENTS AND WORLD PUBLIC ORDER: PRINCIPLES OF CONTENT AND PROCEDURE 35 (1967), 454

DOMINIC MCGOLDRICK, THE HUMAN RIGHTS COMMITTEE, ITS ROLE IN THE DEVELOPMENT OF THE INTERNATIONAL COVENANT ON CIVIL AND POLITICAL RIGHTS (1991), 93, 97, 141, 159

R.D. McKinlay & A.S. Cohan, *Performance and Instability in Military and Nonmilitary Regimes*, 70 AMER. POL. SCI. REV. 850 (1976), 719

R.D. McKinlay & A.S. Cohan, *A Comparative Analysis of the Political and Economic Performance of Military and Civilian Regimes*, 8 COMP. POL. 1 (1975), 719

James C. McKinley, Jr., *Rwanda War Crimes Tribunal Indicts Two Men in Jail in Zambia*, N.Y. TIMES, Feb. 20, 1996, at A9, 297

C. MEDINA QUIROGA, THE BATTLE OF HUMAN RIGHTS: GROSS, SYSTEMATIC VIOLATIONS AND THE INTER-AMERICAN SYSTEM (1988), 448

JUAN E. MÉNDEZ, THE OAS AND HUMAN RIGHTS (1993) (presented as part of the Inter-American Dialogue, Dec. 2-3, 1993), 443, 448

Juan Mendez & José Vivanco, *Disappearances and the Inter-American Court: Reflections on a Litigation Experience*, 13 HAMLINE L. REV. 507 (1990), 246

Juan Méndez & José Vivanco, *Disappearances and the Inter-American Court: Reflections on a Litigation Experience*, 13 HAMLINE L. REV. 507 (1990), **444-448,** 457, 487

Theodor Meron, *Rape as a Crime Under International Humanitarian Law*, 87 AM. J. INT'L L. 424 (1993), 296

Theodor Meron, *Acts of State, Imputability, Private Acts, in* HUMAN RIGHTS AND HUMANITARIAN NORMS AS CUSTOMARY LAW 155 (1989), 675

Theodor Meron, *Editorial Comment: War Crimes in Yugoslavia and the Development of International Law*, 88 AM. J. INT'L L. 78 (1994), 287-288

THEODOR MERON, HUMAN RIGHTS AND HUMANITARIAN NORMS AS CUSTOMARY LAW (1989), 275, 304

Theodor Meron, *On a Hierarchy of International Human Rights*, 80 AM. J. INT'L L. 1 (1986), 83

Theodor Meron, *Rape as a Crime Under International Humanitarian Law*, 87 Am. J. Int'l L. 424 (1993), **528-529**

Theodor Meron, *The Case for War Crimes Trials in Yugoslavia*, Foreign Aff., Summer 1993, at 122, 298

Theodore Meron, *State Responsibility for Violations of Human Rights*, 83 Am. Soc'y Int'l L. Proc. 372 (1989), 303

John Merrills, The Development of International Law by the European Court of Human Rights 34-41 (1988), 481

Middle East Watch, *Guardians of Thought: Limits on Freedom of Expression in Iran* (1993), 147

Stanley Milgram, *Behavioral Study of Obedience*, 67 J. Abnormal Soc. Psychol. 371 (1963), 167

Larry Minear et al., *Humanitarianism and War: Learning the Lessons from Recent Armed Conflicts*, Occasional Paper 8 (Inst. for Int'l Stud., Brown U., 1991), 242

Larry Minear, *The Forgotten Human Agenda*, 73 Foreign Policy 76 (1988-89), 389

Neil J. Mitchell & James M. McCormick, *Economic and Political Explanations of Human Rights Violations*, World Politics 476 (July 1988), **705-711**

James Moeller, Comment, *Human Rights and United States Security Assistance: El Salvador and the Case for Country-Specific Legislation*, 24 Harv. Int'l L.J. 75 (1983), 395

John Norton Moore, *The U.S. Action in Grenada: Grenada and the International Double Standard*, 78 Am. J. Int'l L. 145 (1984), 254

John Norton Moore, *The Secret War in Central America and Future of World Order*, 80 Am. J. Int'l L. 43 (1986), 253

Virginia Morris & Michael Scharf, An Insider's Guide to the International Criminal Tribunal for the Former Yugoslavia: A Documentary History and Analysis (1995), 298

Johannes Morsink, *The Philosophy of the Universal Declaration*, 6 Hum. Rts. Q. 309 (1984), 692

Langhorne A. Motley, *The Decision to Assist Grenada*, Department of State Bulletin, Mar. 1984, at 70, 249, n.2

A. Glenn Mower, Human Rights and American Foreign Policy: The Carter and Reagan Experience (1987), 66, 389, 414

Edward N. Muller, *Dependent Economic Development, Aid Dependence on the United States, and Democratic Breakdown in the Third World*, Int'l Stud. Q. 29 (1985), 751

Edward N. Muller, *Income Inequality, Regime Repressiveness, and Political Violence*, 50 Amer. Soc. Rev. 47 (1985), 749

Joshua Muravchik, The Uncertain Crusade: Jimmy Carter and the Dilemmas of Human Rights Policy (1986), 66, 389

Dean E. Murphy, *Serb General Indicted by U.N. Tribunal*, L.A. Times, Mar. 2, 1996, at A1, 295

Kim Murphy, *Islamic Militants Target Arab Intellectuals, Artists*, L.A. Times, Nov. 28, 1994, at A1, 171

Sean D. Murphy, *The Security Council, Legitimacy, and the Concept of Collective Security After the Cold War*, 32 Colum. J. Transnat'l L. 201 (1994), 242

Makau wa Mutua, *The Banjul Charter and the African Cultural Fingerprint: An Evaluation of the Language of Duties*, 35 Va. J. Int'l L. 339 (1995), 465

Winston P. Nagan, *African Human Rights Process: A Contextual Policy-Oriented Approach*, 21 Sw. U. L. Rev. 63 (1992), 683, 692

Winston P. Nagan, *Economic Sanctions, U.S. Foreign Policy, International Law and the Anti-Apartheid Act of 1986*, 4 Florida Int'l L.J. 85 (1988), 320

Ved P. Nanda, *Tragedies in Northern Iraq, Liberia, Yugoslavia, and Haiti—Revisiting the Validity of Humanitarian Intervention Under International Law—Part I*, 20 Denv. J. Int'l L. & Pol'y 305 (1992), 242

Marian Nash, *Contemporary Practice of the United States Relating to International Law*, 75 Am. J. Int'l L. 142 (1981), 451

David L. Neal, *Note, Women as a Social Group: Recognizing Sex-Based Persecution as Grounds for Asylum*, 20 COLUM. HUM. RTS. L. REV. 203 (1988), 666

Aryeh Neier, *War Crimes Tribunal is an Imperative*, Hum. Rts. Brief (American University Center for Hum. Rts. & Humanitarian L., D.C.), Spring 1994, at 6, 8, **288-289**

Richard W. Nelson, *International Law and U.S. Withholding of Payments to International Organizations*, 80 AM. J. INT'L L. 973 (1986), 240

NEW DIMENSIONS OF PEACEKEEPING (Daniel Warner ed., 1995), 242

FRANK NEWMAN & STANLEY SURREY, LEGISLATION: CASES AND MATERIALS 645 (1955), 454

FRANK NEWMAN, *Civil and Political Rights, in* THE INTERNATIONAL DIMENSIONS OF HUMAN RIGHTS 135 (Karel Vasak & Philip Alston eds., 1982), 18

Frank Newman, *How Courts Interpret Regulations*, 35 CALIF. L. REV. 509 (1947), 454

Frank Newman, *Interpreting the Human Rights Clauses of the U.N. Charter*, 1972 REVUE DES DROITS DE L'HOMME 283, 454

Frank Newman, *Natural Justice, Due Process, and the New International Covenants on Human Rights: Prospectus*, PUB. L. 274 (1967), 454

Frank Newman, *Redress for Gulf War Violations of Human Rights*, 28 DENVER J. INT'L L. S. POL'Y 213 (1992), 273, 488

Frank C. Newman, *United Nations Human Rights Covenants and the United States Government: Diluted Promises, Foreseeable Futures*, 42 DEPAUL L. REV. 1241 (1993), 37

David D. Newsom, *The Diplomacy of Human Rights: A Diplomat's View, in* THE DIPLOMACY OF HUMAN RIGHTS 3 (David D. Newsom, ed., 1986), **411-413**

Fionnuala Ni Aolain, *The Emergence of Diversity*, 19 FORDHAM INT'L L.J. 101 (1995), 159

JAMES W. NICKEL, MAKING SENSE OF HUMAN RIGHTS: PHILOSOPHICAL REFLECTIONS ON THE UNIVERSAL DECLARATION OF HUMAN RIGHTS (1987), 683

ALAN NICHOLS & PAUL WHITE, REFUGEE DILEMMAS: REVIEWING THE COMPREHENSIVE PLAN OF ACTION FOR VIETNAMESE ASYLUM SEEKERS (1993), 642

HAROLD L. NIEBURG, POLITICAL VIOLENCE: THE BEHAVIORAL PROCESS (New York: St. Martin's Press, 1969), 750

Carlos S. Nino, *The Duty to Punish Past Abuses of Human Rights Put Into Context: The Case of Argentina*, 100 YALE L.J. 2619 (1991), 275, 370

Cathal Nolan, *The Influence of Parliament on Human Rights in Canadian Foreign Policy*, 7 HUM. RTS. Q. 373 (1985), 399

Robert Norris, *Observations In Loco: Practice and Procedure of the Inter-American Commission on Human Rights, 1979-1983*, 19 TEX. INT'L L.J. 285 (1984), 357

Robert Norris, *The Individual Petition Procedure of the Inter-American System for the Protection of Human Rights, in* GUIDE TO INTERNATIONAL HUMAN RIGHTS PRACTICE 108 (Hurst Hannum ed., 1984), 448

Manfred Nowak, *Country-Oriented Human Rights Protection by the UN Commission on Human Rights and its Sub-Commission*, 22 NETHERLANDS Y.B. INT'L L. 39 (1991), 216

MANFRED NOWAK, U.N. COVENANT ON CIVIL AND POLITICAL RIGHTS: CCPR COMMENTARY (1993), 100, **155-156**

Manfred Nowak, *U.N. Human Rights Committee: Survey of Decision Given Up Till July 1990*, 10 HUM. RTS. L.J. 139 (1990), 159

Norwegian Refugee Council & Refugee Policy Group, *Norwegian Government Roundtable Discussion on United Nations: Human Rights Protection for Internally Displaced Persons* (1993), 199

Note, Human Rights Practices in the Arab States: The Modern Impact of Shari'a Values, 12 GA. J. INT'L & COMP. L. 55 (1982), 170

Note, Mental Suffering Under Sentence of Death: A Cruel and Unusual Punishment, 57 IOWA L. REV. 814 (1972), 628

Note, What's Culture Got to Do With It? Excising the Harmful Tradition of Female Circumcision, 106 HARV. L. REV. 1944 (1993), 674

NOW Legal Defense and Education Fund, *Fact Sheet: Sex Discrimination Under the International Covenant on Civil and Political Rights* (1994), 126

ROBERT NOZICK, ANARCHY, STATE, AND UTOPIA (1974), 692

Daniel D. Ntanda Nsereko, *Rules of Procedure and Evidence of the International Tribunal for the Former Yugoslavia,* 5 CRIM. L.F. 507 (1994), 298

NEILL NUGENT, THE GOVERNMENT AND POLITICS OF THE EUROPEAN UNION (3d ed. 1994), 493

James C. O'Brien, *The International Tribunal for Violations of International Humanitarian Law in the Former Yugoslavia,* 87 AM. J. INT'L L. 639 (1993), 530

Colleen O'Connor, *Mutilation Custom,* CHI. TRIB., Jun. 27, 1994, at C7, 672

DANIEL O'DONNELL, PROTECCIÓN INTERNACIONAL DE LOS DERECHOS HUMANOS (2d ed. 1989), 448

MICHAEL O'FLAHERTY, HUMAN RIGHTS AND THE UN: PRACTICE BEFORE THE TREATY BODIES (1996), 100

Michael O'Flaherty, *The Reporting Obligation under Article 40 of the International Covenant on Civil and Political Rights: Lessons to be Learned from Consideration by Human Rights Committee of Ireland's First Report,* 16 HUM. RTS. Q. 515 (1994), 100

ROSEMARY H.T. O'KANE, THE LIKELIHOOD OF COUPS (Brookfield, VT: Gower, 1987), 751

John O'Manique, *Human Rights and Development,* 14 HUM. RTS. Q. 78 (1992), 87

Anselm Chidi Odinkalu, *Proposals for review of the Rules of Procedure of the African Commission on Human and Peoples' Rights,* 15 HUM. RTS. Q. 533 (1993), 465

Michael A. Olivas, *Unaccompanied Refugee Children: Dentention, Due Process, and Disgrace,* 2 STAN. L. & POL'Y REV. 159 (1990), 557, n.2

Covey T. Oliver, *Problems of Cognition and Interpretation in Applying Norms of Customary International Law of Human Rights in United States Courts,* 4 HOUS. J. INT'L L. 59 (1981), 579

H.W.O. Okoth-Ogendo, *Human and Peoples' Rights: What Point is Africa Trying to Make?, in* HUMAN RIGHTS AND GOVERNANCE IN AFRICA 74 (Ronald Cohen et al. eds., 1993), 465

Joe Oloka-Onyango, *Beyond the Rhetoric: Reinvigorating the Struggle for Economic and Social Rights in Africa,* 27 CAL. WEST. INT'L L.J. 1 (1995), 392

Mancur Olson, *Rapid Growth as a Destabilizing Force,* 23 J. ECON. HIST. 529 (1963), 749

ON HUMAN RIGHTS: THE OXFORD AMNESTY LECTURES 1993 at 83 (Stephen Shute & Susan Hurley eds., 1993), 531

One Year Later, Rwandans on Trial, WASH. POST, Apr. 7, 1995, at A33, 297

LASSA OPPENHEIM, INTERNATIONAL LAW: A TREATISE (Hersch Lauterpacht ed., 8th ed. 1955), 21

Torkel Opsahl, *The Human Rights Committee, in* THE UNITED NATIONS AND HUMAN RIGHTS (Philip Alston ed., 1992), 100

Mike Oquaye, *Human Rights and the Transition to Democracy Under the PNDC in Ghana,* 17 HUM. RTS. Q. 556 (1995), 275

Diane Orentlicher, *Bearing Witness: The Art and Science of Human Rights Fact-Finding,* 3 HARV. HUM. RTS. J. 83 (1990), 330

Diane Orentlicher, *Settling Accounts: The Duty to Prosecute Human Rights Violations of a Prior Regime,* 100 YALE L.J. 2537 (1991), **259-262**, 370

Organization of African Unity, *Review of the African Commission on Human and Peoples' Rights* (1991), 217

THE ORGANIZATION OF AFRICAN UNITY AFTER THIRTY YEARS (Yassin El Ayouty ed., 1994), 465

Ebere Osieke, *The Legal Validity of Ultra Vires Decisions of International Organizations,* 77 AM. J. INT'L L. 239 (1983), 240

David Ottaway, *Bosnia Convicts 2 Serbs in War Crimes Trial; U.N. Officer Seeks Amnesty to Promote Peace,* WASH. POST, Mar. 31, 1993, at A21, 296

OURS BY RIGHT: WOMEN'S RIGHTS AS HUMAN RIGHTS (Joanna Kerr ed., 1996), 675

Winston Pan, *The Confucian Tradition and its Implications for Human Rights in China,* 3 GLOBAL JUST. 9 (1993), 682

Panel, *World Court Jurisdiction and U.S. Foreign Policy in Latin America,* 78 AM. SOC'Y INT'L L. PROC. 321 (1986), 253

Han S. Park, *Correlates of Human Rights: Global Tendencies*, 9 HUM. RTS. Q. 405 (1987), 719

Penny Parker & David Weissbrodt, *Major Developments at the UN Commission on Human Rights in 1991*, 13 HUM. RTS. Q. 573 (1991), 216

Penny Parker, *A Summary of the Major Developments at the 1995 Session of the U.N. Commission on Human Rights, Held in Geneva, Switzerland, From January 30 to March 10, 1995*, World Wide Web (http://www.umn.edu/humanrts) (1995), 184, 202

John Embry Parkerson, Jr., *United States Compliance with Humanitarian Law Respecting Civilians During Operation Just Cause*, 133 MIL. L. REV. 31 (1991), 254

Jo M. Pasqualucci, *The Whole Truth and Nothing But the Truth: Truth Commissions, Impunity and the Inter-American Human Rights System*, 12 B.U. INT'L L.J. 321 (1994), 275

Jo M. Pasqualucci, *The Inter-American Human Rights System: Establishing Precedents and Procedure in Human Rights Law*, 26 U. MIAMI INTER-AM. L. REV. 297 (Winter 1994-95), 448

GUY J. PAUKER, THE INDONESIAN DOCTRINE OF TERRITORIAL WARFARE AND TERRITORIAL MANAGEMENT (Santa Monica: RAND Corporation, RM-3312-PR, November 1963), 751

Michael S. Paulsen, *Is Lloyd Bentsen Unconstitutional?*, 46 STAN. L. REV. 907 (1994), 621

Jordan Paust, *Suing Saddam: Private Remedies for War Crimes and Hostage-Taking*, 31 VA. J. INT'L L. 351 (1991), 274

Jordan J. Paust, *Applicability of International Criminal Laws to Events in the Former Yugoslavia*, 9 AM. U. J. INT'L L. & POL'Y, 499 (1994), 298

Jordan J. Paust, *On Human Rights: The Use of Human Rights Precepts in U.S. History and the Right to an Effective Remedy in Domestic Courts*, 10 MICH. J. INT'L L. 543 (1989), 520, n.8

Jordan J. Paust, *Litigating Human Rights: A Commentary on the Comments*, 4 HOUS. J. INT'L L. 81 (1981), 579

Jordan J. Paust, *Self-Executing Treaties*, 82 AM. J. INT'L L. 760 (1983), 594

Kelly K. Pease & David P. Forsythe, *Human Rights, Humanitarian Intervention, and World Politics*, 15 HUM. RTS. Q. 290 (1993), 242

Jelena Pejic, *The International Criminal Court: Issues of Law and Political Will*, 18 FORDHAM INT'L L.J. 1762 (1995), 305

Deborah Perluss & Joan F. Hartman, *Temporary Refuge: Emergence of a Customary Norm*, 26 VA. J. INT'L L. 551 (1986), 509, 623

JULIE STONE PETERS, WOMEN'S RIGHTS, HUMAN RIGHTS: INTERNATIONAL FEMINIST PERSPECTIVES (1994), 675

Physicians for Human Rights, *Operation "Just Cause:" The Human Cost of Military Action in Panama* (1991), 254

Physicians for Human Rights, *Cruel and Inhuman Treatment: The Use of Four-Point Restraint in the Onondaga County Public Safety Building Syracuse, New York* (May, 1993), 606

C. A. Pinderhughes, *Differential Bonding: Toward a Psychophysiological Theory of Stereotyping*, 136 AMER. J. PSYCHIATRY 33 (1979), 167

Jeong Hwa Pires, *North Korean Time Bomb: Can Sanctions Defuse It? A Review of International Economic Sanctions as an Option*, 24 GA. J. INT'L & COMP. L. 307 (1994), 420

Joe Pitts & David Weissbrodt, *Major Developments at the UN Commission on Human Rights in 1992*, 15 HUM. RTS. Q. 122 (1993), 216

Richard Plender, *The Legal Basis of International Jurisdiction to Act with Regard to the Internally Displaced*, 6 INT'L J. REFUGEE LAW 345 (1994), 677

Steven Poe et al., *Human Rights and US Foreign Aid Revisited: The Latin American Region*, 16 HUM. RTS. Q. 539 (1994), 399

Steven C. Poe & C. Neal Tate, *Repression of Human Rights to Personal Integrity in the 1980s: A Global Analysis*, 88 AM. POL. SCI. REV. 853 (1994), **715-718**

Steven C. Poe, *Human Rights and the Allocation of U.S. Military Assistance*, 28 J. PEACE RESEARCH 205 (1991), 415

Steven C. Poe, *Human Rights and Economic Aid Allocation under Ronald Reagan and Jimmy Carter*, 36 AMER. J. POLITICAL SCIENCE 147 (1992), 415

Steven C. Poe, *Human Rights and Foreign Aid: A Review of Quantitative Research and Prescriptions for Future Research*, 12 HUM. RTS. Q. 499 (1990), 751

Steven C. Poe & Rangsima Sirirangsi, *Human Rights and U.S. Economic Aid to Africa*, 18(4) INT'L INTERACTIONS 1 (1993), 75

THE POLITICS OF HUMANITARIAN INTERVENTION (John Harriss ed., 1995), 242

THE POLITICS OF PAIN, TORTURERS AND THEIR MASTERS (Ronald D. Crelinsten & Alex P. Schmid eds.) (Boulder, CO: Westview Press, 1994), 168

John Pomfret, *The Dayton Hurrahs vs. Bosnian Reality: Can Serbian Leader Deliver Peace?*, WASH. POST, Nov. 23, 1995, at A35, 420

Margaret Popkin & Naomi Roht-Arriaza, *Truth as Justice: Investigatory Commissions in Latin America*, 20 L. & SOCIAL INQUIRY 79 (1995), 275

Population Crisis Committee, *International Human Suffering Index* (Washington: PCC, 1987), 749

Michael Posner & Cathy Zavis, *Human Rights Priorities for a New Administration and Congress*, 28 VA. J. INT'L L. 893 (1988), 398

Tom Post et al., *Crimes of War: A Pattern of Rape in Bosnia*, NEWSWEEK, Jan. 4, 1993, at 32, 501, n.2

ABBAS POULGERAMI, DEVELOPMENT AND DEMOCRACY IN THE THIRD WORLD (Boulder, CO: Westview Press, 1991), 750

Vincent Power, *Human Rights and the EEC*, in HUMAN RIGHTS A EUROPEAN PERSPECTIVE, 81 (Liz Heffernan ed., 1994), 493

Jonathan Pratter & Joseph R. Profaizer, *A Practitioner's Research Guide and Bibliography to International Civil Litigation*, 28 TEX. INT'L L.J. 633 (1993), 521

Julia Preston, *Massive World Body Resists Shaping Up: Reform Efforts at U.N. Meet Opposition*, WASH. POST, Jan. 3, 1995, at A1, 240

Julia Preston, *Recognition of Kuwait Expected; But Iraq's Grudging Acknowledgment May Not Be Enough to Ease Sanctions*, S.F. EXAMINER, Oct. 20, 1994, at A17, 419

Julia Preston, *Tribunal Set on Rwanda War Crimes; Kigali Votes No on U.N. Resolution*, WASH. POST, Nov. 9, 1994, at A44, 296

Julia Preston, *U.N. Aide Proposes Rapid-Reaction Unit; In Face of U.S. Congressional Opposition, Boutros-Ghali's Plan Appears to Have Little Chance*, WASH. POST, Jan. 6, 1995, at A23, 239

Julia Preston, *U.N. Offers Plan to Ease Oil Embargo on Iraq for Humanitarian Reasons*, WASH. POST, Apr. 14, 1995, at A28, 419

Dana Priest, *House Votes to Reduce Payments to U.N.*, WASH. POST, Feb. 17, 1995, at A1, 240

Kathleen Pritchard, *Human Rights Reporting in Two Nations: A Comparison of the United States and Norway*, id. at 259, 333

Robert N. Proctor, *Nazi Doctors, Racial Medicine, and Human Experimentation*, in THE NAZI DOCTORS AND THE NUREMBERG CODE: HUMAN RIGHTS IN HUMAN EXPERIMENTATION 17 (George J. Annas & Michael A. Grodin eds., 1992), 728

Nigel Purvis, *Critical Legal Studies in Public International Law*, 32 HARV. INT'L L.J. 81, 88-110, 113-14 (1991), **687-69**

KENNETH QUINN, EXPLAINING THE TERROR, IN CAMBODIA 1975-1978: RENDEZVOUS WITH DEATH (Karl Jackson ed.) (Princeton: Princeton University Press, 1989), 167

Robert J. Quinn, *Note, Will the Rule of Law End? Challenging Grants of Amnesty for the Human Rights Violations of a Prior Regime: Chile's New Model*, 62 FORDHAM L. REV. 905 (1994), 275

B.G. RAMCHARAN, THE CONCEPT AND PRESENT STATUS OF THE INTERNATIONAL PROTECTION OF HUMAN RIGHTS (1989), 216

Jonathan C. Randal, *Algerian Leader Quits, Imperiling Power Shift to Muslims*, WASH. POST, Jan. 12, 1992, at A23, 275

KENNETH C. RANDALL, FEDERAL COURTS AND THE INTERNATIONAL HUMAN RIGHTS PARADIGM (1990), 579

Kenneth C. Randall, *Federal Jurisdiction Over International Law Claims: Inquiries into the Alien Tort Claims Statute*, 18 N.Y.U. J. INT'L L. & POL. 1 (1985), 521

Kenneth C. Randall, *Universal Jurisdiction Under International Law*, 66 TEX. L. REV. 785 (1988), 523

Kenneth C. Randall, *Federal Questions and the Human Rights Paradigm*, 73 MINN. L. REV. 349 (1988), 521

Berhane Ras-Work, *Traditional Practices That Inflict Disability, in* WOMEN AND DISABILITY 23 (Esther Boylan ed., 1991), 633

Karen Rasler, *War, Accommodation, and Violence in the United States, 1890-1970*, 80 AMER. POL. SCI. REV. 921 (1986), 719

JOHN RAWLS, A THEORY OF JUSTICE (1971), 692

JOHN RAWLS, THE LAW OF PEOPLES, IN ON HUMAN RIGHTS: THE OXFORD AMNESTY LECTURES 1993 41 (Stephen Shute & Susan Hurley eds., 1993), 692

A. REBECCA CARDOZO, A MODERN AMERICAN WITCH-CRAZE, IN WITCHCRAFT AND SORCERY 369 (Max Marwick ed., 1970), 747-749

Kevin Reed et al., *Race, Criminal Justice and the Death Penalty*, 15 WHITTIER L. REV. 395 (1994), **118-121**

Eric G. Reeves, *Note*, United States v. Javino: *Reconsidering the Relationship of Customary International Law to Domestic Law*, 50 WASH. & LEE L. REV. 877 (1993), 579

Refugee Studies Programme, *Directory of Research on Refugees and Other Forced Migrants* (1993), 642

Robbyn Reichman-Coad, *Note, Human Rights Violations in China: A United States Response*, 15 N.Y.L. SCH. J. INT'L & COMP. L. 163 (1994), 390

W. Michael Reisman, *Peacemaking*, 18 YALE J. INT'L L. 415 (1993), 242

W. Michael Reisman, *American Human Rights Diplomacy: The Next Phase*, 28 VA. J. INT'L L. 899 (1988), 403

Karin L. Remmer, *Exclusionary Democracy*, 20 COMP. INT'L DEMOCRACY 64 (Winter 1985-86), 718

Margherita Rendel, *Abortion and Human Rights*, 141 NEW L.J. 1270 (1991), 436

Patricia L. Rengel, *Ratification of International Human Rights Treaties: Progress and Prospects in the Clinton Administration*, 1994 Proc. of the Ann. Meeting-Am. Soc'y Int'l L. 363, 390

Alison D. Renteln, *The Unanswered Challenge of Relativism and the Consequences for Human Rights*, 7 HUM. RTS. Q. 514 (1985), 683

ALISON D. RENTELN, INTERNATIONAL HUMAN RIGHTS: UNIVERSALISM VERSUS RELATIVISM (1990), 683

Report of the Secretary General as Requested by the General Assembly in Resolution 48/251, U.N. Doc. A/C.5/49/42 (1994), 296

Judith Resnik, *On the Bias: Feminist Reconsiderations of the Aspirations for Our Judges*, 61 S. CAL. L. REV. 1877 (1988), 694

Review & Outlook: The State of PC, WALL ST. J., Sept. 9, 1994 at A14, **103-104**

Keith Richburg, *Criticism Mounts Over Somali Raid; 'Pack Up, Go Home,' U.S. Troops Urged*, WASH. POST, July 15, 1993, at A21, 240

Stefan Riesenfeld & Frederick Abbott, *Foreword: Symposium on Parliamentary Participation in the Making and Operation of Treaties*, 67 CHI-KENT L. REV. 293 (1992), 42

Stefan Riesenfeld, *The Doctrine of Self-Executing Treaties and GATT: A Notable German Judgment*, 65 AM. J. INT'L L. (1971), 22

Stefan A. Riesenfeld & Frederick M. Abbott, *The Scope of U.S. Senate Control Over the Conclusion and Operation of Treaties*, 67 CHI.-KENT L. REV. 571 (1991), 596

Ronald M. Riggs, *The Grenada Intervention: A Legal Analysis*, 109 MIL. L. REV. (1985), 52

THE RIGHT TO KNOW: HUMAN RIGHTS AND ACCESS TO REPRODUCTIVE HEALTH INFORMATION (Sandra Coliver ed., 1995), 84

THE RIGHT TO FOOD: GUIDE THROUGH APPLICABLE INTERNATIONAL LAW (Katarina Tomasevski ed., 1987), 84

A.H. Robertson & John Merrills, Human Rights in Europe: A Study of the European Convention on Human Rights (3d ed. 1993), 237

Jacob Robinson, Human Rights and Fundamental Freedoms in the Charter of the United Nations: A Commentary, From War to Peace Series No. 4 (1946), 7

Nehemiah Robinson, Convention Relating to the Status of Refugees: Its History, Contents and Interpretation (1953), 642

Nigel Rodley, The Treatment of Prisoners under International Law (1987), 166, 201, 208

Nigel Rodley, *United Nations Action Procedures Against "Disappearances," Summary or Arbitrary Executions, and Torture*, 8 Hum. Rts. Q. 700 (1986), 159, 202

Nigel S. Rodley, *On the Necessity of United States Ratification of the International Human Rights-Conventions*, in U.S. Ratification of the Human Rights Treaties: With or Without Reservations? 3 (Richard B. Lillich ed., 1981), **35-37**

George C. Rogers, *Argentina's Obligation to Prosecute Military Officials for Torture*, 20 Colum. Hum. Rts. L. Rev. 259 (1989), 276

Naomi Roht-Arriaza, *State Responsibility to Investigate and Prosecute Grave Human Rights Violations in International Law*, 78 Calif. L. Rev. 449 (1990), 303

Naomi Roht-Arriaza, *State Responsibility to Investigate and Prosecute Grave Human Rights Violations in International Law*, 78 Calif. L. Rev. 449 (1990), 310

Celina Romany, *Women as Aliens: A Feminist Critique of the Public/Private Distinction in International Human Rights Law*, 6 Harv. Hum. Rts. J. 87 (1993), 675

Robert Rosenstock, *Current Development: The Forty-sixth Session of the International Law Commission*, 89 Am. J. Int'l L. 390 (1995), 302

Rossiter & Smith, *Human Rights: The Carter Record, The Reagan Reaction*, Int'l Pol'y Rep., Sept. 1984, 389

Louis K. Rothberg, *Sections 402 and 403 of the Comprehensive Anti-Apartheid Act of 1986*, 22 George Washington J. Int'l L. & Econ. 117 (1988), 420

Alfred P. Rubin, *An International Criminal Tribunal for Former Yugoslavia?*, 6 Pace Int'l L. Rev. 7 (1994), 298

R.J. Rummel, *Democide in Totalitarian States: Mortacracies and Megamurderers* in The Widening Circle of Genocide 3 (Israel W. Charny, ed., 1994) (Vol. 3 in Genocide: A Critical Bibliographic Review), 721

Rudolph. J. Rummel, *Libertarianism and International Violence*, 27 J. Conflict Resol. 27 (1983), 750

Rwanda Asks for Ex-officer's Return, Boston Globe, Mar. 13, 1996, at 36, 297

Rwanda, Human Rights Watch World Report 41 (1995), 313-314

Rwandan Army Puts 14 on Trial, Wash. Post, May 3, 1995, at A24, 297

Leila Sadat Wexler, *The Interpretation of the Nuremberg Principles by the French Court of Cassation: From Touvier to Barbie and Back Again*, 32 Colum. J. Transnat'l L. 289 (1994), 280

Abdul Aziz Said, *Human Rights in Islamic Perspectives*, in Human Rights: Culture and Ideological Perspectives (A. Pollis & P. Schwab eds., 1979), 171

John P. Salzberg, *The Carter Administration and Human Rights*, in The Diplomacy of Human Rights 61 (David Newsom ed., 1986), 414

Douglas Sanders, *The UN Working Group on Indigenous Populations*, 11 Hum. Rts. Q. 406 (1989), 89

Yves Sandoz, A Consideration of the Implementation of International Humanitarian Law and the Role of the International Committee of the Red Cross in the Former Yugoslavia (Geneva, Sept. 28, 1993), 530

Jonathan Earl Sanford, *U.S. Policy Toward the Multilateral Development Banks: The Role of Congress*, 22 George Washington J. Int'l L. & Econ. 1 (1988), 415

David G. Savage, *INS Detention of Children Upheld*, L.A. Times, Mar. 24, 1993, at A3, 557, n.2

Leila P. Sayeh & Adriaen M. Morse, Jr., *Islam and the Treatment of Women: An Incomplete Understanding of Gradualism*, 30 Tex. Int'l L.J. 311 (1995), 171

Oscar Schachter, *International Law in Theory and Practice: General Course in Public International Law*, 178 COLLECTED COURSES OF THE HAGUE ACAD. OF INT'L LAW 1, 21-39 (1982), 697

Michael P. Scharf, *The Jury is Still Out on the Need for an International Criminal Court*, 1991 DUKE J. COMP. & INT'L. L. 135 (1991), 300

Michael P. Scharf, *The Role of the Judiciary in Foreign Policy Litigation*, 86 AM. SOC'Y INT'L L. PROC. 211 (1992), 403

David Scheffer, *Use of Force After the Cold War: Panama, Iraq, and the New World Order, in* RIGHT V. MIGHT: INTERNATIONAL LAW AND THE USE OF FORCE (Louis Henkin et al. eds., 1991), 254

Richard Schifter, *Building Firm Foundations: The Institutionalization of United States Human Rights Policy in the Reagan Years*, 2 HARV. HUM. RTS. Y.B. 3 (1989), 389

David J. Scheffer, *Toward a Modern Doctrine of Humanitarian Intervention*, 23 U. TOL. L. REV. 253 (1992), 239

A. SCHMID, RESEARCH ON GROSS HUMAN RIGHTS VIOLATIONS (1989), 370

ALEX P. SCHMID, RESEARCH ON GROSS HUMAN RIGHTS VIOLATIONS: A PROGRAMME (2d ed. 1989), 749

Eric Schmitt, *House Votes Bill to Cut U.N. Funds for Peacekeeping*, N.Y. TIMES, Feb. 17, 1995, at A1, 239

Eric Schmitt, *Righting Wrongs of War: Billions in Claims Against Iraq*, N.Y. TIMES, Nov. 18, 1994, at B9, 273

Steven M. Schneebaum, *International Law as a Guarantor of Judicially-Enforceable Rights: A Reply to Professor Oliver*, 4 HOUS. J. INT'L. L. 65 (1981), 579

Lars Schoultz, *U.S. Foreign Policy and Human Rights*, 13 COMP. POL. 149 (1980), 751

Minna Schrag, *The Yugoslav Crimes Tribunal: A Prosecutor's Views*, 6 DUKE J. COMP. & INT'L L. 187 (1995), 298

Peter H. Schuck, *The Transformation of Immigration Law*, 84 COLUM. L. REV. 1 (1984), 568

Amy Schwartz, *Brought Together by Bosnia*, WASH. POST, May 14, 1993, at A31, 296

Herman Schwartz, *War Crimes Trials—Not a Good Idea*, HUM. RTS. BRIEF (The Center for Hum. Rts. & Humanitarian L., D.C.), Spring 1994, at 7-8, **289-291**

Stephen M. Schwebel, *Human Rights in the World Court*, 24 VAND. J. TRANSNAT'L L. 945 (1991), 253

Egon Schwelb, *The International Measures of Implementation of the International Covenant on Civil and Political Rights and the Optional Protocol*, 12 TEX. INT'L L.J. 141 (1977), 159

Elaine Sciolino, *Clinton is Stern with Indonesia on Rights but Gleeful on Trade*, N.Y. TIMES, Nov. 17, 1994, at A1, 398

James C. Scott, *Who is the Audience for the Performance?, in* DOMINATION AND THE ARTS OF RESISTANCE: HIDDEN TRANSCRIPTS 68 (1990), **736**

James C. Scott, *The Value and Cost of the Public Transcript, in* DOMINATION AND THE ARTS OF RESISTANCE: HIDDEN TRANSCRIPTS 45 (1990) 700 n.1, **723-726**, 726

Cesar Sepulveda, *The Inter-American Commission on Human Rights of the Organization of American States*, 28 GERMAN Y.B. INT'L. L. 65 (1985), 448

Cesar Sepulveda, *The Inter-American Commission on Human Rights (1960-1981)*, 12 ISRAEL Y.B. HUM. RTS. 46 (1982), 448

Serb is Indicted as War Criminal; Jailed General Spurned Court Request to Testify, CHICAGO TRIB., Mar. 2, 1996, at 10, 295

Stan Sesser, *A Reporter at Large: A Rich Country Gone Wrong*, NEW YORKER, Oct. 9, 1989, at 55, **176-180**

Don Shannon, *Shultz Calls U.S. Debt to U.N. "a Disgrace"*, L.A. TIMES, Aug. 17, 1988, at 1, 240

Gene Sharpe, *The Politics of Nonviolent Action, in* POWER AND STRUGGLE 43 (1973) (Boston: Porter Sargent), 128

John Shattuck, Assistant Secretary of State for Democracy, Human Rights, and Labor, *Introduction, in* CIVIL AND POLITICAL RIGHTS IN THE UNITED STATES: INITIAL REPORT OF THE UNITED STATES OF AMERICA TO THE U.N. HUMAN RIGHTS COMMITTEE UNDER THE INTERNATIONAL COVENANT ON CIVIL AND POLITICAL RIGHTS (July 1994), **100-103**

John Shattuck, *Human Rights and Democracy in Asia,* U.S. DEP'T OF STATE DISPATCH, July 18, 1994 (Vol. 5, No. 29), 420

PARVEEN SHAUKAT ALI, HUMAN RIGHTS IN ISLAM (1980), 170

Dinah Shelton, *Abortion and the Right to Life in the Inter-American System: The Case of* "Baby Boy", 2 H.R.L.J. 309 (1981), 433

Dinah Shelton, *Improving Human Rights Protections: Recommendations for Enhancing the Effectiveness of the Inter-American Commission and Inter-American Court of Human Rights,* 3 AM. U. J. INT'L L. & POL'Y 323 (1988), 449

Dinah Shelton, *International Law, in* U.S. RATIFICATION OF THE INTERNATIONAL COVENANTS ON HUMAN RIGHTS 27 (Hurst Hannum & Dana D. Fischer eds., 1993), **33-34**

Dinah Shelton, *Private Violence, Public Wrongs, and the Responsibility of States,* 13 FORDHAM INT'L L.J. 1 (1989-90), 675

Dinah Shelton, *The Inter-American Human Rights System, in* GUIDE TO INTERNATIONAL HUMAN RIGHTS PRACTICE 119 (Hurst Hannum 2d ed. 1992), 449

Dinah Shelton, *Utilization of Fact-Finding Missions to Promote and Protect Human Rights: The Chile Case,* 2 HUM. RTS. L.J. 1 (1981), 370

GEORGE W. SHEPHERD, JR., EFFECTIVE SANCTIONS ON SOUTH AFRICA: THE CUTTING EDGE OF ECONOMIC INTERVENTION (1991), 415

Jerome J. Shestack, *The Jurisprudence of Human Rights, in* HUMAN RIGHTS IN INTERNATIONAL LAW: LEGAL AND POLICY ISSUES 70 (Theodor Meron ed., 1984), 692

Jerome J. Shestack, *An Unsteady Focus: The Vulnerabilities of the Reagan Administration's Human Rights Policy,* 2 HARV. HUM. RTS. Y.B. 25 (1989), 389

Helen Signy, *Rwanda: It Was Planned This Way—News Review,* SYDNEY MORNING HERALD, June 4, 1994, 297

Kathryn Sikkink, *Human Rights, Principled Issue-Networks and Sovereignty in Latin America,* 47 INT'L ORG. 411 (1993), 390

Kathryn Sikkink, *The Power of Principled Ideas: Human Rights Policies in the United States and Western Europe, in* IDEAS AND FOREIGN POLICY: BELIEFS, INSTITUTIONS AND POLITICAL CHANGE 139 (J. Goldstein & R. Keohane eds., 1993), 370, 751

Jean-Marie Simon, *The Alien Tort Claims Act: Justice or Show Trials?,* 11 B.U. INT'L L.J. 1 (1993), 521

THEDA SKOCPOL, STATES AND SOCIAL REVOLUTIONS: A COMPARATIVE ANALYSIS OF FRANCE, RUSSIA, AND CHINA (London: Cambridge University Press, 1979), 167

SIGRUN I. SKOGLY, HUMAN RIGHTS IN THE NEW EUROPE: PROBLEMS AND PROGRESS (David P. Forsythe ed., 1994), 391

Alison T. Slack, *Female Circumcision: A Critical Appraisal,* 10 HUM. RTS. Q. 437 (1988), 674

Peter Slevin, *America Will Enter Bosnia with Eyes Open to Problems,* PORTLAND OREGONIAN, Nov. 23, 1995, at A4, 295

MELVIN SMALL & J. DAVID SINGER, RESORT TO ARMS: INTERNATIONAL AND CIVIL WARS, 1816-1980 (Beverly Hills: Sage, 1982), 751

Robyn C. Smith, *Note, Female Circumcision: Bringing Women's Perspectives into the International Debate,* 65 S. CAL. L. REV. 2449 (1992), 674

Pieter Smits, *The Right to Life of the Unborn Child in* INTERNATIONAL DOCUMENTS, DECISIONS AND OPINIONS (1992), 436

Abraham D. Sofaer, *International Law and the Use of Force,* NAT'L INTEREST, Fall 1988, at 54, **245-247**

Louis B. Sohn, *The Human Rights Movement: From Roosevelt's Four Freedoms to the Interdependence of Peace, Development and Human Rights* (1995), 33

Some Conditions of Obedience and Disobedience to Authority, 10 HUM. REL. 57 (1965), 730

Lim Soon Neo, *Clinton's new policy towards China working, says Brown,* BUSINESS TIMES, Sept. 3, 1994, at 4, 410

Theodore Sorenson, *United States Policy on United Nations Peace-Keeping Operations*, 18 YALE J. INT'L L. 429 (1993), 242

SOUTH AFRICA: THE SANCTIONS REPORT: DOCUMENTS AND STATISTICS (Joseph Hanlon ed., 1990), 415

Ed Sparer, *Fundamental Human Rights, Legal Entitlements, and the Social Struggle: A Friendly Critique of the Critical Legal Studies Movement*, 36 STAN. L. REV. 509 (1984), 693

MICHAEL SPENCER, STATES OF INJUSTICE, A GUIDE TO HUMAN RIGHTS AND CIVIL LIBERTIES IN THE EUROPEAN UNION (1995), 481, 494

Elizabeth P. Spiro, *Front Door or Back Stair: U.S. Human Rights Policy in the International Financial Institution, in* HUMAN RIGHTS AND U.S. FOREIGN POLICY 133 (Barry M. Rubin & Elizabeth P. Spiro eds., 1979), 392

Peter J. Spiro, *New Global Communities: Nongovernmental Organizations in International Decision-Making Institutions*, 18 WASHINGTON Q. 45 (1994), 402

Barbara Stark, *Economic Rights in the United States and International Human Rights Law; Toward an "Entirely New Strategy,"* 44 HASTINGS L.J. 79 (1992), 579

Barbara Stark, *Nurturing Rights: An Essay on Women, Peace, and International Human Rights*, 13 MICH. J. INT'L L. 144 (1991), 694

Barbara Stark, *Urban Despair and Nietzsche's "Eternal Return:" From the Municipal Rhetoric of Economic Justice to the International Law of Economic Rights*, 28 VAND. J. TRANSNAT'L L. 185 (1995), 65

STATE CRIMES: PUNISHMENT OR PARDON (Alice Henkin ed., 1989), 370

THE STATUS OF HUMAN RIGHTS IN THE UNITED STATES: AN ANALYSIS OF THE INITIAL U.S. GOVERNMENT REPORT TO THE HUMAN RIGHTS COMMITTEE OF THE UNITED NATIONS UNDER THE INTERNATIONAL COVENANT ON CIVIL AND POLITICAL RIGHTS (Morton Sklar ed., March 2, 1995), **126**

Ervin Staub, *The Psychology of Perpetrators and Bystanders*, POL. PSYCHOL. 61 (1985), **729**, 737, 738

Henry J. Steiner, *Political Participation as a Human Right*, 1 HARV. HUM. RTS. Y.B. 77 (1988), 389

Ralph G. Steinhardt, *The Role of International Law as a Canon of Domestic Statutory Construction*, 43 VAND. L. REV. 1103 (1990), 579

Ralph G. Steinhardt, *The United Nations and Refugees: 1945-1988*, AIUSA LEGAL SUPPORT NETWORK NEWSL., Fall 1988, at 103, 623

Ralph G. Steinhardt, *The United Nations and Refugees: 1945-1988, in* THE UNIVERSAL DECLARATION OF HUMAN RIGHTS 1948-1988: HUMAN RIGHTS, THE UNITED NATIONS AND AMNESTY INTERNATIONAL 77, 86-87 (1988), 648

Ralph G. Steinhardt, *Fulfilling the Promise of Filartiga: Litigating Human Rights Claims Against the Estate of Ferdinand Marcos*, 20 YALE J. INT'L L. 65 (1995), 521

ALFRED STEPAN, THE MILITARY IN POLITICS: CHANGING PATTERNS IN BRAZIL (Princeton: Princeton University Press, 1971), 721

Alfred Stepan, *The New Professionalism of Internal Warfare and Military Role Expansion, in* ARMIES AND POLITICS IN LATIN AMERICA 134 (Abraham Lowenthal & J. Samuel Fitch eds., 1989), 751

BETH STEPHENS ET AL., SUING FOR TORTURE AND OTHER HUMAN RIGHTS ABUSES IN FEDERAL COURT: A LITIGATION MANUAL (1993), 521

Beth Stephens, *The Civil Lawsuit as a Remedy for International Human Rights Violations Against Women*, 5 HASTINGS WOMEN'S L.J. 143 (1994), 274

Mattie L. Stevens, *Note, Recognizing Gender-Specific Persecution: A Proposal to Add Gender as a Sixth Refugee Category*, 3 CORNELL J.L. & PUB. POL'Y 179 (1993), 666

David Stewart, *U.S. Ratification of the Covenant on Civil and Political Rights: The Significance of the Reservations, Understandings, and Declarations*, 14 HUM. RTS. L.J. 77 (1993), 41

Todd Stewart Schenk, *Note, A Proposal to Improve the Treatment of Women in Asylum Law: Adding a "Gender" Category to the International Definition of "Refugee,"* 2 IND. J. GLOBAL LEGAL. STUD. 301 (1994), 666

JOHN. G. STOESSINGER, WHY NATIONS GO TO WAR (New York: St. Martin's Press, 1982), 751

Michael Stohl & David Carleton, *The Foreign Policy of Human Rights: Rhetoric and Reality from Jimmy Carter to Ronald Reagan,* 7 HUM. RTS. Q. 205 (1985), 751

Michael Stohl, David Carleton, George Lopez & Stephen Samuels, *State Violations of Human Rights: Issues and Problems of Measurement,* 8 HUM. RTS. Q. 592 (1986), 749

Michael Stohl, David Carleton & Steven E. Johnson, *Human Rights and U.S. Foreign Assistance: From Nixon to Carter,* 21 J. PEACE RES. 215 (1984), 751

Michael Stohl, *The Nexus of Civil and International Conflict, in* THE HANDBOOK OF POLITICAL CONFLICT: THEORY AND RESEARCH (Ted Robert Gurr ed.) (New York: Free Press, 1980), 751

MICHAEL STOHL, WAR AND DOMESTIC POLITICAL VIOLENCE: THE AMERICAN CAPACITY FOR REPRESSION AND REACTION (Beverly Hills: Sage, 1976), 751

Michael Stohl, *War and Domestic Violence: The Case of the United States, 1890-1970,* 19 J. CONFLICT RESOL. 379 (1975), 751

ERIC STOVER & ELEANOR O. NIGHTINGALE, THE BREAKING OF BODIES AND MINDS: TORTURE, PSYCHIATRIC ABUSE AND THE HEALTH PROFESSIONS (New York: W.H. Freeman, 1985), 168

NADINE STROSSEN, RECENT U.S. AND INTERNATIONAL JUDICIAL PROTECTION OF INDIVIDUAL RIGHTS: A COMPARATIVE LEGAL PROCESS ANALYSIS AND PROPOSED SYNTHESIS (1989), 630

Nadine Strossen, *United States Ratification of the International Bill of Rights: A Fitting Celebration of the Bicentennial of the U.S. Bill of Rights,* 24 U. TOLEDO L. REV. 571 (1992), 37

Symposium on Human Rights: An Agenda For the New Administration, 28 VA. J. INT'L L. 827 (1988), 410

Symposium, Transitions to Democracy and the Rule of Law, 5 AM. U. J. INT'L L. & POL'Y 965 (1990), 276

Paul Szasz, *The International Legal Aspects of the Human Rights Program of the United States,* 12 CORNELL INT'L L. J. 161 (1979), 420

Margaret H. Taylor, *Detained Aliens Challenging Conditions of Confinement and the Porous Border of the Plenary Power Doctrine,* 22 HASTINGS CONST L.Q. 1087 (1995), 568

FERNANDO TESÒN, HUMANITARIAN INTERVENTION: AN INQUIRY INTO LAW AND MORALITY 5 (1988), 252

Fernando R. Tesòn, *International Human Rights and Cultural Relativism,* 25 VA. J. INT'L L. 869 (1985), 683

Dorothy Q. Thomas & Michele E. Beasley, *Domestic Violence as a Human Rights Issue,* 15 HUM. RTS. Q. 36 (1993), 533

Pamela Theodoredis, *Comment, Detention of Alien Juveniles:* Reno v. Flores, 12 N.Y.L. SCH. J. HUM. RTS. 393 (1995) 557, 568

AWA THIAM, BLACK SISTERS, SPEAK OUT: FEMINISM AND OPPRESSION IN BLACK AFRICA (1986), 674

HANS THOOLEN & BERTH VERSTAPPEN, HUMAN RIGHTS MISSIONS: A STUDY OF THE FACT-FINDING PRACTICE OF NON-GOVERNMENTAL ORGANIZATIONS (1986), 330

Melissa Thorme, *Establishing Environment as a Human Right,* 19 DEN. J. INT'L L. & POL'Y 301 (1991), 82

Brenda Sue Thornton, *The New International Jurisprudence on the Right to Privacy: A Head-On Collision with* Bowers v. Hardwick, 58 ALB. L. REV. 725 (1995), 476

James Thyden, *An Inside View of United States Foreign Policy Under the Reagan Administration,* 7 WHITTIER L. REV. 705 (1985), 414

CHARLES TILLY, FROM MOBILIZATION TO REVOLUTION (Reading, MA: Addison-Wesley, 1978), 167

TO LOOSE THE BANDS OF WICKEDNESS: INTERNATIONAL INTERVENTION IN DEFENCE OF HUMAN RIGHTS (Nigel S. Rodley ed., 1992), 242

Howard Tolley, *International Human Rights Law in U.S. Courts, Public Interest Groups and Private Attorneys,* 1987 Annual Meeting, American Political Science Association, 630

HOWARD TOLLEY, JR., THE U.N. COMMISSION ON HUMAN RIGHTS (1987), 143, 216

Howard Tolley, *The Concealed Crack in the Citadel: The United Nations Commission on Human Rights' Response to Confidential Communications,* 6 HUMAN RTS. Q. 420 (1984), 191, 216

KATARINA TOMASHEVSKI, DEVELOPMENT AID AND HUMAN RIGHTS 50 (1989), 392

KATARINA TOMASHEVSKI, FOREIGN AID AND HUMAN RIGHTS: CASE STUDIES OF BANGLADESH AND KENYA (1988), 392

Alan Tonelson, *Jettison the Policy*, FOREIGN POL'Y, Dec. 1994, at 121, 390

NAHID TOUBIA, FEMALE GENITAL MUTILATION: A CALL TO ACTION (1993), 674

TRANSITIONAL JUSTICE: HOW EMERGING DEMOCRACIES RECKON WITH FORMER REGIMES (vol. I-III) (Neil J. Kritz ed., 1995), 276

TRANSITION TO DEMOCRACY IN LATIN AMERICA: THE ROLE OF THE JUDICIARY (Irwin P. Stotzky ed., 1993), 276

Ian Traynor, *Serb War Crime Hearing Makes Legal History*, GUARDIAN, Oct. 10, 1995, at 13, 295

H. R. Trevor-Roper, *The European Witch-Craze, in* WITCHCRAFT AND SORCERY 121 (Max Marwick ed., 1970), **743-45**

TRIBAL PEOPLES AND DEVELOPMENT ISSUES: A GLOBAL OVERVIEW (John H. Bodley ed., 1988), 720

David M. Trubek, *Where the Action Is: Critical Legal Studies and Empiricism*, 36 STAN. L. REV. 575 (1984), 693

David M. Trubek, *Economic, Social, and Cultural Rights in The Third World: Human Rights Law and Human Needs Programs, in* HUMAN RIGHTS IN INTERNATIONAL LAW: LEGAL AND POLICY ISSUES (Theodor Meron ed., 1984), 51

Charles Trueheart, *Canadian Peace Keepers Accused: Cases of 2 Killings in Somalia Spark Criticism of Revered Forces*, WASH. POST, May 22, 1993, at A18, 229

Charles Trueheart, *Tapes Embarrass Canada Airborne Unit Shown as Violent, Racist*, WASH. POST, Jan. 21, 1995, at A17, 229

Mark Tushnet, *An Essay on Rights*, 62 TEX. L. REV. 1363 (1984), 693

Patrick E. Tyler, *Abuses of Rights Persist in China Despite U.S. Pleas*, N.Y. TIMES, Aug. 29, 1994, at A1, 410

U.N. Centre for Hum. Rts., *Advisory Services and Technical Assistance in the Field of Human Rights*, Fact Sheet No. 3 (1988), 272

U.N. Centre for Human Rights, *Enforced or Involuntary Disappearances*, Fact Sheet No. 6 (1989), 202

U.N. Centre for Human Rights, *How do the Procedures Differ, Communications Procedures*, Fact Sheet No. 7 (1989), 215

U.N. Centre for Hum. Rts., *United Nations Action in the Field of Human Rights* at 345, U.N. Doc. ST/HR/2/Rev.4 (1994), 272

U.N. Centre for Human Rights, *The Committee on Economic, Social and Cultural Rights*, Fact Sheet No. 16 (1991), 79, 272

U.N., *Multilateral Treaties Deposited with the Secretary-General: Status as at 31 December 1993* (1994), 42

U.S. Dep't of State, *Country Reports on Human Rights Practices for 1992* at 314 (1993), 634

UNESCO, *Access to Human Rights Documentation: Documentation, Databases and Bibliographies on Human Rights* (1991), 642

UNHCR, *An Introduction to the International Protection of Refugees* 6-7 (1992), 647

United Nations Centre for Human Rights, *Human Rights Machinery*, Fact Sheet No. 1 (1988), **149-150**

UNITED NATIONS CODIFICATIONS OF STATE RESPONSIBILITY (Marina Spinedi & Bruno Simma eds., 1987), 304

UNITED NATIONS, THE BLUE HELMETS: A REVIEW OF UNITED NATIONS PEACE-KEEPING (2d ed. 1990), **219-222**

United Nations, *Workshop on International Human Rights Instruments and Reporting Obligations: Preparation of Reports to United Human Rights Treaty Bodies*, HR/PUB/91/5 (1992), 100

Detlev F. Vagts, *The U.S. Action in Grenada: International Law under Time Pressure: Grading the Grenada Take-Home Exam*, 78 AM. J. INT'L L. 169 (1984), 254

Jon M. Van Dyke & Gerald W. Berkley, *Redressing Human Rights Abuses,* 20 DENV. J. INT'L L. & POL'Y 243 (1992), 276, 370

PIETER VAN DIJK & G.J.H. VAN HOOF, THEORY AND PRACTICE OF THE EUROPEAN CONVENTION OF HUMAN RIGHTS (2d ed. 1990), 237

PIETER VAN DIJK & G.J.H. VAN HOOF, THEORY AND PRACTICE OF THE EUROPEAN CONVENTION ON HUMAN RIGHTS 218 (1990), 436, 481

Pieter van Dijk, *The Treatment of Homosexuals under the European Convention on Human Rights, in* HOMOSEXUALITY: A EUROPEAN COMMUNITY ISSUE 179 (Kees Waaldijk & Andrew Clapham eds., 1993), 476

Pieter van Dyke, *Prospects for the Development of Intergovernmental Human Rights Bodies in Asia and the Pacific, in* NEW DIRECTIONS IN HUMAN RIGHTS 51 (Ellen Lutz, Hurst Hannum & Kathryn Burke eds., 1989), 466, n.3

Alain Van Hamme, *Human Rights and the Treaty of Rome, in* HUMAN RIGHTS A EUROPEAN PERSPECTIVE 70 (Liz Heffernan ed., 1994), 494

GERALDINE VAN BUEREN, THE INTERNATIONAL LAW ON THE RIGHTS OF THE CHILD 210 (1995), 574

Katherine Van Wenzel Stone, *The Post-War Paradigm in American Labor Law,* 90 YALE L.J. 1509 (1981), 692

Theo Van Boven, *Fundamental Rights and Nuclear Arms,* 19 DEN. J. INT'L L. & POL'Y 55 (1990), 84

Cyrus Vance, *Human Rights and Foreign Policy,* 7 GA. J. INT'L & COMP. L. 223 (1977), 66

Cyrus Vance, *The Human Rights Imperative,* 63 FOREIGN POL'Y 3, 9 (1986), 388

TATU VANHANEN, THE PROCESS OF DEMOCRATIZATION: A COMPARATIVE STUDY OF 147 STATES, 1980-88 (New York: Crane Russak, 1990), 750

Edmundo Vargas, *Visits on the Spot: The Experience of the Inter-American Commission on Human Rights, in* INTERNATIONAL LAW AND FACT-FINDING IN THE FIELD OF HUMAN RIGHTS 137 (Bertie G. Ramcharan ed., 1982), **348-351**, 457

W. Gary Vause, *Article: Tibet to Tienanmen: Chinese Human Rights and United States Foreign Policy,* 42 VAND. L. REV. 1575 (1989), 410

BERTH VERSTAPPEN, HUMAN RIGHTS REPORTS: AN ANNOTATED BIBLIOGRAPHY OF FACT-FINDING MISSIONS (1987), 330

Herman von Hebel, *An International Tribunal for the Former Yugoslavia: An Act of Powerlessness or a New Challenge for the International Community,* 11 NETH. Q. HUM. RTS. 437 (1993), 286, 287

George K. Walker, *United States National Security Law and United Nations Peacekeeping or Peacemaking Operations,* 29 WAKE FOREST L. REV. 435 (1994), 253

ALICE WALKER, POSSESSING THE SECRET OF JOY (1992), 674

ALICE WALKER & PRATIBHA PARMAR, WARRIOR MARKS: FEMALE GENITAL MUTILATION & THE SEXUAL BLINDING OF WOMEN (1993), 674

Charles P. Wallace, *Indonesia's Labor and Human Rights Practices Fray U.S. Ties,* L.A. TIMES, Sept. 24, 1993, at A5, 398

Wallace F. Warriner, *USMC, The Unilateral Use of Coercion Under International Law: A Legal Analysis of the United States Raid on Libya on April 14, 1986,* 37 NAVAL L. REV. 49 (1988), 254

RUTH E. WASEM, ASYLUM AND TEMPORARY PROTECTED STATUS UNDER U.S. IMMIGRATION LAW (1991), 649

Wave of Repression in Shanghai, Dissidents Say, AGENCE FRANCE PRESSE, Oct. 19, 1993, 421

Mary Anne Weaver, *A Fugitive from Injustice,* NEW YORKER, Sept. 12, 1994, at 48, 171

Herbert Wechsler, *The Issues at the Nuremberg Trial, in* PRINCIPLES, POLITICS, AND FUNDAMENTAL LAW: SELECTED ESSAYS 138 (1961), 280

Claudia Weinstein, *The Children San Diego Forgot,* AMERICAN LAWYER, Sept. 1987, at 102, 558

PAUL WEIS, COMMENTARY ON THE CONVENTION RELATING TO THE STATUS OF REFUGEES (1992), 642

THOMAS G. WEISS ET AL., THE UNITED NATIONS AND CHANGING WORLD POLITICS 17-100 (1994), 242

David Weissbrodt & Paul Fraser, *Report of the Chilean National Commission on Truth and Reconciliation,* 14 HUM. RTS. Q. 601 (1992), **264-266**, 370

David Weissbrodt & Georgina Mahoney, *International Legal Action Against Apartheid,* 4 Law & Ineq. J. 485 (1986), 420

David Weissbrodt & James McCarthy, *Fact-Finding by International Nongovernmental Human Rights Organizations,* 22 Va. J. Int'l L. 1 (1981), 330

David Weissbrodt & Beth Andrus, *The Right to Life During Armed Conflict:* Disabled Peoples' International v. United States, 29 Harv. Int'l L.J. 59 (1988), 439

David Weissbrodt & Paul W. Fraser, *Book Review,* 14 Hum. Rts. Q. 601 (1992), **264-266**

David Weissbrodt, *Domestic Legal Activity in Furtherance of International Human Rights Goals, in* Implementing International Human Rights Through the Domestic Legal Process 10 (John Bassett Moore Soc'y of Int'l Law, 1975), 521

David Weissbrodt, *Ethical Problems of an International Human Rights Law Practice,* 7 Mich. Y.B. Int'l Legal Stud. 217 (1985), 433, 630

David Weissbrodt, *Execution of Juvenile Offenders by the United States Violates International Human Rights Law,* 3 Am. U. J. Int'l L. & Pol'y 339 (1987), 439

David Weissbrodt, *Human Rights Legislation and U.S. Foreign Policy,* 7 Ga. J. Int'l & Comp. L. 231 (1977), 332, 399

David Weissbrodt, *International Trial Observers,* 18 Stan. J. Int'l L. 1 (1982), 370

David Weissbrodt, *International Factfinding in Regard to Torture,* 57 Nordic J. Int'l L. 151 (1988), 330

David Weissbrodt, *Strategies for Selection and Pursuit of International Human Rights Objectives,* 8 Yale J. World Pub. Ord. 62 (1981), 630

David Weissbrodt, *The Three "Theme" Special Rapporteurs of the UN Commission on Human Rights,* 80 Am. J. Int'l L. 685 (1986), **192-196**

David Weissbrodt, *United States Ratification of the Human Rights Covenants,* 63 Minn. L. Rev. 35 (1978), 37, 596

Art Weitzhandler, *Comment, Temporary Protected Status: The Congressional Response to the Plight of Salvadoran Aliens,* 64 U. Colo. L. Rev. 249 (1993), 649

Claude Welch, *The African Commission on Human and Peoples' Rights: A Five-Year Report and Assessment,* 14 Hum. Rts. Q. 43 (1992), 465

Lawrence Weschler, A Miracle, A Universe 64 (1990), 722

Peter Westen, *The Place of Foreign Treaties in the Courts of the United States: A Reply to Louis Henkin,* 101 Harv. L. Rev. 511 (1987), 594

Burns Weston et al., *Regional Human Rights Regimes: A Comparison and Appraisal,* 20 Vand. J. Transnat'l L. 585 (1987), 489

Burns Weston, *Human Rights, in* Encyclopedia Britannica (15th ed. 1985), 83

Burns Weston, *U.S. Ratification of the International Covenant on Economic, Social and Cultural Rights: With or Without Qualifications, in* U.S. Ratification of the Human Rights Treaties: With or Without Reservations? 27 (Richard B. Lillich ed., 1981), **68-72**

Ralf Wetzel, *Introduction, The Vienna Convention of the Law of Treaties,* Travaux Préparatoires 12 (1978), 452

Linda A. Whisman, *Selected Bibliography: Articles and Cases on International Human Rights Law in Domestic Courts,* 18 Int'l Law. 83 (1984), 630

Marjorie M. Whiteman, Digest of International Law § 17, at 137 (1970), 595

James D. Wilets, *Using International Law to Vindicate the Civil Rights of Gays and Lesbians in United States Courts,* 27 Colum. Hum. Rts. L. Rev. 33 (1995), 630

Ann M. Williams, *United States Treaty Law, in* U.S. Ratification of the International Covenants on Human Rights (Hurst Hannum & Dana D. Fischer eds., 1993), **30-31**

Patricia Williams, The Alchemy of Race and Rights (1991), 693

Rick Wilson, *Litigation at the Inter-American Human Rights Commission and Court,* ACLU International Civil Liberties Report, July 1994, at 28, 450

Rick Wilson, *Race, Criminal Justice and the Death Penalty in the Inter-American Human Rights System,* 15 WHITTIER L. REV. 395 (1994), 440

MORTON WINSTON, THE PHILOSOPHY OF HUMAN RIGHTS (1989), 692

ROBERT K. WOETZEL, THE NUREMBERG TRIALS IN INTERNATIONAL LAW 17 (1962), 280

ROBERT K. WOETZEL, THE NUREMBERG TRIALS IN INTERNATIONAL LAW 2 (1962), 277

LAWRENCE WOOD, ALONE AMONG ITS PEERS: THE UNITED STATES REFUSAL TO JOIN THE INTERNATIONAL MOVEMENT TO ABOLISH CAPITAL PUNISHMENT (1991), 579

WORLD JUSTICE?: U.S. COURTS AND INTERNATIONAL HUMAN RIGHTS (Mark Gibney ed., 1991), 579

Robin Wright & Jim Mann, *Clinton Outlines Program Aimed at Human Rights in China,* L.A. TIMES, May 31, 1994, at A6, 410

Stephen L. Wright, *Note, Diplomatic Immunity: A Proposal for Amending the Vienna Convention to Deter Violent Criminal Acts,* 5 B.U. INT'L L.J. 177 (1987), 547

Yolanda S. Wu, *Note, Genocidal Rape in Bosnia: Redress in United States Courts Under the Alien Tort Claims Act,* 4 UCLA WOMEN'S L.J. 101 (1993), 533

Margot C. Wuebbels, *Note, Commercial Terrorism: A Commercial Activity Exception Under § 1605(a)(2) of the Foreign Sovereign Immunities Act,* 35 ARIZ. L. REV. 1123 (1993), 539

Richard Wydeven, *Note, The Foreign Sovereign Immunities Act of 1976: A Contemporary Look at Jurisdiction Under the Commercial Activity Exception,* 13 REV. LITIG. 143 (1993), 539

Hiroko Yamane, *Approaches to Human Rights in Asia,* in INTERNATIONAL ENFORCEMENT OF HUMAN RIGHTS 99 (R. Bernhardt & J. Jolowicz, eds., 1987), 466, n.3

EDWARD YAMBRUSIC, TREATY INTERPRETATION: THEORY AND REALITY 9 (1987), 454

José Zalaquett, *Balancing Ethical Imperatives and Political Constraints: The Dilemma of New Democracies Confronting Past Human Rights Violations,* 43 HASTINGS L.J. 1425 (1992), **262-264**

Alan Zarembo, *In Ethiopia, Time to Settle Accounts,* SAN FRANCISCO CHRONICLE, Apr. 29, 1995, 272

EDUARD A. ZIEGENHAGEN, THE REGULATION OF POLITICAL CONFLICT (New York: Praeger, 1986), 750

Adrien-Claude Zoller, *Analytical Report of the 44th Session of the Sub-Commission,* 17 HUM. RTS. MONITOR 6 (1992), 372

Elisabeth Zoller, *The "Corporate Will" of the United Nations and the Rights of the Minority,* 81 AM. J. INT'L L. 610 (1987), 240

DANIEL ZOVATTO, LOS ESTADOS DE EXCEPCIÓN Y LOS DERECHOS HUMANOS EN AMERICA LATINA (1990), 449

TOM ZUIJDWIJK, PETITIONING THE UNITED NATIONS (1982), 216

TOM ZWART, THE ADMISSIBILITY OF HUMAN RIGHTS PETITIONS: THE CASE LAW OF THE EUROPEAN COMMISSION OF HUMAN RIGHTS AND THE HUMAN RIGHTS COMMITTEE (1994), 481

OTHER

8 C.F.R. § 103, 208, 236, 242, 274, 640

8 C.F.R. § 208.13(b), 645

8 C.F.R. § 242.24 (1988), 557, **561-562**

102 Cong. Rec. S4781-4784 (daily ed., April 2, 1992), 41, 99, 571

132 Cong. Rec. S1377 (daily ed., Feb. 19, 1986), 39

136 Cong. Rec. S17486-92 (daily ed., Oct. 27, 1990), 40

138 Cong. Rec. S2668 (daily ed. Mar. 3, 1992), 552

138 Cong. Rec. S4783 (daily ed., April 2, 1992), **105**

140 Cong. Rec. S13927-28 (daily ed., Oct. 3, 1994), **43-45**

140 Cong. Rec. S7634 (daily ed., June 24, 1994), **42-43**

59 Fed. Reg. 62,284 (1995) (codified at 8 C.F.R. §§ 208, 236, 242, 274a, and 299), 640

14 Refugee Reports (U.S. Comm. on Refugees, Washington, D.C.), Apr. 23, 1993, 649

2 Y.B. Int'l L. Comm'n 374-78, U.N. Doc. A/CN.4/SER.A/1950/Add.1 (1950), 279

2 Y.B. Int'l L. Comm'n 1976 (pt. 2) 95, art. 19 (1), U.N. Doc. A/CN.4/SER.A/1976/Add.1 (Part 2), 303, 304

2 Y.B. Int'l L. Comm'n 1980 (pt. 2) 31, art. 10, U.N. Doc. A/CN.4/SER.A/1980/Add.1 (Part 2), 303

2 Y.B. Int'l L. Comm'n 1985 (pt. 2) 20, U.N. Doc. A/CN.4/SER.A/1985/Add.1 (Part 2), 304

Address by President Clinton to the 49th U.N. General Assembly, September 26, 1994, 377

Advisory Opinion OC-14, Inter-Am Ct. H.R. 101, OEA/Ser.L/V/III.29 doc. 4 (1994), 463

Advisory Opinion on Reservations to the Genocide Convention, 1951 I.C.J. 16, 595

American Bar Association, Report on the International Tribunal to Adjudicate War Crimes Committed in the Former Yugoslavia (1993), 297

American Civil Liberties Union, *amicus brief, Matter of Medina*, Interim Decision No. 3078 (BIA 1988), 591

American Jewish Committee, A.J.C. News Release, June 13, 1945, 7

Analytical Report of the Secretary-General on Internally Displaced Persons, U.N. ESCOR, 48th Sess., 23d mtg., at 5, U.N. Doc. E/CN.4/23 (1992), 676, 677

Annual Report of the Inter-American Court of Human Rights, OAS/Ser.L/V/III.29, doc. 4 (1994), 488

Argument for the Prosecution and Punishment of the Major War Criminals of the European Axis, 58 Stat. 1544, E.A.S. No. 472, 82 U.N.T.S. 280, **276**

Armed Conflict and Iran, U.N. Doc. E/CN.4/1987/NGO 51 (1987), 147

ASYLUM BRANCH, OFFICE OF GENERAL COUNSEL, IMMIGRATION & NATURALIZATION SERV., BASIC LAW MANUAL: ASYLUM, SUMMARY AND OVERVIEW CONCERNING ASYLUM LAW 25 (1991), **675-76**

James Baker, Secretary of State, Hearing of the Senate Foreign Relations Committee, Feb. 2, 1990, **385-386**

Basic Documents Pertaining to Human Rights in the Inter-American System, OAS Doc. OEA/Ser/L/V/II.82 (1992), 437, 457

The Belgrade Minimum Rules of Procedure for International Human Rights Fact-finding Visits, 75 AM. J. INT'L L. 163 (1981), 322

Boutros Boutros-Ghali, *Advisory Services in the Field of Human Rights*, at 24-31, U.N. Doc. E/CN.4/1995/89 (1995), 272

Boutros Boutros-Ghali, *Report of the Board of Trustees of the Voluntary Fund for Technical Cooperation in the Field of Human Rights*, U.N. Doc. E/CN.4/1995/89/Add.1 (1995), 272

C.H.R. dec. 1995/107, U.N. Doc. E/CN.4/1995/L.42 (1995), 234

C.H.R. res. 1987/16, U.N. Doc. E/CN.4/1987/60 (1987), 197

C.H.R. res. 1990/68, U.N. Doc. E/CN.4/1990/94 (1990), 198

C.H.R. res. 1991/42, U.N. Doc. E/CN.4/1991/91 (1991), 199

C.H.R. res. 1992/73, U.N. Doc. E/CN.4/1992/84 (1992), 199

C.H.R. res. 1993/20, U.N. Doc. E/CN.4/1993/L.11/Add.3 (1993), 200

C.H.R. res. 1993/22, U.N. Doc. E/CN.4/1993/L.11/Add.4 (1993), 200

C.H.R. res. 1993/45, U.N. Doc. E/CN.4/1993/L.11/Add.5 (1993), 200

C.H.R. res. 1993/95, U.N. Doc. E/CN.4/1993/L.11/Add.9 (1993), 199

C.H.R. res. 1994/41, 201

C.H.R. res. 1995/23, U.N. Doc. E/CN.4/1995/L.31 (1995), 197

C.H.R. res. 1995/32, U.N. Doc. E/CN.4/1995/L.62 (1995), 274C.H.R. res. 1995/37, U.N. Doc. E/CN.4/1995/L.52 (1995), 197

C.H.R. res. 1995/5, U.N. Doc. E/CN.4/1995/L.12 (1995), 198

C.H.R. res. 1995/81, 201

C.H.R. res. 8 (XXIII), U.N. Doc. E/CN.4/940, (1967), 183 n.2

Commission on Human Rights, *Report of the Seminar on Extreme Poverty and the Denial of Human Rights—Note by the Secretariat*, U.N. Doc. E/CN.4/1995/101 (1994), 87

Commission on Human Rights, *Report on the Human Rights Situation in the Islamic Republic of Iran by the Special Representative of the Commission, Mr. Reynaldo Galindo Pohl*, U.N. Doc. E/CN.4/1987/23 (1987), 145, **146**

Commission on Human Rights, *Study Concerning the Right to Restitution, Compensation, and Rehabili-*

tation for Victims of Gross Violations of Human Rights and Fundamental Freedoms, U.N. Doc. E/CN.4/Sub.2/1993/8 (1993), 488

Commission on Human Rights, Sub-Commission on Prevention of Discrimination and Protection of Minorities, *Human Rights and the Environment: Final Report Prepared by Mrs. Fatma Zohra Ksentini, Special Rapporteur*, U.N. Doc. E/CN.4/Sub.2/1994/9 (1994), **84-85**

U.N. Doc. A/49/514 (1994), 145, 147

Commission on Human Rights, *Violation of Human Rights in the United States as a Result of Racism and Racial Discrimination Persisting in United States Society*, U.N. Doc. E/CN.4/1995/L.26/Rev.2 (1995), 184

Commission on Sustainable Development, *Adoption of the Agenda*, U.N. Doc. E/CN.17/1993/1 (1993), 87

Committee on Economic, Social and Cultural Rights, *Report on the Seventh Session*, U.N. Doc. E/1993/22 (1993), 99

Committee on Economic, Social and Cultural Rights, *Report on the Sixth Session, General Comment No. 4 (1991)*, Supp. No. 3, Annex III, U.N. Doc. E/1992/23 (1992), **77-78**

Committee on Economic, Social and Cultural Rights, *Report on the Eighth and Ninth Sessions*, Supp. No. 3, U.N. Doc. E/1994/23 (1994), **75-77**

Committee on the Rights of the Child, *Concluding Observations of the Committee on the Rights of the Child: Canada*, at 4, U.N. Doc. CRC/C/15/Add.37 (1995), 574

Committee on the Rights of the Child, *Report on Seventh Session*, U.N. Doc. CRC/C/34 (1994), 99

Communication No. R.1/6 (*Sequeira v. Uruguay*), U.N. GAOR, Hum. Rts. Comm., 35th Sess., Supp. No. 40, at 127, U.N. Doc. A/35/40 (1980), *reprinted in* HUMAN RIGHTS COMMITTEE, SELECTED DECISIONS UNDER THE OPTIONAL PROTOCOL (SECOND TO SIXTEENTH SESSIONS), vol. 1 at 52, U.N. Doc. CCPR/C/OP/1, (1985), 572

Communication No. R.8/33 (*Carballal v. Uruguay*), U.N. GAOR, Hum. Rts. Comm, 36th Sess., Supp. No. 40, at 125, U.N. Doc. A/35/40 (1981), *reprinted in* SELECTED DECISIONS, *supra*, vol. 1 at 63, 572

Communication to the U.N. Commission on Human Rights and Subcommission on Prevention of Discrimination and Protection of Minorities: Human Rights Violations by the Police Against Blacks in the U.S.A., submitted by A. Ray McCoy, Black American Law Student Ass'n, U. of Minn. Chapter, June 10, 1982, 371

Communication to the U.N. Commission on Human Rights and Sub-Commission on Prevention of Discrimination and Protection of Minorities: Human Rights Violations of Black People in the U.S., submitted by Theophous Reagans, President, Black American Law School Ass'n, U. of Minn. Law School Chapter, June 22, 1981, 371

Consideration of Reports Submitted by States Parties Under Article 40 of the Covenant: Comments of the Human Rights Committee, U.N. Doc. CCPR/C/79/Add.50 (1995), **123-126**

Consideration of Reports Submitted by States Parties Under Article 40 of the Covenant; Initial Report of the United States of America, U.N. Doc. CCPR/C/81/Add.4 (1994), **105-111**

Core Document Forming Part of the Reports of States Parties: United States of America, U.N. Doc. HRI/CORE/1/Add.49 (1994), **113-115**

PHYLLIS COVEN, OFFICE OF INT'L AFFAIRS (INS), MEMORANDUM: CONSIDERATIONS FOR ASYLUM OFFICERS ADJUDICATING ASYLUM CLAIMS FROM WOMEN (1995), **658-61**

Jacques Cuenod, *Report on Refugees, Displaced Persons and Returnees*, U.N. Doc. E/109/Add.1 (1991), 676

Declaration of Frank C. Newman in Support of Defendants, filed June 12, 1989, in *People v. Wylie, et al.*, Santa Clara Municipal Court, California, No. E8849052, **608-609**

Definition of Aggression, G.A. res. 3314 (XXIX) (Annex-Definition of Aggression), 29 U.N. GAOR Supp. (No. 31) at 142, U.N. Doc. A/9631 (1974), 279

Department of State, *Letter of Submittal to the President*, S. Exec. Doc., 92nd Cong., 1st Sess. 1 (1971), 451

Draft Report of the Committee on Economic, Social and Cultural Rights to the Economic and Social Council, Annex V, U.N. Doc. E/C.12/1992/CRP.2/Add.3 (1992), 78

E.S.C. res. 1235 (XLII), 42 U.N. ESCOR Supp. (No.1) at 17, U.N. Doc. E/4393 (1967), 183 n.3, **184**

E.S.C. res. 1503 (XLVIII), 48 U.N. ESCOR Supp. (No.1A), U.N. Doc. E/4832/Add.1 (1970), 185 n.4, **185-186**

Enhancing International Cooperation for Development: The Role of the United Nations System, U.N. Doc. E/1992/82 (1992), 87

Establishment of an International Criminal Court, G.A. res. 49/53, 49 U.N. GAOR, U.N. Doc. A/RES/49/53 (1994), 302

Establishment of an International Criminal Court: Report of the Sixth Committee, U.N. Doc. A/50/639 (1995), 302

Executive Committee of the High Commissioner's Programme, *Note on International Protection*, U.N. Doc. A/AC.96/815 (1993), 648

Fifth Meeting of Chairpersons of Treaty Bodies, *Improving the Operation of the Human Rights Treaty Bodies: Report of the Secretary-General*, U.N. Doc. HRI/MC/1994/2 (1994), 80

Fifth Meeting of Chairpersons of Treaty Bodies, *Status of the International Human Rights Instruments and the General Situation of Overdue Reports*, U.N. Doc. HRI/MC/1994/3 (1994), 80

Final Report on the Situation of Human Rights in the Islamic Republic of Iran by the Special Representative of the Commission on Human Rights, Mr. Reynaldo Galindo Pohl, U.N. Doc. E/CN.4/1993/41 (1993), **146**

Four Treaties Pertaining to Human Rights: Message From the President of the United States, 95th Cong., 2d Sess. (1978), **66-68, 452-453**

G.A. res. 38/7, 38 U.N. GAOR (No.47), U.N. Doc. A/38/47 (1984), 249 n.3

G.A. res. 95(I), 1 U.N. GAOR at 188, U.N. Doc. A/64/Add.1 (1946), 279

G.A. res. 177(II), 2 U.N. GAOR at 111-12, U.N. Doc. A/519 (1947), 279

G.A. res. 729 (VIII), 8 U.N. GAOR Supp. (No. 17), U.N. Doc. A/2630 (1953), 271

G.A. res. 730 (VIII), 8 U.N. GAOR Supp. (No. 17), U.N. Doc. A/2630 (1953), 271

G.A. res. 839 (IX), 9 GAOR Supp. (No. 21), U.N. Doc. A/2890 (1954), 271

G.A. res. 926 (X), 10 U.N. GAOR Supp. (No. 19), U.N. Doc. A/3116 (1955), 271

GAOR Supp. (No. 20) at 46, U.N. Doc. A/1775 (1950), 646

General Comment 18 Adopted by the Human Rights Committee, *reprinted in Compilation of General Comments and General Recommendations Adopted by Human Rights Treaty Bodies*, U.N. Doc. HRI/GEN/1/Rev.1 (1994), **112-113**

General Comment No. 24, U.N. Doc. CCPR/C/21/Rev.1/Add.6 (1994), 596

General Comment on Article 7, Adopted by the Human Rights Committee, HRI/GEN/1 (1992), at 6 (Sixteenth session, 1982), 571

H.R. 1561, 104th Cong., 1st Sess. (1995), 596

H.R. 934, 103d Cong. 1st Sess. (1993), 539

Hearing on the International Convention on the Eliminaiton of All Forms of Racial Discrimination Before the Committee on Foreign Relations of the United States Senate, S. Hrg. Rep. No. 659, 103d Cong., 2d Sess. (1994), 43

High Commissioner for the Promotion and Protection of All Human Rights, G.A. res. 48/141, 48 U.N. GAOR (No. 49), U.N. Doc. A/48/49 (1993), 12

Human Rights Committee, *Consideration of Reports Submitted by States Parties Under Article 40: Comments of the Human Rights Committee*, U.N. Doc. CCPR/C/79/Add.50 (1995), 571

Human Rights Committee, *Consideration of Reports Submitted by States Parties Under Article 40 of the Covenant: Second Periodic Reports of States Parties Due in 1983. Addendum Islamic Republic of Iran*, U.N. Doc. CCPR/C/28/Add.15 (1992), **138-139**

Human Rights Committee, *Consideration of Reports Submitted by States Parties Under Article 40 of the Covenant: Iran*, U.N. Doc. CCPR/C/1/Add.58 (1982), **135-136**

Human Rights Committee, *General Comment No. 24*, U.N. Doc. CCPR/C/21/Rev.1/Add.6 (1994), 45, **46-47**

Human Rights Committee, *General Comments*, U.N. Doc. CCPR/C/21/Rev.1 & Add.1 (1990), 141

Human Rights Committee, *Guidelines Regarding the Form and Content of Periodic Reports from States Parties*, U.N. Doc. CCPR/C/20/Rev.1 (1991), 141

Human Rights Committee, *Selected Decisions under the Optional Protocol—Volume 2 (Seventeenth to thirty-second sessions)*, U.N. Doc. CCPR/C/OP/2 (1990), 159

Human Rights Committee, *Selected Decisions under the Optional Protocol (Second to sixteenth sessions)*, U.N. Doc. CCPR/C/OP/1 (1985), 159

Human Rights Committee, *Summary Record of the 1194th Meeting*, U.N. Doc. CCPR/C/SR.1194 (1993), **139**

Human Rights Committee, *Summary Record of the 1196th Meeting*, U.N. Doc. CCPR/C/SR.1196 (1993), **139-140**

Human Rights Committee, *Summary Record of the 1230th Meeting*, U.N. Doc. CCPR/C/SR.1230 (1993), **140-141**

Human Rights Field Operation in Rwanda, Modus Operandi for the Human Rights Field Officers, U.N. Doc. CER/MISC.16 (1994), 315

The Human Rights Field Operation in Rwanda, Operational Plan, U.N. Doc. HR/FOR/Misc.1 (1994), 315

IMMIGRATION AND REFUGEE BOARD, GUIDELINES ISSUED BY THE CHAIRPERSON PURSUANT TO SECTION 65(3) OF THE IMMIGRATION ACT: WOMEN REFUGEE CLAIMANTS FEARING GENDER-RELATED PERSECUTION 1 (1993), 665

Information Office of the State Council, Human Rights in China (1991), 681

Inter-American Commission on Human Rights(IACHR), *Report on the Situation of Human Rights in Argentina*, O.A.S. Doc. OEA/Ser.L/V/II.49, doc. 19 corr. 1 (1980), **334-341**

International Covenant on Civil and Political Rights: Note by the Secretary-General, U.N. Doc. E/1992/58 (1992), 141

INTERNATIONAL CRIMINAL TRIBUNAL FOR THE FORMER YUGOSLAVIA, BASIC DOCUMENTS 1995 (1995), 298

The International Dimensions of the Right to Development as a Human Right, U.N. Doc. E/CN.4/1334 (1979), 84

Interpretation of the American Declaration of the Rights and Duties of Man in the Context of Article 64 of the American Convention on Human Rights, Advisory Opinion OC-10/89, Inter-Am. Ct. H. R., 50 (1989), 463

Interrelationship Between Human Rights and International Peace, U.N. Doc. E/CN.4/Sub.2/1988/2 (1988), 84

INTRODUCTION OF REPORT OF UNITED STATES, U.N. Press Release HR/CT/1/400 (1995), 122

Letter dated 1 June 1977 from Deputy Secretary of State Warren Christopher to President Carter accompanying transmission of the American Convention on Human Rights, 45

Letter dated 9 February 1993 from the Secretary-General Addressed to the President of the Security Council, U.N. Doc. S/25274 (1993) (transmitting "Interim Report of the Commission of Experts Established Pursuant to Security Council Resolution 780 (1992)"), 281

Letter dated 10 February 1993 from the Permanent Representative of France to the United Nations Addressed to the Secretary-General, U.N. Doc. S/25266 (1993) (transmitting a report of the Committee of French Jurists on the establishment of an international tribunal), 282 n.3

Letter dated 10 May 1988 from Secretary of State George Shultz to President Reagan, Message From the President of the United States transmitting the Convention against Torture and Other Cruel, Inhuman or Degrading Treatment or Punishment, 100th Cong., 2d Sess. (1988), 40

Letter dated 11 September 1995 from Michel de Bonnecorse, French Ambassador to the United Nations, to the Center for Human Rights, 49

Letter dated 16 February 1993 from the Permanent Representative of Italy to the United Nations

Addressed to the Secretary-General, U.N. Doc. S/25300 (1993) (transmitting a draft statute for a war crimes tribunal for the former Yugoslavia), 282 n.3

Letter dated 18 February 1993 from the Permanent Representative of Sweden to the United Nations Addressed to the Secretary-General, U.N. Doc. S/25307 (1993) (transmitting "Proposal for an International War Crimes Tribunal for the Former Yugoslavia" by Rapporteurs under the Conference on Security and Cooperation in Europe (CSCE)), 282 n.3

Letter dated 27 January 1993 from Robert A. Bradtke, Acting Assistant Secretary for Legislative Affairs, to Senator Arlen Specter, 529 n.9

Letter dated 28-29 March 1995 from Conrad Harper to Francisco José Aguilar-Urbina, Chairman, U.N. Human Rights Committee, **47-49**, 596

Letter dated 30 April 1992 from the International Human Rights Association of American Minorities to United Nations Secretary General Boutros Boutros Ghali, **372**

Tadeusz Mazowiecki, *Report of the Special Rapporteur to the Commission on Human Rights of 28 August 1992*, U.N. Doc. E/CN.4/1992/S-1/9 (1992), 281

Tadeusz Mazowiecki, *Report on the Situation of Human Rights in the Territory of the Former Yugoslavia*, U.N. Doc. E/CN.4/1993/50 (1993), 281

Frank Newman, *amicus brief, Matter of the Requested Extradition of Suarez-Mason*, 694 F. Supp. 676 (N.D. Cal. 1988), **518**

Claire Palley, Sub-Commission on Prevention of Discrimination and Protection of Minorities, *Implications of Humanitarian Activities for the Enjoyment of Human Rights*, ¶ 12, U.N. Doc. E/CN.4/Sub.2/1994/39 (1994), **229-233**, 286

Petition to the U.N. Commission on Human Rights and Sub-Commission on Prevention of Discrimination and Protection of Minorities: Human Rights Violations in the U.S., submitted by The National Conference of Black Lawyers, The National Alliance Against Racist and Political Repression, & United Church of Christ Commission for Racial Justice, Dec. 13, 1978, 371

The Plan of Activities of the Centre for Human Rights for the Implementation of the Vienna Declaration and Programme of Action, 79

Preliminary Report by the Special Representative of the Commission on Human Rights on the Human Rights Situation in the Islamic Republic of Iran, U.N. Doc. E/CN.4/1985/20 (1985), **143-145**

Realization of Economic, Social and Cultural Rights, Report Submitted by Mr. Danilo Turk, Special Rapporteur, U.N. Doc. E/CN.4/Sub.2/1992/16 (1989) (report of a study for the Sub-Commission on Prevention of Discrimination and Protection of Minorities), 58

The Regional and National Dimensions of the Right to Development as a Human Right, U.N. Doc. E/CN.4/1488 (1981), 84

Regulations of the Inter-American Commission on Human Rights in Basic Documents Pertaining to Human Rights in the Inter-American System, OAS Doc. OEA/SER.L.V/II.71, at 75 (1988), 436

Report by Mr. Maurice Glélé Ahanhanzo, Special Rapporteur on Contemporary Forms of Racism, Racial Discrimination, Xenophobia and Related Intolerance On His Mission to the United States of America, U.N. Doc. E/CN.4/1995/78/Add.1 (1995), 112

Report Int'l L. Comm'n, 43 U.N. GAOR Supp. (No. 10) at 140, U.N. Doc. A/43/10 (1988), 279

Report of International Jurists Visit with Human Rights Petitioners in the United States, August 3-20, 1979 3, 9

Report of the High Commissioner for Human Rights, U.N. Doc. E/CN.4/1995/98 (1995), 309

Report of the Human Rights Committee, 36 U.N. GAOR Supp. (No. 40), Annex IV, U.N. Doc. A/36/40 (1981), 94, 95

Report of the Human Rights Committee, 37 U.N. GAOR Supp. (No. 40), U.N. Doc. A/37/40 (1982), **136-137**

Report of the Human Rights Committee, 39 U.N. GAOR Supp. (No. 40) U.N. Doc. A/39/40 (1984), **151-155**

Report of the Human Rights Committee, 41 U.N. GAOR Supp. (No. 40), U.N. Doc. A/41/40 (1986), 96

Report of the Human Rights Committee, 46 U.N. GAOR Supp. (No. 40), Annex VII, U.N. Doc A/46/40 (1992), **92-93**, 95

Report of the Human Rights Committee, 47 U.N. GAOR Supp. (No. 40), U.N. Doc. A/47/40 (1992), **94**

Report of the Human Rights Committee, 48 U.N. GAOR Supp. (No. 40), Annex X, U.N. Doc. A/48/40 (1993), 95, 96

Report of the Human Rights Committee, 50 U.N. GAOR Supp. (No. 40), U.N. Doc. A/50/40 (1995), 49

Report of the Human Rights Committee, General Comments on Article 7 of the Covenant, 37 U.N. GAOR Supp. (No. 40), U.N. Doc. A/37/40 (1982), 137-138

Report of the Independent Expert on El Salvador, U.N. Doc. E/CN.4/1993/11 (1993), 331

Report of the International Law Commission on the Work of its Forty-fifth Session, 48 U.N. GAOR Supp. (No. 10), U.N. Doc. A/48/10 (1993), 302

Report of the International Law Commission on the Work of its Forty-sixth Session, 49 U.N. GAOR Supp. (No. 10), U.N. Doc. A/49/10 (1994), 302

Report of the Mission Dispatched by the Secretary-General on the Situation of Prisoners of War in the Islamic Republic of Iran and Iraq, U.N. Doc. S/20147 (1988), 147, 331

Report of the Secretary-General: An Agenda for Peace, U.N. Doc. A/47/277, S/24111 (1992), 332

Report of the Secretary-General Pursuant to Paragraph 2 of Security Council Resolution 808 (1993), Annex: Statute of the International Criminal Tribunal, U.N. Doc. S/25704 and Add.1 (1993), 282, 284-286

Report of the Special Rapporteur, Mr. Peter Kooijmans, U.N. Doc. E/CN.4/1993/26 (1992), **150**

Report of the Special Rapporteur on Violence Against Women, its Causes and Consequences, U.N. Doc. E/CN.4/1996/53 (1996), 533

Report of the Special Rapporteur on the Situation in Equatorial Guinea, U.N. Doc. HR/95/38 (1995), 370

Report of the Special Rapporteur on the Situation of Human Rights in Haiti, U.N. Doc. E/CN.4/1993/47 (1993), 331

Report of the Special Rapporteur on the Situation of Human Rights in Rwanda, U.N. Doc. E/CN.4/1995/7 (1995), 331

Report of the Sub-Commission on Prevention of Discrimination and Protection of Minorities, 37th Session, U.N. Doc. E/CN.4/1985/3 (1985); E/CN.4/Sub.2/1994/43, 166

Report of the United Nations High Commissioner for Refugees, at 19, U.N. Doc. E/1994/41 (1994), 632, 649

Report of the Working Group on Enforced or Involuntary Disappearances, U.N. Doc. E/CN.4/1987/15/Add.1 (1986), **205-207**

Report of the Working Group on Enforced or Involuntary Disappearances, U.N. Doc. E/CN.4/1986/18/Add.1 (1986), **202-205**

Report on the Mission to the Democratic People's Republic of Korea, the Republic of Korea and Japan on the Issue of Military Sexual Slavery in Wartime, U.N. Doc. E/CN.4/1996/53/Add.1 (1996), 533

Report on the Situation of Human Rights in Rwanda, U.N. Doc. E/CN.4/1996/68 (1996), 319

Restatement (Third) of the Foreign Relations Law of the United States (1987 & Supp. 1988), 14, 18 n.6, n.7, 19 n.10, n.12, 145, **165-166**, 437 n.2, 452, 453, 509, 547, 575, 580, 586, 599

Restrictions to the Death Penalty, Advisory Opinion OC-8/83, 3 Inter-Am. Ct. H.R. (Ser.A) 54 (1983), **459-463**

Franklin D. Roosevelt, *State of the Union*, 90-I Cong. Rec. 55 (1944), 50

Franklin D. Roosevelt, *"Four Freedoms" Speech*, 87-I Cong. Rec. 44 (1941), 49

S. 72, 103d Cong., 1st Sess. (1993), 584

S. Exec. Doc., 92d Cong., 1st Sess. 1 (1971), 31

S.C. res. 687, 46 U.N. SCOR, U.N. Doc. S/RES/687 (1991), *reprinted in* 30 I.L.M. 846 (1991), 273

S.C. res. 778, 47 U.N. SCOR, U.N. Doc. S/RES/778 (1992), 273

S.C. res. 780, 47 U.N. SCOR at 36, U.N. Doc. S/INF/48 (1992), 273

S.C. res. 808, 48 U.N. SCOR at 1, U.N. Doc. S/RES/808 (1993), 282, 531

S.C. res. 827, 48 U.N. SCOR at 2, U.N. Doc. S/RES/827 (1993), 282

S.C. res. 955, 49 U.N. SCOR at 1, U.N. Doc. S/RES/955 (1994), 296

Security Council, *Report of the Secretary-General Pursuant to Paragraph 2 of Security Council Resolution 808 (1993)*, U.N. Doc. S/25704, Annex, at 37-38 (1993), 531

John Shattuck, Assistant Secretary of State for Democracy, Human Rights and Labor, testimony before the Senate Appropriations Subcommittee on Foreign Operations, April 19, 1994, **390**

The Situation of Democracy and Human Rights in Haiti, U.N. Doc. 1/47/908 (1993), 321

Special Investigations Unit: Final Report on the Genocide Investigation, Apr. 12, 1995, 316, 331

Special Rapporteur on Violence Against Women Submits Preliminary Report, 9 Interights Bulletin 7 (Spring 1995), 202

Sub-Comm'n res. 1 (XXIV), U.N. Doc. E/CN.4/1070 (1971), 190 n.6

Sub-Comm'n res. 1994/45, at 103, U.N. Doc. E/CN.4/1994/2 (1994), 274

Sub-Comm'n res. 1994/45, U.N. Doc. E/CN.4/1994/2 (1994), 274

Sub-Commission on Prevention of Discrimination and Protection of Minorities, *Review of Further Developments in Fields with Which the Sub-Commission Has Been Concerned*, at 15, U.N. Doc. E/CN.4/Sub.2/1994/10 (1994), 671

Trials of War Criminals Before the Nuernberg Military Tribunals Under Control Council Law No. 10, Nuernberg, October 1946-April 1949 (1949-1953), 280

U.N. Doc. A/50/22 (1995), 302

U.N. Doc. A/C.6/50/SR.25-31 and 46 (1995), 302

U.N. Doc. A/CN.4/460 (1994), 279

U.N. Doc. A/CN.4/L.436 (1989), 279

U.N. Doc. A/CN.4/L.480 and Add.1 (1993), 303

U.N. Doc. A/CN.4/L.482 (1993), 279

U.N. Doc. A/RES/50/46 (1995), 302

U.N. Doc. E/CN.4/1988/14 (1988), 197

U.N. Doc. E/CN.4/1989/14 (1989), 198

U.N. Doc. E/CN.4/1989/26 (1989), 145

U.N. Doc. E/CN.4/1991/35 (1991), 145

U.N. Doc. E/CN.4/1992/34 (1992), 145

U.N. Doc. E/CN.4/1992/55 (1992), 198

U.N. Doc. E/CN.4/1993/24 (1993), 199

U.N. Doc. E/CN.4/1993/41 (1993), 145

U.N. Doc. E/CN.4/1994/31 (1994), 197

U.N. Doc. E/CN.4/1994/50 (1994), 145, 147

U.N. Doc. E/CN.4/1994/NGO/40 (1994), 147

U.N. Doc. E/CN.4/1995/31 (1995), 199

U.N. Doc. E/CN.4/1995/36 (1995), 196

U.N. Doc. E/CN.4/1995/39 (1995), 200

U.N. Doc. E/CN.4/1995/55 (1995), 145, 147

U.N. Doc. E/CN.4/1995/78 (1995), 200

U.N. Doc. E/CN.4/1995/98 (1995), 214

U.N. Doc. E/CN.4/1995/L.103 (1995), 198

U.N. Doc. E/CN.4/Sub.2/1991/55 (1991), 531

U.N. GAOR, Hum. Rts. Comm., 49th Sess., U.N. Doc. CCPR/C/49/D/469 at 21 (1991), 477

U.N. Office at Vienna, Centre for Social Dev. & Humanitarian Affairs, *Violence Against Women in the Family, 1989*, at 21, U.N. Doc. ST/CSDHA/2 (1989), 671

U.N. OFFICE AT VIENNA, CTR. FOR SOCIAL DEV. AND HUMANITARIAN AFFAIRS, STRATEGIES FOR CONFRONTING DOMESTIC VIOLENCE: A RESOURCE MANUAL (1993), 675

U.N. Res. 1995/29 (1995), 531

U.N. Secretary-General, *An Agenda for Peace: Preventive Diplomacy, Peacemaking and Peace-keeping*, U.N. Doc. A/47/27 (1992), **223-224**

U.N. Secretary-General, *Supplement to an Agenda for Peace: Position Paper of the Secretary-General on the Occasion of the Fiftieth Anniversary of the United Nations*, U.N. Doc. A/50/60 (1995), **235-239**

U.S. Army Field Manual 27-10, The Law of Land Warfare § 498 (1956), 279

U.S. Army, SC FORM 165, June 16, 1995, 241

U.S. DEPARTMENT OF STATE, BUREAU OF PUBLIC AFFAIRS, CURRENT POLICY NO. 551 (1984), 397

U.S. DEPARTMENT OF STATE, COMMENTS OF THE GOVERNMENT OF THE UNITED STATES OF AMERICA ON DRAFT ARTICLES FOR A STATUTE OF AN INTERNATIONAL CRIMINAL COURT, (1994), 303

U.S. DEPARTMENT OF STATE, COUNTRY REPORTS ON HUMAN RIGHTS PRACTICES FOR 1977, REPORT SUBMITTED TO THE SENATE COMMITTEE ON FOREIGN RELATIONS, 95th Cong., 1st Sess. (1977), 332

U.S. DEPARTMENT OF STATE, COUNTRY REPORTS ON HUMAN RIGHTS PRACTICES FOR 1980, 97th Cong., 1st Sess. (Joint Comm. Print 1981), 341

U.S. DEPARTMENT OF STATE, COUNTRY REPORTS ON HUMAN RIGHTS PRACTICES FOR 1988, REPORT SUBMITTED TO THE SENATE COMMITTEE ON FOREIGN RELATIONS AND THE HOUSE COMMITTEE ON FOREIGN AFFAIRS, 101st Cong., 1st Sess. (1989), **383-385**

U.S. DEPARTMENT OF STATE, COUNTRY REPORTS ON HUMAN RIGHTS PRACTICES FOR 1993 (1994), 632, 635

U.S. DEPARTMENT OF STATE, COUNTRY REPORTS ON HUMAN RIGHTS PRACTICES FOR 1994, 104th Cong., 1st Sess. 1269 (1995), **332-333**

UN Documents Establishing an International Tribunal for the Former Yugoslavia, 32 I.L.M. (1993), 298

UNHCR, COLLECTION OF INTERNATIONAL INSTRUMENTS CONCERNING REFUGEES (1990), 642

UNHCR, GUIDELINES ON THE PROTECTION OF REFUGEE WOMEN 7 (1991), **656-57**

UNHCR, HANDBOOK FOR EMERGENCIES (1982), 649

UNHCR, HANDBOOK ON PROCEDURES AND CRITERIA FOR DETERMINING REFUGEE STATUS, U.N. Doc. HCR/IP/4/Eng. Rev.1 (1988), 642, **643-645**

UNHCR, THE STATE OF THE WORLD'S REFUGEES 1995: The Challenge of Protection (1993), 649

UNITAR/CENTRE FOR HUMAN RIGHTS, MANUAL ON HUMAN RIGHTS REPORTING, HR/Pub/91/1 (1991) (Revised and republished in 1995 with a "Trainers' Guide"), 100, 142

United Nations Action in the Field of Human Rights, U.N. Doc. ST/HR/2/Rev.3 (1988), 58, 216

United Nations, Human Rights and Pre-Trial Detention, U.N. Doc. HR/P/PT/3 (1994), 148

UNITED NATIONS, INTERNATIONAL COVENANT ON CIVIL AND POLITICAL RIGHTS; AIDE-MÉMOIRE DATED 15 MARCH 1994 FROM THE PERMANENT MISSION OF CROATIA TO THE UNITED NATIONS, Annex, at 2 (1994), 501

United States Mission to the United Nations, Press Release, *Statement by the Honorable Conrad K. Harper*, USUN 171-(93) (1993), 303

United States Mission to the United Nations, Press Releases, *Statements of John Shattuck, Conrad K. Harper, and Ada Elizabeth Deer Before the United Nations Human Rights Committee at its Fifty-third Session*, USUN 48-(95)-50-(95) (1995), 122

Update on the Activities of the HRFOR 13 July 1995-28 July 1995, 315

Vienna Convention on the Law of Treaties S. Exec. Doc., 92nd Cong., 1st Sess. 1 (1971), 580

Views of the Human Rights Committee under Article 5, paragraph 4, of the Optional Protocol to the International Covenant on Civil and Political Rights (Fifty-first session) concerning Communication No. 414/1990, U.N. Doc. CCPR/C/51/D/414/1990 (1994), **156-58**

Violation of Human Rights in the United States as a Result of Racism and Racial Discrimination Persisting in United States Society, U.N. Doc. E/CN.4/1995/L.26/Rev.2 (1995), 372

War Crimes Tribunal Indictments, November 1994 and February 1995, 34 I.L.M. 996 (1995), 295

World Conference on Human Rights, *Interim Report on Updated Study by Mr. Philip Alston*, at 9, U.N. Doc. A/CONF.157/PC/62/Add.11/Rev.1 (1993), **80**

OTHER INSTRUMENTS

American Declaration of the Rights and Duties of Man, 57

Bangkok Declaration, *in* Our Voice: Bangkok NGO Declaration on Human Rights 242 (1993), 466

Body of Principles for the Protection of All Persons under Any Form of Detention or Imprisonment, G.A. res. 43/173, 43 U.N. GAOR Supp. (No. 49), U.N. Doc. A/43/49, (1988), **150**

Charter of Economic Rights and Duties of States, G.A. res. 3171, 29 U.N. GAOR, Supp. (No. 31), U.N. Doc. A/9631 (1974), 420

Control Council Law No. 10, Punishment of Persons Guilty of War Crimes, Crimes Against Peace and Against Humanity, 3 Official Gazette Control Council for Germany 50-55 (1946), **277-278**, 526

Declaration of Fundamental Rights and Freedoms, European Communities, O.J. (C 120/52) Doc. A 2-3/89 (May 16, 1989), 493

Declaration on Fact-finding by the U.N. in the Field of the Maintenance of International Peace and Security, U.N. Doc. A/RES/46/59, Annex (1992), 321

Declaration on the Elimination of Violence Against Women, G.A. Res. 104, U.N. GAOR, 48th Sess, U.N. Doc. A/48/629 (1993), **528, 533**

Declaration on the Protection of All Persons from Being Subjected to Torture and Other Cruel, Inhuman or Degrading Treatment or Punishment, G.A. res. 3452, 30 U.N. GAOR Supp. (No. 34) at 91, U.N. Doc. A/10034 (1976), **148**

Declaration on the Protection of All Persons from Enforced Disappearances, G.A. res. 47/133, 47 U.N. GAOR Supp. (No.49) at 207, U.N. Doc. A/47/49 (1992), 444

Declaration on the Right to Development, G.A. res. 41/128, Annex, 41, U.N. GAOR Supp. (No. 53) at 186, U.N. Doc. A/41/53 (1986), 23, **85-86**

Declaration on the Rights of Disabled Persons, G.A. res. 3447 (XXX), 30 U.N. GAOR Supp. (No. 34) at 88, U.N. Doc. A/10034 (1975), 23

General Act and Declaration of Brussels of 1890, 24 n.19

General Recommendation No. 19, HRI/GEN/1 (1992), at p. 74 (Eleventh session, 1992), 40

Priciples for the Protection of Person with Mental Illness and the Improvement of Mental Health Care, G.A. res. 119, U.N. GAOR, 46th Sess., Supp. No. 49, at 189, U. N. Doc. A/46/49 (1991), 629

Standard Minimum Rules for the Treatment of Prisoners, *adopted* Aug. 30, 1955, by the First United Nations Congress on the Prevention of Crime and the Treatment of Offenders, U.N. Doc. A/CONF/611, ANNEX I *adopted* July 31, 1957, E.S.C. res. 663C, 24 U.N. ESCOR Supp. (No. 1) at 11, U.N. Doc. E/3048 (1957), *amended* E.S.C. res. 2076, 62 U.N. ESCOR Supp. (No. 1) at 35, U.N. Doc. E/5988 (1977) (adding Article 95), **147-148**

Universal Declaration of Human Rights (1948), 51, 57, 148

Vienna Declaration and Programme of Action (June 25, 1993), **79**, 86

STATUTES

101 Stat. 1343, 582

5 U.S.C. § 702, 621

8 U.S.C. § 1101(a)(42), 641

8 U.S.C. § 1252 (1952), **560-561**

8 U.S.C. § 1254(a), 648

8 U.S.C. § 1357 (1952), **561**

18 U.S.C. § 1203, 522

22 U.S.C. § 2151n, 332

22 U.S.C. § 5202(3), 581, 582, 583

28 U.S.C. § 1346(b), 621

28 U.S.C. § 1350, 505, 550, 584

28 U.S.C. § 1603(a) and (b), 540

28 U.S.C. § 1605(a), **534-535,** 539

Age Discrimination Act of 1975, 42 U.S.C. §§ 6101-6107 (1982), preface n.7

Age Discrimination in Employment Act of 1967, 29 U.S.C. §§ 621-634 (1988 & Supp. III 1991), preface
   n.4

Americans with Diabilities Act of 1990, 42 U.S.C. §§ 12010-12117 (Supp. V 1993), preface n.8

Civil Rights Act of 1962, Pub. L. No. 88-352, 78 Stat. 241 (codified as amended at 42 U.S.C. §§ 2000e-
   2000e-17 (1988 & Supp. IV 1992)), preface n.3

Comprehensive Anti-Apartheid Act of 1986, 22 U.S.C. §§ 5001-16 (Supp. IV 1986), 420

Equal Pay Act of 1963, 29 U.S.C. § 206 (1988), preface n.2

Foreign Assistance Act of 1961, 22 U.S.C., 332, 376, 518

Genital Mutilation Bill, 1994 Minn. Laws Ch. 636, Art. 2, § (criminal penalty) (codified at Minn. Stat.
   § 609.2245), 673

Genocide Convention Implementation Act of 1987, P.L. 100-606; 102 Stat. 3045, 39

Refugee Act of 1980, 21

Rehabilitation Act of 1973, 29 U.S.C. §§ 701-796 (1988), preface n.6

The Federal Torts Claims Act, 28 U.S.C. § 2674, 621

Title IX in the Education Amendments of 1972, 20 U.S.C. §§ 1681-1686 (1982), preface n.5

U.S. Constitution, 111, 125, 161, 555, 581

TREATIES

Abolition of Forced Labour Convention (ILO No. 105), 320 U.N.T.S. 291, *entered into force* Jan. 17,
   1959, 38

Additional Protocols I and II to the Geneva Conventions of 12 August 1949, 1125 U.N.T.S. 3, *entered
   into force* Dec. 7, 1978, 38

African [Banjul] Charter on Human and Peoples' Rights, OAU Doc. CAB/LEG/67/3 rev. 5, 21 I.L.M.
   58 (1982), *entered into force* Oct. 21, 1986, 464

American Convention on Human Rights, O.A.S. Off. Rec. OEA/Ser.L/V/II.23, doc. 21, rev. 6 (1979),
   entered into force July 18, 1978, 38, 57, 89, 486

Atlantic Charter, August 14, 1941, 6

Charter of the Organization of African Unity, 479 U.N.T.S. 39, *entered into force* Sept. 13, 1963,

Commission of Experts Established Pursuant to Security Council Resolution 780 (1992), *Final Report*,
   U.N. Doc. S/1994/674, at 27 (1994), 501 n.3, 530

Common Article 3(1)(b) of the Geneva Conventions of 1949, Conventions I-IV, *adopted* Aug. 12, 1949,
   6 U.S.T. 3114, 574

Convention against Discrimination in Education, 429 U.N.T.S. 93, *entered into force* May 22, 1962**,** 17

Convention against Torture and Other Cruel, Inhuman and Degrading Treatment or Punishment, G.A.
   res. 39/46, Annex, 39 U.N. GAOR Supp. (No. 51) at 197, U.N. Doc. A/39/51 (1984), *entered into
   force* June 26, 1987, 38, **148-149,** 395 n.3, 531, 580 n.5, 670

Convention of Saint-Germain-en-Laye of 1919, 24 n.19

Convention on Consent to Marriage, Minimum Age for Marriage and Registration of Marriages, 521
   U.N.T.S. 231, *entered into force* Dec. 9, 1964, 38

Convention on the Elimination of All Forms of Discrimination against Women, G.A. Res. 34/180, U.N.
   GAOR, 34th Sess., Supp. No. 46, at 193, U.N. Doc. A/34/46 (1980), *reprinted in* 19 I.L.M. 33
   (1980), *entered into force* Sept. 8, 1981, 38, **97-99, 527-528**

Convention on the Political Rights of Women, 193 U.N.T.S. 135, *entered into force* July 7, 1954, 38

Convention on the Prevention and Punishment of the Crime of Genocide, 78 U.N.T.S. 277, *entered
   into force* Jan. 12, 1951, 38

Convention on the Rights of the Child, 166, U.N. Doc. A/RES/44/49, 28 I.L.M. 1448 (1989), *entered
   into force* Sept. 2, 1990, 572

Convention Relating to the Status of Refugees, 189 U.N.T.S. 150, *entered into force* Apr. 22, 1954, 39

Dayton Peace Agreement, U.S. State Department World Wide Web site http://dosfan.lib.uic.edu/WWW/current/bosnia/bosagree.html, 295

European Convention for the Protection of Human Rights and Fundamental Freedoms, 213 U.N.T.S. 222 (1950), *entered into force* Sept. 3, 1953, 468

Four Geneva Conventions for the Protection of Victims of Armed Conflict, 75 U.N.T.S. 31, 85, 135, 287, *entered into force* Oct. 21, 1950, 37, **165**

Geneva Convention for the Protection of Civilian Persons in Time of War, 6 U.S.T. 3516, T.I.A.S. No. 3365, 75 U.N.T.S. 287, *entered into force* Oct. 21, 1950, **524-525**

Geneva Conventions of 1949, Conventions I-IV, *adopted* Aug. 12, 1949, 6 U.S.T. 3114, 3217, 3316, 3516; T.I.A.S. No. 3362-3365; 75 U.N.T.S. 31, 85, 135, 287, *entered into force* Oct. 21, 1950, **523-524**

Hague Convention Respecting the Laws and Customs of War on Land, Oct. 18, 1907, 36 Stat. 2277, 619

Inter-American Convention on the Prevention, Punishment and Eradication of Violence Against Women, 27 U.S.T. 3301, *entered into force* Apr. 22, 1949, 39

Inter-American Convention to Prevent and Punish Torture, 25 ILM 519, Dec. 9, 1985, *entered into force* Feb. 28, 1987, 39

International Convention on the Elimination of All Forms of Racial Discrimination, G.A. res. 2106 (XX), Annex, 20 U.N. GAOR Supp. (No. 14) at 47, U.N. Doc. A/6014 (1966), 660 U.N.T.S. 195, *entered into force* Jan. 4, 1969, 38, 395 n.3

International Convention on the Protection of the Rights of All Migrant Workers and Members of Their Families, G.A. res. 45/158, Annex, 45 U.N. GAOR Supp. (No. 49A) at 262, U.N. Doc. A/45/49 (1990), 39

International Covenant on Civil and Political Rights, G.A. res. 2200A, (XXI), December 16, 1966, 21 U.N. GAOR Supp. (No. 16) at 52, U.N. Doc. A/6316 (1966), 999 U.N.T.S. 171, *entered into force* March 23, 1976, *entered into force in the U.S.* September 8, 1992, 38, 51, 57, 83, 91, **104-105**, 376, 395 n.3, 523, **526-527, 568-570**, 575, 601

International Covenant on Economic, Social and Cultural Rights, G.A. res. 2200A (XXI), 21 U.N. GAOR Supp. (No. 16) at 49, U.N. Doc. A/6316 (1966), 993 U.N.T.S. 3, *entered into force* Jan. 3, 1976, 38

O.A.S. Charter, 119 U.N.T.S. 3, *entered into force* Dec. 13, 1951, *amended* 721 U.N.T.S. 324, *entered into force* Feb. 27, 1970, 37, 57

Optional Protocol to the International Covenant on Civil and Political Rights, G.A. res. 2200A (XXI), 21 U.N. GAOR Supp. (No. 16) at 59, U.N. Doc. A/6316 (1966), 999 U.N.T.S. 302, *entered into force* Mar. 23, 1976, 39

Protocol Additional to the Geneva Conventions of 12 August 1949, and Relating to the Protection of Victims of Non-International Armed Conflicts (Protocol II), U.N. Doc. A/32/144, Annex II, 16 I.L.M. 1442 (1977), *entered into force* Dec. 7, 1978, **525-526**

Protocol Additional to the Geneva Conventions of 12 August 1949, and Relating to the Protection of Victims of International Armed Conflicts (Protocol I), U.N. Doc. A/32/144, Annex I, 16 I.L.M. 1391 (1977), *entered into force* Dec. 7, 1978, 525

Protocol Amending the Slavery Convention, 182 U.N.T.S. 51, *entered into force* July 7, 1955, 37

Protocol Relating to the Status of Refugees, 606 U.N.T.S. 267, 19 U.S.T. 6223, T.I.A.S. No. 6577, *entered into force* Oct. 4, 1967, 38, 597, 641

Second Optional Protocol to the International Covenant on Civil and Political Rights, Aiming at the Abolition of the Death Penalty, G.A. res. 44/128, Annex, 44 U.N. GAOR Supp. (No. 49) at 207, U.N. Doc. A/44/49 (1989), *entered into force* July 11, 1991, 39

Single European Act, O.J. (L 169/1) (1987), [1987] 2 C.M.L.R. 741, 492

Slavery Convention of 1926, 60 L.N.T.S. 253, *entered into force* March 9, 1927, 24 n.19, 37

Supplementary Convention on the Abolition of Slavery, the Slave Trade and Institutions and Practices Similar to Slavery, 226 U.N.T.S. 3, *entered into force* Apr. 30, 1957, 37

T.I.A.S. No. 3362-3365, 574

Treaty on European Union, Feb. 7, 1992, O.J. (C 224/1) (1992), [1992] 1 C.M.L.R. 791, reprinted in 1 I.L.M. 247, 492

U.N. Charter, 59 Stat. 1031, T.S. 993, 3 Bevans 1153, *entered into force* Oct. 24, 1945, 4, 13, **13-14**, 37

Universal Declaration of Human Rights, G.A. Res. 217 A (III), adopted by the U.N. Doc. A/810 (Dec. 10, 1948) 23

Vienna Convention on Diplomatic Relations, 23 U.S.T. 3227, T.I.A.S. No. 7502, 500 U.N.T.S. 95, 547

Vienna Convention on the Law of Treaties, 1155 U.N.T.S. 331, U.S. No. 58 (1980), 8 I.L.M. 679 (1969), *entered into force* January 27, 1980, 15, **29-30**, **31-33**, 83, 145, 437, **450-451**, 537, 580, 585, 594, 601

SUBJECT INDEX

References are to Pages in the Preface and Chapters 1-15

ABORTION, 44, 102, 104, 424-36, 612-13
See Life, right to
Act of state doctrine, 547
ADVISORY OPINION
See European Court of Human Rights; Inter-American Court of Human Rights; International
    Court of Justice
Afghanistan, 11, 142, 185, 195, 213, 246-47, 398, 411, 641
Africa, 19, 187-88, 236, 259, 404, 463, 467, 632-33, 648, 680-81, 739
African Charter on Human and Peoples' Rights, 21, 464-66
African Development Bank, 413
African Commission, 21, 464-66
African-American, 1-7, 101, 104, 110, 113-21, 124, 372
**AGREEMENT FOR THE PROSECUTION AND PUNISHMENT OF THE MAJOR WAR
    CRIMINALS OF THE EUROPEAN AXIS (LONDON AGREEMENT)**
  In general, 7, 276-79, 284, 287
See Nuremberg Charter
Albania, 398, 496
Alien Tort Claims Act, 505-09, 511-23, 531-32, 534-39, 551-52, 599, 622
Alien Tort Litigation, 504-23, 534-41
ALIENS
  In general, 560-68, 574, 610, 636, 645
Rights of, 610-11
Detention of, 122, 558, 561-68, 571, 574, 600, 610-11
Algeria, 274, 736-37
American Bar Association, 43, 300
American Convention on Human Rights, 20, 34, 39, 45, 262, 348, 351, 387, 424, 428, 430,
    436-39, 442-44, 449, 454-63, 486-89, 693
American Declaration of the Rights and Duties of Man, 18, 20, 25-6, 64, 78, 341, 346, 351,
    436-39, 444, 452, 458-59, 463, 506-08
American Jewish Committee, 7
AMERICAS WATCH, 358, 361
See Human Rights Watch
Amnesty International (AI), 11, 131-34, 166, 214, 224, 229, 234, 256, 305, 316-19, 357-58,
    360-61, 364-65, 367, 372, 409, 413, 500, 530, 707, 719-20
Amputation, 129, 131-133, 140, 146 156, 166
Andorra, 495
Angola, 10, 40, 96, 197, 398, 411
Anti-Terrorism Act (ATA), 581-83
APARTHEID
  In general, 142, 420, 719
See South Africa
Arab Charter on Human Rights, 466
Arab Organization for Human Rights, 466
Arbitrary arrest or detention, 191, 265-66, 282, 300, 343, 441-43, 599-600

ARBITRARY KILLING
See Summary or arbitrary executions
Argentina, 20, 93, 187, 264, 266, 272, 311, 334-42, 361-71, 414, 429, 445, 510-15, 535-39, 620, 648
Argentine League for the Rights of Man, 363-64
Arusha Accords, 312
ASIA WATCH, 129, 352, 355, 358-61
See Human Rights Watch
Asian Development Bank, 413
Assembly, freedom of, 8
Association, freedom of, 8, 41-2, 44, 146
Association of Southeast Asian Country, 466
Asylum, 124-26, 233, 556-57, 570, 636-640, 649-56, 658-61, 668-69, 676
Atlantic Charter, 6
Australia, 64, 90-1
Austria, 21, 277, 366, 481, 490-91, 575
Bangladesh, 171, 608
Barbados, 249, 608
Barbuda, 249
Belgium, 3-4, 296-97, 311, 313, 485, 491, 496, 575
Bhutan, 199
Black American Law Student Association, 216
Board of Immigration Appeals, 622, 627, 639, 651-55, 665
BODY OF PRINCIPLES FOR THE PROTECTION OF ALL PERSONS UNDER ANY FORM OF DETENTION OR IMPRISONMENT
  In general, 150
Excerpt, 150
Bolivia, 20, 142, 155-56, 185, 213, 273, 348, 396
Brazil, 198, 264-66, 282-83, 414, 429, 722
British (See United Kingdom)
Brunei, 179
Bulgaria, 737
Burma (see Myanmar)
Burundi, 10, 96, 179, 185, 313-15
Bush, President G., 40, 42-43, 59, 65, 103, 250-52, 379, 396, 399, 402, 404-10, 600
Cairo Declaration on Human Rights, 466
Cambodia (also Democratic Kampuchea), 10-11, 185, 246, 370, 398, 648, 735
Cameroons, 4, 297
Canada, 19, 229, 283, 293, 434-35, 477, 494, 496, 584, 600, 663-65, 669, 671, 673, 676
Carter, President J., 29, 34, 37, 43, 56, 62, 64, 66, 69-71, 103, 246-74, 365, 368, 379-383, 387-88, 393, 397, 403, 405, 410, 413-441, 452
CENTRE FOR HUMAN RIGHTS, U.N., 85, 93, 79-80, 188, 227, 271-72, 317
See United Nations (U.N.)
Center for Constitutional Rights, 296, 509, 520.
Center for Legal and Social Studies, 364
CHILD, RIGHTS OF
See Committee on the Rights of the Child; Convention on the Rights of the Child
Chile, 4, 10, 20, 91, 142, 185, 195, 213, 266, 283, 358, 366, 393, 395, 400, 416-17, 444, 489, 542
Chilean National Commission on Truth and Reconciliation, 266-67

China, People's Republic of, 6-7, 177, 179, 214, 220, 277, 283, 293, 355, 388, 398, 401, 409-10, 421, 542-45, 581, 662, 681-82

Civil Rights Act of 1964, 108

Civil Rights Act of 1968, 117

Clinton, President W., 42-43, 45, 47, 104, 239-41, 253, 303, 376-79, 391, 398, 409-10, 414, 419-21, 613, 630

CLOTHING, RIGHT TO, 8, 14, 50, 74

See International Covenant of Economic, Social and Cultural Rights

Cold War, 3, 66, 223-24, 235, 253, 288, 298, 377, 494-96, 647, 672, 728

Colombia, 20, 155-56, 196, 348, 350, 396, 400, 440-43

Colonialism, 706-07, 709-12

Colville, Lord, 358-61

COMMISSION ON HUMAN RIGHTS, U.N.

In general, 8-11, 53, 86, 134-35, 142, 166, 174, 182-83, 186-201, 208-10, 271-72, 274, 281, 308, 313, 315, 334, 358, 361, 366-69, 371-72, 410, 491, 528

Communications, 182-91

ECOSOC 1235, 142, 184-86, 208-14

Special Rappateurs, 184, 191-202, 281

Thematic Procedures, 174, 181, 191-202

Working Group on Arbitrary Detention, 192, 198-99

Working Group on Disappearances, 192-93, 196, 208, 214, 359-61, 366-69

Working Group on Situations, 186-91

Commission on the Status of Arab Women, 12

COMMITTEE AGAINST TORTURE

In general, 13, 15, 149-50, 308

See Convention against Torture and Other Cruel, Inhuman or Degrading Treatment or Punishment

Committee on Crime Prevention and Control, 12

COMMITTEE ON ECONOMIC, SOCIAL AND CULTURAL RIGHTS

In general, 11, 13, 15, 72-80, 99

Establishment of, 73-4

Function of, 74

General Comments, 76-7

State Reports, 75-6

Committee on the Elimination of All Forms of Racial Discrimination (CERD), 13, 15

Committee on the Elimination of Discrimination against Women (CEDAW), 13, 15

Committe on the Rights of the Child, 13, 15, 17, 198

COMMUNICATIONS

In general, 12-15, 128, 143, 149-59

ECOSOC, 182-91

Human Rights Commission, 182-91

Human Rights Committee, 150-59

Inter-American Commission on Human Rights, 445-47

Sub-Commission Working Group on Communications, 182, 184-91

See Committee against Torture; Confidentiality; ECOSOC resolution 728; ECOSOC resolution 1235; ECOSOC resolution 1503; Human Rights Committee

Comoros, 195

COMPENSATION COMMITTEE

See United Nations (U.N.)

CONFERENCE ON SECURITY AND COOPERATION IN EUROPE (CSCE; Helsinki process)

In general, 58, 389, 494, 528
See OSCE
CONFIDENTIALITY, 183-86, 190-91, 211-12, 216
See ECOSOC resolution 1503; Communications
CONFLICT OF LAWS
Choice of law, 548-49
Damages, 548-50
Congress, U.S., 3, 36, 391-99
CONTRAS
See Nicaragua
Control Council of Germany, 256, 277-78, 287-88, 526
CONVENTION AGAINST TORTURE AND OTHER CRUEL, INHUMAN OR DEGRAD-ING TREATMENT OR PUNISHMENT
In general, 39-41, 74, 90, 149-50, 229, 262, 387, 518, 531, 668, 670
Excerpt, 148-49
U.S. Ratification, 40-1, 90
Convention and Protocol Relating to the Status of Refugees, 568, 585, 597-98, 641-42, 653, 656, 664-65, 668
CONVENTION ON THE ELIMINATION OF ALL FORMS OF DISCRIMINATION AGAINST WOMEN
In general, 43-5, 37, 78, 80, 90, 656, 658, 666, 669, 685, 693
Excerpt, 527-28
U.S. Ratification, 43-5
See Committee on the Elimination of Discrimination against Women; Discrimination (sex)
Convention on the Political Rights of Women, 34-5
CONVENTION ON THE PREVENTION AND PUNISHMENT OF THE CRIME OF GENOCIDE
In general, 33-5, 39, 41, 90, 183, 261-62, 284, 287, 531-32, 568
Ratification, 34-35
U.S. Ratification, 39
See Genocide
CONVENTION ON THE RIGHTS OF THE CHILD
In general, 78, 80, 90, 98-99, 656, 668-69, 673
Excerpt, 98-9, 572-74
CONVENTION ON THE SUPPRESSION AND PUNISHMENT OF THE CRIME OF *APARTHEID*
In general, 90
See *Apartheid*
Corporal punishment, 164-65, 478, 525, 571
Costa Rica, 91, 283, 429, 448, 455
Council of Europe, 19, 468, 472, 479-80, 490-91, 495
Crimes against Humanity, 220, 276-80, 286, 288, 300, 516, 526, 608
Crimes against Peace, 276, 278-79, 300
Critical legal studies, 687-93
CRUEL, INHUMAN, OR DEGRADING TREATMENT OR PUNISHMENT (ALSO ILL-TREATMENT)
See Convention against Torture and Other Cruel, Inhuman or Degrading Treatment or Punishment; Declaration on the Protection of All Persons from Being Subjected to Torture and Other Cruel, Inhuman or Degrading Treatment or Punishment; Torture
Cuba, 11, 185, 268, 372, 388, 398, 400, 411, 429, 545, 567, 610, 662
CULTURAL RELATIVISM

In general, 677-97
Iran, 143-46, 171
CULTURAL RIGHTS, 8, 12, 20, 28, 50, 58, 60, 62, 65, 68
See International Covenant of Economic, Social, and Cultural Rights
CUSTOMARY LAW
In general, 18-9, 47-48, 165-66, 261, 284, 447, 506, 509-10, 559, 581-84, 598, 630, 687-97
Effect of subsequent, inconsistent statutes, 519, 523, 581-83, 617-18
General principles of law recognized by the community of nations, 580-81, 601
Identification of customary norms, 580, 599-601
International Covenant on Civil and Political Rights, 57
International torts, 584-85, 612-13
Judicial enforceability of customary norms, 577-80
Obstacles to application, 612-24
Peremptory norms (see *jus cogens*), 18-19, 83, 144-45, 437-43, 537, 576-77, 601-02, 616, 618-20
Relationship to federal statutes, executive orders, self-executing treaties, 575-76, 584-94, 612-13, 622-23
"Self-executing custom," 559, 575-76, 585, 591
State responsibility, 580-81, 616-17
Universal Declaration of Human Rights, 577
Use for indigenous people, 606-08
Use in deportation proceedings, 589-94, 622-23
Use in state and federal courts, 559, 575-80, 583-84, 597-98, 600-01, 610-12
Cyprus, 91, 474, 490-91
Czechoslovakia, 400, 495
Damages, 478-89
Dayton Peace Agreement, 295, 495, 497
DEATH PENALTY, 40-42, 102-104, 107, 118-19, 121-22, 124-26, 147, 155, 429, 437-39, 448, 459-63, 468, 476-78, 607-08, 628
See United States (U.S.)
Declaration of Fundamental Rights and Freedoms for European Communities, 493
DECLARATION ON THE ELIMINATION OF VIOLENCE AGAINST WOMEN
In general, 533, 658, 667, 669, 685, 693
Excerpt, 528
DECLARATION ON THE PROTECTION OF ALL PERSONS FROM BEING SUB-JECTED TO TORTURE AND OTHER CRUEL, INHUMAN OR DEGRADING TREAT-MENT OR PUNISHMENT
In general, 506-08
Excerpt, 148-49
Declaration on the Right to Development, 85-86
Denmark, 3, 355, 490-91, 496
Deportation, 560, 591
DEROGATION
See Nonderogable rights
DETENTION
In general, 558-75
Of aliens, 558, 561-68, 571, 574, 600, 610-11
See Arbitrary arrest and detention
DISAPPEARANCES
In general, 191, 259
Argentina, 335-42, 362-65, 510-11, 514
Columbia, 440-43

Customary law, 165-66, 513-16
El Salvador, 289
Guatemala, 359-61
Honduras, 443, 487
Iran, 147
Mexico 208,
Peru, 202-08, 396-97
See Working Group on Enforced or Involuntary Disappearances
DISCRIMINATION
    In general, 113,
Racial, 102, 104-113, 115-23, 126, 184, 437-39, 588
Religion, 147
Sex (gender), 126, 147, 656-62, 666, 683-87, 693
Doctors Without Borders, 318, 648
Dominican Republic, 156, 246, 350, 410, 416
Dualist approach to international law, 21-22, 575
Due Process, 107, 109, 146, 338, 434, 436, 556, 564-67, 603, 606, 629
East Timor, 196, 210, 398, 401
Eastern Europe, 6, 19, 187-88, 259, 285, 388, 632
ECONOMIC AND SOCIAL COUNCIL (ECOSOC)
    In general, 9-11, 72-5, 86, 96-7, 99, 174, 182-83, 186, 209, 366, 685
Role in state reports, 96-7
ECOSOC RESOLUTION 728F
    In general, 185-6
Text, 182-83
ECOSOC RESOLUTION 1235
    In general, 11, 142, 174-76, 181, 183-86, 208-14, 366
Text, 184
ECOSOC RESOLUTION 1503 PROCEDURE
    In general, 11, 21, 35, 174-76, 181, 183, 185-91, 208-15, 366-69, 371-72, 491
Commission's Working Group, 187-216
Sub-Commission's Working Group, 187-216
See Confidentiality
ECONOMIC, SOCIAL, AND CULTURAL RIGHTS, 8, 12, 20, 28, 50, 58, 60, 62, 65, 68
See International Covenant of Economic, Social, and Cultural Rights
Ecuador, 91, 156, 195, 429, 448
Ecumenical Movement for Human Rights, 363-64
Egypt, 91, 283, 409
El Salvador, 10-11, 20, 142, 185, 195, 199, 213, 247-48, 267-71, 273, 288-90, 294, 348, 370, 395, 400-01, 676
EMIGRATION
See Leave and return, right to
England (See United Kingdom)
Equal protection, 106-11, 121, 593
Equatorial Guinea, 157-58, 185, 189, 213, 272
Estonia, 11, 495-96
Ethics, 262-64
Ethiopia, 272, 551
Ethnic cleansing, 281, 290-96, 501
Export-Import Bank (EXIM Bank), 365
EUROPE, 6, 19, 187-88, 404, 463, 467, 633, 739

See Conference on Security and Cooperation in Europe, Eastern Europe, European Commission of Human Rights, European Community, European Court of Human Rights

EUROPEAN COMMISSION OF HUMAN RIGHTS
In general, 19, 159-61, 164-65, 435-36, 449, 452, 468, 470-74, 479-80, 490-91, 630, 693
European Committee of Ministers, 468, 479-80
European Community (EC), 177, 293, 315, 468, 491-93, 495-97
European Committee for the Prevention of Torture, 20
European Convention for the Prevention of Torture and Inhuman or Degrading Treatment or Punishment, 20

EUROPEAN CONVENTION OF HUMAN RIGHTS
In general, 19-20, 159, 262, 452, 468-93, 495, 595, 629, 693
Article 3, 159-65

EUROPEAN COURT OF HUMAN RIGHTS
In general, 19, 159, 161-69, 274, 435-36, 439, 478-86, 488-91, 598, 600, 629-30
Damages, 481-86
Death penalty, 476-77, 629-30
Homosexuality, 468-76, 478, 485
Inter-State cases, 489-91
Procedures, 479-80
Remedies, 478-86
European Court of Justice, 20, 491-93
European Parliament, 20, 491-93
European Social Charter, 20

EXECUTIONS
See Death penalty, Extrajudicial executions, Summary or arbitrary executions
Expression, freedom of (speech), 8, 41-2, 44, 101-02, 144
Extradition, 538, 583-84, 600

EXTRAJUDICIAL EXECUTIONS (POLITICAL KILLINGS), 146, 191, 259, 296, 359-61, 513-14
See Summary or arbitrary executions

FACT-FINDING
In general, 358-61
Argentina, 334-42, 361-71
Election observation, 328
Impact, 358-70
Interviews, 323-24
Korea, Democratic People's Republic, 352-58
On-site, 320-29, 348-51
Prison visit, 326-28
Reporting, 330-34
Korea, Republic of, 354-58
Role of IGO's and NGO's, 308, 319-20
Rules, 319-21
Rwanda, 311-19
State Department, 332-34
Suriname, 343-48
Terms of reference, 320
Trial observation, 324-26
Use by OAS, 341-42, 349, 363-65
U.S., 371-72
Without on-site visit, 351-58

See Inter-American Commission on Human Rights, Nongovernmental organizations

Fair Housing Act, 104, 108, 117-18

Federal Tort Claims Act, 621-22

FEMALE GENITAL MUTILATION (FMG)

   In general, 632, 657, 662, 667-70

Canada, 672-73

Cultural Relativism, 677-78, 680-82

France, 673-74

Ghana, 633-35

Nigeria, 672-73

Somalia, 873

U.S., 633-34, 672-73

Finland, 42, 491

Food and Agricultural Organization (FA0), 12

FOOD, RIGHT TO, 9, 14, 50, 68, 74, 85

See International Covenant of Economic, Social and Cultural Rights

FOREIGN AID

   In general, 383-86, 391, 394, 405, 409-21, 721

Country-specific legislation, 395-96

Peru, 369-97

Termination of aid, 365, 408-09, 420

See Section 116, Section 502B, State Department, United States (human rights policy)

FOREIGN POLICY

In general, 379, 614-22

See Congress, U.S.; Foreign aid; United States (human rights policy)

Foreign Service, 404-05

FOREIGN SOVEREIGN IMMUNITIES ACT

   In general, 534-49, 622

"Commercial activity" exceptions, 534, 537, 539

Excerpt, 534

Interaction with Act of State Doctrine, 547

FORMER YUGOSLAVIA

   In general, 10-11, 185, 199, 227, 230, 232-34, 237, 240-41, 280-98, 303, 419-20, 480, 495,
      497, 500-02, 524 528-31, 648

Human Right Violations, 281

NGO, 528

See United Nations (U.N.)

Four Freedoms Speech, 49

France, 3-4, 6, 9, 57, 64, 91, 201, 276-77, 283, 293, 355, 366, 475, 481-82, 490-92, 496-97,
      673-74, 736-37

Freedom of Information Act, 216

Gabon, 93

Gaza Strip, 272

General Assembly, U.N., 9-10, 12, 14, 40, 49, 51, 73, 83, 93, 97, 215, 217-22, 233, 240, 444,
      516, 518, 572, 547-48

GENEVA CONVENTIONS OF 1949

   In general, 17, 24, 228-29, 284-87, 522-23, 529, 532

Common Article 3, 165, 287, 523-24, 574, 592

**GENEVA CONVENTION RELATIVE TO THE PROTECTION OF CIVILIAN PER-
      SONS IN TIME OF WAR (Fourth Convention)**

   In general, 589-94, 622

Excerpt, 524-25

Geneva Conventions, Additional Protocol I, 17, 24, 228-29, 287, 525

Geneva Conventions, Additional Protocol II, 17, 24, 228-29, 287, 523, 525-26

Geneva Convention of 1864 for the Amelioration of the Condition of the Wounded and Sick in Armies in the Field, 3, 17

GENOCIDE, 285-87, 296-97, 313-16, 530, 734-35, 742

See Convention on the Prevention and Punishment of the Crime of Genocide

Germany (German), 5-6, 49, 91, 277, 293, 296, 426, 491-92, 496, 629, 727-28, 732-35, 738

Ghana, 632-35, 676

Greece, 57, 61, 245, 485, 490-91, 496

Grenada, 246, 248-49, 253-54, 438

GUATEMALA

In general, 10, 20, 142, 185, 195, 213, 264, 266, 272, 358-61, 400-02, 414, 417, 421, 460-61, 648, 676

Special Rapporteurs, 359-61

Habeas corpus, 195, 214, 351, 439

Hague Convention of 1899, 3, 17, 24, 299

Hague Regulations of 1907 (Regulations Respecting the Laws and Customs of War on Land), 3, 17, 24, 284, 321, 619

Haiti, 10-11, 20, 93, 185, 213, 232, 253, 272, 348, 388, 401, 416, 419, 450, 541, 552, 556, 567, 585

HEALTH, 50, 68, 84

See World Health Organization

HELSINKI FINAL ACT (ACCORDS)

In general, 19, 58, 494-96

See Conference on Security and Cooperation in Europe (CSCE)

HELSINKI WATCH, 358-61

See Human Rights Watch

High Commissioner for Minorities, 19

HOLOCAUST, 5-6

See World War II

Homosexuality, 124-25, 468-76, 478, 485, 662

Honduras, 20, 195, 247, 400, 443, 487

Hong Kong, 601

Hostage Taking Act, 522-23

HOUSING, RIGHT TO (HABITAT; SHELTER), 9, 14, 50, 74, 77-78

See International Covenant on Economic, Social and Cultural Rights

HUMAN RIGHTS BUREAU

See State Department

HUMAN RIGHTS COMMITTEE

In general, 13, 15, 28, 36-7, 41, 45-6, 49, 97, 102, 112, 122, 129, 142, 308, 355, 475, 520, 571-72

Adjudicative function, 155-59

Communications, 150-59

Examination of State Reports, 100

Examination of Iran's Report, 136-41

Examination of U.S. State Report, 122-26

General comments, 45-9, 94-7, 112-13, 137-38, 141, 570, 595-96, 613

Iran's report, 134-36

Juvenile, 574

Procedure, 91-7, 151-55

State reports, 91-7

Structure, 91

U.S. Report, 100-15

See International Covenant on Civil and Political Rights

HUMAN RIGHTS WATCH, 11, 180-81, 256, 313-14, 399-402, 608

See Africa Watch, Americas Watch, Asia Watch, Helsinki Watch

Humanitarian intervention, 230-52

HUMANITARIAN LAW

In general, 10, 17-18, 23-24, 224-33, 240-41, 252-53, 261, 263, 272, 281-84, 291-92, 294, 296, 303, 528-33

See Geneva Conventions, Nuremberg tribunal

Hungary, 91, 495

HUNGER, FREEDOM FROM

See food

Iceland, 496

Immigration and Nationality Act, 644

Immigration and Naturalization Service, 558-68, 611, 635-46, 651, 657-61, 665-67, 675-76

India, 91

Indian Law Resource Center, 216, 449

INDIGENOUS PEOPLES

In general, 606-08, 620

Indians, 102, 109, 123-25

Rights of, 448

See Working Group on Indigenous Populations; ILO

Indonesia, 179, 195-96, 210, 398, 401, 414

Inter-African Committee on Traditional Practices Affecting the Health of Women and Children, 680

INTER-AMERICAN COMMISSION ON HUMAN RIGHTS

In general, 20, 154, 308, 321, 364, 380, 424, 427-35, 444-50, 453-63, 516

Argentina, 334-41, 364-71

Communications, 445-47

Emergency procedure, 445, 447

Fact-finding, 20, 308-21, 334-51, 346-65, 367-71

Procedures, 436-46

Suriname, 343-48

Inter-American Commission on Women, 12

INTER-AMERICAN COURT OF HUMAN RIGHTS

In general, 20, 274, 443-45, 447, 452, 454, 457, 486-89

Advisory Opinions, 454-63, 452

Damages, 486-89

Death Penalty, 459-63

Suriname, 348

Inter-American Convention on Forced Disapearances of Persons, 448

Inter-American Convention on the Granting of Political Rights to Women, 34

Inter-American Convention on the Prevention and Punishment of Torture, 413

Inter-American Development Bank, 413

Internal Flight, 675-77

INTERNATIONAL BILL OF HUMAN RIGHTS

In general, 8-9, 14, 17, 19, 23-24, 28, 35-36, 376, 576, 588

See International Covenants, Universal Declaration of Human Rights

International Commission of Jurists, 11, 413

INTERNATIONAL COMMITTEE OF THE RED CROSS (ICRC)

In general, 3, 16-17, 146, 261-62, 287, 318, 326-28, 500, 529-30, 648

Commentary on the Fourth Geneva Convention, 241

Fact-finding, 326-28

See Geneva Conventions of 1949

INTERNATIONAL CONVENTION ON THE ELIMINATION OF ALL FORMS OF RA-CIAL DISCRIMINATION

In general, 34-35, 42-43, 45, 78, 80, 90, 693

Excerpt, 97-99

U.S. as signatory, 43

INTERNATIONAL COURT OF JUSTICE (ICJ)

In general, 18-19, 39, 42-43, 45-46, 252-53, 299, 303, 452, 500, 509, 580, 588-89, 598, 601, 615-20

Advisory Opinions, 33, 240, 595

Article 38, 18

Statute of the International Court of Justice, 509, 580, 598

INTERNATIONAL COVENANT ON CIVIL AND POLITICAL RIGHTS

In general, 8, 13-14, 21, 28, 33, 45, 51-52, 54, 60, 65-66, 74, 83, 91, 115-16, 121, 126, 142-45, 150-51, 183, 262, 353, 355-56, 376, 429, 440, 475, 477, 520, 571-82, 574, 600, 613, 656, 669-70, 673, 693

Article 2, 104-05, 376, 526-27, 569

Article 7, 129, 131, 155-59, 527, 571, 669

Article 10, 569

Article 22, 126

Article 23, 669-70, 569

Article 24, 569-70, 670

Article 26, 105, 570

Iran, 129-31, 155, 159

General Comment, 137-38, 141

Optional Protocol, 8, 13-14, 35, 150-59, 215, 326, 520

Peru, 204

Reporting Requirement and Procedures, 90-100

State reports, 100-26, 135-41

U.S. ratification, 14, 30-31, 34-35, 41-42, 468

U.S. reservations, 33-34, 39, 41, 47-49, 66-72, 594-97

U.S. report, 100-15

See Human Rights Committee, Ratifications of human rights treaties, U.S. Report

INTERNATIONAL COVENANT ON ECONOMIC, SOCIAL AND CULTURAL RIGHTS

In general, 8, 11, 14-15, 21, 28-29, 33-35, 51-87, 183, 230, 353, 355-56, 376, 656

Article 2, 52-6, 62, 67, 70

Article 10, 59

Article 11, 56, 59, 67, 77

General comment, 76-78

Obligation of state parties, 51-57

Ratification, 22, 33, 58-66, 84

Reservations, 33, 66-72

State reports, 75-77, 143

U.S. as signatory, 58-72, 376, 387

See Committee on Economic, Social and Cultural Rights; Ratifications of human rights treaties; Reservations

International Financial Institution Act, 391-92

International Human Rights Conformity Act, 571

International Human Rights Law Group, 43

International Humanitarian Law (See Geneva Conventions of 1949)

International Labor Organization (ILO), 3, 12, 16, 49, 80, 97, 102

International Law Commission, 279, 299-305

International League for Human Rights, 11

International Military Tribunal (Nuremberg), 6-7, 227, 256, 262, 276-80, 286-87, 290, 294, 299, 529, 608, 727

International Monetary Fund (IMF), 12, 391-92, 386

International Narcotics Control Act, 396

INTERNATIONAL RED CROSS

See International Committee of the Red Cross (ICRC)

INTERNATIONAL TRIBUNAL FOR THE FORMER YUGOSLAVIA

In general, 10, 227, 230, 234, 276-80, 284-98

Power of, 281-83

Efficacy, 288-98

IRAN

In general, 11, 128-50, 168-71, 185, 195, 209, 213, 246, 358, 398, 411, 414, 608, 651-56, 662, 681, 695-96

Amputation, 129-46, 166

Corporal Punishment, 131, 133-34, 140

Crucifixion, 130-32

Human Rights Commission, 142-46

Human Right violations, 131-34, 146-47, 150

International Covenant on Civil and Political Rights, 129, 131, 142-45, 155, 159

Mutilation, 131-33

Special Rapporteurs, 142-49

State Report, 134-41

United States, 171-72

Iraq, 10-11, 19, 96, 147, 185, 119-32, 234, 273, 388, 398, 401, 411, 419, 488, 608

Ireland, 159-62, 220, 470-75, 486, 490-91

Islamic Penal Code of Iran, 129, 131-34, 681

Israel, 91, 273, 401, 409

Italy, 6, 73, 91, 277, 283, 293, 481-82, 490-91, 496, 737

Jamaica, 91, 155, 249

JAPAN, 6, 91, 177-80, 277, 355, 381, 413, 725

See Tokyo tribunal

Jews, 5-6, 727-29, 732-35, 738-39, 742

Jordan, 398, 523

JUS COGENS, 18-19, 83, 144-45, 437-43, 537, 576-77, 601-02, 616, 618-20

See Customary law (peremptory norms)

JUVENILES

Detention of alien children, 558, 561-68, 571, 574, 600

Execution of, U.S. Supreme Court opinions, 607-08

United States, 41-42, 118, 122, 437-39, 607-08

Kazakhstan, 19

Kenya, 401

Korea, Democratic People's Republic of Korea (North Korea), 352-58, 398

Korea, Republic of (South Korea), 353-56, 381, 393, 417

Kosovo, 11

Kuwait, 229-32, 234, 273, 419, 488

Lao, 199

Latin America, 259, 265, 404, 408

Latvia, 11, 496

Law of Nations, 506-09, 519-52, 556

Lawyers Committee for Human Rights, 11, 333, 364, 367, 399, 403, 411, 415, 571, 590, 646

League of Arab States, 466

League of Nations, 3-4, 299-300, 506-09, 519-22, 556

Leave and Return, Right to, 8, 14, 146

Lebanon, 4, 245, 411, 523

Legal Age of Majority Act, 634

Liberia, 3, 225-26, 401

Libya, 246-47, 249-50, 389, 411, 416-17, 419

LIFE, RIGHT TO, 2, 8, 14, 144-45, 168-69, 346, 424-35, 438-39

See Summary or arbitrary executions

Lithuania, 495-96

Lobola, 634-35

LONDON AGREEMENT (Agreement for the Prosecution and Punishment of the Major War Criminals of the European Axis)

See Nuremberg Charter

Luxembourg, 491, 496

Maastricht Treaty, 493

Madagascar, 156

Malaysia, 179, 401

Matrimonial Causes Act, 634

Mauritania, 91

McCarthyism, 747-49

MERCENARIES

See Special Rapporteurs

Mexico, 64, 429, 450, 552, 557, 583-84, 611

MILITARY, 721-23, 750-51

See International Military tribunal

Military Staff Committee, 220

MINORITIES

See Minority Rights Group, Sub-Commission on Prevention of Discrimination and Protection of Minorities

MISSING PERSONS

See Disappearances

Mongolia, 272

Mozambique, 10, 648

Monist approach to international law, 22, 575

Mothers of Plaza de Mayo, 318, 648

MUTILATION, 131-33

See Female Genital Mutilation

MYANMAR (formerly Burma),

In general, 11, 174-80, 185, 411

Human Rights violations, 178-81

Sanctions, 175

See United States (U.S.)

Namibia, 10, 225, 626

National Association for the Advancement of Colored People (NAACP), 7

NATIVE AMERICAN, 102, 109, 123-25

See Indigenous

Natural law, 166-67, 678, 683, 687

Netherlands, 3, 10, 61, 83, 198, 490-91, 496

New Zealand, 64, 93, 293

Nicaragua, 10, 20, 78, 197, 247, 252-53, 267, 351, 411, 416, 418, 448, 614-629, 348, 350-51

Nigeria, 283, 544, 608, 672-73

Nonderogable rights, 46-48, 83, 437

NONGOVERNMENTAL ORGANIZATIONS (NGOs)

In general, 7, 11, 23-24, 75, 81, 83, 96, 112, 126, 191, 197, 209, 227, 256, 265, 271, 446, 500, 528, 671, 719

Communication under ECOSOC 1505, 366-68

Critique of country reports, 399

Evaluation on U.N. peace-keeping, 224-26, 229

Fact-finding, 308, 316-321, 328, 332, 357, 360-64, 371-72

Iran, 174, 147

Rwanda, 316-19

On violence against women, 671

North Atlantic Treaty Organization (NATO), 468, 496-97, 624

Norway, 3, 293, 490, 496,

Nuremberg Charter (London Agreement), 277-78, 287, 608-10

NUREMBERG CRIMES

See International Military Tribunal

NUREMBERG TRIBUNAL

See International Military Tribunal

Nuremberg rules, 608-610

Organization for Security and Cooperation in Europe (OSCE), 19, 179, 468, 494-96

ORGANIZATION OF AMERICAN STATES (OAS)

In general, 20, 45, 195, 241, 341-42, 349, 363-65, 396, 411, 424, 427, 444, 455, 516, Charter, 20, 38, 78, 251, 376, 433, 452, 458-60, 587-89

See Inter-American Commission on Human Rights

ORGANIZATION OF AFRICAN UNITY (OAU)

In general, 20-21, 45, 195, 241, 321, 464-65, 580, 648

African Charter on Human and Peoples' Rights, 20-21, 38, 78, 251, 464-65

African Commission, 464-466

Organization of Eastern Caribbean States, 248

Organization of the Islamic Conference, 466

Pacific Charter on Human Rights, 466

Pacta sunt servanda, 109, 145

Pakistan, 170, 283, 293, 392, 400, 608, 641

Palestine, 185

Panama, 20, 250-53, 350, 448-49, 545, 619

Panama Canal Treaty, 250-52

Paraguay, 20, 93, 348, 400, 505-09, 447-59, 612

Paris Peace Conference, 3

PEACE-KEEPING

Attacks on peace-keepers, 227-28

Characteristics, 221-22

Holding Action, 220-21

Instruments, 237-39

Liberia, 226

Role of the military, 220-22, 224

Rwanda, 226
Somalia, 228-29
U.N. Charter, 219-20
Personal Jurisdiction, 523
Persecution, 643-45, 667-69, 650-69, 672-73, 675
PERU
  In general, 96, 202-208, 214, 396, 429, 445, 458
Disappearances, 202-208, 396-97
U.S., 396-97,
Philippines, 179, 264-66, 272, 277, 326, 381, 400, 489, 519, 540, 693
Poland, 185, 213, 324, 358, 495, 727
Political prisoners, 180
Political question doctrine, 614-21
POPULATION
See Abortion; Life, right to
Portugal, 61, 491, 496
Positivism, 167-68, 687
PRISON CONDITIONS
  In general, 571, 602-607
Female guards and male prisoners, 606
See Standard Minimum Rules for the Treatment of Prisoners
PRIVACY,
See European Court of Human Rights
Property, right to, 71
Racial discrimination, 102, 104-113, 115-23, 126, 184, 437-39, 588
RAPE
  In general, 296, 528-33, 488, 635, 670-71
As a tort, 531-33
In the former Yugoslavia, 528-33
In Myanmar, 179
International humanitarian law, 528-31
International Rules Governing Rape, 523-33
Role of Geneva Convention, 524-25
RATIFICATION OF HUMAN RIGHTS TREATIES
  In general, 33-34, 45-49
Advantages, 35-37
United States, 58-72, 90, 104-11
See International Covenant on Civil and Political Rights, International Covenant on Economic, Social and Cultural Rights, and other treaties; Treaties
Reagan, President R., 30-31, 40, 42-43, 65, 246-50, 379, 388-89, 398-99, 403, 410, 414, 613
REFUGEE ACT OF 1980
  In general, 21, 593, 612, 622, 641-42, 653, 697-98
Interpretation of, 597-98
REFUGEE LAW
  In general, 636-46
Country-wide persecution, 675-76
Department of Justice, 638-39
Employment authorization, 679
Procedural issues, 636
Well-founded fear of persecution, 641-47, 662-67
See Immigration and Naturalization Service, Asylum

REFUGEES

In general, 382, 567, 632, 636, 638-39

Definition of, 640-41, 645

Gender-based claims, 650-69

Rights of, 124-26, 448

See Asylum, U.N. High Commissioner for Refugees

RELIGION, FREEDOM OF

In general, 8, 101-102, 144

Role in witch-hunting, 742-47

See Special rapporteurs

REMEDIES

In general, 273-75

Damages, 548-50

Private cause of action in international law, 519-20, 585, 597-98

Right to a remedy, 478-89

U.N. Charter, Article 94, 612, 619

RESERVATIONS

See Treaties

RHODESIA, 588, 617

See Zimbabwe

Romania, 142, 185, 414, 418, 495, 727

Roosevelt, President F., 7, 49-50, 67

RWANDA

In general, 4, 10-11, 185, 196, 225-26, 234, 241, 296-97, 303, 311-19, 361, 519, 549, 608

Role of U.N. Security Council, 314-16

Special Rapporteurs, 314-15

See U.N. International Tribunal for Rwanda

Russia, 19

RUSSIAN FEDERATION, 199, 220, 236, 495

See, U.S.S.R.

Salvadoran Peace Accords, 267

Sanctions, 289, 415-21, 588

Saudi Arabia, 535, 608, 673

SECTION 116

In general, 383-84, 393, 403

SECTION 502B

In general, 21, 332, 383-84, 391, 393, 396-97, 403-10, 612-13

SECURITY COUNCIL, U.N.

In general, 7, 9-10, 217, 230-39, 289, 293, 647

Former Yugoslavia, 282-83

Humanitarian intervention, 230-34

Permanent members of, 220

Power, 219-22

Role in peace-keeping, 219-22, 226-30, 237-39

Rwanda, 314-16

See United Nations (U.N.)

Self-determination, 4, 8, 208-14, 232

Self-executing treaty, 22, 41, 48, 71, 585-98, 619-80, 622-23

Shariah, 168-70

Shattuck, John, 100-04, 111, 122, 390, 410

SHELTER

See Housing

Singapore, 171, 179, 401

Slavery, 110, 135

Slavery Convention, 34, 568

Somalia, 10-11, 185, 199, 228-29, 232-33, 237, 140, 673

SOUTH AFRICA, 10, 108, 142, 185, 195, 213, 321, 361, 398, 400, 414, 416-18, 289, 626, 648, 719

See *Apartheid*

South Asia Association for Regional Cooperation, 466

South Pacific Commission, 466

South Pacific Forum, 466

South West Africa (See Namibia)

SOVEREIGN IMMUNITY, 620

See Foreign Sovereign Immunities Act

SOVIET UNION

See U.S.S.R.

Spain, 3, 61, 157, 491, 496

SPECIAL RAPPORTEURS, U.N.

  In general, 185-87, 191-92, 198, 200-01, 211-16

Country rapporteurs, 208-11, 281

On mercenaries, 192, 197

On racism, 112, 184, 192, 200, 372

On religious intolerance, 192, 196-97

On summary or arbitrary executions, 192-94, 196-97, 214, 313

On torture, 192, 194-95, 197, 208, 210

On violence against women, 192, 201, 533

Visits, 180, 199

See, Guatemala, Iran, Rwanda

Spousal Abuse, 635, 657, 662, 666-75, 670-72, 677-83,

Sri Lanka, 210, 215

STANDARD MINIMUM RULES FOR THE TREATMENT OF PRISONERS

  In general, 11, 74, 612

Excerpt, 147-48

STATE DEPARTMENT

  In general, 23, 31, 40-41, 47, 60, 91-92, 100, 104, 122, 216, 295, 365, 380, 383-85, 391, 393, 400-03, 411, 414, 451-52, 530, 578, 583, 718

Amicus curiae brief, 590

Bureau of Human Rights and Humanitarian Affairs, 104-12, 380, 394, 405-06, 414

Country reports on human rights practices, 60, 332-34, 383-85, 394, 400-03, 411

Human rights officer, 100-115, 380

Protection of U.S. citizens abroad, 365

Role in U.S. ratification of American Convention on Human Rights, 352-53

U.S. Report, 100-15

STATE REPORTS

See Committee on the Elimination of Racial Discrimination; Human Rights Committee, United States

Statistics, 113-22, 707-10, 712-15

Statutes of limitations (effect on international human rights law), 548-50

SUB-COMMISSION ON PREVENTION OF DISCRIMINATION AND PROTECTION OF MINORITIES, U.N.

  In general, 9, 11, 84, 166, 182, 186, 208-10, 229-34, 274, 366-69, 371-72, 491

Argentina, 366-68
Communications, 182, 184-91
See ECOSOC resolution 1503
SUBSISTENCE
Right to, 14, 50, 68
See International Covenant on Economic, Cultural, and Social Rights
Sudan, 11, 166, 185, 199, 400
SUMMARY OR ARBITRARY EXECUTIONS,
Guatemala, 359-61
See Special rapporteurs
SUPREME COURT, U.S.
  In general, 39-40, 69, 101-08, 116-17, 121, 427, 430, 433-34, 535-39, 541-45, 555-58, 562-
    68, 570, 584, 598, 603, 612, 615, 621-22, 728
International law sources discussed, 21-23, 505-08, 556-57, 562-68, 570, 584-85, 598-99, 607-
    08, 622-23, 641, 645-46
Homosexuality, 75, 468-69
Suriname, 20, 334-48, 487-88
Sweden, 3, 42, 366, 482-85, 490-91
Switzerland, 61, 639, 739
Syria, 4, 288, 298, 401, 417
Tanzania, 10, 297, 314
Thailand, 179-80
THEMATIC PROCEDURES
  In general, 11, 174, 181, 191-202, 210-11, 214
See also Mercenaries, Religious intolerance, Special rapporteurs, Summary or arbitrary execu-
    tions, Torture
Third generation of human rights, 81-3
Togo, 4, 185
Tokyo tribunal, 6, 227, 256, 276-77, 287, 294, 299, 329
TORT
Claims, 489, 612-22
International common law, 509-15
Of causing disappearance, 510-19
Private right of action for international torts, 519-20, 585, 597-98
Violation of international law, 504, 531
TORTURE
  In general, 159-65, 191-92, 259, 526
Argentina, 361-63, 510-11, 513-15, 536-28
Chile, 266
Columbia, 441-43
Equatorial Guinea, 157-58
European System, 159-65
Former Yugoslavia, 281, 284-96
Guatemala, 359-61
Myanmar, 178-81
Paraguay, 488, 505-09, 612
Phillippines, 489
Right to be free from, 8, 14, 128-31, 135, 137-38, 140, 144-45, 147, 155-57
Saudi Arabia, 535-36
Suriname, 343-47, 487
Uruguay, 265, 267

See Convention against Torture and Other Cruel, Inhuman or Degrading Treatment or Punishment; Declaration on the Protection of All Persons from Being Subjected to Torture and Other Cruel, Inhuman or Degrading Treatment or Punishment; Special rapporteurs

Torture Victim Protection Act, 519-20, 522-23, 532-33, 550-52, 584, 626

TRAVAUX PRÉPARATOIRES

In general, 15, 55, 428-30, 453, 590

See Vienna Treaty on Treaties

TREATIES

In general, 16, 28

Effect on domestic law, 21, 39-49, 58-72

Enforcement by private parties in U.S., 505-23

Interpretation, 21, 52-57, 426-33, 437-44, 450-54, 580-85

In U.S. law, 453, 555, 581-83

Reservations, understandings, and declarations, 31-34, 39-49, 66-72

U.S. as party to treaties with human rights provisions, 15, 30-31

See Ratification of human rights treaties; Self-executing, Travaux préparatoires, Treaty by name

TREATY AGAINST TORTURE

See Convention against Torture and Other Cruel, Inhuman or Degrading Treatment or Punishment

Treaty of Rome, 493

TRIAL

Fair trial, 8, 14, 46, 144-45, 338

Trial observation, 324-26

Turkey, 231, 400, 409, 490-91, 496

Uganda, 189, 195, 272, 297, 311-12, 416

United Kingdom, 3-4, 6-7, 9, 22, 91, 159-62, 170, 220, 276-77, 291-92, 368, 435, 470-76, 478, 481, 490-91, 496, 575, 629, 643-47

UNITED NATIONS (U.N.)

In general, 6-9, 15, 23, 31, 51, 72, 90, 178, 211-12, 219-21, 223-41, 243, 278-79, 288-89, 293-94, 296, 300, 314, 321-22, 377-80, 396, 497, 500, 514, 528, 581-83, 678, 719

Assistance Mission to Rwanda, 308, 315-19, 321

Ad Hoc Commission, 268-71

Commission on the Truth for El Salvador, 256, 258, 267-71, 273, 294, 289-90

Compensation Committee, 10, 273, 468, 488

General Assembly (See General Assembly, U.N.)

Field Operations in Rwanda, 308, 315-19, 321

Headquarters Agreement, 581-83

High Commissioner for Human Rights, 10, 12, 35, 215, 308, 315-16

International Tribunal for the Former Yugoslavia, 10, 227, 230, 234, 281-98, 531

International Tribunal for Rwanda, 10-11, 234, 296-98, 311, 316

Observer Mission in Liberia, 225-26

Peacekeeping force, 222-41, 253

Permanent International Criminal Court, 227, 256, 298-305

Procedures for human rights violations, 181-91

Protection Force, 232

Security Council (See Security Council, U.N.)

Specialized agencies, 190, 226-27

Trusteeship System, 4

Unilateral Intervention, 224-29, 232-40, 243-45, 253

See Centre for Human Rights, Commission on Human Rights, Economic and Social Council, General Assembly, Secretary-General, Special rapporteurs, Sub-Commission on Prevention of Discrimination and Protection of Minorities

U.N. CHARTER
In general, 7, 8, 18, 218-21, 283, 286, 291, 299-300, 321-22, 375-76, 454, 496, 506, 509, 538, 577, 581, 587-89, 609, 613, 615-19, 719
Article 1, 230, 233, 240, 243, 375
Article 1(3), 8, 13, 243, 375
Article 1(7), 243
Article 2(2), 145, 375
Article 2(4), 232, 243-44, 247
Article 2(7), 10, 217-18, 231-32
Article 29, 286
Article 33, 218-20
Article 39, 219-20, 227-28, 232, 234, 282-83, 286
Article 41, 217, 219-21, 231
Article 43(3), 587
Article 45, 587
Article 51, 218-220, 227-28, 232, 234, 245-48, 250-51, 282-83, 286
Article 55, 8, 10, 13-15, 50, 144, 182, 233, 240, 243, 375-76, 507, 588-89
Article 56, 8, 10, 13-14, 16, 50, 144, 182, 230, 233, 240, 243, 373-75, 507, 557, 588-89
Article 92, 509, 580
Article 94, 612, 619
Article 103, 13, 376
Preamble, 8, 10, 13, 243
U.N. Centre for Social Development and Humanitarian Affairs, 670-71
U.N. Children's Fund (UNICEF), 12, 180
U.N. Educational, Scientific, Cultural Organization (UNESCO), 12, 16-17
U.N. HIGH COMMISSIONER FOR REFUGEES (UNHCR), 12, 21, 179, 226, 363, 570, 642-50, 656-59, 667-69, 671
See Refugee
UNITED STATES (U.S.)
In general, 6, 9, 14, 21-22, 35-37, 91, 170, 177, 184, 220, 240-41, 245, 283, 290, 300, 305, 321, 365-68, 448-53, 488-89
Abortion, 102, 424-35, 612-13
Bilateral relations, 347
Corporal punishment, 478
Country reports, 332-34, 383-85, 400-03
Courts, 559, 575-80, 583-84, 597-98, 300-01, 310-12
Death penalty, 40-42, 102, 107, 118-19, 121-22, 124, 476-77, 607-08, 628
El Salvador, 268
Fact-finding, 332-34, 371-72
Grenada, 248-49, 253-54
Head of State Immunity, 541-47
Homosexuality, 468-69, 475
Human rights policy, 379-83, 385
Human rights violations, 123-26
Implementing human rights policy, 391-415
Incorporating international law in U.S. statutes, 21-22, 379-91
International law as a guide to interpretation of U.S. law, 22, 504-23, 556-58, 574-80, 581-85, 602-30

International Covenant on Civil and Political Rights, 14, 30-35, 39, 41, 39-49, 58-72, 90-126, 372

International Covenant on Economic, Social, and Cultural Rights, 14, 55-72, 376, 387

Invasion of Panama, 250-52

Juveniles, 41-42, 118, 122, 437-39, 607-08

Libya, 249-50

Myanmar, 177-80

Nicaragua, 253, 247-48, 614-20

Obligations under human rights treaties, 375-79

Party to human rights treaties, 14-15, 37-39, 581

Peace-keeping, 239-41

Peru, 396-97

Ratification of Human Rights Treaties, 30-31, 34-49, 58-72, 90, 104-11, 539-30, 568-74, 581-85,

Refugees, 382-83

Report, 100-15

Sanctions, 415-21

Somalia, 240-41

Unilateral Intervention, 245-52

See Congress, U.S.; Indigenous People; North Atlantic Treaty Organization; Ratifications of human rights treaties; State Department

U.S. CONSTITUTION

In general, 23, 40-43, 67-69, 101-02, 105-12, 116, 121, 123, 376, 399, 438, 453, 477-78, 508, 518, 546, 555, 560, 581, 585, 600, 611, 618-22

Eighth amendment, 40-41, 107, 438, 478, 560, 571, 586, 600, 628-29

Fifth amendment, 40-41, 106, 560, 564-65, 567, 584, 600, 603, 606, 629

First amendment, 69, 106

Fourteenth amendment, 40-44, 106, 109-10, 121, 438, 564, 584, 300, 628-29

Thirteenth amendment, 108, 110

Supremacy clause, 555-56, 560, 581, 592

See Due process; Equal protection

UNIVERSAL DECLARATION OF HUMAN RIGHTS

In general, 8-9, 14, 16, 21, 28, 35-36, 51, 64, 78, 81, 143-45, 166, 169, 183, 376, 380, 387, 506, 517, 519, 538, 577, 609, 668

Article 3, 168-69

Article 5, 129-31, 166

Cultural Relativism, 678-80

Drafting, 51

Universalism, 678-80, 682

Uruguay, 20, 155-56, 164-66, 348, 429, 448

U.S.S.R., 6-7, 9, 49, 66, 103, 195, 236, 240, 268, 276-77, 300, 367-68, 382, 384-85, 400, 414, 416, 496, 723, 729

Venezuela, 91, 429, 448

VIENNA CONVENTION ON THE LAW OF TREATIES

In general, 15, 18, 29-33, 46-49, 83, 424, 437, 452-54, 462-63, 572, 580, 585, 594-95, 601-02,

Article 18, 30

Article 19, 20-33, 46, 48

Article 21, 32-33, 48

Article 53, 83, 602

Article 64, 602

Definition of reservation, 31-33

Text, 29-30, 450-52

Vietnam, 199, 213, 288, 398, 400-01, 735

Voting Rights Act of 1965, 109

War crimes, 276-78, 292, 300, 530

Western Sahara, 10

Witchcraft, 739-42

Witch-hunts, 739-47

WOMEN

Effect of International Law, 683-87, 693

See Commission on the Status of Women; Committee on the Elimination of Discrimination
against Women; Convention on the Elimination of All Forms of Discrimination against
Women; Discrimination; Discrimination based on sex; Female Genital Mutilation; Rape;
Refugee; Spousal abuse

Women Refugee Project, 667

WORKER RIGHTS, 3, 392

See Forced labor; International Labor Organization

Working Group on Communications, 366, 368, 372

WORKING GROUP ON ENFORCED OR INVOLUNTARY DISAPPEARANCES

In general, 192-92, 196, 210, 212, 359, 360-61, 366, 368

Peru, 202-08

See Disapearances

Working Group on Indigenous Populations, 216, 274

World Bank, 12, 386, 391, 413

World Conference on Human Rights, 79-80, 86, 682

World Health Organization (WHO), 12, 648, 668

World War II, 3, 23, 49-50, 220, 262, 276, 288, 290, 324, 539, 641, 647, 672, 732-35, 737, 742

Yemen, 608

Yugoslavia, (see Former Yugoslavia)

Zaire, 156, 185, 214-15, 314

ZIMBABWE, 668, 671, 676

See Rhodesia